COMPARATIVE LAW

COMPARATIVE LAW

GEORGE E. GLOS

Professor of Law
St. Mary's University of San Antonio
School of Law

FRED B. ROTHMAN & CO.
Littleton, Colorado   80123

ISBN: 0-8377-0610-6

Library of Congress Catalog Card Number: 79-66013

Printed in the U.S.A.

To Blanka,
an understanding and helpful wife

Summary Table of Contents

Table of Contents xi
Acknowledgments xxxv

INTRODUCTION *1*

GENERAL PART

AN OVERVIEW OF THE LAW *5*
    I. *The System and Administration of Civil Law 5*
    II. *The System and Administration of Criminal Law 17*
    III. *The System and Administration of Administrative Law 24*
    IV. *Legal Officers 28*
        Footnote 31

SPECIAL PART

THE FRENCH LAW *35*
    I. *Introduction 35*
    II. *The System and Administration of Civil Law 36*
    III. *The System and Administration of Criminal Law 128*
    IV. *The System and Administration of Administrative Law 159*
    V. *Legal Officers 176*
    VI. *Decisions of French Courts 183*
        Footnotes 210

THE GERMAN LAW *223*

    I.   *Introduction 223*
   II.   *The System and Administration of Civil Law 224*
  III.   *The System and Administration of Criminal Law 289*
  IV.   *The System and Administration of Administrative Law 318*
   V.   *Legal Officers 343*
  VI.   *Decisions of German Courts 350*
        Footnotes 379

THE ITALIAN LAW *386*

    I.   *Introduction 386*
   II.   *The System and Administration of Civil Law 387*
  III.   *The System and Administration of Criminal Law 428*
  IV.   *The System and Administration of Administrative Law 452*
   V.   *Legal Officers 483*
  VI.   *Decisions of Italian Courts 489*
        Footnotes 527

THE SPANISH LAW *535*

    I.   *Introduction 535*
   II.   *The System and Administration of Civil Law 536*
  III.   *The System and Administration of Criminal Law 595*
  IV.   *The System and Administration of Administrative Law 623*
   V.   *Legal Officers 649*
  VI.   *Decisions of Spanish Courts 655*
        Footnotes 681

NOTES ON LEGAL SYSTEMS OF ADDITIONAL COUNTRIES

THE AUSTRIAN LAW *689*

    I.   *Introduction 689*
   II.   *The System and Administration of Civil Law 690*
  III.   *The System and Administration of Criminal Law 692*
  IV.   *The System and Administration of Administrative Law 694*
   V.   *Legal Officers 696*

THE SWISS LAW *698*

    I.   *Introduction 698*
   II.   *The System and Administration of Civil Law 699*
  III.   *The System and Administration of Criminal Law 703*
  IV.   *The System and Administration of Administrative Law 707*
   V.   *Legal Officers 708*

THE MEXICAN LAW *711*

    I.   *Introduction 711*
   II.   *The System and Administration of Civil Law 712*
  III.   *The System and Administration of Criminal Law 714*
  IV.   *The System and Administration of Administrative Law 717*
   V.   *Legal Officers 719*

THE LAW OF OTHER SPANISH- AND PORTUGUESE-SPEAKING COUNTRIES OF THE AMERICAN CONTINENT *724*

THE GEOGRAPHIC EXTENT OF THE COMMON LAW AND ITS DOMINANT FEATURES *726*

THE LAW OF THE SOVIET UNION AND THE COUNTRIES OF THE SOVIET UNION IN CENTRAL AND EASTERN EUROPE *729*

APPENDIX

THE ADMINISTRATIVE STRUCTURE AND LEGAL SYSTEM OF MALAYA *735*
    I. *Introduction 735*
    II. *The* Adat *736*
    III. *Hindu and Muslim Influences 738*
    IV. *The Evolution of Law and State 738*
    V. *The Presently Applicable Law 742*
    VI. *Conclusion 745*
    Footnotes 746

CONTEMPORARY TRENDS IN CONTINENTAL AND BRITISH LEGAL EDUCATION *755*
    I. *Introduction 755*
    II. *Prelegal Education 756*
    III. *Admission to Law School 756*
    IV. *Law Schools 758*
    V. *The Degree and Admission to the Bar 766*
    VI. *Selection and Appointment of Judges 767*
    VII. *Selection and Appointment of Law Teachers 769*
    VIII. *Conclusion 770*
    Footnotes 771

INDEX *781*

Table of Contents

Summary Table of Contents   *vii*
Acknowledgments   *xxxv*

INTRODUCTION   *1*

GENERAL PART

AN OVERVIEW OF THE LAW   *5*

   I. *The System and Administration of Civil Law*   *5*
      A. The Substantive Civil Law   *5*
          1. The Law of Persons   *6*
          2. The Law of Property   *6*
          3. The Law of Succession   *6*
          4. The Law of Obligations (Contracts and Torts)   *7*
      B. The Commercial Law   *7*
          1. Merchants   *8*
          2. Partnerships and Corporations   *8*
          3. Mercantile Transactions   *9*
          4. The Law of Exchange   *9*
          5. Bankruptcy   *9*
          6. Maritime Law   *10*
      C. The System of Civil and Commercial Courts   *11*
          1. Courts of Limited Jurisdiction   *11*
          2. Courts of General Jurisdiction   *12*

3. Appellate Courts *13*
4. Supreme Courts *13*
5. Commercial Courts *14*
D. The Law of Civil Procedure *14*
   1. Jurisdiction and Venue *15*
   2. Parties and Legal Representation *15*
   3. Writs, Citations, the Service of Process, and General Rules Concerning Procedure *15*
   4. Procedings in Trial Courts, Judgments, Rulings and Orders *15*
   5. Appellate Procedings and Further Means to Attack the Validity of Judgments *16*
   6. Execution of Judgments *17*
   7. Specialized Proceedings *17*

II. *The System and Administration of Criminal Law* *17*
A. The Substantive Criminal Law *17*
   1. Offenses against the State *18*
   2. Offenses against the Person and Personal Liberty *18*
   3. Offenses against the Family and Honor *18*
   4. Offenses against Property and Acts Creating Public Danger *19*
B. The System of Criminal Courts *19*
   1. Courts of Limited Jurisdiction *19*
   2. Courts of General Jurisdiction *20*
   3. Appellate Courts *20*
   4. Supreme Courts *20*
C. The Law of Criminal Procedure *21*
   1. Public Authorities Entrusted with the Prosecution of Crime, Courts, and Parties *21*
   2. Preliminary Investigation and the Initiation of Criminal Prosecution *22*
   3. Preparation for Trial *22*
   4. Trial and Judgment *22*
     (a) Persons accused of simple offenses (infractions and usually some lesser misdemeanors) *22*
     (b) Persons accused of lesser crimes (usually lesser felonies and some more serious misdemeanors) *22*
     (c) Persons accused of serious felonies *22*
   5. Proceedings on Appeal and for the Cassation and Revision of Judgments *23*
   6. Execution of Judgments *23*
   7. Specialized Proceedings *24*

III. *The System and Administration of Administrative Law* *24*
A. The Substantive Administrative Law *25*
B. The System of Administrative Authorities (Offices and Courts) *25*
C. The Law of Administrative Procedure and Procedure before Administrative Courts *27*

IV. *Legal Officers* *28*
A. Judges *28*
B. The Public Ministry *29*
C. Attorneys *29*
D. Notaries *30*

Footnote *31*

SPECIAL PART

The French Law 35

  I. *Introduction* 35
 II. *The System and Administration of Civil Law* 36
      A. The Substantive Civil Law 36
          1. Domicile 37
          2. Marriage 38
              (a) Capacity to marry 38
              (b) Celebration of marriage 38
              (c) Opposition to marriage 39
              (d) Petition for annulment of marriage 39
              (e) Obligations arising out of marriage 40
              (f) Duties and rights of spouses 40
              (g) Dissolution of marriage 41
              (h) Second marriages 41
          3. Divorce 42
              (a) Types of divorce 42
                   (i) Divorce by mutual consent 42
                        (aa) Divorce on joint petition of spouses 42
                        (bb) Divorce demanded by one spouse and accepted by the other 42
                   (ii) Divorce on the ground of separation 42
                   (iii) Divorce because of fault 43
              (b) Divorce procedure 43
              (c) Consequences of divorce 44
                   (i) Effects of divorce 44
                   (ii) Compensation 45
                   (iii) Alimony 46
                   (iv) Family home 46
                   (v) Custody 46
              (d) Judicial separation 47
              (e) Conflict of laws applicable to divorce and judicial separation 48
          4. The Law of Property 49
              (a) Classification of property 49
                   (i) Immovables 49
                   (ii) Movables 49
                   (iii) Property and its owner 49
              (b) Ownership 50
                   (i) Right of accession of that which is produced by the thing 50
                   (ii) Right of accession of that which is united with or incorporated in the thing 50
                        (aa) Right of accession to immovables 50
                        (bb) Right of accession to movables 51
              (c) Usufruct, use, and right to use premises 51
                   (i) Usufruct 51
                        (aa) Rights of the usufructuary 52
                        (bb) Obligations of the usufructuary 52
                        (cc) Termination of the usufruct 53

      (ii) Use and right to use premises *53*

  (d) Easements *54*

      (i) Easements that come into being due to the location of land *54*

      (ii) Easements imposed by law *54*

         (aa) Party walls *55*

         (bb) Distances of certain works from boundary lines *55*

         (cc) Easements of view, light and air *55*

         (dd) Dripping of water from roofs *56*

         (ee) Way of necessity *56*

      (iii) Easements established by the parties *56*

         (aa) Kinds of easements *56*

         (bb) Creation of easements *56*

         (cc) Rights of owners of dominant tenements *56*

         (dd) Termination of easements *57*

5. Modes in Which Property May Be Acquired *57*

6. Intestate Succession *58*

  (a) Devolution of property *58*

  (b) Capacity to inherit *58*

  (c) Order of succession *58*

      (i) General provisions *58*

      (ii) Representation *58*

      (iii) Succession of descendants *59*

      (iv) Succession of ascendants *59*

      (v) Succession of collaterals *59*

      (vi) Succession of illegitimates *60*

      (vii) Succession of the surviving spouse *60*

  (d) Succession of the state *60*

  (e) Acceptance and renunciation of inheritance *61*

      (i) Acceptance *61*

      (ii) Renunciation *61*

      (iii) Benefit of inventory, its effect, and the liability of an heir so taking *61*

      (iv) Unclaimed estates *62*

  (f) Partition and contribution *63*

      (i) Suit for partition *63*

      (ii) Contribution *64*

      (iii) Payment of debts *64*

      (iv) Property involved in the partition and warranty of individual shares *65*

      (v) Recission of partition *65*

7. Gifts *inter vivos* and Testamentary Succession *66*

  (a) General provisions *66*

  (b) Capacity to give and to take by gift *inter vivos* or testamentary disposition *66*

  (c) Disposable portion and reduction *67*

      (i) Disposable portion of property *67*

      (ii) Reduction of gifts and legacies *68*

  (d) Gifts *inter vivos* *69*

      (i) Form of gifts *inter vivos* *69*

      (ii) Exceptions from the rule of the irrevocability of gifts *inter vivos* *69*

(e) Testamentary succession *71*
    (i) General rules concerning the form of wills *71*
    (ii) Special rules with respect to the form of some wills *72*
    (iii) Appointment of an heir and of legacies in general *72*
    (iv) Universal legacy *72*
    (v) General legacy *73*
    (vi) Specific legacies *73*
    (vii) Executors *74*
    (viii) Revocation of wills and their invalidity *74*
(f) Provisions by the donor or testator in favor of his grandchildren or the children of his brothers and sisters *75*
(g) Distribution of property made by ascendants *75*
(h) Gifts made by marriage contract to the spouses and the children of the marriage *75*
(i) Dispositions between spouses by marriage contract or during marriage *76*

8. Contracts and Contractual Obligations in General *77*
(a) Introductory provisions *77*
(b) Elements essential to the validity of contracts *78*
    (i) Consent *78*
    (ii) Capacity of the contracting parties *78*
    (iii) Object and subject matter of contracts *78*
    (iv) Cause of contracts *79*
(c) Effect of obligations *79*
    (i) General provisions *79*
    (ii) Obligation to give *79*
    (iii) Obligation to do or not to do *79*
    (iv) Damages and interests resulting from nonperformance of obligations *80*
    (v) Interpretation of agreements *80*
    (vi) Effect of agreements on third parties *81*
(d) Various types of obligations *82*
    (i) Conditional obligations *82*
        (aa) Conditions in general and various types of conditions *82*
        (bb) Suspensive conditions *82*
        (cc) Resolutory conditions *83*
    (ii) Obligations subject to time *83*
    (iii) Alternative obligations *83*
    (iv) Joint and several obligations *84*
        (aa) Among creditors *84*
        (bb) Among debtors *84*
    (v) Divisible and indivisible obligations *85*
        (aa) Effects of a divisible obligation *85*
        (bb) Effects of an indivisible obligation *85*
    (vi) Obligations with penal clauses *86*
(e) Extinction of obligations *87*
    (i) Payment *87*
    (ii) Novation *87*
    (iii) Remission of debt *87*
    (iv) Set-off *88*
    (v) Merger *88*
    (vi) Destruction of the subject matter of the obligation *88*

(vii) Action for annulment or recission of contracts *88*
(f) Proof of obligations and of payment *89*
9. Obligations Formed without Agreement *89*
(a) Quasi-contracts *89*
(b) Torts *90*
(i) Insurance code and uninsured motorists fund *90*
(ii) Airplanes *91*
(iii) Animals *91*
(iv) Owners of buildings *91*
10. Marriage Contracts and Matrimonial Property Systems *92*
(a) General provisions *92*
(b) Community property *92*
(i) Assets and liabilities of the community *92*
(ii) Administration of community and
of separate property *93*
(iii) Dissolution of the community *94*
(c) Community property by agreement *95*
(d) System of separation of property *95*
(e) System of participation in acquired property *96*
11. Prescription and Possession *97*
(a) General provisions *97*
(b) Possession *98*
(c) Causes that prevent prescription *98*
(d) Causes that interrupt prescription, and those that suspend the
course of prescription *98*
(i) Causes that interrupt prescription *98*
(ii) Causes that suspend the course of prescription *99*
(e) Time required for prescription *99*
(i) General provisions *99*
(ii) Prescription of thirty years *99*
(iii) Prescription of ten and twenty years *99*
(iv) Special prescriptions *100*
(f) Protection of possession *100*
B. The Commercial Law *101*
1. Merchants *101*
2. Books of Commerce *102*
3. Register of Commerce *102*
4. Partnerships and Corporations *103*
(a) General partnership *103*
(b) Commandite partnership *104*
(c) Corporation with limited liability *104*
(d) Stock corporation *105*
(e) Commandite stock partnership *106*
5. The Law of Exchange *107*
6. Bankruptcy *107*
(a) Cessation of payments and composition with creditors *108*
(b) Liquidation of property *108*
(c) Personal bankruptcy *108*
(d) Rehabilitation *108*
(e) Criminal offenses *109*

7. Maritime Law *109*
    (a) Ships *109*
        (i) Form of contracts *109*
        (ii) Liens *109*
        (iii) Ship mortgages *110*
        (iv) Limitation of liability *110*
    (b) Personnel *110*
    (c) Charter parties and maritime transport *111*
    (d) Maritime sales *111*
    (e) Marine insurance *111*
    (f) Collision, salvage and average *111*
        (i) Collision *111*
        (ii) Salvage *112*
        (iii) Average *112*
    (g) Maritime offenses and courts *112*

C. The System of Civil Courts *113*
  1. Courts of Instance *113*
  2. Courts of Grand Instance *114*
  3. Courts of Commerce *114*
  4. Courts of Appeal *116*
  5. Court of Cassation *116*

D. The Law of Civil Procedure *118*
  1. Procedure before Courts of Instance *118*
  2. Procedure before Courts of Grand Instance *119*
    (a) Initiation of proceedings *119*
    (b) Preparation for trial *120*
    (c) The trial *122*
    (d) Judgment *122*
  3. Procedure before Courts of Commerce *123*
  4. Procedure before Courts of Appeal *124*
  5. Procedure before the Court of Cassation *126*

III. *The System and Administration of Criminal Law* *128*
A. The Substantive Criminal Law *128*
  1. Preliminary Provisions to the Penal Code *129*
  2. Punishment for Felonies and Misdemeanors *129*
  3. Repeaters *130*
  4. Accomplices *131*
  5. Minors *131*
  6. Murder and Assassination *132*
  7. Involuntary (Negligent) Homicide *132*
  8. Excusable Homicide *133*
  9. Homicide Not Qualified as a Crime *133*
  10. Wounding and Voluntary Infliction of Injuries *133*
  11. Theft *134*

B. The System of Criminal Courts *135*
  1. Police Courts *135*
  2. Correctional Courts *135*
  3. Assize Courts *136*
  4. Courts of Appeal *137*
  5. Court of Cassation *138*

C. The Law of Criminal Procedure *138*
   1. Prescription of Prosecution *139*
   2. Preparatory Proceedings *140*
     (a) Preliminary investigation *140*
     (b) Preparatory instruction *140*
        (i) General provisions *140*
        (ii) Appearance of the suspect *141*
        (iii) Orders issued by the judge of instruction *141*
        (iv) Judicial supervision and preventive detention *142*
           (aa) Judicial supervision *142*
           (bb) Preventive detention *142*
        (v) Experts *143*
        (vi) Decisions of the judge of instruction *143*
        (vii) Appeal against decisions of the judge of instruction *144*
        (viii) Reopening of preparatory instruction *144*
   3. Chamber of Accusation *145*
   4. Procedure before Assize Courts *146*
     (a) Preliminary proceedings *146*
     (b) Selection of jury *146*
     (c) General trial procedure *146*
     (d) The trial *147*
     (e) Judgment *148*
   5. Procedure before Correctional Courts *149*
     (a) General trial procedure *149*
     (b) The trial *150*
     (c) Judgment *150*
     (d) Default judgment *150*
   6. Procedure on Appeal from Judgments of Correctional Courts *151*
   7. Procedure before Police Courts and Appeal from Their Judgments to Courts of Appeal *152*
     (a) Ordinary procedure *152*
     (b) Simplified procedure *153*
     (c) Payment of a fine *153*
   8. Procedure before the Court of Cassation *154*
     (a) Petition for cassation *154*
        (i) Conditions and form of the petition *154*
        (ii) Opening of cassation *155*
        (iii) Trial and judgment *155*
        (iv) Cassation in the interest of law *156*
     (b) Petition for revision of a conviction *156*
   9. Reprieve *157*
     (a) Simple reprieve *157*
     (b) Reprieve with probation *157*
   10. Parole *158*

IV. *The System and Administration of Administrative Law* *159*
  A. The Substantive Administrative Law *159*
   1. Religions *159*
   2. Eminent Domain *160*
   3. Printing and Periodical Publications *161*

4. Foreigners *162*

B. The System of Administrative Authorities *164*

    1. Local Administration *164*

        (a) Communities and cities *164*

        (b) City of Paris and Region of *Ile-de-France* *165*

    2. Intermediate Administration *166*

        (a) Departments *166*

        (b) Regions *167*

    3. Central Administration *168*

    4. Administrative Courts *169*

    5. Council of State *170*

        (a) Composition and function of the Council of State *171*

        (b) Judicial function of the Council of State *171*

C. Administrative Procedure and Procedure in Administrative Courts *173*

    1. Administrative Procedure *173*

    2. Procedure in Administrative Courts *174*

    3. Procedure in the Council of State *175*

V. *Legal Officers* *176*

A. Judges *176*

B. The Public Ministry *178*

C. Lawyers *179*

    1. Attorneys *179*

    2. Legal Practitioners *180*

    3. Legal Councilors *181*

D. Notaries *181*

VI. *Decisions of French Courts* *183*

A. Decisions of Civil and Commercial Courts *183*

B. Decisions of Criminal Courts *195*

C. Decisions of Administrative Courts *203*

Footnotes *210*

THE GERMAN LAW *223*

I. *Introduction* *223*

II. *The System and Administration of Civil Law* *224*

A. The Substantive Civil Law *224*

    1. Residence *224*

    2. Prescription *225*

    3. Obligations *226*

        (a) Contents of obligations *226*

        (b) Contracts *228*

            (i) Formation of contracts *228*

            (ii) Performance of contract *230*

            (iii) Recission of contract *231*

        (c) Extinction of obligations *234*

            (i) Performance *234*

            (ii) Deposit (Payment into court) *235*

            (iii) Set-off *236*

            (iv) Release *236*

    4. Property *237*

(a) Possession *237*
(b) Ownership *237*
 (i) Substance of ownership *237*
 (ii) Acquisition and loss of ownership of land *237*
 (iii) Acquisition and loss of ownership of movables *238*
5. Marriage *241*
(a) Entering into marriage *241*
(b) Annulment of marriage *243*
 (i) Nullity of marriage *243*
 (ii) Annulment of marriage *243*
(c) Dissolution of marriage *244*
6. Wills and Estates *246*
(a) Succession on intestacy *246*
(b) Last will *247*
 (i) Testamentary capacity *247*
 (ii) Types of wills *248*
 (iii) Revocation of wills *249*
(c) Forced share *250*
(d) Unworthiness to inherit *251*
B. The Commercial Law *251*
1. Merchants *252*
2. Mercantile Register *253*
3. Commercial Books *253*
4. Partnerships and Corporations *254*
(a) General partnership *254*
(b) Commandite partnership *255*
(c) Silent partnership *256*
(d) Stock corporation *257*
 (i) General provisions *257*
 (ii) Setting up the corporation *257*
 (iii) Organization of the corporation *258*
 (iv) Dissolution of the corporation *259*
(e) Commandite partnership by shares *259*
(f) Corporation with limited liability *261*
5. The Law of Exchange *262*
6. The Law of Bankruptcy *263*
(a) Bankruptcy *263*
 (i) Initiation of bankruptcy proceedings *263*
 (ii) Compulsory composition with creditors *264*
 (iii) Distribution of proceeds *264*
 (iv) Criminal provisions *264*
(b) Composition with creditors *265*
 (i) Initiation of proceedings *265*
 (ii) Composition of proceedings *265*
 (iii) Termination of proceedings *266*
7. Maritime Law *267*
(a) The shipowner *267*
(b) The master *267*
(c) Carriage of goods and passengers by sea *268*
(d) Average, collision, salvage, maritime liens, and marine insurance *268*
(e) Limitation of time *269*

C. The System of Civil Courts *271*
    1. County Courts *271*
    2. District Courts *272*
    3. Courts of Appeal *274*
    4. Supreme Court *274*
    5. Labor Courts *276*
        (a) Trial level labor courts *276*
        (b) Appellate level labor courts *276*
        (c) Error level labor court *277*
D. The Law of Civil Procedure *278*
    1. Procedure before County Courts *278*
    2. Procedure before District Courts *279*
        (a) Initiation of proceedings and proceedings up to trial *279*
        (b) The trial *280*
        (c) Judgment *281*
        (d) Proceedings on appeals from *Amtsgerichte* *283*
    3. Procedure before Courts of Appeal *284*
    4. Procedure before the Supreme Court *286*
    5. Reopening of Proceedings *287*
        (a) Petition of nullity *287*
        (b) Petition of restitution *288*
        (c) Procedure on petitions *288*
    6. Procedure before Labor Courts *289*

III. *The System and Administration of Criminal Law* *289*
A. The Substantive Criminal Law *289*
    1. Penal Law *290*
    2. Minors and Adolescents *291*
        (a) Minors *291*
        (b) Adolescents *292*
    3. Accomplices *292*
    4. Punishment *293*
    5. Repeaters *294*
    6. Probation *295*
    7. Parole *296*
    8. Murder *297*
    9. Manslaughter *297*
    10. Negligent homicide *297*
    11. Wounding and Bodily Harm *298*
    12. Theft and Embezzlement *298*
    13. Robbery and Extortion *299*
B. The System of Criminal Courts *301*
    1. County Courts *301*
    2. District Courts *302*
    3. Courts of Appeal *304*
    4. Supreme Court *304*
C. The Law of Criminal Procedure *306*
    1. Procedure before Trial Courts *307*
        (a) Preliminary proceedings *307*
        (b) Indictment *308*
        (c) Preparation for trial *309*
        (d) The trial *309*
        (e) Judgment *311*

2. Appellate Procedure *313*
3. Procedure on Error *314*
4. Reopening of Proceedings *316*

IV. *The System and Administration of Administrative Law* *318*
  A. The Substantive Administrative Law *318*
    1. Passports *318*
    2. Protection of the Environment against Pollution *319*
    3. The Law of Public Assembly *321*
      (a) Public meetings in enclosed premises *321*
      (b) Open-air public meetings and processions *322*
  B. The System of Administrative Authorities (Offices and Courts) *323*
    1. State Administrative Authorities (Offices) *323*
      (a) Administrative authorities in *Flächenstaaten* *323*
        (i) Local public administration *323*
          (aa) Communities *323*
          (bb) Districts *324*
        (ii) Intermediate public administration *325*
        (iii) Central public administration *326*
      (b) Administrative authorities in *Stadtstaaten* *327*
        (i) State of Berlin *327*
        (ii) Free Hansetown of Hamburg *328*
        (iii) Free Hansetown of Bremen *328*
          (aa) City of Bremen *329*
          (bb) City of Bremerhaven *329*
    2. Federal Administrative Authorities (Offices) *330*
      (a) Federal offices of the lower level *330*
      (b) Federal offices of the intermediate level *330*
      (c) Federal offices of the central level *330*
    3. Administrative Courts *331*
      (a) Trial level administrative courts *332*
      (b) Appellate level administrative courts *332*
      (c) Error level administrative court *333*
    4. Other Administrative Courts *335*
      (a) Welfare courts *335*
        (i) Trial level welfare courts *335*
        (ii) Appellate level welfare courts *335*
        (iii) Error level welfare court *336*
      (b) Taxation courts *336*
  C. Administrative Procedure and Procedure before
    Administrative Courts *337*
    1. Administrative Procedure *337*
    2. Procedure before Administrative Courts *339*
      (a) Procedure before trial level administrative courts *339*
      (b) Procedure before appellate level administrative courts *340*
      (c) Procedure before the error level administrative court *341*
    3. Procedure before Welfare Courts and Taxation Courts *342*

V. *Legal Officers* *343*
  A. Judges *343*
  B. The Public Ministry *344*
  C. Attorneys *345*
  D. Notaries *348*

VI. *Decisions of German Courts* *350*
    A. Decisions of Civil Courts in Civil and Commercial Matters *350*
    B. Decisions of Criminal Courts *363*
    C. Decisions of Administrative Courts *370*
        Footnotes *379*

THE ITALIAN LAW *386*

I. *Introduction* *386*

II. *The System and Administration of Civil Law* *387*
    A. The Substantive Civil Law (Including Commercial Law) *387*
      1. Domicile and Residence *388*
      2. Marriage and Divorce *389*
        (a) Marriage entered into before a minister of the Catholic Church or before a minister of another church recognized by the state *389*
        (b) Marriage entered into before the registrar of marriages *389*
        (c) Nullity of Marriage *390*
        (d) Dissolution of marriage *391*
        (e) Judicial separation of spouses *391*
        (f) Proprietary regime of spouses *392*
          (i) Patrimonial property *392*
          (ii) Community property *393*
          (iii) Community property by contract *394*
          (iv) Separation of property *394*
          (v) Family enterprise *394*
      3. Wills and Estates *396*
        (a) Portion of the estate reserved to unavoidable heirs *396*
        (b) Testaments *396*
      4. Property *398*
        (a) General provisions *398*
        (b) Rights of ownership *398*
        (c) Acquisition of ownership *398*
      5. Obligations *400*
        (a) Provisions common to obligations *400*
        (b) Contracts in general *401*
        (c) Void and voidable contracts *402*
        (d) Rescission of contracts *402*
        (e) Dissolution of contracts *403*
        (f) Payment made by mistake (Money had and received) and unjust enrichment *403*
        (g) Obligations arising from unlawful acts (Compensation for damage caused intentionally or negligently) *403*
      6. Partnerships and Corporations *406*
        (a) Informal partnership *406*
        (b) General partnership *407*
        (c) Commandite partnership *408*
        (d) Stock corporation *408*
        (e) Commandite partnership by shares *410*
        (f) Corporation with limited liability *411*
      7. Limitation of Actions *413*

    8. The Law of Exchange *415*
    9. Bankruptcy *415*
      (a) Settlement with creditors *416*
      (b) Voluntary administration *416*
   10. Maritime Law *417*
  B. The System of Civil Courts *418*
    1. Justices of the Peace *418*
    2. Praetors *419*
    3. Civil Courts *419*
    4. Courts of Appeal *419*
    5. Supreme Court of Cassation *419*
  C. The Law of Civil Procedure *421*
    1. Procedure before Justices of the Peace and Praetors *421*
    2. Procedure before the *Tribunale* *422*
      (a) Initiation of proceedings *422*
      (b) Procedure before the instructing judge *422*
      (c) Final hearing and judgment *424*
      (d) Proceedings on appeal from the *pretura* *424*
    3. Procedure before Courts of Appeal *425*
    4. Procedure before the Supreme Court of Cassation *426*

III. *The System and Administration of Criminal Law* *428*
  A. The Substantive Criminal Law *428*
    1. Penal Law *429*
    2. Punishment *429*
    3. Minors *430*
    4. Repeaters *431*
    5. Accomplices *432*
    6. Homicide *432*
    7. Unintentional Homicide *433*
    8. Homicide as a Consequence of Another Crime *433*
    9. Negligent Homicide *433*
   10. Wounding and Bodily Harm *434*
   11. Theft *434*
   12. Probation *435*
   13. Parole *436*
  B. The System of Criminal Courts *437*
    1. Praetors *437*
    2. Penal Courts *437*
    3. Assize Courts *438*
    4. Courts of Appeal *439*
    5. Assize Courts of Appeal *439*
    6. Supreme Court of Cassation *439*
  C. The Law of Criminal Procedure *440*
    1. Procedure before Praetors *440*
    2. Procedure before Penal Courts *441*
      (a) Preliminary proceedings *441*
      (b) Proceedings before the judge of instruction *442*
      (c) Summary proceedings *442*
      (d) The trial *443*
      (e) Judgment *443*
      (f) Trial in the absence of the accused *444*

(g) Summary proceedings and judgment in cases where the accused
     was apprehended in the commission of a crime   *444*
(h) Procedure on appeal from decisions of the *pretore*   *444*
3. Procedure before Assize Courts   *444*
4. Procedure before Courts of Appeal   *446*
5. Procedure before Assize Courts of Appeal   *447*
6. Procedure before the Supreme Court of Cassation   *448*
    (a) On a petition for the annulment of a judgment   *448*
    (b) On a petition for the revision of a conviction   *449*
7. Bail   *451*

IV. *The System and Administration of Administrative Law*   *452*
A. The Substantive Administrative Law   *452*
    1. Protection of Objects of Artistic and Historical Interest   *452*
    2. Civil Employees of the State   *454*
    3. Care of Roads and Public Thoroughfares   *456*
    4. The System of Taxation   *457*
        (a) IRPF   *457*
        (b) IRPG   *457*
        (c) ILOR   *457*
        (d) INVIM   *458*
        (e) IVA   *458*
        (f) Other indirect taxes   *458*
B. The System of Administrative Authorities (Offices and Courts)   *459*
    1. Local Administration   *459*
    2. Intermediate Administration   *461*
        (a) Provinces   *461*
        (b) Regions   *462*
    3. Central Administration   *465*
    4. Regional Administrative Courts   *466*
    5. Council of State   *468*
        (a) Advisory function of the Council of State   *468*
        (b) Judicial function of the Council of State   *468*
    6. Other Administrative Courts   *469*
        (a) Court of Accounts   *470*
        (b) Water Courts   *470*
        (c) Tax commissions   *471*
            (i)   Tax commissions of the first level   *471*
            (ii)   Tax commissions of the second level   *472*
            (iii) Central tax commission   *472*
C. Administrative Procedure and Procedure before Administrative
    Courts   *474*
    1. Administrative Procedure   *474*
    2. Procedure before First-Level Administrative Courts   *476*
    3. Procedure before the Council of State   *478*
    4. Procedure before Tax Commissions   *481*
        (a) Procedure before first-level tax commissions   *481*
        (b) Procedure before second-level tax commissions   *481*
        (c) Procedure before the central tax commission   *482*

V. *Legal Officers*   *483*
A. Judges   *483*
B. The Public Ministry   *485*

C. Legal Practitioners *486*
   1. Attorneys *486*
   2. Advocates *486*
D. Notaries *488*

VI. *Decisions of Italian Courts* *489*
  A. Decisions of Civil Courts in Civil and Commercial Matters *489*
  B. Decisions of Criminal Courts *507*
  C. Decisions of Administrative Courts *517*

    Footnotes *527*

THE SPANISH LAW *535*

I. *Introduction* *535*

II. *The System and Administration of Civil Law* *536*
  A. The Substantive Civil Law *536*
   1. Domicile *536*
   2. Marriage *537*
     (a) Provisions applicable to both kinds of marriage *537*
     (b) Canonical marriage *538*
     (c) Civil marriage *538*
     (d) Nullity of marriage *539*
     (e) Separation of spouses *539*
   3. Civil Register *540*
   4. Property *541*
     (a) Ownership of property *541*
     (b) Land register *541*
     (c) Acquisition of property *541*
   5. Wills and Estates *542*
     (a) Kinds of wills *542*
     (b) Revocation *543*
     (c) Capacity to inherit *543*
     (d) Forced heirs *544*
     (e) Disinheritance *544*
     (f) Intestacy *545*
   6. Obligations *546*
     (a) Contracts *546*
     (b) Rescission of contracts *546*
     (c) Nullity of contracts *547*
   7. Marriage Contracts *548*
     (a) Dowry *548*
     (b) Paraphernal property *550*
   8. Marital Property *550*
     (a) Community property *550*
     (b) Separate property *551*
     (c) Separation of marital property *551*
   9. Prescription *553*
     (a) Prescription of title and other property rights *553*
     (b) Limitation of actions *554*
  B. The Commercial Law *555*
   1. Merchants *555*

2. Commercial Register *556*
3. Commercial Books *557*
4. Partnerships and Corporations *559*
   (a) General partnership *559*
   (b) Commandite partnership *560*
   (c) Stock corporation *561*
   (d) Corporation with limited liability *562*
   (e) Dissolution of partnerships and corporations *563*
5. The Law of Exchange *565*
6. The Law of Bankruptcy *565*
   (a) Suspension of payments *566*
   (b) Bankruptcy *566*
      (i) General provisions *566*
      (ii) Classes of bankruptcy *566*
      (iii) Accord of settlement *566*
      (iv) Rights of creditors *567*
      (v) Rehabilitation of the bankrupt *567*
7. Maritime Law *568*
   (a) Vessels *568*
   (b) Persons *568*
      (i) The owner and the ship's husband *568*
      (ii) The master *569*
      (iii) Ship's officers and crew *569*
   (c) Maritime contracts *569*
   (d) Risks, damages, and accidents of maritime commerce *570*
C. The System of Civil Courts *571*
   1. Courts of the Peace *571*
   2. Municipal and Country Courts *572*
   3. Courts of First Instance *572*
   4. Courts of Civil Appeal *572*
   5. Supreme Court of Justice *573*
   6. Labor Courts *574*
D. The Law of Civil Procedure *575*
   1. Procedure in Municipal and Country Courts *576*
      (a) Summary proceedings *576*
      (b) Regular proceedings *577*
   2. Procedure in Courts of First Instance *578*
      (a) Regular proceedings *578*
         (i) Pleadings *578*
         (ii) Proceedings on proof *579*
         (iii) Final statements and final hearing *581*
         (iv) Judgment *581*
      (b) Summary proceedings *582*
      (c) Procedure on appeal from municipal and country courts *583*
   3. Procedure in Courts of Civil Appeal *584*
      (a) Summary proceedings *584*
      (b) Regular proceedings *585*
         (i) Procedure up to the final hearing *585*
         (ii) Final hearing and judgment *586*

4. Procedure in the Supreme Court of Justice *588*
(a) Petitions for the cassation of judgments *589*
(i) Petitions for the cassation of judgments for breach of law or legal doctrine *589*
(aa) Procedure on admission of petitions *589*
(bb) Hearing on the merits *590*
(ii) Petitions for the cassation of judgments for breach of form *591*
(iii) Petitions for the cassation of judgments for breach of form and at the same time for breach of law or legal doctrine *592*
(iv) Petitions for the cassation or annulment of arbitration awards *592*
(v) Petitions for the cassation of judgments initiated by the public ministry *593*
(b) Petitions for the revision of judgments *593*
III. *The System and Administration of Criminal Law* *595*
A. The Substantive Criminal Law *595*
1. Crimes and Infractions *595*
2. Punishment *596*
3. Minors *597*
4. Repeaters *598*
5. Accomplices *598*
6. Homicide *599*
7. Wounding and Bodily Harm *600*
8. Theft *600*
(a) Robbery *601*
(b) Larceny *601*
(c) Robbery and larceny in the use of motor vehicles *602*
9. Probation *603*
10. Parole *603*
B. The System of Criminal Courts *604*
1. Courts of the Peace *604*
2. Municipal and Country Courts *604*
3. Courts of Instruction *604*
4. Courts of Criminal Appeal *605*
5. Supreme Court of Justice *606*
C. The Law of Criminal Procedure *607*
1. Procedure in Courts of the Peace and Municipal and Country Courts *608*
2. Procedure in Courts of Instruction *609*
(a) Appellate proceedings *609*
(b) Original jurisdiction proceedings *609*
(c) Preparation of cases for decision of the *audiencia provincial* *609*
(i) Initiation of proceedings *609*
(ii) Person proceeded against *610*
(iii) Testimony of witnesses and experts *611*
(iv) Conclusion of the proceedings *612*
3. Procedure in the *Audiencia Provincial* *613*

(a) Regular proceedings *613*
    (i) Proceedings preliminary to trial *613*
    (ii) The trial *614*
    (iii) Judgment *615*
(b) Urgent (summary) proceedings *616*
4. Procedure in the Supreme Court of Justice *617*
(a) Cassation proceedings *617*
    (i) Petition for cassation of a judgment *617*
    (ii) Petition for leave to file a petition for cassation *617*
    (iii) Proceedings on the petition for cassation *619*
(b) Revision proceedings *620*
5. Bail *622*

IV. *The System and Administration of Administrative Law* *623*
A. The Substantive Administrative Law *623*
1. Spanish Code of Food Supply *623*
2. Spanish Universities *625*
3. Eminent Domain *628*
(a) General safeguards *628*
(b) Proceedings *628*
(c) Provincial jury of expropriation *629*
(d) Payment and taking of possession *630*
B. The System of Administrative Authorities (Offices and Courts) *630*
1. Local Administration *631*
(a) Localities *631*
(b) Municipalities *631*
(c) Large cities *632*
2. Intermediate Administration *633*
3. Central Administration *635*
(a) Offices of central public administration *635*
    (i) Prime Minister *635*
    (ii) Council of ministers *635*
    (iii) Ministers *636*
    (iv) Undersecretaries and directors general *636*
    (v) Provincial delegates *636*
(b) Central consultative offices and offices of control *636*
    (i) Council of State *636*
    (ii) Directorate general of litigation and offices of
    government counsel *637*
    (iii) Legal departments in the various ministries *637*
    (iv) Court of Accounts *637*
4. Administrative Courts *638*
(a) Administrative chambers within *audiencias territoriales* *638*
(b) Administrative chambers within the Supreme Court of
Justice *639*
(c) Administrative revision chamber within
the Supreme Court of Justice *640*
(d) Other administrative courts *641*
    (i) Taxation juries *641*
    (ii) Economic-administrative courts *642*
        (aa) Minister of Finance *642*

(bb)   Central economic-administrative court   *642*

(cc)   Provincial economic-administrative courts   *642*

(dd)   Customs courts   *643*

C.   Administrative Procedure and Procedure before Administrative Courts   *644*

1.   Administrative Procedure   *644*

(a)   *Recurso de alzada*   *644*

(b)   *Recurso de reposición*   *644*

(c)   *Recurso de súplica*   *645*

(d)   *Recurso de revisión*   *645*

2.   Procedure before Administrative Courts   *645*

(a)   Preliminary proceedings   *645*

(b)   Procedure before courts of the first or the only level   *646*

(c)   Appellate procedure   *647*

(d)   Procedure for the revision of judgments   *648*

V.   *Legal Officers*   *649*

A.   Judges   *649*

B.   The Public Ministry   *650*

C.   Legal Practitioners   *651*

1.   Attorneys   *651*

2.   Advocates   *652*

D.   Notaries   *653*

VI.   *Decisions of Spanish Courts*   *655*

A.   Decisions of Civil Courts in Civil and Commercial Matters   *655*

B.   Decisions of Criminal Courts   *667*

C.   Decisions of Administrative Courts   *674*

Footnotes   *681*

NOTES ON LEGAL SYSTEMS OF ADDITIONAL COUNTRIES

THE AUSTRIAN LAW   *689*

I.   *Introduction*   *689*

II.   *The System and Administration of Civil Law*   *690*

A.   The Substantive Civil Law   *690*

B.   The Commercial Law   *690*

C.   The System of Civil Courts   *691*

D.   The Law of Civil Procedure   *692*

III.   *The System and Administration of Criminal Law*   *692*

A.   The Substantive Criminal Law   *692*

B.   The System of Criminal Courts   *693*

C.   The Law of Criminal Procedure   *694*

IV.   *The System and Administration of Administrative Law*   *694*

A.   The Substantive Administrative Law   *694*

B.   The System of Administrative Authorities and Courts   *695*

C.   The Law of Administrative Procedure   *695*

V.   *Legal Officers*   *696*

    A. Judges and the Public Ministry *696*
    B. Attorneys *696*
    C. Notaries *697*

THE SWISS LAW *698*

  I. *Introduction* *698*

  II. *The System and Administration of Civil Law* *699*
    A. The Substantive Civil Law *699*
    B. The System of Civil Courts *699*
      1. Civil Courts in German-Speaking Cantons *700*
      2. Civil Courts in French-Speaking Cantons *701*
      3. Civil Courts in the Canton of Ticino *701*
      4. Federal Court *702*
    C. The Law of Civil Procedure *703*

  III. *The System and Administration of Criminal Law* *703*
    A. The Substantive Criminal Law *703*
    B. The System of Criminal Courts *703*
      1. Criminal Courts in German-Speaking Cantons *703*
      2. Criminal Courts in French-Speaking Cantons *705*
      3. Criminal Courts in the Canton of Ticino *705*
      4. Federal Criminal Courts *706*
    C. The Law of Criminal Procedure *707*

  IV. *The System and Administration of Administrative Law* *707*
    A. The Substantive Administrative Law *707*
    B. Administrative Authorities *707*
    C. The Law of Administrative Procedure *708*

  V. *Legal Officers* *708*
    A. Judges *708*
    B. The Public Ministry *709*
    C. Attorneys *709*
    D. Notaries *709*

THE MEXICAN LAW *711*

  I. *Introduction* *711*

  II. *The System and Administration of Civil Law* *712*
    A. The Substantive Civil Law *712*
    B. The Commercial Law *712*
    C. The System of Civil Courts *712*
    D. The Law of Civil Procedure *714*
    E. The *Amparo* Legislation *714*

  III. *The System and Administration of Criminal Law* *714*
    A. The Substantive Criminal Law *714*
    B. The System of Criminal Courts *715*
    C. The Law of Criminal Procedure *716*
    D. The *Amparo* Legislation *716*

  IV. *The System and Administration of Administrative Law* *717*
    A. The Substantive Administrative Law *717*

      B.   The System of Administrative Authorities and Courts *717*
      C.   The Law of Administrative Procedure *718*
      D.   The *Amparo* Legislation *719*
  V. *Legal Officers* *719*
      A.   Judges *719*
          1.   Judges of Federal District Courts *720*
          2.   Judges of Federal Circuit Courts *720*
          3.   Judges of the Federal Supreme Court *720*
      B.   The Public Ministry *720*
      C.   Attorneys *721*
      D.   Notaries *722*

THE LAW OF OTHER SPANISH- AND PORTUGUESE-SPEAKING COUNTRIES OF THE AMERICAN CONTINENT *724*

THE GEOGRAPHIC EXTENT OF THE COMMON LAW AND ITS DOMINANT FEATURES *726*

THE LAW OF THE SOVIET UNION AND THE COUNTRIES OF THE SOVIET UNION IN CENTRAL AND EASTERN EUROPE *729*

APPENDIX

THE ADMINISTRATIVE STRUCTURE AND LEGAL SYSTEM OF MALAYA *735*
    I. *Introduction* *735*
   II. *The* Adat *736*
      A. *Adat Perpateh* *736*
      B. *Adat Temenggong* *737*
  III. *Hindu and Muslim Influences* *738*
  IV. *The Evolution of Law and State* *738*
      A.   The Straits Settlements *739*
      B.   The Malay States *740*
      C.   The Federation of Malaya *741*
  V. *The Presently Applicable Law* *742*
      A.   The Law of Property and Succession *743*
      B.   The Law of Marriage and Divorce *744*
  VI. *Conclusion* *745*
        Footnotes *746*

CONTEMPORARY TRENDS IN CONTINENTAL AND BRITISH LEGAL EDUCATION *755*
    I. *Introduction* *755*
   II. *Prelegal Education* *756*
  III. *Admission to Law School* *756*
  IV. *Law Schools* *758*
      A.   Law Schools in Continental Europe *758*
      B.   Law Schools in Britain and the Commonwealth *759*
      C.   Teaching Methods *760*
      D.   Courses and Examinations *762*

E. The Student and Law School *765*

V. *The Degree and Admission to the Bar 766*

VI. *Selection and Appointment of Judges 767*

VII. *Selection and Appointment of Law Teachers 769*

VIII. *Conclusion 770*

Footnotes 771

INDEX *781*

Acknowledgments

I am grateful to Professor Myres S. McDougal of Yale University for his helpful criticism, suggestions and evaluation of the manuscript. I am greatly indebted to Professor Covey T. Oliver of the University of Pennsylvania who read and criticized the leading parts of the manuscript and made valuable suggestions which were incorporated into the final version. I am very thankful to Professor Igor I. Kavass of Vanderbilt University for evaluation and criticism of the manuscript and for his encouragement.

I am also indebted to Mr. Jan White, late Associate Law Librarian, for generously giving his time, providing suggestions and making available material in the St. Mary's University Law Library.

I also wish to acknowledge the help of Professor Roy M. Mersky, Law Librarian, and Mr. Guido F. Olivera, Foreign Law Librarian, and the library staff of the Law Library of the University of Texas at Austin for making available to me the pertinent materials.

I also wish to thank the Max-Planck-Institut für ausländisches öffentliches Recht und Völkerrecht of Heidelberg, Germany, and the South Texas Law Journal of Houston, Texas, for their permission to reprint in the appendix to this book my articles published in their journals.

GEORGE E. GLOS

Introduction

The present work deals with the laws of a number of countries. From the historical point of view, the laws of all countries have become more comprehensive, detailed and exhaustive. This trend is due not only to the continuously increasing skill and expertise of the legal profession in regulating the manifold relations of people in all aspects of human endeavor, but also to the steadily growing intervention and control that respective governments exercise over interpersonal relations, with such intervention being increasingly felt by the law.

The law of every country under discussion in this book has attained such an enormous scope that it cannot be encompassed in a single treatise nor in a number of treatises.

The various civil law countries are governed by codes that systematically cover the law in their particular areas. The laws are legislative enactments and are subject to amendment or repeal by other such enactments. For better comprehension of the codes, and especially for the benefit of those who study the law to become members of the legal profession, treatises explaining and commenting on the codes are being published in the respective areas of the law. The treatises present the law in a commentary form and attempt to give a succinct explanation of the points raised so as to bring out the meaning of the legal provisions written in the codes, the true meaning of which cannot sometimes be readily grasped because of its interrelationship with other provisions appearing elsewhere in the code or in other codes and statutes.

This work adopts such a method of presentation. Obviously, it cannot encompass more than a fraction of the law in existence. It therefore concentrates on selected major areas of the law. It also gives an overview of the whole law, which basically falls into the three traditionally distinct areas: civil law, criminal law, and administrative law. Within these areas it deals with the substantive law, the system

1

of courts administering such law, and the law of procedure with whose assistance the substantive law is applied.

The work opens with the General Part, which gives and overview of the law generally applicable in civil law countries. This serves as an introduction to the Special Part (main body of work).

The Special Part deals with the laws of France, Germany, Italy and Spain. Each country is handled in five sections: civil law, criminal law, administrative law, law applicable to legal officers, and decided cases. The cases are translated from the law reports of the four above-mentioned countries in the civil, commercial, criminal and administrative law fields. Under civil law, the work deals also with commercial law.

With respect to substantive civil and criminal law, the work deals basically with the same topics in the French, the German, the Italian and the Spanish law. Varying topics are used in the section on subtantive administrative law. This is due to the great variety of topics that may be selected for discussion in administrative law. Different topics are used here to allow for the treatment of more topics than would be possible if identical topics in the law of all four countries were discussed.

The several topics are similarly treated in all of the four above-mentioned countries. Occasionally, a topic considered in the law of one country will be elaborated upon more than in that of another country in order to bring out its particular features. Within substantive civil law only, the topics dealt with in French law are discussed in greater detail to give an example of the full scope of the law.

Following the sections on civil, criminal and administrative laws, the law pertaining to legal officers, who are instrumental in the application and administration of the law, is given. It is followed by decided cases in all three areas of the law, thus illustrating the ʼpractical application of the law to actual controversies.

The notes and questions following the text provide guides to exploration and cross-sectional learning. They are by no means exhaustive. They indicate rather the technique that may be used in their formulation. The teacher may devise his own technique.

Following the Special Part are Notes on Legal Systems of Additional Countries. They deal chiefly with the laws of Austria, Switzerland and Mexico.

In the Appendix, a survey of the law of Malaya is given to illustrate the way in which English law was adopted by other nations. A survey of Continental and British legal education is also included in the Appendix.

It is hoped that this work will be helpful in the teaching of comparative law, and that it will be useful to the legal profession as well as to anyone seeking information on foreign laws.

GENERAL PART

An Overview of the Law

I. THE SYSTEM AND ADMINISTRATION OF CIVIL LAW

The term *civil law* may be understood in several ways and convey several meanings. In its broadest sense, it denotes the entire civil law system, as contrasted, for instance, with the common law system or the Soviet system. In a more restrictive sense, however, it connotes that part of the civil law system which deals with relations of citizens with other citizens (subject-subject, private law relationships) to the exclusion of relations of criminal and administrative law (public law). In the narrow sense, civil law means that part of private law within the civil law system which is purely substantive law, as contrasted with the law of civil procedure and usually also with commercial law. Here, civil law is taken in the above-mentioned sense of private law and is further discussed under the headings of Substantive Civil Law, Commercial Law, the System of Civil and Commercial Courts, and the Law of Civil Procedure.

Civil law taken in the widest sense has its direct ancestor in Roman law, which set the pattern for the systems presently existing in the many civil law countries and also greatly influenced the legal structure of common law countries.

A. THE SUBSTANTIVE CIVIL LAW

The original model for all existing civil codes is the code of Emperor Justinian (527–565 A.D.), which is known as the *Corpus iuris civilis*. It entered in operation in 533 A.D., as to the *Institutiones* and the *Digesta*, and in 534 A.D., as to the *Codex*

(*Codex repetitae praelectionis* to replace the *Codex Justinianeus* of 529 A.D.); it codified and consolidated the Roman law then in force. All civil codes of the nineteenth century, as well as the presently applicable codes, rely to a greater or lesser degree on this great legal work. Even if the contents of modern codes differ widely from the text of the Roman law, they are inspired by it and adopt the structure of the Justinian code. They generally deal with the various topics of the law by subdividing them into the law of persons (including family law), the law of property (both real and personal), the law of succession, and the law of obligations (contracts and torts). The great part of all substantive civil law fits within this fundamental framework.

In countries where there are no separate commercial codes, the civil code also contains the bulk of the commercial law. Civil codes do not, however, cover the whole field of substantive civil law. In addition to the codes, there exists a vast array of statutes that deal with a multitude of topics not carried in the codes. The codes thus deal with the bulk of the substantive civil law; that is, with the more fundamental rules, which are not likely to be changed very often. The statutes, on the other hand, are subject to more frequent changes and handle new, emerging topics. More fundamental statutes are usually printed as appendices to the codes.

1.   The Law of Persons

The law of persons deals invariably with the acquisition and loss of legal personality by natural and juridical persons and generally with capacity, incapacity, legal personality, minority and majority, domicile and marriage. In the latter case, the law regulates the capacity of parties to marry, the preliminary formalities, and the celebration of the marriage, as well as the effects and the very institution of marriage. It further deals with void and voidable marriages, with the separation of the parties and the dissolution of the marital bond, and with alimony. It then turns to the rules of paternity and affiliation, legitimation and adoption, the parent-child relationship, and guardianship and emancipation.

2.   The Law of Property

The law of property covers a wide range of topics. The codes usually begin with a classification of things into movables and immovables and discuss possession and ownership, including the various modes of acquisition and loss of property by succession, gifts *inter vivos* and *causa mortis*, marriage, and contract. They then proceed with a treatment of usufruct, easements and adverse possession in both movables and immovables.

3.   The Law of Succession

The treatment of the law of succession is usually introduced by a statement of general principles regarding the capacity to succeed to property, the acceptance and renunciation of inheritance, the inventory and limited liability of an heir, the final distribution of the property, and the rules of procedure that are common to both testamentary and intestate succession. The code then deals separately with testamentary succession, namely, with wills, with capacity to make a will, and the formal requirements of wills. As to form, wills are usually classified as public, private, holographic, wills made by members of the armed forces, those made abroad, and those made on vessels and airplanes. The code further deals with heirs, legatees, the office and function of the executor of a will, and with the nullity and revocation of a will. Then follows the treatment of intestate succession in sections discussing succession by lineal ascendants and descendants, by the spouse, by collaterals, and by the state. The codes also carry provisions as to a compulsory portion, the contract of inheritance, and the purchase of an inheritance.

4. The Law of Obligations (Contracts and Torts)

Every civil code has detailed provisions concerning obligations. They come into existence either by contract or by means other than by contract. As to contracts, the codes deal with the creation, effect, transfer and extinction of contractual obligations. A contract comes into being by agreement of the parties, and the parties are bound to comply with the obligations entered into. The obligation incurred can be transferred by assignment, and a party may be subrogated to the rights of another party. Obligations may be extinguished by performance, set-off, and release. Obligations may also come into existence by unilateral promise of performance and can arise out of quasi-contracts and torts. The codes also deal with the breach of obligation, including its consequences and effects, and with void and voidable contracts. The codes sometimes classify obligations into conditional, alternative, to do or to abstain, etc., and deal with the formal requirements of contracts. After dealing with the more general aspects of obligations, the codes treat separately all the various types of obligations. Thus, they deal with sales (covering the entire law of sales), barter agreements, with leases, loans, bailments, suretyship, pledges, liens and mortgages, partnership and agency agreements, contracts for service and to carry out a certain work, brokerage contracts, marriage contracts, gaming and betting contracts, unjust enrichment, and so on.

As to torts, the civil codes deal with negligence and the duty of the tortfeasor to pay damages, usually under the heading of a duty to compensate the injured party to the extent of his loss. The provisions are rather of a general character and apply to all torts.

B. THE COMMERCIAL LAW

Although commerce is as old as society itself, and although commerce must have been regulated by definite rules in antiquity, no comprehensive commercial codes existed before the nineteenth century. In ancient Rome, basic commercial transactions were governed by civil law. These rules were later incorporated in the *Corpus iuris,* together with a few special rules dealing with bankers and some dealing with maritime trade that were taken from the *lex Rhodia.* The reason for the paucity of known rules lies in the fact that traders governed themselves by customs of their trade and had their disputes decided by other traders acting as judges to the best advantage of the trade. Consequently, there was no need for the state to impose its own rules upon them.

With the exception of the Laws of Oléron, which date from the end of the eleventh or the beginning of the twelfth century and which embodied customary maritime law as defined by the maritime tribunal of Oléron, and with the further exception of the *Consolato del Mare*, which originated in the twelfth or thirteenth century and which embodied the commercial practices of the nations then trading in the Mediterranean Sea, there did not exist any other general collections of commercial law and practice until the nineteenth century, apart from laws and ordinances dealing with particular topics that have been enacted from time to time in the several European countries. The first commercial code appeared in France in 1807, and others soon followed suit. Some countries do not have any separate commercial code, however, but instead have the pertinent rules of commercial law embodied in the civil code and in separate statutes.

Existing commercial codes usually contain some treatment of the following topics: merchants as parties to mercantile transactions, partnership and the several types of corporations, the several types of mercantile transactions, the law of exchange, bankruptcy, maritime law and, where applicable, the special rules of procedure in commercial cases. Commercial codes never cover the entire field of commercial law; they deal only with the traditional, classical topics of commercial transactions. The remainder of the field is regulated by additional statutes. Those of particular importance frequently appear in the appendix to the commercial codes.

1.   Merchants

The codes start by giving a definition of merchants, i.e., persons who are bound by the provisions of the commercial code. They then deal with trading under a firm name, and firm registration, with the stock and commodities exchange, and with brokers and commercial agents, like factors or commission merchants.

2.   Partnerships and Corporations

A partnership is defined in the codes as an association, the members of which are jointly and severally responsible for the acts of any one or more members. Their responsibility is personal, and they are liable for the acts and obligations of the partnership with their private property. Corporations are associations that have legal personality separate of their individual members. There are three basic types of corporations: a corporation with limited liability, a commandite corporation, and a stock corporation.

A corporation with limited liability is in fact a partnership with the liablity of the partners limited to the extent of a stipulated, definite amount, which each partner brings into the business. The commandite corporation (a general and limited partnership corporation) is founded upon an idea of a combination of partnership and limited liability. It has some members as partners liable jointly and severally and other members whose liability is limited to a definite amount, which they contribute as capital to the common stock, and who are not liable beyond the sum so contributed. It is thus a limited partnership. These companies are suited for relatively small business ventures, with only a small number of members, even though they may in fact control large sums of money and large property holdings.

The only company suited to practically unlimited membership, and consequently to large holdings of property, is the stock corporation. In such a corporation, the members have their individual interests in the corporation expressed in the holding of shares. The liability of a stockholder is limited to the shares he holds. He does not risk anything except the money he paid for those shares, up to their full value. Apart from the partnership, all the above types of corporations are current in the countries of the civil legal system. The stock corporation and the corporation with limited liability are the most popular types of business associations.

3.   Mercantile Transactions

The codes deal specifically and in detail with the several most current mercantile transactions. They are mainly sales, transactions of commission merchants, contracts for the carriage of goods, warehouse contracts, and insurance contracts. Most of these transactions were known in antiquity and were regulated by Roman law.

4.   The Law of Exchange

The use of bills of exchange is of a very ancient origin, traceable to ancient Babylonia. Bills of exchange were used in ancient Rome, as well as in the Middle Ages, to facilitate trade relations among nations. Gradually, ordinances were made in all countries of Europe regulating their use. When comprehensive commercial codes made their appearance in the nineteenth century, the law of exchange was embodied therein. Although quite similar, the rules of the various codes differed in details, with the result that less certainty existed after the enactment of the various ordinances than before, when the law of exchange depended wholly on mercantile custom. A movement for a uniform regulation of the law of exchange was thus created, which eventually led to an international regulation of the subject by the Geneva convention of June 7, 1930, whereby a uniform law of bills of exchange was agreed upon by the contracting parties. Similarly, a uniform check law was agreed upon in the Geneva convention of March 19, 1931. Practically all civil law countries of Europe and the rest of the world acceded to these two conventions, with the result that today there are two systems of the law of bills of exchange and check law existing in the world: the Geneva Convention system, and the Anglo-American system which, as the English common law, applies only in English-speaking countries.

The commercial codes of the several civil law countries, parties to the Geneva Conventions, carry the provisions of the conventions. They deal with capacity of parties, form and interpretation of a bill of exchange, drawing, negotiation, acceptance, guarantee, payment, protest, acceptance and payment for honor, rights, duties and liabilities of parties, and prescription. They further deal with promissory notes and checks along the same lines.

5.   Bankruptcy

The problem of recovery of money from a debtor unable to pay is known to have existed in the commerce of antiquity. The rules for recovery, as far as it is known, turned against the person of the debtor, and he was exposed to cruel physical punishment, slavery, and even death. This was the law of Assyria, Babylonia, and Egypt, and also of ancient Rome. Thus the Law of XII Tables, Table III 6 (451–449 B.C.) apparently allowed creditors to cut shares out of the body of a debtor in accordance with the size of the claim and absolved them of liability for cutting more or less. The exact meaning of the provision is, however, in doubt.

The cruelty of these provisions was somewhat mitigated by the gradual removal of corporal punishments, so that, from the eighteenth century, a debtor would be punished by imprisonment only. The remnants of this approach can still be found in modern law, which exposes a fraudulent debtor to imprisonment.

The origins of the modern law of bankruptcy, however, can be found in the Roman law dealing with debtors who were unable to meet their obligations in cash but had more or less sufficient assets to satisfy the claims. The method used in the Roman Republic was an institution of the pretorian law, known as *missio in possessionem* (universal succession), whereby all of a debtor's property was sold to a *bonorum emptor* by the creditors, who would then distribute the proceeds among themselves. In Imperial Rome, an additional method developed whereby the creditors appointed a *curator bonis distrahendis,* who was entitled to sell pieces of the debtor's property individually (*venditio bonorum*). Since, however, as a consequence of these proceedings, the debtor was always declared an infamous person, he inevitably did his best to avoid such proceedings. He actually was able to do so by voluntarily ceding his assets to his creditors (*cessio bonorum*). By so doing, he also escaped physical punishment if the sum realized by the sale of his property fell short of the sum due to his creditors. This privilege of being free from physical punishment was extended, however, only to debtors who were found free of any lack of due care in the conduct of their business.

The Middle Ages did not bring anything new, and the ordinances of the various states applied primarily Roman methods. The idea of the rehabilitation of the debtor was fully developed only in the commercial codes of the nineteenth century. There, an honest bankrupt, after the distribution of his assets among his creditors, would be absolved of all liability and given a new start in life.

The codes deal with the subject in logical order. They begin with the concept and declaration of bankruptcy, and the effects of such a declaration, and proceed with bankruptcy courts and officers, the administration of the estate, proof and priority of debts, property available for the payment of debts, realization and distribution of property among creditors, and the discharge of the bankrupt. The code also provides for the avoidance of bankruptcy in proper cases by composition or arrangement of the debtor with his creditors. The codes usually carry provisions with respect to offenses with the object of punishing fraudulent and dishonest bankrupts.

6.   Maritime Law

As mentioned above, maritime law was the relatively best regulated part of commercial law in antiquity and the Middle Ages. Reference has already been made to the *lex Rhodia.* It originated probably around 400 B.C. and in later form dealt most likely with all aspects of maritime trade. It consisted of the customary law of the traders operating from the island of Rhodes and was later adopted by the Romans. It is known, however, that both the Phoenicians and the Carthaginians had comprehensive codes of maritime law. In the Middle Ages, the Laws of Oléron (eleventh or twelfth century) and the *Consolato del Mare* (twelfth or thirteenth century) were the established rules of maritime trade, that is, apart from the rules governing maritime trade that existed in individual countries, like the Statutes of Marseilles (circa 1253 A.D.), the *Capitulare nauticum* of Venice (circa 1255 A.D.), the *Ordenanza de los Reyes Católicos sobre el comercio marítimo* (1480–1500 A.D.), the *Ordenaçoēs Filipinas* (1603 A.D.), the *Jus anseaticum maritimum* (1614 A.D.), the *Ordonnance de la marine de Louis XIV* (1681 A.D.) and a later Venetian code, the *Codice per la marina mercantile veneta* (1786 A.D.).

Many provisions dealing with maritime trade were incorporated into commercial codes during the nineteenth century. They deal with the ships; with owners, captains, officers, crew and passengers; with maritime contracts (affreightment), charterparties and bills of lading; with bottomry (respondentia), and bonds; and with risks, damage and loss in maritime commerce (accidents, jettisoning of cargo, shipwrecks), and maritime insurance.

C. THE SYSTEM OF CIVIL AND COMMERCIAL COURTS

The institution of courts or tribunals is of very ancient origin, for laws had to be enforced by public authority. Thus references to courts exist in the known history of ancient nations. It is well known that the Romans established an efficient system of administration of justice. The system of courts administering Roman law served then as a model for the administration of justice in the European countries. Yet courts in their present-day form developed gradually over the centuries, and the currently existing system dates from the end of the eighteenth century at the earliest. The formative era of courts administering codes is the nineteenth century. When comprehensive civil and commercial codes were enacted, courts were set up to administer them.

The presently existing system of courts in civil law countries follows a uniform pattern that is very similar to the one existing in common law countries. Division between courts is both territorial and hierarchical. There are always several courts of limited jurisdiction and several of general jurisdiction, as well as several appellate courts. There is only one supreme court in both civil and criminal matters, however, which is the highest tribunal in the country and a court of final resort. Civil and commercial courts are staffed by judges; there are no juries.

1. Courts of Limited Jurisdiction

Courts of limited jurisdiction are limited to hear disputes where the claim does not exceed a certain sum of money. Expressed in dollars, this currently begins in some countries at approximately $1,000 and runs up to about $2,000 in others. The sum limiting the court's jurisdiction is, however, increased to keep in step with rising prices and to maintain the area of limited jurisdiction at a more constant level. In addition to jurisdiction expressed by the sum of the claim or the value of the matter in dispute, courts of limited jurisdiction are empowered to hear disputes of a definite nature and an anticipated limited extent and value, such as those arising between landlord and tenant, travelers and innkeepers, travelers and carriers, and two neighbors (as to the boundaries of their land), as well as those disputes concerning defects in purchased animals, damage done by wild animals, support and alimony suits, and the like.

Cases in courts of limited jurisdiction are always heard by one judge, who is often relatively young, possibly just over thirty years of age, and at the beginning of his judicial career. Every limited jurisdiction court as a territorial unit is staffed with several judges. The court is headed by a president and has one or several vicepresidents, all of whom are judges of higher rank and corresponding age.

Since the courts of limited jurisdiction are courts of first resort and deal with cases that are both minor and from a legal point of view not particularly complex, the parties involved are always free to bring their disputes before the court rather informally and present them in person without being represented by a counsel. Legal representation is thus not required; but should the parties elect to be represented, they must, as a rule, employ the services of a fully qualified lawyer who is admitted to practice in the particular court or country, as the case may be.

2.   Courts of General Jurisdiction

Courts of general jurisdiction are courts that are empowered to hear disputes without any upper limit as to the value of the subject matter and, generally, all civil disputes that are not by special enactment referred to specially designated tribunals. Further, they do not transact business that falls within the competence of courts of limited jurisdiction. They are frequently called courts of first instance, because they are trial courts where cases are brought for trial. In addition to their function of trying cases, they frequently act as courts of appeal from the courts of limited jurisdiction.

Courts of general jurisdiction are, as a rule, collegiate courts, with cases being heard by a panel of three judges. In some countries, easier cases are tried by a single judge, and only the more important ones by a senate of three judges. The tribunal always has several judges on its staff from whom the actual senates are formed. The court is headed by a president, and every senate by a senate president. Members of the court are usually older judges with many years of judicial experience.

Although in some European countries juries were in existence in the remote past, the civil law system as developed from the Roman system does not have juries (apart from certain criminal cases). The judge thus finds the facts and applies the law to these facts; he acts as both judge and jury in an Anglo-American trial. The proceedings are thus cheaper, faster and less cumbersome than in jury trials.

Parties appearing before courts of general jurisdiction must be represented by counsel. An action can be filed only by a fully qualified lawyer, admitted to practice in the court or in the country, as the case may be. A party who for some reason is unable to retain an attorney, in proper cases will be assigned one by order of the court. The chief reason for this rule lies in the fact that the parties involved should have obtained legal advice before bringing an action. By appearing, the attorney warrants that his client's claim is properly brought for the court's consideration. In this way, obviously unfounded claims never reach the court, and also, many valid claims may be settled out of court on advice of counsel. When an action is brought, the attorney presents it in the proper form and proceeds with it in accordance with the law and the rules of court. He thus performs an essential function in the administration of justice, one which no layman could perform.

3. Appellate Courts

Appellate courts are those that hear appeals from decisions of lower tribunals. Usually, courts of general jurisdiction handle appeals from decisions of courts of limited jurisdiction. Separate appellate tribunals are set up to hear appeals from decisions of courts of general jurisdiction.

Where courts of general jurisdiction act as appellate courts from decisions of courts of limited jurisdiction, the appeal is always handled by a senate of three judges (appellate senate), even though the court may be formed by a single judge to hear cases of general jurisdiction in the first instance. No further appeal lies against the decision of the appellate senate; and in some civil law countries, the decision is not subject to any further proceedings in error. Cases that originate in courts of limited jurisdiction are, due to their limited scope, not of fundamental importance and do not qualify for proceedings in the highest tribunals.

Appellate tribunals, which hear appeals from decisions of courts of general jurisdiction, are high tribunals of great prestige. They are staffed with a president, several senate presidents, and appellate judges. Appeals are heard by senates composed of three, and in some countries five, members. In countries where general jurisdiction courts do not act as courts of appeal from decisions of courts of limited jurisdiction, these appeals are also heard by the appellate tribunals.

As in courts of general jurisdiction, the parties involved in appellate proceedings must be represented by properly admitted attorneys.

4. Supreme Courts

Every civil law country has one highest tribunal that acts as the court of final resort. Recourse to this tribunal is, as a rule, by leave only and only by way of error, called revision or cassation, and not by way of an appeal. Since appeal is excluded, the error is concerned with matters of law only.

The function of the court is to interpret the law in an authoritative manner and to maintain uniformity of interpretation and application of the law throughout the whole country. The court sees to it that the law is understood and applied in all courts in the same way and that no discrepancies arise.

The court is headed by a president and has several senate presidents and justices on its staff. Cases are heard by senates (chambers) of five, and in some countries seven, members. In certain cases (e.g., for the purpose of overruling a previous decision of the court), the court will form larger senates having many more members, and may, ultimately, have all the justices of the court on the deciding panel.

Parties must be represented by counsel, who must, as a rule, meet additional requirements to qualify for appearance before the supreme court. They usually have to be admitted to practice before the court in addition to a previous admission to practice before lower courts.

5.   Commercial Courts

Commercial courts are special courts administering the commercial codes and commercial law in general. Commercial courts have a long history that can be traced to the twelfth century. They were set up by associations of merchants for the purpose of settlement of commercial disputes. They were staffed by merchants who were elected by the entire body of merchants. The elected judges were frequently called "consuls" and the tribunals "consulates." Merchants of the nations trading in the Mediterranean Sea, and especially Italian traders, contributed most to the development of medieval commercial courts. These courts proceeded informally, in accordance with the established customs of the trade, handing down their decisions speedily, usually the same day, or within two or three days at the latest.

The medieval commercial courts gradually came under the supervision of the states in which they sat until, in the eighteenth and nineteen centuries, they became courts administering commercial law embodied in the commercial codes and statutes. At present, in some civil law countries, separate commercial courts exist in those commercial centers having adequate court business. In cities that would not warrant the setting up of a commercial court, a judge or a chamber in commercial matters functions within the existing courts of limited and general jurisdiction. At the court of appeal level, commercial cases are dealt with by ordinary appellate tribunals handling civil appeals. In other civil law countries, commercial law is administered by ordinary civil law courts together with other civil matters. This is so especially in countries that do not have separate commercial codes (e.g., Italy).

Where commercial courts exist, they apply simplified rules of procedure to achieve a speedier transaction of business, as contrasted with ordinary civil law business. Parties have to be represented by counsel only in cases transacted at and above the general jurisdiction level. In cases transacted at the limited jurisdiction level, legal representation is not required. In some countries, legal representation is not required even at the general jurisdiction level.

D.   THE LAW OF CIVIL PROCEDURE

The law of civil procedure is the law that implements the civil law. It is designed to enable a party to enforce the rights given to him by the civil law. It contains the rules that govern the procedure before civil and commercial courts.

Since no court could function without definite rules of procedure, it is plain that the law of procedure is as ancient as the substantive law itself. Thus, proceedings before the courts of ancient Rome were conducted in accordance with detailed rules of procedure. As in substantive law, the Roman law of procedure served as a model for the rules of procedure adopted in the civil law countries, and it also greatly influenced the procedure adopted by ecclesiastical courts. Just like the substantive law, the law of procedure was not uniform in any given country. With the movement for the codification of the substantive law in the late eighteenth and nineteenth centuries, the law of procedure also was codified and embodied in codes of civil procedure.

The codes of civil procedure govern all aspects of civil procedure and contain the rules with respect to jurisdiction and venue; parties and legal representation;

writs, citations, the service of process, and general rules concerning procedure; proceedings in the trial courts; judgments, rulings and orders; and appeal and appellate proceedings, recourse against decisions on appeal, further means to attack the validity of judgments, and the execution of judgments. The codes also carry provisions concerning specialized proceedings, as in family relations (divorce, alimony, child support, etc.), devolution of estates, voluntary (non-contentious) jurisdiction, and arbitration. In addition to the matters dealt with in the codes, separate statutes exist that independently handle other aspects of specialized procedure, as in bankruptcy, attachment and garnishment, forcible sale, procedure in landlord-tenant actions, and the like. Some of these specialized procedures are, however, included in the codes.

1.   Jurisdiction and Venue

The codes deal with jurisdiction with respect to subject matter and territorial jurisdiction. They further deal with the settlement of disputes as to jurisdiction; with judicial officers (judges), non-judicial staff, and experts and officers appointed to assist judges; and with the disqualification of judges and other officers.

2.   Parties and Legal Representation

The codes define the capacity of parties to sue and be sued. They deal with plurality of parties and third party proceedings, with representation of parties by attorneys, with costs of proceedings, with bonds, and with indigent parties, etc.

3.   Writs, Citations, the Service of Process, and General Rules Concerning Procedure

The codes contain detailed provisions as to the form of documents made by the court and those made by the parties, as to the process and the service of process within and out of the court's jurisdiction. They further deal with the time within which any action of the parties must be taken and with the computation of time, with the setting of a day for hearing and possible postponement, with the effects and consequences of nonappearance and the expiration of the time set, with reinstatement, and with adjournment. The general provisions concerning procedure deal with such items as the principle of publicity of hearings, conduct of hearings, functions of the court and the parties at a hearing, records made at a hearing, and maintenance of order in the courtroom.

4.   Proceedings in Trial Courts, Judgments, Rulings and Orders

The codes carry provisions as to the pleadings (statement of claim, plea, replication, etc.) and the joinder of issues, the burden of proof (by documents, witnesses, experts, the parties themselves), and the preservation of evidence (depositions), etc. There are further provisions on court decisions, such as final judgements, rulings and interlocutory orders, including their form and content.

The actual proceedings in a court of general jurisdiction differ slightly from those in a court of limited jurisdiction in that cases tried in a court of general jurisdiction are usually heard by a senate of three judges and are more elaborate and formal, whereas those tried in a court of limited jurisdiction are heard by a single judge and are less elaborate and more informal. In a court of general jurisdiction, the presiding judge, the chairman, is the authority in the trial room. He directs the trial in accordance with the rules of civil procedure embodied in the code. No one can speak or ask questions without his permission.

After the case is called, the plaintiff has to present his case, i.e., to prove his allegations in the pleadings by the proper methods of proof. Witnesses are presented by the plaintiff. They are examined by the chairman and, with his permission, by other members of the court and the counsel for the plaintiff and cross-examined by the counsel for the defendant. After evidence is given by the plaintiff, it is the defendant's turn to do likewise. Since the chairman does all the questioning, and practically exhausts the field, there is not much scope left for either counsel in the examination of witnesses. Documents presented as proof by either party must be submitted to the court before trial so that they may be examined at trial.

In some countries, evidence of witnesses is not given under oath. Only when the court so orders is a witness invited to repeat under oath the essential part of his evidence he gave informally. This usually indicates that the court believes the witness but has no other evidence to support his statements, so it wishes to increase the weight of his evidence. Such oath is in the nature of a "decisive oath." Should the witness refuse to give evidence on oath, he will usually not be compelled to do so; but the court will draw the conclusion that his evidence was probably false and will not rely on it.

As the evidence is taken, the chairman dictates *viva voce* a verbal account of the proceedings to the court recorder, who types it word for word. This typewritten record is the official transcript of the proceedings. Both parties, their counsel, and the witnesses listen to what the chairman dictates and may request him to rephrase a sentence so as to express more accurately what has been said. In addition to this official record, a stenographer may be present to record word for word all that has been said, or a tape recording of the proceedings can be made, so as to assist the chairman in the recording of the official transcript.

When all the evidence has been taken and when both counsel and the parties themselves have had an opportunity to speak to the questions raised, the chairman will close the hearing. The court will then retire to the deliberation room to discuss the case and give judgement. Usually, however, the court will announce that the judgement is being reserved and will be given at a later day. As soon as the court has made its decision, the judgement is written down and proclaimed in open court.

5. Appellate Proceedings and Further Means to Attack the Validity of Judgments

An appeal from the decision of the trial court and the appellate proceedings are minutely regulated. The codes deal with judgment on appeal, the ordering of a new trial, and further means to attack the validity of the appellate decisions. Appellate decisions may be subject to a further appeal, but they are always subject to cassation (declared null and void because of nonobservance of the law). A judgment may also be attacked in revision proceedings on the ground that new facts have come to light since the case was definitively decided and became *res judicata*. Appellate proceedings deal with new facts, which for some legitimate reason could not have been presented at trial, but are mainly concerned with questions of law. The appeal usually alleges that the trial court erred in its application of law to the facts found.

6. Execution of Judgments

If the judgment debtor does not voluntarily comply with the terms of the court decision, the judgment can be executed by official action. The codes provide for and regulate the various methods of execution. There are special rules as to the execution of money judgments, execution against personal belongings and real estate of the debtor, forcible sale, attachment and garnishment proceedings, and the like.

7. Specialized Proceedings

Specialized proceedings concern proceedings in family relations, divorce, alimony and child support, and legitimation and adoption. They also deal with proceedings regulating the devolution of estates, both testamentary and on intestacy; noncontentious jurisdiction, e.g., entry in official records, registration of land, and appointment of guardians, etc.; and also arbitration proceedings including the appointment of arbitrators, awards and the means of attacking an award. They may also deal with landlord and tenant proceedings and with the complex bankruptcy proceedings, etc.

II. THE SYSTEM AND ADMINISTRATION OF CRIMINAL LAW

The civil law countries have an efficient system of criminal law. Under the phrase "criminal law and its administration" is understood the totality of substantive law by these tribunals.

Criminal law differs widely from civil law in that it has the statute as its only source and in that it is enforced by public authority, the state, acting on behalf of the entire community. Whereas in a dispute of civil law the dispute exists between persons or between a person and the state acting as a private citizen and not in the exercise of sovereign authority, in a criminal action the state acts as the prosecuting authority. All persons within the state territory are bound to observe the criminal laws, and they expose themselves to criminal prosecution in the case of their breach.

A. THE SUBSTANTIVE CRIMINAL LAW

Today, all criminal law is embodied in criminal codes and statutes, but this has not always been so. In the remote history of mankind, the principles of vengeance, retribution and composition were applied by private persons and public authorities against offenders. These principles were prominent in the fragmentary ancient legislation. Since law was closely knit with religion, the offense was not only to the law of man, but also to the law of God. This much appears from the law of ancient Babylonia, India and Persia, as well as from the Mosaic law. In ancient Greece and Rome, criminal justice was motivated by public interest in the maintenance of order and tranquility—*salus populi suprema lex*. To that end, the state would resort to appropriate punishments that would deter potential offenders from the commission of crime. As a rule, the penalty meted out to apprehended offenders grossly exceeded the injury caused to society. This motivation of criminal law was carried over and further elaborated in the medieval practice of crime suppression, which relied mostly on terror and cruelty. A strong opposition to this approach built up from the seventeenth century and resulted in great humanitarian reforms undertaken during the eighteenth and nineteenth centuries.

The contemporary criminal codes, which originated in the nineteenth century, are based on a scientific approach to the problem of crime and rely on the ideas of prevention and rehabilitation rather than on those of deterrence and suppression. Criminal law is based on the strict observance of the principle *nulla poena sine lege*. There is no offense unless it has been made an offense by the law, and if committed, it may be followed only by punishment provided for by the law and imposed upon the offender by procedures stipulated by law.

The codes approach the subject in two parts, the general and the particular. The general part deals with: the division of punishable acts into infractions, misdemeanors and felonies; the person of the offender and criminal responsibility; juvenile offenders; attenuating and aggravating circumstances; grounds on which an otherwise punishable act may be excused; attempt and participation in the act; accessories before and after the act; and punishments and their application. The particular part deals systematically with individual types of offenses and their punishment, usually as follows:

1. Offenses against the State

These are provisions with respect to offenses against the external and internal security of the state, against international law, public administration and the administration of justice, against public order, and the like. In particular they comprise treason, avoidance of military duty, espionage, piracy, rebellion, sedition, riot, falsification of official documents and seals, and counterfeiting of currency, etc.

2. Offenses against the Person and Personal Liberty

Offenses against the person comprise murder, manslaughter, and bodily injuries in their various forms; those against personal liberty deal with false imprisonment, abduction, threats, and compulsion.

3. Offenses against the Family and Honor

Offenses against the family deal with bigamy and the various sexual offenses and with offenses against good morals. Offenses against honor comprise the law of slander and libel.

4. Offenses against Property and Creating Public Danger

These provisions deal with larceny and robbery, swindling and obtaining property by false pretenses, willful damage to property, usury, etc. Acts creating public danger include arson, commission of crimes involving the use of explosives, and causing of damage by means of explosives or gas.

The codes further carry many other detailed provisions concerning offenses, including those against public health and religion. They also deal with the suppression of cruelty to animals, etc. The actual sequence adopted varies from code to code, but the codes strictly maintain the principle *nulla poena sine lege*. The division of offenses into those against the state, the person, the family, and property also is substantially maintained.

B. THE SYSTEM OF CRIMINAL COURTS

In its history, the system of criminal courts follows closely that of civil courts. In antiquity, kings exercised both civil and criminal jurisdiction over their subjects. In later times, this power became vested in the state. The state maintains, however, a separate system of civil and criminal courts. The division into civil and criminal jurisdiction existed in ancient Rome and has since then been systematically maintained. There are several limited jurisdiction, general jurisdiction, and appellate courts; but there is only one supreme court having both civil and criminal jurisdiction. Only when the volume of business warrants it do criminal courts have their own buildings separate from the civil court of the same jurisdictional area and level. Otherwise, they constitute only one of the two branches of the administration of justice, which they in fact are, and share the same building with the corresponding civil court. The supreme court forms civil and criminal chambers. The courts are staffed with judges, but in most civil law countires jury trials are held in cases involving serious offenses. In general, criminal courts are a replica of civil courts of the same jurisdictional level.

1. Courts of Limited Jurisdiction

Courts of limited jurisdiction usually deal only with infractions, although sometimes they deal with misdemeanors. Their powers are also limited with respect to the punishment they can impose. Since the criminal codes indicate the punishment for individual offenses, the courts are restricted to the area of cases brought before them. By a proper jurisdictional norm, the courts of limited jurisdiction can impose fines up to a certain maximum (e.g., the equivalent of $500) and terms of imprisonment up to a certain maximum (e.g., one year), but must stay within the limits of punishment provided by the criminal codes for the particular offense charged (special limit) if its maximum is less than the jurisdictional limit. Sometimes there is no jurisdictional limit on fines, but only the special limit. The limits run usually between $200-$500, expressed in American dollars, for fines and from two months to three years for imprisonment.

Cases in courts of limited jurisdiction are heard by single judges, but in some countries (e.g., Germany), provision is made for jurors (lay judges) to sit with the judge in some cases. Judges in criminal courts of limited jurisdiction have the same qualifications, and usually are the very same persons as the judges in the civil courts of limited jurisdiction. The criminal court, if separate from the civil court, has its own president. If the courts are not separate, there is just one president who will assign judges to hear civil and criminal cases.

Legal representation is not required, but if the accused wishes to be represented, he has to be represented by a fully qualified attorney.

2.   Courts of General Jurisdiction

Courts of general jurisdiction hear cases that exceed the limits imposed on courts of limited jurisdiction. They thus hear cases of more serious misdemeanors and of felonies. The provisions differ, however, from country to country. Cases are usually heard by senates of three judges, but in most civil law countries provisions are made for jury trials either in all cases or only in the case of specially enumerated felonies. Jury trials also differ from country to country, but they are basically of two types. In some countries, the jury sits separately from the panel of judges and the trial proceeds much along the lines of an English or American felony trial. In other countries, the jurors sit and vote together with the judges as lay judges.

As to its internal organization, the court has a president and several senate presidents and judges. Legal representation is mandatory in trials in courts of general jurisdiction. If the accused for some reason is unable to retain an attorney, the court will appoint one.

3.   Appellate Courts

Appellate courts hear appeals against decisions of trial courts. In some countries (e.g., Germany and Italy), appeals against decisions of criminal courts of limited jurisdiction go to the appellate senate of a criminal court of general jurisdiction. In other countries (e.g., France), all appeals go to a separate court of appeal.

Courts of criminal appeal correspond in all respect to courts of civil appeal. In fact, in most civil law countries, appellate courts function as both courts of civil and criminal appeal. Each court of appeal has several civil and criminal senates. The senate hearing an appeal is composed of three, but in some countries, (e.g., Italy) of five judges. The accused must be represented by counsel.

4.   Supreme Courts

There is one supreme court in every civil law country that is the highest tribunal in the country and the court of final resort in both civil and criminal matters. All that has been said previously in Section C.4 of Part I, dealing with supreme courts within the system of civil courts applies with equal strength to their criminal business.

C. THE LAW OF CRIMINAL PROCEDURE

The law of criminal procedure contains the rules that provide for the application of criminal law. Since substantive criminal law cannot be applied without definite rules of criminal procedure, it is plain that such rules must have existed in antiquity together with those of criminal law. It is known that ancient nations had such rules of procedure dealing with the application of criminal law.

Criminal procedure is basically of two types: accusatory and inquisitory. The early criminal procedure in ancient Rome was accusatory, but it gradually changed into inquisitory in the late years of the Republic and became inquisitory during the Empire. The system of Roman criminal procedure based on inquisitory principles was handed down to posterity and adopted by various kingdoms in the Middle Ages as the Roman law of criminal procedure and as a model for their own rules. This approach continued for a considerable time, but it was eventually replaced by the accusatory system. Hand in hand with the advent of modern criminal law at the beginning of the nineteenth century, the modern law of criminal procedure made its appearance. Like the substantive criminal law, it was codified in the nineteenth century when the presently existing codes of criminal procedure came into being.

The various codes of criminal procedure arrange their subject matter in logical order. They first carry provisions as to the public authorities entrusted with prosecution of crime, with jurisdiction of criminal courts, and with parties, witnesses and experts. They then deal with preliminary investigation and the initiation of criminal prosecution. The next step is to regulate preparation of the case for trial and the trial itself, including judgment in the case of infractions, misdemeanors, lesser felonies and serious crimes. Another part of the codes deals with appeals and proceedings for the cassation and revision of judgments. Yet another handles the execution of judgments, and a further section deals with specialized proceedings.

1. Public Authorities Entrusted with the Prosecution of Crime, Courts, and Parties

The codes contain detailed provisions as to jurisdiction with respect to subject matter and territorial jurisdiction and with respect to parties to criminal proceedings and their legal representatives. These parties include the public ministry, private prosecutors, the accused and his legal representative. The public ministry is a constitutionally created department entrusted with the prosecution of persons accused of having committed criminal offenses. It is an independent department of public administration under the supervision of the ministry of justice. Since preliminary examination of the suspect is conducted at the request of the public ministry while the suspect is under arrest, an independent judicial authority supervising and directing the examination is necessary to protect the constitutional rights of the suspect. Such an authority is the judge of instruction, who directs the examination while at the same time he is safeguarding the rights of the suspect. In addition to the public ministry, which takes the part of the prosecutor, the person injured (damaged) by the criminal offense may join in the prosecution. On the part of the defense stands the suspect, legally represented by his attorney. The codes also have provisions dealing with the role of witnesses and experts in criminal proceedings, and with the presentment and collection of evidence.

2. Preliminary Investigation and the Initiation of Criminal Prosecution

The codes have provisions as to the investigation of crimes, the giving of information leading to the arrest of a suspect, the arrest, the investigation of the suspect, the viewing of the place of crime, and the corpus delicti. They also deal with the search of premises and persons, seizure of documents and material evidence, taking of evidence of witnesses, and securing of expert evidence, e.g., medical, ballistic, etc.

3. Preparation for Trial

Should the suspect not be cleared at the end of the preliminary investigation but, on the contrary, appear to be involved in the crime, the public prosecutor may request the court under whose supervision the preliminary investigation was conducted to order him to stand trial. If the court issues the order, the suspect becomes the accused, and preparation for the trial will begin. The case will be set for trial and notice of the fact will be given to prosecution and defense. The procedure at the trial itself depends on the seriousness of the offense that the accused is alleged to have committed. Even the court that will try the case will be determined in accordance with the offense charged. A court of limited jurisdiction will try persons accused of having committed infractions and sometimes some misdemeanors. A court of general jurisdiction will usually try misdemeanors and lesser felonies, and a jury trial before a court of general jurisdiction will usually be held in capital offenses and cases of serious felonies.

4. Trial and Judgment

(a) Persons accused of simple offenses (infractions and usually some lesser misdemeanors).   Persons accused of infractions and some minor misdemeanors are tried by a court of limited jurisdiction composed of a single judge. There usually is no jury. For that reason, the proceedings are also much simpler and less formal than those before higher courts. Otherwise, the rules are substantially the same as those applied before courts of general jurisdiction.

(b) Persons accused of lesser crimes (usually lesser felonies and some more serious misdemeanors).   Lesser crimes are tried before a court of general jurisdiction, usually composed of three judges. There is no jury. Otherwise, the trial follows the same rules applied in trials of serious crime. The senate president is the chairman and the authority directing the trial. He examines the accused and the witnesses. Other members of the court and parties may speak and ask questions only with his permission. The court rules on facts and law and gives judgment.

(c) Persons accused of serious felonies.   Since the trial of a person accused of a serious crime is by jury (except in Spain, where there are no juries), the codes contain provisions as to the office of the juror and the formation of juries. As a rule, jurors now sit together with judges, although in some countries they sit separately. Where they sit together with judges, they decide together with them as lay judges. Where they sit separately, they decide questions of fact, whereas the court decides questions of law.

The court is nearly always a senate of several, usually three, judges. The senate president is the chairman and presides over the trial. He is the moving power of the trial; he directs, in accordance with the rules of criminal procedure, the entire proceedings. No one may speak, be it the parties or members of the court, without permission of the chairman. After the case is called, the accused is interrogated by the chairman as to his identity and the generalia. Then the prosecution presents its case, and then the defense. Witnesses are examined by the chairman and cross-examined by the prosecution and by the defense counsel. When all the evidence has been presented, the prosecutor makes his final address. Then the defense addresses the court and the prosecution replies. The last word always belongs to the defense and to the accused himself.

If the jury sits together with the judges forming the court, the court retires to the deliberation room where voting takes place after discussion. If the accused is found guilty, sentence is imposed after further deliberation. Judgment is usually reserved on the punishment; but if the accused is acquitted, he is set free at once.

If the jury sits separately from the court, the court will set questions of fact for the jury's decision, and the jury will retire to the jury room and, after its decision, it will inform the court of the results of its vote. If the jury finds the accused not guilty, the court will acquit him and will set him free. If he is found guilty, the court will impose punishment after deliberation or, most likely, will reserve judgment which will be pronounced at a later session of the court.

5. Proceedings on Appeal and for the Cassation and Revision of Judgments

Decisions of trial courts are, in general, subject to appeal. The codes carry detailed provisions regulating appellate proceedings. In the rare instances where decisions of trial courts are not subject to appeal (as, for instance, with some jury trials on the ground that the verdict of the jury representing the country cannot be modified), they are always subject to cassation. Judgments of appellate courts are, in general, not further appealable but are subject to cassation. Cassation is a proceeding in error with its only object the breaking of the judgment on formal grounds, i.e., nonobservance of the rules of procedure or misapplication of the law. It thus deals with points of law only, whereas an appeal deals with both points of fact and law. Judgments of criminal courts are further subject to revision on the ground that new facts have come to light since the trial which show the innocence or lesser responsibility of the accused. The codes of criminal procedure have provisions regulating cassation and revision proceedings.

6. Execution of Judgments

The codes of criminal law and of criminal procedure provide for the execution of judgments. There are also several separate statutes and regulations dealing with the matter. Fines imposed in criminal proceedings are collected much like judgment debts in civil proceedings by civil execution. Only if they are uncollectible because of lack of assets on which execution could be levied may an alternate term of imprisonment be imposed. Terms of imprisonment are served in institutions set up and maintained by the government for that purpose. The order for the commitment of the convict is issued to the proper government prison authority by the criminal court pronouncing the conviction. Further proceedings, such as application by the convict to be placed on probation rather than have a term of imprisonment imposed, are regulated by the codes of criminal procedure or special statutes.

7. Specialized Proceedings

Specialized proceedings usually deal with the prosecution of minors, rehabilitation, extradition of criminals, etc. They may also provide for proceedings on the application for parole by convicted offenders after they have served a sufficient part of their terms to so qualify.

III. THE SYSTEM AND ADMINISTRATION OF ADMINISTRATIVE LAW

Although public administration (i.e., the administration of a state) is, of course, as ancient as the existence of states, and many states in antiquity (e.g., Rome) and in the Middle Ages (e.g., England under Henry II) were known for their public administration, administrative law is of a very recent origin and is a creation of the nineteenth century. Before modern administrative law came into being, public administration was carried out by the government in a purely discretionary way. This type of public administration existed in Europe until the early nineteenth century when it was supplanted by the newly created "police state," which was only a more sophisticated version of the old form. Only in the second half of the nineteenth century, with the introduction of administrative law, were government and public administration carried out according to law and not at the government's discretion.

The body of rules to be followed by the government and its subordinate administrative bodies in the exercise of their administrative functions is termed administrative law. Sources of administrative law are administrative statutes, decrees and regulations of the administrative authorities, and decisions of administrative tribunals.

Substantive administrative law includes both uncontested administrative procedure and contested administrative procedure. In the exercise of public administration, the state acts as the holder of sovereign authority, but in accordance with law. If the legality of its actions is contested by a citizen, the administrative act is reexamined by the proper state authorities at the several levels of state administration; if the citizen still contests the final decision adopted by the administration, the dispute is submitted for the decision of independent administrative tribunals. There the state is only a party, just like any citizen.

A. THE SUBSTANTIVE ADMINISTRATIVE LAW

The fundamental rules of administrative law are embodied in the constitutions of the several civil law countries. These documents lay down the framework of the administrative system in the country. The principles enunciated there are then further elaborated in a number of statutes that contain a detailed treatment of the functions of the various administrative branches of government, define their rights and duties, and the procedures to be followed. Public administration is carried out strictly in accordance with the law, and the constitution and statutes of any given country contain the appropriate law. On the strength of this law, the government is empowered to make further regulations to put the law into effect and to apply it in proper and relevant circumstances. The body of administrative law is very extensive, and it is a definite advantage to have it consolidated in an administrative code. Consolidations of this type exist in all advanced European countries.

Administrative law deals with the various subject matters of public administration, with the authorities exercising the powers of public administration, and with the procedures applied.

With respect to subject matter, virtually all activity of public interest, and in any event all activity subject to licensing, is a proper matter of public administration. So administrative law deals with the possession of fire arms, licensing of liquor, affixing of posters in public places, betting, lotteries, fishing and hunting, public amusement places, roads and vehicles, newspapers and printing, public libraries, hotels, restaurants, public assemblies, racing, supply of water, gas and electricity, expropriation for public purposes, public education, funeral parlors, cemeteries, hospitals, fairs and shopping centers, telephones, telegraphs, railroads and other means of transport (such as bus lines and air lines), banks and savings banks, insurance companies, the exercise of trade and professions, public service, and the like.

As far as the authorities exercising the powers of public administration are concerned, there are central authorities at the ministerial level and subordinate authorities at provincial, district and local levels comprising all facets of public administration. Basically, there is only one money-raising department, the ministry of finance and its system of tax-collecting offices. All other departments disburse money so raised, although they also collect fees for certain services offered to the general public. All these authorities themselves are governed by administrative law.

The procedures applied by administrative authorities in the exercise of their functions are also determined, prescribed and set by administrative law.

B. THE SYSTEM OF ADMINISTRATIVE
AUTHORITIES (OFFICES AND COURTS)

The system of administrative authorities differs slightly from country to country, but the general pattern of public administration is quite uniform. On the top of the structure are the heads of the state and the government. Their positions are defined by both constitutional and administrative law. They are the top administrators. At the ministerial level, there are departments of public administration, each handling matters falling within the area of their competence, i.e., the ministry of finance on one hand and the prime minister's office and all other departments on the other. The basic department among them is the ministry of interior, which is charged with all general public administration not specifically assigned to other specialized ministries. These other ministries include defense, foreign affairs, trade, agriculture, food and supply, welfare, education, health, transport and communication, etc. These central administrative authorities ensure uniformity in public administration.

The territory of every country is subdivided into larger administrative units, usually called provinces, which are directly subordinated to the ministry of interior in matters of general administration and to the other ministries with respect to business falling within their specialized functions. Extensive administration offices, situated in the seat of every province, are in charge of public administration within the territory of the province.

The territory of every province is further subdivided into smaller administrative units, usually called districts. There are administrative offices in every district responsible for its administration. They are subordinated to the proper provincial administrative authority.

Individual townships and communities have their own communal administration headed by the mayor and the city council. In accordance with their size, they either fall within a district or form a district themselves. Larger towns always form a district; and if they are big enough, they form a unit equivalent to a province with their several subdivisions being districts. This is always so in the case of a nation's capital and other very large cities.

The several ministries, provincial, district and communal authorities exercise the administrative functions of public administration.[1]

In addition to the executive offices of public administration, in every European country there is a supreme administrative court and, in some, there are lower level administrative courts. Judges of these tribunals are appointed under the same conditions as those of civil courts and must hold the same qualifications. They are usually appointed from among experts in their field of specialty within public administration. Cases are heard by panels composed of usually three judges at a lower level and five judges at the final level. Parties have generally to be represented by counsel properly admitted to practice in administrative tribunals. The supreme administrative court is a court of great prestige and ranks equally with the supreme court in civil and criminal matters. No further appeal lies against its decisions. It is headed by a president and has a vice-president and several justices on its judicial staff.

In countries where there is only one administrative tribunal, i.e., the supreme administrative court, it hears appeals against decisions of the central executive authorities (ministries), which are not otherwise appealable to any other executive authority. In countries where there are lower administrative courts, they hear appeals from the decisions of executive offices of public administration of an intermediate level, with further appeal possible to the supreme administrative court. Even in these countries, however, appeals against decisions of the central executive authorities (ministries) are made only to the supreme administrative court.

C. THE LAW OF ADMINISTRATIVE PROCEDURE AND PROCEDURE BEFORE ADMINISTRATIVE COURTS

Administrative procedure is based on statutes, government decrees and regulations. It is composed of rules designed to apply the provisions of substantive administrative law. Administrative procedure is thus an essential part of administrative law. Administrative procedure is fundamentally of two types: uncontested and contested.

Uncontested, administrative procedure is the day-to-day routine of administrative authorities. The measures taken by these authorities are not contested by those who may be affected by them. The great majority of administrative decisions are not contested. The procedure applied to arrive at these decisions is governed by the principles of informality, ex officio investigation, privacy, opportunity of any interested party to be heard and to inspect official documents, written proceedings, reasonably speedy handling, and a reasoned decision.

Uncontested administrative procedure is informal in the sense that it is not bound by any specific formalities, such as proceedings in a court of justice. Proceedings are initiated ex officio or at the request of an interested party and are proceeded with by official authority. The authority must search for, collect and assemble all relevant facts and information. The proceedings are held in private and are not open to the general public; only interested parties may attend. Interested parties are entitled to be notified of any proceedings that may affect them and must be given opportunity to give the authority the benefit of their views. They are usually entitled to inspect official documents dealing with such matters. Administrative proceedings are transacted in writing, i.e., all component parts of the transaction must be in writing. Administrative proceedings must be conducted with reasonable speed and culminate with a reasoned decision on the matter.

Even though uncontested, administrative decisions must comply with the law and are subject to review by superior administrative authorities in the exercise of their official functions.

Contested administrative proceedings are governed by the same principles as the uncontested proceedings but are more formal. The party contesting the official measure may act in person or through a representative, who may be a legal counsel. The party must present his views and requests in writing and must present evidence, if any, to support his claim. In addition, the party should discuss the matter orally with the proper officers of the deciding authority so that the issue is sufficiently clarified and no misunderstanding or unclarities exist.

Once the administrative authority has made a decision, it must be served in the form of an order on the contesting party, who can appeal it to the proper superior administrative authority within a fixed time limit. The proceedings there follow the same rules. After the superior authority has made its decision, the contesting party may appeal it to the next higher superior administrative authority until the central, i.e., the highest, administrative authority is reached. The decision of this authority if final in the sense that it cannot be appealed to any other administrative authority, since there is none. Yet the decision is appealable.

The appeal goes to an administrative tribunal. The particular system varies from country to country. In some, the matter may be submitted to the tribunal only as an appeal from the decision of the central administrative authority; in others, it may reach the tribunal at an earlier stage. Accordingly, there may be only one supreme administrative tribunal for the entire country or a hierarchy of administrative tribunals with the supreme administrative tribunal at the top of the structure. It is always assumed, however, that the matter is important enough to warrant these proceedings. Matters of limited importance and value are usually restricted, insofar as appeal is concerned, to the decision of an authority or a tribunal beyond which no futher appeal lies.

Proceedings before administrative tribunals are much like proceedings before civil courts. Parties are represented by counsel, and the matter is presented to the court just as it would be in a civil court with similar rules of evidence applicable. Parties prepare and file written pleadings; witnesses and experts give evidence, are examined, cross-examined, and re-examined; detailed records of the proceedings are kept; and the court deliberates and pronounces a reasoned judgment, which is delivered in written form to the parties. No further appeal lies against decisions of a supreme administrative court.

IV. LEGAL OFFICERS

No legal system can function without proper legal officers. The office of the judge is the most ancient of all legal offices; judges held office in biblical times. In modern times, the system has grown much more complex. Apart from judges, there are officers of the public ministry, attorneys and notaries. These people are the moving power of the legal system in every country, and no legal business could be transacted without their assistance.

A. JUDGES

In civil law countries, candidates for judgeships are usually drawn from law graduates who seek entry into the judicial service. Applications are processed by the department of justice and selection is made on merit. The successful applicant must undergo rigorous training to prepare himself for a judicial career. For about three years, he will have to work in succession as an assistant to a judge, to a procurator, and to a government counsel. He may also spend part of the training time in a lawyer's office as a junior counsel. After completing his training, he must pass an examination; he is then appointed to a subordinate position within the legal system. Only after another three to five years will he be appointed an independent judge, procurator, or government counsel and assigned to discharge these functions. This appointment is usually for life, that is, until retirement, which is generally at the age of seventy.

The first judicial appointment is usually to a judgeship in a court of limited jurisdiction. In time, the young judge will be promoted to a judgeship in a court of general jurisdiction. Then, on a merit and seniority basis, he may ascend to the appellate and final resort courts. Even if he is not appointed to the bench of one of the highest courts, he will ascend within the hierarchy of the court of general jurisdiction to hold the position of senate president, vice-president, or president of the court.

The above system ensures that very experienced judges hold high judicial positions. Thus, a judge of the supreme court must have risen through the entire judicial system and must have held a whole string of judgeships in his twenty to thirty years on the bench before being appointed to the supreme court.

These appointments and promotions are handled by the ministry of justice in cooperation with the judges themselves. The appointments are then formally made by the minister of justice (concerning lower positions) or the head of state (concerning higher positions).

In the exercise of their judicial functions, the judges are independent and are bound only by law. They cannot be removed except for misconduct, and they cannot even be moved (promoted) to the bench of a higher court without their consent. Disciplinary proceedings against a judge may usually be instituted in the court of final resort, and he may be disciplined only in accordance with its decision.

B.   THE PUBLIC MINISTRY

The courts being independent in the handling of their judicial business, the state can appear before them only as a party. In civil actions, the state is represented by the office of the government counsel, who can sue on behalf of the state and who will defend actions brought against the state. In criminal matters, the state must prosecute persons suspected or accused of having committed criminal offenses. This is done by the office of the procurator.

These two branches of the public ministry are constituted as independent authorities, just like the courts. Like the courts, they are maintained out of public funds alloted to them through the ministry of justice, which takes care of their separate budgets.

The offices of the public ministry are centrally organized, with a head office for the whole territory of the state. The advocate-general and procurator-general are at the top of the hierarchy. These offices then have their representatives at all hierarchical levels of jurisdiction. In the exercise of their functions, they are subordinate to the ministry of justice and through it to the government. They take instructions from the branch of government they represent in a particular suit. In criminal matters, the procurators have to see to it that offenders are brought to justice and law-abiding persons are protected.

In some countries (e.g., France), a representative of the public ministry has to be present in court in civil actions dealing with subject matters as stipulated by law (e.g., in actions against persons absent), thus ensuring an additional protection of the interests of the parties, and he may be present in all actions. He may, and in some cases must (e.g., when one of the parties is in a mental institution), address the court at the conclusion of the proceedings, giving the court the benefit of his independent opinion and advice on the subject matter.

C.   ATTORNEYS

Legal representation of parties to litigation is of very ancient origin and was well developed in early Greece and Rome. Roman advocacy flourished again in Italy in the eleventh century, and after several centuries of arbitrary rule and absolutism, which is not a desirable atmosphere for a legal profession to exist in, it was again brought to life at the end of the eighteenth and during the nineteenth centuries. Genuine legal representation can exist only in a government by law, so that when the form of government within a nation is arbitrary absolutism, there is no order of law in existence that the legal profession could uphold and maintain. In such states, attorneys become quite useless, since they cannot assist a party by legal means. As a consequence of the French revolution in 1789, European states gradually became legal states, and advocacy again found its due place within the law.

The legal profession is organized today either as a unitary profession, everyone being basically admitted to practice in every capacity in all courts in the entire country (as in Austria) or as a divided profession, where a lawyer is admitted to practice only in a certain capacity and only before the court of the bar to which he was admitted (as in France before, and to some extent after, the 1971 reform of the legal profession); or the system may take a middle course between these two positions (as in Italy or Spain). Where the profession is united, the advocate deals with clients himself. If he represents a party in litigation, he prepares the case for trial, tries it, and proceeds to appellate proceedings and finally to the court of final resort, if necessary. Where the profession is divided, the client deals with one lawyer in the matter, while another lawyer, a trial lawyer, is hired to argue the case in court. An additional trial lawyer may be needed to argue the case on appeal, and yet another in the court of final resort.

To be admitted into the profession, the candidate must have a law degree from a university and successfully undergo a period of about three years of further preparatory training as an assistant to a fully qualified legal practitioner of senior standing. He must then pass an examination that qualifies him to full membership within the legal profession. Once admitted, the European attorney practices on his own in a one-man practice. There are also partnerships, but they are usually limited to a few partners only. Legal firms are thus generally small with two or a few partners and the necessary clerical staff.

D. NOTARIES

Notaries are public officers discharging important functions. They are appointed from legal pracitioners or from law graduates who immediately after graduation enter the profession and undergo a period of several (usually three to seven) years of preparatory training. Once fully qualified, the candidate may exercise his profession; but to become an independent notary, he must succeed to a vacant position by government appointment.

The notary is a public officer and holds public office. The number of these offices is determined by the government in accordance with public need. Every judicial district must have a notary, but due to the amount of business, several are appointed. Each of them is usually appointed for life (like a judge) within a definite territory (e.g., that of a court of limited jurisdiction) and all notarial business within that territory is to be performed by the notary or notaries of that district. When appointed, the notary must take out a bond as security for monies held by him in the exercise of his official functions.

Notaries have their own offices, often with several fully qualified candidates for notarial appointment in their employ. They also employ those who are doing their preparatory practice and the necessary clerical staff. Their offices are thus larger than those of an attorney and are generally quite profitable, since notaries hold a virtual monopoly within their territory on all dealings falling within their competence.

Notaries execute and make authentic all documents that by law must be so executed. Such documents are mainly contracts for the sale of land, which must be notarized in order to be registered in the public records. Notaries establish the identity of the parties in such transactions and officially certify the transaction. Parties usually prefer to have their more important transactions reduced to writing and officially certified even if the law does not exact such formality. Notaries legalize documents and issue certified copies. Their most important business is centered, however, on wills, powers, and generally probate and administration of estates. Parties frequently have their wills drawn by a notary and ask his advice on the distribution of the estate. The notary is thus the legal adviser to persons making testamentary dispositions, since they prefer to have these documents properly drawn, executed, and certified by the public authority of which the notary is the representative.

Being a legal officer of the state, the state uses the notary's services in the area in which he is most active in his day-to-day practice, namely, in the probate and administration of estates jurisdiction. The notary is generally appointed to perform the functions of a probate court commissioner under the supervision of the court for which he is acting, thus relieving the court of this function.

FOOTNOTE

1. In connection with administrative authorities, it is interesting to mention the office of the ombudsman, which currently exists in such countries of Northern Europe as Sweden, Finland, Denmark and Norway, and which was recently adopted in some British countries. The office is based on the idea of a royal inspector, a king's eye, whose duty it is to watch the royal officers in the performance of their duties and report his findings to the king. Such was the office of the king's eye in ancient Babylonia and the office of the inspector-general in some European countries and the office of the first ombudsman in Sweden in 1713, when it was set up by King Charles XII.

   The function of the contemporary Swedish ombudsman is to supervise the application of law by public authorities and thus to supervise public servants in the exercise of their official duties. The ombudsman is appointed by the House of Parliament for a term of four years and is answerable to it. Although he has the power to inspect the work of public servants, he acts chiefly on the strength of complaints received from the general public. He cannot, however, override any official decision or correct any wrong done. He can bring the matter to the attention of the proper officer, convey to him his findings, and request him to proceed accordingly. This reminder brings about a new official action in the matter, and if warranted, the previous decision will be rescinded and the wrong corrected. The ombudsman may, however, institute disciplinary proceedings against public servants for breach of official duty. The office of the Finnish, Danish and Norwegian ombudsman is modeled on that of Sweden.

It is apparent from the duties and functions of the ombudsman that his office is in existence for the purpose of correcting the inadequate functioning of public authorities, especially because of the lack of an effective appeal against decisions made by these authorities. It is thus an admission of inadequacy and an attempt to provide some remedy.

A properly functioning system admitting complaints to administrative superiors with a further recourse to administrative courts would appear to provide an effective safeguard against erring officialdom without the need for an ombudsman. Yet, due to the human element involved, no administrative system is flawless. Consequently, an officer of the type of an ombudsman may fulfill a useful public function. The institution of ombudsman is particularly appealing to the general public, which prefers a simple approach to public administration and is distrustful of administrative machinery. It is thus often this element of gaining more public trust that causes a government to set up an office of ombudsman.

The recently introduced office of the French *médiateur* falls into this category. The office was set up in 1973 (Law of January 3, 1973, J.O., January 4, 1973, *Recueil Dalloz* 1973, *Législation*, p. 65; and Decrees of Application of March 9, 1973, J.O., March 10, 1973, p. 2619) to receive complaints from members of the general public concerning the functioning of the organs of public administration arising out of their relations with members of the general public. The function of the mediator consists of looking into the matter and, where he finds the complaint meritorious, recommending a solution to the proper authority favoring the person involved. Where the public authority complies with the recommendation, the matter will be settled to the satisfaction of the person involved, and consequently all further administrative proceedings and proceedings in administrative courts will be avoided. The mediator is thus in the position both to assist the general public in its dealings with public authorities and to help smooth the functioning of public administration.

The French mediator has yet further powers; that is, where he finds that a particular public officer has committed a breach of his official duties, he may recommend the institution of disciplinary proceedings by the proper public authority against such public officer.

SPECIAL PART

The French Law

I. INTRODUCTION

The present legal system of France is directly based on that established by Napoleon in the early years of the nineteenth century. Napoleon's order in turn goes back to the 1789 revolution, which gradually reshaped the old pre-revolutionary order and enabled Napoleon and the legal profession of his time to make a modern legal system out of a medieval one. The ancient era of French law began at the dawn of the French state. It developed gradually until 1789, when this slow process was interrupted and the then existing system forcibly remodeled.

Prior to 1789, France had basically two legal systems. One in the north, which comprised the so-called *pays de droit coutumier*, and another in the south, the *pays de droit écrit*. As the names themselves suggest, the north was ruled by customary law and the south by written law. The customary law was more fluid. The influence of Roman law on it was not too pronounced, and it was not in writing. In contrast, the southern law relied heavily on Roman law and was in writing. The written law in the south was, due to the Roman law it contained, much more uniform than the customary law in the north, which varied from province to province (*coutume générale*) and from place to place (*coutume locale*). The most important among them was the customary law of Paris (*coutume de Paris*), which gradually overshadowed all other customary laws.

In 1453, King Charles VII had the Ordinance of Montil-iès-Tours enacted, which provided for the compilation and reduction to writing of all customary law. As a result, by the end of the sixteenth century, the customary law was in writing. The diversity in customary law still continued, however, and was perpetuated somewhat by the pronouncements of provincial Parliaments. There were fourteen

35

Parliaments in existence. They were courts of law, but they also exercised legislative and administrative functions. In addition to their judicial functions, these Parliaments issued policy statements called *arrêts de règlement*, which ostensibly defined and interpreted the existing legal rules, but which in fact amounted to judicial legislation.

A unifying factor in French law was exercised by the law of the Church, that is, by canon law. It governed the law dealing with births, marriages, deaths and the devolution of estates, areas of law that traditionally belonged to the ecclesiastical jurisdiction. Another unifying factor in French law was present in the Royal Ordinances, which were applicable to the whole country. They were too few, however, to have a marked effect until the second half of the seventeenth century when, due to the efforts of Colbert (1619–1683), ordinances of Louis XIV enacted a unified law of civil procedure (*Ordonnance de 1667 sur la procédure civile*), criminal procedure (*Ordonnance de 1670 sur l'instruction criminelle*), commercial law (*Ordonnance de 1673 sur le commerce*), and maritime law (*Ordonnance de 1681 sur la marine*). In the first half of the eighteenth century, parts of civil law were unified in several ordinances under Chancellor D'Aguesseau (1668–1751), namely the law of gifts (*donations*) in 1731, the law of wills (*testaments*) in 1735, and the law of family settlements (*substitutions*) in 1747.

This is where the French law stood in 1789. From then on, until the Napoleonic codes, a period of complete overhaul of the French law (*période de droit intermédiare*) took place. The Napoleonic codes were enacted in spite of opposition, and they may have never been enacted but for the strong determination of Napoleon. They are the Civil Code (1804), the Code of Civil Procedure (1807), the Commerical Code (1808), the Code of Criminal Procedure (1808), and the Penal Code (1810). They are still in power as amended by later legislation with the exception of the Code of Civil Procedure and the Code of Criminal Procedure, both of which have been completely replaced by new enactments.

French administrative law is found chiefly in the Administrative Code, which is of recent origin, but a considerable part of administrative law is embodied in separate codes and enactments.

All codes are supplemented by a great number of statutory provisions.

II. THE SYSTEM AND ADMINISTRATION OF CIVIL LAW

A. THE SUBSTANTIVE CIVIL LAW

The Civil Code of 1804 is in power as amended. Its provisions are supplemented by a great many statutes, which appear in the Code under pertinent articles. The Code, which has 2283 articles, is introduced by six articles dealing with the publication of laws and their effect and application.[1]

The Code is then presented in three books: Book 1. The law of persons; Book 2. The law of property; and Book 3. The various modes of acquisition of property.

Book 1 (The law of persons) has the following titles: I. Enjoyment of civil rights and their loss; II. Registration of births, marriages and deaths; III. Domicile; IV. Persons absent; V. Marriage; VI. Divorce; VII. Paternity and affiliation; VIII.

Adoption; IX. Paternal authority; X. Minority, guardianship and emancipation; and XI. Majority and guardianship of insane persons and spendthrifts.

Book 2 (The law of property) has the following titles: I. Classification of property; II. Ownership; III. Usufruct, use, and right to use premises; and IV. Easements.

Book 3 (The various modes of acquisition of property) has the following titles: I. Intestate succession; II. Gifts *inter vivos* and testamentary succession; III. Contracts; IV. Obligations that arise without agreement; V. Marriage contracts and matrimonial property systems; VI. Sales; VII. Barter; VIII. Leasehold; IX. Partnership; X. Loan; XI. Depositum and sequestration; XII. Aleatory contracts; XIII. Agency; XIV. Suretyship; XV. Settlement of disputes; XVI. Compromise; XVII. Pledge; XVIII. Priorities and mortgages; XIX. Execution sales and order of preference among creditors; and XX. Prescription and possession.

The following are topics selected from the French substantive civil law.

1. Domicile (*Domicile*)[2]

The domicile of every Frenchman with respect to the exercise of his civil rights is the place where he has his principal seat.[3]

A change of domicile is effected by actually living in another place together with the intention to make it the principal seat; intent is shown by a declaration made at the municipal office of the place abondoned as well as at the municipal office in the place where domicile of choice is acquired. Failing these declarations, proof of intent to acquire new domicile will depend on the circumstances.

Citizens appointed to temporary public office retain their existing domiciles, unless they take proper steps to acquire new ones; those appointed to public office for life automatically acquire new domiciles at the new places where they must exercise their functions.

A husband and wife may have separate domiciles without affecting thereby their marriage relationship. Where the spouses live separately and institute proceedings for divorce or separation, their separate residences become their separate domiciles as of right.

An unemancipated minor is domiciled with his father and mother. Where they have separate domiciles, the minor is domiciled with that parent with whom he resides. An adult under guardianship is domiciled with his guardian. Persons of full age who are habitually in the service of another and who live in his house also have his domicile.

Succession to the estate of a decedent will take place in the decedent's domicile.

Where a party elects a domicile which is not his true domicile for the purpose of a particular business, all actions with respect to that business can be undertaken at the place so elected.

QUESTIONS

1. Consider the provisions concerning residence and domicile in the German, the Italian, and the Spanish law. Is there a distinction between the two in all these systems?

2. Does the French term *domicile* include both residence and domicile as understood in Anglo-American law? Does the French law make a distinction between domicile and residence? Is there a significant difference between the French meaning of domicile and residence on the one hand and the Anglo-American meaning of the two terms on the other? See White v. Tennant, 31 W.Va. 790, 8 S.E. 596 (1888).

---

2.   Marriage (*Mariage*)[4]

(a)   Capacity to marry (*Qualités et conditions requises pour pouvoir contracter mariage*).[5]   A man under eighteen and a woman under fifteen years of age may not marry, but a dispensation may be obtained for good reason. Marriage is based on the consent of the parties to enter into it. No one can enter into a second marriage before the dissolution of a first marriage. Minors may not enter into marriage without the consent of their parents, but if there is disagreement between the father and mother, the division of opinion amounts to consent. If one of the parents is dead or is unable to manifest his will, only the consent of the other parent is required.[6]

Marriage between lineal ascendants and descendants is prohibited. Between collaterals, marriage is prohibited between brother and sister, uncle and niece, and aunt and nephew. A dispensation may be obtained for marriage between uncle and niece, however, and between aunt and nephew.

Where a foreigner temporarily staying in France is a party to a proposed marriage, he must secure an authorization from the prefect of the department within the territory in which the marriage is to be celebrated.[7]

(b)   Celebration of marriage (*Célébration du mariage*).[8]   The first step toward the celebration of marriage consists of the future spouses submitting to the registrar of marriages a medical certificate, not more than two months old, stating that they were medically examined with a view to contracting marriage. Having received the certificate, the registrar will display a notice of their intention on the registry's notice board and keep it so affixed for ten days.[9] The marriage may be celebrated only after the tenth day, not counting the day on which the notice was posted. If the marriage is not celebrated within one year from the first day on which the marriage could have been celebrated, a new publication is required.

If opposition to the proposed marriage is filed with the registrar, he must await the outcome of the proceedings. If there is no opposition, or if the matter has been settled by order of the court, the registrar may proceed. The future spouses must file with him an extract from the register of births, not more than three months old if issued in France and not more than six months old if issued abroad, certifying their births. If such an extract cannot be produced, a certificate of notoriety (*acte de notoriété*) must be filed.[10] No remedy lies against the issuance or the refusal to issue the certificate of notoriety.

In the case of a minor spouse, consent of the parents or their representatives must be filed with the registrar.[11]

The marriage must be celebrated in a public ceremony before the registrar of marriages in the locality where one of the spouses has been continously domiciled or residing for at least one month at the date of the publication of the notice of their intention to marry.

The marriage ceremony takes place at the town hall in the presence of two witnesses. The registrar will read to the spouses articles 212, 213, 214 (paragraph 1) and 215 (paragraph 1) of the Code dealing with the duties of husband and wife and will ask the parties whether they have made a marriage contract; if so, he will record the date of such contract and the name and address of the notary who certified it. He will then receive the declaration of the parties that they take one another as husband and wife, and shall declare them married, and shall make a record of the fact.[12] He will also note on the record of birth of each spouse that the marriage was celebrated and the name of the other spouse.[13]

Marriage entered into abroad between French parties or between a French party and a foreign party is valid if it was celebrated in accordance with the rules there applicable and if it did not contravene the provisions as to capacity to marry contained in the French Civil Code. Also valid is a marriage celebrated abroad by French diplomatic or consular officers between a French citizen and a foreigner, if it was celebrated in accordance with French law.

(c) Opposition to marriage (*Opposition au mariage*).[14] Opposition to the celebration of marriage may be taken by a person married to one of the parties or by parents and ascendants of the parties. Failing ascendants, opposition may be taken by brothers, sisters, uncles, aunts, and cousins, if they are of age. Opposition may be taken only when the consent of the family council to the marriage of a minor has not been obtained, as required in Article 159, or when the opposition alleges mental incompetency.

Such opposition is to be submitted to a court of grande instance, which will rule on it. The future spouses may, however, petition the court to lift the opposition and the court must give its decision on the petition within ten days. An appeal from the court's decision must be decided within ten day. If the opposition is overruled, the opposing party, other than ascendants, may be held liable in damages.

(d) Petition for annulment of marriage (*Demande en nullité de mariage*).[15] A spouse whose consent to the marriage was not voluntary, or who did not give his consent, or who was in error as to the person of the other spouse, may petition for annulment of the marriage. Action for annulment will not, however, be maintained after the petitioning spouse cohabited with the other spouse for six months after having acquired full liberty of action or after he became aware of the error in the person of the other spouse.

Only those persons (father, mother, etc.) whose consent to the marriage was required but not obtained can dispute the validity of the marriage; but no one, including the spouses, can petition for nullity after having approved of it expressly or tacitly. Action must be brought within one year after having acquired notice of the marriage, and in the case of a spouse, after he attained the age when he could give his consent to the marriage.

The validity of marriage entered into in violation of Articles 144 (minimum age), 146 (consent), 147 (second marriage), and 161-63 (affinity) may be attacked by the spouses and by interested parties, and it must be attacked by the procurator.[16]

A marriage that was not celebrated publicly and before the proper registrar of marriages may be attacked by the spouses, all interested parties, and the public ministry.

No one can claim to be the spouse of another person unless there is a record of the celebration of the marriage in the register of marriages, except when such records were destroyed or lost.

A marriage that is declared null will nonetheless take effect concerning spouses and their children if it was contracted in good faith. If only one of the spouses entered into the marriage in good faith, it will take effect only in favor of that spouse and the children of the marriage. If none of the spouses entered into the marriage in good faith, it will take effect only in favor of the children of the marriage.

(e)   Obligations arising out of marriage (*Obligations qui naissent du mariage*).[17] By entering into marriage, the spouses bind themselves to feed, maintain, and educate their children.[18]

On the other hand, the children are bound to support their parents and other ascendants if they are in need.[19] The estate of a deceased spouse is bound to support the surviving spouse if he is in need. A person who is bound to support another person may be ordered by the court to receive such person into his home and support him in lieu of support payments.

(f)   Duties and rights of spouses (*Devoirs et droits respectifs des époux*).[20]   The spouses have a mutual obligation of fidelity, support and assistance. Together they ensure the moral and material needs of the family.

If the marriage contract does not provide otherwise, both spouses contribute to the costs of the marriage according to their ability. If one spouse fails to carry out this obligation, the other spouse can hold him to it by proceedings provided for in Article 864 of the Code of Civil Procedure.[21]

The spouses are obligated to live together. They determine the place of their residence by mutual agreement.

Each spouse has full legal capacity. Each spouse may authorize the other to act for him in the exercise of the power conferred on him by the law of matrimonial property. Each spouse may enter on his own into contracts for the maintenance of the household and for the education of the children. The other spouse is jointly liable on such contracts. He will not be liable, however, where the expense is clearly excessive. Installment contracts may be entered into only by both spouses acting in agreement.

Each spouse may open a bank account or a stock account in his own name without the consent of the other. Each is presumed to have the right to dispose freely of the money or valuable paper so deposited.

The wife is free to exercise her profession without the consent of her husband and she can, in the course of that profession, dispose of and bind the private property she owns individually.

Each spouse is entitled to his income and salary and may freely dispose of it after having discharged his share in the expenses of the marriage.

The property acquired by the wife with her income and salary from the exercise of her profession is under her administration, and she may freely enjoy it and dispose of it.

(g) Dissolution of marriage (*Dissolution du mariage*).[22]   Marriage is dissolved by the death of one of the spouses or by divorce.

(h) Second marriages (*Seconds mariages*).[23]   A woman cannot enter into a new marriage before three hundred days have elapsed from the dissolution of her previous marriage. This does not apply to a woman who gives birth after the death of her husband, nor to a woman who produces a medical certificate attesting that she is not pregnant. The president of a court of grande instance may lift this limitation upon evidence that the woman has not cohabited with her previous husband for the last three hundred days.

NOTES AND QUESTIONS

1. The minimum age for entering into marriage in France is not the same for men and women. What are the minimum age requirements in Spain and in Italy? For Anglo-American law, compare, e.g., Illinois S.H.A. ch. 89, §3-3.2. A person reaches his majority at eighteen in France (Civil Code, Art. 488). What is the age of majority in Germany and in Spain? Who then needs parental consent?

French law grants the usual dispensation from prohibition of consanguinity. Compare the German law. Is the French law more liberal in this respect than Anglo-American law? *See,* e.g., Illinois S.H.A. ch. 89, §1.

2. French law now requires a medical examination for venereal disease. This is still not generally required in other civil law countries. Is an examination required in the United States? *See,* e.g., Illinois S.H.A. ch. 89, §6a.

The publication of bans is standard in all civil law countries. Compare, e.g., the Italian law.

French law insists on a marriage ceremony held before the registrar of marriages, a government officer. Parties are, of course, free to enter into a church marriage thereafter if they so desire. How does this requirement of a government marriage compare with the Spanish, the Italian and the German law? Who may celebrate marriages in Anglo-American law? *See,* e.g., Illinois S.H.A. ch 89, §4.

Note the additional requirements required of foreigners to enter into marriage in France. Compare them with the requirements of the German and Italian law.

3. A petition for the annulment of a marriage is subject to the rules generally applicable in the law of civil law countries. Compare, e.g., the Spanish and the Italian law. What are the grounds for the annulment of marriages in Anglo-American countries? *See,* e.g., Calif. C.C.A. §4400ff.

4. Obligations arising out of marriage and duties and rights of spouses are similarly regulated in the German law, German Civil Code, §1353ff.; in the Spanish law, Spanish Civil Code, Arts. 56ff.; and in the Italian law, Italian Civil Code, Arts. 143ff. As to Anglo-American law, *see,* e.g., Texas Family Code §4.01ff.

5. Note the French rule as to second marriages of women after dissolution of a prior marriage. Is the three hundred day waiting period an identical requirement in all civil law countries? Compare, e.g., the German and the Spanish law. What is the purpose of these rules? Are the waiting periods imposed by Anglo-American law

similarly motivated? *See,* e.g., Calif. C.C.A. §§4512 and 4514, and Texas Family Code §3.66.

---

3. Divorce (*Divorce*)[24]

(a) Types of divorce (*Cas de divorce*).[25]   Divorce may be granted in the case of: (i) mutual consent, (ii) separation, and (iii) fault.

(i) DIVORCE BY MUTUAL CONSENT (*Divorce par consentement mutuel*).

(aa) Divorce on joint petition of spouses (Divorce sur demande conjointe des époux).   Spouses petitioning for divorce by mutual consent need not state any reasons for the petition, but they must present to the judge an agreement of settlement. Each party may appoint an advocate (*avocat*), but they each may appoint only one advocate to handle the case. Divorce by mutual consent may not be demanded within the first six months of marriage.

The judge will in private, separately consult with each of the spouses, then with both of them, and thereafter with them in the presence of their advocates. If they persist in their demand for divorce, the judge will instruct them to think the matter over and renew their petition after three months. If the spouses do not renew their petition within six months after the term of the three months set by the judge has run, the petition will lapse.

The judge will make a decree of divorce where he is convinced that both spouses indeed demand it. In his decree he will approve the agreement of settlement presented by the parties. He will, however, not grant the divorce and will not approve the settlement where the settlement does not adequately provide for the children or for one of the spouses. The settlement must completely dispose of and settle all the consequences of the divorce, especially the matrimonial property.

(bb) Divorce demanded by one spouse and accepted by the other (Divorce demandé par un époux et accepté par l'autre).   A spouse may request divorce by mutual consent alleging facts that make the continuation of the marriage intolerable. If the other spouse admits the facts, the judge makes a decree of divorce without deciding the respective faults of the spouses. The decree has the effect of a divorce because of the fault of both spouses.

Where the other spouse would not admit the facts, the judge will not grant a divorce. Statements made by the parties in this proceeding may not be used as proof in any other proceedings.

(ii) DIVORCE ON THE GROUND OF SEPARATION (*Divorce pour rupture de la vie commune*).   A spouse may petition for divorce on the ground of living apart for six years.

The petition may be brought also where for six years the mental faculties of a spouse have been so impaired as to amount to a discontinuation of family life and where it appears that the mental disorder is not likely to adjust in the future. The judge may deny the petition where the divorce would have an adverse effect on the condition of the sick spouse.

The petitioning spouse must prove his case. He must state in his petition how he plans to discharge his duties of support toward the other spouse and the children. Where the other spouse can show that the divorce would have adverse financial or moral consequences for him, especially due to his age and the duration of the marriage, or for the children, the judge will deny the petition.

The petition for divorce on the ground of separation may be brought only by the petitioning spouse. The responding spouse may then present his petition, known as *demande reconventionnelle,* in which he relies on the fault of the petitioner and petitions for divorce on that ground. He must petition for divorce; a petition for judicial separation only is inadmissible in this context. If he can prove his case, the judge will deny the petition of the petitioner for divorce on the ground of separation and will grant divorce to the respondent on his petition because of the fault of the petitioner.

(iii) DIVORCE BECAUSE OF FAULT (*Divorce pour faute*). A petition for divorce may be brought because of acts committed by the other spouse that constitute a serious or a repeated violation of the duties and obligations of marriage that make the continuation of the marriage relationship intolerable. The petition may also be brought on the ground that the other spouse has been convicted of a felony.

Where a reconciliation takes place, the facts alleged in the petition prior to reconciliation may not be used subsequent to the reconciliation, and the petition will lapse.

A new petition, however, may be founded on new facts or on prior facts that were discovered only after the reconciliation. The prior facts may then be cited only in additional support of the new petition. The continuation or the temporary reestablishment of the marriage relationship is not considered a reconciliation if it is brought about by necessity, a conciliation effort, or by the need to attend to the children.

A spouse may petition for divorce even though he is also not free of fault. The respondent spouse may bring a counter-petition (*demande reconventionnelle*) and ask for a divorce because of the fault of the petitioner. Where both parties prove their cases, divorce because of the fault of both parties is pronounced. Divorce because of the fault of both parties will be pronounced whenever it appears that both parties are in fault, even if the respondent spouse does not file a counter-petition.

Whenever a spouse brings a petition for divorce and the court has not yet made a decision, the spouses may amend the single petition to a joint petition for a divorce by mutual consent and proceed accordingly.

(b) Divorce procedure (*Procédure du divorce*).[26] Courts of grande instance (*tribunaux de grande instance*) have jurisdiction in divorce cases. They are general jurisdiction courts. The court appoints a judge in matrimonial cases (*juge aux affaires matrimoniales*), who has exclusive jurisdiction to hear and pronounce on petitions for divorce by mutual consent and also to determine custody of children and pronounce on modification of alimony payments irrespective of the type of divorce. He must protect ex officio the interests of children upon divorce of their parents.

Hearings in divorce cases on the causes and consequences of divorce, and on temporary dispositions, are not open to the public.

In a divorce for fault, where the parties so request, the court may in its reasons for divorce declare that there are facts which constitute a cause for divorce without listing such facts and grievances.

Where a spouse is under guardianship, he must be represented by his guardian. Where a spouse suffers from a mental or physical disorder that impairs the faculties of his will, a petition for divorce by mutual consent may not be brought.

Where a petition for divorce is brought on the ground of separation or fault, one attempt to reconcile the spouses must be made by the court. It is made along the lines of the attempt in a divorce by mutual consent on the joint petition of spouses, but the judge is free to determine the length of the term given the parties to consider the matter. He may always order a suspension of up to eight days; where he thinks a longer time would be beneficial, he may order a suspension of up to six months. Where conciliation fails, the judge then attempts to have the parties make an amicable settlement of the consequences of divorce, concerning especially the custody of the children and the distribution of property. Statements made by the parties in the conciliation proceedings may not be used in the following divorce proceedings.

Where the spouses petition jointly for divorce, they must submit an agreement on the temporary regulation of family relations along with the petition. The judge may modify or delete those provisions he considers contrary to the interests of the children.

In other cases, the judge will make temporary orders that will stay in force until the decree of divorce enters in the power of law. He may especially authorize the spouses to separate, grant one of them the use of the family dwelling and its furnishings or partition its use between them, order the delivery of clothing and personal effects, determine alimony and other payments one spouse must make to the other, and whenever necessary grant a spouse the benefit of his share of community property. Where there are minor children, the judge will make provisional orders as to their custody, visitation rights, and lodgings. He also determines the support payments to be made by the spouse who does not have their custody.

The judge may also make urgent orders concerning the preservation of property and any other matter.

Where the petition for divorce is denied, the judge may pronounce on the contributions the spouses have to make to family expenses, on family residence, and on the custody of minor children.

Proof in divorce proceedings may be made by all means of proof, including admission. The spouses have to disclose all information necessary to determine alimony and support payments, the distribution of property, and the dissolution of the marriage relationship.

(c) Consequences of divorce (*Conséquences du divorce*).[27]

(i) EFFECTS OF DIVORCE (*Effets du divorce*). The decree of divorce dissolves the marriage as from the day on which it becomes *res judicata*.

Where the divorced spouses desire to remarry, they must contract a new marriage.

Each spouse has to use henceforeward his own surname. In the case of a divorce on the ground of separation, the wife may keep the name of her husband where he has petitioned for divorce. In all other cases, she may keep her husband's name only with his consent, or by authorization of the judge where she can prove a special interest of her own or of the children.

A divorce is reputed to have been given against a spouse where it was granted because of his exclusive fault. Divorce is also reputed to have been given against the spouse who obtained a divorce on his petition on the ground of separation. Such spouse loses all rights which the law or a contract with a third party gives to a divorced spouse. Such rights are not lost in the case of divorce because of the fault of both parties or by mutual consent.

Where the divorce is pronounced because of the exclusive fault of one of the spouses, he may be held liable for damages (*dommages-intérêts*) for the loss, both tangible (*matériel*) and intangible (*moral*), caused to the other spouse by the dissolution of the marriage. The guilty spouse will also forfeit all gifts and profits given to him by the other spouse at or after the entering into marriage. The other spouse keeps all such gifts and profits, even though they were reciprocal and there was no reciprocity.

Where the divorce is pronounced because of the fault of both parties, each spouse may revoke gifts and profits given to the other. Where divorce is pronounced on a joint petition, the parties have to make an agreement on the matter. Where they make no agreement, they are presumed to keep what they have received. Where divorce is pronounced on the petition of one spouse in which the other joined, each spouse may revoke the gifts and profits given to the other. Where divorce is pronounced on the ground of separation, the petitioner forfeits all gifts and profits given to him by the other spouse, and the other spouse keeps all gifts and profits received from the petitioner.

(ii) COMPENSATION (*Prestation compensatoire*). As a consequence of divorce, one spouse may be required to grant to the other compensation (*prestation compensatoire*) intended to make good, as much as possible, the imbalance in the standard of living of that spouse created by the dissolution of the marriage. The amount of compensation is determined by the needs of the receiving spouse and the resources of the giving spouse at the time of the divorce, with a view to future developments. The judge must take into consideration the age and health of each spouse, their professional qualifications, their employment possibilities, their present incomes, the possibility of their losing entitlements to benefits, their financial standings as to capital and income after the dissolution of the marriage, the time for which they are required to support their children, and so forth.

The compensation consists primarily of one single payment, and the amount may not be modified. It is acquitted by payment in cash, a grant of movables or immovables, or the grant of valuable papers to a trustee to pay the income thereof to the entitled spouse for a determined time. Where the obligated spouse is not able to pay the whole amount immediately, he may do so in three installments. Where the obligated spouse is unable to pay at all, he will have to make periodical payments. The payments are in the nature of support payments (*rente alimentaire*) to be made for a specified time or for the life of the entitled spouse. In the case of the death of the obligated spouse, the obligation to pay passes to his estate.

Where the spouses petition jointly for divorce, they must determine by agreement the amount and method of payment of the compensation, but the judge may refuse to approve of it if he finds that it is inequitable.

Where divorce is pronounced because of the exclusive fault of one spouse, he is not entitled to any compensation. In exceptional cases, however, he may obtain some compensation where, due to the length of the marriage relationship and his contribution to the business of the other spouse, it would be inequitable to deny him any.

(iii) ALIMONY (*Pension alimentaire*).   Where divorce is decreed on the ground of separation, the petitioning spouse is bound to support the respondent spouse if he is in need. He must pay alimony (*pension alimentaire*), which is set but may always be modified in view of the financial capability of the obligated spouse and the need of the entitled spouse. Alimony comes to an end as of right when the entitled spouse remarries. It will be determined where the entitled spouse notoriously cohabits in concubinage without getting married. In the case of the death of the obligated spouse, the obligation to pay passes to his estate. Where the obligated spouse is possessed of sufficient property to discharge his obligation in a lump sum payment, it will be so ordered in lieu of alimony. If it becomes inadequate, it may be increased later by a further lump sum or by alimony payments.

Both the payment of the compensation (*prestation compensatoire*) and of alimony (*pension alimentaire*) is uniformly enforced on application to the procurator (*procureur de la République*) at the court of grande instance within whose jurisdiction the entitled spouse resides. The procurator enforces the payment through officers of the treasury (*comptables du trésor*), who pass the matter to those in charge at the place of the residence of the obligated spouse.[28]

(iv) FAMILY HOME (*Logement*).   As a consequence of divorce, where the family home belongs to one of the spouses, the judge may grant a leasehold therein to the other spouse where: (1) that spouse has custody of a child, and also where (2) the divorce was decreed on the ground of separation on the petiton of the spouse who owns it. On ground (1), the lease may extend until the youngest child reaches majority. On ground (2), it may not exceed nine years but may be further extended. It comes to an end as of right when the entitled spouse remarries, and it will be determined where the entitled spouse notoriously cohabits in concubinage without getting married. The lease may, however, be determined at any time by order of the judge where it appears proper because of changed conditions.

(v) CUSTODY (*Garde*).   Custody of each minor child is given to one or the other spouse as the interests of the children demand. In exceptional cases, when it is in the best interest of the child, custody may be given to another relative or an institution. Before ordering custody, the judge may request an inquiry (*enquête sociale*) into the circumstances of the case, and a spouse who contradicts the results of such an inquiry may request that another independent inquiry be made.

The spouse who does not have custody (*garde*) of the children has the right to supervise their maintenance and education. He must contribute thereto in accordance with his ability. Visitation rights and temporary possession of a child may not be denied to him except for serious reasons. The judge rules on matters regarding exercise of parental power at the request of a spouse, a family member, or the public ministry. The judge must take into account any agreement made by the spouses, the information obtained by the inquiry into the circumstances of the case, and the wishes of the children where he considers it necessary to hear them. All orders made may be modified by the judge at any time at the request of one of the spouses, a family member, or the public ministry. Where custody was granted at the joint request of the spouses, its conditions may be modified at the request of one of the spouses or the public ministry.

The payment of support is made by the spouse who does not have custody to the spouse who has custody. It takes the form of periodic payments (*pension alimentaire*), payment of a lump sum, assignment of property, or a grant of valuable papers to a trustee to pay the income as support. It is handled in the same way as the payment of compensation (*prestation compensatoire*) or alimony to a former spouse (*pension alimentaire*). It is governed by the same rules and enforced in a like manner.

A parent who takes charge of adult children who cannot take care of themselves is entitled to a proper contribution from the other parent for their support and education.

(d) Judicial separation (*Séparation de corps*).[29] Judicial separation may be decreed on the petition of one of the spouses on the same grounds and conditions as a divorce. Where one spouse petitions for divorce and the other for judicial separation, and the judge finds both petitions well founded, he will decree a divorce because of the fault of both parties.

Judicial separation does not dissolve the marriage, but it terminates the duty of the spouses to cohabit. The wife keeps the surname of her husband, although she may be prohibited from keeping it by decree or a later order. Where the husband has added his wife's surname to his own, she may demand that he be prohibited from using it.

Where one of the spouses dies after judicial separation, the survivor has the rights of a surviving spouse. He loses them, however, where the separation has been granted in favor of the deceased spouse.

Judicial separation always provides for the separation of property. It leaves intact the duty to support one another. The decree or a later order determines the amount of alimony to be paid by one spouse to the other if he is in need, irrespective of fault. Alimony is governed by the general rules applicable to it.

Judicial separation comes to an end when the spouses resume cohabitation. To have effect against third parties, the termination thereof must be declared in a notarized act, or to an officer of the civil registry. The regime of separation of property continues unless the spouses make other arrangements.

Where the separation has continued for three years, the decree of judicial separation may be converted into a decree of divorce at the request of one of the spouses as a matter of right. It may be so converted also at the joint request of both spouses. Where judicial separation was decreed on a joint petition of the spouses, it may be converted into divorce only on their joint request. The consequences of divorce are determined by the law applicable to divorce. The wife may enter into a new marriage as soon as the decree of conversion becomes *res judicata*.

(e) Conflict of laws applicable to divorce and judicial separation (*Conflit des lois relatives au divorce et à la séparation de corps*).[30]   Divorce and judicial separation are governed by French law where both spouses have French nationality, where both spouses are domiciled on French territory, and where French courts have jurisdiction and do not consider a foreign law applicable.

NOTES AND QUESTIONS

1. Compare the French grounds for divorce with those in the German and in the Italian law. Note that French law has divorce by mutual consent. Does such a ground exist in the laws of other countries? *See*, e.g., Texas Family Code §3.01ff.; Calif. C.C.A. §4506ff.; Illinois S.H.A. ch. 40, §1.

2. French divorce procedure proceeds along the lines of the standard civil procedure. This is so in all civil law countries. The special procedural rules in German law concerning dissolution of marriage are contained in the German Code of Civil Procedure §606ff. For Anglo-American law, compare, e.g. Illinois S.H.A. ch. 40, §7.

3. Note the French rule as to the name of the wife upon divorce. Compare it with the German rule. *See*, e.g., Illinois S.H.A. ch. 40, §17.

4. Consider the French provisions as to compensation and alimony. How do they compare with the German provisions? *See also* Illinois S.H.A. ch. 40, §§19 and 19a; Texas Family Code §§3.59 and 3.63.

5. The custody and support of minors after divorce is minutely regulated in French law. In German law, it is chiefly regulated in articles 1601ff. of the German Civil Code. In both the French and the German law the principle obtains that both parents must support their minor children irrespective of divorce. How is the matter regulated in Anglo-American law? *See*, e.g., Illinois S.H.A. ch. 40, §§14 and 19; Calif. C.C.A. §196ff.

Are French parents bound to support an adult child who cannot take care of himself? Compare the German Civil Code §1601, which provides that relatives in the direct line are bound to support each other. The Spanish law and the Italian law carry similar provisions, *see* the Spanish Civil Code, Art. 143, and the Italian Civil Code, Arts. 433ff. How does the matter stand in Anglo-American law? *See*, e.g., Illinois S.H.A. ch. 40, §19; Freestate v. Freestate, 244 Ill. App. 166 (1927); Calif. C.C.A. §210; Texas Family Code §14.05; Wells v. Wells, 227 N.C. 614, 44 S.E. 2d 31 (1947).

6. Judicial separation still exists in French law although the parties may obtain a divorce. Compare the Italian and the Spanish Law. *See also* Calif. C.C.A. §4508.

4. The Law of Property (*Biens*)[31]

(a) Classification of property *(Distinction des biens).*[32] All property is either movable or immovable.

(i) IMMOVABLES *(Immeubles).* Property is immovable by its nature or by the purpose which it serves or to which it is applied. Land and buildings are immovable by their nature as are agricultural produce and fruits not yet picked. Once they are cut or detached, they are movables. Trees become movables when they are cut. Pipes bringing water to buildings or land are immovables and are part of the land.

Things that the owner of land has placed upon it for the enjoyment thereof are immovables by the purpose that they serve.[33] Movables that their owner attached to the land with the intent they become permanently so attached are fixtures.

The owner is taken to have attached to his land as fixtures movables that are affixed with plaster, mortar or cement, or that cannot be detached without damage to them or to the base to which they are attached. Mirrors are considered fixtures if the base to which they are attached is embedded in the woodwork. The same applies to pictures and other ornaments. Statues are fixtures if they are placed in a niche built expressly for that purpose, even if they can be removed without damage.

The following are immovables by the purpose to which they are applied: usufruct of immovables; easements; and suits to recover immovables.

(ii) MOVABLES *(Meubles).* Property is movable according to its nature or by provision of law. Movables by their nature are pieces of property that can move themselves, like animals, or those that cannot be moved otherwise than by external force, like inanimate things.

Debentures and shares in corporations are movables by provision of law. They are regarded movables vis-a-vis a debenture holder or shareholder only as long as the corporation exists. Annuities in perpetuity or for life, payable by the state or by individuals, are also movables by provision of law.[34]

Ships, boats, vessels, and all floating structures not supported by pillars nor forming part of a building are movables. Building materials recovered from a demolished building are movable until used again in the construction of a building.[35]

(iii) PROPERTY AND ITS OWNER *(Biens dans leur rapports avec ceux qui les possèdent).* Individuals may freely dispose of property they own, subject to limitations established by law. Property that does not belong to individuals may be alienated in accordance with its own rules.

All ways, roads and streets under the care of the state, rivers navigable by boats or rafts and their banks, seashores, land between the high and low watermarks, ports, harbors, roads, and generally all French territory not susceptible to private ownership are part of the public domain. All property vacant and ownerless, as well as that which belonged to persons who died without heirs or which was abandoned by its heirs, is part of the public domain. All military fortifications are also part of the public domain. Former military fortifications and the land on which they stand belong to the state, unless they were sold by the state or unless the statute of limitations has run against the state.

Communal property is such property or its produce in which the inhabitants have a vested interest. An interest in property may consist in full ownership, in the right to use the same, or in an easement therein.[36]

(b)   Ownership (*Propriété*).[37]   Ownership is the right to enjoy and dispose of property absolutely, limited only by law. No one can be compelled to surrender his property except for public use and for a just compensation paid in advance. Ownership of property, movable or immovable, carries with it the right of accession, i.e., the right to all that it produces and to all that becomes united with it naturally or artificially.

(i)   RIGHT OF ACCESSION OF THAT WHICH IS PRODUCED BY THE THING (*Droit d'accession sur ce qui est produit par la chose*).   Natural produce of the land (*fruits naturels*) and the produce of work or cultivation of the land (*fruits industriels*), rents and interests (*fruits civils*), and new born animals belong to the owner by accession. That which is produced by the thing belongs to the owner after he has compensated third persons for their work and seed, the value of which is assessed at the time of payment of compensation. A possessor (*simple possesseur*) acquires the produce only if he acts in good faith. If not, he must restitute the produce, together with the substance, to its owner. If the produce is not readily found in a natural state, its value is assessed at the time of payment of compensation. A person is a possessor in good faith when he holds possession as an owner on the strength of a marketable title, the defects of which are not known to him. He ceases to hold in good faith as soon as he becomes aware of said defects.

(ii)   RIGHT OF ACCESSION OF THAT WHICH IS UNITED WITH OR INCORPORATED IN THE THING (*Droit d'accession sur ce qui s'unit et s'incorpore à la chose*).   All that is united with or incorporated in the thing belongs to its owner in accordance with the rules set below.

(aa)   *Right of accession to immovables (Droit d'accession relativement aux choses immobilières).*   Ownership of land carries with it the ownership of all below and above the surface. The owner may plant or build above the surface whatever he thinks proper as long as he observes existing easements. He may build and dig below the surface and remove all that he finds as long as he complies with the laws of mining and of the police.[38]

All construction, plantation or other work done on the land is presumed to have been done by the owner at his expense, unless the contrary is established subject to the rights of third parties who may have acquired or can acquire title to land or buildings by adverse possession. An owner of land who erected a structure, made a plantation, or did other work with material not belonging to him must pay its value to its owner. He may also be required to pay damages, if any. The owner of the material used cannot, however, remove it from the land.

When planting, construction or other work was done by a third party with material owned by him, the owner of the land may either keep it or require such third person to remove it. If he requires its removal, the third party must do so and may also be liable for damages suffered by the owner of the land, if any. If he decides to keep it, he must compensate the third party.[39] If the planting, construction or other work was done by a third person who was evicted from the land but had held it in good faith and therefore could not be required to remove what he had planted, constructed or done, the owner of the land must compensate him.[40]

Alluvion is the accretion that is imperceptibly formed in a river bed. The accretion belongs to the owner of the bank. The same applies where the river exposes one bank while it inundates the opposite one. Alluvion does not apply to lakes and ponds.[41]

Islands and sand bars formed in the bed of a navigable or floatable river or stream belong to the state, unless another person holds title thereto. Islands and sand bars formed in unnavigable or unfloatable rivers belong to the owners of the banks divided by a line drawn down the middle of the river.[42]

If a river changes its course so that a piece of former firm land becomes an island, such land still belongs to its previous owner whether the river is navigable or not. If a navigable river abandons its riverbed, the riparian owners may acquire title to the uncovered river bed up to its middle, for a price determined by experts.[43]

(bb) Right of accession to movables (Droit d'accession relativement aux choses mobilières). If two chattels belonging to different owners are joined together, the owners' rights in the property are governed entirely by equity.[44]

NOTES AND QUESTIONS

1. The French law classifies property into immovables and movables and gives a detailed analysis of the two concepts. Compare the French approach with that of the Italian law. These concepts come from the Roman law and are common to all civil law. Compare also Calif. C.C.A. §654ff.

Consider the French rules as to public domain. Compare the Italian law. What is the rule in the law of your state? *See,* e.g., Calif. C.C.A. §§669-70.

2. The French law defines ownership as the right to enjoy and dispose of property. Compare the Spanish law. Ownership includes the right of accession. *See,* e.g., Calif. C.C.A. §732. As to accession to immovables, including alluvion and islands, compare Calif. C.C.A. §1013ff. As to accession to movables, compare Calif. C.C.A. §1025ff. *See also* the German law.

(c) Usufruct, use, and right to use premises (*Usufruit, l'usage et l'habitation*).[45]

(i) USUFRUCT (*Usufruit*). Usufruct is the right to use as its owner the property of another person without affecting its substance. Usufruct comes into existence by operation of law or by a voluntary act of a person. Usufruct may be set up for a fixed term only or it may depend upon a condition. It may be set up in movables and immovables.[46]

(aa) *Rights of the usufructuary (Droits de l'usufruitier).* The usufructuary has title to the natural, industrial and civil produce of the property.[47]
Natural and industrial produce connected with branches or roots at the creation of
the usufruct belong to the usufructuary; those so connected at the termination
thereof belong to the owner of the property. Civil produce accrues from day to day
and belongs to the usufructuary for the term of the usufruct.

If consumable goods (e.g., money, grain or liquor) are subject to a usufruct, the
usufructuary must restitute goods of the same quality and quantity or their value at
the time of the restitution.

If things that are likely to deteriorate, such as wearing apparel and furniture,
are subject to a usufruct, the usufructuary can use them only for the purposes for
which they were intended and is bound to return them in the existing state at the
expiration of the usufruct. He is answerable, however, for their deterioration due to
intent or negligence.[48]

The usufructuary may lease his right of usufruct to another person, or he may
sell it or give it away as a gift. He is entitled to all rights to which the owner is
entitled. He may operate those mines and quarries that were operational at the
creation of the usufruct, but he has no right to open new ones; nor is he entitled to
treasure-trove.

The owner cannot detract from the rights of usufruct. On the other hand, the
usufructuary cannot, at the termination of the usufruct, claim any indemnity for his
improvements. He may remove mirrors, pictures and other ornaments, but he must
return the place in its previous state.

(bb) *Obligations of the usufructuary (Obligations de l'usufruitier).*
The usufructuary takes the property as he finds it. He must, and in the presence of
the owner, make an inventory of all movables and a record of all immovables. He
must give security that he will use the property as a responsible person, unless he is
exempted from giving security by a stipulation in the document of usufruct.[49] If he
is unable to give security, then the immovables are rented or sequestered; all money
is invested; all consumable goods are sold and the proceeds invested. The
usufructuary then draws interest on the invested principal and the income derived
from the land. The owner may also request the sale of all movables subject to
depreciation and the investment of the proceeds. The court may order, however, at
the request of the usufructuary, that those movables which are necessary for his
enjoyment be left to him on the condition that he will replace them at the
termination of the usufruct.

Even if the usufructuary delays giving security, he is still entitled to the benefit
of the usufruct from the time of its creation. He is bound to make all tenantable
repairs. Substantive structural repairs fall on the owner. If, however, due to the
failure of the usufructuary to keep up the property, substantive repairs will have to
be made, the usufructuary will have to make them.[50]

Neither the owner nor the usufructuary are bound to rebuild that which
collapses because of decay or is destroyed by accident or an act of God.

The usufructuary must pay all the annual rates and charges assessed on the
property during his enjoyment that, according to usage, are considered charges on
the enjoyment of the property. When extraordinary assessments are made on the
property subject to a usufruct, the owner must pay them, but the usufructuary must

pay him interest on the sum paid. If they are paid by the usufructuary, he is entitled to have the money refunded at the termination of the usufruct.

If a testator bequeaths a usufruct in his land subject to an annuity, the usufructuary must pay that annuity. If two or more persons are entitled to the usufruct, they must pay the annuity in proportion to their interests. A usufructuary in a particular piece of land is not bound to discharge a mortgage encumbering that land. If he is actually compelled to discharge it, he is to be compensated by the owner of the land. A person who becomes a usufructuary by the bequest to him of all or part of a testator's property must share in the discharge of any debts of the estate.[51]

The usufructuary is responsible for legal expenses incurred in connection with the usufruct. If a third person causes damage to the property or infringes upon the rights of the owner, the usufructuary must advise the owner. If he fails to do so, he will be liable for all losses caused to the owner in the same way as he is liable for waste.

(cc) *Termination of the usufruct (Fin de l'usufruit).* Usufruct comes to an end by the death of the usufructuary, by the lapse of time for which it was granted, by merger with the title to the property, by nonuse for thirty years, or by the destruction of the property. It may be terminated in consequence of waste committed by the usufructuary or because of his failure to keep up the property.[52]

Usufruct other than that granted to particular persons runs only for thirty years. Usufruct granted with the provision for its termination when a third person attains a certain age runs for that period of time even though the third person may die before attaining that age.

The owner of the property may sell it subject to the usufruct, and the sale does not affect any rights of the usufructuary. The usufructuary may renounce his rights under it, however, and bring about its termination. His creditors may have such renunciation declared void if it is made to their prejudice.

If only a part of the property subject to the usufruct is destroyed, the usufruct will be preserved on the remainder. If the usufruct extends only to a building and the building is destroyed by fire or another accident, or if it collapses due to age, the usufructuary has a right neither to the land nor to the building material.

(ii) USE AND RIGHT TO USE PREMISES (*Usage et l'habitation*). The right of use and the right to use premises are created and terminated in the same way as a usufruct. On his entry, the person entitled must give security and make an inventory of the property, and he must use the property as a responsible person. These rights are defined in the instrument that creates them.[53]

NOTES AND QUESTIONS

Usufruct comes from the Roman law and the concept is current in all civil law countries. Usufruct may be created in immovables or movables, or it may take the form of use of premises. Italian law deals with the subject in the Italian Civil Code, Arts. 978ff.; Spanish law in the Spanish Civil Code, Arts. 1030ff. What is the institution of common law that comes closest to a usufruct? Would it be the life estate? Consider the legal relationship between a fee simple holder and a life tenant in the same land. How do the rights and duties of the parties compare with a relationship of a usufruct? For life estates, compare, e.g., Burby on Real Property, 3rd ed. Ch. 16, Life Estates.

(d) Easements (*Servitudes*).[54]   An easement is a burden imposed on land for the use and benefit of land belonging to another person. Easements come into existence due to the location of land. They also may be imposed by law or may arise by a contract with the landowner.

(i) EASEMENTS THAT COME INTO BEING DUE TO THE LOCATION OF LAND (*Servitudes qui derivent de la situation des lieux*).   Lower lying lands must receive surface waters in their natural condition, flowing from upper lands without the interference of man. The owner of a lower estate cannot build a dam to prevent such flow of water. The owner of the upper estate cannot do anything that would make the burden imposed on the lower estate more onerous.

Every owner has the right to use the rainwater that falls on his land. If such use or direction given to the water makes the burden imposed on the lower estate more onerous, the owner of the lower estate must be compensated. The same applies to water that rises to the surface in springs.

If the owner, by his work, causes underground water to rise to the surface, the owner of the lower estate must receive such water and must be compensated for any damage caused by its flow.[55]

Disputes arising out of the above easements must be brought to a court of instance (*tribunal d'instance*). In giving its decision, the court must consider and balance the interests of agriculture and industry with the right of ownership.

An owner who has a spring on his land can use all the water he needs for his land. If the owner of a lower estate has used such spring water for more than thirty years and has constructed permanent conduits to carry it to his land, the owner of the land on which the spring is located cannot use it to the prejudice of the owner of the lower estate. The owner of a spring cannot deprive the inhabitants of a village or settlement of access to the water, but if the inhabitants did not acquire the use of such spring water by prescription, the owner of the spring is entitled to an indemnity.

If such spring water, on leaving the land where it rises to the surface, becomes a watercourse, the owner of the land cannot change its natural course to the prejudice of the lower water user.

The owner of land bordering upon a watercourse, other than a navigable or floatable river, may use the water for irrigation. If the watercourse actually runs through the land, the owner may make full use of such water but must return it to its ordinary course upon leaving his land.[56]

A landowner may compel his neighbor to define and mark the boundaries of their adjoining lands. The expenses thereof are shared equally.

(ii) EASEMENTS IMPOSED BY LAW (*Servitudes établies par la loi*).   The law imposes easements for the benefit of either the general public at large or that residing in a community, or for the benefit of private persons. Easements for the benefit of the general public are easements of way along navigable or floatable rivers and easements connected with the construction or repair of public roads and other public works.[57]

Easements for the benefit of landowners are imposed by law apart from agreements. They are: party walls; easements of view, light, and air; dripping of water from roofs; and way of necessity.

(aa) Party walls (Mur et fossé mitoyens). Every wall separating one property from another is presumed a party wall unless proved otherwise.[58] Coowners must repair and reconstruct their party walls in proportion to their interests. A co-owner may renounce his right in the wall, however, and then henceforward he is not bound to contribute to its upkeep; he cannot do so if the wall supports his building.[59] An adjoining landowner may make a wall separating his property from that of his neighbor a party wall by paying the neighbor half of its cost and half of the value of the land on which it stands. Every owner of property located in townships can make his neighbor contribute to the construction and repair of walls separating their buildings, yards and gardens. The nature of such walls is determined by local custom and regulations. Failing such determination, in towns with more than 50,000 inhabitants the wall must be at least 3.20 meters (10 feet) high, and in smaller towns it must be at least 2.60 meters (8 feet) high.

Properties may be separated by fences, hedges or ditches. They may be shared by the adjoining owners or may be privately owned. If a hedge is a party hedge, its produce will be shared equally by the neighbors. Trees standing on the dividing line are also owned equally as is their fruit.

Trees and shrubs growing to a height greater than 2 meters must be planted at least 2 meters from the boundary and smaller plants at least .5 meters.

A neighbor may cut the roots of trees and shrubs penetrating into his land and may compel his neighbor to cut branches extending over the boundary. The fruit that falls from such branches belongs to the owner of the land on which it falls.

(bb) Distances of certain works from boundary lines (Distance requis pour certaines constructions). The landowner who excavates on his land to make a well or ditch, who builds a chimney, fireplace, forge, stove or furnace, who sets up a stable, or who stores salt or corrosive substances, must build such structures at a distance from the boundary line so as not to give offense to his neighbor. The distance is determined by special regulations.

(cc) Easements of view, light and air (Vues sur la propriété de son voisin). A landowner cannot make a window or opening in the party wall without the consent of his neighbor.

The owner of a dividing wall standing on his land may make windows or openings in it. The windows cannot open outside, however, only inside, and must be fitted with an iron grill with bars 10 centimeters apart. Nothing can extend into the airspace of the neighbor, or hang over his land. Balconies and other protruding openings may be built, however, if there is still a distance of 1.90 meters (6 feet) left between them and the boundary line, unless there is an easement in favor of the dominant tenement.[60]

(dd) Dripping of water from roofs (Egout des toits). Roofs must be so built that rainwater from them should drain or drip on land owned by the owner of the roof or on a public way, and not on the neighbor's land.

(ee) Way of necessity (Droit de passage). A landowner whose land is fully enclosed and has no access to a public road, or only inadequate access in view of its agricultural, commercial or industrial use, or a structure on an allotment, can demand passage through the land of his neighbors for reasonable compensation. The passage will normally lead to a public road at a place located closest to the enclosed land, but it must be so drawn that it causes the least possible injury to the land over which it runs.

When land is enclosed in consequence of a sale, exchange or partition of land, the right of way is imposed only on the land so sold, exchanged or partitioned.[61]

Where the land is no longer enclosed, the owner of the servient tenement may demand the extinction of the easement to be admitted by the owner of the dominant tenement or to be declared by a judicial decision.

(iii) EASEMENTS ESTABLISHED BY THE PARTIES (*Servitudes établies par le fait de l'homme*).

(aa) Kinds of easements (Diverses espèces de servitudes). A landowner may grant an easement over his land. The easement is governed by its grant, and failing such provision, by the provisions of the Civil Code. Easements relate to **buildings** *(servitudes urbaines)* or to land *(servitude rurales).*[62]

(bb) Creation of easements (Comment s'établissent les servitudes). Continuous and apparent easements are created by express grant or by thirty years of adverse possession. Continuous but nonapparent easements and discontinuous easements, whether apparent or not, can be created only by express grant.

A landowner can create continuous and apparent quasi-easements on his land resulting in a quasi-dominant and quasi-servient tenement. Upon disposal of one of the tenements, so that each of them is owned by a different person, the quasi-easement becomes an easement.

Easements that cannot be created by adverse possession must be created by express grant by the owner of the servient tenement. The grantor cannot derogate from his grant and is deemed to have granted all the rights necessary to a meaningful enjoyment of the easement.[63]

(cc) Rights of owners of dominant tenements (Droits du propriétaire du fonds auquel la servitude est due). The owner of the dominant tenement must undertake, at his own expense, all work necessary for the enjoyment of the easement. If the owner of the servient tenement is bound to undertake such work, he can always exonerate himself by surrendering the servient tenement to the owner of the dominant tenement.

A partition of the dominant tenement cannot make the burden imposed on the servient tenement more onerous.[64] The owner of the servient tenement can request the owner of the dominant tenement to exercise his right over another portion of his land so as to enable him to make better use of his land or make repairs, and the owner of the dominant tenement must accede to such demand. The owner of the dominant tenement, on the other hand, cannot exercise his right over a different portion of the servient tenement than that assigned for such exercise nor make the burden imposed on the servient tenement more onerous.

(dd) Termination of easements (Comment les servitudes s'éteignent). Easements come to an end when they become unusable. They revive, however, when they are again susceptible of enjoyment, unless they were lost by prescription in the meantime. All easements are extinguished by merger and by nonuse for thirty years.[65] The kind of easement may be lost by prescription in the same way as the easement itself.[66]

NOTES AND QUESTIONS

Easements are well known to both civil and common law. What different types of easements are there in French law? How are easements created and how are they extinguished? What are the respective rights and duties attached to dominant and servient tenements.

Spanish law deals with easements in the Spanish Civil Code, Arts. 530ff.; Italian law in the Italian Civil Code, Arts. 1027ff.; and German law in the German Civil Code, Arts. 1018ff.

Compare easements in civil law with those in common law. *See*, e.g., Calif. C.C.A. §801ff., and Burby on Real Property, 3rd ed. Ch. 7, Profits and Easements.

---

5. Modes in Which Property May be Acquired[67] (*Différentes manières dont on acquiert la propriété*)

Title to property is acquired by intestate succession, gifts *inter vivos*, testamentary succession, contract, accession, and prescription.

Ownerless property belongs to the state.[68] Treasure trove belongs to the finder, if he finds it on his own land; if he finds it on someone else's land, only one half belongs to him, and the other half belongs to the owner of the land.[69] Rights to property thrown into the sea or thrown out by the sea and to plants growing on seashores are governed by special laws. The same applies to property lost where the owner remains unknown.

NOTES AND QUESTIONS

Compare the French means of acquisition of title to property with those of the Spanish and the German law. Note that the French law limits itself to pointing to large areas of law applicable and does not enter into details. Is title to property acquired by the same methods in common law?

Note that the French law expressly mentions treasure trove. Does this doctrine still exist in American law? *See*, e.g., Brown on Personal Property, 3rd ed. p. 28. On finding treasure trove, compare, e.g., Calif. C.C.A. §2080ff., and the German and the Italian law.

---

6.   Intestate Succession (*Successions*)[70]

(a)   Devolution of property (*Ouverture des successions et la saisine des héritiers*).[71]
Devolution of property takes place on the death of a person. If several persons who
would inherit one from the other perish as a result of the same event and there is no
indication who died first, presumption of survival depends on the facts of the case
and, failing such facts, then on the age and sex of the persons deceased.[72]

The order of succession to property by legitimate heirs, illegitimate heirs and
the surviving spouse is regulated by law. Failing such heirs, the property passes to
the state. Legitimate and illegitimate heirs and a surviving spouse have a vested
right in the property and in the rights and actions of the deceased, and they are
bound to discharge all the debts of the estate.

(b)   Capacity to inherit (*Qualités requises pour succéder*).[73]   In order to inherit,
one must be alive at the time of death of the person from whom he inherits.
Consequently, persons not yet conceived and newly born children incapable of
living cannot inherit.

The following are debarred from succeeding as unworthy: (1) those convicted
of having killed or having attempted to kill the deceased; (2) those who accused the
deceased of a capital crime with the accusation adjudged false; and (3) an heir of full
age who knows that the deceased was murdered but who fails to inform legal
authorities. The failure to inform authorities does not operate to the detriment of
the ascendants and descendants of the murdered, his relatives of the same degree, his
spouse, or his brothers, sisters, uncles, aunts, nephews and nieces.

(c)   Order of succession (*Divers ordres de succession*).[74]

(i)   GENERAL PROVISIONS (*Dispositions générales*).   Property devolves upon the
children and descendants of the deceased, upon his ascendants, upon collaterals,
and upon the surviving spouse in the order and according to rules herein set forth.

The nature and origin of property subject to devolution has no importance as
to its distribution. All property that devolves to ascendants and collaterals is divided
into two equal parts, one for the heirs in the paternal line and the other for those in
the maternal line. Paternal and maternal heirs are not postponed to first cousins but
take only within their respective lines. First cousins inherit in both lines. If there are
not ascendants or collaterals in one line, the property devolves to the other line.
Within the two lines of succession, the property devolves to closest relatives.

Proximity of kinship is established by generations, which are called degrees.
The sequence of degrees forms a line.[75]

(ii)   REPRESENTATION (*Représentation*).   Representation is a fiction of the law
whereby the descendants of a person take the place of that person and succeed to
property as he would have succeeded had he survived the deceased. Living persons
cannot be represented. Representation takes place only when a person who would
have succeeded to property had he survived the deceased, predeceased him, or when
he renounced his inheritance. For purposes of representation, there is no
distinction between legitimate and illegitimate heirs. Representation takes place in

the direct descending line,[76] but not in favor of ascendants. The nearest relative in each of the two lines excludes the more remote one. Among collaterals, representation takes place in favor of children and descendants of brothers and sisters of the deceased.

When representation takes place, the succession is per stirpes. If there are several branches within one stirps, the succession in each branch is also per stirpes but the members of each branch inherit per capita.

(iii) SUCCESSION OF DESCENDANTS (*Successions déférées aux descendants*). Children and their descendants succeed to the property of their father and mother, grandfather and grandmother, and other ascendants regardless of sex and of primogeniture, and also regardless of the fact that they were not born out of the same marriage. They succeed equally and per capita if they are descendants in the first degree. They succeed per stirpes if all or some of them inherit by representation.

(iv) SUCCESSION OF ASCENDANTS (*Successions déférées aux ascendants*). If the deceased leaves no descendants, nor brothers, sisters or their descendants, his estate devolves equally on his paternal and maternal ascendants. The ascendant nearest to the deceased takes the entire one half of the estate allotted to his line to the exclusion of all others. Ascendants of the same degree take per capita.

If the parents, brothers, sisters or their descendants survive a deceased who dies without issue, the estate is divided in two equal parts, one of which goes to the father and mother equally. The other half goes to the brothers and sisters, or their descendants. If the father and mother predeceased the deceased, their half of the estate also goes to the brothers, sisters or their descendants.

(v) SUCCESSION OF COLLATERALS (*Successions collatérales*). If the father and mother predecease the deceased, who dies without issue, his brothers and sisters, or their descendants, succeed to the estate to the exclusion of all other collaterals. They succeed either themselves or by representation. If both the father and mother survive the deceased, the brothers and sisters of the deceased or their descendants take one half the estate; if only the father or only the mother survives, they take three fourths. They take equally if they have the same father and mother. If they are half brothers and half sisters, their share of the estate is dividied into two equal portions, one for the paternal and the other for the maternal line. Full brothers and sisters take only in their line. If there are brothers and sisters only in one line, they take the whole to the exclusion of all other relatives in the other line.

If there are neither brothers nor sisters nor their descendants, and if there are no ascendants in one line, the ascendants in the other line take the whole. Failing ascendants in both lines, the closest relatives within each line succeed to the half of the estate allotted to their line. If such relatives are in the same degree, they take per capita.

Collaterals beyond the sixth degree do not take except descendants of brothers and sisters of the deceased. They, however, take up to the twelfth degree if the deceased was incapacitated but was not under guardianship. If there are no relatives within one line nor a spouse who has not been judicially separated, the relatives in the other line take the whole.

(vi) SUCCESSION OF ILLEGITIMATES (*Droits successoraux résultant de la filiation naturelle*). Illegitimacy does not create any rights of intestate succession unless it is legally established. An illegitimate child generally inherits from his father and mother and from his other ascendants, as well as from his brothers and sisters and his other collaterals, in the same manner as would a legitimate child. Reciprocally, the father and mother and other ascendants of an illegitimate child, as well as his brothers and sisters and other collaterals, inherit from him as if he were a legitimate child.[77]

(vii) SUCCESSION OF THE SURVIVING SPOUSE (*Droit du conjoint survivant*). If the deceased is not survived by relatives of a degree capable of succeeding, or if he is survived only by collaterals other than his brothers and sisters or their descendants, the surviving spouse succeeds to the entire estate, if he was not divorced nor judicially separated from the deceased. If the deceased is not survived by any relatives capable of succeeding within just one line of succession, either the paternal or maternal, or if he is survived in that line only by collaterals other than brothers and sisters or their descendants, the surviving spouse succeeds to one half of the estate if he was not divorced nor judicially separated from the deceased.

The surviving spouse who does not succeed to the whole estate of the deceased, and who has not been divorced nor judicially separated from the deceased, has a usufruct in the estate of the deceased. This right of usufruct is to the extent of one quarter of the estate if the deceased is survived by one or more children, whether legitimate or illegitimate and whether or not born out of marriage, or to the extent of one half if the deceased is survived by brothers and sisters and their descendants or by ascendants or by illegitimate children conceived during the marriage. The surviving spouse has no right of usufruct in property that the deceased has disposed of *inter vivos* or by will. If the surviving spouse obtained gifts from the deceased equivalent to the value of the usufruct, he cannot claim any usufruct; if the gifts amounted to less, he can claim only such usufructuary interest that implements the value of the usufruct provided for by law.

(d) Succession of the state[78] (*Droits de l'état*). Failing heirs, the estate falls to the state. The administration of state property has to make an inventory of the estate and must be invested with possession of the estate by order of the territorially competent court of grande instance.

NOTES AND QUESTIONS

1. Consider the French provisions as to inheritance in the case of simultaneous death. Compare them with the American Uniform Simultaneous Death Act, which has been adopted in most states, e.g., Illinois S.H.A. ch. 3, §3-1.

2. Who are considered unworthy to inherit in French law? Compare the French rules with those of Spain and Germany. Does a similar provision exist in Anglo-American law? *See,* e.g., Illinois S.H.A. ch. 3, §2-6.

3. Intestate succession is very uniform in all civil codes. Compare the German law. *See also,* e.g., Illinois S.H.A. ch. 3, §2.

Note that an illegitimate child, where paternity is established, inherits both from his father and mother. Compare, e.g., Illinois S.H.A. ch. 3, §2.2; Calif. Prob. C.A. §255.

4. Failing heirs, the estate escheats to the state. *See,* e.g., the German law. Compare also, e.g., Illinois S.H.A. ch. 3, §2-1; Calif. Prob. C.A. §231ff.

(e) Acceptance and renunciation of inheritance[79] (*Acceptation et la répudiation des successions*).

   (i) ACCEPTANCE (*Acceptation*). An inheritance may be accepted unconditionally or with the benefit of an inventory. Nobody is bound to accept an inheritance due to him. An inheritance due to minors or persons under guardianship may be accepted only in accordance with the provisions of title 10 of the Civil Code on Minority, Guardianship and Emancipation.[80]

The effect of an acceptance relates back to the devolution of property, i.e., to the time of the death of the deceased. Acceptance is express when a person expressly accepts the inheritance, formally or informally; it is tacit when the heir takes steps which necessarily imply his intention to accept the inheritance and which only an heir can take. Acts of simple maintenance and protection of the inheritance do not constitute tacit acceptance, but the gift, sale or assignment of his right to inherit by a co-heir implies acceptance. If a person dies without having renounced or accepted his inheritance, his heirs may do so in his stead. If they cannot agree whether to accept or to renounce, they must accept with the benefit of an inventory. Once accepted, a person of full age cannot renounce his inheritance except in case of fraud practiced on him. He may, however, do so when the inheritance is diminished by over one half of its value due to the discovery of a testament after the acceptance.

   (ii) RENUNCIATION (*Renonciation*). Renunciation of inheritance cannot be presumed. It must be made before the clerk of the court of grande instance in the district where the succession to the estate is opened, and it must be recorded in a book kept for that purpose. The heir who renounces his inheritance is reputed never to have been an heir. The portion of the heir who renounces his inheritance accrues to his co-heirs, and if there are none, it passes to those in the next degree.[81]

The creditor of an heir who renounces his inheritance to the detriment of the creditor's rights may be authorized by the court to accept it in the stead of his debtor. The option to take or repudiate an inheritance lapses after thirty years.[82] No one can even by a marriage contract renounce the succession to the estate of a living person nor dispose of any future rights he may have to the inheritance. Heirs who have removed or concealed property belonging to an estate have the option of renouncing and remain heirs notwithstanding their renunciation. They have no share in the property so removed or concealed.

   (iii) BENEFIT OF INVENTORY, ITS EFFECT, AND THE LIABILITY OF AN HEIR SO TAKING (*Bénéfice d'inventaire, ses effets, et les obligations de l'inhéritier bénéficiaire*). The statement by an heir that he intends to take under the benefit of inventory must be made to the clerk of the court of grande instance in the district where the succession to the estate is opened, and it is entered in a book in which declarations of renunciation are recorded. This declaration is effective only if an inventory of the estate is made within three months from the death of the deceased. The heir has forty days allowed to him to decide whether to accept or renounce the inheritance, counted from the making of the inventory if it is made within the three months.

The heir may obtain court authorization to sell perishable items of the estate by public sale. The heir is to be paid reasonable expenses out of the estate. After all the above time has run, the heir may still request more time if he is exposed to litigation, and the court may grant or refuse such request.[83] In any event, the heir may, even after the expiration of the time allowed to him, qualify as heir with the benefit of an inventory, unless he has already become heir without such benefit.

An heir who has concealed property of the estate or who has intentionally omitted to include some property in the inventory is deprived of the benefit of the inventory.

The benefit of an inventory consists in that the heir is not responsible for the debts of the estate beyond its value and he is also fully discharged if he abandons the estate to creditors and legatees; property of the estate is thus not mixed with that of the heir and the heir may demand payment of his claims against the estate.

An heir under the benefit of inventory is charged with the administration of the estate and must account to creditors and legatees. He may not be required to pay debts of the estate out of his own pocket so long as he is not in default in submitting an account of his administration. Once the account of his administration has been approved, he cannot be required to pay any amount out of his own pocket unless such an amount was not accounted for. In the administration of the estate, he is responsible only for gross negligence.

The heir can sell movables of the estate only by public auction and immovables only in accordance with the provisions of the Code of Civil Procedure, and he must pass the proceeds thereof to the mortgagees, if there are any. If the creditors request it, he must give security equivalent to the value of the movables comprised in the inventory and to the value of that portion of immovables the price of which was not passed on to the mortgagees. If he fails to take out a bond or to give other security, the movables will be sold, as well as the above-mentioned portion of immovables, and the proceeds will be applied to discharge the liabilities of the estate. If the creditors oppose the heir's handling of the administration, he can pay only by order of a judge and only in accordance with the provisions of such an order. If there is no opposition, he pays creditors and legatees in the order they present themselves. Nonopposing creditors who present themselves after the account of the administration has been approved and payment made can present their claims only against the legatees. Their claims lapse three years from the date of the settling of the account and the payment of the balance. The costs of sealing the estate, the inventory, and the account of administration are charged to the estate.

(iv) UNCLAIMED ESTATES (*Successions vacantes*). If the time allowed to make an inventory (three months) and that allowed to an heir whether to accept or renounce (forty days) has run, and no one claims to succeed to the estate, and there are no known heirs or they have renounced their inheritance, the estate is reputed unclaimed. The court of the grande instance in the district where the succession is opened will appoint an administrator at the request of any interested person or at the request of the procurator. The administrator must make an inventory. He then must convert the estate into money and pay it into the Treasury.

(f) Partition and contribution (*Partage et les rapports*).[84]

(i) SUIT FOR PARTITION (*Action en partage*). No one can be compelled to hold property with another. Partition may always be obtained notwithstanding its prohibition or an agreement to the contrary. Parties may, however, agree not to partition the property within a certain time, not exceeding five years, and the agreement may be renewed. Minor co-heirs, or those under guardianship, may bring action through their guardians authorized by the family council. Relatives in possession may sue on behalf of absent co-heirs. A husband may not without the consent of his wife cause partition of property inherited by her which becomes community property, or of property which becomes his own and of which he has the administration. Any partition of such property he may undertake on his own is only provisional.

If all heirs are present and are of full age, the estate need not be sealed and distribution may be made in such form as the heirs deem proper. If all heirs are not present or if some of them are minors or persons under guardianship, the estate must be sealed at the request of the heirs, or at that of the procurator, or ex officio by a judge of the court of instance of the district where the succession is opened. Creditors may also have the estate sealed by virtue of an execution order or by leave of the court.

The suit for partition and all oppositions thereto must be brought in the court where the succession of the estate is opened. If one of the co-heirs does not consent to the partition or if the distribution is contested, the court will proceed to judgment in a summary manner or it will appoint a judge to study the matter and will render judgment on the strength of his report.

Valuation of the immovables is made by experts chosen by the parties or, upon their refusal to chose experts, by experts appointed ex officio by the court. Movables are valued by experts in the field if such movables were not valued when the inventory was made. Each co-heir may request his share in movables and immovables in kind, but if there are creditors or if the majority of co-heirs deems the sale of property necessary in order to discharge debts and defray the costs of the succession, the movables are sold by public auction. If the immovables cannot conveniently be partitioned or allotted, they must be sold by public auction held by the court. The parties, if they are of full age, may agree that the auction be held by a notary of their choice, or one appointed ex officio if they fail to agree on one, to proceed to distribution.

Each co-heir must bring in what he has received as gifts and what he owes to the estate. If this is not done, the other co-heirs can take an equal share from the estate in property of the same kind and quality, as far as possible. After this has been done, the remainder of the estate is divided into as many equal shares as there are heirs or roots (*souches*) entitled to a share. In order to prevent the breaking up of real estate and of farms, each share must, as much as possible, be formed entirely or partly of movables or immovables, rights, or interests of equal value. The surviving spouse or the co-owning heir may request to be accorded as his share farmland forming an economic unit. Failing agreement, the request is brought to the proper court. The value of the farm is taken as of the day of partition and any surplus in value exceeding the share of the recipient must be paid by him in cash unless the co-heirs agree to defer the payment. If there are more requests, the court of grande instance may determine which petitioner is best suited to run the farm, or it may refuse to grant any request altogether.

All inequality in shares will be compensated in cash, paid in a lump sum or by installments. The division of the estate into shares is undertaken by one of the co-heirs, if they can agree among themselves on the selection, otherwise by an expert appointed by the court. They are then allotted to the heirs by drawing lots. Each heir may file a protest against the composition of the shares before the drawing. The heirs, or any one of them, may prevent a person, even a relative not entitled to succession, from taking a share in the estate if such person acquired the share by purchase or otherwise from an heir by paying him the value thereof. After the distribution, each of the heirs will receive title to the property allotted to him as his inheritance.

(ii) CONTRIBUTION (*Rapports*). Every heir must bring in all that he had received from the deceased by gift *inter vivos* unless the deceased expressly stipulated that such gifts should not be brought in. Legacies made to heirs are not to be brought in unless the testator provided otherwise, in which case the legatee can take his legacy only when his share of the estate is proportionally reduced. An heir can retain gifts which the deceased stipulated not be brought in and legacies up to the amount which the deceased could freely dispose of, but any excess is subject to reduction. The heir who renounces his inheritance may retain gifts *inter vivos* and claim legacies given to him up to the amount the testator could freely dispose of.[85]

All that the deceased gave to an heir to set him up in life or expended in payment of his debts must be brought in. But what the deceased expended on an heir for his upkeep, education, learning of a trade, and objects of daily use need not be brought in.[86] Property lost by accident and without fault of the heir is not to be brought in. The natural produce, accession, and interest from property that is to be brought in are computed only from the time of the death of the deceased. Contribution operates only to the benefit of co-heirs and not to the benefit of legatees or creditors of the estate.[87]

(iii) PAYMENT OF DEBTS (*Payement des dettes*). Co-heirs must contribute among themselves to the payment of debts of the estate and to the expenses of the succession in proportion to what they take. A universal legatee contributes together with the heirs in proportion to his legacy. Simple legatees are not responsible for the payment of debts and expenses with the exception of mortgages on immovables devised to them. If the immovables are subject to mortgages, each co-heir may demand that they be discharged before the estate is divided into inheritable shares. If the co-heirs partition the estate as it stands, the immovable is valued as if unencumbered, but the sum due on the mortgage is deducted from its price so that the heir who actually inherits the immovable is responsible only for the payment of interest on the sum of the mortgage. The heirs are liable for all debts of the estate and costs of the succession. They are responsible personally up to the value of their share, and secondarily for the whole. They have a claim, however, against all coheirs and universal legatees for their contribution to the estate.

If a simple legatee discharges a debt encumbering an immovable devised to him, he is subrogated to the rights of the creditor as against the heirs and universal successors. A co-heir or a successor under a universal title who, in discharging a mortgage, pays more than his share of the debt of the estate has no regress against other co-heirs or successors under a universal title except against the portion for which they are liable personally, even if the co-heir caused himself to be subrogated to the rights of the creditor. This does not apply to an heir with the benefit of inventory who is entitled, like a creditor, to payment of his personal claims against the estate. In the case of insolvency of one of the co-heirs or the successors under a universal title, his share in the mortgage debt is equally divided among all others. Orders of execution subsisting against the deceased are also enforceable against the heir personally, but execution on them against the heir can be had only eight days after the notification.[88]

(iv) PROPERTY INVOLVED IN THE PARTITION AND WARRANTY OF INDIVIDUAL SHARES (*Effets du partage et la garantie des lots*). Each co-heir is considered to have succeeded immediately to the property comprised in the share allotted to him and not to have ever had any interest in the other property of the estate.

The co-heirs warrant to indemnify one another against actions and evictions resulting in the heir being deprived of the property and originating from causes that arose prior to partition. There is no warranty where the kind of eviction suffered was expressly excepted from the warranty in the deed of partition. There is also no warranty if the co-heir is deprived of the property due to his own fault.

Each of the co-heirs is personally bound in proportion to his hereditary share to indemnify his co-heir for the loss caused to him by the eviction. If one of the coheirs is insolvent, his portion of the indemnity is divided equally among the remaining solvent co-heirs.

(v) RESCISSION OF PARTITION (*Rescision en matière de partage*). A partition may be rescinded because of duress or fraud. There may also be rescission when a co-heir establishes a shortage greater than one fourth.[89] The omission of an item of the estate in the partition is not a ground for rescission; it gives rise, instead, to a supplementary partition. An action for rescission may be brought against any act that is intended to divide the property among co-heirs even if it is called a sale, an exchange, a settlement, or otherwise. After a partition, or a disposition that takes its place, action for rescission cannot be brought against a transaction designed to dispose of a problem arising out of such partition or disposition.

Action cannot be brought to rescind the sale of hereditary rights made by some co-heirs, or one of them, at their own risk and without fraud to any other co-heir. A defendant in a suit for rescission may have it dismissed and may prevent a new partition by offering to supplement the plaintiff's share in cash or in kind. A co-heir who has alienated his share of the inheritance in part or in its entirety cannot bring suit for rescission for fraud or duress if he disposed of the property after discovery of the fraud or after cessation of the duress.

NOTES AND QUESTIONS

1. Consider the French provisions as to an unconditional acceptance of an inheritance and of its acceptance subject to an inventory. What is the purpose of accepting subject to an inventory? Acceptance of an inheritance is similarly treated in the Italian Civil Code, Arts. 470ff.; in the Spanish Civil Code, Arts. 988ff.; and in the German Civil Code, Arts. 1967ff.

Compare the French provisions above with Calif. Prob. C.A. §§190ff., 300, 600ff.

2. Partition of property is a universal right and no one may be compelled to hold property in co-ownership irrespective of how such property was acquired. Consequently, an inheritance may be partitioned.

Partition is similarly treated in the Italian Civil Code, Arts. 713ff.; in the Spanish Civil Code, Arts. 1035ff.; and in the German Civil Code, Arts. 2032ff.

As to the Anglo-American law of partition, *see*, e.g., Calif. Prob. C.A. §1100ff.

---

7. Gifts *inter vivos* and Testamentary Succession[90] (*Donations entre vifs et testaments*)

(a) **General provisions** (*Dispositions générales*).[91] No one can dispose of his property gratuitously except by a gift *inter vivos* or by a testamentary provision in the forms laid down in the following provisions of the Civil Code.

A gift *inter vivos* is an act by which the donor parts immediately and irrevocably with the property given to the donee, who accepts it. A testament is an act by which the testator disposes of all or part of his property to take effect at such time when he will be no more, and it is an act that he is free to revoke.

Substitutions are prohibited. Every disposition whereby the donee, heir, or legatee is charged to preserve the property and to transfer it to another is void even as to the donee, heir, or legatee.[92] A disposition whereby another person is called upon to take a gift, inheritance, or legacy in case the donee, appointed heir or legatee does not take it is not considered a substitution and is valid. The same applies to an *inter vivos* or a testamentary disposition whereby the usufruct in a piece of property is given to one person and the bare title to it to another.

In all *inter vivos* and testamentary dispositions, conditions that are impossible or contrary to law and morals are reputed not to be written.

(b) **Capacity to give and to take by gift *inter vivos* or testamentary disposition** (*Capacité de disposer ou de recevoir par donation entre vifs our par testament*).[93] To make a gift *inter vivos* or a testamentary disposition one must be of sound mind. All persons may give and take by gift *inter vivos* or by will except those who are declared incapable by law.

A minor below the age of sixteen years is incapable of such disposition except to his spouse with the consent of those whose consent is required for the minor to enter into marriage. A minor of sixteen years of age can dispose of his property only by will, and only of up to one half of the property that a person of full age can dispose of.[94]

In order to take *inter vivos*, one must be conceived at the time the gift is made. In order to take by will, one must be conceived at the time of the death of the testator; but the gift or testamentary disposition will take effect only if the child is born capable of living.

A minor, although he is sixteen years of age, cannot make a disposition in favor of his tutor, even by will.[95]

Physicians, health officers and pharmacists who treat a person during an illness from which he died cannot take anything from him by way of gift *inter vivos* or a testamentary disposition made during such illness. The same applies to a minister of religion.[96]

Gifts *inter vivos* and by will made to public bodies will be effective only when they are accepted by the proper authority.[97]

A gift made to a person who lacks the capacity to take is void even if it is disguised as a contract or if it is made to an intermediary who takes for the person lacking capacity. The following are presumed to be such intermediaries: the father, the mother, the children, the descendants and the spouse of the person lacking capacity to take. The presumption is irrebuttable.

(c) Disposable portion and reduction (*Portion de biens disponible et la réduction*).[98]

(i) DISPOSABLE PORTION OF PROPERTY (*Portion de biens disponible*). Gifts, whether *inter vivos* or by will, cannot exceed one half of the donor's property if he is survived at his death by one child; one third if he is survived by two children; or one fourth if he is survived by three or more children. No distinction is made between legitimate and illegitimate children except as follows: where an illegitimate child whose father or mother was at the time of his conception married to another person succeeds to the estate of his parent together with the legitimate children of that marriage, he is included in the calculation of the above portion of the property of which the testator may dispose, but his share in the inheritance is only one half of what he would have received if all the children, including him, were legitimate. The amount by which his share is reduced accrues exclusively to the legitimate children of that marriage in equal shares. Where an illegitimate child succeeds to the estate of his parent alone or together with other children who were not born out of the marriage under the above circumstances, the above-mentioned exception does not apply.

Gifts *inter vivos* or by will cannot exceed one half of the property if, failing children, the deceased is survived by one or more ascendants in both the paternal and maternal lines; they cannot exceed three fourths of the property if the deceased is survived by ascendants in only one of the two lines. The ascendants take in the order determined by law. They are exclusively entitled to this share if a partition, together with collaterals, would not give them the share of the estate to which they are entitled.[99]

Failing ascendants and descendants, gifts *inter vivos* and by will may dispose of the totality of the estate.

If the gift grants a usufruct or an annuity the value of which exceeds the portion of the estate the donor may dispose of, the heirs for whom property is set aside by law may either honor such gift or surrender to the donee all the property the donor was entitled to dispose of.

The value of the property disposed of as a life annuity or a sinking fund annuity, or property disposed of with the reservation of a usufruct in favor of a person in the direct line of succession and capable to succeed to the property, is computed as part of the disposable portion. If such value exceeds the disposable portion, the excess is added to the mass of the estate. This computation cannot be demanded by persons in the direct line of succession who consented to such alienation of property. It can never be demanded by persons in the collateral line of succession. The donor may dispose of the disposable portion *inter vivos* or by will in favor of his children or other persons entitled to the succession, and such donees and legatees are not required to bring such gifts in before they succeed to the estate of the donor if the donor expressly declared that the gift should not be so brought in. Such declaration may be made in the document of gift or later in a document made *inter vivos* or by will.

(ii) REDUCTION OF GIFTS AND LEGACIES (*Réduction des donations et legs*). Gifts *inter vivos* or by will made in excess of the disposable portion will be reduced so as not to exceed it at the time of death of the donor. Reduction of gifts *inter vivos* may be demanded only by those for whom a share of the estate is set aside by law and by their heirs or assigns. The donees, legatees and creditors of the deceased cannot request the reduction nor benefit therefrom.

The reduction is made as follows: all property of the donor or testator existing at the time of his death forms an entity. To that is mathematically added, after deducting the debts, the value of all property that the donor gave away by gift *inter vivos*, said value taken at the time of his death. The portion which the deceased could have disposed of is then determined by taking into account the ranking of the heirs entitled to the estate. If a reduction must be made, the testamentary gifts are reached first. Only when they are exhausted, a reduction of gifts *inter vivos* is resorted to, beginning with the most recent gift and so on, reducing an earlier gift only when a gift made later in point of time is completely eliminated.

When the value of gifts *inter vivos* equals the disposable portion of the estate, all testamentary gifts are extinguished and lapse. When testamentary gifts exceed the disposable portion, or the part that remains after deducting the gifts *inter vivos*, they are reduced pro rata without any distinction being made between a universal legacy and individual legacies. However, if the testator expressly stipulated that a particular legacy was to be paid preferentially, it shall not be reduced unless the value of the other legacies is equal to the share reserved for the heirs.

An action for reduction or repossession is maintainable by the heirs against third parties who hold immovables that were transferred to them by a donee. They take the place of the donee. The most recent transfer is attached first and so on.

(d) Gifts *inter vivos* (*Donations entre vifs*).[100]

(i) FORM OF GIFTS *INTER VIVOS* (*Forme des donations entre vifs*). A gift *inter vivos* made in writing must be made before a notary public observing the formalities of contracts, and a record of the transaction must be made. If these requirements are not met, the gift is null and void.[101] A gift *inter vivos* takes effect only when it is expressly accepted by the donee and his acceptance is communicated to the donor. If the donee dies before notification is given, the gift is void. The acceptance must be made by a notarized act.[102]

Gifts made to charitable institutions must be accepted by administrators duly authorized by the institution.

A gift duly accepted is fully effective by consent of the parties; no further transfer of the property is required. In the case of a gift of property that is subject to a mortgage, notification of the notarized act of donation and of the acceptance must be made to the registry of mortgages in the district where the property is situated.

All existing property of the donor may be the subject of a gift *inter vivos;* a gift of futures is void. A gift made on a condition, the execution of which depends solely on the donor, is void. A gift is void if it is made on the condition that the donee shall discharge debts or obligations other than those existing at the time of the making of the gift or such as are stipulated in, or annexed to, the document of gift.

If the donor reserves the right to dispose of one of the items of property given, or of a fixed sum levied on the property given, and if the donor dies without having disposed of such reserved interest, it passes to the heirs of the donor irrespective of any provision to the contrary.

A gift *inter vivos* of movables that is made in writing is not valid unless a statement identifying the movables given, and assessing their value, is signed by both the donor and the donee and annexed to the document of donation. The donor may reserve to himself or to another person the right of enjoyment or of usufruct in the immovables or movables given. If movables are given with the reservation of usufruct, the donee must take them as he finds them when the usufruct expires. He may take action, however, against the donor or his heirs for the value of movables, as indicated in the statement assessing their value, if such movables are not handed over to him by the person entitled to the usufruct. The donor may reserve the right to retake the property given in case the donee or his descendants predecease the donor. The right enures only to the benefit of the donor himself. The donor is then entitled to retake such property irrespective of any alienation of such property by the donee and free of any charges or mortgages, with the only exception being a mortgage that secures a dowry and then only when the gift was made by a marriage contract from which the mortgage originates.

(ii) EXCEPTIONS FROM THE RULE OF THE IRREVOCABILITY OF GIFTS *INTER VIVOS* (*Exceptions à la règle de l'irrévocabilité des donations entre vifs*). A gift *inter vivos* may be revoked only because of nonfulfillment of a condition on which it was made, because of ingratitude, and because of the subsequent birth of children.

When a gift is revoked because of nonfulfillment of a condition, the property must be returned to the donor free of any charges or mortgages created by the donee.

In the case of immovables, the donor can exercise against third parties holding such immovables all the rights that he has against the donee himself.

A gift may be revoked for ingratitude in the following cases: (1) where the donee makes an attempt on the life of the donor; (2) where he is guilty of serious ill-treatment, crime or grievous injuries toward him; or (3) where he refuses to support the donor.

An action to revoke a gift because of ingratitude must be brought within one year from the day of the offense or from the time when the offense could have been discovered by the donor. The action cannot be brought against the heirs of the donee nor by the heirs of the donor unless, in the latter case, the action was brought by the donor or the donor died within one year from the injury. The revocation will not affect any alienation of property given nor any incumbrances imposed thereon before the announcement of the revocation. The donee will have to restitute the value of the property alienated, together with its produce, as from the date of the suit. Nuptial gifts cannot be revoked because of ingratitude.

All gifts *inter vivos* of any type whatsoever made by persons who did not have any children or living descendants at the time of the making of the gift are revoked by force of the law when a legitimate, even posthumous, child is born to the donor, as well as when an illegitimate child born after the making of the gift is legitimated by subsequent marriage. This is so even if such child of the donor or the donatrix was already conceived at the time of the making of the gift, or if the donee entered in possession of the property given only after the birth of such child.

Property subject to a gift that is revoked by force of the law revests in the donor free of any charges or mortgages of the donee. The gift once revoked cannot be revived, and it is not revived even by the death of the donor's child; but if the donor desires to give such property to the donee, whether before or after the death of the child by the birth of whom the gift was revoked, he must do so by a new gift. The donor cannot contract out of the revocation, and any arrangement by which the donor renounces the revocation is void.

Revocation of a gift because of a subsequently born child is prescribed and cannot be enforced against the donee, his heirs or assigns after thirty years, counted from the day of the birth of the last child of the donor, even if born posthumously.

NOTES AND QUESTIONS

1. Note the approach of the French law to gifts *inter vivos* and testamentary succession. Both are treated alike as to what they have in common, and after this has been done, they are treated separately for their differing aspects. Is a similar approach taken in the laws of other civil law countries? The Italian Civil Code deals with gifts in Art. 769ff., and the Spanish Civil Code in Arts. 618ff.; in both these codes, gifts are treated in connection with successions, but separately. The German Civil Code treats gifts in Art. 516ff. within the law of obligations and completely separate from the law of acquisition of property or of successions as a means of acquiring property. The actual provisions of the above Codes as to gifts are, of course, very similar. How are gifts and testamentary succession treated in Anglo-American law? *See*, e.g., Calif. C.C.A. §1146ff. for gifts and Calif. Probate Code for testamentary succession.

2. What is the minimum age required for making a French will? Compare the Spanish and the German law. Note that a French minor over the age of sixteen may dispose of only one half of his property under further limitations. What is the minimum age for making a will in Anglo-American law? *See,* e.g., Illinois S.H.A. ch. 3, §4-1.

3. What are the French provisions concerning the disposable portion? Are these the rules otherwise known as forced shares? Compare them with forced shares in Italian and in Spanish law. Do forced shares exist in Anglo-American law? What about community property; could the share of community property be considered a forced share in the same sense as in civil law countries? Note the French provision as to succession of illegitimate children. Compare, e.g., Illinois S.H.A. ch. 3, §2-2.

4. As to gifts *inter vivos,* refer to note 1 above. Compare, e.g., Calif. C.C.A. §1146ff and Brown on Personal Property, 3rd ed., ch. VII and VIII on gifts.

(e) Testamentary succession (*Dispositions testamentaires***).**[103]

(i) GENERAL RULES CONCERNING THE FORM OF WILLS (*Règles générales sur la forme des testaments*). A person may dispose of his property by will by naming an heir, by making legacies, or in any other form. A will cannot embody testamentary dispositions of two or more persons whether for the benefit of a third person or for their mutual benefit. A will may be holographic, made by public act, or in the mystic form.

A holographic will must be entirely written, dated and signed by the hand of the testator.

A will by public act is made before two notaries or before one notary and two witnesses. The will is reduced to writing as it is dictated by the testator. It is then read to him and the fact is expressly stated in the will. The will must be signed by the testator in the presence of the notary and the witnesses, who must also sign. If the testator cannot sign, the reason must be given in the will. Legatees and their relatives up to the fourth degree, clerks of the notary, and the notaries before whom the will is made cannot act as witnesses.

A will in the mystic form is made by the testator and is handed by him to a notary in a closed, sealed envelope and in the presence of two witnesses, or it may be so sealed by the testator in the presence of a notary and two witnesses. The testator must make a declaration that the paper contains his last will and testament, signed by him and written by his hand or by that of another person or typewritten. If it was not written by his own hand, the testator must declare that he has read and examined the writing. The notary shall draw up a minute of the testator's declaration and have it written on a bigger envelope in which the envelope containing the will is enclosed and sealed by the notary. The endorsement contains, in addition to the declaration of the testator, the date and place of its execution. It is signed by the testator, the notary and the witnesses.[104]

Witnesses must be French citizens of full age and capacity. They may be male or female, but a husband and wife may not witness the same will.

(ii) SPECIAL RULES WITH RESPECT TO THE FORM OF SOME WILLS (*Règles particulières sur la forme de certains testaments*).   Persons in the armed forces may make a will before a senior officer or senior medical officer in the presence of two witnesses. Two originals of the will must be made and forwarded separately, by different mailings, to the Department of Defense to be deposited for safekeeping with a notary indicated by the testator or, failing such indication, with the president of the chamber of notaries in the district of the testator's last domicile. A will made in the above form will be void after the testator has lived for six months in a place where he could have made a will in the usual form.

In a place with which all communication has ceased because of the outbreak of a contagious disease, wills may be made before a judge of the court of instance or a municipal officer of that community and two witnesses. The same applies to French islands in European waters where there is no notary and when it is not possible to reach the French mainland. Wills made in this form will be void six months after the reestablishment of communication or after the testator has come to a place where he can make a will in the usual form.

Aboard a ship, even in a port where there is no French consulate or French agent, wills may be executed before the master assisted by an officer and two witnesses. Aboard a ship owned by the state, wills may be executed before the administrative officer or, failing such officer, before the commanding officer in the presence of two witnesses. Two originals of the will are made. One is given to a French diplomatic or consular officer in the next port of call to be forwarded to the ministry of the navy. The other, or both if the ship calls in a French port, is deposited with the registrar of ships, or in the case of a government ship, with the ministry of the navy, to be forwarded for safekeeping to the notary indicated by the testator or, failing such indication, to the president of the chamber of notaries in the district of the testator's last domicile.

A will made aboard a ship is valid only if the testator dies aboard or within six months after he has disembarked in a place where he could have made a will in the usual form. All provisions made in favor of members of the crew, except the testator's relatives, are void even if the will is holographic. The testator must be advised that the will shall become void six months after the above events take place, and the fact must be so stated in the will.

A Frenchman may make his will in a foreign country in the holographic form or in accordance with the form prescribed by the law of the place where the will is made. Wills made abroad must be registered at the place of the testator's domicile in France and at the place where immovables owned by the testator are situated. If not so registered, the will has no effect on property situated in France.

The above formalities concerning wills must be observed. Failure to do so will result in nullity.

(iii) APPOINTMENT OF AN HEIR AND OF LEGACIES IN GENERAL (*Institution d'héritier et des legs en général*).   Testamentary disposition may be universal, general, or specific and shall produce the results indicated by the following rules whether the technique of appointing an heir or that of making legacies is adopted.

(iv) UNIVERSAL LEGACY (*Legs universel*).   Universal legacy is a testamentary disposition by which the testator leaves to one or more persons the whole of the property he owns at the time of his death.

If at the time of the testator's death there are heirs to whom the law reserves a portion of the estate, they are seized of the estate as of his death and the universal legatee must request them to surrender to him the property comprised in the will.[105] If there are no such heirs, the universal legatee is himself seized of the estate as of the time of the testator's death and no request for its surrender is necessary. If in such a case the will by which a universal legatee is appointed was made in the holographic or in the mystic form, the universal legatee will be invested with possession of the estate by order of the president of the proper court of grande instance.

A universal legatee who shares the estate with a person to whom the law has reserved a portion thereof is responsible for the debts and obligations of the estate personally to the extent of his interest and as a surety for all such debts and obligations. He is also bound to pay out all legacies except when they are subject to reduction.

(v) GENERAL LEGACY (*Legs à titre universel*). A general legacy is such by which the testator leaves a certain portion of the property of which the law permits him to dispose, e.g., one half, one third, or all of his immovables, or all his movables, or a fixed portion of his immovables or movables. Every other type of legacy is a specific devise or bequest.

A general legatee must request that the heir to whom the law reserves a portion of the estate surrender to him the property left to the heir by the testator; failing such an heir, he must direct his request to the universal legatee or, failing even a universal legatee, to the heirs entitled on intestacy. A general legatee is liable for the debts and obligations of the estate in the same manner as a universal legatee, namely, personally to the extent of his interest and as a surety for all such debts and obligations.

When the testator has disposed of only a fraction of the portion of the estate of which he can lawfully dispose, and if such disposition is made in the form of a general legacy, such legatee is bound, together with the heir or heirs, to discharge proportionally all specific bequests and devises.

(vi) SPECIFIC LEGACIES (*Legs particuliers*). A specific legacy gives the legatee a right to the property bequeathed or devised to him as of the testator's death. This right is inheritable and assignable. The legatee is entitled to actual possession of the property, together with its proceeds or interest, as of the day of his request for the surrender of such property to him.[106]

The heirs, or those responsible for the discharge of legacies, are personally responsible to discharge the same in proportion to what they receive from the estate. As a surety, they are liable to discharge all the legacies up to the value of the immovable estate held by them.

The property bequeathed must be surrendered, together with its accessions, in the condition in which it was on the day of the testator's death.

Where the testator devised certain immovables to a legatee and later acquired further contiguous property, the later acquired property is not considered part of the devise. However, improvements and structures erected on a devised land form part of the devise.

If before or after the making of the will, the property bequeathed or devised has been mortgaged or encumbered with a usufruct, the person bound to discharge the legacies is not required to discharge such encumbrances unless expressly directed by the testator.

Should the testator bequeath or devise property not belonging to him, the provision is void whether he knew or not that it did not belong to him. If the property bequeathed is identified only by description, the heir is not bound to surrender one of the best quality, nor can he give one of the poorest quality. A bequest made to a creditor is not considered to have been made in lieu of payment of the debt, nor is a bequest to a servant taken to have been made in lieu of wages.

A specific legatee is not responsible for the debts of the estate, except for a possible reduction of the legacies and the possible claims made by mortgagees with respect to land owned by the estate.

(vii) EXECUTORS (*Exécuteurs testamentaires*). The testator can appoint one or more executors of his will. He may invest them with possession of all or a part of his movable property, but they cannot hold it beyond a year and a day from his death. If the testator did not so invest them, they cannot themselves demand possession. An heir may divest them of possession by offering to hand over to them a sum of money sufficient to discharge all legacies of movables.

A person lacking full legal capacity cannot hold the office of executor. A minor cannot hold the office even with the consent of his guardian.

If there are minor heirs, heirs under disability, or absent heirs, the executors must seal the estate. They must make an inventory of the estate in the presence of the heir apparent. If there is not enough cash to discharge legacies, they must sell movables to obtain it. They are responsible for the execution of the testator's last will; and if its validity is contested, they may take legal action to sustain its validity. They must render account of their administration one year after the testator's death.

The office of the executor is not inheritable. If several executors accept the apointment, any one of them may act alone in default of the other or others. They are, however, jointly responsible for the movable property entrusted to them unless the testator divided their functions. In that case, each of them is liable for the property entrusted to him.

The expenses incurred by the executor in sealing the estate, taking inventory, rendering his account, and exercising his official functions are to be paid out of the estate.

(viii) REVOCATION OF WILLS AND THEIR INVALIDITY (*Révocation des testaments et leur caducité*). A will may be revoked, whether in full or in part, only by a later will or by a declaration made before a notary.[107] A later will that does not expressly revoke an earlier one does not make in invalid. Only such provisions of the earlier will that are incompatible with, or in contradiction to, those made in the later will are abrogated.

A revocation made in a later will is effective even though the property involved remains undisposed of because the later will gives it to a person who is incapable of taking it, or because he declines to take it.

Every alienation made by the testator in full or in part of the property given, even with the right of repurchase or exchange, operates as a revocation of the gift to the extent of the alienation. This is so even if alienation is void and the testator resumes title to the property.

A testamentary disposition lapses if the beneficiary does not survive the testator. A testamentary disposition made subject to a condition depending on an event that may or may not occur, and with such disposition not operative until the occurrence or nonoccurrence of that event, lapses if the heir or legatee appointed to take thereunder dies before the condition is fulfilled. If only the enjoyment of a testamentary gift is postponed, however, the right of the appointed heir or legatee to take thereunder, once acquired, descends to his heirs.

A legacy lapses if the property bequeathed is destroyed during the life of the testator or after his death but without any fault of the heir. If the heir delays its surrender to the legatee, the legacy lapses if the property would have also perished in possession of the legatee.

A testamentary disposition lapses if it is repudiated by the heir or the legatee, as the case may be, or if they lack testamentary capacity.

If property is given to several legatees jointly, the right of survivorship applies. This is so always when the testator does not indicate the shares in the property to be held by individual legatees, or if the property is not susceptible of partition without damage.

A testamentary disposition may be revoked on the same grounds on which gifts *inter vivos* may be revoked. A demand for revocation on the ground of a grievous injury to the memory of the testator must be made within one year from the commission of the offense.

(f) Provisions by the donor or testator in favor of his grandchildren or the children of his brothers and sisters (*Dispositions permises en faveur des petits-enfants du donateur ou testateur, ou des enfants de ses frères et soeurs*).[108] Fathers and mothers may give *inter vivos* or by will all or part of the property of which they may lawfully dispose to one or more of their children for their grandchildren living or to be born. A similar disposition made by a person who dies childless in favor of the children living or to be born of his brothers and sisters is also valid. The above provisions are valid only if no distinction or preference is made among the children with respect to age or sex. If the person bound to surrender the property to his children dies but is predeceased by one or more of his children who are again survived by their children, these children take the share of their parent by representation.[109]

(g) Distribution of property made by ascendants (*Partages faits par les ascendants*).[110] Fathers, mothers, and other ascendants may distribute their property among their descendants by gift *inter vivos* or by will. Distribution by gift *inter vivos* is subject to the law of gifts *inter vivos*, and that by will is subject to the law of testamentary succession.[111]

(h) Gifts made by marriage contract to the spouses and the children of the marriage (*Donations faites par contrat de mariage aux époux, et aux enfants à naitre du mariage*).[112] Gifts *inter vivos* of presently existing property made by marriage contract to spouses or to one of them are subject to the general rules of gifts *inter vivos*. If such gift is made to children to be born of the union it must comply with Articles 1048-1074 of the Civil Code.[113]

Fathers, mothers, other ascendants, collateral relatives of the spouses, and even strangers may by marriage contract dispose of all or some of the property that they might have at the time of death in favor of their spouses or in favor of the children to be born of the union in case the spouse or spouses predecease the donor. Such gift is always presumed to have been made in favor of the children and descendants of the union if the spouse or spouses predecease the donor.[114]

A gift by marriage contract may be made on condition that that donee pays the debts of the donor's estate or on other conditions. The donee must either comply with the condition or renounce the gift. If the donor reserves the right to dispose of a piece of property or a fixed sum of money comprised in the gift but dies without disposing of it, it belongs to the donee.

A gift by marriage contract lapses if the marriage does not take place. A gift by marriage contract made to one spouse only, lapses if the donor survives the donee and his issue.

(i) Dispositions between spouses by marriage contract or during marriage (*Dispositions entre époux, soit par contrat de mariage, soit pendant le mariage*).[115]

Spouses may by marriage contract make gifts one to the other as they think proper and as further provided. All gifts made between spouses by marriage contract must comply with Articles 1081-1090 of the Civil Code[116] as to gifts made to spouses by third persons,but a gift between spouses does not pass to the children born of the union in case of the death of the donee spouse before the donor spouse.

A spouse, by marriage contract or during marriage to the other spouse, may dispose of all property he could dispose of to third parties as well as the share of his property reserved to his ascendants by Article 914 of the Civil Code[117] in the event he leaves no children or other descendants, legitimate or illegitimate, on his death. If he is survived by children or descendants, legitimate or illegitimate, he may grant to the other spouse all that he could grant to third parties, or one fourth of his property in full ownership and three fourths in usufruct, or he may grant the other spouse a usufruct in all of his property. A minor spouse may make the same dispositions with the consent of those whose consent is required for the celebration of the marriage.

All gifts made between spouses during marriage are revocable.

One spouse cannot grant to the other spouse indirectly what he cannot give him directly in accordance with provisions of the Civil Code. Any concealed gift or a gift to intermediaries is void.[118]

NOTES AND QUESTIONS

1. Compare the types of French wills with those of the Italian and the Spanish law. Consider the qualifications of witnesses. Must they be of full age and capacity? The Spanish law has provisions similar to the French law in Spanish Civil Code, Art. 681; and in the case of an epidemy, it reduces the age to sixteen years fully completed in Art. 701. The Italian Civil Code has provisions identical to the

Spanish Civil Code. *See* Italian Civil Code, Arts. 601ff. and 609. In German law, the witnesses must be of full age and capacity, *Beurkundungsgesetz* §26. Must witnesses in Anglo-American law be of full age and capacity to attest a will?

2. Note the French provisions as to universal, general, and specific legacies. The Italian law deals with the topic in Civil Code, Arts. 624ff.; the Spanish law in Civil Code, Arts. 763ff.; and the German law in Civil Code, Arts. 2087ff. As to legacies in Anglo-American law, *see,* e.g., Calif. Prob. C.A. §160ff.

3. The function of an executor is similar in civil law and Anglo-American law. The Italian law deals with executors in Civil Code, Arts. 700ff.; the Spanish law in Civil Code, Arts. 892ff.; and the German law in Civil Code, Arts. 2197ff. For Anglo-American law, *see,* e.g., Illinois S.H.A. ch. 3, §6 and 9.

4. Note the rules concerning revocation of wills. Compare them with those of the Italian and the German law. Compare also Illinois S.H.A. ch. 3, §4-7.

5. Ancestors may donate as a gift *inter vivos* to their descendants property of which they may lawfully dispose. There is no rule preventing such gifts, although they tend to attract a gift tax if over the tax-free minimum. The gift tax is, however, much lower than an inheritance tax so that such gifts are fairly common in civil law countries.

6. Note the French provisions as to gifts between spouses. The Spanish law deals with the subject in Civil Code, Art. 1327ff. and the Italian law in Civil Code, Art. 781. Both the Italian and the Spanish law hold such gifts void. These rules are brought about by the existence in these countries of the law of community property and also by the law of forced shares. Are there any special rules concerning gifts between spouses during marriage in Anglo-American law?

---

8. **Contracts and Contractual Obligations in General (*Contrats ou les obligations conventionnelles en général*)[119]**

(a) Introductory provisions (*Dispositions préliminaires*).[120] A contract is an agreement whereby one or more persons obligate themselves with respect to another person or to other persons to give, to do, or not to do something. The contract is bilateral when the contracting parties incur reciprocal obligations toward one another. It is unilateral when one or more persons have entered into an obligation towards one or more other persons without any obligation on the part of the latter. It is commutative when each party obligates himself to give or do something that is taken as an equivalent for what is given to or done for him. When the equivalent consists in a chance of gain or loss for each of the parties upon an uncertain event, the contract is aleatory.

A gratuitous contract is that by which one party provides to the other an advantage for free. An onerous contract is that by which each of the parties is obligated to give or do something.

All contracts, whether specifically classified or not, are governed by the general rules of contracts. Special rules governing certain contracts are set forth under pertinent headings in the Civil Code. Special rules applicable to commercial transaction are set forth in the commercial law.

(b)   Elements essential to the validity of contracts (*Condition essentielles pour la validité des conventions*).[121]   To be valid, a contract must contain four elements: consent of the obligated party; capacity to contract; a certain object that forms the substance of the agreement; a lawful purpose.

(i) CONSENT (*Consentement*).   There is no valid consent if it is given by mistake, or if it is obtained by force or by fraud.

Mistake is a ground for the annulment of a contract only if it relates to the very substance thereof. It is not a ground for the annulment of a contract if it relates only to the person with whom one intended to contract, unless the identity of the person is of essence.

Force applied against a contracting party is a ground for annulment even if it was applied by a person other than the one deriving an advantage under the contract. By force, it is meant that which is likely to produce in the mind of a reasonable person the apprehension of the infliction upon his person or property of a substantial and immediate harm. The age, sex and condition of the person is considered in this connection. Force is a ground for annulment even if it is exerted against the spouse, descendants or ascendants of the contracting party.[122] A contract cannot be set aside on the ground of force if the contract was expressly or tacitly ratified after the force ceased, or if the time set by law to bring an action for rescission has run.

Fraud is a ground for the annulment of a contract when it is evident that without the practices applied by one party, the other party would not have entered into the contract. Fraud cannot be presumed, it must be proved. An agreement entered into by mistake, force or fraud is not void in itself; it only gives rise to an action for its annulment or rescission. The lack of an adequate consideration vitiates only some contracts or contracts entered into by certain persons as explained in the Civil Code. As a general rule, a person may in his own name enter into agreements and act only for himself. Yet a person may promise the performance of another, and in case such person refuses to perform, he will answer in damages. A person may also provide for the benefit of a third party, which provision may be contained in a declaration or in a statement of gift to another person. The provision cannot be revoked after the third party has declared that he wishes to take advantage thereof. A person is reputed to have provided for himself, his heirs, and his assigns unless a contrary intention is manifested or unless it appears from the agreement.

(ii) CAPACITY OF THE CONTRACTING PARTIES (*Capacité des parties contractantes*). Every person may enter into contracts unless declared incapable by law. Minors and persons under disability specified by law lack capacity to contract. Persons having capacity to contract cannot have a contract set aside on the ground that the person with whom they contracted lacked capacity.

(iii) OBJECT AND SUBJECT MATTER OF CONTRACTS (*Objet et la matière des contrats*). Every contract has for its object something that one of the parties obligates himself to give, to do, or not to do. The mere use or the mere possession of a thing, as well as the thing itself, may be the object of a contract. Only things *intra commercium* may become the object of contracts. An obligation must have for its object a thing ascertained at least as to its kind. The quantity of a thing may be uncertain so long as it can be ascertained. Futures (things not yet in existence) may be the object of obligations. One cannot, however, renounce an inheritance during the lifetime of the person from whom it would be forthcoming, nor make any provisions with respect to such inheritance even with the consent of that person.

(iv) CAUSE OF CONTRACTS (*Cause*). An obligation without a cause, or one with a false or an unlawful cause, is void. The agreement is valid even though the cause is not expressed. The cause is unlawful when it is prohibited by law, or when it is contrary to good morals or to the public order.

(c) Effect of obligations (*Effet des obligations*)[123]

(i) GENERAL PROVISIONS (*Dispositions générales*). Agreements lawfully entered into have the power of law over those who made them. They can be revoked only by mutual consent or for causes stipulated by law. They must be performed in good faith. Contracts hold a party not only to that which is expressed therein, but also to that which by equity, custom, and the law is incidental to the obligation in accordance with its nature.

(ii) OBLIGATION TO GIVE (*Obligation de donner*). The obligation to give embodies the obligation to deliver the thing and to care for it until delivery. Failure to do so makes the giving party liable in damages to the other party. The obligation to care for the thing requires the person so obligated to apply the care of a responsible person irrespective of whether the agreement benefits only one of the parties or both of them. The proper standard of care may be higher or lower as provided in specific contracts treated under the proper headings of the Civil Code. The obligation to deliver the thing is incurred by the mere consensus of the contracting parties. It makes the person to whom it is due the owner of the thing and places it at his risk from the time it should have been delivered even though it may not have been handed over, unless the obligated person failed to deliver it in time, in which case the thing remains at the latter's risk. The obligated person is put in default by a writ of summons or any equivalent act or by the simple running of time provided for in the contract for performance.[124] If a person is bound to give or deliver a movable to two persons in succession, the one of them who is actually put in possession is preferred over the other and is regarded the owner thereof, even though his title is posterior in date to that of the other person, as long as he holds the property in good faith.

(iii) OBLIGATION TO DO OR NOT TO DO (*Obligation de faire ou de ne pas faire*). If a person obligated to do or not to do does not perform, he is liable in damages. Yet the person entitled under the obligation has the right to demand that all that has been done in contravention of the agreement be undone; and he can obtain authorization to undo it himself at the expense of the obligated person without forfeiting his right to damages. In case of nonperformance, the person entitled under the obligation may also be authorized to carry out the obligation himself at the expense of the obligated person. If the obligation is to abstain from doing something, the person who contravenes it is answerable in damages by the mere act.

(iv) DAMAGES AND INTEREST RESULTING FROM NONPERFORMANCE OF OBLIGATIONS (*Dommages et intérêts résultant de l'inexécution de l'obligation*). Damages are due only when the obligated person defaults in the performance of his obligation, or when the thing that the obligated person had bound himself to give or to do could have been given or done only at a certain time, which he has allowed to run. The obligated person will be ordered to pay damages and interest because of his failure to perform or delay in performance unless he can show that his nonperformance was due to an extraneous cause for which he was not responsible and provided that there was no bad faith on his part. No damages are payable when the obligated person was prevented from giving or doing what he was bound to give or do, or did what he was prohibited from doing, by an act of God or by an unavoidable accident.

Damages and interests are payable to the entitled person ordinarily to make good the loss he suffered and the profit of which he was deprived, subject to the exceptions and modifications hereinafter set forth. If the nonperformance of the obligation was not due to his fraud, the obligated person is liable only for damages that were foreseen or that could have been foreseen at the time of contracting. Even where nonperformance of the contract was caused by the fraud of the obligated person, damages and interest due to the entitled person for the loss he suffered and for the profit of which he was deprived can extend only to the immediate and direct consequences of nonperformance of the contract.

When the contract provides that the party who shall fail to perform will have to pay a certain sum as damages, the other party can recover neither a larger nor a smaller sum. The court may, however, increase such contractual penalty when it is obviously inadequate or decrease it when it is manifestly excessive.

In obligations consisting of the payment of a certain sum, the damages arising from a delay in performance are limited to the legal rate of interest, subject to special rules applicable to commerce and suretyship. Such damages and interest are due without the entitled person being obligated to prove any loss. They are due only from the day of the demand for payment, except in the case where the law causes them to run. An entitled person to whom a delaying obligated person has, by his bad faith, caused a loss that is unconnected with the delay, may obtain damages and interest in addition to those allowed for the delay in payment.

Interest due on capital will also bear interest as from the legal demand for payment or by special agreement as long as it is due for at least one full year. Yet amounts, the payments of which are overdue, like rents and arrears of rents and annuities, bear interest from the day of the demand or from the date of the agreement. The same rule applies to the restitution of fruits and to interest paid by a third person to the entitled person on behalf of the obligated person.

(v) INTERPRETATION OF AGREEMENTS (*Interprétation des conventions*). In interpreting agreements, the common intention of the parties to the agreement is to be ascertained beyond the literal meaning of the terms. When a provision is susceptible of two meanings, it must be understood in that sense in which it may have some effect, rather than in a sense which would make it meaningless. Terms that can have two meanings must be taken in the sense that fits best within the subject matter of the contract. Ambiguous provisions are to be interpreted in accordance with the usage of the place where the contract was made.

In contracts, usual provisions are to be implied, even though they are not expressly stipulated. All provisions in an agreement are to be interpreted with due regard to all the other provisions, and each of them in accordance with the contract as a whole. In case of doubt, the agreement is interpreted against the person entitled and in favor of the person obligated under the agreement. Regardless of how general the terms used in a contract are, the contract concerns only matters with which it appears the parties intended to deal. Where an example is given in a contract for the better explanation of the obligation, the parties are not taken to have intended thereby to limit its scope so as not to extend it to situations that it would otherwise cover by law.

(vi) **EFFECT OF AGREEMENTS ON THIRD PARTIES** (*Effet des conventions à l'égard des tiers*). Agreements affect only the contracting parties; they neither adversely nor beneficially affect third parties, with the exception of agreements for the benefit of third parties. Yet, creditors may take over and exercise the rights to which their debtors were entitled, with the exception of purely personal rights. They may also, in their own name, dispute the validity of acts made by their debtors in fraud of their rights. In exercising these rights, creditors must abide by provisions of the Civil Code on intestate succession and on marriage contracts and the rights of spouses.

NOTES AND QUESTIONS

1. Note the French definition of a contract. How is a contract defined in the Spanish and the Italian law? What is the definition of contract in Anglo-American law? *See,* e.g., Restatement, Contracts, §1; Calif. C.C.A. §1549.

2. What are the essential elements of contracts? Compare the Spanish and the Italian law. *See also* Restatement, Contracts, §19; Calif. C.C.A. §1550. Consider the French treatment of consent, capacity, object, and cause of contracts. *See* Calif. C.C.A. §1565ff. for a comparison.

What is the effect of an obligation as understood by French law? Note the effect of obligations to give, to do, or not to do. The primary obligation for the breach of such an obligation is liability for damages and interest. May specific performance then be obtained in French law? Compare the Italian, the Spanish, and the German law where specific performance is readily obtainable.

Specific performance of a contract may, in the discretion of the court, be obtained in the French law by the procedure known as *astreinte.* The Law of July 21, 1949, and Law No. 72-626 of July 5, 1972, as amended, deal with *astreintes.* It is limited chiefly to the obtaining of possession of premises and immovables.

For specific performance in Anglo-American law, *see,* e.g., Restatement, Contracts, §358ff.; Calif. C.C.A. §3384ff.

3. Compare the French rule on interpretation of contracts with that of the German law. What is the Anglo-American rule? *See*, e.g., Restatement, Contracts §226ff., Calif. C.C.A. §1635ff.

(d)   Various types of obligations (*Diverses especes d'obligations*).[125]

(i)   CONDITIONAL OBLIGATIONS (*Obligations conditionnelles*).

(aa)   Conditions in general and various types of conditions (Condition en général, et ses diverses espèces).   An obligation is conditional when it depends on a future uncertain event, whether it is suspended until the happening of the event or it is terminated if the event does not take place. Fortuitous condition is that which depends purely on chance and which is controlled neither by the entitled nor the obligated party. Potestative condition is that which makes the performance of the agreement depend on an event which one or the other party may bring about or prevent from arising. Mixed condition is that which depends at the same time on the will of one of the parties and on that of a third person.

The condition of something impossible, contrary to good morals, or prohibited by law is void and makes void an agreement that depends on it. The condition not to do something impossible does not make void the obligation entered into under that condition.

Any obligation entered into by the obligated party on a potestative condition is void.[126]

A condition must be performed in the way intended by the parties. When an obligation is entered into on condition than an event occur within a definite time, the condition is broken when the time has run without the event taking place. If no time has been set, the condition may yet be performed and it is considered broken only when it is certain that the event will not take place. When an obligation is entered into on condition that a particular event not occur within a certain time, such condition is fulfilled when the time has run without the event taking place. The condition is also fulfilled if it is certain before the time has run that the event will not take place. When no time has been set, the condition is fulfilled when it is certain that the event will not take place.

A condition is deemed fulfilled when the party obligated under it prevents it from being fulfilled. A fulfilled condition has retroactive effect from the day of contracting. If the entitled party dies before the condition has been fulfilled, his rights pass to his heirs. Before the condition is fulfilled, the entitled party may take all steps to protect his rights.

(bb)   Suspensive condition (Condition suspensive).   An obligation entered into subject to a suspensive condition depends either on the happening of a future uncertain event or on an event that has already occurred without it being known to the parties. In the first case, the obligation can be performed only after the happening of the event. In the second case, the obligation takes effect on the day of contracting.

When an obligation has been entered into subject to a suspensive condition, the thing that constitutes the subject matter of the agreement is at the risk of the obligated party, who is not required to deliver it until the fulfillment of the condition. If the thing perishes without the fault of the obligated party, the obligation is extinguished. If the thing deteriorates without any fault of the obligated party, the entitled party can either rescind the obligation or take the thing in its existing condition without any reduction in price. If the thing deteriorates due to the fault of the obligated party, the entitled party can either rescind the obligation or take the thing in its existing condition together with damages and interest.

(cc) Resolutory condition (Condition résolutoire). A resolutory condition, when fulfilled, rescinds the obligation and places matters in the same state as though the obligation had not been incurred. The condition does not suspend the performance of the obligation. It only requires the entitled party to refund all that he received in case the event contemplated by the condition takes place.

A resolutory condition is always implied in bilateral contracts when one of the parties does not perform. In such a case, the contract is not dissolved by operation of law. The party who is entitled to the performance of the other party has the choice either to compel the other party to perform, if performance is possible, or to rescind the contract and claim damages and interest. A petition for rescission must be made in court, and the defendant may obtain additional time if it is warranted by the circumstances of the case.

(ii) OBLIGATIONS SUBJECT TO TIME *(Obligations à terme).* A stipulation of time differs from a condition in that it does not suspend the obligation but merely delays its execution. What is due at a certain time cannot be demanded at an earlier date, and what was paid in advance cannot be reclaimed. Time is always deemed stipulated in favor of the obligated party, unless it appears from the agreement or the attending circumstances that it was also meant to operate in favor of the entitled party. The obligated party cannot claim the benefit of time if he becomes a bankrupt or after he reduces the security provided for in the contract to the entitled party.

(iii) ALTERNATIVE OBLIGATIONS *(Obligations alternatives).* The party obligated under an alternative obligation is discharged from his obligation by the delivery of one of the two things comprised in the obligation. The choice belongs to the obligated party, unless it has been expressly granted to the entitled party. The obligated party must give up one of two things, but he cannot make the entitled party accept a part of one and a part of the other.

An obligation is not an alternative obligation, even if so contracted, if one of the two things promised cannot form the subject matter of the obligation.

An alternative obligation becomes pure and simple if one of the two things perishes and cannot be delivered, even if this is due to the fault of the obligated party. The price of the thing cannot be offered in its stead. If both things perish and one does so due to the fault of the obligated party, he must pay the price of the one that perished last. If in the above-described situation the entitled party has the choice and one of the things perishes without any fault of the obligated party, the entitled party must take the remaining one. If it perishes due to the fault of the obligated party, the entitled party may take the remaining one or the price of the one that perished. If both things perish due to the fault of the obligated party, or if any one of them perishes due to his fault, the entitled party may take the price of either of the two.

If both things perish without any fault of the obligated party and without his being in default, the obligation is extinguished. The same rules apply where more than two things are comprised in an alternative obligation.

(iv) JOINT AND SEVERAL OBLIGATIONS (*Obligations solidaires*).

(aa) *Among creditors (Solidarité entre les créanciers).* An obligation is joint and several among several creditors when it expressly gives each of them the right to payment of the whole debt, and when payment made to one of them will discharge the debtor even though the substance of the obligation is divisible among the creditors. The debtor has the choice to pay any one of the creditors as long as he is not sued by one of them. However, a discharge that is given by one of the joint and several creditors, discharges the debtor only for the share and interest of that creditor.

Every act that stops a limitation from running against one of the joint and several creditors stops it from running against all the others.

(bb) *Among Debtors (Solidarité de la part des débiteurs).* There is joint and several liability where all of the debtors are liable for the same debt, so that each may be made to pay the whole and where payment by one of the debtors discharges all of them. Liabilility may be joint and several even though the obligation of one of the debtors may differ from that of the other debtors, such as where the obligation of one of the debtors is only conditional, or where one debtor is granted a time for payment that the other debtors have not been accorded. Joint and several liability cannot be presumed but must be expressly stipulated. This rule applies in all cases except where joint and several liability is provided for by law.

The creditor may demand payment from any one of the debtors according to his choice, and a suit brought against one of the debtors does not bar the creditor from proceeding against the others.

If the subject matter of the obligation has perished due to the fault of one or more debtors, or while he or they were in default, the other co-debtors are not discharged from their obligation to pay the price of the thing, but they are not liable for damages. The creditor can claim damages only from the debtors by whose fault the thing perished, or who were in default while it perished.

Proceedings instituted against one of the debtors stop time from running with regard to all. Similarly, a demand for interests made against one debtor is a demand against all.

A co-debtor who is being sued by a creditor may use in his defense all exceptions arising out of the obligation and all personal defenses and such as are common to all of the co-debtors. He may not use any defense personal to another co-debtor.

If one of the debtors becomes the sole heir of the creditor, or if the creditor becomes the sole heir of one of the debtors, the union discharges only the share of the particular debtor or creditor. A creditor who agrees to the division of a debt with respect to one co-debtor retains his action against all other co-debtors for the entire debt, less the share of the co-debtor whom he so discharged from joint and several liability. A creditor who receives separately the part of one co-debtor, without reserving in the receipt his right to claim the whole amount of the debt from all co-debtors, discharges only that particular co-debtor. A creditor is not deemed to have discharged a co-debtor after accepting from him his part of the debt as long as the receipt does not so indicate. A creditor who accepts separately and without reservation the portion of one co-debtor in the arrears or interest of the debt loses his joint and several claim only with respect to the arrears and interest already due, but not to that which will become due nor to his claim to the principal, unless he keeps accepting separately the co-debtor's portion of arrears or interest for ten consecutive years.

As among themselves, joint and several co-debtors are liable only for their respective portions, and a co-debtor who pays the whole debt can recover from each other co-debtor his respective portion. If one of them is insolvent, the loss must be equally shared by all the other solvent co-debtors. If the creditor discharges one or more co-debtors and one or more other co-debtors becomes insolvent, the portion of the insolvent co-debtors will have to be paid equally by all the solvent co-debtors, including those who were discharged. If only one of the co-debtors was actually interested in the deal, the co-debtor so interested is liable to the others for the whole debt and they are only his sureties.

(v) DIVISIBLE AND INDIVISIBLE OBLIGATIONS (*Obligations divisibles et indivisibles*). Whether an obligation is divisible or indivisible depends on whether its subject matter, be it a physical thing or a thing in action, is physically or ideally divisible or not. An obligation is indivisible even though its subject matter is divisible if, in its proper relation, it cannot be performed by installments. Joint and several liability does not make an obligation indivisible.

(aa) *Effects of a divisible obligation (Effets de l'obligation divisible).* An obligation susceptible of division must be made by the parties as if it were indivisible. This is so since divisibility applies only to the parties' heirs who can claim payment or be required to pay only their respective portions of the debt. This rule does not apply to the debtor's heirs in the following cases: (1) when it is a mortgage debt; (2) when the amount of the debt is a certain sum; (3) when the debt consists of an alternative obligation and the creditor has the choice to select one of two things, one of which is indivisible; (4) when only one of the heirs is bound to perform the obligation; and (5) when the parties intended that the debt not be discharged by installments. The intention of the parties may be implied from the nature, the subject matter, or the purpose of the transaction.

In the first three eventualities, the heir who is in possession of the thing or of the mortgaged land may be proceeded against for the whole amount of the debt, but he has recourse against his co-heirs. Under (4), the heir alone may be proceeded against; under (5), any one of the heirs may be proceeded against for the whole amount of the debt, but the one sued has his recourse against the co-heirs.

(bb) *Effects of an indivisible obligation (Effets de l'obligation indivisible).* Every person who incurs an indivisible debt together with another person or persons is liable for the entire debt, even if the obligation was not joint and several. This applies also to the heirs of such a person.

A creditor's heir can demand the performance of an indivisible obligation. But he cannot discharge the whole debt or take value in lieu of the thing. If he does it, however, his co-heir cannot demand the indivisible thing unless he accounts for the portion of his co-heir who gave the discharge or who accepted the price.

A debtor's heir who is being sued for the whole debt may request time to implead his co-heirs unless the debt cannot be discharged but by him. In such a case, he will be held liable but shall have a recourse against his co-heirs.

(vi) OBLIGATIONS WITH PENAL CLAUSES (*Obligations avec clauses pénales*). A penal clause is that by which a party, in order to secure performance of another party, enters into an obligation to become effective in case of his nonperformance. If the principal obligation is void, the obligation embodied in the penal clause is also void; but nullity of the penal clause does not affect the validity of the principal obligation.

A creditor may proceed to the enforcement of the principal obligation rather than enforce the obligation embodied in the penal clause.

The penal clause provides compensation for the loss a creditor has suffered due to the nonperformance of the principal obligation. A creditor cannot demand at the same time the performance of the principal obligation and that embodied in the penal clause, unless the penalty was stipulated for a mere delay. Whether or not the principal obligation contains a provision as to the mode of performance, the obligated party can incur the penalty only when he is in default. The penalty may be modified by the judge when the principal obligation has been performed in part. When the original obligation is indivisible, the penalty is incurred by the breach thereof by any one of the debtor's heirs and may be demanded from him in full, or it may be demanded from each co-heir as to his respective portion. In such a case, each co-heir stands as surety for the payment of the entire penalty and has a recourse against his co-heirs for what he has paid over his respective portion. When the original obligation is divisible, the penalty is incurred only by such debtor's heir or heirs who did not perform, and only as to his respective portion. No action lies against those who performed the principal obligation as to their respective portions. The rule as to payment in part does not apply when it is excluded by a provision to that effect in the penal clause, or when a co-heir prevented the performance of the entire obligation. In this case, the whole penalty may be demanded from such a co-heir; but from other co-heirs, the demand may be only as to their respective portions, and these co-heirs have a recourse for what they have paid in excess of their portions.

NOTES AND QUESTIONS

1. Consider the French law dealing with conditions, alternative obligations, joint and several obligations, and divisible and indivisible obligations. The matter is dealt with in the Italian law in Civil Code, Arts. 1277ff. and 1353ff.; in the Spanish law in Civil Code, Arts. 1113ff.; and in the German law in Civil Code, Arts. 158ff. and 420ff.

How is the topic treated in Anglo-American law? *See*, e.g., Restatement, Contracts §250ff.; Calif. C.C.A. §§1430ff. and 1434ff.

2. As to penal clauses, compare the German law. The topic is dealt with in the Spanish law in Civil Code, Arts. 1152ff., and in the Italian law in Civil Code, Arts. 1382ff.

What is the Anglo-American view on penal clauses? *See*, e.g., Restatement, Contracts §339ff.; Calif. C.C.A. §1670–1671; UCC 2-718.

(e) Extinction of obligations (*Extinction des obligations*).[127] Obligations are extinguished by: payment, novation, remission, set-off, merger, destruction of the subject matter of the obligation, nullity or rescission, operation of a resolutory condition, and prescription.

(i) PAYMENT (*Payement*). Every payment presupposes a debt. Anything paid without being owed may be recovered, but a voluntary discharge of a moral obligation is not recoverable. Payment must be made to the creditor or to a person authorized by him, or to a person authorized by a court or by law to receive payment for him. Payment must be made at the place specified in the agreement. If no place is specified and if the subject matter of the obligation is a definite thing, payment must be made at the place where the thing was located at the time the obligation arose. Support payments are to be made at the residence of the recipient unless otherwise directed by the court. In all other cases, payment is to be made at the debtor's residence.

Should the creditor refuse to accept payment, the debtor can formally tender what is due to the creditor, and upon his refusal to accept the tender, the debtor can pay the money into court or place the thing in the custody of the court. Formal tender followed by payment into court discharges the debtor, and the thing placed in the court's custody is at the creditor's risk.

(ii) NOVATION (*Novation*). Novation takes effect in the following cases: when a debtor contracts a new debt from his creditor and the new debt is substituted for the old one, which is extinguished; when a new debtor is substituted for the old one, who is discharged by the creditor; and when by new agreement, a new creditor is substituted for the old one with respect to whom the debtor is discharged.

Novation is never presumed. The intent to effect it must be clearly manifested on the face of the act.

(iii) REMISSION OF DEBT (*Remise de la dette*). The voluntary surrender of documents of title by the creditor to the debtor is evidence of discharge. The voluntary surrender of a certified copy of title raises a presumption of discharge or of payment of the debt unless it is shown otherwise. The surrender of the documents of title or of a certified copy of the title to one of several co-debtors inures to the benefit of all co-debtors.

The discharge of one co-debtor discharges them all unless the creditor expressly reserves his rights against them. If he so reserves his rights, he can enforce payment of the debt against them less the part of the discharged co-debtor.

The release of a thing given as security does not amount to a presumption of discharge of the debt.

The discharge of the principal debtor discharges the sureties. The discharge of a surety does not discharge the principal debtor, and the discharge of one of the sureties does not discharge the other sureties. All that a creditor has received from a surety toward his discharge inures to the benefit of the principal debtor and the other sureties and is to be deducted from the debt.

(iv) SET-OFF (*Compensation*). Whenever two persons are indebted to each other, a set-off takes place that extinguishes both debts in accordance with the rules set forth. Set-off takes place by operation of law, even if the debtors are not cognizant of the rule. Both debts are extinguished to the respective amount the moment they come into existence side by side. Set-off takes place only with respect to debts of money or of goods of the same kind sold by description and which are equally liquid and demandable. Uncontested advances of grain or other commodities, having a current market price, may be set off against money. A delay granted does not bar a set-off.

Set-off does not take place against a claim for the restitution of a thing of which its owner was unjustly deprived; against a claim for the return of a deposit and of a loan for use; and against a debt representing support payments that cannot be seized by creditors.

(v) MERGER (*Confusion*). When the qualities of creditor and debtor are united in one person, merger takes place by operation of law and extinguishes the obligation. Merger affecting the principal debtor inures to the benefit of his sureties. That affecting a surety does not, however, extinguish the debt. That affecting the creditor inures to the benefit of joint and several co-debtors only as to their respective portions.

(vi) DESTRUCTION OF THE SUBJECT MATTER OF THE OBLIGATION (*Perte de la chose due*). When the subject matter of the obligation perishes, is taken out of commerce, or is lost, the obligation is extinguished if the thing perishes or is lost without any fault of the debtor and before he is in default. Even if the debtor is in default, the obligation is extinguished if the thing would have likewise perished had it been delivered to the creditor, unless the debtor has assumed responsibility for accidental loss. The debtor must prove loss by unavoidable accident if he alleges that the property so perished.

Irrespective of how a stolen thing perishes or is lost, the person who appropriates it is not relieved from restitution of its value.

When the thing perishes, is placed out of commerce, or is lost without any fault of the debtor, he must assign to the creditor any rights or claims for indemnity he may have in connection with the thing.

(vii) ACTION FOR ANNULMENT OR RESCISSION OF CONTRACTS (*Action en nullité ou en rescision des conventions*). An action for annulment or rescission of contracts may be brought within five years, unless a shorter time is provided in a particular statute.

In the cases of duress, time begins to run from the day on which it ceased, and in the case of error or fraud from the day on which it was discovered. As against a minor, time runs from the day of his majority or emancipation. As against the heirs of an incompetent, time runs from the day of his death if it was not already running prior to his death.

(f) Proof of obligations and of payment (*Preuve des obligations et du payement*).[128]   A person who demands performance of an obligation must prove its existence. Conversely, a person who claims to have been released from his obligation must show payment or proof extinguishing his obligation. Proof is governed by the rules of the Civil Code applicable to proof by documents, witnesses, presumptions, admission of a party, and oath.[129]

NOTES AND QUESTIONS

The methods of discharge of obligations are standard in civil law countries. Compare the German and the Italian law.

Are the methods of discharge the same in Anglo-American law? *See,* e.g., Restatement, Contracts, Chapter 13; Calif. C.C.A. §§1473ff. and §1682ff.

---

9. Obligations Formed without
    Agreement (*Engagements qui se
    forment sans convention*)[130]

There are obligations that arise without any agreement on the part of either the obligated or the entitled party. Some arise purely by operation of law, others arise from acts of the obligated party. The first mentioned are formed involuntarily, like those among owners of adjoining land or those imposed on guardians and administrators who are not allowed to decline the duties imposed on them. Obligations that arise from acts of the obligated party spring up either from quasi-contracts or from torts.

(a) Quasi-contracts (*Quasi-contrats*).[131]   Quasi-contracts are the voluntary acts of man that result in obligations with respect to third parties, and sometimes in reciprocal obligations of two parties.

A person who voluntarily attends to the business of another, whether with or without the knowledge of the other, tacitly enters into an obligation to continue to attend to such business until the other shall be able to attend to it himself. He must also attend to all business that depends on the business to which he is attending. He assumes all the obligations that would have arisen had the owner given him an express authority. If the owner dies, he must proceed with the business until an heir is in the position to take over. He must attend to the business with the care of a responsible person. Yet, having regard for the circumstances that induced him to attend to the business, a judge may mitigate any damages that result from his errors or from his negligence. The owner whose business was well attended to must honor all the engagements negotiated by the person attending to his business. He must indemnify such person against all personal obligations incurred and must compensate such person for all useful and necessary expenses.

A person who knowingly or in error receives that which is not due to him incurs the obligation to restitute it to the person from whom he received it. Whenever a person erroneously assumes he is indebted to a creditor and discharges a debt, such person is entitled to a refund of what he paid. This right to a refund from the creditor is extinguished, however, if the creditor has disposed of the money; but such person is entitled to payment from the true debtor. When there is bad faith on the part of the recipient of the money, he must repay the capital together with interest or profit from the date of payment.

If the thing unduly received is an immovable or a chattel, the recipient is bound to return it if it still exists. He must refund its value if the thing deteriorates or perishes by his fault. If he receives the thing in bad faith, he is liable even if the thing is lost by accident. If a recipient in good faith sells the thing, he must refund only the price of the sale. The person to whom the thing is restored must compensate even a possessor in bad faith for all necessary and useful expenses made for the preservation of the thing.

(b) Torts (*Délits et quasi-délits*).[132] Every act of man that causes damage to another obligates the person by whose fault the loss arose to make it good. Everyone is liable for the damage caused not only by his acts but also by his negligence or lack of prudence. Every person is liable for the damage caused not only by his own acts but also by the acts of those for whom he is answerable, and by property under his control.

A person who holds, in any capacity whatsoever, an immovable, or any part of it, or movables, within which a fire originates is not liable to third parties for the loss caused by that fire, unless it is proved that the fire arose due to his fault or due to the fault of persons for whom he is answerable. This provision does not apply, however, to the landlord-tenant relationship, which is governed by Articles 1733 and 1734 of the Civil Code.

A father and mother are jointly responsible for the damage caused by their minor children in their custody living in their household. Masters and principals are liable for the damage caused by their servants and agents in the exercise of their duties. Teachers and craftsmen are liable for the damage caused by their pupils and apprentices under their supervision. Fathers, mothers, and craftsmen are liable as mentioned above unless they can show that they were unable to prevent the act which gives rise to their liability. With respect to teachers, whenever it is alleged that their fault, lack of prudence, or negligence was the cause of the damage, such fault, lack of prudence, or negligence must be established by the claimant according to law.

(i) INSURANCE CODES AND UNINSURED MOTORISTS FUND (*Code des assurances et le fonds de garantie*). Article L.420 of Decree No. 76-666 of July 16, 1976, set up a fund from which persons who suffer personal injuries as a result of accidents involving motor vehicles will be compensated if the person responsible for the injury is unknown or insolvent. Damage to property also may be compensated. The fund is formed by compulsory contributions made by all insurers engaging in covering automobile risks. Payments out of the fund are directed by order of the court.

(ii) AIRPLANES (*Aéronefs*).   Article L.141-2 of Decree No. 67-333 of March 30, 1967, which codifies provisions dealing with civil aviation, provides that the operator of an airplane is liable for the damage caused to people and property on the ground by the aircraft or by anything falling from the aircraft. This liability cannot be reduced nor can the operator be relieved of the liability except on proof that the damage arose due to the injured party's own fault.

(iii) ANIMALS *(Animaux)*.   The owner of an animal is liable for the damage the animal causes whether the animal is under his control or whether the animal is lost or escapes. A person making use of the animal is so liable while the animal is being used.

(iv) OWNERS OF BUILDINGS (*Propriétaires des bâtiments*).   The owner of a building is liable for damage caused by its ruinous condition whether it arises due to lack of maintenance or by a defect in its construction.

NOTES AND QUESTIONS

1. The French law deals here with quasi-contracts and torts. Compare the Italian law. The Spanish law deals with the subject in Civil Code, Arts. 1887ff. and the German law in Civil Code, Arts. 812–853. Is quasi-contract part of Anglo-American law? *See*, e.g., Corbin on Contracts, One Volume Edition, 1952, §19.

2. Consider the French rule that the person who causes damage to another by his fault must make it good. Compare it with the mandate of the Italian law. The Spanish Civil Codes states the same rule in Art. 1902 and the German Civil Code in Art. 823. Is there such a sweeping rule embodied in Anglo-American law? *See*, e.g., Prosser on Torts, 4th ed., Ch. 1.

With respect to fire, compare Prosser on Torts, 4th ed., Ch. 1.

With respect to responsibility of parents for damage caused by their minor children, compare, e.g., Texas Family Code, Section 33; Calif. C.C.A. §1714ff.

3. Note the French rules as to uninsured motorists. Compare, e.g., Calif. Ins. C. §11580.2; Texas Motor Vehicle Safety Responsibility Act, Vernon's Ann. Civ. St. Art. 6701(h).

With respect to liability for damage done by airplanes or anything falling from them, compare, 49 U.S.C.A. §1301ff.

As to liablity for animals, the Spanish law deals similarly with the matter in Civil Code, Arts. 1905–1906; the Italian law in Civil Code, Art. 2052; and the German law in Civil Code, Arts. 833ff. *See also* Calif. C.C.A. §3341ff.

Liability of owners of ruinous buildings is similarly treated in the Spanish Civil Code, Arts. 389ff.; in the Italian Civil Code, Arts. 2053; and in the German Civil Code, Arts. 836ff. Compare Prosser on Torts, 4th ed., Ch. 10.

10.   Marriage Contracts and Matrimonial
Property Systems (*Contrats de marriage et les
régimes matrimoniaux*)[133]

(a)   **General provisions** (*Dispositions générales*).[134]   The spouses may make arrangements with respect to matrimonial property as they deem fit, but such agreements may not be contrary to good morals and the provisions of the Civil Code applicable thereto. The spouses cannot contract out of legal provisions governing their rights and duties in marriage and out of those governing parental power and custody. They may make gifts both *inter vivos* and testamentary, but they may not provide for any modification of the succession on intestacy.

The spouses may declare before celebration of the marriage that they wish their property to be governed by any of the matrimonial property systems provided for in the Civil Code. Failing any declaration that would displace the applicability of the system of community property, or modify it, their property will be governed by the rules of community property (*communauté légale*).

A marriage contract must be made by notarized act before the celebration of the marriage. A certificate issued by the notary that a marriage contract has been made must be handed to the office of the registry of marriages before the celebration of the marriage. The certificate of marriage notes whether a marriage contract was made or not. Where a marriage contract was made, it becomes operative upon the celebration of marriage; where none was made, the spouses are presumed to have their property governed by the rules of community property. After the celebration of the marriage, the system of matrimonial property under which the spouses were married may be changed only by order of the court.

After two years of marriage under any of the matrimonial property systems, the spouses may modify or completely change it by a notarized act, which must be approved by the court. The change is effective upon the spouses as of the date of the court order, and upon third parties three months after the change has been endorsed on the record of the marriage in the registry of marriages.

A minor who is capable of entering into marriage may make all such marriage contracts with the consent of those whose consent is required for him to be married.

(b)   **Community property** (*Communauté légale*).[135]   Community property is set up automatically where the spouses fail to make a marriage contract, and also where they declare without any formality that they are entering into marriage under the system of community property.

(i) ASSETS AND LIABILITIES OF THE COMMUNITY (*Actif et le passif de la communauté*).   Community assets are all property acquired by the spouses together and individually during marriage as a product of their labor or as income from their separate property. All property, whether movable or immovable, is presumed community property unless it is shown that it is the separate property of one of the spouses.

Each spouse keeps title to his separate property. Only that income from separately owned property which a spouse does not use up falls into the community. Upon dissolution of the marriage, the spouse has a claim against the community for the return of such income for the last five years.

Personal clothing, proceeds of a claim in damages, money due to him from his debtor, recurring benefits due him (like retirement benefits), and generally all property of a personal nature and all rights that attach to his person are also part of the separate property of a spouse. Property owned by the spouses at the time of the celebration of the marriage, as well as that which they each acquire during marriage by inheritance or gift, is separate property. Only gifts made to them jointly fall into community property. Any accession to separate property is separate property, as is property acquired by exchange for separate property.

The liabilities of the community are comprised of payments in support of children, debts contracted by the spouses to run the household and educate the children, and all other debts incurred by one or the other spouse during the community system as further elaborated below.

Debts owed by the spouses on the day of the celebration of the marriage, and those that encumber any property inherited or obtained as a gift during marriage, are their separate liabilities.

All debts incurred by the husband during community are satisfied from community property, subject to compensation of the community property by the husband in proper cases.

All debt incurred by the wife during community that arise without any contract, those which arise by contract to which the husband consented or which were authorized by a court order, and those incurred for the purpose of running the household or educating the children are satisfied from the community property. Any other debts incurred by the wife are satisfied from her separate property.

A debt that has been incurred by one of the spouses and is entered into the community may not be satisfied from the separate property of the other spouse. Such debt enters the community only by consent of the other spouse, and his separate property does not answer for it. Where, however, the debt is incurred by the wife with the consent of the husband, it may be satisfied from community property or the separate property of either spouse. If it is satisfied from the community or the separate property of the husband, these funds may be compensated in proper cases from the separate property of the wife.

The wife who exercises a profession binds only her separate property by her professional activity. The community or the separate property of the husband can be bound only by an express agreement to be so bound.

(ii) ADMINISTRATION OF COMMUNITY AND OF SEPARATE PROPERTY (*Administration de la communauté et des biens propres*). The husband alone administers the community property. He is responsible for negligence. He may alienate community property with the limitations imposed on him by law, as mentioned below. He may not make gifts *inter vivos* of community property, even to set up his children, without the consent of his wife. His testamentary dispositions may not exceed his share in the community. If he bequeaths a chattel owned by the community, the donee can obtain possession of it only if on partition of the community property it is allotted to the husband's heirs. If it is not so allotted, the donee has a claim for the full value of the chattel on the share of community property allotted to the husband's heirs and on the separate property of the husband. The husband may not without the consent of the wife sell, encumber, or lease immovables and commercial property of the community.

Where one of the spouses is incapacitated and so unable to administer the community, the other spouse may, by order of the court, be invested with his powers. Such spouse has then the powers of the spouse for whom he acts. He must obtain court authorization for dispositions for which he would need the consent of the incapacitated spouse.

Where a spouse exceeds his powers with respect to community property, the other spouse may, unless he has ratified such act, demand its annulment within two years from the day on which he acquired notice thereof, but not later than two years from the dissolution of the community.

Each spouse has full title and administration of his separate property. If one spouse entrusts the other with the management of his separate property, the rules of agency apply. Where one of the spouses is incapacitated and so unable to administer his separate property, the other spouse may, by order of the court, be authorized to administer it. The community must indemnify the separate property of the spouses for any advantage taken therefrom and vice versa.

(iii) DISSOLUTION OF THE COMMUNITY (*Dissolution de la communauté*). The community is dissolved by the death of one of the spouses, the declaration of disappearance of one of the spouses, divorce, judicial separation, separation of property, or a change in the system of matrimonial property.

As to the separation of property, it may be demanded by one of the spouses where, due to the bad administration of the other spouse, the interests of the demanding spouse are endangered. Where a decree of separation of property is made, it takes its effect from the day on which the petition was filed. The order will be noted on the record of the marriage in the office of the registry of marriages. The spouse who obtains separation of property must contribute, together with the other spouse, to the support of the household and the education of the children. He must bear such expenses alone if the other spouse is unable to contribute.

The decree of separation of property places the spouses under the system of separation of property regulated by the Civil Code.[136]

Where due to the fault of one of the spouses their cohabitation comes to an end, the other spouse may demand that separation of property be decreed as of the day of such end of cohabitation.

In the case of divorce, the spouses may make an agreement for the dissolution and partition of community property. The agreement must be made in a notarized act and must be approved by the court.

Upon dissolution of the community, each spouse takes his separate property and the community property is partitioned. Each spouse must list his claims against the community and what he owes to the community. If there is a balance in favor of the community, it must be brought in. If there is a balance in favor of the spouse, he can take it out. It will be first levied on ready cash, then on movables, and finally on immovables of the community. If both spouses have a balance against the community, the wife's is taken out first. The husband may levy only against the community property, whereas the wife may, in case of insufficiency, levy also against the separate property of her husband. All claims bear interest from the day of the dissolution of the community. After all claims have been satisfied, the remaining community property is partitioned equally between the spouses. A spouse who conceals or diverts an asset is not entitled to share in it.

Where the community is dissolved by the death of one of the spouses, the surviving spouse has a right to have food and habitation and expenses of the sorrow paid from community property for the following nine months. It is a personal right of the surviving spouse.

Where the debts of the community have not been fully paid at the time of distribution of community property, each spouse is liable in full for the community debts incurred by him and up to one half for the community debts incurred by the other spouse. Each spouse must pay one half of the debts of community property and also one half of the expenses incurred in the partition (e.g., those of an inventory or sale of property). A spouse who pays more than his share of community debts may recover the excess from the other spouse.

(c) Community property by agreement (*Communaté conventionnelle*).[137]   The spouses may by marriage contract modify the provisions governing community property (*communauté légale*), and especially may provide that community property will comprise only movables and property acquired by them (*communauté de meubles et acquêts*); that the rules as to the administration of community property shall not apply; that one of the spouses will have the option of taking certain property out of community property upon dissolution for an indemnity (*clause de prélèvement moyennant indemnité*); that the surviving spouse shall have a preferential claim on community property (*préciput*); that the spouses shall hold uneven shares in the community property (*stipulation de parts inégales*); or that the community will comprise all their property (*communauté universelle*). Where the spouses do not make a different provision, the rules applicable to *communauté légale* will apply.

As to administration, the spouses may provide that they will administer community property jointly (*clause de la main commune*). In that case, all acts disposing of and administering community property must be undertaken and signed by both spouses. The spouses may provide that they will mutually administer community property (*clause de représentation mutuelle*). In that case, one may act for the other in the administration of community property, but any act disposing of the property must be made by the consent of both spouses. The spouses may provide that the husband will administer the separate property of the wife (*clause d'unité d'administration*). In that case, both spouses may use and enjoy the separate property of both. The husband is also liable to the wife for negligence in administration.

(d) System of separation of property (*Régime de separation de biens*).[138]   Where the spouses provide in the marriage contract that their property relationship will be governed by the system of separation of property, each of them retains the administration, enjoyment, and free disposition of his property. They contribute to the expenses of marriage in accordance with the provisions of the marriage contract, and failing such provisions, in accordance with their capabilities. Each spouse may prove, by all means of proof, that he is the owner of a particular property. Property to which neither spouse can show title belongs to them equally as tenants in common (*indivisément, à chacun pour moitié*).

Where one of the spouses entrusts to the other the management of his property, the law of agency applies.

Upon dissolution of the marriage by death of one of the spouses, by divorce, or by judicial separation, the partition of property they hold as tenants in common proceeds along the rules of distribution upon intestacy among co-heirs established by the Civil Code.[139]

(e) System of participation in acquired property (*Régime de participation aux acquêts*).[140]   Where the spouses declare that they enter into marriage under the system of participation in acquired property, each of them retains the administration, enjoyment, and disposition of his property. The system operates like the system of separation of property until its termination. Upon dissolution of the system, each spouse is entitled to one half of the net value of acquisitions of the other spouse. Where the system is terminated by the death of a spouse, his right of participation passes to his heirs. The net value of acquisitions is obtained by subtracting the value of the property of a spouse at the celebration of the marriage from that at the termination of the system.

The original property (*patrimoine originaire*) includes all property belonging to a spouse at the celebration of the marriage and that which he acquired later by inheritance or gift. It is established by a written document listing such property and signed by the other spouse. Where no such document exists, the original property is presumed to have been none. Original property is valued as of the day of termination of the system. Where original property has been alienated, its value is taken as of the day of alienation.

The final property (*patrimoine final*) includes all property belonging to a spouse at the termination of the system. In the case of divorce, judicial separation, or termination of the system of participation in the property acquired, the system is terminated as of the day of the filing of the petition. Final property is established by a written document listing such property and made in the presence of the other spouse or his heirs. To this property is added the value of gifts made *inter vivos*. The property is valued as of the date of the termination of the system.

Where the final property exceeds in value the original property, a case of participation arises. The gains of both spouses are compared, and the spouse whose gain was smaller participates in one half of the excess realized by the other spouse. The amount to which the spouse is thus entitled is due in cash. Where the debtor spouse is unable to pay, he may obtain an extension of up to five years and, by agreement with the creditor spouse or by order of the court, he may also surrender property rather than pay in cash.

NOTES AND QUESTIONS

1. Consider the several choices spouses have on entering into marriage with respect to the system of property by which their property relationship would be governed in marriage. Which system will the law select for them if they do not exercise their choice? Compare the Italian and the Spanish law. *See also*, e.g., Calif. C.C.A. §5100ff., Texas Family Code, Ch. 5.

2. Community property was introduced to the United States by the French and the Spanish law. Which are the American community property states? English law

does not know the concept of community property and most American states apply the same rule. The German law has a provision for community property in the Civil Code, Arts. 1415–1518, but the spouses must make it applicable to their property upon marriage through a marriage contract. Virtually no one does this. German spouses may also make a marriage contract for the regulation of their property relationship during marriage in a way similar to that as occurs in France, but again this is rarely done. Consequently, upon a German marriage, the parties are governed by a property system determined by law in the German Civil Code, Arts. 1363–1390, which is similar to the English system and that current in most American states. When compared with the French system, it comes closest to the French concept of separation of property with features of the French system of participation in acquired property. It is called in German *Zugewinngemeinschaft*.

3. Consider the French system of community property and compare it with those of Italy, Spain, Texas and California. After the celebration of the marriage, French law, until recently, did not allow any change in the system. However, new French legislation now provides for a complete change of the system after two years under one system. Compare the Italian law, under which a change is still impossible. What is the position in Texas and in California? *See* Texas Family Code §5.42; Calif. C.C.A. §5104.

4. The French, Spanish and Italian community property systems were envisaged for the protection of the interests of the wife under conditions existing centuries ago. Such conditions no longer exist to the same extent, and the French and Italian systems have been greatly modernized and made purely elective, with similar modifications expected in Spain. It may in fact be asserted that the system of separation of property as applied in English law and the law of most American states protects the interests of the wife as well as or even better than the system of community property under presently existing conditions. Do you agree? *See*, e.g., In re Estate of Crichton, 20 N.Y. 2d 124, 228 N.E. 2d 799 (Ct. App. 1967).

---

11. Prescription and Possession *(Prescription et Possession)*[141]

(a) **General provisions** *(Dispositions générales)*.[142] Prescription is the means of acquiring title to property or of discharging debts by the running of time on conditions laid down by law. One cannot renounce a prescription before it is acquired, but one can renounce a prescription already acquired. The renunciation of a prescription is either express or tacit. A tacit renunciation arises from a fact that presupposes the abandonment of acquired rights. Only a person who has the capacity to alienate property may renounce a prescription. Prescription must be pleaded, the court cannot apply it ex officio. Prescription may be pleaded at any stage of the proceedings, even on appeal, unless the party who does not plead it is considered, in accordance with the circumstances of the case, to have renounced it. Creditors and all other persons who may have an interest in the accrual of prescription may plead it even though the debtor or the owner has renounced it.

Prescription does not run against property not *in commercium*. The state, public institutions, and municipalities are subject to the same prescriptions as private persons and may also plead them.

(b) Possession (*Possession*).[143]   Possession is the holding or the enjoyment of property or of a right. A person may hold or exercise possession himself or through another person who holds or exercises it in his name. To acquire title by prescription, the possession must be continuous, uninterrupted, peaceable, open, unequivocal, and under a claim of title. A person is always presumed to hold possession for himself and under a claim of title, unless it is proved that he entered to hold for another. When a person enters to hold for another, he is presumed to hold under the same claim of title unless shown otherwise.

Acts of permission or forbearance are insufficient to bring about possession or prescription. Possession obtained by force does not make time run. Only after the force ceases is possession established. A present possessor who can show that he was in possession at a certain time in the past will be presumed to have been in possession for all the intermediate time unless shown otherwise. To complete one's term of prescription, a person may tack his possession onto that of his predecessor, whether he succeeded him by inheritance, by gift, or by purchase.

(c) Causes that prevent prescription (*Causes qui empêchent la prescription*).[144] Those who hold property for another cannot acquire title to it by prescription. Thus a *fermier*,[145] a depositary, a usufructuary, and all those who hold property of another by agreement cannot acquire title to it by prescription. Equally, the heirs of such persons who held property as above cannot acquire title to it by prescription. Yet, the above persons may acquire title to the property by prescription, if the nature of their possession is changed either by the act of a third person or by their refusal to recognize the title of the owner. Those to whom the *fermiers,* depositaries, and other persons holding the property of another by agreement have transferred the same, by a document capable of transferring property, may acquire title to it by prescription. One cannot acquire title by prescription against his own title, in the sense that one cannot change by his own act the nature and the origin of his possession. One can acquire title by prescription against his own title, in the sense that one may obtain the discharge of an obligation he himself contracted.

(d) Causes that interrupt prescription, and those that suspend the course of prescription (*Causes qui interrompent ou qui suspendent le cours de la prescription*)[146]

(i) CAUSES THAT INTERRUPT PRESCRIPTION (*Causes qui interrompent la prescription*).   Prescription may be interrupted either naturally or legally. Natural interruption occurs when the possessor is deprived of the enjoyment of the property for more than one year, either by the former owner or by a third person. A legal summons, a demand of payment, or an attachment made against the person whom one wishes to prevent from acquiring title by prescription constitutes a legal interruption. A legal summons to appear even before a court lacking jurisdiction interrupts the running of the prescription. If the summons is void because of a defect in form, if the plaintiff withdraws his claim, if he allows the suit to be dismissed for want of prosecution, or if his suit is dismissed, the interruption is taken as not having occurred. Prescription is interrupted by the recognition of the debtor or the possessor of the right of the person against whom he holds. A demand made in accordance with the above rules against one of several joint debtors, or an admission made by him, interrupts the prescription against all others, and even against their heirs. A demand made on the principal debtor, or his recognition of the debt, will interrupt the running of time against his surety.

(ii) CAUSES THAT SUSPEND THE COURSE OF PRESCRIPTION (*Causes qui suspendent le cours de la prescription*). Prescription runs against all persons, unless they are protected by an exception established by law. Prescription does not run against minors and persons under guardianship, except as provided in the Civil Code, Article 2278, [147] and in other cases stipulated by law. Prescription does not run between spouses.

Prescription does not begin to run with respect to a claim depending on a condition, until the condition is complied with; with respect to an action in warranty, until eviction takes place; or with respect to a debt due on a certain day, until that day. Prescription does not run against the beneficiary of an estate, with respect to debts due to him by the estate. But it runs against an estate, the inheritance of which is not yet accepted or renounced by the heir, even though no administrator has been appointed to administer it. It also runs during the three months that the law allows for the making of an inventory and for the forty days allowed for deliberation on whether to accept or renounce an inheritance.

(e) Time required for prescription (*Temps requis pour prescrire*)[148]

(i) GENERAL PROVISIONS (*Dispositions générales*). Prescription is reckoned by days and not by hours. It is acquired after the last day of the term has run.

(ii) PRESCRIPTION OF THIRTY YEARS (*Prescription trentenaire*). After thirty years, all actions, whether real or personal, are prescribed, and the person claiming prescription is not required to show any title, nor can it be alleged against him that he acted in bad faith.

(iii) PRESCRIPTION OF TEN AND TWENTY YEARS (*Prescription par dix et vingt ans*). A person who acquires an immovable in good faith and by lawful means acquires title to it by possession of ten years, if the true owner thereof resides within the jurisdiction of the court of appeal where the immovable is situated; or by possession of twenty years, if he resides out of that court's jurisdiction. If the true owner resided partly within and partly out of the court's jurisdiction, the time he resided within the jurisdiction is counted, and if it is less than ten years, the time required to make it ten years is added twice to complete the ten years of residence. A title voided because of a defect in form cannot serve as the basis for acquisition of title by prescription of ten and twenty years. Good faith is always presumed. The person who alleges bad faith has the burden of proof. It is sufficient that there was good faith at the time of the acquisition of the property.

Architects and builders are released of all responsibility for the structural parts of buildings they constructed, or the construction of which they directed, after the expiration of ten years where their work is of a fundamental nature and after the expiration of two years where their work is of a subsidiary nature.[149]

(iv) SPECIAL PRESCRIPTIONS (*Prescriptions particulières*). Actions of teachers in the arts and sciences for lessons given by the month and actions of innkeepers for lodging and board supplied are prescribed in six months. Actions of bailiffs for payment for their services are prescribed in one year. Actions of medical practitioners, surgeons, dentists, nurses and pharmacists for their services and medicaments and actions of merchants for goods sold to non-merchants are prescribed in two years. Actions of attorneys for their fees and expenses are prescribed in two years from the judgment in the suit, from the settlement of the parties, or from the discharge of the retainer. For unfinished business, however, they can sue for their fees and expenses for the last five years. In the above cases, the prescription takes effect even though the supplies, deliveries, services or work may continue. It ceases to run only when a bill is acknowledged, a note or bond is given, or an action is instituted and not discontinued.

Judges and attorneys are discharged of liability for papers in their possession five years after the giving of the judgment. Bailiffs are discharged of liability for the service of process in two years from such service.

Salaries, arrears of annuities in perpetuity and for life, arrears of support payments, rents of premises and of farmland, interest on money borrowed, and generally all amounts payable yearly or in shorter terms are prescribed in five years.

The prescriptions mentioned in this section run against minors and persons under guardianship subject to their claim in damages against their guardians.[150]

With respect to movables, possession is equivalent to title. The person who loses property, however, or whose property is stolen, may reclaim it within three years from the day of loss or theft from anyone holding such property. That person has a claim for damages against the person from whom he obtained the property. If the present possessor of stolen or lost property bought it at a fair, at a public market, at public auction, or from a merchant dealing in the commodity, the owner of the property cannot obtain restitution of it without paying the possessor the amount he paid to acquire it.

(f) Protection of possession (*Protection possessoire*).[151] Possession is protected against any disturbance irrespective of how it was acquired. The possessor is protected against everybody except the one from whom he obtained possession. Possessory actions are regulated by the Code of Civil Procedure.[152]

NOTES AND QUESTIONS

The law of prescription is governed by statutory enactments even in common law countries. Under prescription, civil law statutes cover a subject treated in common law countries under both limitation and acquisition of title by adverse possession.

Compare the provisions of the French law of prescription with those of the German, the Italian and the Spanish law. Do you find any significant differences?

Do the French and Spanish provisions make a clearer distinction between adverse possession and limitation than the German and Italian provisions?

Is suspension and interruption of prescription treated uniformly in all four laws?

Does prescription run against the state?

Consider the wide spectrum of different terms of limitation in the provisions of the various laws. Select a particular, e.g., two-year term, and follow it through the several laws. Does it generally cover similar claims? How does it compare with the law of your state? *See*, e.g., Calif. C.C.P.A. §312ff.

Note the protection of possession in French law. Compare the Anglo-American possession doctrine as developed in Armory v. Delamirie, [1722], 1 Strange 505; Elwes v. Brigg Gas Co. [1886], 33 Ch. D. 562; South Staffordshire Waterworks Co. v. Sharman, [1896] 2 Q.B. 44.

B. THE COMMERCIAL LAW

The French Code of Commerce dates from 1807, as supplemented and amended by later enactments. It has 644 articles presented in four books: Book 1. Commerce in general; Book 2. Maritime commerce; Book 3. Bankruptcy; and Book 4. Commercial courts.

Book 1 (Commerce in general) has the following titles: I. Merchants; II. Books of Commerce; III. repealed; IV. repealed; V. The exchange and brokers; VI. Pledges and commission merchants; VII. Purchases and sales; VIII. Commercial paper; and IX. Prescription.

Book 2 (Maritime commerce) has the following titles: I. Ships; II. Personnel; III. Charter parties and maritime transport; IV. Maritime sales; V. Marine insurance; VI. Maritime events; VII. Maritime offenses and courts; and VIII. Diverse provisions.

Book 3 (Bankruptcy) is now governed by the Law of Bankruptcy, No. 67-563 of July 13, 1967, as amended.

Book 4 (Commercial courts) has the following titles: I. Organization of commercial courts; II. Jurisdiction; III. Proceedings; and IV. Proceedings on appeal.

Further important statutes appear in the appendix to the Commercial Code. They deal, for instance, with regulation of commerce, commercial sales, banking and credit, patents, trademarks, copyrights, and corporations.

The following are topics selected from the French commercial law.

1. Merchants (*Commerçants*)[153]

Merchants are persons who habitually engage in acts of commerce in the exercise of their profession. Minors, even when emancipated, may not engage in commerce.

A married woman may freely engage in commerce. She is not reputed a merchant if she only assists her husband in his business. To be a merchant, she must engage in business on her own, independent of her husband. A wife who is a merchant binds her separate property under any of the systems of matrimonial property. She may also bind community property with the consent of her husband.

Merchants must keep the usual commercial books and must be registered in the register of commerce.

2. Books of Commerce (*Livres de commerce*)[154]

Each person, whether physical or corporate, having the quality of a merchant must keep books in which are entered the daily operations of the business. He may enter therein only a monthly summary of such operations, but in that case he must retain documents from which his operations may be traced day by day. He must also make each year a statement of assets and liabilities of his business (*inventaire des actifs et passifs*), a balance sheet (*bilan*), and a profit and loss statement (*compte de pertes et profits*). The statement of assets and liabilities is entered in a book of inventory (*livre d'inventaire*), in which the balance sheet and the profit and loss statement are also entered. The book of daily entries and the book of inventory are kept chronologically, without gaps or alterations of any kind. They are checked and initialed in the usual form and without cost, by a judge of a court of commerce, a judge of a court of instance, or the city mayor or his assistant. All the books and documents mentioned above must be preserved for ten years. All correspondence received and copies of correspondence dispatched also must be filed and preserved for ten years.

Books of commerce properly kept may be admitted by the court as proof of acts of commerce between merchants. Books of commerce that have not been properly kept may not be produced in court or made proof to the benefit of the person who keeps them without prejudice of provisions on bankruptcies. The disclosure of entries in books and inventories may not be ordered by the court except in matters of succession, community property, partition of partnership property, and bankruptcy. In the course of judicial proceedings, the court may order the books to be produced.

3. Register of Commerce (*Registre du commerce*)[155]

The following are registered in the commercial register: all merchants; all foreign partnerships and corporations that open a branch, agency or any other office in France; all French entities of industrial or commercial nature with legal personalities and financial autonomy; and every commercial agency or representation of foreign states or foreign public entities operating in France.

The register of commerce is kept by the clerk of court (*greffier*) of every commercial court and of every court of grand instance sitting in commercial matters. There also is a national register of commerce (*registre national du commerce*), which holds the information supplied to the various courts on a national basis.

Every person or entity required to register must so register with the proper court within fifteen days from the beginning of commercial activity. The proper court is that within the jurisdiction of which the person or entity has his or its seat. The court clerk causes the information to be published within eight days in the

Bulletin officiel des annonces commerciales, which is a commercial supplement to the *Journal Officiel* and is published on a national basis.

Upon ceasing commercial activity, every person or entity entered in the register must request the deletion of such registration within fifteen days of the discontinuation of such activity.

NOTES AND QUESTIONS

1. The French commercial law is consolidated in the Code of Commerce. It comprises the law covered in the American law in the Uniform Commercial Code and also such other subjects as the laws of admiralty, bankruptcy, partnerships, and corporations. Compare it with the German and the Spanish commercial law. How is commercial law treated in Italian law?

2. How does the definition of a merchant in French law compare with that of German law? A merchant must be registered in the register of commerce. The register is kept by commercial courts or by those courts of grand instance that form commercial chambers. All merchants, including partnerships and corporations, must register. Compare the Anglo-American system.

3. Merchants must keep the usual commercial books. What commercial books must be kept? Compare the Spanish and the German requirements. Do the books make proof of the transactions recorded?

---

4.   Partnerships and Corporations (*Sociétés commerciales*)[156]

There are general partnerships, commandite partnerships, corporations with limited liability, stock corporations, and commandite stock partnerships.

(a)   General partnership (*Société en nom collectif*).[157]   A general partnership is a partnership of two or more persons who are jointly and severally liable for the debts of the partnership. Names of all partners must appear in the firm name, or only the name of one or more partners with the additional words "and company," but the partnership may have only a firm name and operate thereunder.

The partnership contract determines the relations among partners, especially when all are also managing partners. Unless otherwise provided, all partners may individually undertake acts on behalf of the partnership. Essential matters that exceed the scope of management must be decided by all partners.

The partnership comes to an end by the death or bankruptcy of a partner, but the other partners may continue the partnership. A partner may dispose of his interest in the partnership only with the consent of the other partners.

A creditor may not sue an individual partner unless he has first made a demand for payment on the partnership.

The partnership must keep the usual commercial books and must be registered in the register of commerce.

(b) Commandite partnership (*Société en commandite simple*).[158]   A commandite partnership has two types of partners: one or more general partners (*associés commandités*) and one or more commandite partners (*associés commanditaires*). The partnership is governed by the rules applicable to general partnership, with the exception of provisions applicable to the commandite partners.

Only the names of general partners may appear in the firm name. Should the name of a commandite partner appear in the firm name, he would be liable in the same manner as a general partner.

The partnership contract must list the financial interest of every partner in the partnership with the indication of whether he is a general or a commandite partner.

Commandite partners may not take part in the management of the partnership, not even under a power of attorney.

The partnership contract may provide that the commandite partners may dispose of their interests to any other partner. It may also provide for such disposition to strangers with the consent of the general partners and with that of the majority of commandite partners and of the capital held by them. The death or bankruptcy of a commandite partner has no effect on the partnership. The partnership must keep the usual commercial books and must be registered in the register of commerce.

(c) Corporation with limited liability (*Société à responsabilité limité*).[159]   A corporation with limited liability is a commercial corporation and is subject to the laws and usages of commerce. It is created by a notarized document or by an act under private signature. The number of its members may not exceed fifty. Its capital must be at least twenty thousand francs, and the shares must be of equal value not inferior to one hundred francs. It is definitively set up only after all the shares have been allotted among members as is provided in the memorandum of association. A corporation with limited liability that is constituted in contravention of the above provisions is void and considered not validly constituted. Its nullity, however, cannot be pleaded to the detriment of third parties.

The name of the corporation may be derived from its activity, or it may embody the names of one or more of its members. It must register with the register of commerce, which is kept by the court of commerce or, failing one, by the court of grand instance within the jurisdiction of which it is situated. It must trade under its name, which must be followed with the words "corporation with limited liability" and with the sum of its capital. The shares of the corporation may be freely alienated to existing members, but to third persons only with the consent of the majority of members who hold at least three fourths of the corporation's capital. The members respond only with their shares for the debts of the corporation.

The corporation is managed by one or more directors or managers, taken from among its members or from other persons, who are paid for their services or who perform them free. They are appointed by the members in the memorandum of association, or in a later document, for a fixed time or indefinitely. They can act for the corporation. Any limitation imposed on their power to act is of no effect against third persons. They can be removed only for good reason, unless they are appointed for a fixed time. They are responsible to the corporation and third parties for any breach of law and defaults committed in the course of their management. Most decisions of the members are made at meetings, but less important decisions may be made by correspondence. All decisions must be made by members holding a majority of the corporation's capital. Each member has the right to as many votes as he holds shares. At least one annual meeting must be held. Where the corporation's capital exceeds 300,000 francs, an auditor (*commissaire aux comptes*) must be appointed. The auditor or auditors are appointed by the members for three commercial years.

The corporation may convert itself into another type of partnership or corporation with the consent of all members. The death or bankruptcy of a member has no effect on the corporation. Dissolution of the corporation requires an affirmative vote of three fourths of the capital.

(d) Stock corporation (*Société anonyme*).[160] A stock corporation has its capital expressed in shares. It must have at least seven members who are liable only with their shares. Its capital must be at least 500,000 francs, where it offers its shares to the general public, and 100,000 francs otherwise. Its shares must be of equal value, not below 100 francs. It is registered in the register of commerce kept by the court of commerce or, failing one, by the court of grand instance within the jurisdiction of which it is situated. Its name must incorporate the words "stock corporation."

It is administered by the board of administration (*conseil d'administration*), which has between three and twelve members elected by the general assembly for a term of six years. They may be reelected. They may be revoked any time by the general assembly. Each member of the board must hold a number of shares determined by the charter. For meetings, there must be a quorum of one half of the board members, and decisions are made by a simple majority of those present unless the charter requires a larger majority. The president of the board, who is elected by the board, has a casting vote. The board of administration has all the powers of administering the corporation and its president is the chief officer of the corporation. It may appoint one or two directors general to assist its president.

The corporation is directed by a board of directors (*directoire*) whose members are appointed by the supervisory board. There may be one to five directors, one of whom is president of the board of directors, appointed to his office directly by the supervisory board. The corporation deals with third parties only through its board of directors or the directors general.

The supervisory board (*conseil de surveillance*) watches over the running of the corporation by the board of directors. It has between three and twelve members elected by the general assembly for six years. They are reeligible and may be removed by the general assembly at any time. The board elects its own president and vice-president. A quorum is one half of its members and decisions are made by a simple majority of those present unless the charter requires a larger majority.

The corporation must have one or more auditors (*commissaires aux comptes*) who are not otherwise associated with the corporation. A corporation that offers its shares to the general public must have at least two auditors.

The general assembly meets in a regular or ordinary session and in an extraordinary session. In an extraordinary session (*assemblé générale extraordinaire*), at least one half of the capital must be represented at the first call, and at least one quarter at the second call. It decides by a two-thirds majority. It may change the charter (*statut*) of the corporation and make fundamental decisions. In an ordinary session (*assemblé générale ordinaire*), at least one quarter of the capital must be represented at the first call with no requirement of a minimum at the second call. It decides by simple majority. It makes all other decisions except those of a fundamental nature. An ordinary assembly is held at least once a year to hear reports of all the boards and the auditors and to approve the balance sheet and the profit and loss account.

(e) Commandite stock partnership (*Société en commandite par actions*).[161] This is a variation of the commandite partnership and a combination of the general partnership and the stock corporation. There must be at least one general partner and at least three commandite partners whose interest is expressed in shares. The general partners are governed by the rules applicable to general partnership and the commandite partners by the rules applicable to stock corporation, which are modified, however, to fit the occasion. The partnership must have a charter (*statut*) and a supervisory board (*conseil de surveillance*), which must have at least three members elected by the general assembly. The supervisory board exercises supervision over the management. The general assembly elects a manager or several managers with the consent of the general partners. It also appoints at least one auditor (*commissaire aux comptes*).

The commandite stock partnership must keep the usual commercial books and must be registered in the register of commerce.

NOTES AND QUESTIONS

1. How does the French general partnership compare with the Spanish general partnership? How does a partnership come into existence? Compare the Italian law. For Anglo-American partnerships, *see* the Uniform Partnership Act, e.g., Illinois S.H.A. ch. 106½, §6.

Does every partner have the authority to act for the partnership? Compare, e.g., Illinois S.H.A. ch. 106½, §9.

How is a partnership dissolved? Compare the German law and Illinois S.H.A. ch. 106½, §29ff.

Are there any notable distinctions between the French general partnership and the American partnership as consolidated in the Uniform Partnership Act?

2. How does the French commandite partnership compare with the Anglo-American concept of limited partnership? *See*, e.g., the American Uniform Limited Partnership Act, Illinois S.H.A. ch. 106½, §44ff.

Compare the authority and liability of a commandite partner under the French law with those of a limited partner under the Uniform Limited Partnership Act.

Is the French commandite partnership virtually identical with those of other civil law countries?

3. Compare the French corporation with limited liability with those of Italy, Germany and Spain. What are the specific features of this type of corporation that make it most popular in civil law countries all over the world?

The French law limits the number of members to fifty. Is there a similar limitation in the Italian, the German and the Spanish law?

The corporation with limited liability is designed to allow a very small group of persons to obtain the advantages of limited liability while controlling a corporation with large capital holdings. Is there a counterpart to the French corporation with limited liability in Anglo-American law? Would an American corporation or an English company of "Proprietary Limited" be able to perform the same function? *See*, e.g., Illinois S.H.A. ch. 32, §157.46ff.

4. The French stock corporation is the standard type of corporation as understood in Anglo-American law. Compare the Model Business Corporation Act and the corporation law in power in your state.

The stock corporation must have a minimum capital. Does the law of the other civil law countries have a similar requirement? Must an American corporation have a minimum capital? *See*, e.g., Illinois S.H.A. ch. 32, §157.47-14.

With respect to incorporation compare, e.g., Illinois S.H.A. ch. 32, §157.47.

Compare the authority and functions of the French board of administration, board of directors, supervisory board, and auditors with the authority and functions of the various organs of an American corporation. Compare also a meeting of French shareholders and the powers they exercise with the corresponding authority of shareholders in an American corporation.

As to dissolution of the stock corporation, *see*, e.g., Illinois S.H.A. ch. 32, §157.74ff.

5. Compare the French commandite stock partnership with those under the Italian and the German law. What are the advantages of such an association? Does a similar type of partnership exist in Anglo-American law?

---

5. The Law of Exchange (*Droit de change*)[162]

The French law of exchange is governed by the Geneva Convention of June 7, 1930. The French law of checks is governed by the Geneva Convention of March 19, 1931. Since these two conventions have been adopted in nearly all the countries of civil law, as distinguished from the English-speaking countries, only two systems of the law of exchange and the law of checks exist in the world, namely, the law of the Geneva conventions and the law of the English-speaking world.

NOTES

The English-speaking world has not adopted the above Geneva conventions unifying the law of bills of exchange and the law of checks. As a result, there is a difference, although not a substantial one, between the law of the conventions and that of the United States. For American law, *see* UCC, Arts. 3, 4, and 5.

---

6. Bankruptcy (*Faillites*)[163]

The French scheme of bankruptcy proceeds first to cessation of payments and composition with creditors and then to liquidation of the debtor's property if no composition with creditors can be reached. It also deals with personal bankruptcy and offenses.

(a) Cessation of payments and composition with creditors (*Cessation de paiements et règlement judiciaire*).   Every businessman, including a corporation, who ceases making payments must within fifteen days make a declaration to that effect with a view to composition with creditors or to the liquidation of property before a court of commerce (*tribunal de commerce*), if a merchant, or before a court of grand instance (*tribunal de grande instance*), if not a merchant. The proceedings may also be initiated at the request of a creditor. The court will grant the debtor's request for composition with creditors where it appears feasible and the debtor seems to be making a sincere effort. The debtor will then have to meet with his creditors and make them approve his plan of composition. The creditors must approve it by a simple majority; however, such majority must represent two thirds of their claims. Where so approved, the plan then must be approved by the court in order to become binding on the creditors. The court will approve it if it is in accordance with the law. The plan may be set aside where the debtor does not keep it, or for fraud.

When making the declaration of cessation of payments, the court immediately appoints a commissioner (*juge-commissaire*) to supervise the process and one to three trustees (*syndics*) who actually handle the business of the debtor. The commissioner may also appoint two controlers (*contrôleurs*) from among the creditors.

(b) Liquidation of property (*Liquidation des biens*).   Where the court does not grant the petition for composition, the debtor does not obtain the required majority of creditors, or the composition is set aside by the court, the liquidation of property takes over.

The property is liquidated by the trustee, who reports to the commissioner, and the final liquidation is pronounced by the court.

Property given as security to creditors is sold first, and any surplus in any particular sale over the claim of that particular creditor is added to the assets. In case of a deficiency, the secured creditor ranks as an unsecured creditor for the remainder of his claim. Unsecured creditors rank equally and get dividends.

(c) Personal bankruptcy (*Faillite personnelle*).   Businessmen or managers of corporations will be declared personally bankrupt where it appears that they ran their businesses in breach of the commercial custom, acted with inexcusable imprudence or in bad faith, did not carry books properly, or dissipated assets, and so on. Where so declared personally bankrupt, they may not engage in or manage a business until they are rehabilitated.

Those declared personally bankrupt will be rehabilitated only when they have paid in full all debts due to their creditors.

(d) Rehabilitation (*Réhabilitation*).   A businessman, including a corporation, who ceases making payments, will be declared rehabilitated only after fully performing the agreement of composition with his creditors, after obtaining a release of debts from his creditors, or after obtaining the individual consent of his creditors to his rehabilitation.

(e) Criminal offenses (*Banqueroutes et autres infractions*).   Fraudulent bankruptcy and other offenses may be prosecuted by order of the criminal law.

NOTES AND QUESTIONS

1. The French scheme of bankruptcy prefers composition with creditors, but the case may proceed directly to liquidation. Compare it with the Italian and Spanish schemes.

Where the person who ceases to make payments is a merchant, the proceedings will take place in a court of commerce. In which courts are bankruptcy cases heard in the United States? *See* F.C.A. 11 §11.

Procedure in bankruptcy is governed by the French Law of Bankruptcy, a special statute. It is a procedure of civil law. Are there special bankruptcy rules in American law?

2. Note the French officers administering the law of bankruptcy. Compare them and their powers with those of the German law. *See also* F.C.A. 11 §61ff.; Bankruptcy Rules, Rule 501ff.

As to creditors, *see* F.C.A. 11 §91ff.; Bankruptcy Rules, Rule 204.

3. Consider the French rule as to rehabilitation. How does it compare with the Spanish rule? *See also* F.C.A. 11 §32ff.; Bankruptcy Rules, Rules 404–409.

4. Note the French rule of personal bankruptcy. Would it compare with Spanish culpable bankruptcy?

------

7. Maritime Law (*Droit maritime*)[164]

The French law deals with maritime law under ships; personnel; charter parties and maritime transport; maritime sales; marine insurance; collision, salvage and average; maritime offenses; and courts.

(a) Ships (*Navires*)[165]

(i) FORM OF CONTRACTS (*Forme des actes relatifs à la propriété des navires*).   Contracts for the building of a vessel, sale and purchase or chartering of a vessel, and affreightment must be made in writing. Such contracts not made in writing are null and void. Vessels may be owned by a partnership or a corporation.

(ii) LIENS (*Privilèges sur les navires*).   Privileged maritime liens rank as follows: (1) expenses of justice; (2) taxes and rates, including port taxes, pilotage fees, expenses of guarding, and the conservation of the vessel in the last port; (3) wages of master and crew; (4) salvage and contribution of the vessel in general average; (5) damages for collision, damage done to harbors and waterways, personal injuries to passengers and crew, and damage to cargo and luggage, including the participation of such claims in average; and (6) contract claims.

Privileged maritime liens rank above ship mortgages. Liens in any of the above classes rank equally, but in groups (4) and (6) they rank in inverse order, with the later liens before earlier ones. The whole ranking applies to a particular voyage and a later voyage ranks ahead of an earlier voyage. Claims arising from the same event are reputed as arising at the same time.

Privileged maritime liens expire one year after their creation with the exception of contract liens, which expire in six months. Privileged maritime liens are extinguished by confiscation of the vessel for breach of customs or police laws or by the judicial sale of the vessel. In case of a sale of the vessel, they are extinguished two months after the publication of the document of sale.

(iii) SHIP MORTGAGES (*Hypothèques maritimes*). Ship mortgages must be made in writing and recorded in the home port of the ship. They attach to the ship and all its accessories. They rank in accordance with the date of their recording, those recorded on a given day rank equally. In case the ship is lost or damaged, the ship mortgage extends to money due the ship owner for damage to the ship, for money due in average, for services performed by the ship in salvage, and for money due under a policy of insurance. Privileged maritime liens rank above ship mortgages.

(iv) LIMITATION OF LIABILITY (*Limitation de responsabilité*). The shipowner may limit liability for damage caused aboard ship or by the ship to any interest, including cargo, in accordance with provisions of the Brussels Convention on Limitation of Liability of October 10, 1957, unless he is personally at fault. The limitation of liability applies also to claims advanced by the state. It may not, however, be applied against claims for salvage and average, against claims for wages of the master and the crew, and against claims for wages of any person employed to work aboard ship by virtue of a labor contract. The owner may abandon his ship to claimants; or he may post bond in the amount due in the limitation proceedings, whereupon the ship is freed from arrest.

(b) **Personnel** (*Armement*).[166] French law deals principally with an *armateur*, the master and the pilot. In French law, an *armateur* is a person who runs the ship, whether he is the owner or not. The owner is presumed to be the *armateur*. The charterer is an *armateur* if it is so provided in the charter party and the charter party is properly made public.

The master (*capitaine*) is appointed by the owner or charterer. He is in command of the ship. He must keep aboard all required documents, especially the ship registration, a list of the crew, documents on charter parties, all commercial documents, and any other documents concerning the ship and cargo. He must keep the log book (*journal de mer*) where he writes, day by day, all entries relating to the navigation and events that take place.

As to pilots, the ship is liable for the navigation of the pilot unless it shows the pilot to be at fault. The pilot must post bond and is himself not civilly liable beyond its value for any loss caused by him. He is, however, criminally liable if he is guilty of acts that bring about criminal responsibility.

(c) Charter parties and maritime transport (*Affrètement et transport maritimes*).[167] The French law recognizes a voyage charter, a time charter, a bareboat charter, and subchartering.

Provisions of the law as to maritime transport deal with the Carriage of Goods by Sea as per the Brussels Convention of 1924. Carriage is effected under bills of lading (*connaissement*). Where the owner makes the ship seaworthy for a particular voyage and a given cargo, he is not responsible for supervening defects in the vessel, fault in navigaton by the master and crew, fire, strikes and lockouts, defects in the cargo, and salvage or attempted salvage of life and property and deviation connected therewith. In any event, the liability of an owner is limited to two thousand francs per bale, or other unit, unless there is fraud or unless the shipper declared a higher value and such value was accepted by the vessel. Suits against the vessel or owner must be brought within one year.

Transport of passengers is governed by similar rules. The ship owner is liable for the injury or death of a passenger unless he can show that the accident was not due to his fault nor to that of his subordinates. Damages are limited, however, to 82,000 francs per person. There is no limit in the case of intent or inexcusable negligence. Action to recover damages must be brought within two years.

(d) Maritime sales (*Ventes maritimes*).[168] The French law recognizes the following sales customary in maritime trade:

1. F.A.S. free alongside (*vente au départ*), where property passes to the buyer on delivery of goods alongside the vessel, and *franco-bord*, where the seller must deliver on board the vessel and property in the goods passes then;

2. F.O.B. point of destination (*vente à l'àrrivée*), where the seller bears the risk of transport; and

3. C.I.F. cost, insurance, freight, port of destination (*C.A.F. coût, assurance, fret*), where the price quotation includes the price of the goods, insurance and freight to the named port of destination.

(e) Marine insurance (*Assurances maritimes*).[169] French law recognizes all types of insurance customary in maritime trade. Every legitimate interest is insurable.

(f) Collision, salvage and average (*Abordage, assistance et avaries*)[170]

(i) COLLISION (*Abordage*). Where collision is accidental or by *force majeure*, or where the cause of the accident cannot be determined, the loss lies where it falls. Where the collision is caused by one vessel, she is liable for the loss of the other. Where the collision is caused by the fault of both vessels, the loss is apportioned in proportion to their respective faults.

Damage caused to cargo and property carried aboard is made good by the ships in proportion to their respective faults. Both vessels are jointly liable for the personal injury or death of persons in the collision; however, a ship that pays above the proportion of her fault may recover that portion from the other ship.

The ship is liable for the fault of a compulsory pilot. Suit to recover damages due to collision must be brought within two years from the collision.

(ii) SALVAGE *(Assistance)*.   French law of salvage is governed by the Brussels Assistance and Salvage Convention of 1910. Salvagers are entitled to liberal remuneration, to be determined by the parties involved, or failing agreement, by the court. In determining remuneration, the court will consider the success of the operation; the efforts of the salvagers; the danger run by salvaging the property and cargo salvaged, by the crew and passengers salvaged, and by the salvagers and the ship giving assistance; the time expended; the expense and loss suffered by the salvagers; the value of the property salvaged; freight and passage money; and the value of the ship giving assistance.

Suit to recover salvage must be brought within two years after salvage operations have been concluded, but time does not run in favor of a ship outside of the jurisdiction of a French court.

(iii) AVERAGE *(Avaries)*.   Average may be general *(avaries communes)* or special *(avaries particulières)*. Special average is that which is not classified as general. Sacrifices for the general good are decided by the master. Ship, freight, and cargo all contribute in general average. The value is taken at the end of the voyage. Suit to recover general average must be brought within five years after the end of the voyage.

(g)   Maritime offenses and courts *(Infractions maritimes, tribunaux maritimes)*.[171] The statute governing maritime offenses is the Disciplinary and Penal Code of the Merchant Marine *(Code disciplinaire et pénal de la marine marchande)*. It contains detailed provisions concerning discipline, administration of the law, and procedure.

The decree on Maritime Courts, known as *Les tribunaux maritimes commerciaux et la forme de procéder devant ces tribunaux*, sets up admiralty courts in all major French ports and regulates the procedure before them.

NOTES AND QUESTIONS

1. The French law of admiralty is governed by a number of statutes which combined present a cohesive whole. Compare the French law with the Spanish and the German law. How is admiralty law dealt with in Anglo-American countries?

2. French admiralty law embodies a number of international conventions unifying admiralty law. The United States is not a party to these conventions, but statutes have been enacted with a similar effect. Compare, e.g., the Limitation of Shipowners' Liability Act, 46 U.S.C.A. §§181-189; the Harter Act, 46 U.S.C.A. §§190-195; and the Carriage of Goods by Sea Act, 46 U.S.C.A. §§1300-1312.

3. As to maritime liens, compare the German law. Note the ranking and enforcement of liens. Anglo-American maritime liens are governed mainly by decisions of admiralty courts. *See also* the Federal Maritime Lien Act, 46 U.S.C.A. §§971-975.

4. Compare the French provisions as to collision, salvage and average with those of Spain and Germany. As to Anglo-American law, *see*, e.g., Gilmore and Black, The Law of Admiralty, 2nd ed., Chapters VII, VIII, and IV.

C. SYSTEM OF CIVIL COURTS

In France there are courts of limited jurisdiction, known as courts of instance (*tribunaux d'instance*); courts of general jurisdiction, known as courts of grand instance (*tribunaux de grande instance*); commercial courts, known as courts of commerce (*tribunaux de commerce*); appellate courts, known as courts of appeal (*cours d'appel*); and one court of final resort, known as the Court of Cassation (*Cour de Cassation*).

1.   Courts of Instance (*Tribunaux d'instance*)[172]

Courts of instance are courts of limited jurisdiction. There is one such court in every *arrondissement*.[173] Cases are heard and decided by single judges. Courts of instance have judges on their staffs delegated to them from courts of grand instance. The highest ranking judge is appointed to head the administration of the court. If some judges are of the same rank, the office of the administrator judge is held by the one having seniority of service at that particular court. The administrator judge administers the court business and directs judicial assignments.

The jurisdiction of courts of instance is limited to a certain value of the subject matter in dispute. In addition, they exercise jurisdiction over certain specifically enumerated types of claims. They decide finally, without any appeal from their decisions, all suits *in personam* and transitory actions not exceeding the value of 3,500 francs. They have jurisdiction to decide such suits up to the value of 10,000 francs, but their decisions above the value of 3,500 francs are subject to appeal. They decide finally, without any appeal, suits arising out of leaseholds and distraint where the value of the claim does not exceed 3,500 francs; where the value of the claim exceeds that sum, their decisions are subject to appeal. Courts of instance also exercise jurisdiction over matters assigned to them by various statutes.

In suits *in personam* and in those concerning movables, as well as in those where the statute does not otherwise provide, action is brought in the court within whose jurisdiction the defendant habitually resides. If he has no known permanent home, then at the place where he is found. If there are several defendants, action is to be brought in the court within whose jurisdiction one of the defendants habitually resides. In landlord-tenant cases and in cases dealing with immovables, action is to be brought in the court where the immovables are situated. In tort cases, action is to be brought where the damage was caused or where it ensued.

Judgments of a court of instance that are subject to appeal may be appealed to the proper court of appeal within one month from notification of the judgment on the parties. Judgments that may not be appealed are subject to cassation on the ground that the court exceeded its powers or for violation of law. A petition for cassation must be filed with the Court of Cassation within two months from notification of the judgment.

Judgments of all courts that entered into the power of law are subject to petition for revision on the ground of fraud. The petition must be filed within two months from discovery with the court that pronounced the judgment.

Parties appearing before courts of instance may appear without the assistance of lawyers or they may be assisted or represented by attorneys (*avocats*). They may also be represented or assisted by their spouses, by their lineal relatives, or by collateral relatives up to and including the third degree. The state, government, departments, communities, and public establishments may be represented by their own officers. All such representatives require and must produce a special retainer in writing from the party whom they represent. Attorneys (*avocats*) do not require any such express authority.

The public ministry is represented by one of its officers designated by the procurator (*procureur de la République*) in the court of grand instance within whose territory the court of instance is situated.

2. Courts of Grand Instance (*Tribunaux de grande instance*)[174]

Courts of grand instance are courts of general jurisdiction. They hear all cases that exceed the power of courts of instance. There is at least one such court in every department,[175] but in many departments there are two or more courts of grand instance. The court is presided over by a president and has a number of judges on its staff. One or more vice-presidents are always appointed.

Cases are heard by panels composed of three judges. Decision is by majority vote. The court may order, however, that a case be heard by a single judge (*juge unique*); but the case will be heard by a panel of three judges when one of the parties so desires. Also, the judge who is assigned to hear the case may refer it back to the panel with the approval of the presiding judge of the panel. All matters dealing with the execution of judgments, recognition of foreign judgments, and the enforcement of French or foreign arbitral awards are heard by a single judge. The territorial jurisdiction of courts of grand instance is defined in the same terms as that of courts of instance.

Judgments of courts of grand instance are subject to appeal. The appeal must be filed with the proper court of appeal within one month from notification thereof on the parties. All judgments that enter into the power of law are subject to petition for revision on the ground of fraud under conditions applicable to such petitions.

Parties appearing before the court must be represented by attorneys (*avocats*). The public ministry is represented by the procurator (*procureur de la République*) and by his deputies.

3. Courts of Commerce (*Tribunaux de commerce*)[176]

Courts of commerce are courts dealing with commercial matters at the level of courts of grand instance. An independent court of commerce is set up in every department if there is enough business to justify it. If not, a commercial chamber is set up within the proper court of grand instance to attend to such business.

The court is headed by a president and is staffed by judges, all of whom are lay judges. They are known as consular judges (*juges consulaires*). The court sits in chambers of at least three members, one of whom must be a *juge titulaire*. The president of the court, who serves for a term of three years, and the judges, who serve terms of two years, are elected by all merchants entered in the register of commerce in the district, such merchants are themselves eligible for the office. To be eligible for the position of president, the candidate must have served for at least three years as a titulary judge (*juge titulaire*); for the position of a *juge titulaire*, the candidate must have served at least three years as a supplemental judge (*juge suppléant*). All judges may serve for three consecutive terms in any rank, but then they must step down and are not eligible for office for one year. A titulary judge who serves his three terms as titulary judge may be elected president without the one year intermission.

The court has jurisdiction over all disputes arising between merchants, and between members of a commercial partnership or corporation, as well as those arising from acts of commerce between any persons. A commercial act is so defined that it covers any purchase for resale, any manufacture, transport by land or water, banking, obligations from bills of exchange, construction and sale of ships, carriage of goods by sea, marine insurance, charter parties and all maritime contracts, and wages and salaries of seamen and their service on ships. Courts of commerce also have bankruptcy jurisdiction over merchants.[177]

Suit is to be brought at the discretion of the plaintiff in the court of commerce within whose jurisdiction the defendant resides, or the promise of the defendant was made and the goods delivered, or the payment was to have been made.

Courts of commerce dispose of their business without any appeal if the parties to the dispute so agree, and also in claims not exceeding the value of 3,500 francs. Appeals against appealable decisions of courts of commerce must be brought to the proper court of appeal and must be filed within one month from notification of the judgment being appealed.

Parties appearing before courts of commerce may appear in person without legal assistance or they may be represented by any person holding a special power of attorney.

NOTES AND QUESTIONS

1. Courts of instance are limited jurisdiction courts. How does their jurisdiction compare with that of Spanish, Italian and German courts of limited jurisdiction?

Compare their powers with those of the limited jurisdiction courts in your state. *See*, e.g., Illinois Supreme Court Rules 281–288 (Circuit court practice for small claims).

To which courts may parties appeal from decisions of courts of instance? Compare the German and Spanish rules.

Is legal representation required in courts of instance? Compare the Italian and Spanish rules.

2. Courts of grand instance are general jurisdiction courts. Compare their powers with their Spanish, Italian and German counterparts. How do they compare with the Anglo-American courts of general jurisdiction? *See*, e.g., Illinois S.H.A. ch. 37 §72.1ff. as to Illinois Circuit Courts.

Note that courts of grand instance form commercial chambers in those districts where there is no separate court of commerce.

To which court may an appeal be lodged against decisions of courts of grand instance? Compare the Italian rule as to appeals from courts of general jurisdiction. As to Anglo-American courts, *see*, e.g., Illinois S.H.A. ch. 37 §25ff. for Illinois appellate courts.

Is legal representation compulsory in courts of grand instance? Compare the German rule as to legal representation in courts of general jurisdiction.

3. Courts of commerce are separate courts. Where there is no separate commercial court, a commercial chamber is constituted in the court of grand instance to sit as a court of commerce. How are commercial cases handled in Italy and in Spain?

What qualifications must judges of courts of commerce have? Compare them with the qualifications of judges who hear commercial cases in Germany.

What is the jurisdiction of French courts of commerce? Which courts hear commercial cases in Anglo-American jurisdictions?

Is legal representation required in French courts of commerce? For judges and attorneys, *see* the section on legal officers below.

---

4.   Courts of Appeal (*Cours d'appel*)[178]

Courts of appeal hear appeals against appealable judgments given by courts of instance, against judgments given by courts of grand instance, and against judgments given by courts of commerce. The appeal is made to the court of appeal within whose jurisdiction the court that gave the judgment being appealed is situated. Each court of appeal has about six to seven courts of grand instance within its jurisdiction. The appeal must be filed within one month from notification of the judgment.

The court is staffed by a first president, by as many presidents of chambers as there are chambers, and by a number of justices, called *conseillers*. Appeals are heard by chambers[179] composed of three members (*audience ordinaire*), and in special cases by five members (*audience solennelle*), the presiding justice included. Decisions are by majority vote.

No further appeal lies against decisions of a court of appeal. Its judgments may only be attacked by cassation on the ground that the court exceeded its powers or violated the law. The petition for cassation must be filed with the Court of Cassation within two months from notification of the judgment on the parties. Judgments of courts of appeal that enter into the power of law are subject to petition for revision on the ground of fraud under conditions applicable to such petitions.

Parties appearing before the court must be represented by legal practitioners (*avoués*), admitted to practice in that court. Parties may also be represented by counsel (*avocats*). The public ministry is represented by a procurator general (*procureur général*) and several advocates general (*avocats généraux*).

5.   Court of Cassation (*Cour de Cassation*)[180]

The Court of Cassation, with its seat in Paris, is the supreme court of France. It has one first president, as many presidents of chambers as there are chambers, and a number of justices called *conseillers*. It is composed of six chambers: five civil chambers, one being a welfare chamber, and one criminal chamber. Each chamber is headed by a president of chamber and has a number of justices. The chamber in session has a quorum of seven members.

The court may sit in full assembly (*assemblée plénière*). The full assembly is presided over by the first president or his deputy and must comprise all presidents of chambers and their deputies, or, failing them, those who exercise their functions, and two justices of each chamber designated annually by the first president.

The court may also sit as a mixed chamber (*chambre mixte*). It is presided over by the first president or his deputy, who is the most senior president of a chamber, and comprises the presidents of those chambers taking part in the mixed chamber, their deputies, and two justices of every participating chamber. Where the mixed chamber is presided over by the president of a chamber that takes part in it, another justice from that chamber is called to sit.

The mixed chamber and the full assembly may not sit unless all their members are present. If such members are unable to sit, their places are taken by substitutes.

The chambers of the Court of Cassation may also sit in solemn session (*audience solennelle*) or in general assembly (*assemblée générale*).

The Court of Cassation reviews final judgments of all lower courts if they are attacked on the ground that the court pronouncing them exceeded its powers or violated the law. Cassation cannot be brought against interlocutory judgments. A petition for cassation must be brought by the parties within two months from the notification of the judgment on the parties. The procurator general (*procureur général*) may bring a petition on his own initiative irrespective of time. If the petition is successful and the judgment attacked is annulled, the matter is remitted to the jurisdictional level from where it originated, but not to the same court, if there remains something to be determined on the merits.[181]

No remedy lies against decisions of the Court of Cassation, but those of its judgments that enter into the power of law are subject to petition for revision on the ground of fraud under conditions applicable to such petitions, namely, the petition must be filed within two months from discovery with the court that pronounced the judgment, in this case with the Court of Cassation.

Parties before the Court of Cassation must be represented by counsel (*avocats*) taken from those who are admitted to practice in the court. There are only sixty counsel so admitted.

The public ministry is represented by a procurator general (*procureur général*), a first advocate general (*premier avocat général*) and several advocates general (*avocats généraux*).

NOTES AND QUESTIONS

1. What is the jurisdiction of French courts of appeal? What is the composition of their panels? Compare the German and Spanish appellate courts. Compare also the powers of French courts of appeal with those of Anglo-American appellate courts. *See*, e.g., Illinois S.H.A. ch. 37 §§25ff. and 32.1.

What remedies lie against decisions of French courts of appeal? What are the comparable rules in Germany, Italy and Spain? What is the rule in your state? *See*, e.g., Illinois S.H.A. ch. 37 §32.2.

2. What is the jurisdiction of the French Court of Cassation? In what different panels may it sit? Compare it with courts of final resort in Germany, Italy and Spain. How does it compare with Anglo-American courts of final resort? *See*, e.g.,

Illinois S.H.A. ch. 37 §1ff. as to the Illinois Supreme Court, and 28 U.S.C.A. §1251ff. as to the U.S. Supreme Court.

For French judges, public ministry and attorneys, *see* the section on legal officers below.

D.   THE LAW OF CIVIL PROCEDURE

The French Code of Civil Procedure dates from 1975, as supplemented and amended by later enactments. It is presented in five books: Book 1. Provisions applicable to all courts; Book 2. Provisions applicable to particular courts; Book 3. Special procedure in accordance with the subject matter; Book 4. Arbitration; and Book 5. Execution of judgments.

Book 1 (Provisions applicable to all courts) has the following titles: I. Preliminary provisions; II. Suit; III. Jurisdiction; IV. Statement of claim; V. Means of defense; VI. Conciliation; VII. Presentation of proof; VIII. Plurality of parties; IX. Intervention; X. Disqualification, recusation and renvoi; XI. Incidents of a suit; XII. Legal representation; XIII. Public ministry; XIV. Judgment; XV. Execution of judgment; XVI. Means of review; XVII. Time, acts of bailiffs, and notices; XVIII. Costs and expenses; XIX. Court records; XX. Letters rogatory; and XXI. Final provisions.

Book 2 (Provisions applicable to particular courts) has the following titles: I. Special provisions applicable to courts of grand instance; II. Special provisions applicable to courts of instance; III. Special provisions applicable to courts of commerce; IV. Special provisions applicable to conciliation; V. Special provisions applicable to courts of rural leasehold (*tribunal paritaire de baux ruraux*); VI. Special provisions applicable to courts of appeal; and VII. Procedure in the Court of Cassation.

Books 3, 4 and 5 have as yet no special titles.[182]

Further important provisions appear in the appendix to the Code of Civil Procedure, such as provisions concerning courts, judges, attorneys, notaries, court clerks, bailiffs, and tariffs of costs and expenses.

The following are selected topics from the French law of civil procedure.

1.   Procedure before Courts of Instance
(*Tribunaux d'instance*)[183]

Procedure before courts of instance follows that applicable to all courts and proceeds along the lines of procedure in courts of grand instance unless otherwise provided. The procedure is simplified and as informal and speedy as possible.

Proceedings are initiated by a citation (*assignation*), which is served on the defendant by the court bailiff (*huissier*). It must contain the name, occupation, and address of the plaintiff; indicate the court before which the case is brought; include a statement of claim and means of proof; state the date and hour of the hearing; and provide a warning that should the defendant not appear, a default judgment would be entered against him. It must be served at least fifteen days before the day on which the case is to be heard. A copy of the citation must be filed with the court at least eight days before the day of the hearing. In urgent cases, the time may be shortened by order of the court.

Parties may always appear voluntarily before the court, even though the court would otherwise lack jurisdiction because of the value of the subject matter in dispute. The parties or any one of them may first initiate conciliation proceedings before the court and proceed to trial only where they are unsuccessful.

At the hearing, the judge first makes a conciliation attempt; where it is not successful, he may proceed to trial immediately or set a day for trial at a later day. The trial is oral. A record of the proceedings and of the judgment is made by the court clerk (*sécretaire-greffier*). The judge may make urgent dispositions (*ordonnances de référé*) whenever necessary.

NOTES AND QUESTIONS

The French Code of Civil Procedure applies to procedure in all civil courts. It lists all the rules applicable generally and then gives the rules that apply specifically to procedure in particular courts, like courts of instance, courts of grand instance, courts of commerce, courts of appeal, and the Court of Cassation. Procedure in courts of instance is thus the standard procedure with special simplifications provided for by special rules.

Compare the French approach with procedures in German, Italian and Spanish courts of limited jurisdiction.

How do Anglo-American jurisdictions deal with the matter? *See*, e.g., Illinois S.H.A. ch. 110 (Civil Practice Act) and ch. 110 A (Practice Rules), which provide for trial and appellate practice with special provisions for small claims (ch. 110 A §281ff.).

---

2. Procedure before Courts of Grand Instance (*Tribunaux de grande instance*)[184]

Procedure before courts of grand instance follows that applicable to all courts unless otherwise provided.

(a) Initiation of proceedings (*demande initiale*). Proceedings are initiated by service on the defendant (*défendeur*) of a citation (*assignation*) issued by the court. It is prepared by the plaintiff's attorney. The citation must contain the name, occupation, and address of the plaintiff (*demandeur*); the name and address of his attorney; the name of the court before which the case is brought; a statement of claim and means of proof; a warning that should the defendant not appear, a default judgment would be entered against him; and a notice that the defendant must appoint an attorney within fifteen day. Service is effected by the court bailiff (*huissier*) at the place where the defendant resides, but process may be served on him wherever he is found. Juridical persons are served at their offices or, failing one, service is made on a member who has the authority to receive service of process.

The attorney for the defendant notifies the attorney for the plaintiff of his appointment and also notifies the court. The case is pending as soon as any one of the parties files a copy of the citation with the court clerk (*sécretaire-greffier*). The copy must be so filed within four months of the service or the service is void.

In urgent cases, the president of the court, at the request (*requête*) of the plaintiff, may set a day for hearing the case before a chamber of the court, and this order is communicated to the defendant together with the citation. The date set must allow the defendant sufficient time to appoint an attorney and prepare his defense. The case may be decided at the hearing or, by order of the court, it will be handled as would be other less urgent cases.

The president of the court assigns the case to a particular chamber and sets a day and hour for the case to be called before the president of that chamber. At that time, the attorneys for the parties involved must appear and discuss the case with the president. Where the case appears to be ready, the president of the chamber, having discussed the matter with the attorneys, sets the case for trial. He will also do so in cases where the defendant does not appear, unless he decides to issue another summons to him. The president may order the attorneys to undertake certain acts and appear before him again when he feels that the case will then be ready for trial. When the president of the chamber sets the case for trial, it may be held the same day.

Where the case is not suitable to be set for trial, the president assigns the handling of the case to a judge who is a member of his chamber to prepare the case for trial; this judge is known as the *juge de la mise en état*.

The president of the chamber may direct that the case be handled and decided by a single judge (*juge unique*). Such judge then has all the powers of the court, including those of the *juge de la mise en état*. The order is communicated to the parties, who may object to it within fifteen days. Where an objection is made, the case will be heard by the entire chamber. The président of the chamber may ex officio or at the request of the single judge remove the case to the entire chamber at any time.

Objections to jurisdiction, allegations of improper service of process, the lack of capacity, and any other objections to form, known as *exceptions de procédure*, must be made at the first opportunity before any pleading to the merits. If they are not made, they are waived.

Urgent matters that require immediate action without any delay, like the prevention of imminent damage or the cessation of an obviously illicit activity, may be submitted before a special judge, known as the *juge des référés*, for his provisional order. The *juge des référés* may hold court on Sundays and holidays in court or at his home when required. His orders are provisional and he may make his order subject to a bond given by the petitioner as security for any loss caused to the other party.

(b) Preparation for trial (*Instruction*). Preparation for trial (*instruction*) is handled by the delegated judge, the *juge de la mise en état*. He has to direct and supervise the steps taken by the parties and watch over their compliance with the time limits imposed on them for filing their briefs and other communications. He sets the time within which any measure is to be undertaken and may grant extensions. He has to meet with the attorneys and discuss matters conducive to the speedy conclusion of the proceedings. He may also summon the parties themselves. He should attempt a settlement of the case. He has all the powers required to order the production of any documents and evidence he deems necessary. He will rule on motions of the parties and on admissibility of evidence. He may order provisional measures. His rulings are not subject to any remedy, but they may be ultimately challenged by appeal or a petition for their cassation after a judgment is given. The challenge is included in the appeal or petition for cassation, which attacks the judgment itself. His orders to discontinue proceedings and his provisional measures in divorce or separation proceedings are subject to appeal, however.

The delegated judge hears all evidence in the case. It is given by witnesses, experts, documents, or judicial oath. The judge may also view the parts.

The parties must indicate whom they wish to call as witnesses and the judge summons them to appear before him in the presence of the parties. Notice of the hearing is given at least eight days before the hearing. Any person may be a witness except those who have been judicially declared incompetent. Even such persons may be heard, but not on oath. Children may never be heard as witnesses in support of any claims in the divorce or separation suit of their parents. Persons related in direct line with one of the parties and the spouses and former spouses of the parties may refuse testimony in any event.

Witnesses give testimony on oath. Persons who may not be heard under oath are admonished to tell the truth. Witnesses are heard and questioned by the judge. He may ask them any pertinent question. He may reexamine them and confront them with other witnesses and the parties. Parties may not directly ask questions, only through the judge after the judge has completed his questioning of the witness. Witnesses who fail to appear or refuse to testify without any legitimate excuse may be fined from one hundred to ten thousand francs. A record of the proceedings is kept.

Without going into the formalities of expertise, the judge may appoint any person knowledgeable in the field under consideration to state certain facts (*constatations*) or give advice (*consultations*) on any matter. After consideration of the matter, such a person, who is known as a *technicien*, makes certain findings or gives his expert advice. The matter is handled like one of expertise but without all the attending formalities. The judge will appoint an expert only when the matter cannot be handled in this less formal way of a finding or consultation by *technicien*.

The judge may appoint one or more experts to report to him within a fixed time determined by him. The parties must cooperate with the expert and give him all the information he needs. The report of the expert is given orally to the judge at a hearing in the presence of the parties and a record thereof is made. Usually, however, and always in more involved cases, the report is submitted in writing to the court clerk. Only one report is given, even if there is more than one expert. On points on which they differ, the experts state their opinions separately. Where the judge is not clear about matters reported in the written report, he may summon the expert or experts to a hearing to clarify such matters. The report is a sworn report given on oath.

Documents that are challenged as to their authenticity are subject to special proceedings. The judge first inquires of the party for whom the document is produced or in the cause of whom it is used whether he wishes to rely on it in the proceedings. If the party withdraws the document or if it is irrelevant for a decision in the case, it will be removed from further consideration. If the party wishes to rely on it, however, its authenticity must be established. The party must give a sample of his writing and produce other papers for comparison. The authenticity may be established by a *technicien* or an expert or experts.

Proof may also be made by an oath known as the *serment judiciaire*.[185] Either it is requested by one party that the other swear to the truth of his allegations, known as the *serment décisoire* since the matter is decided on the stength thereof, or it is ordered by the judge on his own motion, known as the *serment déféré d'office*. The oath is taken by the first party at a hearing in the presence of the other party. The oath is ordered by the judge and his order is subject to an appeal. The party who is requested by the other party to take the oath may refer it back to the first party. A party who refuses to take the oath or refer it back loses the point asserted.

When the delegated judge has concluded his work and the case is ready for trial, he will declare the preparation for trial (*instruction*) concluded and will advise the president of the chamber, who will set the case for trial. The delegated judge is in charge of the case until the opening of the trial.

(c) The trial (*Débats*). The trial (*débats*) is public. It is, however, held in private chambers in uncontested matters. The court may exclude the public where the parties so request, where it is in the interest of public order, or where intimate matters of private life are to be discussed.

The presiding judge keeps order in the court room. He may expell any person who disturbs the proceedings. Such person may be prosecuted in separate proceedings if he actually commits an act for which he may be proceeded against in criminal or disciplinary proceedings.

The presiding judge directs the proceedings. No one may speak without his permission.

After the case is called, the presiding judge asks the delegated judge to give his report. This is done only in cases heard by the entire chamber and only when the presiding judge thinks it necessary. It is regularly done when a delegated judge is appointed to prepare the case for trial. The report is prepared in writing and the delegated judge presents it orally in open court without giving his opinion on the case.

After the delegated judge has given his report, the plaintiff's attorney takes the floor and pleads his case. Then the defendant's attorney presents the case for the defense. The parties themselves may also speak. At any stage of the trial, the presiding judge or the other judges may ask questions of the attorneys or the parties themselves in order to clarify an issue. When the court feels that the case is ready for judgment, the presiding judge will declare the trial closed. He may, however, reopen it if he thinks it necessary.

(d) Judgment (*Jugement*). The court considers judgment in private. Only judges who were present at the trial may participate in the discussion, known as the *délibéré*. The decision is by majority vote.

The judgment is given in the name of the French people.[186] It contains the name of the court; the names of the judges; its date, which is that date of its pronouncement; the name of the representative of the public ministry, if he took part in the trial; the name of the secretary; the names, surnames and addresses of the parties; and the names of the attorneys and other persons who assisted the parties.

The judgment must contain the claims of the parties and their demands for relief. It must give reasons for the decision. It must contain the actual order (*dispositif*).

The judgment is signed by the presiding judge or, if he cannot sign it, by another judge who took part in the trial. It is also signed by the secretary. The judgment is then publicly pronounced in open court by one of the judges who gave it.

The judgment becomes executory when it enters into the power of law. It is then executed by the *juge d'exécution.*

NOTES AND QUESTIONS

1. The first step in the proceedings is the preparation of papers by the plaintiff's attorney. He then has a citation issued by the proper court and served on the defendant, unless an attorney for the defendant is already constituted and accepts service. Compare the initiation of proceedings with that of the German law. How are proceedings initiated in Anglo-American law? *See,* e.g., F.R.C.P. Rules 3 and 4.

Note the French provision for a summary trial where the matter is simple and appears ready for trial.

The standard case goes to the instructing judge to prepare it for trial. Note also the French rule for a single judge to handle and to decide the case. Compare it with the Spanish procedure.

2. The instructing judge hears all evidence in successive hearings. Means of proof are standard in all civil law countries. Compare, e.g., the Italian preparation for trial.

Since there are no instructing judges in Anglo-American proceedings, how is the case prepared for trial? Do the attorneys for the parties undertake preparatory steps similar to those taken before the judge of instruction? *See* F.R.C.P. Rules 12, 15, 16, 26, 34.

Note the French provision for an oath taken by a party to decide a certain point or virtually the whole case. Compare the Spanish and the Italian law.

3. The trial takes place before a panel of judges and is conducted by the presiding judge. There is no jury. Since the case has been thoroughly prepared for trial, the attorneys for the parties stress mainly the law applicable to the facts already established before the instructing judge. Compare it with a German trial. How does a French trial differ from an Anglo-American trial? *See,* e.g., F.R.C.P. Rule 38ff.

4. The court must deliberate on the judgment. Decision is by simple majority. The form of the judgment must comply strictly with the law, otherwise it is void. For actual judgments, *see* the section on judgments below.

Note that the judgment must be publicly pronounced in open court. It is not executory until it becomes *res judicata.* Compare the Italian and the Spanish law.

As to American judgments, *see,* e.g., F.R.C.P. Rule 54ff.

---

3. Procedure before Courts of Commerce (*Tribunaux de commerce*)[187]

The procedure before courts of commerce is governed by the rules of procedure applicable to all courts unless otherwise provided.

Proceedings may be initiated by summons, by a joint request of the parties, or by the voluntary appearance of the parties in court.

Proceedings are usually initiated by the service on the defendant of a citation (*assignation*) issued by the court. It must contain the same information as a citation issued by a court of instance. Where the plaintiff resides abroad, it must give the name, surname, and address of the person with whom he elects to be domiciled in France for purposes of the suit. The citation must be served at least fifteen days before the hearing. The case is pending when one of the parties files a copy of the citation with the office of the court clerk (*greffe*). The copy must be so filed at least eight days before the hearing. In urgent cases, the president of the court may shorten these terms. In urgent matters in maritime and aviation cases, terms may be set from hour to hour without any authorization from the president of the court.

Where the case is not ready for trial, the panel to which the case is assigned will set a date for trial or will appoint one of its members as rapporteur to prepare the case for trial.

The rapporteur has the same powers and proceeds along the same lines as the *juge de la mise en état* in a court of grand instance.

In urgent cases, the president of the court may issue orders on the request of a party (*ordonnances sur requête*), or he may submit an urgent matter to the *juge des référés* as done in other courts.

The case is instructed by the rapporteur; it is tried, and a judgment is given by the court of commerce in accordance with the same rules as in the court of grand instance. The court of commerce does not execute its judgments, they are executed by the *juge d'exécution* in the court of grand instance.

NOTES AND QUESTIONS

How does the procedure in French courts of commerce differ from the ordinary procedure in courts of grand instance? Are the proceedings less formal and speedier? How are commercial cases handled in German and Italian law? How are they handled in Anglo-American law?

Note that under the rules of procedure in civil law countries, the speed of the proceedings depends largely on the handling of the case by the parties themselves. If they state their case with precision and take advantage of summary proceedings, the matter may be decided in a very short time. The French procedure in commercial courts stresses this approach.

----

4. Procedure before Courts of Appeal
(*Cours d'appel*)[188]

Procedure before courts of appeal is governed by the rules of procedure applicable to all courts unless otherwise provided.

The notice of appeal (*déclaration d'appel*) must contain the name, surname, address, nationality, and date and place of birth of the appellant (*appellant*), and if he is a juridical person, his name, seat, and nature and the organ representing him. The notice of appeal must further contain the name, surname, and address of the appellee (*intimé*), and if he is a juridical person, his name and seat. It must also give the name of the legal representative (*avoué*) who, acting for the appellant, actually prepared and signed the notice of appeal. It further identifies the judgment appealed from and the court of appeal to which the appeal is brought. It must also indicate to which parts of the judgment the appeal is limited, if it is so limited, and should give the name of the counsel (*avocat*) who will be pleading the case.

The filing of the notice of appeal will prevent the judgment from entering into the power of law, but a provisional execution thereof may be obtained.

The notice of appeal is handed to the office of the court clerk (*sécretariat-greffe*) of the court of appeal in as many copies as there are appellees, plus two. The court clerk will mail them to the appellees. As soon as an appellee appoints his legal representative (*avoué*), he will notify the *avoué* of the appellant and the court clerk of the appointment. The case is pending as soon as one of the parties requests the office of the court clerk to put it on the court calendar (*inscription au rôle*). This must be done within two months from filing the notice of appeal, otherwise the appeal is considered abandoned.

Where the appellee does not appoint an *avoué*, the *avoué* of the appellant will have to arrange for the service of the notice of appeal on the appellee, with a warning that if he does not appoint an *avoué* within fifteen days, a judgment would be given against him based only on the allegations of the appellant.

As soon as the case is pending, the first president assigns it to a chamber. Where is appears to the first president that the case seems ready for trial and could be more speedily handled, he may, together with its assignment to a chamber, fix a day on which it will be called before the president of that chamber. This is known as the shortened procedure (*procédure abrégé*).

In urgent cases and upon an appellant's motion (*requête*), which must explain why the rights of the appellant are in peril, the first president may order that the case be called on a given day before the president of a chamber to which it is assigned. The notice of appeal, together with the order, is served on the appellee by the bailiff; the notice must instruct him to appoint an *avoué*. At the hearing, the president of the chamber may have the case heard before the chamber immediately, or he may fix another day, or he may handle it as a less than urgent case when the matter turns out not to be urgent. This procedure is known as the fixed day procedure (*procédure à jour fixe*).

Where the case proceeds normally, the president of the chamber will assign the handling of it to one of the judges (*conseillers*) of his chamber. The judge, known as the *conseiller de la mise en état*, prepares it for trial. He has the same powers and proceeds along the same lines as the *juge de la mise en état* in courts of grand instance.

The parties must file their briefs, present evidence, and undertake all acts as requested by the *conseiller de la mise en état*. The *avoués* send all communications to the court and directly to each other.

The case is before the court of appeal for a trial *de novo* as to both facts and law. It deals, however, only with those parts of the case requested by the parties expressly or implicitly. It deals with the case *in toto* where annulment of the judgment is sought. The parties may bring new facts and points of law or offer new proof in support of the claims they made in the trial court. They may elaborate and clarify such claims. They may not, however, raise entirely new claims.

The case is instructed by the *conseiller de la mise en état,* it is tried, and a judgment is given by the court of appeal in accordance with the same rules as in courts of grand instance. The court may affirm, modify, or reverse the judgment of the court below. Where it reverses the judgment, it gives its own judgment on the merits. Where the appeal is found dilatory or frivolous, the appellant may be fined up to ten thousand francs.

The judgment of the court of appeal is executed by the original trial court, but the court of appeal may execute it itself if it so decides, or it may assign it for execution to another proper court.

NOTES AND QUESTIONS

Which rules govern the procedure in courts of appeal? As to appellate procedure, compare the Spanish and Italian laws of procedure. Compare also the Federal Rules of Appellate Procedure.

Note that the appeal must be filed within one month from notification of the judgment on the parties. Compare the German law of procedure. *See also* F.R.A.P. Rule 4.

Note the procedure that provides for the appointment of a legal representative for the appellee. The procedure is initially in the hands of the legal representatives of the parties. After the parties appear, the moving power shifts to the president of the chamber who will make provisions for the preparation of the case for trial.

When the case is heard by the chamber, is the trial a trial *de novo?* What dispositions may the court make in giving judgment? Compare the Italian procedure. *See also* 28 U.S.C.A. §2106.

What remedies lie against the decisions of French courts of appeal? Compare the German and Spanish laws of procedure. *See also* U.S.C.A. §2101ff.

---

5.   Procedure before the Court of
     Cassation (*Cour de Cassation*)[189]

Procedure before the Court of Cassation is governed by the rules of procedure applicable to all courts unless otherwise provided.

A petition for the cassation of an order or of a judgment of a court must be filed with the office of the clerk of court (*greffe*) within two months from notification of the order or judgment on the parties. The petition must be signed by an attorney (*avocat*) who has the right of appearance before the Court of Cassation and the Council of State. A copy of the order or judgment attacked must be attached to the petition. The clerk of court (*greffier*) will notify the respondent by registered letter within fifteen days and will request the files from the court below.

Within five months from filing the petition, the petitioner must file a complete brief with the clerk of court, and a copy thereof must be given to the respondent's counsel. The respondent must file his brief, signed by counsel, within three months from the filing of the petitioner's brief. As soon as the respondent files his brief or, failing the filing of such brief, as soon as time allowed him to file it has run, the matter is considered in issue and is transmitted to the proper chamber of the Court of Cassation.

The president of the chamber appoints a rapporteur from among the justices of his chamber. The rapporteur will study the case and submit a report to the Court within the time stipulated by the Court. After the justice files his report with the clerk of court, the parties cannot file any more supplementary briefs. The record of the case is then transmitted to the procurator general (*procureur général*), who assigns the study of the case to the advocates general (*avocats généraux*). As soon as the advocates general prepare their brief, the record is returned to the clerk of court and the case may be set for hearing.

At the hearing, the parties are heard through their counsel, but the Court may allow the parties to address the Court. The hearing is under the control of the president of the chamber, who is the presiding justice. First the rapporteur gives his report, then counsel for the parties address the Court and make their comments. With permission of the president, members of the Court may then ask questions. Finally, the advocate general addresses the Court. The decision of the Court is by majority opinion. The rapporteur votes first, then the justices in order of seniority of appointment, the senior before the junior. The president votes last. The Court in session has a quorum of seven.

The defeated party is required to pay the costs. A losing petitioner is required to pay a fine set by the Court in addition to the costs, but the Court may exempt him from paying it.

The Court must hear preferentially petitions in certain matters, classified as urgent. These include matters of divorce, alimony, and industrial accidents. The periods of time allowed in the proceedings are then shortened with the exception of the time allowed to file the petition itself, which remains two months.

A hearing in the Court of Cassation may be held before a plenary assembly (*assemblé plénière*), with the first president or by his deputy presiding. The hearing may be ordered by the first president. It is so ordered when an order or judgment is annulled by the Court of Cassation and referred by it to another court for further proceedings, and where the order or judgment of that court in the same matter is again attacked by a petition for its cassation. The rapporteur in this case is a judge from another chamber than that which heard the first petition. If the Court decides to annul the order or judgment, the court to which the case is then referred for further proceedings must follow the ruling of the Court of Cassation.

The first president may order a hearing before the mixed chamber (*chambre mixte*) when the matter raises points that fall within the competence of several chambers or when the decision of one chamber may give rise to different decisions by other chambers. The first president orders the hearing at his own motion or at the request of the chamber handling the case. He must issue the order if the procurator general requests it.

The Court may uphold or annul the judgment of the court below. Where it annuls the judgment, it will remit the case for further proceedings to the jurisdictional level against the decision of which the petition was brought; not to the same court, but to the nearest neighboring court. It will so remit the case to a trial or appellate court, as the case may be.

Judgments of the Court of Cassation are published in its bulletin.

NOTES AND QUESTIONS

Is the French Court of Cassation purely a court of error? Compare the Spanish and Italian courts of final resort.

Within what time must the petition be filed? Compare the German procedure. *See also* 28 U.S.C.A. §2101; R.R. Rules 11 (1) and 22(1).

Note that the case is prepared for trial by a rapporteur, as is done in French trial and appellate courts. Compare the German procedure.

Upon decision, will the Court remit the case to a lower court for further proceedings? Compare the Spanish and Italian procedures. *See also* 28 U.S.C.A. §2106.

III. THE SYSTEM AND ADMINISTRATION OF CRIMINAL LAW

A. THE SUBSTANTIVE CRIMINAL LAW

The French Penal Code dates from 1810, as supplemented and amended by subsequent provisions. It has 477 articles presented in four books: Book 1. Punishment for felonies and misdemeanors and the effect thereof: Book 2. Persons liable to punishment, persons to be excused or held responsible for felonies and misdemeanors; Book 3. Felonies, misdemeanors, and their punishment; and Book 4. Infractions and their punishment.

Book 1 (Punishment for felonies and misdemeanors and the effect thereof) has the following chapters: I. Punishment for felonies; II. Punishment for misdemeanors; III. Other punishment that may be imposed for felonies and misdemeanors; and IV. Punishment for the repeated commission of felonies and misdemeanors.

Book 2 (Persons liable to punishment, persons to be excused or held reponsible for felonies and misdemeanors) has only one chapter dealing with its topic.

Book 3 (Felonies, misdemeanors, and their punishment) has two titles: I. Felonies and misdemeanors against particular persons. Title I has the following chapters: (i) Felonies and misdemeanors against the security of the state; (ii) Unlawful assembly; (iii) Felonies and misdemeanors against the constitution; and (iv) Felonies and misdemeanors against the public peace. Title II has the following chapters: (i) Felonies and misdemeanors against the person and (ii) Felonies and misdemeanors against property.

Book 4 (Infractions and their punishment) has two chapters: I. Punishments and II. Infractions and punishments.

Further important statutes are listed in the appendix to the Penal Code. They deal with such topics as: alcoholism, banking, identity cards, hunting, railroads, traffic (road traffic), sale of liquor, protection of children, state of siege, state of emergency, aliens, frauds, public drunkenness, medicine and pharmacy, fisheries, mail and communications, press and publications, price control and supply of food and services, sequestration of property, poisons, usury, and veterinarians.

The following are topics selected from the French substantive criminal law.

1. Preliminary Provisions to the Penal Code (*Dispositions préliminaires*)[190]

A breach of the law punished with a police punishment is an infraction (*contravention*). A breach of the law punished with a corrective punishment is a misdemeanor (*délit*). A breach of the law punished with a punishment involving affliction or dishonor is a felony (*crime*).

An attempt to commit a felony (*crime*) manifested by the beginning of its realization is treated as a completed felony, even though it was not completed or it did not achieve its objective because of circumstances beyond the control of the actor. An attempt to commit a misdemeanor (*délit*) is considered a misdemeanor only when specially indicated in the law.

No infraction, misdemeanor or felony may be punished by penalties that were not in effect before the acts were committed.

In the case of conviction of several felonies or misdemeanors, only the penalty for the most serious act is imposed.

NOTES AND QUESTIONS

What are the French categories of offenses? Compare them with the Spanish and the Italian law. *See also*, e.g., Calif. Pen. C.A. §16; Illinois S.H.A. ch. 38 §1005-5.1.

How is attempt treated in French law? Compare the Spanish and Italian law. *See also*, e.g., Illinois S.H.A. ch. 38, §8-4.

Note the fundamental principle of law that no one may be punished by a law which was not in effect at the time of the commission of the offense. The law has no retroactive application. Compare the German law. *See also*, e.g., Calif. Pen. C.A. §3.

Note that the French law does not cumulate punishment in the case of conviction for several offenses. The offender is punished for the most serious offense within the framework of that offense and the actual maximum may be imposed. Compare the German law. The Italian Penal Code deals with the matter similarly in Arts. 71ff.; the Spanish Penal Code allows, however, the cumulation of punishment to a certain extent as provided in Arts. 69ff. of the Spanish Penal Code. May concurrent sentences be imposed in Anglo-American law? *See*, e.g., Illinois S.H.A. ch. 38 §1005-8-4.

----

2. Punishment for Felonies and Misdemeanors (*Peines en matière criminelle et correctionnelle*)[191]

Punishment for felonies involves affliction and dishonor, or only dishonor. Punishment involving affliction and dishonor includes (1) death; (2) reclusion for life; (3) detention for life; (4) reclusion for a certain time; and (5) detention for a certain time. Punishment involving dishonor includes: (1) banishment and (2) civil degradation.

Punishment for misdemeanors includes: (1) imprisonment for a certain time; (2) loss of certain civil rights for a certain time; and (3) fines.

The assessment of punishment does not affect the right of victims of crime to compensation or damages.

Reclusion for a certain time and detention for a certain time may be assessed for a term ranging from ten to twenty years, or from five to ten years in accordance with the provisions of the particular statute. A conviction of felony carries with it civil degradation.

Imprisonment for a certain time may be assessed for a term ranging from two months to five years, except in the case of a repeated offense or in special cases where the law prescribes different limits. The court imposing the punishment of imprisonment may also pronounce the loss of certain civil rights, like the right to vote and to run in elections. It may do so only where it is authorized to do so by a special provision of the law and for not more than ten years unless otherwise provided.

A convicted person may be prohibited from staying in certain localities for a time, ranging from two to five years in case of a misdemeanor and from five to ten years in the case of a felony.

NOTES AND QUESTIONS

What are the punishments in French penal law? *See also* the Italian, German and Spanish systems of punishments.

France still has the death penalty. Compare the German and the Spanish law.

What are the punishments in Anglo-American law? *See*, e.g., Illinois S.H.A. ch. 38 §1005-5-3ff.

----

3. Repeaters (*Récidive*)[192]

A person previously convicted of a felony who commits another felony punishable with reclusion or detention for ten to twenty years will be assessed the maximum term, which may be raised up to twice the usual maximum. If the second felony is punishable with reclusion or detention for five to ten years, for instance, a term of up to twenty years may be imposed. A person previously convicted of a felony or misdemeanor with a term exceeding one year who commits another felony or misdemeanor within five years from his release will be assessed the maximum term provided for by law, which again may be raised up to twice the usual maximum. A person previously assessed a term of one year or less who commits the same misdemeanor within five years from his release must be assessed a term twice as long as the first, but it may not exceed twice the maximum allowed by the law.

Criminal detention (*tutelle pénale*) may be imposed against hardened recidivists, i.e., those who within a period of ten years after attaining twenty-one years of age and excluding time spent in custody are convicted twice for felony, or are convicted four times for felony or misdemeanor with terms exceeding six months imprisonment for wounding, lewd conduct, pandering, theft, robbery, embezzlement, abuse of confidence, receiving stolen property, extortion, and forgery. Criminal detention is imposed in the judgment convicting the recidivist for an offense committed. It is pronounced for a term of ten years and takes effect when the convict finishes serving the term to which he is convicted. It will come to an end when the convict reaches sixty-five years of age irrespective of how much of it he has served. Criminal detention is served in a penitentiary and is subject to parole.

NOTES AND QUESTIONS

Compare the French handling of repeaters with that of the Spanish and the German law. How does Anglo-American law treat repeaters? *See*, e.g., 18 U.S.C.A. §3575.

Note the French provisions as to criminal detention for hardened criminals. Compare it with the Italian law. Do French courts have sufficient powers to handle repeaters? Compare the French measures with those applicable in your state.

----

4. Accomplices (*Complices*)[193]

Accomplices in the commission of a felony or a misdemeanor incur the same punishment as principals unless the law otherwise provides. Accomplices are those who by gifts, promises, threats, abuse of authority, machinations, or trickery procure the commission of the act or give instructions to commit it; those who procure weapons, instruments, or any other means to be used in the act, with knowledge that they would be so used; and those who purposely aid and assist the principal or principals in the act, or in the preparation of the act, or in its facilitation. Those who are aware of the criminal conduct of criminals, as well as those who supply them habitually with lodgings, a hiding place, or a place for meeting, will be punished like accomplices.

NOTES AND QUESTIONS

Consider the definition of accomplices in the French law. How do the French provisions compare with those of the Italian and the German law? Note the Spanish law on the matter. Do these laws make a clear distinction between accessories before and after the fact?

How are accomplices treated in Anglo-American law? *See*, e.g., Illinois S.H.A. ch. 38 §5-1.

----

5. Minors (*Mineurs*)[194]

Persons below eighteen years of age who are accused of having committed a felony, a misdemeanor or an infraction are proceeded with as minors before courts for minors.

Criminal responsibility begins at the age of thirteen years, fully completed. Persons who are at least thirteen years of age but less than eighteen years of age at the time of the commission of the criminally punishable act are responsible as minors. The court for minors may, however, for good reasons, remove the protection of minority from any offender over sixteen years of age at the time of the commission of the act.

Where the criminal act committed is a felony for which an adult would incur the death penalty, reclusion or detention for life, a minor will be punished with imprisonment from ten to twenty years. Where an adult would incur reclusion or detention for ten to twenty years or five to ten years, a minor will be punished with imprisonment for one half of that time as a maximum. Where the criminal act committed is a misdemeanor or an infraction for which an adult would be punishable with imprisonment for more than ten days, a minor will be punished with imprisonment for one half of that time as a maximum.

NOTES AND QUESTIONS

At what age does criminal responsibility begin in French law? Compare the German and the Spanish law. *See also,* e.g., Calif. Pen. C.A. §26.

Note the French provision for the removal of the protection of minority. How does it compare with the German approach, which tends to stretch the protection of minority to adults? How is the subject treated in Italian law? Are there significant differences in the above-mentioned laws?

---

6.   Murder and Assassination (*Meurtre et assassinat*)[195]

An intentional homicide is murder. Murder committed with premeditation or while lying in wait is assassination. Premeditation consists in the intent formed before the act of making an attempt on the life of a particular person, or even on a person found or encountered. The intent may depend on circumstances or on some condition. Lying in wait consists of waiting for a longer or shorter time in one or several places to kill or assault a person.

A person guilty of assassination or poisoning is punished with death. All criminals will be punished as if guilty of assassination if, in the course of committing felonies, they commit acts of torture or barbarism on their victims.

Murder is punishable by death when it precedes, is committed simultaneously with, or follows the commission of another felony. It is equally punishable by death when its object is to prepare, facilitate, or carry out a misdemeanor, or to facilitate an escape, or to assure the impunity of principals or accomplices of that misdemeanor. In all other cases, murder is punished with reclusion for life. A person assessed the death penalty shall have his head cut off.

7.   Involuntary (Negligent) Homicide (*Homicide involontaire*)[196]

Whoever shall involuntarily commit a homicide by lack of skill, imprudence, inattention, negligence, or inobservance of safety rules, will be punished with imprisonment from three months to two years, and with a fine.

8. Excusable Homicide (*Homicide excusable*)[197]

Murder is excusable when it is provoked by blows and serious acts of violence against persons. It is also excusable when it is committed in the course of repelling a break-in into inhabited premises at daytime.[198] Whenever the circumstances that make the murder excusable are established, the commission of a felony which carries the death penalty, or reclusion or detention for life, is punishable only with imprisonment for one to five years.

9. Homicide not Qualified as a Crime (*Homicide non qualifié crime*)[199]

There is no crime committed when the homicide is ordered by the law and commanded by legitimate authority. There is no crime committed when the homicide is brought about by an actual necessity in the course of the legitimate defense of oneself or another person. An actual necessity of legitimate defense comprises the two following cases: (i) when the homicide is committed in the course of repelling a break-in into inhabited premises at night; and (ii) when it is committed in the course of defending oneself against theft or looting by violent means.

NOTES AND QUESTIONS

How does the French treatment of homicide compare with the traditional Anglo-American division into murder and manslaughter? How many different types of homicide are listed in the French law? Compare the French approach with that of the Italian and the Spanish law. Is the French approach more elaborate than that of the German law?

Compare the French approach with the law of your state. *See,* e.g., Illinois S.H.A. ch. 38, §§9-1, 9-2, 9-3, distinguishing murder, voluntary manslaughter, involuntary manslaughter, and reckless homicide.

Compare the individual definitions of the various types of homicide in the French law with those of the other above-mentioned laws.

---

10. Wounding and Voluntary Infliction of Injuries (*Blessures et coups volontaires*)[200]

Whoever shall voluntarily inflict wounds, blows or violence to another person from which a total disability to work for eight days or more shall result, shall be punished with imprisonment from two months to five years, and with a fine. Where there was premeditation or lying in wait, the punishment is reclusion from five to ten years.

Where the application of violence results in mutilation, loss of an eye or the use of a bodily function, or permanent disability, the punishment is reclusion from five to ten years. Where the voluntary infliction of injuries without any intent to kill results in death, the punishment is reclusion from ten to twenty years.

Where there is premeditation or lying in wait, and where death then ensues, the punishment is reclusion for life. Where under the same circumstances the application of violence results in mutilation, loss of an eye or the use of a bodily function, or permanent disability, the punishment is reclusion from ten to twenty years.

NOTES AND QUESTIONS

Consider the French provisions and compare them with those of the Spanish law. The French law provides for the punishment of acts ranging from minor bodily harm to serious injuries including maiming. Is this the standard approach taken by the laws of Italy and Germany? *See also* the law of your state. Compare, e.g., Illinois S.H.A. ch. 38 §12-1.

---

11.   Theft (*Vol*)[201]

Whosoever shall fraudulently take anything not belonging to him shall be guilty of theft. Those guilty of theft shall be punished by death if they carried a weapon, whether openly or not, even though the theft was committed in daylight by only one person. The same punishment is obtained where one of them had a weapon in the motor vehicle that brought them to the place of the crime or that they used in their escape. Those guilty of theft shall be punished with reclusion for life when the crime was committed with the concurrence of four out of the five following circumstances: (i) where the theft was committed at night; (ii) where it was committed by two or more persons; (iii) where it was committed in inhabited premises or in those serving for habitation and the entry therein was obtained by breaking in, by scaling walls, by the use of false keys, by pretending to be a public officer (whether civil or military), by wearing the uniform of a public officer, or in pursuance of a false warrant allegedly issued by civil or military authorities; (iv) where it was committed with violence and (v) where a motor vehicle was used to facilitate the commission of the act or to facilitate the escape.

A person guilty of theft with violence (robbery) shall be punished with reclusion from ten to twenty years. Wherever the application of violence has resulted in wounds or marks, the punishment is reclusion for life.

All thefts not specifically dealt with shall be punished with imprisonment from one to five years, and with a fine.

NOTES AND QUESTIONS

The French law treats theft and robbery together. How is the subject treated in the Spanish and the German law? Note the severity of French punishments. Are milder punishments foreseen in the German law? *See also* the Italian law.

Note the definition of theft and robbery in the French law. How does it compare with those of the other laws?

Anglo-American law usually approaches theft and robbery separately. The modern approach is to list them as offenses against property. *See*, e.g., Illinois S.H.A. ch. 38 §15ff. Compare Illinois S.H.A. ch. 38 §16-1 for theft, and §18-1 for robbery.

———————

B. THE SYSTEM OF CRIMINAL COURTS

There are courts of limited jurisdiction, known as police courts (*tribunaux de police*), courts of general jurisdiction, known as correctional courts (*tribunaux correctionnels*) and assize courts (*cours d'assises*), appellate courts, known as courts of appeal (*cours d'appel*), and one court of final resort, known as the Court of Cassation (*Cour de Cassation*). The system of criminal courts is the criminal counterpart of the civil court system.

1. Police Courts (*Tribunaux de police*)[202]

Police courts are courts of limited criminal jurisdiction. They are a counterpart of courts of instance. They are set up in the seats of courts of instance. Their jurisdiction extends over infractions (*contraventions*) committed within the area of their territorial jurisdiction.[203] The court is constituted by a judge of the court of instance who sits as a single judge.

An appeal against judgments of the court lies only when a term of imprisonment exceeding five days or a fine exceeding 160 francs was imposed. It must be made to the proper court of appeal within ten days from the pronouncement of the judgment or, where the party appealing was not present in court, then from the notification thereof.

Parties before the court may represent themselves, but they may engage the services of an attorney (*avocat*). The public ministry is represented by one of its officers, usually by the local police commissioner (*commissaire de police*).

2. Correctional Courts (*Tribunaux correctionnels*)[204]

Correctional courts are trial courts of misdemeanors (*délits*).[205] They are a counterpart of courts of grand instance. They are set up in the seats of courts of grand instance. They are territorially competent to try any person for a misdemeanor (*délit*), as well as an infraction (*contravention*) connected therewith, if it was committed within its jurisdiction, or if the person accused resides within its jurisdiction, or if he was arrested within its jurisdiction.

The court is composed of a presiding judge and two judges. Decisions are made by majority vote. In cases dealing with checks, insurance of motor vehicles, involuntary (negligent) homicide or injury, transport, or hunting and fishing, the president of the court of grand instance may order the case to be tried by a single judge.

Judgments of the court are appealable to the court of appeal. The appeal must be made within ten days from the pronouncement of the judgment or, if the party appealing was not present in court, from the notification thereof.

The accused may defend himself, but he may engage the services of an attorney (*avocat*). If he has not appointed an attorney and demands one be appointed, the court will appoint one ex officio. The public ministry is represented by the procurator (*procureur de la République*) or by one of his deputies.

NOTES AND QUESTIONS

1. The police court is in fact the court of instance sitting as a criminal court. It is a court of limited jurisdiction. What is the limit of its authority?

Compare the jurisdiction of French police courts with that of Italian praetorial courts and German *Amtsgerichte*. How is the court constituted and to which court may its decisions be appealed?

How do French police courts compare with Anglo-American criminal courts of limited jurisdiction, like courts of petty sessions or municipal courts?

2. The correctional court is in fact the court of grand instance sitting in the exercise of its criminal jurisdiction. What is its jurisdiction? Compare it with the jurisdiction of the Italian *tribunale* and the Spanish *juzgados de instrucción*. How does its jurisdiction differ from that of the German *Landgericht*? Note that the correctional court is purely a court of trial jurisdiction and that it is in fact also a court of limited jurisdiction.

With which Anglo-American court can it be compared? Can it be compared with the English Crown Court, the California Superior Court or the Illinois Circuit Court?

Must the accused be represented by counsel in proceedings before the correctional court?

---

3. Assize Courts (*Cours d'assises*)[206]

Assize courts are trial courts of felonies (*crimes*), as well as of misdemeanors (*délits*) and infractions (*contraventions*) connected therewith. They are courts of full criminal jurisdiction. They are set up periodically (every three months) in every department in the seat of a court of appeal or, failing such court of appeal, in the seat of a court of grand instance.

The court is composed of a presiding justice, who is a president of a chamber or a justice of a court of appeal, and of two justices appointed from among the justices of a court of appeal or from among the president, vice-president, or judges of the court of grand instance of the place where the court sits. The court is further composed of a jury of nine persons. Court and jury form one unit and deliberate and decide together as one court. Any decision disfavorable to the accused must be taken by at least eight votes. On the question of punishment, a simple majority vote is required. If there are several opinions, the most disfavorable to the accused is eliminated, and a new vote is taken until a simple majority is reached. Votes are taken by secret ballot.

The judgment of the assize court is not subject to appeal, but it may be attacked by a petition for its cassation. Such a petition must be filed in the Court of

Cassation within five days from the pronouncement of the judgment or, if the petitioning party was not present in court, from the notification thereof.

The accused must be represented by an attorney (*avocat*). If the accused does not appoint one, the court will appoint one ex officio. The public ministry is represented by a procurator general (*procureur général*) and several advocates general (*avocats généraux*) if the court sits in the seat of a court of appeal, and by a procurator (*procureur de la République*) or one of his deputies if it sits in the seat of a court of grand instance.

NOTES AND QUESTIONS

What kind of offenses does the assize court try? Note the composition of the court. May not the jurors be called rather lay judges? Note that the lay judges may outvote the professional judges. How is the vote actually taken? Compare the voting procedure with that in Italian assize courts.

Compare French assize courts with Italian assize courts and with Spanish *audiencias provinciales*. How does the French assize court compare with the German *Landgericht*?

What are the remedies against decisions of French assize courts? Compare them with those available against decisions of Italian assize courts and Spanish *audiencias provinciales*.

Is legal representation mandatory in assize courts?

How would the French assize court compare with an Anglo-American trial court, like the Texas District Court, the California Superior Court, the Illinois Circuit Court, or the U.S. District Court?

––––––––––––

4. Courts of Appeal (*Cours d'appel*)[207]

The criminal chamber of the court of appeal (*chambre des appels correctionnels*) hears appeals against judgments of police courts and correctional courts situated within its jurisdiction. The criminal chamber is composed of a president of chamber and two justices (*conseillers*). They decide by majority vote. No further appeal lies against judgments of the court of appeal, but they may be attacked by a petition for their cassation. The appeal must be filed within five days from the pronouncement of the judgment or, if the petitioning party was not present in court, from the notification on the parties.

The accused must be represented by an attorney (*avocat*). The public ministry is represented by a procurator general (*procureur général*) and several advocates general (avocats généraux).

NOTES AND QUESTIONS

What is the jurisdiction of the court of appeal in criminal matters? Note that the court of appeal has both civil and criminal jurisdiction. Its criminal chamber hears criminal appeals. Why is there no appeal against judgments of French assize courts?

Compare the functions of French courts of appeal with those of Italian courts of appeal, German *Oberlandesgerichte* or Spanish *audiencias provinciales*.

How does the French court of appeal compare with an Anglo-American court of criminal appeal?

What remedies lie against judgments of French courts of appeal?

----

5. Court of Cassation (*Cour de Cassation*)[208]

The criminal chamber (*chambre criminelle*) of the Court of Cassation is headed by a president of chamber and has a number of justices (*conseillers*). The chamber in session has a quorum of seven members. It hears petitions for the annulment of judgments on the ground that the lower court exceeded its power or that it violated the law. Judgments of all lower courts may be so attacked. If the petition is successful and the judgment attacked is annulled, the case is remitted to the jurisdictional level from where it originated, but not to the same court, if there remains something to be determined on the merits. The procurator general (*procureur général*), on his own initiative and irrespective of time, may file a petition purely in the interest of the law.

Parties before the Court must be represented by counsel (*avocats*) taken from those who are admitted to practice before the Court. There are only sixty counsel so admitted. The public ministry is represented by the procurator general (*procureur général*), a first advocate general (*premier avocat général*), and several advocates general (*avocats généraux*).

NOTES AND QUESTIONS

Is the French Court of Cassation purely a court of error? Note that its criminal jurisdiction is exercised by one chamber only, the criminal chamber. Compare the function of the French Court of Cassation with that of the Italian Court of Cassation, the Spanish Supreme Court and the German Supreme Court. How does its function compare with that of the highest criminal court in your state? How does it compare with that of the United States Supreme Court?

Note the special representation required in the French Court of Cassation. Is there special legal representation required in the courts of final resort in other countries?

For judges, prosecutors and attorneys in the French courts, *see* the section on legal officers below.

C. THE LAW OF CRIMINAL PROCEDURE

The French Code of Criminal Procedure dates from 1958.[209] It has 802 articles presented in a preliminary title, which deals with public and private prosecution and five books, which include: Book 1. Public prosecution and instruction; Book 2. Procedure to judgment; Book 3. Extraordinary means of recourse; Book 4. Special procedures; and Book 5. Execution procedures.

Book 1 (Public prosecution and instruction) has the following titles: I. Authorities entrusted with public prosecution and with instruction; II. Preliminary investigation; and III. Instruction. Title I has the following chapters: I. Judiciary police; II. Public ministry; and III. Judge of instruction. Title II has the following chapters: I. Flagrant felonies and misdemeanors and II. Preliminary investigation. Title III has the following chapters: I. Judge of instruction and the procedure of instruction and II. Chamber of accusation and procedure before it.

Book 2 (Procedure to judgment) has the following titles: Title I. The assize court; Title II. Proceedings in misdemeanors; Title III. Proceedings in infractions; and Title IV. Service of process and notification of judgments. Title I has the following chapters: I. Jurisdiction of the assize court; II. The seat of the assizes; III. Composition of the assize court; IV. Preliminary proceedings; V. Opening of trial; VI. Trial; and VII. Judgment. Title II has the following chapters: I. Correctional court and II. Appeal from its judgments. Title III has the following chapters: I. Jurisdiction of police courts; II. Simplified procedure; II. Payment of fine to avoid proceedings; III. Scope of business transacted; IV. Proceedings before the police court; V. Judgment and judgment by default; and VI. Appeal from judgments of police courts. Title IV has no separate chapters.

Book 3 (Extraordinary means of recourse) has the following titles: I. Petition for cassation and II. Petition for revision. Title I has the following chapters: I. Decisions that may be attacked by cassation and the conditions thereof; II. Form of the petition; III. Preconditions of cassation; IV. Proceedings; V. Orders made by the Court of Cassation; and VI. Petition for cassation in the interest of the law. Title II has no separate chapters.

Book 4 (Special procedures) has the following titles: I. Proceedings in absentia; II. Proceedings in case of forgery; III. Proceedings in case of disappearance of records of procedure; IV. Proceedings for the taking of depositions from members of the government and from representatives of foreign governments; V. Conflicts of jurisdiction; VI. Transfer of the case from one court to another; VII. Disqualification of judges; VIII. Proceedings for criminal acts committed in the courtroom; IX. Felonies and misdemeanors committed by judges and some other officers; X. Felonies and misdemeanors committed abroad; and XI. Felonies and misdemeanors against the security of the state. The above titles have no separate chapters.

Book 5 (Execution procedures) has the following titles: I. Execution of sentences; II. Detention; III. Parole; IV. Probation; V. Proof of identity of convicted persons; VI. Imprisonment in lieu of payment of fine; VII. Prescription of penalties; VIII. Criminal records; IX. Rehabilitation of prisoners; and X. Legal costs. Title II has the following chapters: I. Execution of preventive detention; II. Execution of sentences of imprisonment; III. Provisions common to penitentiaries; and IV. Preparation for parole. Title IV has the following chapters: I. Simple probation and II. Conditional probation. The other titles have no separate chapters.

The following are topics selected from the French law of criminal procedure.

1. Prescription of Prosecution
    (*Prescription de l'action publique*)[210]

Prosecution for felonies (*crimes*) is prescribed ten years from the day on which the felony was committed, if no prosecution was ever instituted, or ten years from the last act of prosecution. Prosecution for misdemeanors (*délits*) is prescribed in three years, and that for infractions (*contraventions*) in one year, under the same conditions. Private prosecution cannot be initiated after the time for the initiation of public prosecution has expired.

NOTES AND QUESTIONS

1. The French Code of Criminal Procedure deals first with those areas of public prosecution and preparation of the case for trial that are common in proceedings before all courts. It then proceeds to rules applicable to procedure in particular courts, like the assize and correctional courts, which deal mainly with the trial, appeal and error.

2. No action may be instituted if it is barred by the statute of limitations. The Spanish law deals with prescription in Penal Code, Arts. 113ff.; the Italian law in Penal Code, Arts. 157ff.; and the German law in Penal Code, Arts. 78ff. Compare Calif. Pen. C.A. §799ff. Note that the French law carries the provisions of the statute of limitations in the Code of Criminal Procedure while the above-mentioned countries have them in their penal codes.

---

2. Preparatory Proceedings (*Enquête préliminaire et l'instruction*)[211]

(a) Preliminary investigation (*Enquêtes*).[212]   Preliminary investigation is carried out by officers of the judiciary police (*police judiciaire*) on their own initiative or at the request of the procurator. The judiciary police may hold any person for twenty-four hours without authority, and with the authorization of the procurator for another period of twenty-four hours, for the purpose of investigation of crime. Whenever it appears that a felony or a misdemeanor has been committed, or a highway accident has occurred under the influence of alcohol, the judiciary police are bound to have a blood sample taken from the presumed offender. Any person who refuses to submit to the blood test is punishable with imprisonment from one month to one year and/or a fine.

(b) Preparatory instruction (*Instruction préparatoire*)[213]

(i) GENERAL PROVISIONS (*Dispositions générales*).   Preparatory instruction is obligatory in felonies, facultative in misdemeanors and infractions. The judge of instruction may initiate his investigation only at the request of the procurator, but he then proceeds on his own initiative to obtain all the information useful and necessary to find out the truth of the matter. He may also order a medical examination of the person investigated. The procurator may request the judge of instruction to take certain steps in the investigation which appear to him useful. If the judge of instruction does not wish to take them, he must make a ruling giving his reasons within five days from such request. The judge of instruction may order a search to be made and the seizure of objects useful in the investigation. He may summon any person to appear before him as a witness. If such person does not appear voluntarily, he may order him to be brought in by force and fine him for nonappearance.

(ii) APPEARANCE OF THE SUSPECT (*Comparution de l'inculpé*). At the first appearance of the suspect before him, the judge of instruction satisfies himself of the suspect's identity and announces to the suspect which acts are imputed to him, and that he is not required to make any statement unless he so desires. If the suspect makes a statement, it is immediately taken down in writing by order of the judge of instruction. Before receiving the statement, the judge of instruction must advise the suspect of his right to appoint counsel from among the attorneys (*avocats*). If the suspect does not appoint counsel but demands one to be appointed, counsel will be appointed ex officio. The suspect may, however, make a statement without being assisted by counsel, if he so desires.[214] In urgent cases, the judge may receive a statement from the suspect and confront him with witnesses without informing him of his right to remain silent or of his right to appoint counsel.

The judge of instruction may hold the suspect incommunicado for ten days and may renew the term once, but this does not apply to the suspect's communications with his counsel, with whom he may freely communicate.

After the first appearance of the suspect, he may be heard or confronted only in the presence of his counsel unless he expressly renounces this right.[215] The procurator may be present at the hearing, and if he desires to be present, he must be notified by the judge of instruction of any hearing. The procurator, counsel for the suspect, and counsel for the civil party may ask questions of the suspect only with the permission of the judge of instruction.

Inobservance of Articles 114 and 118, mentioned above, requiring the judge of instruction to tell the suspect that he may make a statement or remain silent and that he may appoint counsel, and further requiring the judge of instruction to hear the suspect only in the presence of his counsel unless he expressly renounces such right, results in nullity which may be pronounced by the judge of instruction or by the chamber of accusation. Proceedings affected by nullity are erased from the record.

(iii) ORDERS ISSUED BY THE JUDGE OF INSTRUCTION (*Mandats decernés par le juge d'instruction*). The judge of instruction may issue an order for the appearance of the suspect (*mandat de comparution*). He may also issue an order for the suspect to be brought before him by force (*mandat d'amener*). If he cannot hear the suspect at once, the judge of instruction may order him to be detained for a time not exceeding twenty-four hours. If the time has run without the suspect having been heard, the officer in charge of the detention house must bring the suspect before the procurator who will immediately contact the judge of instruction, and failing him, the president of the court or his deputy and request the immediate hearing of the suspect. If the suspect is not heard then and there, the procurator must order his immediate release. Failure to observe these rules will expose the judges and other officers to criminal prosecution and to an action for damages.[216]

The judge of instruction may also issue an order for the arrest of the suspect (*mandat d'arrêt*). The suspect is arrested and brought into the house of detention. He must be heard within forty-eight hours from such arrest. If he is not so heard, the officer in charge of the detention house must undertake the above-mentioned steps to have him heard, indicated in Articles 125 and 126, or he must be set free. If the suspect is arrested at a place outside the jurisdiction of the judge of instruction who issued the order, the suspect is brought immediately before the procurator at the place of his arrest who will hear him. The procurator will notify the judge of instruction who issued the order that the arrest was made and will request the transfer of the suspect. Arrests on private premises must be made only between the hours of 6A.M. and 9P.M., as the agents may not enter private premises at other hours.

(iv) JUDICIAL SUPERVISION AND PREVENTIVE DETENTION (*Contrôle judiciaire et détention provisoire*).

(aa) Judicial supervision (Contrôle judiciaire). Judicial supervision may be ordered by the judge of instruction whenever the suspect is proceeded against for a misdemeanor or a more serious breach of the law. The judge of instruction may impose on the suspect one or more limitations, e.g., to stay at a given place, not to leave his residence, to inform the judge of instruction of any change of address, to appear periodically at a given office, to surrender his passport (or identity card or driver's license) to the custody of the court, to avoid meeting certain persons, to submit to medical treatment, or to give bail, etc. The amount of bail is freely determined by the judge of instruction, taking into account the capability of the suspect. The judge of instruction may modify or revoke his order at any time.

Where the suspect is ordered to give bail, it is given to ensure: (1) his appearance whenever required and (2) the payment of costs of the proceedings and of fines. The order determines the portions allotted to each purpose. The first part is refunded when he complies with the order, if proceedings against him are discontinued, or if he is acquitted. The second part is refunded if proceedings against him are discontinued or if he is acquitted. If he is convicted, only a surplus, if any, is refunded.

The suspect may demand at any time to have the judicial supervision lifted. The judge of instruction must rule on the request within five days. If the judge of instruction fails to make a ruling, the suspect may bring the matter before the chamber of accusation which must rule on it within fifteen days after having obtained and considered the advice of the procurator general. If it fails to act within that time, the judicial supervision is lifted as of right.

Where the suspect does not abide by the order submitting him to judicial supervision, the judge of instruction may issue a warrant for his arrest (*mandat d'arrêt*), or for his being taken into custody (*mandat de depôt*), and impose preventive detention.

(bb) Preventive detention (Détention provisoire). Preventive detention may be ordered where the suspect is proceeded against for a misdemeanor for which he could be imprisoned, if convicted, for two years or more and where the measure of judicial supervision is inadequate to preserve proof, or to prevent interference with witnesses or contact between accomplices. Preventive detention may also be ordered on the above conditions to safeguard public order, to protect the suspect, to prevent him from committing further offenses, or to ensure his appearance when required.

Preventive detention may not exceed four months, but when it has lasted that long, the judge of instruction may extend it a further term not exceeding four months. However, where the suspect has not been previously convicted of a felony or a misdemeanor, or where he has not been assessed a term of imprisonment exceeding three months, and where the offense for which he is proceeded against is not punishable with imprisonment exceeding five years, preventive detention may be extended only once and only for a term not exceeding two months.

Preventive detention is always ordered when the suspect is proceeded against for felony. If it appears, however, that the suspect can be proceeded against only for a misdemeanor, he may be set free or subjected to preventive detention or judicial supervision as mentioned above.

The suspect may demand at any time that the judge of instruction set him free. The judge of instruction must rule on the request within five days after having obtained and considered the advice of the procurator. If he fails to do so, the suspect may bring the matter before the chamber of accusation, which must rule on it within fifteen days after having obtained and considered the advice of the procurator general. If the chamber of accusation fails to rule on the matter within that time, the suspect must be set free as of right.

A person proceeded against may demand his release at any time and stage of the proceedings. Where the case is already pending before a court, that court will have to rule on the motion. If the case is not yet pending before a court but the handling of the case has passed out of the hands of a judge of instruction, the request has to be made to the chamber of accusation.

(v) EXPERTS (*Expertise*). The judge of instruction, or another judge, may order an expert opinion on any matter on his own initiative, or at the request of the public ministry or of the parties. If a request for the appointment of an expert is made and the judge of instruction does not wish to grant it, he must give a reasoned ruling for his refusal. Experts are selected from a national list of experts kept in the Court of Cassation or from one of the lists kept by the courts of appeal. In exceptional instances, a person not so listed may be appointed. Whenever the decision in the case may depend on the opinion of experts, at least two experts must be appointed. In urgent cases, however, the opinion of only one expert will be sufficient.

The experts are under the control of the judge of instruction and their task is delimited by the order appointing them. If they require to question the accused, such questions are put to the accused by the judge of instruction in their presence and that of his counsel and of the procurator. After the experts have concluded their work, they have to submit their report to the judge of instruction. They may submit a joint report or as many reports as there are experts. The judge of instruction will then summon the parties and will communicate to them the opinion of the experts. He has to give time to the parties to present their comments on the report. At the trial, if it takes place, the experts will have to appear in person and explain what research they undertook and they will have to answer questions put to them by the court, the parties and the public ministry.

(vi) DECISIONS OF THE JUDGE OF INSTRUCTION (*Ordonnances de règlement*). As soon as his preparatory instruction is terminated, the judge of instruction transmits the file to the procurator who has to submit his comments within three days. The judge of instruction must then determine whether there is enough evidence to charge the suspect with violation of criminal law. If he thinks that there is no case, he must make a ruling to that effect and order the release of the suspect if he is being detained. If the judge rules that the facts constitute an infraction, he orders the matter be taken up by the proper police court (*tribunal de police*). If he rules that the facts constitute a misdemeanor, the matter is submitted to the proper correctional court (*tribunal correctionnel*). If he rules that the facts constitute a felony, the matter is submitted to the procurator general at the proper court of appeal (*cour d'appel*) for submission to the chamber of accusation for further action. Notice of these rulings is given to all parties within twenty-four hours by registered mail.

(vii) **APPEAL AGAINST DECISIONS OF THE JUDGE OF INSTRUCTION** (*Appel des ordonnances du juge d'instruction*). Appeal against decisions of the judge of instruction may be made to the chamber of accusation. The procurator must file his appeal within twenty-four hours, and the procurator general within ten days, from the making of the decision. The suspect and the civil party must file their appeal within three days from the notification of the decision on them. The civil party may appeal only such decisions that affect its interests. The president of the chamber of accusation will decide within eight days whether the appeal will be heard. If the appeal is not substantiated, he will deny it. If the appeal is substantiated, he will transmit the file to the procurator general. A hearing will then be held before the chamber that will decide the appeal.

(viii) **REOPENING OF PREPARATORY INSTRUCTION** (*Reprise de l'information sur charges nouvelles*). Where the judge of instruction has ruled that there is no case against the suspect, no new proceedings can be instituted against him in connection with the same facts unless there is new evidence. New evidence consists of statements by witnesses and new facts that have since appeared and which could not have been presented to the judge of instruction in the previous preparatory instruction proceedings. It must be of the nature to strengthen the case against the suspect or to give it a new turn toward finding out the truth in the matter. Only the public ministry may request the reopening of the proceedings.

NOTES AND QUESTIONS

1. Preliminary investigation is undertaken by the judiciary police. Note that the police may hold a person on suspicion of crime for twenty-four hours without any authority. Preparatory instruction is initiated at the request of the procurator, who is informed by the judiciary police. It is undertaken by the judge of instruction. The suspect is thus arrested by the police on its own initiative or under a warrant issued by the judge of instruction. Note the various orders the judge of instruction may issue to have the suspect brought before him. Is the judge of instruction required to have the suspect arrested in order to make him appear? How is the matter handled in the Italian and the German law? For Anglo-American law, *see*, e.g., Illinois S.H.A. ch. 38 §107ff.

2. Must the judiciary police or the judge or instruction first advise the suspect

of his right to remain silent and to appoint counsel? Compare the German and Italian systems.

3. What are the French provisions concerning bail? Compare them with the Spanish and Italian rules. For Anglo-American law, *see,* e.g., Illinois S.H.A. ch. 38 §110.

Note that the judge of instruction may release the suspect without bail or, on the other hand, impose preventive detention. How do the powers of the judge of instruction compare in this respect with those of the Spanish, Italian and German investigating judges?

4. After the judge of instruction has completed his investigation, what orders will he make? Who decides in the Anglo-American law whether the suspect should stand trial? *See,* e.g., Illinois S.H.A. ch. 38 §§111 and 112.

---

3. Chamber of Accusation (*Chambre d'accusation*)[217]

A chamber of accusation is set up in every court of appeal. It is composed of a president of chamber and two justices. The public ministry is represented by the procurator general and his deputies. The chamber of accusation hears appeals against decisions of judges of instruction and decides whether a suspect should stand trial in cases referred to it.

The procurator general must place the matter before the chamber within forty-eight hours from its reception in cases of preventive detention, and within ten days in all other cases. The chamber sets a date for a hearing, and the procurator general must give notice thereof to all parties by registered mail forty-eight hours before the hearing in cases of preventive detention, and a minimum of five days in other cases. The files of the case are accessible to all parties during that time, and they may file their comments thereto and their communications.

At the hearing, first the rapporteur, who is one of the justices, gives his report; then the procurator general and counsel for the parties present their views in the matter. The chamber may order the personal appearance of the parties (the suspect and the victim of crime) and the presentation of exhibits. After the hearing, the chamber deliberates in private. It may order any further steps to be taken to find out the truth in the matter. It may decide that there is no case and order the release of the suspect if he is being detained. The chamber may order the transfer of the case before a proper police court (*tribunal de police*), if it is of the opinion that the facts amount to an infraction, and before a proper correctional court (*tribunal correctionnel*), if it thinks that the facts amount to a misdemeanor. If it is of the opinion that the facts constitute a felony, it will order the suspect to stand trial in the proper assize court (*cour d'assises*). Such an order must give reasons for the making thereof, otherwise it is null and void. The order is signed by the president of the chamber and by the court clerk (*greffier*).

The decisions of the chamber of accusation are subject only to a petition for their cassation directed to the Court of Cassation (*Cour de Cassation*).

The president of the chamber of accusation exercises supervision over the functioning of the judges of instruction within the jurisdiction of the court of appeal at which the chamber is set up. The chamber of accusation also exercises supervision over the functioning of the judiciary police within its jurisdiction.

NOTES AND QUESTIONS

What is the function of the chamber of accusation? Which court exercises supervision over judges of instruction in the Spanish and Italian systems? How is the matter handled in the German criminal procedure?

Are decisions of the chamber of accusation final? Are they subject to any remedy? Note that the final decision concerns only the question of whether the suspect should or should not stand trial. The suspect thus has another opportunity to obtain his release and have the case against him dropped.

---

4.   Procedure before Assize Courts (*Cours d'assises*)[218]

Proceedings are initiated by an order of the chamber of accusation that the suspect should stand trial for felony. No other way of bringing a case before an assize court is available. The court is composed of three judges and nine jurors who act together as one unit. The jurors thus act as lay judges.

(a) Preliminary proceedings (*Procédure préparatoire*).[219]   The president of the court or one of its members hears the accused (*accusé*). He must assure himself of the identity of the accused and that he received copy of the accusation made by the chamber of accusation. The trial cannot take place in less than five days from the hearing. The accused is requested to appoint counsel if he has not yet done so. If he does not do so, the court will appoint one ex officio. Counsel must be selected from attorneys (*avocats*). As an exceptional measure, the president of the court may allow the accused to appoint a relative or a friend as counsel. The parties must submit to each other, at least twenty-four hours before trial, a list of persons whom they wish to be heard as witnesses. At the latest, a list of jurors selected by law must be delivered to the accused the day before the trial.[220] The president may strike from the list of cases to be tried any case that does not appear ready for trial.

(b) Selection of jury (*Formation du jury de jugement*).[221]   The president of the court asks the accused his name, date and place of birth, occupation and address. The court clerk calls the jurors, whose names are written on cards and placed in a receptacle. At least twenty-three jurors are in attendance. The trial jury is composed of nine jurors. The court clerk draws the cards by chance, and the accused or his counsel, and then the public ministry, may reject any of them as the names are called. The defense may reject five and the prosecution four. The jury is formed as soon as nine jurors are seated. The president then administers the oath to the jurors and declares the jury formed.

(c) General trial procedure (*Débats, dispositions générales*).[222]   The trial is public. The court may exclude the public because of danger to public order or morals. It may exclude minors from any public hearing. The use of cameras and television or recording devices is prohibited. The president conducts the trial. He may reject any question that may compromise the court's dignity or delay the proceedings. He may take any measures to arrive at the truth of the matter. He may summon any person who may be likely to shed new light on the matter as it develops before the court. Persons so called are not heard on oath and their statements are taken only as information. Members of the court and jurors may ask questions of the accused and witnesses by leave of the president. The prosecution, the defense and the civil party may ask questions of the accused, the co-accused, witnesses and of any other person through the president only.

The public ministry may make motions and requests to the court, and the court is bound to consider them and rule on them. The accused and the civil party may also submit motions and requests to the court and obtain rulings. All disputed motions and requests must be ruled on by the court, after hearing the public ministry and the parties. These rulings may be attacked by a petition for their cassation, but such petition may be made only together with a petition for the cassation of the final decision made by the court in the case.

The accused must be represented by counsel at the trial. If the appointed counsel does not show up, the president will appoint and bring in one ex officio. Any person who disturbs the order in the courtroom at trial will be expelled. He may also be tried on the spot for the offense and convicted to imprisonment of from two months to two years, without prejudice of further proceedings against him. If the accused causes the trouble, identical measures are applicable against him. The trial will proceed in his absence. After every session, the court clerk will read to him the record of the proceedings, and will give him copies of requests made by the prosecution and orders of the court.

(d) The trial (*Débats*).[223] The president directs the court clerk to read the list of witnesses called to give evidence by the parties. They are called and directed to retire to another room to await their turn. A witness who does not appear may be brought in by force. In any event, he will be fined. The court clerk then reads aloud the charge made against the accused by the chamber of accusation. The president then hears the accused and receives any statement made by him. Witnesses give evidence on oath in the order determined by the president. Ascendants, descendants, brothers and sisters, husband or wife of the accused, the civil party, and children below the age of sixteen years may not give evidence on oath. They may, however, be heard without oath. The same applies to any person who was not properly called to give evidence. The witnesses give cohesive evidence, without interruption, on the alleged facts that the accused had committed, on his personality and character. After they have concluded, the president, and with his leave other court members, jurors, the prosecution and the defense and the civil party may ask questions.

After all evidence is heard, the civil party takes the floor, then the prosecution. Then the accused and his counsel present their defense. The civil party and the prosecution have the right of reply, but the defense always has the last word.

The president then declares the trial concluded. After he has done so, it cannot be reopened. He then announces the questions which will be presented for the court's decision. The questions must deal with all the facts specified in the charge presented by the chamber of accusation. A question must be asked on every aggravating circumstance as well as on every excuse submitted. If objection to a question is made by the parties, the court must rule on it. The ruling is subject to a petition for cassation joined with a petition for the cassation of the final judgment. The president then orders the accused removed from the courtroom and adjourns the hearing.

(e) Judgment (*Jugement*).[224]   The court then retires to the conference room and it cannot leave it before the decision is made. After deliberation, the vote is taken by separate ballot in writing, first on the main question, and then on the question of aggravating circumstances, on subsidiary questions, on the question of legal excuse, and finally, when the accused was found guilty, on the question of attenuating circumstances. Questions are answered yes or no. The members write their answer onto the ballots and hand them to the president, who places them in a receptacle. After having received all the ballots, the president opens them one by one in the presence of the court, who may verify the ballots and announces the result. A blank ballot or one declared void by a majority of the court is taken as favorable to the accused. Every decision taken against the accused must obtain at least eight votes, including the rejection of attenuating circumstances.

If the accused is found guilty, a vote on punishment to be assessed is taken immediately after discussion thereof. Vote is by secret ballot just as on the question of guilt. Decision is taken by simple majority of votes. If after two separate ballotings, a majority has not been obtained, the punishment most disfavorable to the accused appearing on the second ballot is eliminated, and a new vote is taken. If there is still no majority, the procedure is repeated by eliminating the now most disfavorable punishment and by taking a new vote until a majority on punishment is arrived at.

If the accused is found not guilty, the court pronounces his acquittal. If the act of the accused has been found excusable, he is pronounced absolved of criminal liability.

The answers given by the court to the questions are noted on the sheet containing the questions, and the sheet is signed by the president and the first juror, who is selected by chance. The answers given by the court to the questions are irrevocable.

The court then returns to the courtroom, the accused is brought in, and the president reads the answers given by the court to the questions. He then pronounces the conviction, absolution, or acquittal of the accused. If the accused is absolved or acquitted, he is immediately set free, unless he is held for another cause. A person acquitted can never again be proceeded against for the same cause. The accused has to pay the costs of the case if he is found guilty or if he is absolved of liability.

The court, without jury and after hearing the parties, then rules on the claim of the civil party (the victim of crime) for damages, or on the claim of the acquitted accused against the civil party for damages.

The court clerk prepares the judgment in writing. The record thereof is signed by the president and by the court clerk.

NOTES AND QUESTIONS

1. A trial before the assize court is a trial for a felony, and it is a jury trial. How does the jury compare with an Anglo-American jury?

What are the different successive stages of the trial?

How do the preliminary proceedings compare with those in German and Spanish felony trials?

As to the formation of the jury, compare the Italian procedure. Are there juries or lay judges in German and Spanish felony trials?

2. Note the proceedings at the trial. The trial is minutely regulated by the law, and the court must follow the rules of criminal procedure step by step. Compare the French felony trial with those in Spanish and Italian courts. For Anglo-American law, *see*, e.g., Illinois S.H.A. ch. 38 §115ff.

3. How does the court make its decisions? Note the procedure for determination of questions to be answered by the court and the balloting procedure. Compare it with the procedure in Italian and German felony trials. *See also*, e.g., F.R. Crim. P. Rules 23-36. As to judgments, *see* the section on judgments below.

---

5. Procedure before Correctional Courts (*Tribunaux correctionnels*)[225]

Cases are brought before the court usually by direction of a judge of instruction, but they may also be brought by a voluntary appearance of the parties, by a citation served on the suspect, or by procedures provided for prosecution of persons caught in the act. A person caught in the act of committing a misdemeanor is brought before the procurator and is presented for trial on the same day. If the court is not in session, he will be tried the next day. If this is not possible, he will be tried as soon as practicable. If the case is not ready for trial, the court may postpone trial until the required investigation has been made. In the meantime, the person proceeded against is kept in detention or under judicial supervision.

(a) General trial procedure (*Débats, dispositions générales*).[226] The trial is public, but the court may exclude the public on the ground of public order or morals. Minors may always be excluded. The use of cameras and television or recording devices is prohibited. The president conducts the trial. Any person who would disturb order in the courtroom will be expelled. He may also be tried on the spot for the offense and convicted to imprisonment of from two months to two years, without prejudice of further proceedings against him. If the accused causes the trouble, identical measures are applied. The trial will proceed in his absence and he will only be brought in for the pronouncement of judgment.

The president satisfies himself of the identity of the accused. If the breach of the law of which the accused is being charged is punishable only with a fine, or with imprisonment for less than two years, he may request, by letter addressed to the president of the court, that he be tried in his absence. However, he must be represented by counsel. If the court regards the presence of the accused necessary, it may refuse the request.

The accused has the right to be assisted by counsel. If he does not appoint one but demands one be appointed, the president appoints one ex officio. Counsel must be appointed from among the attorneys (*avocats*). The accused must have legal representation if he is suffering from an infirmity that may affect his defense. Any person who claims to have been injured by the misdemeanor may appear as the civil party and claim damages. The civil party may always be represented by counsel, but may not be heard as a witness.

(b)   The trial (*Débats*).[227]   Trial proceeds along the lines of that before the assize courts. The president first cites the authority on the strength of which the court has to try the accused (e.g., the order of the judge of instruction). He also takes notice of the presence of the civil party, the witnesses, experts and interpreters. The case against the accused is to be made by any method of proof. Proof (by witnesses, etc.) is given on the same principles as before assize courts. The prosecution, the defense, and the civil party may submit requests to the court and obtain rulings thereon. After all the evidence has been presented, the civil party is heard, then the prosecution. The accused and his counsel present the defense. The civil party and the prosecution have the right of reply, but the defense always has the last word.

(c)   Judgment (*Jugement*).[228]   The court may give judgment immediately at the close of the proceedings, or it may reserve judgment. If the court finds that the accused committed a misdemeanor, it pronounces him guilty and assesses punishment. It also rules on the claim of the civil party and may award damages. If the court finds that the accused had committed only an infraction (*contravention*), it assesses the punishment and rules on the claim of the civil party. If the accused is convicted of a misdemeanor and of a connected infraction, the court pronounces only one judgment and assesses punishment. If the act of the accused is found excusable, he is pronounced absolved of criminal liability. If the court finds the accused not guilty of the charge, it gives the judgment of not guilty.

The accused who is acquitted, who is absolved of criminal liability, or who is convicted but put on probation is immediately set free. The same applies to the accused who was assessed a term of imprisonment equal to the time he has already spent in detention.

The accused who was found guilty is required to pay the court costs. If the accused is acquitted, the civil party is required to pay the court costs, but may be relieved of the requirement by the court.

The judgment is composed of the reasons, the order, and the reasons forming the ground for the order. The order lists the acts of which the accused was found guilty, the punishment assessed, and the legal provisions applied. The president reads the judgment in open court. The record of the judgment (*minute du jugement*) is dated; it gives the names of the judges who sat on the court and the names of the officers who represented the public ministry. The record is signed by the president and by the court clerk and is filed with the office of the court (*greffe*) within three days from the pronouncement of the judgment.

(d)   Default judgment (*Jugement par défault*).[229]   If an accused who was properly cited does not appear without a proper excuse, he will be tried in his absence and a default judgment will be given against him. The judgment will be served on him by a court bailiff. A default judgment is vacated if the accused files an objection within ten days from the notification thereof. The objection is considered as not having been made if the accused does not appear at a new date set for trial.

NOTES AND QUESTIONS

What cases do correctional courts try? Since the court sits without a jury, the procedure is less formal. Also, the offenses tried are of a much less significant nature than those tried in assize courts. The trial procedure follows, however, that in assize courts. It proceeds through identical stages from preliminary proceedings to judgment.

---

6. Procedure on Appeal from Judgments of Correctional Courts (*Cour d'appel en matière correctionnelle*)[230]

Judgments of correctional courts are subject to appeal to the criminal chamber of the court of appeal. The parties, including the prosecutor, may appeal within ten days from the pronouncement of the judgment, and where the party appealing was not present in court, then from the notification thereof. Where the judgment was rendered by default, time runs only from the notification. If only one of the parties appeals, the other party or parties have an additional time of five days to file an appeal. The procurator general may appeal within two months from the pronouncement of the judgment. The appeal is filed with the court clerk of the court which pronounced the judgment, who transmits it to the criminal chamber of the court of appeal. If no appeal is filed by any party, the judgment does not enter into the power of law until the time to appeal (ten days) has run. If an appeal is filed, the judgment will not enter into the power of law except in accordance with the judgment of the court of appeal. The judgment of the court of appeal will enter in force in accordance with the rules of criminal procedure.

Rules applicable to the procedure before correctional courts apply also before the criminal chamber of the court of appeal unless otherwise provided. The court is composed of a president and two justices and decides by majority vote.

At the hearing, first the rapporteur, who is one of the justices, gives his report. Then the accused is heard. Witnesses are heard only if they are ordered to appear by the court. Then the appellant takes the floor, then the respondent or respondents. If there are several appellants and respondents, the order is set by the president. The defense always has the last word.

The court of appeal may reject an appeal filed out of time or one that does not conform to the rules of procedure. If the appeal is formally in order, the court will consider it on the merits. If the court finds the appeal unfounded, it will affirm the judgment of the trial court. In that case, the appellant has to pay the costs of the appeal.

The court may, on the appeal of the prosecution, increase or decrease the punishment; it may affirm the judgment in full or in part, or reverse it in full or in part, whether the effect is favorable or disfavorable to the accused. The court may not, on the sole appeal of the accused or of a person civilly responsible for him, increase the punishment or reform the judgment so as to make it more disfavorable to the accused or to the person civilly responsible for him. The same principle holds good in case of a sole appeal by the civil party.

The court will acquit the accused if it finds that he commited neither a felony, nor a misdemeanor, nor an infraction. It will immediately rule on his claim for damages. If the court finds that the accused is entitled to a legal excuse, it will absolve him of criminal liability. If the court finds that the accused committed only an infraction (*contravention*), it will annul the judgment and convict the accused of the infraction and assess punishment. It will also rule on the claim of the civil party for damages, if any. If the court finds that the accused is in fact to be charged with having committed a felony, it will annul the judgment, and will transfer the files to the public ministry for further action. If it appears to the court that the judgment must be annulled because of an error in the procedure which makes it void, it will annul the judgment and will pronounce a new judgment on the merits.

NOTES AND QUESTIONS

Judgments of correctional courts are subject to appeal. Does an appeal lie from judgments of French assize courts? Is the appeal an appeal on the merits? Does it amount to a trial *de novo*?

Consider the hearing before the court of appeal. How does it compare with hearings before Italian and Spanish courts of criminal appeal? Do all appellate courts appoint a rapporteur to prepare the case for trial?

May the court of appeal increase the punishment imposed on the accused by the trial court?

What remedies lie against judgments of French courts of appeal?

For appellate procedure in Anglo-American courts, *see*, e.g., Federal Rules of Appellate Procedure, Rule 3ff.

---

7.   Procedure before Police Courts (*Tribunaux de police*) and Appeal from Their Judgments to Courts of Appeal (*Cours d'appel*)[231]

(a) Ordinary procedure (*Instruction définitive*).[232]   The court is composed of a single judge of the court of instance. Cases are brought before it by order of the judge of instruction, by summons issued to the suspect, or by voluntary appearance of parties. The procedure is the same as that applicable in correctional courts unless otherwise provided. It is, however, less formal.

If the court finds that the accused committed an infraction (*contravention*), it will convict him and will assess punishment. It will also rule on the claim of the civil party. If it finds that the act charged amounts to a felony or to a misdemeanor, it will declare itself incompetent, and will transmit the case to the public ministry for further action. If no breach of law was committed, or cannot be proved, or cannot be imputed to the accused, it will acquit the accused. If the court finds that the accused is entitled to a legal excuse, it will declare him absolved of criminal liability, and it will rule on the claim of the civil party.

Judgments of police courts are subject to appeal to the criminal chamber of the court of appeal whenever imprisonment exceeding five days or a fine exceeding 160 francs is imposed. The appeal and the appellate procedure are governed by the same rules as those governing an appeal from correctional courts. If an appeal is brought from an order by which the police court declared itself incompetent on the ground that the act charged constituted a misdemeanor (*délit*), and the court of appeal concurs, it will immediately pronounce a conviction and assess punishment, and will also rule on the claim of the civil party for damages.

(b) Simplified procedure (*Procédure simplifiée*).[233] The public ministry, which prosecutes infractions, in a case where it would prosecute a person and request only the payment of a fine, may adopt a simplified procedure (*procédure simplifiée*). This procedure may not be used where the offense arose from the Labor Code (*Code du Travail*), where the offense is punishable with imprisonment exceeding ten days or a fine exceeding six hundred francs and was committed by a person below the age of eighteen years at the time of its commission, or where the victim has already initiated proceedings.

Under the rules of simplified procedure, the public ministry presents the matter before a judge of the police court and requests him to consider it and either dismiss it or assess a fine. The judge may return the matter to the public ministry and recommend that normal prosecution should be held. If the judge assesses a fine, he will make an order to that effect which will be communicated to the public ministry. The public ministry may contest the order within ten days, whereupon the simplified proceedings are terminated and normal proceedings are held. If the public ministry does not oppose the order, it is communicated by registered mail to the person proceeded against. He may within thirty days from the day on which the letter was mailed, either pay the fine or oppose payment. Payment of the fine closes the matter. Opposition terminates the simplified proceedings and normal proceedings may be initiated. Where the person proceeded against does neither, the sum of the fine will be executed against him.

(c) Payment of a fine (*amende forfaitaire*).[234] In the case of minor infractions punishable only by fine not exceeding a certain amount (600 francs), the procedure of the *amende forfaitaire* takes place. This is so especially in infractions arising out of the breach of the traffic code by motor vehicles (*circulation routière*). The procedure may not be used where the person proceeded against is also liable in damages for personal injuries or damage to property, nor where he has, by the same act, committed another infraction (or infractions) that may not be dealt with by an *amende forfaitaire*.

The proper authorities set up a tariff of fines by which certain infractions are punishable and determine which officers may levy them. The fine is levied on the spot and against a receipt upon apprehension by the proper officer. It may be also paid by letter, the sum being paid in duty stamps affixed to the letter within fifteen days. Where the person proceeded against does not pay the fine, the simplified procedure or the ordinary procedure is instituted.

NOTES AND QUESTIONS

What are the three types of procedure that may be instituted in police courts?

The regular procedure follows that used in correctional courts. Can you indicate its development from information until judgment? The procedure is much simplified, however.

How would you characterize the simplified procedure and the procedure on the payment of a fine in police courts? How does it compare with procedure in Anglo-American courts of limited criminal jurisdiction?

How does the procedure in French police courts compare with that in Italian praetorial courts or in German *Amtsgerichte*?

Does an appeal lie against the decisions of police courts?

---

8.   Procedure before the Court of Cassation (*Cour de Cassation*)[235]

(a)   Petition for cassation (*Pourvoi en cassation*).[236]

(i) CONDITIONS AND FORM OF THE PETITION (*Conditions et formes du pourvoi*). Orders of the chamber of accusation, as well as orders and judgments of courts of final resort in prosecution of felonies, misdemeanors and infractions, are subject to a petition for their cassation on the ground that the court exceeded its powers or violated the law. Both the parties and the public ministry may petition. The petition must be filed within five days from the pronouncement of the judgment or, where the petitioning party was not present in court, from the notification thereof. In case of a judgment by default, time runs against the accused only from the day following the last day for the filing of objections. The public ministry must petition within ten days from the notification of the default judgment. The judgment does not enter in the power of law until the time for filing of the petition expires. If the petition is filed, the judgment does not enter in the power of law until the Court of Cassation rules on the matter. If the accused is acquitted, absolved of criminal liability, or convicted to a term of imprisonment but put on probation, he must be set free irrespective of the filing of a petition for annulment. The same applies when the term of imprisonment assessed is coextensive with the time for which the accused has been held until judgment.

An order of acquittal made by an assize court is subject to a petition for its annulment only in the interest of the law, and the filing of the petition will not affect the accused. The civil party, however, may petition for the annulment of an order dealing with his claim for damages after the accused has been acquitted or absolved of criminal liability.

The petition is filed with the clerk of the court that pronounced the decision being attacked. It must be signed by the petitioner or his attorney (*avocat*). If the petitioner is being detained, he may petition by letter, which he hands to the officer in charge of the house of detention. The petitioner must notify all parties of his petition by registered mail within three days. Together with the petition, or within ten days from its filing, the petitioner must file with the clerk of court a brief containing his reasons and grounds for attack. The clerk of court will then, within twenty days from the filing of the petition, transmit the files to the public ministry for further transmittal to the procurator general at the Court of Cassation, who will in turn hand them over to the clerk of the criminal chamber of the Court of Cassation. The president of the chamber then assigns the case to one of the justices who will act as rapporteur. The rapporteur fixes a time for the parties to file their briefs with the clerk. A brief, or an additional brief, filed after the time fixed may be rejected.

 (ii) OPENING OF CASSATION (*Ouvertures à cassation*). Orders of the chamber of accusation, as well as orders and judgments of courts of last resort, may be annulled only for violation of law if they are correct as to form. They are annulled if they were rendered by a court composed of a smaller number of judges than prescribed, if all the judges were not continuously present at the trial, if the judgment was given without the public ministry having been heard, or if the rules as to publicity of trial and pronouncement of judgment were infringed. They will also be annulled if they do not contain grounds for decision, or if the grounds given are inadequate so that the Court of Cassation cannot establish whether the decision is properly founded in law. The same obtains if the court did not, or refused to, rule on a request or motion submitted by a party or by the public ministry.

 In convictions for felony, if the accused has been assessed punishment other than that prescribed by law, the petition for annulment may be filed by the accused and by the public ministry. In misdemeanors, the accused cannot use as a ground for annulment any alleged irregularity that he failed to contest on appeal to the court of appeal.

 (iii) TRIAL AND JUDGMENT (*Instruction des recours et des audiences*). The general rules as to publicity of hearings, conduct of hearings and order in the courtroom applicable to criminal trials apply also to the Court of Cassation.

 At trial, first the rapporteur gives his report, then the counsel for the parties are heard, then the public ministry takes the floor.

 The voting of the court proceeds under the direction of the president. First the rapporteur votes. Then the justices vote in the order of seniority of their appointment, the most senior first and the most junior last. The president votes last.

 The court may render its decision in any matter of felonies, misdemeanors or infractions after ten days have elapsed from the receipt of the files in the Court of Cassation. It must decide all urgent cases within three months from such receipt. Urgent cases include petitions for the annulment of orders directing the trial of the accused in the assize court and petitions for the annulment of a judgment of the assize court pronouncing the death penalty.

 Before deciding on the merits, the Court of Cassation considers whether the petition for cassation is in order as to form. If it is not, the Court will deny it. The Court will reject a petition that it holds unfounded on the merits. The petitioner whose petition is denied must pay the costs and a fine. This does not apply to persons convicted of felony and to officers of public administration.

 When the court annuls an order or judgment in misdemeanors or infractions, it will remit the case for further proceedings to another court of the same category and standing as the one that rendered the annulled decision. In felonies, the matter is remitted to another chamber of accusation than that which made the order, if the order emanated from a chamber of accusation. If the order or judgment attacked was made by an assize court, the case is remitted to another assize court.

A copy of the order annulling an order or judgment and remitting the case to another court for further proceedings is delivered to the procurator general at the Court of Cassation within three days for transmittal to the new court. The procurator general will send another copy to the officer in charge of the public ministry at the court that pronounced the annulled order or judgment.

A copy of the order denying the petition for cassation, or annulling an order or judgment without remission of the case for further proceedings to another court, is delivered to the procurator general at the Court of Cassation for transmittal to the officer in charge of the public ministry at the court that pronounced the order or judgment attacked or annulled, as the case may be. The officer in charge of the public ministry will notify the parties of the decision by registered mail.

When a petition for cassation is denied, the party bringing it cannot bring another petition against the same order or judgment under any circumstances.

When an order or judgment is annulled by the Court of Cassation and the matter is remitted to another court for further proceedings and a new order or judgment is pronounced in the second proceedings, which is again attacked by a petition for its cassation, and the second proceedings are in the same matter and between the same parties acting in the same capacity with the attack based on the same grounds, the next hearing will take place before the plenary assembly (*assemblée plénière*) of the Court of Cassation. If the order or judgment is again annulled, the court to which the matter is now remitted for further proceedings must follow the decision of the Court of Cassation on the point of law decided.[237]

(iv) CASSATION IN THE INTEREST OF LAW (*Pourvoi dans l'intérêt de la loi*). The Minister of Justice may direct the procurator general at the Court of Cassation to attack any order or judgment alleged to have been rendered in contravention of law, and the criminal chamber of the Court of Cassation is bound to hear the case.

The procurator general at the Court of Cassation may bring a petition for the cassation of any order or judgment pronounced in felonies, misdemeanors or infractions against which the parties failed to bring the petition in the prescribed time. The petition is solely in the interest of the law, and if the attacked order or judgment is annulled, the parties are not affected thereby. They cannot oppose the execution of the annulled decision.

(b) Petition for revision of a conviction (*Demande en révision*).[238] A revision of a conviction of a felony or a misdemeanor may be initiated in the interest of the person convicted. Proceedings may be brought whenever new evidence appears pointing to the innocence of the convicted person. Such proceedings may be brought by the Minister of Justice or by the convicted person or his legal representative. After the death of the convicted person, or in his absence, proceedings may be brought by his spouse, children, parents, universal legatees or anybody having his authorization. Proceedings are brought in the criminal chamber of the Court of Cassation by the procurator general at the direction of the Minister of Justice, who in turn acts at the request of the interested parties. The Minister may act on his own initiative, however, after hearing the opinion of a commission composed of three justices of the Court of Cassation.

If the petition is held founded, the Court of Cassation will annul the conviction, and if new proceedings are warranted, it will remit the matter to another court of the same category and standing as the one that rendered the annulled decision for further proceedings. If no further proceedings are warranted, the Court of Cassation will so indicate. If the innocence of a convicted person is established, the court may allow him damages, which will be paid by the state.

NOTES AND QUESTIONS

1. Proceedings take place before the criminal chamber of the Court of Cassation. The case may reach it only on error. Against the decisions of which courts may error be taken? On what grounds may error be taken?

Consider the proceedings in the criminal chamber and follow them through trial and judgment. Note the voting of the Court to arrive at its judgment. Compare the French procedure with that in the Italian Court of Cassation and in the Spanish Supreme Court. How does it compare with procedure in an Anglo-American criminal court of final resort?

Note the rules concerning remission of the case to a lower court. Compare the French rules with those of Italy and of Germany. *See also* 28 U.S.C.A. §2106.

2. French proceedings for the revision of a conviction must be initiated in the Court of Cassation. On what grounds may the petition be brought? Who may bring it and within what time?

Compare the French proceedings with those of the Italian, Spanish, and German criminal procedures. *See also* F.R. Crim. P. Rule 33.

---

9. Reprieve (*Sursis*)[239]

A court that pronounces a conviction to imprisonment or to a fine may reprieve the person proceeded against. Reprieve may be a simple reprieve (*sursis simple*) or a reprieve with probation (*sursis avec mise à l'épreuve*).

(a) Simple reprieve (*Sursis simple*).[240] A person may be reprieved if he has not been convicted within the five preceding years of a felony, or of a misdemeanor with a term exceeding two months imprisonment. Reprieve is applicable to all convictions of felony or misdemeanor and to additional measures, like the suspension of a driver's license. It is also applicable to infractions exceeding ten days of imprisonment or six hundred francs of fine. The court may reprieve the person only with respect to a part of the imprisonment or fine.

If, within five years from the conviction that was reprieved, the reprieved person has not committed any felony or misdemeanor and has not incurred a conviction for felony or misdemeanor without reprieve, the conviction reprieved is considered as not having been pronounced. If the reprieved person has committed such an offense, the punishment imposed for the offense will be carried out, but the court, for good reasons, need not revoke the original reprieve.

(b) Reprieve with probation (*Sursis avec mise à l'épreuve*).[241] Reprieve with probation is applicable to all convictions to imprisonment for felony or misdemeanor. The term of probation may not fall below three years nor exceed five years. The court may reprieve the person only with respect to a part of the imprisonment. The court may extend the term of probation if the person reprieved does not comply with the conditions of reprieve imposed on him, or if he was convicted of another offense where the reprieve was not revoked.

Where the person proceeded against complies with the conditions of the reprieve, the conviction will be declared as not having been imposed. Where he commits another felony or misdemeanor while on probation and incurs another conviction, the court may revoke the reprieve in full or in part. In that case, the conviction will be executed independently of the second conviction.

NOTES AND QUESTIONS

What are the conditions of simple reprieve and of reprieve with probation? French law allows probation in certain cases and gives the court power to entirely dispense with punishment. Compare the German and the Italian law. *See also* Illinois S.H.A. ch. 38 §1005-6-1 as to probation and conditional discharge.

---

10.   Parole (*Libération conditionnelle*)[242]

Parole may be granted to all prisoners who serve one half of their terms. Repeaters may be paroled after serving two thirds of their terms. Persons convicted to criminal detention (*tutelle pénale*) may be paroled after serving three fourths of their terms. Those convicted to life imprisonment may be paroled after serving fifteen years.

Where the conviction imposed is below three years of imprisonment, parole may be granted by a judge of supervision (*juge de l'applicaton des peines*)[243] after he hears the commission on supervision (*commission de l'application des peines*). Where the conviction exceeds three years, parole may be granted by the Minister of Justice on the recommendation of the judge of supervision who heard the commission.

Once the convict has served the time making him eligible for parole, his case is reviewed once a year with a view to parole.

If he is paroled, he will be subjected to conditions and to supervision. Supervision will extend over the remainder of his term of imprisonment and may exceed it by one year. In the case of parole granted to a person convicted to imprisonment for life, supervision is imposed for a term between five and ten years.

Where the paroled complies with all the conditions of parole, his release is final and his imprisonment is deemed to have ended on the day of his release on parole.

Where the paroled person does not comply with the conditions of parole or where he is convicted of a new offense, parole may be revoked in full or in part. He will then have to serve the remaining time or a part thereof as determined by the particular authority that paroled him.

NOTES AND QUESTIONS

What proportion of his sentence must a prisoner serve to be eligible for parole?

Consider the provisions dealing with supervision of paroled persons and with revocation of parole. Compare the French rules with those of the Spanish and the German law. For Anglo-American law *see*, e.g., Illinois S.H.A. ch. 38 §1003-3-1ff.

IV. THE SYSTEM AND ADMINISTRATION OF ADMINISTRATIVE LAW

A. THE SUBSTANTIVE ADMINISTRATIVE LAW

The French substantive administrative law is composed of a great number of statutes, the more important of which are embodied in the Administrative Code (*Code administratif*). They regulate the relationship between the state as the holder of public authority and the citizen. The areas dealt with comprise: manufacture and sale of weapons, registration of land titles, horse racing, religions, sale of liquor, gas and electricity, markets, foreigners, hotels and guests, gambling, lotteries, mining and quarries, historical monuments and sites, hunting and fishing, printing and press, public meetings, public health, public welfare, fire brigades, cemeteries, shows (theatrical, movie, etc.), tourism, public transport, construction of buildings, public roads, and so on.

The Administrative Code deals in detail with public administration and especially with: communities and their administration, accounting of public authorities, rights and duties of citizens, national defense, the departments and their administration, the public domain, public education, public officers, civil pensions, police, mail and telecommunications, expropriation, administrative courts, the Council of State, the Court of Accounts, and the City of Paris and its administration.

Some of the topics are of such an extent that they are dealt with separately in independent codes, which include: The Rural Code, The Code of Forests, The Code of Social Security, The Code of Public Health, The Code of Labor, The Code of Taxation, The Code of Transport, and The Electoral Code, and so on.

The following are topics selected from the French substantive administrative law.

1. Religions (*Cultes*)[244]

The republic assures the liberty of conscience and guarantees the free exercise of religion. The republic does not recognize, pay for, or support any religion.

Meetings for the purpose of religious services are open to the general public. They must comply with the rules of public order. No political meetings may be held on premises dedicated to religious service. The ringing of bells is regulated by regulations issued by the municipality in agreement with the particular religious body or, failing agreement, by regulations issued by the authority of the prefect.

NOTE

The French approach to churches is governed by the principle of separation of state and church. Other countries may take a different approach. Compare Amendment I to the U.S. Constitution and the voluminous law made thereunder.

---

2.   Eminent Domain (*Expropriation*)[245]

Expropriation of immovables may be ordered only in the public interest and for the public good. A declaration that the expropriation is so required may be made only in the proper proceedings. The declaration of public interest is made by decree of the Council of State, by a ministerial order, or by a prefectoral order.

The procedure is as follows: The expropriating entity (e.g., a public utility, like the electricity board or the highway department) submits a petition to the prefect requesting expropriation of a given land. The request must state the public interest involved in the work, a plan of the work, and an estimate of the expense. The prefect submits the request to a commission of enquiry (*commission d'enquête*) set up in the department for its recommendation. The commission is composed of members appointed by the prefect from among persons eligible to serve on the commission. A list of eligible persons is set up annually by the ministry of public works and comprises retired judges and procurators, active and retired administrative officers, architects, engineers-designers, and members of the chambers of agriculture, commerce, and trade. The commission actually set up by the prefect must have an odd number of members, usually seven or nine. The commission studies the matter and hears the parties and other persons who it thinks should be heard. The work of the commission must take at least fifteen days but not more than thirty days. The commission then submits its report to the prefect. On the strength of the report, the prefect may declare the land subject to expropriation. If he so declares, the matter is submitted to the court for an order of expropriation to be made by a judge.

In every department, the court of grand instance with its seat in the departmental capital has jurisdiction in expropriation matters. The judges who act as expropriation judges are appointed by the president of the court of appeal. A single judge hears the case. He is bound to make the expropriation order if all the conditions and requirements of the expropriation are met. The order is subject to appeal to the expropriation chamber of the court of appeal.

If the parties fail to agree on compensation, it is determined by the judge in separately held compensation proceedings. Already in the proceedings before the prefect, the petitioner must make an offer of compensation, and the owner of the land is requested to disclose a sum for which he would be willing to sell the land. These two sums form the basis in the compensation proceedings. The judge may not appoint experts. In exceptional instances, however, he may appoint a notary, from among those appearing on a list set up for that purpose by the president of the court of appeal, or any other person, to study the matter and make a valuation of the land. A recommendation is also made to the judge by the government counsel (*commissaire du gouvernement*). The parties themselves must make their recommendation. The judge then makes an award, which is appealable within fifteen days from its notification on the parties to the chamber of expropriation in the court of appeal.

NOTES AND QUESTIONS

Expropriation of property falls within administrative law and the procedure applied is administrative. The proceedings are held before administrative authorities. After conclusion of the administrative proceedings, the case is referred to the court for its order. The court must make the order where the administrative authorities handled the matter in accordance with law. Note that the question of compensation is handled separately. Are the proceedings designed to lead to a fair and reasonable award?

Compare the French expropriation proceedings with the scheme designed in the Uniform Eminent Domain Code. Note that the American proceedings are governed by the rules of civil procedure. Trial is by the court or by court and jury as requested by the parties. The award is made by the court. What are the chief differences between the French and American approaches to eminent domain? Do you find any traces of administrative procedure in the American approach?

Compare also the French approach with the Spanish approach.

---

3. Printing and Periodical Publications (*Presse*)[246]

Printing and publishing do not require any permits whatsoever and are free. Any publication must indicate the name and address of the publisher. Failure to do so is punishable with a fine. On second conviction, imprisonment from one to six months may be imposed.

A daily newspaper or a periodical publication may be published without any authorization or security deposit after a declaration has been filed with the procurator giving its name and frequency of publication, the name and address of the responsible director, and an indication of where and by whom it is published. If the director is entitled to parliamentary immunity, a co-director who is not so protected must be appointed.

The director must publish free of charge on the front page of the next issue any rectification directed to him by public authorities with respect to any statement appearing in the publication concerning such public authorities which was incorrectly reported. The rectification may not exceed twice the size of the article originally published.

The director must publish within three days the answer of any person who was referred to in the publication. The answer must appear at the same place and in the same size of print as the article that gave rise to the answer. Failure to publish such statement or answer is punishable with a fine and may in addition give ground to a suit for damages.

Foreign periodicals and publications, whether in French or a foreign language and whether printed in France or abroad, may be prohibited in France by the Minister of the Interior.

Any allegation or imputation of a fact injurious to the honor of a person or of an entity to whom or to which it is imputed is defamatory. The original publication, as well as a publication by way of repetition, is punishable even if it is published in a dubitative form, and even if it does not name the person or entity, as long as he or it may be identifed from the general tenor. Defamation committed against the courts, the armed forces, the authorities of government or public administration is punishable with imprisonment of from eight days to one year and/or a fine. Defamation against private persons or entities is punishable with imprisonment of from five days to six months and/or a fine.

The use of any outrageous expressions and terms of contempt or invective that do not contain any allegation or imputation of fact is an insult. An insult committed against the above-enumerated public authorities is punishable with imprisonment of from six days to three months and/or a fine, and that committed against private persons or entities with imprisonment of from five days to two months and/or a fine.

Defamation or insult committed against the memory of deceased persons is punishable only if it is intended to injure the honor of the decedents, living heirs, spouses or universal legatees.

Truth of an allegation or imputation may always be shown, relieving the persons otherwise responsible of liability except when the imputation or allegation concerns the private life of a person, when it relates to facts that occurred more than ten years ago, or when it relates to facts that constitute an offense which was amnestied, or which cannot be prosecuted because of prescription, or for which its author was convicted and suffered punishment.

Prosecution for offenses committed by the printed word is directed first against the directors or editors then, failing satisfaction, against the authors, printers, and distributors, in that order. Authors may always be prosecuted as accomplices. Should the directors not be liable because of parliamentary immunity, the printers may be prosecuted as accomplices.

NOTES AND QUESTIONS

Printing and the daily press are regulated by special laws. Note that printing and publishing do not require any permits. They are controled only by standards of good taste and common decency as understood by the general public and incorporated into the law of defamation.

Defamation by periodicals and publications is specially treated in the law.

Compare the French approach with that prevailing in the United States. *See* Amendment I to the United States Constitution on freedom of speech and the press. State constitutions have similar provisions. Compare, e.g., Illinois Const. Art. 1, §4.

Libel committed by the printed word is governed by the law of libel as it is understood in the Anglo-American common law. *See,* e.g., Prosser on Torts, 4th ed., Ch. 19.

What are the main differences between the French and the Anglo-American approaches?

----

4.   Foreigners (*Étrangers*)[247]

Foreigners are all persons who do not have French citizenship, whether they have any other citizenship or not.

To enter France, foreigners must be in possession of a valid passport or another valid travel document and a French visa. No visa is required of citizens of a foreign state that has concluded with France a treaty dispensing with visas on reciprocal conditions for a stay not exceeding three months. The exemption does not apply to persons who were previously expelled or denied a permit to stay or whose permit to stay was withdrawn. No visa is required of foreigners who are in a French port aboard a vessel calling at the port, as long as they do not leave the vessel, or of foreigners in transit by air who are at a French airport, as long as they do not leave the airport. No visa is required of citizens of neighboring states for the purpose of entering the border zone on reciprocal basis to facilitate small border traffic.

Foreigners entering France to stay longer than three months must, within eight days from their entry, apply to the department of police (*commissariat de police*) at the place of their residence for a permit to stay (*carte de séjour*). Members of diplomatic and consular missions and their families, as well as foreigners who do not stay longer than three months, do not require a *carte de séjour*.

There are three types of foreigners who may stay in France: temporary residents (*résidents temporaires*), ordinary residents (*résidents ordinaires*), and privileged residents (*résidents privilégiés*).

Temporary residents are tourists, students, seasonal workers and all those who do not intend to stay permanently. They receive a permit to stay temporarily (*carte de séjour temporaire*), which may not exceed one year, provided their passports and visas are valid for the time of the permit. They must leave at the expiration of the permit unless they obtain a new permit or a permit of residence.

Ordinary residents are those who wish to establish residence in France. They must apply to the prefecture for a permit (*carte de résidence ordinaire*). If they wish to work, they must obtain an authorization from the ministry of labor (*ministère du travail*). If not, they must give evidence of resources. They must present a medical certificate regarding their health from a medical practitioner determined by the public administration. The permit is for a stay of three years and is renewable.

Privileged residents are those who have stayed in France without interruption for at least three years. A stay of only one year is required of foreigners married to French women who kept their French citizenship upon marriage, of fathers and mothers of French children, and of those who lost French citizenship upon marriage to foreigners. A decree of the Minister of the Interior (*Ministre de l'intérieur*) determines the conditions under which the permit is issued to foreigners who rendered important services to France and to those who served in French or allied armed forces. The permit (*carte de résident privilégié*) is valid for ten years and is renewable as of right. It may be withdrawn only by a decree of the Minister of the Interior.

Foreigners who enter France without complying with the above provisions may be punished by imprisonment of up to one month and a fine between 180 and 3,600 francs.

Foreigners may be expelled by order of the Minister of the Interior if they present a danger to public order or if they must be supported at public expense. Those holding a *carte de séjour* must be advised of the order and may challenge it within eight days. Their objections are heard by a commission set up at the prefecture for that purpose. They may be assisted by counsel. The commission is presided over by the president of the court of grand instance in the seat of the department and has another two members, namely the head of the section dealing with foreigners at the prefecture and a prefectoral councilor. The commission reports its findings to the Minister of the Interior, who will then make a decision. A foreigner who is unable to leave because he cannot return to the country of his origin, and whom no other country would accept cannot be expelled. He may be required to live in a designated place and report periodically to the police.

NOTES AND QUESTIONS

What is the definition of a foreigner in the French law? Compare 8 U.S.C.A. §1101(3) for American law. What documents are required of foreigners to enter France? What is the visa requirement and what are the exemptions? For issuance of visas to enter the United States, *see* 8 U.S.C.A. §1201ff.

Compare the French provisions as to admission of certain persons without a visa, like foreign crewmen on vessels and passengers arriving by air who depart without leaving the airport, with the provisions of 8 U.S.C.A. §1101 (15).

Note that a foreigner who intends to stay in France longer than three months must obtain a special permit and that there are several kinds of such permits. Is there any counterpart to those permits in American law?

Under United States law, aliens may be admitted to permanent residence and issued an immigration visa. Does the French law provide for a comparable immigration visa? Is the status of a French privileged resident comparable to the status of an American permanent resident?

Note the penal provisions of the French law. Compare them with those of the United States law. *See* 8 U.S.C.A. §1321ff.

What is the French procedure concerning the deportation of aliens? Compare the American procedure in 8 U.S.C.A. §1251ff.

B. THE SYSTEM OF ADMINISTRATIVE AUTHORITIES (OFFICES AND COURTS)

Administrative authorities are local (communities and cities), intermediate (departments and regions), and central (highest offices of public administration, like ministries and the presidency). Administrative courts are at two levels: the administrative courts at the lower level and the Council of State at the final level.

1. Local Administration

(a) Communities and cities (*Communes*).[248]   City administration is governed by the Code of Community Administration (*Code des communes*). It regulates all the facets of communal activity. It deals with the names and territorial limits of communities, with municipal councils, with mayors, with city government, with financing (including the budget, income and expenditure, city taxes, and accounting), and with services which the city provides to citizens (e.g., markets and stores, public works, supply of water, gas and electricity, public transport, maintenance of streets, protection against fire, and regulation of funeral parlors and cemeteries). It also contains the statutes of municipal employment, including recruitment, promotion, and retirement.

Every community is governed by a municipal council (*conseil municipal*) and a mayor (*maire*) and his deputies (*maires adjoints*). The municipal council has at least nine members in communities below one hundred inhabitants, and proportionally more in larger communities. Large cities, like Lyon and Marseilles, have over sixty members on their municipal councils. Municipal councilors are elected in elections held in accordance with the provisions of the Electoral Code. They are elected for a term of six years. Elections are held always in March, and all seats are to be filled, irrespective of whether a member actually serves a full term or not. Municipal councilors elect the mayor and his deputies from among themselves.

The municipal council is presided over by the mayor. A quorum is a simple majority of its members. Decisions are taken by a simple majority of members present. The presiding officer (the mayor or an assistant mayor) has a casting vote in case of a tie. The municipal council lays down the policy of the community in its rulings. It gives its opinion on any matter required by statutes and regulations. It also gives its opinion on any matter of local interest.

The mayor and assistant mayors are elected by the municipal council from among its members by secret ballot and an absolute majority. If no one has obtained an absolute majority in two successive ballotings, a third ballot is taken and a relative majority suffices for an election. In case of a tie, the older candidate is elected. In every community below 2,500 inhabitants, there are two assistant mayors, in communities over 2,500 inhabitants but below 10,000, there are three. The number of assistant mayors increases in line with the size of the city population to thirteen in cities over 300,000 inhabitants. Large cities, like Lyon and Marseilles, have over twenty assistant mayors. Mayors and assistant mayors are elected for their terms as municipal councilors.

The mayor is the head of the city administration; he attends to his business under the control of the municipal council and under the supervision of higher administrative authorities. He is required to administer city property, to manage its assets and accounting, to prepare the budget, to direct public works, to represent the community in court, to exercise police powers, and to carry out laws and regulations. The mayor and assistant mayors are also registrars of births, deaths and marriages.

(b) City of Paris and Region of *Ile-de-France* (*Ville de Paris et la région d'Ile-de-France*).[249] The City of Paris (*Ville de Paris*) has an exceptional position in local administration. The same territory is administered coextensively by the City and by the Department of Paris (*Département de Paris*). The City is governed by the general provisions applicable to municipalities, and the Department by those generally applicable to departments, unless otherwise provided. The Department of Paris is headed by the Prefect of Paris (*Préfet de Paris*) and has its own departmental organization.

The two organizations have the Council of Paris (*Conseil de Paris*) in common. The Council has both the powers of a city council (*conseil municipal*) and of the general council (*conseil général*). It has 109 members elected in municipal elections. The members elect from among themselves the mayor (*maire*) and eighteen assistant mayors (*maires adjoints*). They also may elect up to nine supplementary assistant mayors.

The City is divided into twenty districts, called *arrondissements*. The mayor may delegate his powers to his deputies to exercise them in particular *arrondissements*. In every *arrondissement*, there is a commission (*commission d'arrondissement*) composed in equal parts of city councilors elected in that *arrondissement*, municipal officers appointed by the mayor (to act as registrars of births, deaths and marriages), and members elected by the city council from among prominent citizens active in that *arrondissement* in social, educational, cultural and other public activities. The commission gives advice to the city council and to the mayor on topics submitted to it by the city council or by the mayor.

The City of Paris extends its influence beyond the boundaries of the Department of Paris, however, and affects as its outlaying suburbs the neighboring departments of *Essone, Hauts-de-Seine, Seine-et-Marne, Seine-Saint-Denis, Val-de-Marne, Val-d'Oise,* and *Yvelines*. In conformity with the regional organization, the region of Paris, which is known as the Region of *Ile-de-France*, comprises all these departments and its administration is headed by the Prefect of the Region of *Ile-de-France*. The Prefect of Paris is ex officio the Prefect of the Region of *Ile-de-France*. The police within the Paris region is headed by the Prefect of Police (*Préfet de Police*).

NOTES AND QUESTIONS

1. French municipalities are governed by a uniform system of city administration. The subject is dealt with in great detail in the law, so that the bodies formed to administer communities, their election and powers are uniformly regulated throughout the country.

Compare the French system with the systems existing in Germany, Italy and Spain. *See also* Illinois S.H.A. ch. 24, as to American cities.

2. How is the City of Paris governed? Note that the regime applicable to all municipalities applies also to Paris with some minor modifications as mentioned above. Compare the administration of Paris with that of German city-states and that of large Spanish cities. How does the administration of Paris compare with that of large American cities, like New York, Chicago or Los Angeles?

---

2.   Intermediate Administration

(a)   **Departments** (*Départements*).[250]   The authorities in the departments are the prefect, the general council, and the departmental commission.

The prefect (*préfet*) is the head of the department. He is the representative of the government in the department. He is assisted by vice-prefects (*sous-préfets*), one in charge of each *arrondissement*, by a secretary-general, and by administrative officers and the staff of the prefecture. He is appointed by the President of the Republic in the council of ministers at the recommendation of the Minister of the Interior. The prefect is the chief executive officer in the department. He must enforce the laws and decisions of the government, as well as the decisions of the general council and of the departmental commission. His direct superior is the Minister of the Interior, but he is also subordinated to every other minister in matters falling within the competence of a particular ministry.

The general council (*conseil général*) is the policy making and supervisory body in the department. Members of the council are elected for six years, one in every canton.[251] Elections are held in March every three years, with one half of the members elected. This ensures continuity of the council. After every election, the council elects from among its members a president, several vice-presidents and secretaries. All are reeligible to membership in the council as well as to offices within it. The council decides all fundamental questions concerning the department, it approves the budget presented by the prefect, who is charged with the execution of decisions taken by the council. The council holds two regular sessions every calendar year, the first lasts the entire month of April and the second runs from September 1 to January 15 of the following year. The council may be called into extraordinary session by the prefect, who must call such a session if it is requested by two thirds of the councilors or by the departmental commission. A quorum is the majority of members and decisions are taken by a simple majority. In case of a tie, the president has a casting vote.

The departmental commission (*commission départementale*) is elected every year by the general council from among its members at the end of the second ordinary session of the council. It has four to seven members who are reeligible. The commission elects its president and secretary. It holds at least one meeting every month. A quorum is the majority of members, and decisions are taken by a simple majority. In case of a tie, the president has a casting vote. The commission is thus a committee of the council. It may meet at any time. Its function is to carry on the business otherwise dealt with by the council when the council is not in session. The commission also has functions of its own, namely to assist the prefect in the exercise of his official functions. The commission submits a report of its activities to the council for the council's approval.

(b) Regions (*Régions*).[252] In order to promote better administration and economic development in the country, larger territorial divisions are set up covering several departments. The seat of the region is selected by a government decree. It is always the seat of a departmental administration. The prefect of the department so selected is the prefect of the region. His function is to coordinate activities in his region and ensure the cooperation of the departments forming part thereof. In the exercise of the economic programs set up for the region, he is assisted by the prefects of the departments forming part of the region and by officers of the central administration taking part therein. He is also assisted by the regional council and by the economic and social committee.

The regional council (*conseil régional*) is composed of all members of the House of Parliament and senators elected in the region, of members of local representative bodies elected by the general councils, and of representatives of municipal and communal councils elected from among themselves. All the representatives other than the members of Parliament and the senators elected in the region together hold a number of seats equal to the seats held by the members of Parliament and the senators. All hold office for the term for which they were elected.

The regional council elects its president and other officers. Its function is to give advice on the problems of development and management of the region. Each year, the prefect of the region gives an account of his work of regional planning for the advancement of the region to the regional council. The regional council also sets a regional tax which is levied on motor vehicles and land to finance the activities of the region.

The economic and social committee (*comité économic et social*) has between 35 and 60 members. At least 50 percent of the membership comes from organizations representing employers and employees, those representing persons active in agriculture, and those representing chambers of commerce, industry, agriculture, trade and crafts. At least 10 percent comes from persons exercising activities particular to the region. At least 25 percent comes from persons representing health and welfare, family, education, science, culture, sport, and independent professions. The representatives are delegated by the organizatons they represent. Finally, not more than 10 percent of the membership is appointed by the Prime Minister after consultation with the prefect of the region from among personalities prominent in the region.

All members are appointed for a term of five years. The committee elects its president and other officers and functions along the lines of the regional council. The function of the committee consists of advising and promoting regional development. The prefect of the region must submit matters for the advice of the committee before they are submitted for advice to the regional council. The regional council and the economic and social committee or their committees may hold joint meetings, but they always vote separately.

NOTES AND QUESTIONS

1. Departments are the fundamental units of the French administrative system. How are they administered? Compare them with Spanish provinces, Italian provinces and German districts. *See also* the organization of Anglo-American counties, e.g., Illinois S.H.A. ch. 34.

2. Regions were set up in France to promote economic growth and development. Note the emphasis on economic development of regions in the French law. How do French regions compare with Italian regions? How do they compare with German states?

3. Central Administration

Central administration is conducted by the ministries headed by members of the government. All intermediate and local administration is directed through them, and they assure uniformity of treatment throughout the country. The ministries are also the authorities of final resort against measures taken by the authorities of local and intermediate administration. No further appeal lies against their decisions. In contested proceedings, however, there is a further remedy, namely an action initiated in the Council of State, which acts as the supreme court in administrative matters. Legal proceedings may already be initiated against decisions of the intermediate authorities in the administrative courts, from the decisions of which a further appeal lies to the Council of State.

NOTES AND QUESTIONS

Which authorities exercise the French central adminstration? Would you consider the French public administration eminently centralized? Compare the French central administration with those of Italy, Spain and Germany. How would it compare with the administration of the American states or of the United States?

The organs of public administration administer the country in accordance with the law. Note that the French central administration is also subject to control that is both political, exercised by Parliament, and legal, exercised by administrative courts.

---

4. Administrative Courts (*Tribunaux administratifs*)[253]

Administrative courts are composed of a president, a vice-president and several judges known as councilors (*conseillers*). They are appointed under the same conditions as other judges; that is, for life. They hear cases in panels of an odd number, the minimum being three. They decide by majority vote. The government is represented before the court by at least one government counsel (*commissaire du gouvernement*). Parties before the court must be represented either by an attorney (*avocat*) admitted to practice in the Council of State or in any other French court, or by a legal practitioner (*avoué*) admitted to practice in the court of appeal where the administrative court has its seat. In exceptional cases, no legal representation is required. This is so in petitions of annulment for excess of power, in matters of retirement benefits, and in personnel matters of public officers (e.g., appointments or promotions).

An administrative court hears appeals against decisions of administrative authorities having their seats within the area of the jurisdiction of the court. These are chiefly departmental authorities. An appeal must be filed within two months from notification of the decision on the parties. Decisions of administrative courts are appealable to the Council of State within two months from notification of the judgment on the parties.

Matters chiefly dealt with by administrative courts are connected with taxation and the regulation of building, trade and industry; but other matters, like electoral complaints and complaints connected with public appointments, may also occur.

At present, there are twenty-five administrative courts in France and four in French possessions overseas.[254]

NOTES AND QUESTIONS

What is the functions and authority of French administrative courts? What is their jurisdiction? What is their composition and how are their decisions arrived at? Compare them with Italian regional administrative courts. How do they compare with Spanish administrative chambers in *audiencias territoriales* and with German administrative courts?

Note that French administrative courts provide a full administrative review and decide on the merits. The parties must be represented by counsel.

Does a similar uniform system of review by administrative courts exist in Anglo-American countries? Compare, e.g., 5 U.S.C.A. §701ff.

---

5. Council of State (*Conseil d'État*)[255]

(a) Composition and function of the Council of State. The Council of State has two functions, advisory and judicial. As an advisory body, it advises the government on any matter submitted to it; as a judicial body, it is the supreme court in administrative matters. It has five sections, four administrative i.e., the section of the interior (*intérieur*), the financial section (*finances*), the section of public works (*travaux publics*), and the welfare section (*sociale*) and one judicial (the *section du contentieux*).

The head of the Council of State is its vice-president. There is no president. This is so in deference to an old custom dating from pre-revolutionary times when the king was nominally its president. It is further composed of presidents of its sections, of councilors of state in the ordinary, of councilors of state in the extraordinary, of masters of requests (*maîtres des requêtes*), of assessors of first class (*auditeurs de 1re classe*), and of assessors of second class (*auditeurs de 2e classe*). The secretariat of the Council of State is headed by a secretary-general. The vice-president, the presidents of sections, and the councilors of state are appointed by the President of the Republic in the council of ministers at the recommendation of the Minister of Justice. Masters of requests and assessors are appointed by the President of the Republic at the recommendation of the Minister of Justice. Councilors of state in the extraordinary are selected from nationally known personalities, specialists in their particular field of public administration. At least two thirds of the councilors of state in the ordinary are selected from masters of requests. The vice-president of the Council and the presidents of sections are selected only from councilors of state in the ordinary. At least three fourths of the masters of requests are selected from assessors first class, and all assessors first class are taken from assessors second class. The remainder of councilors and masters is taken from distinguished officers of public service, especially from the ministries. They hold office until retirement age, which is sixty-eight for councilors of state and sixty-five for lower ranks.

The four administrative sections transact business falling within the area of their competence. Each section has a president, at least seven councilors of state in the ordinary, and a number of councilors of state in the extraordinary, masters and assessors. Only the president and the councilors may vote. Masters and assessors vote only when they act as rapporteurs. However, their opinion may be heard on any matter. Decisions are taken by majority vote and the presiding officer has a casting vote. The president and at least three councilors, two of them in the ordinary, must be present for a valid decision. In the absence of the president, four councilors, three of them in the ordinary, must be present.

The Council of State may sit in a general assembly, and it forms a standing commission.

The general assembly of the Council meets either in its full assembly or in its ordinary session.

The full assembly (*assemblée générale plénière*) meets at least twelve times per year and twice per trimester. It may be presided over by the Prime Minister or by the Minister of Justice, but it is usually presided over by the vice-president of the Council. It transacts important business reserved by the Council for its decision. All officers of the Council may attend, but only those holding the rank of councilor of state and higher may vote. Any minister may attend and vote when matters falling within the area of his ministry are being discussed.

The ordinary assembly (*assemblée générale ordinaire*) is presided over by the vice-president of the Council and is composed of the president of the research commission, the presidents of all sections, one assistant president of the judicial section, twelve councilors of the judicial section, three councilors of each of the administrative sections, and three councilors of the research commission. Other members of the Council of State may attend, but they may vote only if they act as rapporteurs. The ordinary assembly discusses all proposals of legislation, whether laws, decrees or ordinances, and all business reserved for its decision by the vice-president.

Decisions in the general assembly of either form are taken by majority vote. In case of a tie, the presiding officer has a casting vote.

The Council of State also has a standing commission (*commission permanente*) to transact urgent business. It is presided over by the vice-president and is composed of the president of one of the administrative sections, ten councilors (two from each section), and masters and assessors appointed by the vice-president. Decision is by majority vote and the presiding officer has a casting vote.

(b) Judicial function of the Council of State. The judicial section (*section du contentieux*) has nine subsections. It is headed by a president and three assistant presidents. The subsections handle the usual business of the Council of State acting as the supreme court in administrative matters. Each subsection has a president and two assistant presidents, and several masters and assessors. The president of the section allocates the cases to the several subsections. They prepare them for hearing and judgment. A rapporteur is appointed for each case by the president of the subsection. For purposes of judgment, two or three subsections may be united in any given case. The united subsections are presided over by an assistant president of the section, or by the most senior president of the participating subsections. The quorum for judgment is five voting members. The number of voting members must be an odd number; if there is an even number, the most senior councilor, master or assessor present at the hearing will become a voting member.

Difficult cases are reserved for hearing and judgment before the entire section by order of the vice-president or at the request of the president of the judicial section, the presiding officer of the united subsections, or the president of the subsection handling the case. For the purpose of hearing and deciding a case, the section is composed of the president of the section, all three assistant presidents, presidents of the subsections, two councilors, and the rapporteur. The quorum is nine voting members. Decision is by majority vote and the presiding officer has a casting vote.

Cases of special importance are decided by the assembly of the section (*assemblée du contentieux*). It is comprised of the vice-president, presidents of all sections, two most senior assistant presidents of all sections, two most senior assistant presidents of the judicial section, the president of the subsection that handled the case, and the rapporteur. In the absence of the vice-president, the assembly is presided over by the president of the judicial section. The presidents of the four administrative sections may be represented by councilors of state appointed as their substitutes. The quorum of the assembly is nine voting members. Decision is by majority vote and the presiding officer has a casting vote.

The government is represented at every hearing by a government counsel (*commissaire du gouvernement*). Government counsel are appointed for a limited time, not exceeding three years, from among masters and assessors of the Council of State. They then revert to their functions within the Council.

The sections united to form a panel are selected every year by order of the vice-president on the advice of the president of the judicial section. In making these selections, the object of the pairing is to set up a panel composed of those who have thoroughly studied the case (i.e., members of the subsection to which the case was assigned to prepare it for hearing and judgment) and those who are dealing with the matter for the first time at the hearing (i.e., members of another subsection or subsections). Thus the blending of the results of a thorough study with the reflex of first impression of minds freshly brought in is achieved. The higher ranking panels of the entire judicial section, and of the assembly of the judicial section, apply the same principle.

In its judicial capacity, the Council of State hears petitions for annulment of decrees, including those dealing with a change of name; disputes concerning appointment, promotion, salary and other matters affecting public officers, civil and military, appointed by decree of the President of the Republic; appeals against unilateral administrative acts, the functional or territorial application of which exceeds the powers of an administrative court; petitions for annulment of administrative orders of ministers on the ground that they exceeded their powers; appeals against decisions of administrative courts; petitions for the annulment of final decisions of central administrative jurisdictions, e.g., the Court of Accounts; petitions for annulment of decisions of national professional organizations; and petitions for annulment of administrative decisions of collegiate organs of national competence.

Parties before the Council of State must be represented by counsel (*avocat*) specially admitted to appear in the Court of Cassation and in the Council of State. There are only sixty counsel so admitted.

NOTES AND QUESTIONS

1. What are the functions of the Council of State? How many sections does it have? What business is transacted by the individual sections? Compare the French Council of State with the Italian Council of State.

Note the composition of the several panels of the Council of State. Is there any comparable body in Anglo-American countries that would exercise the functions that are exercised in France by the Council of State?

2. What is the function of the judicial section of the Council of State? What is its composition and in what different panels does it sit? Name the comparable courts in Italy, Spain and Germany.

Note the unique French feature in the composition of the panels that combine members who have thoroughly studied the case pending before them with members who come to the hearing on the matter for the first time. Is this system used in other countries?

C. ADMINISTRATIVE PROCEDURE AND PROCEDURE IN ADMINISTRATIVE COURTS

1. Administrative Procedure

What was said previously on administrative procedure in the General Part, Section III. C. on the law of criminal procedure applies also to the French administrative procedure. The administrative system operates basically at three levels: municipal, departmental, and ministerial. Process may be initiated at any level depending on the nature of the matter. Most of it, however, is initiated at the departmental level with appellate proceedings conducted before the central authorities. If he so chooses, the dissatisfied citizen may appeal directly to an administrative court from decisions of departmental authorities, thus removing the matter from purely administrative proceedings to judicial administrative proceedings.

The proceedings are informal and in writing, i.e., the authority must keep a written record thereof. Any order given by the authority to the citizen must be in writing, including a reasoned decision of the action taken. It must also advise the citizen to which authority and within what time the order may be appealed. There is no appeal from decisions of the central authorities, but the matter may be taken to the Council of State sitting as the supreme court in administrative matters.

The appeal to administrative courts and to the Council of State has no suspensive effect unless so ordered by them. Apeals to administrative courts and to the Council of State from decisions of administrative authorities must be taken within two months from the notification. A four month administrative silence equals a denial and an appeal to administrative courts or to the Council of State may be taken, as the case may be.

NOTES AND QUESTIONS

What are the salient features of French administrative procedure? At which levels may administrative proceedings by initiated? May each case reach the central administrative offices in Paris? Compare the Italian, Spanish, and German systems of administrative procedure. How does the French administrative procedure compare with the Anglo-American administrative procedure? *See*, e.g., 5 U.S.C.A. §500ff.

---

2. Procedure in Administrative Courts
(*Tribunaux administratifs*)[256]

The proceedings are initiated by a private party complaining about some action of the public authorities. The petition, called *requête*, is filed with the registrar of the court within the prescribed time, usually within two months from the notification of the order complained of. The petition must be signed by counsel, with the exception of petitions of annulment for excess of power and those dealing with retirement benefits or personnel matters of public officers (e.g., appointments and promotions). The registrar notifies the president of the court who immediately appoints a rapporteur from among the judges. The rapporteur prepares the case for trial. The respondent authority is given a copy of the petition together with the request for any action ordered by the rapporteur or by the court. The respondent must file his answer within the time stipulated by the court. A copy thereof is passed on to the petitioner with a time limit for his reply, and so on until the position of the parties is determined. If the petitioner does not file his statement within the time limit, he is understood to have abandoned his suit. If it is the respondent who does not file, the case will proceed to trial and judgment.

The court may, at the request of the parties or on its own motion, order an expertise to be undertaken and appoint experts. Only one expert is to be appointed unless the court thinks it necessary to appoint more. The court also may delegate a judge to view the place of the dispute (*visite de lieux*), or may view the place itself. The court also may order an inquiry (*enquête*) into specifically determined matters to be made either at the request of the parties or on its own motion. It may summon witnesses and examine documents. It may direct interrogatories to the parties as requested by them or on its own motion.

When all preliminary steps have been completed and the case is ready for trial, the president of the court makes an order to that effect (*clôture de l'instruction*) and sets a date for the trial. The order is communicated to the parties and to the government counsel at least five days before the trial. In urgent cases, the time may be reduced to two days.

The trial (*séance*) is public unless otherwise directed. First the rapporteur gives his report, then the parties and/or their counsel present oral statements in support of their cases. Finally, the government counsel gives his opinion on all disputed points. The court then adjourns the hearing. The court deliberates in private and renders its judgment in open court. The judgment is in writing and is delivered to the parties by registered mail. It is very exhaustive. It lists all laws relevant to the matter, the position taken by the parties, the relevant evidence given, and the reasons for the decision. The defeated party is required to pay the court costs. The judgment is immediately executory. It may be appealed to the Council of State within two months from the notification thereof on the parties but the appeal has no suspensive effect unless the Council of State so orders.

NOTES AND QUESTIONS

Procedure in French administrative courts is similar to that in the Council of State. It is based on the French Code of Civil Procedure. How does it compare with procedure in Italian, Spanish and German administrative courts?

Is a judgment given by the administrative court immediately executory?
For American administrative procedure, *see,* e.g., 5 U.S.C.A. §500ff.

---

3. Procedure in the Council of State (*Conseil d'État*)[257]

The petition (*requête*) submitted to the Council of State must be signed by counsel except in those cases in administrative courts, as mentioned above, where it needs not be so signed. The registrar transmits the petition to the president of the judicial section (*section du contentieux*), who assigns the case to one of the subsections. The president of the subsection appoints a rapporteur to study the case. The rapporteur communicates with the parties and they file their statements, as is done in proceedings in administrative courts. The rapporteur reports to the president and if the subsection is of the opinion that the case is ready for trial, it so rules; it sets a date for the trial and transmits the files to the government counsel so that he may prepare himself for the trial. If further proceedings are necessary, the court may order an expertise, view the premises, order an inquiry, summon witnesses, examine documents, and so forth, in the same way as is done in proceedings before administrative courts. When the matter is ready for trial, it is so set by the president of the subsection if the case is being heard by two or three united subsections, by the president of the section if it is being heard by the section, or by the vice-president if it is being heard by the assembly of the section. At least four days' notice of the trial must be given to the parties, although in urgent cases it may be reduced to two days.

The hearing is open to the public unless declared private. First the rapporteur gives his report, then counsel for the parties present their oral arguments, then the government counsel gives his opinion. The court gives its decision in open court only if the hearing is open to the public.

Since each case is thoroughly prepared for trial, and since the steps that are normally taken at trial in civil proceedings are undertaken prior to trial in administrative courts and in the Council of State, the final hearing is rather short. To save time, the hearing comprises a number of cases, which are heard one after the other. The rapporteurs change from case to case; parties and their counsel appear only at the hearing of their respective cases; but the composition of the court remains the same. To protect the court against the possibility of a lack of quorum, several additional members are always present so that even if a member suddenly drops out, e.g., because of illness, the cases are heard as scheduled with sufficient members present for a decision.

The judgment is in writing and is delivered to the parties by registered mail. It is very exhaustive. It lists the laws relevant to the matter, the position taken by the parties, the evidence given, and the reasons for the decision. The court indicates whether one or the other party must pay the court costs, or whether each will pay his own. Costs are taxed before one of the masters at a later hearing. Where the public authority is defeated, the particular minister or ministers may ask the Council of State for clarifications as to the execution of the judgment.

The decision is not susceptible to any appeal, but opposition (*opposition*) may be filed against a judgment given by default. The petition must be filed within two months from notification of the default judgment on the parties.

A petition for the revision (*revision*) of a judgment on the merits may be filed within the same two months in cases where the judgment is alleged to have been based on falsified documents, where the defeated party lost the case because he was unable to produce a document which was in fact held by the opponent, or where prescribed formalities were not complied with (e.g., improper composition of the court).

NOTES AND QUESTIONS

How does the French procedure in the Council of State compare with that in French administrative courts? Note that the Council of State hears appeals from judgments of administrative courts.

Compare the procedure in the Council of State with that in the Italian Council of State, the Spanish Supreme Court, and the German Supreme Administrative Court.

For judgments of French administrative tribunals, *see* the section on judgments below.

V. LEGAL OFFICERS

A. JUDGES (*Magistrats*)[258]

The French system of judicial appointments follows the scheme discussed previously in the General Part, Section IV. A., on judges. The time to join judicial service is, as a rule, immediately after graduation from law school. After a period of further training, the candidate is appointed to his first judicial office. He then ascends within the hierarchy by promotion based on seniority and merit and may reach the highest judicial office. As a judge, he is irremovable and serves until he reaches the retirement age, which is sixty-eight for magistrates above the hierarchy and sixty-five for all other judges. Judges may not engage in any sort of political activity, nor may they disclose their political opinions. They are truly impartial.

Candidates for judicial office must hold the degree of *licencié en droit*, must hold French citizenship for more than five years, must be in possession of their civil rights and of good moral character, and must have complied with the requirements of military service. If successful in the entrance examinations, they are required to undergo training under the care of the National School of the Magistracy (*école nationale de la magistrature*). They are called *auditeurs de justice*. Attorneys (*avocats*), legal representatives (*avoués*), notaries (*notaires*), bailiffs (*huissiers*), and court clerks (*greffiers*) of at least three years standing may be appointed *auditeurs de justice* without taking part in the entrance examinations. The training of *auditeurs de justice* takes three years. They are assigned to civil and criminal courts and to the office of the prosecutor. They assist judges and officers of the public ministry. They are present at the deliberation of the various courts. After completing their training, they are placed on a list in order of merit which is published in the *Journal officiel*. Successful candidates are then appointed to judicial functions in the second grade of the lower division by the President of the Republic at the recommendation of the Minister of Justice.

Officers in the second grade, lower division, are chiefly judges of courts of instance and the courts of grand instance, and deputy procurators. In the upper division are chiefly judges of the Court of Grand Instance in the Department of Paris, the presidents, vice-presidents, procurators and deputy procurators of courts of grand instance, and judges-directors in courts of instance. In the lower division of the first grade are mainly judges of courts of appeal; in the upper division are mainly judges of the Court of Appeal of Paris, the vice-president of the Court of Grand Instance in the Department of Paris, presidents of chambers and advocates general in courts of appeal. Above these two grades are placed chiefly judges of the Court of Cassation, first presidents of courts of appeal and procurators general in these courts, and presidents of chambers in the Court of Appeal of Paris and advocates-general in that court.

Judicial officers thus serve either as judges or as procurators who form the *parquet*. They may move freely from one function to another. Those who actually hold judicial position may be transferred or even promoted only with their consent. Promotions are given every year. A commission of promotion (*commission d'avancement*) is set up to prepare a list of officers eligible for promotion, and a list of merit. Every officer must stay in a rank for a certain minimum time, usually two years, before being eligible for promotion. The list of merit is compiled on the basis of reports submitted by the heads of courts and by the ministry of justice. The commission is presided over by the first president of the Court of Cassation and includes the procurator general at the Court of Cassation as a permanent member. Further, there are two members selected from the Court of Cassation (one from the judges and the other from the procurators), two first presidents and two procurators general from courts of appeal, and nine judges (three of the first grade, three of the upper division of the second grade, and three of the lower division of the second grade). All these nonpermanent members are appointed for a term of three years and they cannot be immediately reappointed.

Appointments are made at the recommendation of the Superior Council of the Magistracy (*Conseil supérieur de la magistrature*). It is composed of nine members appointed by the President of the Republic for four years. They may be reappointed for one more term. Three members of the Council are taken from the Court of Cassation, one of them from among the advocates general; another three are taken from judges of lower courts; one member is taken from among the councilors of state; and the last two are not judicial officers. Officers recommended by the Council are then appointed by the President of the Republic. The Council also has disciplinary powers over judicial officers.

Certain persons who hold all the qualifications required for admission to apprenticeship and who are lawyers of long standing may be appointed directly to judicial office of the first and second grade on application to the ministry of justice. Their application is referred to the commission of promotion, which determines the grade and the function to which they might be appointed. These persons are government legal officers of eight years standing, lecturers in law who have taught at least two years in state law schools, attorneys (*avocats*) and legal practitioners (*avoués*) admitted to practice in any court who have exercised their profession for at least eight years, and notaries who have exercised their profession for at least eight years. Also chief court clerks (*greffiers en chef*) may be appointed to the second grade after serving for at least fifteen years, eight of them as chief clerks.

Judges are subject to discipline exercised by the Superior Council of the Magistracy, which then sits as the Council of Discipline (*Conseil de discipline*). After judicial proceedings before the Council, they may be reprimanded, transferred, demoted, retired or removed. At the hearing before the Council, the judge is confronted with charges levied against him. He may defend himself, and he may be assisted by another judge or by counsel. The council deliberates in private and gives a reasoned decision. The decision is not susceptible of any remedy.

NOTES AND QUESTIONS

How are French judges appointed? What are their qualifications? How are the judges of superior courts selected? How does the French system compare with those of Italy, Germany and Spain?

As to American judges, *see*, e.g., Calif. Gov. C.A. §68120ff.; 28 U.S.C.A. §§1ff., 41ff., 81ff.

B. THE PUBLIC MINISTRY (*Ministère public*)[259]

All that was said above about judges applies equally to officers of the public ministry since they form one group of legal officers. They are selected by the ministry of justice in the manner discussed above and serve as officers of public ministry and as judges. There is a procurator general in charge of the *parquet* at the Court of Cassation and at the several courts of appeal, and a procurator at the courts of grand instance and at the courts of instance. The *parquet* is composed of all the officers of public ministry assigned to serve in a particular court. They act as prosecutors and government counsel in criminal matters and as government counsel in civil matters. When acting as government counsel, they give the court the benefit of their opinion on the merits of the case.

As to discipline, they are subject to their own commission of discipline (*commission de discipline du parquet*). It is presided over by the procurator general at the Court of Cassation and has as members a judge and two advocates general at the Court of Cassaton, as well as fifteen procurators of lower courts selected from special lists. They hold office for a term of three years. The quorum of the commission is five. It decides by simple majority. Its decision is passed on to the Minister of Justice who may then impose the punishment recommended by the commission.

NOTES AND QUESTIONS

How do officers of the French public ministry compare with French judges?

How are they appointed? Compare them with the officers of public ministry in Germany, Spain and Italy. How do they compare with the American prosecutors? *See,* e.g., Calif. Gov. C.A. §26500ff., and 28 U.S.C.A. §541ff.

C. LAWYERS

There are presently three kinds of lawyers in France: attorneys (*avocats*), legal practitioners (*avoués*), and legal councilors (*conseils juridiques*). This is the result of changes enacted in 1971 that reorganized the legal profession.[260]

1. Attorneys (*Avocats*)[261]

Avocats are general legal practitioners who give legal advice and plead cases in court. They practice on their own or they may practice in partnership. When they practice in partnership, they are subject to the law governing professional partnerships.[262]

Membership in the bar is compulsory. All attorneys having offices within the jurisdiction of a particular court of grand instance form a chapter of the bar (*barreau*). A chapter of the bar may comprise all attorneys practicing in two or more courts of grand instance situated within the jurisdiction of a particular court of appeal. This is usually done when the number of members is small.

The organs of the bar are the council and the *bâtonnier.*

Members of a chapter (*barreau*) elect the council of the bar (*conseil de l'ordre*) by secret ballot in general assembly comprising all the members of that particular chapter. The *conseil de l'ordre des avocats* has three to twenty-one members in accordance with the size of the chapter. The council of the Paris chapter has thirty-three members. Members of the council are elected for three years and may be immediately reelected, but then they are ineligible for reelection for two years. One third of the councilors is elected every year.

The head of the chapter is known as the *bâtonnier.* He is elected in general assembly by secret ballot for a term of two years and is not immediately reeligible. Only in small chapters, those with no more than thirty members, may the *bâtonnier* succeed himself once. The *bâtonnier* presides over the meetings of the council and attends to the day-to-day business of the chapter.

The council is the governing body of the chapter. It handles any matter of importance to the chapter and protects the interests of the profession. It also acts as a disciplinary body of the chapter. In this capacity it may, after proper proceedings, impose the following penalties: a warning, censure, suspension not exceeding three years, or disbarment. An appeal against its decisions lies to the court of appeal and must be filed with that court within one month from notification of the decision.

A candidate for admission to the bar must file with the *bâtonnier* an extract from the criminal records showing that he has never been convicted of any offense, a certificate of French citizenship showing that he has been a citizen for more than five years, his diploma of *licencié en droit,* and his certificate of aptitude to become an attorney. He must further show that he is of good moral character (never proceeded against in bankruptcy).

The certificate of aptitude is obtained upon successfully passing a course held in French law schools. Students in their last year of studies and law graduates are eligible to enter. The course includes professional conduct, the preparation of legal documents, giving oral and written legal advice, and the preparation of briefs.

After being accepted, the candidate must undergo training for three years under the direction of a center of admission to the bar (*centre de formation professionnelle*). The centers are regional centers, but they may be established in the area of every court of appeal. Several bars may participate in one center. The center is governed by a council of administration (*conseil d'administration*). In accordance with the size of the bar or bars that it serves, the council has up to twenty attorneys and one additional attorney for every fifty members of the bar. It also has from one to three judges and from one to three professors of law. The council directs the training of the candidates.

As a trainee (*avocat stagiaire*), the candidate must master the art of advocacy. He must spend the three years in the chambers of an attorney, in the office of an *avoué* or a notary, or at the *parquet* of a court. He usually works in several of these offices as directed by the center. He also must listen in court and undertake any further training given by the center. After successfully passing his training, he will be given a certificate to that effect from the center and will be admitted to the bar as a full member. Judicial officers (judges of civil, criminal and administrative courts, and officers of the public ministry) and professors and lecturers of state law schools are admitted directly without the three years of training (*stage*).

After being admitted to practice, the candidate may engage in practice as an attorney. He will set up his office and practice within the jurisdiction of the court of grand instance where he is a member of the bar. He may appear in any court anywhere in the country, however, with the exception of the five courts in which only advocates admitted to practice in the Court of Cassation and the Council of State may appear. These five courts are: the Court of Cassation, the Council of State, the Court of Conflicts, the Court of Accounts, and the Prize Court.[263] Only sixty advocates are admitted to practice in these courts.

The attorney must take out an insurance policy of not less than 500,000 francs protecting him against claims arising out of his practice.

2.   Legal Practitioners (*Avoués*)[264]

Avoués are ministerial officers who represent parties in courts of appeal. They are considered officers of the court, and thus they may practice only in the court in which they are admitted. In addition to an *avoué*, a party may also appoint counsel (*avocat*).

To become an *avoué*, a person must hold French citizenship, be at least twenty-five years of age, have complied with laws governing military service and have a clean police record. He must be of good character, having never declared bankruptcy or been unable to pay his debts. He must hold the degree of *licencié en droit* or *docteur en droit*, and must undergo further training, called *stage*, for three years if he is *licencié en droit* and for two years if he is *docteur en droit*. During the *stage*, the candidate clerks in the office of an *avoué*. He must pass an examination at the end of his training and is then admitted to practice in a court of appeal. The examination is both written and oral, especially emphasizing civil law and procedure, commercial law, criminal law and procedure, and also professional conduct and accounts.

All *avoués* practicing in a given jurisdiction of a court of appeal form a regional bar chapter. There is also a national bar chapter comprising all *avoués* practicing in France. The chapters and their officers transact the business of the bar, they exercise disciplinary powers over their members and supervise admission to the bar.

3. Legal Councilors (*Conseils juridiques*)[265]

Legal councilors give legal advice and draft legal documents. They must be registered with the procurator (*procureur de la République*) within the jurisdiction of the court of grand instance where they establish their office.

To be registered, a person must hold the degree of *licencié en droit* or *docteur en droit* or a degree recognized as an equivalent, must have clerked in the office of a legal councilor for three years, and must comply with the moral requirements required of attorneys (*avocats*). Also, a foreigner may be so registered if his practice is concerned with foreign or international law.

A legal councilor may specialize as a legal and tax councilor (*conseil juridique et fiscal*), a tax councilor (*conseil fiscal*), a legal councilor in welfare law (*conseil juridique en droit social*), or a legal councilor in corporation law (*conseil juridique en droit des sociétés*).

Once registered, a legal councilor may exercise his profession anywhere in France. He must be registered, however, with the procurator of the place where he has his office, as mentioned above. He may practice on his own or in partnership. He must also be insured against claims arising out of his practice for a sum of not less than 500,000 francs.

A legal councilor is subject to the discipline of the court of grand instance within the jurisdiction of which he has his office.

Thus legal councilors may not represent a party in court, they may only give legal advice and draft legal documents.

NOTES AND QUESTIONS

What different kinds of lawyers are there in France? What was the situation in France before the 1971 reform? Who are the *avocats* and what business do they attend to? In what area of law do *avoués* and *conseils juridiques* practice?

Compare French lawyers with those of Germany, Italy and Spain.

How does a person become an *avocat* in France? How do the French requirements compare with those in Germany?

Note the organization of the French bar. How does it compare with those of Italy and Spain?

How does the French bar compare with the English bar and the several American state bars? *See*, e.g., Illinois S.H.A. ch. 13.

D. NOTARIES (*Notaires*)[266]

Notaries are public officers who prepare and notarize documents that have to be notarized by provision of law, or which the parties wish to have notarized. They are depositaries of notarized documents of which they make certified copies.

To become a notary, a candidate must hold French citizenship, hold a law degree (*licence en droit*), have no criminal record, have never been removed from any office or disciplined, and have never have been proceeded against for bankruptcy.

To be accepted into the profession, the candidate must acquire the certificate of aptitude (*certificat d'aptitude aux fonctions de notaire*) or the superior diploma of notarial studies (*diplôme supérieur de notariat*). He also must undergo a term of clerkship, called *stage*, for three years if he is a candidate for the diploma. The *stage* is done in the office of a notary and consists of practical training. To obtain the certificate of aptitude, the candidate must take written and oral examinations within the last three months of the term of the *stage*. To obtain the diploma, the candidate must attend courses in a university for three years and take examinations. In both cases, the examinations are on preparation of notarized documents and on the law with which these documents usually deal.

The *stage* is undertaken under the direction of the regional center of admission to the office of notary (*centre de formation professionnelle*). The centers are established in every region and are supervised by the regional council of notaries (*conseil regional de notaires*). The center issues to every candidate a certificate attesting that he has completed his training.

Judges, officers of public ministry, and professors and lecturers of law are exempted from the above requirements if they wish to become notaries, but they will have to undergo a clerkship for a time of not less than one year in the office of a notary. *Avocats, avoués,* and *conseils juridiques* must have practiced for at least two years to be exempted from the above requirements, and they must also serve a clerkship of at least one year.

After successfully complying with all the requirements, the notary must apply for an appointment to the ministry of justice. Appointments are made only to existing vacancies. Until appointment, the new notary usually works in the office of an established notary.

Notaries have their offices within a given locality determined by the ministry of justice. Their number within the jurisdiction of each court of instance is limited by decree of the said ministry. They may practice on their own or in partnership. Notaries must contribute annually a sum prescribed by law to a special fund for security. Should they be found to owe money to parties and unable to pay, parties can receive compensation from the fund. If no claim is made against them, the money paid in is refunded to them or to their heirs two years after they cease practicing.

Notaries form chambers of notaries at the departmental level, and councils of notaries at the regional and national levels. Departmental chambers are set up in the capital city of every department. Regional councils are elected by the chambers located within the jurisdiction of each court of appeal. The national council (*Conseil supérieur du notariat*) is located in Paris, its members are elected by the regional councils. Chambers of notaries deal with all the business affecting them, they exercise disciplinary powers over their members, and they supervise the admission of new members. The councils coordinate actions of the chambers and function as advisory bodies to public authorities.

The exercise of the office of notary is strictly regulated by law. Notaries must keep books in which they must enter every document prepared and notarized. They must keep accounts of all sums received for their clients. Committees of inspection are set up throughout the country to audit all the books and accounts of notaries. They are composed of notaries selected by the chambers of notaries under the supervision of the public ministry and the ministry of justice. All offices of notaries are inspected annually. In addition, a spot inspection may be made.

NOTES AND QUESTIONS

How does a person qualify to become a notary? Is it more difficult to become a notary than to become an *avocat*? Compare the French notary with German, Spanish and Italian notaries as to their training, qualifications and methods of appointment.

What is the chief business of a notary?

For a comparison with American notaries, *see*, e.g., Illinois S.H.A. ch. 99.

VI. DECISIONS OF FRENCH COURTS

NOTE: *Cases have been selected to allow an insight into the legal system and the life of the country under consideration.*

Note the approach taken by the various courts in handling the matters considered.

Note also the time needed to bring the case from the trial court through the several hierarchically superimposed courts to the court of the last resort.

A. DECISIONS OF CIVIL AND COMMERCIAL COURTS

SPOUSES GOUBEAU v. ALIZAN

Court of Cassation, Mixed Chamber, April 30, 1976, President Monguilan, Rapporteur Rouquet, Advocate-General Aymond, Advocates Garaud and Remond. (*Gazette du Palais*, 1976, 2nd semester, Jurisprudence, p. 459).

Petition for the cassation of the decision of the Court of Appeal of Rennes of January 4, 1974.

Decision of the Court

Sitting as a Mixed Chamber, the Court gave the following decision:

On the only ground for cassation:

Having considered Art. 1382 of the Civil Code and Arts. 2, 3, and 10 of the Code of Criminal Procedure, and Arts. 731 and 732 of the Civil Code.

Considering that the above provisions state that a person who suffers loss of whatsoever nature is entitled to compensation from the one who caused it by his fault; that the right to compensation for the loss resulting from mental suffering caused to the parents by the death of their son who was the victim of an accident for which a third party was liable, having become part of their property, it passes on their death to their heirs.

Considering that Alizan was found guilty by a criminal court of an involuntary homicide committed on January 17, 1971, on the person of Patrick Goubeau; that the father of the latter died on July 12, 1972; that the reason given in the decision for the denial of the claim of the heirs of the father of Patrick Goubeau to indemnity for his mental suffering because of the accidental death of his son was the fact that the father Goubeau did not bring suit prior to his death.

Considering that in so holding the Court of Appeal violated the above-mentioned provisions.

For these reasons: This Court quashes and sets aside the decision given on October 26, 1973, by the Court of Appeal of Poitier (Correctional Chamber), but only to the extent to which it denies the claim for damages brought by the spouses Goubeau in compensation for the mental suffering caused to the father by the death of Patrick Goubeau; it restitutes consequently the case and the parties to the state where they stood prior to the said decision, and it remits them for further proceedings to the Court of Appeal in Angers.

NOTES AND QUESTIONS

The Mixed Chamber heard the case in order to settle a conflict between holdings of the Criminal Chamber and the Civil Chambers of the Court of Cassation. While the Civil Chambers held that the claim would pass to the heirs upon death of the entitled party, the Criminal Chamber held that it would not if the entitled party failed to initiate proceedings in his lifetime. The Mixed Chamber ruled in favor of the interpretation of the Civil Chambers. The same rule applies to physical injuries and damage to property.

The contents of the provisions mentioned appear in the text of the decision.

For courts of appeal and the Court of Cassation, *see* the section on the system of civil and criminal courts above.

To which court did the Court of Cassation remit the case for further proceedings? Would an Anglo-American court of final resort have remitted the case on the above facts? Are there separate civil and criminal courts or chambers at the appellate level in Anglo-American jurisdictions? Are there such separate courts or chambers at the final resort level? May a conflict of the French type arise where the court has both civil and criminal jurisdiction, like, e.g., the United States Supreme Court?

———————

B. v. HIS WIFE

Court of Grand Instance of Paris, Order of the Judge in Matrimonial Causes of May 5, 1976, President Desjardins, Advocates L. Halimi and N. Nikiforoff. (*Gazette du Palais*, 1976, 2nd semester, Jurisprudence, p. 466).

Decision of the Court

Mr. B., by his counsel Lucien Halimi, filed a petition for divorce pursuant to Art. 237 of the Civil Code. Parties were properly summoned for a conciliation attempt held on April 28, 1976, and both parties and their counsel appeared.

Mrs. B. there asserted that the petition for divorce could not be considered since the parties lived together from time to time within the preceding six years.

Then the Judge in Matrimonial Causes made an attempt at reconciliation as prescribed by law. Heard separately, and then together, the spouses declined to reconcile. The Judge then requested them to settle amicably the consequences of divorce by an agreement which the Court could consider.

The Judge then heard the counsel on their motions concerning provisional orders and set a hearing for May 5, 1976, to give them time to study the objection of the respondent to the petition for divorce.

The counsel submitted to the Judge their observations in writing. They considered the question of the duration of the separation of the spouses a question of substance to be decided by the court, one that exceeded the powers of a conciliation judge. The parties agreed on the amount of alimony *pendente lite* to be paid to the wife.

Consequently, we, the Judge in Matrimonial Causes, declare the petition for divorce admissible. We hold that the Court will have to rule on the question of duration of the separation of the spouses. We authorize the petitioner to petition for divorce and we draw the attention of the spouses to the provisions of Art. 42 of Decree 75-1124 of December 5, 1975, which reads as follows: "If the spouse has not petitioned for divorce within three months from the authorization, the other spouse may so petition within a new term of three months and may demand judgment. If neither spouse has so petitioned within six months, the provisional dispositions lapse." We make the provisional dispositions and base them on the agreement of the parties: We authorize the spouses to live separately; the husband in Bezons with Mr. Ben Mohamed, 88, Jean-Jaurès Street; the wife in Paris 11, 2, Basfroy Street; we grant the wife the use and enjoyment of the apartment and of the household furniture; we order that each party takes his clothing and personal effects; we set temporary alimony at 500 francs, which Mr. B. must pay in cash to his wife for her own needs; we order provisional execution of the above dispositions.

NOTES AND QUESTIONS

Article 237 of the Civil Code provides that each of the spouses may petition for divorce on the ground of six years of actual separation of the spouses.

For the law of divorce and the appropriate procedure, consult the section on divorce above.

Note that the fundamental question of whether the parties actually lived apart for six years will have to be decided by the whole court.

How do the French grounds for divorce and the divorce procedure mentioned in this case compare with the divorce law and divorce procedure of your state? *See,* e.g., the Texas Family Code or the California Civil Code.

MORIN v. LOUISE-ADÈLE

Court of Appeal of Colmar, 2nd Civil Chamber, March 12, 1976, President Mazarin, Deputy Advocate-General Segret, Advocates Beckers, Sinay and Perrad. (*Gazette du Palais, 1976, 2nd semester, Jurisprudence, p. 526*).

Decision of the Court

Considering that on June 25, 1971, at about 8:30 P.M., a collision occurred in the parking lot of the Bagg store in Illkirchen-Graffenstaden between the automobile Simca 1100 of Louise-Adèle and the Opel vehicle driven by Morin.

Considering that by judgment of February 6, 1975, the Court of Grand Instance of Strasbourg held Morin exclusively responsible for the accident and adjudged him to pay to Louise-Adèle the sum of 460 francs and to the company "La Mutuelle Assurance Artisanale de France" the sum of 11,564.98 francs with interest; that the counterclaim of Morin and his insurer, the company "La Mutuelle," was denied and they were adjudged to pay the costs of the proceedings.

Considering that on April 10, 1975, Morin and the company "La Mutuelle" filed an appeal against the judgment; they assert that the trial court should have taken into account the negligence of Louise-Adèle, who failed to give the right of way to the automobile coming from his right; they claim that the judgment should be set aside, and that it should be held that the claim of their opponents was unfounded and should be denied, that their claim was well founded and that judgment should be given on their counterclaim against their opponents, who should be held liable to pay Mr. Morin the sum of 310 francs with interest from the decision and to the company "La Mutuelle" the sum of 6,450 francs with interest from the decision, and that their opponents should be adjudged to be jointly liable for the costs of the proceedings in both instances.

Considering that on January 30, 1976, Louise-Adèle and "La Mutuelle Assurance Artisanale de France" filed their brief demanding that the judgment be affirmed and the appeal be dismissed. They impute the collision to the improper entry of Morin on the main driveway of the parking lot.

Having considered the files of the case, the briefs of the parties and their additional briefs which state the facts and their claims.

Considering that since only property damage was caused in the accident, the police did not enter the case and made no report; that the expert Loir-Mongazon made a report at the request of Louise-Adèle and heard all parties and that his report and his sketch are uncontested.

Considering that it appears therefrom that Louise-Adèle proceeded at a speed of fifteen kilometres an hour along the main driveway of the parking lot from which it is possible to turn into sideways or to proceed to the public road; that Morin took his car, which he had parked to the right of the main driveway; that he put it into first and then into second gear and emerged between two sideways on the main driveway; that the front of his car collided with the right front side of the car of Louise-Adèle; that the two automobiles came to rest in an individual parking space located at the left side of the main driveway after each of them damaged two other vehicles.

Considering that since the accident occurred in a private parking lot, the Highway Code was not applicable but each driver had to observe the general rules of prudence.

Considering that Louise-Adèle was not in fault in proceeding slowly in the proper direction along the main driveway.

Considering that Morin should not have entered the main driveway without caution, but should have been ready to give right of way to vehicles already on it; that obstruction of vision caused by parked vehicles and the white lines on the ground at the entry of the sideways should have made him increase his caution; that on the contrary, Morin was very careless in having briskly entered the main driveway without making certain that it was free, he himself having stated that he did not see the Simca.

Considering that his imprudence and lack of caution were solely responsible for the collision, his appeal is consequently unfounded.

For these reasons and others not contrary to those of the trial court, this Court declares the appeal of Morin and of the company "La Mutuelle" properly brought but unfounded; it dismisses the appeal and affirms the judgment attacked, and holds the appellants jointly liable for the costs of the appeal.

NOTES AND QUESTIONS

The French law applies the principle of proportional negligence, but in this case the court held the defendant fully and exclusively liable. For torts, *see* the section on torts above. Note the Highway Code, which contains all the rules of automobile traffic was held not to apply in a private parking lot.

Does the rule of proportional negligence apply generally in Anglo-American law? Would it apply to accidents on public roads and also on private property? Do Anglo-American Highway Codes apply to traffic on private property? How would an Anglo-American court decide the case?

PREHAUT AND THE TRANSPORT CORPORATION CITROËN v. PÉRON

Court of Cassation, 1st Civil Chamber, July 15, 1975, President Bellet, Rapporteur Devismes, Advocate-General Granjon, Advocates Le Prado and Lyon-Caen. (*Gazette du Palais*, 1976, 1st semester, Jurisprudence, p. 199).

Petition for the cassation of the decision of the Court of Appeal of Riom of November 15, 1973.

Decision of the Court

On the first ground for cassation:

Having considered Art. 1147 of the Civil Code.

Considering that the obligation to transport the passenger safely to his destination provided for in this article is imposed upon the carrier only in the course of the performance of the contract of carriage.

Considering that Jean-Marc Péron traveled in a motor coach of the Transport Corporation Citroën when, at a stop the driver asked him to take a parcel to a café; that in crossing the highway Péron was hit and injured by an automobile.

Considering that in order to hold the driver of the motor coach and the Transport Corporation Citroën liable for the accident, the Court of Appeal relied on the contract of carriage and held that the responsibility for the accident fell on the carrier.

Considering that in so holding, although they found that the accident occurred when the passenger alighted from the vehicle for a reason unconnected with his carriage, the judges of the Court of Appeal have by its erroneous application violated the above-mentioned article of the Civil Code.

For these reasons and without any need to consider the second ground for cassation, this Court sets the judgment aside and remits the case to the Court of Appeal of Limoges for further proceedings.

NOTES AND QUESTIONS

Article 1147 of the Civil Code provides that the debtor is liable in damages because of nonperformance or delay in the performance of his obligation unless he can show that the nonperformance or delay was due to a reason which cannot be imputed to him so long as he did not act in bad faith.

This article is applied to assure safe carriage of passengers, professional treatment of patients by physicians, care taken of children by baby-sitters, care taken of spectators at public shows, and so forth. To escape liability, the debtor must show that an act of God or accident in which he bears no fault made it impossible for him to perform his contractual obligation.

The court found as a fact that the passenger left the vehicle at the express request of the driver to carry a parcel to a café. It also found that this had nothing to do with the contract of carriage. Consequently, the protection of Art. 1147 of the Civil Code does not apply.

How would an Anglo-American court approach the problem? Was the passenger a mere volunteer in carrying the parcel at the express request of the driver? Did the driver act within the scope of his authority when he requested the passenger to carry the parcel? Would the employer answer for the driver's conduct on the theory of *respondeat superior*? What about remoteness? Was the accident too remote an event, thus causing the chain of causation to snap? Was the accident foreseeable or was it the direct consequence of the request of the driver?

GLEIZE v. GLEIZE

Court of Appeal of Nimes, 1st Chamber, October 29, 1975, President Brunel. (*Gazette du Palais*, 1976, 1st semester, Jurisprudence, p. 366).

Decision of the Court

Considering that by a notarized act made on February 1, 1963, before Fauconnet, a notary in Carpentras, Charlot Gleize partitioned between his two sons, Elian and Josian, as a gift, all that he inherited from the estate of his first wife, Edmée Marie Sauvan, who had died on July 27, 1954, and that the total value of the property so inherited, partitioned and donated amounted to 12,000 francs.

Considering that it was provided in the act under the heading "Renunciation of the donor," that the donor renounced his right to revoke the gift and also renounced all rights of whatsoever nature that may have come into existence in consequence of the gift, and that he further renounced the prohibition against alienation and encumbrance of the property donated, intending that the donees were free to dispose of the property given to them.

Considering that on January 13, 1971, Charlot Gleize brought suit against his two sons for the revocation of the gift for ingratitude.

Considering that on December 3, 1971, the rapporteur judge ordered an inquiry, which was held on February 8, 1972, and on March 6, 1972, pursuant to letters rogatory.

Considering that by judgment of July 4, 1972, the Court of Grand Instance of Carpentras ordered a new inquiry, which was held on October 17, 1972.

Considering that by judgment of October 1, 1974, the Court of Grand Instance of Carpentras held: (1) that suit for the revocation of the gift of February 1, 1963, was properly brought; (2) that the conduct of Elian and Josian Gleize toward their father was one of ingratitude; (3) that the gift was revoked for ingratitude; (4) that restitution of the property donated was to be effected only after the conclusion of the probate proceedings of the estate of Edmée Marie Sauvan, the spouse of Gleize; (5) that Elian and Josian Gleize had to pay the costs of the proceedings.

Considering that on November 19, 1974, Elian and Josian Gleize filed an appeal against that judgment and that Charlot Gleize moved that the judgment be affirmed.

Considering that Elian and Josian Gleize request: (1) a declaration that the suit could not be brought because of the renunciation clause in the act of donation of February 1, 1963; (2) alternatively, that the claim be denied as unfounded.

Considering that we must first consider whether the renunciation clause is all inclusive and includes also revocation for ingratitude and for failure to carry out imposed obligations.

Considering that the trial court was of the opinion that revocation for ingratitude was not included in the renunciation clause on the only ground that revocation for ingratitude was founded on reasons of public order.

But considering that revocation for ingratitude is construed by the law as a private penalty, and is left purely to the sole discretion of the donor as against the donee and is subject to strict conditions as to time, and that this aspect prevents the public order to enter the matter.

Considering that if Art. 953 of the Civil Code allows revocation of gifts in three definite cases, namely, for failure to carry out obligations imposed by the donor on the donee, for ingratitude, and because of the subsequent birth of a child, it is only on the ground of the subsequent birth of a child that Art. 965 of the Civil Code prohibits a renunciation that extends beyond the provisions of the law; that the legislator expressed his desire to assure succession to estates, which is a matter involving public order, and that he provided for the revocation for ingratitude of which the donor could become the victim; that no provision analogous to Art. 965 of the Civil Code was made for the case of ingratitude of the donee; that to annul a renunciation that the law leaves entirely to the discretion of the donor would amount to an addition to the law.

Considering also that although the Civil Code does not contain any prohibition of a renunciation to bring an action for the revocation of a gift for ingratitude, it prohibits, on the contrary, in Art. 959, the revocation for ingratitude of gifts made in view of marriage; this provision implies that revocation of gifts for ingratitude is not affected by the doctrine of public order.

Considering that the action of Charlot Gleize consequently may not be brought, and that the defeated party is to pay the costs of the suit.

For these reasons, this Court holds the appeal properly brought and declares it well founded on the merits; modifying the judgment appealed from, it declares that the suit of Charlot Gleize for the revocation of his gift of February 1, 1963, for ingratitude may not be brought; and it holds him liable for all the costs of the suit.

NOTES AND QUESTIONS

Article 953 of the Civil Code provides that a gift *inter vivos* may be revoked only for failure to carry out a condition on which the gift was made, for ingratitude, and because a child is subsequently born to the donor.

Article 965 of the Civil Code provides that any provision whereby the donor renounces his right to revoke a gift because of the subsequent birth to him of a child is null and void.

Article 959 of the Civil Code provides that marriage gifts may not be revoked for ingratitude.

The court thus held valid the renunciation of the donor's right to revoke the gift for ingratitude.

As to gifts *inter vivos* and the question of revocation, consult the section on gifts above.

Does Anglo-American law have provisions comparable to those of the civil law concerning the revocation of gifts? May a gift be revoked for ingratitude in Anglo-American law? How would an Anglo-American court handle the matter?

CITY OF NICE v. MARQUES

Court of Cassation, 2nd Civil Chamber, June 12, 1975, President Drouillat, Rapporteur Bequet, Advocate-General Mazet, Advocates Peignot and Lesourd. (*Gazette du Palais*, 1976, 1st semester, Jurisprudence, p. 104).

Petition for the cassation of the decision of the Court of Appeal of Aix-en-Provence of May 2, 1973.

Decision of the Court

On the first ground for cassation:

Considering that it appears from the decision attacked that three children, upon leaving school, descended into a steep ravine owned by the city of Nice and to which neither barrier nor sign prohibited access; that one of the children, the minor Philippe Marques, fell and was injured while climbing back out of the ravine; that Bernard Marques, acting both for himself and for his minor son, brought civil action for damages against the city of Nice; that [the insurance company] intervened.

Considering that the judgment held the city of Nice liable on the strength of Art. 1382 of the Civil Code, the city alleges that the judgment violated the principle of *res judicata* of a judgment pronounced by the Administrative Court, and also that it was not shown that a barrier could have prevented the accident from occurring, since it did not occur on the descent into the ravine but only on the ascent after the descent was successfully accomplished.

But considering that although the Court of Appeal held, identically with the Administrative Court in which the father first sued, that no legal rule imposed a duty upon the city of Nice to enclose the rim of the ravine, it still held the city liable on the strength of Art. 1382 of the Civil Code on the ground that it was in fault for not having taken proper security measures in order to prevent the danger created by the presence of the ravine on its property in the proximity of a school frequented by young children; that the Court of Appeal in no way interfered with the effect of *res judicata* of the judgment of the Administrative Court, which held the city not responsible for an alleged failure to carry out public works and to render police services, and which declared itself without jurisdiction to hear a claim for damages brought by Marques.

Considering that contrary to the allegations made in the petition for cassation, the Court of Appeal held that the existence of the unprotected ravine within the fully built up area of the city created a definite risk of fall for all persons who would come too close to the rim and that it was risky to come close to it. It follows that the petition is unfounded.

On the second ground for cassation:

Considering that the judgment is also attacked on the ground that while the Court of Appeal held that the parents of the young accident victim were at fault for lack of his supervision, it further held that their fault could not be attributed to the child and that the city of Nice was fully liable for the injury, even though the fault of parents may be attributed to their children; and that by finding the parents at fault, the Court of Appeal could not have legally justified the imposition of full liability for the accident on the city.

But considering that when the liability of the one who causes an accident is based on the provisions of Art. 1382 of the Civil Code, only the concurrence of the victim's fault in the bringing about of the damage may partially exonerate the one who caused the accident.

And considering that the Court of Appeal made a distinction between the loss suffered by the father and that suffered by the child; and with respect to the first, it found that the father and the mother of the victim were at fault for not having properly supervised their child in view of his young age, and held that this fault could justly be invoked by the city and could discharge it of part of its liability; with respect to the injury suffered by the child, it held the child not himself at fault and this holding was not challenged by the petition for cassation, and it further held that the fault of his parents was not attributable to him. Consequently, the petition is unfounded.

For these reasons this Court denies the petition.

NOTES AND QUESTIONS

Article 1382 of the Civil Code provides that whosoever shall cause damage to another due to his fault is obligated to make it good.

The court thus held that the loss caused to the parents was to be apportioned between them and the city in proportion to their respective faults in causing the accident. But the loss suffered by the child fell entirely on the city because the child was not at fault.

The father proceeded against the city in the Administrative Court claiming that the city should have constructed rails on the rim of the ravine and that it should have given proper warning of the danger to passers-by. The Administrative Court denied the claim since no rule of law imposed such a duty on the city. The Administrative Court lacked jurisdiction, however, over a claim sounding in damages, which fell within the jurisdiction of the civil courts.

Supposing the facts took place in an Anglo-American jurisdiction, what would the cause of action be? Would it lie in negligence or in nuisance? Could contributory negligence be found on the part of a child of tender years? Would not the ravine constitute an attraction to youngsters to explore? Would the alleged lack of parental supervision be held against the parents? Unless the parents were required to meet the child in school and take him home, how else could they have prevented him from exploring the ravine? Would in your opinion the city be held liable similarly to the holding of the French courts?

BROCARD AND DELÉPINE IN THEIR OFFICIAL CAPACITIES v. MARTIN AND DERAIN IN THEIR OFFICIAL CAPACITIES

Court of Cassation, Commercial Chamber, March 2, 1976, President Cenac, Rapporteur Delpech, Advocate-General Laroque, Advocates Peignot and de Grandmaison. (*Gazette du Palais*, 1976, 2nd semester, Jurisprudence, p. 456).

Petition for the cassation of a decision of the Court of Appeal of Dijon of October 29, 1974.

Decision of the Court

On the second ground for cassation:

Having considered the principle of *res judicata* applicable to judgments pronouncing composition with creditors and liquidation of assets.

Considering that according to facts found in the attacked judgment, Delépine, who was appointed provisional administrator of the corporation Brocard and Son after the resignation of its president and director general, Georges Brocard, declared the cessation of payments by that corporation to the office of the Clerk of Court of the Court of Commerce of Paris, which declared composition with creditors by its judgment of March 28, 1974, and appointed Gourdain a trustee; that on April 18, 1974, the Court of Commerce of Beaune, acting ex officio, also declared the composition with creditors of the corporation Brocard and Son, and appointed Martin and Derain as trustees; that Delépine and Gourdain appealed that decision and that Georges Brocard intervened; they claimed that since the judgment of March 28, 1974, of the Court of Commerce of Paris entered into the power of law, the decision of the Court of Commerce of Beaune infringed the principle of *res judicata* and should be annulled; that the Court of Appeal denied the appeal and affirmed the decision on the ground that on October 24, 1974, an appeal was filed by Martin and Derain against the judgment of March 28, 1974.

Considering that having so held while the first judgment of March 28, 1974, which declared composition with creditors of the corporation Brocard continued in effect with respect to all parties and operated as a bar to the institution of new proceedings in the same cause even though it was being appealed, the Court of Appeal lacked legal justification for its decision.

For these reasons, and without need to consider other grounds for cassation, this Court sets aside the said judgment.

NOTES AND QUESTIONS

The court thus held that the institution of bankruptcy proceedings in a proper Court of Commerce was a bar to the subsequent institution of identical proceedings in another competent Court of Commerce. That was so even though the first judgment did not become *res judicata* because it was being appealed. There was no reason why the same matter should have been simultaneously transacted in two different courts; the court that was earlier in time would keep its jurisdiction.

For bankruptcy, consult the section on bankruptcy above.

In view of the fact that bankruptcy is federally regulated in America, is a similar conflict of competence likely in the United States? What are the steps to be taken by the parties and by the courts in bankruptcy proceedings in French and in Anglo-American law? Consult the section on bankruptcy above. When does a judgment become *res judicata*? What is the effect of *res judicata* and how does it operate?

MERONNEAU v. VASSEUR DENIS

Court of Appeal of Paris, 3rd Chamber, October 24, 1975, President Jourdan, Justices Bergeret and Duval, Advocate-General Lacoste, Advocates Babout (of the Melun bar) and Simonnet. (*Gazette du Palais*, 1976, 1st semester, Jurisprudence, p. 106).

Decision of the Court

Considering that by suit of June 4, 1974, Meronneau brought suit against Vasseur Denis in the Court of Commerce of Melun for the repayment of the sum of 56,507.40 francs advanced as a loan together with interest, and for the sum of 1,500 francs as damages, and for the sale of the commercial establishment of café-grocery-haberdashery-restaurant run by Vasseur Denis in Valence-en-Brie; that to challenge the jurisdiction of the Court of Commerce of Melun, Vasseur Denis alleged that the document on which Meronneau relies in his suit and which is entitled "Obligation with the commercial establishment as collateral security" was made in Paris on the 17th and 20th of January 1967 and contained the following clause: "The present obligation having arisen in Paris out of an express agreement of the parties, all disputes arising out of the present agreement will be submitted to the Court of Commerce of Seine"; that in order to obtain the dismissal of the claim of lack of jurisdiction, Meronneau relied on the provisions of Art. 16 of the Law of March 17, 1909; that without considering this argument, the Court held the clause applicable, declared itself without jurisdiction and held that Meronneau should bring his suit in the Court of Commerce of Paris.

Considering that Meronneau alleges in this Court that the decision contravenes Art. 16 of the Law of March 17, 1909, which gives jurisdiction to the court of commerce where the commercial establishment is located to consider demands for the sale of commercial establishments; that it was held in prior decisions that parties may not contract out of this jurisdictional rule; that Vasseur Denis claims that the decision should be affirmed since the suit of Meronneau did not demand the sale of his commercial establishment as its principal claim but requested the repayment of the sum allegedly due and damages; that the claim for the sale of the commercial establishment appeared only as his third claim subsidiary to the first two claims; that he contests the amount of the debt alleged by Meronneau which dispute falls, in accordance with the agreement of the parties, within the competence of the Court of Commerce of Paris, and that any sale of the commercial establishment depends on the outcome of the dispute.

Considering that the action brought by Meronneau is not governed by Art. 16 of the Law of March 17, 1909, which deals only with the sale of commercial establishments demanded as a principal claim, but it is governed by Art. 18 of the same Law, which provides that a court of commerce having jurisdiction over the payment of a debt that is secured on a commercial establishment may order the sale of such commercial establishment in one judgment; that in this article there is no reference to the mandatory provisions of Art. 16; that Art. 16 does not apply to a case where a clause giving jurisdiction to the Court of Commerce of Paris is valid and should be given full effect.

Considering that since the case is not ready for judgment, the merits of the case may not now be dealt with as it is demanded by Meronneau.

For these reasons, this Court holds the appeal of Paul Meronneau admissible but unfounded; it affirms the judgment appealed from and assesses the costs against Meronneau.

NOTES AND QUESTIONS

Article 16 of the Law of March 17, 1909, provides that a vendor or a creditor who has his claim recorded upon a commercial establishment, may cause the sale of such property which constitutes his collateral security. The suit is brought in the court of commerce within the jurisdiction of which the property is situated.

Article 18 of the same Law provides that a court of commerce in which a suit is brought for the payment of a debt secured on a commercial establishment as collateral security may, upon giving judgment at the request of the creditor, order in the same judgment the sale of such property.

The Court thus held the forum selection clause valid because it did not contravene any mandatory rule of jurisdiction.

How does Anglo-American law treat forum selection clauses? Would an Anglo-American court hold the clause valid on the above facts? *See*, e.g., Bremen v. Zapata Off-Shore Co., 407 U.S. 1 (1972) and Scherk v. Alberto-Culver Co., 94 S.Ct. 2449 (1974).

B. DECISIONS OF CRIMINAL COURTS

BERTAULT JEANNE, MARRIED SINOU

Court of Cassation, Criminal Chamber, March 10, 1976, President Combaldieu, Rapporteur Dauvergne, Advocate-General Davenas. (*Gazette du Palais*, 1976, 2nd semester, Jurisprudence, p. 460).

Petition for the cassation of a decision of the Court of Appeal of Rennes of November 18, 1975.

Decision of the Court

Deciding on the petition for cassation of Bertault Jeanne, married Sinou, brought against the decision of the Court of Appeal of Rennes, Criminal Chamber, of November 18, 1975, which convicted her to six months imprisonment for the conversion of collateral security.

Having considered the petition.

On the only ground for cassation based on the alleged violation of Art. 400 of the Penal Code.

Considering that it appears from the findings of the attacked decision, and from the judgment, which is based on uncontradicted evidence, that Bertault Jeanne, married Sinou, bought on March 15, 1973, an automobile for 32,000 francs; that she obtained a loan of 19,000 francs from the Société de crédit universel, which took the automobile as collateral security; that Mrs. Sinou sold the automobile on May 2, 1974, for 12,500 francs without giving any notice to the lender.

Considering that unimpressed by the argument of the defense that the collateral was not registered with the prefecture, the trial court has rightly found the accused guilty of conversion of the collateral; the formality of publicity has the only purpose of notifying third parties of the contract and of protecting them against further dealings; the consequence of nullity in the case of failure to record has no effect on the relation of the lender, as holder of the secured interest, and the borrower, as the grantor thereof, who has notice of the secured interest and of the obligations flowing therefrom by the contract itself; consequently, the petition for cassation should not have been admitted.

And considering that the decision is regular as to its form.

For these reasons, this Court denies the petition.

NOTES AND QUESTIONS

Article 400 of the Penal Code appears in the part of the Code dealing with larceny. It provides, among other things, that the punishment of Art. 401 of the Penal Code also applies to any debtor, borrower or pledger who destroys, converts or attempts to destroy or convert the collateral.

The failure of the lender to record his interest in the collateral resulted in the loss of his claim against the purchaser of the automobile from the borrower. The claim is purely of civil law. The registration or failure thereof has no effect on the criminal liability under Art. 400 of the Penal Code. The Court of Cassation thus let the conviction stand.

Would the acts committed by the accused constitute a criminal offense in Anglo-American law? Is there any offense sounding in conversion of collateral security known to Anglo-American law? Could a person be guilty of theft on the facts of the above case?

BESSE JACQUES

Court of Appeal of Angers, Correctional Chamber, June 22, 1976, President Auran, Justices Blach and Petit, Deputy Procurator-General Jacquemin, Advocate James. (*Gazette du Palais*, 1976, 2nd semester, Jurisprudence, p. 486).

Decision of the Court

Considering the appeal lodged by the public ministry against a judgment given on March 22, 1976, by the Court of Police of Bauge, which relieved Besse Jacques of responsibility for exceeding the lawful speed on an open highway outside of city limits on the ground that the owner of the vehicle denies having been the driver of his automobile on the day and place of the infraction, and that he was within his right to decline to name the driver who could not be ascertained.

Considering that the facts are correctly stated in the judgment given.

Considering that Art. L. 21 and Art. R. 232 of the Highway Code are directed expressly against the driver of an automobile and make him criminally responsible for infractions committed by him in the driving of that automobile; that the only exception foreseen in Art. L. 21-1 deals with parking infractions; and that no legal rule analogous to that contained in Art. 62 of the Penal Code requires the owner of an automobile to name the driver who was guilty of the infraction.

For these reasons, this Court affirms the judgment of the trial court on the grounds there given. Costs are to be taxed against the Treasury.

NOTES AND QUESTIONS

Article L. 21 of the Highway Code provides that the driver of a vehicle is criminally responsible for all infractions committed by him in the driving of the vehicle.

Article L. 21-1 of the Highway Code provides that in derogation of the above rule, the holder of the certificate of registration of a vehicle is financially responsible for parking infractions for which only a fine is imposed, unless he shows an act of God or unless he supplies information permitting the identification of the person who actually committed the infraction.

Article R. 232 of the Highway Code provides that the driver of a vehicle who infringes the provisions of Book I of the Code shall be punished with a fine between 160 and 600 francs and with imprisonment not exceeding eight days, or with only one of the penalties where the infringement deals with: (1) one-way traffic, (2) speed of motor vehicles, (3) driving (to the right) and overtaking, (4) entering intersections and right of way, (5) signaling, (6) stop signs, (7) prohibition or restriction of use of certain roads by certain types of vehicles, or (8) prohibited manoeuvers.

In the case of a second offense, imprisonment not exceeding ten days may be imposed. Also, the fine may be increased up to 1,500 francs.

Article 62 of the Penal Code provides for the punishment of those who, knowing that a felony has been attempted or committed . . . do not immmediately inform administrative or judicial authorities.

Note the severity of punishment provided in the French Highway Code for the above offenses.

Compare the above traffic regulations with the corresponding regulations in the Traffic Code of your state. May the owner of an automobile, rather than the driver, be prosecuted in the case of speeding? Does it follow that if the driver is not apprehended and identified, no prosecution may be held? Is the exception with respect to parking infractions well founded? May the owner of an automobile be required to disclose the name of the driver in such cases.

EGAZAN MICHEL

Court of Cassation, Criminal Chamber, February 18, 1976, President Combaldieu, Rapporteur Vergne, Advocate-General Davenas, Advocate Rocques. (*Gazette du Palais*, 1976, 1st semester, Jurisprudence, p. 330).

Petition for the cassation of the decision of the Court of Appeal of Paris, 11th Chamber, of July 3, 1975.

Decision of the Court

Deciding on the petition for cassation of Egazan Michel brought against the decision of the Court of Appeal of Paris, 11th Chamber, of July 3, 1975, which convicted him to six months imprisonment with probation for five years and to damages for violence with premeditation.

Having considered the petition.

On the only ground for cassation based on the alleged violation by improper application of Arts. 309 and 311 of the Penal Code, . . . for lack of evidence and lack of legal grounds, in that the attacked decision held the accused guilty of violence with premeditation for having made telephone calls to the two spouses, on the ground that these acts constituted repeated assaults although the trial court found that the improper calls did not cause serious stress to the persons who were the object thereof and did not result in a serious mental condition of those persons, and that the failure to establish such a condition resulted in that the commission of the misdemeanor of violence has not been legally demonstrated.

Considering that it appears from the findings of facts of the attacked decision that from November 1971 to February 1972, Egazan maliciously made numerous telephone calls to the spouses Marteau, which the judges found disturbing, aggressive, and occasionally even threatening, and that the calls brought the spouses into a state of anguish and that the mental state of Mrs. Marteau was thereby especially affected.

Considering that in view of these authoritative findings, the Court of Appeal was correct in holding that these acts, because of their considerable number and their aggressive nature, constituted the misdemeanor of premeditated violence foreseen and punished by Art. 311 of the Penal Code.

Considering that in enacting Arts. 309, 311 and R. 40-1 of the said Code, the legislature aimed at voluntary violent acts and intended to punish specifically those acts which, without physically touching the person were nonetheless of a nature able to cause mental shock; in the light of that, the attacked decision far from violating the provisions mentioned in the petition, applies them correctly; from which it follows that the petition should not have been admitted.

And considering that the decision is regular as to its form.

For these reasons, this Court denies the petition.

NOTES AND QUESTIONS

Article 309 of the Penal Code provides that whosoever shall voluntarily inflict wounds, blows or apply violence to another person from which a total disability to work for eight days or more shall result will be punished with imprisonment of from two months to five years and with a fine of from 500 to 10,000 francs.

Article 311 of the Penal Code provides that where the wounds, blows or other acts of violence do not cause a total disability to work in excess of eight days but are inflicted with premeditation, lying in wait, or with arms, the offender is to be punished with imprisonment of from two months to five years and with a fine of from 500 to 10,000 francs.

Article R. 40-1 provides that the individuals and their accomplices who voluntarily inflict wounds, blows or apply violence to another person from which an illness or a total disability to work exceeding eight days does not result and where there is no premeditation, lying in wait or use of arms, will be punished with imprisonment of from ten days to one month and with a fine of from 600 to 1,000 francs or with one of the penalties only.

The Court thus held that the above articles of the Penal Code apply to acts of violence which are likely to cause a mental shock.

Is the making of annoying telephone calls punishable in Anglo-American law? Would a statutory provision comparable to Art. 311 of the French Penal Code likely be held to embrace the subject of annoying telephone calls or would a specific provision expressly defining the offense be necessary? Compare, e.g., Calif. Pen. C.A. §653m. Would you say the the French courts are stretching the law to its utmost limits in order to make annoying telephone calls punishable in view of the legal provisions applied?

PEIGNOT MICHEL

Court of Cassation, Criminal Chamber, January 27, 1976, President Chapar, Rapporteur Crevy, Advocate-General Aymond, Advocate Galland. (*Gazette du Palais*, 1976, 1st semester, Jurisprudence, p. 291).

Petition for the cassation of a decision of the Court of Appeal of Grenoble of February 21, 1975.

Decision of the Court

Deciding on the petition for cassation of Peignot Michel brought against the decision of the Court of Appeal of Grenoble, Correctional Chamber, of February 21,

1975, which found him guilty of swindling and convicted him to thirteen months of imprisonment with probation, and to a 1,000 francs fine and to damages.

Having considered the petition.

On the only ground for cassation based on the alleged violation of Art. 405 of the Penal Code, . . . for lack of evidence and lack of legal grounds, in that the decision attacked held the accused guilty of swindling on the ground that the accused lied and made the young woman, whom he met through a marriage advertisement, believe that he would marry her, and on the strength of that promise she bought him an apartment and gave him money, although a false promise to marry does not constitute a fraudulent act characteristic of the misdemeanor of swindling if it is not accompanied by external acts designed to give it credit, and that the presence of such external acts was not found by the court, and consequently, contrary to the holding of the judges trying the merits of the case, the accused did not commit any fraudulent act.

Considering that it appears from the findings of facts of the attacked judgment, which is founded on uncontradicted evidence that Peignot, who was in serious financial difficulties, met Miss Demaison-Mermet early in 1969 in response to a marriage advertisement that he had placed in a weekly magazine; that he promised to marry her, the marriage ceremony having been planned for the latter part of 1970; that the promise was false; that Peignot has been for a number of years living with a mistress whom he has never left; that he pretended to Miss Demaison that he was divorced and the father of several children; the he never intended to marry Miss Demaison; that before the marriage project came to an end, Peignot had Miss Demaison buy him the apartment where he was living and that he participated with her in 1970 in its renovation as if it were to become their future home; that having thereby persuaded Miss Demaison-Mermet of the sincerity of his intentions, she handed over to him money and took over an obligation of his debt.

Considering that on these facts the Court of Appeal has rightly convicted Peignot of swindling Miss Demaison-Mermet; that it appears from the findings made in the decision that in order to make his false promise of marriage creditable, the petitioner used diverse techniques which constituted acts which instilled in the victim the hope of a chimeric event, and made her give the accused funds; it follows that the petition should not have been admitted.

And considering that the decision is regular as to form.

For these reasons, this Court denies the petition.

NOTES AND QUESTIONS

Article 405 of the Penal Code provides that any person who shall assume a false name or identity, or shall use deceptive practices so as to make belief in the existence of nonexistent ventures or in fictitious powers or credit, or who shall instill hope or fear of success, accident or another fictitious event, and thereby obtains or attempts to obtain any money, movables, obligations, releases, notes, promises, receipts or discharges, and by any such practices shall swindle or attempt to swindle another out of his property, in whole or in part, will be punished by imprisonment of from one year to five years and with a fine of from 3,600 to 36,000 francs.

Applying the above provision, the court holds that a false promise to marry is not criminally punishable, but when the offender applies fraudulent practices to instill belief in his victim that he would marry her and extracts money from her, he will be guilty of swindling.

Do Anglo-American penal codes carry provisions similar to Art. 405 of the French Penal Code? Consider the offense of obtaining money, property or labor by false pretenses. *See,* e.g., Calif. Pen. C.A. §532. Would an Anglo-American court pronounce a similar decision on the facts of the case?

DARDEL GEORGES

Court of Cassation, Criminal Chamber, February 11, 1976, President Combaldieu, Rapporteur Vergne, Advocate-General Aymond, Advocate Calon. (*Gazette du Palais,* 1976, 1st semester, Jurisprudence, p. 437).

Petition for the cassation of a decision of the Court of Appeal of Paris of June 28, 1975.

Decision of the Court

Deciding on the petition for cassation of Dardel Georges brought against a decision of the Court of Appeal of Paris, 11th Chamber, of June 28, 1975, which passed only on the civil claim in proceedings for false defamatory accusation and convicted him to damages.

Having considered the petition.

Considering that the attacked decision passed only on the civil claim, the petition is without substance insofar as it extends beyond damages to a criminal conviction.

On the only ground for cassation based on the alleged violation of Art. 373 of the Penal Code, . . . for lack of evidence and lack of legal grounds, in that the attacked decision held the accused guilty of false defamatory accusation and convicted him to damages payable to the two civil parties on the ground that the proof of truth of the facts alleged was unsuccessful; that the accused assumed that the old reprehensible practices were being continued while he did not have any proof thereof, and that the bad intent which constituted the offense was based on the knowledge at the time of the making of the accusation that the alleged facts were false; that nothing of the sort appears from the above facts, but on the contrary, the assumption of the perpetuation of the old reprehensible practices shows that the accused believed in their truth, and also, that the judgment did not take into account evidence tending to show that the accused was misled by the apparent state of city affairs which made him believe that the old practices were being continued, which shows his good faith.

Having considered the above-mentioned article of the Penal Code.

Considering that every judgment or decision must give its reasons; that insufficient reasons or their contradiction amounts to lack of reasons.

Considering that the attacked decision recites that on April 26, 1972, Dardel wrote a letter to the Public Ministry of Paris in which he accused Ceccaldi-Reynaud, the mayor of Puteaux, and others of breach of Art. 174 of the Penal Code, in that he employed in the management, publication and distribution of the newspaper *Notre*

Commune one Touboul and one Bouaouina whose positions were fictitious and who were paid from city funds; . . .

Considering that deciding only on the appeal of the civil parties Touboul and Bouaouina, after the accused was discharged in the trial court, the decision held Dardel guilty of false defamatory accusation and convicted him to damages.

Considering that in answer to the allegations of the defense that the accused acted in good faith, the decision limited itself to a statement that Dardel simply assumed that the old practices current while he was mayor were being continued at city hall under his successor, and that if he arrived at that conclusion from the appearance of some laxity in the management of the city finances it was unfounded as far as the civil parties were concerned.

But considering that these grounds are insufficient to show intent in the offense held to have been committed, since to constitute the offense it is not enough to show the lack of good ground on the part of the accused, but it must be shown that he knew that the facts imputed by him to his opponents were false; and that consequently the decision must be set aside on this ground.

For these reasons, this Court sets aside and annuls the decision of the Court of Appeal of Paris of June 28, 1975, and remits the case to the Court of Appeal in Amiens to give a new decision in accordance with the law.

NOTES AND QUESTIONS

Article 373 of the Penal Code provides that any person who by any means whatsoever makes a false defamatory accusation against any other person or persons, to judicial officers or to officers of the administrative or judiciary police or to any prosecuting authority or to any authority having the power to pass the matter to a competent authority, or to the superiors or employers of the person so accused, will be punished by imprisonment from six months to five years and with a fine from 500 to 15,000 francs.

To constitute the offense, the prosecution must prove that the accuser knew that the fact imputed to his opponent were false.

Is any offense similar to that described in Art. 373 of the French Penal Code known in Anglo-American law? Could criminal prosecution be instituted against the accuser? Could the accuser be sued for malicious prosecution? Could an action in defamation for libel be brought against him?

CALVAGRAC v. THE PUBLIC MINISTRY

Court of Cassation, Criminal Chamber, March 4, 1976, President Combaldieu, Rapporteur Monzein, Advocate-General Aymond, Advocate Coutard. (*Gazette du Palais*, 1976, 1st semester, Jurisprudence, p. 417).

Petition for the cassation of a decision of the Court of Appeal of Dijon of June 26, 1975.

Decision of the Court

On the only ground for cassation and on the additional ground for cassation based on the alleged violation of Arts. 44-1 and 44-2 of the Law of December 27, 1973, . . . for failure to recognize the legal nature of the facts in the information, lack and contradiction of reasons in that the attacked decision held the petitioner, the director of a corporation producing fruit juice and fruit drinks, guilty of the misdemeanor of false advertising on the ground that advertisements reading: "Poker, made of fruit ready to drink," without giving any other details, manifestly contained an allegation and representation likely to mislead the public in giving to understand that it referred to fruit juice while in fact the beverage contained only 50 percent fruit juice; that the prosecution is based purely on subjective prejudice and is not supported by any proof so that the reasons for the decision do not make it possible for the Court of Cassation to review the case.

On the additional ground based on the alleged violation . . . of Art. 44-1 of the Law of December 27, 1973, . . . for lack of evidence and lack of legal grounds in that the attacked decision held the petitioner . . . guilty of the misdemeanor of false advertising but failed to inquire whether the accused acted with intent to defraud, on the ground that bad faith on the part of the accused was not required by the law for the commission of the offense; but that although bad faith is not expressly mentioned in the Law of December 27, 1973, it is implicitly and necessarily an element constituting the offense with which the accused is charged, and that an inquiry into the intent which is characteristic of the offense is thus required to be undertaken by the trial court, which in this case did not base the conviction on any legal grounds.

Considering that it appears from the attacked decision that the corporation V.J.F., of which Calvagrac is the director general, placed advertisements in 127 buses that run in the city of Grenoble, and such advertisements were so displayed from the 9th to 15th of April, 1974, bearing the words "Poker—made of fruit ready to drink"; that the beverage called Poker, made and marketed by the said corporation, contains only 50 percent fruit juice while the statement "made from fruit ready to drink" makes one believe it is a fruit juice without any addition of water; that the judges trying the case on the merits found that in accordance with the information supplied by the Department for the Suppression of Fraud, the corporation V.J.F. was already previously notified that these advertisements concerning the product were unfair; that the corporation took no notice of the recommendation made by the National Union of Producers of Fruit Juice and Vegetable Juice for truthful advertising; and that the judges thus concluded that . . . the labeling of the product constituted proof of intent to mislead the consumers.

Considering that these findings are neither insufficient nor contradictory with respect to all the elements of the misdemeanor of false advertising, and that the statement was of the nature to mislead, the Court of Appeal properly substantiated its decision, from which it follows that the petition must be denied.

And considering that the decision is regular as to form.

For these reasons, this Court denies the petition.

NOTES AND QUESTIONS

Article 44-1 of Law No. 73-1193 of December 27, 1973, provides that all advertising is prohibited which contains false claims, indications or representations of any kind or of a nature to mislead, whenever they refer to the following elements: the existence, nature, composition, quality, kind, origin, quantity, means and date of making, properties, or price and terms of sale of the goods or services that are the object of the advertising; conditions of use that may be understood from their use; method of sale or the rendition of services understood from the obligations undertaken by the advertiser; or the identity or nature of the maker, distributor, promoter, or the one rendering the service.

Article 44-2 of the same Law provides that the officers of the Directorate-General or Internal Commerce and Prices in the Ministry of Trade and Finance, officers of the Department for the Suppression of Fraud and of Quality Control in the Ministry of Agriculture and Rural Development, and officers of the Department of Weights and Measures in the Ministry of Industrial and Scientific Development must report in writing all offenses against provisions of Art. 44-1. They may require that the advertiser make available to them any facts in order to justify such allegations, indications, claims or representations made in advertising. The report is transmitted to the Procurator.

The Court of Cassation thus left standing the decision of the Court of Appeal convicting the accused to a fine of 5,000 francs.

Did the French courts properly apply the provisions of the law prohibiting false advertising? Is similar legislation in power in Anglo-American jurisdictions? Compare, e.g., Calif. Business and Professions Code Ann. §17500ff. Is it in the public interest that false advertising be prosecuted? Is it the object of consumer protection laws to prevent unfair business practices and to protect the consumer?

C.   DECISIONS OF ADMINISTRATIVE COURTS

MRS. ELISE C. v. C.N.A.S.E.A.

Court of Instance of Orléans, October 21, 1975, President Mrs. Dufour, Advocates Plison and Bernard of the Paris Bar. (*Gazette du Palais*, 1976, 1st semester, Jurisprudence, p. 328).

Decision of the Court

Considering that Mrs. C. brought suit on June 28, 1975, against the C.N.A.S.E.A. for the payment of 30,000 francs as damages for breach of her contract of employment.

Considering that the defendant contests the jurisdiciton of the court on the ground that the C.N.A.S.E.A. is a public institution, that the conditions of employment of its personnel are set by decree, and that its personnel participates directly in the exercise of public service.

Considering that while Mrs. C. agrees that a dispute of the above-mentioned kind falls within the jurisdiction of administrative courts, she nonetheless claims that since her contract of employment deals expressly with rights of private law and since the nature of her duties in the C.N.A.S.E.A. was not in conflict with such rights, the jurisdiction of civil courts was well founded.

Considering that the uncontested function of the public institution C.N.A.S.E.A. is defined in Art. 59 of the Law of November 29, 1965, as "the application of legislative and regulatory provisions for the improvement of agriculture."

Considering that the conditions of employment of its personnel are determined by Decree No. 72-111 of February 3, 1972, and that Mrs. C. as a secretary participated in the exercise of public service carried out by the C.N.A.S.E.A.

Considering that in such a case any dispute concerning the contract of employment is of an administrative nature unless the conditions determining relations between the C.N.A.S.E.A. and Mrs. C. refer directly to a contract of private law.

Considering that the plaintiff relies on the decision of the Council of State of December 23, 1955, which declared itself incompetent to hear a case dealing with a dispute arising out of a contract that defined the conditions of employment as "such which generally govern the relations between employers and employees."

Considering that no similar provision appears in the contract of service of Mrs. C. . . .

Considering that the contract of Mrs. C. does not contain any express reference to a contract of private law; that in the exercise of her duties she participated in the public service exercised by the C.N.A.S.E.A., a public institution; it follows that the dispute arising out of the dismissal of Mrs. C. falls within the jurisdiction of administrative courts.

Considering that the C.N.A.S.E.A. does not contest the jurisdiction of the Administrative Court of Orléans.

For these reasons, this Court upholds the objection to its jurisdiction brought by the C.N.A.S.E.A.; it declares itself incompetent as to the subject matter; it agrees with the C.N.A.S.E.A. that the proper court in this matter is an administrative court, either the Administrative Court of Orléans or that of Paris; it consequently directs Mrs. C. to bring her case in one of these courts, and it assesses the costs against her.

NOTES AND QUESTIONS

The case was brought in the civil system but the civil court declined jurisdiction and held that the matter fell within the jurisdiction of administrative courts.

C.N.A.S.E.A. stands for *Centre national pour l'aménagement des structures des exploitations agricoles* (National Center for the Improvement of Agriculture). Mrs. C. was employed by the above public institution in its offices in Orléans. The court found that her employment contract was one of administrative law.

Are employment contracts of public servants in Anglo-American jurisdictions considered contracts of administrative law? Does the legislation regulating public service provide for administrative commissions to hear employment disputes? Having exhausted the administrative way, may the employee bring suit in ordinary civil courts?

MOREY v. THE SUPER HIGHWAY CORPORATION PARIS-LYON

Council of State, (6th) Judicial Section, March 19, 1976, Government Counsel

Frane, Rapporteur Cazin d'Honincthun, Advocates Cail and Galland. (*Gazette du Palais*, 1976, 2nd semester, Jurisprudence, p. 495).

Decision of the Council of State

Considering that on October 25, 1971, Mr. Morey, while driving his automobile, collided with a wild boar crossing the road at the 319th kilometre of the super highway Paris-Lyon.

Considering that with respect to conditions of traffic on super highways, the lack of any device intended to prevent big wild animals from entering super highways does not constitute negligence in their upkeep. This is so whether the super highway is located in the proximity of large forests in which such animals live or in areas where such animals habitually cross the road. Further, the present accident took place in the forest of Demigny, which does not fall into any of the above categories. Consequently, no negligence in the upkeep of the super highway may be imputed to the corporation, even though it did not take any special precautions on that particular spot of the super highway to prevent such animals from straying onto the road. The corporation is correct when it asserts that the Administrative Court of Dijon has wrongly held it liable and ordered it to pay Mr. Morey a compensation for the loss he suffered in the collision.

With respect to costs of proceedings in the trial court:

Considering that the costs of the proceedings in the trial court must be assessed against Mr. Morey.

This Court holds: (1) Arts. 2 and 3 of the judgment of the Administrative Court of Dijon of November 5, 1975, are set aside; (2) The suit brought by Mr. Morey in the Administrative Court of Dijon is dismissed; (3) Mr. Morey must bear the costs of the proceedings in the trial court and on appeal.

NOTES AND QUESTIONS

Since the suit arose from the maintenance of public roads that are owned by the state and built from public funds, the matter falls within administrative law and a dispute arising therefrom must be handled by the administrative system. For administrative offices and courts and for proceedings before them, *see* the proper sections on administrative courts and administrative procedure above.

Does a system of administrative courts similar to that in France exist in Anglo-American countries? In which court could the plaintiff bring his suit in Anglo-American jurisdictions on the same facts? Would he be likely to succeed?

COMPANY SAADA FATHER AND SON AND THE SPOUSES SAADA

Council of State, 2nd and 6th United Subsections, October 22, 1975, Government Counsel Rougevin-Baville, Rapporteur Legatte, Advocates Calon and Sourdillat. (*Gazette du Palais*, 1976, 1st semester, Jurisprudence, p. 163).

Decision of the Council of State

On the rights that the petitioners claim to derive from the Interministerial Order of April 20, 1966:

Considering that the compensation foreseen by the Interministerial Order of

April 20, 1966, to be paid to French persons and companies constituting a family enterprise for material loss suffered in Algeria between November 1, 1954, and July 3, 1962, is not founded on the general principles governing the liability of the state, nor on any provision of an international treaty which would apply to France, nor on any statutory provision; under these circumstances, the Order of April 20, 1966, which was never properly published, could not confer on interested parties any right to the benefits provided therein; consequently, the Company Saada Father and Son may not claim that the Administrative Court of Paris has wrongly dismissed their suit for the setting aside of the decision of the Director of the Agency for the protection of property and interests of repatriated persons, dated March 2, 1967, and affirmed February 9, 1972, and for an order to the Agency to pay them 61,013.28 francs.

On the claims against the state:

Considering, on the one hand, that the loss for which the Company Saada and the Spouses Saada claim compensation was not caused by the Interministerial Order of April 20, 1966, pursuant to which some persons and companies situated in Algeria derived benefits, but that it was caused by acts of terrorism perpetrated by Algerians or by Frenchmen; consequently, the petitioners may not rely on the inequality of treatment meted out to French enterprises located in Algeria by the Order of April 20, 1966, to make the state liable.

Considering, on the other hand, that the acts of terrorism of which the petitioners were the victims on July 1, 1962, in Algiers cannot be regarded as having occurred in consequence of a gross failure of police protection; further, in view of the conditions prevailing at the time and place where the acts were committed, the state is not responsible for them on the ground of inequality of treatment by public authorities.

Considering that it follows from the above that the Administrative Court of Paris has properly denied relief to the Company Saada Father and Son and to the Spouses Saada in their suit against the state.

This Court holds: (1) The petition of the Company Saada Father and Son and of the Spouses Saada is denied; (2) Costs are assessed against the petitioners.

NOTES AND QUESTIONS

The Interministerial Order was a purely internal provision of the public administration and was not meant to vest any rights in anyone. For these reasons, it was never published. Such internal administrative measures cannot become the subject of administrative review. Responsibility of the public administration for such measures is purely political.

With respect to the claim against the state, it should be noted that the state is not liable by any provision of law for acts of terrorism that its forces are unable to prevent. The state is not an insurer.

Does Anglo-American law hold the state liable for acts of terrorism that its forces are unable to prevent? Is it correct to say that such responsibility could be imposed upon the state only by statute? Would an Anglo-American court dismiss a similar claim for lack of a cause of action?

TALBOURDEAU v.
PUBLIC OFFICE OF THE H.L.M. OF MONTLUÇON

Council of State, 1st and 4th United Subsections, November 27, 1974, Government Counsel Dondoux, Rapporteur Dandelot, Advocates Boulloche, Arminjon and Defrenois. (*Gazette du Palais*, 1976, 1st semester, Jurisprudence, p. 165).

Decision of the Council of State

Considering that the specifications in the contract made between the Public Office of Housing of Montluçon and the firm Mirocalor for the installation of heating units in two apartment buildings located in Villar and Nerdré, respectively, required the heating units to heat the apartments to the temperature of 18 degrees centigrade when the outside temperature would be minus 10 degrees centigrade; that the units were unable to perform as required, and the Office declined to accept the work performed and obtained a decision in the Administrative Court of Clermont-Ferrand which held the firm Mirocalor and the architect Mr. Talbourdeau jointly liable and ordered them to make good the loss; that Mr. Talbourdeau petitions to be discharged of the liability; that he does not contest the inadequacy of the performance of the heating units and does not allege that the contractor was solely responsible for the defect in the work done, but he claims that it was the sole responsibility of the contractor to carry out the work so as to comply with the specifications.

Considering that unless otherwise provided, the function of an architect is not limited to the stipulation of objectives to be attained pursuant to a contract made between the owner and the contractor; that the architect must direct how the work should be carried out and the contractor must follow his directions; that the architect must supervise the work done by the contractor; if the architect does not comply with this obligation, which is to be considered in the light of the work to be done and the competence of the contractor, he becomes contractually liable to the owner; that in this case, Mr. Talbourdeau inserted in the specifications directions only of a general nature and made only minor modifications in the plans submitted to him by the contractor; that he did not properly discharge his duties; that since the work done is defective, he is responsible therefor; and that consequently, since Mr. Talbourdeau does not dispute the allocation of fault as determined by the Administrative Court of Clermont-Ferrand, he may not claim that the said court has wrongly held him jointly liable with the contractor Mirocalor.

This Court holds: (1) The petition of Mr. Talbourdeau is denied; (2) Mr. Talbourdeau is liable for costs of the proceedings in the Council of State.

NOTES AND QUESTIONS

The name of the housing authority is *Office public d'habitations à loyer modéré de Montluçon* (Public Office of Housing at Moderate Rental in Montluçon). It is a government agency. The dispute is therefore administrative and belongs to administrative courts. Note the liability of the architect as defined by the court.

Considered under Anglo-American law, does the liability of the architect sound in contract or in tort? How would an Anglo-American court approach the matter? Is it likely that the action of the housing authority against the architect and the contractor would be based solely on negligence? Does the case against the contractor sound in contract whereas that against the architect sounds in tort? Since there was no clear evidence available as to the proportion of the fault of the two defendants, is it likely that they would be held jointly liable in much the same way as in the French administrative court system?

PETITION NO. 94799

Council of State, (8th) Judicial Section, March 3, 1976, Government Counsel Mrs. Latournerie, Rapporteur Schricke. (*Gazette du Palais*, 1976, 1st semester, Jurisprudence, p. 347).

Decision of the Council of State

Considering that, on the one hand, Art. 163 of the Taxation Code provides: "If during one year, the taxpayer had an exceptional income . . . and the amount of this exceptional income exceeds the average net income on which the taxpayer was taxed in accordance with the taxation of physical persons in the last three years, the taxpayer may request that in order to determine the tax on the exceptional income in the year in which it was derived, it should be distributed among the year of its realization and the preceding years not yet affected by prescription." That, on the other hand, Art. 6-1 of the Taxation Code provides: "Income tax is imposed on the family head with respect to his personal income as well as to that of his wife and his dependant children;" and that Art. 6-3 of the Taxation Code provides that "a married woman is taxed separately: . . . (a) if separation of property has been effected between her and her husband and she does not live with her husband."

Considering that it appears from the facts found that Mrs. L. signed, on May 3, 1968, a contract of sale, subject to certain conditions, for a piece of land belonging solely to her, and that the conditions having been fulfilled, the sale became effective on November 22, 1968; that at that time, Mrs. L., whose property was separated from that of her husband, did not live with her husband having been ordered to leave the matrimonial home on May 15, 1968; that in consequence of these facts, Mrs. L. was considered personally liable for the payment of tax with respect to the excess-value of 311,648 francs which she derived from the above-mentioned sale; that Mrs. L. requested the benefit of the provisions of Art. 163 of the Taxation Code; that this was denied on the ground that she could not be regarded as a taxpayer in the years preceding the year in which she derived the said excess-value.

Considering that Art. 163 of the Taxation Code provides that a taxpayer who derives an exceptional income is entitled to the benefit provided therein for the averaging of the amount; that the fact that a taxpayer did not qualify as a taxpayer with respect to the income tax of physical persons in the years preceding the one in which the income was derived cannot have the effect of depriving him of the right given to him by Art. 163 of the Taxation Code to effect such averaging.

Considering that Mrs. L. became personally liable for the income tax imposed on physical persons as of May 15, 1968, on which date she fully complied with the provisions of Art. 6-3 (a) of the Taxation Code; that it is not contested that the excess-value she derived due to the sale of her land on November 22, 1968, was an exceptional income; that consequently, the taxation authorities wrongly denied her the benefit of averaging provided for in Art. 163 of the Taxation Code.

Considering that Mrs. L. requested in her income tax return for 1968 the averaging of the excess-value over the years 1965, 1966, 1967 and 1968; that since these years are not affected by prescription, the excess-value must be allotted in equal parts to the four years mentioned in the request of Mrs. L.; that consequently, the part to be allotted to 1968 is 77, 912 francs.

Considering that it follows from the above that Mrs. L. rightly asserts that the Administrative Court of Paris has wrongly denied her claim for a reduction of the tax.

This Court holds: (1) The judgment of the Administrative Court of Paris of July 9, 1974, is set aside. (2) The amount of taxable income to be included in the base for the imposition of the income tax of physical persons is assessed at 77,912 francs. (3) Mrs. L. is discharged of liability for the difference between the amount on which tax was imposed against her in the assessment of the city of Paris and the amount determined under (2) above.

NOTES AND QUESTIONS

The provisions of the Taxation Code appear in the text of the decision. Note that the administrative courts have jurisdiction in taxation. For administrative courts and administrative procedure, *see* the proper sections under administrative courts and procedure above.

Do the provisions of the French Taxation Code dealt with in the above decision differ substantially from those of the United States Internal Revenue Code? Would a wife have to file a separate income tax return when she is separated and lives apart from her husband? *See,* 26 U.S.C.A. §6012ff. Would she be entitled to averaging under the United States law? *See,* 26 U.S.C.A. §1301ff. In which court would she have to bring her action? *See,* 26 U.S.C.A. §7441ff. To which court could she then appeal such decision? *See,* 26 U.S.C.A. §7482ff.

AFFAIRE MORIZOT

Administrative Court of Nancy, March 11, 1976, President Delevalle, Justices Petitdemange and Mrs. Le Foulon, Government Counsel Baradel, Advocate J. Megret. (*Gazette du Palais*, 1976, 2nd semester, Jurisprudence, p. 498).

Decision of the Court

Considering that by decision of November 28, 1974, the prefect of the department of Meuse, on the advice of the departmental committee of experts, denied the application of Mr. Morizot for an indemnity for the loss of his crops of corn due to the natural disaster mentioned below. The land affected is situated in the community of Tannois in the department of Meuse. The application was based on the provisions of the Interministerial Order of November 20, 1973, which conferred the character of a natural disaster upon losses suffered by crops of corn in the months of September and November of 1973. The application was denied on the ground that the applicant, a farmer who also raises crops in the department of Aube, did not, in accordance with Arts. 188-1 and 188-8 of the Rural Code, apply for a license to grow crops in addition to those grown in the other department and found himself in breach of those provisions at the time when the disaster occurred.

Considering that . . . Art. 8 of the Law of July 10, 1964, which set up a fund to provide for agricultural disasters, gives authority to the prefect assisted by a departmental committee of experts to allow a certain amount to each claimant, but no provision of that Law, nor of the Decree of July 29, 1970, which sets regulations for the application of the Law, makes the award of an indemnity depend on the condition that the recipient is not in breach of legislation concerning the simultaneous growing of crops in several departments. It follows that by denying indemnity to Mr. Morizot, who properly contributed to the fund set up by the Law of July 10, 1964, on the ground that he was in breach of the legislation concerning simultaneous growing of crops, the prefect of the department of Meuse added another condition to those set up by law, and his decision is devoid of any legal ground.

Considering that Mr. Morizot is within his right to demand the annulment of the decision of the prefect of the department of Meuse of November 28, 1974.

This Court holds: (1) The decision of the prefect of the department of Meuse dated November 28, 1974, is set aside; (2) Costs of the proceedings are assessed against the state.

NOTES AND QUESTIONS

The applicable provisions of the Rural Code and that of Art. 8 of the Law of July 10, 1964, appear in the text of the decision. Note that it is the function of the prefect to see to it that all administrative provisions are properly applied in his department. Since prefectoral decisions and orders are subject to administrative review, the dispute falls properly within administrative law.

To which government office could the farmer have appealed the decision of the prefect in lieu of bringing suit in the Administrative Court? The suit having been brought in the Administrative Court, to which court may the prefect appeal its judgment? For administrative courts, *see* the section on such courts above.

FOOTNOTES

1. The most important of them are Arts. 4 and 5. Article 4 provides that a judge who would refuse to give judgment on the ground that the law was silent on the matter or obscure or inadequate can be proceeded with for denial of justice. Article 5 forbids judges to make general and regulatory dispositions on matters submitted for their decision. Judges must, therefore, decide all matters properly brought before them; but they cannot lay down general rules of conduct, i.e., they cannot resort to judicial legislation.

2. Civil Code, Arts. 102-111.

3. Domicile is in fact the place of permanent residence; if a person has several residences, the principal residence is his domicile. As far as business establishments are concerned, it is the head or principal establishment. A person, both physical and legal, can have only one domicile. Persons living on boats and persons having no permanent residence must select a location within the area of their circulation as their domicile. (Civil Code, Art. 102, and the Ordinance of October 7, 1958, on the domicile of persons having no permanent residence).

4. Civil Code, Arts. 144-228.

5. *Ibid.*, Arts. 144-164. The age of majority begins at eighteen years. (Civil Code, Arts. 388 and 488).

6. The consent to the marriage of a minor is further elaborated in Arts. 149-160 of the Civil Code.

7. Petition for the authorization must be directed to the prefecture through the municipal office of the place of celebration. It must indicate: the place of celebration; the given names, surnames, citizenship, date and place of birth of the future spouses; and their residences. The prefecture will then grant the authorization and deliver it to the proper registrar of marriages authorizing him to celebrate the marriage. (The Decree of February 21, 1946, on the application of Art. 13 of the Ordinance of November 2, 1945, on the marriages of foreigners temporarily residing in France.)

8. Civil Code, Arts. 63-76, 165-171.

9. A dispensation from the production of the medical certificate, from the publication of the notice of intention to marry, and from the ten-day period for which the notice should be affixed to the notice board is obtainable from the procurator. (Civil Code, Art. 169).

10. The *acte de notoriété* must contain a declaration made by three witnesses concerning the name, surname, occupation and domicile of the spouse and of his father and mother; it must give the place and date of his birth and the reason for not producing an extract from the register of births. In addition to the three witnesses, a judge of a court of instance must sign the document. (Civil Code, Art. 71).

11. The consent must be given in a document prepared by a notary public, an officer of the registry of marriages, or a French diplomatic or consular officer. (Civil Code, Art. 74).

12. The certificate of marriage must contain (1) name, surname, occupation, age, date and place of birth, domicile and residence of both spouses; (2) name, surname, occupation and domicile of fathers and mothers of the spouses; (3) consents, if required; (4) name and surname of the preceding spouse of each of the spouses, if any; (5) [abrogated]; (6) declaration of the parties that they take each other in matrimony and the declaration of the officer who pronounced them married; (7) name, surname, occupation and domicile of witnesses and a statement that they are of age; and (8) declaration concerning a marriage contract, and if made, its date and the name and address of the notary who certified it. (Civil Code, Art. 76).

13. The President of the Republic may authorize the celebration of marriage if one of the future spouses dies after having formally indicated his consent to the marriage. Such a marriage gives no right to succeed to the estate of the deceased and the matrimonial relation between the spouses is not regarded as ever having existed. (Civil Code, Art. 171).

14. Civil Code, Arts. 172-179.

15. *Ibid.*, Arts. 180-202.

16. The validity of the marriage entered into in prohibition of Art. 144 (minimum age) cannot be challenged after six months have run from the point of time when the spouse or spouses attained the required minimum age, or when the underage wife conceived

before six months elapsed. (Civil Code, Art. 185). Civil Code, Arts. 186-189 give further details as to the annulment of marriage.

17. Civil Code, Arts. 203-211.
18. Children have no cause of action against their parents to be set up in life by marriage or otherwise. (Civil Code, Art. 204).
19. The obligation of support is reciprocal between ascendants and descendants. Even sons-in-law and daughters-in-law are bound to support their parents-in-law, but this obligation comes to an end upon the death of the spouse who created this relationship and upon that of the children born of that union. (Civil Code, Art. 206, 207).
20. Civil Code, Arts. 212-226.
21. The proceedings take place in a court of instance and may result in a decree attaching part of salary, wages, product of the work, or income of the delinquent spouse. (Code of Civil Procedure, Art. 864).
22. Civil Code, Art. 227.
23. *Ibid.*, Art. 228.
24. *Ibid.*, Arts. 229-310.
25. *Ibid.*, Arts. 229-246.
26. *Ibid.*, Arts. 247-259-3; Decree No. 75-1124 of December 5, 1975, on the reform of the procedure of divorce and judicial separation.
27. Civil Code, Arts. 260-295.
28. The obligated spouse may also be fined for nonpayment. The enforcement is governed by Decree No. 73-216 of March 1, 1973, Law No. 75-618 of July 11, 1975, and Decree No. 75-1339 of December 31, 1975, as amended.
29. Civil Code, Arts. 296-309.
30. *Ibid,* Art. 310.
31. *Ibid.*, Arts. 516-710.
32. *Ibid.*, Arts. 516-543.
33. They are: farm animals, farm equipment, pigeons in pigeon houses, wild rabbits, beehives, fish in ponds, straw and manure, utensils and machinery. (Civil Code, Art. 524).
34. Equitable conversion sets in immediately upon a contract for the sale of immovables becomes binding on the parties.
35. Civil Code, Arts. 533-535 give a definition of the terms *meuble, meuble meublants, biens meubles, mobilier* and *effets mobiliers.*
36. Literary and artistic property is governed by the Law of March 11, 1957, as amended. It deals with the rights of authors and the use of such rights.
37. Civil Code, Arts. 544-577.
38. Mining is governed by the Mining Code (*Code minier*) of August 16, 1956, as amended. Law No. 509 of September 27, 1941, as amended, regulates archeological excavations and finds.
39. The amount of compensation is, at the option of the owner of the land, either the sum by which the value of the land was enhanced or the price of the material supplied and labor done, valued at the time of the payment of compensation. (Civil Code, Art. 555 (3)).
40. The sum of the compensation is arrived at in accordance with the provisions of Art. 555 (3) of the Civil Code.
41. If a river suddenly carries away an identifiable piece of the bank and deposits it on the same or on the opposite bank downstream, the owner of the piece can claim it within one year. (Civil Code, Art. 559).
42. The owner of the bank of a not-navigable river owns the river bed up to the middle of the watercourse. He therefore owns all islands existing or formed in his half. (Rural Code, Art. 98).

43. Civil Code, Art. 563 and Rural Code, Arts. 99-100 provide for the sale of the land to other applicants should the riparian owners fail to buy the land. Civil Code, Art. 564 provides that pigeons entering a wrong pigeon house, rabbits a wrong enclosure, and fish a wrong pond belong to the owner of the contraption entered into unless they were lured there by design. The Rural Code carries further provisions with respect to lost animals.

44. Civil Code, Art. 566-577 give examples of decisions for the guidance of the judge in such circumstances. The chattels may be separated or the owner of the principal chattel has to compensate the owner of the other chattel. The Code also carries provisions for an equitable solution of cases where material not owned by a person is worked into a new product by that person, etc.

45. Civil Code, Arts. 578-636.

46. Usufruct comes very close to a life estate or to a determinable life estate, e.g., to X for thirty years if he lives so long.

47. By natural produce (*fruits naturels*), it is meant the produce that comes into existence spontaneously by natural processes of the land. Animal products and new born animals are also natural produce. By industrial produce (*fruits industriels*) of land, it is meant the produce obtained by cultivation. (Civil Code, Art. 583). By civil produce (*fruits civils*), it is meant the rent of land or premises, interest and dividend. (Civil Code, Art. 584).

48. Civil Code, Arts. 590-593 deal with the usufructuary's right to timber. The usufructuary must replace fruit trees that die or are destroyed. (Civil Code, Art. 594).

49. The father and mother who have a legal usufruct in the property of their children, and the vendor or donor who reserves a usufruct upon the transfer of his property, are not required to make a bond. (Civil Code, Art. 601).

50. Substantive repairs are those of main walls and pillars, of all beams and the whole roof, or of all supporting walls and all enclosing walls. All other repairs are considered current upkeep. (Civil Code, Art. 606).

51. The method of his contribution is as follows: first the value of the estate subject to the usufruct is assessed; then the contribution of the usufructuary to the discharge of debts of the estate is assessed in proportion to the value of the estate. If the usufructuary decides to pay his portion of the debts, the owner of the land will have to refund to him the money at the termination of the usufruct without interest. If he does not make the contribution, the owner may either pay the debts himself, in which case the usufructuary will have to pay interest on that sum to the owner until the termination of the usufruct, or the owner may sell a portion of the property subject to the usufruct corresponding to the contribution of the usufructuary.

52. Creditors of the usufructuary may intervene in the proceedings to safeguard their rights. (Civil Code, Art. 618).

53. If the instrument does not define these rights, the basic provisions incorporated in Civil Code, Arts. 630-636 apply. If the use consists in the use of produce of land, the person entitled can take only what he needs for himself and his family. He cannot transfer or lease his right to another person. The right to use premises extends to the family of the person entitled even though he was single at the creation of the right. It is limited to him and his family and cannot be transferred or let to another person. If the person entitled uses all the produce of the land or occupies the entire premises, he must bear the expenses of cultivation or those of upkeep of the premises and must make the required contribution in money as a usufructuary. If he uses or occupies only a part, he contributes only pro rata. The use of forests is governed by special laws. (Civil Code, Arts. 629-636).

54. Civil Code, Arts. 637-710.

55. The burden to receive surface water in its natural condition, untouched by the hands of

man, cannot be made more onerous in the case of buildings, gardens, parks and enclosures adjoining buildings forming the lower estate. (Civil Code, Art. 641).

56. Civil Code, Arts. 538, 644. The Rural Code of April 16, 1955, as amended, contains a detailed treatment of the topic.

57. These easements are governed by special laws and regulations. (Civil Code, Art. 650).

58. In certain cases, the wall is presumed owned by one landowner only. (Civil Code, Art. 654).

59. The Civil Code deals with party walls in detail in Arts. 653-668. Co-ownership of apartment houses, i.e., condominiums (*copropriété des immeubles bâtis*) is governed by Law No. 65-557 of July 10, 1965, and Decree No. 67-223 of March 17, 1967, as amended.

60. The distance of 1 meter 90 centimetres is taken from the wall, if windows open outside, and from the balcony or other protrusion at a point closest to the boundary line. (Civil Code, Arts. 678, 680).

61. But if no adequate way is so provided, the right of way will be granted in accordance with the above rules. (Civil Code, Arts. 682-684).

62. Easements are further continuous (*continues*) as water conducts, drains or easements of view, or discontinuous (*discontinues*) as a right of way. They are apparent (*apparentes*) as windows, or nonapparent (*non apparentes*) as a prohibition to build on a given land or a prohibition to build above a fixed elevation. (Civil Code, Arts. 688,689).

63. So, for instance, the grant of a right to draw water from a well contains the right to enter the servient tenement for that purpose. (Civil Code, Art. 696).

64. So, for instance, a right of way will still benefit all the parts of the dominant tenement but must be exercised through the same road as before. (Civil Code, Art. 700).

65. The thirty year period begins to run from the first day of nonuse, in the case of discontinuous easements, and from the act adverse to the easement, in the case of continuous easements. (Civil Code, Art. 707).

66. If the dominant tenement is owned by co-owners jointly or in common, the enjoyment by one is the enjoyment by all. If adverse possession cannot run against one of them, e.g., because of his minority, neither can it run against the other co-owners. (Civil Code, Arts. 709-710).

67. Civil Code, Arts. 711-717.

68. There are things that do not belong to anyone and may be enjoyed by the general public. The right of their enjoyment is governed by police laws. Hunting and fishing is also regulated by special laws. (Civil Code, Arts. 714-715).

69. By treasure-trove, it is meant a thing of value which is hidden and to which no one can show title and which is discovered by chance. (Civil Code, Art. 716). Archeological finds are governed by Law No. 509 of September 27, 1941, as amended.

70. Civil Code, Arts. 718-892.

71. *Ibid.*, Arts. 718-724.

72. If those who perished together were below the age of fifteen, the oldest is presumed to have survived. If all were over the age of sixty, the youngest is presumed to have survived. If some were below fifteen and some over sixty, the first are presumed to have survived. If those who perished together were over the age of fifteen and below the age of sixty, the male is presumed to have survived, the age being equal or the difference in age not being greater than one year. If they were of the same sex, the younger is presumed to have survived. (Civil Code, Arts. 721-722).

73. Civil Code, Arts. 725-730.

74. *Ibid.*, Arts. 731-767.

75. There is a direct line between persons who descend from one another, and a collateral line between those who do not so descend but who have a common ancestor. The lines are descending and ascending lines. In the direct line, there are as many degrees as there

are generations; so the son, with respect to his father, is within the first degree. In a collateral line, degrees of kinship are counted by generations from one parent up to and not counting the common ancestor, and from the common ancestor down to the other parent. So two brothers are related in the second degree; uncle and nephew in the third degree, first cousins in the fourth degree, and so on. (Civil Code, Arts. 735-738).

76. So the descendants of a child who predeceased the deceased take the child's share and rank with the other children of the deceased. (Civil Code, Art. 740).

77. Civil Code, Arts. 756-764 contain further provisions concerning the matter.

78. Civil Code, Arts. 768-773.

79. *Ibid.*, Arts. 774-814.

80. *Ibid.*, Arts. 388-487.

81. The doctrine of representation does not apply, and if the only heir or all co-heirs within a degree renounce, their children take in their stead per capita. (Civil Code, Art. 787).

82. Within this time, an heir who renounced may still accept unless the inheritance has been already accepted by other heirs and, without prejudice to rights acquired in the property, by third parties. (Civil Code, Art. 790).

83. The costs connected therewith are charged to the estate where the heir shows that he was unaware of the death of the deceased or that the time given was inadequate, otherwise he will have to pay them himself. (Civil Code, Art. 799).

84. Civil Code, Arts. 815-892.

85. A donee who was not an apparent heir at the time of the donation, but who becomes an heir at the time of the decedent's death, must also bring in the value of the gift unless the donor provided otherwise. Gifts made to the son of an heir are not to be brought in. When the son becomes the donor's heir in his own right, he is not required to bring in gifts made to his father even if he inherited from his father. But if the son inherits only by representation, he must bring in all that which the donor gave to his father even if he renounced the inheritance due to him from his father. Gifts and legacies made to the spouse of an apparent heir are not to be brought in. If such gifts and legacies were made to the spouses jointly, one of whom is an heir, the heir brings in only one half. If the gifts were made to the apparent heir, he must bring them in in their entirety. Contribution is made only to the estate of the donor. (Civil Code, Arts. 846-850).

86. Also not brought in are any profits the heir derived from contracts made with the deceased if such contracts did not give the heir any indirect advantage when they were made. The same applies to profits from partnerships and associations between the deceased and the heir if they were made by a notarized document. (Civil Code, Arts. 853-854).

87. Detailed rules as to contribution appear in Civil Code, Arts. 843-869.

88. The heirs may insist, as against creditors, that property of the estate of the deceased is kept separate from the property of the heirs. They cannot do so, however, if the heir admitted the claim and became substituted for the deceased as a debtor. The heirs must exercise this right within three years as to movables; with respect to immovables, they can exercise it for as long as the immovable is held by the heir. Creditors of an heir cannot avail themselves of this right as against creditors of the estate. Creditors of a person taking part in the distribution of an estate may be heard and may intervene in the partition, but they may not attack a completed partition unless they filed an opposition to it and partition ensued without their being heard and in prejudice to their rights. (Civil Code, Arts. 878-882).

89. To establish shortage, the value of the item is taken as at the time of the partition. (Civil Code, Art. 890).

90. Civil Code, Arts. 893-1100.

91. *Ibid.*, Arts. 893-900-1.

92. The dispositions that fathers, mothers, brothers and sisters may make in accordance

with the provisions of Civil Code, Arts. 1048-1074 are an exception from the general prohibition. (Civil Code, Art. 897).

93. Civil Code, Arts. 901-912.

94. If he is serving in the armed forces during hostilities, he may, as long as hostilities exist, dispose of his property as an adult in favor of one or more relatives up to and including the sixth degree or in favor of his spouse. Failing relatives including the sixth degree, he can dispose of his property as an adult. (Civil Code, Art. 904).

95. Even on attaining majority, a minor cannot make a gift *inter vivos* or by will to his guardian unless the guardianship account is rendered and approved. Ascendants of a minor who were his guardians are not affected by the prohibition. (Civil Code, Art. 907).

96. The prohibition does not affect remuneration for services rendered and general provisions to relatives up to and including the fourth degree unless there are heirs in the direct line. It does not apply to a beneficiary who is one of the heirs. (Civil Code, Art. 909).

97. See, e.g., Code of Communal Administration, the Decree of May 22, 1957, Arts. 299-305 as to gifts made to cities; Code of State Domaine, Decree No. 62-298 of March 14, 1962, Arts. 11-21 as to gifts made to the state.

98. Civil Code, Arts. 913-930.

99. *Ibid.*, Art. 914.

100. *Ibid.*, Arts. 931-966.

101. The provisions of Arts. 931 and 932 do not affect gifts *inter vivos* where the subject matter of the gift passes from hand to hand, i.e., where the donor manually delivers the gift to the donee and the donee accepts it on the spot.

102. If the donee is of full age, acceptance must be made by him or by another person under his authority. Authorization must be given in a notarized act and a copy thereof must be attached to the record of the acceptance. A gift made to a nonemancipated minor or to a person under guardianship must be accepted by the guardian. Parents and ascendants of a nonemancipated minor may accept a gift for the minor. (Civil Code, Arts. 933, 935).

103. Civil Code, Arts. 967-1047.

104. If the testator who had signed the will cannot for some reason sign the declaration, the declaration must mention the fact and give reason therefor. A will in the mystic form cannot be made by a person who is unable to read, but it may be made by a person who can write without being able to speak. (Civil Code, Arts. 976-979).

105. The universal legatee has the enjoyment of the property comprised in the will as of the testator's death if he requests surrender of the property within one year from the death of the testator. If not, his enjoyment begins only on the day on which he brings action or on the day on which a promise to surrender the property was obtained. (Civil Code, Art. 1005).

106. The interest or proceeds of the property bequeathed or devised will run, however, as of the testator's death if the testator so ordered in his will or if he bequeathed to the legatee an annuity or pension for the legatee's support. (Civil Code, Art. 1015).

107. Destruction of a will by the testator does not necessarily indicate the intent to revoke it.

108. Civil Code, Arts. 1048-1074.

109. Civil Code, Arts. 1051-1074 contain further details as to the surrender of the property given to the ultimate donees, i.e., the grandchildren of the donor or the children of his brothers and sisters.

110. Civil Code, Arts. 1075-1080.

111. Civil Code, Arts. 1075-1080 contain further details concerning the distribution.

112. Civil Code, Arts. 1081-1090.

113. See section (f) above.

114. A gift made by marriage contract is irrevocable in that the donor cannot transfer the property comprised in the gift to another person without consideration. He may, however, dispose of such property for valuable consideration. (Civil Code, Art. 1083).
115. Civil Code, Arts. 1091-1100.
116. See section (h) above.
117. See section (c) above.
118. All gifts made by one spouse to the child or children of the other spouse by another marriage, and gifts made to the ascendants of the other spouse when the said spouse is the heir apparent of such ascendant, are reputed to have been made to intermediaries and are void. (Civil Code, Art. 1100).
119. Civil Code, Arts. 1101-1369.
120. *Ibid.*, Arts. 1101-1107.
121. *Ibid.*, Arts. 1108-1133.
122. Esteem toward the father, mother and other ascendants on its own, without any force, is not a ground for the annulment of a contract. (Civil Code, Art. 1114).
123. Civil Code, Arts. 1134-1167.
124. The effect of an obligation to give or to transfer title to immovables is regulated in the titles "On sales" and "On preferred creditors and mortgages" in the Civil Code. (Civil Code, Art. 1140).
125. Civil Code, Arts. 1168-1233.
126. Only a potestative condition on the part of the obligated party makes the obligation void. A potestative condition on the part of the entitled party is permissible and does not affect the validity of the obligation. (Civil Code, Art. 1174).
127. Civil Code, Arts. 1234-1314.
128. *Ibid.*, Arts. 1315-1369.
129. The Civil Code carries detailed provisions as to proof in Arts. 1315-1369.
130. Civil Code, Arts. 1370-1386.
131. *Ibid.*, Arts. 1371-1381.
132. *Ibid.*, Arts. 1382-1386.
133. *Ibid.*, Arts. 1387-1581.
134. *Ibid.*, Arts. 1387-1399.
135. *Ibid.*, Arts. 1400-1496.
136. *Ibid.*, Arts. 1536-1542.
137. *Ibid.*, Arts. 1497-1527.
138. *Ibid.*, Arts. 1536-1542.
139. *Ibid.*, Arts. 815-892.
140. *Ibid.*, Arts. 1569-1581.
141. *Ibid.*, Arts. 2219-2283.
142. *Ibid.*, Arts. 2219-2227.
143. *Ibid.*, Arts. 2228-2235.
144. *Ibid.*, Arts. 2236-2241.
145. A *fermier* is a tenant of agricultural land. His relationship with his landlord is governed by Art. 1764-1778 of the Civil Code.
146. Civil Code, Arts. 2242-2259.
147. See section (e)(iv) below.
148. Civil Code, Arts. 2260-2281.
149. Work of a fundamental nature means the very structure of a building or its main parts.
150. Civil Code, Art. 2278.
151. *Ibid.*, Arts. 2282-2283.
152. Code of Civil Procedure; Art. 23ff.
153. Code of Comemrce, Arts. 1-5.

154. *Ibid.*, Arts. 8-17.
155. The register of commerce is governed by Decree No. 67-237 of March 23, 1967, and by Decree No. 67-238 of March 23, 1967, as amended.
156. Partnerships and Corporations are governed by Law No. 66-537 of July 24, 1966, and by Decree No. 67-236 of March 23, 1967, as amended.
157. Law No. 66-537 of July 24, 1966, Arts. 10-22; Decree No. 67-236 of March 23, 1967, Arts. 6-16.
158. *Ibid.*, Law, Arts. 23-33; Decree, Arts. 17-19.
159. *Ibid.*, Law, Arts. 34-69; Decree, Arts. 20-53.
160. *Ibid.*, Law, Arts. 70-353; Decree, Arts. 54-299.
161. *Ibid.*, Law, Arts. 251-262; Decree, Arts. 202-203.
162. Code of Commerce, Arts. 110-189; Decree-Law of October 30, 1935, unifying the law of checks.
163. The French law of bankruptcy is governed by Law No. 67-563 of July 13, 1967, and by Decree No. 67-1120 of December 22, 1967, as amended.
164. Maritime law is governed by a number of statutes listed below.
165. The law of ships is governed by Law No. 67-5 of January 3, 1967, and by Decree No. 67-967 of October 27, 1967, as amended.
166. Personnel is governed by Law No. 69-8 of January 3, 1969, and by Decree No. 69-679 of June 19, 1969, as amended.
167. Charter parties and maritime transport are governed by Law No. 66-420 of June 18, 1966, and by Decree No. 66-1078 of December 31, 1966, as amended.
168. Maritime sales are governed by Law No. 69-8 of January 3, 1969, and by Decree No. 69-679 of June 19, 1969, as amended.
169. Marine insurance is governed by Law No. 67-522 of July 3, 1967, and by Decree No. 68-64 of January 19, 1968, as amended.
170. Collision, salvage and Average is governed by Law No. 67-545 of July 7, 1967, and by Decree No. 68-65 of January 19, 1968, as amended.
171. The subject is governed by the Law of December 17, 1926 (Disciplinary and Penal Code of the Merchant Marine), as amended, as to maritime offenses, and by the Decree of November 26, 1956 (Maritime Commercial Courts), as amended, as to maritime courts.
172. Courts of instance are governed chiefly by Decree No. 58-1284 of December 22, 1958, as amended, on the jurisdiction of courts of instance, courts of grand instance, and courts of appeal in civil matters.
173. An *arrondissement* is a territorial administrative unit of a relatively small size, like a city district or precinct or the subdivision of a county. Each French department has two or more *arrondissements*.
174. Courts of grand instance are governed chiefly by Decree No. 58-1284 of December 22, 1958, and by Law No. 70-613 of July 10, 1970, as amended.
175. A department is a territorial administrative unit corresponding roughly to an Anglo-American county but usually larger in size.
176. Courts of commerce are governed by Decree No. 61-923 of August 3, 1961, by Code of Commerce, Arts. 853-878, as amended.
177. Code of Commerce, Arts. 631-634. If all parties to a bill of exchange payable to order are not merchants and the bill is not drawn in the course of commerce, the action must be transferred to a court of grand instance at the request of the defendant. But if one party to a bill is a merchant, a court of commerce has jurisdiction. (Code of Commerce, Arts. 636,637).
178. Courts of appeal are governed by a number of provisions dating from the early nineteenth century to the present and especially by Decree No. 58-1284 of December 22, 1958.
179. The court has chambers of civil appeal and criminal appeal and one welfare chamber

(*chambre sociale*). The welfare chamber hears appeals in cases of social security, labor law and connected statutory provisions.

180. The Court of Cassation is governed by a number of provisions dating from the eighteenth century to the present and especially by Decree No. 67-523 of July 3, 1967, and Decree No. 67-1208 of December 22, 1967, as amended.

181. Thus, a matter coming from a court of appeal is remitted for further proceedings to the court of appeal nearest to that which pronounced the judgment attacked. The same obtains with courts of grand instance, and so on.

182. The Code of Civil Procedure of 1975 is still in the process of development.

183. Procedure in courts of instance is governed by Code of Civil Procedure, Art. 827-852, and by the general rules of procedure applicable to all courts contained in Book I of the Code.

184. Procedure in courts of grand instance is governed by Code of Civil Procedure, Arts. 750-826, and by the general rules of procedure applicable to all courts contained in Book I of the Code.

185. The judicial oath is regulated by Civil Code, Arts. 1357-1369, and by Code of Civil Procedure, Arts. 317-322.

186. All judgments and orders are headed: "Republic of France," and begin with the formula: "In the name of the French people." They conclude as follows: "Consequently, the Republic of France directs and orders all bailiffs to carry out this [judgment, order], and all procurators to uphold them, and all officers of the forces of public order to assist in the execution thereof, if properly requested to give their assistance. In witness thereof this [judgment, order] is signed by the court."

187. Procedure in courts of commerce is governed by Code of Civil Procedure, Arts. 853-878.

188. Code of Civil Procedure, Arts. 542-578, 899-972.

189. *Ibid.,* Art. 973ff.

190. Penal Code, Arts. 1-5.

191. *Ibid.,* Arts. 6-55-1.

192. *Ibid.,* Arts. 56-58-3.

193. *Ibid.,* Arts. 59-63.

194. *Ibid.,* Arts. 66-67; the Ordinance of February 2, 1945, on delinquent children; and Ordinance No. 58-1274 of December 22, 1958, on children's courts, as amended.

195. Penal Code, Arts. 295-304.

196. *Ibid.,* Art. 319.

197. *Ibid.,* Arts. 321-326.

198. *See* Homicide not qualified as crime, Section A.9, following.

199. Penal Code, Arts. 327-329.

200. *Ibid.,* Arts. 309-315.

201. *Ibid.,* Arts. 379-401.

202. Code of Criminal Procedure, Arts. 521-523.

203. Infractions are offenses that the law punishes with imprisonment for not more than two months, or with a fine of not more than 2,000 francs. (Code of Criminal Procedure, Art. 521).

204. Code of Criminal Procedure, Arts. 381-405.

205. Misdemeanors are offenses that the law punishes with imprisonment for more than two months, or with a fine exceeding 2,000 francs. (Code of Criminal Procedure, Art. 381).

206. Code of Criminal Procedure, Arts. 231-379.

207. *Ibid.,* Arts. 496-520.

208. *Ibid.,* Arts. 567-621.

209. It is based on the Law of December 31, 1957, instituting the Code of Criminal Procedure, and on Ordinance No. 58-1296 of December 23, 1958, completing the Code of Criminal Procedure.

210. Code of Criminal Procedure, Arts. 6-10.
211. *Ibid.,* Arts. 75-190.
212. *Ibid.,* Arts. 75-78.
213. *Ibid.,* Arts. 79-190.
214. *Ibid.,* Art. 114.
215. *Ibid.,* Art. 118.
216. *Ibid.,* Arts. 125, 126.
217. *Ibid.,* Arts. 191-230.
218. *Ibid.,* Arts. 231-380.
219. *Ibid.,* Arts. 268-287.
220. An annual list of jurors is prepared in the seats of assize courts from among eligible persons. In the Assize Court of Paris, the list has 1,200 jurors; in assize courts in the departments of Hauts-de-Seine, Seine-Saint-Denis, and Val-de-Marne, it has 500 jurors; elsewhere it must have between 160-240 jurors. All must reside within the jurisdiction of the particular assize court. One juror is taken from each 1,300 inhabitants. The lists are prepared by the several courts of instance, and the annual list is prepared therefrom by a special commission. At least 15 days before the opening of the term, the president of the particular court of appeal, or the president of the particular assize court draws by chance 27 jurors and 6 supplementary jurors from the annual list who will act as jurors during the term. This is the final list delivered to the accused. (Code of Criminal Procedure, Arts. 259-267).
221. Code of Criminal Procedure, Arts. 293-305.
222. *Ibid.,* Arts. 306-322.
223. *Ibid.,* Arts. 323-354.
224. *Ibid.,* Arts. 355-380.
225. *Ibid.,* Arts. 381-520.
226. *Ibid.,* Arts. 400-405.
227. *Ibid.,* Arts. 406-461.
228. *Ibid.,* Arts. 462-486.
229. *Ibid.,* Arts. 487-495.
230. *Ibid.,* Arts. 496-520.
231. *Ibid.,* Arts. 521-549.
232. *Ibid.,* Arts. 531-549.
233. *Ibid.,* Arts. 524-528-2.
234. *Ibid.,* Arts. 529-530.
235. *Ibid.,* Arts. 567-626.
236. *Ibid.,* Arts. 567-621.
237. See procedure in the Court of Cassation in civil matters above.
238. Code of Criminal Procedure, Arts. 622-626.
239. *Ibid.,* Arts. 734-747.
240. *Ibid.,* Arts. 734-1-737.
241. *Ibid.,* Arts. 738-747.
242. *Ibid.,* Arts. 729-733.
243. In every court of grand instance, there is a judge of supervision (*juge de l'application des peines*) who supervises the execution of the punishment imposed by the criminal courts. (Code of Criminal Procedure, Arts. 709-1, 722).
244. The Law of December 9, 1905, on separation of state and church, as amended.
245. Ordinance No. 58-997 of October 23, 1958; Decree No. 59-701 of June 6, 1959; Decree No. 59-1335 of November 20, 1959; Decree No. 61-164 of February 13, 1961; Decree No. 62-1112 of September 21, 1962; Law No. 65-561 of July 10, 1965; Law No. 70-612 of July 10, 1970; Decree No. 77-392 of March 28, 1977.
246. The Law of July 29, 1881, as amended.

247. The subject is regulated by numerous provisions, especially by Ordinance No. 45-2658 of November 2, 1945; Decree No. 46-1574 of June 30, 1946; Decree No. 70-29 of January 5, 1970; and Decree No. 76-56 of January 15, 1976.

248. *Code des communes*, Decree No. 77-90 and No. 77-91 of January 27, 1977; Decree No. 77-240 and No. 77-241 of March 7, 1977; Decree No. 77-732 and No. 77-373 of March 28, 1977, all as amended.

249. Law No. 64-707 of July 10, 1964, on reorganization of the Paris region, as amended; Decree No. 66-614 of August 10, 1966, on organization of state services in the Paris region; Law No. 75-1331 of December 31, 1975, on administrative reform in the City of Paris; Law No. 76-394 of May 6, 1976.

250. Departments are governed by numerous provisions, e.g., the law of August 10, 1871, on general councils; and Decree No. 64-250 of March 14, 1964, on prefects, etc.

251. A canton is a territorial division of an *arrondissement*. Every *arrondissement* has several cantons. The only significance of a canton is for purposes of police and elections.

252. Regions are governed chiefly by Decree No. 64-251 of March 14, 1964, on organization of state services in the regions; Law No. 72-619 of July 5, 1972, on creation and organization of regions; Decree No. 73-854 of September 5, 1973, on regional councils.

253. Administrative courts are governed by the Code of Administrative Courts, Decree No. 73-682 and No. 73-683, both of July 13, 1973, and Law No. 76-521 of June 16, 1976, as amended.

254. Administrative courts have functioned from the establishment of the republic in the eighteenth century. They were then known as prefectoral councils (*conseils de préfecture*), one in every department. In 1926, they were reorganized. They were then known as interdepartmental prefectoral councils (*conseils de préfecture interdéparte-mentaux*). Some included the territory of only two departments and some of up to seven departments, in order to comprise an approximately equal size population. Their names were those of the cities where they were situated. The prefectoral council in the department of Seine was left as it was, so that there were twenty-two interdepartmental prefectoral councils and one prefectoral council in France. Since 1953, they are known as administrative courts, the one in the department of Seine (since 1964 in the department of Paris), known as the administrative Court of Paris (*Tribunal Administratif de Paris*).

255. The Council of State is governed chiefly by Ordinance No. 45-1708 of July 31, 1945, and by Decree No. 63-766 of July 30, 1963; also by Decree No. 75-791 of August 28, 1975, as amended.

256. Procedure in administrative courts is governed by the Code of Administrative Courts, Decree No. 73-682 and No. 73-683, of July 13, 1973, as amended.

257. Procedure in the Council of State is governed by Ordinance No. 45-1708 of July 31, 1945, and by Decree No. 63-766 of July 30, 1963, as amended.

258. Judges are governed chiefly by Ordinance No. 58-1270 of December 22, 1958; Ordinance No. 58-1271 of December 22, 1958; Decree No. 58-1277 of December 22, 1958; Decree No. 59-305 of February 19, 1959; all as amended; and by Law No. 70-642 of July 17, 1970; and Law No. 76-120 of February 5, 1976.

259. Officers of the public ministry are governed by the same provisions as judges.

260. Prior to changes in the legal profession, *avocats* were actually pleaders, fulfilling the functions of English barristers. Parties in courts of grand instance had to employ an *avoué* admitted to practice in that particular court, and *avoués* performed functions similar to those performed by English solicitors. They could not plead in court. An *avocat* had to be employed to do so. In the courts of commerce, parties had to employ the services of an *agréé*, who performed the function of an English solicitor in a particular court of commerce. The case had to be pleaded by an *avocat*. The reform act of 1971 removed all these requirements and replaced *avocats*, *avoués* and *agréés* with the single

profession of *avocat*, known as the new profession of advocacy (*nouvelle profession d'avocat*).

261. The profession of *avocat* is governed chiefly by Law No. 71-1130 of December 31, 1971; Decree No. 72-468 of April 9, 1972; Decree No. 72-669 of July 13, 1972; and Decree No. 72-783 of August 25, 1972.

262. Law No. 66-879 of November 29, 1966, on professional partnerships (*sociétés civiles professionnelles*).

263. The Court of Conflicts (*Tribunal des Conflits*) is a special court presided over by the Minister of Justice and composed of judges of the judiciary as well as judges of administrative courts. The Court decides conflicts of competence between judicial courts and administrative courts where both courts assumed jurisdiction or where both denied jurisdiction. It decides on the merits in cases which were brought before both judicial and administrative courts and where inconsistent judgments were obtained.

 The Prize Court (*Conseil des Prises*) is a court of maritime jurisdiction dealing with prize law. It is of a very limited importance. It is presided over by a councilor of state and has six other members taken from the masters of requests and officers of the ministry of the navy and of the ministry of external affairs. It is an administrative court. Appeal against its decisions lies to the Council of State.

 The Court of Accounts (*Cour des Comptes*) is an important tribunal in matters of public accounting. It hears disputes arising out of the accounting of public authorities, like the state, departments and public enterprises.

264. The profession of *avoué* is governed chiefly by the Decree of December 19, 1945, as amended.

265. The profession of legal councilor is governed chiefly by Law No. 71-1130 of December 31, 1971; Decree No. 72-670 and No. 72-671, both of July 13, 1972; and Decree No. 72-698 of July 26, 1972.

266. Notaries are governed chiefly by the Ordinance of November 2, 1945, on notaries; the Decree of December 19, 1945, on notaries; Decree No. 67-868 of October 2, 1967; and Decree No. 73-609 of July 5, 1973; all as amended.

The German Law

I. INTRODUCTION

German law originally developed from the tribal law (*Stammrecht*) applicable to each Germanic tribe. It was customary law. It was gradually supplanted by Roman law of the *Corpus Iuris Civilis* in the process referred to as the reception of Roman law. This process was already under way as early as in the eleventh century and was completed in the sixteenth century. The Roman law took the place of the customary law, but there was a great body of statutory provisions that differed from place to place. The law known as *Landrecht* applied in each *Land* and differed widely so that the law was very splintered, notwithstanding the reception of Roman law. Each township had its own law independent of the law of the particular *Land*, and the township law prevailed over the *Land* law in case of a conflict. Similary, in the case of a conflict, the *Land* law prevailed over the law meant to apply in the entire country, known as *Reichsrecht*.

The law was thus very fragmentary. The trend toward unification of the law gained momentum only at the end of the eighteenth and during the nineteenth century. The forerunners of the presently applicable codes were especially the Bavarian Code (*Codex Maximilianeus Bavaricus*) of 1756, the Prussian Land Law (*Allgemeines Landrecht für die Preussischen Staaten*) of 1794, the Baden Land Law (*Badisches Landrecht*) of 1809, the Bavarian Criminal Code (*Bayerisches Strafgesetzbuch*) of 1813, and the Uniform Negotiable Instruments Law (*Deutsche Wechselordnung*) of 1848.

The presently applicable codes are: the Civil Code of 1896, the Commercial Code of 1897, the Penal Code of 1871, the Code of Criminal Procedure of 1877, and the Code of Civil Procedure of 1877, all as amended.

II. THE SYSTEM AND ADMINISTRATION OF CIVIL LAW

A.   THE SUBSTANTIVE CIVIL LAW

The Civil Code (*Bürgerliches Gesetzbuch*) of 1896 is in power as amended. It has 2385 articles given in five books: Book 1. General Part; Book 2. Obligations; Book 3. Property; Book 4. Family Law; and Book 5. Law of Succession.

Book 1 (General Part) has the following sections: 1. Persons; 2. Things; 3. Legal transactions; 4. Computation of time; 5. Prescription; 6. Exercise of rights, self defense, self help; and 7. Giving of security.

Book 2 (Obligations) has the following sections: 1. Nature of obligations; 2. Obligations out of contracts; 3. Extinction of obligations; 4. Assignment of claim; 5. Assumption of debt; 6. Plurality of debtors and creditors; and 7. Individual obligations.

Book 3 (Property) has the following sections: 1. Possession; 2. General provisions concerning rights in land; 3. Ownership; 4. (repealed); 5. Easements; 6. Preemption; 7. Charges on land; 8. Mortgage, land charge, annuity charge; and 9. Pledge of movables and rights.

Book 4 (Family Law) has the following sections: 1. Civil marriage; 2. Family relationship; and 3. Guardianship.

Book 5 (Law of Succession) has the following sections: 1. Order of succession; 2. Legal status of the heir; 3. Last will; 4. Contract of inheritance; 5. Forced share; 6. Unworthiness to inherit; 7. Renunciation of inheritance; 8. Certificate of heirship; and 9. Purchase of Inheritance.

Further important statutes are usually carried in the appendix to the Civil Code. They include, for example, the marriage and divorce law, illegitimate children law, change of name, land register, and landlord and tenant law.

The following are topics selected from the German substantive civil law.

1.   Residence (*Wohnsitz*)[1]

A person who continuously resides in a place establishes therein his residence. The residence may exist simultaneously in several places. The residence is abandoned when it is abandoned with the intent to terminate it. An incompetent person or a person with limited capacity may neither establish nor abandon residence without the consent of his legal representative. A married or formerly married minor may establish and abandon his residence on his own.

A person serving in the armed forces has his residence at the place where he is stationed. When he is not stationed in the country, the place where he was last stationed in the country is deemed to be his residence. These provisions do not apply to persons serving in the armed forces who are performing their compulsory military duty nor to those who may not establish a residence on their own.

A minor has the residence of his parents. He does not have the residence of the parent who lacks the right to possession of the minor. Where neither parent has the right to take possession of the minor, the minor has his residence with the person who has that right. The minor retains his residence until he legally abandons it.

An association has its seat at the place where its management is carried out unless otherwise provided.

QUESTIONS

Consider the provisions concerning residence and domicile in the French, the Italian and the Spanish law. Is there a distinction between the two in all these systems?

Does the German term *Wohnsitz* include both residence and domicile as understood in Anglo-American law? Why should a distinction be made between domicile and residence? May not both terms be fused?

Is there a significant difference between the legal meaning of *Wohnsitz* in German law and domicile or residence in Anglo-American law? *See* In re Estate of Jones, 192 Iowa 78, 182 N.W. 227 (1921). Also, F.R.C.P. Rule 17 (b).

---

2. Prescription (*Verjährung*)[2]

The right to demand an act or an omission from another person is subject to prescription. A claim arising out of a family law relationship is not subject to prescription insofar as it is directed to the reestablishment of the position appropriate to the relationship.

The regular period of prescription is thirty years. There are, however, two shorter periods of limitation of two and four years in specially enumerated cases.[3]

The two-year prescription applies mainly to the claims of merchants, manufacturers, artisans and those engaging in handicrafts for the delivery of goods, performance of work, and the attendance to the business of others, including disbursements, unless the performance is rendered for the business of the debtor; claims of carriers, shippers, and the like for fares; claims of innkeepers for food and lodging; claims of workmen and employees for wages and salaries; claims by institutions for instruction, education, care of the sick, and nursing; claims of medical practitioners, veterinarians and midwives for their services; and claims of attorneys and notaries for their fees.

The four-year prescription applies mainly to the claims to arrears of interest, rent, annuities, salaries, pensions, support payments and all other periodical payments.

The regular thirty-year prescription begins to run the moment the claim arises. The shorter two- and four-year prescriptions begin to run only from the end of the calendar year in which the particular claim has arisen.

The running of prescription is suspended in the case of deferment of performance, the cessation of administration of justice, and an act of God. Between spouses, prescription is suspended for the duration of the marriage; between parents and children, it is suspended during the minority of the children; and between guardian and ward, it is suspended during the guardianship. The effect of suspension is that the time for which the running of prescription is suspended is not counted. A prescription running against incompetents or persons of reduced capacity who are without legal representation will run for another six months after the defect has been corrected. Also, a prescription running in favor of or against an estate will run for another six months after the acceptance of the inheritance by the heir, after bankruptcy proceedings are instituted against the estate, or after a claim by or against an agent might be enforced.

The running of prescription is interrupted by acknowledgement, the filing of suit, the service of an order for payment, the filing of a claim in bankruptcy, the assertion of a set-off or the impleading of a third party in legal proceedings, and the institution of execution proceedings. Interruption continues until the termination of the proceedings that brought it about. If the action or the proceedings are withdrawn or dismissed, there is no interruption. The effect of interruption is that the time which has run before the interruption is not counted, and a new period of prescription will begin to run only from the termination of the interruption.

A claim embodied in a judgment prescribes in thirty years, even if the claim itself was subject to a shorter period of prescription.

When the period of prescription has run, the obligated party may refuse performance. If he performs, however, he may not recover what he has performed even if he was unaware of the fact that the prescription has run. The same applies to the acknowledgment of a claim or the giving of security.

Parties may not provide for the nonapplication or a more onerous application of prescription, but they may provide for its less onerous application and especially for the shortening of prescription time.

NOTES AND QUESTIONS

The law of prescription is governed by statutory enactments even in the common law countries. Civil law statutes cover the subject of prescription under both limitation and acquisition of title by adverse possession.

Compare the German provisions with those of the Italian law. Does the definition of prescription given in these two systems differ, or is it the expression of an identical idea in different words?

What is the shortest term used in any of the four systems? What is the longest term? Is the term for acquisition of title by adverse possession uniform in all four systems? Many common law countries apply different terms of adverse possession under different circumstances. Do any of the four civil law systems do likewise? Compare, e.g., the New York Statute of Limitation of Actions, Civil Practice Law and Rules §211ff. *See also* UCC 2-725, 3-122, 4-406, 6-111.

The German law provides that a person who performs an obligation unaware of the fact that the limitation has run may not recover his performance. Does the same rule apply in all four systems? Does it apply in the law of your state?

------

3. Obligations (*Schuldverhältnisse*)[4]

(a) **Contents of obligations** (*Inhalt der Schuldverhältnisse*).[5]   On the strength of an obligation the creditor (*Gläubiger*) is entitled to demand performance

(*Leistung*) of the debtor (*Schuldner*). The performance may consist of refraining from acting. The debtor is bound to perform in good faith and with regard to local custom.

A debt expressed in a foreign currency payable in the country may be paid in German currency unless payment in the foreign currency is expressly stipulated. The rate of exchange is that applicable at the time and place of payment.

Where the place of performance is not stipulated and where it cannot be deduced from the circumstances, performance is to be effected at the place where the debtor had his residence at the time of the creation of the obligation. Where the obligation arose in the course of the debtor's business and his business is located elsewhere, that place is substituted for his residence. It is not to be concluded from the mere fact that the debtor has assumed the cost of delivery that the place to which delivery is to be made is the place of performance.

When in doubt, money is payable by the debtor to his creditor at the creditor's residence and at the debtor's risk and expense. Where the claim arose in the course of the creditor's business and his business is located elsewhere, that place is substituted for his residence. Where the creditor changes his residence or his place of business after the creation of the obligation, resulting in a higher cost or risk of effecting payment there, the creditor must bear the additional cost or risk.

Where the time of performance has neither been stipulated nor can it be deduced from the circumstances, the creditor may demand performance at once and the debtor may also perform at once. Where the time for performance has been stipulated, it is understood, in case of doubt, that the creditor may not demand performance before the stipulated time but that the debtor may perform his part earlier.

Where the debtor does not perform, although performance is due and the creditor has requested performance, the creditor's request for performance places the debtor in default. The bringing of an action for performance or the service of an order for payment are equivalent to the request for performance. Where the time of performance is stipulated in accordance with the calendar, the debtor is in default if he does not perform at the stipulated time and no request for performance is necessary. The same applies where a notice must be given to induce performance and the time of performance is so stipulated that it may be calculated by the calendar from the time of the notice.

The debtor must compensate the creditor for any damage that arises from his default. Where the creditor is no longer interested in the debtor's performance because of his default, the creditor may reject performance and demand compensation for nonperformance, which is governed by the provisions of Articles 346-356 dealing with rescission.[6] A debtor in default is liable for negligence and also for the impossibility of performance arising accidentally, unless the damage would have arisen even if he had performed in time.

The creditor is in default when he does not accept the performance actually offered to him in the proper manner. An oral offer of performance is adequate where the creditor has indicated that he would not accept performance or where an act of the creditor is necessary to performance, such as where the creditor must take away the thing due. The request to the creditor to undertake the necessary act is equivalent to the offer of performance. Where the time for the act to be undertaken by the creditor is stipulated by the calendar, an offer of performance is required only when the creditor has undertaken the act in time. The same applies where notice is required to induce the act and the time for the act is so stipulated that it may be calculated by the calendar from the time of the notice.

When the creditor is in default, the debtor is liable only for willful conduct and gross negligence. Where the thing owed is determinable by description, the risk passes to the creditor from the time when he fell in default because of nonacceptance of the thing offered.

Where the creditor is in default, the debtor may demand compensation for expenses incurred by the fruitless offer and for the safekeeping of the thing due.

NOTES AND QUESTIONS

Obligations in German law have the same meaning as in Roman law. They regulate the relationship between creditor and debtor irrespective of how this relationship arose (by sale, advance of money, etc.). The technique used by the Civil Code is to deal first with the general provisions common to all such relationships. This introductory treatment thus precedes the more detailed treatment of contracts. Compare this approach, e.g., with that used in the Italian Civil Code.

Note the German rule on payment in foreign currency. Does the same rule apply in American law? *See* Hicks v. Guiness, 269 U.S. 71, 46 S. Ct. 46 (1925) and Die Deutsche Bank Filiale Nurnberg v. Humphrey, 272 U.S. 517, 47 S. Ct. 166 (1926).

The provisions dealing with the place and time of performance are generally dealt with under the heading of tender. English law defines tender as attempted performance. Parties must perform as contracted. Failing such an agreement, the rules provided in the Civil Code take over.

Where money is due and payable under a contract, the debtor must pay the creditor at the creditor's residence and at the debtor's risk and expense. Does the same rule obtain in Anglo-American law? *See* Walton v. Mascall (1844) 13 M & W. 458; also UCC 2-511.

Where tender of goods is made, the seller must deliver the goods to the buyer. The contract governs, but when in doubt, the Civil Code fills the gap. Is Anglo-American law in line with this proposition? *See*, e.g., Startup v. Macdonald (1843) 6 M & G. 593, UCC-2-503, 504.

Note the detailed provisions of the German Civil Code as to the time of performance. Once performance is properly tendered by either party and is not accepted, the other party is in default. The consequences of default are also regulated by the Code. For Anglo-American law, *see*, e.g., UCC 2-309, 2-601-616, 2-701-725.

(b) Contracts (*Verträge*).[7]

(i) FORMATION OF CONTRACTS (*Vertragsschliessung*). Whosoever offers to enter into a contract (*Vertrag*) with another is bound by the offer unless he indicates that he is not to be so bound. The offer (*Antrag*) expires when it is refused to the offeror, or when it is not accepted in due time. An offer made to a person present may be accepted only on the spot. The same applies to an offer made by one person to another by telephone. An offer made to a person not present may be accepted only up to a point of time when the offeror may expect to receive an answer under normal conditions. Where the offeror fixes a time for the acceptance offer, it may be accepted only within that time.

Where the acceptance (*Annahme*) reaches the offeror late, but it was sent so that it should have arrived in time under normal conditions of transport, and this fact is known to the offeror, he must notify the acceptor at once of the delay, unless he has already done so. If he delays sending the notification, the acceptance is deemed to have been made in time.

The late acceptance of an offer is deemed to be a new offer. An acceptance with additions, limitations or other alterations is deemed a rejection together with a new offer.

The contract is concluded by the acceptance of the offer without it being necessary to notify the offeror of the acceptance if by local custom such notification is not to be expected, or if it is waived by the offeror. The point of time when the offer expires is determined by the intent of the offeror, discoverable from the offer or the circumstances.

Where a contract is certified by a notary without both parties being simultaneously present, the contract is concluded on certification of the acceptance unless provided otherwise. The making of the contract is not prevented by the supervening death or incompetency of the offeror before acceptance, unless a contrary intent of the offeror may be presumed.

In case of doubt, a contract is not made until the parties reach agreement on all points concerning which, according to even only one party, an agreement must be reached. An agreement on individual points is not binding even where it is taken down and noted. Where the parties agree to have the contract certified, the contract is, in case of doubt, not concluded until such certification.

Where the parties to a contract that they consider binding have in fact not agreed on a point on which they intended to contract, the contract is valid as made if it can be assumed that they would have made the contract even without inserting in it a provision with respect to such point.

At an auction, the contract is made only with the fall of the hammer. A bid expires when a higher bid is made, or where the auction is terminated without knocking down the object on which the bid was made.

Contracts must be interpreted in accordance with good faith and with regard to local custom.

A contract between the parties is necessary for the creation of an obligation by legal transaction, as well as for the modification of an obligation, unless otherwise provided by law.

A contract is void if its performance is impossible (*unmöglich*). Where a party to a contract knows, or should have known at the time of the making of the contract, that its performance is impossible, he must make good any damage the other party suffered due to his reliance on the validity of the contract but not beyond the value of the interest of the other party in its validity. The duty to make good the damage does not arise when the other party knew, or should have known, of the impossibility of the performance. The same applies *mutatis mutandis* where the performance is only partially impossible and the contract is valid as to that part of its performance which is possible, or where one of several optional acts of performance is impossible of performance.

The above-mentioned rules dealing with impossibility of performance apply *mutatis mutandis* to contracts contrary to law (*gesetzwidriger Vertrag*).

A contract whereby a party undertakes to transfer his future property or a part thereof, or to charge it with an usufruct, is void. A contract whereby a party undertakes to transfer his present property or a part thereof, or to charge it with an usufruct, must be executed in a notarized act.

A contract concerning the estate of a living third person, as well as a contract concerning the forced share or a devise or a bequest from the estate of a living third person, is void. The provisions do not apply to a contract made among future statutory heirs concerning the statutory share or the forced share of one of them, but such a contract must be executed in a notarized act.

A contract whereby a party undertakes to convey or to acquire title to land must be executed in a notarized act. A contract made without observance of the prescribed form becomes fully valid when the transfer is actually made and is recorded in the land register.

(ii) PERFORMANCE OF CONTRACT (*Vertragserfüllung*). A party to a mutual contract (*gegenseitiger Vertrag*) may withhold performance until the other party performs his part, unless the former party is bound to perform first. Where performance is due to several persons, the part due to one of them may be withheld until the entire counter-performance has been effected. Where one party has performed in part, the other party may not withhold his counter-performance to an extent which would be contrary to good faith in the circumstances, especially where the remaining part to be performed by the former party is unsubstantial. Where a party is obligated to perform first, he may withhold performance until counter-performance is made, or security for it is given by the other party, if a substantial deterioration of the financial strength of the other party, which may affect his ability to counter-perform, occurs after making the contract.

Where a party to a mutual contract is in default (*Verzug*) as to his performance, the other party may give him reasonable time to perform and declare that he will not accept performance after the time has run. Where the first party does not perform within the given time, the other party may demand compensation (*Schadensersatz*) for nonperformance or may withdraw from the contract but may not demand performance. Where due to the default, the other party is no longer interested in the performance, he may demand compensation for nonperformance or withdraw from the contract without being required to give the first party any time for performance. Articles 346-356 of the German Civil Code, dealing with rescission,[8] apply *mutatis mutandis* to the right to withdraw from the contract. Where the other party rescinds the contract on a ground for which the first party is not responsible, the first party is liable only for unjust enrichment (*ungerechtfertigte Bereicherung*).

A contract may provide for performance to a third party and give him the right to demand performance. Failing an express stipulation to this effect, it is to be deduced from the circumstances, especially from the purpose of the contract, whether the third party shall acquire the right, whether the right shall arise forthwith or only under certain conditions, or whether the contracting parties have reserved the right to take away or modify the right of the third party without his consent.

Where the debtor promises the creditor the payment of a sum of money as it is deemed to be an indication of the conclusion of the contract. In case of doubt, the earnest is not deemed to be a forfeit (*Reugeld*). In case of doubt, the earnest is to be credited to the performance of the giver, or when this cannot be done, it must be returned on performance of the contract. The earnest is also to be returned in case the contract is rescinded.

Where the debtor promises the creditor the payment of a sum of money as penalty (*Vertragsstrafe*) in case he does not meet or does not properly meet his obligation, the penalty is forfeited on his default. Where the performance consists of refraining from an action, forfeiture takes place on breach of the obligation.[9]

Where the debtor promises to pay a penalty in the case of nonperformance, the creditor may demand the payment of the penalty in place of performance. Where the creditor declares that he demands the payment of the penalty, he may not claim performance. Where the creditor has a claim for compensation for nonperformance, he may demand the payment of the penalty as the minimum amount of damages but may claim additional damages.[10]

Where the debtor promises to pay a penalty in case he does not properly meet his obligation, especially in case he does not perform at the stipulated time, the creditor may demand the payment of the penalty in addition to performance. Where the creditor has a claim for compensation for improper performance, he may demand the payment of the penalty as the minimum amount of damages and may claim additional damages. Where the creditor accepts the performance, he may demand the payment of the penalty only if he reserved the right to do so at the time of the acceptance.[11]

Where something else rather than the payment of money is promised as penalty, the provisions of Articles 339 to 341 of the German Civil Code (see footnotes 7-9 above) are applicable. Where the creditor demands the penalty in such a case, he may not claim damages.[12]

A disproportionally high penalty may be reduced to an appropriate amount by judicial decision on the application of the debtor. In considering what is appropriate, the court must consider every legitimate interest of the creditor, not only his proprietary interest. No reduction of the amount of the penalty is possible after it has been paid.

(iii) RESCISSION OF CONTRACT *(Rücktritt)* Where a party to a contract has reserved the right of rescission *(Rücktritt)*, the parties are, in the case of rescission, obligated to restitute whatever they have received. For services rendered or for the use of a thing, the value of these services or of that use must be given; where the contract provides for payment in money, it must be paid. In case of rescission, the claim to damages for the deterioration, destruction, or impossibility of return of a thing is determined as of the acceptance of performance in accordance with provisions governing the relationship between an owner and a possessor as from the initiation of a suit to determine title. The same applies to the claim for the return of the fruits of a thing, or compensation for their use, and to the claim for compensation for expenses incurred in connection with a thing. Money bears interest from the time of its receipt.

The obligations of the parties arising from rescission must be fulfilled without delay (*Zug um Zug*). Rescission is effected by declaration to the other party.

The right of rescission is not barred because of the accidental destruction of the object received by the party entitled to rescission. The right of rescission is barred, however, where the party entitled to rescission is responsible for the significant deterioration, destruction, or impossibility of return of the object received. The right of rescission is barred also where the party entitled to rescission transforms the thing received into another thing by processing or remodeling, alienates the object received or a considerable part thereof, or encumbers it with a right in favor of a third party. The right of rescission is barred where a third party acquiring the object or the interest therein is responsible for its above-described significant deterioration, destruction, impossibility of return, or transformation.

Where the party entitled to rescission is in default with the return of the object received or a significant part thereof, the other party may give him reasonable time to so do and may declare that he will refuse to accept it after the time has run. The rescission will be ineffective if the object is not returned before the time has run.

Where a time for the exercise of the right of rescission is not agreed upon, the party entitled to rescission may be given reasonable time to exercise such right by the other party. The right of rescission is extinguished if the rescission is not declared before the time has run.

Where a party reserves the right of rescission in case of nonperformance of the other party, rescission is ineffective where the other party could have discharged his obligation by a set-off and actually declares a set-off promptly after rescission.

Where a party reserves the right of rescission on the payment of a forfeit, the rescission is ineffective if the forfeit is not paid before or at the time of the declaration of rescission, and the other party promptly rejects the declaration for this reason. Rescission is effective, however, if the forfeit is paid promptly after the rejection.

Where a contract provides that the debtor shall forfeit his rights thereunder upon his nonperformance, the creditor is entitled to rescind the contract on the occurrence of that event.

Where a mutual contract provides that one of the parties must perform at a determined time or within a determined period of time, it is assumed, in case of doubt, that the other party is entitled to rescind the contract if performance is not made accordingly.

NOTES AND QUESTIONS

After providing the framework for all obligations, the German Civil Code proceeds to the treatment of contracts in particular. This is the approach taken by all other civil codes. Compare, e.g., the French Civil Code.

1. As to the formation of contracts, contracts are formed by offer and acceptance. Do the terms required by German law for the formation of contracts coincide with those in Anglo-American law? *See*, e.g., UCC 2-206; Owen v. Tunison, 131 Me. 42, 158 A. 926 (1932). Suppose the acceptance arrives late due to

delay in transport, is the German rule in accordance with the English rule? *See* Adams v. Lindsell (1818) 1 B. & Ald. 681; Household Fire Ins. Co. v. Grant, (1879) 4 Ex. D. 216.

Does the death or incapacity of the offeror terminate the offeree's power of acceptance? *See* Corbin, Offer and Acceptance, and Some of the Resulting Legal Relations, 26 Yale L.J. 169, 198 (1917); Restatement Second, §35 A, §48; Jordan v. Dobbins, 122 Mass. 168 (1877).

What about auction sales? Is the German rule also good in the United States and Britain? *See* UCC 2-238; Payne v. Cave (1789) 3 T.R. 148.

Article 157 of the German Civil Code provides that contracts must be interpreted in accordance with good faith and with regard to local custom. Anglo-American law stresses the same point. *See,* e.g., UCC 1-203, 205; Summers, "Good Faith" in General Contract Law and the Sales Provisions of the Uniform Commercial Code, 54 Va.L. Rev. 195 (1968).

Like the Statute of Frauds of 1677, Stat 29, Car. II, c.3,. which requires certain agreements to be made in writing to be enforceable, the German law also requires some agreements and acts be made in writing. The German law goes even further, though, and requires some acts to be executed in a notarized form. It does not list all such transactions in one comprehensive rule, however, but states each requirement individually, as it deals with a particular subject. Thus, a debtor is entitled to a receipt in writing upon payment of his debt (BGB §368), the making of a contract of lease of premises for a term exceeding one year must be made in writing (BGB §566), the notice to determine a lease must be given in writing (BGB §564(a)), and a contract whereby a person agrees to become the surety for another must be in writing (BGB §766), etc. General rules as to documents in writing and to notarized acts appear in BGB §§125-129. For instance, a contract for the transfer of property must be notarized (BGB §§311-313); a promise to make a gift must be notarized (BGB §518); and a marriage contract must be notarized (BGB §1410). Compare, e.g., the Italian provisions dealing with the same subject matter.

The physical or legal impossibility of performance makes the contract void. The same rule obtains in Anglo-American law. Where the promise is impossible of performance, there is no contract since such a promise is no real consideration for any promise given in respect of it. *See,* e.g., Scott v. Coulson [1903] 2 Ch. 249; Harvey v. Gibbons, (1675) 2 Lev. 161, UCC 2-613; Mineral Park Land Co. v. Howard, 172 Cal. 289, 293, 156 P. 458, 460 (1916). A supervening impossibility will not necessarily absolve the promisor. *See,* e.g., International Paper Co. v. Rockefeller, 161 App. Div. 180, 146 N.Y.S. 371 (3d Dept., 1914); Cargill, Inc. v. Commodity Credit Corp., 275 F. 2d 745, 751-753 (2d Cir. 1960).

2. As to performance of contracts, the German Civil Code elaborates on the performance in mutual contracts. It demands performance as promised by the parties. Is the Anglo-American law in accord? *See,* e.g., Browning v. Johnson, 70 Wash. 2d 145, 422 P. 2d 314 (1967); Sylvan Crest Sand & Gravel Co. v. United States, 150 F2d 642 (2d. Cir. 1945).

As a consequence of breach of contract, the German Civil Code lists a claim for damages, rescission, and unjust enrichment. It also deals with deposits, forfeits and penalties. Compare UCC 2-718. Deposits are usually given in contracts for the sale of land. Penalties may be provided for in the case of nonperformance. The German law seems to be more liberal than the Anglo-American law, which would allow the recovery of liquidated damages agreed upon by the parties but is distrustful of penalties. *See,* e.g., UCC 2-718; Dunlop v. New Garage Co., [1915] A.C. 79; Cellulose Acetate Silk Co. Ltd. v. Widnes Foundry Ltd., [1933] A.C. 20; Acme Process Equipment Co. v. United States, 347 F. 2d 509 (Ct. Cl. 1965); Dave Gustafson & Co. v. State 83 S.D. 160, 156 N.W. 2d 185 (1968).

German law may also enforce performance along the lines of Anglo-American specific performance. The rule is built in Art. 241 of the Civil Code, which gives the creditor the right to demand performance of the debtor. The method of enforcement resembling the Anglo-American specific performance is provided for in Arts. 883-898 of the Code of Civil Procedure. It provides for both specific performance and enforcement of injunctions. The actual enforcement, if necessary, is done by a court officer. He may thus seize and hand over chattels to the creditor or put him in possession of premises, as the case may be. Injunctions are enforced by fines and imprisonment, which may not exceed two years.

3. As to rescission of contracts, the German law deals here with a contractually reserved right of rescission. Rescission leads to restitution. It originates in the Roman doctrine of *restitutio in integrum. See,* e.g., Hulton v. Hulton, [1917] 1 K.B. 813 at p. 821. In Anglo-American law, restitution is linked to quasi-contracts and unjust enrichment. *See,* e.g., Callano v. Oakwood Park Homes Corp. 91 N.J. Super. 105, 219 A2d 332 (1966). Compare also UCC 2-209. Is it correct to say that in Anglo-American law rescission is thought of as an equitable remedy granted for cause (e.g., in the case of mistake or misrepresentation) rather than a contractually reserved right?

(c) **Extinction of obligations** (*Erlöschen der Schuldverhältnisse*).[13]   Obligations are extinguished (*erlischt*) by performance, by deposit (payment into court), by setoff, and by release.

(i) PERFORMANCE (*Erfüllung*).   An obligation is extinguished by performance (*Erfüllung*) made to the creditor. Where the creditor accepted as performance an act of performance offered to him as such, the burden of proof is on him to show that it was not the due performance or only an incomplete performance when he does not want to recognize it as valid performance on that ground.

An obligation is extinguished where the creditor accepts something other than the due performance in lieu of performance. Where a thing, a claim against a third party, or any other right is given in lieu of performance, the debtor must give warranty against a defect in title or in the thing as a seller.

Where the debtor is obligated to effect to the creditor similar acts of performance arising out of several obligations, and the performance effected is insufficient to discharge all of the debts, that debt specified by the debtor on making performance will be discharged. Where he makes no specification, a debt already due will be discharged first; among several due debts, the one that gives the creditor least security will be discharged; among several equally secure debts, the one most burdensome to the debtor will be discharged; among several equally burdensome debts, the oldest will be discharged; and where they are equally old, each debt will be discharged pro rata.

Where the debtor must pay interest and costs apart from his performance and his payment is insufficient to discharge the whole debt, his payment is first applied to the costs, then to the interest, and lastly to the principal. Where the debtor specifies another application, the creditor may refuse to accept performance.

The creditor must give the debtor, at his request, a written receipt of the acceptance of performance. The debtor must prepay and bear the costs of the receipt, unless a different practice developed in his relationship with the creditor. Where several creditors are substituted for the original creditor because of an assignment of the claim or because of succession upon death, the additional costs must be borne by the creditors.

Where a document of indebtedness has been issued with respect to the claim, the debtor may demand its surrender together with the receipt. Where the creditor claims he is unable to surrender it, the debtor is entitled to demand an officially certified acknowledgment that the debt has been extinguished.

(ii) DEPOSIT (PAYMENT INTO COURT) (*Hinterlegung*).   Where the creditor is in default in accepting performance, the debtor may deposit money, securities, or other documents and valuables for him in a public place provided for that purpose.

The same applies where the debtor cannot discharge or cannot safely discharge, his obligation due to a ground concerning the person of the creditor, or because of an uncertainty as to the identity of the creditor that is not due to the debtor's negligence.

The deposit (*Hinterlegung*) must be made at the deposit office (*Hinterlegungsstelle*) in the place of performance. If the debtor makes the deposit at another place, he must compensate the creditor for any damages arising therefrom. The debtor must notify the creditor of the deposit without delay. He is liable in damages if he fails to do so. No notification is required if it is impracticable.

The debtor has the right to take out the thing deposited. His right to do so is barred if he declares to the deposit office that he waives his right to withdraw it; if the creditor declares to the deposit office his acceptance of the deposit; or if an enforceable judgment between the creditor and the debtor, which holds the making of the deposit proper, is presented to the deposit office.

Where the right to withdraw the deposit is barred, the debtor's obligation is discharged as if he had performed to the creditor at the time of making the deposit.

Where the right to withdraw the deposit is not barred, the debtor may refer the creditor to it. The thing deposited is at the creditor's risk, and the debtor is not obligated to pay interest or compensation for the fruits of a thing which the creditor does not draw. Where the debtor withdraws the deposit, it is deemed not to have been made.

The creditor bears the costs of the deposit, but such costs fall on the debtor if he withdraws the deposit.

The right of the creditor to the deposit expires thirty years from the receipt of the notice of deposit, unless the creditor appears at the deposit office within that time. The debtor may withdraw the deposit even if he has waived the right to withdraw it.

Where the creditor is in default and where the thing due to the creditor is a movable unsuitable for deposit, the debtor may sell it by public auction and deposit the proceeds. The same applies when the thing is likely to perish or where its custody would involve disproportionate expense. The auction (*Versteigerung*) may take place only after notice thereof has been given to the creditor. No notice needs to be given where the thing is deteriorating and there is risk in delay. The debtor must give notice of the auction to the creditor without delay. He is liable in damages if he fails to do so. Both the above notices need not be given when they are impracticable.

Where the thing has an exchange or a market price, the debtor may have it sold by a licensed broker or a licensed auctioneer at the current price. The costs of the sale or auction fall on the creditor, but they fall on the debtor if he withdraws the proceeds thereof from the deposit.

(iii)   SET-OFF (*Aufrechnung*).   Where two parties mutually owe each other acts of performance of the same kind, each party may set-off his claim against that of the other party as soon as he can demand the performance due to him and effect the performance due by him. The set-off (*Aufrechnung*) is effected by a declaration to the other party. The declaration is ineffective (*unwirksam*), if it is made subject to a condition (*Bedingung*) or stipulation of time (*Zeitbestimmung*).

The set-off extinguishes the mutual claims that are suited for a set-off as of the time on which they arise against each other.

The set-off is not made inapplicable because different places were stipulated for performance or delivery. The party effecting the set-off, however, must compensate the other party for the loss he suffers because he does not receive or cannot effect performance at the stipulated place. Where by agreement the performance is to be effected at a determined time and place, it is understood in case of doubt that a claim which is to be performed at another place may not be set-off.

A disputed claim may not be set-off. Prescription does not make set-off inapplicable if the prescribed claim was not yet prescribed at the time when set-off could have been effected. A set-off is not permissible against a claim arising out of a willfully committed tort.

(iv)   RELEASE (*Erlass*).   An obligation is extinguished when the creditor by agreement releases the debtor from his debt. The same applies when the creditor by agreement with the debtor acknowledges the obligation as nonexistent.

NOTES AND QUESTIONS

The German Civil Code deals here mainly with the discharge of an obligation by payment. Payment in accordance with a contract will amount to the *solutio obligationis*. The contract is thus discharged by performance.

As to payment into court, the Civil Code makes detailed provisions as to the handling of such payments. In Anglo-American law, is not payment into court considered a procedural device? *See*, 28 U.S.C.A. §§2041, 2042.

Set-off is intended to simplify dealings between parties. It expresses the idea of a current account. Compare the doctrine of merger in French law. How does it compare with the so-called account stated in American law? *See*, Restatement, Contracts §422.

A release will discharge a debt. This is a universal rule of law. *See*, e.g., Restatement, Contracts §§402-404. UCC 1-107.

4.   Property (*Sachenrecht*)[14]

(a)   Possession (*Besitz*).[15]   The possession of a thing is acquired by the acquisition of actual power over it. An agreement between the present possessor and the person acquiring possession suffices for the acquisition of possession of a thing where the person acquiring possession is capable of exercising power over it.

Possession comes to an end when the possessor gives up the actual power over a thing or when he loses it in some other manner. Possession does not come to an end where the possessor is temporarily prevented from exercising power over the thing. Possession devolves upon the heir.

It is unlawful to deprive the possessor of his possession against his will or to interfere with his possession. Possession so obtained is defective and continues to be defective in the hands of an heir or in that of a successor in possession who knew of the defect on his acquisition of possession.

A possessor may repel by force an attempt to unlawfully deprive him of possession. Where an attempt to unlawfully deprive him of possession of a movable is successful, he may retake it by force from an offender caught in the act or in hot pursuit. Where he is unlawfully deprived of his possession of land, he may immediately dispossess the offender and recover possession.

Where a possessor is unlawfully deprived of possession or is being unlawfully disturbed in his possession by a person whose possession against him is defective, he may claim restitution of his possession or the cessation of the interference. A person whose posession or whose predecessor's possession was defective against the present possessor or the person disturbing him in his possession has no such claim. The claim is extinguished one year after the unlawful dispossession or disturbance and is also extinguished by a final judgment holding for the person dispossessing or disturbing him.

(b)   Ownership (*Eigentum*).[16]

(i)   SUBSTANCE OF OWNERSHIP (*Inhalt des Eigentums*).[17]   An owner may deal with a thing as he pleases and prevent others from dealing with it, unless it is contrary to law or the rights of third parties. The owner may not prohibit the interference with the thing where it is necessary to avert a present danger and the damage likely to ensue is disproportionally high as compared to that caused by the interference. The owner has a claim to compensation for his loss.

The right of ownership in land extends to the airspace and to the ground under the surface. The owner may not, however, prohibit an interference occurring at such a height or depth that he has no interest in preventing it.[18]

(ii)   ACQUISITION AND LOSS OF OWNERSHIP OF LAND (*Erwerb und Verlust des Eigentums an Grundstücken*).[19]   A transfer of title to land (*Auflassung*) must be made by the transferor and the transferee in a written document that provides for the transfer and its registration in the land register (*Grundbuch*). It must be executed in the presence of both parties before a proper authority. A notary or an officer of the land registry office is such an authority. A transfer of title to land may also be made as a part of a court approved settlement. A transfer of title to land may be made only on the strength of a contract (*Vertrag*) in writing made by the parties involved in the transfer of the land. The contract must be certified by a notary and made before or at the same time with the transfer. A transfer of title to land that is made subject to a condition or a stipulation of time is void and has no effect.

An owner of land who does not register his title in the land registry office may lose his land by thirty years of adverse possession. Time is computed in the same way as in adverse possession of movables. If an owner registers his title, the proceedings to take away his title by adverse possession (*Aufgebotsverfahren*) may be instituted only when he has died or has been missing and no entry in the land register which would require his consent has been made for the last thirty years. The adverse possessor who is successful in the proceedings and who obtains a judgment to this effect acquires title by recording of the judgment in the land register.

A person who does not own the land, but has registered his title in the land registry office, will acquire title by thirty years of adverse possession.

(iii) ACQUISITION AND LOSS OF OWNERSHIP OF MOVABLES (*Erwerb und Verlust des Eigentums an beweglichen Sachen*).[20]   Ownership in movables is acquired and lost by delivery; adverse possession; annexation, confusion or processing; acquisition of fruits or products; occupation; and finding.

For the acquisition of ownership in a movable by delivery (*Übertragung*), it is necessary that the parties agree that ownership should be so transferred; and the owner must deliver the movable to the acquiring party. A document directing delivery may be substituted for physical delivery.

To acquire title to a movable by adverse possession (*Ersitzung*), the adverse possessor must hold it in his uninterrupted possession as an owner (*im Eigenbesitze*) for ten years. Adverse possession does not run in favor of a person who lacks good faith (*bona fides*) at the time of acquisition or who later finds out that he is not entitled to ownership. Where a bona fide adverse possessor transfers possession of a movable to another bona fide adverse possessor, the time for which the transferor held possession enures to the benefit of the transferee and is tacked onto it. The same applies to succession upon death.

Title to movables may also be acquired by annexation (*Verbindung*), confusion (*Vermischung*), and processing (*Verarbeitung*).

Where a movable is attached to a piece of land so that it becomes a part thereof, it becomes a part of the land—a fixture.

Where two movables are so joined as to become one, their owners become co-owners of the thing in proportion to the value each movable had at the time of their joining. Where one of the movables is to be considered the principal, the owner thereof acquires sole title to the thing. The same applies where movables are inseparably commingled. The commingling is considered inseparable where separation would result in a disproportionately high expense.

A person who produces a new movable thing by processing or transforming one or more materials becomes the owner of the new thing, unless the cost of the processing or transforming is substantially less than the value of the material.

A person who suffers a loss in consequence of an annexation, confusion or processing may demand, from the person who gained thereby, compensation in money in accordance with principles governing unjust enrichment. *Restitutio in integrum* may not be demanded.

Fruits and products of a thing (*Erzeugnisse und Bestandteile einer Sache*) belong to the owner thereof, even after separation, unless otherwise provided. Where a person has the right to acquire the fruits or the products of a thing belonging to another, he will acquire ownership of them upon separation. The same applies to the possession of a thing by a bona fide adverse possessor. Where the owner of a thing permits another to appropriate its fruits or products, that person acquires title to them upon taking possession of them or, where he is in possession of the thing itself, upon separation. Where the owner is bound to grant permission, he may not revoke it so long as the other is in possession of the thing.

A person who takes possession as an owner (*Eigenbesitz*) of an ownerless movable acquires title to it by occupation (*Aneignung*). Title is not acquired where the occupation is prohibited by law or where the right of another to appropriate the movable is violated thereby. A movable becomes ownerless when the owner gives up the possession thereof with the intent to abandon ownership.

Title to movables may also be acquired by finding (*Fund*). A person who finds a lost thing and takes possession thereof must immediately notify the person who lost it, its owner, or a person entitled to it. Where the finder does not know the person entitled to it, he must immediately notify the police of the finding and of any circumstances that may be of importance for ascertaining the person entitled. Where the value of the thing does not exceed 3 German marks, there is no need to notify the police.

The finder must keep the thing in safe custody. Where there is a risk of deterioration or where the cost of the safekeeping would be disproportionately high, the finder must have the thing sold by public auction and hold the proceeds in its stead. He must notify the police of the auction. The finder may deliver the thing or the proceeds to the police rather than keep them, and must so deliver them if the police request it.

The finder is liable only for willfull conduct and for gross negligence.

The finder is absolved of any liability by returning the thing to the person who lost it. He is entitled to compensation for necessary expenses incurred for the safekeeping and preservation of the thing, or for the purpose of ascertaining the person entitled to it. He may also request a finder's fee from the person entitled to it. The finder's fee amounts to 5 percent of the value of the thing up to 300 German marks, and 1 percent of the value thereof exceeding 300 German marks. The finder's fee with respect to animals amounts to 1 percent of the value. Where the thing has only a personal value, a reasonable finder's fee should be given. The finder forfeits his claim to the finder's fee when he fails to give notice of the finding or conceals having found the thing. The finder may hold the thing found until he is paid his expenses and his finder's fee, as above.

The finder acquires title to the thing found one year after notifying the police of the finding, unless the person entitled to it becomes known to the finder or such person notifies the police before that time. The acquisition of ownership extinguishes all other rights to and in the thing.

Where the value of the thing found does not exceed 3 German marks, the one year term runs as from the finding. The finder does not acquire title if he conceals having found the thing, but notification of the police by the person entitled does not stand in the way of the finder acquiring title.

Where the finder waives his right to acquire title in the thing found, his right passes to the community of the place where the thing was found.

A person who loses his title to a thing because the finder or the community acquired title therein may demand the delivery of the thing pursuant to the provisions governing unjust enrichment. The claim is extinguished after three years have run from the passing of the title in the thing to the finder or to the community unless a timely suit is filed.

Special rules apply to chattels found on the premises of public authorities and in the means of transportation providing public transport. The above-mentioned rules applicable to finding do not apply in such cases, but the finder must surrender the thing found to the authority. Persons who have lost chattels under such circumstances may claim them from the public authorities. Unclaimed articles will be sold by public auction after public notification that the articles found and unclaimed would be sold. Proceeds of the sale will be held for three years from the public notification, and if the person entitled does not appear, they will fall into the state treasury.

Treasure trove (*Schatzfund*) is governed by a special rule. Where a movable thing is discovered which has been hidden for so long that its owner cannot be ascertained, the title to one half of it will be acquired by the person who discovered it, and that to the other half by the owner of the thing or land in which it was hidden.

NOTES AND QUESTIONS

1. Possession is a doctrine of Roman law from which it entered into the modern law of European countries. For Anglo-American law, compare, e.g., Salmond on Jurisprudence, Chapters 13 and 14, and Brown on Personal Property, 3d ed., pp. 19-23. Note the extent of protection given to possession in German law. Not only may a possessor repel by force any attempt to unlawfully deprive him of possession, but he may also forcibly retake the possession of which he was so deprived provided he acts promptly. The rule applies both to the possession of chattels and possession of land. Does modern American law sanction similar self-help? *See*, e.g., New York, Real Prop. Actions & Proceedings Law, §§711-713; Vernon's Texas Stat., Arts. 3973-3975, dealing with forcible entry and detainer. Compare also the German law of possession with that of France.

2. The fundamental rights of ownership are common to all civil codes. *See*, e.g., the Italian law. The same rule applies *mutatis mutandis* to both chattels and land. With respect to chattels, the owner may use and enjoy the thing. He may also consume it. Limitations on use of property affect especially the ownership of land. *See*, e.g., Burby, Real Property, 3d ed., p. 13. Note the German provision concerning the use of the airspace. Compare Rest. Torts §§159, 194; also 49 U.S.C.A. §1301ff.

3. As to acquisition of title to land, the German law requires a contract for the sale of land and a directive to the land registry to record the transfer of title in the books of records. How does it compare with the traditional Anglo-American requirement for a contract of sale and for a conveyance or a transfer? The German registration of title gives a strong, virtually absolute, certainty of title. Compare it e.g., with the certainty afforded by the Australian Torrens system. The Torrens system is also used in some areas of the United States, e.g., in Cook County in Illinois.

As to acquisition of title to movables, title normally passes by delivery. Delivery usually takes place in pursuance of a contract or a gift. It may also be acquired by accession, confusion, and adverse possession. Compare Brown on Personal Property, 3d ed., Chapters IV, VI, and VII. Compare also the Italian law.

4. Note the provisions of the German law with respect to finding. Compare Brown on Personal Property, 3d ed., Chapter III. How does the German rule concerning the finding of valuables on the land of another person compare with that prevailing in England and in the United States? See Brown on Personal Property, 3d ed., p. 25; *See also*, e.g., Armory v. Delamirie (1722) 1 Strange 505; Hannah v. Peel, [1945] 1 K.B. 509; McAvoy v. Medina (1866) 11 Allen (Mass.) 548, 87 Am. Dec. 733; Schley v. Couch, 155 Tex. 195, 284 S.W. 2d 333 (1955). Compare also the Italian law.

---

5. Marriage (*Ehe*)[21]

(a) **Entering into marriage** (*Eheschliessung*).[22] A person may not marry before he or she is of full age (eighteen years). The court may grant a dispensation from this requirement on the petition of a petitioner who is at least sixteen years of age and whose future spouse is of full age.[23]

An incompetent also may not marry. A minor and a person of limited competence require parental consent, or that of the guardian. Where the consent is refused without a good ground, the court may grant it on motion.

A person may not marry an ancestor or descendant, a brother or sister of the whole or half blood, or a person related by marriage in the direct line (uncle-niece, nephew-aunt). A court may grant dispensation from the prohibition against the marriage of persons related by marriage.[24]

A person may not marry unless his prior marriage has been annulled or dissolved.

A person whose marriage was dissolved because of his adultery may not marry the person with whom he committed it where the divorce decree dissolved the marriage on that ground. The court may, however, grant a dispensation from this prohibition.[25]

A woman may not marry before ten months have run from the annulment or the dissolution of her prior marriage, unless she gives birth in the meantime. The registrar of marriages may grant a dispensation from this prohibition.

A foreigner may not marry unless he produces a certificate issued by the proper authority of the country of his citizenship that there is no impediment. The chief judge of the court of appeal (*Präsident des Oberlandesgerichts*) of the judicial district where the marriage is to be celebrated may grant dispensation from this requirement. The dispensation is given mainly where the foreigner is stateless or where the state of his citizenship does not issue the required certificate.

The marriage must be celebrated before the registrar of marriages (*Standesbeamte*) within six months of the publication of banns. The registrar of marriages may grant a dispensation from the publication of banns. The registrar asks each of the parties in their presence and in the presence of two witnesses whether they wish to marry each other, and after they have answered in the affirmative, he declares them married to each other in the name of the law.[26] The registrar then records the marriage in the register of marriages.

The proper registrar of marriages to celebrate a marriage is the one in whose district one of the parties to the marriage has his residence. Where several registrars are territorially competent, the parties to the marriage have a choice. Where neither of the parties has his residence in Germany, the proper registrar is the one in the Registry of Marriages No. I in Berlin or in the Main Registry of Marriages in Munich, Baden-Baden, or Hamburg. The proper registrar may grant a written authority to any other registrar to celebrate a particular marriage.

Where both parties to the marriage are foreigners, the marriage may be celebrated by a properly appointed officer of the country of the citizenship of one of the parties in accordance with the law of that country. A certified copy of the marriage certificate, issued to the spouses by that country, makes full proof of the marriage. Where the registrar of marriages of the district where the marriage was celebrated is handed such a certified copy, he will record the marriage in the register of marriages and will keep the said copy as evidence.

NOTES AND QUESTIONS

The German law sets a uniform minimum age for entering into marriage. This is in accordance with the view of equality of the sexes. Does the same rule apply in the law of your state? *See,* e.g., Texas Family Code §§1.5.—1.53; Duley v. Duley, 151 A. 2d 255 (D.C. 1959). Compare it also with the French rule.

Mentally incompetent persons may not enter into marriage. Compare, e.g., Larson v. Larson, 42 Ill. App. 2d 467, 192 N.E. 2d 594 (1963). In some jurisdictions, such marriages are merely voidable. *See,* e.g., Colo. Rev. Stat. Ann. 46-3-1 (Supp. 1960); Texas Family Code §2.45. Compare also the German provisions with those of Spain and Italy.

Marriages in breach of the consanguinity rule are prohibited in Germany, and the prohibition holds good in the laws of other countries. *See,* e.g., California Civil Code §4400; Texas Family Code §2.21. Only some jurisdictions, like Germany, grant dispensation from the prohibition of marriage between uncle and niece, and between nephew and aunt. *See,* e.g., In re May's Estate, 305 N.Y. 486, 114 N.E. 2d 4 (Ct. App. N.Y., 1953). Compare also the Italian law on the matter. May a dispensation be obtained in your state?

Is the prohibition of marriage during the existence of a prior marriage valid in most countries? What about countries whose religious laws allow polygamy?

The prohibition against remarriage of a woman before ten months have run from the annulment or dissolution of her prior marriage is not a penalty but a rule to make the legitimacy of children more certain. Compare Texas Family Code §3.66, which says: "Neither party to a divorce may marry a third party for a period of thirty days immediately following the date the divorce is decreed, but the parties divorced may marry each other at any time."

The celebration of marriages is rather uniform throughout the Western world. Germany requires a marriage to be entered into before a registrar of marriages, a government officer. Does the same rule apply in Italy or in your own state? *See*, e.g., Texas Family Code §1.83.

(b) Annulment of marriage. The marriage law (*Ehegesetz*) deals with annulment of marriage under two separate headings: (i) nullity of marriage (*Nichtigkeit der Ehe*) and (ii) annulment of marriage (*Aufhebung der Ehe*).[27]

(i) NULLITY OF MARRIAGE (*Nichtigkeit der Ehe*).[28] A marriage is void because of lack of form if it is not celebrated in accordance with the provisions of Article 13 of the *Ehegesetz*. The marriage is valid, however, from the very beginning where the spouses live together for five years after the celebration of the marriage. Where one spouse dies, the marriage is valid from the very beginning where the spouses lived together until such death, but at least for three years. A petition for the annulment of marriage may not be brought after the above-mentioned time has run.

The marriage is also void where one of the parties is incompetent, unconscious or temporarily insane at the time of the celebration of the marriage. The marriage is valid, however, from the very beginning where the other party makes it clear after removal of the impediment that he wishes to continue the marriage relationship.

The marriage is void where one of the parties is married to another person at the time of its celebration.

The marriage is void when it is entered into in prohibition of Article 4 of the *Ehegesetz*, dealing with consanguinity and affinity. The marriage is valid, however, from the very beginning where a dispensation is subsequently obtained from the prohibition of marriage between parties related by marriage.

The marriage is void if it is entered into in prohibition of Article 6 of the *Ehegesetz*. The marriage is valid, however, from the very beginning where dispensation is subsequently obtained.

No one may rely on the nullity of a marriage until it is declared void by judgment. The procurator (*Staatsanwalt*), the spouses, and in the case of bigamy also the spouse of the prior marriage may petition for the annulment of the marriage. Where the marriage is terminated by death or by divorce, only the procurator may petition for its annulment. A petition for annulment of marriage may not be brought after the death of both spouses.

(ii) ANNULMENT OF MARRIAGE (*Aufhebung der Ehe*)[29] A spouse may petition for annulment of marriage where his capacity was limited at the time of the celebration of marriage and his guardian did not give his consent to its celebration. A spouse may petition for annulment of marriage where he did not understand the nature of the marriage ceremony, or where, although he understood it, he did not want to give his consent to the marriage. Also, a spouse may petition for annulment where he was mistaken as to the person of the other spouse, or where he was mistaken as to the personal qualities of the other spouse in that, had he known the facts, he would not have married him. A petition for annulment of marriage may also be brought where a spouse was induced to enter into the marriage by fraud or duress.

The petition may not be brought where after the removal of the impediment, discovery of the error or fraud, or the ceasing of the duress, the spouse indicates that he wishes to continue the marriage relationship. In the case of fraud, the petition may not be brought where the fraud was perpetrated by a third person without the knowledge of the other spouse, or where it concerned property.

The suit must be brought within one year from the removal of the impediment, discovery of the error or fraud, or ceasing of the duress.

NOTES AND QUESTIONS

The German Civil Code lists the standard grounds which make a marriage void or voidable following the above-discussed distinction between *Nichtigkeit* and *Aufhebung* of marriage. The grounds fall, however, into the generally applied groups familiar to Anglo-American law as to void and voidable marriages. The German law requires a marriage to be declared void by judgment. Does the same rule obtain in other countries? *See,* e.g., Texas Family Code §2.24.

———————————

(c) **Dissolution of marriage** (*Ehescheidung*).[30] A marriage may be dissolved because of the fault of one of the spouses, or on grounds other than fault. Grounds involving fault are adultery, other gross breach of the marriage relationship, and dishonorable or immoral conduct. A spouse forfeits his right to petition for dissolution of marriage on the ground of adultery where he consents to it, or where he, by his deliberate conduct makes it possible or easier for the other spouse to commit it. He may not petition on the other above grounds where he is himself also at fault and where, due to the nature of his own fault, his claim would not be morally justifiable.

Grounds other than fault are mental disturbance, mental sickness, a contagious or repulsive disease with no hope for recovery in the foreseeable future, and three years of separation. In the case of separation, the marriage may not be dissolved at the petition of the spouse who is exclusively or predominantly to blame for the separation where the other spouse opposes the dissolution, unless such other spouse appears not to be ready to continue the marriage relationship. It may also not be dissolved where it would not be in the best interest of the child or children of the marriage.

The grounds for dissolution of marriage that are based on fault are extinguished by condonation. The suit must be brought within six months from the time when the spouse became aware of the ground. Time does not run, however, where the spouses are separated. It begins to run only from the request of the guilty spouse to the innocent spouse urging him to resume cohabitation or to bring suit. In any event, the claim is extinguished when ten years have run from the time when the cause of action accrued.

Where the marriage is dissolved because of fault, the decree must state that it is dissolved because of the fault of one of the spouses, or both of them, or because of the predominant fault of one of the spouses.

Upon dissolution of the marriage, the wife keeps the name of her husband. She is free, however, to resume her maiden name. She may do so by a declaration to the registrar of marriages. She may also resume her married name from a previous marriage if there are children living out of that previous marriage. She may not do so, however, where the marriage was dissolved because of her fault or her predominant fault.

Where the marriage is dissolved because of the fault or predominant fault of the wife, the husband may, by a declaration to the registrar of marriages, prohibit her from keeping his name. She is then required to resume her maiden name.

Where the wife keeps the name of her husband after the dissolution of the marriage, the husband may petition the court to take it away from her if, after the marriage is dissolved, she leads a dishonorable or immoral way of life. If the court finds for the husband, it will order her to resume her maiden name.

Where the marriage is dissolved because of the fault or the predominant fault of the husband, he must pay the wife proper alimony if she does not have sufficient income from her property or her work. Where it is dissolved because of the fault or predominant fault of the wife, she must pay the husband proper alimony if he is unable to support himself. In both of the above cases, the court must consider the payment capabilities of the spouse making the payments, especially his obligation to support a minor child or a new family after remarriage, and the amount of the alimony must be equitably adjusted.

Where the marriage is dissolved because of the fault of both spouses, neither being predominantly at fault, the court may award the spouse who is unable to support himself a contribution from the other spouse if it appears equitable.

Where the marriage is dissolved on grounds other than fault, but the decree dissolving it contains a finding of fault on the part of one of the spouses, the abovementioned rules as to alimony apply. Where the decree contains no finding of fault, the court may award alimony to the respondent for the dissolution of the marriage if it appears equitable.

Alimony is paid monthly in advance. The obligated spouse may be required to give security. Alimony may also be paid in a lump sum. It is paid until the death or remarriage of the entitled spouse. The obligation to pay alimony is not extinguished by the death of the obligated spouse, but passes to his estate. The entitled spouse may lose his claim to alimony by order of court if, after the dissolution of the marriage, he leads a dishonorable or immoral way of life or is guilty of serious misconduct toward the obligated spouse.

Both parents must support their minor children.

NOTES AND QUESTIONS

The German law distinguishes between divorce because of fault and divorce on grounds other than fault. There is no divorce by consent, and there is no such ground as incompatibility. Compare the German provisions with those of the French law. Does your state recognize divorce by consent? Does it have incompatibility as a ground for divorce? *See, e.g.,* Texas Family Code §§3.01-3.07.

Consider the detailed provisions concerning the name of the wife after divorce. Do such provisions exist in Anglo-American law? *See, e.g.,* Texas Family Code §3.64. *See also* the provisions of the French law.

Compare the German provisions as to alimony with those of the French law. Note that a German court may award alimony to a husband if he is unable to support himself. How does this compare with the law of your state? Some states have no provision for alimony for a former wife, *See,* e.g., Texas Family Code §3.59.

------

6. Wills and Estates (*Erbrecht*)[31]

(a) Succession on intestacy (*Gesetzliche Erbfolge*).[32] Heirs of the first degree are the descendants of the deceased. A descendant living at the time the inheritance accrues (the death of the intestate) excludes from the succession all the descendants related to the deceased through him. For a descendant no longer living at that time, the descendants related to the deceased through him take by substitution and per stirpes. Children inherit in equal shares.

Heirs of the second degree are the parents of the deceased and their descendants. If the parents are living at the time the inheritance accrues, they take in equal shares. If the father or the mother is no longer living at the time the inheritance accrues, his or her descendants take by substitution in accordance with the provisions applicable to succession of heirs of the first degree. If there are no descendants, the surviving parent takes alone.

Heirs of the third degree are the grandparents of the deceased and their descendants. If the grandparents are living at the time the inheritance accrues, they take in equal shares. If, among the paternal or maternal grandparents, the grandfather or grandmother are no longer living at the time the inheritance accrues, the descendants of the deceased take by substitution. If there are not such descendants, the share of the deceased grandparent goes to the surviving grandparent on that side, and if he is no longer living, to his or her descendants. If the paternal or the maternal grandparents are no longer living at the time the inheritance accrues, and there are no descendants of the deceased grandparents, the grandparents on the other side, or their descendants, take alone. Where the descendants inherit in place of their parents or grandparents by substitution, they take in accordance with the provisions applicable to succession of heirs of the first degree.[33]

Heirs of the first, second, or third degree who belong to several stirpes, will receive the share due to them in each particular stirps. Each share is a separate share of the estate.

Heirs of the fourth degree are the great-grandparents of the deceased and their descendants. If the great-grandparents are living at the time the inheritance accrues, they take alone. If only some are living, they take in equal shares irrespective of whether they belong to the same or to a different line. If the great-grandparents are no longer living at the time the inheritance accrues, the descendant most closely related to the deceased inherits. Descendants equally closely related take in equal shares.

Heirs of the fifth degree and of further degrees are the remoter ascendants of the deceased and their descendants. The rules of inheritance applicable to heirs of the fourth degree apply *mutatis mutandis.*

The surviving spouse of the deceased takes one quarter of the estate where there are heirs of the first degree, and one half of the estate where there are heirs of the second degree or grandparents. Where there are grandparents and the descendants of grandparents, the surviving spouse also takes the share in the other half which would have passed to the descendants under Article 1926. Where there are neither heirs of the first or second degree, nor grandparents, the surviving spouse takes the whole estate.

Where no relative nor the spouse of the deceased is living at the time the inheritance accrues, the estate passes to the treasury of the particular state of the federation of which the deceased was a subject at the time of his death. If he was a subject of several states, the treasuries of those states take in equal shares. If the deceased was a German who was not a subject of any state of the federation, the estate passes to the federal treasury.

The deceased may exclude, by will, a relative or his spouse from intestate succession without leaving his estate to any heir.

NOTES AND QUESTIONS

Succession on intestacy is uniformly regulated in codes throughout the world. The German Civil Code adopts the distribution in accordance with the degrees of relationship to the decedent. Compare the German approach with those of the Spanish and French Civil Codes. What approaches do they follow? How is the matter regulated in the law of your state? *See,* e.g., New York Estates, Powers and Trusts Law §4-1.1.

On what occasions does the German law provide for succession per capita, and on what per stirpes? Does the law of your state also have such a provision? Compare, e.g., the above-mentioned New York rule.

When are the great-grandparents and their descendants called to succeed? Compare the German rule with, e.g., New York Estates, Powers & Trusts Law §4-1.1 (9).

When does the estate pass to the Treasury? *See,* e.g., New York Abandoned Property Law §200.

(b) **Last will** (*Testament*).[34]

(i) TESTAMENTARY CAPACITY (*Testierfähigkeit*).[35] A minor may make a will only if he is over sixteen years of age. Minors who are at least sixteen years old and adults under temporary guardianship do not require the consent of their legal representatives in order to make wills.

A person under guardianship may not make a will. The incapacity sets in as of the filing of the petition on the strength of which the declaration of guardianship is made. Where such a person makes a will before the order placing him under guardianship becomes *res judicata,* the will is valid if he dies before the order so becomes. Where a person already under guardianship makes a will after the petition to remove the guardianship has been filed, the will is valid if the guardianship is actually removed on the strength of the petition.

A person who, because of an impairment of mental capacity, weakness of

mind, or an impairment of consciousness, is incapable of realizing the significance
of a declaration of intention made by him, and of acting accordingly, may not make
a will.

(ii) TYPES OF WILLS (*Testamentsformen*).[36] Wills are either regular or emergency. Regular wills are either public or holographic.

A public will is made before a notary. It may be declared orally by the testator to
the notary who draws it up; or the testator may hand it over to the notary in writing,
enclosed in a sealed or an unsealed envelope. Where the testator hands the will
already written to the notary, the will need not be handwritten by the testator. It may
be handwritten by another person, or typewritten. A minor may make a will only by
oral declaration to the notary or by delivering to him, in an unsealed envelope, his
will already written. Where the notary draws up the will or receives it unsealed, he
must make certain that it is valid. The notary must draw up a notarial act of the
proceedings. The act must identify the testator, state that he has the capacity to
make a will, and indicate whether the will was drawn up by the notary or handed
over to him by the testator sealed or unsealed. The notary must read to the testator
the contents of the act, and it must be signed by the testator and the notary. The
notary then places the will and the notarial act in an envelope, which he seals with
his official seal. He then writes on the envelope what it contains, as well as the place
of making and the date, and affixes his signature thereto. He must then file it for
safekeeping with the county court (*Amtsgericht*) within the district of which the
notary has his office. The *Amtsgericht* issues the testator a receipt of the filing.

A holographic will must be written in longhand by the testator and must be
subscribed by him. It should give the place, day, month and year of making. The
signature should contain both his first name and his family name. The omission of
the indication of the place and date and of the full name of the testator will not
render the will invalid if these facts and the identity of the testator may otherwise be
ascertained. Minors and persons unable to read may not make holographic wills.
The testator may deposit the will for safekeeping with the *Amtsgericht*.

Emergency wills may be made only where, due to the imminent danger of death
of the testator, a public will cannot be made. Emergency wills may be made before a
mayor of a community (*Bürgermeister*), who takes the place of a notary, and two
witnesses, or only before three witnesses. During a sea voyage aboard a German
ship, a will may be made before three witnesses. In all these cases, minutes of the
proceedings must be drawn up and signed by all present. If the testator is unable to
sign, the minutes must so state. The witnesses may not be given any benefit in the
will nor may they be appointed to the office of executor. If they are given a benefit or
if they are appointed to the office of executor, their witnessing of the will is void.
Emergency wills are taken as not having been made if the testator survives three
months from their making. The time does not run while the testator is unable to
make a will before a notary. If the testator embarks on a new sea voyage before the
time has run, the running of time is interrupted and an entirely new time begins to
run from the conclusion of the new sea voyage.

In all wills made before a notary or an official taking his place, the notarial
authentication is void if the notary himself, his spouse or former spouse, or a person
related to him by blood or by marriage in the direct line, or a person related to him

collaterally by marriage up to the second degree is or are given any benefit thereunder.

(iii) REVOCATION OF WILLS (*Widerruf des Testaments*).[37]   The testator may revoke his will, or a particular disposition contained therein, at any time. He may revoke a will even after he has been placed under guardianship because of weakness of mind or alcoholism or because he was declared a spendthrift.

The will is revoked by a later will. It is also revoked by the destruction of the will with the intent to revoke it, or by making alterations or erasures therein with the intent to revoke it in full or in part. Where the testator destroys the will, it will be presumed that he intended to revoke it. Where he makes alterations or erasures therein, it will be presumed that he intended to revoke it in full or in part in accordance with the alterations or erasures. Where a later will does not expressly revoke an earlier will, the earlier will will be revoked only to the extent of any inconsistency. If the later will is revoked, the earlier will is, in the case of doubt, valid as if it had not been revoked. Similarly, if the revocation by will of a testamentary disposition is itself revoked, the will or the disposition is, in the case of doubt, valid as if it had not been revoked.

A will made before a notary or an emergency will made before a *Bürgermeister* and two witnesses is revoked when the testator withdraws it from the *Amtsgericht* where it was placed for safekeeping. The proper officer at the *Amtsgericht* must inform the testator of the consequences of the withdrawal, note it on the will, and make a record thereof in his files. The testator may withdraw the will from the *Amtsgericht* at any time.

A holographic will, however, which the testator in his discretion deposited with the *Amtsgericht* for safekeeping, will not be automatically revoked when the testator withdraws it from the *Amtsgericht*.

NOTES AND QUESTIONS

1. What is the minimum age for making a will? May it be still less than sixteen years of age? *See*, e.g., the Spanish law. Is full age usually required for a person to make a will? Compare, e.g., New York Estates, Powers & Trusts Law §3-1.1.

2. Persons of unsound mind are disqualified from making wills. May persons under guardianship make wills? Compare the German rule with, e.g., New York Estates, Powers & Trusts Law §3-1.1. *See also* In re Signorelli's Will, 46 Misc. 2d 849, 260 N.Y.S. 2d 889 (1965); In re Coe's Will, 47 App. Div. 177, 62 N.Y.S. 376 (1900).

3. The German law distinguishes between regular and emergency wills, and further between public and holographic wills. How does this scheme compare with those of the Italian and the Spanish law?

Public wills require the attestation of a notary and are kept in the proper custody of a court or of the notary. *See* the Italian law on the topic. Does Anglo-American law require a notarial attestation? Where the will is made before a notary, is the presence of witnesses dispensed with? *See*, e.g., the Spanish law. Where no witnesses as in German law are required, the prohibition against a witness being given any benefit under the will applies rather to the notary. Anglo-American law uniformly prohibits a witness from receiving anything under the will. *See*, e.g., New York Estates, Powers and Trusts Law §3-3.2.

The required number of witnesses may vary from country to country. *See*, e.g., the Spanish law. Compare, e.g., New York Estates, Powers and Trusts Law §3-2.1 (4).

Does Anglo-American law recognize holographic wills? *See*, e.g., The English Wills Act, 1963, 11 & 12 Eliz., 2, Ch. 44. May holographic wills be made by the law of your state? *See*, e.g., New York Estates, Powers and Trusts Law §3-2.2. Note the formalities of a holographic will.

Does a noncupative will equal the German emergency will? *See*, e.g., New York Estates, Powers and Trusts Law §3-2.2.

4. How do German provisions as to the revocation of wills compare with Anglo-American law? *See*, e.g., New York Estates, Powers and Trusts Law §3-4.1.

Since in Germany every will made before a notary must be filed for safekeeping with the proper *Amtsgericht*, its withdrawal from custody amounts to a revocation. How does this compare with the Italian law?

Methods of revocation seem to be standard in most laws. Consider the question of the revival of an earlier will revoked by a later disposition. Is the German rule the same as the Italian rule? May a revoked will be so easily revived in Anglo-American law? *See*, e.g., New York Estates, Powers and Trusts law §3-4.6.

(c) **Forced share** (*Pflichtteil*).[38]   The descendants of a testator, his parents, and his spouse may demand a forced share if they are excluded (omitted) from inheritance by the testator in his will. The forced share amounts to one half of the statutory share that they would have received on intestacy. Where any of them is left in the will less than his forced share, he may demand the balance. The claim must be made within three years from the time the beneficiary has knowledge of the accrual of the inheritance, and within thirty years of the accrual of the inheritance irrespective of such knowledge.

The testator, by a direct provision in his will, may deprive a descendant of his forced share on specifically stated grounds that exist at the time of the making of the will and are stated therein. The burden of proof falls on the person enforcing the provision. The grounds are: (1) an attempt on the life of the testator, his spouse or his descendant; (2) the willful physical mistreatment of the testator or of his spouse where the offending descendant also descends from such spouse; (3) a felony (*Verbrechen*) or a serious willful misdemeanor (*Vergehen*) committed against the testator or his spouse; (4) a malicious breach of the statutory duty of the descendant to support the testator; and (5) a dishonorable or immoral way of life led by the descendant contrary to the wishes of the testator. The acts must be committed by the offending descendant.

The testator may similarly deprive his parents of their forced share on grounds (1), (3) and (4) above. The testator may further deprive his spouse of his forced share in a similar way where the offending spouse is guilty of an offense against the testator that entitles the testator to sue for dissolution of marriage. He may do so even where his claim to bring the action is barred by lapse of time.

The right to deprive an unavoidable heir of his claim to a forced share is extinguished by condonation. A testamentary disposition already made will be without effect where the testator forgives the offense.

(d) Unworthiness to inherit (*Erbunwürdigkeit*).[39] A person may not inherit, not even the forced share, when he has been declared unworthy. The declaration of unworthiness is made by a court on the petition of any person who would benefit thereby. Where the decree is made, the benefit falling to the unworthy heir is taken as not having accrued. The benefit then falls to those who would have been entitled to it had the unworthy heir been dead at the time of the accrual of the inheritance.

A person is unworthy to inherit if he has: (1) willfully and unlawfully killed or attempted to kill the testator or the intestate, or has reduced him to a condition whereby he became incapable, up to the time of his death, of making or revoking a testamentary disposition; (2) willfully and unlawfully prevented the testator or intestate from making or revoking a testamentary disposition; (3) by fraud or duress induced the testator or intestate to make or revoke a testamentary disposition; or (4) been guilty of forgery or destruction of a testatmentary disposition of the testator.

The unworthiness does not arise under (1), (3) and (4) above, where the testamentary disposition becomes inoperative before the time the inheritance accrues.

The suit to declare an heir unworthy may not be brought when the testator or intestate has forgiven the heir.

The action to declare an heir unworthy must be brought within one year from the time when the person bringing the action acquired knowledge of the ground of unworthiness, but not later than thirty years from the time the inheritance accrued.

NOTES AND QUESTIONS

Forced shares have their origin in Roman law. The object was to protect the family against excessive generosity of the testator in disposing of his property on his death. Compare, e.g., the Italian law. English law preferred to leave the testator his freedom of testamentary disposition.

Since the civil law provides for forced shares, it then must provide for disinheritance in specifically determined cases to deprive an unworthy heir of his forced share. Compare the German grounds for disinheritance with those of the Spanish law.

How does Anglo-American law deal with the matter? *See,* e.g., New York Estate, Powers & Trusts Law §§4-1.4 and 5-1.1; In re Weiss' Estate, 33 Misc. 2d 773, 227 N.Y.S. 2d 378 (1962); Crum v. Bliss, 47 Conn. 592 (1880); Healy v. Reed, 153 Mass. 197, 26 N.E. 404 (1891).

What is the distinction in German law between disinheritance and unworthiness to inherit?

B. THE COMMERCIAL LAW

The Commercial Code (*Handelsgesetzbuch*) of 1897 is in power as amended. It has 905 articles presented in four books: Book 1. Merchants; Book 2. Partnerships; Book 3. Commercial transactions; and Book 4. Maritime commerce.

Book 1 (Merchants) has the following sections: 1. Merchants; 2. Mercantile register; 3. Mercantile firm; 4. Commercial books; 5. Agency and authority to act; 6. Commercial employees and apprentices; 7. Commercial agents; and 8. Brokers.

Book 2 (Partnerships) has the following sections: 1. General partnership; 2. Commandite partnership; 3. repealed; 4. repealed; and 5. Silent partnership.

Book 3 (Commercial transactions) has the following sections: 1. General provisions; 2. Commercial purchase and sale; 3. Commission merchants; 4. Forwarding agency; 5. Warehousemen; 6. Carriers (bills of lading); and 7. Carriage of goods and persons by rail.

Book 4 (Maritime commerce) has the following sections: 1. General provisions; 2. The shipowner; 3. The master; 4. Carriage of goods; 5. Carriage of passengers; 6. repealed; 7. Average; 8. Salvage and assistance in distress; 9. Maritime liens; 10. Marine insurance; and 11. Limitation of time.

Further important statutes usually appear in the appendix to the Commercial Code. They include, for instance, the law of corporations, the law of exchange; the law of unfair competition, the law of bankruptcy, and the law of patents and trademarks.

The following are selected topics from the German commercial law.

1. Merchants (*Kaufleute*).[40]

A merchant is a person, a partnership or a corporation who or which engages in commerce as his or its profession. The following are deemed acts of commerce: (1) procurement and resale of goods or securities irrespective of whether the goods are resold in the form in which they were acquired or after processing; (2) processing of goods for others, unless the business is one of handicrafts; (3) writing of insurance in return for premiums; (4) banking and moneychanging; (5) carriage of goods and passengers by sea, carriage under bills of lading, carriage of goods and passengers on land and inland waterways, and towage; (6) business of commission merchants, forwarding agents, and warehousemen; (7) business of commercial agents and brokers; (8) business of publishing and trading in books and works of art; and (9) business of printing, unless it is run as a craft.

When a business is not already considered commerce under the above rules, it will be so considered where, because of its character and size, it is required to be run in a businesslike manner, and where its firm name is entered in the mercantile register. The entrepreneur is under a duty to have it so registered.

The above provisions concerning merchants do not apply to farming and forestry.

The provisions of the Commercial Code concerning firm name, commercial books and agency do not apply to persons whose business, because of its character and size, is not required to be run in a businesslike manner. Where such persons join for the purpose of running such a business, they may not form a general or a commandite partnership.[41]

Where the firm name is registered in the mercantile register, the entrepreneur may not claim against a party relying on the registration that the business is not governed by the Commercial Code or that it is a busines to which Article 4 of the Commercial Code applies.

2. Mercantile Register (*Handelsregister*)[42]

The mercantile register is kept by the courts. Any person may search the register and obtain certified copies therefrom.

All instruments submitted for recording must be executed in the form of a notarized act. All registration must be published in full in the Official Gazette (*Bundesanzeiger*) and at least in one other newspaper determined by the court. The recording must be made with the court (*Amtsgericht*) where the merchant has his seat of business, that is, his main office. Where there are branch offices, all instruments concerning them must be filed with the *Amtsgericht* of the main office. One copy is kept there, and another is forwarded through official channels to the proper *Amtsgericht* where the branch office is located. Where a merchant has his seat of business (his main office) abroad, the branch office in Germany must register all instruments concerning the branch office with the *Amtsgericht* of its location.

The merchant who causes an instrument to be registered may not rely on its registration against third parties until the registration is published as mentioned above, unless the third party knows of the facts contained therein. The publication is effected when the day on which it is published in the Official Gazette and in the newspaper or newspapers determined by the court has run. This does not apply to notices of the transaction of legal business to take place within fifteen days from the publication where the third party shows that he did not know nor should have known the fact.

3. Commercial Books (*Handelsbücher*)[43]

Every merchant must keep books that are in accordance with the principles of proper bookkeeping and reflect both his dealings and the condition of his business.

At the opening of his business, he must take an inventory and make a balance sheet. He must do so again at the end of every business year. The balance sheet must be made in German currency. The value of all assets and liabilities is taken as of the date of the making of the balance sheet. The inventory and the balance sheet must be signed by the merchant.

The books must be kept in a living language. They must be bound and the pages numbered. No space intended for contents may be left blank. No erasures may be made, and crossed out writing must leave the text legible. No changes in an entry may be made that would leave the date of the change uncertain.

Every merchant must keep his books, inventories and balance sheets, copies of all letters sent out, all letters received, and any documents on the strength of which entries in the books are made. Books, inventories and balance sheets must be preserved for ten years; copies of letters sent out, letters received, and the documents on the strength of which entries are made must be preserved for seven years. Time runs from the end of the calendar year in which the last entry was made in a book, in which the inventory or balance sheet was made, in which the letter was sent out or received, or in which the document was made.

NOTES AND QUESTIONS

1. The German Commercial Code is a counterpart of the American Uniform

Commercial Code. It is, however, more extensive and deals with many matters not covered by the UCC. Compare the contents of the German Commercial Code with that of the UCC. Note that it comprises the law of admiralty. Compare also the German Commercial Code with those of France and Spain.

The topics of merchants, mercantile register and commercial books are closely connected. Merchants must be registered in the mercantile register and must keep commercial books.

A merchant engages in acts of commerce, which are defined in the Code. *See* the definition of a merchant in UCC 2-104.

2. Mercantile registers are kept by the *Amtsgerichte.* In them is entered all relevant information concerning merchants whether they are physical persons, partnerships or corporations. Does such a uniform registration system exist in the Anglo-American law? Compare also the Spanish law. Does the Anglo-American system require the registration of individual merchants trading under a family name?

3. Commercial books must be kept by law. The books required to be kept are universally kept by businessmen in all countries. Compare the French and the Spanish law. Failure to keep books properly may result in their being denied proof of the transactions recorded and it may also constitute an offense, e.g., in bankruptcy. *See* criminal provisions in bankruptcy below.

---

4.   Partnerships and Corporations
(*Handelsgesellschaften*)

There are the following types of partnerships and corporations: general partnership, commandite partnership, silent partnership, stock corporation, commandite partnership by shares, and corporation with limited liability.

(a)   General partnership (*Offene Handelsgesellschaft*).[44]   This is a partnership engaging in business under provisions applicable to merchants, under a firm name, and with unlimited liability of the partners.

The partnership must be registered with the *Amtsgericht* within the district of which it has its seat. The registration must give the following information: The full names, occupations and addresses of the partners; the firm name of the partnership and its seat; and the date of the setting up of the partnership. Any changes must be filed for registration. The documents must be signed by all partners. The partners who act for the partnership must also file a specimen of firm signature.

The relationship among the partners is governed by the partnership contract. Where the contract does not provide otherwise, the provisions of Articles 109-122 of the Commercial Code apply. They deal chiefly with the conduct of partnership business and the sharing in profits and losses. All partners are bound to run the business; but where the partnership contract leaves the management to only some partners, the others are excluded from its management. Where all partners take part in the management, each may act alone; if another partner is opposed to a particular act, however, it may not be undertaken. Every partner, whether managing or not, may inquire into the firm's business and inspect the books and papers thereof. The profit or loss established at the end of the business year is credited or debited to the capital of each partner in the business. Every partner is entitled to draw from the profit an amount equal to four percent of his capital investment, and may do so during the business year.

The relationship of the partnership to third parties is governed by the Commercial Code. The partnership is in existence as of the moment of its registration in the mercantile register. If it undertakes business before the registration, it is fully responsible therefor.

The partnership may acquire title to movables and immovables, acquire rights and incur obligations in its firm name and may also sue and be sued thereunder. The partners are liable personally, jointly and severally for the debts of the partnership. A judgment against the partnership is enforceable only against the partnership assets. To reach a partner, judgment must be given against him personally. Where a new partner enters into an existing partnership, he is liable for the debts thereof incurred prior to his entry.

The partnership is dissolved by the running of time, if it was set up for a time only; by the decision of the partners; by the declaration of bankruptcy of the partnership; by the death of a partner, unless provided otherwise in the partnership contract; by the declaration of bankruptcy of an individual partner; by any one of the partners leaving the partnership; or by a court order.

A partner must give notice of his intention to leave the partnership at least six months before the end of the business year in order to become effective at the end of that business year. A judgment creditor of a given partner may levy on the partner's share in the partnership after his levy on the movable property of the partner proved fruitless. The levy is effected by giving notice of his intention to do so at least six months before the end of the business year of the partnership, and the share of the partner is then available to the judgment creditor at the end of that business year.

The partnership contract may provide for the continuation of the partnership by the remaining partners after the death, bankruptcy or leaving of a partner. It may also provide for the continuation of the partnership with the heir of a partner who dies.

When a partnership is dissolved, it must be wound up. The winding up occurs in bankruptcy proceedings, if such proceedings have been instituted, or by the partners themselves in other cases. The partners then become liquidators. They must conclude the business of the partnership, convert all assets into money, pay all creditors, and distribute the remainder among themselves in accordance with their investment in the partnership. They must prepare a balance sheet at the beginning of the winding up and again a final balance sheet after the winding up.

All claims against the partners in connection with the partnership are extinguished five years from the dissolution thereof. The same limitation time applies to claims against a leaving partner, namely five years from his leaving the partnership.

(b) Commandite partnership (*Kommanditgesellschaft*).[45] This is a kind of commercial partnership where one or more partner's liability is limited to the amount he or they brought into the partnership, whereas the liability of the other partners is unlimited. Unless otherwise provided in the Commercial Code, the partnership is governed by the provisions applicable to general partnership.

The commandite partners (*Kommanditisten*), i.e., those whose liability is limited, are not entitled to take part in management of the partnership and cannot represent it. They are entitled to receive the balance sheet and may verify its correctness by inspecting the books of the partnership. They are not entitled to inspect the books generally. Their liability is limited to a fixed amount, which must be recorded in the mercantile register. When a limited partner enters the partnership, he is liable up to the stated amount for the debts of the partnership incurred before his entry. The death of a limited partner does not cause dissolution of the partnership.

(c) Silent partnership (*Stille Gesellschaft*).[46] Silent partnership may occur with a commercial partnership or with an individual merchant. The interest of the silent partner (*stiller Gesellschafter*) in the business is represented by the amount he brings in, which passes into the property of the merchant. It is an agreement between him and the merchant, and it is not recorded. The merchant alone is responsible for the running and liabilities of his business.

The share of the silent partner in the profit and loss of the business is determined by the agreement. It may provide that the silent partner does not share in the loss, but it may not exclude him from profit. The profit of the silent partner is paid to him at the end of every business year. He partakes in the loss only to the amount of his investment under the agreement. He may not be required to repay what he was paid as profit against later loss. He is entitled to the balance sheet of the business and may verify its correctness by inspecting the books. He is not entitled to inspect the books generally.

The silent partner may leave the partnership under the provisions applicable to a general partnership. In the case of bankruptcy of the merchant, the silent partner becomes creditor in bankruptcy for the amount for which he was not, by his agreement, liable in the loss.

NOTES AND QUESTIONS

1. The German general partnership is very much like an Anglo-American general partnership. Compare the Uniform Partnership Act, which has been enacted with minor modifications in the various states of the United States.

Note that the partnership must register with the *Amtsgericht*. Are such records kept by the courts in British countries and in American states? *See*, e.g., New York General Business Law §130.

Is a new partner who joins the partnership liable for the existing debts of the partnership? Compare, e.g., New York Partnership Law, §72.

How is a partnership dissolved? *See*, e.g., New York Partnership Law, Art. 6.

How do you sue a partnership? Do you reach individual partners by suing only the partnership firm? Compare, e.g., Fed. Rules of Civil Procedure, Rule 17(b), and Rule 4(d)(3) as to service on partnerships.

What is the liability of a retiring partner? *See*, e.g., New York Partnership Law §67.

Compare the provisions of the German general partnership with those of French, Italian and Spanish general partnerships.

2. How would you define a commandite partnership by reference to the Anglo-American concept of a limited partnership? Is the German commandite partnership the counterpart of the Anglo-American limited partnership? Are there any significant differences? *See* the Uniform Limited Partnership Act. May commandite partners inspect the books of the partnership? *See,* e.g., New York Partnership Law §99. What is the liability of a commandite partner in German law and that of a limited partner in Anglo-American law? *See,* e.g., New York Partnership Law §106. What effect does the death of a limited partner have on the partnership? *See,* e.g., New York Partnership Law §110.

Compare also the provisions of French, Italian and Spanish commandite partnerships.

3. A silent partnership lies on the borderline between a partnership of some sort and a loan of money to be used in business. The German law regulates silent partnerships in detail. This is not often done in other laws. Does the Uniform Partnership Act or the Uniform Limited Partnership Act mention the silent partnership? Compare, e.g., Rosenblum v. Springfield Produce Brokerage Co., 243 Mass. 111, 137 N.E. 357 (1922); Petition of Williams, 297 F. 696 (1st Cir. 1924).

In Italian law, the so-called *associazione in partecipazione,* Arts. 2549-2554 of the Italian Civil Code, comes close to the German silent partnership.

(d) Stock corporation (*Aktiengesellschaft*).[47]

(i) GENERAL PROVISIONS (*Allgemeine Vorschriften*).[48]   The stock corporation has a legal personality. It is liable to its creditors with all its property. Its capital is expressed in shares (*Aktien*). It is a commercial corporation even if it does not engage in commerce. Its name must include the word "*Aktiengesellschaft.*" Its seat, determined by its charter,[49] is the place where it carries on business, where it has its management or its administration. The capital and the shares must be expressed in German marks. The minimum capital is 100,000 German marks, the minimum nominal value of a share is 50 German marks but any higher denominations must be in multiples of 100 German marks. Shares may be of different kinds. Every share gives the right to a vote, but preferred shares may be issued without such right.

(ii) SETTING UP THE CORPORATION (*Gründung der Gesellschaft*).[50]   At least five persons must be parties to the corporation's charter (*Satzung*). They take shares for value. The charter must be made in a notarized act. It must indicate the corporate name, the seat of the corporation, its objects, the amount of share capital, the face value and the kinds of shares, and the form of the corporation's public announcements. The shares are issued to bearer (*Inhaberaktien*) unless otherwise provided. The shareholders who are parties to the charter are the founders of the corporation. The corporation is formed when the founders take all the shares. The founders must set up a provisional supervisory board (*Aufsichtsrat*) which appoints the provisional management (*Vorstand*). They hold office until the end of the first meeting of shareholders (*Hauptversammlung*). The founders must issue a written report of the founding of the corporation (*Gründungsbericht*). The report must be examined by the management and the supervisory board, as well as by professional examiners, as to the correctness of the facts and compliance with the law. The corporation must then be registered in the mercantile register. It may be registered only after all the shares have been subscribed and one fourth of the nominal value of the shares has been paid.

The corporation is registered with the *Amtsgericht* within the jurisdiction of which it is located. The court examines the application and will register the corporation only if it has complied with all the requirements provided for by law. The corporation enters into existence only with the registration. Those who act for the corporation before its registration are personally and jointly liable.

(iii) ORGANIZATION OF THE CORPORATION (*Verfassung der Aktiengesellschaft*).[51] The corporation is run by the management (*Vorstand*), composed of one or several members. If the corporation's capital exceeds three million German marks, there must be at least two managers, unless the charter provides for only one. Where there are several managers, they run the corporation jointly, although the charter or the supervisory board may provide otherwise; however, no provision may be made that one or more managers may decide differences of opinion within the management against the majority of its members. The management represents the corporation in its dealings with third parties. The powers of the management may be restricted internally by provisions of the supervisory board, the meeting of shareholders, the charter, or provisions of the management itself; but they may not be restricted against third parties.

The managers are appointed by the supervisory board for a term not exceeding five years and they may be reappointed. Where there are several managers, the supervisory board may appoint a chairman of the management. The supervisory board may remove a manager or the chairman of the management at any time for a good reason.

The management must report to the supervisory board on the business. It must see to it that all proper commercial books are kept. It must run the business of the corporation with the care of a reasonable businessman (*Sorgfalt eines ordentlichen und gewissenhaften Geschäftsleiters*). The managers are liable to the corporation for the loss caused to it by breach of their duties.

The supervisory board (*Aufsichtsrat*) must have at least three members. The charter may provide for a greater number, however, with the board not exceeding nine members where the corporation's capital is below three million German marks, fifteen where it exceeds that sum, and twenty-one where it exceeds twenty million German marks. The number of its members must be divisible by three. Members of the supervisory board are elected by the meeting of shareholders, although some are designated by trade unions and holders of special shares. At least two thirds of the members must be elected by the shareholders' meeting. Their term of office may not exceed the date of the meeting of shareholders held in the fourth business year after they take office. The business year in which they take office is not counted.

The supervisory board elects its own chairman and vice-chairman. A quorum is one half of its members, but not less than three. They hold meetings as required, but at least once a year. Meetings are called by the chairman; he must call a meeting whenever requested by the management or by two of its own members. Minutes of meetings must be kept. The supervisory board represents the corporation against the management and must use the care of a reasonable businessman.

The meeting of shareholders appoints and removes members of the supervisory board; it appoints auditors and passes on the distribution of profits, on reports of the management and the supervisory board, on the increase and reduction of capital, on amendments to the charter, and on the dissolution of the corporation. It is called as required by law and the charter. A one-month notice of the meeting must be given. The meeting of shareholders decides by majority vote, unless the law or the charter requires a larger majority. An amendment of the charter, the increase or reduction of capital, and the dissolution of the corporation require a three-fourths majority, unless the charter requires a larger majority. Each share has one vote. All resolutions are reduced to notarized writing and recorded in the mercantile register.

(iv) DISSOLUTION OF THE CORPORATION (*Auflösung der Gesellschaft*).[52] A corporation may be dissolved by the expiration of the time for which it was set up, by a resolution of the meeting of shareholders, or by a declaration of bankruptcy. It is then liquidated either by the management or, in the case of bankruptcy, in bankruptcy proceedings. The managers become liquidators (*Abwickler*). They must conclude the corporation's business, convert all assets into money, pay all creditors, and distribute the remainder among shareholders. They prepare a balance sheet at the beginning of liquidation (*Abwicklung*) and again at its conclusion. The conclusion of the liquidation is recorded in the mercantile register. Books of the corporation must be preserved for ten years at a place determined by the court.

(e) Commandite partnership by shares (*Kommanditgesellschaft auf Aktien*).[53] A commandite partnership by shares combines the features of a commandite partnership and a stock corporation. It must have at least one general partner whose liablity for the obligations of the partnership is personal and unlimited, and nominal capital expressed in shares for which the shareholders are not personally liable. The relationship of the general partners to the shareholders (*Kommandit-aktionäre*) and to third parties is governed by the provisions of the Commercial Code applicable to commandite partnerships. In all other respects, the provisions of the Code applicable to stock corporations apply unless the Commercial Code provides otherwise.

The firm name must contain the words "*Kommanditgesellschaft auf Aktien.*" At least five persons must be parties to the charter, including all general partners and those shareholders who take the shares. They are the founders of the partnership. The charter is made in a notarized act. The partnership must be registered in the mercantile register.

The provisions of the Commercial Code applicable to stock corporations with respect to the corporation's management (*Vorstand*) apply *mutatis mutandis* to the general partners.

At the meeting of shareholders, the general partners who hold shares may not vote on the appointment and removal of members of the supervisory board (*Aufsichtsrat*), on the removal of general partners, on the appointment of auditors and special auditors, and on the claims for damages made against them.

The supervisory board represents the shareholders against the general partners. The latter may not sit on the supervisory board.

The partnership may be dissolved on the grounds applicable to commandite partnerships. Dissolution other than in bankruptcy must be approved at a meeting of shareholders by a three-fourths majority, unless the charter requires a larger majority. The bankruptcy of a shareholder does not terminate the partnership, nor may the creditor in bankruptcy of a shareholder cause the dissolution of the partnership. The liquidation is carried out by the general partners together with representatives of the shareholders appointed by the meeting of shareholders.

NOTES AND QUESTIONS

1. The German *Aktiengesellschaft* is the counterpart of the English limited company under the Companies Act and of the American corporation. Compare the French, Italian and Spanish counterparts. The *Aktiengesellschaft* is a corporation suitable for large enterprises with a great number of shareholders and the greatest financial resources. Compare the Model Business Corporation Act and the corporation law of your state.

The corporation must be registered with the *Amtsgericht*. Is an American corporation registered only with the county clerk?

Is there a requirement for minimum capital and minimum nominal value of a share in Anglo-American law? *See,* e.g., New York Business Corporation Law §§501, 504, 506.

As to incorporation of the corporation compare, e.g., New York Business Corporation Law §§201, 202, 401 and 402.

2. The organs of the German corporation are the management, the supervisory board and the meeting of shareholders. Are three such separate bodies in existence in an Anglo-American corporation? *See,* e.g., New York Business Corporation Law §§701-720. Is the function of an American board of directors comparable to that of the German supervisory board? If so, who then holds the function of the German management in an American corporation? Are auditors appointed by the meeting of shareholders in both the German and Anglo-American systems? What is the power of the meeting of shareholders? Compare, e.g., New York Business Corporation Law §602ff.

How is a corporation dissolved? Compare, e.g., New York Business Corporation Law §1001ff.

3. The German commandite partnership by shares is in fact a partnership, the limited partners of which have their holding expressed in shares like in a stock corporation. It is still only a type of partnership, and it is not used for large holdings of capital. Compare the provisions applicable in French and Italian law to commandite partnerships by shares. Does a similar type of partnership exist in Anglo-American law? What is the special advantage of limited partners holding shares like shareholders in a stock corporation?

(f) Corporation with limited liability (*Gesellschaft mit beschränkter Haftung*).[54]
The corporation is set up by a contract made in a notarized act to which all of its
partners are parties. Only two incorporators are required. The contract of
association must state the firm's name and its seat, the nature of the business, the
size of the capital, and the interest of each partner in the corporation. The firm's
name must be taken from the type of business conducted, or it must use the name of
one or more of its members and must contain the words *"mit beschränkter
Haftung."* The corporation's capital must be twenty thousand German marks as a
minimum. The respective shares of the members may be of different amounts, but
they must not be less than five hundred German marks and must be in multiples of
one hundred German marks. There must be at least one manager (*Geschäftsführer*);
he may be one of the partners, although another person may be appointed. The corporation must be registered in the mercantile register at the *Amtsgericht* within the
jurisdiction of which it has its seat. It comes into existence by the registration.
Those who act for the corporation before its registration are personally and jointly
liable.

The corporation has a legal personality. It is liable for its obligations with all
its property. It is a business corporation within the meaning of the Commercial
Code.

The shares of the members are inheritable and may be disposed of with the
permission of the corporation. The transfer must be made in a notarized act. The
members are entitled to profits in accordance with their interests in the corporation.

The corporation is represented by the managers (*Geschäftsführer*). They are
appointed and removed by the members. They conduct the business of the
corporation and are bound to keep the books. They must prepare a profit and loss
account and a balance sheet within three months after the expiration of every
business year. They must use the care of a reasonable businessman (*Sorgfalt eines
ordentlichen Geschäftsmannes*) and are jointly liable to the corporation for its
breach.

The corporation does not need to have a supervisory board (*Aufsichtsrat*). The
contract of association should make the provision; if it provides for a supervisory
board, the board is governed by the provisions of the *Aktiengesetz* applicable to the
supervisory board unless otherwise provided in the contract of association.

The members of the corporation approve the balance sheet, appoint and
remove the managers, supervise the management, represent the corporation against
the management, and so on. They decide by majority vote in the meeting of
members. Every one hundred German marks of the corporation's capital has a vote.
The meetings are called by the managers, but members holding 10 percent of the
capital may request a meeting to be called. If it is not so called, they may call it themselves.

The contract of association may be amended by the decision of the members.
The vote requires a three-fourths majority.

The corporation is dissolved by the running of time, if it was set up only for a
particular time; by the decision of its members having a three-fourths majority; by
order of a court or of an administrative court; or by the declaration of bankruptcy.
After being dissolved, the corporation is then liquidated either by the managers or,
in the case of bankruptcy, in bankruptcy proceedings. Where the corporation is
liquidated by its managers, they must conclude the corporation's business, convert

all assets to money, pay all creditors, and distribute the net surplus among the members in accordance with their interests in the corporation. They must prepare a balance sheet at the beginning of the liquidation and at the end of every year. The books and records of the corporation must be preserved for ten years in the custody of one of its members or another person as determined by the court.

NOTES AND QUESTIONS

This is a very widely used type of German corporation. It is the counterpart of the English company called proprietary limited. It is suitable for a family holding; at the same time, its capital may be very substantial. The law thus enables a small group of persons, like a family, to have the advantages of individual holding while absolving them of personal liability. Like the English proprietary limited company, the German corporation with limited liability is modeled on the stock corporation, but its provisions are made suitable to ownership by a small group. It must have only one manager and does not need to have a supervisory board. All decisions are made by the members.

Compare the German corporation with limited liability with its French, Italian and Spanish counterparts.

Does the American law provide for a similar type of corporation? Is an American stock corporation also suitable for a family or small group holding? *See*, e.g., New York Business Corporation Law §§701, 702.

---

5. The Law of Exchange (*Wechselrecht und Scheckrecht*)

Germany is party to the Geneva convention of June 7, 1930, concerning bills of exchange (*Wechsel*). The provisions of the convention were incorporated into German law by the *Wechselgesetz* of June 21, 1933 (RGBl. I S. 399). Germany is also party to the Geneva convention of March 19, 1931, concerning checks (*Scheck*). The provisions of that convention were incorporated into German law by the *Scheckgesetz* of August 14, 1933 (RGBl. I S. 597).

NOTES

Since the Geneva conventions on bills of exchange and on checks have not been adopted in the English-speaking world, there are two systems in existence in the world: (1) the system of the Geneva conventions, which extends virtually over the whole world with the exception of the English-speaking countries, and (2) the individual systems in power in the various English-speaking countries. Both systems are founded on the commercial practice that developed centuries ago in Europe and are therefore very similar. There are, however, differences. For the American law, *see* UCC, Arts. 3, 4, and 5. *See also*, e.g., United States v. Guaranty Trust Co. of New York, 293 U.S. 340, 55 S. Ct. 221, (1934); Weissman v. Banque de Bruxelles, 254 N.Y. 488, 173 N.E. 835 (Ct. App. N.Y. 1930); and UCC 4-102 (2).

---

6. The Law of Bankruptcy
(*Konkursrecht*)

The law deals separately with bankruptcy and with composition with creditors.

(a) Bankruptcy (*Konkurs*).[55]

(i) INITIATION OF BANKRUPTCY PROCEEDINGS (*Eröffnungsverfahren*). Bankruptcy proceedings are initiated on the petition of the debtor or one of his creditors to the *Amtsgericht* within the jurisdiction of which the business of the debtor has its seat. The proceedings are governed by provisions of the Code of Civil Procedure unless otherwise provided.

The court makes a declaration of bankruptcy and notes the hour of the declaration. Failing the determination of the hour, the declaration is considered to have been made at noon. The order appoints a receiver (*Verwalter*) whose duty it is to take possession of the assets and convert them into money. He acts under the supervision of the court. He must prepare an inventory of the assets and a balance sheet. The declaration of bankruptcy is published in the daily press and is recorded in the proper registers as the case demands, e.g., in the mercantile register, the land register, the ship register, and so forth.

The creditors must submit their claims within a term of from two weeks to three months, as directed by the court. A claim is admitted if it is not disputed by the debtor, the receiver or a creditor. Disputed claims are settled by the court.

The receiver is assisted by a committee of creditors elected by the meeting of creditors. The meeting of creditors is called and conducted by the court. Creditors whose claims have been admitted take part. The meeting of creditors decides by majority of claims and, in the case of a tie, by majority of creditors. The meeting of creditors decides on the size of support payments to the debtor and whether the business should be salvaged and operated or wound up. It may give the receiver authority to sell certain assets or the entire business of the debtor.

The creditors may challenge all dealings of the debtor undertaken after the discontinuation of payments or after the date of the bankruptcy petition. They may also challenge all dealings of the debtor made with a party who knew that they were undertaken in order to damage the creditors. They may further challenge all uncompensated dealings of the debtor undertaken within one year before the declaration of bankruptcy with his spouse, whether before or after the celebration of marriage, and with his or his spouse's lineal relatives, with his and his spouse's brothers and sisters of the half or full blood, or with the spouses of such persons. They may challenge all gifts made by the debtor in the last year before the declaration of bankruptcy, and all gifts made to his spouse in the last two years before the declaration of bankruptcy. Dealings undertaken earlier than six months before the declaration of bankruptcy may not be challenged on the ground that the other party knew that the debtor had discontinued payments.

Bankruptcy proceedings may be discontinued when it appears that there are not enough assets to pay for the costs of the proceedings. In that case, title to the assets passes to the debtor. The proper order to discontinue the proceedings is made by the court.

(ii) COMPULSORY COMPOSITION WITH CREDITORS (*Zwangsvergleich*). After the claims of the creditors are established, the debtor may request a compulsory composition with ordinary creditors. To achieve this, the debtor must propose a reasonable way of settlement with the creditors and must offer at least a 20 percent dividend. The offer may not be accepted where the debtor has absconded or is being prosecuted for, or was convicted of, a fraudulent bankruptcy. The offer must be accepted by a three-fourths majority of the claims and a majority of the creditors. It then must be approved by the court. Where so approved, the composition is effected and is binding on all ordinary creditors. The bankruptcy proceedings are then terminated.

(iii) DISTRIBUTION OF PROCEEDS (*Verteilung*). Preferred creditors are paid independently by the receiver with approval of the court. Ordinary creditors are paid a dividend from the mass.

The debts of the bankruptcy proceedings (*Masseschulden*), like claims arising out of the acts of the receiver, are paid first. Then the costs of the bankruptcy proceedings (*Massekosten*) are paid. These are mainly court costs, expenses of the administration, sale of the assets and distribution of the proceeds, and support payments to the bankrupt and his family.

Then come the actual claims against the debtor. Where they cannot be paid in full, they are paid in equal dividend within each rank. The wages of employees of the bankrupt accrued in the last year before the declaration of bankruptcy rank first. Taxes and rates rank second. The claims of public institutions and fire insurance premiums for the last year before the declaration of bankruptcy rank third. The claims of physicians, veterinarians, pharmacists, nurses, and others for medical care incurred in the last year before the declaration of bankruptcy rank fourth. The claims of children or persons in the care of the bankrupt to recover their property administered by the bankrupt rank fifth. All other claims rank sixth.

The distribution, which takes places as soon as the assets have been converted into money, must be approved by the court.

The court then sets a time between three weeks and one month for the receiver to present his final balance sheet, for objections to be filed, and for the decision of the creditors to be made with respect to those asssets that the receiver was unable to convert into money. Thereafter the court makes an order lifting the bankruptcy. The order is made public in the daily press and recorded in the proper registers. After the bankruptcy is lifted, all bankruptcy creditors who were not paid in full may proceed against the debtor individually.

(iv) CRIMINAL PROVISIONS (*Strafbestimmungen*). A debtor may be held guilty of fraudulent bankruptcy (*betrügerischer Bankrott*) if he conceals assets, admits to nonexisting debts, does not carry books that he is bound to carry by law, or destroys or alters such books.

A debtor may be held guilty of a simple bankruptcy (*einfacher Bankrott*) if he squanders his property by excessive spending, gaming and betting, or speculation on the stock exchange; if he delays the institution of bankruptcy proceedings by selling property below its value to obtain cash; if he does not carry, or properly carry, books that he is required to carry by law, or if he does not prepare a balance sheet at the proper time.

A debtor may further be found guilty of favoritism to creditors (*Gläubigerbe-*

günstigung) if he pays a particular creditor after he discontinues other payments or after the declaration of bankruptcy.

A creditor, on the other hand, may be found guilty of favoritism to a debtor (*Schuldnerbegünstigung*) if, after the debtor discontinues payments or after the declaration of bankruptcy, the creditor conceals assets of the debtor or makes unfounded claims in the bankruptcy proceedings in order to favor the bankrupt. A creditor may also be found guilty of selling his vote, i.e., of voting in a way favoring the debtor or other persons for value (*Stimmenverkauf*).

The prosecution takes place in criminal proceedings before criminal courts.

(b) Composition with creditors (*Vergleich*).[56]

(i) INITIATION OF PROCEEDINGS (*Eröffnung des Verfahrens*).   Proceedings are initiated on the debtor's petition. The petition must state whether, within the last five years, the debtor already had a composition with his creditors. It must further provide information on the situation of the debtor's business, including a profit and loss account and a balance sheet; give a list of his creditors and debtors; indicate whether within the last year there was a settlement of property between him and his spouse or his close relatives; and show whether within the last two years he made gifts to his spouse or his close relatives.[57] The petition must further contain a proposal for the composition that may not offer less than 35 percent of the claims. Where the debtor proposes to make payment only a year or more from the approval of the composition, he must offer at least 40 percent, and where he proposes to pay after eighteen months, he must offer more than 40 percent.

The petition is submitted to the *Amtsgericht* within the jurisdiction of which the debtor's business has its seat. The court will immediately appoint a provisional trustee (*vorläufiger Verwalter*) and consults with the professional association of the industry, trade or craft within which the debtor's business falls.

The court will deny the petition where the debtor did not comply with the above requirements; where he has absconded or is being proceeded against because of fraudulent bankruptcy, where his business went bankrupt or where he petitioned for composition with his creditors within the last five years from the day of the petition; where there are not enough assets to pay the costs of the proceedings; where his records are not well kept so that the position of his business cannot be properly assessed; where he brought about the failure of his business by lack of honesty, selling below the price, or lack of care; where he delayed in bringing the petition; where his offer is not realistic in that it offers too little or too much in view of the financial condition of his business; and where his business is not expected to survive.

If the court denies the petition, it must also decide whether bankruptcy proceedings should be initiated. If it grants the petition, the court appoints a trustee (*Vergleichsverwalter*) and sets a date for a hearing on the composition proposal. It also gives the hour of the initiation of the composition proceedings. If the hour is not given, the proceedings are considered initiated at noon on the day on which the order was made. The order is recorded in the mercantile register and published by the court.

(ii) COMPOSITION PROCEEDINGS (*Vergleichsverfahren*).   Secured creditors do not take part in the proceedings. Unsecured creditors must make known their claims. A claim is admitted when it is not contested by the debtor, the trustee, or another creditor. A contest is decided by the court.

The trustee must supervise the conduct of the debtor's business and report to the court. He stands under the supervision of the court. He is assisted by a committee of the creditors (*Gläubigerbeirat*) appointed by the court.

The meeting of creditors considers the composition proposal of the debtor. To be accepted, it must receive the approval of the majority of the debtors representing at least three-fourths of all claims. Where the debtor offers less than 50 percent, at least four-fifths of the claims must approve of the plan. Where only one of the majorities is reached, the debtor may request a new vote at a later day. Three fourths of the claims must approve of the adjournment.

Where the composition proposal is accepted by the creditors, it then must be approved by the court. The court will consult with the trustee and the committee of creditors before making a decision. It must disapprove of the plan where the debtor has absconded or is being proceeded against for fraudulent bankruptcy; where the approval of the creditors was improperly obtained, especially where it favors some creditors; and where it is not to the general good of all the creditors. If the court denies approval, it must immediately decide whether bankruptcy proceedings should be initiated. If it does not declare bankruptcy, the office of the trustee and the committee of creditors come to an end. If it declares bankruptcy, bankruptcy proceedings take over from then on. They are known as bankruptcy annexed to composition proceedings (*Anschlusskonkurs*).

If the court approves the composition as accepted by the creditors, the composition is valid against all creditors. The creditors are entitled to have their claims paid in the proportion defined in the composition plan.

(iii) TERMINATION OF PROCEEDINGS (*Aufhebung des Verfahrens*). Where the court approves the composition, the trustee and the committee of creditors see to it that the debtor pays in accordance with the plan. Composition proceedings are terminated by order of the court when the trustee reports that the debtor has performed the agreement.

The court may, however, terminate the composition proceedings upon request of the creditors after the composition plan is approved by the court.

The court must terminate the composition proceedings when the debtor requests it. He may do so any time before the conclusion of the voting of the creditors on his composition proposal. The court must also terminate the proceedings where the debtor has absconded, where he does not abide by the limitations imposed on him by the court, where he does not allow the trustee or members of the committee of creditors to inspect his books or does not provide them with information, where he does not live modestly, or where his composition proposal does not obtain the required majority in the meeting of creditors.

NOTES AND QUESTIONS

1. The German law makes a fundamental distinction between bankruptcy and composition with creditors. Is this distinction made in the same strong fashion in the laws of France? Bankruptcy acts in English-speaking countries do not usually make such strongly worded distinctions, instead they allow the debtor to make a

proposal for composition or arrangement with his creditors. *See*, e.g., F.C.A. (Federal Code Annotated) 11 §701ff.

2. In Germany, the petition is filed with the *Amtsgericht.* Are there special bankruptcy courts in other countries? Compare, e.g., France and Italy. *See also* F.C.A. 11 §11.

The bankruptcy procedure is governed in Germany by the Code of Civil Procedure. Does the same rule obtain in France? Compare also USCS (U.S. Code Service) Rules of Bankruptcy.

3. Who are the officers in bankruptcy? Compare F.C.A. 11 §61ff.; Bankruptcy Rules, Rule 501ff.

What are the powers of the creditors? *See*, e.g., the Italian law. Compare F.C.A. 11 §91ff.; Bankruptcy Rules, Rule 204.

Is there any provision in the law of other countries comparable to the German compulsory composition with creditors?

4. Note the German rules as to final distribution of the proceeds. Compare, e.g., F.C.A. 11 §§104-106; Bankruptcy Rules, Rules 301-310.

What is the effect of the discharge of the bankrupt? *See*, e.g., the French law. Compare also F.C.A. 11 § 32ff.; Bankruptcy Rules, Rules 404-409.

5. Bankruptcy offenses are usually listed in the bankruptcy statutes and also in the penal codes. *See*, e.g., the Spanish law. *See also* 11 U.S.C.A. §11 (4); New York Penal Law §185.00; 18 U.S.C.A. §151ff.

---

7.   Maritime Law (*Seerecht*)[58]

(a)   The shipowner (*Reeder*).[59]   The shipowner may be a partnership or a corporation. Where there are several co-owners (*Mitreeder*), the ownership is known as a *Reederei.*

The shipowner may appoint a ship's husband (*Korrespondentreeder*) to manage the ship. He then represents the owner against the ship and third parties and must use the care of a reasonable shipowner (*Sorgfalt eines ordentlichen Reeders*).

The owner is liable to third parties for loss or damage caused by the ship and the ship's personnel, including a pilot. He may limit liability in accordance with the provisions of the Brussels convention of October 10, 1957 (BGBl. 1972 II S. 653) concerning limitation of liability of owners of seagoing vessels. The amount to which liability may be limited is 3,100 units (gold francs) per ton, containing 65.5 milligrams of gold of 900/1000 gold content for claims including death, bodily injury or property damage; and 1,000 units (gold francs) of the same description for claims for property damage only.

(b)   The master (*Kapitän*).[60]   The master is in charge of the ship. He is required to use the care of a reasonable master (*Sorgfalt eines ordentlichen Kapitäns*). He is liable for all losses that arise due to his fault, and especially for those arising due to his breach of provisions of the Commercial Code. He is liable not only to the owner but also to the shipper, the consignee, the stevedores, the passengers, and the crew. He cannot escape liability if he acted on the instruction of the owner. The owner is also liable if he knew the facts at the time he gave the instruction.

It is the duty of the master to see to it that the ship is seaworthy, properly stocked and equipped, with a proper crew and with all required documents aboard at the beginning of the voyage. He must make sure that the ship is not overloaded, and he must comply with all foreign regulations when abroad. In case of danger, he may call the ship's council (*Schiffsrat*), even though it has only an advisory capacity. He must make all the decisions and is liable for them. He must enter into the logbook (*Tagebuch*) all accidents that occur.

Dealings undertaken by the master in the home port are binding on the owner only if he gave the master a power of attorney. Outside of the home port, however, the master may bind the owner in all matters falling within his apparent authority.

The master is appointed and removed by the owner, but where the owner has appointed a ship's husband, the power to appoint and remove the master passes to him. The master then deals only with the ship's husband, who represents the owner.

(c) **Carriage of goods and passengers by sea** (*Frachtgeschäft zur Beförderung von Gütern und Reisenden*).[61]   The Commercial Code has detailed rules as to carriage of goods and passengers by sea. It provides for charter parties (*Charterpartien*), for the liability of the charterer (*Verfrachter*) and for rules governing the carriage of goods, including delivery to the vessel, loading, unloading, dangerous cargo, and bills of lading.

A passenger may not assign his right entitling him to transport to another person. He is not entitled to any refund if he misses the departure of the vessel. Where the passenger dies or is unable to undertake the voyage before the beginning of the voyage and the fact is properly communicated to the vessel, he is liable only for one half of the fare. He may not obtain any refund after the beginning of the voyage. Where the ship must undergo repairs during the voyage, the passenger must be taken care of by the ship. He may be offered equivalent transport; if he refuses it, the duty of the ship to furnish food and lodging comes to an end.

(d) **Average, collision, salvage, maritime liens, and marine insurance.**[62]   The Commercial Code carries detailed provisions concerning general and special average (*grosse und besondere Haverei*).[63] Both ship and cargo take part in general and special average.

With respect to collision (*Zusammenstoss von Schiffen*),[64] in a collision caused by accident or *force majeure*, or where the cause cannot be ascertained, the loss lies where it falls, and no claim with respect to damage to ship and cargo or personal injury to persons aboard may be made against the other ship. Where the collision is caused by the fault of one of the ships, the owner thereof must make good the loss of the other. Where the collision occurs due to the concurrent faults of both ships, their owners are liable in proportion to their respective faults in causing the collision. Where such faults appear equal, or where the respective proportions of fault cannot be ascertained, they are liable equally. Where personal injury or death occurs in a collision caused by the concurrent faults of both ships, the shipowners are liable to the injured or dead jointly; among themselves, however, they are liable only in proportion to the respective faults of the ships in causing the collision. The ship is liable for the negligence of a pilot. The owner may limit liability in accordance with the provisions of the Brussels convention, mentioned above.

With respect to salvage (*Bergung*),[65] the Commercial Code has detailed provisions concerning salvage and the reward paid to salvors. The reward is determined equitably. Where a ship or cargo is salvaged by another ship, the reward is determined for the salvage as a whole. Out of the amount so set, the owner of the ship engaged in the salvage operation is compensated first for any damage or loss occasioned thereby; the remainder then is partitioned among the owner, who receives two thirds, the master, one sixth, and the crew, one sixth. The one sixth going to the crew is distributed by the master in accordance with a scheme rewarding the individual effort of particular crewmembers. Those who engaged in saving persons participate in the fund. Persons saved are not required or expected to pay for the help given to them.

With respect to maritime liens (*Pfandrechte der Schiffsgläubiger*),[66] they are extinguished after one year has run from the moment of their creation unless they are enforced against the vessel. The order of priority is as follows: (1) claims of the master and the crew; (2) maritime taxes, rates, harbor taxes, and claims of pilots for their services; (3) claims for death or injury of persons and loss or damage of property arising out of the operation of the ship; (4) salvage claims, contributions of ship and cargo to general average, and claims for removal of shipwreck; and (5) claims of persons entitled under social security, including unemployment claims against the shipowner. Claims listed under (4) have priority over all claims arising earlier. Claims listed under (1), (2), (3), and (5) rank equally within their respective groups without regard to the point in time when they arose. Claims under (4) rank among themselves in inverted order, so that those arising later outrank those arising earlier, and those arising simultaneously rank equally.

The Commercial Code has exhaustive provisions concerning marine insurance (*Versicherung gegen die Gefahren der Seeschiffahrt*).[67] Any interest that may be expressed in money is insurable. Policies may be written for the account of whom it may concern. The insurer needs not pay for a loss that arises to ship or cargo when the ship was unseaworthy, not properly stocked or equipped, not properly manned, or without the required documents aboard at the beginning of the voyage. He does not need to pay for any damage to the ship and its appurtenances that arises through usual wear and tear, aging, rot or worms. He does not need to pay for damage to cargo that occurs through spoilage, shrinkage, leakage and the like, results from improper packing, or that is due to rats or mice.

(e) Limitation of time (*Verjährung*).[68]   With respect to limitation of time, the Commercial Code provides for a one-year limitation on claims for maritime taxes, rates, and harbor taxes; claims of pilots for their services; contributions to general average; claims against the owner or charterer out of contracts for the carriage of goods and out of bills of lading; and the claim of a shipowner against another shipowner to recover monies paid in excess of his share of fault in a collision for personal injuries or death.

A two-year limitation applies to claims against the owner or charterer out of contracts for the carriage of passengers, claims for damages arising out of collision, claims for salvage, and claims for compensation for having removed a shipwreck.

A five-year limitation applies to claims arising to the insurer and the insured from a contract of marine insurance. The time begins to run from the end of the year in which the insured voyage came to an end or, in time insurance, from the end of the day on which the insurance period ended. In the case of disappearance of the ship, limitation begins to run from the end of a period of time determined by the Commercial Code within which the ship should have arrived at its destination, known as *Verschollenheitsfrist.*[69]

The one-year and two-year limitations begin to run from the end of the year within which the claim accrued. Limitation with respect to claims for damages arising out of collision begins to run from the end of the day on which the event took place. Limitation with respect to claims arising out of salvage or for compensation for having removed a shipwreck begins to run from the end of the day on which the work was completed.

NOTES

1. While the German law of admiralty is codified, the Anglo-American law of admiralty is founded overwhelmingly on decisions of admiralty courts.

Due to large sums of money needed in shipping, the owners are always corporations. Note the limitation of liability of owners for loss of life and property at sea pursuant to the Brussels convention. The United States is not a party to the convention, but a comparable effect was achieved by legislation. *See* the Limitation of Shipowners' Liability Act, 46 U.S.C.A. §§181-189; the Harter Act, 46 U.S.C.A. §§190-195; and the Carriage of Goods by Sea Act, 46 U.S.C.A. §§1300-1312.

Note the German provisions concerning the master. Compare them with those of the French and the Spanish law. As to the so-called Home Port Doctrine, *see*, e.g., The Lottawana, 88 U.S. 558 (1875) and The Federal Maritime Lien Act, 46 U.S.C.A. §§971-975.

2. Carriage of goods and passengers by sea is probably the bulk of admiralty law. The Anglo-American law rests on innumerable court decisions and on a number of statutes, among them the above-referred to Harter Act and Carriage of Goods by Sea Act.

3. The German rules with respect to collision conform to the Brussels International Convention of September 23, 1910. The United States is not party to the convention, but a similar effect was achieved by the decision of the United States Supreme Court in United States v. Reliable Transfer Co. 421 U.S. 397, 95 S. Ct. 1708 (1975), which overruled the long standing rule in The Schooner Catharine v. Dickinson, 58 U.S. 170 (1854).

4. Salvage is governed in Anglo-American law by the decisions of admiralty courts and by statutes, *see*, e.g., The Salvage Act, 46 U.S.C.A. §§727-731.

The same applies to maritime liens. Compare The Federal Maritime Lien Act, 46 U.S.C.A. §§971-975.

5. As to limitation of actions, the Anglo-American law does not have any generally applicable statute of limitation but relies rather on the doctrine of laches, which also holds that every claim must be enforced within reasonable time. There are, however, statutes of limitation built in particular statutes dealing with

individual situations, like the Death on the High Seas Act, 46 U.S.C.A. §§761-766 and The Salvage Act, 46 U.S.C.A. §§727-731.

C. THE SYSTEM OF CIVIL COURTS

There are county courts (*Amtsgerichte*), district courts (*Landgerichte*), courts of appeal (*Oberlandesgerichte*), and one court of final resort (*Bundesgerichtshof*). *Landgerichte* form commercial chambers in commercial matters. There is also an independent system of labor courts (*Arbeitsgerichte*).

1. County Courts (*Amtsgerichte*)[70]

Amtsgerichte are limited jurisdiction courts whose territorial jurisdiction is determined by law. Each *Amtsgericht* is headed by a presiding judge (*Präsident*) and has a number of judges (*Richter*) on its staff. The court actually hearing a case consists of a single judge. The court hears cases up to a value determined by law (3,000 German marks) as well as specially designated cases irrespective of the value of the subject matter involved, e.g., those dealing with disputes between landlord and tenant, disputes between travelers on the one hand and innkeepers and carriers on the other arising out of payment for services or the damage or loss of luggage or property, disputes between travelers and repairmen arising in connection with travel, and disputes concerning alleged defects in animals, damage done by wild animals, and paternity cases.

Within *Amtsgerichte* determined by the state ministries of justice in every German state, a family court (*Familiengericht*) is set up to handle all family matters. Family matters are all matrimonial matters, including nullity and divorce, alimony for the former spouse, disputes concerning property of the spouses, and custody and support of children. The family court is staffed by family judges (*Familienrichter*).[71]

An appeal (*Berufung*) against judgments of an *Amtsgericht* must be filed with the proper Landgericht within one month from notification of the judgment. When the jurisdiction of the *Amtsgericht* is founded on the value of the subject matter, an appeal may be filed only where the judgment orders the payment of a sum exceeding a minimum determined by law (500 German marks). A complaint (*Beschwerde*) against rulings of the *Amtsgericht* must be filed with the court within a time provided by law in accordance with the nature of the ruling, usually within two weeks from its notification. The *Amtsgericht* may grant the request and rescind or modify its ruling, or it must transmit the complaint within one week to the proper *Landgericht* for its decision, which is final. In paternity and family cases, the appeal or the complaint goes to the proper *Oberlandesgericht* under the same conditions, thus by-passing the *Landgericht*.

A judgment of an *Amtsgericht* is also subject to a petition of nullity (*Nichtigkeitsklage*) and a petition of restitution (*Restitutionsklage*). Such petitions must be brought within one month from discovery of the ground for nullity or restitution and may not be brought after five years have elapsed from the time when the judgment entered into the power of law.

Parties before an *Amtsgericht* may appear by themselves, they may appoint another person under a power of attorney to represent them, or they may engage the services of an attorney (*Rechtsanwalt*) admitted to practice before it.

2.   District Courts (*Landgerichte*)[72]

The *Landgericht* is a general jurisdiction court whose territorial jurisdiction is determined by law. It is headed by a president (*Präsident*) and has a number of presiding judges (*vorsitzende Richter*) and judges (*Richter*) on its staff. The court hearing a case is a chamber (*Kammer*) of three judges, including the presiding judge. Decision is by simple majority. In the exercise of its original jurisdiction, and in cases that are not too involved and do not deal with a legal matter of fundamental importance, the court may, ex officio, appoint a single judge to hear and decide the case.

In the exercise of its original jurisdiction, the court hears cases, irrespective of value, that exceed the jurisdiction of the *Amtsgericht*, and all other cases that are not specifically assigned to the *Amtsgericht*.

In its appellate jurisdiction, the *Landgericht* hears appeals (*Berufungen*) against judgments (*Urteile*) and complaints (*Beschwerden*) against rulings (*Beschlüsse*) of the particular *Amtsgerichte* located within the area of its territorial jurisdiction, with the exception of paternity and family cases.

In the exercise of its original and appellate jurisdiction in commercial cases, the *Landgericht* forms a commercial chamber (*Handelskammer*). The chamber is presided over by a presiding judge and has two businessmen as its members. Decision is by simple majority. The businessmen are appointed for a term of three years at the recommendation of the Chamber of Industry and Commerce. They must be registered merchants, or members of management of a corporation that is so registered, and must be thirty years of age or older. Commercial cases are those based on provisions of the Commercial Code.[73] They are brought before the commercial chamber at the petition of the plaintiff. A defendant may have a case removed to the commercial chamber only if he is a registered merchant.

No further appeal nor error lies against judgments of *Landgerichte* given in the exercise of their appellate jurisdiction. A judgment of a *Landgericht* is subject, however, to a petition of nullity (*Nichtigkeitsklage*) and a petition of restitution (*Restitutionsklage*). Such petitions must be brought within one month from discovery of the ground for nullity or restitution and may not be brought after five years have elapsed from the time when the judgment entered into the power of law.

Against judgments (*Urteile*) of *Landgerichte* in the exercise of their original jurisdiction, an appeal (*Berufung*) lies to the proper court of appeal (*Oberlandesgericht*). It must be filed with the *Oberlandesgericht* within one month from notification of the judgment. Similarly, a complaint (*Beschwerde*) lies against rulings (*Beschlüsse*) of the *Landgericht*. It must be filed, however, with the *Landgericht* within a time provided by law in accordance with the nature of the ruling, usually within two weeks from its notification. The *Landgericht* may grant the request and rescind or modify the ruling, or it must transmit the complaint within one week to the proper *Oberlandesgericht* for its decision, which is final.[74]

The parties may agree, however, to by-pass the *Oberlandesgericht* and bring an error, known as *Sprungrevision*, directly to the *Bundesgerichtshof*. It must be filed with the *Bundesgerichtshof* within one month from notification of the judgment. The *Bundesgerichtshof* may deny admissibility of the error where the legal problem involved is not of fundamental importance. The error may not be founded on procedural defects.

Parties before a *Landgericht* must be represented by attorneys (*Rechtsanwälte*) admitted to practice before it.

NOTES AND QUESTIONS

1. *Amtsgerichte* are limited jurisdiction courts, but they exercise jurisdiction exceeding that of the British petty sessions courts or the American city courts, justice's courts, or corporation courts. Are they roughly comparable to the Anglo-American county courts? What about the family court which sits within the German *Amtsgericht* and has full jurisdiction of an Anglo-American divorce court?

Compare the powers of the *Amtsgericht* with those of the Italian *pretura* and the French court of instance. Which of these three courts has the most extensive powers?

How does the German *Amtsgericht* compare with the county court of your state? *See*, e.g., New York Judiciary Law §190ff.

Note that appeals against *Amtsgerichte* go to *Landgerichte* and not to courts of appeal. Each *Landgericht* has an appellate chamber to hear such appeals. How is the matter handled in France? To which court does an appeal go from the decision of an American county court? *See*, e.g., New York Civil Practice Law and Rules §5701.

Note that parties may always appear by themselves without any legal representation.

2. *Landgerichte* are typical general jurisdiction courts in civil matters with respect to their original jurisdiction. They do not have jurisdiction in family matters. Compare their powers with the Spanish courts of first instance or with the French courts of grande instance. How do they compare with the Anglo-American courts of general jurisdiction, like the Texas District Courts, British Supreme Courts, and the supreme courts of many American states? Do these Anglo-American courts also exercise appellate jurisdiction or are they purely trial courts?

The *Landgericht* also forms a commercial chamber to hear commercial cases. Does the same practice exist in Italy or in Spain? Does it exist in any of the Anglo-American jurisdictions? Which courts hear commercial cases in Britain and in the American states?

How does the jurisdiction of a *Landgericht* compare with that of a United States District Court? *See* 28 U.S.C.A. §1330ff.

To which court may the parties appeal from the decisions of a *Landgericht*? How does it compare with appeals from the French court of grand instance? To which courts do you appeal from decisions of an Anglo-American trial court of general jurisdiction?

Note that parties must be represented by attorneys in the *Landgericht*. Does the same rule obtain in other civil law countries? Must parties be represented by attorneys in the Anglo-American general jurisdiction courts? *See*, e.g., 28 U.S.C.A. §1654.

As to the judges and attorneys in the German system, consult the section on legal officers below.

---

3. Courts of Appeal (*Oberlandesgerichte*)[75]

A court of appeal (*Oberlandesgericht*) is headed by a president (*Präsident*) and has a number of presiding judges (*vorsitzende Richter*) and judges (*Richter*) on its staff. The court hearing a case is a panel (*Senat*) of three judges, including the presiding judge. Decision is by simple majority.

The court hears appeals (*Berufungen*) against judgments (*Urteile*) and complaints (*Beschwerden*) against rulings (*Beschlüsse*) of *Amtsgerichte* in paternity and family cases, and appeals against judgments and complaints against rulings of *Landgerichte* given by them in the exercise of their original jurisdiction. The appeals and complaints reach an *Oberlandesgericht* from the *Amtsgerichte* and *Landgerichte* located within its area of territorial jurisdiction.

No further appeal lies against judgments of the court, but error (*Revision*) may be brought in cases involving property rights where the value of the subject matter exceeds a certain minimum sum (40,000 German marks) or with leave of the *Oberlandesgericht* granted in the judgment. The *Oberlandesgericht* must grant the leave where the legal problem involved is of fundamental importance, or when its decision differs from a previous decision of the *Bundesgerichtshof*. Error without leave and without regard to the value of the subject matter may be brought against those final judgments of an *Oberlandesgericht* that deny admissibility of an appeal from judgments of a *Landgericht* given in the exercise of its original jurisdiction. In cases involving property rights where the value of the subject matter exceeds 40,000 German marks, the *Bundesgerichtshof* may deny admissibility of the error when the legal problem involved is not of fundamental importance. A two-thirds majority of votes is required for the denial.

Against decisions of an *Oberlandesgericht* on complaints (*Beschwerden*) in family matters, a further complaint (*weitere Beschwerde*) may be brought directly to the *Bundesgerichtshof* within one month from the notification.

Error (*Revision*) against judgments of an *Oberlandesgericht* must be filed with the *Bundesgerichtshof* within one month from the notification.

A judgment of an *Oberlandesgericht* is subject to a petition of nullity (*Nichtigkeitsklage*) and to a petition of restitution (*Restitutionsklage*) under standard conditions applicable to these petitions.

Parties before an *Oberlandesgericht* must be represented by attorneys (*Rechtsanwälte*) admitted to practice before it.

4. Supreme Court (*Bundesgerichtshof*)[76]

This is the supreme court of the law; it is located in the city of Karlsruhe.[77] It is headed by a president (*Präsident*) and it has several presiding judges (*vorsitzende Richter*) and judges (*Richter*) on its staff. The Court hears a case as a panel (*Senat*) of five judges, including the presiding judge. Decision is by simple majority.

The Court also forms a large senate (*grosser Senat*) in civil matters and another in criminal matters. The *grosser Senat* is presided over by the president of the court or his deputy and has another eight members. Decision is by simple majority. Since the presiding judge of the *Senat* from which the matter was referred to the *grosser Senat* may also sit on the *grosser Senat* and thus produce an even number of members, the president has a casting vote in the case of a tie. The Court further forms a united large senate (*vereinigte grosse Senate*), which is presided over by the president of the court or his deputy and has all members of both large senates as members. Decision is by simple majority and the president has a casting vote.

The large senate in civil matters (*grosser Senat für Zivilsachen*) has jurisdiction where a senate in civil matters (*Zivilsenat*) wishes to give a decision that would differ from a previously given decision of another *Zivilsenat* or the *grosser Senat für Zivilsachen*, or where a *Zivilsenat* considers the matter of fundamental importance and refers it to the *grosser Senat für Zivilsachen* for its decision.

The united large senate (*vereinigte grosse Senate*) has jurisdiction where a senate in civil matters (*Zivilsenat*) wishes to give a decision that would differ from a previously given decision of a senate in criminal matters (*Strafsenat*) or the large senate in criminal matters (*grosser Senat für Strafsachen*), or vice versa, or where a *Zivilsenat* or *Strafsenat* wishes to give a decision that would differ from a previously given decision of the *vereinigte grosse Senate*.

One of the chief functions of the *Bundesgerichtshof* is thus to uphold the uniformity of the application of the law in the country.

The Court hears error (*Revision*) against judgments (*Uteile*) of *Oberlandesgerichte* and *Sprungrevision* against judgments of *Landgerichte*. It also hears complaints (*Beschwerden*) against the denial of appeal by an *Oberlandesgericht* and further complaints (*weitere Beschwerden*) against a decision on complaints (*Beschwerden*) by an *Oberlandesgericht* in family matters.

No further remedy lies against decisions of the *Bundesgerichtshof,* but its judgments are subject to petitions of nullity (*Nichtigkeitsklagen*) and petitions of restitution (*Restitutionsklagen*) under standard conditions applicable to these petitions.

In hearing error, the Court may uphold the judgment attacked, or it may quash it. When it quashes a judgment where no further proceedings are required, it will give its own judgment in the matter. Otherwise it will remit the matter for further proceedings to the *Oberlandesgericht* against whose judgment the error was brought. In the case of *Sprungrevision*, it may remit the matter to the *Landgericht* or to the *Oberlandesgericht* within whose territorial jurisdiction the *Landgericht* is situated.

Parties before the Court must be represented by attorneys (*Rechtsanwälte*) admitted to practice before it.

NOTES AND QUESTIONS

1. The *Oberlandesgericht* is a court of appeal. Note that it also hears appeals in family matters. Compare its jurisdiction with that of the Spanish *audiencias territoriales.* How does it compare with the appellate courts in your state? *See,* e.g., New York Judiciary Law §70ff.; New York Civil Practice Law and Rules §5701ff.; 28 U.S.C.A. §1291ff.

What remedies lie against decisions of the *Oberlandesgericht*? Compare, e.g., remedies against decisions of Italian courts of appeal. To which court may an Anglo-American suitor proceed with his case in comparable circumstances?

2. The German Supreme Court is a federal court, but the German system of courts is as unitary as, e.g., the system in France. Note the elaborate system of panels to give consistent decisions and to keep the law uniform throughout the country. It is a court of error. Compare its function with the Italian Court of Cassation. How does the *Bundesgerichtshof* compare with the highest court in Anglo-American jurisdictions, like the highest state courts, the English House of Lords and the U.S. Supreme Court? *See*, e.g., New York Const., Art. VI. §2; New York Civil Practice Law and Rules §5601ff.; U.S. Const., Art. III. sec. 1; 28 U.S.C.A. §1251ff.

As to judges and attorneys in the German system, consult the section on legal officers below.

---

5. Labor Courts (*Arbeitsgerichte*)[78]

Labor courts form an independent system of courts. They operate on three levels: trial, appellate and error. They are modeled on ordinary civil courts, and procedure before them is governed by the Code of Civil Procedure. They handle disputes between employers and employees arising out of the employment relationship, and those concerning the existence and the consequences of such a relationship. They also handle disputes between employers arising out of labor relations. They further hear cases arising out of tariff agreements between parties to such agreements or between them and third parties.

(a) Trial level labor courts (*Arbeitsgerichte*). *Arbeitsgerichte* are set up on the district level. Each court has a president (*Präsident*), a number of presiding judges (*vorsitzende Richter*), and lay judges (*Arbeitsrichter*) who are selected from and represent the interests of either employers or employees. The court hears cases in chambers (*Kammern*) that are presided over by a presiding judge and have another two lay judges, one representing the employers, and the other the employees. In cases arising out of tariffs, the court is composed of five members, namely, the presiding judge, two lay judges representing employers, and two representing employees. Decision is by simple majority.

Appeals (*Berufungen*) against judgments (*Urteile*) and complaints (*Beschwerden*) against rulings (*Beschlüsse*) of the court lie to the proper appellate level labor court (*Landesarbeitsgericht*) under the same rules as in the civil court system.

Parties before the court may represent themselves, or employees may be represented by representatives of the trade unions (*Gewerkschaften*) and employers by representatives of the associations of employers (*Vereinigungen der Arbeitsgeber*). Lawyers are admitted to represent parties only where the value of the subject matter in dispute exceeds a certain minimum, or by leave of the court.

(b) Appellate level labor courts (*Landesarbeitsgerichte*). *Landesarbeitsgerichte* are set up on the appellate level. They have a president (*Präsident*), a number of presiding judges (*vorsitzende Richter*), and a number of lay judges (*Landesarbeits-*

richter) who are selected from and represent the interests of either employees or employers. The court hears cases in chambers (*Kammern*) consisting of three members, namely the presiding judges and two lay judges, one representing employers and the other employees. In tariff cases, the court has another two lay judges, one representing employers and the other employees. The composition of the court is thus identical with those at the trial level.

The court hears appeals (*Berufungen*) and complaints (*Beschwerden*) against judgments (*Urteile*) and rulings (*Beschlüsse*) of the subordinated *Arbeitsgerichte* located within its appellate jurisdiction.

No further appeal lies against judgments of the court, but error (*Revision*) may be brought to the *Bundesarbeitsgericht* in cases where the value of the subject matter in dispute exceeds a certain minimum sum. Error may also be brought by leave of the *Landesarbeitsgericht* or, without such leave, where the judgment differs from a previously given judgment of the *Bundesarbeitsgericht* or another *Landesarbeitsgericht*. The error is brought under the same rules as in the civil court system.

Parties before the court must be represented by representatives of the trade unions (*Gewerkschaften*) or the associations of employers (*Vereinigungen der Arbeitsgeber*), as the case may be, or they must be represented by attorneys (*Rechtsanwälte*) admitted to practice before the court.

(c) Error level labor court (*Bundesarbeitsgericht*). This is the supreme court in labor matters; it is located in the city of Kassel. The court has a president (*Präsident*), a number of presiding judges (*vorsitzende Richter*), judges (*Richter*), and lay judges (*Bundesarbeitsrichter*) who are selected from and represent the interests of either employees or employers. The court hears cases in panels (Senate), which are presided over by a presiding judge and have two judges and two lay judges, one representing employers and the other employees. Decision is by simple majority.

The court also forms a large senate (*grosser Senat*), which is presided over by the president of the court or his deputy and has another eight members, namely, four judges and four lay judges, two representing employers and two employees. The large senate hears cases of fundamental importance and cases that will ensure a uniform application of the law throughout the country. Decision is by simple majority.

The court hears error (*Revision*) against judgments (*Urteile*) of *Landesarbeitsgerichte*. The error is brought under the same rules as in the civil court system.

Parties before the court must be represented by attorneys (*Rechtsanwälte*) admitted to practice before it.

NOTES AND QUESTIONS

Labor courts are a special feature of the German legal system. The object is to provide specialized courts for labor disputes and channel them through a legal system rather than to leave them to ordinary courts. The participation of the representatives of employees and employers inspires confidence in a thorough exploration of the problem and in a just solution.

Compare the German labor courts with those of Spain.

Do labor courts exist in Anglo-American jurisdictions? Do they exist in other civil law countries? Can ordinary civil courts handle labor cases as efficiently as specialized labor courts?

D. THE LAW OF CIVIL PROCEDURE

The German Code of Civil Procedure (*Zivilprozessordnung*)[79] of 1877 is in power as amended and supplemented by further provisions. It has 1048 articles presented in ten books: Book 1. General provisions; Book 2. Proceedings in trial courts; Book 3. Remedies against decisions; Book 4. Nullity and restitution petitions; Book 5. Claims based on documents, bills of exchange or checks; Book 6. Family, paternity, support and guardianship matters; Book 7. Orders for payment; Book 8. Execution of judgments; Book 9. Public notice proceedings; and Book 10. Arbitration proceedings.

Book 1 (General provisions) has the following sections: 1. Courts; 2. Parties; and 3. Procedure.

Book 2 (Proceedings in trial courts) has the following sections: 1. Proceedings in *Landgerichte* and 2. Proceedings in *Amtsgerichte*.

Book 3 (Remedies against decisions) has the following sections: 1. Appeal; 2. Error; and 3. Complaint.

Books 4 and 5 have no separate sections.

Book 6 (Family, paternity, support and guardianship matters) has the following sections: 1. Proceedings in family matters; 2. Paternity proceedings; 3. Proceedings concerning support of minors; and 4. Proceedings placing a person under guardianship because of lack of mental capacity.

Book 7 has no separate sections.

Book 8 (Execution of judgments) has the following sections: 1. General provisions; 2. Execution of money judgments; 3. Execution of judgments for the delivery of movables, and those ordering an act or an omission; 4. Declaration on oath by the debtor as to his assets and arrest for refusal to do so; and 5. Arrest and interim orders.

Books 9 and 10 have no separate sections.

Further important statutes appear in the appendix to the Code, including the introductory law to the Code (*Einführungsgesetz zur Zivilprozessordnung*), the Judiciary Act (*Gerichtsverfassungsgesetz*), the Courts Costs Act (*Gerichtskostengesetz*), and the Compensation of Witnesses and Experts Act (*Gesetz über die Entschädigung von Zeugen und Sachverständigen*).

The following are topics selected from the German law of civil procedure.

1. Procedure before County Courts (*Amtsgerichte*)[80]

The rules of procedure applicable before *Landgerichte*, which are general jurisdiction courts, apply also before *Amtsgerichte* unless otherwise provided. The procedure is simplified, however, and less formal. The parties need not be represented by an attorney and they may make their statements orally to the court clerk who will reduce them to writing.

After the statement of claim of the plaintiff is submitted in writing or reduced to writing by the court clerk, it is handed to a judge who will set a day for the hearing. A summons is then issued by the court and delivered, together with the statement of claim, to the defendant under the same rules as in a *Landgericht*.

Where the court lacks jurisdiction, it must point it out ex officio to the defendant before he answers the merits of the case.

A written record of the proceedings is made by the court.

In all other respects, the procedure is identical with that in a *Landgericht*. Procedure in family, paternity, support and guardianship matters is governed by Book 6 of the Code of Civil Procedure.

2. Procedure before District Courts (*Landgerichte*)[81]

(a) Initiation of proceedings and proceedings up to trial. Proceedings are initiated by the plaintiff's attorney filing a statement of claim (*Klageschrift*) with the clerk of court. The statement of claim must contain the names of the parties and of the court, the subject matter of the dispute and its value, and the reasons for the claim and the petition. The clerk of court hands the papers to the presiding judge of the proper chamber which will handle the case. A summons is then issued and served on the defendant together with the statement of claim. Service is effected by the court bailiff. The summons must instruct the defendant to appoint an attorney, if he wishes to defend the action, and to advise the court through the attorney within a term of not less than two weeks whether he has any objections to the case being heard and decided by a single judge.

The presiding judge may appoint a day for an early oral hearing, or he may order that the proceedings preliminary to trial proceed in writing.

Where he orders an early oral hearing (*Früher erster Termin zur mündlichen Verhandlung*), the day of that hearing will already appear in the summons which is served on the defendant together with the service of process. At least two weeks must elapse between the service on the defendant and the day of the hearing. In cases arising out of dealings in fairs and markets, the term is at least twenty-four hours. Where service is made abroad, the court will set an appropriate time. The same rule applies to a summons to trial. Where the case is not disposed of at the early oral hearing, the court orders a trial to be held.

Where the presiding judge orders preliminary proceedings in writing (*schriftliches Vorverfahren*), he orders the defendant to file an appearance within two weeks from service of the summons and to file an answer (*Klageerwiderung*) within another two weeks, or longer if so determined.

The presiding judge may always appoint one of the judges to handle the case and prepare it for trial. In commercial cases, the presiding judge must handle the case himself as the others are lay judges.

The parties must then file their briefs, offering proof for their allegations and filing any documents relevant to the proceedings that they have in their possession.

The appointed single judge (*Einzelrichter*) will see to it that the case is prepared for trial in a manner which should, whenever possible, dispose of the case in one hearing without adjournment. He may ask the parties to submit additional briefs containing clarifications, to produce documents, and to appear personally at the trial; he may also summon witnesses and experts to appear at the trial, etc.

At any stage of the proceedings, the court may make an attempt to produce a settlement. It may order the personal appearance of the parties for that purpose. If the case is not disposed of without trial, it must proceed to trial.

(b)   The trial.   The trial takes place under the chairmanship of the presiding judge of the particular chamber (*Kammer*). The presiding judge opens and conducts the trial. He carries on discussions with the attorneys for the parties, witnesses, experts, etc. No one may speak without his permission. Members of the court are free to ask questions of the parties, witnesses and experts after requesting permission to do so from the presiding judge. He also keeps order in the court room. The court may order any person who disobeys its orders to be removed and may impose a fine of up to 2,000 German marks or imprisonment of up to one week.[82] Where the trial takes place before a single judge, he exercises all the above powers.

After the trial opens, the parties make presentations of their positions through their attorneys, first the plaintiff and then the defendant. The parties themselves may speak after requesting permission from the presiding judge. Parties need not be present, but the court may order them to appear in person.

Where the court declines jurisdiction, it must transfer the case to the proper court. Where several courts have jurisdiction, the court will transfer the case to the court selected by the plaintiff. No remedy lies against the transfer and the order is binding on the court to which the case is transferred.

The parties must raise issues and make their statements, motions, replies and defenses at the proper time and in the proper order in accordance with the progress of the hearing. Motions, claims and defenses that the other party is not likely to be in the position to answer without prior notice must be made in writing before the oral hearing, thus allowing the opponent proper time to make his preparations. Where such a matter is raised at the oral hearing without prior notice giving sufficient time to prepare, the court may adjourn the hearing. The court may do so where it is of the opinion that the adjournment would not unduly delay the proceedings or where the delay in raising the matter is excusable. Otherwise it will reject such motions, claims and defenses. It will always reject them where their admission would unduly delay the proceedings or where the delay in raising such matters arose due to gross negligence of the party.

Proof is then made by the parties, first by the plaintiff and then by the defendant. It is made by order of the court. Proof may be made by viewing parts, by witnesses, by experts, by documents and by hearing the parties themselves.

Viewing parts (*Augenschein*) may be ordered in proper cases. The court may appoint a single judge to conduct it.

Witnesses are summoned by the court. A witness who does not appear may be fined and, in the case of nonpayment, imprisoned. He will have to also pay the costs caused by his nonappearance. In the case of a second nonappearance, another punishment may be imposed and the witness may be forcibly brought before the court.

Witnesses are requested to give an account of the matters known to them in a cohesive presentation. They are not sworn in, but they are reminded that they may be required to take an oath. No hearsay rule applies. The court and the parties may ask questions. The spouse, a lineal relative, or a collateral relative up to the third degree of a party need not testify. A witness need not answer questions where his answers might cause him or such related persons as listed above a proprietary loss, expose him or the above-enumerated related person to criminal prosecution, or cause him to disclose an art or trade secret. Where the witness refuses to give his testimony without a valid excuse, the court may fine him and imprison him in the case of nonpayment in the same way as in the case of nonappearance.

Where the court considers it appropriate, it may make a witness take an oath after he has given his testimony, unless the parties dispense with it. Witnesses below sixteen years of age and those who do not understand the binding nature of an oath may not be required to take an oath.

Experts are appointed by the court. The provisions applicable to witnesses generally apply also to experts. Experts give evidence on oath taken before or after giving the evidence. They give evidence orally at the trial, but they are usually required by the court to submit their opinions in writing before the trial in addition to their oral testimony.

The court may order the parties to produce all documents relevant to the proceedings. Public documents are presumed authentic unless proved otherwise. Private documents are presumed authentic unless their authenticity is contested. When contested, their authenticity must be established.

A party may request the court to order his opponent to testify. Where the opponent refuses to testify, the court may draw its conclusions therefrom and may consider the claims of the proponent as established. The court may order either party or both parties to testify on its own motion where the testimony given in the case is not adequate proof of the claims asserted. The rules applicable to witnesses apply, unless otherwise provided. The court may order a party to take an oath after he has given testimony where the court does not regard the unsworn testimony as full proof. Where both parties give testimony, only one of the parties may be required to take an oath. Where a party refuses to testify or refuses to take an oath, the court may draw its conclusions therefrom.

The court freely evaluates the evidence presented. After all the evidence has been presented, the court again discusses the questions of fact and of law of the case with the parties. When the court considers the case ready for judgment, it will declare the trial concluded.

A court record is kept of the trial and of the entire proceedings. The court may order a stenographic record to be made of the trial.

(c) **Judgment.** Judgment must be given in the same session of the court or, in cases of special difficulty, within a term that should not exceed three weeks from the conclusion of the trial. The deliberation is held in private and is presided over by the presiding judge. The court determines the issues to be decided and the order in which they are to be decided. Any difference of opinion is decided by the court. The court decides by simple majority. Where the court must determine a sum of money and there are more than two opinions, the vote for the largest sum is added to that of the next smaller sum to produce a majority.

Judges vote in inverted order of seniority. Where they are of the same seniority, the younger judge votes before the older. The presiding judge votes last. Lay judges vote before professional judges, the younger before the older. Judges giving judgment must have been present at the trial.

Judgment is given in the name of the people. It must contain the description of the parties, their attorneys, and the court; it must indicate the names of the individual judges and the day on which the trial was concluded; it must include the actual order (*Urteilsformel*) made by the court and the facts (*Tatbestand*), namely, a summary of the case on the basis of the presentation of the parties at trial, with emphasis on the motions and matters raised. Finally, it must give the reasons for the decision (*Entscheidungsgründe*) as to both facts and law. All the parts of the judgment must appear clearly separated one from the other.

The judgment may not grant a party anything beyond the petition of that party.

The judgment must be signed by all of the judges. If a judge is incapacitated and cannot sign the judgment, the fact must be noted at the foot thereof. If the judgment has not been completely worked out at the time of its pronouncement, it must be handed in its final form to the court clerk within three weeks from its pronouncement. Writing or spelling errors, calculation errors, or any other obvious error in judgment are corrected at the motion of the parties or at the court's own motion. Where there are incorrect or unclear statements, omissions or contradictions in the summary of the facts (*Tatbestand*) that go beyond the above-described rule of correction of obvious errors, either party may file a motion with the court within two weeks from notification of the judgment to have the matter corrected. The statement is served on the other party and a day for a hearing is set by the court. After the hearing, the court will rule on the motion. Only the judges who gave the judgment may participate. If one of the judges is incapacitated and there is a tie, the presiding judge has the casting vote. If the presiding judge is incapacitated, the senior judge has the casting vote.

The judgment may not be executed until the time for an appeal has run without an appeal being filed. However, before the end of the trial, the plaintiff may move to have the court order provisional execution. Both parties are heard on the matter. The court may grant the petition where the plaintiff would be seriously affected by the delay and may not grant it where the defendant would suffer an irreparable loss. It may require the plaintiff to give bond as a condition for granting the motion.

A default judgment may be given when a party does not appear at an oral hearing held in the proceedings. When the plaintiff does not appear, the court may dismiss the action if the defendant so moves. If the defendant does not appear, the court may give a default judgment against him after oral presentation of the plaintiff. The plaintiff's statement of facts is taken as admitted. In both these cases of nonappearnce, the appearing party may move for judgment on the pleadings (*Entscheidung nach Aktenlage*) rather than for a default judgment. The motion may be granted only when the case is sufficiently advanced to warrant a final judgment and where both parties already participated in the proceedings.

The court will deny a motion for a default judgment where it is of the opinion that the time between the original service of process on the defendant and the date of the trial was rather short or that too short a time was allowed between the service of the summons to appear at the trial and the date thereof. A complaint (*Beschwerde*) lies against a ruling denying default judgment. No remedy lies against a denial of the motion to give judgment on the pleadings, Where the motion for a default judgment is denied, the court will set a new day for the hearing.

Where neither party appears, the court may give judgment on the pleadings, it may set a new date for the hearing, or it may adjourn the hearing *sine die*.

A party against whom a default judgment is given may, within two weeks from notification of the judgment, file a motion with the court to set the default judgment aside. Where notification takes place abroad, a longer time may be set by the court. Upon the filing of the motion, which must give good reasons therefor, the court will set a day for hearing the motion. After hearing the parties, the court will decide ex officio whether to grant or deny the motion. If the motion is denied, the court will further declare that the default judgment is upheld. If the motion is granted, the case will be returned to the state where default took place. A party who is successful in setting aside a default judgment given against him, but who defaults for the second time, may not make a motion to set aside a second default judgment given against him.

(d) Proceedings on appeals from *Amtsgerichte*. The rules of procedure governing the handling of appeals in appellate courts are identical irrespective of whether the appeal is heard in a *Landgericht* from a judgment of an *Amtsgericht* or in an *Oberlandesgericht* from a judgment of a *Landgericht*.[83]

NOTES AND QUESTIONS

1. The procedure before an *Amtsgericht* is governed by the general rules of civil procedure with specifically indicated simplifications whose object is to make the proceedings less formal and more speedy, appropriate to the occasion of minor claims. In all other respects, the generally applicable rules govern. This is the approach taken by limited jurisdiction courts in all civil law countries. *See*, e.g., the Italian procedure. Does the same rule hold good in Anglo-American jurisdictions?

2. The procedure before a *Landgericht* applies the standard rules of civil procedure.

(a) Proceedings are initiated by the filing of a writ with the court; process is then served on the defendant by a court officer. Is service of process effected by a court officer in Anglo-American jurisdictions or do the parties rather use the services of professional process servers? *See* F.R.C.P. Rules 3 and 4. *See also* procedure in Spanish courts of general jurisdiction.

In civil law systems, a single judge is generally appointed to prepare the case for trial. The trial court is usually composed of three judges; but even when the trial is conducted by a single judge, he prepares the case for trial. Compare, e.g., the French procedure. Does this practice exist in the Anglo-American law of procedure?

The defendant must file an appearance within two weeks from the service of process under normal circumstances. Compare, e.g., the Italian procedure. *See also* F.R.C.P. Rule 12.

Parties then file their pleadings. This is done between attorneys. A copy of all filings with the court is also delivered to the attorney for the opponent or opponents so that every party to the suit receives a copy. *See*, e.g., F.R.C.P. Rule 5. The single judge watching over the case studies the pleadings and communicates with the parties with a view to the preparation of the proof. Eventually, all evidence is produced to the judge and the respective positions of the parties are clarified so that the issues to be decided on trial clearly emerge. Compare the preparation for trial in German civil procedure with that in French civil procedure. How does it compare with the American procedure? *See*, e.g., F.R.C.P. Rules 12, 15, 16, 26, 34.

(b) No jury trials exist and all civil cases are tried without a jury. The judge or the court under the chairmanship of the presiding judge conducts the trial. Does the same rule obtain in Anglo-American courts? Compare, e.g., Herron v. Southern Pacific Co., 283 U.S. 91, 95, 51 S. Ct. 383, 384 (1931).

Means of proof are standard in all jurisdictions. *See*, e.g., the Spanish procedure. Compare also the Federal Rules of Evidence, Arts. VI-X. Note that no hearsay rule exists. Compare the German rule on evidence of witnesses under oath with Rule 603 of the Federal Rules of Evidence.

A court record of the proceedings is kept. The presiding judge dictates a summary to the court clerk who types it as the trial proceeds. There is no word-for-word record of the proceedings. Should this be desired, the court may order a stenographic record or a taped record to be made. Is a word-for-word record of the proceedings necessary?

(c) Since the court is usually a collegiate court, deliberation is held and then followed by voting. Compare, e.g., the Italian procedure. Judgment is by simple majority.

For examples of actual judgments, consult the section on judgments below. Compare the form of such judgments with those given by the courts of record in your state. For a simple form of a judgment, *see* F.R.C.P., Appendix of Forms, Form 32. *See also* F.R.C.P. Rule 54.

May an American court correct errors in a judgment in a similar way as does a German court? *See* F.R.C.P. Rule 60.

Note that a judgment may not be executed until it enters into the power of law, i.e., until it becomes *res judicata*. Does the same rule obtain in Anglo-American courts? *See* F.R.C.P. Rule 62.

Note the provisions concerning judgment by default. How can a default judgment be set aside? *See* F.R.C.P. Rule 55.

---

3.   Procedure before Courts of Appeal (*Oberlandesgerichte*)[84]

An appeal against the judgment of a *Landgericht* must be filed with the proper *Oberlandesgericht* within one month from notification of the judgment. Default judgments may not be attacked by appeal, except where it is alleged that a default judgment should not have been given because the party was not in default. The appeal (*Berufungsschrift*) must identify the judgment appealed from and it must declare that the appellant is appealing that judgment. It must include a certified copy of the judgment and give evidence of the day of notification.

The appeal may also contain the reasons for the appeal (*Berufungsbegründung*), but they may be contained in a separate brief filed within one month from the filing of the appeal (*Berufungsschrift*). An extension of this time may be obtained. The brief must give the reasons singly and in detail, indicating which changes in the judgment are demanded. It must offer proof, including facts and means of proof substantiating the allegations.

The appeal and the appellate brief are served on the appellee, who may join in the appeal even where the time for its filing has run.

Within twenty-four hours from filing the appeal, the clerk of court of the *Oberlandesgericht* must request the transfer of the files from the *Landgericht*.

The *Oberlandesgericht* must examine the appeal as to its admissibility; that is, whether it is substantiated and filed in time and in the proper form. Where it lacks such a requirement, the *Oberlandesgericht* may issue a ruling (*Beschluss*), without any oral hearing, rejecting the appeal. A complaint (*Beschwerde*) lies against the rejection. It must be filed with the *Oberlandesgericht* within two weeks from the notification thereof. Where the court upholds its denial, it will transmit the complaint to the *Bundesgerichtshof* within one week for its decision. The *Oberlandesgericht* may set a day for an oral hearing on the admissibility by judgment. Error (*Revision*) to the *Bundesgerichtshof* lies against such judgment as of right.

Where the appeal is admitted, the proceedings follow the same course and are governed by the same rules that govern the procedure before *Landgerichte* unless otherwise provided.

The court thus usually appoints a member of the court to act as single judge (*Einzelrichter*) who holds hearings with the parties and prepares the case for trial. The parties may agree to let the single judge decide the merits of the case.

The case will be heard *de novo* within the limits of the petitions of the parties. Parties may bring new facts and new proof, but the court will not allow such means of either offense or defense which could have been used in the trial court and which, in the court's opinion, were not used there because of gross negligence. All such means that were already rightfully rejected in the trial court because of delay and gross negligence are inadmissible. A counterclaim may be made only with the consent of the opponent. The court may order a party to give evidence, or to give evidence on oath, when such party refused to do so at the trial only where the court is of the opinion that the reasons for the party's refusal no longer subsist. Where a party gave evidence on oath in the trial court, the court of appeal may order his opponent to give evidence on oath only where the taking of the evidence of the first party or the taking of it on oath in the trial court was inadmissible.

The appellate court may modify the judgment appealed from only as far as this is requested. The appellate court may deal with issues that must be decided even when such issues were not discussed and not decided in the trial court.

The appellate court will usually give a new judgment in the case. It may, however, set aside the judgment of the court below and remand the case to it for further proceedings where the proceedings below suffered from a procedural defect, the judgment below rejected the suit as inadmissible, the court below decided only on the admissibility of the suit or did not give a decision on the merits, or the judgment below was a default judgment.

NOTES AND QUESTIONS

Proceedings before appellate courts are governed by the rules of civil procedure applicable to trial courts unless otherwise provided. The trial is *de novo* within the scope of the petition of the parties.

Within what time must the appeal be filed? *See,* e.g., the French law, also F.R.A.P. Rule 4. How is the record of the case transmitted to the court of appeal? *See,* e.g., the Italian law, also F.R.A.P. Rule 11.

Note that the German court of appeal may affirm, modify, or set aside the judgment appealed from. It will nearly always give a new judgment without remission, which is provided for only in the specially enumerated cases. Compare, e.g., 28 U.S.C.A. §2106, and the Spanish appellate procedure.

---

4.   Procedure before the Supreme Court (*Bundesgerichtshof*)[85]

Error (*Revision*) against a judgment of an *Oberlandesgericht* must be filed with the *Bundesgerichtshof* within one month from notification of the judgment.

The petition for revision (*Revisionsschrift*) must identify the judgment against which error is brought and declare that error is brought against it. It must include a certified copy of the judgment and state the day of notification.

The petition may also contain the reasons for the petition (*Revisionsbegründung*), but they also may be contained in a separate brief filed within one month from the filing of the petition. An extension of this time may be obtained. The brief must indicate to what extent the judgment is being attacked and state the individual reasons. It must indicate the legal provisions violated and whether they are substantive or procedural. No new reasons may be added after the time for giving the reasons for the petition has run.

The reasons that the Court must hold violative of the law (*Absolute Revisionsgründe*) include: improper composition of the court, participation in the decision on the part of a judge who was not authorized to sit or who was disqualified, improper assumption or denial of jurisdiction, lack of proper representation of a party, improper exclusion of the general public at trial, and failure of the court to give grounds for its decision.

The petition for revision and the brief of the plaintiff in error (*Revisionsklager*) are served on the defendant in error (*Revisionsbeklagte*), who may join in the petition within the time for the filing of the reasons for revision.

The *Bundesgerichtshof* must examine the petition as to its admissibility; that is, whether it is substantiated and filed in time and in the proper form. Where it lacks such a requirement, it will be rejected. This may be done without an oral hearing. No remedy lies against the rejection.

Where the petition is admitted, the proceedings follow the same course and are governed by the same rules as in a *Landgericht*, unless otherwise provided. The rules governing appellate procedure also apply as far as practicable.

All proceedings take place before the proper senate of the *Bundesgerichtshof*. No single judge may be appointed. The court's examination will extend to matters within the framework of the petitions made by the parties. The Court is not bound, however, by the reasons for the revision stated by the parties and may find the law violated on other grounds.

Where the Court finds that the law was violated but that the decision of the court below was still correct, it will affirm the judgment.

Where the *Bundesgerichtshof* grants the petition, it will set aside the judgment of the court below and will remit the case to it for further proceedings. It may so remit the case to another senate of the appellate court against whose judgment error was taken. That court is bound by the decision of the *Bundesgerichtshof* and must use its reasoning in deciding the case.

The *Bundesgerichtshof* will, however, decide the case itself without remitting it, where the judgment of the court below was set aside only because of misapplication of a statute to particular facts and the case is ready for judgment, or where the court below lacked jurisdiction.

NOTES AND QUESTIONS

The Federal Supreme Court is a court of error. To bring a matter before it requires the allegation of violation of the law, which occurs usually in proceedings before a court of appeal. Error occuring in lower courts will be remedied on appeal without recourse to the Federal Supreme Court. The error is brought as of right. Compare, e.g., the French Court of Cassation. Are American state courts of final resort purely courts of error, i.e., reviewing purely questions of law? Compare, e.g., New York Civil Practice Law and Rules §5601ff. with respect to the New York Court of Appeals, which is the New York state court of final resort. *See also* 28 U.S.C.A. §2101ff. with respect to the United States Supreme Court.

The error must be filed within one month. Compare, e.g., the Italian rule to bring a case before the Italian Court of Cassation. *See also* U.S.C.A. §2101; R.R. Rules 11 (1), 22 (1).

The case is heard by a proper senate, and no single judge may be appointed to prepare the case for trial. Compare, e.g., the procedure before the Spanish Supreme Court. Does the practice of appointing a rapporteur judge exist in any Anglo-American court of final resort?

Note the rule as to the remission of a case to a lower court. How does it compare with the French rule? *See also* 28 U.S.C.A. §2106.

---

5. Reopening of Proceedings
   (*Wiederaufnahme des Verfahrens*)[86]

Proceedings terminated by a judgment that has entered into the power of law may be reopened on the strength of a petition of nullity or of restitution. These are two independent, although closely related, petitions with identical rules of procedure applicable to each. Where both petitions are raised by any party in the same case, the nullity petition is handled first with the petition of restitution handled only after the decision in the nullity proceedings enters into the power of law.

(a) Petition of nullity (*Nichtigkeitsklage*). The petition of nullity may be brought where: (1) The court that pronounced the decision was improperly composed; (2) a judge participated in the decision who was not authorized to sit; (3) a disqualified judge participated in the decision; and (4) a party to the proceedings was improperly represented.

The petition may not be brought on grounds (1) and (3) where the matter could have been raised in regular proceedings by appeal, complaint or error.

(b) Petition of restitution (*Restitutionsklage*). The petition of restitution may be brought where: (1) The opponent gave false evidence on oath and the judgment was based on that evidence; (2) a document on which the judgment was based was false or falsified; (3) a witness or expert in giving evidence on which the judgment was based committed a punishable breach of duty to tell the truth; (4) the judgment was brought about by a criminally punishable act undertaken by the representative of the party or by the opponent or his representative; (5) a judge participated in the decision who was guilty of a criminally punishable breach of his official duties towards the party in the proceedings; (6) a prior judgment of a court or an administrative court on which the judgment was based was set aside by another judgment that entered into the power of law; and (7) a party becomes aware of a prior judgment given in the case that entered into the power of law, or a party finds or is able to use a document the presentation of which would have resulted in a more favorable decision.

On grounds (1) through (5), the petition may be brought only where the offender was actually convicted or where criminal proceedings cannot be instituted or continued because of other reasons, like lack of proof.

The petition of restitution may be brought only when the ground on which it is brought could not have been raised in the prior proceedings, especially by a motion to set the judgment aside, by appeal, or by joining in an appeal.

(c) Procedure on petitions (*Verfahren*). The above petitions must be brought in the court that decided the case on the trial level. They must be brought in the court that decided the case on the appellate level where the judgment complained of was given by the appellate court, or where it was given by the court of error and is being attacked on the grounds for restitution described in numbers (1) through (3), (6) and (7). They must be brought in the court that decided the case on the error level where the judgment complained of was given by the court of error and is being attacked on the grounds for nullity, or on the grounds for restitution described in numbers (4) and (5). Where the petitions are directed against a judicial order to pay a sum of money (*Vollstreckungsbescheid*), they must be brought in the court that would have had jurisdiction in the matter had regular proceedings been instituted.

The petitions are governed by the rules generally applicable to civil procedure unless otherwise provided.

The petitions must be brought within one month from the day on which the party becomes aware of the ground for the petition; if at that time, however, the judgment complained of has not yet entered into the power of law, then the time runs from the day on which it so entered. The petitions may not be brought after five years have run from the day on which the judgment complained of entered into the power of law. The above-mentioned rules as to time do not apply to a nullity petition brought on the ground of lack of representation. There time runs from the day on which the party is notified of the judgment or, in the case where the party lacks legal capacity, from the day on which his legal representative is so notified.

The petition must identify the judgment complained of and declare that it is brought against it. It must state the ground for the petition, the means of proof of the facts on which the petition is founded, and the time when the party became aware of the ground. It must indicate the relief requested. All relevant documents must be attached to the petition; if they are not in possession of the petitioner, the petition must indicate what motion or motions must be made by the petitioner to obtain their production.

The court in which the petition is brought must examine it to determine whether it is substantiated and brought in time and in the proper form. The petition will be rejected if it lacks any of these requirements. The court may order that the hearing on the admissibility of the petition be held prior to the hearing on the merits. Where this is done, the hearing on the merits is considered as further proceedings on the ground and admissibility of the reopening of the proceedings. The merits of the petition are heard *de novo* within the limits of the petition.

Against decisions of the court on the petitions, the parties may use all of the remedies generally available to contest such decisions.

NOTES AND QUESTIONS

This is the standard procedure to reopen judgments that have already entered into the power of law. Compare, e.g., the Spanish petition for the revision of a judgment in the Spanish Supreme Court. Note the elaborate German rules that designate the court to hear the petition. Compare the Spanish rule which requires that the petition be made to the Supreme Court.

In Italian law, the matter is dealt with in Arts. 395-403 of the Italian Code of Civil Procedure. In Italy, the petition must be brought in the court that pronounced the judgment attacked.

Note that in German law the petition may generally not be brought after five years have run from the day on which the judgment entered into the power of law. What is the Spanish rule on the matter?

On which grounds and within what time may judgments of Anglo-American courts be reexamined after they became *res judicata*? *See* F.R.C.P. Rule 60.

---

6. Procedure before Labor Courts
   (*Arbeitsgerichte*)[87]

Procedure before labor courts is governed by the Code of Civil Procedure (*Zivilprozessordnung*) and proceeds along the lines of procedure before civil courts.

III. THE SYSTEM AND ADMINISTRATION OF CRIMINAL LAW

A. THE SUBSTANTIVE CRIMINAL LAW

The Penal Code of 1871 is in power as amended. It has 358 articles in two parts: the general part and the particular part.

The general part has the following sections: 1. The penal law; 2. The act; 3. Legal effects of the act; 4. Private prosecution; and 5. Prescription.

The particular part has the following sections: 1. Preparation for the waging of an offensive war, high treason, endangering of the democratic form of government; 2. Treason and the endangering of the external security of the state; 3. Offenses against foreign states; 4. Offenses against high officers of state and electoral offenses; 5. Offenses against national defense; 6. Resistance to state authority; 7. Offenses against the public order; 8. Counterfeiting of currency, stamps and securities; 9. False unsworn testimony and perjury; 10. False accusation; 11. Offenses against religion and creed; 12. Offenses against personal status, marriage and family; 13. Sexual offenses; 14. Defamation; 15. Offenses against privacy; 16. Homicide; 17. Bodily harm; 18. Offenses against personal freedom; 19. Theft and embezzlement; 20. Robbery and extortion; 21. Accessories after the fact and receiving stolen property; 22. Fraud and breach of trust; 23. Forgery; 24. [deleted]; 25. Punishable frauds (gaming, poaching, fishing in territorial waters, usury, etc.); 26. Willful damage to property; 27. Criminally punishable acts endangering the public (arson, explosives, atomic energy, radiation, flooding, endangering of rail, ship, air and road traffic, etc.); and 28. Criminally punishable acts in office (bribery, favoritism, prosecution of innocent persons, disclosure of official secrets, etc.)

Further important statutes are carried in the appendix to the Penal Code. They deal with: hunting, weapons, explosives, protection of animals, contagious diseases, military duty, military penal justice, minors, and the like.

The following are topics selected from the German substantive criminal law.

1.   Penal Law (*Strafgesetz*)[88]

An act is punishable only when it was made punishable by law before it was committed. German penal law applies to acts committed in Germany. It also applies to acts committed aboard vessels or aircraft that are authorized to display the flag of the Federal Republic of Germany, independently of the law of the country where the act was committed. German penal law also applies, independent of the law of the country where the act was committed, to preparation for the waging of an offensive war, high treason, treason, some offenses against the national defense, kidnapping, etc.[89] German penal law further applies, independent of the law of the country where the act was committed, to genocide; offenses committed with atomic energy, explosives, or radiation; attacks on air traffic; trafficking in narcotics; counterfeiting of currency and securities, etc.[90] German penal law also applies to acts committed abroad against a German when the act is punishable in the country where it was committed, or when the place of commission is not subject to the authority of any state. Under the same circumstances, it applies to acts committed by a German, or by a foreigner, if he is apprehended in Germany but not extradited because his extradition is not requested, is denied, or is not possible.[91]

The law distinguishes between felonies and misdemeanors. Felonies (*Verbrechen*) are criminal acts punishable with imprisonment of not less than one year. Misdemeanors (*Vergehen*) are criminal acts that are punishable with a lesser term of imprisonment, or with a fine.[92]

NOTES AND QUESTIONS

The German criminal law stresses the point that a person may be punished only in accordance with a statute in power at the time of the commission of the act. It applies the principle *Nullum crimen sine lege* and also prohibits the retroactive effect of criminal laws. It generally subscribes to the principle of territorial application of criminal law with noted exceptions. It also extends its jurisdiction over German nationals abroad in stipulated cases. Compare this jurisdiction with that generally applied by Anglo-American jurisdictions, especially by the American states which adhere to the territorial application of state criminal law. Does the United States claim exterritorial criminal jurisdiction in certain cases? *See* 18 U.S.C.A. §2381, and Rivard v. U.S. 375 F. 2d 882 (5th Cir. 1967) Cert. denied 389 U.S. 884 (1967). As to extradition, compare 18 U.S.C.A. §3182ff. and note the various treaties of extradition between the United States and foreign countries.

Note that the German law distinguishes only two categories of offenses, i.e., felonies and misdemeanors. Compare the French categories of offenses. Compare also the rule in the criminal law of your state. *See,* e.g., New York Penal Law, Art. 55; Calif. Penal Code Annotated §16.

---

2. Minors (*Jugendliche*) and Adolescents (*Heranwachsende*)[93]

A person who, at the time of the commission of the act, is not yet fourteen years of age is not imputable. A minor (*Jugendliche*) is a person who was fourteen but not yet eighteen years of age at the time of the commission of the act. An adolescent (*Heranwachsender*) is a person who was eighteen but not yet twenty-one years old at the time of the commission of the act. Anyone who has completed that age is fully imputable.

(a) Minors (*Jugendliche*). A minor is criminally imputable when, at the time of the commission of the act, he is mature enough in his moral and mental development to realize that his act is wrong and to act accordingly. Where he is not imputable because he lacks this degree of maturity, the judge may act as in guardianship matters. Where the minor is found imputable, the judge may, in any case, give directions as to the place of his residence, place of work or education, avoidance of certain persons or places, and the like. The judge may impose a type of correction (*Zuchtmittel*) upon the minor, such as a warning, the duty to make good the damage caused, or an obligation to apologize. He may order the minor's arrest for the period of his weekly free time (*Freizeitarrest*), for a short arrest (*Kurzarrest*), or for a longer arrest (*Dauerarrest*). A *Freizeitarrest* is an arrest for the two days in a given week during which the minor has no school or employment. It may be so imposed for up to four consecutive weeks. A *Kurzarrest* is an arrest for up to six consecutive days. A *Dauerarrest* is an arrest for a minimum of one week and up to, and including, four weeks. Any number of days of arrest between the minimum and maximum may be imposed.

Where due to the nature of the act, the judge is of the opinion that more severe measures should be taken, he may impose punishment (*Jugendstrafe*) rather than a mere correction. The minimum punishment is imprisonment for six months and the maximum is imprisonment for five years. Where the minor has committed a felony punishable with more than ten years imprisonment, the maximum is ten years. The judge may also impose imprisonment of an undetermined duration, with a maximum of four years and a minimum term that must be at least two years less than the maximum actually ordered.

Where the term of imprisonment imposed does not exceed one year, or in proper cases two years, the minor may be admitted to probation. The minimum term of probation is two years and the maximum three years. In his discretion, the judge may not impose any sentence and admit the minor to probation on the finding of his guilt only. In such a case, the term of probation is one year as a minimum and two years as a maximum. If probation is revoked, the judge imposes the term of imprisonment that he would have originally imposed.

The imprisonment is served in an institution for juveniles. The judicial proceedings are held in a juvenile court.

(b)   Adolescents (*Heranwachsende*).   An adolescent may be treated as a minor where the court is of the opinion that in view of his moral and mental development at the time of the commission of the act, he was at the level of a minor, or where the offense is of a juvenile nature. If the adolescent is treated as a minor, the maximum term of imprisonment imposed may not exceed ten years.

Where the adolescent is treated as an adult, the court may impose imprisonment of between ten and fifteen years rather than life imprisonment, and may not impose preventive detention (*Sicherungsverwahrung*).

NOTES AND QUESTIONS

German law makes persons criminally imputable as from the age of fourteen years fully completed. Compare the Italian and the Spanish law. *See also*, e.g., Calif. Pen. C.A. §26.

Note the elaborate provisions of the German law with respect to minors between fourteen and eighteen years of age. May they still be held not imputable?

Consider the German provisions with respect to adolescents. Note that a person reaches full age and capacity in Germany at the age of eighteen. Why should a special privilege be extended by the criminal law to persons over that age? Note that the full age in Germany stood at twenty-one until it was reduced to eighteen in 1974 by the Law of July 31, 1974 (BGBl. I S. 1713). Compare the German approach with the French approach. What are the main differences?

How are juvenile offenders treated in the criminal law of your state? Compare also the Federal Youth Corrections Act, 28 U.S.C.A. §5005ff., where a "youth offender" is defined in §5006 as a person under the age of twenty-two years at the time of conviction.

---

3.   Accomplices (*Teilnahme*)[94]

Where two or more persons commit a criminal act together, each of them will be punished as a principal. An instigator who instigates a person to commit a criminally punishable act will be punished as a principal.

A person will be punished as an accomplice if he intentionally aids another person in the commission of a criminally punishable act. Punishment is based on that of the principal, but it is reduced in accordance with the provisions of Article 49 (1).[95] Every accomplice will be punished in accordance with his guilt without regard to that of another.

An accessory after the fact is punished with imprisonment of up to five years or with a fine. The punishment may not exceed that for the commission of the act itself.

NOTES AND QUESTIONS

German law first defines the principal and then proceeds to define accomplices who are liable in accordance with the law, which stresses the act of the principal and virtually treats helpers like principals. Compare the Italian approach. How is participation in the commission of crime treated in Anglo-American law? *See,* e.g., Calif. Pen. C.A. §§30-33; People v. Stein (1942) 55 CA2d 417, 130 P2d 750. *See also* 18 U.S.C.A. §§2-4.

---

4.   Punishment *(Strafen)*[96]

Punishment may be imprisonment and/or a fine. Imprisonment is for life or for a term of from one month to fifteen years. A fine is assessed at a daily rate and its multiples. The daily rate will be set by the court at what the offender earns net per day. It may be any amount between 2 and 10,000 German marks. The fine is assessed at 5 to 360 multiples. A fine that is not recoverable is converted into imprisonment at the rate of one day imprisonment for a daily rate of the fine. The minimum term of imprisonment is one day.

As a supplementary punishment in the case of a driving offense, the court may impound the offender's driver's license from one to three months.

The guilt of the offender forms the basis for the assessment of punishment. The court must consider the effect of the punishment on the future life of the offender and must look into the circumstances of the commission of the offense, balancing against each other those that are mitigating and those that are aggravating. The circumstances to be considered are chiefly the motives and objectives of the offender, his attitude and determination appearing from the act, the manner in which the act was carried out and its effects, the prior way of life of the offender and his personal and economic conditions of life and, also his conduct after the commission of the act, especially any endeavor to make good the damage caused.

Imprisonment under six months will be assessed only exceptionally when necessary in the interest of law and order, otherwise the punishment will consist of the assessment of a fine.

Where there are mitigating circumstances, life imprisonment may be reduced to imprisonment not under three years. In the case of a term of imprisonment, the term actually imposed may not exceed three fourths of the statutory maximum. The same applies to fines. The increased minimum of imprisonment will be reduced from ten or five years to two years, from three or two years to six months, from one year to three months, and in other cases to the statutory minimum. Where a statute provides for mitigation, the court may reduce the punishment to the statutory minimum or commute imprisonment into a fine.

As to aggravating circumstances, where the same act infringes several criminal provisions, or the same provision several times, only one punishment will be assessed. Where several provisions are infringed, punishment will be assessed on the basis of the most serious of the offenses. Again, where a person is tried for several independent offenses, only one punishment will be assessed. A fine may be imposed in addition to imprisonment. The punishment for the most serious offense will be increased in these cases, but it may not equal the total of the punishments that might be assessed for individual offenses. The punishment actually assessed may not exceed fifteen years of imprisonment, or 720 multiples of daily earnings.

NOTES AND QUESTIONS

German punishments run from a fine to life imprisonment. There is no death penalty in German law. The assessment of the actual punishment is left to the court within a determined frame of statutorily prescribed punishment. Within that statutory frame, the court considers aggravating and attenuating circumstances and assesses the actual punishment.

How is punishment assessed in other systems? Compare the French system of assessment of punishment. *See also* the Spanish system. Compare, e.g., Calif. Pen. C.A. §15ff.

Note especially the German method of calculating fines in accordance with the earnings of the offender.

---

5.   Repeaters (*Rückfälligen*)[97]

A person will be treated as a repeater (*Rückfällige*) if he has been convicted twice and suffered imprisonment for at least three months, and then he commits another intentional criminal act for which the maximum punishment is at least one year. The minimum punishment for the new offense will be set at six months imprisonment, unless the new offense is of a nature for which the law provides a higher minimum. A prior offense will not be considered in this connection if five years have elapsed between its commission and that of the subsequently committed offense.

A person over twenty-five years of age who commits an intentional criminally punishable act for which he is convicted to at least two years imprisonment may be held in preventive detention (*Sicherungsverwahrung*) by order of the court. The court may order such confinement where the person was previously convicted twice to imprisonment of at least one year on each occasion and he has actually spent two years in prison or in another institution, like a mental hospital for criminals, and where, in view of his criminal inclination, he is considered dangerous to society. Where a person has committed three criminally punishable acts, at least one of them after completing 25 years of his age, and has incurred imprisonment of at least one year for each, and where at least one of the convictions was to a minimum of three years imprisonment, the court may order preventive detention if the offender is considered dangerous to society. The confinement takes place usually after the offender has suffered the punishment. At that time, the court may put the offender on probation if it thinks that the confinement is no longer necessary. Where the confinement takes place before the imprisonment, the time spent in confinement is credited towards the term of imprisonment. Whenever preventive detention is ordered for the first time with respect to a particular person, it may not exceed ten years. The court must consider every two years whether the detention should be continued or the remaining term should be probated.

When the repeater is eventually released, he is placed under the supervision (*Führungsaufsicht*) of a probation officer (*Bewährungshelfer*). The time of supervision is set by the court at a period of between two and five years. The court may give the offender directives for his conduct, as mentioned under probation below. The probation officer reports to the court. Where the offender behaves well, the court may terminate his supervision after two years, or any time thereafter. If he misbehaves, the court may order his preventive detention.

NOTES AND QUESTIONS

German law provides an elaborate scheme of punishment for repeaters. It also provides for preventive detention but, on the other hand, aims at the rehabilitation of an offender with release under supervision. How does this approach compare with those of the French and the Italian law? How does the law of your state handle repeaters? *See,* e.g., New York Penal Law §§70.06, 70.10; 18 U.S.C.A. §3575.

---

6. Probation (*Bewährung*)[98]

Where a person is convicted to imprisonment not exceeding one year, the court may admit him to probation if it is of the opinion that he will not commit any further offenses. The court will arrive at this conclusion by considering the personality of the offender, his prior life, the circumstances of the act he committed, his conduct after the commission of the act, and the conditions under which he lives and would live if placed on probation. In exceptional cases, the court may admit a person to probation who is convicted to imprisonment not exceeding two years. The time of probation will be determined by the court, between the statutory minimum of two years and a maximum of five years.

The court may impose on the offender the obligation to make good the damage he caused, to pay a given amount to a charitable or other institution or to the public treasury, or to do some good as instructed by the court.

The court may give the offender directives for his conduct while on probation. They may relate to his place of abode, training, work, or the way he spends his free time; or they may instruct him not to associate with certain persons or not to have certain instruments in his possession, etc.

During the time of probation, the offender will be placed under the supervision of a probation officer who will report to the court on his conduct.

The court will revoke probation where the offender commits a criminally punishable act during the time of probation, where he acts contrary to the directives given to him by the court, where he avoids the supervision of the probation officer, or where he does not perform the obligations imposed on him by the court.

Where the time of probation runs without probation being revoked, the court will remit punishment.

Where the offender has paid a fine equivalent to up to 180 multiples of a daily fine, and where the court is of the opinion that he will not commit further criminal acts, that in view of the personality of the offender he should not be convicted to imprisonment, and that the imposition of imprisonment is not necessary to uphold the legal order, the court will determine the punishment, but will not impose it on the offender and will hold it suspended until the time of probation has run. The court will set the time of probation as a period between the statutory minimum of one year and a maximum of three years. The court may impose on the offender the performance of obligations as mentioned above. The court will revoke the probation and impose the punishment on the offender if he is found guilty of a breach of the terms of probation as mentioned above.

In proper cases, the court may dispense with any punishment where the consequences of the act committed by the offender already weigh against him and where any further punishment which the court might impose would be inappropriate. This provision does not apply where the offender has incurred a term of imprisonment exceeding one year.

7.   Parole (*Aussetzung des Strafrestes*)[99]

A convicted offender who has served two thirds of the term of imprisonment imposed upon him may be paroled when the court finds that the risk may be taken to see whether or not he will behave. The court may parole an offender after he has served one half of his punishment if he has actually served one year and there are special circumstances favoring his release. In both cases, before the court will parole an offender, it will consider his personality, and the conditions of life into which he would return upon release. The offender must also consent to being paroled.

The term of parole may not fall below the remainder of the term of imprisonment and will be set between two and five years. The offender will be placed under the supervision of a parole officer who will report on his conduct. The conditions of parole are governed by the same rules as probation in all respects, namely, the imposition of obligations, directives for conduct, and provisions for termination and revocation.

NOTES AND QUESTIONS

1. As to probation, only persons assessed a term of imprisonment not exceeding one (exceptionally two) years may be admitted to probation. What is the rule in Italian law?

The court imposes a number of conditions to be complied with by the offender in order to be placed on, and to continue on, probation. In proper cases, the court may dispense entirely with punishment. Compare, e.g., New York Penal Law §65.00ff. and 18 U.S.C.A. §3651ff.

Where the person does not comply with the conditions, probation will be revoked. When is revocation of probation effected in Italian law? Compare, e.g., 18 U.S.C.A. §3653.

2. As to parole in Germany, the offender must actually serve two thirds (exceptionally one half) of his term of imprisonment before he is eligible for parole. What is the rule in French law? If he is actually paroled, the offender is placed under supervision virtually identical with that for probation. The same applies to revocation of parole.

Compare the law of your state. *See,* e.g., Calif. Pen. C.A. §3040ff. and 18 U.S.C.A. §4201ff. *See also* the Spanish law.

---

8. Murder (*Mord*)[100]

A murderer is a person who kills a human being out of a desire to kill, out of a sexual desire, out of covetousness, or out of any base motives, and who kills treacherously or cruelly, or with generally dangerous means, or in order to further or to cover up another criminal act. Murder is punished with imprisonment for life.

9. Manslaughter (*Totschlag*)[101]

Whosoever shall kill a person without being a murderer will be guilty of manslaughter and will be punished with imprisonment of not under five years. In especially serious cases, the punishment will be life imprisonment. In less serious cases, or where the offender was provoked, without any fault on his part, by ill treatment or a serious insult to his own person or to one of his relatives given by the killed person so that the offender was inflamed by anger and acted on the spur of the moment, the punishment is imprisonment of from six months to five years.

10. Negligent Homicide (*Fahrlässige Tötung*)[102]

Whosoever shall bring about the death of a person by negligence will be punished with imprisonment of up to five years or with a fine.

NOTES AND QUESTIONS

The German law retains the classical distinction between murder, manslaughter and negligent homicide. How does this division compare with the French and the Italian law? How does the Anglo-American law approach homicide? *See,* e.g., Calif. Pen. C.A. §187ff., 18 U.S.C.A. §1111ff. Compare the German definition of murder with that of your own state. *See,* e.g., Calif. Pen. C.A. §187. Compare the German definition of manslaughter and negligent homicide with that current in American law. *See,* e.g., Calif. Pen. C.A. §192. *See also* the Spanish law.

---

11. Wounding and Bodily Harm (*Körperverletzung*)[103]

Where a person bodily harms or affects the health of another person, he will be punished with imprisonment of up to three years or with a fine. Where the offense is committed against ancestors, the punishment is imprisonment of up to five years or a fine.

Dangerous bodily harm (*gefährliche Körperverletzung*) occurs where the bodily harm is caused by a weapon (especially by a knife or another dangerous tool), by a treacherous attack, by several persons acting together, or by treatment dangerous to life. The punishment is imprisonment of up to five years or a fine. The attempt is also punishable.[104]

Aggravated bodily harm (*schwere Körperverletzung*) occurs where the victim loses an important part of the body (e.g., the sight in one or both eyes, hearing, speech, or capability of procreation), is permanently disfigured in a serious way, or becomes sickly, paralysed or insane. The punishment is imprisonment of from one to five years. In less serious cases, the punishment is imprisonment of up to five years or a fine. Where one of the above-enumerated consequences of the injury was intended and actually occurred (*beabsichtigte schwere Körperverletzung*), the punishment is imprisonment of from two to ten years. In less serious cases, the punishment is imprisonment of from six months to five years.

Where death occurs as a consequence of the injury (*Körperverletzung mit Todesfolge*), the punishment is imprisonment of not less than three years. In less serious cases, the punishment is imprisonment of from three months to five years.

Where bodily harm occurs due to the negligence of another person (*fahrlässige Körperverletzung*), the punishment is imprisonment of up to three years or a fine.

NOTES AND QUESTIONS

Note that the German provisions move from simple bodily harm to more serious injuries up to injury resulting in death. They thus cover a wide spectrum of offenses. Compare, e.g, the Italian law. How does the Anglo-American law treat the matter? *See*, e.g., 18 U.S.C.A. §111ff.

Does the German bodily harm provision compare with assault in the third degree in New York Penal Law §120.00 or with battery in Calif. Pen. C.A. §242?

Does German dangerous bodily harm compare with assault in the second degree in New York Penal Law §120.05?

Does German aggravated bodily harm compare with assault in the first degree in New York Penal Law §120.10, or mayhem in Calif. Pen. C.A. §203?

Does the German provision for death as a consequence of bodily injury compare with Calif. Pen. C.A. §194? What was the reason in Anglo-American law to provide that death must occur within a certain time after injury to qualify as murder or manslaughter? Compare, e.g., R. v. Dyson, [1908] 2 K.B. 454; Head v. State, 68 Ga. App. 759, 24 S.E. 2d 145 (1943).

---

12.   Theft and Embezzlement (*Diebstahl und Unterschlagung*)[105]

Theft (*Diebstahl*) is defined as follows: Whosoever shall take someone else's movable thing with the intent to unlawfully appropriate it, shall be punished with imprisonment of up to five years or with a fine. An attempt is punishable.

An especially serious case of theft (*besonders schwerer Fall des Diebstahls*) will be punished with imprisonment of from three months to ten years. Such a case occurs where: (1) The offender, in order to commit the act, breaks into a building, an apartment, office or business premises, or any other enclosure, entering by means of false keys or other tools not designed for lawful opening, or where he hides in the enclosure; (2) a thing specially protected against a theft in a locked container or by another device is stolen; (3) the offender steals professionally; (4) the offender steals from a church or from a building or premises used for religious services a thing dedicated to such services; (5) a thing important to science, the arts, history or technical development which is located in a publicly accessible collection or is publicly displayed is stolen; or (6) the offender steals in taking advantage of the helplessness of another person, an accident, or a state of general danger. A case is not an especially serious case where the value of the thing is unsubstantial.

Theft while armed (*Diebstahl mit Waffen*) and theft by a gang (*Bandendiebstahl*) are punished by imprisonment of from six months to ten years. Theft while armed is committed when the offender or his accomplice carry a firearm, or where the offender or his accomplice carry a weapon or a tool for the purpose of overcoming the resistance of another person by violence or the threat of violence. Theft by a gang is committed where a member of a gang steals with the assistance of another member of the gang. The attempt to commit these acts is punishable.

Embezzlement (*Unterschlagung*) is defined as follows: Whosoever shall unlawfully appropriate someone else's movable thing while it is in his possession or custody will be punished with imprisonment of up to three years or with a fine, and if the thing has been entrusted to him, with imprisonment of up to five years or with a fine. The attempt is punishable.

The theft (*Diebstahl*) and embezzlement (*Unterschlagung*) of things of small value will be prosecuted only on private prosecution, unless public prosecution is instituted because of a special public interest in the prosecution.

The unauthorized use of motor vehicles and of bicycles (*unbefugter Gebrauch eines Fahrzeugs*) is punishable with imprisonment of up to three years or with a fine, unless a more severe punishment is provided in other laws. The attempt is punishable. The offense is prosecuted only on private prosecution.

The tapping of electric energy (*Entziehung elektrischer Energie*) is punishable by imprisonment of up to five years or with a fine. The attempt is punishable.

13. Robbery and Extortion (*Raub und Erpressung*)[106]

Whosoever shall take away from another person, with force against the person or with threats of immediate injury to life or limb, someone else's movable thing, with the intent to unlawfully appropriate it, shall be punished for robbery (*Raub*) with imprisonment of not under one year. In less serious cases, the punishment is imprisonment of from six months to five years.

An aggravated robbery (*schwerer Raub*) is punishable with imprisonment of not under five years. This is the case where: (1) The offender or an accomplice taking part in the robbery carry a firearm; (2) the offender or an accomplice taking part in the robbery carry a weapon, a tool, or a device for the purpose of overcoming the resistance of another person by violence or the threat of violence; (3) the offender or an accomplice taking part in the robbery place another person in the danger of death or of an aggravated bodily harm; or (4) the offender commits the robbery as a member of a gang, together with another member of the gang, which has for its object the commission of robbery or theft. In less serious cases, the punishment is imprisonment of from one to five years.

Where death occurs as a consequence of the robbery (*Raub mit Todesfolge*), the punishment is imprisonment for life or imprisonment for not less than ten years.

Theft in the nature of robbery (*räuberischer Diebstahl*) is committed where the offender is surprised in the act of theft and he applies force to another person or threatens him with an immediate injury to life or limb in order to retain possession of the thing stolen. The offender is punished as a robber.

A person is guilty of extortion (*Erpressung*) who, by force or by threats of a grievous evil and in order to unlawfully enrich himself or a third person, compels another to do an act, to acquiesce to an act, or to omit to do an act, and thereby causes a financial loss to the person so compelled or to another person. Extortion is punishable with imprisonment of up to five years or with a fine. In especially serious cases, it is punishable with imprisonment for not less than one year. The act is unlawful where the use of force or the threatened evil is reprehensible in view of the end to be attained thereby. The attempt is punishable.

An extortionary robbery (*räuberische Erpressung*) is committed where the extortion is committed against a person by the use of force or by the threat of an immediate injury to limb or life. The offender will be punished as a robber.

In all cases of robbery and extortion, the court may order that the offender be placed under supervision after he has suffered punishment and is released from prison.[107]

NOTES AND QUESTIONS

1. As to theft, the German law provides for several kinds of theft. Compare, e.g., the Spanish law. Note that it covers the offense of burglary as it is defined in the Anglo-American law. See, e.g., New York Penal Law §140.00ff. Note further that it especially mentions the tapping of electric energy. Does this provision usually appear in American penal statutes, since it clearly amounts to larceny? See, e.g., Calif. Pen. C.A. §499(a).

Note also that the German law specifically defines embezzlement. Compare, e.g., Calif. Pen. C.A. §503ff., 18 U.S.C.A. §641ff.

The German law also has a specific provision as to the unauthorized use of motor vehicles. See also the Spanish law. Compare, e.g., Calif. Pen. C.A. §499(b).

2. As to robbery, the German law provides for a number of offenses falling under robbery. Compare it with the Spanish law. How is robbery treated in the law of your state? See, e.g., Calif. Pen. C.A. §211ff., 18 U.S.C.A. §2111ff. Compare also the various degrees of robbery in German law with those in the New York Penal Law §§160.05-160.15.

Note the German provision for death in consequence of robbery. See also the Spanish law. Would not Anglo-American law approach the subject the other way around, like homicide (murder) in the furtherance of a felony (robbery)? See, e.g., New York Penal Law §125.25 (3); People v. Carter (1975) 50 A.D.2d 174, 377 N.Y.S. 2d 256.

Note also the German rule as to extortion. How is extortion treated in the law of your state? *See, e.g.,* Calif. Pen. C.A. §518ff., 18 U.S.C.A. §871ff.

B. THE SYSTEM OF CRIMINAL COURTS

The German system of criminal courts comprises courts of limited jurisdiction, known as *Amtsgerichte* (county courts), courts of general jurisdiction, known as *Landgerichte* (district courts), appellate courts, known as *Oberlandesgerichte* (courts of appeal), and one court of final resort, known as the *Bundesgerichtshof* (Supreme Court).[108]

1. County Courts (*Amtsgerichte*)[109]

Amtsgerichte are courts of limited jurisdiction. They exercise their criminal jurisdiction within the territory determined by law. The court is constituted by a single judge when it hears cases of misdemeanors (*Vergehen*) that are prosecuted on private prosecution and are not punishable by imprisonment exceeding six months, or when the public prosecutor brings the misdemeanor case before a single judge and the punishment to be imposed is not expected to exceed one year imprisonment.

In other cases of misdemeanors (*Vergehen*) and felonies (*Verbrechen*), the court sits as the *Schöffengericht* and is constituted by a presiding judge and two lay judges, known as *Schöffen*. Decisions of the *Schöffengericht* are by simple majority.[110] The public prosecutor brings before the *Schöffengericht* cases where the expected punishment will not exceed imprisonment for three years since the *Amtsgericht* may not impose imprisonment exceeding three years, nor confinement in a mental hospital or preventive detention (*Sicherungsverwahrung*). It also cannot hear cases that are reserved for the *Landgericht* sitting as the *Schwurgericht* or for the *Oberlandesgericht*, irrespective of the term of imprisonment requested by the public prosecution.

The lay judges are selected in accordance with rules generally used throughout the world for the selection of jurors. A list of prospective lay judges is made every four years by the public administration of the county where the court sits. It must contain three persons per one thousand inhabitants. It must properly represent the population with respect to sex, age, occupation and standing in society. The lay judges must be between twenty-five and seventy years of age and of full capacity. No one convicted of an offense committed intentionally and to imprisonment exceeding six months may be listed. The list will be open to inspection by the general public for one week. It is then submitted to a committee consisting of a judge of the *Amtsgericht*, who is the chairman, an officer of the public administration, and ten members elected in the county. The committee elects from the list, by a two-thirds majority, as many persons as are required for service in the opinion of the presiding judge of the *Amtsgericht*, taking care that all strata of the population are properly represented. The *Amtsgericht* makes a list of those elected and determines by lot the order in which they must serve.

An appeal (*Berufung*) against judgments (*Urteile*) of the single judge and of the *Schöffengericht* may be filed with the *Amtsgericht* for transmittal to the

Landgericht within one week from pronouncement of the judgment or, where the accused was not present, from notification.

Judgments of the *Amtsgericht* also may be attacked by error (*Revision*), known as *Sprungrevision*. The error must be filed with the *Amtsgericht* within one week from its pronouncement or notification, as the case may be, for transmittal to the proper *Oberlandesgericht*, thus by-passing the *Landgericht*.

A complaint (*Beschwerde*) against the ruling (*Beschluss*) of an *Amtsgericht* must be filed within a time provided by law in accordance with the nature of the ruling, usually within one week from its pronouncement. The *Amtsgericht* may grant the request and rescind or modify its ruling, or it must transmit the complaint within three days to the proper *Landgericht* for its decision, which is final.

The accused may defend himself or he may appoint an attorney (*Rechtsanwalt*) admitted to practice before the court. He must be represented by an attorney when he is accused of a felony (*Verbrechen*) or when he is deaf or mute. The prosecution (*Staatsanwaltschaft*) is represented by the proper *Staatsanwalt* or *Amtsanwalt*.

2. District Courts (*Landgerichte*)[111]

Landgerichte are general jurisdiction courts. In the exercise of their criminal jurisdiction, they sit in chambers (*Kammern*) of three judges (*Richter*).

At a hearing of a case (*Hauptverhandlung*), they are constituted in one of the following forms. When hearing appeals (*Berufungen*) from a single judge of the *Amtsgericht*, the court is presided over by a presiding judge, has two lay judges (*Schöffen*) as members, and is known as the small criminal chamber (*kleine Strafkammer*). When hearing any other case, i.e., on appeal (*Berufung*) from the *Schöffengericht* and as a trial court, the court is presided over by a presiding judge, has two other judges and two lay judges (*Schöffen*) as members, and is known as the large criminal chamber (*grosse Strafkammer*). When hearing specially enumerated serious crimes, the large criminal chamber is also known as the *Schwurgericht*. Decision is by simple majority, except that decisions which are prejudicial to the accused and concern his guilt and the legal consequences of his act, including the circumstances which exclude, decrease or increase punishment, require a two-thirds majority of the votes.

The *Landgericht* thus hears appeals (*Berufungen*) from judgments (*Urteile*) of the *Amtsgericht*, and also complaints (*Beschwerden*) against rulings of the *Amtsgericht*. Where the judgment of the *Amtsgericht* is set aside, the *Landgericht* will give judgment in the matter. Yet, where the defect in the judgment was such that error because of breach of law occurred, the *Landgericht* may remit the case to the *Amtsgericht* for further proceedings.

In its trial jurisdiction, it hears cases of felonies (*Verbrechen*), unless the *Amtsgericht* or *Oberlandesgericht* has jurisdiction, cases of offenses where the punishment that is likely to be assessed may exceed imprisonment for three years or where commitment to a mental hospital or preventive detention may be ordered, or cases that are brought before the court by the public prosecution because of their special importance. Like the *Schwurgericht*, it also hears cases of specially enumerated serious crime.[112]

The lay judges (*Schöffen*) of the *Landgericht* are selected in the same way as they are in the *Amtsgericht*.

No appeal lies against judgments (*Urteile*) of the *Landgericht,* but error (*Revision*) may be brought within one week from pronouncement of a judgment or, where the accused was not present, from the notification. The error must be filed with the *Landgericht* for transmittal to the proper *Oberlandesgericht* or to the *Bundesgerichtshof,* as the case may be.

A complaint (*Beschwerde*) against rulings (*Beschlüsse*) of the *Landgericht* may be brought to the *Landgericht* for eventual transmittal to the *Oberlandesgericht* under the same conditions as a complaint against rulings of the *Amtsgericht* is brought to the *Amtsgericht* for eventual transmittal to the *Landgericht.*

The accused must be represented by an attorney (*Rechtsanwalt*) admitted to practice before the court in all cases heard by the *Landgericht* in its trial jurisdiction. In its appellate jurisdiction, the accused must be so represented only if he was represented already when the case was heard in the *Amtsgericht.* The prosecution (*Staatsanwaltschaft*) is represented by the proper *Staatsanwalt.*

NOTES AND QUESTIONS

1. As to county courts, they exercise both civil and criminal jurisdiction. Here they sit as criminal courts. Note the jurisdiction of the court. A single judge may not impose a sentence exceeding one year imprisonment. The *Schöffengericht* may imprison up to three years, but not for any longer term. Compare the jurisdiction of the *Amtsgericht* with that of the Italian *pretura.* Do German *Amtsgerichte* exercise greater powers than Spanish municipal courts or French police courts? How do German county courts compare with California municipal courts?

Note that the *Schöffengericht* also has two lay judges who are comparable to Anglo-American jurors in the method of their selection. On the bench, however, they are endowed with the powers of judges and together they may outvote the presiding professional judge. Do lay judges sit on the limited jurisdiction criminal courts in other countries? Are trials in American municipal courts or justice courts trials by jury? Compare, e.g., trial before U.S. Magistrates, 18 U.S.C.A. §3401ff., and Rules of Procedure for the Trial of Minor Offenses before U.S. Magistrates.

An appeal against judgments of the *Amtsgericht* goes to the *Landgericht.* Compare appeals from French police courts.

Note the German rule as to legal representation of the accused. Compare it with the Spanish rule. As to legal representation in American criminal trials, *see,* e.g., 18 U.S.C.A. §3006A.

2. As to district courts, consider the system of different panels formed in the German *Landgericht* in the exercise of its criminal jurisdiction. Compare it with the composition of French correctional courts and assize courts, and Italian penal courts and assize courts. How do they compare with Anglo-American general jurisdiction trial courts, like the Texas District Courts or the California Superior Courts?

Note that the accused must be represented by an attorney in the trial jurisdiction of the *Landgericht.*

For German judges, prosecutors and attorneys, consult the section on legal officers below.

3.   Courts of Appeal (*Oberlandesgerichte*)[113]

In the exercise of its criminal jurisdiction, an *Oberlandesgericht* hears error (*Revision*) against judgments (*Urteile*) of the small criminal chamber (*kleine Strafkammer*) and the large criminal chamber (*grosse Strafkammer*) of the *Landgericht* situated within its area of territorial jurisdiction, and also against judgments (*Urteile*) pronounced by such *Landgerichte* in the exercise of their trial jurisdiction where the error is founded exclusively on the alleged breach of state law (as contrasted with federal law).

Where the judgment of *Landgericht* is set aside, the *Oberlandesgericht* will give judgment when no further proceedings are required, such as when the accused is acquitted, a determined punishment is to be assessed, the prosecution agrees that the statutorily determined minimum punishment should be imposed, or where no punishment will be imposed. In other instances, the case will be remitted for further proceedings to another chamber of the *Landgericht* that pronounced the judgment or to another *Landgericht* in the same state.

Oberlandesgerichte also hear complaints (*Beschwerden*) against rulings (*Beschlüsse*) of *Landgerichte*. In all of the above capacities the panel (*Senat*) hearing a case is composed of three judges, one of whom presides.

The *Oberlandesgericht* within whose territorial jurisdiction the seat of the government of a particular state is situated has further jurisdiction over certain offenses as a trial court. These are mainly offenses against peace and the state.[114] In this capacity, the panel (*Senat*) hearing a case is composed of five judges, one of whom presides.

Decisions of *Oberlandesgerichte* are by simple majority, except that decisions which are prejudicial to the accused and concern his guilt and the legal consequences of his act, including the circumstances which exclude, decrease or increase punishment, require a two-thirds majority of the votes.

No further remedy lies against judgments (*Urteile*) or rulings (*Beschlüsse*) of an *Oberlandesgericht* pronounced in the exercise of its jurisdiction on error (*Revision*). Against judgments (*Urteile*) pronounced in the exercise of its trial jurisdiction, however, error (*Revision*) lies to the *Bundesgerichtshof*. It must be filed within one week from pronouncement of the judgment or, where the accused was not present, from notification, with the *Oberlandesgericht* for transmittal to the *Bundesgerichtshof*.

A complaint (*Beschwerde*) may be brought against some of the rulings (*Beschlüsse*) of an *Oberlandesgericht* pronounced in the exercise of its trial jurisdiction.[115] The complaint is filed with the *Oberlandesgericht* for eventual transmittal to the *Bundesgerichtshof* under the same conditions as mentioned above applicable to complaints.

The accused must be represented by an attorney (*Rechtsanwalt*) admitted to practice before the court. In cases heard in the error jurisdiction of the *Oberlandesgericht*, the prosecution (*Staatsanwaltschaft*) is represented by the proper *Staatsanwalt*; in cases heard by the court in its trial jurisdiction, the prosecution is represented by the *Generalbundesanwalt*.

4.   Supreme Court (*Bundesgerichtshof*)[116]

In the exercise of its criminal jurisdiction, the Supreme Court sits in panels

(*Senate*) of five judges. There also is a large senate in criminal matters (*grosser Senat für Strafsachen*), composed of the president of the Court and his deputy and eight members. The large senate in criminal matters hears cases in which a criminal senate wishes to deviate from a previous decision of another criminal senate or of the large senate in criminal matters.

The *Bundesgerichtshof* hears error (*Revision*) against judgments (*Urteile*) of *Oberlandesgerichte* given in the exercise of their trial jurisdiction, and also against judgments (*Urteile*) of *Landgerichte* given in the exercise of their trial jurisdiction where an *Oberlandesgericht* does not have jurisdiction, namely, where the error is founded on the alleged breach of federal law (as contrasted with state law).

The *Bundesgerichtshof* further hears complaints (*Beschwerden*) against those rulings (*Beschlüsse*) of an *Oberlandesgericht* against which this remedy is available.[117]

Where judgment (*Urteil*) of the court below is set aside, the *Bundegerichtshof* will give judgment when no further proceedings are required, such as when the accused is acquitted, the prosecution agrees that the statutorily determined minimum punishment should be imposed, or no punishment will be imposed. In other instances, the case will be remitted for further proceedings to another chamber of the court of the same rank in the same state. In the case of an *Oberlandesgericht*, the case is remitted to another senate of the particular *Oberlandesgericht*.

Decisions are by simple majority, except that decisions which are prejudicial to the accused and concern his guilt and the legal consequences of his act, including the circumstances which exclude, decrease or increase punishment require a two-thirds majority of the votes.

No further remedy lies against decisions of the *Bundesgerichtshof*.

The accused must be represented by an attorney (*Rechtsanwalt*) admitted to practice before the Court. The prosecution (*Staatsanwaltschaft*) is represented by the *Generalbundesanwalt*.

NOTES AND QUESTIONS

1. As to courts of appeal, the German *Oberlandesgericht* in the exercise of its criminal jurisdiction is not a court of appeal but a court of error only. Error means the nonapplication or improper application of law. It thus hears error in cases that originate in an *Amtsgericht* as a trial court and come to a *Landgericht* on appeal. The error is alleged to occur in the judgment of the *Landgericht*. The *Oberlandesgericht* also hears error against judgments of the *Landgericht* pronounced in its trial jurisdiction dealing with state law only. These cases are rather rare. The trial jurisdiction of the *Oberlandesgericht* is also rare.

Compare the German system with that of Spain. Compare it also with the systems in France and Italy. They all differ with respect to appeal and error. What are the differences?

Being a court of error in criminal matters, is the German *Oberlandesgericht* functionally comparable to the court of final resort in the several American states, like the New York Court of Appeals, or the United States Supreme Court? *See*, e.g., 28 U.S.C.A. §§1254 and 1257.

2. As to the Supreme Court, in the exercise of its criminal jurisdiction, the

Bundesgerichtshof chiefly hears error against the judgments given by *Landgerichte* acting as trial courts in matters of national (federal) law. Since the German Penal Code is federal, virtually any penal case that is tried in a *Landgericht* may go to the *Bundesgerichtshof* on error. Compare this system with the Spanish system. How does the German setup differ from the Italian system?

Being the court of final resort in both civil and criminal cases, the *Bundesgerichtshof* may be compared with the courts of final resort in the Anglo-American system.

For judges, prosecutors and attorneys of the courts of appeal and the Supreme Court, *see* the section on legal officers below.

C. THE LAW OF CRIMINAL PROCEDURE

The Code of Criminal Procedure of 1877 is in power as amended. It has 473 articles presented in seven books: Book 1. General provisions; Book 2. Procedure at trial level; Book 3. Means of review; Book 4. Reopening of proceedings terminated by a judgment in the power of law; Book 5. Participation of the victim of the crime in the proceedings; Book 6. Special types of proceedings; and Book 7. Execution of punishment and costs of the proceedings.

Book 1 (General provisions) has the following sections: 1. Jurisdiction of courts as to subject matters; 2. Territorial jurisdiction of courts; 3. Disqualification and challenge of judicial officers; 4. Judicial decisions and their publication; 5. Calculation of time and reinstatement of time; 6. Witnesses; 7. Experts and view; 8. Seizure, recording of communications, and search; 9. Arrest and provisional detention; 9(a) Other means to ensure criminal prosecution and execution of judgments; 9(b) Preliminary prohibition to exercise a calling; 10. Examination of the suspect; and 11. Defense.

Book 2 (Procedure at trial level) has the following sections: 1. Indictment; 2. Preparation of the indictment; 3. [deleted]; 4. Decision as to holding of the trial; 5. Preparation of the trial; 6. Trial; and 7. Proceedings against absentees.

Book 3 (Means of review) has the following sections: 1. General provisions; 2. Complaint; 3. Appeal; and 4. Error.

Book 4 (Reopening of proceedings terminated by a judgment in the power of law) has no separate sections.

Book 5 (Participation of the victim of crime in the proceedings) has the following sections: 1. Private prosecution; 2. Intervention; and 3. Indemnification of the victim of crime.

Book 6 (Special types of proceedings) has the following sections: 1. Procedure concerning penal orders; 2. Procedure in cases of preventive detention; 3. Procedure in confiscations and seizures of property; and 4. Procedure concerning the imposition of fines against juridical persons and associations.

Book 7 (Execution of punishment and costs of the proceedings) has the following sections: 1. Execution of punishment; and 2. Costs of the proceedings.

Further important statutes appear in the appendix to the Code, such as the introductory law to the code (*Einführungsgesetz zur Strafprozessordnung*), the Judiciary Act (*Gerichtsverfassungsgesetz*), the Juvenile Courts Act (*Jugendgerichtsgesetz*), the Extradition Act (*Auslieferungsgesetz*), the Court Costs Act

(*Gerichtskostengesetz*), the Compensation of Witnesses and Experts Act (*Gesetz über die Entschädigung von Zeugen und Sachverständigen*), and the Criminal Records Act (*Bundeszentralregistergesetz*).

The following are topics selected from the German law of criminal procedure.

1. Procedure before Trial Courts (*Verfahren im ersten Rechtszug*)[118]

Trial courts include *Amtsgerichte, Landgerichte,* and to a certain extent also *Oberlandesgerichte.* Trial procedure before all these courts is governed by the same rules.

(a) Preliminary proceedings. Information on the commission of an offense is communicated to the police, an office of the public prosecution, or an *Amtsgericht.* A suspect may be apprehended in the act. Anyone may arrest a suspect in the act or on hot pursuit when his identity is not immediately known. Police officers may arrest suspects without a warrant also in circumstances under which a warrant of arrest would be issued.

Where the suspect is not arrested, the information is related to a judge of the *Amtsgericht,* who will order the suspect in writing to appear before him. In cases that justify the issuance of a warrant of arrest, the judge may issue the warrant or he may order the suspect brought before him immediately without issuing such a warrant. He may then issue the warrant after hearing the suspect. Under an order to appear, the suspect may not be held longer than the day on which he is to appear.

Where the suspect is already under arrest, he must be brought before the judge at the latest on the day following the day of his arrest.

The judge must hear the suspect and give him the opportunity to clear himself of suspicion. First, he must tell the suspect what act he is supposed to have committed and which provisions of the criminal law apply, then the judge must inform the suspect that he may speak or remain silent, that he is free to appoint counsel immediately, and that he may offer proof to clear himself.

A warrant of arrest may be issued where the suspect has absconded or is likely to abscond or where he is likely to destroy evidence, influence witnesses and generally interfere with the prosecution of his case. It also may be issued where the alleged offense is of a serious nature, like murder, manslaughter, aggravated theft, robbery, or arson.[119] Where the offense is punishable only with imprisonment of up to six months or with a fine of up to 180 multiples of the daily rate of fine, the suspect may not be held under arrest on the ground of his likelihood of interfering with the prosecution. He may be held on the ground of his likelihood of absconding only where he has already once absconded or made preparations to abscond, or where he does not reside or stay in Germany, or where he cannot prove his identity.

The judge may not hold a suspect in confinement who is held only because of his likelihood to abscond where this danger does not exist any more, or where his presence may be insured by other means, such as a direction not to leave town. The judge may similarly not hold a suspect who is held only because he might interfere with the prosecution where the direction not so to interfere is deemed sufficient. The judge may release a suspect without any security or on bail. Bail is given in cash, valuable papers, or deposit of valuables with or without sureties. The amount and type of bail is determined freely by the judge.

The suspect who is held under arrest may request his release at any time. A hearing on the petition must be held as soon as possible within two weeks. Where the petition is denied, it may be repeated every two months. No suspect may be held in confinement generally over six months. If he is held longer, a decision of the *Oberlandesgericht* to hold him is required. In any case, he may not be held longer than one year; he must be tried or released.

The police is under a duty to investigate the commission of offenses and to report to the office of the public prosecutor (*Staatsanwaltschaft*). The same duty falls on the office of the public prosecutor. Where the police or the office of the public prosecutor hears the suspect, it must give him the same instructions as a judge, namely, what offense he is supposed to have committed, which provisions of the law apply, that he may speak or remain silent, that he may appoint counsel, and that he may offer proof to clear himself.

The office of the public prosecutor may also summon witnesses and appoint experts and obtain their evidence like a court. The evidence it takes is unsworn. Only a court can take sworn evidence.

(b) Indictment. Judicial proceedings are initiated by the public prosecution filing an indictment (*Anklageschrift*) with the proper court. It must identify the suspect, describe the offense, give the place and time of commission, cite the applicable law, and indicate the proof that will be offered. It must designate the court before which the trial should be held, and give the name of the counsel for the suspect.

The presiding judge of the court with which the indictment is filed will have a copy of the indictment delivered to the suspect. He will also inquire whether the suspect wishes to offer immediate proof to clear himself. The court may order ex officio that proof be offered for the better clarification of the case.

The court will study the indictment, the reports of the police and the prosecution, and the evidence given by the defense, if any. It then will order that the suspect stand trial where the suspect appears to stand under sufficient suspicion of having committed a criminally punishable act. Where the suspect has not been apprehended, the court will discontinue the proceedings.

Where the court refused to act on the indictment and does not order the suspect to stand trial, it must state whether the order is based on questions of fact or law. No remedy lies against a decision that the suspect must stand trial, but a complaint (*Beschwerde*) may be brought by the public prosecutor against a decision not to act on the indictment.

Where the court orders that the suspect must stand trial, it will designate the proper court where the trial is to be held. A *Landgericht* may designate any other *Landgericht* or *Amtsgericht*, but it may not designate an *Oberlandesgericht*. If it considers an *Oberlandesgericht* to be the proper trial court, it must submit the matter to it for a decision.

Where in the opinion of the public prosecutor a given *Amtsgericht* is the proper court to try a particular case, he will bring the case before such *Amtsgericht*. He may present a suspect for trial in summary proceedings (*beschleunigtes Verfahren*) in such *Amtsgericht* where the punishment will not exceed one year imprisonment and where no order for preventive detention will be made. In summary proceedings, the indictment may be communicated to the court orally and the trial may be held promptly. The judge or the *Schöffengericht* before whom the case is so brought will rule on the motion. Where he feels that regular proceedings should be held, he will deny the motion. No remedy lies against the denial.

Once the court has ruled that the suspect must stand trial, the suspect becomes the accused and preparation for trial begins.

(c) Preparation for trial. The presiding judge of the court will set the case for trial. A summons will be issued to the accused, his counsel and the prosecution. At least one week must lie between service of the summons and the trial date. The court will also summon the witnesses requested to be summoned by the parties and gives both parties a list of all the witnesses so summoned. If the court does not summon a witness because it does not consider his presence of importance, the party that requested him summoned may summon him himself. The prosecution is obligated to properly prepare its case and to produce all evidence in its possession, including the tools with which the offense was committed and other incriminating objects.

(d) The trial. The trial (*Hauptverhandlung*) is held in the continuous presence of the judges who will decide the case, and also in the presence of officers of the public prosecution and the defense counsel. The accused may appoint up to three defense counsel. He may freely communicate with them. They may inspect the court files.

The object is to proceed with the trial without interruption. Short adjournments, e.g., for lunch, are ordered by the presiding judge. Longer adjournments are ordered by the court. The trial may be adjourned for up to ten days. Where the trial has lasted ten days already, it may be interrupted once for up to thirty days, and where it has been resumed and continued for ten days, it may be again interrupted for up to ten days. Where the day on which the trial was to resume is a Saturday, Sunday, or holiday, the trial may be resumed on the next business day.

A trial may not be held against an absent accused. Evidence against him will be preserved so that he may be tried when apprehended.

Where the accused disrupts the orderly proceedings of the trial, he may be removed from the courtroom and the trial may proceed in his absence.

A trial may be held in the absence of the accused, if he is properly summoned but does not appear and is advised in the summons that the trial will be held in his absence. This may be done only where the punishment imposed does not exceed 180 multiples of the daily rate of fine or consists only in the confiscation of objects or the revocation of a driver's license. A driver's license may be revoked only where the possibility of its revocation was mentioned in the summons.

A trial may also be held in the absence of the accused at his request, but the maximum punishment imposed in such a case may not exceed six months imprisonment or 180 multiples of the daily rate of fine. The confiscation of objects and the revocation of a driver's license may be ordered.

The presiding judge directs the proceedings at the trial. Any objection to his direction (*Anordnung*) will be decided by the court.

The trial opens with the case being called. Thereupon the presiding judge makes certain that the accused and his counsel are present, as well as all the summoned witnesses and experts, and all evidence is ready to be produced. The witnesses are requested to leave the courtroom.

The presiding judge interrogates the accused as to the generalia. Then the public prosecutor (*Staatsanwalt*) reads the charges (*Anklagesatz*). The presiding judge advises the accused that he may comment on the charges to clear himself or he may remain silent. If the accused desires to speak, he must be heard.

Proof is then offered. The court must see to it that the truth appears in the matter. The court may reject evidence which is improper, superfluous, or designed to delay the proceedings. Where evidence is offered of which the opponent has not yet been advised, it may not be rejected, but the opponent may request an adjournment to enable him to prepare to meet it. The court decides on all motions. Witnesses testify and are sworn in only after giving testimony. Persons under the age of sixteen and persons who are themselves under suspicion of participation in the offense may not give sworn testimony. The court, in its discretion, needs not swear in witnesses who are older than sixteen but younger than eighteen years of age, persons who may refuse to testify because of their relationship to the accused or to the victim of the crime, persons whose testimony the courts considers not essential, persons who have previously been convicted of perjury, and persons whose testimony by agreement of the prosecution and the accused and his counsel need not be taken on oath. The following may refuse to testify: the person engaged to marry the accused, his spouse or former spouse, his relatives in the direct line, those related to him by marriage or adoption, collaterals related by blood up to the third degree, and those related by marriage up to the second degree even if the marriage upon which the relationship is based no longer subsists.

A witness who refuses to testify or to testify on oath without any legal ground for refusal will be ordered to pay the costs caused by his refusal, he will be fined, or be imprisoned for up to six months. A witness who does not appear, although he was properly summoned, will be subject to the payment of costs of the spoiled proceedings and to the payment of a fine or imprisonment. He may be brought into the court by force.

The presiding judge calls the witnesses, first those for the prosecution and then those for the defense. Each witness is asked to give a cohesive account of what he knows about the matter. The presiding judge and the other judges, and thereafter the prosecution and the defense may agree to do the questioning themselves rather than leave it chiefly to the presiding judge. In such a case, each side questions its witnesses and only after it finishes will the other side be free to ask questions. The court always has the duty to clarify the issue by asking questions. Persons below the age of sixteen are questioned first by the presiding judge. Objections to admissibility of a question are resolved by the court.

Documents presented in evidence are read. This includes extracts from registers (like the registers of births, deaths and marriages) and records of prior convictions of the accused. Evidence given by witnesses before a commissioner may be read when the witness has died, or when he has been excused from personal appearance because of illness or for any other reason, or when both parties agree that such evidence may be given.

After hearing every witness, expert or codefendant, and after reading any documents, the presiding judge must ask the accused whether he has any comments. The prosecution and the defense may also comment.

When all the evidence has been given, the presiding judge asks the prosecution to make its final statement and thereafter the defense. The prosecution may reply, but the defense has the last word. Then the presiding judge asks the accused whether he still has anything to say in his defense. The trial having thus come to an end, the presiding judge declares it closed. The court then retires to consider judgment.

The proceedings at the trial are recorded by the court recorder. The record (*Protokoll*) is signed by the presiding judge and the recorder. The record must be completed and signed before judgment is declared.

(e) Judgment. The presiding judge directs the discussion of the court and determines the topics for debate and the order in which the questions are to be decided. He records the decisions of the court. Any difference of opinion will be decided by the court. The court freely evaluates the evidence and decides in accordance with its free conviction.

The court decides by simple majority of its members, but on the question of the guilt of the accused and on the legal consequences of the act, including attenuating and aggravating circumstances, a two-thirds majority of votes is required.

In questions that are decided by simple majority, if there are more than two opinions, neither of which has a majority, the votes most unfavorable to the accused are added to the next less unfavorabe until majority is reached. Where there are two opinions and neither has the majority, the more favorable opinion to the accused prevails. If a *Schöffengericht* composed of two judges and two lay judges hears the case and a tie results, the presiding judge has the casting vote.

Judges vote in inverted order of seniority; if of equal seniority, the younger votes before the older. Lay judges vote before the judges, the younger before the older. Where there is a rapporteur, he votes first. The presiding judge votes last.

The judgment (*Urteil*) must be publicly pronounced within eleven days from the closing of the trial, otherwise a new trial must be held. The judgment is read in open court.

The judgment is given in the name of the people. It contains the actual order acquitting or convicting the accused (*Urteilsformel*), followed by the reasons for the decision (*Urteilsgründe*).

Where the accused is convicted (*verurteilt*), the decision must state the facts that the court found as established and the law infringed thereby and on which the conviction relies. It must also state the reasons for the assessment of the punishment actually pronounced, taking into account attenuating and aggravating circumstances, if applicable.

Where the accused is acquitted (*freigesprochen*), the decision must state whether he was found not guilty and of what acts, or whether the acts were not punishable.

A judgment where the court could have imposed preventive detention or the withdrawal of the driver's license must state why such an order was made or was not made, as the case may be. Where the court releases the convicted person on probation, it must make all the convenient provisions with respect to supervision.

The judgment is signed by all the judges who heard the case. If a judge cannot sign, it will be noted by the presiding judge indicating the reason for the inability; if the presiding judge is so incapacitated, it will be noted by the senior judge. Lay judges need not sign the judgment.

The judgment is filed with the record of the case. The record officer of the court (*Urkundsbeamte*) issues copies thereof under his signature and the court seal.

NOTES AND QUESTIONS

The German law of criminal procedure has a unified system of procedure before all trial courts, irrespective of whether the proceedings take place in a limited or general jurisdiciton court or, exceptionally, in the *Oberlandesgericht*.

1. Arrest is made usually by the police. Where it is effected with a warrant, such warrant of arrest may be issued only by a judge. Who may order the arrest of a person in the French system? Compare also the Italian system. Who may issue warrants of arrest in the Anglo-American system? *See*, e.g., Calif. Pen. C.A. §813ff.; F.R. Crim. P. Rules 4 and 5. How is the arrest made? *See*, e.g., Calif. Pen. C.A. §833ff.

Note that the suspect must be brought before a judge at the latest the next day after his arrest. Compare the French law. What is the Anglo-American rule? *See*, e.g., Calif. Pen. C.A. §821ff., F.R. Crim. P. Rule 5.

Note the German provisions concerning release on bail or without bail. Compare the Italian or Spanish law. *See also*, e.g., 18 U.S.C.A. §3141ff., F.R. Crim. P. Rule 46.

2. Formal judicial proceedings open with the indictment. It is prepared by the prosecution and is filed in the proper court in which, in the opinion of the prosecutor, the suspect should be tried. The court will then decide whether there is enough evidence against the suspect to order him to stand trial. It is thus the court that orders a person to stand trial. Note that German criminal procedure abandoned the institution of an investigating judge, and that investigation of the suspect is done by the police and the prosecution. Compare the German approach with those of Spain and France.

When the court orders the suspect to stand trial, it will consider whether it is territorially and functionally competent, i.e., whether the prosecution filed the indictment in the proper court. If the court feels that it is not competent, it will pass the case to the proper court.

The indictment is for the offense that appears from the investigation to have been committed. No plea bargaining exists. Compare it with, e.g., F.R. Crim. P. Rule 11 (e).

3. Preparation for trial begins when the court orders the suspect to stand trial. This is done by the court and the prosecution while the defense is preparing its case.

The trial is directed by the presiding judge. The court is always a panel of several judges with the exception of a trial for minor offenses before a single judge in the *Amtsgericht*. Consequently, the burden of conducting the trial falls on the presiding judge. Compare, e.g., the Italian procedure.

The trial usually lasts a few hours only, but there may be adjournments and it may even take several days in involved cases, especially if there are several defendants.

Note that an accused who is not apprehended may not be tried in his absence. Compare, e.g., the Italian and the Spanish law. An accused present in court who disrupts the proceedings may be removed from the courtroom and the trial will proceed in his absence. Compare, e.g., the French law. Do the same rules apply in Anglo-American courts? *See*, e.g., F.R. Crim. P. Rule 43; Calif. Pen. C.A. §1043.

Proof is offered by all of the standard means of proof. Note the German rule concerning testimony of witnesses. What is the minimum age required of a witness to give sworn testimony in Spanish law? Are witnesses in an Anglo-American trial sworn in only after they have given evidence? *See*, e.g., Fed. Rules of Evidence, Rule 603.

Note that the trial ends with the final address of the prosecution and the defense and that the defense always has the last word. Compare, e.g., the Italian law; also F.R. Crim. P. Rule 29.1.

Note that the accused may be represented by as many as three defense counsel. Is this the standard rule in criminal trials in other countries? *See*, e.g., the Italian rule, Art. 125 of the Italian Code of Criminal Procedure, which limits the accused to two counsel. Does any such rule exist in Anglo-American law?

A record of the trial is continuously made. When completed, it is certified by the presiding judge and the recorder. Compare the Italian rule. *See also* F.R. Crim. P. Rule 55.

4. As to judgment, the court, being composed of several members, must deliberate and then proceed to voting. Compare the German voting procedure with that of France. Note the German rule requiring a two-thirds majority on the main questions. Does a similar requirement exist in other countries? *See*, e.g., the Spanish rule. Note also that there is no rapporteur in the German trial court. Compare the Italian and French requirements.

The actual judgment must be drawn up strictly in accordance with the law, otherwise it would be void. Compare, e.g., the Italian rule. *See also* F.R. Crim. P. Rule 32, and Form 25.

---

2. Appellate Procedure *(Berufung)*[120]

Appellate courts are the *Landgerichte* that hear appeals from judgments of the *Amtsgerichte*.

Both the accused and the prosecution may appeal. Notice of appeal is to be given orally or in writing to the court that pronounced the judgment within one week from its pronouncement or, where the accused was not present, from the notification. The appellant must file his brief within another week. Where notice of appeal is given in time, the judgment does not enter into the power of law.

The court office hands over the files to the office of the public prosecutor, which sends them to the office of the public prosecutor at the proper appellate court. That office will hand them over to the appellate court within one week. Where the appeal has been filed by the prosecution, it will send a copy of the appeal to the defense.

The court of appeal considers whether the appeal was filed in time, and if so, it will hear the appeal. If not, it will reject the appeal by its ruling *(Beschluss)*, which may be attacked by a complaint *(Beschwerde)*.

The presiding judge of the chamber *(Kammer)* hearing the case will appoint a rapporteur *(Berichterstatter)* from among the judges, or he will act as rapporteur himself. The preparatory proceedings and the trial proceed in accordance with the rules of procedure before trial courts. New evidence may be presented. The appellate review is, however, limited to the issues raised on appeal. Where an accused who is not under arrest does not appear at the hearing, nor does his counsel, and the appeal was filed by the defense, the court will summarily dismiss the appeal. Where the appeal was filed by the prosecution, it will be heard even in the absence of the defense.

At the hearing, first the rapporteur (*Berichterstatter*) gives his report on the proceedings up to the time of his report. This is done in the absence of the witnesses. Then the judgment appealed from is read; the presiding judge hears the accused; and proof is given by witnesses, experts, documents, and so forth, in accordance with the rules of trial in trial courts. When all proof has been given, the appellant addresses the court and then the appellee. The defense always has the last word. The presiding judge declares the hearing closed and the court retires to consider judgment.

Judgment is given in accordance with the rules applicable to trial courts. Where the court considers the appeal justified, it will set aside the judgment of the court below and give its own judgment. Where the court finds that the judgment appealed from suffers a defect which gives ground to error proceedings (*Revision*), it may, where it finds it advisable, remit the case to the court below for further proceedings rather than give judgment. The judgment of the appellate court may not increase the penalty in any way where only the accused appealed or on an appeal of the prosecution brought solely for the benefit of the accused.

3.   Procedure on Error (*Revision*)[121]

Courts of error include the individual *Oberlandesgerichte* and the *Bundesgerichtshof,* each within the sphere of its jurisdiction.

Notice of error must be given orally or in writing to the court that pronounced the judgment within one week from its pronouncement or, where the accused was not present, from the notification. Where the notice is given in time, the judgment does not enter into the power of law.

The plaintiff in error must file his brief within one month from the expiration of the time to give notice of error. He must indicate in what respect he attacks the judgment and give his reasons. Error may be brought only for breach of the law. A breach of the law occurs when a rule of the law was not applied or when it was improperly applied.

A judgment is conclusively considered as suffering from error in the following cases: (1) where the court was not properly constituted; (2) where a disqualified judge or lay judge was sitting on the court; (3) where a judge or lay judge was sitting on the court who was successfully challenged for cause or where the challenge was improperly dismissed; (4) where the court improperly assumed jurisdiction; (5) where the trial took place in the absence of the prosecution or in the absence of a person whose presence is prescribed by law; (6) where the judgment is based on oral proceedings with respect to which the provisions concerning the publicity of proceedings were infringed; (7) where the judgment does not give any reasons for the decision or where such reasons were not filed with the record of the case within the prescribed time; and (8) where by a ruling of the court, the defense was improperly restricted with respect to an issue material for the decision.[122]

Where the plaintiff in error gives the notice of error in time and files his brief in a timely fashion and in the proper form, a copy thereof is delivered to the defendant in error who has one week to file his reply. Where the reply is filed in time, or the time for reply runs, the court passes the files to the office of the public prosecutor, which will channel them to the proper court of error.

The court of error will summarily dismiss the error where the error was not brought in time or where it was not brought in the proper form. It may also summarily dismiss the error at the motion of the prosecution where it unanimously finds the error obviously unfounded. The prosecution must deliver its motion requesting such ruling to the plaintiff in error, who has two weeks to file his reply.

Where the court of error unanimously finds the error well founded, it will summarily set aside the judgment complained of. Summary decisions are made by a ruling (*Beschluss*). In all other cases, the court of error wil decide by judgment (*Urteil*).

The presiding judge of the panel (*Senat*) hearing the error will appoint a rapporteur (*Berichterstatter*) from among the judges to study the case and will set a day for the hearing. A proper summons will issue to the parties.

At the hearing, first the rapporteur gives his report on the proceedings up to the time of his report. Then the plaintiff in error takes the floor and thereafter the defendant in error. The defense always has the last word. The presiding judge declares the hearing closed, and the court retires to consider judgment.

Judgment is given in accordance with the rules applicable to trial courts. The review of the court of error is, however, limited to matters raised by the error. Where the court considers the error well founded, it will set aside the judgment of the court below.

The court of error will give its own judgment in the matter where the accused is acquitted, where the prosecution is discontinued, where a statutorily determined punishment is assessed, where the court on a motion of the prosecution decides to assess the minimum punishment provided for by law, or where the court does not impose any punishment. Otherwise, the case will be remitted for further proceedings to another section or chamber of the court whose judgment was set aside or to another court of the same level within the same state. Where the judgment set aside was given by an *Oberlandesgericht* in the exercise of its trial jurisdiction, the case is remitted to another panel (*Senat*) of that *Oberlandesgericht*. The case may be remitted to a court of yet lower level in the event that that court has jurisdiction over the matter still to be dealt with.

The court to which the case is remitted for further proceedings is bound by the decision of the court of error and must apply its reasoning in the judgment to be given in the case. The judgment may not increase the penalty in any way where only the accused brought the error or where it was brought by the prosecution solely for the benefit of the accused.

NOTES AND QUESTIONS

1. As to appellate procedure, it governs procedure on an appeal from an *Amtsgericht* to a *Landgericht*.

The appeal is as of right. The entire procedure proceeds along the lines of that before the trial court. Grounds for error, if any, are included in the appeal since the court may correct such defects on appeal. How does the German appellate procedure compare with the French appellate procedure? Compare it also with the Italian appellate procedure.

The German appeal is an appeal from the limited jurisdiction trial court to the appellate division of the general jurisdiction trial court. How does it compare with the Anglo-American practice. *See*, e.g., Calif. Pen. C.A. §1466ff. as to appeals from inferior courts.

2. As to procedure on error, error is brought as of right on grounds specifically enumerated in the law. The usual error court is the *Bundesgerichtshof* in the exercise of its criminal jurisdiction. The procedure is based on that existing in trial courts while it embodies all applicable features of appellate procedure. The error court will in most cases give a judgment without any remission. Compare these dominant features of the German error procedure with those of Italy or France. How can a criminal case reach the Anglo-American court of final resort? *See*, e.g., 28 U.S.C.A. §§2101ff., 1254ff.

As to remission to lower courts, compare the French system. How is remission effected in the Italian system? *See*, e.g., 28 U.S.C.A. §2106 as to the United States Supreme Court and United States Courts of Appeal.

---

4. Reopening of Proceedings
(*Wiederaufnahme des Verfahrens*)[123]

Proceedings terminated by a judgment that has entered into the power of law may be reopened on the strength of a petiton for their reopening brought for the benefit of a convicted person or to the disadvantage of the accused.

The petition may be brought in favor of the convicted person where: (1) A document presented to his disadvantage at the trial was not genuine or was falsified; (2) a witness or an expert, on giving testimony or rendering an opinion to the disadvantage of the convicted person, made himself guilty of an intentional or negligent violation of the duty imposed on him by the oath, or of intentionally giving false unsworn testimony; (3) a judge or a lay judge who participated in the passing of the judgment made himself guilty of a criminally punishable breach of his official duties with respect to the matter, unless the breach was caused by the convicted person himself; (4) a judgment of a civil court on which the criminal judgment was based was set aside by another judgment that entered into the power of law; and (5) new facts or proof appeared which alone, or in conjunction with the evidence previously given, seem to justify the acquittal of the accused, or a lesser punishment in view of the application of a milder provision of the law, or a substantially different decision concerning supplemental orders, like confinement to a mental hospital or to preventive detention.

The petition does not produce a stay of execution of the judgment, but the court may order a postponement or a stay of execution. The petition may be brought even where the person suffered punishment or died. Where the convicted person has died, his spouse, his lineal and collateral relatives, as well as his brothers and sisters, may petition.

The petition may be brought to the detriment of the accused where: (1) A document presented to his advantage at trial was not genuine or was falsified; (2) a witness or an expert, on giving testimony or rendering an opinion to the advantage of the accused, made himself guilty of an intentional or negligent violation of the duty imposed on him by the oath, or of intentionally giving false unsworn testimony; (3) a judge or a lay judge who participated in the passing of the judgment made himself guilty of a criminally punishable breach of his official duties with respect to the matter; and (4) an acquitted person made a credible confession, in or out of court, of having committed a criminally punishable act.

The petition may not be brought in order to bring about a different punishment on the strength of the same provisions of the law.

The petition must state the legal ground for the reopening of the proceedings and must offer proof. The petition may be filed with the proper court or with the court that pronounced the judgment attacked, but it will then be channelled to the proper court.

Before the opening of each judicial year, each *Oberlandesgericht* will determine the courts within its judicial district that are designated to hear petitions for reopening of proceedings. The petition is heard by another court of the same level as that which gave the judgment attacked. Where the judgment attacked was given in error proceedings, the petition will be heard by another court of the same level as that which gave the judgment against which the error was brought. Where there is only one court of the particular level within the district of the *Oberlandesgericht,* or only one *Oberlandesgericht* within a given state, the petition will be heard by another chamber or section of the same court.

The proper court will consider the petition and will summarily reject it where it is not in the proper form, where it does not state a proper ground, or where it does not offer any proof. Otherwise, it will admit the petition and pass a copy thereof to the opponent. The court will also appoint a judge to hear the proof offered by the petitioner. The judge will set a day for taking evidence, and after it has been received, he will request that the parties make their motions within a specific time set by him.

The court will then consider the petition in view of the evidence received and will summarily reject it if it finds the proof insufficient to have the case reopened. Otherwise it will grant the petition and order a new trial. The court may, however, summarily acquit the convict or uphold the conviction where the convict dies in the meantime. It may also summarily acquit the convict with the consent of the prosecution in any other case where there is sufficient evidence for an acquittal. Summary decisions are made by rulings (*Beschlüsse*) subject to complaints (*Beschwerden*).

Where a new trial is ordered, the rules applicable in trial courts apply.

The judgment given after a new trial may either uphold the judgment complained of or set it aside. Where the court sets the judgment complained of aside, it must give a new decision in the case in the same judgment. The new decision may not in any way modify the judgment complained of to the detriment of the convict where only he has petitioned or where the prosecution brought the petition solely for his benefit.

NOTES AND QUESTIONS

This is the standard procedure to obtain a revision of a conviction after the judgment has entered into the power of law. To which court is such a petition directed? Compare the French and Italian provisions. Note that the petition may be made both to the advantage or disadvantage of the person proceeded against.

On which grounds may such a petition be brought? *See*, e.g., the Spanish provisions.

May the petition be made at any time, even after the person has served his term or died? Compare the Italian rules. *See also* F.R. Crim. P. Rule 33.

IV. THE SYSTEM AND ADMINISTRATION OF ADMINISTRATIVE LAW

A. THE SUBSTANTIVE ADMINISTRATIVE LAW

The German substantive administrative law is composed of a great mass of statutes and regulations. It comprises the wide area of public administration, both state and federal; public servants; the police; mails and telecommunications; public transport; highway traffic; aviation; passports; aliens; medicaments; narcotics; contagious diseases; inoculations; pollution; associations; public places; weapons and explosives; atomic energy; protection of animals; public welfare; public education; and taxation.

The substantive administrative law is founded on provisions of the German constitution (*Grundgesetz*) and on those of the statutes regulating the particular subject matters.

The following are topics selected from the German substantive administrative law.

1. Passports (*Pässe*)[124]

Germans who leave or enter the Federal Republic of Germany must prove their identity by producing a passport.[125] The federal government may make exceptions from this requirement. It may also, on the ground of public security or public order, issue instructions concerning the prohibition of entry and departure as well as the granting of passports and visas. In areas located at the national boundary, especially for purposes of local border traffic and excursions, a state government may permit the crossing of the national boundary by persons holding other identity documents and may dispense with the visa requirements, if any.

A German is entitled to be issued a passport on proof of his German citizenship.

A passport will be denied where it appears that the applicant would endanger the inner or outer security or the interests of the Federal Republic or of a German state; where he intends to escape criminal prosecution or the execution of a criminal judgment; where he intends to avoid his tax liability or intends to avoid or by-pass customs or currency regulations; where he intends to avoid his legal duty of support; where he intends to enter without permission into a foreign military service; where he does not personally appear before the proper passport office, although he was requested so to do; or where a minor applicant does not obtain the consent of his guardian.

A passport for the purpose of returning to the Federal Republic may not be denied on any ground except on that concerning the endangering of the inner or outer security or of the interests of the Federal Republic or of a German state.

A passport may be withdrawn where it appears that conditions exist under which an applicant would not be entitled to be issued a passport on the grounds mentioned above.

Passports are issued by passport office (*Passbehörden*), which also have the authority to deny passports, to withdraw passports, and to cancel visas already granted. Official passports and diplomatic passports are issued by the Foreign Office. The authorized agencies of the Foreign Office abroad exercise the functions of passport offices.

A German who leaves or enters the Federal Republic without having a passport may be punished by imprisonment of up to one year or with a fine. The attempt is punishable.

A German may be fined up to 5,000 German marks if he crosses the federal boundary at places other than those provided for its crossing or at times other than the designated business hours; if he avoids the official passport examination; if he acts contrary to regulations concerning border traffic issued by the proper authorities; or if he improperly obtains or uses several German passports.

NOTES AND QUESTIONS

German passports are issued as of right to German citizens. Note the reasons for which a passport may be denied. *See*, e.g., 22 U.S.C.A. §211a ff.; Schachtman v. Dulles (1955) 225 F. 2d 938, 96 U.S. App. D.C. 287; Zemel v. Rusk, 381 U.S. 1, 85 S. Ct. 1271 (1965).

Who issues passports? *See*, e.g., 22 U.S.C.A. §211a.

Note the various offenses in connection with passports. For offenses in connection with United States passports, *see* 18 U.S.C.A. §1541ff.

---

2. Protection of the Environment against Pollution (*Schutz vor schädlichen Umwelteinwirkungen*)[126]

The purpose of the antipollution law is to protect persons, animals, plants and other things against detrimental environmental influences, and to prevent such detrimental influences from arising.

The provisions of the statute apply to: the setting up and operation of enterprises; the manufacture, bringing into operation and introduction of enterprises, fuels, substances and products; the nature, equipment, operation and examination of motor vehicles and their trailers, and of rail, air, and water crafts; and construction of public roads, railroads and tramways.[127]

Detrimental environmental influences include air pollution, noise, tremors, light, heat, and rays. Air pollution comprises those alterations in the natural composition of the air that are produced by smoke, soot, dust, gas, aerosol, steam or odorous substances.

The setting up and operation of enterprises that are likely to cause detrimental environmental influences, or otherwise injuriously affect or annoy the general public or the neighborhood, require a permit. The federal government, after hearing the interested parties and with the consent of the upper House of Parliament (*Bundesrat*), determines by regulation (*Rechtsverordnung*) the enterprises that are required to have a permit.

Those enterprises requiring permits must be so set up and operated that detrimental environmental influences do not arise. They must take all technically feasible measures to limit emissions and dispose of all waste. The federal government, after hearing the interested parties and with the consent of the *Bundesrat*, may make regulations (*Rechtsverordnungen*) applicable to the setting up, the nature, and the operation of such enterprises; may require them to comply with determined technical requirements; and may order them not to exceed certain levels of emissions.

The permit may be issued on certain conditions of compliance. Also, any changes in the location, the nature or the operation of an enterprise requiring a permit, requires a permit. Further directives (*Anordnungen*) may be issued after the permit is granted, if it appears that the general public or the neighborhood is not sufficiently protected. Particular directives may not, however, be issued where the enterprise could not absorb the additional expense connected therewith or where their execution would not be technically feasible.

Where the enterprise does not comply with the regulations, the proper authority may prohibit its operation, partially or completely. An enterprise that has been set up, operated or modified without the necessary permit may be ordered by the proper authority to discontinue its operations, or the proper authority may order its closing and removal.

Also, enterprises that do not require a permit must be set up and operated in such a way as to avoid such detrimental environmental influences as are technically avoidable. Those which are not so avoidable must be reduced to a minimum. The enterprises must properly dispose of all waste. The federal government may make regulations (*Rechtsverordnungen*) with respect to enterprises that do not require a permit under the same conditions as those that do require a permit. It may require them to comply with determined technical requirements and order them not to exceed certain levels of emissions. Where they do not comply with the regulations, the proper authority may order the enterprise closed and removed.

The federal government, after hearing the interested parties and with the consent of the *Bundesrat*, may make regulations concerning the manufacture, distribution, and use of fuels (and substances and products made therefrom) so as to prevent detrimental environmental influences, especially air pollution. It may similary make regulations governing the construction and operation of motor vehicles, rail, air, and water crafts so that avoidable emissions are prevented and unavoidable ones are reduced to a minimum.

State governments may issue regulations (*Rechtsverordnungen*) for the protection of certain areas against detrimental environmental influences caused by air pollution or noise. In particular specially designated areas, such regulations may prohibit the operation of enterprises, not allow their construction, or allow them to operate only during certain hours or under stricter requirements. State governments may also prohibit the use of certain fuels in such areas or impose a limit on their use.

The proper authorities are required to monitor the compliance with provisions of the antipollution law and regulations made thereunder.

Breaches of the antipollution law and regulations made thereunder are punishable with fines and imprisonment.

NOTES AND QUESTIONS

Note the scope of application of the German antipollution law. It applies to all entities that are likely to cause air pollution. How is the U.S. Air Pollution Control Law worded? *See* 42 U.S.C.A. §1857ff. Note that the German law also includes noise, tremors, light, heat, and rays, etc.

How is the prevention of pollution accomplished? *See* 42 U.S.C.A. §1857c.

What are the provisions controlling air pollution resulting from the combustion of fuels in vehicle engines? *See* 42 U.S.C.A. §1857b, and f-5.

What are the enforcement provisions concerning the prevention of air pollution? *See* 42 U.S.C.A. §1857f-3,4.

---

3. The Law of Public Assembly (*Versammlungsgesetz*)[128]

The statute regulating the right of public assembly develops the provision laid down in the Federal Constitution (*Grundgesetz*) which provides that all Germans have the right to assemble peacefully and unarmed without any prior notification or permission, and that this right may be restricted by law with respect to open-air meetings.[129]

The statute provides that everyone has the right to organize public meetings and processions and to take part in them.

Such rights do not apply to: those who have abused these rights and their forfeiture of them has been pronounced by the Federal Constitutional Court (*Bundesverfassungsgericht*); a political party that seeks to impair or destroy the free democratic order or to endanger the existence of the Federal Republic when its unconstitutionality has been upheld by the Federal Constitutional Court; those who promote the objectives of such an unconstitutional political party; and associations whose objectives or activities are in conflict with the criminal law or are directed against the constitutional order or the concept of international understanding.[130]

The organizer of a public meeting must give his name in the invitation. All persons taking part should avoid any disruptions; no one should carry arms, except public officers who have such right. No one may appear in uniform or dress alike to give thereby an expression of a political motivation. Youth organizations may be exempted from the prohibition against uniforms.

(a) **Public meetings in enclosed premises** (*Öffentliche Versammlungen in* *geschlossenen Räumen*).   Public meetings in enclosed premises may be prohibited only in individual cases on the grounds mentioned above; and also where the organizer allows armed persons to enter, where it appears that the organizer or his followers will attempt to promote violence or a riot at the meeting, or where it appears they will make or tolerate statements to be made which are criminally punishable.

The invitation to the meeting may exclude certain persons or groups of persons. Newsmen may not be excluded.

Every meeting must have a chairman, who is normally the organizer. Where the meeting is called by an association, its president is the chairman. The chairman is in charge of the meeting. He may place another person in charge in his stead. The person in charge directs the meeting and is responsible for public order. He may adjourn or dismiss the meeting at any time. He may appoint a reasonable number of deputies to assist him. They must be of full age and must wear white armbands. Persons taking part must obey the directions of the chairman and his deputies designed to maintain order. Persons who disrupt the meeting may be requested to leave and they must then do so immediately. Where police officers are assigned to be present at a public meeting, they must make known their presence to the chairman who must provide seats for them.

A public meeting may be adjourned or dismissed by the police on any of the grounds mentioned above on which it could have been prohibited from taking place.

(b) Open-air public meetings and processions (*Öffentliche Versammlungen unter freiem Himmel und Aufzüge*).   Persons intending to call a public meeting or hold a procession in the open must notify the proper authority at the latest forty-eight hours before such event and indicate the name of the presiding person responsible therefor. The proper authority may, in the interest of public order and security, prohibit the event or allow it on certain conditions only. A meeting or procession may be dissolved where no notice of its holding was given, where it is being held otherwise than indicated in the notice, where the conditions imposed have been disregarded, or where it contravenes public order and security. No meetings or processions may be held in the vicinity of federal or state parliaments or the Federal Constitutional Court.

The above-mentioned provisions concerning the notification and dissolution of meetings and processions do not apply to religious services, religious processions and pilgrimages, funerals, wedding processions and established festivals. The provisions applicable to indoor meetings apply to outdoor meetings and processions *mutatis mutandis.*

Infractions of the provisions applicable to all meetings and processions are punishable by fines and imprisonment.

NOTES AND QUESTIONS

How does the German constitutionally guaranteed right to public assembly compare with that in U.S. Const. Amendment I? *See,* e.g., De Jonge v. Ore., 299 U.S. 353 (1937).

Most provisions regulating public assemblies in other countries may be found in traffic laws and city ordinances. This is so especially in Anglo-American law. *See* the law of your state and the city ordinances of your city dealing with traffic and public assembly.

As to limitations imposed on assemblies and parades, *see also*, e.g., 18 U.S.C.A. §1507, Calif. Pen. C.A. §§403,407.

B. THE SYSTEM OF ADMINISTRATIVE AUTHORITIES (Offices and Courts)

There are both state and federal German administrative authorities. State offices of public administration function generallly on three levels: local, intermediate and central. There may, however, be more than one set of offices within a particular level, so that there may be in fact four levels of offices or, vice versa, there may be only two levels. Federal offices of public administration function generally on three levels: lower, intermediate and central. Federal administration deals with federal matters as contrasted with state matters, but it also uses state offices of public administration to administer the application of federal laws. Thus, while federal offices deal with only federal matters, state offices deal with both state and federal matters. Administrative courts are also state and federal, but they appear as one unitary system with the first and second levels being state and the final third level being federal.

1. State Administrative Authorities (Offices) (*Staatliche Verwaltungsbehörden*)

By provision of the federal constitution,[131] the states must conform to principles of republican, democratic and social government. In the states, their districts and communities, the people must be represented by a body chosen in general, direct, free, equal, and secret elections. Although they conform in this respect, state administrative authorities are different in open-country states (*Flächenstaaten*) and city-states (*Stadtstaaten*).

(a) Administrative authorities in *Flächenstaaten* (*Verwaltungsbehörden in den Flächenstaaten*).[132] Administrative authorities in *Flächenstaaten* differ from state to state; yet, in all of them, public administration is exercised at three levels (local, intermediate and central), with the exception of *Saarland* and *Schleswig-Holstein*, where it is exercised at only two levels (local and the central).

(i) LOCAL PUBLIC ADMINISTRATION (*Untere Verwaltungsbehörden*). Local public administration is exercised by communities and districts. By provisions of the federal constitution,[133] they administer their own affairs on the principle of self-government within the limits set by law.

(aa) Communities (Gemeinden).[134] Communities may be small or large. Larger communities carry the title cities (*Städte*). Large cities may themselves be districts (*Stadtkreise*). The administration of a community differs considerably from state to state, but it usually has two main organs: the assembly and the mayor; or three main organs: the assembly, the council, and the mayor.

The assembly, which is known as the *Gemeinderat* or the *Rat* or the *Gemeindevertretung*, is elected by the inhabitants for a term of usually four, five, or six years. It is the highest organ of the community and has both legislative and executive powers. It is responsible for administration during its term of office. From among its members, it elects the mayor, the council (if any), and the first, second, or third, etc. councilors (*Beigeordnete*) as well as committees. It is presided over by the mayor.

The council, if there is any, is known as the *Gemeindevorstand* or the *Verwaltungsausschuss* and in the cities as the *Magistrat*. It is presided over by the mayor and has as members the first councilor and other councilors (usually not more than ten), elected by the assembly, and the bureaucratic head of the community or city offices, known as the *Gemeindedirektor* or *Stadtdirektor*. The council attends to the day-to-day business of the community.

The mayor is generally elected by the assembly; in *Baden-Württemberg* and in *Bayern*, however, he is elected directly by the voters. He is elected for the term of the assembly. He presides over the assembly and the council, if any. He is the head and the moving power of the communal or city administration. He is the direct superior of the bureaucratic head of the city offices, who is known as the *Gemeindedirektor* or *Stadtdirektor* and is elected by the assembly. Under the mayor's authority, the *Gemeindedirektor* or *Stadtdirektor* runs the city offices. In larger cities, there is a first mayor and a mayor. The first mayor is known as the *erste Bürgermeister* or the *Oberbürgermeister*.

The communities pass ordinances (*Satzungen*) for their self-government within the existing state law. They run their community enterprises, like waterworks, electricity and gas works, and city transport, and they have their city employees. They regulate activities within community limits, like health and welfare care, public education, sports, and entertainment.

To finance their activities, they levy communal (city) rates (*Gemeindesteuern*), especially on the land (*Grundsteuer*), on enterprises (*Gewerbesteuer*), on liquor (*Getränkesteuer*), on entertainments (*Vergnügungssteuer*), and on dogs (*Hundesteuer*), etc.

(bb) *Districts*.[135] Districts are entities of both local government and state administration. They thus combine features both of self-government and public administration. There are many communities within each district, but a large town may itself form a district. The district has its name, usually the name of the city where its administration is located, and its seal, coat of arms and flag. The organs and the administration of districts follow the lines of the communal administration.

The administration of districts differs considerably from state to state, but it always has three main organs: the district assembly (*Kreistag*), the district committee (*Kreisausschuss*), and the district head (*Kreisvorsteher*).

The *Kreistag* is elected by the inhabitants of the district for a term equal to that for which the communal (city) assemblies are elected in that particular state. Elections are held together with city elections. The members are known as district deputies (*Kreistagabgeordnete*, *Kreisverordnete*, or *Kreismitglieder*, and in Bavaria as *Kreisräte*). The *Kreistag* is usually presided over by the district head (*Kreisvorsteher*), who either can or cannot vote in accordance with the provisions in power in the particular state. In *Hessen, Niedersachsen, Nordrhein-Westfalen,* and *Schleswig-Holstein,* the *Kreistag* elects its own president, who is known as the *Kreispräsident,* the *Kreistagvorsitzender,* or the *Landrat.* The *Kreistag* is the legislative and supreme decision-making body of the district within the limits of local self-government.

The district committee (*Kreisausschuss* or *Kreisrat*) is the directive body of the district. Its composition varies greatly from state to state. In some states, it consists exclusively of district deputies elected to the district committee by the *Kreistag.* In others, it consists of the district deputies elected to the district committee by the *Kreistag* and the district head (*Kreisvorsteher*) who presides over it. In some states, it consists of the above plus other persons who may vote. In yet others, it consists of persons who are not district deputies.

The district head (*Kreisvorsteher*) is always a professional administrator. His title is usually *Landrat,* but in *Niedersachsen* and in *Nordrhein-Westfalen* his title is *Oberkreisdirektor.* He is the executive officer of the district. He forms the link between self-government and state administration. Consequently, he must be acceptable to both local interests and the state government. The manner of his selection varies greatly from state to state, as does the term of his office, which varies from six to twelve years. In *Rheinland-Pfalz* and in *Saarland,* he has no fixed term. In *Bayern,* he is elected by the electorate. In *Hessen,* he is elected by the *Kreistag.* In *Baden-Württemberg,* the state ministry of the interior and the *Kreistag* jointly select three candidates from whom the *Kreistag* elects the *Landrat.* In *Niedersachen,* the *Kreistag* may elect only a person who has judicial qualifications and it requires the prior consent of the state to elect a person lacking such qualifications. In *Nordrhein-Westfalen* and *Schleswig-Holstein,* the district head is elected by the *Kreistag* but must be confirmed by the state. In *Rheinland-Pfalz* and *Saarland,* the district head is appointed by the state with the consent of the *Kreistag.* The district head is in charge of district offices, which are organs of state administration and directly subordinated to higher offices of state administration.

Districts pass ordinances (*Satzungen*) for their self-government within the existing state law along the lines of city administration. To finance their activities, they levy district rates (*Landkreissteuern*), especially in the form of a percentage added to the *Grundsteuer* and the *Gewerbesteuer* levied by the communities located in the district. This is known as the *Kreisumlage.*

(ii) INTERMEDIATE PUBLIC ADMINISTRATION (*Landesmittelbehörden*).[136] Intermediate, regional public administration is exercised by state regional offices (*regionale Landesmittelbehörden*), which are known as regional governments (*Regierungen*). They are the offices of state administration that are the direct superiors of the district administration and they are directly subordinate to the state central administration. They are a regional replica of the central administration. Their direct superior is the ministry of the interior with respect to matters of general administration, and the proper ministry with respect to matters of particular subject matter. Their number differs from state to state, generally in accordance with the size of the particular state. So there are, e.g., three in *Hessen,* four in *Baden-Württemberg,* and seven in *Bayern.* The head of a *Regierung* is known as the *Regierungspräsident.* There are many districts within the territory of every region, usually eleven to twenty-four districts per region.

(iii) CENTRAL PUBLIC ADMINISTRATION (*Oberste Landesbehörden*).[137] Central public administration is carried out by the individual state governments (*Landesregierungen*).[138] The central offices are the ministries (*Ministerien*). Each state has a prime minister's office (*Ministerpräsidium*) and ministries of the interior (*Inneres*), commerce and transport (*Wirtschaft und Verkehr*), education (*Kultus*), justice (*Justiz*), treasury (*Finanzen*), labor and welfare (*Arbeit und Sozialverwaltung*), food (*Ernährung*), agriculture and forestry (*Landwirtschaft und Forsten*), and so on. The ministries are headed by ministers responsible to the state parliament (*Landtag*). Each state also has a court of accounts (*Landesrechnungshof*), which supervises and controls the spending of public monies.

Directly subordinated to the ministries are the individual central offices (*Landesoberbehörden*) which exercise authority over the entire state territory and handle specialized government business. The state office of statistics (*Statistische Landesamt*) and the state office for highway construction (*Landesstrassenbauamt*) are examples of *Landesoberbehörden*.

NOTES AND QUESTIONS

The German organization of state authorities differs widely from state to state. The sometimes referred to distinction between city-states and so-called *Flächenstaaten* (open-country states) is only for convenience, namely, to deal separately with the largest cities in the country.

1. As to communities, these comprise small localities and very large cities. There is always a mayor and a city assembly. Usually there are city councilors elected by the assembly. There are city administrative offices headed by bureaucrats.

How does the German setup compare with that in French or Italian communities? *See also* Calif. Gov. C.A. §34000ff.

Elections are held to elect officers for stipulated terms, which may differ from city to city. Every resident has the right to vote. The various candidates for office run on tickets of national political parties, thus municipal elections are only a replica of national elections. How is the matter regulated in Anglo-American cities? *See*, e.g., Calif. Gov. C.A. §§34051 and 34879.

Cities issue ordinances for their self-government and run their community enterprises. They must levy local rates to finance their activities. Compare the French and the Spanish law. Compare the ordinances of your city for the subject matters dealt with. Compare the Italian city rates. *See*, e.g., Calif. Gov. C.A. §43000ff.

2. As to districts, some districts have only a small district town and a few villages within their boundaries, whereas some cities are so large that they themselves form separate districts. Note the differences in the administrative structure of the various districts. May German districts be compared with French departments or Italian provinces? Are they similar to Anglo-American county authorities? How are counties governed in your state? *See*, e.g., Calif. Gov. C.A. §23000ff.

Note the combination of elections and appointments in the selection of district officers. How does the German district system compare with the systems used in Italian and Spanish provinces? What are the Anglo-American county authorites? How are counties governed in your state? *See*, e.g. Calif. Gov. C.A. §2400ff.

German districts pass ordinances and levy rates to finance their activities. Compare these taxes with Italian local taxes. What taxes are levied by Anglo-American counties? *See,* e.g., Calif. Gov. C.A. §29000ff.

3. As to the regional public administration, regions are divisions of state administration. How do they compare with French departments or Spanish provinces? Do they have a counterpart in the Anglo-American administrative system?

4. As to the central administration, this is the administration exercised by state governments. The administration is centrally organized. How do the German states compare with French or Italian regions? How do they compare with American states?

(b) **Administrative authorities in** *Stadtstaaten (Verwaltungsbehörden in den Stadtstaaten).* The German Federal Republic has three big cities that are so large they themselves form states. They are Berlin, Hamburg and Bremen. Although their rank within the public administration is that of states, their administrative setup follows the pattern prevalent in large cities, which they in fact are.

(i) STATE OF BERLIN *(Land Berlin).*[139] It comprises that part of Berlin which is attached to the Federal Republic and is known as West Berlin.

The chief organs of the state are the senate *(Senat)* and the parliament *(Abgeordnetenhaus).* The parliament is elected by the voters of the state in state elections. It then elects from among its members the governing mayor *(regierende Bürgermeister),* mayor *(Bürgermeister)* and senators *(Senatoren).* The senate corresponds to the state government. Each senator is in charge of a particular department and has the rank of a state minister. The individual central offices *(Landesoberbehörden),* such as the state archives office *(Landesarchiv),* the state office for statistics *(Statistische Landesamt)* and the state supply office *(Landesversorgungsamt),* are subordinate to the particular departments.

Directly subordinate to the state central offices are the twelve districts *(Bezirke)* into which the state is subdivided. Each district has three main organs: the district assembly *(Bezirksverordnetenversammlung),* district committees *(Deputationen),* and the district office *(Bezirksamt).*

The district assembly is elected by the inhabitants of the district in district elections. The assembly is the legislative and the supreme decision-making body of the district within the limits of local self-government. It elects the officers of district committees *(Deputationen)* and of the district office *(Bezirksamt).*

District committees *(Deputationen)* are setup by the district assembly to administer all matters of the district administration. A number of such committees is setup in accordance with the subject matter. Each individual committee *(Deputation)* is headed by a district councilor *(Bezirksstadtrat)* and is composed further of six assemblymen *(Bezirksverordeneten)* and four expert officers *(Bürgerdeputierten).* All are elected by the district assembly. Decisions of the committees are binding on the district office, but the district office may object to them and submit them to the district assembly, which decides the matter.

The district office (*Bezirksamt*) is the executive organ of the district. It is headed by the district mayor (*Bezirksbürgermeister*) and five to seven district councilors (*Bezirksstadträte*). Each district councilor heads a specialized department of the district office. They act individually and as a body. All are elected by the district assembly. The district mayors of all twelve districts form the council of mayors (*Rat der Bürgermeister*), which is an advisory body to the state senate.

(ii) FREE HANSETOWN OF HAMBURG (*Freie Hansestadt Hamburg*).[140] The organization of the city of Hamburg is similar to that of Berlin. The chief organs are the senate (*Senat*) and the state parliament (*Landtag*). The parliament is elected by the inhabitants of the city in city elections. It then elects from among its members two mayors (*Bürgermeister*) and ten senators. The senate corresponds to the state government. Each senator is in charge of a particular department, known as a *Fachbehörde,* and each department is run by a committee (*Deputation*) presided over by a senator. Each committee has fifteen additional members who are elected by the *Landtag* from among the citizens and whose offices are honorary. The senator may object to any decision made by the committee and submit it to the senate for its decision.

The senate sets up commissions (*Senatskommissionen*), which are headed by the senators, and separate offices (*Senatsämter*), which are headed by a particular senator. Both the commissions and the offices may deal with any designated matter of public administration, like justice, city public service or archives. Thus, there is a justice commission (*Senatskommission für Justizverwaltung*) and a number of other commissions and offices, such as those for personnel (*Personalamt*), the press (*Pressamt*), sports (*Sportamt*), and statistics (*Statistisches Landesamt*).

The chief advisor to every senator is a *Senatssyndicus*. The *Senatssyndici* are professional administrative officers. They are the bureaucratic heads of the various departments (*Fachbehörden*) and offices (*Senatsämter*) headed by the mayors and senators, for whom they also act as deputies.

The city is subdivided into seven districts (*Bezirke*). The administration of every district is exercised by a district office (*Bezirksamt*). Each *Bezirksamt* has three main organs, namely, the district assembly (*Bezirksversammlung*), the district committee (*Bezirksausschuss*), and the district head (*Bezirksamtsleiter*).

The *Bezirksversammlung* is elected by the inhabitants of the district in district elections. It is the legislative and the supreme decision-making body of the district within the limits of local self-government. It elects from among its members a number of committees and one district committee (*Bezirksausschuss*). The district committee is the directive body of the district.

The district head (*Bezirksamtsleiter*) prepares and carries out the decisions of the district committee and attends to the day-to-day business of the district office. He is appointed by the senate with the consent of the district assembly.

In some districts, there are detached localities. They are headed by a local head (*Ortsamtsleiter*), who is appointed by the *Senatsamt für Bezirksverwaltung*, and by a local committee (*Ortsausschuss*) appointed by the proper district committee (*Bezirksausschuss*).

(iii) FREE HANSETOWN OF BREMEN (*Freie Hansestadt Bremen*).[141] The chief organs of the city-state are the state parliament (*Landtag*) and the senate (*Senat*).

The parliament is elected by the inhabitants in state elections. It then elects from among its members the president (*Präsident*), his deputy, and ten senators, who form the state government. Each senator heads a particular department of state administration.

In every department there is a committee (*Deputation*) that consists of the senator in charge of the department and a number of members of parliament (*Abgeordneten*) elected by the parliament (*Landtag*). This is the directive body of each individual department. The senator in charge may object to its decisions and submit the matter for the decision of the senate (*Senat*). In addition to the departments, the city-state of Bremen has a state court of accounts (*Rechnungshof*), which is also one of the highest state offices (*oberste Landesbehörden*).

The *Landesoberbehörden* are state commissions for supply (*Landesversorgungsamt*), taxation (*Obverfinanzdirektion*), health (*Hauptgesundheitsamt*), and so on.

The state administration is further subdivided into two separate city organizations, namely, the city of Bremen and the city of Bremerhaven.

(aa) City of Bremen (Stadtgemeinde Bremen). The city administration consists of the city assembly (*Stadtbürgerschaft*), its members being the members of the state parliament coming from the city, and the state senate (*Senat*) The city is governed by twelve specialized committees (*Deputationen*) elected by the city assembly from among its members and also from professional administrators.

The city also has fourteen local offices (*Ortsämter*). They are headed by a head (*Amtsvorsteher*) and a local council (*Beirat*) of citizens.

(bb) City of Bremerhaven (Stadtgemeinde Bremerhaven). The city of Bremerhaven is more detached from the state administration. It has three main organs: the city assembly (*Stadtverordnetenversammlung*), the city council (*Magistrat*), and the first mayor (*Oberbürgermeister*).

The city assembly is the legislative and supreme decision-making body of the city. It is elected by the inhabitants in city elections. It elects from among its member the first mayor (*Oberbürgermeister*), mayor (*Bürgermeister*), and city councilors (*Stadträte*).

The city council (*Magistrat*) consists of the *Oberbürgermeister*, the *Bürgermeister* and the councilors (*Stradträte*). It is the directive body of the city.

The *Oberbürgermeister* is elected by the city assembly for a term of twelve years. He is the chief officer of the city and the head of the city offices.

NOTES AND QUESTIONS

Germany has three city-states: Berlin (i.e., its West portion), Hamburg and Bremen. Their systems of administration are in fact large-scale city administration. Note the slight differences in the systems of administration. Their administration is comparable with that of large cities in other countries. *See,* e.g., the administration of the French capital city of Paris, or that of the big Spanish cities. How does the administration of large German cities compare with the administration of large Anglo-American cities? Compare, e.g., the special laws applicable in the government of New York City, including the New York City Charter; New York

City Local Laws; New York Code, Rules and Regulations; and New York City Administrative Code.

---

2. Federal Administrative Authorities (Offices) (*Bundesverwaltungsbehörden*)

Although the federal offices of public administration may function on three levels (lower, intermediate and central),[142] only a very few do so. This is because the federation uses the state offices of public administration to administer federal laws. In accordance with the provisions of the Federal Constitution (*Grundgesetz*), the function of the federation is chiefly legislative, whereas the states are invested with the task of administering federal laws. Consequently, the federation has a great number of offices at the central level but relatively few at the intermediate and lower levels. The federation supervises the administration of its laws by the state administrative offices through its central administrative offices.

(a) **Federal offices of the lower level** (*Bundesunterbehörden*).   Very few branches of federal public administration have offices operating on the lower level. They concern activities which are purely federal and into which the states do not venture and which must be functionally widely decentralized. They include passport control offices (*Passkontrolämter*), customs offices (*Hauptzollämter*), district military reserve offices (*Kreiswehrersatzämter*), post offices (*Postämter*), and federal railways offices (*Bundesbahn-Betriebs-Verkehrs-und Maschinenämter*). They are subordinated to the federal intermediate level offices.

(b) **Federal offices of the intermediate level** (*Bundesmittelbehörden*).   Generally only those branches of federal public administration that operate offices on the lower level operate offices on the intermediate level. They include passport control directorates (*Passkontrolldirektionen*), regional military reserve offices (*Bereichswehrersatzämter*), postal directorates (*Oberpostdirektionen*), federal railway directorates (*Bundesbahndirektionen*), and regional taxation offices (*Oberfinanzdirektionen*). Regional taxation offices, which are at the same time also state taxation offices, have two branches, namely, a federal and a state branch (*Bundes- und Länderabteilung*). Federal offices of the intermediate level are subordinate to the federal central level offices, usually a federal ministry.

(c) **Federal offices of the central level** (*Bundeszentralbehörden*).   The highest offices of federal central administration (*Oberste Bundesbehörden*) are the Federal President (*Bundespräsident*) and the Office of the Presidency (*Bundespräsidialamt*), the Presidium of the Federal Parliament (*Präsidium des Bundestages*) headed by a director, the Federal Government (*Bundesregierung*), the Federal Chancelor (*Bundeskanzler*), the various federal ministers (*Bundesminister*) at the head of the ministries (*Bundesministerien*), the Federal Constitutional Court (*Bundesverfassungsgericht*) and the Federal Court of Accounts (*Bundesrechnungshof*).

Directly subordinate to the ministries are the individual federal central offices (*Bundesoberbehörden*), which exercise their authority over the entire federal territory and handle specialized government business. Each *Bundesoberbehörde* is subordinate to a particular ministry in accordance with the subject matter of its specialization. Thus, for instance, the Federal Criminal Office (*Bundeskriminalamt*) and the Federal Office of Statistics (*Statistisches Bundesamt*) are subordinate to the Federal Ministry of the Interior (*Bundesministerium des Innern*); the German Patent Office (*Deutsches Patentamt*) is subordinate to the Federal Ministry of Justice (*Bundesministerium der Justiz*); the Federal Health Office (*Bundesgesundheitsamt*) is subordinate to the Federal Ministry of Health (*Bundesministerium für Gesundheitswesen*); and the Office of the Federal Government for Press and Information (*Presse- und Informationsamt der Bundesregierung*) is subordinate to the Federal Chancellor (*Bundeskanzler*).

In addition, there are several federal institutes (*Bundesanstalten*) without any legal personalities of their own that operate under the supervision of a particular federal ministry. These include, for example, the Federal Printing Office (*Bundesdruckerei*), the Federal Archive (*Bundesarchiv*), and the Federal Institute for Highway Construction (*Bundesanstalt für Strassenbau*).

Further, there are several federal institutes with legal personalities of their own that also operate under the supervision of a particular federal ministry. These include, for example, the German Federal Bank (*Deutsche Bundesbank*); the Federal Employment Office (*Bundesanstalt für Arbeitsvermittlung und Arbeitslosenversicherung*), to which are subordinated the State Employment Offices (*Landesarbeitsämter*), and to which are further subordinated the Employment Offices (*Arbeitsämter*); and the German Radio System (*Deutschlandfunk und Deutsche Welle*).

NOTES AND QUESTIONS

Federal authorities administer, from the highest to the lowest level, only those activities into which the states do not venture, like the mail system, railways, the military, and currency. In all other matters, the federal offices of the central level are virtually the superiors of the state offices, which at the lower level administer federal laws. The entire system of administrative law and administrative courts is national in scope and the individual states enact only provisions necessary for carrying out the law. The fundamental rules set in the German Federal Constitution are of uniform application everywhere and are further carried into effect by national (federal) laws enacted by the Federal Parliament.

Note the scope of the federal administration at the three different levels. The central level has the widest scope of administrative activity, since it is the highest level of administrative authority administering the law made by the Federal Parliament. How does the German system compare with the French or Italian systems? How does it compare with the American system?

---

3. Administrative Courts
(*Verwaltungsgerichte*)[143]

Administrative courts operate on three levels: trial, appellate and error. Trial and appellate level administrative courts are state courts and the error level court is a federal court. Yet the system is a unitary one. Administrative courts hear disputes of public law (*öffentlich-rechtliche Streitigkeiten*) unless they are submitted by federal law to another court system.[144]

(a) Trial level administrative courts. Trial courts of the administrative system are known as administrative courts (*Verwaltungsgerichte*). They are state courts and are set up by state legislation, usually on a regional basis. In some states, especially in the city-states, there may be only one *Verwaltungsgericht*.

The court has a president (*Präsident*), several presiding judges (*vorsitzende Richter*), and a number of judges (*Richter*). The court hears cases in chambers (*Kammern*) consisting of three judges and two lay judges.

The lay judges are elected from a list prepared by the districts (*Kreise*). The election is made by a committee that is presided over by the president of the court and is composed of an administrative officer and seven inhabitants of the court district, who are themselves elected by the state parliament (*Landtag*). Lay judges are elected for a term of four years and the order in which they serve is determined for every particular year.

The court hears suits brought against the decisions of the public administration made on any level, though usually on the regional or state level. The decision of the panel is by simple majority vote. Lay judges have the same rights as professional judges.

An appeal (*Berufung*) against judgments (*Urteile*) of the court may be brought by either party. It must be lodged with the court that pronounced the judgment within one month from the notification for transmittal to the proper *Oberverwaltungsgericht*. If there is ground for error (*Revision*), the judgment of the *Verwaltungsgericht* also may be attacked by error, known as *Sprungrevision*. It must be lodged with the court that pronounced the judgment within one month from the notification for transmittal to the *Bundesverwaltungshof*.

Against rulings (*Beschlüsse*) of a court, a complaint (*Beschwerde*) may be brought to the court that made the ruling within two weeks. If the court does not comply with the request, it will immediately transmit the complaint to the proper *Oberverwaltungsgericht* for its decision, which is final.

Judgments of *Verwaltungsgerichte* are also subject to petitions of nullity (*Nichtigkeitsklagen*) and petitions of restitution (*Restitutionsklagen*) under standard provisions applicable to these petitions in the civil courts system. Such provisions are contained in the Code of Civil Procedure (*Zivilprozessordnung*).

Parties before the court may appear by themselves or they may be represented by other persons under a power of attorney (*Vollmacht*).

(b) Appellate level administrative courts. Appellate courts of the administrative system are known as *Oberverwaltungsgerichte*. They are state courts, with one in every state, except *Niedersachsen* and *Schleswig-Holstein*, which by agreement have a joint *Oberverwaltungsgericht*. In *Baden-Württemberg*, *Bayern* and *Hessen*, the court is called the *Verwaltungsgerichtshof*.

The court has a president (*Präsident*), several presiding judges (*vorsitzende Richter*), and a number of judges (*Richter*). The court hears cases in panels (*Senate*) consisting of three judges. In *Bayern*, the *Senat* consists of five judges. In *Berlin*, *Hamburg*, *Hessen*, *Niedersachsen*, *Nordrhein-Westfalen*, *Rheinland-Pfalz*, and *Schleswig-Holstein*, two lay judges sit together with the three professional judges.

The lay judges are selected in the same way as in trial level administrative courts. Decision is by simple majority.

A large senate (*grosser Senat*) is formed in cases where a question of fundamental importance must be decided or where the senate wishes to differ from a previous opinion of another senate or of the large senate. The large senate is composed of the president of the court or his deputy and at least six other professional judges. Decision is by simple majority. In case of a tie, the presiding judge has a casting vote.

The court hears appeals (*Berufungen*) against judgments (*Urteile*) and complaints (*Beschwerden*) against rulings (*Beschlüsse*) of the trial level administrative courts situated within its territorial jurisdiction.

No further appeal lies against judgments of the court, but error (*Revision*) may be brought to the *Bundesverwaltungsgericht*. It must be filed with the *Oberverwaltungsgericht* that pronounced the judgment within one month from the notification for transmittal to the *Bundesverwaltungsgericht*. Against a denial of leave to bring error, a complaint (*Beschwerde*) may be filed with the *Oberverwaltungsgericht* within one month from notification of the ruling. Where the *Oberverwaltungsgericht* denies the complaint, it will transmit it to the *Bundesverwaltungsgericht*, which will decide it by a ruling (*Beschluss*).

Judgments of the *Oberverwaltungsgerichte* are also subject to a petition of nullity (*Nichtigkeitsklage*) and a petition of restitution (*Restitutionsklage*) under standard provisions applicable to these petitions in the civil courts system. Such provisions are contained in the Code of Civil Procedure (*Zivilprozessordnung*).

Parties before the court may appear by themselves or they may be represented by other persons under a power of attorney (*Vollmacht*).

(c) Error level administrative court. This is the final resort error court. Known as the *Bundesverwaltungsgericht*, it has its seat in Berlin. It is a federal court.

The court has a president (*Präsident*), several presiding judges (*vorsitzende Richter*), and a number of judges (*Richter*). The court hears cases in panels (*Senate*) of five judges. In rulings (*Beschlüsse*) made otherwise than during an oral hearing, it is composed of three judges only. Decision is by simple majority.

A large senate (*grosser Senat*) is formed in cases where a question of fundamental importance must be decided or where the senate wishes to differ from a previous opinion of another senate or of the large senate. The large senate is composed of the president of the court or his deputy and at least six other judges. Decision is by simple majority. In case of a tie, the presiding judge has a casting vote.

The court hears error (*Revision*) against judgments of *Oberverwaltungsgerichte*, *Sprungrevision* against judgments of *Verwaltungsgerichte*, and complaints (*Beschwerden*) against the denial of leave to bring error. Error may be brought only on the ground of an alleged violation of federal law.

The *Bundesverwaltungsgericht*, as a first and final level administrative court, also hears cases of an administrative nature arising between the Federation and the individual states, or between states, and other matters enumerated in article 50 of the *Verwaltungsgerichtsordnung*.[145]

No further remedy lies against decisions of the court, but its judgments are subject to a petition of nullity (*Nichtigkeitsklage*) and a petition of restitution

(*Restitutionsklage*) under standard provisions applicable to these petitions in the civil courts system. Such provisions are contained in the Code of Civil Procedure (*Zivilprozessordnung*).

Parties before the court must be represented by attorneys (*Rechtsanwälte*) admitted to practice before the court.

NOTES AND QUESTIONS

1. As to trial courts, the system of German administrative courts is as unitary as the system of civil and criminal courts. Trial level administrative courts hear suits brought against decisions of any office of public administration after the administrative way of procedure has been exhausted. *See* the section on administrative procedure below. Resort to the trial level is as a matter of right. Note that the jurisdiction of these courts is very wide, comprising virtually all administrative cases with the exception of those to be brought in specialized administrative courts, such as tax or welfare courts. How does the jurisdiction of German administrative trial courts compare with that of Italian or French administrative trial courts?

Note that there are lay judges on the panel, but they are in a minority as compared with the professional judges. Compare the Spanish and Italian systems.

Note also that parties need not have professional representation by attorneys. Is professional representation required in the French system?

Does a comparable system of administrative courts exist in Anglo-American countries? Is there any right to appeal against the final decisions of the public administration? *See*, e.g., 5 U.S.C.A. §701ff.

2. As to appellate courts, the appeal from trial level administrative courts is as of right. The German appellate level is also the final level with respect to state law. However, most of the law is national (federal) law and a further recourse to the error level is possible in such cases. The court decides on the merits; it is a full administrative review.

Are they any appellate level administrative courts in the Italian and French systems? On how many levels do French and Italian administrative courts operate?

Note that in some German states there are lay judges present on the appellate panel. How does this compare with the composition of Spanish and French panels?

Note also that parties may represent themselves and do not need attorneys. Is this a usual rule for appellate administrative courts in other countries?

3. As to the error level court, this is the highest administrative court in the country. Error is only on federal law and is as of right only on some specially enumerated formal grounds. Otherwise, it is by leave only. How does the German *Bundesverwaltungsgericht* compare with the French Council of State and the Spanish Supreme Court hearing administrative cases?

Does the German error court give the government advice along the lines of the French and Italian Councils of State?

Note the composition of the panels and compare it with that of Italian panels. Must the parties be represented by attorneys?

In what way would the German error court compare with Anglo-American courts of final resort?

---

4. Other Administrative Courts

These are chiefly welfare and taxation courts. There is also a disciplinary system dealing with the discipline of public employees (*Disziplinargerichtsbarkeit*), but it is affiliated with the ordinary administrative court system. Disciplinary chambers (*Disziplinarkammern*) are formed in the *Verwaltungsgerichte*, and disciplinary senates (*Disziplinarsenate*) within the *Oberverwaltungsgerichte* and the *Bundesverwaltungsgericht*. It should also be noted that the Federal Court of Accounts (*Bundesrechnungshof*) and the state courts of accounts (*Landesrechnungshöfe*) are not courts but the highest authorities, namely, the *oberste Bundesbehörde* and the *obersten Landesbehörden*, respectively.

(a) Welfare courts (*Sozialgerichte*).[146] Welfare courts operate on three levels: trial, appellate and error. Trial and appellate level courts are state courts and the error level court is a federal court. Yet the system is a unitary one. Welfare courts hear cases dealing with disputes arising out of social security (*Sozialversicherung*), unemployment benefits (*Arbeitslosenversicherung*), health insurance (*Krankenversicherung*), and other welfare programs. The welfare courts system is only a replica of the ordinary administrative courts system.

(i) TRIAL LEVEL WELFARE COURTS. These are known as the *Sozialgerichte*. They are state courts and are set up on the regional basis. They are constituted along the lines of the *Verwaltungsgerichte*. They hear cases in chambers (*Kammern*) consisting of a presiding judge (*vorsitzende Richter*) and two lay judges (*Sozialrichter*), one representing the welfare authority and the other welfare recipients. Decision is by simple majority.

An appeal (*Berufung*) lies to the proper appellate level welfare court (*Landessozialgericht*) against judgments (*Urteile*) of the court and also a complaint (*Beschwerde*) against rulings (*Beschlüsse*) of the court under the same rules as in the administrative court system.

Parties before the court may appear by themselves or they may be represented by other persons under a power of attorney (*Vollmacht*).

(ii) APPELLATE LEVEL WELFARE COURTS. These are known as the *Landessozialgerichte*. They are state courts, one in every state. They are constituted along the lines of the *Oberverwaltungsgerichte*. They hear cases in panels (*Senate*) consisting of three professional judges, one of whom presides, and two lay judges (*Landessozialrichter*), one representing the welfare authority and the other welfare recipients. Decision is by simple majority.

The court hears an appeal (*Berufung*) against judgments (*Urteile*) and a complaint (*Beschwerde*) against rulings (*Beschlüsse*) of the subordinated *Sozialgerichte* located within its appellate jurisdiction.

No further appeal lies against judgments of the court, but error (*Revision*) may be brought to the *Bundessozialgericht* under the same conditions as in the administrative court system.

Parties before the court may appear by themselves or they may be represented by other persons under a power of attorney (*Vollmacht*).

(iii) ERROR LEVEL WELFARE COURT.   This is the final resort error court, known as the *Bundessozialgericht*. It has its seat in the city of Kassel. It is a federal court. It is constituted along the lines of the *Bundesverwaltungsgericht*.

The *Bundessozialgericht* hears cases in panels (*Senate*) consisting of a presiding judge (*vorsitzende Richter*), and two other judges (*Richter*), and two lay judges (*Bundessozialrichter*), one representing the welfare authority and the other welfare recipients. Decision is by simple majority.

The large senate (*Grosser Senat*) of the court is presided over by the president of the court or his deputy; it has six more judges (*Richter*) and four lay judges (*Bundessozialrichter*), two representing the welfare authority and two welfare recipients. Decision is by simple majority. The large senate hears cases of fundamental importance and cases that will ensure a uniform application of the law throughout the country.

The court hears error (*Revision*) against judgments (*Urteile*) of *Landessozialgerichte*. The error is brought under the same rules as in the administrative courts system.

Parties before the court must be represented by attorneys (*Rechtsanwälte*) admitted to practice before it.

(b)   Taxation courts (*Finanzgerichte*).[147]   Taxation courts operate on two levels, the appellate (intermediate) and error (central) levels. Appellate level courts (*Finanzgerichte*) are state courts while the error level court (*Bundesfinanzhof*) is a federal court. The system is a unitary one. The courts hear taxation cases on appeal from final decisions of the taxation authorities (*Finanzbehörden*) on state and federal taxation. They have no authority with respect to taxation cases arising out of communal taxation (*Kommunale Abgabensachen*). Such cases are heard by ordinary administrative courts (*Verwaltungsgerichte*).

The *Finanzgerichte* are constituted along the lines of the *Oberverwaltungsgerichte*. They hear cases in panels (*Senate*) consisting of three professional judges, one of whom presides, and two lay judges. Decision is by simple majority. No further appeal lies against decisions of the court, but error (*Revision*) may be brought to the *Bundesfinanzhof* under the same conditions as in the administrative court system. Parties before a *Finanzgericht* may appear by themselves or they may be represented by any person under a power of attorney (*Vollmacht*).

The *Bundesfinanzhof* is the final resort error court. Its seat is in the city of Munich. It is a federal court. It is constituted along the lines of the *Bundesverwaltungsgericht*. It hears cases in panels (*Senate*) consisting of a presiding judge (*vorsitzende Richter*) and another four professional judges (*Richter*). Decision is by simple majority. The court hears error (*Revision*) against judgments (*Urteile*) of *Finanzgerichte;* it is brought under the same rules as in the administrative courts system. Parties before the *Bundesfinanzhof* must be represented by attorneys (*Rechtsanwälte*) admitted to practice before it.

NOTES AND QUESTIONS

1. As to welfare courts, they are a replica of the general administrative courts but specialize in welfare cases. How are lay judges represented on these courts? What are the requirements for legal representation? Must parties be represented by attorneys?

Are there any separate welfare courts in other administrative systems, like those of France or Spain? Which courts would handle similar cases in Anglo-American jurisdictions?

2. As to taxation courts, they are special administrative courts in taxation cases. Note that they operate only on two levels. Is a three-level system of administrative courts actually necessary in taxation or any other administrative cases? Compare the French system. Note that *Finanzgerichte* also have lay judges, and that legal representation before them is not required.

The *Bundesfinanzhof* is fully comparable to the *Bundesverwaltungsgericht* within its taxation jurisdiction.

How does the German system of taxation courts compare with that in Italy?

Are there any special taxation courts in Anglo-American jurisdictions? *See,* e.g., the U.S. Tax Court, 26 U.S.C.A. §7441ff. Compare the function of the U.S. Tax Court with the German taxation courts.

C. ADMINISTRATIVE PROCEDURE AND PROCEDURE BEFORE ADMINISTRATIVE COURTS

1. Administrative Procedure

Whatever has been said previously on administrative procedure in Section III. C. of the chapter "An Overview of the Law" applies generally to German administrative procedure. German public administration operates on three, and in some instances on four or only two, levels. The differences are due to different subject matters of public administration and to the approach traditionally taken by the several states. Process may be initiated on any level. The higher level offices exercise general supervision of the functioning of the subordinate levels, so that the central offices of public administration, whether state or federal, are the highest directive and decisionmaking offices within the spheres of their competence.

Procedure is based on the principle of informality. The public authority must ex officio study the facts and the applicable law pertaining to any matter before it and must make a proper determination. To establish the facts, it must gather proof. It may summon witnesses and hear them, but it may not administer oaths unless it has the power to do so in particular proceedings. It may freely evaluate the proof. The party or parties involved in the proceedings should be heard and they are heard even if no particular statute so orders. The authority usually allows the party to inspect its files; unless it is bound to allow it by statute, however, it is within its discretion to allow it or not. The proceedings are not open to the general public. Only the parties concerned may attend. The proceedings are conducted in writing, and oral statements made by a party are reduced to writing by the public authority.

Proceedings are initiated ex officio or at the request of a party. In many instances, printed forms are used. The party may be requested to appear, and if he fails to appear, the authority may make a decision in accordance with its files. If so authorized by a particular statute, it may order the appearance of a party by public force. All communications to the party must be properly delivered. In accordance with the subject matter of the business, delivery may be effected by regular mail, by registered mail, or by personal service effected by an officer.

Administrative acts (both decisions and orders) must contain reasons and must give instructions on the right of the party to challenge the decision or order, especially within what time and to which office the challenge should be brought.

An administrative act (*Verwaltungsakt*) may be attacked by an objection (*Widerspruch*), which must be filed with the authority that pronounced it within one month from its delivery. If it does not contain instructions as to the rights of the party to challenge the act, or if it contains an erroneous instruction, the party may file its objection within one year from the delivery. The filing of the objection prevents the execution of the administrative act unless a particular statute provides that it may be executed notwithstanding the filing of an objection.

The authority must reconsider the matter, and it may comply with the objection. If it refuses to do so, it will forward the matter to the next superior authority (*Widerspruchbehörde*) for its decision. Where the next superior authority is the highest federal or highest state authority (*oberste Bundes- oder oberste Landesbehörde*) the matter is not so forwarded and the decision is made by the same authority, which itself becomes the *Widerspruchbehörde*. In that case, the matter is decided usually by a committee set up to consider the objection (*Widerspruch*). The examination by the *Widerspruchbehörde* always involves not only the question of the legality of the administrative act issued, but also its propriety.

Where the administrative act (*Verwaltungsakt*) is made by the highest federal or highest state authority (*oberste Bundes- oder oberste Landesbehörde*), the above-mentioned procedure of bringing an objection (*Widerspruchsverfahren*) is not necessary and the matter may be immediately taken to the proper administrative court. In all other cases, i.e., where the administrative act (*Verwaltungsakt*) is issued by a lower authority, the procedure of bringing an objection (*Widerspruchsverfahren*) must be undertaken before the matter can be taken to an administrative court.

Where the objection (*Widerspruch*) is properly filed but no decision is delivered to the objecting party within three months, the party is free to take the case directly to the proper administrative court but must do so before one year has run from the filing of the objection.

NOTES AND QUESTIONS

German administrative procedure is uniformly applicable throughout the country. It is based on broad principles of sound administrative action of offices of public administration and the differences from one branch of public administration to another are slight. There is an appeal available to the hierarchical superior, if any, against decisions of any administrative authority. Once the administrative way has been exhausted, the party may turn to the administrative court system. Note the steps required to be undertaken by a party before bringing suit in an administrative court.

How does the German administrative procedure compare with that of Italy or of France? How does it compare with that of the United States? *See*, e.g., 5 U.S.C.A. §500ff.

Note that the decision is on the merits and that the review by administrative courts is also a review on the merits.

Note the German provision as to silence of the administrative authority. If the authority does not reply, the case is deemed resolved against the party and he may proceed further. Compare the Spanish procedure. How would the matter be handled in Anglo-American countries? Would mandamus be a proper remedy? *See*, e.g., 28 U.S.C.A. §1361; Rules of App. Proc., Rule 1.

---

2. Procedure before Administrative Courts

Procedure before administrative courts is governed by the Law on Administrative Courts (*Verwaltungsgerichtsordnung*).[148] It applies the Code of Civil Procedure (*Zivilprozessordnung*) to procedure before administrative courts unless otherwise provided in the *Verwaltungsgerichtsordnung*. The instances where special rules are provided for the procedure before administrative courts are quite rare so that the *Zivilprozessordnung* virtually governs without any significant changes.

The proceedings are oral and public, and the proof is made in the same way as before civil courts. Administrative courts, however, are bound to investigate the matter before them ex officio and are not limited to the presentation of the matter by the parties. The courts give rulings (*Beschlüsse*) and judgments (*Urteile*), just like civil courts.

The nature of actions brought before administrative courts is of three distinct types: It may demand the rescission of the administrative act (known as the *Anfechtungsklage*); it may demand that the public authority be ordered to issue a particular administrative act (known as the *Verpflichtungsklage*); or it may demand a declaration that a certain legal relationship does or does not exist, or a declaration that the administrative act is void (known as the *Feststellungsklage*).

(a) Procedure before trial level administrative courts (*Verwaltungsgerichte*).[149] Procedure before trial level administrative courts proceeds along the lines of procedure before trial level civil courts.

The suit must be initiated by filing it in writing with the proper *Verwaltungsgericht* within the time provided for. It may also be initiated by a statement made orally to the proper court officer who will reduce it to writing. As many copies as there are participants to the proceedings must be filed.

The suit will be channelled to the proper chamber (*Kammer*). The statement of claim must be complete in all respects. It must offer proof and contain a definite request for relief. The original or a copy of the administrative act (*Verwaltungsakt*) and the final order issued by the public authority on the objection of the party (*Widerspruchsbescheid*), if any, which are being challenged must be attached.

The presiding judge (*vorsitzende Richter*) of the chamber will make certain that the papers filed are in order, and if not, he will request the plaintiff to file further materials completing his statements within a fixed term. The process is then served on the defendant by order of the court. The defendant is free to file his answer within a time set by the court, and he may also bring a counter action (*Widerklage*).

The presiding judge appoints a rapporteur (*Berichterstatter*) from among the judges or acts as the rapporteur himself. The court studies the matter ex officio and is not limited to materials brought in by the parties. The parties must file their briefs in preparation for trial. Parties are free to inspect the court files. When the court feels that the case is ready for trial, it will set a day for trial. Notice of trial is sent to the parties at least two weeks before the date of trial.

At trial, after the case is called, first the rapporteur gives his report on the development of the case up to then. Thereafter, the plaintiff presents his case and then the defendant. The court must discuss all relevant matters with the parties from the point of view of both the facts and the law. When the parties have rested and the court feels that the case is ready for judgment, the presiding judge will declare the trial closed.

The court then retires to consider judgment. Judgment must be given in the term within which the trial took place, and, in special cases, within the time set by the court, which may not exceed two weeks. Judgment is read in open court, but it may be handed over to the court office without having been read in open court within two weeks from the close of the trial.

The consideration of the judgment and the form and contents of the judgment follow the rules governing the same in proceedings before civil courts. The judgment must contain instructions concerning remedies which may be taken against the judgment.

The court may affirm the administrative act complained of, or it may set it aside or modify it. Where the court sets the administrative act aside, but where it has already been carried out, the court may order a *restitutio in integrum;* in that case, it must indicate how the restitution is to be brought about. Restitution may be ordered only where the public authority is able to bring it about. An action for damages (*Schadensersatz*) caused thereby to the party must be brought against the public authority in an ordinary civil court.[150]

Where the administrative act has ordered the payment of a sum of money or the delivery of things identifiable by description (*vertretbare Sachen*), or has made a declaration, the court may modify the sum or number of such things, or may make a new declaration. Where the public authority has refused to issue a particular administrative act (*Verwaltungsakt*), the court may order it to issue such an act.

(b) Procedure before appellate level administrative courts (*Oberverwaltungsgerichte*).[151] Appellate administrative procedure is governed by the rules regulating trial in administrative courts unless otherwise provided.

The appeal must contain the grounds for appeal and must offer proof. The appeal is channeled to the proper senate (*Senat*) of the *Oberverwaltungsgericht.* The senate must make certain that the appeal has been filed in the proper form and within the proper time. If the appeal is defective in these respects, the court, after hearing the parties, will reject it by a ruling (*Beschluss*). The rejection may be attacked by a complaint (*Beschwerde*), whereas a judgment having the same contents would be attacked by error (*Revision*).

Where the appeal is in order, the court will study the case, it will appoint a rapporteur (*Berichterstatter*) from among the judges, and it will prepare the case for a hearing. The *Oberverwaltungsgericht* considers the case in the same manner as a trial court but only within the scope of the appeal as presented by the appellant and the appellee. New facts and new proof are admissible.

The oral hearing proceeds like a trial in the trial level administrative court. The judgment given may affirm the decision of the *Verwaltungsgericht*, it may modify it, or it may set it aside. Where the judgment of the court below is set aside, the *Oberverwaltungsgericht* gives a new judgment in the case. It may, however, remit the case to the court below for further proceedings in instances where the *Verwaltungsgericht* has not as yet decided the case, where the proceedings in the *Verwaltungsgericht* were defective as to form, or where new facts or new proof essential for a decision in the case came to light in the meantime. Where the case is remitted, the *Verwaltungsgericht* is bound by the decision of the *Oberverwaltungsgericht*.

(c) Procedure before the error level administrative court (*Bundesverwaltungsgericht*).[152] Error may be brought basically only with the leave of the *Oberverwaltungsgericht*. Leave will be granted where the matter is of fundamental importance, where the judgment of the *Oberverwaltungsgericht* differs from a previous judgment of the *Bundesverwaltungsgericht*, or where a rule of procedure was broken. The denial of leave to bring error may be attacked by a complaint (*Beschwerde*), which must be filed with the *Oberverwaltungsgericht* within one month from the notification. Where the *Oberverwaltungsgericht* does not grant the leave, it will forward the files to the *Bundesverwaltungsgericht*, which will decide by a ruling (*Beschluss*).

Error may be brought without any leave where the *Oberverwaltungsgericht* was not properly constituted, where a judge who was not authorized to sit or who was disqualified participated in the decision, where a party was not properly represented, where the public was improperly excluded at the hearing, and where no grounds for the decision were given.

Error from the trial level administrative court (*Verwaltungsgericht*), which is known as *Sprungrevision*, may be brought only on the ground that the matter is of fundamental importance or that the decision of the *Verwaltungsgericht* differs from a previously given decision of the *Bundesverwaltungsgericht*. It needs leave of the *Verwaltungsgericht*. No remedy lies against denial of the leave, but the error will be treated as an appeal (*Berufung*). The error may be brought only on the alleged breach of federal law.

Federal law is considered to have been broken and no leave to bring error is required in instances where the court that pronounced the judgment was not properly constituted, where a judge who was not authorized to sit or who was disqualified participated in the decision, where a party was not properly heard, where the public was improperly excluded at the hearing, and where no grounds for the decision were given.

Procedure on error is governed by the rules regulating appellate administrative procedure unless otherwise provided.

The error must be filed in the proper form and within the proper time. The brief containing the grounds for error must be filed within another month. The court against the judgment of which the error is brought will transmit the files to the *Bundesverwaltungsgericht*.

The error is channeled to the proper senate of the *Bundesverwaltungsgericht*. The senate must make certain that the error has been properly filed.

Where the error was not filed in the proper form or within the proper time, the *Bundesverwaltungsgericht* will reject it by a ruling (*Beschluss*).

Where the error is in order, the court will study the case, it will appoint a rapporteur (*Berichterstatter*) from among the judges, and it will prepare the case for a hearing. The court considers the case within the scope of the petition of error. The hearing and judgment proceed along the lines of appellate procedure.

The *Bundesverwaltungsgericht* will deny the error where it finds it groundless. Where the error succeeds, the court will set aside the judgment of the court below and will either decide the matter itself, or it will remit the case for further proceedings to the *Oberverwaltungsgericht* against the judgment of which the error was brought. In case of a *Sprungrevision*, the *Bundesverwaltungsgericht* may also remit the case to the particular *Oberverwaltungsgericht* that is the proper appellate court from the *Verwaltungsgericht* against the judgment of which the *Sprung-revision* was brought. The court to which the case is remitted is bound by the decision of the *Bundesverwaltungsgericht*.

3.   Procedure before Welfare Courts
     (*Sozialgerichte*)[153] and Taxation Courts
     (*Finanzgerichte*)[154]

Procedure before the three different levels of welfare courts (*Sozialgerichte*) and the two levels of taxation courts (*Finanzgerichte*) proceeds along lines applicable to the corresponding levels of administrative courts (*Verwaltungsgerichte*).

NOTES AND QUESTIONS

The procedure before all administrative courts is governed by the rules of administrative procedure contained in the Law on Administrative Courts (*Verwaltungsgerichtsordnung*). It relies on the Code of Civil Procedure. Consequently, the procedure before the three different levels of administrative courts and other special administrative courts is very similar to that before the corresponding levels of civil courts. Note that judgments of administrative courts become executory only after they enter into the power of law, as is the case in civil courts. Compare this rule with that in the Italian administrative procedure.

Compare the procedure before German administrative trial courts with that before German civil trial courts. *See also* the procedure before Italian trial level administrative courts. Are there any significant differences in the German and Italian procedures?

Compare the procedure in German administrative appellate courts with that in German civil courts of appeal. Compare it also with the appellate procedure in administrative matters before the Spanish Supreme Court. How does the German three-level administrative procedure compare with the two-level procedures in France and Italy?

Compare the German procedure in the administrative error court with that before the German civil error court. How does the procedure before the *Bundesverwaltungsgericht* compare with procedures before the French and Italian Councils of State sitting as courts of final resort in administrative matters?

Is the procedure in the *Bundesverwaltungsgericht* comparable to that in Anglo-American courts of final resort, like the United States Supreme Court?

V. LEGAL OFFICERS

A. JUDGES (*Richter*)[155]

Whatever has been said previously on judges in Section IV. A. of the chapter "An Overview of the Law" applies also to the German legal system.

The time to join the judicial service is immediately after a person has fully qualified legally.[156] He must apply to the ministry of justice of his state for an appointment; and if he is admitted into the service, his first appointment is only probationary (*Richter auf Probe*). After three years of judicial experience, usually at a county court (*Amtsgericht*), he is eligible for a permanent appointment, which must be granted not later than five years after his probationary appointment or he must be removed from office. Permanent appointment is for life (*Richter auf Lebenszeit*), which means until the compulsory retirement age.[157]

In addition to his legal qualifications, the applicant for a judicial appointment must hold German citizenship, be of full age and capacity and be free of any criminal conviction. Having been appointed to a permanent judgeship, he is then promoted to higher judicial positions and may in due time reach the highest state and federal courts. Appointments to the highest federal courts are made from among judges of the highest state courts.[158]

In the exercise of their judicial functions, judges are independent and are subject only to the law.[159]

In every court, the judges form a council of judges (*Richterrat*) and a council of the presidency of the court (*Präsidialrat*).[160]

The *Richterrat* consists of three to five judges who are elected by the judges at a particular court from among themselves by a secret ballot for a term of four years. The president of the court and his deputy may not be on the *Richterrat*. The *Richterrat* represents the judges as a body in matters concerning the conditions of their employment.

The *Präsidialrat* consists of the president of the court and his deputy plus another three to five judges elected by the judges of the court from among themselves by secret ballot for a term of four years. The *Präsidialrat* must be consulted with respect to any appointments and promotions of judges in the court. It gives a written statement in every such matter.

Service courts (*Dienstgerichte*)[161] are set up within the state courts and the *Bundesgerichtshof* to act as disciplinary courts. In the states, the courts are chambers and senates created in the general jurisdiction courts, respectively. They have jurisdiction over state judges only. For federal judges, a special senate is set up in the *Bundesgerichtshof*. The presidents of courts and their deputies may not sit on the *Dienstgerichte*. The senate in the *Bundesgerichtshof* is composed of three judges of the *Bundesgerichtshof*, one of them presiding, and two judges of the particular branch of federal jurisdiction to which the judge whose case is being considered belongs. They are appointed for a term of five years by the respective highest federal courts. Composition of the chambers and senates in the state courts is analogous. The *Dienstgerichte* have the power to discipline judges; they also decide on the forcible transfer of judges, on the validity of their appointments, and on their retirement or dismissal. As a disciplinary court, they may discipline a judge by a reprimand, a fine, or dismissal.

B. THE PUBLIC MINISTRY (*Staatsanwaltschaft*)[162]

Officers of the public ministry and judges form one group of legal officers. Consequently, they have the same qualifications and are selected and appointed in the same manner. The offices of the public ministry are centrally organized. There is an office of public ministry at every court. At the *Bundesgerichtshof*, the office is headed by the *Generalbundesanwalt* and a number of *Bundesanwälte*; at *Oberlandesgerichte* and *Landgerichte*, by one or more *Staatsanwälte*; and at *Amtsgerichte* by one or more *Staatsanwälte* or *Amtsanwälte*. The office of the *Generalbundesanwalt* is subordinate to the Federal Ministry of Justice, and the offices of the *Staatsanwaltschaften* in every particular state to the ministry of justice of that state.

Officers of the public ministry prosecute offenders before criminal courts, but they also represent the interests of their respective states or of the federation before civil courts.[163] In the exercise of their functions, they are subordinate to their proper superiors.

Like judges, officers of the public ministry are subject to the discipline of service courts (*Dienstgerichte*). In the respective chambers or senates, the members, who must be drawn from the branch to which the person proceeded against belongs, are thus drawn from the officers of the public ministry.[164]

NOTES AND QUESTIONS

1. As to judges, the German system of appointment of judges is in line with such systems in other civil law countries. Fully legally qualified persons usually apply for admission into the service promptly after they become so qualified. If they are accepted and then satisfactorily comply with the requirements of their probationary appointment, they become permanent judges and are promoted on merit and on seniority until they reach the highest positions within the system and are eventually retired. Compare the German system with the Italian system. How does the German system compare with the French system of judicial careers?

Note the provisions on judicial discipline and conduct. How do these provisions compare with similar Spanish provisions?

How does the German method of judicial appointment compare with such methods in Anglo-American countries? Are judges in British countries elected? For American states, compare, e.g., the system in power in California, Calif. Gov. C.A. §68120ff.; for the United States, *see* 28 U.S.C.A. §§1ff., 41ff., and 81ff.

2. As to the public ministry, it forms one integral service with the judges. Services of public ministries are similarly organized in all civil law countries. *See,* e.g., the Italian public ministry. While judges are independent, officers of the public ministry are hierarchically subordinate to the ministry of justice.

See also the Anglo-American system of public prosecution for comparative purposes. *See,* e.g., Calif. Gov. C.A. §26500ff. and Texas Vernon's Ann. Civ. St. Arts. 321 ff. as to district attorneys. *See also* 28 U.S.C.A. §541ff. as to United States Attorneys.

C. ATTORNEYS (*Rechtsanwälte*)[165]

To become an attorney (*Rechtsanwalt*) a person must be fully legally qualified. The qualifications are the same as those required to hold judicial office (*Befähigung zum Richteramt*).[166] Like a candidate for judicial office, he must hold German citizenship, be of full age and capacity, and be free of any criminal conviction.

The candidate must then apply for admission to the ministry of justice of the state where he wishes to practice. He must specify in which *Amtsgericht* he wishes to practice, and he may also request to be admitted to practice in the *Landgericht* within the district of which the *Amtsgericht* of his choice is located. As a rule, admission to these two courts is always granted. The ministry of justice must obtain an opinion from the chamber of attorneys (*Rechtsanwaltskammer*) of which the applicant would become a member on his admission as to his admissibility, but he has a legal right to be admitted if he complies with the statutory requirements. Both the ministry of justice and the proper *Rechtsanwaltskammer* consider only whether the applicant has complied with the statutory requirements. Admission may not be denied on any other ground, especially not on the ground that there are already too many attorneys in practice and no further attorneys are needed.

The applicant is issued by the ministry of justice a document of admission to practice (*Zulassung zur Rechtsanwaltschaft*) and also admission to practice in a particular court (*Zulassung bei einem Gericht*). He will then take an oath of office in the court of his admission and his name will be placed on the list of attorneys admitted to practice in that court. He will have to reside within the district of the *Oberlandesgericht* within which the court of his admission is located, and he will have to open his office in the place where the court to which he is admitted is located. Where he is admitted to an *Amtsgericht* and its *Landgericht* and they are located in different places, he must open his office in the locality of the *Amtsgericht*. The ministry of justice may grant exceptions from all these residence requirements.

An attorney may at any time request the ministry of justice in any state to be admitted to practice in any *Amtsgericht* and its superior *Landgericht*. He has a legal right to be so admitted. Once he is so admitted, he will have to relinquish his previous admission in the court or courts to which he was previously admitted. He only changes from court to court and his admission to practice in general (*Zulassung zur Rechtsanwaltschaft*) once obtained in a state is good in all states.

An attorney who has practiced for five years in an *Amtsgericht* or a *Landgericht* may request the state ministry of justice to be admitted to practice in an

Oberlandesgericht. He has a legal right to be so admitted. He must on admission, however, relinquish his previous admission to practice in any other court.

Admission to practice in the Federal Supreme Court (*Bundesgerichtshof*) is obtained only through a special procedure of admission. It is obtained by the decision of an election committee (*Wahlauschuss*), presided over by the president of the *Bundesgerichtshof*. Its members are the presiding judges of the civil senates thereof, members of the council of the presidency. (*Präsidium*) of the Federal Chamber of Attorneys at the Federal Supreme Court (*Rechtsanwaltskammer bei dem Bundesgerichtshof*). A quorum is a simple majority of members and decisions are by simple majority vote.

The election committee admits only as many attorneys as are needed to handle the volume of work. The names of candidates for admission are submitted on lists presented exclusively by the Federal Chamber of Attorneys (*Bundesrechtsanwaltskammer*) and the Chamber of Attorneys at the Federal Supreme Court (*Rechtsanwaltskammer bei dem Bundesgerichtshof*). The names of candidates are suggested to the above two bodies by the several chambers of attorneys from all over the country. Such candidates must have practiced for at least five years and be thirty-five years old or older. The candidates elected by the election committee are then admitted by the Federal Minister of Justice. They must relinquish their right to practice before all lower courts. The admission to practice at the *Bundesgerichtshof* includes also admission to practice before all federal high courts (*obere Bundesgerichte*) and before the Federal Constitutional Court (*Bundesverfassungsgericht*).

German attorneys exercise their profession usually as a one man practice, but partnerships of two or three attorneys also exist. The profession is unitary and strictly localized.

Attorneys must be members of the proper chamber of attorneys.

All attorneys exercising their profession in the district of an *Oberlandesgericht* form a chamber of attorneys (*Rechtsanwaltskammer*). Attorneys admitted to practice in the Federal Supreme Court form their own chamber. All the chambers form the Federal Chamber of Attorneys (*Bundesrechtsanwaltskammer*).

The organs of the chambers are the assembly (*Versammlung*), which consists of all members, the council (*Vorstand*), which consists of at least seven members elected by the assembly, and the council of the presidency (*Präsidium*), which consists of at least four members elected by the council from among its members. All terms of office are for four years.

To be elected to the council, an attorney must have practiced for five years and be at least thirty-five years old. The council is the advisory body of the chamber. The Chamber of Attorneys at the Federal Supreme Court may have a council of less than seven members.

The council of the presidency (*Präsidium*) is composed of the president, vice-president, recorder and treasurer. The council may elect additional members to the council of the presidency. It is the governing body of the chamber. It reports to the council. The president presides over meetings of the council of the presidency, of the council, and of the assembly.

The Federal Chamber of Attorneys (*Bundesrechtsanwaltskammer*) has only two organs: the council of the presidency (*Präsidium*) and the assembly (*Hauptversammlung*). The *Präsidium* consists of a president, vice-president and treasurer. It is elected by the assembly. The assembly is composed of the presidents of all the chambers of attorneys. It decides by simple majority. The president has a casting vote. The various chambers of attorneys represent the interests of the profession in their respective areas.

Discipline in the profession is maintained by disciplinary courts (*Ehrengerichte*), which are set up at three levels: trial, appellate, and error.

At the trial level, a disciplinary court (*Ehrengericht*) is set up for each chamber of attorneys. It is set up by the state ministry of justice and its members are appointed from among members of that chamber suggested by the chamber. The panel hearing a case has three members and decides by simple majority.

At the appellate level, usually one disciplinary court (*Ehrengerichtshof*) is set up in a state, but one may be set up at every *Oberlandesgericht*. Its members are appointed by the state ministry of justice from among attorneys and judges. The panel hearing a case has a president, who is an attorney, and four members, of whom two are judges and two are attorneys. Decision is by simple majority.

At the error level, a senate is set up within the *Bundesgerichtshof* to hear error in disciplinary matters. It is known as the *Bundesgerichtshof in Anwaltssachen*. It is presided over by the president of the *Bundesgerichtshof* or his deputy and has another six members, of whom three are judges of the *Bundesgerichtshof* and three are attorneys. The attorneys are appointed by the Federal Minister of Justice from a list submitted by the Federal Chamber of Attorneys. The court decides by a simple majority. All appointments are for a term of four years.

The procedure in disciplinary matters is basically a criminal procedure. The prosecution is handled by the office of the public ministry (*Staatsanwaltschaft*). The disciplinary court (*Ehrengericht*) may acquit or convict, or it may discontinue proceedings. Upon conviction, the court may impose the following penalties: a warning (*Warnung*), a censure (*Verweis*), a fine (*Geldbusse*) of up to 10,000 marks, or disbarment (*Ausschliessung*). The censure and the fine may be assessed simultaneously.

NOTES AND QUESTIONS

German attorneys hold the same qualifications as judges and officers of the public ministry. They will then be admitted to practice in the limited and general jurisdiction courts of their choice. In distinction to the usual practice in other countries, German attorneys are very localized. Compare them with French attorneys.

Note that to qualify for legal office, the candidate must pass an apprenticeship which, in distinction to other countries, is fitted into the study of law and is not undertaken after graduation.

Note also that the German attorney is admitted to practice in the court of appeal as of right. Admission to practice in the highest national (federal) courts is purely discretionary. How does this rule compare with similar rules in Spain and Italy?

Membership in the bar is compulsory, as it is in virtually all civil law countries. Note the elaborate organization of the German bar. How does it compare with the French bar?

Note also that there is only one type of attorney in Germany. How does this rule compare with similar rules in other countries, such as France, Italy or Spain?

Compare also the German attorney with an American attorney. *See*, e.g., Texas Vernon's Ann. Civ. St. Arts. 304ff. as to Texas attorneys; *see also* the rules as to attorneys in your state.

As to disciplinary provisions, compare the German rules with those of Italy.

D. NOTARIES (*Notare*)[167]

Notaries are public officers who certify acts of any nature as well as signatures and copies. They hold the originals and issue copies and extracts therefrom. They also act in probate proceedings and perform further functions assigned to them by law.

To become a notary, a person must be qualified to hold judicial office (*Befähigung zum Richteramt*).[168] Like a candidate for judicial office, he must hold German citizenship, be of full age and capacity, and be free from any criminal conviction.

The candidate must then apply to the ministry of justice of the state where he wishes to be appointed for admission into the service. The state admits only as many as are required for the proper functioning of the service. If admitted, the candidate will be assigned to a notary by the president of the chamber of notaries (*Notarkammer*) to serve a three-year term of candidacy (apprenticeship) as a candidate (*Notarassessor*). After completion of his apprenticeship and whenever a vacancy exists, the candidate is appointed to the office of a notary.

The appointment is by a decree of the state ministry of justice. It designates the place where he must set up his office. He may exercise his office only within his district, which is the district of an *Oberlandesgericht*. He may not undertake any notarial acts outside of his district except when the business is urgent and there is danger in delay. However, even the acts undertaken by him in breach of this rule are valid. The appointment to the office of a notary is for life.

Notaries either exercise their office (*Nurnotare*) exclusively or they exercise it together with the profession of an attorney (*Anwaltsnotare*).

All notaries within a particular notarial district, i.e., the judicial district of an *Oberlandesgericht*, form a chamber of notaries (*Notarkammer*). The state may, however, provide for the formation of only one chamber of notaries in the state. The chamber of notaries has two organs: the assembly (*Versammlung*) and the Council (*Vorstand*). The council is composed of the president and his deputy and several members whose number is determined by the charter (*Satzung*) of the particular chamber and who are elected by the assembly for a term of four years. The council handles the business of the chamber and reports to the assembly. The president presides over the council and the assembly.

All chambers of notaries form a Federal Chamber of notaries (*Bundesnotarkammer*). Its organs are the assembly of representatives (*Vertreterversammlung*) and the council of the presidency (*Präsidium*). Every chamber of notaries sends a representative to the assembly and has one vote for every district of an *Oberlandesgericht* it comprises. The assembly decides by a simple majority vote and the president has a casting vote. The council of the presidency counsists of the president, two deputy presidents and four members. The president, one deputy president, and two members must be notaries who are exclusively notaries (*Nurnotare*); the other deputy president and two members must be notaries who are at the same time attorneys (*Anwaltsnotare*). They are all elected by the assembly for terms of four years. The council of the presidency handles the business of the *Bundesnotarkammer* and reports to the assembly of representatives. The various chambers of notaries represent the interests of notaries within their respective areas.

Notaries are subject to the supervision of the presidents of the *Landgerichte* and *Oberlandesgerichte* and the state ministries of justice. In accordance with the location of his office, each notary is supervised by all three of these hierarchically superimposed supervisory authorities.

Discipline over notaries is exercised by the disciplinary courts, which are the *Oberlandesgerichte* at the trial level and the *Bundesgerichtshof* at the appellate level. Only one *Oberlandesgericht* may be designated by the state ministry of justice to handle the cases in the whole state territory.

At the trial level, the panel of the *Oberlandesgericht* hearing the case is presided over by a presiding judge and has another judge and a notary as members. Decision is by simple majority. The notary is appointed for a term of four years by the state ministry of justice from a list submitted by the chamber of notaries.

At the appellate level, the panel of the *Bundesgerichtshof* hearing the case is presided over by a presiding judge and has another four members, of whom two are judges and two are notaries. The notaries are appointed for a term of four years by the Federal Minister of Justice from a list submitted by the Federal Chamber of Notaries. Decision is by simple majority.

The procedure in disciplinary matters is basically a criminal procedure. The prosecution is handled by the office of the public ministry. The disciplinary court may acquit or convict, or it may discontinue proceedings. Upon conviction, the court may impose the following penalties: a warning (*Warnung*), a censure (*Verweis*), a fine (*Geldbusse*) of up to 10,000 German marks, or removal from office (*Entfernung aus dem Amt*). The censure and the fine may be assessed simultaneously.

In disciplinary proceedings conducted against a notary who is at the same time an attorney (*Anwaltsnotar*), it must first be decided whether his breach of duties falls within the sphere of his notarial functions or within that of his functions as an attorney. The decision is made by the state ministry of justice after hearing the opinion of the respective chambers of attorneys and notaries. The *Anwaltsnotar* is then proceeded against as a notary or as an attorney, as the case may be. The removal from office of a notary also has the effect of disbarment.

NOTES AND QUESTIONS

Notaries in Germany are fully qualified lawyers. They hold the same legal qualifications as are required for persons who become judges, officers of the public ministry, or attorneys.

They hold public office and their functions are similar in all civil law countries. Are there any noticeable differences between German and French notaries?

Note that a German notary may be at the same time an attorney. Is this possible in other countries?

How do German notaries compare with American notaries public? *See,* e.g., Calif. Gov. C.A. §8200ff. and the law of your state.

VI. DECISIONS OF GERMAN COURTS

NOTE: *Cases have been selected to allow an insight into the legal system and the life of the country under consideration.*

Note the approach taken by the various courts in handling the matters considered.

Note also the time needed to bring the case from the trial court through the several hierarchically superimposed courts to the court of the last resort.

A. DECISIONS OF CIVIL COURTS IN CIVIL AND COMMERCIAL MATTERS

H. AND S. SCH. v. J.R.

Federal Supreme Court, 7th Civil Senate, Judgment of October 10, 1974, 1st Instance: *Landgericht* Freiburg, 2nd Instance: *Oberlandesgericht* Karlsruhe/ Freiburg. (Decisions of the Federal Supreme Court in Civil Matters, Vol. 63, 1975, p. 96, Case 14).

Decision of the Court

By a notarized contract of February 23, 1965, the defendants purchased from the plaintiff a lot of land, located at Karl Street No. 6, together with the vendor's interest in the family home that was being constructed on the land. They paid the agreed purchase price of 85,000 German marks with the exception of the last 3,800 German marks. They list a number of defects in the building and claim damages.

The plaintiff brought suit for the remaining 3,800 German marks. The defendants counterclaimed for damages exceeding that sum.

The *Landgericht* and the *Oberlandesgericht* held partially for the defendants. The defendants brought a petition of error and the plaintiff a counterpetition. The error brought by the defendants succeeds to a large extent.

The reasons:

(1) The Court of Appeal approaches the contractual relation between the parties exclusively from the point of view of the law of sale and applies the statute of limitations of §477 of the Civil Code to the claim for damages of the defendants.

(2) This cannot be upheld.

   (a) In accordance with the prior decisions of the Federal Supreme Court, the claim for damages by a purchaser of land on which a building is being built by the vendor is governed by the law for the carrying out of the work. . . . How far the construction has advanced at the time of making the contract of sale is of no importance (the V. Civil Senate so held in judgment WM 1969, 96). Whether another rule applies where the contruction was fully completed or where minor work of little importance was still to be done needs not be decided, since in this case, on uncontradicted evidence, extensive painting and installation work was still to be done and the doors were yet to be installed. This was not minor work of little importance to be left out of consideration.

(b) How much the work has advanced at the time of making a contact of sale is, as a rule, of no importance because that point of time is frequently purely fortuitous. This is so because the work is frequently already in progress before the contract is finalized. How much the work has progressed at the time when the contract is notarized is of no importance to the duty assumed by the vendor in the contract to construct the building. In accordance with the law concerning the carrying out of work, the liability for defects in the thing attaches purely to this duty.

This clearly appears from the present case. It is stated in the offer to sell submitted to the defendants that some of the buildings were still to be built. In a section headed "Sale and Building Contract," the builder directly states that he obligates himself to hand over to the purchaser a family home built in accordance with specifications and the building plan for a determined price. Under these circumstances, it is of no importance how far the construction of the building has progressed at the time of the notarization of the contract.

(3) Since the claim to damages for defects in the building brought by the defendants is governed by §633ff. of the Civil Code, it is prescribed in five years from the acceptance of the building (Civil Code, §638).

NOTES AND QUESTIONS

The court thus held that a claim for damages brought by the purchaser of land on which the vendor undertakes to build a building is governed, as a rule, by the law applicable to the carrying out of work if at the time of making the contract of sale the building is already partially built.

The law as to the carrying out of work is contained in §§631-651 of the Civil Code.

§633ff. of the Civil Code deals with the removal of defects by the builder.

§638 of the Civil Code provides for a five-year limitation, which runs from the acceptance of the building.

§477 of the Civil Code applicable to sales provides for a six-month limitation in the case of movables and a one-year limitation in the case of immovables as from delivery or entering into possession.

Compare also the section on property and on prescription above.

Compare Calif. C.C.P.A. §§337.1 and 337.15.

Would the rule of *caveat emptor* apply in such a case in Anglo-American law or would the case be governed by the law applicable to the construction of buildings? Would the contract require notarization in Anglo-American law? Would the fact that the building was already partially constructed at the time when the contract was made be of any importance?

H. AG. v. K.

Federal Supreme Court, 8th Civil Senate, Judgment of December 18, 1974, 1st Instance: *Landgericht* Braunschweig, 2nd Instance: *Oberlandesgericht* Braunschweig. (Decisions of the Federal Supreme Court in Civil Matters, Vol. 63, 1975, p. 333, Case 48).

Decision of the Court
The plaintiff was a guest in the defendant's hotel during the night of July 11-12, 1973. He parked his automobile in the parking lot of the defendant. The automobile was seriously damaged when a beech tree, which stood at the edge of the parking lot and which forked directly from the ground, fell apart in the forking in good weather without wind and one of its trunks fell on the automobile. The tree was rotten inside and about two thirds of the forking was decayed. The defendant denied liability for the damage on the ground that the accident did not occur through his fault. The *Landgericht* denied plaintiff's claim. The Court of Appeal reversed and held for the plaintiff on the ground that the defendant was liable without any fault on his part in accordance with §538 of the Civil Code. The error brought by the defendant is denied.

The reasons:
(1) The plaintiff was instructed by the defendant to park his automobile in the parking lot owned by the hotel. We agree with the Court of Appeal that under these circumstances the accommodation contract extended also to the space used in the parking lot. The fact that the plaintiff was free to select the particular parking space is of no importance. The space in the parking lot was provided not as a courtesy but pursuant to a contractual obligation and as a part of the accomodation contract.

In the present case, the defendant is liable for the breach of his obligation not only under the law of safekeeping but also under that of landlord and tenant. Liability under the landlord-tenant relationship applies since the damage was caused by the defective condition of the parking lot, i.e., by a defect in the thing given to the use of the guest, and not by the lack of care on the part of the innkeeper to protect the property of the guest.

(2) The defendant displayed a notice in the parking lot reading: "Parking at one's own risk," and he thus declined any responsibility for the automobiles parked therein. In the opinion of this Court, the notice does not absolve the defendant of liability for any possible kind of damage but only for that due to typical risks, like theft, breaking into the vehicle, and damage to the vehicle caused by other users of the parking lot. In view of local conditions, the effect of the notice was limited to the above. . . .

It is, however, doubtful whether the notice could have had any effect in this particular case since the accommodation contract was already made when the plaintiff brought his automobile in the parking lot and saw the notice.

(3) The Court of Appeal did not consider the question of whether the defendant had examined the condition of the trees lining the parking lot. In its opinion, the defendant was liable in accordance with §538, Subs. (1) of the Civil Code. Pursuant to that provision, the tenant is entitled to damages when the premises at the time of the giving of possession suffer from a defect that reduces their suitability or makes them unsuitable to the use contemplated in the agreement. This view is in

accordance with the opinion of this senate (see the judgment of January 20, 1959-VIII ZR 22/58-S. 26; . . .). The landlord warrants that the premises are without any defect at the time when the tenant obtains possession. The fact that the landlord is without fault does not relieve him of liability.

(4) We agree with the Court of Appeal that §701 Subs. (4), of the Civil Code does not relieve the innkeeper of liability for damages to the automobiles of his guests to the extent asserted by the defendant. . . . The liability of innkeepers for things brought in by their guests provided for in §701ff. of the Civil Code is a statutory liability which applies irrespective of contract, and makes the innkeeper liable irrespective of fault. . . . An accommodation contract is subject to the general and special rules governing the law of obligations. It is important to note that the accommodation contract is basically a landlord-tenant contract even though it frequently displays elements of a contract of sale, a contract of safekeeping, or a contract of work and labor, etc.

Applying the landlord-tenant law, . . . the liability in accordance with §538 of the Civil Code is a contractual liability that cannot exist without the making of a contract. In this case, it is not denied that an accommodation contract, including the providing of a parking space for the automobile of the plaintiff, was made. The liability provided for in §538, Subs. (1) of the Civil Code consequently applies.

(5) The Court of Appeal has properly upheld the claim of the plaintiff in accordance with §538, Subs. (1), of the Civil Code.

NOTES AND QUESTIONS

§538, Subs. (1) of the Civil Code provides that a tenant may claim damages from the landlord when at the time of the making of the contract the premises are suffering from a defect that reduces their suitability or makes them unsuitable for the use contemplated in the contract, and when the landlord fails to remove such defect. Subs. (2) provides that the tenant may remove the defect himself when the landlord fails to do so and may demand compensation for the expense.

§§701-704 of the Civil Code deal with the liability of innkeepers for things brought in by their guests.

§701, Subs. (1) of the Civil Code provides that the innkeeper is liable for loss, destruction or damage to things brought in by his guests. Subs. (4) provides that the liability does not extend to vehicles, to things left in vehicles, and to live animals.

Would the law of innkeepers or that of landlord and tenant apply to the subject matter in Anglo-American law? Could it be argued in Anglo-American law that a contract of bailment was in existence between the parking lot operator (the innkeeper) and the guest? May is be asserted that the guest rented only a parking space in the parking lot and that the car was parked there at his own risk? What would be the effect in Anglo-American law of a notice displayed in the parking lot disclaiming liability? *See*, e.g., Calif. C.C.A. §1859ff. as to innkeepers; Brown on Personal Propery, 3d ed. p. 218ff. and p. 374ff.; Governor House v. Schmidt (DC Mun.App.), 284 A2d 660 (1971). As to damage caused to a motor car by a tree, *see*, e.g., Noble v. Harrison [1926] 2 K.B. 332.

S.T. v. VEW AG

Federal Supreme Court, 8th Civil Senate, Judgment of June 4, 1975, 1st Instance: *Landgericht* Münster, 2nd Instance: *Oberlandesgericht* Hamm. (Decisions of the Federal Supreme Court in Civil Matters, Vol. 64, 1975, p. 355, Case 51).

Decision of the Court

The plaintiff takes electric power for his chicken farm from the defendant. The contract incorporates the regulations for the supply of electricity applicable by law. Section II, No. 5, of the regulations provides that no damages will be paid in the case of decrease in the voltage or interruption of power. During the night of July 19-20, 1972, the supply of power was interrupted because two wires carrying electricity touched each other on the property of the plaintiff, broke and fell to the ground.... The supply of electricity for lighting was not affected thereby and the plaintiff did not notice the interruption. The interruption produced the stoppage of supply of fresh air to the chicken houses and 1933 chickens died, causing a loss to the plaintiff in the amount of 14,955.50 German marks. He claims damages from the defendant. The *Landgericht* held for the plaintiff. The *Oberlandesgericht* reversed and denied the claim. The petition of error is denied.

The reasons:

The Court of Appeal held that the loss was caused by a typical interruption of supply of power as provided in Section II, No. 5, of the regulations. No claim for damages consequently lies against the defendant. It is irrelevant whether the interruption of supply arose due to impossibility, default, breach of contract or tort. It is also irrelevant whether the interruption arose due to the defendant's fault. The petition of error unsuccessfully challenges this reasoning.

(1) Suppliers of electric power are exempt by the law of liability for damages caused by interruption in the supply of power. This senate has repeatedly held that this exemption may not be challenged. The risk of interruption in the supply of power falls on the consumer.

(2) All damage caused by the interruption in the supply of power falls within the exemption. The cause of the interruption is irrelevant, whether it is caused by accident, by avoidable technical reasons or by human error.

(3) Any differentiation concerning the cause of the interruption in the supply of power would bring about an increase in the price of electricity. . . . The exemption applies even when the interruption amounts to a tort.

(4) The type of damage which is caused to the consumer by the interruption of power is of no importance. It may be direct or indirect damage, damage to property, etc.

(5) It needs not be decided whether the exemption of Section II, No. 5, of the regulations also applies in the case when the interruption in the supply of power occurs due to gross negligence of the supplier. On the facts of the case, no such negligence occurred. . . . The interruption in supply was only of a short duration. The line was repaired in the morning of July 20. The exemption fully covers such cases.

NOTES AND QUESTIONS

The defendant is a stock corporation (the letters AG stand for *Aktiengesellschaft*). *See* the section on stock corporations under commercial law above.

The court thus held the statutory exemption fully applicable.

Does a similar exemption protect electricity suppliers in countries other than Germany? Are there no exceptions? Does a similar rule apply in your state?

IN THE MATTER OF THE MARRIAGE OF B.

Federal Supreme Court, 4th Civil Senate, Judgment of September 20, 1974, 1st Instance: *Landgericht* Itzehoe, 2nd Instance: *Oberlandesgericht* Schleswig. (Decisions of the Federal Supreme Court in Civil Matters, Vol. 63, 1975, p. 78, Case 10).

Decision of the Court

The petitioner was married to the former police officer B. The respondents are the two children of the marriage. B. returned from military service in the last war with an injury to his brain. The petitioner petitioned for divorce in 1955 but withdrew her petition with the consent of her husband. Divorce was granted, however, on the counterpetition of B. on October 27, 1955, by judgment of the *Landgericht* in accordance with §48 of the Marriage Law without pronouncement on fault. The judgment entered into the power of law.

B. then died. The petitioner claims that her late husband lacked capacity to sue in 1955 due to his brain injury. He was therefore not properly represented in the divorce proceedings, and he was not properly notified that a divorce decree was granted.

The petitioner brought an annulment suit in accordance with §579, Subs. (1), No. 4 of the Code of Civil Procedure and requests: (1) annulment of the judgment of the *Landgericht,* and (2) dismissal of the counterpetition brought in the above-mentioned proceedings.

The respondents approve of the petition.

The *Landgericht* denied the petition. The *Oberlandesgericht* affirmed but authorized a petition in error. The petitioner brought error, which is denied.

The reasons:

(1) There is no need to decide whether, pursuant to §628 of the Code of Civil Procedure, a divorce decree may be attacked by a petition for its annulment after the death of a party to the divorce proceedings, since the petition may not be brought for other reasons. The petitioner relies on the ground for annulment given in §579, No. (4) of the Code of Civil Procedure. She claims that her late former husband, due to his mental illness, lacked capacity to sue at the time when he instituted divorce proceedings.

The petitioner may not rely on that ground. As it has been previously decided in a decision of the *Bundesfinanzhof* (BFH 96, 385, 387), this ground may be relied upon only by the party who lacked proper representation in the proceedings, but not by the opponent. The requirement of proper representation applies only to the party in need of such representation. The defeated opponent, in this case the petitioner, did not suffer any prejudice due to the lack of proper representation of the other party. It is not impossible in divorce proceedings, though, for an improperly represented party, on whose petition the decree dissolving the marriage was made, to attack such decree with a petition for its annulment in order to obtain the dismissal of the divorce suit. This, however, does not give the other party any grounds for complaint. . . . Where such other party wishes to be certain that the divorce decree will continue in power, he must take care that the divorce decree is served on the legal representative of the improperly represented party so as to make the time run as indicated in §586, Subs. (1) of the Code of Civil Procedure (§586, Subs. (3) Code of Civil Procedure).

(2) Since the petition for annulment lacks a cause of action, it is unimportant whether it was possibly brought too late as it should have been brought within one month from the time on which the petitioner acquired notice of the ground for an annulment as provided in §586, Subs. (1) of the Code of Civil Procedure. . . . The petition was therefore properly denied.

NOTES AND QUESTIONS

§48 of the Marriage Law provides for the dissolution of a marriage on the ground of separation of the parties for three years.

§579 (1), No. 4 of the Code of Civil Procedure provides that a petition for annulment may be brought when a party to the proceedings lacked proper representation, unless he has expressly or tacitly approved of the handling of his case.

§586 (1) of the Code of Civil Procedure provides that a petition for the annulment of a judgment must be brought within one month.

§586 (3) provides that the time mentioned in Subs. (1) runs in the case of improper representation of a party lacking legal capacity only from the day on which the judgment was delivered to his legal representative.

§628 of the Code of Civil Procedure provides that should one of the spouses die before the judgment [decree] enters into the power of law, the judgment [decree] lapses. (§628 was renumbered and presently appears as §619 of the Code of Civil Procedure).

For petitions for the annulment of judgments, *see* the section above on civil procedure dealing with the reopening of proceedings.

Compare the German provisions with F.R.C.P. Rule 60, and 28 U.S.C.A. §1655.

May a final judgment that becomes *res judicata* be further challenged in Anglo-American law? Within what time and on what grounds may the judgment be so attacked? Would the lack of proper representation amount to a denial of due process? May a party attack a judgment for lack of proper representation of the opponent?

B. v. K.

Federal Supreme Court, 8th Civil Senate, Judgment of October 9, 1974, 1st Instance: *Landgericht* Münster, 2nd Instance: *Oberlandesgericht* Hamm. (Decisions of the Federal Supreme Court in Civil Matters, Vol. 63, 1975, p. 94, Case 13).

Decision of the Court

The Court of Appeal dismissed the appeal of the defendant by a default judgment. At the hearing set on the motion of the defendant to set the default judgment aside, both parties appeared and made their motions. Thereupon the properly summoned witness C. gave evidence on oath. Immediately thereafter the attorney for the defendant declared that he would not represent the defendant any longer and withdrew from the case. The plaintiff then moved for judgment on the pleadings or for a default judgment. The Court of Appeal then dismissed the defendant's motion to set aside the default judgment by a second default judgment. The defendant's petition of error succeeds.

The reasons:

(1) The Court of Appeal erred in pronouncing the second default judgment on the ground that the defendant took part in the proceedings at first but did not continue to do so at the conclusion of the hearing.

A party who makes a motion to set aside a default judgment is in default in accordance with §345 of the Code of Civil Procedure when he does not appear at the hearing or when he does not plead to the merits of his case. Since the attorney for the defendant made the proper motions and, as stated by the Court of Appeal, proceeded with his case, there was no case of default at the beginning of the proceedings.

(2) The statement made by the defendant's attorney, after the witness had given evidence, that he was withdrawing from the case did not bring the defendant into default. The making of motions and pleading to the merits at the beginning of the hearing keeps its effect beyond the proceedings on proof. The situation contemplated in §332 of the Code of Civil Procedure does not arise.

(3) §285, Subs. (1) of the Code of Civil Procedure does not require the repetition of the already made motions. It only gives the parties an opportunity to debate the results of proof. The parties may waive this right. The provision is not mandatory. . .

(4) Since the defendant was not in default, a judgment on the merits should have been given. Plaintiff's motion for a judgment on the pleadings or for a default judgment does not prevent the court from giving a judgment on the merits.

NOTES AND QUESTIONS

§345 of the Code of Civil Procedure provides that a party who makes a motion to set aside a default judgment given against him but who does not appear at the hearing on the motion, or who does not plead to the merits of the case at such hearing, may not make a motion to set aside a default judgment which denies his motion.

§332 of the Code of Civil Procedure provides that a hearing means also an adjourned hearing.

Compare the section above on judgments under the law of procedure before district courts.

Compare the German provisions with F.R.C.P. Rule 55. *See also* the Code of Professional Responsibility of the American Bar Association, Disciplinary Rule 2-110, Withdrawal from Employment.

Would an Anglo-American appellate court give a default judgment on the facts of the case? Would it rather adjourn the case upon withdrawal of counsel? Would it be proper for an Anglo-American counsel to withdraw from a case during a hearing?

B. v. T.

Federal Supreme Court, 2nd Civil Senate, Judgment of September 30, 1974, 1st Instance: *Landgericht* Paderborn, 2nd Instance: *Oberlandesgericht* Hamm. (Decisions of the Federal Supreme Court in Civil Matters, Vol. 63, 1975, p. 214, Case 30).

Decision of the Court

The defendant and tax adviser H. were members in the plaintiff corporation with limited liability. On April 10, 1970, the defendant transferred his interest in the corporation to H. All parties agreed that the defendant would continue in the service of the plaintiff until the end of 1970, and that he would not accept any clients of H., nor of the plaintiff, until the end of 1972. Plaintiff brought suit against the defendant for damages and for a contractual penalty on the ground that the defendant violated the agreement.

The defendant challenged the jurisdiction of the court and demanded the transfer of the case to the proper labor court as it involved a labor dispute, or alternatively, to the commercial chamber of the court.

The civil chamber of the *Landgericht* ruled on June 14, 1972, that the case was to be transferred to its commercial chamber as requested by the defendant. The reasons for the ruling were that the case did not present labor dispute. Instead, the claim of the plaintiff was founded on the membership of the parties in the corporation, and consequently, the dispute was one of commercial law pursuant to §95, Subs. (1), No. 4a, of the Judiciary Law. Thus, the case had to be transferred to the commercial chamber.

The presiding judge of the commercial chamber assumed jurisdiction, whereupon the defendant filed an appeal against the decision of the civil chamber claiming that the case should have been transferred to the proper labor court.

The Court of Appeal held the appeal admissible but denied it as unfounded. It held that the *Landgericht* had jurisdiction in the case and that the case was to be heard by the commercial chamber of the *Landgericht*.

The error brought by the defendant is denied. The judgment of the Court of Appeal is set aside and the appeal against the ruling of the civil chamber of the *Landgericht* is dismissed as inadmissible.

The reasons:

The ruling of the civil chamber of the *Landgericht* contains an order for the transmittal of the case to the commercial chamber. The order is binding and is not subject to any challenge as provided in §102 of the Judiciary Law. Further, the civil chamber considered the subject matter of the dispute between the parties, namely the question whether it was a civil law or a labor law dispute, and ruled in favor of the jurisdiction of the civil courts. Its decision is binding and is not subject to any challenge. This is explained as follows:

(1) When a court assumes jurisdiction and gives an interlocutory judgment (Code of Civil Procedure, §303), or a final judgment to that effect, the decision is subject to the usual means of challenge. It is, however, different when the court transmits the case because of lack of jurisdiction. In that instance, the ruling of the court is binding with respect to all points of jurisdiction considered and ruled upon.

This applies to any transfer made in accordance with §102 of the Judiciary Law. . . . The reason for the difference between the assumption of jurisdiction and the denial of jurisdiction lies in the fact that, in the case of a denial, after the question of jurisdiction has been considered and the case transferred, it would not be in the interest of justice to have the same matter reconsidered by a second court with a view to a retransfer. Such jurisdictional disputes would cause only delay and expense and should be avoided.

The consideration that a transfer to the labor jurisdiction involves two different courts while a transfer from the civil to the commercial chamber involves only one and the same court has no importance. Similarly, it is of no importance that a transfer to the labor jurisdiction is made only on the motion of the plaintiff (Federal Labor Courts Law, §48, Subs. (1)), whereas a transfer between civil and commercial chambers is generally made on the motion of the defendant.

(2) [omitted]

(3) The fact that the defendant moved for a transfer to the commercial chamber only in the alternative is also of no importance. This court has held in similar cases that the decision on the primary motion is not subject to any challenge when the court has considered the matter and found it unfounded and then ordered a transfer on the alternative motion. §98, Subs. (1) of the Judiciary Law applies.

NOTES AND QUESTIONS

For corporations with limited liability, *see* the section on commercial law above. As to the transfer to a commercial chamber, *see* the section on district courts above.

§95, Subs. (1), No. 4 of the Judiciary Law provides that a dispute which arises between members of a commercial partnership or members of a corporation, between a member of a partnership and the partnership, or between a member of a corporation and the corporation is a dispute of commercial law.

§102 of the Judiciary Law provides that a transfer from a civil chamber to a commercial chamber and vice versa is not subject to any remedy and is binding on the chamber to which the case is referred.

§303 of the Code of Civil Procedure provides that a court may give an interlocutory judgment whenever appropriate.

The Court thus held that an order for the transfer of a case from a civil to a commercial chamber was binding and was not subject to any remedy. The rule also applied to a case where the court in its decision has found the labor courts without jurisdiction.

What is the Anglo-American counterpart of a German corporation with limited liability? Are there any special commercial courts in the Anglo-American system? Are there any commercial courts in civil law countries other than Germany?

R.H. KG v. A.V.

Federal Supreme Court, 2nd Civil Senate, Judgment of December 1, 1975, 1st

Instance; *Landgericht* Hamburg, 2nd Instance: *Oberlandesgericht* Hamburg. (Decisions of the Federal Supreme Court in Civil Matters, Vol. 65, 1976, p. 304, Case 51).

Decision of the Court

On January 13, 1970, the vessel M.V. "Anjo" (423 BRT) was lying at anchor in heavy fog in the Baltic Sea near the Gedser-Revs outside of the traffic channel. While there, she was run into by the dredge "Heinrich Hupfeld" (654 BRT) and was damaged. The plaintiff, an insurance company, brought suit to recover payments made to his insured, the M.V. "Anjo," from the defendant, the owner of the "Heinrich Hupfeld." The only point in dispute is whether M.V. "Anjo" bears one fourth of the fault in the collision because she did not make use of her radar at the time of the collision. It is alleged that had she made use of it, she could have warned the other ship by signals or by radio once the danger became apparent on the radar screen. Both the trial court and the appellate court found no fault on the part of the M.V. "Anjo." The petition for error brought by the defendant is denied.

The reasons:

(1) The appellate court stressed that the entire Baltic sea is used for shipping, although the traffic channel is heavily used in this particular stretch. The appellate court is of the opinion that vessels should make use of radar and that the safety of the M.V. "Anjo" and of other shipping would have been enhanced had she used it. She could have warned, with a great chance of success, any ship that was coming too close by ringing the bell, and especially by horn or by radio. Yet her failure to use radar did not constitute a breach of Rule 29 of the International Rules pursuant to which a ship has to take all precautions required by custom or by the circumstances of the case. We agree with the expert testimony of Captain B. that ships lying at anchor in the Baltic Sea outside the traffic channel are not required to take any steps beyond and above those required by International Rules, Rule 11 (the use of anchor lights) and Rule 15 (c)(iv) (the ringing of the bell in proper intervals). . . . The International Rules do not require ships at anchor to use their radar.

(2) We wish to add our comments to the above assertions.

The International Rules do not carry any express provisions concerning the use of radar. Yet it has long been recognized that ships under way should use their radar under conditions calling for the application of Rule 16 (a) (reduction of speed because of poor visibility). This also appears from Rule 29, dealing with the general care of the officer in charge. He should make use of any available device on board which enables him to ascertain his position in the traffic earlier than by visual observation in order to enhance the safety of his ship and that of other traffic. No other provision would be applicable to ships lying at anchor on the high seas. . . . Consequently, even a ship at anchor on the high seas should make use of her radar in case of poor visibility and should not limit herself to the prescribed signals. . . . This should be done even if it means stationing an additional man on the bridge to handle the radar since there must, in any event, be as many persons on the bridge as the security of the ship and that of other traffic demands. . . . The Court is therefore of the opinion that the M.V. "Anjo" was under a duty to use her radar.

(3) The petition is nonetheless denied. The Court agrees with the defendant that no blame for the collision may be placed on the M.V. "Anjo," since the use of radar in poor visibility while the ship is at anchor on the high seas has not yet

become part of shipping practice. This appears not only from the High Sea Rules but also from the evidence given by the expert B. Nor did any court express any other opinion in the matter. The Court of Appeal therefore correctly held the M.V. "Anjo" not liable for the damage caused to the dredge nor for that caused to her.

NOTES AND QUESTIONS

The Court thus held that a ship lying at anchor on the high seas in poor visibility has to watch the traffic situation also with her radar.

The applicable International Rules are given in the text of the decision. These rules are also called the "Rules of the Road at Sea" or the "Collision Regulations." In United States law, they are embodied in 33 U.S.C.A. §§1051-1094. *See also* Afran Transport Co. v. The Bergechief, 274 F. 2nd 469 (2d Cir. 1960); Gilmore and Black, The Law of Admiralty, 2d ed. p. 511ff.; Compare also the section on maritime law above.

The petitioner in error, R.H. KG, is a commandite partnership. The letters KG stand for *Kommanditgesellschaft*.

How are collisions of ships treated in Anglo-American law? Does the rule of proportional fault apply? Is a ship at anchor bound to use her radar? Would the outcome of the case be similar had it been brought in an American court?

S. v. P. KG

Federal Supreme Court, 2nd Civil Senate, Judgment of December 1, 1975, 1st Instance: *Landgericht* Limburg/Lahn, 2nd Instance: *Oberlandesgericht* Frankfurt/Main. (Decisions of the Federal Supreme Court in Civil Matters, Vol. 65, 1976, p. 309, Case 52).

Decision of the Court

The defendant and the merchant K. were general partners in B. KG, which operated a machine factory. According to the partnership contract, which was properly recorded in the mercantile register, the partners could act for the partnership only jointly. The defendant left the partnership as of October 1, 1972, but the fact was recorded in the mercantile register only in November of 1973. In the meantime, B. KG ordered goods from the plaintiff who submitted two bills to B. KG, which remained unpaid. The plaintiff then obtained a default judgment for the whole sum of 3,109.55 German marks against the defendant, and the defendant filed an objection.

The plaintiff alleged that the defendant was liable because the fact that he had left the partnership was not on record in the mercantile register at the time when the goods were ordered and delivered. The defendant claimed that when relying on the mercantile register, the plaintiff had to take the record as he found it, and therefore, had the plaintiff still been a partner at the time the contract was made, he would have been a necessary party thereto, and since he did not act for the partnership, the contract was invalid. Both the *Landgericht* and the *Oberlandesgericht* upheld the default judgment. The petition of error filed by the defendant does not succeed.

The reasons:

(1) The Court of Appeal upheld the liability of the defendant in accordance with §15, Subs. (1), and §128 of the Commercial Code since the defendant could not charge the plaintiff with notice of his leaving the partnership without having recorded the fact in the mercantile register. The fact that had the defendant not left the partnership, the partner K. would have been entitled to act for the partnership only jointly with the defendant, was considered unimportant by the Court of Appeal because only the true conditions existing at the time of making the contract were of importance to the validity of the contract. The Court of Appeal futher held that pursuant to §15, Subs. (1) of the Commercial Code, a person who should have recorded could not be relieved of liability to the detriment of a third party. We agree with the reasoning of the Court of Appeal.

(2) The view that the contents of the mercantile register may be considered only in their totality, and that a person who relies on the mercantile register with respect to a particular fact is bound by the totality of the registration entered therein, finds no support in the law; §15, Subs. (1) of the Commercial Code takes the opposite view. It provides that an unrecorded fact may not be used against a third party, but that it may be used against the person who should have recorded it. Consequently, an outsider may always rely on the true facts. . . . The view on which the petition for error relies is based on the proposition that a person who relies on a fact recorded in the mercantile register may not be heard to say that he had failed to notice all the other pertinent entries while searching, and consequently, he must be held to have acquired notice of all the entries. This reasoning is founded on a wrong premise. The Commercial Code, §15, Subs. (1), protects confidence in the correctness of the entries in the mercantile register concerning a business establishment. This, however, does not require the person relying on the mercantile register to have actually searched it. The law considers the opportunity to search the register as a sufficient basis for the protection afforded. For these reasons, it is impossible to restrict or to extend the protection afforded by §15, Subs. (1) of the Commercial Code beyond the limits set thereby.

NOTES AND QUESTIONS

The partnership is a commandite partnership. *See* the section on commercial law above.

§128 of the Commercial Code provides that partners are jointly liable to creditors for partnership debts and that any agreement to the contrary has no effect with respect to third parties.

§15, Subs. (1) of the commercial Code provides that a fact which should have been recorded in the mercantile register but which was not so recorded cannot be held against a third party by the one who should have recorded it unless the third party had actual knowledge thereof.

Do commandite partnerships exist in Anglo-American jurisdictions? What is the effect of recording in the proper register of partnerships in Anglo-American law? Would a failure to record an event like the leaving of a partner have a similar effect in Anglo-American law? Would the defendant be liable on the above facts in Anglo-American law?

B. DECISIONS OF CRIMINAL COURTS

PEOPLE v. B.

Federal Supreme Court, 2nd Criminal Senate, Ruling of September 19, 1973, 2 StR 165/73, From the *Schwurgericht* Darmstadt. (Decisions of the Federal Supreme Court in Criminal Matters, Vol. 25, 1975, p. 229, Case 58).

Decision of the Court

The accused, a Yugoslav, one night met a group of ten to fifteen of his compatriots who were arguing and who obviously intended to fight. He had in his possession an automatic revolver with at least seven rounds of ammunition which he shortly before had obtained from a friend for safekeeping. With the intent of mediating the dispute, he spoke to the group to settle the matter. At first, he succeeded in making them disperse. Three of the group—one Z., one Zd., and one C.—returned, however, and approached the accused saying that blood will now be shed. C. held a screwdriver in his hand, pointed at the accused. The accused retreated at first but seeing that he would be attacked from several directions, he stood firm, produced the revolver and said that he would open fire if the three continued to advance towards him. He then fired a shot or two in the air. His pursuers did not heed the warning and continued their advance. The accused lowered his hand holding the revolver with the intent of firing a few shots into the ground ahead of his pursuers. He rapidly fired all his remaining shots but contrary to his intention not all the shots hit the ground. One hit Z. in the neck and he died the same day from internal bleeding.

The *Schwurgericht* found the accused guilty of negligent homicide and of unauthorized possession of a gun. The conviction cannot stand since the accused acted in self-defense.

The accused was being attacked by three men without any provocation. His pursuers demonstrated by their conduct that their threats were not idle and that they intended to cause the accused serious bodily harm. The accused was therefore entitled to use any means of defense to ward off the danger. This means that he was entitled to fire at the men after his warnings remained unheeded. He caused Z. a deadly injury in the exercise of his right of self-defense.

The *Schwurgericht* was of the opinion that the accused should have aimed at the legs of the men and that he killed Z. because of his negligent handling of the revolver. This Court does not agree. . . . There is not enough evidence to find the accused negligent. . . . As the three men would not desist from advancing on the accused, even though he fired warning shots, and since they spoke of the shedding of blood and since one of them pointed a screwdriver at the accused, he was entitled to aim at them and to make them stop their attack. He was free, of course, to aim only into the ground. He should not lose his defense of self-defense, however, because he unintentionally hit one of the attackers, since he was entitled to aim at him and hit him deliberately. A person attacked in the circumstances of the present case may not be punished for a negligent injury to his attacker when he acted in accordance with §53, Subs. (2) of the Penal Code and when he did no more than he was entitled to do.

The fact that the accused did not intend to kill Z. does not reflect on his intent to defend himself.

NOTES AND QUESTIONS

The Court thus held that an act is undertaken in self-defense when the person attacked uses more moderate means of defense than he is entitled to use and he thereby negligently brings about an effect which he is entitled to bring about deliberately.

§53, Subs. (1) of the Penal Code provides that an act committed in self-defense is not punishable. Subs. (2) defines self-defense as any defense that is necessary to repel a present unlawful attack on oneself or another person. Note that the new German Penal Code carries the same provisions in §32.

For homicide, *see* the section on criminal law above. For the *Schwurgericht*, *see* the section on the system of criminal courts above.

Was there enough evidence in this case to justify self-defense? Was the accused negligent in the handling of the weapon? Would an Anglo-American court uphold self-defense in this case? Compare, e.g., Calif. Pen. C.A. §197.

PEOPLE v. B.

Federal Supreme Court, 2nd Criminal Senate, Judgment of August 29, 1973, 2StR 268/73, From the *Schwurgericht* Darmstadt. (Decisions of the Federal Supreme Court in Criminal Matters, Vol. 25, 1975, p. 222, Case 56).

Decision of the Court

The *Schwurgericht* convicted the accused to imprisonment for seven years for bodily harm followed by death. At a meeting with his wife from whom he was separated, the accused became very agitated when she bitterly complained about his management of her several fashion stores. After she had made an improper remark concerning his sons from his previous marriage, the accused lost all control of himself, seized her by the throat with both hands, and began strangling her. He meant only to hurt her but the strangling led to her instant death.

The sentence cannot stand.

Serious objections are raised already against the reasoning by which the court declined to give effect to attenuating circumstances pursuant to §228 of the Penal Code. While married, the parties had frequent disagreements, as found by the trial court. The dispute that led to the act and the improper remark of the victim concerning the sons of the accused that made him lose his temper may be considered on the basis of the previous record of the marriage. The trial court itself stated that the remark was the last drop which made the cup run over as far as the accused was concerned. It was not disposed, however, to see the circumstances of the case in a more benevolent way and to consider that the accused was repeatedly offended by his wife so that he became agitated to a degree which made him commit the violent act.

This court does not agree. Had the accused acted with an intent to kill, the court should have considered, in accordance with §212 of the Penal Code dealing with manslaughter, whether the remark that made the accused lose self-control was a gross provocation, which by the provision of §213 of the Penal Code brings the attenuating circumstances into play and limits the sentence to be imposed to a maximum of five years imprisonment. Since the accused acted only with the intent to cause bodily harm, it is difficult to understand why he was deprived of the opportunity to have his act considered under a milder provision of the law. It is also obvious that in cases of bodily harm followed by death dealt with in §266 of the Penal Code, when considering the question of attenuating circumstances in accordance with §228 of the Code, the attenuating ground of provocation given in §213 of the Code must be applied. Only in this way may a conflict be avoided between the maxima in punishments provided for in cases of manslaughter and bodily harm followed by death. Should therefore the trial court hold at the new trial that the accused was provoked without any fault on his part by the grossly offensive insult by the victim, he must be given the benefit of the milder provisions of §228 of the Penal Code.

NOTES AND QUESTIONS

For §§212 and 213 of the Penal Code, *see* the section on manslaughter under substantive criminal law above. For §226 of the Penal Code dealing with death as a consequence of bodily injury, *see* the section on wounding and bodily harm above.

§228 of the old Penal Code provided for the application of attenuating circumstances in the cases of bodily harm. The new Penal Code deals with the matter in §49.

Does Anglo-American law provide for bodily harm followed by death comparable to §226 of the German Penal Code or would it rather treat the matter as manslaughter? Does Anglo-American law recognize the killing following a sudden quarrel or in the heat of passion as an attenuating circumstance? What is the usual punishment for manslaughter under such attenuating circumstances? *See*, e.g., Calif. Pen. C.A. §§192 and 193; 18 U.S.C.A. §112.

PEOPLE v. W. AND OTHERS

Federal Supreme Court; 5th Criminal Senate; Judgment of January 15, 1974; 5 StR 602/73; From *Landgericht* Kiel. (Decisions of the Federal Supreme Court in Criminal Matters, Vol. 25, 1975, p. 261, Case 69).

Decision of the Court

The reasons:
The conviction of insurance fraud pursuant to §265 of the Penal Code cannot stand.

The accused, who was in financial trouble, decided in September 1970 to sink his yacht, which was insured for 80,000 German marks against accidents at sea and total loss, and then to claim the sum from the insurer. He sunk the yacht on September 23, 1970, at sea and on October 2, 1970, he reported the alleged theft of the yacht to the insurance company. The above facts leave the possibility open that at the time of the sinking of the yacht, the accused intended to claim compensation for an alleged theft of the yacht to which he was not entitled. If that is so, he is not punishable for insurance fraud for the following reasons:

§265 of the Penal Code imposes punishment of from one to ten years imprisonment and a fine upon a person who sets a thing afire or who sinks or runs aground
an insured vessel, while §263 of the Penal Code provides for imprisonment of only
up to five years and a fine to punish the fraud committed by a person in breach of
§265. The severe punishment provided for in §265 leads to the conclusion that the
protection of §265 does not apply to property. The purpose of the provision, as far
as it concerns the setting ablaze of a thing insured against fire, is the prevention of
the general loss that would occur if fire insurance is improperly obtained. . . . The
same applies also to the sinking of a vessel when it is insured against such risk. . . .

It follows from the interest protected by §265 that the intent to defraud required
by the article demands that the person must intend to obtain payment of the
insurance policy by deceiving the insurer with respect to the reason for the fire of the
thing insured or the sinking of the vessel and thereby obtain money to which he is
not entitled. Only such act preparatory of fraud affects the interest protected by
§265. The intent of the person to obtain compensation for theft by pretending a
theft is not sufficient.

The above applies also in this case where the insurance against accident at sea
is combined with that against the total loss of the ship. Such combinations are
common. They do not detract from the principle that the interest protected by §265
is affected only when the person intends to claim improperly for fire or ship
accident at sea.

NOTES AND QUESTIONS

The contents of §§265 and 263 of the Penal Code appear in the text of the case.
As to theft, *see* the section dealing with theft above. The court held that the allegation of theft would not suffice to make §265 applicable to the case in question.

How is insurance fraud treated in Anglo-American law? What is the definition
of insurance fraud and what is the protected interest in Anglo-American law? *See*,
e.g., Calif. Pen. C.A. §§450a and 548.

PEOPLE v. H. AND OTHERS

Federal Supreme Court; 5th Criminal Senate; Judgment of February 13, 1968; 5
StR 706/67; From the *Landgericht* Berlin. (Decisions of the Federal Supreme Court
in Criminal Matters, Vol. 22, 1969, p. 83, Case 22).

Decision of the Court

The reasons:

The petitions of error brought by the accused Jürgen H. and U., the violation
of the law of procedure and of the substantive criminal law, bring us to set aside the
judgment with respect to these accused.

Both petitions of error rightfully allege the violation of §169, sentence 2, of the
Judiciary Law, which provides that no television pictures may be taken of court
proceedings. It appears from the reports of the three professional judges and of the
procurator that the presiding judge authorized the taking of television pictures at

the pronouncement of judgment, that this was known to the accused and to their counsel before the event was televised, and that it was so televised. The Criminal Chamber thus violated §169, sentence 2, of the Judiciary Law. Under "proceedings before the court" are understood in criminal cases the trial proceedings, which in accordance with §260 Subs. (1) of the Code of Criminal Procedure end with the pronouncement of judgment.

The parties may still request permission to make a motion during the pronouncement of judgment. The presiding judge is, of course, not required to grant the permission. . . . The knowledge that the pronouncement of the judgment would be televised or broadcasted may influence the proceedings and the deliberation of the court. . . . In the present case, the interference is obvious. Since the proceedings were in progress when the televising began, the presiding judge ordered the suspension of the televising rather than devote his attention to the proceedings of the court. It is irrelevant whether any part of the proceedings that did not belong to the pronouncement of judgment was televised. What is important is that the presiding judge tolerated a gross interference with the proper course of the proceedings, contrary to the express prohibition of the law, which the law terms inadmissible.

All of the judges reported that the defense counsel had not objected to the televising. This is irrelevant. Even if all defense counsel and all the accused expressly consented, or even if the televising was undertaken at their own initiative, the televising was still inadmissible and they could have brought error on that ground. As far as the accused are concerned, it is the object of §169, sentence 2, of the Judiciary Law to take all precautions to prevent that they become martyrs. For this reason, the consent of the accused to the televising is irrelevant. The accused may not suffer because the defense counsel overlooked or misunderstood a mandatory provision of the law, which was also overlooked by the court.

NOTES AND QUESTIONS

§169, sentence 1, of the Judiciary Law provides that proceedings before a court, including the pronouncements of judgments and rulings, are public. §169, sentence 2, of the Judiciary Law provides that sound, television and radio recording and motion picture taking for the purpose of public screening, broadcasting or publication are inadmissible.

§260, Subs. (1) of the Code of Criminal Procedure provides that the trial concludes with the pronouncement of judgment after deliberation.

Do you agree with the rule generally applicable in all countries that proceedings in court may not be broadcasted, filmed or televised for public viewing? Is the object of the prohibition to prevent the court proceedings from becoming a public show with all the logical consequences arising therefrom? Does the prohibition hold good in Anglo-American countries? *See* F.R. Crim. P. Rule 53.

PEOPLE v. B.

Federal Supreme Court; 4th Criminal Senate; Judgment of January 19, 1968; 4

StR 559/67; From *Landgericht* Mönchengladbach. (Decisions of the Federal Supreme Court in Criminal Matters, Vol. 22, 1969, p. 80, Case 21).

Decision of the Court

The reasons:

The assumption of the *Landgericht* that the accused made two attempts (§43 of the Penal Code) at an unauthorized use of a motor vehicle does not raise any legal problems. . . . On both occasions, the act of the accused constituted an attempt because he shook the front wheels of the vehicles, which amounted to the beginning of the realization of the punishable act. To constitute the beginning of the realization of a punishable act, the completion of one of the elements of the completed act is not necessary. It suffices that the accused made a determined direct attack on the legally protected concept, which is thereby compromised, and the bringing about of the final result is brought nearer to realization. The unauthorized use of the vehicles required their taking. The legal characterization of the act of the accused as an attempt depends therefore, like in theft, on the fact of whether or not he already affected the possession of the owner with the intent to take. The trial court answered the question rightly in the affirmative.

The trial court found that the act of the accused had been directed against a particular vehicle. In both cases, the accused was determined to take a particular motor car for his proposed trip to D. He shook the front wheels to find out whether the steering wheel was locked. If found unlocked, he was determined to immediately seize that vehicle. In view of this conduct, the trial court was right in holding that the accused had begun to bring about a taking. It was an intentional attack on a particular thing which suited the accused and which came very close to the violation of the possession of another person.

The accused had not contemplated making a choice between several motor cars by shaking their front wheels to find out which of them would be easy to take. Had he intended that, it would have amounted only to a preparatory act. He, moreover, directed his attention to one particular vehicle at a time. The fact that the possession of the owner was affected appears also from the connection in point of time between the shaking of the front wheels and the intended taking of the vehicle. The Federal Supreme Court, in its judgment of September 28, 1956 (5 StR 332/56), decided in this context that when a pickpocket touches the pocket of a street car passenger in order to find out whether it contains a wallet, it is not merely a preparatory act, but it amounts to an attempted theft. Similarly in this case, the trial court attached considerable importance to the connection in point of time between the act of the accused and the intended theft in order to draw a line between a preparatory act and an attempt.

NOTES AND QUESTIONS

§43 of the Penal Code provides that an attempt was made when the determination of the actor to commit a felony or a misdemeanor is manifested by acts which amount to the beginning of the bringing about of that felony or misdemeanor. The new German Penal Code deals with attempt in §22 and provides that there is an attempt when the person proceeds to the bringing about of the punishable act.

How is an attempt defined in Anglo-American law? Did the act of the accused amount to an attempt? How does Anglo-American law define the distinction between preparatory acts and an attempt? *See,* e.g., Calif. Pen. C.A. §§663 and 664; R. v. Robinson [1915] 2 K.B. 342.

PEOPLE v. M.

Federal Supreme Court; 2nd Criminal Senate; Judgment of Februry 13, 1974; 2 StR 552/73; From *Landgericht* Bad Kreuznach. (Decisions of the Federal Supreme Court in Criminal Matters, Vol. 25, 1975, p. 285, Case 75).

Decision of the Court

The reasons:

The indictment charges the accused with two completed acts of arson and with one attempted arson. He was acquitted by the trial court. The error brought by the public ministry succeeds.

In the opinion of the trial court, there is considerable evidence that the accused committed the act against the property of farmer G. Yet the trial court held that the accused must be acquitted because, on the evidence of witness C., the accused left his inn in the locality of K. in his tractor at about 1:15 A.M., while the fire at the barn of farmer G. in the locality of B. had already been noticed at 1:10 A.M.. The court thus applies an alibi in favor of the accused.

In considering the alibi, the trial court should have considered all the facts from which conclusions could have been drawn for or against the accused and it should have evaluated them in the reasons for its decision. This it did not do. Other witnesses stated that the accused arrived in B. from a direction other than from K. at a time at which he could not yet have arrived there had the evidence given by the innkeeper C. been correct. The trial court, however, accepted the version of C. without even mentioning in this connection the contradictory evidence given by other witnesses, which should have been evaluated.

From this error, it clearly appears that the trial court misunderstood the substance of the proof of an alibi. Under the circumstances of the case stated by the trial court, it held that the guilt of the accused had not been established. Yet upon the successful proof of an alibi, the accused must be declared free of any guilt and must be found not guilty. The trial court could not have found so. It is generally known that only proof of an alibi may influence a decision. Otherwise the inadmissible result would follow that an unproven allegation of the absence of the accused from the place of the act would necessarily lead to an acquittal, even though the trial court was convinced of the guilt of the accused. Any doubts concerning the alibi are therefore resolved against the accused. This was not fully recognized by the trial court as it appears from its contradictory pronouncements on the alibi.

The petition of error brought by the public ministry succeeds.

Concerning a new trial to be held in the case, this court wishes to point out that the failure of the proof of an alibi does not amount, on its own, to an element of proof of the guilt of the accused.

NOTES AND QUESTIONS

The court held that a trial court has to state in the reasons for its decision all the facts from which conclusions may be drawn for or against the accused. It further held that the principle *in dubio pro reo* does not apply to the proof of an alibi.

Alibi is a good defense in criminal prosecution. How is it treated in Anglo-American law? *See*, e.g., F.R. Crim. P. Rule 12.1.

C. DECISIONS OF ADMINSTRATIVE COURTS

IN AN ENLISTMENT MATTER

Federal Supreme Administrative Court; Judgment of the 8th Senate of September 11, 1974; BVerwG VIII C 2.74; From the Administrative Court Augsburg. (Decisions of the Federal Supreme Administrative Court, Vol. 47, 1975, p. 41, Case No. 7).

Decision of the Court

The plaintiff, who was born in 1949, was drafted as "able" in March 1968. He obtained a postponement first until July 31, 1971, and then until June 30, 1972. In April 1972, he requested a further medical examination and in June, 1972, a further postponement. After the examination, the District Military Reserve Office decided, by order of August 1, 1972, that the grading of the plaintiff as "able" had not been changed and granted him postponement until June 30, 1973.

The complaint brought by the plaintiff against the grading was denied. He did not challenge the denial.

By order of April 24, 1973, the plaintiff was summoned to present himself for military service on July 2, 1973. The Administrative Court set aside the order, as well as the order which denied the plaintiff's above complaint, on the ground that the plaintiff should have been given another hearing before the summons was issued. Upon a petition of error brought by the military, the matter is remitted to the Administrative Court.

The reasons:

We agree with the Administrative Court that a new hearing in accordance with §13 Subs. (3), sentence 1, of the Enlistment Regulations was not held. It was, however, not required.

Pursuant to §13 Subs. (3), sentence 1, of the Enlistment Regulations, persons subject to military service who are not actually called up within two years from the enlistment must be heard before they are called up and they must be medically examined, if they so desire, or they may be so examined ex officio.

The prescribed hearing pursuant to §13 Subs. (3), sentence 1, of the Enlistment Regulations is directly related to the prescribed medical examination; such examination must be held at the request of the person subject to military service after two years have run since his enlistment. The reason for this is that the health condition of the person may have changed in that time. This provision does not apply when the person was medically examined within that time. At the hearing, the person is given an opportunity to raise the issue of his health as well as any other issues that may speak against his being called up. The reason is that a person who has not been called up for two years after enlistment may have made undertakings in the meantime which may make his joining the military difficult, and he must be given an opportunity to point that out. This provision does not apply when the person has been newly examined within that time.

There is no need for a new hearing nor for a new medical examination when two years have not yet elapsed from the last examination of the case by the military authorities.

The plaintiff was not only medically examined in 1972, but also his availability was newly examined and he was granted another postponement. Contrary to the opinion of the Administrative Court, he was not entitled to another hearing before his being called up in 1973. The judgment must therefore be set aside.

A final decision cannot be made in this case since the Administrative Court has not examined the medically motivated objections of the plaintiff to his being called up.

NOTES AND QUESTIONS

The contents of the section of the Enlistment Regulations appear in the text of the decision. For administrative courts, *see* the section on Administrative Courts above. Germany, like most European countries, has a compulsory military service for all men. Note that the problem handled in the decision is a proper subject for administrative courts and is not left to the military authorities for their decision.

Was the plaintiff treated fairly within the meaning of Anglo-American law? Did the decision of the Federal Supreme Administrative Court comply with due process as understood in Anglo-American law?

IN THE MATTER OF CUSTOMS DUTIES AND EXAMINATION FEES

Federal Supreme Administrative Court; Judgment of the 7th Senate of March 8, 1974, BVerwG VII C 34.71; From the Bavarian Administrative Court Munich. (Decisions of the Federal Supreme Administrative Court, Vol. 45, 1975, p. 72, Case No. 9).

Decision of the Court
The plaintiff imported on April 16, 1970, oranges from Italy. They were examined at the border by the Bavarian State Institute of Plant Protection, for which the Institute charged and obtained from the plaintiff the fee of 22.10 German marks. The plaintiff alleges that the assessment of the fee was contrary to law because it offends the provisions of the European Common Market.

The Bavarian Administrative Court Munich denied the claim. The petition of error brought by the plaintiff directly to this courts succeeds. The State of Bavaria is ordered to refund the fee of 22.10 German marks with 6 percent interest.

The reasons:

Pursuant to §9, Sentence 1, of the Plant Inspection Regulation of August 23, 1957 (BGBl.I S. 1258), together with the appendix to the Regulation, all imported citrus fruits must be inspected prior to the customs inspection. Pursuant to §1, Subs. (1), No. 2, of the Plant Protection Fees Law of August 26, 1969 (BGBl. I S. 1406), the inspecting agencies may levy fees to cover their costs connected with the inspection. This authority is given because the inspection is in the public interest.

Yet, the provision is ineffective since it is contrary to the applicable law of the European Community, which overrides the law of the individual states. It offends against Art. 9, Subs. (1), of the Treaty on the Foundation of the European Common Market of March 25, 1957 (BGBl. II S. 766), which prohibits the levying of customs duties and fees of an identical nature by member states. Article 13, Subs. (2) of the Treaty provides for the discontinuation of such duties as of April 16, 1970. The fee for plant inspection is such a customs duty or fee.

The fee is of an identical nature as a customs duty since it is levied at the occasion of importation of goods. It is not a fee for actually performed services nor a compensation for fees levied inland.

The fee is not a fee levied for actually performed services since the fee does not increase the value of the imported goods. . . . The European Court, in its judgment of October 11, 1973 (Case 39/73), held that an act of the state administration in the area of health inspection in the common interest may not be regarded as a service to the importer which would justify the levying of a fee.

The fee does not represent a compensation for fees levied inland. Nationally produced plants and plant products are not subject to any inspection. They are checked only selectively in the area of their production. Imported plants and plant products, however, are subject to inspection prior to the customs inspection, even though they have been examined in the country of their origin and treated against disease. It is important to note that the inspection of plants grown nationally is performed free. Consequently, the fee levied against the plaintiff at the occasion of the importation of oranges has no counterpart in the national system. It is therefore a fee of an identical nature as a customs duty in the sense of Arts. 9 and 12 of the Treaty, even if it does not have any discriminatory or protectionist effect. It is of no importance that no oranges are grown in Germany since the fee does not have the purpose of equalizing inland fees. The European Court so held in its above-mentioned judgment.

Since the defendant has already levied the fee, this court may order him to reimburse it pursuant to §113, Subs. (1), Sentence 2, of the Administrative Courts Law. Since the dispute concerned the reimbursement of a fee, the plaintiff is entitled to 6 percent interest in accordance with §111 of the Taxation Courts Law.

NOTES AND QUESTIONS

The contents of the various provisions cited in the decision are given in the decision. For administrative courts, *see* the section on administrative courts above.

Note that the matter went directly to the Federal Supreme Administrative Court on a *Sprungrevision*, thus by-passing the appellate administrative court.

May the law of the European Community be likened to the American federal law? May the law of the individual member countries of the European Community be likened to that of the American states? Do Anglo-American countries examine plants and plant products before they are imported? Do they charge fees for the examination?

IN THE MATTER OF A PRIVATE SCHOOL

Federal Supreme Administrative Court; Ruling of the 7th Senate of March 27, 1974; BVerwG VII C 3. 73; 1st Instance: Administrative Court Würzburg; 2nd Instance: Appellate Administrative Court Munich. (Decisions of the Federal Supreme Administrative Court, Vol. 45, 1975, p. 117, Case No. 16).

Decision of the Court

The plaintiff petitions for a determination that the defendant, who runs a school for interpreters in Bavaria and holds a state permit to operate it as a private school, has improperly denied her the right to take part in the examinations in French held July 13-17, 1970. The Administrative Court upheld the plaintiff's claim. The Appellate Administrative Court, by judgment of November 20, 1972, set the judgment of the Administrative Court aside, held that the case was improperly brought in the administrative court system, and remitted it to the proper civil court. The plaintiff brought error and moved that it be handled *in forma pauperis*. This court denied her motion, whereupon the plaintiff withdrew her petition altogether.

The reasons:

The error is not likely to succeed. (§166, Subs. (1) of the Administrative Courts Law; §114 Subs. (1), Sentence 1, of the Code of Civil Procedure.)

The Appellate Administrative Court is rightly of the opinion that the subject matter of this case, concerning a private school which is permitted but not recognized in Bavaria, may be dealt with only in the ordinary civil courts and not in the administrative courts. . . . It is not a dispute of public law as defined in §40 Subs. (1), Sentence 1 of the Administrative Courts Law, which would fall within the jurisdiction of the administrative courts. The dispute is rather of a civil law nature. This court has already held in its judgment of October 18, 1963 (BVerwGE 17, 41) . . . that a private school recognized by the state could be sued in the administrative courts. That cannot apply to schools which are only permitted. The distinction made in the state laws between schools recognized and those only permitted by the state was held permissible by the Federal Constitutional Court (Ruling of November 14, 1969—1 BvL 24/64—BVerfGE 27, 195). A school that is only permitted by the state cannot exercise the powers of a public authority. The permit . . . only declares that there are no objections to setting up the school. The Federal Constitutional Court expressly declared such activity to fall within the scope of civil law. . . .

The Bavarian law does not invest the defendant with the powers of a public authority and consequently, the jurisdiction of administrative courts may not be invoked. . . .

The Appellate Administrative Court has correctly remitted the case to the proper civil court (§41 Subs. (3), Sentence 1, VwGO, §13 GVG).

NOTES AND QUESTIONS

§166 of the Administrative Courts Law and §114 of the Code of Civil Procedure deal with the standing of a party *in forma pauperis*. The standing is granted only when the court rules that the case offers a sufficient likelihood of success.

§40 Subs. (1), Sentence 1, of the Administrative Courts Law gives jurisdiction to administrative courts in all disputes of public law that do not fall within constitutional law, unless another court has jurisdiction by express provision of the federal law.

§41 Subs. (3), Sentence 1, of the Administrative Courts Law provides that administrative courts decide the question of their jurisdiction.

§13 of the Judiciary Law provides that all disputes of civil law and all criminal matters must be handled by ordinary courts if they do not fall within the jurisdiction of the administrative authorities and administrative courts, or if they are not assigned to other courts by federal law.

For jurisdiction of the administrative system, *see* the section on administrative law and the system of administrative courts above.

Does the Anglo-American legal system have a separate hierarchy of administrative courts? How are civil law matters distinguished from administrative law matters in Anglo-American law?

IN THE MATTER OF A TAX REDUCTION AND THE HOUSE BUILDING LAW

Federal Supreme Administrative Court; Judgment of the 8th Senate of March 27, 1974; BVerwG VIII C 21.73; 1st Instance: Administrative Court Koblenz; 2nd Instance: Appellate Administrative Court Koblenz. (Decisions of the Federal Supreme Administrative Court, Vol. 45, 1975, p. 120, Case No. 17).

Decision of the Court

Plaintiff purchased a lot in 1968 on which, at that time, his predecessor in title completed the construction of a house. The land is zoned "W"—Weekend houses. The well-built house was approved by the building authority as a weekend house. The plaintiff lived in the house as in his "second house" until 1971 when he sold it. His request that the premises be declared eligible for a tax reduction was denied since, by law, no tax reduction may be granted to weekend houses.

The Administrative Court upheld the plaintiff's claim. The Appellate Administrative Court denied it. Plaintiff's petition of error does not succeed.

The reasons:

We agree with the Appellate Administrative Court that the house is not eligible for a tax reduction since it was approved only as a weekend house and may be used only for that purpose.

The Appellate Administrative Court also found that the use to which the house was put by the plaintiff was contrary to the permit of the building authority, which approved it only as a weekend house.

To be considered for a tax reduction, the actual use of the building must be permitted by the building authority.

The encouragement of house building by tax reduction in accordance with §82 II. of the House Building Law must be considered within the framework of proper building planning. . . . Since only the building of structures constructed in accordance with the applicable law may be encouraged, a use other than approved may not become the basis for a tax reduction.

The Appellate Administrative Court found that the plaintiff obtained a permit only for the construction of a weekend house and not for the construction of a permanent building, and that the change in the use of the building required a new permit. The use to which the house was put by the plaintiff was not approved.

Since the house at the time of its completion could not have been permanently inhabited, it does not qualify for a tax reduction.

The tax reduction provided for in §82 II. of the House Building Law does not apply to weekend houses.

Had the plaintiff intended to live in the house permanently in accordance with the law, he should have applied for a permit to build a permanent house, and were such permit denied, he should have brought suit. He has not done so.

NOTES AND QUESTIONS

§82 II. of the House Building Law provides for tax reduction for the construction of permanent premises. The plaintiff faced the further problem of having the house built in an area zoned for weekend houses only. Consequently, a permit to build a permanent structure could not have been obtained without an exception.

For jurisdiction of the administrative courts, *see* the section on administrative courts above.

Does the case present a tax problem or rather a zoning oriented problem? How is zoning handled in Anglo-American law? Would the dispute eventually reach the courts in the Anglo-American legal system?

IN THE MATTER OF ADMINISTRATIVE PROCEDURE

Federal Supreme Administrative Court; Ruling of the 2nd Senate of June 28, 1974; BVerwG II B 81.73; 1st Instance: Administrative Court Schleswig; 2nd Instance: Appellate Administrative Court Lüneburg (Decisions of the Federal Supreme Administrative Court, Vol. 45, 1975, p. 260, Case No. 38).

Decision of the Court

The complaint based on §132, Subs. (2), No. 3, of the Administrative Courts Law does not succeed.

The plaintiff alleges that the Appellate Administrative Court committed a procedural error in that at the trial held on August 28, 1973, it did not read aloud a motion made by his attorney and have it approved (or not approved) by him. It thus contravened §173 of the Administrative Courts Law and §162, and 160, Subs. (2), No. 2, of the Code of Civil Procedure. The plaintiff alleges that had the Court proceeded correctly, he would have noticed the defect and would have made his attorney raise the issue so that the Court would have been bound to rule thereon.

No such error was in fact committed because the above-referred to provisions of the Code of Civil Procedure do not apply to administrative procedure. The Court was not required to read the motion and to have it approved by the plaintiff's attorney.

§173 of the Administrative Courts Law provides for the application of the Code of Civil Procedure to administrative procedure only when the Administrative Courts Law does not have its own provisions and when such application is not excluded by a fundamentally different premise of administrative procedure.

The Administrative Courts Law has its own provision on the matter. It provides in §105, Subs. (3): "The record of evidence given by witnesses, experts and parties must be read to them, or given to them so that they can read it. It must be noted in the record that this took place and that the record was approved by them or what objections they have made."

The provision differs from that of §162 of the Code of Civil Procedure in that there the following additional items must be read and approved: admissions, waivers and settlements, motions and declarations, and the report of viewing parts.

In view of the special regulation of the matter by the Administrative Courts Law, the provision of the Code of Civil Procedure is not applicable as far as it concerns the reading and approval of motions. . . . In administrative proceedings, motions need not be read aloud by the court and require no approval of the person concerned.

The correctness of this approach appears from the different treatment of motions in civil procedure and in administrative procedure.

In civil procedure, the plaintiff's statement of a claim must contain a definite demand (§253, Subs. (2), No. 2, Code of Civil Procedure); in administrative procedure, it only should contain it (§82, Subs. (1), Administrative Courts Law). In civil procedure, the trial begins with the parties making their motions (§137, Subs. (1), Code of Civil Procedure); in administrative procedure, the rapporteur first gives his report, including the claims made by the parties (§103 Subs. (2), Administrative Courts Law). In civil procedure, the decision of the court may not go beyond the claims of the parties (§308, Subs. (1), Code of Civil Procedure); in administrative procedure, the decision of the court may not go beyond the claims of the parties, but the court is not bound by the form of the motions (§88 Administrative Courts Law).

From the above, the importance attached by the law of civil procedure to motions made by the parties is apparent since the law relies on the adversary system of procedure. In contrast, administrative procedure holds to the subject matter of the claim and is based on the inquisitorial system of procedure. The claims of the parties appear usually from the report of the rapporteur and the parties need not make their motions at trial, nor is the court required to read them aloud.

It appears from the above that in administrative procedure the form of the motions is of a considerably lesser importance than it is in civil procedure. The particular method of examination of motions by having them read aloud by the court and their approval by the parties may be dispensed with in administrative procedure and is consequently not required. The respective provisions of the Code of Civil Procedure are therefore inapplicable.

NOTES AND QUESTIONS

§132, Subs. (2), No. 3 of the Administrative Courts Law provides that an Appellate Administrative Court may grant leave to bring error against its judgment on the ground of a procedural defect from which the judgment is alleged to suffer.

The contents of the other provisions appear in the text of the decision.

For administrative procedure, *see* the section on administrative procedure above.

How does administrative procedure differ from civil procedure in Anglo-American law? Do most Anglo-American jurisdictions have any rules of administrative procedure? Is Anglo-American administrative procedure founded on the inquisitorial principle of procedure?

IN THE MATTER OF ROAD TRAFFIC

Federal Supreme Administrative Court; Judgment of the 7th Senate of May 23, 1975; BVerwG VII C 43.73; 1st Instance: Administrative Court Hamburg; 2nd Instance: Appellate Administrative Court Hamburg. (Decisions of the Federal Supreme Administrative Court, Vol. 48, 1976, p. 259, Case No. 33).

Decision of the Court

Early in 1972, the plaintiff parked his car almost daily in front of the building at Pilatuspool Street No. 2, in Hamburg, within a ten-metre long strip that begins at a point where the said street enters the Karl-Muck-Square and ends with a no-stopping traffic sign erected at the curb. This sign also displays a white arrow pointing away from the driveway. No other no-stopping sign has been erected ahead of this sign on Pilatuspool Street.

After the plaintiff ignored several warnings not to park there, he was advised that his car would be towed away if found parked there again. Soon thereafter, when he had once more parked his car there, the police ordered the car to be towed away and demanded from the plaintiff the payment of the towing costs of 65.98 German marks.

The plaintiff brought suit for a declaratory judgment that the towing away of his car was contrary to law and for the cancellation of the payment order. Both the Administrative Court and the Appellate Administrative Court denied his claim. The petition of error to this Court succeeds.

The reasons:

The contested judgment violates federal law.

The Appellate Administrative Court, applying the Hamburg Law of Public Security and Order of March 14, 1966 (BVBl. S. 77), held that since the plaintiff parked his car in a no-stopping zone, it amounted to a disturbance of public order and the towing away of the car was justifiied. This question, however, must be decided in accordance with federal law, namely, by the Street Traffic Regulations of November 16, 1970 (BGBl. I S. 1565).

In contradiction to the opinion of the Appellate Administrative Court, the spot where the plaintiff parked his car was not subject to any no-stopping order. The Appellate Administrative Court is of the opinion that the no-stopping sign with the white arrow pointing away from the driveway standing a few metres in front of the plaintiff's car had the effect of creating a no-stopping zone running back to the point where the street enters the square.

This view is contrary to the wording of §12, Subs. (1), No. 6, (a), of the Street Traffic Regulations, which provides that the beginning of a no-stopping zone must be marked and declares that no vehicle may stop when stopping is prohibited by a traffic sign.

Also §41, Subs. (2), Sentence 3, of the Street Traffic Regulations, which deals with traffic signs, provides that traffic signs must be erected at a point where, from that point on, the order given thereby must be obeyed.

The arrow in the sign pointing away from the driveway cannot have the effect of moving the prohibited zone ahead of it. . . . An arrow pointing away from the driveway marks the end of a no-stopping zone. It has no other meaning.

This ambiguous sign could not create any legally binding obligation as against the plaintiff. The effect of a prohibition may begin only at a point where the sign setting up the prohibition is erected. A traffic sign that marks the end of a nonexistent no-stopping zone is meaningless because it does not indicate what it ends. The sign has no legal significance and is therefore ineffective. . . . It does not give the driver any order, but rather indicates that it terminates an order which has never been given.

The legality of the order to tow away the plaintiff's car may not be deduced from the fact that the police had, on several occasions, orally stated to the plaintiff not to park his car there. This did not amount to a directive pursuant to §36 of the Street Traffic Regulations. Such directives are given only in particular cases and serve a momentary necessity of the traffic. The directive given to the plaintiff was not of that kind. . . . The oral directives pointed to a no-stopping order which, in the opinion of the police, was in effect at the location.

Since no legal basis for the towing away of the plaintiff's vehicle (i.e., the disturbance of public order) has been established, the plaintiff's suit for a declaratory judgment succeeds.

The order requiring the plaintiff to pay for the towing away of his car must also be set aside.

NOTES AND QUESTIONS

The contents of the several articles of the German traffic law appear in the text of the decision. Note that the regulation of road traffic falls within administrative law in Germany and in other civil law countries. For administrative courts and administrative procedure, *see* the pertinent sections above. Note also the rule that federal law overrides state law.

Does the regulation of road traffic fall within administrative law in Anglo-

American jurisdictions? Which courts would hear a similar case in the Anglo-American court system. *See* the laws of your own state for the applicable road traffic regulations.

FOOTNOTES

1. Civil Code, Arts. 7-11, 24. The German law does not recognize the concept of domicile as it is known in Anglo-American law. It deals simply with residence. Jurisdictionally, however, the function performed by domicile in Anglo-American law is performed by citizenship in German law. *See*, e.g., *Einführungsgesetz zum BGB* (Law of Introduction to the Civil Code) Art. 25. (The property of an alien who had his residence in Germany at the time of his death descends in accordance with the law of the country of his citizenship.)
2. Civil Code, Arts. 194-225.
3. Other periods of limitation apply in special cases, e.g., a six-month period of limitation applies to claims for the removal of a defect in a work and for the rescission, reduction of the price, or compensation for such defect; a one-year limitation applies to the above claims in the case of work on land. Civil Code, Art. 638.
4. Civil Code, Arts. 241-432.
5. *Ibid.*, Arts.241-304.
6. *See* Section 3(b)(iii) below on rescission of contract.
7. Civil Code, Arts. 145-157, 305-361.
8. *See* Section 3(b)(iii) below on rescission of contract.
9. Civil Code, Art. 339.
10. *Ibid.*, Art. 340.
11. *Ibid.*, Art. 341.
12. *Ibid.*, Art. 342.
13. *Ibid.*, Arts.362-397.
14. *Ibid.*, Arts.854-1296.
15. *Ibid.*, Arts. 854-872.
16. *Ibid.*, Arts. 903-1011.
17. *Ibid.*, Arts. 903-924.
18. The Civil Code further deals with the rights and duties of adjoining landowners concerning nuisance (smoke, noise, etc.), natural support (excavation), overhanging branches of trees, boundaries, right of way, etc.
19. Civil Code, Arts. 873-902, 925-928.
20. *Ibid.*, Arts. 929-984.
21. *Ibid.*, Arts. 1297-1588; Marriage Law (*Ehegesetz*) of February 20, 1964, No. 16, as amended.
22. *Ehegesetz*, Art. 1-15a.
23. A person is of full age and capacity upon reaching his eighteenth year of age. Civil Code, Art. 2; *Ehegesetz*, Art. 1; *Gesetz zur Neuregelung des Volljährigkeitsalters vom 31. Juli 1974 (BGBl. I, S. 1713)*.
24. *Ehegesetz*, Art. 4.
25. *Ibid.*, Art. 6.
26. *Ibid.*, Art. 13.
27. The grounds for annulment of marriage under both headings are such as are traditionally given for annulment of marriage in American law. The term *nichtig* (void) in the *Ehegesetz* has the meaning of both void and voidable in American family

law. Under (i) *Nichtigkeit der Ehe* (Nullity of marriage), the marriage is invalid unless declared valid by the provisions of the *Ehegesetz*. No one may, however, rely on, or take advantage of, the invalidity until the marriage has been declared null and void by judgment. Under (ii) *Aufhebung der Ehe* (Annulment of marriage), the marriage is valid until annulled by judgment. Consequently (i) deals chiefly with void marriages and (ii) chiefly with voidable marriages, as the terms are understood in American family law.

28. *Ehegesetz*, Arts. 16-27.
29. *Ibid.*, Arts. 28-37.
30. *Ibid.*, Arts. 41-76.
31. Civil Code, Arts. 1922-2385.
32. *Ibid.*, Arts. 1924-1938.
33. *Ibid.*, Art. 1926.
34. *Ibid.*, Arts. 2064-2273.
35. *Ibid.*, Arts. 2229-2230.
36. *Ibid.*, Arts. 2231-2252; the Notarial Authentication Law (*Beurkundungsgesetz*) of August 28, 1969 (BGBl. I. S. 1513), as amended.
37. Civil Code, Arts. 2253-2258.
38. *Ibid.*, Arts. 2303-2338a.
39. *Ibid.*, Arts. 2339-2345.
40. Commercial Code, Arts. 1-7.
41. *Ibid.*, Art. 4.
42. *Ibid.*, Arts. 8-16.
43. *Ibid.*, Arts. 38-47a.
44. *Ibid.*, Arts. 105-160.
45. *Ibid.*, Arts. 161-177.
46. *Ibid.*, Arts. 335-342.
47. The Corporation Law (*Aktiengesetz*) of September 6, 1965 (BGBl. I.S. 1089), as amended, Arts. 1-277.
48. *Ibid.*, Arts. 1-22.
49. The German law of corporations does not distinguish between a memorandum of association and articles of association or by-laws. Every corporation must have a charter (*Satzung*), which embodies all the provisions usually found in the above documents current in the English and American law. In addition to the *Satzung*, the management (*Vorstand*) may issue and always issues a regulation (*Geschäftsordnung*) for its own management. The *Geschäftsordnung* may be issued by the supervisory board (*Aufsichtsrat*) rather than by the management.
50. *Aktiengesetz*, Arts. 23-53.
51. *Ibid.*, Arts. 76-147.
52. *Ibid.*, Arts. 262-274.
53. *Ibid.*, Arts. 278-290.
54. The Law of April 20, 1892 (*RGBl. S. 477*), as amended.
55. The law of bankruptcy is governed by the *Konkursordnung* of February 10, 1877 (*RGBl. S. 351*), as republished on May 20, 1898 (*RGBl. S. 612*), as amended.
56. The law of composition with creditors is governed by the *Vergleichsordnung* of February 26, 1935 (*RGBl. I. S. 321, ber. S. 356*), as amended.
57. The close relatives of the debtor are: his and his spouse's lineal relatives, his and his spouse's brothers and sisters of the half or full blood, and the spouses of such persons.
58. Commercial Code, Arts. 476-905, deal with the topic under the heading maritime trade (*Seehandel*).
59. Commercial Code, Arts. 484-510.
60. *Ibid.*, Arts. 511-555.

61. *Ibid.*, Arts. 556-678.
62. *Ibid.*, Arts. 700-905.
63. *Ibid.*, Arts. 700-733.
64. *Ibid.*, Arts. 734-739. The Federal Republic of Germany is party to the international convention for the unification of certain rules relating to collisions between vessels, signed at Brussels on September 23, 1910.
65. Commercial Code, Arts. 740-753.
66. *Ibid.*, Arts. 754-764.
67. *Ibid.*, Arts. 778-900.
68. *Ibid.*, Arts. 901-905.
69. The time differs with respect to motor propelled vessels and sailing ships and also with respect to the port of departure and the port of destination and is fixed at periods ranging from six to twelve months. Commercial Code, Arts. 862, 863.
70. The Judiciary Act (*Gerichtsverfassungsgesetz*) of January 27, 1877 (*RGBl. S. 41*), as republished on September 12, 1950 (BGBl. S. 513), as amended, Arts. 22-27.
71. Arts. 23 and 23a-c of the *Gerichtsverfassungsgesetz* determine in full detail the jurisdiction of the *Amtsgerichte*.
72. *Gerichtsverfassungsgesetz*, Arts. 59-75.
73. *Ibid.*, Art. 95, defines commercial matters in full detail.
74. As to proceedings on admissibility of appeals, *see* procedure before courts of appeal.
75. *Gerichtsverfassungsgesetz*, Arts. 115-122.
76. *Ibid.*, Arts. 123-140.
77. By provision of Art. 8 of the Introductory Law to the Judiciary Act (*Einführungsgesetz zum Gerichtsverfassungsgesetz*) of January 27, 1877 (*RGBl. S. 77*), as amended, any German state (*Land*) within the territory of which there are two or more *Oberlandesgerichte* may set up a supreme court of the state (*oberstes Landesgericht*) to hear error that would otherwise go to the *Bundesgerichtshof*, but only in cases involving the law of that particular *Land*. The court would thus ensure the uniformity of application of law in that *Land*. Only Bavaria took advantage of the legislation and set up an *oberstes Landesgericht* by enactment of the *Bayerisches Gesetz zur Ausführung des Gerichtsverfassungsgesetzes* of November 17, 1956 (*BayBS III. S. 3*).
78. Labor courts have been set up pursuant to the authority of the Federal Constitution (*Grundgesetz*) Art. 96(1), and are regulated by the Federal Labor Courts Law (*Bundes-Arbeitsgerichtsgesetz*) of September 3, 1953 (*BGBl. III. Nr. 32*), as amended.
79. *Zivilprozessordnung* of January 30, 1877, as republished on September 12, 1950 (BGBl. S. 533), as amended.
80. ZPO (*Zivilprozessordnung*), Arts. 495-510b.
81. *Ibid.*, Arts. 253-494, 128-165, 214-238; *Gerichtsverfassungsgesetz*, Arts. 192-197.
82. *Gerichtsverfassungsgesetz*, Arts. 176-183. Acts committed in the courtroom that are criminally punishable are dealt with by the criminal courts.
83. *See* procedure before the courts of appeal.
84. ZPO (*Zivilprozessordnung*), Arts. 511-544.
85. *Ibid.*, Arts. 545-566a.
86. *Ibid.*, Arts. 578-591.
87. Federal Labor Courts Law (*Bundes-Arbeitsgerichtsgesetz*) of September 3, 1953 (*BGBl. III. Nr. 32*), as amended.
88. *Strafgesetzbuch* (*StGB*), Arts. 1-10.
89. All the instances are enumerated in *Strafgesetzbuch* (*StGB*), Art. 5.
90. All the instances are enumerated in *Strafgesetzbuch* (*StGB*), Art. 6.
91. *Strafgesetzbuch* (*StGB*), Art. 7.
92. *Ibid.*, Art. 12. German criminal law thus recognizes only two types of offenses. The former division into felonies, misdemeanors and infractions (*Übertretungen*) was

abolished as of January 1, 1975. Introductory Law to the Penal Code (*Einführungs-gesetz zum Strafgesetzbuch*) of March 2, 1974, Art. 300.

93. *Strafgesetzbuch* (*StGB*), Art. 10, and the Penal Law of Minors (*Jugendgerichtsgesetz*) of December 11, 1974 (BGBl. I. 3427; III. 451-1), as amended.

94. *Strafgesetzbuch* (*StGB*), Arts. 25-31, as to accomplices and accessories before the act; Arts. 257-258a, as to accessories after the act.

95. *See* the section on punishment below.

96. *Strafgesetzbuch* (*StGB*), Arts. 38-55.

97. *Ibid.*, Arts. 48, 66-67g, 68-68g.

98. *Ibid.*, Arts. 56-56g, 58-60.

99. *Ibid.*, Arts. 57, 56-56g.

100. *Ibid.*, Art. 211.

101. *Ibid.*, Arts. 212, 213.

102. *Ibid.*, Art. 222.

103. *Ibid.*, Arts. 223-233.

104. The attempt (*Versuch*) of a felony (*Verbrechen*) is always punishable, the attempt of a misdemeanor (*Vergehen*) is punishable only when determined by law. The punishment for an attempt may be less than for the completed act. *Strafgesetzbuch* (*StGB*), Arts. 22-24.

105. *Strafgesetzbuch* (*StGB*), Arts. 242-248c.

106. *Ibid.*, Arts. 249-256.

107. *See* the section on repeaters above.

108. *Amtsgerichte, Landgerichte, Oberlandesgerichte* and the *Bundesgerichtshof* exercise both civil and criminal jurisdiction. Whatever has been said about them concerning the exercise of their civil jurisdiction applies *mutatis mutandis* to the exercise of their criminal jurisdiction.

109. *Gerichtsverfassungsgesetz* (*GVG*), (Judiciary Act), Arts. 22-58.

110. Decisions of all collegiate courts that are prejudicial to the accused and concern his guilt and the legal consequences of his act, including circumstances which may exclude, decrease or increase punishment, require a two-thirds majority of votes. In the case of the *Schöffengericht*, it is equal to a simple majority.

111. *Gerichtsverfassungsgesetz* (*GVG*), Arts. 59-78b.

112. These cases are enumerated in the *Gerichtsverfassungsgesetz*, Art. 74 (2), and comprise all cases of homicide and some cases of arson, explosion of atomic energy, and misuse of radiation.

113. *Gerichtsverfassungsgesetz* (*GVG*), Arts. 115-122.

114. They are particularly the offenses of: preparation for the waging of an offensive war, high treason, treason, attacks against representatives of foreign states, offenses against high officers of state, failure to inform authorities of the planning of such offenses, and genocide. *Gerichtsverfassungsgesetz*, Art. 120.

115. These are rulings which: disqualify the defense attorney from further participation in the defense; deal with the arrest and confinement of the accused, seizures and searches; or refuse to set the case for trial, discontinue the proceedings, order a trial in the absence of the accused, transfer the case to a lower court, deal with inspection of court files, revoke probation, deal with reopening of proceedings, etc. *Gerichtsverfassungsgesetz*, Art. 135(2).

116. *Gerichtsverfassungsgesetz* (*GVG*), Arts. 123-140.

117. *See* footnote 115 above.

118. *Strafprozessordnung* (*StPO*) (Code of Criminal Procedure), Arts. 151-295, 48-93.

119. The circumstances under which a warrant of arrest may be issued are enumerated in *StPO*, Arts. 112-113.

120. *StPO*, Arts. 312-332.

121. *Ibid.*, Arts. 333-358.

122. *Ibid.*, Art. 338.
123. *Ibid.*, Arts. 359-373a, *GVG*, Art. 140a.
124. The statute governing German passports is the Law Concerning Passports (*Gesetz über das Passwesen*) of March 4, 1952 (BGBl. I. 290; III. 210-2), as amended, and the regulations made thereunder of April 16, 1968 (*Bundesanzeiger Nr. 85*), and of February 25, 1969 (*Bundesanzeiger Nr. 44*), as amended.
125. The entry into the Federal Republic by foreigners and the requirement that they hold and produce passports is regulated by the Law Concerning Foreigners (*Ausländergesetz*) of April 28, 1965 (*BGBl. I. 353; III. 26-1*), as amended.
126. The Federal Antipollution Law (*Bundes-Immissionsschutzgesetz*), of March 15, 1974 (*BGBl. I. 721, ber. 1193; III. 2129-8*), as amended, forms the basis of pollution control.
127. The provisions of the statute do not apply to airports or to radioactive materials, atomic fuels and enterprises that are governed by the Atomic Law (*Atomgesetz*) of December 23, 1959 (*BGBl. I. S. 814*), as amended.
128. *Versammlungsgesetz* of July 24, 1953 (*BGBl. I. 684; III. 2180-4*) and of March 2, 1974 (*BGBl. I. 469, 555*), as amended.
129. German Constitution (*Grundgesetz*), Art. 8.
130. *Versammlungsgesetz*, Art. 1 (2); *Grundgesetz*, Arts. 9 (2), 18, 21 (2).
131. *Grundgesetz*, Art. 28 (1).
132. The open-country states (*Flächenstaaten*) are: *Baden-Württemberg, Bayern, Hessen, Niedersachsen, Nordrhein-Westfalen, Rheinland-Pfalz, Saarland* and *Schleswig-Holstein*.
133. *Grundgesetz*, Art. 28 (2).
134. In all states, the administration of the communities is uniformly regulated by a state statute governing the same, known as the *Gemeindeordnung*.
135. In all states, the administration of the districts is uniformly regulated by a state statute governing the same, known as the *Landkreisordnung*.
136. The regional public administration is governed by a statute that governs the entire public administration in a given state; it is usually known as the *Landesorganisationsgesetz* or the *Landesverwaltungsgesetz*.
137. *See* footnote 136 above.
138. In Bavaria, the state government is known as the *Staatsregierung* and the ministers as *Staatsminister*.
139. Public administration in the state of Berlin is governed by a number of state statutes similar to those in the other German states, like the state constitution (*Verfassungsgesetz*), state administrative law (*Verwaltungsgesetz*), and state public service law (*Landesbeamtengesetz*).
140. Public administration in the state is governed by a number of state statutes similar to those in other German states.
141. *See* footnote 140 above.
142. The system and powers of federal administrative authorities are founded on the Federal Constitution (*Grundgesetz*), e.g., Articles II. The Federation and the States, V. The Federal President, VI. The Federal Government, and VIII. The Execution of Federal Laws of the Federal Administration, and on a number of federal statutes.
143. They are based on provisions of the Federal Constitution (*Grundgesetz*) in Art. 96, and they are set up and regulated by the Federal Law on Administrative Court (*Bundes-Verwaltungsgerichtsordnung*) of January 21, 1960 (*BGBl. I. S. 17*), as amended. All German states have enacted laws concerning the application of the Federal Law on Administrative Courts (*Gesetze zur Ausführung der Verwaltungsgerichtsordnung*). They supply the details applicable in the particular states, set the number and location of the lower level administrative courts, determine the location of the intermediate level administrative court, etc.
144. Pursuant to the authority of the Federal Constitution (*Grundgesetz*), Art. 96 (1), there

are separate tax, labor, and welfare court systems in addition to the ordinary judicial and administrative court systems.

145. Cases of a constitutional nature are handled by the Federal Constitutional Court (*Bundesverfassungsgericht*). The fundamental provisions concerning the *Bundesverfassungsgericht* appear in Arts. 93, 94, 99 and 100 of the Federal Constitution (*Grundgesetz*). The court decides on the interpretation of the Federal Constitution in the case of disputes concerning the extent of rights and duties of the highest federal organs, the compatibility of federal or state law with the Federal Constitution, and the rights and duties of the Federation and the states, as well as disputes involving public law between the Federation and the states and between different states.

146. They are based on provisions of the Federal Constitution (*Grundgesetz*) in Art. 96, and they are set up and regulated by the Federal Welfare Courts Law (*Bundes-Sozialgerichtsgesetz*) of September 3, 1953, as amended, and by the respective state laws.

147. They are based on provisions of the Federal Constitution (*Grundgesetz*) in Art. 96, and they are set up and regulated by the Federal Tax Courts Law (*Bundes-Finanzgerichtsordnung*) of October 6, 1965, as amended.

148. *Verwaltungsgerichtsordnung* of January 21, 1960 (*BGBl. I. S. 17*), as amended.

149. *Verwaltungsgerichtsordnung*, Arts. 81-123.

150. This is pursuant to the provision of the German Constitution (*Grundgesetz*), Art. 34.

151. *Verwaltungsgerichtsordnung*, Arts. 124-131.

152. *Ibid.*, Arts. 132-145.

153. Procedure before the *Sozialgerichte* is founded on provisions of the Federal Welfare Courts Law (*Bundes-Sozialgerichtsgesetz*) of September 3, 1953, as amended.

154. Procedure before the *Finanzgerichte* is founded on provisions of the Federal Tax Courts Law (*Bundes-Finanzgerichtsordnung*) of October 6, 1965, as amended.

155. The office of a judge is based on provisions of the Federal Constitution (*Grundgesetz*), Chapter IX, The Administration of Justice, especially Articles 97 and 98. It is further regulated by the German Law on Judges (*Deutsches Richtergesetz*), as republished on April 19, 1972 (*BGBl. I. S. 713*), as amended. On the strength of these two fundamental provisions, each state enacted its own State Law of Judges (*Landesrichtergesetz*).

156. To qualify, a person must study law for seven semesters in a university and pass a number of written examinations and an oral examination, which are grouped together and referred to as the first juridical state examination (*erste juristische Staatsprüfung*). Thereafter he must spend two years in practical training with civil courts, criminal courts, the office of the public prosecutor, administrative courts, an attorney in an attorney's office, or, in accordance with his wishes, in one out of a number of possible courts and government offices, like welfare courts, taxation courts, or labor courts, or even with a foreign government or a foreign attorney in a foreign country. Immediately thereafter, he must pass the second juridical examination (*zweite juristische Staatsprüfung*), which also consists of a number of written examinations and an oral examination. Having successfully passed the second legal examination, a person is fully legally qualified and has the qualifications required for admission into judicial service, known as the *Befähigung zum Richteramt. Deutsches Richtergesetz*, Arts. 5-7.

157. *Deutsches Richtergesetz*, Arts. 10-12, 48, 76. Judges of the Federal Supreme Court retire at 68 years of age, other federal judges at 65. The retirement age of state judges is determined by the individual state laws on judges along the above lines.

158. Judges of the *Bundesgerichtshof* are selected jointly by the Federal Minister of Justice and a committee consisting of the ministers of justice of the states and of an equal number of members elected by the *Bundestag* (Lower House of Parliament). Judges of the *Bundesverwaltungsgericht, Bundesfinanzhof, Bundesarbeitsgericht*, and *Bundessozialgericht* are selected similarly in that the federal ministers competent for the particular matter take the place of the Federal Minister of Justice and the competent

state ministers take the place of the state ministers of justice. The judges are then appointed by the Federal President. *Grundgesetz*, Arts. 95 (3) and 96 (2).

159. *Grundgesetz*, Art. 97 (1), *Deutsches Richtergesetz*, Art. 25.
160. *Deutsches Richtergesetz*, Arts. 49-60, 72-75.
161. *Ibid.*, Arts. 61-68, 77-83.
162. *Gerichtsverfassungsgesetz*, Arts. 141-152, *Deutsches Richtergesetz*, Art. 122.
163. Where the federal state or an individual state appears as a litigant, it is represented by the particular branch of government actually involved. Detailed regulations have been issued by the federal and state governments concerning such representation. At the top, the federal government or an individual state is represented by the particular ministry, and at the lower levels by the appropriate agencies.
164. *See* the section on judges above.
165. The profession of an attorney (*Rechtsanwalt*) is governed by the Federal Law on Attorneys (*Bundesrechtsanwaltsordnung*) of August 1, 1959 (*BGBl. I. S. 565*), as amended. All German states have enacted state laws on attorneys; these state laws must conform to the federal law.
166. *See* the section on judges above.
167. The office of a notary (*Notar*) is regulated by the Federal Law on Notaries (*Bundesnotarordnung*) of February 24, 1961 (*BGBl. I. S. 98*), as amended.
168. *See* the section on judges above.

The Italian Law

I. INTRODUCTION

Italian law is of ancient tradition and distinguished ancestry. The law of ancient Rome, which represents the most accomplished system of law ever produced until the Napoleonic codification in France, belongs to its ancestors. After the fall of the western part of the Roman Empire, Roman law, which was until then the undisputed master, had to compete with the Germanic customary law brought into Italy by the invading Germanic tribes. It was not replaced by such customary law, however, nor by the rapidly developing canon law, but held its own side by side with them.

The Roman law, the canon law and the Germanic law were the governing legal systems in Italy until the end of the eighteenth century. A codification movement began in the second half of the eighteenth century and appeared to be the beginning of a new Italian law being developed in the various Italian states. This promising development was interrupted, however, by the introduction of the French Napoleonic codes into all the Italian states by the victorious French.

After the fall of Napoleon, the French codes continued in power and were first replaced by codes of the various Italian states, which were closely modeled on the Napoleonic codes, and after the reunification of Italy in 1865, by all-Italian codes of civil law, civil procedure, criminal procedure and commercial law. The Code of Commerce was replaced in 1882, and an all-Italian Code of Criminal Law was first enacted in 1890. These five codes, although now applicable throughout all of Italy, were again closely modeled on the Napoleonic codes. They did not meet with the unreserved approval of the Italian legal profession, however. The chief objection leveled against them was that they were only a reproduction of the French

Napoleonic codes and that they did not draw from the rich tradition of pre-Napoleonic Italian law. A movement to produce new codes that would fully reflect the wealth of Italian legal heritage was initiated at the close of the nineteenth century and serious codification work was undertaken after World War I. The new, truly Italian codes were completed in the 1930's and 1940's. The Penal Code and the Code of Criminal Procedure entered in force in 1931; the Civil Code, which comprises also the area previously covered by the Commercial Code, and the Code of Civil Procedure entered in force in 1942.

II. THE SYSTEM AND ADMINISTRATION OF CIVIL LAW

A. THE SUBSTANTIVE CIVIL LAW
(Including Commercial Law)

The Civil Code of 1942 is in power in Italy as amended and supplemented by many statutes. The Code is introduced by thirty-one introductory articles on legal sources and the general application of law. The Code itself has 2969 articles contained in six books: Book 1. Persons and family; Book 2. Succession; Book 3. Property; Book 4. Obligations; Book 5. Labor; and Book 6. Protection of rights.

Book 1 (Persons and family) has the following titles: I. Physical persons; II. Juridical persons; III. Domicile and residence; IV. Absence and the declaration of presumed death; V. Consanguinity and affinity; VI. Marriage; VII. Affiliation; VIII. Adoption; IX. Paternal power; X. Guardianship and emancipation; XI. Publicly or privately supported minors and their affiliation; XII. Mental incompetence, interdiction and disability; XIII. Alimony; and XIV. Vital statistics records (registration of births, deaths and marriages).

Book 2. (Succession) has the following titles: I. General provisions; II. Intestate succession; III. Testamentary succession; IV. Distribution of property; and V. Gifts.

Book 3 (Property) has the following titles: I. Property; II. Ownership; III. Rights in the surface of land; IV. *Emphyteusis* (long-term lease); V. Usufruct, use, and right to use premises; VI. Easements; VII. Concurrent ownership; VIII. Possession; and IX. Injunctions against new constructions and prevention of anticipated damage.

Book 4. (Obligations) has the following titles: I. Provisions common to obligations; II. Contracts in general; III. Individual types of contracts; IV. Unilateral promises; V. Commercial papers; VI. Spontaneous agency; VII. Payment of what is not due; VIII. Unjust enrichment; and IX. Compensation for damages caused intentionally or negligently.

Book 5 (Labor) has the following titles: I. Regulation of professional activity; II. Entrepreneurs; III. Independent labor; IV. Subordinate labor; V. Partnership and corporations; VI. Cooperatives and mutual insurance; VII. Special partnerships; VIII. Business assets, trade names and trademarks; IX. Rights of authorship in literary and artistic works, and patent rights in industrial inventions; X. Regulation of competition and business association; and XI. Penal provisions concerning corporations and business associations.

Book 6 (Protection of rights) has the following titles: I. Recording of documents and titles: II. Proof; III. Liability for debts, collateral security, priorities, and mortgages; IV. Foreclosure sales; and V. Limitation of actions, lapse of time, and forfeiture.

Further important statutes appear in the appendix to the Civil Code. They are grouped as to their subject matter, and are given in alphabetical order. They include, for example, motor vehicles, markets and the stock exchange, patents and trademarks, bills of exchange, citizenship, bankruptcy, land registry, and auditors.

The following are topics selected from the Italian substantive civil law.

1.   Domicile and Residence (*Domicilio e residenza*)[1]

The domicile of a person is the place where he has established the principal seat of his business and interests. Residence is the place where he habitually resides. A change of residence may not be set up against third parties in good faith unless it is declared as required by law. Where a person has both his domicile and residence in the same place, and changes only his residence, as against third parties he is considered to have changed also his domicile unless he declares otherwise in a declaration.

Each spouse has his domicile in the place where he has established the principal seat of his business and interests. A minor has his domicile in the place of residence of the family or in that of his guardian. Where the parents have separated, or where their marriage has been annulled or dissolved, or where they do not reside together, the minor has the domicile of the parent with whom he lives. An incompetent has the domicile of his guardian.

Wherever the law makes certain effects depend on residence or domicile, in the case of juridical persons, reference is made to the place where they have established their seat. Where the seat of the juridical person indicated in the register differs from its actual seat, third parties may take its actual seat for its true seat.

A person may establish a special domicile for specific acts or business. Declaration of a special domicile must be made in writing.

NOTES AND QUESTIONS

1. Consider the provisions concerning residences and domiciles in the French, the German and the Spanish law. Is there a distinction between the two in these systems?

2. The Italian Civil Code gives a definition of both domicile and residence. Is there a similar definition given in the civil codes of any of the other countries? Does the distinction made by Italian law between the two suggest that domicile is the seat of a person's business, where he would deal with third parties, whereas residence is a person's private home?

3. Is the meaning of residence in Italian law coextensive with the meaning of residence in Anglo-American law? Can the same be said of domicile? *See also* In re Dorrance's Estate, 309 Pa. 151, 163 Atl. 303 (1932); and In re Estate of Dorrance, 115 N.J. Eq. 268, 170 Atl. 601 (1934).

4. Is the meaning of residence and domicile in Anglo-American law closer to their meanings in Italian law or in French law?

---

2. Marriage and Divorce (*Matrimonio ed il divorzio*)[2]

(a) Marriage entered into before a minister of the Catholic Church or before a minister of another church recognized by the state. Marriage celebrated before a minister of the Catholic Church and in accordance with provisions of canon law is governed by provisions of the Concordat between the Holy See and Italy of February 11, 1929. It produces the same effects as that celebrated before the registrar of marriages whenever it is recorded with the registrar. The certificate of marriage is executed in two originals, one of which is transmitted to the registrar within five days of the celebration of the marriage. The certificate must indicate that the minister read to the spouses Articles 143, 144, and 145 of the Civil Code on the duties of husband and wife. If it does not so indicate, the registrar must return it to the minister to incorporate therein such indication. If the marriage has for any reason whatsoever not been recorded with the registrar, it may be so recorded at any time on the request of any interested party.

Marriage may also be celebrated on similar conditions before ministers of other churches recognized by the state. It must comply with the provisions of the Civil Code otherwise provided for marriages entered into before the registrars of marriages.

(b) Marriage entered into before the registrar of marriages. Marriages are otherwise celebrated before the registrar of marriages. The minimum age required for entering into marriage is the age of majority, namely, eighteen years for both men and women. The court of general jurisdiction (*tribunale*) may dispense with the above requirement for good reasons and allow a marriage between persons of not less than sixteen completed years of age.[3]

Incompetents because of weakness of mind may not marry.[4] Persons already married may not marry.[5] The following may not marry: (1) direct ascendants and descendants, legitimate or illegitimate; (2) brothers and sisters, half-brothers and half-sisters; (3) uncle and niece, aunt and nephew; (4) father-in-law and daughter-in-law, mother-in-law and son-in-law, with the prohibition continuing even if the marriage which brought about the relationship is annulled; (5) brother-in-law and sister-in-law; (6) an adopting person, the person adopted and his descendants; (7) adopted children of the same person; (8) an adopted child and the children of the adopting person; or (9) the adopted person and the spouse of the adoptant, the adopting person and the spouse of the adopted person. The *tribunale* may grant a dispensation and allow marriage between persons enumerated in numbers (3), (5), (6), (7), (8) and (9) above. It may also grant dispensation of the prohibition of number (4), in the case where the relationship has arisen due to a marriage that has been annulled.[6] A person convicted of homicide or attempted homicide of another person cannot marry the spouse of that person.[7]

A woman may not marry within three hundred days from the dissolution or annulment of her previous marriage, except where the marriage was annulled because of impotency of one of the spouses. The *tribunale* may grant dispensation and allow her to marry. The prohibition ceases the day on which the woman gives birth.[8]

Where a minor petitions to be allowed to marry, the court will assign a special guardian to assist him.[9]

A declaration of intention to marry must be published by being affixed to the door of the town hall for eight consecutive days, including two Sundays, in the locality or localities where the applicants reside. If the duration of a residence is less than one year, publication must be effected also in the locality of a previous residence.[10] Marriage may not be celebrated before the fourth day after publication has been concluded. If it is not celebrated within 180 days after the conclusion of publication, a new publication is required.[11] The *tribunale* may reduce the number of days required for publication for good reason, and it may also dispense with publication entirely.[12]

Opposition to the celebration of a marriage may be made by the parents of the applicants or, failing parents, by other ascendants, by collaterals up to the third degree, and by the public ministry on the ground of an impediment arising out of the provisions of the above-mentioned Articles 84-90 of the Italian Civil Code (*see* footnotes 3-9). It is made with the registrar of marriages and the marriage may not be celebrated unless the opposition is dismissed by judgment of the court. If it is so dismissed, any opponent who is not an ascendant of the petitioners or the public ministry may be made liable in damages.[13]

Marriage is celebrated in the town hall before the registrar of marriages in the presence of two witnesses. The registrar must read to the spouses Articles 143, 144 and 147 of the Civil Code on the duties of husband and wife.[14]

Persons in the armed forces in time of war may be married by proxy. A marriage by proxy may also be held when one of the spouses resides abroad and there are good reasons therefor. The proxy must be executed by a public act.[15] The marriage must be celebrated within 180 days from the execution of the proxy.

A foreigner who desires to marry in Italy must present to the registrar of marriages a document of the proper authority of his own country to the effect that he suffers from no impediment to enter into marriage. He must still comply with the provisions of the above-mentioned Articles 85, 86 and 87, subsections 1, 2 and 4, and Articles 88 and 89. In addition, a foreigner who has his domicile or residence in Italy must proceed to the publication of his intention to marry as provided in Articles 93-101 (*see* footnotes 10-12) of the Italian Civil Code.[16]

(c) **Nullity of marriage** (*Nullità del matrimonio*). Marriage entered into in contravention of the above-referred to Articles 84, 86, 87 and 38 may be annulled. A petition for its annulment may be made by the spouses, their ascendants, the public ministry, or any interested party with respect to Articles 86, 87 and 88, and by the spouses, their parents and the public ministry with respect to Article 84. Marriage may also be annulled on the ground of insanity. The ground of insanity may not be used after the spouse has recovered and the spouses have cohabited for one year after the recovery.

When the marriage was entered into in good faith, it is valid until annulled. If only one spouse entered into the marriage in good faith, the marriage is so valid as to him and the children.

(d) Dissolution of marriage (*Scoglimento del matrimonio*). Marriage is dissolved by the death of one of the spouses or by a decree of dissolution of marriage.[17] Dissolution of marriage may be demanded by a spouse where the other spouse is convicted to imprisonment for fifteen years or more, or where he is found guilty of incest or rape, of homicide of a descendant or of attempted homicide of a descendant or of the spouse, of bodily harm inflicted on the spouse or a descendant, irrespective of the length of imprisonment assessed in all these cases. Dissolution of marriage may also be demanded where the other spouse is acquitted of the above crimes because of insanity.

Dissolution of marriage may further be demanded where a judicial separation of the spouses has previously been decreed and five years of actual separation have preceded the filing of the petition. Dissolution of marriage may be demanded where the spouses have lived separately for five years. The required time of living apart is increased to seven years where the judicial separation was decreed out of the fault of the petitioning spouse. Dissolution of marriage may also be demanded where the other spouse, who is a foreigner, obtains a divorce or annulment abroad and remarries. Dissolution of marriage may be further demanded where the marriage was not consummated. The court will decree the dissolution of marriage on any of the above grounds. Upon dissolution of the marriage, the wife reacquires the use of the name she had before the marriage.

(e) Judicial separation of spouses (*Separazione dei coniugi*). Judicial separation may be demanded on the ground that any further cohabitation of the spouses is intolerable. Judicial separation entitles the spouses to live apart. The innocent spouse is entitled to alimony if he does not have adequate means of support.

NOTES AND QUESTIONS

1. As to marriage, Italian law gives the parties a choice to marry in the church of their religion or before the registrar of marriages. Is there a similar choice in Spain or Germany? Compare also the French law. Who may solemnize marriages by Anglo-American law? *See*, e.g., Calif. C.C.A. §4205.

Note the minimum age for entering into marriage. It is the same for both spouses and may be reduced to age sixteen. Compare the corresponding requirements of the French and the German law. What is the rule of the Spanish law? *See also* Calif. C.C.A. §4101.

Note also the various grounds of prohibition of marriage, especially consanguinity. How does the Italian rule compare with the French and Spanish rules? In Italian law, dispensation may be obtained from the prohibition against consanguinity except in the direct line between brothers and sisters and half brothers and half sisters. Compare the Italian rule with the Anglo-American rule. *See*, e.g., Calif. C.C.A. §4400.

How does the Italian prohibition against a marriage by a woman within three hundred days from the dissolution of her previous marriage compare with the French and German rules? What is the purpose of the provision of the State of California, Calif. C.C.A. §§4512 and 4514, which provide for the entry of a final judgment of dissolution of marriage only after an interlocutory judgment has been entered and six months have expired from the date of service of a copy summons or the date of appearance of the respondent?

2. As to nullity of marriage, a marriage entered into in breach of a prohibition against marriage may be annulled. The grounds for annulment comprise the grounds that in Anglo-American law make a marriage both void and voidable. The annulment must be pronounced by a competent court after proper proceedings. Compare the German and Spanish laws of annulment. *See also,* e.g., Calif. C.C.A. §§4400-4429.

3. As to dissolution of marriage, the Italian divorce law is a relatively recent statute (enacted in 1970), and it provides for dissolution of marriage only in very limited cases. Compare it with the divorce law of France. Note that upon divorce the wife reacquires the use of the name she had upon entering into the marriage. Does this mean her maiden name? Compare the German law. *See* Calif. C.C.A. §4362. As to grounds for dissolution of marriage and proceedings in Anglo-American law, *see,* e.g., Calif. C.C.A. §4501ff.

4. As to judicial separation, before the enactment of the divorce law in 1970, only judicial separation was obtainable in Italy. Judicial separation is still possible in other countries even though divorce is readily available. *See,* e.g., the French law.

(f) Proprietary regime of spouses (*Regime patrimoniale della famiglia*). The proprietary regime of the spouses takes mainly the form of patrimonial property, community property, or separation of property. It is set up by a marriage contract. Marriage contracts (*convenzioni matrimoniali*) may be made between the spouses before the celebration of the marriage or thereafter. Marriage contracts made before the celebration of the marriage may be modified after its celebration only with authorization of the court. Marriage contracts must be made by public act, otherwise they are null and void. When they deal with immovables, they must be recorded. Where the spouses do not make any provisions as to property, their property relationship is governed by the law of community property.

(i) PATRIMONIAL PROPERTY (*Fondo patrimoniale*). Patrimonial property may be set up by one or both spouses in a public act, or by a third person also in a testamentary provision, to serve the needs of the family. Immovables and movables properly described and identified may be so constituted before or after the celebration of the marriage. Both spouses hold title to the corpus unless otherwise provided in the act of settlement, and the fruits of the property are applied to the needs of the family.

The administration of the property is governed by the rules applicable to community property. The property may be alienated, mortgaged, pledged or otherwise dealt with only by agreement of both spouses, and if there are minor children, with the court's authorization on proof of evident need or utility. Execution against the property may not be had for debts that the creditor knew were contracted for purposes other than to meet the needs of the family. Patrimonial property comes to an end when the marriage is annulled or dissolved or when its civil effects are terminated. If there are minor children, the patrimonial property exists until the youngest of them reaches majority. At any time during its existence, the court may assign to the children a portion of patrimonial property, both corpus and income. If there are no minor children, patrimonial property is dissolved in accordance with the rules of dissolution of community property.

(ii) COMMUNITY PROPERTY (*Comunione legale*). Community property is composed of all property acquired by the spouses together or individually during marriage, with the exclusion of personal effects; the fruits of their separate property accrued and not consumed at the dissolution of the marriage; the proceeds of separate efforts of each of the spouses not consumed at the dissolution of the marriage; and the business transacted by both spouses after the celebration of the marriage. Property intended for an undertaking of one of the spouses and set up after the celebration of the marriage and the fruits thereof, even if the undertaking was set up before the celebration of the marriage, fall into community property only if they are in existence at the time of dissolution of the marriage.

Separate property of the spouses is property owned by a spouse before marriage; property acquired during marriage by gift or succession unless otherwise indicated; property of purely personal use; property used in the exercise of the profession of a spouse, even if it is used in an undertaking forming part of community property; property obtained as damages or as compensation for loss of working capacity; and property acquired with the proceeds of the sale of separate property or by exchange for separate property.

Each spouse is entitled to the management of community property. Acts that are beyond ordinary administration must be undertaken jointly. Where one spouse refuses to give his consent to an act that goes beyond ordinary administration, the other spouse may obtain a court order to undertake it, if it is in the interest of the family or in that of the business. One spouse may empower the other to administer community property; in the case of an impediment, such authority may be given by the court. The court may exclude a minor spouse or a spouse who has not properly managed community property from the administration. A spouse who lacks full legal capacity may not manage community property. Acts of management improperly undertaken by one spouse without the consent of the other may be set aside.

Community property answers for all burdens imposed on it at the time of its acquisition; for the expenses of its administration; for maintenance of the family, education of children, and all obligations contracted jointly or individually by the spouses for the benefit of the family; and for any obligation entered into jointly by the spouses.

Community property does not normally answer for obligations of the spouses entered into prior to their marriage. It answers, however, up to the value of the interest of each of the spouses therein, for obligations entered into by a spouse during marriage with respect to acts exceeding the ordinary administration of community property, and undertaken without the consent of the other spouse, where the creditor cannot obtain satisfaction from the separate property of that spouse. Similarly, creditors who are unable to obtain satisfaction from the separate property of a spouse for debts incurred by him prior to the marriage may proceed against his interest in community property. Also, creditors who are unable to obtain satisfaction from community property of the spouses for the debts thereof may proceed against the separate property of each of the spouses for one half of the claim.

Community property is dissolved by the declaration of disappearance or the presumed death of one of the spouses; by annulment, dissolution, or termination of the civil effect of the marriage; by separation of the spouses; by judicial separation of their property; by a contractual modification of their proprietary relations; and by bankruptcy by one of the spouses.

Each spouse must reimburse the community for money taken out for purposes other than for those for which it answers.

Judicial separation of property may be decreed where a spouse is placed under guardianship, where he is unable to adminster community property, or because of his poor administration. The order of judicial separation of property relates back to the time of filing of the petition and has the effect of setting up the regime of separation of property as between the spouses.

The actual division of community property is effected by dividing the assets and debts equally between the spouses. For the benefit of children, the court may impose a usufruct on a part of the property given to one of the spouses in favor of the other spouse.

(iii) COMMUNITY PROPERTY BY CONTRACT (*Comunione convenzionale*). The spouses may modify by contract the terms of community property imposed by law. However, they may not include in community property separate property of purely personal use of the spouses; property used in the exercise of the profession of a spouse, even if it is used in an undertaking forming part of community property; or property obtained as damages or as compensation for loss of working capacity. Nor can they change the rules of administration of community property and the equality of their shares therein. Where the spouses provide that the property owned by them before marriage should enter into community property, the community property then answers for those debts incurred prior to their marriage.

(iv) SEPARATION OF PROPERTY (*Separazione dei beni*). The spouses may provide in a marriage contract or in the act of celebration of the marriage that each shall keep the exclusive title to his property acquired during marriage. Where, in such a case, one spouse uses the property of the other, he has all the obligations of a usufructuary. In case of a dispute, each spouse may prove title to his property by all means at his disposal. Property to which neither spouse is able to show title is owned by them equally as tenants in common.

(v) FAMILY ENTERPRISE (*Impresa familiare*). Unless otherwise provided, a family member who continuously works in a family business has a right to maintenance in accordance with the standing of the family and participates, in proportion to his contribution, in the gains, in the property acquired with them and in the increased value of the business. In a family business, all decisions whether ordinary or extraordinary, with respect to management, the employment of funds, and the abandonment of the business are made by majority vote of those family members participating in the business. Minor family members are represented by those who have parental power over them. The work of a woman is fully equal to that of a man.

Family members are understood as the spouses, lineal relatives up to and including the third degree, and collaterals including the second degree. The right to participate in the family business is transferable from one family member to another with the consent of all participating family members. The interest of the leaving member may be paid out to him in money and in several annual installments. In case of dispute, the court will determine the matter. The same applies in case of a sale of the business. Where the family business is of an agricultural nature, it may be further regulated by local custom. Such customs may not, however, conflict with provisions of the Civil Code.

NOTES AND QUESTIONS

1. As to patrimonial property, it must be set up by a public act. It is meant to perform the function that in older times was performed by the setting up of a dowry. It is a property fund for the support of the family. Compare it with the dowry in Spanish law. Could a similar fund be set up in Anglo-American law for the support of a family? How would it best be effected?

2. As to community property, community property is an institution of the Romance nations. It was introduced to the United States especially through the French and the Spanish law. The present system of Italian community property is closely linked to all these systems and differences between them are slight. Compare, e.g., the California law, Calif. C.C.A. §5102ff. Note that in Italian law, the spouses are automatically under the system of community property if they fail to make another provision upon entering into marriage. Compare the French law. *See*, e.g., Calif. C.C.A. §5134ff.; Texas Family Code §5.41ff.

Note that Italian spouses may regulate their property relationship by a marriage contract upon entering into marriage; but as long as they provide for some form of community property, they may not contravene certain stipulated provisions of the community property provided by law. Compare the French and the Spanish law.

Italian spouses may by contract modify their property relationship during marriage. May such modifications be made under the French and the Spanish law? How does the matter stand in American community property? *See*, e.g., Texas Family Code §5.42.

3. As to separation of property, this system is entered into by a marriage contract or by a later contract modifying the existing system. Compare it with the French system of separation of property. How does it compare with the property relations of spouses in British countries and American common law states?

4. As to family enterprise, this is a new feature of Italian law, which regulates relationships frequently encountered in Italian life. The problems of a family enterprise are now legally regulated on the principle of equality of the sexes.

3.   Wills and Estates[18]

(a) Portion of the estate reserved to unavoidable heirs (*Quota di eredità*).   The law reserves a portion of the succession to legitimate children, legitimate ascendants, recognized illegitimate children, and the surviving spouse. Legitimated and adopted children are treated as legitimate children. A legitimate or recognized illegitimate child is entitled to one half of the estate. If there are two or more such children, they are entitled to two thirds of the estate. If there are no legitimate nor recognized illegitimate children but there are legitimate ascendants, they take one third of the estate. The surviving spouse takes one half of the estate. If one legitimate or recognized illegitimate child and the spouse survive the testator, the child takes one third and the spouse another third of the estate. If there are more children, they take one half of the estate in equal shares and the spouse one fourth.[19]

(b) Testaments. Persons below the age of eighteen years, those under guardianship because of mental weakness, and those actually suffering from mental weakness at the moment of making the testament are incapable of making the same. Testaments are either holographic or made before a notary. A holographic will (*testamento olografo*) must be written in its entirety, dated and subscribed by the hand of the testator. The signature must appear at the end of the will.

Testaments made before a notary (*testamento per atto di notaio*) are either public (*testamento pubblico*) or secret (*testamento segreto*). Public testament is taken by the notary in the presence of two witnesses. The notary reduces it to writing and reads it to the testator in the presence of two witnesses. It is then subscribed by the testator, the witnesses and the notary. It must indicate the place, the day and the time of its execution. A secret testament is written either by the testator or by another person. it must be subscribed by the testator at its end. If it is written by another person, or typewritten, the testator places the will in an envelope, which he seals. He then hands the envelope to a notary in the presence of two witnesses and declares that it contains his testament. He may hand the envelope to the notary unsealed; the notary then seals it in the presence of the testator and two witnesses. The notary then draws up a memorandum of the receipt of the envelope containing the will. The memorandum is then signed by the testator, the witnesses and the notary. The will is then kept by the notary or a public depository. A secret testament that lacks some of its prescribed formalities may take effect as a holographic will.

All testaments may be deposited with a notary or a public depository for safekeeping. They may be withdrawn at any time by the testator.

The testator may revoke the testament at any time. Revocation may be effected by a declaration in a later testament or by a declaration of revocation executed before a notary in the presence of two witnesses. The revocation may itself be revoked and the revoked provisions of the testament will be thus revived. A later will that does not expressly revoke a previously made will annuls the provisions in the previously made will only to the extent of inconsistency. A destroyed, mutilated or cancelled holographic will is considered revoked unless it is shown that it was so dealt with by another person or that the testator had no intention of revoking it. The withdrawal of a secret testament from the safekeeping of the notary or a public depository does not effect its revocation if the will can take effect as a holographic will. A will is also revoked by operation of law when the testator who did not have children at the time of making the will has a child born to him thereafter. The same applies when the testator adopts a child or recognizes an illegitimate child.

NOTES AND QUESTIONS

1. Intestate succession is regulated in the Italian law (in Arts. 566-586 of the Civil Code) in a similar way to the French and the German law and its provisions are not reproduced here. *See* the French and German provisions.

2. As to forced shares, this is an institution of Roman law carried over to the Italian law. A beneficiary who is by law entitled to a forced share may be deprived of it only by disinheritance as not being worthy of his share. Articles 463-466 of the Italian Civil Code give the reasons for unworthiness, such as an attempt on the life of the decedent, inducement by fraud or undue influence to make, modify or revoke a will, or the suppression or alteration of a will. Compare the rules of Italian law with those of the French law.

In view of the fact that Anglo-American law prefers to leave the testator his freedom of testamentary disposition, are there any forced shares in the law of some common law states? Compare, e.g., New York Estates, Powers and Trusts Law 4-1.4 and 5-1.1; Crum v. Bliss, 47 Conn. 592 (1880). Do American community property states provide for forced shares in their laws?

3. As to the testament, note the minimum age required by the testator for making a will. How does the Italian age requirement compare with those in France, Germany and Spain? What is the minimum age required by Anglo-American law? *See*, e.g., Calif. Prob. C.A. §20.

The various types of wills are standard in civil law countries. What are the requirements of the Italian secret will? How does it compare with a French will made in the mystic form or a Spanish closed will? Is this type of will available in the German law? Do similar types of wills exist in Anglo-American countries? Compare, e.g., Calif. Prob. C.A. §50.

Italian law also has special wills, which are made in times of public calamity, aboard a ship, and the like. They are dealt with in Arts. 609-619 of the Italian Civil Code. The form is similar to that of German emergency wills.

Note that apart from holographic and special wills, a will must be executed before a notary in the presence of two witnesses. Compare this rule with similar rules in the German and the Spanish law. What is the Anglo-American rule? *See*, e.g., Calif. Prob. C.A. §50ff.

Must every will be deposited for safekeeping with a notary or a public depository? What about the secret will? Does the withdrawal from safekeeping effect revocation of the will? Compare the German and the French law.

Compare the Italian rule as to revocation of wills with that of France. Is a will automatically revoked when a child is born to the testator after making the will? Compare the French, German and Spanish rules. What is the Anglo-American rule on the matter? *See*, e.g., Calif. Prob. C.A. §71; New York Estates, Powers and Trusts Law §5-3.2. Does the same rule apply to a subsequent marriage? *See*, e.g., Calif. Prob. C.A. §70; New York Estates, Powers and Trusts Law §5-1.3.

4. Property (*Proprietà*)[20]

(a) General provisions. Property is that which may become the object of rights. Property is immovable and movable. Natural energy that has economic value is considered a movable. Fruits of property are either natural or civil. Natural fruits arise directly from the property with or without the intervention of man, like agricultural produce, timber, newborn animals. Until they are separated they form part of the property. Civil fruits are interests, rents and the like.

Beaches, harbors and ports, rivers, lakes, and all other waters declared public form part of the public domain. Roads, highways, and railroads also form part of the public domain in cases where they belong to the state, as do aqueducts and collections in museums, archives and libraries. All property that forms part of the public domain is inalienable.

(b) Rights of ownership. The owner has the right to enjoy and dispose of his property fully and exclusively within the limits stipulated by law. The owner may not undertake acts that have no other purpose than to cause damage or annoy others. The owner may be deprived of his property by expropriation in the public interest. Public interest in the matter must first be declared as provided by law and just compensation must be paid for the property expropriated. The owner also may be deprived of his property by requisition. Both movables and immovables may be requisitioned by military and civil authorities in the case of a grave and urgent need. Requisitions may be made only in accordance with the law, and a just compensation for the property taken must be paid.

Ownership of the surface extends to subsoil and to everything located there. The owner may excavate as long as he does not cause damage to his neighbor. These provisions do not apply to mining. The owner of the surface may not oppose the activities of third parties conducted so deep below the surface of his land or so high above it that he has no reason to prevent them. The owner may enclose his land. He must, however, whenever necessary, allow entry to his land by his neighbor so that the neighbor may build or repair a fence or a wall which is owned jointly or only by the neighbor. He must also allow the entry of a person whose thing or animal found its way accidentally on his land for the purpose of retrieving it. He may, however, retrieve the thing or animal himself and hand it over to its owner.

The owner of land cannot prevent the entry of smoke, heat, fumes, noise, or the like from the neighbor's land as long as they do not exceed the lawful level having regard for local conditions.

(c) Acquisition of ownership. Property is acquired by occupation, finding, accession, commixture or confusion, specification, adverse possession, contract, succession, and acquisition by a bona fide purchaser for value and without notice.

Ownerless movables may be acquired by occupation. They are abandoned chattels and animals that are hunted or fish that are caught.

Found movables must be returned to the owner by the finder, if he is known, and if not, they must be surrendered to the proper officer of the place where found. The officer shall advertise the finding; if the true owner does not claim the chattel within one year from the last day of publication, the chattel, or its value if it must be sold, will be given to the finder. The owner must pay the finder a reward of 10 percent of the value of the thing found, and if the value exceeds 10,000 lire, 5 percent. If the thing found has no commercial value, the reward is determined equitably by a judge. Any movable of value to which no one can show title and which is found hidden or placed underground is a treasure. It belongs to the owner of the land where it lies. If it is found on land owned by another person, it is divided equally between the finder and the owner of the land. The same applies when it is found in a movable.

Where the owner of land builds a structure with materials belonging to another or plants a plant belonging to another, he must pay their value to the other person if such person does not request them in specie or if they cannot be returned without damaging the structure or the plant. He must also pay damages, if any. The other person may not reclaim his materials or plants after six months from the day on which he acquired notice of the annexation. Where a person builds a structure or plants a plant owned by him on someone else's land, the owner of the land can either retain such accession for value or have it removed.

When property belonging to different persons has been mixed so as to form one whole but it is still separable, each owner may retake his own property. If separation is impossible or inconvenient, each one owns a share corresponding to his interest. Where one of the things may be regarded as principal and the other added to it as accessory, the owner of the principal thing acquires title of the whole but must pay the value of the accessory.

Where a person uses material belonging to another person to make a product, the product belongs to him by specification, but he must pay the value of the material to its owner. If the value of the material greatly surpasses the value of the labor, the product belongs to the owner of the material, who then must pay for the value of the labor used in making the product.

Title to immovables and the right to use them is acquired by twenty year continuous possession. The acquisition in good faith of an immovable, even if from a person who was not the owner thereof, by virtue of title adequate to transfer the property and properly recorded matures in good title after ten years of continuous possession from such recording.

An acquisition of movables in good faith followed by a continuous possession of ten years gives title. If the acquisition was in bad faith, twenty year possession is required to give title.

Title to property is acquired by contract in accordance with provisions of the law of contract.[21] Title to property may also be acquired by succession in accordance with provisions of the law of succession.[22]

The purchaser of movables for value and without notice at the time of the purchase that the person from whom the movables were purchased was not the owner thereof acquires good title to them.[23]

NOTES AND QUESTIONS

1. Like all civil laws, the Italian law distinguishes between movable and immovable property rather then between personalty and realty as is done in the common law. *See*, e.g., In re Berchtold [1923] 1 Ch. 192; Calif. C.C.A. §657.

Note the Italian provisions as to the public domain of the state. All such property belongs to the nation and is administered by the administrative authorities of the state. Individual members of the general public may use it by provision of the administrative law. Note that beaches along the shore of the sea are public property. What is the Anglo-American rule? *See,* e.g., Texas Vernon's Ann. Civ. St. Art. 5415d; Calif. C.C.A. §670.

2. The owner may fully use and enjoy his property, both movable and immovable. This is a universal rule. *See,* e.g., Calif. C.C.A. §679. *See* the rights of ownership as defined in the French law.

Any limitation on the use of property is stipulated by law. The owner may be deprived of his property by eminent domain for proper compensation. Eminent domain is handled in the law of the civil law countries traditionally in administrative law. *See,* e.g., the French law in the section on administrative law. Compare also the American Uniform Eminent Domain Code.

The owner must, however, put up with the usual amount of smoke, noise and other interference before he can have recourse to remedies against nuisance. *See* the Italian Civil Code, Arts. 844, 2043. As to Anglo-American law, *see,* e.g., Calif. C.C.A. §3479ff.

3. Title to property, both movable and immovable, is acquired by the standard methods known to the civil law. Compare, e.g., the French and the German law.

Note the Italian rule as to finding. How does it compare with the German provisions? Note that the civil law provides a finder's fee to reward the finder for his efforts. Is a finder's fee a feature of Anglo-American law? *See,* e.g., Calif. C.C.A. §2080; Automobile Ins. Co. of Hartford, Conn. v. Kirby 25 Ala. App. 245, 145 So. 123 (1932). As to finding generally in American law, *see,* e.g., Calif. C.C.A. §2080ff.

Title to land passes usually by succession or by a contract of sale and its recording in the land register (*registro immobiliare*). The matter is dealt with in the Italian Civil Code, Arts. 2643-2682. The procedure is similar to that in other civil law countries, like Germany or France. For American recording of land, *see,* e.g., Texas Vernon's Ann. Civ. St. Arts. 6626ff; Calif. C.C.A. §1169ff.

Note the Italian rule that a purchaser of movables for value and without notice acquires good title. This applies also to negotiable instruments, as provided in Art. 1994 of the Italian Civil Code. What is the rule in Anglo-American law? *See,* e.g., UCC 1-201 (19), (32), (33), (44); UCC 2-403; UCC 8-301, 302.

---

5. Obligations (*Obbligazioni*)[24]

(a) Provisions common to obligations.   Obligations arise from contracts,[25] from unlawful acts,[26] from unilateral promises,[27] from family relationships,[28] and from spontaneous agency.[29] In the performance of an obligation, the debtor must use the care of a responsible person.

The creditor who accepts payment from a third party may subrogate the third party into his rights as against the debtor. The debtor who accepts money from a third party in order to discharge the debt may subrogate the third party into the creditor's rights.

The creditor who does not accept performance offered to him without a lawful reason is in default. He is not entitled to interest or fruits, and he is responsible for any loss caused by his default and for the cost of maintenance and custody of the thing due.

The debtor who does not perform exactly in accordance with his obligations is liable in damages unless he shows that his nonperformance or delayed performance was due to an impossibility to perform for which he was not responsible.

Obligations are extinguished by novation, remission, set-off, and merger. An obligation is extinguished by novation when the parties substitute a new obligation for the old one. The intent to extinguish the old obligation must be clearly apparent. A declaration by the creditor that he remits the debtor's debt extinguishes the obligation when it is communicated to the debtor, unless he refuses to accept the remission. Where two persons are obligated to each other, both debts are extinguished by set-off in the corresponding amounts as of the date of their coexistence. Where the qualities of creditor and debtor are united in the same person, the obligation is extinguished by merger and any third parties who guaranteed the debtor's performance are discharged.

(b) Contracts in general. A contract (*contratto*) is an agreement made by two or more parties to create, regulate or extinguish among themselves a legal proprietary relationship. Parties may freely contract within the limits imposed by law.

The essentials of a contract are: (1) agreement of the parties; (2) lawful purpose (*causa*); (3) lawful object; and (4) proper form.

A contract is made at the moment when the party making the offer is notified of the acceptance by the other party. The acceptance must reach the offeror within the time set by him, or within the time necessary in accordance with the nature of the business or in accordance with custom. The offeror may accept a late acceptance of the offeree. Where the offeror requires acceptance in a particular form, an acceptance in another form is of no effect. An acceptance not made in accordance with the offer is a new offer.

An offer may be revoked before the contract is concluded. An acceptance may be revoked if the revocation reaches the offeror before the acceptance. Where the offeror has intimated that the offer will stand open for a certain time, he cannot revoke it. An offer or an acceptance made by an entrepreneur in the course of his business is not affected by his death or incapacity before the conclusion of the contract except in the case of small traders.

Where contracts are entered into by subscribing to printed forms, any clause actually inserted into the form by the parties shall prevail over the printed clauses to the extent of incompatibility even though the printed clauses may not be cancelled.

The purpose (*causa*) of the contract is unlawful when it is contrary to a positive rule of law, to the public order, or to good morals.

The object of the contract must be possible, lawful, certain or ascertainable.

As to form, the following acts must be executed in writing either by a public act or under private signature, otherwise they are void: (1) contracts for the transfer of title to immovables; (2) contracts that create, modify or transfer the right of usufruct in immovables, the right in the surface of land, or the right to emphyteusis (long-term lease); (3) contracts that create co-ownership in matters mentioned under (1) and (2) above; (4) contracts that create or modify easements, the use of immovables, or the right to use premises; (5) acts renouncing any rights arising out of matters mentioned under (1) to (4) above; (6) contracts dealing with land subject to emphyteusis; (7) contracts of antichresis; (8) lease of land for a term longer than nine years; (9) contracts of partnership or association that confer the right to use land for a term longer than nine years or for an indeterminate term; (10) acts creating annuities in perpetuity or for life; (11) acts of partition of immovables and other rights in immovables; (12) settlements of controversies arising out of any matter mentioned above; and (13) any other acts required by law to be made in writing, e.g., matrimonial contracts, wills, gifts, insurance contracts, mortgages, and powers of attorney.[30]

In interpreting contracts, inquiry as to the common intent of the parties must be made without limiting oneself to the literal meaning of words. In determining the common intent of the parties, their overall demeanor before and after the making of the contract must be considered.

A contract has the force of law between the parties. It may be dissolved only by mutual consent of the parties or for a cause recognized by law. It does not affect third parties except where provided by law.

(c) Void and voidable contracts. A contract is void if it is contrary to a positive rule of law, if it lacks the agreement of the parties, if its purpose (*causa*) is unlawful, if its object is unlawful, or if it is not executed in writing as required for certain contracts in Article 1350 of the Italian Civil Code.[31]

A contract is voidable and may be annulled because of incapacity, mistake, undue influence, and fraud. It may be annulled when one of the parties was legally incapable of contracting. Mistake serves as a cause of annulment when it goes to the essence of the contract and may have been detected by the other party. A mistake is of the essence when it goes to the object of the contract, to the identity or quality of the object, or to the identity or quality of the person of the other party; a mistake of law occurs where such mistake was the only reason for the party to enter into the contract. A mathematical error gives only the right to rectification. A mistake is detectible where, considering the contents and circumstances of the contract as well as the quality of the contracting parties, a person of average diligence should have detected it. Annulment for mistake may not be demanded where, before the party in error has suffered any loss, the other party offers to execute the contract as if the mistake had not arisen.

Undue influence is a ground for annulment even if it is exerted by a third party. Fraud is a ground for annulment where the deception employed by one of the contracting parties is of such a nature that without it the other party would not have contracted. If it is exerted by a third party, the contract may be annulled where the party who derived benefit therefrom knew of the fraud.

Annulment of a contract may be demanded only by the party for whose benefit it is provided for by law. The action is subject to a five-year period of limitation. The time begins to run on the day when the undue influence ceases, when the mistake or fraud is discovered, when the incapacitated party regains his full capacity, or when a minor attains majority. In other cases, time begins to run on the day the contract is made.

(d) Rescission of contracts. Where there is disproportion in the consideration because one party took advantage of the need of the other to his own advantage, the party who incurs the loss may demand rescission of the contract. The action is not admissible unless the loss exceeds one half of the value given or promised by the party suffering the loss at the time when the contract was made. Aleatory contracts may not be rescinded on this ground. The action for rescission is subject to a one-year period of limitation running from the making of the contract.

(e) Dissolution of contracts. Where one of the parties to the contract does not perform his part, the other may demand either performance or dissolution of the contract. Damages may be demanded in either case. Dissolution of the contract for nonperformance has retroactive effect between the parties, except in contracts calling for periodic or term performance where the dissolution does not affect performance already effected. In contracts calling for mutual performance, a party may refuse to perform unless the other party performs or offers to perform at the same time, or unless a different time for performance is agreed upon or appears from the nature of the contract.

Contracts may also be dissolved because of impossibility of performance. In the case of total impossibility, the party who cannot perform because of impossibility of performance may not demand performance of the other party, and he must refund to that party all that he already received under the contract. In the case of partial impossibility, the other party is entitled to reduce his performance proportionately, but he may renounce the contract in its entirety if he is not interested in partial performance.

In contracts calling for periodic or term performance, a party may demand dissolution of the contract if his part of the contract becomes excessively onerous due to extraordinary and unforeseeable events. The party against whom the dissolution is demanded may avoid it by offering to modify the contract.

(f) Payment made by mistake (Money had and received) and unjust enrichment.
Where a person makes a payment which he is not obligated to make, he has the right to recover what he so paid. He also is entitled to fruits and interest from the date of payment where the recipient acted in bad faith, and from the day of the demand for the refund where the recipient acted in good faith. Payments made contrary to good morals may not be recovered.

Where a person enriches himself without a just cause to the detriment of another person, he must indemnify that person for his loss. If the enrichment consists of the acquisition of property, the recipient must return it *in natura* if it is still in existence at the time of the demand. The action for unjust enrichment may be brought only where the party suffering the loss has no other available action to recover.

(g) Obligations arising from unlawful acts (Compensation for damage caused intentionally or negligently). Whosoever causes damage to another, whether intentionally or negligently, is bound to make it good. There is no liability for damage caused in the defense of oneself or of another person. Where the person who caused the damage acted out of necessity to save himself or another from an acute danger to his person, and the danger was not brought about by him voluntarily nor was it otherwise avoidable, the person who suffered the damage is entitled to an indemnity determined by the judge *ex aequo and bono*.

Persons actually incapacitated are not responsible unless they themselves brought about the incapacity. Where damage is caused by an incapacitated person, compensation is due from his guardian or the person exercising supervision over him, unless he can show that he was unable to prevent the act.

Fathers, mothers and guardians are liable for the damage unlawfully caused by minors under their care and guardianship. Teachers, instructors and masters are liable for damage unlawfully caused by their students or apprentices while they are under their care. The above persons are relieved of liability if they can show that they were unable to prevent the act. Employers and masters are liable for damage unlawfully caused by their employees and servants in the course of their employment.

Whosoever causes damage to another in the exercise of an activity dangerous by its nature or because of the means adopted must make it good, unless he can prove that he undertook all proper measures to prevent damage. A person must make good the damage caused by property in his custody, unless he can prove that the damage was caused by unavoidable accident. The owner of an animal must make good the damage caused by it whether the animal was in his custody or had escaped, unless he can prove that the damage was caused by unavoidable accident.

The owner of a building or structure must make good the damage caused by its ruinous condition or collapse, unless he can prove that it was not caused by the lack of its maintenance or by faulty construction.

The driver of a vehicle not riding on rails is liable to make good damage caused to persons and property by its operation, unless he can prove that he did everything possible to avoid the damage. In the case of a collision between vehicles it is presumed, unless shown otherwise, that each driver contributed equally to the damage of every vehicle. The owner or usufructuary of the vehicle is jointly and severally liable with the driver thereof, unless he can prove that the vehicle was operated without his permission. In any case, the driver and the owner or the usufructuary are liable for the damage caused by the faulty construction of the vehicle or by the lack of its maintenance.

NOTES AND QUESTIONS

1. The Italian law first lists matters that are common to all obligations, namely, the creation, performance and discharge of obligations. Compare this approach with the German, Spanish and French approaches. Since the fundamentals of obligations in the law of the various civil law countries are founded on Roman law, the law in these countries is uniform and differs only in some details. In Anglo-American law, the law of contracts was developed entirely by the common law. For a modern approach to contracts, *see*, e.g., the California law of obligations, Calif. C.C.A. §§1427-3268.

2. As to the formation and form of contracts, the Italian law gives a definition of contract. How does it compare with that of the Spanish law? For Anglo-American law, *see*, e.g., Corbin on Contracts, One Volume Ed., §3, 1952; Restatement, Contracts §1; Calif. C.C.A. §1549, UCC 2-106.

What are the essentials of contract in Italian law? Compare the French law. How do the Italian requirements compare with Anglo-American law? *See*, e.g., Calif. C.C.A. §1550.

Compare the formation of contracts in Italian law with the requirements of the German law. Are there any significant differences? Compare also Calif. C.C.A. §1565ff.; UCC 2-206.

Note the Italian rule as to printed forms to the effect that a written clause will override a printed provision if incompatible, even if the printed provision is not deleted. How does this rule compare with the American rule? *See* Restatement, Contracts §236(e).

The Italian counterpart of the Statue of Frauds requires that enumerated acts be made in writing. Note that when the law requires notarization, it directly so provides in a particular article of the law. Thus, e.g., Italian Civil Code, Art. 14, provides that corporations must be set up by a notarized act. Compare the German law.

What is the Italian rule as to interpretation of contracts? Compare the French law. How does the Italian rule compare with American law? *See* Restatement, Contracts §226ff; Calif. C.C.A §1635ff.

3. As to void and voidable contracts, the reasons for making a contract void or voidable are uniform throughout the law of the civil law countries. Compare, e.g., the Spanish law. Are the grounds used in civil law comparable with those in Anglo-American law? *See,* e.g., Calif. C.C.A. §1565ff; Restatement, Contracts §§475ff, 492ff.

4. As to rescission, the Italian Civil Code, Art. 1448, gives a right to rescind for *lesione,* i.e., when one party takes advantage of the other and the loss exceeds one half of the value. In Art. 1447, it provides for rescission when the parties do not negotiate at arm's length and where one takes advantage of the other irrespective of the value of the loss. The German Civil Code contains a similar provision in Art. 138, but it has no corresponding rule to Art. 1448 of the Italian Civil Code and does not set the loss at any fixed rate before the article may be invoked. The French Civil Code, Art. 1674, allows rescission for *lésion* only in the case of the sale of immovables when the loss exceeds seven twelfths of the price. The Spanish Civil Code, Art. 1291(1), restricts *lesión* to contracts made by guardians and the loss must exceed one fourth of the value. Does a similar cause of action exist in Anglo-American law? *See,* e.g., Brooks v. Towson Realty, Inc., 223 Md. 61, 162 A. 2d 431 (C. App. 1960); Marks v. Gates, 154 Fed. 481 (9th Cir. 1907); Brandolino v. Lindsay, 269 Cal. App. 2d 319, 75 Cal. Rptr. 56 (C.A. 1969). How does the Anglo-American approach differ from the civil law approach?

5. As to dissolution of contract, the innocent party may demand damages for nonperformance or he may demand performance plus damages. The demand for performance means specific performance as understood in Anglo-American law. It is based on Arts. 2930-2933 of the Italian Civil Code and is carried out in accordance with Arts. 605-614 of the Italian Code of Civil Procedure. It also includes the Anglo-American injunctions and their execution. The order is issued by the court and is executed by court officers, if necessary with the assistance of the police. Compare the German provisions as to specific performance and injunctions.

As to performance of contracts, compare the German law. How is performance handled in the French law?

As to impossibility, *see also* Restatement, Contracts §454ff; Calif. C.C.A. §1595ff.

6. As to unjust enrichment, the Italian law of unjust enrichment covers the Anglo-American concept of money had and received as introduced by Lord Mansfield in Moses v. Macferlan (1760) 2 Burr. 1005, within the scope of the Roman concept of unjust enrichment. The topic is dealt with the German Civil Code, §812-822; in the French Civil Code, Arts. 1371-1381 (under the heading of quasi-contracts); and in the Spanish Civil Code, Arts. 1887-1901 (also under quasi-contracts). Is unjust enrichment part of Anglo-American law? *See*, e.g., Estok v. Heguy, 44 W.W.R. 167 (Brit. Columbia 1963).

7. As to obligations arising out of unlawful acts, this deals actually with the law of torts as understood in Anglo-American law. Compare the French law.

The German Civil Code deals with the matter in §§823-853; the Spanish Civil Code in Arts. 1902-1910.

Note the Italian rule of proportional negligence in motor vehicle accidents. This rule generally applies in civil law countries; *see*, e.g., German Civil Code §254, and *Strassenverkehrsgesetz* §7ff. It also applies in Britain and the Commonwealth. Does it also apply in the law of your state? *See*, e.g., New York Civil Practice Law and Rules §1411.

---

6.   Partnerships and Corporations[32]

(a)   Informal partnerships (*Società semplice*).   In an informal relationship, the contract of partnership is not subject to any special form. It may be modified only with the consent of all partners unless otherwise provided.

Unless otherwise provided, each partner is entitled to the management of the partnership. Where the management is run by some partners only, each such managing partner may oppose any planned undertakings proposed by any other managing partner before they are put into effect. The dispute is decided by agreement of partners holding majority interest in the partnership. Where the management is carried out by some partners jointly, the consent of all such managing partners is necessary to make a decision. Individual partners may not act except in cases of urgency to prevent impending loss to the partnership. Managing partners are jointly and severally liable to the partnership for their management.

Partners not participating in the management must be informed on the management. They have the right to inspect books and documents and must be given an account of the management at least once each year. Each partner is entitled to his share of the profits. The share of profit and loss of each partner is commensurate with his interest in the partnership. If the contribution of partners is not determined in the partnership contract, their shares are presumed equal. Any agreement that would exclude one or more partners from sharing in the profits or losses is void.

Partnership property is primarily liable for partnership debts. In addition, all partners are jointly and severally liable, unless those partners who did not take part in the management are expressly exempted. The exemption must be brought to the attention of third parties dealing with the partnership, otherwise it will not be valid against them. A partner who is requested to pay may require the creditor to levy first on partnership property. The creditor of a particular partner may obtain satisfaction from his share of the profits in the partnership. If this is not enough to satisfy his claim, the creditor may levy on the partner's actual share in the partnership.

The partnership is dissolved by expiration of the time for which it was set up; by attaining its purpose, or because of the impossibility of attaining it; by decision of all the partners; when only one partner remains and no other partner enters into the partnership within six months; or on any other grounds provided for in the partnership agreement.

Unless provided otherwise in the partnership contract, liquidation of the partnership is undertaken by one or more liquidators appointed by all the partners or, where they fail to agree, by the court. Such liquidators may be removed by all the partners, or by the court at the request of one or more partners, for good reason. The liquidators must pay all the debts of the partnership and distribute the remainder among the partners. Where the partnership property is not sufficient to pay the debts, the individual partners must contribute to their payment in proportion to their shares in the losses. After the debts of the partnership are paid, each partner is refunded his contributions to the partnership. Any further surplus is apportioned among the partners in proportion to their shares in the profits.

When a partner dies, the remaining partners may pay to the heir or heirs of the deceased his share in the partnership, they may dissolve the partnership, or they may continue it with the heir or heirs of the decedent. They may so continue the partnership only with the consent of such heir or heirs.

Each partner may withdraw from the partnership when it is set up for an indeterminate time or for life. A three-month notice must be given. A partner may further withdraw on grounds provided in the partnership contract, or for a good reason.

A partner may also be excluded from the partnership by the decision of the majority of partners, not counting the one being excluded. The exclusion takes effect thirty days after notice thereof is given to the excluded partner. In the meantime, he may petition the court to set aside his exclusion. If there are only two partners, one may be excluded by the court at the request of the other. A partner may be exluded if he fails to honor his obligations to the partnership, if he is incapacitated, or if he is convicted of an offense which carries with it the loss of right to hold public office. A partner who has to bring into the partnership certain property may be excluded if the property perishes before being brought in. A partner who brings in his labor and skill may be excluded if he refuses to exert it. A partner is excluded by provision of law if he is declared a bankrupt or his creditor levies against his whole share in the partnership.

(b) General partnership (*Società in nome collettivo*). In a general partnership, all partners are jointly and severally liable for the obligations of the partnership. Any agreement to the contrary is void. The partnership name may be constituted by the name of one or more partners together with the indication of the partnership relationship. The name of a deceased or a retired partner may be kept in the partnership name with the consent of the heirs of the deceased partner or with that of the partner who has retired. The provisions applicable to informal partnership apply also to the general partnership unless otherwise provided.

The document of partnership must indicate the name, place and date of birth, domicile, and citizenship of each partner; the business name; the names of managing partners; the seat of the partnership and of its branches; the contribution of each partner, their value and method of valuation; the duties of partners bringing their labor and skill into the partnership; the rules in accordance to which profits and losses will be apportioned, and the share of each partner in profits and losses; and the duration of the partnership. The act of partnership with all the signatures of partners properly authenticated, or an authenticated copy thereof, must be filed within thirty days of its execution with the office of the register of enterprises. Failing registration, the rules of informal partnership govern and partners are liable jointly and severally with all their property for the debts of the partnership.

The managing partner or partners may undertake all acts of business of the partnership. Any limitation on their authority must be recorded. The managing partners must keep books required by law.

(c) Commandite partnership (*Società in accomandita semplice*). In a commandite partnership, the general partners are jointly and severally liable with all their property, whereas the special partners are liable only up to the value of their shares in the partnership. The shares of the partners may not be given in stock. The partnership name must comprise at least the name of one of the general partners and must state that it is a commandite partnership. The rules governing general partnerships apply also to commandite partnerships unless displaced by specific provisions.

The act of partnership must indicate who the general partners are and who the special partners. If the act of partnership is not registered in the register of enterprises as against third parties, all partners respond with all their property jointly and severally, and their obligations are governed by provisions applicable to informal partnership (*società semplice*). As within the partnership, however, the special partners are liable only with their contributions brought into the partnership, unless they take part in the management. Only general partners may engage in the management of the partnership business.

Unless otherwise provided in the act of partnership, the consent of the general partners and of as many special partners as necessary to represent the majority of the capital subscribed by the special partners is required for the appointment and removal of the managing partners.

The commandite partnership comes to an end also when there are only general or special partners left in the partnership, unless substitute partners are added within six months.

(d) Stock corporation (*Società per azioni*). In a stock corporation, only the property of the corporation is liable for corporation debts. The shares of members are denoted by their holding corporation stock. The corporate name must indicate that the corporation is a stock corporation. The capital of the corporation may not be less than one million lire.

The corporation must be set up by a public act that must indicate the name, domicile, citizenship, and number of shares held by each stockholder; the name of the corporation and its seat; the object of the corporation; the amount of capital subscribed and paid; the nominal value of shares; the number of shares and whether they are registered or to bearer; the amount of money advanced, and the value of the property brought into the corporation in kind; the rules for the distribution of profits; the number of directors and their powers with the indication of which directors have the power to act for the corporation; the number of members of the board of auditors; and the duration of the corporation. The corporation is not constituted unless all of its capital is subscribed and at least three tenths thereof is paid and deposited in a bank, and unless the necessary government permits, if any, are obtained.

The notary who certifies the act of incorporation must file it, together with evidence that the capital has been subscribed and 30 percent thereof paid, with the register of enterprises within thirty days. The evidence is submitted to the court which, finding the documents in order, orders the inscription of the corporation in the register of corporations. By inscription in the register, the corporation acquires legal personality. Even in case of an annulment of the act of incorporation after the registration of the corporation, acts undertaken on behalf of the corporation are valid.

The shares of the shareholders must be paid in money unless otherwise provided in the act of incorporation. Where the stockholder does not pay his subscribed share, the corporation may sell it at his risk. If it cannot find a buyer, it must reduce the corporate capital in a corresponding sum. Shares may not be issued below their nominal value, and they may not be further subdivided. They must be of equal value and must entitle their holders to equal rights. Preferred stock may be issued, however, by the authority of the act of incorporation. Every share, whether preferred or ordinary, gives the right to one vote.

Organs of the corporation are the meeting of shareholders, the directors, and the board of auditors.

An ordinary meeting must be called by the directors at least once per year. The notice must indicate the place, day and time of the meeting as well as the business to be transacted. It must also be published in the Official Gazette at least fifteen days before the day of the meeting. An ordinary meeting approves the balance sheet of the corporation and appoints directors, auditors and the chairman of the board of auditors. It determines the salary of the directors and auditors and passes upon matters reserved to it in the act of incorporation.

An extraordinary meeting is called by the directors and the notice thereof must indicate the place, day and time of the meeting as well as the business to be transacted. It must also be published in the Official Gazette at least fifteen days before the day of the meeting. An extraordinary meeting must be called to pass upon amendments to the act of incorporation and upon the issue of debentures. It also passes upon the appointment and powers of the liquidators.

An ordinary meeting is properly constituted if shareholders holding at least one half of the corporation's capital are present. It decides by majority vote (one share, one vote), unless a larger majority is required by the act of incorporation. A simple majority of capital is required as a quorum for an extraordinary meeting. If there is no quorum, a new meeting of shareholders must be called within thirty days. Notice thereof must appear in the Official Gazette at least eight days before the meeting. The first notice, however, may provide for a second meeting in case the first meeting lacks a quorum.

The second ordinary meeting may be held irrespective of the size of the capital represented. The second extraordinary meeting requires one third of the corporation's capital to be represented, unless the act of incorporation requires a larger representation. But even at the second extraordinary meeting, a majority of the corporation's capital is required for any decision regarding a change in the business line of the corporation, its dissolution, the transfer of its seat abroad, or the issuance of preferred stock. An extraordinary meeting must be called when it is requested by shareholders holding one fifth of the corporation's capital. Should it not be called promptly, it will be called by order of the court on petition of the shareholders.

There must be at least one director. If there are two or more, they form the board of directors. They select the chairman from among themselves, unless he is appointed by the meeting of shareholders. Even persons not holding any stock in the corporation may be appointed directors. Directors are appointed by the meeting of shareholders for a term not exceeding three years, and they may be reappointed unless provided otherwise in the act of incorporation. Directors may resign at any time with immediate effect. They must give security in the value of one fiftieth of the corporation's capital as a minimum. The act of incorporation may provide that the security may not exceed 200,000 lire. Decisions are taken by the board of directors by a simple majority, and a simple majority is required as a quorum, unless the act of incorporation requires a larger majority.

The board of auditors is composed of three or five members. Persons not holding stock in the corporation may be appointed. They are appointed by the meeting of shareholders for a term of three years and cannot be removed except for cause. The board must meet at least every three months. It supervises the management of the corporation, the observance of the law and of the act of incorporation by the management. It verifies the profit and loss account and the balance sheet of the corporation. The individual members of the board may themselves proceed to inspection and control of the corporation. They are jointly liable with the directors for losses that could have been prevented had they exercised their functions properly. Shareholders holding at least one tenth of the corporation's capital may petition a court to order an investigation of the management on suspicion of irregularities on the part of the directors and auditors.

The corporation must keep records of shareholders, of debentures, and of the proceedings and decisions of meetings of shareholders, board of directors and the board of auditors. It must prepare a profit and loss account and a balance sheet.

The corporation is dissolved by the running out of time, if it was set up for a definite time only; by attaining its objective, or the impossibility of attaining it; by the impossibility of operating; by reduction of its capital below the legal minimum; by decision of the meeting of shareholders; or on any other ground specified in the act of incorporation. Following a decision to dissolve the corporation, the meeting of shareholders must appoint liquidators; failing such appointment, liquidators are appointed by the court at the request of shareholders. The liquidators must liquidate the corporation and present a final statement indicating the payment each share will receive as final distribution. Following liquidation, the books and records of the corporation must be handed over to the office of the register of enterprises where they will be kept for ten years.

(e)   Commandite partnership by shares (*Società in accomandita per azioni*).   In a commandite partnership by shares, the general partners are liable jointly and severally with all their property. The special partners respond only with the capital brought into the partnership and held in stock. The partnership trades under a firm name that must embody the name of at least one general partner and state that it is a commandite partnership. The rules otherwise applicable to stock corporations (*società per azioni*) apply also to the commandite partnership by shares unless displaced by a specific provision to the contrary.

The act of partnership must indicate who the general partners are. They are the directors of the firm as of right and are subject to the provisions applicable to directors in a stock corporation with the only exception of provisions relating to security, which they are not required to give. They may be removed from office as per provisions applicable to stock corporations. If there are no general partners acting as directors, the partnership comes to an end unless within six months at least one director is appointed.

(f) Corporation with limited liability (*Società a responsabilità limitata*). In a corporation with limited liability, only the corporation and its property is answerable for liabilities incurred by the corporation. The shares of its members may not be expressed in stock. The name of the corporation must include the words "corporation with limited liability." The capital of the corporation must be 50,000 lire as a minimum, and the interest of a member must not be less than 1,000 lire. Members may hold different size interests in the corporation, but only in multiples of 1,000 lire.

The corporation is constituted by a public act that must indicate: (1) the name, domicile and citizenship of each member; (2) the name and seat of the corporation; (3) the business line of the corporation; (4) the amount of capital subscribed and paid; (5) the interest of each member; (6) rules as to distribution of profits; (7) the number of directors and their powers, with the indication of which directors have authority to act on behalf of the corporation; (8) the number of members on the board of auditors; and (9) the duration of the corporation. The corporation must be registered in the register of enterprises in accordance with provisions applicable to the registration of corporations.

Organs of the corporation are the meeting of members, the directors and the board of auditors. The rules applicable to stock corporations apply to them unless otherwise provided. Every member has at least one vote in the meeting and one vote for each 1,000 lire of his interest. A simple majority of the corporation's capital is necessary for a decision in the ordinary meeting, and a two-thirds majority in an extraordinary meeting, unless provided otherwise in the act of incorporation. The corporation may not issue debentures. There must be at least one director. There must be a board of auditors if the corporation's capital equals 1,000,000 lire. Where there is no board of auditors, each member has the powers of the board of auditors.

The corporation must keep the usual books and records, including: (1) records of members and their respective interests; (2) records of proceedings of meetings of members; (3) records of proceedings of the board of directors; and (4) records of proceedings of the board of auditors, if there is one in existence.

The directors must prepare a profit and loss account and a balance sheet at least fifteen days before the meeting of the members. When approved by the meeting, they are filed with the register of enterprises.

The corporation may modify its act of incorporation, increase or reduce its capital, or dissolve itself in accordance with the provisions applicable to stock corporations.

NOTES AND QUESTIONS

1. As to the informal partnership, this is the basic form of partnership and its rules apply to all other types of partnerships unless excluded by a specific statutory provision. An informal partnership may not engage in commerce and, consequently, it is not required to register in the register of enterprises (*registro delle imprese*), Civil Code, Art. 2200. Commerce is defined in the Civil Code, Art. 2195, as an industrial activity devoted to the making of goods and providing of services; and activity of an intermediary in the distribution of goods; transport by land, water or air; banking and insurance; and other activities in support of the above. The purpose of the institution of an informal partnership is to regulate legally its relationship without submitting it to registration and thus to the publicity requirement.

2. As to the general partnership, this is the counterpart of an Anglo-American partnership. *See* the Uniform Partnership Act.

The partnership must be recorded in the register of enterprises, which is kept in the seat of every court of general jurisdiction (*tribunale*) under the supervision of the court. Who keeps partnership records in Anglo-American countries? *See*, e.g., Calif. Corp. C.A. §15010.5. Note that until it is so recorded, the partnership is subject to the rules governing informal partnerships, but even after it is recorded all the basic rules applicable to informal partnerships apply.

The law applicable to general partnerships is uniform in both the civil and the common law. Compare, e.g., the German law and the American Uniform Partnership Act.

3. As to the commandite partnership, it is a concept identical in all civil law countries. Compare the German, the French and the Spanish law.

How does the commandite partnership compare with the Anglo-American limited partnership? *See* the American Uniform Limited Partnership Act, e.g., Calif. Corp. C.A. §15501ff.

What is the liability of a commandite partner in Italian law as compared with that of a limited partner under the Uniform Limited Partnership Act? *See*, e.g., Calif. Corp. C.A. §15517.

4. As to the stock corporation, this is the counterpart of the German *Aktiengesellschaft*, the French *société anonyme*, and the American corporation. What is its Spanish counterpart?

The stock corporation, like a partnership, must be registered with the register of enterprises. With whom must an American corporation be registered? *See*, e.g., Calif. Corp. C.A. §308.

As to the formation of a corporation in Anglo-American law, *see*, e.g., Calif. Corp. C.A. §300ff.

As to directors and management, compare the French and the Spanish law, and also Calif. Corp. C.A. §800ff.

What is the position of shareholders in the corporation? Compare the German law and Calif. Corp. C.A. §2200ff.

What are the rules concerning the dissolution of a corporation? Compare the French law. *See also,* e.g., Calif. Corp. C.A. §4600ff.

5. As to the commandite partnership by shares, this is a type of partnership used in civil law countries. Compare the German and the French law. It makes investment by the commandite partners more attractive since they are in fact shareholders, as in a corporation, and enjoy similar rights.

6. As to the corporation with limited liability, it is a very popular type of corporation and is widely used because of its versatility, which makes it possible for a large amount of capital to be controlled by a few persons, like a family enterprise. How does it compare with the English company "Proprietary Limited"? How does it compare with the American corporation? *See,* e.g., Model Business Corporation Act §§36, 53; Calif. Corp. C.A. §§300, 301.

Compare the Italian corporation with limited liability with its German and Spanish counterparts.

---

7. Limitation of Actions (*Prescrizione*)[33]

Every right that is not exercised will lapse by prescription, with the exception of certain specifically enumerated rights that are not subject to prescription, such as the action contesting the legitimacy of a person, or the right to be recognized as heir and entitled to a share in the estate of a decedent, or the action for the annulment of a contract. Prescription begins to run on the day on which the right could have been exercised. The provisions as to prescription may not be modified or abrogated by parties. Prescription must be pleaded, it does not operate by force of law. What has been paid in fulfillment of a debt already prescribed may not be recovered.

The running of time is suspended between: (1) spouses; (2) a person exercising parental power and the person subject to it; (3) the guardian and the ward; (4) the curator and the emancipated minor or other disabled person; (5) the heir and an inheritance accepted with the benefit of an inventory; (6) the administrators, executors and trustees appointed by a court and beneficiaries until the settling of the account of their administration; (7) legal persons and their directors; and (8) a debtor who is fraudulently concealing assets and his creditor, until the fraud is discovered.

Time does not run against minors and insane persons if they have no legal representative, and also for six months following the appointment of such legal representative. Time also does not run in time of war against members of the armed forces as provided for by special legislation.

The running of time is interrupted by the service of process following the filing of a lawsuit. It is also interrupted by any act that puts the debtor in default. It is futher interrupted by an admission of the right by the obligated party. When running of time is interrupted, the period of prescription must run all over again from the beginning.

Unless otherwise provided, all rights are prescribed by the running of time for ten years.

An action for damages must be brought within five years, and for damages caused by vehicles within two years.

Actions to recover annuities in perpetuity or for life, annuities for the support of a person, rents, interests, and damages for the breach of a contract of employment are prescribed in five years. Rights derived from partnerships and corporations also are prescribed in five years. The claim of a broker to his commission is prescribed in one year.

Rights derived from bills of lading and contracts for the carriage of goods are prescribed in one year. Where the carriage of goods begins or terminates outside of Europe, the action is prescribed in eighteen months.

Rights derived from a contract of insurance are prescribed in one year, and those derived from a contract of reinsurance in two years.

Claims of innkeepers for food and lodging are prescribed in six months.

Claims of the following are prescribed in one year: teachers for instruction given per hour, day or month; as are claims of workmen for work and labor done not exceeding one month; schools for board and instruction; process servers for their services; merchants for goods sold and delivered; and pharmacists for medicaments supplied.

Claims of the following are prescribed in three years: workmen for work and labor done exceeding one month; professional men for payment of their fees and expenses; notaries public for payment of their services; and teachers for instruction exceeding one month.

Prescription takes effect when the last day of the term has run. Time is computed according to the calendar. The day on which the prescription begins to run is not computed, and the prescription takes effect only when the last moment of the last day of the term has run. If the last day is a Sunday or holiday, the right may be exercised the next working day. Prescription by months expires on the same date in the expiring month. If there is no such day, the term runs out on the last day of the month.

Where a right must be exercised within a stipulated time, the rules as to the suspension and interruption of the running of time do not apply unless otherwise provided. Contracts which stipulate a time in such a way as to make it very difficult for a party to exercise his rights are void.

NOTES AND QUESTIONS

The law of prescription is governed by statutory provisions even in the common law countries. Civil law statutes cover under prescription a subject that is treated in the common law countries under both limitation and acquisition of title by adverse possession.

Compare the provisions of the Italian law as to prescription with those of the Spanish law. How is the running of time interrupted in these two systems? Which of the two systems deals with interruption in more detail? Is the distinction between natural and civil interruptions as written into the Spanish law also present in the Italian law?

Follow the Italian prescription term of five years into the French, German and

Spanish systems. Does this term of prescription occur in any of these systems? If so, does it cover the same type of claims?

Italian law provides that all rights are prescribed by the running of time for ten years unless otherwise provided. Do any of the other three systems have a similar blanket provision? Does the law of your state have a similar provision? *See*, e.g., Calif. C.C.P.A. §§315ff. and 335ff.; *see also* UCC 2-725, 3-122, 4-406, 6-111.

----

8.   The Law of Exchange

Promissory notes and bills of exchange (*cambiale*) are governed by provisions of the International Convention of June 7, 1930, made in Geneva. The provisions of the convention are incorporated into Italian law by Royal Decree-Law of August 25, 1932, No. 1130. Cheques (*assegno bancario*) are governed by the Geneva Convention of March 19, 1931, which is incorporated into Italian law by Royal Decree-Law of August 24, 1933, No. 1077.

NOTES

The law of negotiable instruments and checks is uniformly regulated by the law of the Geneva conventions to which most of the countries of the world acceded, with the notable exception of the English-speaking countries. For the American law, *see* UCC, Arts. 3, 4 and 5. Compare also the German and the Spanish law.

----

9.   Bankruptcy (*Fallimento*)[34]

All traders are subject to the laws of bankruptcy with the exception of public enterprises and individual small traders. Small traders are those whose trading capital is below a certain sum stipulated by law.[35] Public enterprises, like insurance enterprises, savings banks, and cooperative societies are subject to administrative liquidation.

A trader who is insolvent is declared bankrupt. Bankruptcy is declared at the request of the debtor, one or more creditors, or the public ministry. Bankruptcy also may be declared ex officio by the court of the place where the trader has his seat of business. The declaration of bankruptcy also contains the appointment of a trustee in bankruptcy. The declaration further orders the bankrupt to submit records of his business ventures and the creditors to present their claims within not more than thirty days, and it sets a date for the examination of the losses of the bankrupt's business.

The trustee in bankruptcy is a public officer. He acts as a receiver and assesses the assets and liabilities of the bankrupt. Further, a committee of three to five creditors is appointed by the judge to represent the creditors in the proceedings.

All property of the bankrupt is subject to bankruptcy, except: (1) strictly personal property and rights; (2) support payments and any other income which the bankrupt needs for his maintenance and that of his family; (3) income from the usufruct in the property of the children of the bankrupt; (4) income from property given to the bankrupt as a dowry; and (5) property that cannot be seized by provision of the law.

Claims of the creditors are accepted in accordance with the law. Preferred (secured) creditors are entitled to payment in full, ordinary creditors have a claim to a pro-rata payment from remaining assets.

All payments of debts and gifts made by the bankrupt within two years prior to the declaration of bankruptcy are void. The trustee may request that any other acts of the bankrupt be declared void. All abnormal transactions and payments made by the bankrupt within two years prior to bankruptcy also are void, unless the other party can prove that he was not aware of the bankrupt's insolvency. All normal day-to-day transactions and payments made by the bankrupt within one year prior to the declaration of bankruptcy are void if the trustee proves that the other party was aware of the bankrupt's insolvency.

After the bankrupt's assets have been ascertained and secured, and his liabilities ascertained, the bankrupt may petition for a settlement with his creditors. His petition must state his offer of payment to the creditors of a determined percentage of his debt and what security he offers for such payment. The offer must be accepted by the majority of the creditors entitled to two thirds of the debts. If it is not so accepted, or if the bankrupt does not keep the arrangement, regular winding up proceedings follow. Movables and immovables are sold privately or in public auction by order of the judge on the advice of the trustee and the committee of creditors.

(a) Settlement with creditors. A trader who is insolvent may petition for a settlement with his creditors to forestall possible bankruptcy proceedings if: (1) He has been in business for at least two years; (2) he has not been declared bankrupt within the preceding five years; and (3) he has never been convicted of fraudulent bankruptcy or of fraud. He must offer to pay at least 40 percent of all debts due to his creditors within six months of the settlement and sound guarantees of payment, or he must offer all his property in payment of his debts. If the debtor complies with the above rules, the court will order settlement proceedings, otherwise it will make a declaration of bankruptcy. Where settlement proceedings are instituted, the court appoints a judge to handle the case, and also a trustee to handle the administration of the assets. It also sets a hearing where all creditors will have the opportunity to approve or disapprove the settlement. Creditors entitled to two thirds of the debts must assent to the settlement if it is to be accepted. If they give their assent and if the judge approves the plan, then the settlement becomes binding on all parties. If it is not so approved, normal bankruptcy proceedings follow.

(b) Voluntary administration. A trader who finds it temporarily difficult to meet his obligations may apply to the court for temporary administration of his business for a period not exceeding one year. The court will institute the proceedings if the debtor appears worthy of being granted this privilege. It will appoint a judge and a trustee, and it will call a meeting of creditors. At the meeting, the majority of creditors holding the majority of the outstanding claims must approve the plan. If the plan is accepted and if it works satisfactorily, the administration is lifted. If not, or if the business is unable to meet its obligations, the debtor may petition for a settlement with creditors, otherwise a declaration of bankruptcy will be made.

NOTES AND QUESTIONS

The Italian law of bankruptcy gives the trader in financial difficulty several choices. What are they? On what conditions do these schemes depend? Bankruptcy follows only as a matter of last resort. What choices are offered by the French and the Spanish law? Does the Anglo-American law offer similar advantages? *See*, e.g., F.C.A. 11 §701ff.

The petition is filed with the general jurisdiction court (*tribunale*). With which courts is the petition filed in Spain and in France? How is the matter handled in the United States? *See* F.C.A. 11 §11.

The proceedings are regulated by a special statute. Compare, e.g., the German law. For American law, compare U.S. Code Service Rules of Bankruptcy.

As to exemptions of property falling into bankruptcy, compare F.C.A. 11 §25.

Note the several officers administering the proceedings. Who are the officers in the French law? For American law, *see* F.C.A. 11 §61ff. and Bankruptcy Rules, Rule 501ff.

To obtain a settlement with creditors, the insolvent must offer at least 40 percent of the debts due. What is the German rule on the matter? Must the insolvent make a minimum offer as a condition for acceptance of a settlment in the French and American law? *See*, e.g., F.C.A. 11 §701ff.

The bankrupt will be discharged when he pays all his debts or if he complies with the arrangement approved by the court (Italian Civil Code, Arts. 142-145). What are the conditions for the debtor's discharge in the French and in the Spanish law? *See also* F.C.A. 11 §32ff; Bankruptcy Rules, Rules 404-409.

The Italian bankruptcy law provides for punishment for fraudulent bankruptcy and for other offenses in Arts. 216-241. Compare the German law. *See also* F.C.A. 11 §11 (4).

---

10. Maritime Law

Provisions as to maritime law are embodied in the Code of Navigation (*Codice della Navigazione*).[36] The Code is presented in four parts. The first deals with maritime and internal navigation, the second with aerial navigation, the third with penal and disciplinary provisions, and the fourth with transitory and supplementary provisions. Provisions with respect to maritime trade are thus covered in the first part.

The first part, dealing with maritime and internal navigation, is given in four books: Book 1. Administrative regulation of navigation; Book 2. Ownership of ships and charter parties; Book 3. Liabilities arising from navigation; and Book 4. Procedural provisions.

Book 1 (Administrative regulation of navigation) deals with the administrative regulation of maritime and internal navigation; maritime domains, like beaches, ports, rades, bays, mouths of rivers, canals, and their uses; the administration and policing of ports; pilotage and towage; port labor; maritime personnel and the personnel of internal navigation, like captains, other officers, engineers, and seamen; licensing and registration of ships and their seaworthiness; ship documents; supervision of navigation; supervision and policing on board; registration of births, deaths and marriages on board; and maritime fishing.

Book 2 (Ownership of ships and charter parties) deals with shipbuilding; ownership and co-ownership of ships; charter parties; and the captain and crew.

Book 3 (Liabilities arising from navigation) deals with charter parties; carriage of persons and goods; general average; collision; salvage; insurance; and maritime liens and ship mortgages.

Book 4 (Procedural provisions) deals with procedure before port captains, courts, and appellate courts; labor disputes; limitation of liability; enforcement of liens and mortgages; and removal of liens and mortgages.

NOTES

The Italian law deals very comprehensively with maritime law in a special code. In addition, the Code of Navigation deals separately also with the law of the air.

The Italian maritime (admiralty) law corresponds fully to that of other maritime nations. Italy is also party to all major international conventions regulating and unifying maritime law. *See* the German, the French and the Spanish law on the subject, including notes.

B. THE SYSTEM OF CIVIL COURTS

The Italian system of civil courts comprises justices of the peace (*giudici conciliatori*); courts of limited jurisdiction, known as courts of the praetor (*pretore*); courts of general jurisdiction (*tribunali*); courts of appeal (*corti di appello*); and one court of final resort, the Supreme Court of Cassation (*Corte Suprema di Cassazione*).[37]

1. Justices of the Peace (*Giudici conciliatori*)[38]

In every community there is at least one justice of the peace. His office is honorary and his services are free of any charge. His jurisdiction is conciliatory, but he has civil jurisdiction in matters not exceeding a certain fixed value (50,000 lire). His decisions are based on equity and common sense. The justice of the peace must hold Italian citizenship, reside in the community where he exercises his office, be at least twenty-five years of age and be of the male sex. Appointments are made by the president of the court of appeal for a term of three years, and incumbents may be reappointed. Supervision over them is exercised by superior judicial authority. An appeal against decisions of a *conciliatore* goes to the proper *pretore*. It must be lodged within ten days from the notification of the decision. No legal representation is required before the *conciliatore*.

2. Praetors (*Pretori*)[39]

The *pretura* is a limited jurisdiction court staffed by a number of judges and headed by the *pretore titolare*. The court hears appeals against decisions of a *conciliatore* and exercises limited civil jurisdiction up to a certain fixed value (750,000 lire).[40] It also hears cases, irrespective of maximum value, dealing with specifically enumerated matters, such as repossession of movables, trespass of land, and anticipated damage from new structures, unless the matter, because of its small value, falls within the jurisdiction of the *conciliatore*. The court in session is formed by a single judge. Appeal against his decision lies to the proper *tribunale* and must be lodged within thirty days from the notification of the decision. Seats of these courts are determined by law. Parties appearing before the praetor need legal representation, but the praetor may authorize them to appear by themselves. If authorization is not granted, they must engage the services of attorneys (*procuratori*) admitted to practice in that legal district. They may also engage the services of advocates (*avvocati*) admitted to practice anywhere in Italy.

3. Civil Courts (*Tribunali*)[41]

The *tribunale* is a general jurisdiction court. Its trial jurisdiction extends to all matters that are beyond the jurisdiction of the *pretura*, and it also hears appeals against decisions of the *pretura*. The *tribunale* is headed by a president and it has a number of judges on its staff. Cases are heard by panels of three judges. The seats of the several courts are determined by law. Appeals against decisions of the *tribunale* must be lodged within thirty days from notification of the decision. It goes to the proper *corte di appello*. Parties appearing before the *tribunale* must be represented by attorneys (*procuratori*) admitted to practice in that legal district. They may also secure the services of advocates (*avvocati*) admitted to practice anywhere in Italy.

4. Courts of Appeal (*Corti di appello*)[42]

Appellate courts hear appeals against decisions of *tribunali*. The court is headed by a president and has several judges on its staff. The title of the judge is *consigliere* (counselor). The court hears appeals in panels of five judges. Seats of these courts are determined by law. There is no further appeal against decisions of a court of appeal; however, error, known as the *ricorso per cassazione*, is available to the *Corte Suprema di Cassazione*. It must be lodged within sixty days from notification of the decision. Parties appearing before a court of appeal must be represented by attorneys ((*procuratori*) admitted to practice in the particular legal district headed by that court of appeal, and they may further engage the services of advocates (*avvocati*) admitted to practice anywhere in Italy.

5. Supreme Court of Cassation (*Corte Suprema di Cassazione*)[43]

This is the supreme court of Italy; its seat is in Rome. Its function consists of the enforcement and uniform application of law in the whole country. It also settles conflicts of jurisdiction between subordinate courts. It is headed by a first president and is staffed with presiding justices of the individual sections and with justices called *consiglieri*. The Court hears cases in panels of seven justices. It may also combine two sections and act in a panel of fifteen justices, including the presiding justice who usually is the first president of the Court. Parties appearing before the Court must be represented by advocates (*avvocati*) admitted to practice in the Supreme Court of Cassation.[44]

NOTES AND QUESTIONS

1. Italian justices of the peace perform mainly a conciliatory function and are active especially in small communities. Since such conciliatory offices may well be performed by the local mayor or a police officer, the appointment of special conciliation officers has been discontinued in most civil law countries. Note that their office is strictly honorary. Compare them with Spanish courts of the peace. May their function be compared with that of the ancient Justices of the Peace who held office in England since the reign of King Edward III?

2. The Italian *pretura* is a typical limited jurisdiction court. How does it compare with French courts of instance or Spanish municipal and country courts? Can it be compared with Anglo-American municipal, justice or county courts? *See*, e.g., Calif. C.C.P.A. §81ff. In what respect does the jurisdiction of a *pretura* differ from that of a German *Amtsgericht*?

3. Italian *tribunali* are general jurisdiction courts. How do they compare with French courts of grande instance or German *Landgerichte*? Note that the *tribunale* has an appellate division to hear appeals from the *pretura*. May the Italian *tribunale* be compared with a typical Anglo-American court of general jurisdiction, like the New York Supreme Court, California Superior Court, Texas District Court or U.S. District Court?

Note that the Italian *tribunale* handles civil cases, including commercial cases. Does the same rule obtain in France? What is the position in Spain and the rule in Germany? Which courts try commercial cases in Anglo-American jurisdictions?

Note that the panel hearing a case is composed of three judges. There are no juries. What is the composition of Spanish courts of first instance or German *Landgerichte*?

Legal representation is mandatory. For judges and attorneys, *see* the section on legal officers below.

4. Italian courts of appeal hear appeals against decisions of *tribunali* in their trial jurisdiction. It is a genuine appeal on the merits. The panels are composed of five judges. Compare Italian courts of appeal with French courts of appeal and Spanish *audiencias territoriales*. With which Anglo-American courts may Italian courts of appeal be compared? *See*, e.g., Calif. C.C.P.A. §§41ff. and 77ff., and 28 U.S.C.A. §1291ff.

5. The Italian Supreme Court of Cassation is a court of error only. The error is as of right on grounds enumerated in the law. *See* procedure before the Supreme Court of Cassation below. What is the chief function of the court? Compare it with the French Court of Cassation. Note that it hears cases in panels of seven justices or in larger panels of fifteen justices. Do all courts of final resort in civil law countries increase the number of justices on hearing important cases? Does the same rule obtain in Anglo-American courts of final resort?

Compare the function of the Italian Supreme Court of Cassation with the jurisdiction of the highest court in your state and with that of the U.S. Supreme Court, 28 U.S.C.A. §1251ff.

As to judges and attorneys, *see* the section on legal officers below.

C. THE LAW OF CIVIL PROCEDURE

The Italian Code of Civil Procedure of 1942 is in power, as amended. It has 831 articles and it is given in four books: Book 1. General provisions; Book 2. Civil procedure; Book 3. Execution of judgments; and Book 4. Special proceedings.

Book 1 (General provisions) deals with the jurisdiction of courts, judges, court clerks and other officers; the public ministry; the parties; the institution of legal process; powers of judges; judicial acts; and hearings in civil matters.

Book 2 (Civil procedure) deals with procedure in courts of general jurisdiction and courts of limited jurisdiction; appeal and procedure in appellate courts; error and procedure in the Court of Cassation; and procedure in labor disputes.

Book 3 (Execution of judgments) deals with the procedure governing the execution of judgments; judicial sales; defenses available to the debtor; and the suspension and abandonment of proceedings.

Book 4 (Special proceedings) deals with summary proceedings; proceedings in matters of family law concerning spouses and minors; proceedings affecting the status of persons, including persons under guardianship and the declaration of absence or the death of a person; proceedings governing devolution of property on the death of a person; procedure for the discharge of mortgages; suits brought on judgments obtained abroad; and arbitration.

The following are topics selected from the Italian law of civil procedure.

1. Procedure before Justices of the Peace (*giudici conciliatori*) and Praetors (*pretori*)[45]

The procedure before courts of limited jurisdiction is governed by the rules applicable to procedure before courts of general jurisdiction unless otherwise provided. The procedure is simplified, however, and it is much less formal than that before courts of general jurisdiction.

The suit is initiated by a citation, which must give the day and time of the hearing. It also contains the statement of claim. In very small claims, the plaintiff may make his claim verbally to an officer of the court who will reduce it to writing and prepare the citation. At least three days must elapse between the service of the citation and the return date. The hearing itself takes place before the conciliator, if brought in a court of a justice of the peace, or before the praetor, if brought in the *pretura*, along the lines of procedure before courts of general jurisdiction. The case is heard by a single judge. An appeal against decisions of a *conciliatore* lies to the proper *pretore*. It must be lodged within ten days from the notification of the decision. Neither further appeal nor error are available. An appeal against decisions of the *pretore* lies to the proper *tribunale* and must be lodged within thirty days from notification of the decision. There is no further appeal, but error lies to the *Corte Suprema di Cassazione*.

2. Procedure before the *Tribunale* (General jurisdiction court)[46]

(a) Initiation of proceedings.   Proceedings are initiated by the filing of a copy of a citation on the defendant. The citation is prepared by the plaintiff's attorney (*procuratore*). It must give the following information: (1) name of the court; (2) name, surname and address of the plaintiff and the defendant; (3) object of the claim; (4) facts of the case and the law applicable thereto and the demand made by the plaintiff; (5) means of proof, especially documents that the plaintiff will use to prove his claim; (6) name and surname of the attorney (*procuratore*) and the power given to him by the plaintiff; and (7) return date of the citation before the instructing judge (*giudice instruttore*).

The citation is signed by the plaintiff or his attorney (*procuratore*). A copy thereof is then served by the plaintiff on the defendant. The return date stipulated in the citation is determined by the plaintiff in accordance with the court calendar. Only dates set by the court may be so selected. The return date must be selected so as to provide for a specified minimum number of days to elapse between the service of the citation and the return date. At least thirty days are required if the defendant is served within the district of the court. At least forty days are required if the defendant is served out of court's jurisdiction but within the district of the court of appeal within which the court is located. At least sixty days are required if the defendant is served within the jurisdiction of another court of appeal. At least ninety days are required if the defendant is notified in European states outside of Italy or in states located in the Mediterranean sea basin. At least one hundred and eighty days are required if the defendant is notified in any other foreign state. In urgent cases, the president of the court, at the request of the plaintiff, may reduce the time required up to one half.

Within ten days of the service of the citation, the plaintiff must file with the court registrar the original citation and all documents listed by him as means of proof, the power of attorney, and a request to place the case on the court calendar. At least five days before the return date of the citation, the defendant must file, through his attorney (*procuratore*), his defense, the copy of the citation served on him, and the power of attorney. His brief must contain all his defenses and claims, the law applicable thereto, the means of proof and his legal conclusions. If he wishes to implead a thirdy party, he must do so in his defense brief. A copy of his brief must be given to the plaintiff.

Having received the brief of the plaintiff or, failing such brief, having received the brief of the defendant, the registrar enters the case on the court calendar, makes a file and delivers it promptly to the presiding judge of the proper court division that will hear the case. The presiding judge appoints an instructing judge (*giudice instruttore*) before whom the parties will have to appear on the return date. If neither party files its brief properly, the return date will be postponed for one year; if neither party proceeds in the meantime, the case will lapse. If only the plaintiff files his brief, a default judgment may be given. If only the defendant files his brief, the plaintiff's claim will be dismissed.

(b) Procedure before the instructing judge (*Giudice instruttore*).   The instructing judge must study the case before the first hearing takes place at the return date.

He is charged with all the proceedings in the matter with the exception of the final hearing, which will be held before the entire trial court composed of three judges of whom he is one. If neither party appears at the first hearing, the instructing judge adjourns the case to a later date, and if they do not appear then, the case is struck out. If the plaintiff does not appear and the defendant does not request further proceedings (e.g., on his counterclaim), the hearing is adjourned to a later date, and if the plaintiff does not appear then, the case is struck out. If the defendant requests proceedings, he may prove his case, and if the case is ready for judgment, the instructing judge will refer it to the entire court for a default judgment. If the defendant does not appear, the plaintiff may prove his case, and if the case is ready for judgment, the instructing judge will refer it to the entire court for a default judgment.

Proceedings before the instructing judge are oral. He first makes sure that all the papers in the dispute have been properly filed and he has the parties correct any defects. At the first hearing the parties may modify, supplement and clarify their claims and statements. The instructing judge must explore the situation with the view to a possible settlement of the dispute. If the case is ready for proof, the instructing judge will set a hearing for that purpose. He may also appoint experts to give their opinions on any matter. He rules on any motions of the parties. His rulings are not appealable; however, they are submitted to the entire court for review, together with the merits of the case, at the final hearing. The court may then overrule such rulings. As an exception, rulings that deal with admissibility of evidence may be appealed to the entire court within ten days of such a ruling.

At the hearing set for proof, the instructing judge hears all the evidence produced by witnesses. He may also order any person to produce documents and property for inspection. If a party denies the authenticity of his signature appearing on a document, or the authenticity of the whole document allegedly made by him, the authenticity must be established. The ruling in this matter is made by the entire court, to whom the matter is referred by the instructing judge. Where a party claims that a document produced by another party is forged, the instructing judge must ask the party who produced the document whether he will rely on it as proof. If the party does not drop the document from his list of proof, its authenticity must be proved. The ruling on its authenticity is made by the entire court, to whom the matter is referred by the instructing judge. The instructing judge may also allow the parties to submit interrogatories for answer by the opponent. Parties must answer such interrogatories and may admit claims made against them. In addition to written answers, parties may be interrogated orally. Where a party does not answer or refuses to answer, the court may take it as an admission.

A party may propose at any time that the opponent swear to the truth of his allegations. The opponent may either accept the proposal or refer it back to the proponent. The decision of whether the oath will be made is made by the entire court. If the court rules in the affirmative, the party accepting or the one to whom the proposal was referred back must swear to the truth of his allegations. If he does so, judgment is given in his favor; if he refuses, judgment is given against him. This institution is known as the decisive oath. The instructing judge may, in the exercise of his judicial power, request one party to make the oath; the party so requested may not refer it to his opponent.

Evidence by witnesses is given orally before the instructing judge. Persons who have an interest in the matter in dispute may not be heard as witnesses. Also, the spouse of a party, even though judicially separated, may not give evidence, nor may any relative in the direct line of consanguinity of affinity, unless the case bears on family matters. Minors below the age of fourteen may be heard only when necessary in the circumstances, and they may give unsworn evidence only. Witnesses give evidence under oath. A witness who does not appear will be fined and a new date for the hearing will be set. He will also have to pay the costs of the hearing. A witness who refuses to testify or, if he does so, is difficult or is suspected of not telling the truth may be prosecuted.

(c)   Final hearing and judgment.   When the case is ready for judgment, the instructing judge sets it for final hearing before the entire court. The hearing is opened by the presiding judge who calls on the instructing judge to give his report. The instructing judge reports on the proceedings. He gives all the relevant facts in the case and indicates all the points that must be decided. The parties then take the floor, first the plaintiff and then the defendant. The presiding judge then declares the proceedings closed and the court retires to its chambers to deliberate and give judgment.

The deliberations are secret. The court may at any time reopen the proceedings if further evidence is required. The court makes a list of points for its decision and votes on them. Decision is by majority vote. First the instructing judge votes, then the other judge, and the presiding judge votes last. The decision having been made, the presiding judge prepares and signs the order of the judgment. The reasons for the judgment and the judgment in its final form will be prepared by the instructing judge. When ready, the judgment is properly typed by the court office and copies are delivered to the attorneys for the parties. Failing attorneys, copies of the judgment are delivered directly to the parties at their respective addresses. Any error in the judgment may be corrected by the court ex officio or on the motion of either party.

An appeal against judgments of the *tribunale* goes to the proper *corte di appello* and must be filed within thirty days from notification of judgment on the parties. The judgment becomes executory only after the time for filing the appeal has run without any appeal being made. On motion of the victorious party, the judgment may be made executory by order of the court founded on good reasons, such as when the delay may adversely affect the chances of the victorious party to recover.

(d)   Proceedings on appeal from the *pretura.*   The rules of procedure governing the handling of appeals in appellate courts are identical irrespective of whether the appeal is heard in the *tribunale* from a judgment of the *pretura* or in the *corte di appello* from a judgment of the *tribunale*.

NOTES AND QUESTIONS

1. Procedure before the *pretura* is a more simplified procedure than that before courts of general jurisdiction. Compare it with procedure before German *Amtsgerichte* or French courts of instance. What rules of procedure apply in Anglo-American courts of limited jurisdiction?

2. Procedure before the *tribunale* is the standard procedure in civil matters.

(a) The attorney for the plaintiff will prepare the papers and will have the original citation issued by the court office. A copy thereof will then be served by a court bailiff on the defendant. Where both parties, e.g., business firms, are in communication and are represented by attorneys on a permanent retainer, no official service is necessary and the attorney for the plaintiff simply forwards a copy of the citation to the attorney for the defendant who accepts service. All futher communications are then made between attorneys. Compare the initiation of proceedings in French courts of grande instance and the contents of the French citation. As to initiation of proceedings in Anglo-American law, *see* F.R.C.P Rules 3 and 4.

(b) The case develops in successive hearings before the instructing judge. All of the evidence is given at such hearings. Failure to follow the time limits set may result in a default judgment for or against the plaintiff. Compare the German procedure, and F.R.C.P. Rule 55 as to the Anglo-American procedure.

The institution of the instructing judge is a pivotal feature of civil procedure in civil law countries. *See also* the Spanish and French procedures.

As to the means of proof, are they identical with those in Anglo-American countries? Consider the decisive oaths. Does decisive oath exist in Anglo-American countries?

Note that parties may use interrogatories. *See*, e.g., F.R.C.P. Rule 33.

Witnesses give evidence on oath and are sworn in to tell the truth. Compare the Spanish and German rules. Compare Federal Rules of Evidence, Rule 603.

(c) The final hearing takes place before a panel of three judges. There is no jury. Note that the court will decide the points which are brought for decision as a result of the proceedings before the instructing judge. The final hearing is opened by the report of the instructing judge, who is a member of the panel. How does this approach compare with the French and German procedures?

After the parties have presented their respective cases on the points so set, the final hearing is concluded. How does the Italian final hearing compare with an Anglo-American trial? Must there be a jury trial in Anglo-American law? *See*, e.g., F.R.C.P. Rules 38, 39; Calif. C.C.P.A. §631ff.

Note the deliberation and voting procedure of the Italian court giving judgment. Compare it with the Spanish procedure. For actual judgments, *see* the section on judgments below.

The judgment becomes executory only after it enters into the power of law. To obtain provisional execution, the victorious party must make a special motion in accordance with Art. 282ff. of the Italian Code of Civil Procedure to that effect and offer proof of impending loss, should immediate execution not be granted. *See also* the German rule.

(d) For procedure on appeal from the *pretura, see* procedure in courts of appeal below.

---

3. Procedure before Courts of Appeal (*Corti di appello*)[47]

The rules of procedure applicable to proceedings before courts of general jurisdiction (*tribunali*) apply also to proceedings before courts of appeal, unless they are displaced by a specific provision of the law applicable to procedure in courts of appeal.

The court of appeal (*corte di appello*) hears appeals in panels of five judges, one of them presiding. The appeal must be filed with the office of the proper court of appeal within thirty days from notification of the judgment pronounced in the *tribunale* on the parties. The appeal must contain a summary of the facts and the specific reasons for the appeal. The office will arrange the transfer of the files from the *tribunale* to the proper panel which will handle the case. The presiding judge of the panel will appoint an instructing judge from among its members who will deal with the matter and prepare it for the final hearing. No new demands may be made on appeal, but new exceptions may be cited and new evidence may be produced. If, however. the party could have availed himself of such exceptions or evidence in the trial court, he will have to pay the costs of the proceedings where they are given on appeal.

The instructing judge will fix a date for the first hearing, and both parties must file their briefs before such hearing along the lines of proceedings before the *tribunale*. At the hearing, the instructing judge makes sure that the parties have complied with the rules and that the appeal is properly filed. If not, he will declare the appeal inadmissible. The rulings of the instructing judge are appealable to the entire panel within ten days of notification of the ruling on the parties. When all additional proof has been offered, and the parties have made all their points, the instructing judge will refer the case for final hearing and decision before the entire panel.

At the final hearing, first the instructing judge gives his report; then the parties take the floor, first the appellant and then the appellee. The presiding judge then declares the proceedings terminated and the court retires to deliberate and give judgment. The court votes on all questions to be decided. First the instructing judge votes, then the other judges in inverted order of seniority; the presiding judge votes last. Decision is by majority vote. The judgment supersedes the judgment appealed from. The case may not be referred back to the trial court except when its judgment is annulled by the court of appeal or when the trial court refused jurisdiction and the court of appeal rules that the refusal was improper.

There is no further appeal against the decision of a court of appeal; but error, known as *ricorso per cassazione*, may be lodged with the *Corte Suprema di Cassazione* within sixty days from notification of the judgment on the parties.

4. Procedure before the Supreme Court of Cassation (*Corte Suprema di Cassazione*)[48]

The Supreme Court of Cassation (*Corte Suprema di Cassazione*) hears cases in panels of seven justices, one of them presiding. It hears error, known as *ricorso per cassazione*, lodged against judgments of courts of appeal as well as against judgments given by *tribunali* on appeal from decisions of *pretori*. Error may be brought on the following grounds: (1) territorial jurisdiction; (2) jurisdiction as to the subject matter in dispute; (3) violation or improper application of law; (4) nullity of the judgment or of the proceedings; or (5) absence of grounds, or insufficiency or contradiction in the reasoning in a judgment. After a judgment is given by the *tribunale* in its trial capacity, the parties may agree to by-pass the court of appeal and file the *ricorso per cassazione;* however, they may do so only on the ground that the court allegedly violated or improperly applied the law.

The procurator general in the Supreme Court of Cassation may bring the *ricorso ex officio* in the interest of the law where the parties do not file error within sixty days. If the judgment attacked is actually set aside in such proceedings, the parties may not take advantage thereof.

The *ricorso* must be filed by an advocate (*avvocato*) admitted to practice before the Supreme Court of Cassation. The brief must give the names of the parties, the judgment attacked, a summary of the facts of the case, the grounds for cassation, and the law on which the grounds are founded. The *ricorso* is filed in the office of the cassation court. The office will arrange the transfer of the files of the case from the lower court to the Supreme Court of Cassation. The party against whom the *ricorso* is directed must file his brief within twenty days from notification of the filing of the *ricorso*. If he does not do so, he may not file his brief later but may take part in the oral proceedings before the Court.

In the proceedings before the Supreme Court of Cassation, the parties may not produce any documents that were not produced before. If nullity is alleged, the parties may produce new documents referring to nullity. The *ricorso* does not suspend execution of the judgment attacked, but the court that pronounced the judgment may, on application of any party, suspend its execution on good grounds, especially where the execution would produce irreparable injury to the defeated party.

The office of the Court channels the *ricorso* to the proper panel by order of the first president of the Court. The first president sets a date for the hearing and appoints a rapporteur (*relatore*) from among the justices of the proper panel. The date and hour of the hearing is communicated to the advocates of the parties at least twenty days before the hearing. The parties may file statements until five days before the hearing. The public ministry receives copies of all dealings and must present its reasoned conclusions on the case. Such conclusions must be communicated to the parties at least twenty days before the hearing.

At the hearing, the rapporteur gives his report first. He gives all the facts relevant for the decision on the *ricorso,* a summary of the judgment attacked, the grounds for the *ricorso,* and the argument of the defendant in error. Then the parties put their cases before the Court, first the plaintiff in error and then the defendant in error. Then the public ministry gives its evaluation and its reasons for a suggested decision. The parties may present to the Court their comments in writing on the report of the public ministry. The hearing is then concluded and the Court retires to deliberate on the judgment.

The Court deliberates in the presence of the public ministry. Decision is by majority vote. First the rapporteur votes, then the justices in inverted order of seniority; the presiding justice votes last.

If the matter turns on the question of jurisdiction and the Court determines the matter, it will determine which court has jurisdiction to hear the case. Any decision on the merits of the case made by a court lacking jurisdiction will be set aside. Equally, if the Supreme Court of Cassation finds that the plaintiff never had any cause of action, it will set aside the judgment. In neither case will the matter be referred to another court for further proceedings. Where the Court sets aside the decision on any other ground than those mentioned above, it will refer the case for further proceedings to a court other than that from which it came but of rank equal thereto. Where the Court finds a violation or erroneous application of law, it will enounce the principle that is to be binding on the lower court to which the case is referred for further action. A copy of the judgment will also be sent to the court that pronounced the judgment against which the *ricorso* has been taken.

Proceedings before the court to which the case is referred by the Supreme Court of Cassation may be initiated by either party within one year from the publication of the judgment in the cassation court. Proceedings are initiated by a citation taken out by the more diligent party. If neither party so moves, the proceedings lapse but the judgment of the Supreme Court of Cassation will stand unimpaired.

NOTES AND QUESTIONS

1. As to procedure before courts of appeal, the Italian appellate procedure exemplifies a typical appellate procedure in civil law countries. Note the function of the instructing judge, who handles the case until the final hearing. How does a case proceed on appeal in the Spanish and in the French law? Compare the function of the Italian instructing judge with the functions of Spanish and French rapporteurs.

Do Italian appellate proceedings amount to a trial *de novo*? Compare the German appellate proceedings. Is an Anglo-American appeal a trial *de novo*?

Note that the appeal is as of right. Does the same rule apply in the Anglo-American law? *See*, e.g., F.R.A.P. Rules 3-5.

2. As to procedure before the Italian Supreme Court of Cassation, proceedings before the Court are purely proceedings in error, reviewing exclusively questions of law. How does the Italian procedure compare with that before the French Court of Cassation?

Does the Italian procedure provide for a rapporteur to prepare the case for the hearing? What is the German rule?

How does the procedure before the Italian Supreme Court of Cassation compare with that before the Supreme Court of the U.S.? *See*, 28 U.S.C.A. §2101ff.

Consider the Italian rules as to remission of the case to a lower court for further proceedings. *See also* the relevant French rule. What is the German rule on the matter? For an Anglo-American rule, *see*, e.g., 28 U.S.C.A. §2106, and Calif. C.C.A. §43.

III. THE SYSTEM AND ADMINISTRATION OF CRIMINAL LAW

A. THE SUBSTANTIVE CRIMINAL LAW

The Penal Code of 1930 is in power as of July 1, 1931, as amended. The code has 734 articles contained in three books dealing with: Book 1. General provisions; Book 2. Particular crimes; and Book 3. Particular infractions.[49]

Book 1 (General provisions) has the following titles: I. Penal law; II. Punishment; III. Penal acts; IV. The offender and the victim; V. Modification, application and execution of punishment; VI. Extinction of the penal act and of punishment; VII. Civil liability; and VIII. Administrative detention.

Book 2 (Particular crimes) has the following titles: I. Crimes against the state; II. Crimes against public adminstration; III. Crimes against the administration of justice; IV. Crimes against religion, disturbing the peace of the deceased; V. Crimes against public order; VI. Crimes against the security of the public at large and against its property; VII. Crimes against public faith (counterfeiting and falsifications); VIII. Crimes against the national economy, industry and commerce; IX. Crimes against public morality and good manners; X. Crimes against bodily integrity and health (abortion, infection with contagious disease); XI. Crimes against the family; XII. Crimes against the person; and XIII. Crimes against property.

Book 3 (Particular infractions) has the following titles: 1. Police infractions; and II. Infractions against the social activity of public administration (truancy, damaging objects of archeological, historical or artistic value, destruction of beauties of nature in protected areas).

Further important statutes are usually carried in the appendix of the Penal Code. They deal with: water and electricity, public notices, amnesty and remission, protection of animals, arms and weapons, autopsies, motor-vehicles, hunting, prisons, institutions of reeducation, theatres, contraband and offenses against the administration of customs, criminal bankruptcy, railroads, tax frauds, venereal diseases, insane persons, road traffic, narcotics, and so on.

The following are topics selected from the Italian substantive criminal law.

1. Penal Law (*Legge penale*)[50]

No one may be punished for an act that has not been expressly made a criminal act by law, nor may he be assessed a punishment not provided therein. Ignorance of the penal law is not an excuse.

2. Punishment (*Pene*)[51]

Principal punishments provided for crimes (*delitti*) are imprisonment for life (*ergastolo*),[52] imprisonment for a time (*reclusione*), and fine (*multa*). Principal punishments provided for infractions (*contravvenzioni*) are arrest (*arresto*) and fine (*multa*).

All prisoners are held in forced labor. Imprisonment for a time (*reclusione*) extends from fifteen days to twenty-four years, and arrest (*arresto*) from five days to three years.

An attempt to commit a crime (*delitto*) that was formerly punishable by death is punished now with imprisonment of from twenty-four to thirty years; an attempt to commit a crime (*delitto*) formerly punishable by imprisonment for life is punished with imprisonment of not less than twelve years. All other cases of attempts to commit a crime (*delitto*) are punishable with the same punishment as for the completed crime, but reduced from one to two thirds.

NOTES AND QUESTIONS

1. The fact that no one may be punished for an act unless such act has been made punishable by law testifies to the statutory nature of Italian penal law. The principle *nulla poena sine lege* (no punishment without law) applies in full force, and by law it is meant a statutory provision. How does this principle apply in Anglo-American law? Anglo-American law was from time immemorial the common law. What is the function of criminal statutes in Anglo-American law? *See* Blackstone, 1 Comm. 86. Is the criminal law mostly codified in English-speaking countries today?

Note that ignorance of the law is not an excuse in Italian law. Does the same rule apply in Anglo-American law? Compare, e.g., New York Penal Law §15.20.

2. Italian criminal law distinguishes between crimes and infractions. Does this duality exist in the French law? Compare also the Spanish law. How does it compare with the traditional division into felonies, misdemeanors and infractions in Anglo-American law? *See*, e.g., New York Penal Law, Art. 55.

The Italian division of punishments into imprisonment for life, imprisonment for a time, and fines is very logical. Compare it, e.g., with the German law. *See* also New York Penal Code, Arts. 70 and 80.

There is no death penalty in Italian law. Does the death penalty exist in the major European systems? *See, e.g., the French and Spanish law. Does it exist in the law of your state? See*, e.g., New York Penal Law §60.06; 18 U.S.C.A. §2381.

3. Note the punishments for an attempt. An attempt to commit a crime (*delitto*) is generally punishable, but an attempt to commit an infraction is punishable only if the law so provides. Compare, e.g., the Spanish law. *See also* New York Penal Law, Art. 110. Attempt is always less punishable than the completed crime. *See*, e.g., the Spanish law, and the New York Penal Law §110.05.

----

3.   Minors (*Minori*)[53]

A person who at the time of the commission of the act has not yet completed fourteen years of age is not imputable. A person who has completed fourteen years of age but has not yet completed eighteen years of age and who has the capacity to understand and to intend the act is imputable, but the punishment is reduced as provided in Article 65 of the Penal Code (life imprisonment that was formerly death is reduced to a term of imprisonment of from twenty-four to thirty years, life imprisonment is reduced to a term of from twenty to twenty-four years, and any other term is reduced up to one third). A person who has completed eighteen years of age is fully imputable.

NOTES AND QUESTIONS

Imputability commences in Italian law at age fourteen. Is fourteen years of age a universally recognized age for imputability to begin? Compare the French and the Spanish law. *See also*, e.g., New York Penal Law §30.00.

Full imputability begins at eighteen in Italian law. *See also* the German rule. What was the common law rule in Anglo-American law?· Compare also the American Law Institute's Youth Correction Authority Act, and the Federal Youth Corrections Act, 18 U.S.C.A. §5005ff.

---

4. Repeaters (*Recidiva*)[54]

A person previously convicted who commits a new breach of criminal law will have the punishment for the newly committed offense increased by up to one sixth. The punishment is increased up to one third in the following cases: The new offense is of the same type; (2) the new offense was committed within five years of the preceding conviction; and (3) the new offense was committed during or after the execution of punishment.

Where two or all three of the above-enumerated circumstances concur, the punishment may be increased up to one half. Where the offender commits yet another offense, the punishment may be increased up to one half; where he commits an offense under the circumstances indicated in numbers (1) or (2) above, the punishment may be increased up to two thirds; and where he commits an offense under the circumstances indicated in number (3) above, the punishment may be increased from one third to two thirds. In no case may the increase in punishment by the application of the provision as to repeaters exceed the total punishment resulting from convictions preceding the commission of the new offense.

A person will be declared a habitual criminal when he has been convicted of crimes (*delitti*) of the same type on three consecutive occasions within ten years to an aggregate term exceeding five years. But he may be so declared upon a third conviction for any crime (*delitto*) having regard to the nature of the crimes and the conduct of the criminal.

Persons convicted of infractions (*contravvenzioni*) on three consecutive occasions who commit a further infraction (*contravvenzione*) of the same type, may be declared habitual offenders. Persons declared habitual criminals or habitual offenders who commit another crime or infraction are declared professional criminals or professional offenders, respectively.

After suffering their punishments, persons declared habitual criminals (*delinquenti abituali*) or professional criminals (*delinquenti professionali*) are held in preventive detention. Habitual offenders (*contravventori abituali*) and professional offenders (*contraventori professionali*) will be subjected chiefly to supervision while free, and/or be prohibited from staying in certain localities.

Persons held in preventive detention are committed to a settlement of farm work (*colonia agricola*) or to a house of labor (*casa di lavoro*). The minimum term of commitment is one year. Habitual criminals (*delinquenti abituali*) are committed for a mandatory term of two years, and professional criminals (*delinquenti professionali*) for a mandatory term of three years.

Persons actually committed may not be released as long as they are regarded as dangerous. After the mandatory term of commitment indicated above has run, the. court will examine the detainee. If he is ruled not dangerous, he will be set free under supervision as the court may direct. If he is ruled dangerous, the court will remand him and will set a later date for his reexamination.

NOTES AND QUESTIONS

Italian criminal law provides a scheme of gradually increased penalties for repeaters. A criminal who works his way up to the standard of a professional criminal may be held in prison indefinitely. How does the French law deal with the matter? Compare also the German law. How does Anglo-American law deal with repeaters? *See*, e.g., New York Penal Law §§70.06, 70.10; 18 U.S.C.A. §3575.

---

5. Accomplices (*Concorso di persone nel reato*)[55]

Where two or more persons concur in bringing about a criminally punishable act, each of them is punishable with the punishment prescribed for the act. The penalty is increased when five or more persons take part in the act; the organizer or directing member incurs an increased penalty irrespective of the number of persons taking part; an organizer or directing member who commanded another person to carry out the act incurs an increased penalty; an organizer or directing member who commanded a minor below the age of eighteen, or a person of reduced mental capacity, to carry out the act incurs an increased penalty. The court may decrease the penalty in the case of a person whose part in the commission of the act was marginal, and also in the case of minors below the age of eighteen and persons of reduced mental capacity.

NOTES AND QUESTIONS

The Italian law punishes accomplices basically as principals. The punishment may be increased or decreased in accordance with the scope of participation of the particular offender in the commission of the offense. The subject may be tackled differently in the law. *See*, e.g., the Spanish law, which makes a distinction between accessories before and after the fact. *See also* the German law.

Consider the traditional English common law division into principals in the first degree, principals in the second degree, and accessories before and after the fact. The principal in the first degree is the actual offender, while the principal in the second degree aids and abets the actual offender at the very time of the commission of the offense; *see*, e.g., Breese v. The State (1861), 12 Ohio 146. An accessory before the fact is always punished more than an accessory after the fact, who generally does not have any part in the commission of the act.

Compare also New York Penal Law, Art. 20, especially §§20.00 and 20.15. *See* 18 U.S.C.A. §§2-4. How are accomplices treated in the law of your state?

---

6. Homicide (*Omicidio*)[56]

Whosoever shall bring about the death of another person will be punished with imprisonment for not less than twenty-one years. Homicide under aggravating circumstances is punishable with imprisonment for life.[57] Aggravating circumstances occur when the homicide is committed: to cover up the commission of another crime; against an ascendant or descendant under circumstances of subsections 1-4 of Article 61,[58] or by poisoning or other base means, or with premeditation; by an escapee to avoid arrest or to obtain provisions; by an accomplice to avoid arrest; or in the course of committing a rape.[59] Homicide under aggravating circumstances is punishable with imprisonment for life when committed: against an ascendant or descendant; by poisoning or by other base means; with premeditation; or under circumstances of subsections 1-4 of Article 61. The punishment is imprisonment of from twenty-four to thirty years when the act is commited on a spouse, brother or sister, an adoptive father or mother, an adopted child, or a lineal relative.[60]

7. Unintentional Homicide (*Omicidio preterintenzionale*)[61]

Whosoever with the intent to cause bodily harm, brings about the death of another person shall be punished with imprisonment of from ten to eighteen years. The term of imprisonment will be increased by one third to one half when there are aggravating circumstances as enumerated in Article 576. It will be increased up to one third when there are aggravating circumstances as enumerated in Article 577 or where the act was committed by arms or corrosives.

8. Homicide as a Consequence of Another Crime (*Morte come conseguenza di altro delitto*)[62]

Whenever death is brought about as an unintended consequence of a crime, the punishment is as in negligent homicide, but the term of imprisonment therein prescribed is increased.

9. Negligent Homicide (*Omicidio colposo*)[63]

Negligent homicide (by negligence, imprudence, inexperience, or inobservance of safety rules) is punishable by imprisonment from six months to five years. When more than one person is killed, or one is killed and another or more persons are injured as a consequence of negligence, the term of imprisonment may be increased up to twelve years.

NOTES AND QUESTIONS

Note the several types of homicide in Italian law. The subject is dealt with beginning with simple homicide, and is followed by homicide under aggravating circumstances, unintentional homicide and negligent homicide. Compare it with the French law. Do these two approaches differ from the German law?

How does the Anglo-American common law approach the subject? Is the division into murder, manslaughter and accidental death still the basis of the Anglo-American approach? *See, e.g.*, New York Penal Law, Art. 125. Note the definition of homicide *ibidem* in §125.00. Compare also 18 U.S.C.A. §1111ff.

Negligent homicide is a relatively modern concept. *See, e.g.*, R. v. Franklin

(1883), 15 Cox 163; Commonwealth v. Welansky, 316 Mass. 383, 55 N.E. 2d 902 (1944); New York Penal Law §125.10.

---

10.   Wounding and Bodily Harm
(*Lesione personale*)[64]

Bodily injury that is the cause of a disability, whether of the body or of the mind, is punishable with imprisonment of from three months to three years. The offense is punishable with imprisonment of from three to seven years where the disability extends over a period of forty days; the impairment of a sense or organ results; or, in the case of a woman, the injury brings about a premature birth. Where an incurable disability results, or where there is the loss of a sense or of an organ, mutilation, deformation, or miscarriage, the punishment is imprisonment of from six to twelve years.

NOTES AND QUESTIONS

This is bodily harm short of homicide. It has a large range from simple wounding to mutilation. *See,* e.g., the German law. How is the offense treated in the law of your state? *See,* e.g., New York Penal Law §§120.00, 120.05, 120.10; 18 U.S.C.A. §111ff. Consider the punishments threatened in the laws of the several countries.

---

11.   Theft (*Furto*)[65]

Whosoever takes from the possession of another person any movable property for his own benefit or for that of another will be punished with imprisonment of from fifteen days up to three years and with a fine. Electric energy and any other energy that has economic value is considered movable property.

The penalty is imprisonment of from one to six years and a fine where there are aggravating circumstances as follows: (1) where the offender enters a building or other premises used for habitation to commit the offense; (2) where he uses force or fraudulent means; (3) where he carries arms or narcotics without using them; (4) where the offense is committed by dexterity or by snatching from the person of the victim; (5) where the offense is committed by three or more persons, or by one person who pretends to be a public officer or an employee of a public utility; (6) where the offense is committed on the luggage of travelers in any means of transport, in stations, ports, hotels or in any place where food and drink is served; (7) where the offense is commited on property held in offices of public establishments, or applied to public service or to public use; or (8) where the offense is commited on three or more heads of animals or a flock or herd, or on cattle or horses. Where any two of the above-enumerated circumstances concur, or any one combined with any one of those enumerated in article 61,[66] the punishment is imprisonment of from three to ten years and a fine.

Theft effected by force or threats is termed robbery (*rapina*) and is punishable by imprisonment of from three to ten years and by a fine. The same applies to cases where force or threats are used by the offender to stay in possession of stolen movables or to assure himself of impunity. The punishment is increased from one third to one half where an offender using violence or threats is armed or disguised, where the offense is committed by more than one person, or where the violence consists in placing the victim in a state of incapacity to will or to act.

NOTES AND QUESTIONS

How does the Italian definition of larceny compare with that of other countries? Compare, e.g., the Spanish law. How does Anglo-American law define larceny? *See*, e.g., Bracton's definition of theft: "The fraudulent handling of another man's thing, without his agreement, and with the intention of stealing it." Lib. 3, c. 32, fo. 150b.; New York Penal Law §155.05.

Italian law especially defines electric energy and any other energy as movables subject to theft. Compare, e.g., the German law. Does the same hold good in Anglo-American law? Is a specific mention of electric or other energy necessary? *See*, e.g., Commonwealth v. Shaw, 86 Mass. 308 (1862); People v. Menagas, 367 Ill. 330, 11 N.E. 2d 403 (1937).

The Italian law then proceeds to aggravating circumstances. Compare, e.g., the French law. Does the Anglo-American law apply the same technique? *See*, e.g., New York Penal Law §§155.30-155.40.

Robbery stresses the use of force. This is so in all penal laws. *See*, e.g., New York Penal Law §160.00. The punishment also increases if there are aggravating circumstances. Compare, e.g., the Spanish law and New York Penal Law §§160.05-160.15.

---

12. Probation (*Sospensione condizionale della pena*)[67]

Whenever a person is convicted to imprisonment (*reclusione*) or to arrest (*arresto*) for a term not exceeding two years, or to a fine that has been converted into imprisonment, the court may order suspension of the sentence for five years in the case of a crime (*delitto*), and for two years in the case of an infraction (*contravvenzione*). The court may so order only where it is of the opinion that the offender will abstain from further criminal activity. The court may not grant probation to a person previously convicted of crime (*delitto*), even though he has been rehabilitated; to a habitual criminal, even though he has been convicted only for infractions (*contravvenzioni*); to a professional criminal; or to a person considered socially dangerous.

Probation may be granted only once, and it may be made conditional upon payment by the offender of damages to the victim of crime. Where the person admitted to probation does not commit a crime (*delitto*) or an infraction (*contravvenzione*) of the same type within the stipulated time, the offense is extinguished and the punishment may not be inflicted. Probation will be revoked where the person commits a crime (*delitto*) or an infraction (*contravvenzione*) of the same type or is convicted of a crime (*delitto*) previously committed to a term of imprisonment which, together with the term probated, exceeds two years. The court may revoke probation, however, even if the cumulative term does not exceed two years.

13.   Parole (*Liberazione condizionale*)[68]

A prisoner who, by his good behavior in prison, gives promise of good behavior after release may be paroled after he has served one half of his term. He must have served, however, at least thirty months, and no more than five years of his sentence may be remitted. In the case of a prisoner previously convicted, he must serve at least three fourths of his term but not less than four years. Prisoners convicted to life imprisonment are eligible for parole after having served twenty-eight years. To be eligible for parole, the prisoner must fully compensate the victim of his crime as required by law.

Parole will be revoked if the person commits a crime (*delitto*) or an infraction (*contravvenzione*) of the same type, or if he violates the conditions of parole. He must then serve all the remainder of his term and is not credited with the time that elapsed while he was free on parole. Furthermore, he cannot again be paroled. Where the person does not commit any offense as mentioned above and successfully completes the remainder of his term while free on parole, or in the case of a person convicted to life imprisonment where five years have elapsed since he was released on parole, the entire term is extinguished.

NOTES AND QUESTIONS

1. Probation is called the suspension of punishment in Italian law. The same approach is taken in French law.

Probation may not be granted to an offender who was convicted to a term exceeding two years of imprisonment. Compare the Spanish and the German law. Must the grant of probation be limited in these terms? *See,* e.g., the French law. Compare also New York Penal Law §§65.00 and 65.05. *See also* 18 U.S.C.A. §§3651 and 3652.

Probation is granted only once. How is the matter regulated in German law? How does Anglo-American law approach the matter? *See,* e.g., New York Penal Law §65.00.

What are the conditions of probation? May the reparation of the loss be required as a precondition? *See,* e.g., New York Penal Law §65.10; 18 U.S.C.A. §3651.

When will probation be revoked? Compare the German law. *See also* New York Penal Law §65.00; 18 U.S.C.A. §3653.

2. Italian law requires the offender to serve at least one half of his term before he is eligible for parole. What are the requirements in the Spanish law? Is the requirement of the service of one half of the time assessed a usual provision in penal

laws? *See,* e.g., the German law. What are the usual requirements in Anglo-American law? *See,* e.g., New York Penal Law §70.40; 18 U.S.C.A. §4205.

What is the minimum time required for a person convicted to life imprisonment to serve before he is eligible for parole? *See,* e.g., the French law. What is the rule applicable in your state? *See also* 18 U.S.C.A. §4205.

It is understood that the prisoner is paroled for good behaviour. This is a general rule of law.

As to revocation of parole, *see also* the German law; New York Penal Law §70.40; 18 U.S.C.A. §4214.

B. THE SYSTEM OF CRIMINAL COURTS

The Italian system of criminal courts comprises courts of limited jurisdiction, known as courts of the praetor (*pretore*), courts of general jurisdiction, known as penal courts (*tribunali penali*), assize courts (*corti di assise*), appellate courts known as courts of appeal (*corti di appello*), and one court of final resort, known as the Supreme Court of Cassation (*Corte Suprema di Cassazione*).

1. Praetors (*Pretori*)[69]

The *pretura* is a limited jurisdiction court staffed by a number of judges and headed by the *pretore titulare*. The court exercises limited criminal jurisdiction within its territory, namely over offenses for which imprisonment not exceeding three years and/or a fine may be imposed. The court is formed by a single judge. Appeal against his judgment must be lodged within three days from the pronouncement of the decision to the proper *tribunale*. The accused must be represented by an attorney (*procuratore*) admitted to practice in that legal district, or by an advocate (*avvocato*) admitted anywhere in Italy whenever the punishment imposed may exceed one month imprisonment. The public ministry acts as the prosecutor. Its functions are carried out by vice-praetors or officers of public security.

2. Penal Courts (*tribunali penali*)[70]

Penal courts are staffed by a number of judges and are presided over by a president. Cases are heard by panels of three judges, one of them presiding. Their jurisdiction extends to all cases beyond the jurisdiction of the *pretura* but does not extend to the specifically enumerated serious offenses reserved to the assize courts (*corti di assise*). In their appellate jurisdiction, they hear appeals against decisions of the *pretura*. No further appeal lies against these decisions. Appeal against their decisions in their original jurisdiction must be lodged within three days from pronouncement of the decision. It goes to the proper *corte di appello*. The accused must be represented by an attorney (*procuratore*) admitted to practice in that judicial district, or by an advocate (*avvocato*) admitted anywhere in Italy. The public ministry acts as the prosecutor. Its functions are carried out by the procurator of the republic (*procuratore della Repubblica*).

3.   Assize Courts (*Corti di assise*)[71]

At least one assize court (*corte di assise*) is set up in every judicial district of a court of appeal. The court has eight members, including the presiding judge who is a judge of the court of appeal. There is another judge on the panel, who is a judge of the penal court, and six lay judges (jurors), of whom at least three must be men. The court hears cases and decides them as one unit by a simple majority vote. First the jurors vote, the younger before the older, then the judge; the presiding judge votes last. In case of a tie, the opinion most favorable to the accused prevails. If there are more opinions, the votes most unfavorable to the accused are added to those less unfavorable until a tie or a majority is reached. The court hears cases of serious offenses specifically assigned to it for trial by the law. Such offenses are mainly homicide, attempted homicide, robbery and kidnapping. An appeal against a decision of the court must be lodged within three days from pronouncement of the decision; it goes to the proper assize court of appeal (*corte di assise di appello*). The accused must be represented by an advocate (*avvocato*) admitted anywhere in Italy. The public ministry, which prosecutes the case, is represented by the procurator general of the republic at the court of appeal (*procuratore generale della Repubblica preso de la corte d'appello*).

NOTES AND QUESTIONS

1. The praetor sits here as a criminal judge in the exercise of his criminal jurisdiction. He has both civil and criminal jurisdiction. The *pretura* is a limited jurisdiction court. Compare its powers with those of German *Amtsgerichte* and French police courts. To which Anglo-American courts can the praetorial courts be compared? Do they exceed the criminal jurisdiction of British petty sessions courts or American justice courts? What about the jurisdiction of the U.S. Magistrates pursuant to 18 U.S.C.A. §3401?

Note that appeals against decisions of the praetor go to the penal court. Compare this rule with the French system. Note also the provision for legal representation. Is legal representation mandatory in the limited jurisdiction courts of Spain and Germany? Must a criminal defendant be represented by an attorney in an Anglo-American limited jurisdiction court? *See,* e.g., 18 U.S.C.A. §3006A.

2. Penal courts are general jurisdiction courts; they may not hear the most serious crimes, however, which are reserved to assize courts. How does their jurisdiction compare with French correctional courts? Compare them also with Spanish courts of instruction.

Note that they have both civil and criminal jurisdiction and that they sit as criminal courts under the name of *tribunali penali*.

Are they more or less the counterpart of an Anglo-American criminal trial court of general criminal jurisdiction?

Note that legal representation is compulsory.

3. Assize courts go back in history to the assize courts of Henry II in France and England. Note the presence of lay judges, who outnumber the professional judges. This is a special criminal court; it has no counterpart in the system of civil courts.

Compare it with the French assize court. How does it compare with the German *Schwurgericht*? How does it compare with Anglo-American criminal trial courts, like, the Texas District Court, New York Supreme Court, U.S. District Court, British Supreme Court, London Central Criminal Court, or English Crown Court?

On judges, prosecutors and attorneys, consult the section on legal officers below.

---

4.   Courts of Appeal (*Corti di appello*)[72]

Appellate courts hear appeals against decisions of *tribunali*. The court is headed by a president and has several judges, known as *consiglieri* (counselors), on its staff. Appeals are heard in panels of five judges, one of whom presides. There is no appeal against decisions of the court of appeal but error, known as *ricorso per cassazione*, is available to the *Corte Suprema di Cassazione*. It must be filed within three days from pronouncement of the decision. The accused must be represented by an advocate (*avvocato*) admitted anywhere in Italy. The public ministry prosecuting the case is represented by the procurator general of the republic at the court of appeal (*procuratore generale della Repubblica preso la corte d'appello*).

5.   Assize Courts of Appeal (*Corti di assise di appello*)[73]

Assize courts of appeal are set up in every district of a court of appeal to hear appeals against decisions of the assize courts sitting in that district. The panel hearing the appeal is presided over by a judge of the *Corte Suprema di Cassazione*. There is another judge on the panel, who is a judge of the court of appeal, and six lay judges (jurors), of whom at least three must be men. Altogether the panel has eight members. The process of decision, as well as the representation of the accused and of the public ministry, is identical with that in assize courts. There is no further appeal against decisions of an assize court of appeal but error, known as *ricorso per cassazione*, is available to the *Corte Suprema di Cassazione*. It must be filed within three days from pronouncement of the decision.

6.   Supreme Court of Cassation (*Corte Suprema di Cassazione*)[74]

This is the supreme court of Italy. All that has been said on its civil-legal structure applies also to its criminal-legal structure. The accused must be represented by an advocate (*avvocato*) admitted to practice before it. The public ministry is represented by the Procurator General of the Republic at the Supreme Court of Cassation (*Procuratore Generale della Repubblica preso la Corte Suprema di Cassazione*).

NOTES AND QUESTIONS

1. Italian courts of appeal hear both civil and criminal appeals in separate

divisions. Criminal appeals come from penal courts, so that courts of appeal do not hear appeals against decisions of assize courts. Compare their functions with those of Spanish *audiencias provinciales* or German *Oberlandesgerichte*. How do Italian courts of appeal compare with English courts of appeal? Do they perform the function of an American state courts of appeal or United States Courts of Appeals?

2. Italian assize courts of appeal are purely courts of criminal appeal. They have a majority of lay judges. They are a unique feature of the Italian administration of criminal law. Do assize courts of appeal exist in France? Do appeals lie against decisions of French assize courts? Is there a counterpart to the Italian assize court of appeal in the German, Spanish and Anglo-American systems?

3. The Italian Supreme Court of Cassation hears error in both civil and criminal cases in separate sections. It is the highest Italian court. How does it compare with the French Court of Cassation? How does it compare with the Spanish Supreme Court? Is it the Italian counterpart of the English House of Lords, the U.S. Supreme Court, or a typical American state supreme court?

For Italian judges, prosecutors and attorneys, *see* the section on legal officers below.

C.   THE LAW OF CRIMINAL PROCEDURE

The Code of Criminal Procedure of 1930 is in power as of July 1, 1931, as amended.[75] The code has 672 articles presented in five books dealing with: Book 1. General provisions; Book 2. Proceedings; Book 3. Trial; Book 4. Execution; and Book 5. Relations with foreign judicial authorities.

Book 1. (General provisions) has the following titles: I. The actions; II. The court; III. The parties; and IV. The processual acts.

Book 2 (Proceedings) has the following titles: I. General provisions; II. Formal proceedings; III. Summary proceedings; and IV. Reopening of proceedings.

Book 3 (Trial) has the following titles: I. Proceedings preliminary to trial; II. The trial; and III. Trial on appeal, on a petition for cassation, on a petition for revision.

Book 4. (Execution) has the following titles: I. General provisions; II. Execution of penal judgments; III. Civil execution in criminal matters; IV. Provisions incidental to execution; and V. Execution of security measures.

Book 5 (Relations with foreign judicial authorities) has the following titles: I. General provisions; II. Letters rogatory; III. Extradition; and IV. Recognition of foreign penal judgments.

The following are topics selected from the Italian law of criminal procedure.

1.   Procedure before Praetors (*Pretori*)[76]

The procedure before the praetor is governed by the rules applicable to proceedings before penal courts (*tribunali penali*) unless otherwise provided. The procedure is simplified, however, much less formal than before the *tribunali*.

The commission of an offense is brought to the attention of the praetor by information or by a police report (*polizia giudiziaria*). Where the offender was apprehended in the commission of the offense, he already will be under arrest. The praetor compiles all the information, orders further information, if necessary from the police, and where criminal proceedings seem warranted, issues a citation. Where the person has been arrested, he must be brought before the praetor within twenty-four hours. The praetor interrogates him before he decides to issue a citation. This interrogation must take place within three days after the suspect is brought in by the police. Where the citation is issued, the arrested person may be admitted to bail.

There is no formal preliminary examination in the *pretura* and the case proceeds immediately to trial on the day and hour indicated in the citation. The hearing is before a single judge, and it is public. After the judge declares the hearing open, preliminary objections, like an objection to jurisdiction, must be made first. The judge then questions the accused, then the victim of crime, if he is not also a witness, next the witnesses, and finally the experts, if any. Witnesses and experts testify on oath. After all the proof has been offered, the final pleadings take place, First the prosecution and the victim of crime speak; then the defense speaks, both through an attorney or advocate and through the accused himself. Parties may reply to statements made by the other party but the defense always has the last word. The judge then declares the proceedings closed and gives judgment. If he finds the accused guilty, he pronounces the sentence.

An appeal against the decision of the judge must be made within three days from pronouncement of the decision to the proper *tribunale*. There is no further appeal from the decision of the *tribunale*; but error, which must also be brought within three days from the pronouncement of the decision, lies to the *Corte Suprema di Cassazione*.

NOTES AND QUESTIONS

Procedure before the *pretura* is based on the same rules and principles as that before courts of general jurisdiction. The procedure is simplified as it deals only with minor offenses. Compare the Italian procedure before the *pretura* with that in French police courts. How does the Italian procedure compare with that in English petty sessions courts or that in American justice, municipal, or county courts? *See*, e.g., Rules of Procedure for the Trial of Minor Offenses before United States Magistrates.

---

2. Procedure before Penal Courts (*Tribunali penali*)[77]

(a) Preliminary proceedings. The commission of a crime is brought to the attention of the procurator of the republic (*procuratore della Repubblica*) by information or by a police report (*polizia giudiziaria*). The police must arrest any person apprehended in the commission of crime for which the maximum punishment exceeds three years imprisonment. In all other cases, the offender is arrested only where there is a likelihood that he would try to escape prosecution. A person arrested must be brought before the procurator within twenty-four hours, and the procurator must interrogate him within three days after he is brought in. The procurator must set the suspect free where there is no ground for prosecution. Otherwise he must transfer the suspect to a judge of instruction for further proceedings.

(b)   Proceedings before the judge of instruction (*giudice instruttore*).   Proceedings before the judge of instruction are always held in cases falling within the jurisdiction of the *tribunale* and the *corte di assise,* with the exception of summary proceedings, which are held where the accused is apprehended in the commission of the act or where he confesses to committing the act.

In every court of appeal there is set up a department of judges of instruction who carry out the investigation and rule whether the suspect must stand trial. Judges of instruction are under the supervision of the procurator general at the court of appeal.

The judge of instruction to whom the case is assigned investigates the matter with the help of the police, the prosecution, and the defense. He hears the informant or person making the complaint, if any, and the victim, and he interrogates the suspect. He may appoint one or more experts in any field, for example, medical practitioners to give an opinion on the mental state of the subject. He may appoint an interpreter, order searches and the sequestration of objects important in the case, summon witnesses and hear their evidence, arrange for a line-up to see whether the victim or witnesses will identify the suspect, and confront witnesses, and so on.

When the suspect appears before the judge of instruction for the first time, the judge will request him to appoint counsel. Where he does not do so, the judge of instruction must appoint one ex officio. Any attorney (*procuratore*) admitted to practice in that judicial district, or any advocate (*avvocato*) admitted anywhere in Italy, may be appointed. The judge must give notice of at least twenty-four hours to the defense counsel and the public prosecutor of any hearings to be held. Both the prosecution and the defense must be present at such hearings. If they do not appear, however, the hearing may proceed in their absence. Both the prosecution and the defense can examine all the court files on the case.

After the judge of instruction concludes his investigation, he will decide by an order whether the suspect should stand trial or be released for lack of evidence. Where he finds, e.g., that the suspect did not commit the act, or that no such act was in fact committed, he will state so in his order as the reason the suspect should not stand trial. The order will further declare that the suspect is to be immediately set free, if he is in custody, and that the proceedings against him have been dropped. Where he finds that the suspect must stand trial, he will so declare in his order and determine the court in which the trial will take place.

The proceedings are carried out in secret so as not to compromise the suspect should he not be charged with any offense and the case be dropped.

(c)   Summary proceedings.   Where the suspect is apprehended in the commission of crime, or where he confesses to having committed it, there is no need to hold any proceedings before the judge of instruction, because it is plain that the suspect will have to stand trial. In such a case, only summary proceedings will be held before the procurator.

(d) The trial. The order of the judge of instruction, or that of the procurator in the case of summary proceedings, that the suspect must stand trial for a given offense is handed to the president of the proper *tribunale,* who after hearing the procurator, orders the case put on the calendar for trial. He issues a citation ordering the accused to appear on a given day and hour for trial. The citation must allow at least eight days between the date of its issue and the day of trial. The prosecutor and the defense counsel are similary notified, and the witnesses are summoned.

The trial is public, unless publicity is excluded for a good reason, e.g., good morals. Order in the courtroom is maintained by order of the presiding judge who questions the accused, the witnesses and the experts, if any, and generally conducts the trial. Nobody can speak without his permission. The trial court is composed of three judges.

After the presiding judge declares the trial open, preliminary questions must be discussed first, including those pertaining to the constitution of the parties, jurisdiction of the court, admissibility of evidence by witnesses, experts, effect of the nonappearance by any person summoned to appear, and admissibility of documents.

After the preliminary questions have been disposed of, the presiding judge interrogates the accused. The accused may consult freely with his counsel, but he may not consult with him before he answers any given question. Counsel may not suggest to the accused, by any means, answers to any questions. The accused must behave civilly in court; if he fails to do so, the court may remove him from the courtroom and try him in his absence.

The presiding judge then hears the victim of crime, examines the witnesses and experts on oath, and has documents pertaining to the case read in open court. All parties and the other judges may ask questions through the presiding judge of all the parties, witnesses and experts. If any question of admissibility arises, the presiding judge makes a ruling immediately.

All proof having been offered, the parties make their final statements. First the victim of crime addresses the court and makes a claim for damages. Then the prosecutor makes his request for the court to find in a certain way, e.g., to find the accused guilty and assess him the penalty of imprisonment for a fixed number of years. Both the accused and his counsel may speak, as well as the person legally responsible for the accused, if any, by himself or through his counsel. The prosecutor and all counsel may reply. In any case, the defense has the last word.

(e) Judgment. The presiding judge declares the proceedings closed and the court retires to the conference room to consider the judgment. The presiding judge makes a list of questions covering all matters of fact and law to be decided. The judges then vote on the questions. First the judge junior in rank votes, then the judge senior in rank; the presiding judge votes last. The decision is by majority vote. If the two associate judges are of equal rank, the junior with respect to his appointment to his rank votes first.

The judgment is headed "In the name of the Italian people." It gives the name of the court that pronounced it, the name and identification of the accused and of the parties, the charge, the facts, and imputations giving rise to the charge, the facts found by the court and the law on which the judgment is founded, and a detailed enumeration of the sections of the law from the Penal Code and statutes actually applied. Then follows the actual order, the date when made, and the signatures of the judges as well as that of the registrar. If the judgment is defective in any of the above points, it is void.

The order will be an acquittal where the court finds that no such act was committed or that the accused did not commit it, or that the accused is not guilty for any other reason. Where the accused is acquitted for lack of evidence against him, the judgment will so state.

Where the accused is found guilty, the judgment will impose punishment. In proper cases, the court may admit the convict to probation. The convict is also assessed the costs of the proceedings. He is also sentenced to payment of damages to the victim.

The registrar prepares a record of the proceedings, which then is signed by the presiding judge and the registrar. Failure to make the record results in nullity of the judgment.

(f)   Trial in the absence of the accused.   Where the accused does not appear at the trial and his nonappearance is due to an absolute impossibility, the court will adjourn the trial. Where the accused does not appear without a proper excuse, the trial will take place in his absence. The court will rule whether the nonappearance of the accused is excusable. Where the accused is not excused, the court will make certain that the accused was properly summoned and that all the rules of procedure have been properly observed. If so, the court will try the accuse in his absence.

(g)   Summary proceedings and judgment in cases where the accused was apprehended in the commission of a crime.   Where the accused was apprehended in the commission of a crime falling within the competence of the *tribunale*, the procurator of the republic may, after interrogating the accused present him for trial before the court within five days from his apprehension. If it is not possible, then normal proceedings will take place.

Where the accused is summarily presented for trial, the victim of crime and witnesses may be cited orally to appear at trial. All parties may also present witnesses without arranging for their proper citation.

(h)   Procedure on appeal from decisions of the *pretore*.   The procedure follows that before courts of appeal as much as possible. The appeal is lodged with the *pretore* who pronounced the judgment within three days of its pronouncement and is transmitted by him to the proper *tribunale*. The citation issued by the *tribunale* must have a minimum return date of ten days.

3.   Procedure before Assize Courts (*Corti di assise*)[78]

Procedure before assize courts is governed by the rules applicable to procedure before *tribunali penali*. The only difference is due to the composition of the court, which includes six lay judges (jurors). The six jurors (*giudici popolari*) are selected from a list made from lists of eligible persons prepared by local administrative officers. A sufficient number of potential jurors is summoned to appear at a hearing held for the only purpose of selecting the six jurors in any particular case. The hearing is presided over by the president of the assize court and the jurors are called in the presence of the prosecution and of the defense. The names are written on cards and inserted in a container from which they are drawn at random. The jury must have at least three men.[79]

NOTES AND QUESTIONS

1. Procedure before penal courts and assize courts is governed by the standard rules of the Code of Criminal Procedure.

May persons be arrested without a warrant? In Italy, the warrant of arrest is issued by the praetor or the procurator (Art. 243 C. Crim. Proc.). Compare it with the German law. What is the position in the Anglo-American law? *See,* e.g., F.R. Crim. P. Rules 4 and 5.

The procurator will set the person free if there is no ground for prosecution. Does a U.S. Magistrate have similar powers? *See,* F.R. Crim. P. Rule 5.1.

2. The main function of the judge of instruction is to determine whether the suspect should stand trial. This is the standard procedure in civil law countries. Compare the Spanish and French proceedings. *See also* the German practice for a different approach. Who decides in Anglo-American criminal proceedings whether the suspect should stand trial? In English countries there is no grand jury. It was abolished in England in 1933 by the Administration of Justice (Miscellaneous Provisions) Act, 1933, 23 & 24 Geo. V, c. 36, s. 1, and other British countries followed suit. As to the American grand jury, *see* 18 U.S.C.A. §3321ff. and F.R. Crim. P. Rules 6 and 7.

Do Italian judges of instruction perform functions other than those performed by British magistrates or American grand juries? Compare also French and Spanish proceedings before judges of instruction.

The major merit of the institution of a judge of instruction is that the investigation of the case is in the hands of an independent judge before whom the prosecution and defense appear as parties. The suspect is thus not at the mercy of the prosecution as he may well be in countries where the criminal investigation procedure does not provide for investigation by an investigating judge.

Where the investigating judge orders the suspect to stand trial for a particular offense, it must be the offense that appears from the evidence as having been committed. He may not charge him with any other offense. There is no plea bargaining. There is no contest between prosecution and defense but a fact-finding by the investigating judge. Any attempt to reduce the offense charged would seem like favoritism and the omission of prosecution in breach of Arts. 361, 378 of the Italian Penal Code.

3. The trial is conducted by the court and since it is a collegiate court, by the presiding judge. He is the moving power of the trial. He determines the order in which evidence is presented and he examines all the documents presented in evidence and the witnesses. Only after he has concluded may the parties ask questions. This approach is generally taken in all criminal trials in civil law countries. *See,* e.g., the French trial procedure.

The witnesses testify on oath (Art. 449 C. Crim. Proc.).

Note that the accused may be removed from the courtroom if he disrupts the proceedings. Compare, e.g., the German law. *See also* F.R. Crim. P. Rule 43.

Note that the accused may be tried in his absence. May trial be held against an absent accused in German law? How does the matter stand in Anglo-American law? *See*, e.g., F.R. Crim. P. Rule 43.

The accused may freely consult with his counsel during trial. This is a rule of general application.

Since the penal court is composed of only professional judges, it is a trial by the court as understood in Anglo-American law and there is no jury. May a trial without jury be held in an Anglo-American criminal court? *See*, e.g., F.R. Crim. P. Rule 23.

After all the evidence has been offered to the satisfaction of the court and the parties, the court asks the parties to make their final statements. Each party may reply to statements made by any other party. Note that the defense always has the last word. This is a fundamental principle of criminal procedure in civil law countries. *See*, e.g., the French law. Does the same rule obtain in criminal trials in Anglo-American law? *See*, e.g., F.R. Crim. P. Rule 29.1.

4. Since the Italian court is a collegiate court, voting of the judges must be held after deliberation. Compare, e.g., the French voting procedure.

The document of judgment must comply strictly with the law. *See*, e.g., the Spanish law. Lack of requirements may make the judgment void. What are the requirements for an Anglo-American judgment? *See*, e.g., F.R. Crim. P. Rule 32, and Form 25.

A record of the proceedings is continuously made; when completed, it is certified by the presiding judge and the court registrar. Compare, e.g., the Spanish requirements. How are records of proceedings kept in Anglo-American trials? *See*, e.g., F.R. Crim. P. Rule 55.

5. Procedure at trial in assize courts is identical with that in penal courts except for the presence of lay judges on the bench. Consequently, the lay judges must be selected in accordance with the process generally used in judicial systems for the selection of jurors. *See* the section on assize courts above. Note that they vote before the professional judges so as not to be influenced by them. Compare the voting procedure before French assize courts.

Italian lay judges then are not jurors in the Anglo-American sense. Do they actually have more influence on the outcome of the case than an Anglo-American jury? What are the respective powers of the judge and the jury? *See*, e.g., F.R. Crim. P. Rules 29, 30 and 31. Note that the decision of the court is by simple majority and that Italian lay judges may outvote the professional judges. No unanimity of verdict is required. Compare, e.g., the French procedure.

---

4. Procedure before Courts of Appeal
(*Corti di appello*)[80]

Procedure before courts of appeal follows the rules applied in trial courts as far as applicable. The same applies to appellate procedure before the *tribunale*.

Appeals against decisions of the *tribunale* must be lodged with the *tribunale* within three days from their pronouncement. As soon as the record of the case is transmitted by the *tribunale* to the proper court of appeal, the registrar of that court hands it over for examination to the public ministry. When the papers are returned, the president of the court of appeal sets a date for the hearing. A proper citation to the parties is issued. The return date must be at least fifteen days after service.

At the hearing, first the rapporteur, who may be the presiding judge, gives his report, which is limited to matters dealing with the appeal. The accused then is interrogated by the presiding judge. Then counsel for the victim of crime takes the floor and is followed by the public prosecutor. Thereafter the defense presents its case. The prosecution may reply but the defense must always have the last word. No witnesses or experts appear at the hearing.

If it appears to the court that no decision can be made on the strength of the evidence presented and the record of the case in the trial court, it may reopen the proceedings. It may summon the witnesses and experts who gave evidence in the trial court, may order new evidence and proof to be presented, and in case of need, may order a new expertise. The new proceedings follow the rules prescribed for trial courts.

A record of the proceedings is kept in accordance with the rules applicable to trial courts.

After the court has declared the proceedings closed, it retires to consider judgment. Where the proceedings in the court below are declared null and void on the ground of judicial incapacity, lack of a quorum, or absence of the prosecution or defense in proceedings where such presence is obligatory, the matter is remanded to the trial court for a new trial. Where the proceedings in the court below are annulled on any other ground, the appellate court will consider the merits of the case and give judgment. The same occurs where the trial court erroneously held that the statute of limitation had run or that the prosecution was not maintainable.

Where no nullity is found, the court of appeal gives a judgment that affirms or reforms the judgment appealed from. Where the accused is acquitted, he is immediately set free. A copy of the judgment is sent to the trial court immediately after the time (three days) for filing a petition for the cassation of the judgment of the court of appeal has run without any such petition being filed.

5. Procedure before Assize Courts of Appeal (*Corti di assise di appello*)[81]

Procedure before assize courts of appeal follows the rules applicable in courts of appeal and includes also those applicable in assize courts.

NOTES AND QUESTIONS

Note that the Italian rules of appellate procedure apply on appeal from the *pretura* to penal courts, from penal courts to courts of appeal, and from assize courts to assize courts of appeal. They are rules of universal application in appellate procedure. Compare, e.g., the German rules. Does the same rule apply in Anglo-American criminal procedure? *See*, e.g., the Federal Rules of Appellate Procedure.

Grounds for appeal may be grounds for error. Appellate courts hear both appeal and error from trial courts. Only when error is alleged to have occurred in proceedings before a court of appeal or an assize court of appeal does the error go to the Supreme Court of Cassation since there is no other court superimposed over these two appellate courts.

Compare the Italian appellate procedure with that of France.

Note that the court first attempts to proceed on the strength of the evidence given in the trial court. Only if it feels that there is not enough evidence for a decision will it reopen the proceedings and in fact try the case *de novo*.

Where the court of appeal hears a case on grounds of appeal as distinguished from those of error, it will always give a new judgment without any remittance. The case is remitted only for specifically enumerated reasons in the law.

The appeal is always as of right. Compare appeals in German law. May appeals be taken as of right from decisions of Anglo-American trial courts of general jurisdiction? Compare the jurisdiction of English courts of appeal (criminal division). *See also* F.R. App. P., Rule 4.

---

6. Procedure before the Supreme Court of Cassation (*Corte Suprema di Cassazione*)[82]

(a) On a petition for the annulment of a judgment (*Ricorso per cassazione*). A petition for the annulment of a judgment (*ricorso per cassazione*) must be filed within three days from the pronouncement of the judgment with the court that pronounced it. The registrar of that court will transmit the record without delay to the registrar of the Supreme Court of Cassation, who will present it to the first president of the Court. The first president will assign the case to a particular section, or to two combined sections where required by law.[83]

The *ricorso* may be brought by both the accused and the prosecution against both a conviction or an acquittal. It may be brought only against a certain feature or provision of the judgment and its filing does not have any suspensive effect.

Grounds for the *ricorso* are: (1) inobservance or erroneous application of law; (2) exercise by the court of legislative or administrative powers; and (3) inobservance of rules provided for in the Code of Criminal Procedure where, by provision of the Code, such inobservance results in nullity, inadmissibility or lapse of time. The petition must be signed by an advocate (*avvocato*) admitted to practice before the Supreme Court of Cassation. Parties before the Court must be represented by such advocates.

As soon as the record of the case arrives at the office of the registrar, he will advise the counsel for the defense that he may examine the papers and make copies therefrom within fifteen days from such notification.

The Court will decide in chambers on the petition without a hearing where the petition is inadmissible because it is based on grounds other than provided for by the law, or where it is manifestly unfounded. It will also so decide on conflicts of jurisdiction, change of venue and recusation of a judge.

In all other cases, the Court will set a day for a hearing and appoint a rapporteur to study the case. After the fifteen days during which the record is at the disposal of the defense counsel has run, the registrar will transmit the record to the procurator general, who must return it at least five days before the day set for the hearing. The registrar will also notify all parties of the day set for the hearing. Notice must be given to the defense at least fifteen days before the hearing.

All rules applicable to proceedings in trial courts and appellate courts apply to proceedings before the Supreme Court of Cassation as far as applicable. The parties may file their briefs at the latest eight days before the hearing.

At the hearing, first the rapporteur, who may be the presiding justice or another justice appointed by the presiding justice, gives his report. then counsel for the victim of crime takes the floor, and then the public ministry makes its request as to how the case should be decided. After that, the defense counsel has his word. There is no right of reply.

The Court then deliberates in private. It may uphold the judgment attacked by the *ricorso* and dismiss the petition. It may annul the judgment partially or *in toto* and either declare the proceedings terminated or remit the case for further proceedings to a lower court. Errors found in the proceedings and the judgment do not produce an annulment if they have not materially influenced the judgment.

The judgment is annulled without any further remission where the act is not punishable by law, where the act is beyond the jurisdiction of criminal courts, where the lower court exceeded its powers, where the judgment is contrary to law, where there is an error in the person of the accused, where the accused was already convicted in previous proceedings for having committed the act (*autrefois* convict, *autrefois* acquit), and also in any case where the court can dispose of the matter without remission. In all other cases, the matter is remitted to a lower court for further proceedings.

Where an interim order of a lower court is set aside, the matter is remitted to the court that pronounced it for further proceedings.

Where a judgment of an assize court of appeal is annulled, the case is remitted to another neighboring assize court of appeal. Where a judgment of a court of appeal is annulled, the case is remitted either to another section of that court of appeal or to a neighboring court of appeal. Where a judgment of an assize court is annulled, the matter is remitted to another assize court within the district of the same court of appeal. Where a judgment of a penal court is annulled, the matter is remitted either to another section of that penal court or to a different penal court within the district of the same court of appeal. Where a judgment of a praetor is annulled, the matter is remitted to another praetor within the same judicial district.

Where a disposition of an instructing judge is annulled, the matter is remitted to the same court but another instructing judge will be appointed to handle the case.

The court to which the matter is remitted is bound by the decision of the Supreme Court of Cassation in that matter. The decisions of the Supreme Court of Cassation are not subject to any further attack.

(b) On a petition for the revision of a conviction (*Revisione*).   Revision of a conviction may be had without any time limit after the time for an appeal or for cassation has run and the conviction thus has entered in the power of law. It may be had even after the convict has fully suffered his punishment. Any conviction for a crime (*delitto*), or for an infraction (*contravvenzione*), is subject to revision.

The petition is made on the following grounds: (1) The facts on which the conviction is founded cannot be reconciled with those which support another conviction that has entered into the power of law; (2) the conviction is based on a prior decision of a civil or administrative court, and that decision was subsequently revoked; (3) new facts became known or new proof became available to the effect that no criminally punishable act was committed or that the convicted person did not commit it, or that he was not imputable; (4) the conviction was obtained by fraud; and (5) in the case of a conviction for homicide, new facts are discovered that make it doubtful the alleged victim died.

Revision may be requested by the convicted person, by his next of kin, or by his guardian. Where the convict has died, it may be requested by his heirs or next of kin. It may be requested by the procurator general at the court of appeal within the jurisdiction of which the conviction was pronounced or the procurator general at the Supreme Court of Cassation, in both cases ex officio in the exercise of their official duties. Revision also may be requested by the Minister of Justice.

The petition may be filed by the petitioner in person or by an advocate (*avvocato*) admitted to practice in the Supreme Court of Cassation. The procedure used follows the rules prescribed for proceedings before the Supreme Court of Cassation.

Where the convict is in prison, the Court may admit him to bail. The Court may either dismiss the petition or annul the conviction without remission, or it may annul the conviction and remit the case for further proceedings. Remission is made to another court of the same rank as the one that pronounced the conviction, and where the conviction was affirmed on appeal, to another court of appeal or assize court of appeal, as the case may be.

Where the matter was remitted for further proceedings, the court to which the case is remitted may either affirm the conviction or set it aside on the grounds for revision referred to above. The decision is subject to a petition for its cassation (*ricorso per cassazione*).

Where the conviction is set aside, the convict is entitled to the refund of all monies he paid in consequence of the conviction (such as court costs and prison costs), as well as to the payment of damages commensurate with the time served in prison. Where the convict has died, his next of kin is entitled to the money. The money is paid in a lump sum or by installments as a pension for life.

NOTES AND QUESTIONS

1. As to petitions for the cassation of judgments, such petitions may be brought on grounds specifically enumerated in the law against decisions of any criminal court. Usually, however, errors committed by trial courts will be corrected on appeal and no petition for cassation is necessary. Compare the French rule on the matter. The petition is brought as of right. Compare, e.g., the Spanish rule. *See also* 28 U.S.C.A. §§1254, 2101ff. as to the United States Supreme Court; New York Criminal Procedure Law §450ff. as to the New York Court of Appeals.

The Italian Supreme Court of Cassation disposes of the case without remission only in specifically enumerated cases, otherwise it will set the judgment aside and remit the case for further proceedings to a lower court. Compare this practice with that in the Spanish Supreme Court. What is the practice in Anglo-American criminal courts of final resort? *See*, e.g., 28 U.S.C.A. §2106.

Note that at the hearing the defense always has the last word.

2. As to petitions for the revision of a conviction, this is the criminal counterpart to the reopening of judgments given in civil cases. In criminal cases, the petition must be brought to the Supreme Court of Cassation. Compare the grounds for revision in the Spanish and the French law.

Within what time period must the petition be made? Is there any time limit? Compare, e.g., the Spanish procedure. Does the same rule apply in Anglo-American criminal procedure? *See,* e.g., F.R. Crim. P. Rule 33.

May the petition be brought even after the convict has died? *See,* e.g., the German procedure.

---

7.   Bail (*Libertà provisoria*)[84]

Bail is not normally obtainable when the accused is charged with a crime (*delitto*) for which the minimum penalty is imprisonment for five years, or when he is charged with trafficking in or possession of narcotics or with counterfeiting of currency irrespective of penalty. But even in those cases, he may be admitted to bail. Bail is purely discretionary and is granted only when the suspect or accused gives sufficient proof that he will appear when required. If he is unsuccessful in doing so, he cannot be admitted to bail.

Bail may be granted at any time during the proceedings. It will usually be granted by the *pretore* or by the *giudice instruttore,* but it may also be granted by the public ministry. Bail may be granted without any security, but usually the person proceeded against is required to deposit with the court a sum of money determined by the authority granting bail. He may also be required to give sureties, who promise to pay a given sum if the person proceeded against does not appear when required. Bail may be revoked by the court when the person proceeded against is in breach of the conditions thereof and the amount forfeited. When the person proceeded against complies with all the conditions, the money will be refunded.

NOTES AND QUESTIONS

Bail generally may be obtained in Italian criminal proceedings, with the exception of serious offenses. It is granted by the praetor or the judge of instruction. On what conditions and by whom may bail be granted in the French law? Compare also the Spanish law.

Note that if security is required, it must come from the suspect's own property. He may not used borrowed money. No bonding companies exist. The property stands as security for the suspect's appearance and when he complies with the terms of the arrangement, the sum will be refunded. Compare, e.g., the French law.

On what conditions are suspects released on bail in Anglo-American law? *See,* e.g., 18 U.S.C.A. §3141ff., and F.R. Crim. P. Rule 46; New York Criminal Procedure Law §§500.10-530.80.

IV. THE SYSTEM AND ADMINISTRATION OF ADMINISTRATIVE LAW

A. THE SUBSTANTIVE ADMINISTRATIVE LAW

The Italian administrative law is composed of a mass of statutes. It regulates relations between the state as holder of public authority and the citizen. The areas dealt with include: the general area of public administration, i.e., communities, cities, provinces and regions and their administration; the public domain (public property); public officers; police; mail and telecommunications; public transport; highways; waterways; maritime and aerial navigation; public welfare; public health; gas and electricity; hotels; tourism; markets; printing and press; and hunting and fishing.

In many cases, the statutes pertaining to a given area of legislation have been consolidated in separate codes, like the Highway Code (*Codice della strada*), Navigation Code (*Codice della navigazione*), and Postal Code (*Codice postale e delle telecomunicazioni*). In other instances, the law scattered through many statutes has been consolidated and republished in one authoritative text, known as the *testo unico* or only text of the law. This occurs for example, in the area of water law (*testo unico acque*), hunting (*t.u. caccia*), fishing (*t.u. pesca*), public health (*t.u. delle leggi sanitarie*), public security (*t.u. di pubblica sicurezza*), direct taxation (*t.u. delle leggi sulle imposte dirette*), communal and provincial administration (*t.u. comunale e provinciale*), local financing (*t.u. per la finanza locale*), and the Council of State (*t.u. sul Consiglio di Stato*).

The following are topics selected from the Italian substantive administrative law.

1. Protection of Objects of Artistic and Historical Interest[85]

The present law encompasses both immovables and movables of artistic, historical, archeological and etnographic interest, including objects of interest to paleontology, prehistory, primitive civilizations, and numismatics. Such objects as manuscripts, autographs, correspondence, rare books, prints and engravings are included as well as residences, parks and gardens of artistic or historical interest.

A register of all such objects is kept in the ministry of public instruction, which is charged with their supervision and protection. Such objects may not be demolished, removed, modified or restored without the authorization of the Minister of Public Instruction. They may not be applied to purposes incompatible with their historical or artistic character or to purposes prejudicial to their conservation. The Minister may order all necessary work for their conservation; in the case of movables, he may order their removal to public institutions. The expense of such conservatory work will be borne by the owners, but if they cannot sustain it, it will be paid by the state. In such cases, the Minister may order the acquisition of the object by the state for a reasonable price paid to the owners. In the case of immovables, any orders made by the Minister will be entered in the records of immovables.

All such objects are inalienable. However, the Minister, after hearing from the Council on Antiquity and Arts, may authorize their alienation from the state or public institutions if the alienation produces no adverse effect on their conservation, and if they are not withdrawn from the public view. The Minister may authorize the alienation of objects publicly owned that are of no interest to the state and public institutions. After hearing from the Council on Antiquity and Arts, he may authorized an exchange of such objects for others belonging to institutions, private persons, and even foreign nationals. such objects owned by private institutions and persons may be alienated with the authorization of the Minister. After hearing from the Council on Antiquity and Arts, he may refuse the authorization where it would result in a loss to the country or would withdraw the object from public view. These rules apply also to transactions other than alienation where alienation may ultimately result, like mortgaging such objects.

Private owners of such objects must obtain authorization of the Minister to any alienation thereof. Where such objects descend by inheritance, the acquiring heir must notify the Minister. Whenever the owner desires to sell such objects, the Minister has a preemptive right and may acquire such objects for the price agreed upon by the buyer. Where several items are sold together for one price, the Minister may determine the price ex officio. Where such price is not accepted by the seller, it will finally be determined by a committee of three members, one of whom is appointed by the Minister, another by the seller, and the third by the president of the *tribunale* (court of general jurisdiction). The Minister must exercise the right of preemption within two months. If so, the objects become the property of the state.

The export of all such objects is prohibited. The Minister, after hearing from the Council on Antiquity and Arts, may grant a permit for their exportation. The application for the permit must indicate the value of the object; if the permit is granted, a progressive tax of from 5 percent up to 30 percent of its value will be imposed in accordance with the value indicated, or with the value determined by the Minister. Where there is disagreement as to the value, it will be finally determined by a committee of three members, one of whom is appointed by the Minister, another by the applicant, and the third by the president of the *tribunale*. The Minister has, however, a preemptive right and may acquire the object for the state for the stipulated price. These rules apply even to an application for a permit for temporary exportation, and an amount equal to the tax imposed in case of permanent exportation is held pending reimportation of the object. The Minister may, however, in agreement with the Minister of Finance, grant a permit for the temporary export free of tax to expositions of art abroad or to Italian diplomatic and consular missions.

The Minister of Public Instruction has the authority to conduct excavations and works for the purpose of discovering objects of artistic and historical interest. He may authorize officers to enter private property, and he must indemnify the owner in case any damage is done. The discovered objects are state property, but the Minister must pay indemnity therefor, which in no case may exceed one fourth of the value of the objects discovered. In case of disagreement as to value, it is finally determined by a committee of three members, one of whom is appointed by the Minister, another by the owner of the land, and the third by the president of the *tribunale*. The Minister may leave the discovered items to the owner of the land, however, if they are not of sufficient interest to the state.

The Minister may also grant a license to public or private entities to conduct work for the purpose of discovering objects of artistic and historical interest. In such case, the licensee is entitled to equal indemnity with the owner of land, i.e., up to one fourth of the value of the objects discovered, under the same rules.

Any owner of land who wishes to conduct work for such purposes must obtain a permit from the Minister. The objects found belong to the state under the same conditions as above, except that the indemnity due to the owner may reach up to one half of their value.

Where a person accidentally finds such objects, he must immediately notify the proper authorities. Immovables are left in place and movables taken into custody, if convenient. All objects found must be properly protected, and the finder may ask the assistance of law enforcement officers. Expenses incurred by the finder will be paid by the Minister of Public Instruction. The objects belong to the state. The finder is entitled to an indemnity of up to one fourth of the value of the objects, and an equal indemnity is due to the owner of the land where the objects were found. The value of the objects will be assessed in accordance with the rules stated above.

The Minister of Public Instruction may order the expropriation of all objects of artistic and historical interest from private ownership and transfer their ownership to the state, the provinces or communities, wherever their conservation or public interest is best served.

Any breach of the provisions of the statute is punishable with fines and imprisonment.

NOTES AND QUESTIONS

Italy, as a country holding innumerable treasures of art, enacted a comprehensive statute dealing with the protection of objects of artistic and historical interest. The public authority charged with the execution of the statute is the ministry of public instruction. Note that the statute deals with all facets of interest, from the excavation and discovery of artistic and historical objects to their safekeeping and preservation.

Most countries have similar statutes for the protection of their national heritage. Compare the statutes of your own state and regulations of your own city. *See also*, e.g., 40 U.S.C.A. §§461 (i), 304a-2, 304-b.

The Italian Minister of Public Instruction relies on the advice of the Council on Antiquity and Arts in the exercise of his functions. Compare, e.g., the functions of the Commission of Fine Arts in the District of Columbia created by 40 U.S.C.A. §104. *See also* 40 U.S.C.A. §72ff. concerning the Commission.

---

2. Civil Employees of the State[86]

The employee must carry out his functions in accordance with the law, to the best of his ability, and in furtherance of the interest of public administration in the general welfare. He must observe provisions of the constitution and those of other statutes and may not engage in activities incompatible with his duties. He must work in cooperation with his superiors and colleagues, and give guidance and example to his subordinates. In his relations with the public, he must conduct himself so as to merit the confidence of the public and to promote happy relations between the public and the administration.

In his official capacity, he must attend to business as it comes, in chronological order, unless there are compelling reasons to the contrary. In his private life, he must conduct himself in accordance with the dignity bestowed on him by his public office. He is bound to keep official secrets and not to divulge matters that may be harmful to the administration or third parties.

The employee must carry out orders given to him by his superior concerning the exercise of his functions. Whenever difficulties arise in connection with such orders, he must make suggestions for the removal of the difficulties to his immediate superior to be forwarded to the hierarchically proper superior. All other communications of the employee to his superiors must be forwarded in the hierarchical order. The employee has the right, however, to present to his immediate superior a sealed envelope containing a communication of particular importance in connection with his official functions to be forwarded to the appropriate minister. Such communications must be forwarded to the minister without delay.

Where the employee is given an order by his superior and he considers such order to be patently illegal, he must protest the order to that superior and give his reasons. Where the order is given to him again in writing, the employee must carry it out. But in no case may he carry out an order that is prohibited by criminal law.

The employee must pay compensation to the state for damage or loss caused to it by breach of his official duties. The Court of Accounts (*Corte dei Conti*) has jurisdiction in these matters. All heads of office who become aware of such damage or loss must report it to the procurator general of the Court of Accounts for further action. Where the employee is bound to carry out the order complained of, he is free of liability, and the superior who gave him the order is liable.

An employee who causes an unjust damage to a third party must make it good. The state is also liable for the acts of the employee and is subrogated to any successful claim against an employee that it had to satisfy. To amount to an unjust damage, the employee must act intentionally or with gross negligence (*per dolo o per colpa grave*). The act by which the employee causes the damage may consist of an omission or an unjustified delay. Where the damage is caused by a collegiate body, all members who participated in the act are jointly and severally liable. Those who dissented, however, are not liable. The employee may be represented by the office of the government counsel (*avvocatura dello stato*). The employee is free of liability if he acted in self-defense or in defense of others.

NOTES AND QUESTIONS

The *testo unico,* or only text, on civil employees of the state contains detailed provisions concerning public servants. The above are excerpts dealing with their performance and their responsibility. Compare these provisions with statutes providing for public servants in your state. Do they contain similar provisions? As to federal civil employees, compare 5 U.S.C.A. Part III.

---

3. Care of Roads and Public Thoroughfares[87]

The statute prohibits any acts that may damage roads and appurtenant structures, including the green strip containing plants, directional indicators and signs. It is prohibited to impede the free flow of water in ditches along the roads and from the roads to lower lying land. It is also prohibited to graze cattle on the shoulders of roads or to water them at lateral canals or ditches. It is prohibited to excavate on adjoining land within a distance of three meters from the outer limits of any road, as well as to construct any building or structure within the same distance so long as the properly applicable building regulations do not stipulate a larger distance within which one may not build. Trees may not be planted within three meters from the outer limits of any road, hedges not taller than one meter within one-half meter, and taller hedges within two and a half meters. The proper authorities may in particular instances prohibit any construction, trees or hedges within a distance of one hundred meters from the outer limits of any road for reasons of good visibility and traffic safety. Any breach of these rules is punishable with fines, and an order for the removal of the structure or obstruction will be issued.

It is prohibited to make any road repairs without a license obtained from the proper highway authority. All those holding a license to run railroads, lay electric and telephonic cables, conduct water and gas along roads, must obey the rules applicable to roads. The irrigation of land adjoining roads must avoid any damage to roads. The owners of adjoining land are bound to trim hedges and prune branches of trees projecting over the roads. All walls and structures adjoining roads must be kept in good condition. The proper highway authority may order their owners to carry out all necessary repairs. Failing such repairs, the authority may order the structure demolished at the owner's expense. Should branches of trees or the trees themselves, or any stone, brick or other material fall on the highway due to bad weather or any case whatsoever, the owners thereof must remove such obstacles without delay. Should an owner fail to do so, the work will be undertaken by the highway authority at the owner's expense. Any activity that may adversely affect the roads and safety of their users may not be carried out within a minimum distance off roads to be determined by the proper authorities. Such activities include factories, shooting ranges, storage of explosives, and so on. Violations of all the above rules are punished by fines.

NOTES

This is an excerpt from the Italian traffic law which provides for the care of roads. The traffic law is consolidated in the Highway Code (*Codice della Strada*), the *testo unico* of June 16, 1959, No. 393, as amended, and highway regulations. It deals with all aspects of road traffic. Compare, e.g., the New York Highway Law, or the highway law of your state.

Note that the law quoted in the excerpt is concerned with the removal of obstructions and the promotion of good visibility. *See also* the provisions concerning federal highways, 23 U.S.C.A. §§131, 152, 153, 302.

----

4.   The System of Taxation (*Sistema delle imposte*)[88]

The state levies four direct taxes and a number of indirect taxes. The direct taxes are the IRPF, the IRPG, the ILOR, and the INVIM. The indirect taxes are the IVA and other taxes.

(a)   IRPF (*Imposta sul reditto delle persone fisiche*).[89]   This is a tax on the income of individuals. All residents are subject to the tax, and nonresidents only with respect to income derived in Italy. There are five types of income: income from land (*redditi fondiari*); income from capital (*redditi di capitale*); income from labor (*redditi di lavoro*), which is subdivided into income from dependent labor performed under the direction of others (*lavoro dipendente*) and income from independent labor performed by professional people (*lavoro autonomo*); income from activity of self-employed persons (*redditi d'impresa*); and income from diverse activity (*redditi diversi*). Each group has its own deductions in addition to an overall personal exemption for the taxpayer, his spouse and children. The total net income is arrived at by adding up the net income in the five groups. The tax is then a percentage rising progressively from 10 to 72 percent.

(b)   IRPG (*Imposta sul reddito delle persone giuridiche*).[90]   This is a tax on the income of legal persons (corporations). All resident corporations are subject to the tax, and nonresident ones only with respect to income derived in Italy. The net income is determined from the profit and loss account of the corporation. The tax is imposed at a fixed rate of 25 percent. Financial institutions are taxed at 7.5 percent and corporations in which the state holds over one-half interest at 6.25 percent.

(c)   ILOR (*Imposta locale sui redditi*).[91]   This is the local income tax. It is imposed automatically and at a fixed rate on incomes already determined by the IRPF and the IRPG. Only some of the income of the IRPF is subject to the ILOR. Thus, the income from dependent labor (*lavoro dipendente*) is exempt, and the income from agriculture (*reddito agrario*), that is a part of the income from land (*reddito fondiario*), as well as the income of self-employed persons (*reddito d'impressa*), is subject to the ILOR only as to 50 percent of the income. The ILOR is a state tax, but it is levied for the benefit of local administration. It is paid directly to the local administration by the state tax collection agencies. The rates levied range from 6 to 8.5 percent for municipalities, from 1.5 to 2.5 percent for provinces, from 1 to 2 percent for regions, from 0.4 to 1.2 percent for chambers of commerce (*camere di commerzio*), and 0.5 percent for the *aziende di cura*. The actual rates within these limits are determined annually by the municipalities, provinces and regions as to the taxes levied within their respective territories, and by the ministry of industry for the chambers of commerce.

(d) INVIM (*Imposta comunale sull'incremento di valore degli immobili*).[92] This is known as the municipal tax on the increased value of immovables. It is a state tax, but it is levied for the benefit of municipalities. It is levied at the time of the transfer of immovables whether by sale, exchange, gift or inheritance. Companies holding immovables as a business (*società immobiliari*) must pay the tax with respect to immovables held for ten years and at intervals of ten years thereafter.

The tax is progressive, ranging from 3 to 5 percent where the increase over the original value is below 10 percent, to 25-30 percent where the increase over the original value exceeds 200 percent. The actual rates are determined annually by the municipalities within these indicated limits. The tax falls on the transferor where the immovable is transferred for value and on the transferee in other cases. The tax is reduced by 75 percent in cases of transfers of immovables of artistic or historical value. Gratuitous transfers to the state and other public entities are exempt.

(e) IVA (*Imposta sul valore aggiunto*).[93]   This is a value added tax. It is levied on the transfer of title to movable and immovable property and on the performance of services in the course of business, on the performance of services to business establishments in the exercise of the arts and the professions, and on imports undertaken by anyone. The tax is collected by the seller who must prepare an invoice for every transfer subject to the tax. It is paid monthly to the tax collection office together with a statement giving all of the details of the transactions and the taxes levied. The normal rate of tax is 12 percent, with a rate of 6 percent imposed on necessities, and 18 percent on luxury goods and services. The rate on the import and sale of food is 3 percent.

(f) Other indirect taxes.   They are chiefly the following: taxes on inheritances and gifts (*imposta sulle successioni e donazioni*); the registration tax (*imposta di registro*), imposed on all documents that have to be registered; the *imposta ipotecaria*, imposed on all transactions in the register of immovables; and the stamp tax (*imposta di bollo*), imposed on documents indicated in the stamp tax law. They are mainly documents executed by the public administration. There also are customs duties (*tributi doganali*).

NOTES AND QUESTIONS

1. Note the five different groups of personal income tax. A person may have separate income of two or more different types, like income from land, from capital and from labor. These incomes are treated separately for deductions; the net income is then added and is subject to tax after deducting the personal exemptions. Compare it with the United State income tax on individuals; *see* 26 U.S.C.A. §1ff.

2. Note the Italian corporation tax. Compare it with the American corporation income tax in the Internal Revenue Code 26 U.S.C.A. §11.

3. The local income tax is comparable to the state income tax in the several

states of the United States. Under the Italian system, the proceeds are shared by local entities from regions to municipalities. How does the Italian local income tax compare with the American state income tax? *See,* e.g., the New York Personal Income Tax.

4. Italian municipalities derive the proceeds of the tax on the transfer of immovables. It is a type of a local land tax. How does it compare with an American land tax? *See,* e.g., New York Real Property Tax Law §400ff. How does it compare with local American county taxes?

5. The value added tax is a tax introduced in European Common Market countries. It replaced the different sales taxes in existence in those countries. How does it compare with the sales taxes imposed in the various American states?

6. The Italian inheritance and gift tax is of considerable importance. Compare it with, e.g., the New York Estate Tax and the New York Gift Tax. Do the other above-mentioned Italian taxes have counterparts in the system of your state? Note that there are no school taxes in Italy and the same holds true for other civil law countries. Schools are financed by the state from the general budget (income from all sources). Since school attendance up to a certain age (usually fourteen or sixteen) is compulsory, every taxpayer must contribute.

B. THE SYSTEM OF ADMINISTRATIVE AUTHORITIES (OFFICES AND COURTS)

Administrative authorities are local (communities and cities), intermediate (provinces and regions), and central (the highest offices of public administration, like ministries and the presidency). Administrative courts are of two levels: the administrative tribunals at the lower level and the Council of State at the final level. In addition, there are several administrative courts exercising jurisdiction over matters specially conferred on them by statute.

1. Local Administration

Communities and cities (*comuni*) are governed by the *testo unico* or only text of communal and provincial law.[94] It regulates all aspects of communal activity. The authorities of municipal administration are the assembly (*consiglio*), and the council (*giunta*), and the mayor (*sindaco*).

The assembly is elected for a term of five years by all citizens eligible to vote in national elections. In communities below 3,000 inhabitants, 15 assemblymen are elected. The number increases with the number of inhabitants to a maximum of 80 assemblymen in cities over 500,000 inhabitants. The assembly is the legislative-deliberative body of the community.

A newly elected assembly first elects the mayor from among its members and immediately thereafter proceeds to the election of the council. The vote is by secret ballot. The number of councilmen is determined by the size of the community, and ranges from two to fourteen, with two to four alternates. Councilmen are elected for the term of the assembly (five years) from among the newly elected assembly members by an overall majority of votes. The quorum is two thirds of the assembly. If the required number of councilmen is not elected in two ballots, a third ballot is held. Only those candidates, up to twice the number of the seats to be filled, who have on the second ballot obtained most votes are eligible. In case of parity, the older ones are elected. The council is the executive body of the community.

The mayor is elected for the term of the assembly (five years) in the first session of the newly elected assembly before the election of the councilmen. Unlike the assembly, the mayor and the councilmen remain in office even after their terms expire until successors are appointed. Should a vacancy occur during term, e.g., by death or resignation, a supplementary election is held to fill it. The quorum is two thirds of the assembly. The mayor is elected by an overall majority of votes. If no candidate reaches such majority in two ballots, a third ballot is held for which only the two candidates who obtained the most votes on the second ballot are eligible. If such majority is not reached, or if the election cannot be held because a quorum is lacking, a new election is held within eight days. The quorum then is one half plus one of the assembly. If no one receives an overall majority of votes, a second ballot is held; the candidate who receives the most votes is elected mayor.

The mayor is the head of municipal administration. He presides over both the assembly and the council. He delegates his powers to the councilmen to handle particular business. This is done in accordance with the subject matter, so that every councilman is in charge of a particular branch of municipal administration, and/or in accordance with the territory, so that the mayor may appoint a councilman to head the administration of a particular district. The districts of a municipality are known as *frazioni*.

The municipality has its offices and its employees. The head of the municipal offices is the municipal secretary (*segretario comunale*), who runs the city offices in accordance with the law and under the supervision of the elected officers.

The municipality has legislative powers within its sphere of competence, mainly in the area of public order and public health. The regulations (*regolamenti comunali*) deal with, e.g., buildings and building permits, supply of water, sewers, food and drink, traffic, streets, and municipal services.

To obtain the necessary funds, the municipalities levy municipal rates allowed by statutes.[95]

NOTES AND QUESTIONS

The statutory provisions as to communities comprise also cities of all sizes. Every city must have the above-mentioned three organs. Compare it with the German city organization. What are the organs of Anglo-American cities? *See*, e.g., California Government Code Annotated §34000ff.

Who may vote in municipal elections? May every resident of the community vote? *See*, e.g., Calif. Government C.A. §34051.

What are the terms of the elected officers? Compare, e.g., the French law. *See also* the rules applicable in American cities; *see*, e.g., Calif. Government C.A. §34879.

How is the mayor elected? Compare, e.g., the German law. *See also*, e.g., Calif. Government C.A. §36801. What are the functions of the mayor? Compare, e.g., the Spanish law. *See also*, e.g., Calif. Government C.A. §36802.

When are the elections usually held? Compare the French law and also Calif. General C.A. §36503.

How many city councilors are there on the city council? Compare, e.g., the French law. How many city councilors are there on the city council of your city? *See,* e.g., Calif. Government C.A. §36501.

Note that municipal elections in Italy are only a replica of national elections and that candidates represent the existing political parties and run on their behalf. The city is then governed in accordance with the law by those representatives of the parties who obtain municipal office.

The cities have city public service, i.e., a number of employees in accordance with their size. Large cities have a sizeable number of employees. *See,* e.g., the Spanish law; compare also Calif. Government C.A. §45000ff.

Cities have local legislative and regulatory powers. They issue local ordinances. *See,* e.g., the German law and Calif. Government C.A. §36900ff.

They also levy municipal rates. *See* the section on Italian taxes above. Compare Italian municipal taxes with those levied in Germany. What city rates do Anglo-American cities levy? *See* the law of your state and the municipal ordinances of your city. Compare, e.g., Calif. Government C.A. §43000ff.

---

2. Intermediate Administration

(a) Provinces *(Provincie).*[96] The province can be viewed from two viewpoints: as a territorial division of state administration and as a unit of local autonomy. In the second capacity, the province is far less important than a community, which enjoys considerable local autonomy. It can be said that the province is principally state oriented. Its territory is determined by statute and it is headed by a prefect *(prefetto)* who is a state officer appointed by a decree of the President of the Republic on the proposal of the Minister of the Interior after consideration of the appointment in the council of ministers. The prefect is thus the head of state administration in the province. His direct superior is the Minister of the Interior and, further, all the other ministers in matters of their competence. He may be removed from office by decision of the council of ministers. His main function is to supervise the application of state laws and the maintenance of peace and order in the province. He is the head of the prefectoral office known as the *prefettura.* It has many divisions handling all state administration in the province. The divisions correspond, in terms of subject matter, to the central offices in Rome. There is thus a division of public health, treasury, public works, industry and trade, and so on. The *prefettura* employs considerable staff. In the exercise of his functions, the prefect is assisted by the prefectoral council *(consiglio di prefettura).* It is a consultatory body presided over by the prefect and having only another two members, who are usually the highest ranking officers of the *prefettura.*

As a unit of local autonomy, the province has the following organs: the assembly *(consiglio),* the council *(giunta),* and the president of the council *(presidente della giunta).* The method of their election and their functions correspond to those of municipal administration. The assembly has a minimum of 24 members in provinces with less than 300,000 population and a maximum of 45 members in provinces with over 1,400,000 population. The council has a minimum of 4 and a maximum of 8 members under the same terms. First the assembly is elected by universal suffrage under the rules applicable to national elections. The assembly in its first session elects from among its members the president of the council and the council members. The president of the council presides over sessions of both the assembly and the council. All are elected for terms of five years, but the councilmen and the president stay in office even after the five years have run until successors are appointed.

The assembly is the deliberative organ and the council the executive with the president of the council the head of the local autonomous organization. The areas of their competence are limited mainly to public health, public works, social services, and communal administration. Within their powers, they may suggest regulations which, if approved by the state authorities, are then promulgated by a decree of the President of the Republic. To finance their activities, they levy provincial rates.[97] In their work, they are assisted by provincial offices, headed by the secretary (*segretario della provincia*), which function along the lines of municipal offices.

(b) Regions (*Regioni*).[98]   Like the province, the region is a part of the state territory and administration as well as a unit enjoying local autonomy. The region is, however, of recent origin. The first, *Valle d'Aosta*, was created only in 1945. Regions were set up to promote regional development and decentralization of state and government authority. There are five regions enjoying special autonomy due to their particular conditions. They are: *Sicilia, Sardegna, Trentino-Alto Adige, Friuli-Venezia Giulia,* and *Valle d'Aosta*. There are another fifteen regions: *Piemonte, Lombardia, Veneto, Liguria, Emilia-Romagna, Toscana, Umbria, Marche, Lazio, Abruzzi, Molise, Campania, Puglia, Basilicata* and *Calabria*. The fundamental provisions as to the regions appear in the Constitution of the Republic. The regions are there defined as autonomous units with their own powers and functions. The areas of their competence include offices of local administration; local police; fairs and markets; public welfare and public health; public instruction; museums and libraries; city development; tourism and hotels; public transport; highways, aqueducts and public works; mineral and thermal water; caves and peat deposits; hunting; fishing; agriculture and forestry; and crafts.

The organs of the region are: the assembly (*consiglio*), the council (*giunta*), and the president of the council (*presidente della giunta*). The method of their election and their functions follow the pattern of the province. In the autonomous regions, with the exception of *Val d'Aosta*, their own regional statutes determine the matter. In ordinary regions and in *Val d'Aosta*, it is determined by a national statute.[99] In the ordinary regions and *Val d'Aosta*, the assembly has a minimum of thirty members in regions of not more than one million population and a maximum of eighty members in those over six million. First the assembly is elected by universal suffrage under the rules applicable to national elections. The assembly in its first session elects the president of the assembly from among its members by secret ballot and an absolute majority. Unlike the provincial and the communal assemblies, the regional assembly thus elects its own president, so that the president of the council is not also the president of the assembly.

Immediately after the assembly elects its president, it similarly elects the president of the council and the council members. The number of council members is determined by regional statutes, as is the majority required for their election. A vice-president of the council is elected by the assembly from among the already elected council members, is elected by the council from among the councilors, or is appointed by the president of the council from among the councilors, all in accordance with the provisions of the particular regional statutes.

The assembly is elected for a term of five years. The terms of office for the president of the council, the vice-president and other councilors are determined by the particular regional statutes. They must stay in office until replaced.

The assembly is the legislative and deliberative organ. It may legislate for the region within the area of its competence, and it may submit proposals for national legislation to the Parliament in Rome. The council is the executive organ, the regional government. The president of the council is the head of the regional administration. He promulgates regional laws and regulations and represents the region in its relations with the state government and other regions.

The state government is represented in the region by the government commissioner (*commissario del governo*). His function is to supervise the government administration within the region and to coordinate it with regional autonomous administration. He is selected, like the prefect in the provinces, from among senior officers of the ministry of the interior. He is appointed by a decree of the President of the Republic on the proposal of the Prime Minister, which is submitted after deliberation in the council of ministers and with the agreement of the Minister of the Interior. The commissioner is assisted by the staff of his office.

All regional laws enacted by the region must be submitted to the government commissioner for government approval. The commissioner refers them to the government with his recommendations, and they will be so approved if they do not exceed the competence of the region and do not clash with national interest or with those of other regions. The approval is then given by the commissioner within thirty days from submission by the president of the assembly. If no answer is received, the measure is considered approved. If the government disapproves, it will return the measure to the assembly with its reasons. If the same measure is again enacted by the assembly and submitted to the government for its approval, the government must either approve or, if there is a question of competence, submit the question to the constitutional court (*corte constituzionale*). If the government disapproves because of conflicting interests, the question is one of merit and it is submitted by the government for decision to the Parliament in Rome. The decision of either the constitutional court or of the Parliament is final. After the measure is approved, it is promulgated by the president of the council and enters into power fifteen days after its publication.

The assembly may be dissolved when it commits breaches of the constitution or serious breaches of the law, or when it does not remove the council or the president of the council after it has been requested by the government to remove them for the same reasons. It may also be dissolved when it cannot form a majority and cannot function. It is dissolved by a decree of the President of the Republic after consultation with the parliamentary committe on the regions. The decree also sets in motion the machinery for new elections to be held within three months.

The constitution also provides for the fusion of regions, for the creation of new regions, and for the detachment of a certain area from one region and its attachment to another. All such changes must be approved by majority vote in a referendum held in the area affected.

To finance their activities, the regions levy rates along the provincial pattern.[100]

The regions also exercise control over the provinces and communities within their area under the supervision of state authorities. The elected organs of the region carry out their functions with the assistance of and through the offices of regional administration.

NOTES AND QUESTIONS

Italian intermediate administration is exercised by the provinces at a lower level and by the regions at a higher level. The provinces are traditional, historically known units of public administration, while the regions are new and were set up to promote development on a larger basis than was possible on the smaller size of a province.

1. As to provinces, they are units of public administration coming from the top, i.e., from the central administration run by the government of Italy. On the other hand, they also have organs of local administration operating in their own spheres of competence. There is thus a duality of function. Compare Italian provinces with French departments and Spanish provinces. With what territorial unit in Germany can the Italian province be best compared? How would the Italian province compare with an Anglo-American county? *See*, e.g., New York County Law and the county law of your state.

The Italian province is headed by the prefect. Who heads the Spanish province? Who heads an Anglo-American county? *See*, e.g., New York County Law §150ff. The prefect and his offices are controlled by superiors in the central and regional governments, and they are also watched over by the locally elected provincial administration. Who controls county commissioners or county supervisors in American counties? What powers does an American board of supervisors hold? *See*, e.g., New York County Law §200ff.

Note that the Italian provincial assembly, council and, council president are elected under similar rules as those applicable to municipalities. Compare, e.g., the French departmental organs.

The Italian province also levies local taxes. Compare them with German local rates. As a general rule, most of the provincial income comes from governmental allotments. What is the position in an Anglo-American county? *See*, e.g., New York County Law §233ff.

2. As to regions, they promote the idea of the decentralization of public administration. Their area of competence is delimited but within it, the administration displays features of local rather than centralized administration. Note that the regional organs are elected in the same manner as those in the provinces and cities. The representatives represent political parties on the ticket of which they ran.

Note also the special autonomous provinces. They are either islands, so that they are natural units, or regions in border areas having special problems, like ethnic minorities.

Compare the Italian regions with those of France. Could they be best compared with German states? Could they be compared with American states, especially the smaller American states?

---

3. Central Administration
(*Amministrazione centrale*)

The head of state is the President of the Republic. His office stands above the government and does not form part of the executive power but is rather a power of its own. The central administration is headed by the government, which is composed of the president of the council of ministers, the council of ministers, and individual ministers. The public administration is carried out by the government through the ministries. The ministries are the highest organs of state administration in areas of their competence and are the superiors of regions, provinces and communities in the hierarchy of public administration. The decision of the government in administrative matters is final. In contested proceedings, however, there is a remedy against decisions of the offices of central administration; namely, an action brought in the proper regional administrative court (*tribunale amministrativo regionale*) with an appeal to the Council of State (*Consiglio di Stato*), which acts as the supreme court in administrative matters. Suit may be brought against decisions of regional authorities to the regional administrative courts (*tribunali amministrativi regionali*) from whose decisions an appeal lies to the Council of State. The administrative jurisdiction reaches administrative acts injurious to legitimate interests, as defined in Article 103 of the Constitution, as well as administrative acts involving some subjective rights as provided by law.[101] In controversies involving subjective rights, as defined in *L. 20 mar. 1865, n. 2248, art. 2,* legal action may be brought in courts of general jurisdiction (*tribunali*) from whose decisions appeals lie to courts of appeal (*corti di appello*).

NOTES AND QUESTIONS

Italian central administration is comparable with that of an American state and also with that of the United States federal government. Italian central administration is headed by the government, which is responsible to Parliament and must resign if it loses majority support of the representatives. Are the Italian ministries comparable to United States departments and Italian ministers to United States secretaries? Compare also the French government. The ministries are staffed by civil servants of the state, who run the offices in accordance with the law. The individual minister heading a particular ministry has only such powers as the law gives him, and they are mainly supervisory. How does the Italian central administration compare with that of Germany? How does it compare with the United States federal administration?

---

4. Regional Administrative Courts
(*Tribunali amministrativi regionali*)[102]

Regional administrative courts were set up in accordance with the provisions of Article 125 of the Constitution. The first to be set up was in *Valle d'Aosta* in 1946, under the name of the *giunta giurisdizionale amministrativa della Val d'Aosta*. It was followed by the one in Sicily in 1948, under the name of the *consiglio di giustizia amministrativa per la regione siciliana*, and then those for the other special regions. Regional administrative courts for all regions were set up only in 1971. Before they were set up, their functions were carried out at the provincial level by provincial administrative councils (*giunte provinciali amministrative*), one in every province.[103]

Regional administrative courts sit in the capital city of every region. Some of them also have a detached section (*sezione staccata*), which sits permanently in another city within the region. The regional administrative court of the Lazio region has, in addition to the detached section, also another three sections sitting in Rome.

Each regional administrative court in the ordinary regions is composed of a chief judge (*presidente*) and at least five other judges (*giudici*). The panel hearing a case has three members, including the presiding judge.

The presiding judge is a president of a section in the Council of State or a councilor of state. In regions with detached sections, the presiding judge is a president of a section in the Council of State. In the regional administrative court in the Lazio region, the presiding judge of each of the three sections in Rome is a president of a section in the Council of State.

Other judges are regional administrative judges (*magistrati amministrativi regionali*). All judges are assigned to individual posts by decree of the President of the Republic at the request of the president of the council of ministers after having heard the council of the presidency of the regional administrative courts.

Judges of regional administrative courts follow careers analogous to those in the Council of State. In both cases, they begin as referendars (*referendari*), who are appointed by public competition from among legally qualified applicants with over five years of legal experience. After six years of service, they are eligible for promotion to first referendars (*primi referendari*), who are appointed from among the referendars on merit as to two thirds and on seniority as to one third. Further promotion is to the rank of councilor (*consigliere*), who are appointed from among first referendars of at least six years' standing by decree of the President of the Republic at the request of the president of the council of ministers after deliberation in the council of ministers and after hearing the council of the presidency of the regional administrative courts.

The council of the presidency of the regional administrative courts (*consiglio di presidenza dei tribunali amministrativi regionali*) must be heard on all appointments, transfers, and other matters concerning judges. It is presided over by the president of the Council of State and has another eight members, namely the two most senior presidents of sections in the Council of State, two presidents of the regional administrative courts, and four judges thereof.

A regional administrative court hears appeals (*ricorsi*) against decisions of regional administrative authorities, further *ricorsi* against decisions of state administrative authorities and state entities having their seats within the region, and also *ricorsi* against decisions of central administrative authorities of the state and state entities of national extent with respect to acts that are limited in their effects to the region. *Ricorsi* against decisions of central administrative authorities of the state and state entities of national extent regarding acts that are national in scope must be brought to the sections of the regional administrative court of Lazio sitting in Rome, also known as the *tribunale amministrativo regionale di Roma*.

The *ricorso* must be filed within sixty days from notification of the administrative decision on the parties. An appeal (*appello*) lies to the Council of State against decisions of regional administrative courts. The appeal must be filed within sixty days from notification of the decision on the parties.

In Sicily, which enjoys special autonomy, there is even a court of appeal from decisions of the Sicilian regional administrative court, known as the *consiglio di giustizia amministrativa per la regione siciliana*. It is presided over by a president of a section of the Council of State and has another four members, namely, two councilors of state and two jurists (advocates or professors of law) designated by the regional council. It hears appeals that in other regions go to the Council of State. It may submit, however, for the decision of the plenary session of the Council of State, cases where differences of opinion have arisen between the individual sections of the Council of State and the Sicilian council of administrative justice. In that case, two judges of the Sicilian council of administrative justice sit as ad hoc members in the plenary session of the Council of State.

The administrative authority is represented by the office of the government counsel (*avvocatura dello stato*) or by a special commissioner (*commissario*) especially appointed for the particular case and selected from among the directors or inspectors general of ministries. Private parties must be represented by advocates (*avvocati*) or attorneys (*procuratori*).

NOTES AND QUESTIONS

Italian regional administrative courts are courts of general administrative jurisdiction hearing appeals against decisions of administrative authorities. After administrative review within the administrative hierarchy has been exhausted, the party may resort to an administrative court as a matter of right. The matters considered encompass every possible facet of public administration. Compare, e.g., French administrative courts.

Note the composition of the courts and the judicial staff sitting on the courts. Compare, e.g., Spanish administrative courts.

Note that an appeal to an administrative court must be filed within sixty days. Compare this, e.g., with the German rule.

Note also that parties must be represented by attorneys. Compare, e.g., the Spanish and German rules.

Do similar administrative courts exist in Anglo-American countries? Is there any appeal against the final decision of an Anglo-American administrative authority, e.g., the head of a United States Department (a United States secretary) or an English cabinet minister? If so, is it an administrative appeal or a purely judicial review in specially stipulated cases? Is there any general right to appeal in the

Anglo-American system against final decisions of the highest government administrative authorities? *See*, e.g., 5 U.S.C.A. §701ff.

---

5.   Council of State (*Consiglio di Stato*)[104]

(a)   Advisory function of the Council of State.   The Council of State is a consultative organ of the state as well as the supreme court in administrative matters. In its consultative function, it gives the government advice on any legal matter concerned with public administration. The advice is that of a disinterested body[105] and the government is not bound to follow it.[106] Its independence from the government is guaranteed by the constitution.[107]

The Council is composed of six sections, the first three are consultative and the other three are judicial. The head of the Council is its president; each section is also headed by a president and is staffed by not less than seven councilors (*consiglieri*) and by first referendars (*primi referendari*) and referendars (*referendari*). The councilors and presidents are appointed by the head of the state on the nomination of the Prime Minister after cabinet debate. One half of the councilors are chosen by a public competition open to civil, criminal and administrative judges and to first class public servants who are fully legally qualified. One quarter is taken from regional administrative councilors (*consiglieri amministrativi regionali*); the last quarter is selected freely by the government, after hearing the Council of State, from among persons well qualified in public administration. Within the last quarter, the government usually selects the highest ranking public servants, like directors general of ministries. The exact personnel composition of each section is made every year by a decree of the President of the Republic. A similar decree provides for the distribution of work among the three advisory sections for the coming year.

The advice (*parere*) is given by a single section; but if the government requests it, or by decision of the Council itself in important matters, the advice is given in a general assembly (*adunanza generale*) presided over by the president of the Council and composed of all the councilors. Decisions in sections and the general assembly are by majority vote; in case of parity, the vote of the president prevails.

(b)   Judicial function of the Council of State.   The judicial function of the Council of State is performed by sections IV, V and VI. Each section has its president and a minimum of seven councilors and a secretary. Their personnel composition is set every year by a decree of the President of the Republic. Each year at least two councilors must be transferred from one section to another. The distribution of work among the sections is made every year by the president of the Council of State with the assistance of the presidents of the three sections. A quorum in a section is seven members, and there must be seven continually present at the hearing. Decisions are made by simple majority. In the case of a tie, the vote of the presiding judge prevails.

The Council also sits in a plenary session (*adunanza plenaria*). In this case, it is presided over by the president of the Council of State and has another twelve councilor members, four from each section. The particular members are appointed every year by a decree of the President of the Republic. Matters submitted for the decision of a plenary session are matters of special importance. They are submitted by the individual sections, or at the request of the parties, or by order of the president of the Council of State. The decisions so made naturally have more force than those made by the individual sections, but they do not bind the sections in their future actions and do not constitute a binding precedent. The Sicilian council of administrative justice may submit, for the decision of the plenary session, cases where differences of opinion have arisen between the individual sections of the Council of State and the Sicilian council of administrative justice. In that case, two judges of the Sicilian council of administrative justice sit as ad hoc members in the plenary session of the Council of State.

The Council hears appeals (*appelli*) from decisions of regional administrative courts.[108] An appeal must be filed within sixty days from notification of the decision.

The government is represented by the State General Legal Counsel (*Avvocatura Generale dello Stato*) or by a special commissioner (*commissario*) especially appointed for the particular case and selected from among the directors or inspectors general of ministries.

The private party must be represented by counsel (*avvocato*) admitted to appear before the Council of State.

NOTES AND QUESTIONS

1. As to the advisory function of the Council of State, it is a most useful function by which the government can obtain independent advice that it cannot obtain from its subordinates in the offices of central administration. The emphasis is on the word "independent." Compare it with the advisory function of the Spanish Council of State. Does any such institution exist in the Anglo-American system of government? Who advises Anglo-American governments?

2. As to the judicial function of the Council of State, this is the Italian supreme court in administrative matters. It hears appeals from decisions of regional adminstrative courts. Note that the Council hears and decides the merits of the case. It is a full administrative review of the case in view of the previous decision of the regional administrative court. Compare it with the judicial functions of the French Council of State and the German *Bundesverwaltungsgericht*.

Does any such court exist in the Anglo-American system? Which courts may hear appeals against decisions of administrative authorities in the Anglo-American system? Would it be only a judicial review, as compared to an administrative review? *See*, e.g., 5 U.S.C.A. §706. Would the Italian Council of State be comparable to the U.S. Supreme Court?

Note the composition of the panel hearing a case. Compare it, e.g., with the Spanish Administrative Chambers in the Supreme Court.

---

6. Other Administrative Courts

They are the Court of Accounts (*Corte dei Conti*), water courts (*tribunali delle acque*), and several other courts, such as those to rule on indemnity due for expropriated property and professional courts set up by the several professions, like advocates and attorneys. Among these courts, the most important are those concerned with taxation.

(a) Court of Accounts (*Corte dei Conti*).[109] The Court of Accounts is an independent organ of state control exercising a neutral, disinterested function.[110] Its function is to ensure that the government and its agencies observe the law. It thus exercises full control, with the exception of the question of the constitutional validity of laws and acts of state, which is reserved to the constitutional court (*corte constituzionale*). It is a companion institution to the Council of State with similar structure, staffing, organization and procedure. It is headed by a president, has presidents of sections, and has a number of councilors, first referendars and referendars on its staff. It also has an extensive secretariat.

It has five basic sections, but many additional sections have been added ad hoc. The sections decide by a quorum of five voting members. In more important matters, the case is heard by two united sections with eleven voting members as a quorum. In addition, the Court maintains a branch office in every region.

The control exercised is preventive and successive. Preventive control is exercised by the Court by the affixing of a *visto* on the measure indicating that it conforms with the government budget. Measures which must be submitted for approval are: (1) all decrees of the President of the Republic, with the exception of political measures and those exercising sovereign prerogative; (2) all measures of individual ministries that contemplate expenditure over 2,400,000 lira or contracts over 4,800,000 lira; and (3) provisions dealing with salaries and pensions of public servants. Where the *visto* is denied by the court, the minister responsible for the measure may submit the matter before the council of ministers, which may request the court to review its decision before two united sections. The court may then either approve the measure or approve it under protest (*con riserva*), still holding it illegitimate. The government may then incur the expenditure, but it may be held responsible for the expenditure in Parliament.

Successive control is exercised by the Court over all financial matters of the state handled by the ministry of treasury (*ministero del tesoro*).

In contested proceedings (*contenzioso contabile*), the Court deals with the fiscal responsibility of adminstrators (elected officers, like ministers) and government officers. It further deals with salaries and pensions of public servants.

There is an appeal (*appello*) available against decisions of the Court to two united sections thereof. Also, on grounds of error of fact or in calculation, or appearance of new facts, a recourse to revoke the decision (*ricorso per revocazione*) may be lodged with the section that pronounced it. For lack of jurisdiction, the decision of the Court is subject to cassation in the Supreme Court of Cassation (*Corte Suprema di Cassazione*).

The government is represented in the court by the procurator general (*procuratore generale*). Private parties must be represented by counsel (*avvocati*) admitted to practice before the court.

(b) Water courts (*Tribunali delle acque*).[111] There are eight regional water courts (*tribunali regionali*) set up within the courts of appeal in *Torino, Milano,*

Venezia, Firenze, Roma, Napoli, Palermo, Cagliari. Such water courts are sections of these courts of appeal with the addition of three technical officers of the department of public works. The trial court is constituted by two magistrates and one technical officer.

These courts decide all disputes concerning the ownership or use of water and the indemnity for expropriation or damage done in the course of building waterworks. Parties may be both private citizens or government instrumentalities. Water courts have all the powers of civil courts and use the Code of Civil Procedure.

An appeal against their decisions may be lodged within thirty days to the superior court of public waters (*tribunale superiore delle acque pubbliche*) situated in Rome. This court is headed by a president and is further composed of four councilors of state, four councilors of cassation, and three technical officers from the superior council of public works (*consiglio superiore dei lavori pubblici*) situated in Rome. This court is headed by a president and is further composed of four councilors of state, four councilors of cassation, and three technical officers from the superior council of public works (*consiglio superiore dei lavori pubblici*). The actual panel hearing an appeal is composed of three councilors of cassation, one councilor of state, and one technical officer.

Decisions of the court are subject to a petition for revocation, which is filed with the court, on grounds of fraud, discovery of new facts, or error. Their decisions are also subject to a petition for cassation on grounds of lack of jurisdiction, excess of power, and violation or misapplication of law. Such petitions are filed with the Supreme Court of Cassation.

Parties appearing before water courts must be represented by advocates (*avvocati*) or attorneys (*procuratori*). In the superior court, parties must be represented by counsel (*avvocati*) admitted to appear before the court. The state, if it is a party, is represented at both levels by the office of government counsel (*avvocatura dello stato*).

(c) Tax commissions (*Commissioni tributarie*).[112] Tax commissions hear appeals from the assessment and imposition of a tax with respect to nearly all types of taxes. The most notable exception concerns customs duties (*tributi doganali*), which go on appeal to a regional administrative court.

The *commissioni tributarie* are of three levels, namely, the first, second and third levels.

(i) TAX COMMISSIONS OF THE FIRST LEVEL (*Commissioni tributarie di primo grado*). They sit in the seat of the general jurisdiction courts (*tribunali*), one in each district of the *tribunale*. Each commission may have several sections. Each section has a president, a vice-president and four members. The panel hearing a case is presided over by the president or vice-president of the section and has two other members. They decide by simple majority. The chief judge (*presidente della commissione*) must be a judge of the civil or administrative system or an intendant of finance or a deputy intendant of finance. Presiding judges must be graduates in law, economics or commerce. Other members may have only a degree of secondary education. One half of the judges must be taken from among persons nominated for appointment by the financial administration, chambers of commerce and professional bodies; another half from persons selected by the commissions themselves and by the assemblies of the communities located within the district of the commission. Judges are selected from among such persons by the chief judge of the court of general jurisdiction (*presidente del tribunale*), and the appointment is made by a decree of the Minister of Finance (*Ministro per le finanze*).

The commission hears *ricorsi* against decisions of taxation authorities on the assessment and imposition of a tax. The commission may uphold, modify or reverse a decision. An appeal (*appello*) from decisions of the commission must be filed with the same commission within sixty days from notification for transmission to the commission of the second level.

(ii) TAX COMMISSIONS OF THE SECOND LEVEL (*Commissioni tributarie di secondo grado*).   Tax commissions of the second level sit in the capital city of a province and hear appeals against decisions of tax courts of the first level located in that province. Their composition and the selection of judges is identical to those of the first level, except that candidates nominated by municipal assemblies in first-level courts are nominated by the provincial assembly (*consiglio provinciale*) in the second-level courts and the actual selection is made by the president of the court of appeal (*presidente della corte d'appello*).

A tax commission of the second level may uphold, modify or reverse the decision appealed from. Where it reverses the decision below on the ground that the parties were not properly cited or constituted, or that the commission was improperly composed, it will remand the case for further proceedings to another section of the same first-level tax commission or, where there is only one section, to another first-level tax commission.

A recourse (*ricorso*) lies against decisions of the commission for violation of law (*violazione di legge*) and in questions of fact (*questioni di fatto*), with the exception of those dealing with valuation and the amount of a fine. The ricorso must be filed with the commission that pronounced the decision within sixty days from notification for transmission to the central tax commission (*commissione tributaria centrale*).

As an alternative to recourse to the central commission, recourse may be taken to the court of appeal (*corte di appello*) on the same grounds. The recourse may be taken only after the time of sixty days for the filing of the recourse to the central tax commission has run. It must be taken within ninety days from that time. The recourse before the court of appeal proceeds under the rules of procedure before that court.

(iii) CENTRAL TAX COMMISSION (*Commissione tributaria centrale*).   The central tax commission sits in Rome. It has a president, presidents of sections, and judges. Each section has a president and six members. The panel hearing a case is presided over by a president of a section or the most senior member and has four other members. The united sections (*sezioni unite*) are presided over by the president of the central commission and have all the presidents of sections as members. Presidents of sections may be replaced by the most senior member of that particular section.

Judges of the central commission are taken from among judges of the Supreme Court of Cassation, councilors of state, councilors of the Court of Accounts, members of the government counsel of the rank of *sostituto avvocato generale* and higher, professors of law or economics, officers of the central financial administration of the rank of director general or inspector general, and advocates who have practiced before superior courts for at least ten years.

Presidents of sections are taken from among senior judges of the central commission who qualify for appointment to presidents of sections of the Supreme Court of Cassation, the Council of State, or the Court of Accounts.

The president of the central commission is taken from among presidents of sections of the Supreme Court of Cassation, the Council of State, or the Court of Accounts.

All appointments are made by a decree of the President of the Republic at the recommendation of the Minister of Finance after deliberation in the council of ministers.

The central tax commission may uphold, modify or reverse the decision below. Where it reverses the decision and cannot give its own decision because the matter requires a new valuation or decision on the amount of a fine, it will remit the case for further proceedings to another section of the same second-level commission or, where there is only one section, to another second-level commission. Where it reverses the decision below on the ground that the parties were not properly cited or constituted, or that the second-level commission was not properly composed, it will remand the case to the second level in the same way. Where the defect arose already before the first-level commission, it will remand the case to the first level in the way mentioned above, thus by-passing the second level. The matter is always remitted to another section of the commission or, where the commission has only one section, to another commission.

No further remedy lies against decisions of the central tax commission except a petition for cassation for violation of law (*violazione di legge*). Such a petition must be filed with the Supreme Court of Cassation within twenty days from notification of the decision.

A petition for revocation (*revocazione*), however, on grounds of fraud, discovery of new documents or facts, or an error of fact, lies against decisions of all tax commissions that involve the determination of fact. The petition is governed by the standard rules applicable to such petitions.[113]

Private parties appearing before any of the tax commissions may represent themselves or may have themselves represented by persons under power of attorney. They may also engage the services of attorneys (*procuratori*), advocates (*avvocati*), and specialists, like industrial or commercial experts. The state is represented by the proper branch of the *avvocatura dello stato*.

NOTES AND QUESTIONS

1. As to the Court of Accounts, it is in fact not a court as the function of a court is understood, but an advisory body and an organ of control over the spending of public monies by the government. In that, it is similar to the French and German Courts of Accounts. Note that it also has some contested jurisdiction. Compare it, e.g., with the Spanish Court of Accounts. Which government office performs similar control over government spending in Anglo-American countries? *See*, e.g., New York Executive Law §40ff. concerning the Department of Audit and Control; 31 U.S.C.A. §41ff. concerning the U.S. General Accounting Office.

2. As to water courts, they are an Italian specialty. There is a relative shortage of water in Italy and the courts specialize in water jurisdiction. They are affiliated with the ordinary civil court system. The court of final appeal is, however, a separate court. No similar courts generally exist in other countries. In Spain, there is a similar court in Valencia only, known as the *tribunal de las aguas de Valencia*, but in every community using irrigation, there are irrigation juries (*jurados de riego*) to administer the irrigation laws. Water laws exist, however, in all countries and are administered with the regular administrative system. Compare, e.g., The Texas Water Commission, which is an administrative agency dealing with the appropriation of state waters. Appeal against its rulings lies to the proper district court; *see* Vernon's Ann. Civ. St. Arts. 7467ff. and 7503ff.

3. As to tax commissions, they are separate administrative courts handling taxation. They provide for the review of decisions of taxation offices. Compare, e.g., the Spanish system. Italian tax commissions operate on three levels. Compare, e.g., the German system. Note that the parties have a choice to appeal either to the central commission or to the court of appeal from the decision of the second-level commission. Note also that there is no compulsory representation by attorneys before any tax commission.

How would Italian tax commissions compare with the U.S. Tax Court? *See* the provisions on organization and jurisdiction of the U.S. Tax Court, 26 U.S.C.A. §7441ff. To which court may the decision of the United States Tax Court be appealed? *See* 26 U.S.C.A. §7482. Is then the Italian first-level tax commission comparable to the United States Tax Court? Compare the composition of Italian tax commissions with that of the United States Tax Court.

C.   ADMINISTRATIVE PROCEDURE AND PROCEDURE BEFORE ADMINISTRATIVE COURTS

1.   Administrative Procedure[114]

Whatever has been said on administrative procedure in the General Part (An Overview of the Law), Section III. C., applies generally to the Italian administrative procedure. The Italian administrative system operates at four levels: communal, provincial, regional and central. Process may be initiated at any level depending on the particular case. Most of it is in fact initiated at the provincial level, with a recourse to the regional level. This is known as hierarchical recourse (*ricorso gerarchico*). It may be brought only once, from the decision of an administrative authority to the immediately superior authority. It must be filed with the authority that pronounced the decision, or with that indicated in the decision, within thirty days from the notification. Where the authority does not decide on the *ricorso gerarchico* within ninety days from its filing, the recourse is considered denied and the party may proceed with its further remedies.

Rather than file the *ricorso gerarchico* immediately, a party may first file the *ricorso in opposizione* in cases where this is expressly admitted. The *opposizione* is filed with the authority that issued the decision on the same conditions as the *ricorso gerarchico*. The authority is requested to cancel or to modify its decision, and where the authority actually does so, the party need not proceed to the hierarchical superior. Where the *opposizione* is denied, the party may then take the *ricorso gerarchico*.

From an unsuccessful *ricorso gerarchico*, and from an administrative decision at any level, a recourse (*ricorso*)[115] may be taken to a regional administrative court, and a further appeal (*appello*) to the Council of State. In Sicily, the *appello* goes to the Sicilian council of administrative justice.

Administrative acts may be attacked either on the ground that they lack formal validity (*vizi di legitimità*) or for alleged defects on the merits (*vizi di merito*).

As to the lack of formal validity, administrative acts may be attacked for lack of jurisdiction in the authority that pronounced them (*incompetenza*), for excess of power (*eccesso di potere*), or for violation of the law (*violazione di legge*) by the issuing authority. Violation of law constitutes a residual ground of attack and covers any lack of formal validity not covered by the preceding two grounds.

The jurisdiction of first instance administrative courts extends both to formal validity and to merits of the administrative acts complained of, while the jurisdiction of the Council of State is limited to the matter brought up on appeal whether formal or substantive or both.

Where the administrative court finds the administrative act defective, it may modify it or outright annul it. It may not, however, award the petitioner damages against the state. If an award of damages is sought, proceedings must be instituted in an ordinary civil court. If proceedings concerning administrative acts are taken in civil courts, such courts may hold them illegal and award damages; they cannot annul such acts, however, as the power for their modification (*riforma*) and annulment (*caducazione*) is exclusively vested in administrative courts.

Suits before administrative courts are of three types: actions of impugnation (*azioni d'impugnazione*); actions for a declaratory judgment (*azioni di accertamento*), also known as *azioni relative a rapporti;* and actions of execution (*azioni di esecuzione*).

An action of impugnation is directed against an administrative act and the petition is for the modification (*riforma*) or the annulment (*caducazione*) of the act. Most actions before administrative courts are of this type.

The action for a declaratory judgment (*azione di accertamento*) does not attack any administrative act but petitions the court to rule on a report (*rapporto*) declaratory of the respective rights and duties of the parties. The matters dealt with are mainly salaries and pensions of public servants, and disputes between municipal and provincial authorities on the apportionment of expenditures in matters of public health and public welfare.

The action of execution (*azione di esecuzione*) is an action brought by a party who obtained a judgment against an administrative authority in an ordinary civil court to enforce such judgment against that authority. The object of the action is to have the administrative act annulled, revoked or modified in accordance with the judgment of the civil court and to enforce the order for the payment of damages, if any, pronounced by that court.

As an alternative to proceedings in administrative courts, an administrative decision may be attacked by an extraordinary recourse to the President of the Republic (*ricorso straordinario al Presidente della Repubblica*). Only lack of formal validity (*vizi di legitimità*) may be so attacked. The recourse must be brought within 120 days from notification to the proper ministry, which will submit it to the Council of State for its decision. The decision is made in the form of a decree of the President of the Republic, and it is subject to a petition for revocation (*ricorso per revocazione*) and to a recourse to a regional administrative court. In Sicily, the recourse may be taken from decisions of the Sicilian regional authorities to the president of the region. Once a recourse is taken to a regional administrative court, the extraordinary recourse to the President of the Republic may not be brought.

NOTES AND QUESTIONS

Italian administrative procedure is a body of rules regulating procedure before all administrative offices. It is of general application throughout the country and applies from the lowest offices of public administration to the office of head of state. The procedure is similar in other civil law countries. Compare, e.g., the Spanish and German administrative procedures.

Usually the party may request the administrative office to reconsider its decision, and only if no result is obtained will the party proceed with an appeal to the hierarchical superior. The hierarchical recourse may be brought only once in the Italian system. What is the position in the German system? How is the matter handled in the French system?

Having exhausted the administrative route, the party may turn to administrative courts. Compare the French rule on the matter. Note the grounds for attack of administrative acts, and the several types of actions before administrative courts.

Compare Italian administrative procedure with American administrative procedure, 5 U.S.C.A. §500ff. Is there any administrative review available under the Anglo-American system? Is there any uniform system of judicial review available in the Anglo-American system? *See* 5 U.S.C.A. §701ff. To which court may a dissatisfied party turn in judicial review of an administrative decision? *See* 5 U.S.C.A. §703. What is the scope of an Anglo-American judicial review? Does it equal the Italian full review on the merits? *See*, 5 U.S.C.A. §706, and, e.g., Lowery v. Richardson, 390 F. Supp. 356 (D.C. Okl. 1973).

----

2.   Procedure before First-Level Administrative Courts (*Tribunali amministrativi regionali*)[116]

The procedure before administrative courts is governed by the Code of Civil Procedure unless otherwise provided. Provisions specially applicable to administrative procedure in derogation of provisions of the Code of Civil Procedure are designed to simplify that procedure.

The procedure in regional administrative courts (*tribunali amministrativi regionali*) is initiated by a recourse (*ricorso*) against an administrative act issued by an administrative authority. It must be filed with the court within 60 days from its notification. The *ricorso* must give the name and address of the petitioner, identify the administrative act complained of and its date, and state a summary of the facts of the case and the demand. It must be signed by an advocate (*avvocato*) or attorney (*procuratore*).[117] The petitioner must deliver a copy to the administrative authority that issued the act attacked within the same sixty days. The original is then deposited by the petitioner in the secretariat of the court within thirty days of service. The cause is pending as soon as the original is so deposited. The respondent authority may file an answer in a similar way within twenty days, and so on; but a party must file with the court a request to set the matter for trial within two years from the deposition of the original of the recourse in the secretariat, otherwise it will be presumed that the petitioner has abandoned the case, and it will be struck out.

The filing of the *ricorso* does not suspend the administrative act complained of and it is fully executory. If the petitioner wishes to have it suspended, he must make a request to that effect either in his petition or separately with the court. The court will hear the request promptly and rule on it, but will grant it only if irreparable loss would ensue to the petitioner.[118]

When the original is filed with the court, the president of the court appoints, from among the judges, a rapporteur (*relatore*) who will handle the case and will report to the court; or he will act as the rapporteur himself.

The procedure before administrative courts is adversary, i.e., the parties must come forward with their motions; it also has an inquisitory feature, however, in that the court may ex officio order the parties to produce documents and supply information, or it may obtain such information itself when it deems as incomplete that which is supplied by the parties. It is the duty of the rapporteur to see to it that the case is ready for trial. To that end, he may hold hearings, appoint experts, request additional information, and so forth. When the rapporteur concludes his work, known as the instruction (*instruzione*), he will deposit the files with the secretariat of the court, which will notify the parties. One of the parties must then request to have the case set for trial. As soon as the request to set the matter for trial is made, the president will do so in chronological order of the cases pending. At least forty days' notice of the hearing will be given to the parties. All documents must be filed twenty days and briefs ten days before the hearing.

At the hearing, first the rapporteur (*relatore*) gives the facts of the case and his report. Then the counsel for the petitioner takes the floor; then the counsel for the respondent authority gives his address. Parties may reply, and when the parties rest, the president of the court panel hearing the case will close the proceedings. The hearing may also be adjourned if further investigation is to be undertaken.

The court then deliberates in private. After deliberation a vote is taken. First the rapporteur votes, then the other judges in the reverse order of seniority. The presiding judge votes last. The decision is adopted by a simple majority. The presiding judge then assigns one of the judges who voted with the majority to prepare the judgment. If the rapporteur is one of the majority, he will be required to prepare it.

The judgment is pronounced in the name of the Italian people and must contain: the names of parties and of their counsel, their petitions, a summary of the facts and the applicable law, the decision, an order to the administrative authority to conform to the decision, the date and place of decision, signatures of members of the court, the name of the judge who prepared the judgment, and the signature of the secretary of the court.

The judgment also orders the defeated party to pay the costs of the proceedings, unless for good reasons the court orders each party to pay its own costs. Once the judgment is signed, it may not be modified. The secretary will announce the decision at the first public hearing following the signing thereof. It is also communicated in writing to the counsel for the parties.

The judgment will either deny the request of the petitioner or it will modify or annul the act complained of. The judgment is immediately executory. If a stay of execution is sought, the petition must be filed with the Council of State.

Remedies against the judgment are either a petition for its revocation (*revocazione*) directed to the court that pronounced it, or an appeal (*appello*) to the Council of State. Both may be joined together.

The petition for the revocation of the judgment may be filed within thirty days from its notification or the discovery of the ground of revocation, which may be on the ground of fraud, discovery of new documents or facts, or discovery of an error of fact. The court will set a hearing on the petition; if the petition is substantiated, the court will revoke its decision and, wherever possible, will give a new judgment in the matter at the same time. Where no new decision is given, the parties are left in the position they were before the judgment in the matter, now revoked, was given, and it is for the petitioner to move. The revocation is not susceptible to a further petition for its revocation.

The appeal to the Council of State must be filed with that court within sixty days of notification of the judgment. Both parties may appeal.

NOTES AND QUESTIONS

Italian administrative courts are courts fully equivalent to courts in the Anglo-American system. They apply the Code of Civil Procedure like ordinary civil courts with minor modifications.

Note that the filing of the recourse does not suspend the administrative act and that it may be executed unless a stay of execution is obtained.

The entire procedure follows that before a civil court. There is a rapporteur to prepare the case for trial and handle the instruction of the case. The hearing, deliberation, voting and decision is the same as in civil courts. The judge who actually writes the judgment is known as the *estensore*, as he is in civil and criminal courts.

Note that the judgment is immediately executory. This is in contradiction to judgments in civil and criminal courts, which become executory only after they enter into the power of law.

How does the Italian procedure before regional administrative courts compare with that before French administrative courts? Compare also the procedure before Spanish administrative chambers in *audiencias territoriales*.

How does this procedure compare with the procedure before Anglo-American courts of judicial review of administrative acts? *See*, e.g., 5 U.S.C.A. §701ff.

---

3. Procedure before the Council of State (*Consiglio di Stato*)[119]

The procedure before the Council of State is very similar to that before first-level administrative courts.

Appeals (*appelli*) against judgments of first-level administrative courts must be filed within sixty days from their notification. The *appello* must be signed by an advocate (*avvocato*) admitted to practice before the Council of State. The appellant must serve a copy of the appeal on the office of the State General Legal Counsel (*Avvocatura Generale dello Stato*) and file the original with the secretariat of the Council of State within thirty days of such service. The cause is pending as soon as the original is so filed. The appellee may file an answer within thirty days from the filing of the original, and so on; but either party must move to have the case set for trial within two years from the filing of the original appeal in the secretariat, otherwise the case will be struck out.

The filing of the *appello* does not suspend the judgment appealed from and it is fully executory. A petition for its suspension may be made to the Council of State either in the *appello* or separately. The Council of State will rule on the petition, but it will grant the suspension only if irreparable loss would ensue to the petitioner.

On the filing of the original of the appeal with the secretariat, the office of the president of the Council of State will assign the matter to one of the three judicial sections, IV, V, or VI. The president of that section will appoint a rapporteur (*relatore*) from among the judges of the section. The rapporteur will handle the case and reports to the section; he is responsible to the section until the case is ready for trial. He may hold hearings, appoint experts, request further information, and so forth. When the rapporteur concludes his work, known as the instruction (*instruzione*), he will deposit the files with the secretariat of the court, which will notify the parties. Either party may then move to have the case set for trial. When such motion is made, the president of the section will set a date for trial. The date so fixed is always two to three months from the making of the order so as to give both parties time to file additional documents, which must be filed at least thirty days before the trial, and briefs, which must be filed at least ten days before the trial.

At the hearing, the rapporteur gives his report first, then counsel for the petitioner addresses the court. Finally counsel for the respondent takes the floor. Parties may reply; judges ask questions; and unless the trial is adjourned in order to undertake further investigation, the president of the court will close the hearing after the parties have rested.

The court deliberates in private and after deliberation a vote is taken. First, the rapporteur (*relatore*) votes, then the judges in the reverse order of seniority. The presiding judge votes last. The decision is adopted by a simple majority, and in case of a tie, the vote of the presiding judge prevails. The presiding judge then assigns one of the judges who voted with the majority to prepare the judgment. If the rapporteur is one of the majority, he will be required to prepare it.

The judgment is pronounced in the name of the Italian people and must contain: names of parties and their counsel, their petitions, a summary of the facts and the applicable law, the decision, an order to the administrative authority to conform to the decision, the date and place of decision, signatures of members of the court, the name of the judge who prepared the judgment, and the signature of the secretary of the court.

The judgment also orders the defeated party to pay the costs of the proceedings, unless for good reasons the court orders each party to pay its own costs. Once the judgment is signed, it may not be modified. The secretary will announce the decision at the first public hearing following the signing thereof. It is also communicated in writing to the counsel for the parties.

The judgment will either deny the petition or modify or annul the act complained of. The judgment is immediately executory. Where the Council of State finds that the regional administrative court lacked jurisdiction or that the recourse taken to it was null and void, the Council will annul the court's judgment without remission. Where the Council of State finds that a procedural defect arose in the proceedings below, or that the judgment of the regional administrative court suffers from a lack of form, it will annul that judgment and remit the case to the regional administrative court for further proceedings. In all other cases, the Council of State will decide the matter itself. Where the case has been remitted to the regional administrative court for further proceedings, the parties must reopen the proceedings before that court within sixty days from notification of the judgment of the Council of State or, failing notification, within one year from the declaration of the judgment in the Council of State, otherwise the case will be considered abandoned.

Remedies against a judgment of the Council of State are a petition for its revocation (*revocazione*) or a petition for its cassation (*cassazione*).

The petition for the revocation of the judgment may be filed with the Council of State within sixty days from its notification or the discovery of the ground of revocation, which may be on the ground of fraud, discovery of new documents or facts, or discovery of an error of fact. The court will set a hearing on the petition and if found substantiated, it will revoke its decision and wherever possible a new judgment will be given at the same time. Where a new judgment is not given, the parties are left where they were before the revoked judgment was given and it is for the parties to move. The revocation is not susceptible to a further petition for its revocation, but a petition for its cassation may be made to the Supreme Court of Cassation (*Corte Suprema di Cassazione*).

A petition for the cassation of the judgment or for that of an order for the revocation of a judgment may be made to the Supreme Court of Cassation (*Corte Suprema di Cassazione*). It must be filed within twenty days from the notification and is limited purely to the question of jurisdiction. In a case where the Supreme Court of Cassation holds that the Council of State has improperly declined jurisdiction, the parties must make their next move in the Council of State within two years from the notification, otherwise the case will be struck out.

NOTES AND QUESTIONS

The procedure before the Council of State and that before a regional administrative court is virtually identical. This is because the newly created regional administrative courts are in fact a lower division of the Council of State and were set up mainly for the purpose of acting as trial courts, leaving the Council of State only with appellate jurisdiction. They therefore adopted the trial procedure of the Council of State, which is again fully based on that before the civil court system. Compare the Italian procedure with that before the French Council of State.

Note that decisions of the Italian Council of State are subject to a petition for their cassation by the Supreme Court of Cassation. Does such a rule exist in other administrative systems? Compare, e.g., the French and German systems.

May the procedure before the Italian Council of State be compared with the Federal Rules of Appellate Procedure and the Revised Rules of the U.S. Supreme Court?

------

4. Procedure before Tax Commissions (*Commissioni tributarie*)[120]

(a) Procedure before first-level tax commissions (*procedimento di primo grado*). The *ricorso* against a decision of the taxation authority must be filed in duplicate with the commission within sixty days of the notification. The secretary of the commission will hand it to the president of the commission who will assign the case to the proper section. The secretary will within ten days, send the copy of the *ricorso* to the taxation authority that issued the decision. The authority must submit its brief in duplicate within 120 days from the day on which the copy of the *ricorso* was transmitted to it. The copy is delivered to the petitioner.

After the time of 120 days for submission of the brief of the tax authority has run, whether the authority filed its brief or not, the presiding judge will set a day for a hearing so that at least thirty days' notice to the parties may be given. He will also appoint a rapporteur (*relatore*) to prepare the case for trial. The petitioner may bring additional submissions up to ten days before the hearing and the tax authority may request a postponement of the hearing if it needs time to reply.

At the hearing, the *relatore* gives his report first, explaining the facts and the questions involved. Then the petitioner presents his case and then the tax administration. The case is further properly discussed by the court and the parties. The presiding judge then declares the hearing closed.

The commission retires to consider judgment. The decision is given promptly and must be given within thirty days.

The entire proceedings are governed by the Code of Civil Procedure unless otherwise provided.

(b) Procedure before second-level tax commissions (*procedimento di appello*). An appeal against a decision of a first-level tax commission must be filed in duplicate with the commission that made the decision within sixty days of the notification. The appellee is given a copy of the appeal by the secretary and has sixty days to reply or to file his own appeal in duplicate from the receipt thereof. After this time has run, the secretary will transmit the appeal and files to the proper second-level tax commission.

Proceedings before second-level tax commissions are governed by the same rules as those before first-level tax commissions.

The decision may uphold, modify or reverse the decision appealed from. Where the decision is reversed on the ground that the parties were not properly cited or constituted, or that the commission was not properly composed, the second-level commission will remand the case to another section of the first-level tax commission or, where it has only one section, to another first-level tax commission for further proceedings.

(c) Procedure before the central tax commission (*procedimento dinanzi alla commissione tributaria centrale*). The *ricorso* must be filed in duplicate with the second-level commission that gave the decision within sixty days of the notification. The copy is served on the other party, who then has sixty days to file his brief in reply, in duplicate, or his own *ricorso*. After this time has run, the parties have thirty days to inspect the files of the commission on the case. Thereafter, the secretary will transmit all of the files to the central commission.

The *ricorso* may be brought only because of an alleged violation of law (*violazione di legge*) or on questions of fact (*questioni di fatto*) with the exception of those dealing with valuation and the amount of a fine.

The president of the central commission will assign the case to a particular section or, where there is conflict of precedents, to the united sections. The section to which the case is assigned may refer it to the united sections on the same ground. The presiding judge of the section handling the case will appoint a *relatore* to prepare the case for judgment and will set the case for decision so that at least sixty days notice of it is given to the parties. Parties may file additional briefs up to ten days before the case is set for decision. No oral hearing is held and the decision is made by the commission on the strength of documents. The commision makes its decision on the appointed day unless it decides to postpone the consideration of the case, but it may not postpone it beyond sixty days.

The decision may uphold, modify or reverse the decision below. Where it reverses the decision and cannot give its own decision because the matter requires a new valuation or decision on the amount of a fine, it will remit the case for further proceedings to another section of the same second-level commission or, where it has only one section, to another second-level commission. Where it reverses the decision below on the ground that the parties were not properly cited or constituted, or that the second-level commission was not properly composed, it will remand the case to the second-level in the same way. Where the defect arose already before the first-level commission, it will remand the case to the first level in the way mentioned above, thus by-passing the second level. The matter is always remitted to another section of the commission or, where the commission has only one section, to another commission.

The proceedings before the central tax commission are otherwise governed by the Code of Civil Procedure.

NOTES AND QUESTIONS

Since tax commissions are special administrative courts dealing with taxation, they apply the usual administrative procedure applied in the other administrative courts, i.e., that before regional administrative courts and the Council of State. What is the procedure applied in German tax courts? How is the matter handled in the Spanish and French systems?

How does the procedure before Italian tax commissions compare with procedure before the U.S. Tax Court, 5 U.S.C.A. §7451ff., the Rules of Practice before the U.S. Tax Court, and the procedure on review of the decisions of the U.S. Tax Court, 5 U.S.C.A. §7481ff.?

V. LEGAL OFFICERS

A. JUDGES (*Magistrati*)[121]

Whatever has been said above on judges in Section IV. A. of the chapter on an overview of the law applies to the Italian legal system.

The time to join the judicial service is immediately after graduation from law school. Admission is by public competition conducted by the ministry of justice. Applicants must hold Italian citizenship and must be in full possession of their civil and political rights, of good moral character (never convicted), and over twenty-one and below thirty years of age at the time of the competition. They must also hold a law degree (*laurea in giurisprudenza*) from an Italian university. The competition takes place in Rome once each year before an examination commission appointed by the Minister of Justice (*Ministro di grazia e giustizia*). It is presided over by a president of a section in the Court of Cassation, and it is further composed of six members of a rank not below that of a judge of a court of appeal, two or whom belong to the public ministry (*pubblico ministero*), and of another two members who are university professors of law.

The examination commission gives a preliminary written examination on Italian law, and those who pass are admitted to an oral examination. Those who pass this are graded by the examination commission in order of merit, and the Minister of Justice appoints as many as are required to fill existing vacancies, beginning with the highest ranked candidate to serve as a judicial trainee, known as *uditore giudiziario*. Those who pass but for whom no vacancy is available may be appointed later. No person may take the examination more than three times.

Trainees must spend at least two years in training with general jurisdiction courts (*tribunali*), with the various offices of the procurator of the republic (*procura della Repubblica*), and with limited jurisdiction courts (*preture*). A commission is set up in every court of appeal to supervise the trainees (*commissione per il tirocinio degli uditori*) undergoing their training in the jurisdiction of the court. It is presided over by the president of the court of appeal, and its further members are the president of the court of general jurisdiction (*tribunale*), the procurator of the republic (*procuratore della Repubblica*), and the presiding justice of the limited jurisdiction court (*pretura*) having its seat in the seat of the court of appeal.

The commission supervises the trainees and allots them to different courts. It appoints a judge to act as supervisor to groups of five trainees and every month hears his report on the progress of the trainees. The commission holds regular instruction sessions for trainees to instruct them on their work as future judges.

After six months of training, the trainees may be appointed to exercise judicial and procuratorial functions at the courts of limited and general jurisdiction and at the offices of the public ministry on a temporary basis. They are promoted to judicial assistants (*aggiunti giudiziari*) after two years of training and after passing a practical examination, both written and oral, on the application of the law in the courts. The commission giving the examination is presided over by a president of a section in the Court of Cassation and has another six members of the rank of judge of the court of appeal. Those who pass are ranked in order of merit and are appointed to exercise the functions of judges in limited and general jurisdiction courts and as assistant procurators. Those who do not pass the examination on two attempts within four years from their appointment as judicial trainees are permanently excluded.

After three years of service as *aggiunti giudiziari*, the candidates are appointed as judges (*magistrati di tribunale*) by the Minister of Justice on the recommendation of the judicial council (*consiglio giudiziario*)[122] of the court of appeal to which they are attached. Against an adverse report denying the recommendation, and within thirty days therefrom, the candidate may file a recourse (*ricorso*) to the superior council of the magistracy (*consiglio superiore della magistratura*), the decision of which is final.

Judges are appointed for life, but they must retire when they reach seventy years of age. They are irremovable and may be transferred only with the consent of the superior council of the magistracy. They may however, be disciplined, and even removed for cause by the superior council of the magistracy.

Promotion of judges to higher ranks is on seniority and merit. All promotions are made with the approval of the superior council of the magistracy. Advocates (*avvocati*) and professors of law may also be appointed to judgeships. Those who have exercised their profession for fifteen years may be appointed to the rank of appellate judge, and those who have done so for eighteen years to the rank of judge at the Court of Cassation.

The superior council of the magistracy (*consiglio superiore della magistratura*)[123] is presided over by the President of the Republic. Its membership includes the president of the Supreme Court of Cassation, the procurator general of the republic at that court, fourteen members elected by judges from among judges, and seven members elected by Parliament from among professors of law and advocates of more than fifteen years standing. The elected members hold office for four years and may not be immediately reelected. The council elects a vice-president from the members elected by Parliament. The council appoints committees as the need arises, among them a standing promotions committee and a disciplinary committee.

The disciplinary committee (*sezione disciplinare*) of the supreme council of the magistracy has fifteen members. It has the power to discipline a judge. Disciplinary proceedings proceed like proceedings in civil matters before ordinary courts. The proceeding is initiated by the Minister of Justice and the case is prosecuted by the procurator general of the republic. The actual trial court is composed of seven members of the disciplinary committee. It is presided over by the vice-president of the superior council of the magistracy and its other members are: the president and three judges of the Supreme Court of Cassation, a judge of the same rank as the one against whom the proceedings are conducted, and one member elected by Parliament. It decides by a simple majority. The court may dismiss the complaint, or it may provide for an admonition, censure, loss of seniority, demotion, or dismissal. Against the decision of the court, an appeal lies to two united sections of the Supreme Court of Cassation. It must be filed within sixty days. The Supreme Court of Cassation decides on questions of legality and merits and its decision is final.

NOTES AND QUESTIONS

The Italian system with respect to the selection and appointment of judges is typical for other civil law countries. Compare, e.g., the Spanish system. The time to join the service is immediately after graduation from law school, that is, at a young age. This does not mean that older jurists would not be eligible to enter with credit for their legal activity since graduation. Thus, attorneys may become judges and judges may abandon the service and become attorneys. Compare, e.g., the French system.

The system has the merit that every judge must start at the bottom and work his way up through the system. Promotions are on seniority and merit. *See,* e.g., the German system.

How are judges selected and appointed in the Anglo-American system? Is the selection from practicing attorneys, as is done in the Anglo-American system, unknown in civil law system? *See,* e.g., the Swiss and Mexican systems. Is the principal method of selection of judges in the Anglo-American system by election? How are English judges appointed?

The standard method of appointment of judges in American states is by election. *See,* e.g., New York Judiciary Law. As to appointment of federal judges, *see* Art. III, Section I, of the United States Constitution, and 28 U.S.C.A. §1ff. for justices of the United States Supreme Court, §41ff. for judges of U.S. courts of appeal, and §81ff. for judges of U.S. District Courts.

For standards of judicial conduct, compare the American Code of Judicial Conduct as promulgated by the American Bar Association.

B.   THE PUBLIC MINISTRY (*Pubblico Ministero*)[124]

All that has been said above about judges applies with equal force to officers of the public ministry, since they form one group of legal officers and hold the office of a judge or of an officer of public ministry as required. There is a procurator general at the Court of Cassation, procurators general at every court of appeal, and procurators of the republic at every court of general jurisdiction (*tribunale*). In every such office, there is a staff of procurators handling the business under the direction of the above-mentioned heads of office. In limited jurisdiction courts (*preture*), the office of the public ministry is exercised by judicial assistants (*aggiunti giudiziari*), judicial trainees (*uditori giudiziari*), or other officers appointed by the public ministry.

The public ministry sees to it that the laws are properly applied and enforced, that justice is speedily and properly done, and that the interests of the state are generally protected.[125]

NOTES AND QUESTIONS

The public ministry is similarly organized in other civil law countries. *See,* e.g., the Spanish system.

How does the Italian system of public ministry compare with the Anglo-American system of public prosecutors? *See*, e.g., New York Executive Law §60ff. on the Department of Law. As to the United States, compare 28 U.S.C.A. §501ff. for the United States Department of Justice and §541ff. for U.S. attorneys.

C. LEGAL PRACTITIONERS[126]

There are two types of legal practitioners: attorneys (*procuratori*) and advocates (*avvocati*).

1. Attorneys (*Procuratori*)

To become an attorney, a person must hold Italian citizenship, must be in possession of his civil rights, must be of good moral character (never convicted), must hold a law degree (*laurea in giurisprudenza*) from an Italian university, must have served the prescribed apprenticeship for at least one year, must have passed the prescribed bar examination, and must reside in the area of the court of general jurisdiction (*tribunale*) where he applies for admission. Advocates (*avvocati*), judges of five years' standing, and law teachers in Italian universities who have taught for two years are admitted without apprenticeship and examination.

The prescribed apprenticeship is undertaken in the office of an attorney (*procuratore*) and in courses given by the bar in the law school of a university as directed by the ministry of justice. All candidates (*praticanti procuratori*) are entered as apprentices in the rolls of attorneys (*procuratori*) and may appear in courts of limited jurisdiction (*preture*) for a period of four years from their enrollment. Within that time they must pass the bar examination.

Bar examinations are given in seats of courts of appeal by examination commissions appointed by the Minister of Justice. Each commission is presided over by a judge of the court of appeal and has another four members, namely, an officer of the public ministry, a professor of law, and two advocates. The examination opens with two written examinations, one on civil and administrative law and the other on civil and criminal procedure. Then follows an oral examination on civil, criminal and administrative law and taxation, and on civil and criminal procedure.

Upon passing the bar examination, candidates are entered on the roll of attorneys (*procuratori*) in the court of general jurisdiction (*tribunale*) where they reside and intend to practice.

Attorneys (*procuratori*) may practice in the court of appeal and in all lower courts of that judicial district within which is located the court of general jurisdiction (*tribunale*) where they were admitted, with the exception of participating in the defense of parties accused in criminal matters before courts of appeal (*corti di appello*) and assize courts (*corti di assise*) where advocates (*avvocati*) have the exclusive right of practice.

2. Advocates (*Avvocati*)

An attorney (*procuratore*) who exercises his profession for six years is eligible to become an advocate (*avvocato*). He may become an advocate after two years, however, if he takes and passes an examination on Italian law geared to the exercise of the profession of an advocate. The examination is given once a year in Rome. Judges and government legal counsel (*avvocati dello stato*) of eight years' standing, judges and legal officers of the rank of judges of appeal of at least three years' standing, former prefects of three years' standing, and professors of law of three years' standing are admitted without examination.

Advocates may exercise their profession in all courts of appeal and lower courts anywhere in Italy. They cannot, however, appear in the highest courts of the land where the right to practice is reserved to advocates entered on a special roll. To be enrolled on that roll, an advocate must practice for eight years. Professors of law of four years' standing, legal officers of the rank of judge of the Court of Cassation, and legal officers of the rank of judge of a court of appeal of three years' standing are entitled to admission. Advocates entered on this special roll may appear before the Court of Cassation, Council of State, and Court of Accounts as well as the supreme military tribunal and superior court of public waters.

The professions of attorney and advocate are two separate professions, but a person may exercise both professions by being on both rolls. Advocates entered on the special roll must also be on the roll of advocates; however, after twenty years, they may restrict their membership only to the special roll.

The bar is organized within the jurisdiction of every court of general jurisdiction. The bar exercises disciplinary powers over its members. Every bar has a directive body, the council of the bar (*consiglio dell'ordine*), which may discipline its members. The proceedings follow the rules of civil procedure and the council may pronounce a sentence of admonishment, censure, suspension for up to one year, or disbarment. Disbarment is mandatory on conviction for contempt of court and for fraud or dishonesty of any kind. Against decisions of the local council, an appeal lies to the National Forensic Council (*Consiglio Nazionale Forense*). It must be filed within twenty days from the notification. From decisions of the National Council, there is an appeal to two united sections of the Court of Cassation, but this appeal is limited to questions of jurisdiction (*incompetenza*), excess of power (*eccesso di potere*), and violation of law (*violazione di legge*). It must be lodged within thirty days from the notification.

NOTES AND QUESTIONS

The Italian division between attorneys and advocates has a rather unique feature in that a person must become first an attorney to later become an advocate and also that a person may then hold both positions at the same time. How does this compare with the British Commonwealth system of barristers and solicitors who are also admitted to perform both functions? How does the Italian system differ from the Spanish division into attorneys and advocates?

Note that the candidate must work as an apprentice and pass a bar examination. How does this compare with the Spanish system? *See also* the Mexican system.

Note that to practice in the highest courts, like the Court of Cassation and the Council of State, special admission is required. Compare the German requirements.

Membership in the bar is compulsory in Italy and in virtually all civil law countries. Compare also the Mexican requirements.

Disciplinary provisions are very similar in all civil law countries. *See*, e.g., the French provisions.

How do the requirements for becoming Italian legal practitioners compare with those in Anglo-American countries? Is apprenticeship still required in American jurisdictions as it is in British jurisdictions?

As to American attorneys, compare the law of your state, and, e.g., the New York Judiciary Law §460ff. and the Code of Professional Responsibility promulgated by the American Bar Association.

D. NOTARIES (*Notai*)[127]

Notaries are public officers who receive and legalize acts *inter vivos* and wills. They hold copies of the documents legalized by them and issue copies and extracts therefrom. They perform all further functions assigned to them by law. They must make a bond so that should there be a claim against them, it may be paid therefrom.

To become a notary (*notaio*) a person must hold Italian citizenship, be over twenty-one years of age, be of good moral character (never convicted), hold a law degree (*laurea in giurisprudenza*) from an Italian university, have served an apprenticeship with a notary for two years, and have passed the prescribed examination.

The examination is held once a year in Rome. Candidates must apply to the Minister of Justice for permission to take the examination; it is given on the recommendation of the procurator of the republic of the judicial district where the candidate resides. The examination is given by an examination commission presided over by a judge of the rank of a judge of the Court of Cassation. Its membership includes one professor of law, one judge holding the rank of a judge in the court of appeal, and two notaries. It decides by majority vote.

The examination is both written and oral. The written examination requires the candidate to prepare a notarial act *inter vivos*, a will, and an appeal against a decision in civil matters. The oral examination has three parts: (a) civil and commercial law with reference to notarial acts; (b) notarial law; and (c) fees a notary may charge for his services. No candidate over the age of fifty is admitted to take the examination. Those who pass the examination are appointed to vacancies as need arises. They hold office until retirement on reaching the age of seventy-five years.

Notaries exercise their office within designated judicial districts. They cannot act outside of their districts. The districts are set by the ministry of justice. Once every two years, the office of a notary is inspected by an inspection commission under the authority of the council of notaries (*consiglio notarile*).

All notaries within a district of a court of general jurisdiction (*tribunale*) belong to the chapter of notaries (*collegio notarile*) and elect a council (*consiglio notarile*). The council has 5, 7, 9, or 11 members in accordance with the size of the membership; that is, whether it is below 30, over 30 but below 50, over 50 but below 70, or over 70. Councilors hold office for three years and may be reelected. One third is elected every year. The chapters of notaries elect the National Council of Notaries

(*Consiglio Nazionale del Notariato*); its seat is in Rome. It has fifteen members who hold office for three years and may be reelected. The National Council of Notaries represents the profession in its dealing with the government and protects its interests.

Every notary is subject to the discipline of the council of his chapter. The punishments are: admonishment, censure, fine, suspension, disbarment. The admonishment and censure may be made by the council with an appeal to the court of general jurisdiction (*tribunale*), the decision of which is final. More serious pronouncements may be made only in proceedings held in the court of general jurisdiction (*tribunale*) following civil procedure. The case is prosecuted by the public ministry at the request of the council. Against a decision of that court, an appeal lies to the court of appeal, and its decision is subject to a recourse (*ricorso*) to the Court of Cassation, but only for lack of jurisdiction (*incompetenza*), violation or misapplication of law (*violazione o falsa applicazione della legge*).

NOTES AND QUESTIONS

Notaries are fully qualified lawyers who specialize in this particular field of law. Their organization is similar to that of attorneys; but unlike attorneys, they are public officers. The education and admission to practice of notaries is fairly uniform in the various civil law countries. *See,* e.g., the Spanish system.

How do Italian notaries compare with Anglo-American notaries public? Must Anglo-American notaries public be fully qualified lawyers? Compare the law of your state. *See,* e.g., New York Executive Law §130ff.

Are the functions of notaries identical in all civil law countries? Compare, e.g., the Italian and German systems. *See also* the Mexican system. Compare also the Anglo-American system. *See,* e.g., New York Executive Law §135.

VI. DECISIONS OF ITALIAN COURTS

> NOTE: *Cases have been selected to allow an insight into the legal system and the life of the country under consideration.*
>
> *Note the approach taken by the various courts in handling the matters considered.*
>
> *Note also the time needed to bring the case from the trial court through the several hierarchically superimposed courts to the court of last resort.*

A. DECISIONS OF CIVIL COURTS IN CIVIL AND COMMERCIAL MATTERS

SUSCA v. DE LILLO

Court of Appeal of Bari; Order of July 11, 1976; President Sammartano. (*Foro Italiano,* Vol. 99, Part I, p. 2716.)

By the Court

It appears that (Mrs.) De Lillo requested the provisional execution of the divorce decree pointing to the danger in delay and stressing that the payment is for alimony. There do not appear any definite signs of the alleged danger in delay, especially considering that the trial judge ordered alimony payments to be made directly to De Lillo by the proper directorate general of the treasury from the benefit normally drawn by the judgment debtor. With respect to the nature of the debt, it is held in the doctrine and in decisions of courts that no finality of alimony payments may be asserted by invoking Art. 282 of the Code of Civil Procedure.

But even if we wanted to overcome these objections as to the merits, the petition may not succeed in view of other objections made by Susca. By Art. 10, second subsection, of the Law No. 898 of December 1, 1970, the decree of divorce produces "all civil effects," and consequently also the order for payment therein made becomes operative as from the day on which the decree of divorce is recorded in the civil register of the community where the marriage was celebrated or recorded. No such recording took place in the present case nor could it have taken place pending appeal.

It must be noted that the decree of divorce cannot produce any effects until it enters into the power of law, and since the order for payment is a part of that decree, a rapporteur judge of the Court of Appeal may not pending appeal decide which parts of the divorce decree may have already entered into the power of law. Since the trial judge has not ordered provisional execution of the decree and since such order may not be made in his place in the present state of the case, the invoked legal provisions may not be applied to this case.

For these reasons, the petition for the provisional execution of the divorce decree is denied.

NOTES AND QUESTIONS

For the function of the court of appeal consult the section on the system of Italian civil courts, and the section on Italian civil procedure above. On marriage, separation and divorce consult the section on that topic above. The *estensore* is the judge who wrote the judgment.

Article 282 of the Italian Code of Civil Procedure deals with provisional execution of judgments. It provides that provisional execution may be obtained at the petition of a party, among other things, when there is danger in delay. Provisional execution of a judgment ordering support payments should be ordered unless there are good reasons for a denial.

Law No. 898 of December 1, 1970, is the law on the dissolution of marriage. Article 10 thereof is reproduced in the text of the decision.

The proposition approved by the court in this decision is that the provisional execution of that part of a divorce decree which awards alimony to the divorced spouse may not be ordered until the decree enters into the power of law.

Does the Anglo-American legal system adhere to the same principle? When are judgments executory in the Anglo-American system? Is a decree of alimony final in the sense that it cannot be subsequently modified? On which grounds may such decrees be modified? Could not the problem in this case be remedied by an award of alimony *pendente lite*? Is alimony considered a debt in Anglo-American law? How are decrees of alimony enforced, as a debt or by contempt proceedings?

SOCIETÀ FERROVIA ROVERETO-RIVA v. BARONI

Supreme Court of Cassation; 3rd Civil Section; judgment of July 20, 1974, No. 2189; President Boccia, *Estensore* Delfini; Public Ministry Antoci; Counsel Biamonti, Franchetti, Gentile for the Società; Counsel Visona for Baroni. (*Foro Italiano*, Vol. 98, Part I, p. 104.)

By the Court

The facts: Following a traffic accident, which took place on May 4, 1962, in which a trailer truck belonging to Romeo Baroni and driven by Vinicio Cottica collided with a motor coach owned by the Società and driven by Mario Dossi, the Società and Dossi brought suit against Baroni and Cottica in the Civil Court of Rovereto claiming damages. The defendant Baroni counterclaimed. Some passengers of the motor coach intervened claiming damages from the owners and drivers of both vehicles. The insurance companies also intervened, claiming from the owners and drivers of both vehicles reimbursement of sums paid to their insured who suffered personal injuries.

The aforementioned court by judgment of July 25, 1968, held both drivers negligent and assessed the proportions of fault ninety percent as to the driver of the trailer truck and ten percent as to the driver of the motor coach and assessed damages accordingly. The judgment, which was challenged by Baroni and by the Società, was modified on appeal by the Court of Appeal of Trento by judgment of February 16, 1971. The Court of Appeal, in view of the lack of objective proof, held that it was impossible to determine with certainty how the accident took place, and applied the presumption of equal fault of the drivers pursuant to Art. 2054, subsection 2 of the Civil Code. It held that Baroni and Cottica must pay one half of the damages suffered by the Società and Dossi, and that the last two must pay one half of the damages suffered by Baroni.

This judgment was attacked by error brought by the Società. Baroni brought counter error.

The reasons:

Both suits in error are considered together by application of Art. 335 of the Code of Civil Procedure.

The Società alleges the violation and false application of Art. 2054 of the Civil Code in view of Art. 360, No. 3 of the Code of Civil Procedure, and the violation and false application of Art. 246 of the Code of Civil Procedure.

The first ground of error concerns the admissibility of evidence given by witness Bruno Spini, which the judgment complained of ruled inadmissible on the ground that by his own testimony the witness had suffered damage in the accident but omitted to consider that he was entitled to compensation. The error is well founded. The judge trying the merits correctly stated the principle that inadmissibility of testimony of those who have an interest in the matter does not affect those who already received full compensation. The judge should have considered whether the witness found himself in that position and should not have omitted from his consideration the statements made by this witness concerning the claims and defenses of the parties.

The second ground of error alleges that the Court of Appeal failed to evaluate the proof presented, and applied the rule as to the absence of proof contained in Art. 2054 of the Civil Code. . . . It must be admitted that the Court of Appeal, in contrast to the trial court, committed an error of law with respect to the interpretation of Art. 2054 of the Civil Code, and that the second ground of error is also well founded.

This court has repeatedly held that the evaluation of proof concerning a traffic accident and the ascertainment of the causal link leading to it in the conduct of the two drivers pertains exclusively to the judge trying the merits of the case and may not be reviewed in a court of error, but this is subject to the assumption that the reasoning of the court is free of error in logic and in law. In this case, however, the judge trying the merits did not apply the proper meaning of Art. 2054 of the Civil Code, but held that the presumption sanctioned by it has a primary and decisive meaning and may not be overcome except by an exceptionally strong proof. Only by erroneously attributing to the presumption of subsection 2 of Art. 2054 a special meaning, may the search by the court for absolute certainty, which is normally unattainable by usual procedural means, and the rejection of proof lacking a strong scientific objectivity be justified.

But this is not what Art. 2054 means. The legislature has not intended in any way to derogate from the usual criteria of search for the truth and of evaluation of proof. Even in cases of vehicular traffic, the judge must attempt, in accordance with his prudent evaluation, to reach a reasonable degree of certainty, which is a completely different matter than an absolute certainty to the exclusion of any doubt, however abstract or hypothetical. To do that, the judge should apply all available means of proof without arbitrarily refusing to recognize that the knowledge of facts may be obtained apart from objective proof, like reports, tracks of vehicles, photographs, and plans, also by an attentive and prudent evaluation of the testimony of persons present at those events.

It must be recognized that the court trying the merits has erred in the application of Art. 2054 by construing the legal presumption of equal fault of drivers of vehicles as absolutely preeminent and practically insuperable, thus ignoring the literal meaning of that provision and the legal principle repeatedly enunciated by this court by which the presumption of equal fault in subsection 2 of Art. 2054 has only a subsidiary function and applies only when it is not possible to determine the actual degree of fault in the event.

The error thus succeeds and the judgment complained of is set aside. The matter is remitted to another judge who, in applying the above-mentioned principles of law and without being bound by the criteria set by the Court of Appeal, will consider with full freedom of examination the capacity of witnesses, the admissibility of testimony, the interpretation of expert reports, and so forth and evaluate the oral and documentary proof in order to reconstrue the facts and to determine the liability of each of the two drivers. The same judge will also decide on the costs of the error proceedings. The Società is entitled to a refund of the deposit in the error proceedings.

NOTES AND QUESTIONS

For the Supreme Court of Cassation, consult the section on the structure of

Italian civil courts and that on Italian civil procedure. The *estensore* is the judge who wrote the judgment.

Article 2054 of the Civil Code deals with damage caused by vehicular traffic. Its first subsection provides that a driver of a vehicle not operating on tracks must make good the damage caused by it to persons and property, unless he can show that he has done everything possible to avert the damage. The second subsection provides that in the case of a collision it is presumed that each of the drivers contributed equally to the damage caused to the vehicles unless proved otherwise. Its third subsection provides that the owner of a vehicle is jointly liable with the driver unless he can show that the vehicle was being used against his will.

Article 335 of the Code of Civil Procedure provides that all remedies brought against the same judgment will be consolidated and heard in one suit.

Article 360, No. 3, of the Code of Civil Procedure provides for the bringing of the petition for the cassation of a judgment because of violation or false application of law.

Article 246 of the Code of Civil Procedure provides that persons who have an interest in the judgment which may bring about their taking part in the suit may not be heard as witnesses.

The proposition approved by the court in this decision is that the presumption of equal fault of both drivers provided in Art. 2054 of the Civil Code operates only when it is not possible to determine which driver was responsible for the accident nor their individual degree of fault.

The party petitioning for cassation must file a deposit with the court which will be refunded if it succeeds or as the court may order. The purpose of the deposit is to discourage groundless petitions.

Does the same proposition hold good in the law of your state? Does the rule of proportional fault apply generally in negligence? What are the other standards commonly used? On which principle is the owner of a vehicle responsible for the damage caused by it while it was driven by an employee or a person with the owner's permission? Is the distinction in the relationship of master-servant, and principal-agent, of importance?

COCCIA v. BERLINGIERI

Supreme Court of Cassation; First Civil Section; judgment of July 12, 1974, No. 2083; President Giannattasio, *Estensore* Santosuosso, Public Ministry Mililotti, Counsel Coccia for Coccia, Counsel Salerni for Berlingieri. (*Foro Italiano*, Vol. 98, Part I, p. 120.)

By the Court

The facts: By summons of February 16, 1967, attorney Giuseppe Berlingieri cited attorney Ivo Coccia before the Civil Court of Rome and alleged that he was liable in accordance with Art. 2043 of the Civil Code of an injury to his reputation and should be ordered to pay damages. He alleged that at a hearing held on April 20, 1963, in a suit against the newspaper *L'Unità*, attorney Coccia made the allegation that Berlingieri had withdrawn an action and then paid to Coccia in a closed envelope one half of the court costs, which were set at 60,000 lire by agreement of the parties.

The defendant appeared and requested interrogatories and testimonial proof, but the motions were denied by the court. Berlingieri then died and the action was continued by his widow and daughter, who also claimed damages in their own right.

The court considered both claims together. It denied the claim for damages brought by the widow and daughter in their own right but upheld the claim for damages in the original action and ordered Coccia to pay 551,000 lire damages and two thirds of the court costs. The Court of Appeal of Rome affirmed and held that the words in question were defamatory and it denied the testimonial proof requested by Coccia. It also excluded applicability of Art. 598 of the Penal Code, which grants immunity to statements contained in briefs of the defense, because the words were not directly linked to the exigencies of defense but constituted an expression of an old personal ill-feeling. It also ordered the payment of interest on the sum awarded as from the making of the injurious statement.

Coccia petitions for cassation on five grounds; the heirs of Berlingieri brought a counter petition.

The reasons:

In his second ground, the petitioner alleges that the judges on the merits were in error to hold that the ground for exclusion of liability provided in Art. 598 of the Penal Code requires a strict logical and causal nexus between the offense and the subject matter of the suit, while the doctrine and decisions hold that any link is amply sufficient.

The allegation is founded. It must be stated that the ascertainment by the judge on the merits of injurious statements made in briefs and orally in pleading before courts and their relation to the subject matter of the suit may not be attacked on error whenever the judgment is supported by sufficient reasoning and is not affected by an erroneous interpretation of the concepts of "relationship" and "subject matter of the suit."

The challenged judgment is defficient on this point in that without inquiring into the subject matter of the suit in which a writing containing the offensive statements was produced, and without considering analytically these statements with reference to the development of the suit, the court limited itself to the statement: "There was no logical nexus between the injurious statements and the subject matter of the suit, in that the first were in the nature of discordant digressions and could not be considered arguments strictly linked to the needs of the defense, but were rather the manifestations of an older personal ill-feeling."

This insufficient reasoning may be criticized also from the point of view of the principle of exclusion of liability provided in Art. 598 of the Penal Code. The law, in order not to hamper the vivacity of pleading and the freedom of expression, provides the special ground of justification in Art. 598 of the Penal Code, which does not demand that the injurious statements be legally necessary or useful in the exercise of the defense of the person who has written or pronounced them, thus supporting the exclusion of liability provided in Art. 51 of the Penal Code, but requires only that the injurious statements be in some way linked to the defense. This "relationship" of the injurious statements to the subject matter of the suit consists in the mere relation of the injurious or defamatory words to the substance in dispute even thought they are not strictly linked to the needs of the defense.

It may be deduced from the legislative intent that to qualify for the exclusion of liability in Art. 598 of the Penal Code it is necessary that the injurious statements made by the parties or their representatives be true and that they do not display features of personal ill-feeling.

In view of these principles, the judge on the merits should have examined the words written by attorney Coccia in the context of the whole dispute that formed the subject matter of the pleading. He should have ascertained whether the story concerning the payment of one half of the costs, the reimbursement of which was agreed upon, had a foundation in the claim for damages or in other claims within the subject matter of the suit. He should have further examined whether all this formed a part of a defensive theory which tended to show "communist disloyalty" for not having complied with the terms set for the withdrawal of the suit. Only after a negative outcome of this examination could the conclusion have been made that the statements were totally unrelated to the questions discussed by the parties at that point of time.

This examination must be held by the judge to whom the case will be remitted after the cassation of the judgment. He will also have to consider whether to admit the means of proof demanded by Coccia. This is the third ground of the error and it is well founded.

The contradiction in the reasoning consists in the irreconcilability of a possible justification in the conduct of Coccia with the evident requirement of malice on the part of the offender. It is not clear why the judges on the merits did not attach any relevance to the circumstance that was the subject of the proof, namely the function of Berlingieri as a mere carrier of the letter in question.

NOTES AND QUESTIONS

Article 2043 of the Civil Code provides that whosoever shall commit an intentional or negligent act which causes unjust damage to another is obligated to make good the damage.

Article 598 of the Penal Code provides that offensive statements made in writing or orally by the parties or their representatives in judicial or administrative proceedings are not punishable if the statements concern the subject matter of the dispute.

Article 51 of the Penal Code provides that the exercise of a right or the implementation of a duty imposed by a legal norm or by a legitimate order of a public authority excludes liability.

The proposition approved by the court in this decision is that it is not necessary for the exclusion of liability that the offensive statements are in the nature of legal necessity or utility in the exercise of the defense by the party who has spoken or written them, but it is sufficient that the offensive statements, even if they are not true and are dictated by the personal motives of ill-feeling of the offender, are related to the subject matter of the suit.

Does the principle announced in Art. 2043 of the Italian Civil Code hold good also in Anglo-American law? Are statements privileged by Art. 598 of the Italian

Penal Code privileged in Anglo-American proceedings? Does the mandate of Art. 51 of the Italian Penal Code exist in Anglo-American law? Does the principle announced by the court obtain also in Anglo-American law? How would a case of defamation be handled on these facts in Anglo-American law?

MAIMONE v. MINISTRY OF THE INTERIOR

Supreme Court of Cassation; Third civil section; judgment of February 1, 1974, No. 281; President La Farina, *Estensore* Gabrieli, Public Ministry Silocchi; Counsel Bottai and Biaggetti for Maimone and Government counsel (*Avvocato dello Stato*) Gozzi for the Ministry of the Interior. (*Foro Italiano*, Vol. 97, Part I, p. 2734.)

By the Court

The facts: Giovanni Maimone, who was employed with the mobile squad of the police of Rome as an officer of public security from February 1, 1958, until February 1, 1961, and who at that time took part in many difficult assignments together with his German shepherd named "Dox," owned and trained by him for detective work, brought suit against his minister in the Civil Court of Rome. He alleged that he had received only a subsidy of 25,000 lire for the maintenance of the dog in all that time and demanded that the ministry should be ordered to pay him 10,800,000 lire for maintenance of the dog, and for the loss of gains he could have made at the rate of 300,000 lire per month by using the dog in public shows.

The ministry appeared and denied the claim. It admitted that the plaintiff was employed as stated but alleged that nothing was due to him with respect to the dog because he used his dog voluntarily on his own initiative and not at the request of the ministry.

The Court, by judgment of December 23, 1966, dismissed the claim on the ground that there was no correlation between the alleged loss and enrichment which would justify a claim for unjust enrichment.

The Court of Appeal of Rome affirmed by judgment of June 24, 1969, and observed that the ministry may have been enriched by not having paid for the maintenance and training of the dog but not by the exceptional results of detection performed by the dog, which did not provide the ministry with any financial gain. Further, Maimone did not suffer any loss since he had to provide for the dog in any event. Maimone could have suffered a loss by not making gains he could have made had he displayed the dog at public shows, but he was not prevented by the ministry from using the dog in that way. There was no correlation between the alleged loss of Maimone and a gain by the ministry, which did not enrich itself even in the slightest from what Maimone claims to have lost.

Maimone filed a petition for the cassation of the judgment and the ministry filed a counter petition.

The reasons:

The petition raises two grounds, which will be considered together: (1) It alleges a violation and false application of Art. 2041 of the Civil Code since the judge on the merits did not award to Maimone the value of the services performed by the dog, and at least the expense of maintenance and training of the dog; and (2) it alleges lack of grounds, inadequate reasoning and contradiction in the reasons of the judgment (Art. 360 No. 5 of the Code of Civil Procedure) in that the judge on the merits failed to consider the gain Maimone could have realized by exhibiting the dog in public shows, and further that he could not have so exhibited the dog because of his employment as a police officer since he was under orders of his superiors even with respect to the dog.

The error is only partially founded. The judgment complained of approaches the matter on the ground of unjust enrichment stated by the claim and requires a causal connection between the gain of one and the loss of the other in full observance of the principle on which both the doctrine and decisions agree, that in order to succeed there must be a simultaneous coincidence of the enrichment of one and the corresponding loss of the other arising from the same causal fact. The judgment is correct in declaring that the ministry could not have been enriched by the exceptional services of the dog since they were of no financial value but only by having made a saving in not paying for the maintenance and training of the dog.

As to the second ground of error, the judgment is correct. Maimone could have actually displayed the dog since he admitted himself that he could have exhibited the dog in public without himself being present. There is thus no evidence of a shift of gain from Maimone to the ministry. The possible gain that he could have realized is purely hypothetical while the law demands an actual financial loss.

The judgment is, however, suffering from an error when it holds that the ministry was not required to pay for the maintenance and the training of the dog since Maimone was bound to do so in any event, even if the ministry had not made any use of the dog. It is a purely one-sided view to consider the interest that the owner has in the maintenance of the life of the animal and to fail to consider the benefit of the dog's services accruing to the ministry.

It must be therefore held that the expense of maintenance of the dog, not for the exclusive use of its owner but chiefly for the benefit of the ministry, constitutes a financial loss susceptible of ascertainment, while the ministry is enriched because at the expense of the owner of the dog it took advantage of the dog's services. Equally, the work exerted by Maimone in the training and development of the special qualities of the dog in relation to his employment cannot be assumed to have been done for free, and he has a claim for compensation within the scope of an action for unjust enrichment.

For these reasons, with respect to the expense of maintenance and training of the dog, the attacked judgment must be set aside and the matter referred to another section of the Court of Appeal in Aquila for a new trial of the case in accordance with the expressed principles.

NOTES AND QUESTIONS

Article 2041 of the Civil Code provides that a person who without a just cause enriches himself at the expense of another person must, within the scope of the enrichment, indemnify the latter for the corresponding financial loss.

Article 360, No. 5 of the Code of Civil Procedure provides that judgments of appellate courts may be attacked by a petition for their cassation on the ground that the court omitted to consider, insufficiently considered, or made contradictions in its reasoning with respect to a decisive point in the controversy raised by the parties or ex officio.

The court thus held that Maimone kept the dog chiefly for the benefit of the ministry. His work expended in the training and use of the dog for the benefit of the ministry was additional to the services he rendered to the ministry as a police officer and he had not received any appropriate corresponding compensation therefor.

Does the concept of unjust enrichment exist in Anglo-American law? In states where such cause of action is unknown, could the suit be founded on *quasicontract* or *quantum meruit*? Did unjust enrichment already exist in Roman law? Is the claim of Maimone for the maintenance of the dog justified in view of the facts of the case? What about his claim for loss of the gain he could have made by displaying the dog in public shows? Is it purely speculative? Suppose Maimone, after leaving the police force, actually displayed the dog in public shows and could prove his annual income therefrom? Would an Anglo-American court resolve the matter differently on the facts presented?

FERRINI *v.* GNASSI

Supreme Court of Cassation, Second civil section; judgment of October 27, 1973, No. 2797; President Pratillo, *Estensore* Lazzaro, Public Ministry Pandolfelli; Counsel Visco and Anza for Ferrini, and Counsel Rosati for Gnassi. (*Foro Italiano*, Vol. 97, Part I, p. 2770.)

By the Court

The facts: By summons of November 10, 1966, (Mrs.) Dorina Ferrini brought suit against (Mrs.) Dirce Gnassi in the Civil Court of Pesaro. She alleged that her maternal uncle Giuseppe Giunta died on October 4, 1963, and that he disposed of all of his property by an holographic will dated June 1, 1963, as follows: "I the undersigned leave at my death all to my wife so long she shall live; on her death one half to her kin and the other half to my kin." His wife, Rosa Mariotti Giunta, also died and assuming that she was only an usufructuary of the estate of her husband, the title to which passed one half to his and the other half to her kin, appointed Gnassi as universal heir in a public testament. Plaintiff demanded that the defendant should hand over to her the property held without title with all fruits perceived since the death of the usufructuary.

Gnassi resisted and claimed that the testator Giunta intended to leave full title to his property to his wife, Rosa Mariotti, with full right to dispose of it in her lifetime, and that the remainder constituted a residuary trust prohibited by law.

The court held that the disposition in favor of the kin of the testator and those of his wife were void and dismissed the action.

Ferrini appealed to the Court of Appeal in Ancona and that court affirmed the decision by judgment of November 14, 1969. It held that the trust of the residue clearly appeared from the language used by the testator.

Ferrini brings error on three grounds.

The reasons:

As to the first ground, Ferrini alleges violation and false application of Arts. 1362, 1363 and 1367 of the Civil Code in that the judgment did not give effect to the wishes of the testator which appeared in his testamentary provision although they were not phrased with precision, namely, to give his widow a usufruct and leave the title one half to his, and the other half to her, kin.

The ground is unfounded. The interpretation of the testamentary scheme is a question of fact and may not be made at the error level when it was made in the courts below in accordance with the law and without lapses in logic. The courts of merit held that the testator intended to leave all his property to his wife as a general heir with a prohibition to dispose of it by testament and then provided a detailed scheme of how the property should descend on her death. He thus excluded any intent to leave her only a usufruct and dispose of the title to the property at the time of his death.

The terms "I leave all" sound clearly as the grant of title without any limitation, not only as to quantity but also as to full title in the property. If he desired to leave his wife a lesser interest he could have easily said so by using usual terms of the commonly used language. The terms "so long as she shall live" may not limit the preceding meaning, transforming a grant of full title into a lesser interest. . . . [Second ground omitted]

In her third ground, Ferrini alleges violation of Art. 692 of the Civil Code in that the court held the provision in the will to the kin to be a residuary trust.

This ground of error cannot be sustained. Since the court on the merits has correctly identified the legal elements that constitute a residuary trust, the question of fact of whether or not the disposition in question amounted to a residuary trust may not be reviewed on error if it is supported by reasoning not failing as to its adequacy and in logic.

Consequently, the court on the merits has correctly determined that the manifest intent of Giunta was to leave full title to all his property to his wife as a general heir without the prohibition of disposing of it by testament, and to render operative the provision in favor of their kin at her death. . . . With respect to the residuary trust, its nullity is directly proclaimed in the last subsection of Art. 692 of the Civil Code. The reason for it is that it inhibits the free alienation of property.

There is no error.

Ferrini is ordered to pay the costs of the cassation proceedings and loses her deposit.

NOTES AND QUESTIONS

For the procedure before the Court of Cassation, consult the section on such procedure above.

For provisions on wills and estates, consult the section so named above.

Article 1362 of the Civil Code states that in the interpretation of contracts one must inquire as to what was the intent of the parties and not be limited to the literal meaning of the words. To determine the intent of the parties, their conduct as a whole, even after making the contract must be considered.

Article 1363 of the Civil Code states that clauses in a contract are interpreted by reference to the others, attributing to each of them the meaning which appears from the whole document.

Article 1367 of the Civil Code provides that in case of doubt, the contract or its individual provisions must be given that meaning which makes them meaningful rather than that which makes them meaningless.

Article 692 of the Civil Code provides that a residuary trust for the benefit of a person under guardianship or a minor is lawful, but it is void in all other cases.

The court thus held that the testator intended to leave his wife full title to his property on his death, appointing her a general heir with a prohibition to dispose of the property inherited by will if some should remain at her death, and that he intended the kin to succeed to it on her death but that such disposition was void as offending against the last subsection of Art. 692 of the Civil Code.

A usufruct may be set up for the life of the usufructuary but not beyond. Usufruct of a legal person may not exceed thirty years. The usufructuary may enjoy the thing subject to limitations imposed on him by law. He must protect the economic value of the thing. He may assign his right if he is not prohibited from doing so by the grantor.

What are the several types of wills a testator may use in Italian law? What are the characteristics of an holographic will and a public will? May a testator make an holographic will in your state? Does Anglo-American law recognize an holographic will? Would the testamentary disposition in this case have the same meaning in Anglo-American law? Would it not rather be interpreted as a devise: to my wife for life, remainder to the respective kin in equal shares? Would an Anglo-American court rather be expected to agree with the petitioner in error? Is life estate in Anglo-American law the corresponding institution of an Italian usufruct?

SOCIETÀ I.R.B.I.A.M. v. SOCIETÀ IMMOBILIARIA ANCUSA AND CONDOMINIO VIA COPERNICO 53—MILANO

Supreme Court of Cassation, Second civil section; judgment of December 14, 1973, No. 3405; President Cortesani, *Estensore* Corasaniti, Public Ministry Mililotti; Counsel Lavena for Società I.R.B.I.A.M. and Counsel Arata for Ancusa. (*Foro Italiano*, Vol. 97, Part I., p. 2739.)

By the Court

The facts: The stock corporation I.R.B.I.A.M., purchaser of premises in a building situated in Milan, Via Copernico 53, brought suit in the Civil Court of Milan against the vendor, a corporation with limited liability Ancusa and the condominium of the building. It alleged that the heating system in the premises was faulty and demanded that the defendants be ordered to repair the heating system and pay damages which arose due to its defectiveness.

The defendants rejected the claim.

The court denied the claim for repairs, holding that the law does not give such a remedy to the plaintiff and that the claim to damages must also be denied since the plaintiff knew of the defects. The court of appeal affirmed. Plaintiff petitions for cassation on three grounds. The defendant filed a counter petition.

The reasons:

In its first ground of error, the plaintiff complains that the court of appeal erroneously denied his claim for the elimination of the defects, holding that the law does not give such a remedy to the purchaser with respect to defects in the thing sold.

The ground fails. The reason why the law does not give such a remedy to the purchaser is the absence of any obligation to do on the part of the vendor. Even if this claim is presented in the form of defective performance of the vendor, it may still not succeed as it demands the exact compliance by the vendor of his primary obligation. . . . . The vendor, in contrast to an independent contractor, is not required to eliminate the defects. This holds good even where the vendor has made the thing sold. . . . The law takes notice of the facts of economic life in that a manufacturer has the facilities to produce but not to repair or remake the thing he makes. This function is undertaken by affiliated enterprises.

The second ground of error succeeds. There the plaintiff complains that the court of appeal denied his claim to damages and failed to admit his proof to show that he was unaware of the defects. It is true that the claim for damages being tied to the so-called warranty against defects may not succed in the case where an action for rescission of the contract or the reduction of the purchase price may not be brought because of the statute of limitation. It is also true that only the party who may demand rescission or reduction of the purchase price may sue for damages, but it is not true, as the court of appeal has erroneously held, that the proof of a claim with respect to a remedy not allowed by the law concerning the defects in the thing precludes also the proof of a contractual remedy. The court of appeal should not have thus denied the claim for damages on this ground and should have examined the reasons for admission of the proof.

The third ground of error is also well founded. The plaintiff complains of the failure of the court to hear his claim to damages arising from the defects. It concerns the loss caused to the purchaser by defects in the thing bought referred to in Art. 1494, subsection 1. The court of appeal should not have failed to consider the claim.

The second and third grounds of error consequently succeed and the judgment is set aside to that extent. The case is remitted to another judge who will be bound by the indicated principles of law. He will also decide on the costs of the error proceedings. The petitioner is entitled to have his deposit refunded.

NOTES AND QUESTIONS

With respect to corporations, consult the section on corporations above. Sales are discussed in the Italian Civil Code in Arts. 1470-1547.

Article 1490 of the Civil Code provides that the seller warrants that the thing sold is free of any defects which make it unsuited for the purpose for which it is intended.

Article 1491 of the Civil Code provides that this warranty (of Art. 1490) does not apply where at the time of the making of the contract the buyer knew of the defects in the thing; the warranty does not equally apply where the defects were easily discoverable, unless the seller declared that there were not defects.

Article 1492 of the Civil Code provides that, pursuant to Art. 1490, the buyer may at his option demand either the dissolution of the contract or the reduction of the purchase price. The option is irrevocable once suit is filed.

Article 1494 of the Civil Code provides that in either case the seller is liable in damages unless he proves that he did not know of the defects in the thing and that he was not negligent in not knowing. He has also to make good the loss arising to the buyer due to the defects in the thing.

Article 1495 of the Civil Code provides that the buyer must notify the seller of defects in the thing within eight days from their discovery, unless a different time is provided for by the parties or the law. If he does not do so, he loses his right to the warranty. In any event the action may not be brought one year after the delivery, but the buyer may still take advantage of the warranty if he notifies the seller before one year of the delivery has run.

The purchaser of the premises did not seek the rescission of the contract nor a reduction of the purchase price, but wanted only the vendor and the condominium to provide proper heating. The court held that the law does not give the buyer such a remedy, but that he may claim damages.

Would the plaintiff be better off had he only leased premises, since the lease has a standard provision providing that the lessor will supply the heat for the premises? He then would have been able to use the standard remedies that the law gives to the lessee. Is it true that the concept of a condominium is more favorable to the vendor than to the purchaser? Since the purchaser of premises is then entitled only to the remedies available to a purchaser, he must denounce any defects within a short period of limitation. But even at the making of the contract, the principle of caveat emptor applies in full force. Is there then any advantage left to the purchaser of a condominium over a lessee of premises? Is the legal position of a purchaser of premises in a condominium in Italy similar to such a purchaser in Britain or America? The Italian law treats the purchase like a purchase of a chattel; is the same true in the Anglo-American law?

CANCRINI v. BARTOLINI AND FAVINO

Supreme Court of Cassation, Third civil section; judgment of April 27, 1973, No. 1150; President Aliota, *Estensore* Miani, Public Ministry Martinelli; Counsel Dente for Cancrini and Counsel Tirone for Bartolini (*Foro Italiano*, Vol. 97, Part I, p. 3158.)

By the Court

The facts: On January 19, 1966, Doctor Leone Cancrini brought suit against Francesco Bartolini and Aldo Favino in the Civil Court of Rome claiming that a partnership should be declared to exist between them and that they as partners should be ordered to repay to the plaintiff the sum of 10,000,000 lire advanced by him to Favino as a loan to be applied to the partnership.

Bartolini appeared and denied the allegations of the plaintiff and claimed that since Favino was declared a bankrupt by judgment of the Civil Court of Rome of February 3, 1966, the suit should have been brought in the bankruptcy court.

Cancrini then limited his claim only to a declaration of the existence of a partnership between the defendants. Favino did not appear.

The Civil Court of Rome, by an interlocutory judgment of November 20, 1967, rejected the exception of inadmissibility of the plaintiff's claim raised by Bartolini, and he appealed. The Court of Appeal of Rome, by a judgment of May 30, 1969, declared the claim of Cancrini inadmissible on the ground that it would, in fact, extend the bankruptcy of Favino to Bartolini, which could be done only by a court having jurisdiction in the matter, namely, the court that declared the bankruptcy of Favino.

Against the judgment, Cancrini filed a petition for its cassation dated September 25, 1969, basing his claim on a single ground of error. Bartolini filed a counter petition. Favino did not appear, although he was properly summoned.

The reasons:

The petitioner in error alleges the violation and false application of Art. 147 of the Bankruptcy Law and Arts. 1290, 1304 and 1954 of the Civil Code, and he further alleges that the judgment complained of has illogically and erroneously held that a petition for a declaratory judgment declaring a partnership to exist among several persons, one of them being already bankrupt, may not be made outside of bankruptcy proceedings.

The error is founded in substance. The court of appeal held that the declaration sought by the plaintiff would amount to an extension of the bankruptcy of Favino, a single trader, to the partnership and to his partner Bartolini, and would make them liable without any limitation.... This interpretation suffers from logical and legal errors.

There is a contradiction in the holding of the court in that it holds that the petition for a declaratory judgment is in fact a petition for the declaration of bankruptcy. It further holds that once it is found that a partnership exists between a bankrupt and a third person, the bankruptcy must be automatically extended to the partnership and to the partner of the bankrupt. This is not correct.

It is one thing to hold that a bankrupt firm owned by a single trader was in fact a partnership which would make them all bankrupt, and another to determine whether there existed a partnership between a bankrupt and another person which would not make the other person bankrupt. In this case, Art. 149 of the Bankruptcy Law applies, which provides that bankruptcy of one or more jointly liable partners does not make the partnership bankrupt and does not thus extend the bankruptcy to the other partners.

From that follows that the further holding of the court of appeal, that the consideration of the question of whether a partnership existed between a bankrupt and another person would invade the jurisdiction of a bankruptcy court, is also erroneous.

Where a declaration of partnership between a bankrupt and another person is sought in order to obtain a judgment against a partner who is not bankrupt so as to make him pay a joint debt without making any claims against the bankrupt, the proceedings do not invade the jurisdiction of the court that made the declaration of bankruptcy.

The reasoning of the court on the merits is thus erroneous, but is harmless to the extent that the court has made a distinction between a court in which the petition for the declaratory judgment was brought and that which has declared the bankruptcy since all these events took place in one and the same territorially competent court, the Civil Court of Rome.

The error therefore succeeds. The judgment is set aside and the case remitted to another section of the Court of Appeal of Rome, which will decide also on the costs of the cassation proceedings and which will abide by the following direction as to the law: "A petition for a mere ascertainment of the existence of partnership between a bankrupt trader and another person does not fall within the exclusive jurisdiction of the court that declared the bankruptcy and may be made outside of bankruptcy proceedings. . . . The bankruptcy of one or more partners with unlimited liability does not, according to Art. 149 of the Bankruptcy Law, make the partnership automatically bankrupt."

Cancrini is entitled to the refund of his deposit, while Bartolini loses his deposit.

NOTES AND QUESTIONS

By bankruptcy court is meant the court that is actually seized of a particular bankruptcy case. There are no separate commercial or bankruptcy courts in Italy. Such cases are handled by the ordinary civil courts.

For partnerships, consult the section on partnerships above. As for bankruptcy, consult the section on bankruptcy above.

Article 147 of the Bankruptcy Law provides that bankruptcy of a partnership which has partners whose liability is limited produces also the bankruptcy of the partners whose liability is unlimited.

Article 149 of the Bankruptcy Law provides that the bankruptcy of one or more partners whose liability is unlimited does not produce bankruptcy of the partnership.

Article 1290 of the Civil Code provides that when both alternative obligations become impossible of performance and the debtor is liable on one of them, he must pay the equivalent of the one which became impossible of performance last, if he has the choice. If the creditor has the choice, he can select the equivalent of either of them.

Article 1304 of the Civil Code provides that a settlement made before any suit is brought between a creditor and one of the jointly liable debtors has no effect on the other debtors unless they declare that they claim the same benefit.

Article 1954 of the Civil Code provides that where several persons have warranted the same debt of the same debtor, the one who has paid the debt may obtain contribution from all the others. If one of them is insolvent, his share must be borne proportionally by the others.

Do most of the Anglo-American jurisdictions have separate bankruptcy courts? If so, would a petition for a declaratory judgment on the facts of the above case have to be made in a bankruptcy court? Does the bankruptcy of a general partner make the partnership bankrupt under Anglo-American law? Does the Anglo-American law recognize the partnership as an entity separate from the individual general partners? What will Cancrini have to show in the further proceedings in order to succeed against Bartolini? Would the same facts have to be shown in an Anglo-American court in order to succeed?

BARTOLINI v. PUCCETTI

Court of Cassation; First civil section; judgment of January 27, 1977, No. 406; President G. Rossi, *Estensore* Zappulli, Public Ministry Gentile; Counsel Belli and

Landi for Bartolini, and Counsel Formiggini for Puccetti. (*Foro Italiano*, Vol. 102, Part I, p. 320.)

By the Court

The facts: Mario Bartolini brought suit on April 21, 1964, in the Civil Court of Bologna against Vittorio Puccetti. He alleged that, in 1936, he formed a general partnership with the defendant for the manufacture of electrical and hydrodynamic equipment for railroads, and that by the provisions of the agreement, the partnership was to exist until December 31, 1960. But prior to the termination of the partnership, Puccetti set up his own enterprise, which was registered with the local chamber of commerce in February 1960, and produced identical equipment and thus caused the partnership not to be invited to bid on contracts for the maintenance of equipment of the state railways. Plaintiff claimed damages caused by the competition of the defendant to the partnership in the sum of 6,000,000 lire with interest.

Puccetti appeared and moved the dismissal of the suit on the ground that he began to exercise the alleged activity only in 1961; that is, only after the termination of the partnership, which was formally dissolved on December 31, 1960, as certified by notary public Grechi on February 13, 1961, in a notarized act.

By preliminary judgment of February 7, 1969, the court ordered Puccetti to make good the loss suffered by Bartolini by infringement of Art. 2301 of the Civil Code, which prohibits competition between partners without their consent. Puccetti appealed, and the Court of Appeal of Bologna, by a judgment of April 30, 1973, denied the claim of the plaintiff. It held that the plaintiff may not bring such suit as an individual, but that only the partnership by its liquidator could bring a suit against Puccetti, and further that such a suit was inadmissible because it amounted to a new claim which was raised for the first time only in the appellate proceedings, namely, a claim for unfair competition defined in Art. 2598 of the Civil Code.

Bartolini petitioned for cassation on three grounds. Puccetti brought a counter petition.

The reasons:

In his first ground of error, Bartolini alleges that the court of merit misapplied Art. 2301 when it held that only the partnership may bring suit for damages under its provisions, since the rule expressed in that article may not apply when there are only two partners in the partnership because then the loss would fall exclusively on one of them.

The error is not well founded since subsection 3 of Art. 2301 of the Civil Code provides that, in the case of a violation of its first subsection, the partnership is entitled to damages apart from provisions of Art. 2286, which deals with the removal of a partner and which confirms this rule. The proposition of the plaintiff concerning the case where the partnership has only two partners is unfounded since the property of a general partnership is a separate entity even though it does not have a separate legal personality, and its existence, separate from the partners, excludes the possibility that the faculties attributed exclusively to it could be exercised by an individual partner.

It may be noted that Art. 2304 of the Civil Code provides that a creditor of a partnership, even in liquidation, may not demand the payment of a partnership debt from an individual partner unless the partnership property has been exhausted. This implies that even in a partnership formed by only two partners, the partnership property is a separate entity.

In his second ground of error, the petitioner alleges violation of Art. 345 of the Code of Civil Procedure since the court did not follow the rule that a modification of a claim is inadmissible only when the very substance of the claim is modified.

This ground is unfounded because Art. 2598 of the Civil Code lists particular cases of unfair competition and requires intent or negligence on the part of the actor. . . . In fact, Bartolini in his statement of claim in his suit in the trial court not only specifically relied on Art. 2301 of the Civil Code, but stated that the loss he suffered was due to the activity exercised by Puccetti in competition with the partnership due to Puccetti's use of the goodwill of the firm name of the partnership. Bartolini asserted that his loss arose due to the activity of Puccetti and from the loss of the goodwill of the firm name of the partnership, but he has not indicated any facts which exceed the scope of ordinary competition and enter that of unfair competition under Art. 1598. . . . . [The third ground is omitted.]

The petition is denied.

NOTES AND QUESTIONS

For partnerships, consult the section on partnerships above. For procedure on appeal, consult the section on appellate procedure above. For notaries, consult the section on notaries, above.

Article 2301 of the Civil Code provides that a partner may not, without the consent of the other partners, exercise an activity in competition with that of the partnership. In case of breach, the partnership has a right to damages apart from Art. 2286.

Article 2286 of the Civil Code provides for the expulsion of a partner from the partnership on several specified grounds.

Article 2598 of the Civil Code lists cases of unfair competition. It defines unfair competition as the improper use of names or signs likely to produce confusion with respect to those used by another, the imitation of the product of another, or any other means which create a confusion with respect to the products or activity of another.

Article 2304 of the Civil Code is reproduced in the text of the decision.

Article 345 of the Code of Civil Procedure provides that no new demand may be made on appeal, and if so made, it will be rejected ex officio.

The court thus held that a partner in a general partnership may not bring suit for damages against another partner for exercising a competing commercial activity with that of the partnership even if the partnership has only two partners and is in liquidation. It further held that a claim which for the first time alleges in the appellate proceedings facts of unfair competition pursuant to Art. 2598 of the Civil Code, is a new claim where in the demand in the trial court the claim was based on allegations of ordinary competition pursuant to Art. 2301 of the Civil Code.

Is the concept of general partnership identical in Italian and Anglo-American law? Under Anglo-American law, may a partner in a general partnership compete individually with the partnership? What is the distinction between ordinary competition, which is a healthy feature of a free commercial system, and unfair competition, which is prohibited by law? On which ground, as alleged by the plaintiff, was the ordinary competition exercised by the defendant unlawful? Was it thus a statutory or a contractual prohibition? May new demands be made in appellate proceedings in Anglo-American courts? Does the definition of a new demand in the Italian system conform to the concept of a new demand in the Anglo-American system?

B. DECISIONS OF CRIMINAL COURTS

REPUBLIC v. MAZZIOTTI

Court of Cassation; Third Penal Section; judgment of January 27, 1975; President Straniero, *Estensore* M. Rossi, Public Ministry Moscarini; petition by the Public Ministry and by Mazziotti. (*Foro Italiano*, Vol. 99, Part II, p. 358.)

By the Court

The facts: Following initiation of proceedings on September 17, 1967, Salvatore Mazziotti, after preliminary proceedings, was ordered to stand trial in the Criminal Court of Naples for rape of the minor Maria Capuano, age seven. The Court by a judgment of May 25, 1972, found Mazziotti guilty and in view of attenuating circumstances convicted him to three years and six months of reclusion.

Both the procurator general of Naples and the accused appealed. The procurator general demanded an increase in the term of imprisonment in that the court, starting from the base of three years, failed to consider the provision concerning the increase of penalty in Art. 523 which is directly referred to in Art. 524 of the Penal Code.

The accused alleged that the facts he had supposedly committed lacked proof and secondarily that the punishment imposed was excessive.

At the hearing on February 8, 1973, before the Court of Appeal of Naples, Mazziotti did not appear and his counsel produced a medical certificate; the Court held that his absence was not due to an absolute impossibility on a legitimate ground, however, and proceeded in the absence of Mazziotti. By judgment of the same date, the Court of Appeal dismissed the appeal of the Public Ministry, and in partial acceptance of the appeal by the accused relying on Art. 523 of the Penal Code and attenuating circumstances, it reduced the penalty to two years of reclusion.

Both the procurator general of Naples and the accused petitioned for cassation, the accused also on the ground that the Court of Appeal erred in proceeding in his absence.

The law:

The public ministry alleges the violation of Art. 524, No. 1, of the Code of Criminal Procedure in relation to Art. 69 of the Penal Code and the erroneous application of the law in that Art. 524 of the Penal Code provides for a separate offense with respect to the possibilities contemplated in Arts. 522 and 523 of the Penal Code, and the court could not have therefore applied the punishment provided in subsection 1 of Art. 523 to which Art. 524 refers, nor should it have considered the attenuating circumstances.

The error is well founded. Article 524 contemplates two different types of crime against a minor below the age of fourteen, or against an incapacitated person. They differ by the purpose for which the offender has seized the victim, i.e., rape with a view to marriage, or rape for lust. Rape for lust is punished by punishment set in subsection 1 of Art. 523. This article punishes a violent or a fraudulent rape for lust against a minor or a woman of full age with reclusion of from three to five years, and provides that the act is aggravated if it is committed against a person below the age of eighteen or a married person.

It follows that rape for lust of a minor below the age of fourteen or an incapacitated person contemplated in Art. 524 is a separate crime and differs from the violent or fraudulent rape for lust contemplated in Art. 523, and it cannot be taken as an aggravating circumstance of the latter crime.

Article 524 thus constitutes a separate crime. It does not, however, follow that the attenuating circumstances which were recognized by the trial court should not be considered since Art. 69 of the Penal Code is applicable only when circumstances of a different nature concur. The court on the merits should have thus applied the reduction of punishment because of the attenuating circumstances only after it had determined the basic punishment for rape under the guidance of the first subsection of Art. 523.

The attacked sentence must be set aside and the case remitted to another chamber of the Court of Appeal of Naples, which will apply the reasoning indicated for the imposition of punishment for rape.

NOTES AND QUESTIONS

For the Court of Cassation, refer to the section on the system of criminal courts above and that on procedure before the Court of Cassation in criminal matters above. *Estensore* is the judge who wrote the judgment.

Article 522 of the Penal Code provides that whosoever shall by force, threats or fraud seize or hold with a view to marriage an unmarried woman will be punished with reclusion of from one to three years. Where the act is committed against an unmarried person of either sex above the age of fourteen but below the age of eighteen, it is punished by reclusion of from two to five years.

Article 523 of the Penal Code provides that whosoever shall by force, threats or fraud seize or hold for the purpose of lust a minor or a woman of full age will be punished with reclusion of from three to five years. The punishment is increased where the act is committed against a person below the age of eighteen or a married woman.

Article 524 of the Penal Code provides that punishment provided in Arts. 522 and 532 will be applied also when the act therein referred to is committed without force, threats or fraud against a person below the age of fourteen, a person mentally incapacitated, or a person who is unable to resist because of physical or mental disability even if this condition was not brought about by the offender.

Article 524, No. 1 of the Code of Criminal Procedure provides that a petition for cassation may be brought for inapplication or the erroneous application of penal law or other legal norms which must be observed in the application of penal law.

Article 69 of the Penal Code contains detailed provisions for application of attenuating and aggravating circumstances when they occur side by side in a particular case.

The court approved the proposition that since rape for lust of a minor below the age of fourteen, or of an incapacitated person, constitutes a separate offense and is not an aggravating circumstance of a rape by force or fraud for lust, the court may not apply attenuating circumstances by reference thereto.

Note the wording of Arts. 522, 523 and 524 attempting not to distinguish as to the sex of the victim. It protects minors of either sex.

Do you know of any other legal system that would provide for rape with a view to matrimony? Has this provision been successful in suppressing the old devise to force an unwilling girl into marriage? Does the Italian law provide an adequate protection against rape in comparison to Anglo-American law? On which ground do you think the accused was free pending appeal? Must the accused be personally present in appellate proceedings? How would a statutory rape be handled in an Anglo-American court on the above facts?

IN RE MORELLINI

Penal Court of Rovereto; decree of October 19, 1976; President Zamboni, *Estensore* Carestia. (*Foro Italiano,* Vol. 99, Part II, p. 360.)

By the Court

The facts: Mario Morellini, presently in the prison of Rovereto in preventive detention, was ordered to stand trial for fraudulent bankruptcy, passing of worthless checks, and fraud. He filed a petition for release under supervision for the forty days of imprisonment into which a fine of 200,000 lire had been converted.

The office of supervision in Trento requested permission of the procurator of the republic in Rovereto in order to grant the release. The procurator passed the request to the Penal Court of Rovereto together with his opinion in the matter. In his opinion, the regime of preventive custody prevails over that of release under supervision. Since it is an order to hold the accused in custody, the permission to release him under supervision may not be granted. It would not make any sense to release an accused under supervision while he finds himself in preventive custody as it would defeat the very purpose of preventive detention.

The law:

The court shares in principle the opinion of the public ministry.

There appears to be a conflict between Art. 271, subsection 4, of the Code of Criminal Procedure and Art. 49 of Law No. 354 of 1975. The first provides that the service of a term of imprisonment for another offense suspends the running of preventive custody. Under the second, whenever a fine is converted into a term of imprisonment, such term of imprisonment is served on release under supervision. This is a mandatory provision and the convict has a right to it.

If the above is correct, there is a conflict since it is inconceivable that the accused subjected to preventive detention for acts which may be very serious could benefit from the provisions of release under supervision with all the inherent opportunity of escape, interference with proof, and so forth.

As observed by the public ministry, a solution cannot be found in subordinating the admission to release under supervision to the leave of judicial authority since it is not subject to judicial discretion. The person convicted to a term of imprisonment into which a fine has been converted has a right to serve it on release under supervision.

We have then to take notice of the conflict and hold Art. 271, subsection 4, partially abrogated in the sense that the suspension therein provided cannot be applied to imprisonment into which a fine has been converted.

It follows that Morellini will begin to serve the term of forty days of reclusion after his preventive detention has ended.

For these reasons, the petition for permission submitted by the office of supervision in Trento is denied.

NOTES AND QUESTIONS

The portent of Art. 271 of the Code of Criminal Procedure and Art. 49 of Law No. 354 of 1975 appears in the text of the decision. For preventive detention (incarceration while under investigation for crime), *see* the section on procedure before penal courts above.

The court thus announced that a person in preventive custody may be admitted to release under supervision with respect to a conviction for another offense to imprisonment into which a fine has been converted only after the end of preventive detention.

Did the court correctly apply the well-known legal principle *lex posterior derogat priori* (later law abrogates the prior one)? May the person proceeded with be released on bail? Would he be so released in proceedings held before an Anglo-American court?

THE REPUBLIC v. VOLTOLINI

Criminal Court of Turin; judgment of April 20, 1976; President Capirossi, *Estensore* Nattero. (*Foro Italiano,* Vol. 102, Part II, p. 26.)

By the Court

Facts and law: In the course of an inspection undertaken on November 2, 1973, by the office of the provincial veterinary of Turin, samples were taken from minced meat of lamb sold by Ernesto Voltolini in the Square of the Republic, one hectogram for 80 lire. An examination in the provincial laboratory of hygiene of Turin revealed the presence of sulphur dioxide at the rate of 2230 milligrams per kilogram. Since the addition of this particular additive was not allowed in meats, Voltolini was invited to request a second analysis of the sample, and was thereafter charged before the Praetor of Turin with violation of Art. 5(g) of Law No. 283 of April 30, 1962, in relation to the Ministerial Decree of March 31, 1965.

The accused did not request a new analysis and was found guilty as charged by the Praetor on May 12, 1975. He was convicted to one month imprisonment and a 200,000 lire fine and was placed on probation to the full extent of the punishment. He stated to the Praetor that he had personally prepared the minced meat in question and added to it white wine and garlic paste as it is customarily done. He denied having added any sulphur dioxide to the meat and asserted that he did not even know such substance; but he mixed it with garlic paste made by the firm "Bellinello Pio e figlio" of Rovigo, which contained sulphur dioxide. The trial judge did not believe the accused because of the substantial percentage of the additive in the sample and held that he must have himself added the substance.

The accused appealed and alleged that the trial judge improperly denied the holding of an expertise to show whether he added the additive or whether it came from the garlic paste. He further stated that the additive in question was allowed in wine and in garlic paste at the rate of 800 milligrams per kilogram. He asserted that it followed that Art. 4 of the Ministerial Decree of March 31, 1965, did not prohibit adding to one product another product to which an additive was lawfully added.

It is the opinion of this court that the judgment of the Praetor should be affirmed for the reasons given by him and also because of further consideration of the above-mentioned legal provisions.

The arguments of the accused must be rejected on two grounds.

As to the first ground. In Art. 5 of Law No. 283 of April 30, 1962, the legislature intended to prohibit any adulteration of food and provide the consumer with as good food as is technically attainable. It follows that the prohibition of additives so decreed must be observed. It is an absolute prohibition in the interest of public health.

As to the second ground. Article 4 of the Ministerial Decree of March 31, 1965, implicitly prohibits the mixing of food to which an additive may lawfully be added with another to which such additive may not be added. It states: "In food products that are made by the mixing of several edible substances to which additives may be added, the maximum quantity of the additive added may not exceed that permitted to be added to each of the substances of which the product is composed." It follows that the adding of additives must be lawful to each and every substance of which the product is composed. The law thus does not allow the mixing of foods that may lawfully contain a particular additive with those that may not contain it. . . . For this reason, the mixture of meat, wine and garlic paste must not contain sulphur dioxide. On the strength of the above considerations, there is no need to hold an expertise to determine the truth of the allegations made by the accused. We may as well believe him. But that does not relieve him of liability since, as a person engaged in business, he should have known and observed the rules prescribed for the making of foods, and since the act is only an infraction, the awareness and voluntary commission of the act is all that is necessary. The judgment is affirmed in all respects.

NOTES AND QUESTIONS

For the function and powers of a criminal court, *see* the section on the structure of criminal courts above. For a distinction between crimes and infractions, *see* the section on substantive criminal law above.

A felony requires intent unless otherwise provided by the law for a particular offense. An infraction requires only that the act be committed knowingly and voluntarily (Art. 42 of the Italian Penal Code).

The statutory provisions referred to in the decision appear in the text of the decision.

A hectogram is one tenth of a kilogram. A milligram is the thousandth part of a gram. A kilogram has 1000 grams.

The accused was prosecuted for an infraction and it suffices in Italian law for the prosecution to show that he committed the act knowingly and voluntarily. Would the same degree of proof be sufficient in an English or in an American court? Is *mens rea* required for a conviction for a statutory offense? In contrast to infractions, in crimes the Italian law requires the proof of intent for conviction. Does the same hold true in Anglo-American law? Does the *mens rea* in Anglo-American law equal to intent in Italian law?

How is the subject of food additives and food adulteration regulated in Anglo-American law? Does the law provide for fines and imprisonment for breach of the proper regulations? Consult the regulations applicable in your state for a comparison.

REPUBLIC v. NICHELE

Court for Minors of Trento; judgment of November 19, 1975; President Capozzi, *Estensore* Giuliano. (*Foro Italiano*, Vol. 99, Part II, p. 365.)

By the Court

Facts and law: By written report of the mobile highway police of the highway of Bolzano of December 26, 1974, the minor Claudio Nichele is reported having committed acts amounting to an infraction in breach of Art. 80 of the Highway Code (driving a motor vehicle without a license) and in breach of Art. 79 of the Highway Code (driving a motor vehicle by a person below the age of eighteen). The procurator of the republic at the Court for Minors prosecuted the minor. Nichele pleaded guilty.

A legal problem arises with respect to the concurrent application of Arts. 80 and 79 of the Highway Code, a problem recently tackled by the Court for Minors in Florence. By judgment of October 9, 1974 (*Foro Italiano*, 1975, II, 246), that court resolved the problem by application of the principle of specifics contained in Art. 15 of the Penal Code and held that driving without a license when imputed to a minor constitutes a violation of Art. 79 because he does not comply with the age requirement, which as a specific norm overrides Art. 80. The provision of Art. 79, which deals with the driving of a motor vehicle by a person not in compliance with the age requirement set by law, comprises fully the provision of Art. 80, since a minor cannot have a driver's license. Article 79 thus provides a specific reason—the lack of required age. . . . The court also stressed that the legislature intended to punish an adult who could obtain a license but would not do so more strictly than a minor who cannot obtain a license for reasons beyond his control.

This court does not agree with the above reasoning. First of all, the person who is of age and can obtain a driver's license but does not do so is less dangerous on the road than a minor who does not hold a license nor may obtain one due to his tender age. It is admitted that the legislation on traffic infractions follows the objective of avoiding serious offenses committed by inexperience, imprudence, and negligence. . . . The minor who wishes to drive cannot obtain a license since the law considers him immature, and if he still drives, it constitutes a more serious violation of the law.

Considering the legal reasons, this court holds that Art. 15 of the Penal Code is not applicable. The concept of specifics is strictly logical. The specific norm contains all the elements of the general norm and still others that are characteristic for the specific norm. . . . With respect to Arts. 79 and 80, the imputed act appears in both but with different prerequisites; in Art. 79 it is age, in Art. 80 it is the license. The age is, of course, a prerequisite for the acquisition of the license but it does not appear in Art. 80, nor does it form part of its ratio. But Art. 80 is more specific than Art. 79, since in addition to the more general prerequisite of age, it lists the holding of a license as a specific requirement. And if Art. 80 were abolished, a minor would still be liable pursuant to Art. 79, while an adult would not be punishable.

But in all truth, these two norms are not related as general and specific norms, because age is not a part of the ratio of Art. 80.

The accused is therefore guilty of the concurrent breach of Arts. 79 and 80 of the Highway Code, although they do not stand to each other in the relation of a general and a specific norm.

NOTES AND QUESTIONS

All offenses committed by persons below the age of eighteen at the time of their commission are handled by the Courts for Minors. (Article 9, Royal Decree Law No. 1404 of July 20, 1934, as amended, on the Courts for Minors).

For minors, *see* the section minors under substantive criminal law above.

The portent of Arts. 79 and 80 of the Highway Code appears from the text of the decision.

Article 15 of the Penal Code provides that where several penal laws or several dispositions of the same penal law regulate the same matter, the specific law, or the specific provision of a law, overrides the general law, or the general provision of a law, unless otherwise provided.

Do separate courts for minors exist in your state? Do they handle the same type of cases as in Italy? Would not, in Anglo-American law, a similar traffic violation be handled rather by a local traffic court (city court, corporation court, petty sessions court) even in the case of a minor? The Italian court considered in detail the well-known rule that a specific rule overrides a general rule. Does this rule have similar application in Anglo-American law? Is this rule limited to criminal law or does it apply to all branches of the law? Is it purely a rule of statutory interpretation or does it extend to the common law? The Italian court inquired into the reasons for the enactment going beyond the meaning conveyed by the individual articles and speculated on the legislative intent. May an Anglo-American court take a similar approach and engage in similar speculation?

REPUBLIC v. FALCIONI

Supreme Court of Cassation; Sixth penal section; President Bartolomei, *Estensore* Ugazzi, Public Ministry De Andreis (*Foro Italiano,* Vol. 98, Part II, p. 141.)

By the Court

Facts and law: The Praetor of Florence, by judgment of October 16, 1972, acquitted Luciano Falcioni because the act of which he was charged, namely, that on August 22, 1971, a Sunday, a day of public rest, he opened his leather goods shop for business, did not constitute an infraction of Art. 665 of the Penal Code and of Decree No. 7209 of the Prefect of Florence of August 13, 1957.

The Praetor held the Decree invalid since it did not refer to the labor unions to which it applied, but referred instead to an association of businessmen that was not empowered to protect the interests of the businessmen in the branch in question.

The procurator of the republic of Florence appealed and the Criminal Court of Florence, by judgment of May 22, 1973, convicted Falcioni to a fine of 10,000 lire. It held that the Decree of the Prefect referred to above was not applicable because the obligation to close places of public work on Sundays derived from Law No. 370 of February 22, 1934, on Sunday and weekly rest.

Falcioni petitions for cassation on the ground the judgment is void because it violates Art. 477 of the Code of Criminal Procedure, and also, because it omits to indicate the articles of the statute that were infringed.

This court holds the act no longer punishable. . . . The act ceased to be punishable by Law No. 558 of July 28, 1971, on the hours of business in retail businesses, which delegated the matter to the regional administration and made such acts punishable by administrative provisions.

The judgment complained of is set aside without remittance and the files are transferred to the Tuscan region, which is competent in this matter.

NOTES AND QUESTIONS

This case illustrates the borderline between civil and criminal law on the one hand and administrative law on the other. Although clearly administrative, infringement of the provisions of this particular administrative law was, in the past, enforced in criminal courts. Since the enactment of the 1971 statute, however, enforcement of even its administrative provisions falls on administrative authorities.

Article 665 of the Penal Code provides that whosoever shall open or operate a public business without the license of the proper authority will be punished by imprisonment of up to six weeks or with a fine up to 200,000 lire. Inobservance of other provisions after a license has been obtained exposes the person to imprisonment of up to three months or to a fine up to 120,000 lire.

Law No. 370 of February 22, 1934, provided for the closing of all businesses on festive days, i.e., Sundays and holidays.

Law No. 558 of July 28, 1971, abolished the requirement to close businesses on

Sundays and public holidays, and transferred the entire matter to administrative law.

Article 477 of the Code of Criminal Procedure provides that a court may apply to a given fact a different legal provision than that indicated in the indictment or in the citation, and proceed accordingly, even if it means the assessment of a higher punishment. But when it appears that the very fact alleged to have been committed is different, then the court must submit the files to the public ministry for further action.

The court thus held that since now the penal provisions in the particular administrative law are not to be regarded as penal norms but as administrative norms, the administration of the statute falls purely within the competence of administrative authorities.

Is a Sunday Observance Act still on the books of your state? Is it considered to be an administrative or a penal statute? Before which court or authority would a person charged with a breach of its provisions be cited? What is the legislative policy behind such statutes? If it is to provide a day of rest per week, must necessarily such a day be Sunday? Christians hold Sunday their holy day, but some other religious denominations honor other days, like Saturday or Friday. In a country with a mixed population, would it not be more appropriate to provide for one day of rest irrespective of the particular day of the week?

REPUBLIC v. BOLZANI

Supreme Court of Cassation; Fifth penal section; judgment of January 29, 1974; President De Rosa, *Estensore* De Fina, Public Ministry was represented. (*Foro Italiano*, Vol. 98, Part II, p. 78.)

By the Court

Facts and law: By order of March 25, 1968, the investigating judge at the Criminal Court of Verona discontinued all proceedings against Vittorio Bolzani, because the offense of which he was charged (altering the date of the holographic will of Alessandro Piccinelli from July 7, 1962, to an earlier date, in breach of Arts. 491 and 482 of the Penal Code) was extinguished by the statute of limitation.

Bolzani petitioned for the cassation of the judgment on the ground that he was not heard. This court, by judgment of March 3, 1971, confirmed the error and, setting aside the judgment, remitted the matter to the same investigating judge for further proceedings.

Bolzani was then heard and stated that he never had the will in his possession so that he could not be assumed to have altered it. He demanded an acquittal since, as he asserted, his innocence appeared from the facts. He renounced the benefit of the statute of limitation and requested an investigation.

The judge of instruction by judgment of October 10, 1972, acquitted the accused because the act he was alleged to have committed was not actionable by the statute of limitation.

The accused petitions for cassation on four grounds.

He claims a violation of Art. 152 of the Code of Criminal Procedure.

The alleged falsity appeared in a handwriting expertise ordered in civil proceedings initiated by Paolo Pulcinelli as a universal heir, but it was not found that the plaintiff was the person who falsified the document.

In his second ground, the plaintiff alleges violation of Art. 475, No. 3, of the Code of Criminal Procedure. He alleges that the instructing judge should have indicated the reasons for his acquittal and should not have limited himself to a statement that there was no ground to prosecute him.

But the defense did not specify any reasons why he should be prosecuted. . . . The judgment complained of dispensed with the reasons stating the facts and holding that on those facts no proof appeared that would justify an acquittal on the merits.

In his third ground, the accused alleges a violation of Art. 544 of the Code of Criminal Procedure. He alleges that by setting aside the preceding judgment, the Court of Cassation indicated to the judge of instruction that the accused had a right to be heard for the purpose of presenting his defense, and that the judge of instruction, by not following that direction, violated the rights of the defense and also the legal principles contained in the judgment of the Court of Cassation. Yet by provisions of the last subsection of Art. 152 of the Code of Criminal Procedure, the judge of instruction was precluded from any investigation as to the merits and could have pronounced an acquittal on the merits only if there was proof making the innocence of the accused evident. . . . [Fourth ground omitted]

For these reasons, the judgment of the judge of instruction of the Criminal Court of Cremona of October 10, 1972, is affirmed.

NOTES AND QUESTIONS

For wills, consult the section on wills above.

For proceedings before the judge of instruction, *see* procedure before criminal courts above.

Articles 491 and 842 of the Penal Code provide for punishment for the alteration of documents, among them holographic wills.

The statute of limitation in the prosecution of criminal offenses is Art. 157 of the Penal Code. Offenses are prescribed in accordance with the maxima if imprisonment threatened for each offense, ranging from twenty years for offenses punishable with reclusion of not less than twenty-four years to eighteen months for offenses punishable with a fine only.

Article 152 of the Code of Criminal Procedure provides that in any stage of proceedings, when the judge finds that the act was not committed or that the accused did not commit it or that it is not punishable or that the liability is extinguished or that no criminal proceedings should have been instituted or continued, he shall so declare ex officio by judgment. Where the liability has been extinguished but there is proof to show that the act was not comitted or that the accused did not commit it or that the act is not punishable, the judge will decide on the merits acquitting the accused.

Article 544 of the Code of Criminal Procedure provides that on remission, the accused may offer new means of defense within the limits indicated by the Court of Cassation.

Article 475, No. 3 of the Code of Criminal Procedure provides that a judgment must contain the statements of facts and circumstances which form the ratio of the offense.

Do holographic wills exist in your jurisdiction? Is an interference, like an alteration of a will by an unauthorized person, criminally punishable? Once it appears in criminal proceedings that an offense may not be prosecuted because of the running of the statute of limitation, is the court bound to discontinue the proceedings? May the accused insist that he be tried for the offense in order to give him an opportunity to show his innocence? Must the person proceeded against be heard or may the proceedings be discontinued immediately once it is established that the act is not punishable? Would a similar decision be given on the above facts in an Anglo-American court?

C. DECISIONS OF ADMINISTRATIVE COURTS

COOPERATIVA TRA GONDOLIERI E ALTRI
v. COMUNE DI VENEZIA

Council of State, Section V.; decision of November 13, 1973, No. 829; President P. Breglia, *Estensore* Vivenzio; Counsel Poguici and Angelucci for the Cooperativa, Counsel Mascarini and Piccardi for the Comune di Venezia. (*Foro Italiano*, Vol. 97, Part III, p. 262.)

By the Section

The facts: The cooperative composed of gondoliers Messrs. Daniele Manin, Bruno Bacci, Giacomo Camera, and other gondoliers petitioned for the annulment of Order No. 750/9 of the municipal council of the City of Venice dated July 28, 1969, which made certain modifications in the regulation of boat traffic adopted by Order No. 28/233 of February 15, 1963, and in the ensuing Ordinance No. 48630 of the mayor of Venice in that in Art. 60 of the new regulation were set new routings for gondolas, flat-bottom boats and motorboats.

The petitioners complain that the mayor of Venice, by Ordinance No. 43381 of July 3, 1968, . . . modified the traffic of privately operated gondolas and boats from the place of embarkation in the Grand Canal at Cà Foscari in the direction to the square of Rome and the railway, and allowed it only in that one direction as one-way traffic; that by the later Ordinance No. 49566 of August 7, 1968, the mayor modified the earlier ordinance and allowed traffic in both directions in fixed periods of time and at particular hours and also determined the distances gondolas had to keep between them when in use; that on July 28, 1969, the municipal council delegated to the mayor the authority to regulate the traffic of boats; that the mayor issued on July 31, 1969, a new regulation which reserved the stretch on Rio Nuovo between the Bridge of Saint Pantaleo and that of Careria between the hours of 8 A.M. and 9 P.M. to publicly operated motorboats; that the mayor reserved to those gondolas and flat-bottom boats holding a city permit to transport passengers as from 9 P.M. the routes further determined.

The petitioners object to these regulations as follows: They allege violation of Royal Decree No. 148 of February 4, 1915, on the division of powers; violation of

Presidential Decree No. 328 of February 15, 1952, on the regulation for putting into effect the Code of Navigation; excess of power in that the city council delegated to the mayor authority which is must exercise itself and which may not be delegated. . . . They also allege that the mayor, by his ordinance, has avoided the control of the city council.

The law:

The objection to the standing of the petitioners made by the City of Venice appears to be founded.

The legal position of the petitioning gondoliers is not different from that of any users of the canals or from that of those who use these water roads within the city of Venice with boats of any description.

The gondoliers use the canals in the exercise of their service of transport as per authorization of the city in the public interest.

A similarity appears between them and taxi drivers who use the city streets in the exercise of their trade. But no sufficient legal distinction may be made between them since both use city property, the one the streets, the others the canals, and their use of the property does not give them any special right to the use of the property beyond that of the general public. They would have to show such right in order to be entitled to challenge adminstrative provisions made by the proper administrative authorities with respect to such property.

The use of vehicles of public roads is a use by the general public without any distinction between public and private use. The same applies to the use of canals in the City of Venice. In both cases, the user of public property has only a factual interest in such use. By exercising such use, his interest does not become a protected interest and does not entitle him to challenge administrative decisions concerning road traffic.

For these reasons, the petition must fail for lack of standing of the petitioners. Each party bears his own costs of the proceedings.

NOTES AND QUESTIONS

This case illustrates the fundamental question of standing in administrative matters. The interest of a party must go beyond that of a member of the general public and he must be able to point to a detriment particular to him personally. Such an interest arises, e.g., with respect to the ownership of property. An owner of a building may challenge an administrative regulation that prescribes, e.g., the materials to be used in the construction of buildings. A member of the general public would not have any standing. The *estensore* is the judge who wrote the judgment.

The various statutes, regulations and ordinances cited in the decision were cited without any success by the petitioners, since they could not and did not in fact even make any attempt to show their unreasonable application by the city.

Does the above-outlined principle as to the standing of a party in court apply equally in Anglo-American law? On which ground could the petitioners further challenge the regulations of the city? Supposing they claimed that the exclusion of gondolas from certain canals unduly discriminated against them? Could the court strike down a city regulation for unreasonableness? What is the principle *delegatus non potest delegare*? Suppose the Venice City Council exercised powers delegated to it by a higher authority in accordance with provisions of the Highway Code, could it then further delegate their exercise to the mayor? Does the same rule apply in Anglo-American administrative law?

MINISTERO DELLA DIFESA v. GAMBACORTA

Council of State, Section IV.; decision of March 30, 1976, No. 233; President De Capua, *Estensore* Pezzana; Government Counsel Azzariti for the ministry of defense, Counsel Piscione for Gambacorta. (*Foro Italiano*, Vol. 102, Part III, p. 75.)

By the Section

The claim of territorial incompetence of the T.A.R. of Abruzzo appears founded. In fact, it appears from the documents produced in court following the interlocutory order, without any doubt, that the order denying an exemption from military conscription was issued directly by the ministry of defense and not by the district military command in Teramo.

Since it is clear that the matter does not deal with public employment, the general rule of Art. 3 of Law No. 1034 of December 6, 1971, must be applied. It provides that all recourses against administrative acts issued by the central administration fall within the competence of the T.A.R. of Lazio, unless the effect of the administrative act is territorially limited to the jurisdiction of another T.A.R.

This is what Gambacorta alleges. He claims that the effect of the administrative act is limited to the territorial jurisdiction of the T.A.R. in Abruzzo since he is listed in the list of conscription in the district of Teramo.

This allegation appears unfounded. The attacked order does not refer to a question concerning the lists of conscription, i.e., whether Gambacorta should be inscribed in the list of Teramo or in that of L'Aquila, but deals with a completely different problem, namely, whether he, being properly listed in a list of citizens subject to military service, has or has not a ground for exemption from the service because of family reasons.

From this exposition, it is clear that the effect of the order is not limited to any particular territorial division but extends over the totality of the national territory.

Further, the duty to serve in the military, which is imposed on all citizens able to bear arms, is in no way localized, but must be complied with wherever the citizen is found, even abroad where the citizen must present himself to the Italian diplomatic and consular authorities.

Since compliance with the service is not territorially limited, an order that grants or denies an exemption from such service is not territorially limited.

For these reasons, the T.A.R. of Lazio must be held to have jurisdiction in the matter.

NOTES AND QUESTIONS

T.A.R. stands for Tribunali Amministrativi Regionali (regional administrative courts). *See* the section on administrative offices and courts, above.

Law No. 1034 of December 6, 1971, deals with the T.A.R.; Art. 3 thereof provides that administrative acts emanating from offices of central administration and having effect over the whole of the national territory may be challenged only in the T.A.R. of Lazio.

For administrative procedure, *see* the section dealing with administrative procedure above. For the function of the Council of State, *see* the section on the Council of State above.

The case thus deals with the question of territorial jurisdiction. Note also that most European countries have compulsory military service for all their citizens.

This case gives an example of the right of a citizen to contest administrative orders. He may appeal to the proper superior offices and then to administrative courts with the Council of State at the top of the structure. How does it compare with the Anglo-American legal structure? Are there any administrative courts in the Anglo-American legal structure to which a person could appeal in the above circumstances? Are there any administrative courts in the Anglo-American legal system? Could a person appeal to an ordinary civil court on these facts? Would not an administrative court, due to its specialization, be better suited to handle the case than a general civil court?

Lazio is the Italian region within which the city of Rome is located.

CAPUCCIO v. MINISTERO DEI LAVORI PUBBLICI

Council of State, Section IV.; decision of February 12, 1974, No. 174; President Benvenuto, *Estensore* Paleologo; Counsel Magrone and Capuccio for Capuccio, Government Counsel Azzariti for the ministry, Counsel Zini Lamberti, Astuti and Voltaggio Lucchesi for the community of Rivoli. (*Foro Italiano*, Vol. 97, Part III, p. 335.)

By the Section

By document in writing delivered to the community of Rivoli on December 14, 1965, and to the ministry of public works on December 17, and filed on January 7, 1966, Pia Capuccio, attorney Ugo Capuccio and Carla Capuccio of Manini, owners of land in the community of Rivoli to the extent of fifteen hectars, ten of which were included in the building zone of the said community, challenge the plan itself as approved by the Ministry of Public Works by Decree No. 160 of September 27, 1965, and adopted by decision of the communal council on September 23, 1964, No. 203. They alleged five grounds as follows: grounds 1-3 allege unconstitutionality and improper cutting in two of their property; ground 4 alleges that while Art. 5 of Law No. 167 of 1962 provides that a building plan must be made together with a financial plan, the attacked plan makes no such provision, and the plan also exceeds by far the needs of the community as to is extent; ... ground 5 alleges ... the building plan relies on a nonexistent general regulatory plan since it has not as yet been approved.

The law:

The petition is founded in grounds 4 and 5 while the other allegations are not relevant including that of unconstitutionality.

In their fourth ground, the petitioners allege that the building plan of Rivoli, which was approved in 1965, did not lead to the construction of a single building although it extends over an area of more than one million square meters.

The law requires that only needed land may be included in the plan in accordance with minute planning. Taking of land beyond these limits would result in useless prejudice to the land owners, in the withdrawal from production of agricultural land, and in the withdrawal of land from building, results which the building plan desired to avoid.

The ministerial decree which approved the building plan was aware of this disproportion when it stated that the plan responds to the needs of the community development although it seems to be excessive with respect to the building needs of the community for the next ten years.

The minister should have denied approval of the plan on this ground, or he should have approved it only after modifications that would have given effect to the actual needs of the community and allowed the owners of land to exercise control over that not needed. Rather than doing this, however, the minister ordered a reduction in the height of the planned buildings and in their size. This is rather illogical, because he did not consider the reduction in the surface of the land taken.

As to the fifth ground, in adopting the building plan, the municipal council of Rivoli tied the plan to a plan of actual contruction that should have indicated the actual building zone.

The minister has not in fact considered and approved the regulatory plan. He only noted that a general plan of urban development was worked out since the municipal council had approved a general regulatory plan, but it has not as yet obtained regular approval.

Such approach is improper. . . . The building plan must be approved together with an actual plan of construction so as to make certain and operative a territorially delimited urban building design at the moment when approval is obtained.

The petition succeeds. The building plan of the community of Rivoli is annulled. The defeated party pays the costs of the proceedings.

NOTES AND QUESTIONS

For the Council of State, *see* the section on the Council of State above.

The Council of State held that the ministry of public works may not approve a building plan which, to its knowledge, exceeds the needs of the community.

Italian administrative courts thus decide on the merits and they ultimately decide what should or should not be done in derogation of the view of the administrative authority constitutionally instituted to make such decision. They do so in accordance with the law.

The above-mentioned law providing for building planning is comprehensive legislation. It provides for expropriation of land for house construction and for the building of housing. The owner of the land that is expropriated may challenge such order by administrative remedies directed to the proper administrative authorities, and if unsuccessful, may then turn to administrative courts.

Is the above scheme the counterpart of the Anglo-American scheme of city renewal? Would such a task be handled by an administrative agency, like the Department of Housing? Would the agency have the power of eminent domain? What would be the function of the particular township within which the activity was to take place? Would there have to be a building plan and a proper zoning ordinance passed by the city council? Would an individual land owner be able to challenge separately the city ordinance and the orders of the housing authority? To which bodies, commissions, etc. could such a complainant appeal? Are there always administrative boards of review to which the complainant may appeal? Since there are no administrative courts on the Italian model in existence in the Anglo-American law, may then the complainant complain to a court of law? If so, what is the nature of the court review? May the court review the case on the merits and substitute its own opinion for that of the administrative body? If not, may the court inquire whether the proceedings and decision of the administrative body complies with its own formal requirements and is not *ultra vires*? Is then the court review only a formal rather than a material review? Which system does, in your opinion, better service to the community?

GRICCIOLI v. CONSORZIO NAZIONALE PER IL CREDITO AGRARIO DI MIGLIORAMENTO

Council of State, Section IV.; decision of January 8, 1974, No. 24; President Potenza, *Estensore* Granato; Counsel Raspa and Falzetti for Griccioli, Counsel Antonuccio for the Consorzio. (*Foro Italiano*, Vol. 97, Part III, p. 392.)

By the Section

The facts: By order of April 23, 1953, the executive committee of the Consorzio with its seat in Rome decided to avail itself of the services of Dr. Giuseppe Griccioli as an external consultant for the processing of loan applications. As of July 1, 1957, Dr. Griccioli has been employed by the Consorzio as a temporary employee. Following the introduction of new regulations as to personnel, which provided for the filling of vacancies from among temporary employees who had been employed for at least one year, the Consorzio appointed Dr. Griccioli as from January 1, 1958, to become an officer of the third class, grade VI.

When Dr. Griccioli retired on June 27, 1967, he had been an officer of the second class, grade III, since January 1, 1963. The decision for his retirement was made pursuant to Art. 38 of the regulation as to personnel and was communicated to Dr. Griccioli on June 28, 1967. He demands the annulment of the decision on two grounds. The first ground alleges that no reason was given for his retirement. The above-mentioned Art. 38 provides for two eventualities: (a) An employee may retire after 35 years of service, or when he reaches 60 years of age; or (b) an employee must retire after 40 years of service, or when he reaches 65 years of age. The petitioner had not completed 40 years of service, nor had he attained 65 years of age. He alleges that the decision is void for not giving a reason for the decision, and that once an employee exceeds 60 years of age (the petitioner was 62 at the time when the decision was made), he may be retired only after 40 years of service, or when reaching 65 years of age. The second ground alleges that his retirement was ordered by the board of directors and not by the executive committee as prescribed by Art. 32 of the regulation on personnel of March 13, 1958.

The law:

The Consorzio objects to the jurisdiction of the Council of State, relying instead on the decision of the Supreme Court of Cassation which held that ordinary civil courts have jurisdiction in matters of employment of the Consorzio because it is a public economic agency.

This objection is well founded.

Public economic agencies are juridical persons set up for the administration of industrial or commercial enterprises. They are agencies which, as government institutions, exercise a true and their own activity as enterprises in the economic field.

The criterion in accordance with which a public agency is qualified as a public economic agency depends on the activity that must be exercised in the economic field and must have for its object the satisfaction of a public interest. The making of profit is not necessary since a public agency is not required to make profit.

Once it appears that a public agency has the above-mentioned characteristics, it is withdrawn from the exclusive jurisdiction of the Council of State. The Consorzio is such an agency, although it does not have all the characteristic features. . . . From its activity, the Consorzio, like other banking institutions, derives a profit, which it pays to other agencies and also applies to increase its reserves.

Since the Consorzio is then a true economic agency competing on the open market, the controversies arising between it and its employees must be decided by ordinary civil courts within the meaning of Art. 429 of the Code of Civil Procedure.

The petition is therefore denied for lack of jurisdiction. The parties bear their own costs of the proceedings.

NOTES AND QUESTIONS

The Consorzio is a public institution for the advance of credit to farmers for improvements. It has a legal personality and acts as a private enterprise.

The Council thus held that the Consorzio is an institution subject to civil rather than administrative law, and it thus must be sued in ordinary civil courts.

The case illustrates the line between civil and administrative law in this particular area.

Article 429 of the Code of Civil Procedure deals with the pronouncement of judgment.

What is the typical characteristic of an institution of public law subject to the administrative system? The retirement provisions set forth in the decision are typical for Italian public service and also for private employers. How do these rules compare with those in power in your state? When the action of the plaintiff has been dismissed because of lack of jurisdiction, may he then bring the action in the proper civil court? What is the hierarchy of such courts? Suppose the Consorzio was a true administrative agency, would the administrative court system have jurisdiction over the matter? To which administrative court would the action be brought? Would it reach the Council of State on appeal? Suppose a similar case on the facts had arisen in your state, could the petitioner bring his case to the ordinary civil court and claim reinstatement?

E.N.EL. v. COMMUNE DI VADO LIGURE

Council of State, Section V.; decision of November 23, 1973, No. 910; President P. Lugo, *Estensore* Catalozzi; Counsel G. Guarino for E.N.EL., Counsel Natali and Aglietto for the Comune. (*Foro Italiano,* Vol. 97, Part III, p. 428.)

By the Section

The second ground of the petition is founded and it comprises all the other grounds brought up by the petitioner.

The construction of power lines for the transmission of electric power is strictly regulated by Arts. 107-129 of the Only Text of December 11, 1933, No. 1775 on water and electric plants, and it is subject to authorization by the Minister of Public Works or by the prefect.

By provisions of the law, the request for such authorization must be lodged with the office of the civil engineer, which will then handle the matter. It will communicate the proposed layout of the power line to all interested bodies (military authorities, highway authorities, railways, civil aviation, mining authorities, all localities through which the power line is to run, forest authorities, and the province); it will publish an announcement in the official gazette of the province; it will send copies of the files to the ministry of posts and telecommunications to obtain their indication that they have no objections concerning any effect the power line may have on telephonic and telegraphic services; it will receive all comments and objections from interested parties made within thirty days from the publication of the above announcement; it will then submit a detailed report to the proper decision-making authority of all its findings.

From the provision above, it appears that the proceedings as to the construction of power lines are fully determined by these provisions and that no other authority has the power of consent over the construction.

The construction of power lines for the conduct of electric current from the place of its production to the place of its distribution is thus not subject to a building permit mentioned in Art. 31 of Law No. 1150 of August 17, 1942, as superseded by Art. 10 of Law No. 765 of August 6, 1967. . . . The above-mentioned law withdraws the construction of power lines from any possible building regulation, and therefore no local body as a community has any authority in the matter, especially not a local mayor whose permission is not required.

It must be stressed that the local bodies of the territories through which the power line is proposed to run have an opportunity to take part in the proceedings and to make their views known to the decision-making authority and object to the final decision by administrative appeal and by recourse to administrative courts. The concentration of the decision-making power in one authority has the purpose of preventing the fragmentation of that authority among several local bodies and preventing a meritorious project of public interest from being delayed by strictly local interests.

It is therefore unnecessary to determine whether the support structures embedded in the ground are buildings in the sense of the building law or whether they fall within the works of local urban development.

It therefore appears that the construction of the power line for the conduct of electric energy from the works located in Vado Ligure (Savona) to the station in Camporosso (Imperia) by the E.N.EL. is not subject to a building permit from the mayor of Vado Ligure, and that the absence of such permit could not have given the said mayor the authority to order the immediate discontinuation of the construction by his order of August 14, 1971. This particular order is hereby declared null and void. The petition therefore succeeds. Each party will bear his costs of the proceedings.

NOTES AND QUESTIONS

E.N.EL. stands for *Ente nazionale per l'energia elettrica*, i.e., the national agency for electric energy. It is a producer and distributor of electricity.

The Only Text on a given topic is the consolidation of the existing law on that particular subject matter. The Only Text on water and electric plants thus consolidates all the law concerning electric plants and the conduct of electric power.

The above-mentioned Law No. 1150 of August 17, 1942, as amended, deals with urban development and building. It provides for permits to be obtained from local authorities for the building of structures to be erected within the territory of a particular locality.

The community of Vado Ligure, which unsuccessfully challenged the construction of the mentioned power line in its planning stage, then took the law in its own hands, and when the construction actually began on its land, it issued, through its mayor an order for the cessation of the construction. The E.N.EL. brought the case before the Council of State, which held the order of the mayor void, i.e., as never issued, and fully immaterial.

The above proceedings are purely administrative. They have for their object the annulment of an administrative act. Can you envisage circumstances under which a recourse to ordinary civil courts in this case would be necessary even in Italian law? Note that the review by the Council of State is not only a formal review but also a review on merits. May an Anglo-American court review an administrative act issued by an administrative body on the merits? Had the above facts arisen in your state and had the case been brought before a court, would not the judge be limited to an examination of whether or not the agency and the mayor stayed within their powers; and could the judge strike down only such an administrative provision issued in excess of power? Did the mayor of Vado Ligure act in excess of his powers?

RIGHETTI v. UNIVERSITÀ DEGLI STUDI DI GENOVA

Regional Administrative Court of Liguria, judgment January 22, 1976, No. 18; President Vivenzio, *Estensore* Mirto. (*Foro Italiano*, Vol. 102, Part III, p. 101.)

By the Court

The complaint of the complainant appears founded when he alleges the violation of Presidential Decree No. 758 of June 5, 1965, and the false and erroneous application of Art. 6, of Decree Law No. 261 of July 8, 1974, which became Law No. 355 of August 14, 1974, with respect to Law No. 336 of May 24, 1970.

By the retirement order of November 30, 1971, the complainant was retired as a public officer under provisions of the then existing law (Art. 1 of Presidential Decree No. 758 of 1965, and Art. 3 of Law No. 336 of 1970). The retirement order allowed the complainant, as a war veteran, to hold the position of a university lecturer and the consequent cumulation of the retirement benefit of a public servant with the active salary of a university lecturer.

The right acquired by the complainant is a subjective public right that is not affected by the later Art. 6 of Decree Law No. 261 of July 8, 1974, which may not have retroactive application and may not affect rights that were perfected under previous legislation. Since in the case before us all the acts necessary for the acquisition of the right to the cumulation of benefits occurred under the previous legislation, Art. 6 of the new law is not applicable. In other words, Art. 11 of the general principles of law in the Civil Code, which prohibits the retroactive application of law, although not always applicable, may be dispensed with only by an express mandate of the legislature.

Thus Art. 6 of Decree Law No. 261 of 1974 undoubtedly constitutes an exception to the principle prohibiting a retroactive effect, since the legislature has allowed the retroactive effect of the law to curb the abuses made possible by the generosity of Law No. 336 of 1970 and ordered the termination of all relations originating after retirement under provisions of that law.

The said Art. 6 sanctions the retroactivity of a provision by which employment was taken after retirement under Law No. 336 of 1970.

Consequently, in order to determine employment taken prior to July 8, 1974, two conditions must be complied with: (1) retirement pursuant to Law No. 336 and (2) the employment was taken after the retirement.

It is evident that a person like the complainant, who took the employment before he was retired under Law No. 336, continues to be governed by the rule of Presidential Decree No. 758 of 1965, which allows the cumulation of a retirement benefit and a salary for active service.

Facts that took place under the law previously in existence may not now be reopened. The legislature considered such facts as fully completed and made the new law to apply only to the taking of employment after retirement.

Since the administrative act attacked appears illegitimate, it must be annulled with costs.

NOTES AND QUESTIONS

The complainant was a public servant in full-time employment. In addition, he held the position of a university lecturer (*docente*), a part-time position. He also was a war veteran, thus benefiting from legislative favoring those who served their country in war. The statutes mentioned in the decision gave the right to war veterans to a government retirement benefit from government employment while at the same time allowing them to be employed by the government in another capacity and draw a salary. Article 6 of Decree Law No. 261 of July 8, 1974, provided that war veterans who were retired with war pensions could not take new employment with the state or state entities after they were retired, and those who have done so could not hold such new employment without renouncing their retirement benefits. The appointed date was July 8, 1974, and those affected by the provision had to make a decision within the next six months.

Universities in Italy are state institutions of learning and are fully subject to administrative law. Their decisions may be challenged administratively with a final recourse to the administrative courts.

The University of Genova terminated the employment of the complainant under the assumption that he cannot at the same time draw a university salary and a state retirement benefit. The court held the termination illegitimate since the complainant was entitled to both.

The effect of the above-mentioned statutes appears from the text of the decision and from the explanation given in this note.

Government employment in Italy is life employment (until retirement), so that a person retired is not likely to seek any further employment. The only exception occurs in the case of war veterans. How does this compare with the so-called double dipping whereby U.S. military retirees in their forties find new civil employment with the government and draw both their military retirement and the new salary, and after their retirement from the second, civil employment, a second government retirement benefit? The Italian law stopped this practice (although it was limited to actual war veterans) as of July 8, 1974.

What is the effect of the present decision of the T.A.R. (Tribunale Amministrativo Regionale) of Liguria? What further remedies are now open to the defeated party? To which court may he still appeal?

FOOTNOTES

1. Civil Code, Arts. 43-47.
2. *Ibid.*, Arts. 79-158. Law No. 847 of May 27, 1929.
3. *Ibid.*, Art. 84.
4. *Ibid.*, Art. 85.
5. *Ibid.*, Art. 86.
6. *Ibid.*, Art. 87.
7. *Ibid.*, Art. 88.
8. *Ibid.*, Art. 89.
9. *Ibid.*, Art. 90.
10. *Ibid.*, Arts. 93-95.
11. *Ibid.*, Art. 99.
12. *Ibid.*, Art. 100.
13. *Ibid.*, Arts. 102-104.
14. *Ibid.*, Art. 143. *Mutual rights and duties of the spouses.* In marriage, the husband and the wife acquire the same rights and undertake the same duties. From marriage derive

the mutual obligations of fidelity, moral and material support, cooperation in the interest of the family, and cohabitation. Both spouses are obligated to contribute to the needs of the family, each in accordance to his ability and his professional or household work capability.

Ibid., Art. 144. *The course of family life and the family residence.* The spouses agree among themselves on the course of family life and determine the family residence in accordance with their needs and with those of the family. Each of the spouses has the right to bring about such an agreement.

Ibid., Art. 147. *Duties toward children.* Marriage imposes on both spouses the obligation to support, instruct and educate their children taking into account their capabilities, natural inclinations and aspirations.

15. A public act is a document drawn up and certified by a notary or by another public officer authorized to execute public acts (Civil Code, Art. 2699).
16. Civil Code, Art. 116.
17. Law No. 898 of December 1, 1970, on dissolution of marriage.
18. Civil Code, Arts. 456-768.
19. Article 544 of the Civil Code regulates the share of the above heirs in the estate in the other available eventualities.
20. Civil Code, Arts. 810-1172.
21. *Ibid.*, Arts. 1321-1986.
22. *Ibid.*, Arts. 456-712.
23. *Ibid.*, Arts. 1153-1157.
24. *Ibid.*, Arts. 1173-2059.
25. *Ibid.*, Arts. 1321-1469.
26. *Ibid.*, Arts. 2043-2059.
27. *Ibid.*, Arts. 1987-1991.
28. *Ibid.*, Art. 433.
29. *Ibid.*, Arts. 2028-2042.
30. *Ibid.*, Art. 1350.
31. See section 5(b) Contracts in general above.
32. Civil Code, Arts. 2247-2510.
33. *Ibid.*, Arts. 2934-2969.
34. The law of bankruptcy is governed by Royal Decree No. 267 of March 16, 1942.
35. The sum is at present set at 900,000 lire by Law No. 1375 of October 20, 1952.
36. *Codice della navigazione, Regio Decreto 30 marzo 1942, n. 327,* as amended.
37. The authority, powers and jurisdiction of courts are laid down in the *Ordinamento Giudiziario, Regio Decreto 30 gennaio 1941, n. 12,* as amended by subsequent legislation.
38. *Ordinamento Giudiziario,* Arts. 22-29.
39. *Ibid.*, Arts. 30-41.
40. The value of the matter in dispute falling within the competence of the justice of the peace and of the praetor is raised from time to time to keep it in line with the price index.
41. *Ordinamento Giudiziario,* Arts. 42-51.
42. *Ibid.*, Arts. 52-64.
43. *Ibid.*, Arts. 65-68.
44. To be admitted, the applicant must show that he has practiced for at least eight years as an advocate in courts of appeal and general jurisdiction courts. *Ordinamento delle professioni di avvocato e procuratore, R.D.L. 27 nov. 1933, n. 1578,* Art. 33.
45. Code of Civil Procedure, Arts. 311-322.
46. *Ibid.*, Arts. 163-310.
47. *Ibid.*, Arts. 323-359.
48. *Ibid.*, Arts. 360-403.
49. Italian penal law distinguishes between crimes, called *delitti*, and infractions, termed

contravvenzioni. Delitti correspond to felonies but include also some lesser breaches of the law that would fall within the classification of misdemeanors if the Italian penal law had such a class of acts; *contravvenzioni* correspond to infractions but include similarly some more serious breaches of the law that would elsewhere be termed misdemeanors. The Italian penal law thus has a twofold division of breaches of criminal law, namely *delitti* and *contravvenzioni*, rather than the traditional threefold division into felonies, misdemeanors and infractions.

50. Penal Code, Arts. 1-16.
51. *Ibid.*, Arts. 17-38, 39-84.
52. There is no death penalty as punishment for crimes provided for in the *Codice penale.* Wherever it was formerly provided, the punishment of imprisonment for life will be imposed (*Decreto legislativo luogotenenziale 10 agosto 1944, n. 224*).
53. Penal Code, Arts. 97-98.
54. *Ibid.*, Arts. 99-109.
55. *Ibid.*, Arts. 110-119.
56. *Ibid.*, Arts. 575-577.
57. The death penalty, which formerly applied to this crime, has been abolished. See footnote 52.
58. These circumstances are: (1) with a base motive; (2) to cover up the commission of another crime; (3) having acted recklessly although the outcome was clearly foreseeable; and (4) with cruelty. Penal Code, Art. 61 (1-4).
59. *Ibid.*, Art. 576.
60. *Ibid.*, Art. 577.
61. *Ibid.*, Arts. 584-585.
62. *Ibid.*, Art. 586.
63. *Ibid.*, Art. 589. Where the act is committed by breach of rules of driving, or by breach of rules set to prevent labor accidents, the punishment is imprisonment of from one to five years.
64. Penal Code, Arts. 582-583.
65. *Ibid.*, Arts. 624-628.
66. The first four circumstances are those enumerated in footnote 58; the other circumstances are: (5) having taken advantage of circumstances of time, place or person to obstruct private or public means of defense against the commission of such an offense; (6) where the offense is committed by a fugitive from justice; (7) where the offense causes the victim serious damage; (8) where the offender has aggravated the consequences of the act; (9) where the offense is committed by a public officer or a minister of religion abusing his official authority; (10) where the offense is committed against a public officer, a minister of religion, or a diplomatic officer of a foreign state while they are attending to their official business; and (11) where the offense is committed by abusing family authority, official authority, master-servant relationship, cohabitation or hospitality. Penal Code, Art. 61 (5-11).
67. *Ibid.*, Arts. 163-168. Where the act has been committed by a minor below the age of 18 years, the sentence may be probated when it does not exceed 3 years. Where the act has been committed by a person older than 18 but below 21, or by a person aged 70 and older, the sentence may be probated when it does not exceed 2 years and 6 months.
68. Penal Code, Arts. 176-177.
69. Code of Criminal Procedure, Arts. 31, 125, 199. *Ordinamento Giudiziario*, Arts. 30-41, 72, 74. *Ordinamento delle professioni di avvocato e procuratore, R.D.L. 27 nov. 1933, n. 1578*, Art. 4.
70. Code of Criminal Procedure, Arts. 30, 125. *Ord. Giudiziario*, Arts. 42-48, 70. *Ord. delle professioni di avvocato e procuratore, R.D.L. 27 nov. 1933, n. 1578*, Arts. 4-6.
71. Code of Criminal Procedure, Art. 29. *Ord. Giudiziario*, Art. 70. *Ord. delle professioni di avvocato e procuratore, 27 nov. 1933, n. 1578*, Arts. 4-6.

72. *Ord. Giudiziario*, Arts. 52-59. *Ord. delle professioni di avvocato e procuratore, R.D.L. 27 nov. 1933, n. 1578*, Arts. 4-6.

73. Code of Criminal Procedure, Art. 199. Law No. 287 of April 10, 1951. *Riordinamento dei giudizi di Assise*, Arts. 4-12.

74. *Ord. Giudiziario*, Arts. 65-70. *R.D.L. 27 nov. 1933, n. 1578*, Arts. 4, 33.

75. By Law No. 108 of April 3, 1974, the Italian legislature delegated to the government the power to prepare a new Code of Criminal Procedure.

76. Code of Criminal Procedure, Arts. 7, 8, 199, 231, 245, 254, 277, 398, 406-409, 423, 440-468.

77. Code of Criminal Procedure, Arts. 219-505.

78. *Ibid.*, Arts. 405-496 and Law No. 287 of April 10, 1951, as amended.

79. The rules as to selection of jurors are contained in Law No. 287 of April 10, 1951, as amended.

80. Code of Criminal Procedure, Arts. 511-523.

81. *See* System of Criminal Courts, Assize Courts of Appeal, Code of Criminal Procedure, Procedure before Assize Courts, Procedure before Courts of Appeal.

82. Code of Criminal Procedure, Arts. 524-552.

83. This is so in case of doubt as to the jurisdiction of a single section or two combined sections, and also in case of a petition for the revision of a conviction on the ground that it cannot be reconciled with another conviction.

84. Code of Criminal Procedure, Arts. 277-294.

85. Law No. 1089 of June 1, 1939, as amended, on the protection of objects of artistic and historical interest.

86. The Only Text of provisions concerning the statute of civil employees of the state. Decree No. 3 of the President of the Republic of January 10, 1957, as amended.

87. The Only Text of provisions concerning the care of roads and traffic. Royal Decree No. 1740 of December 8, 1933, as amended.

88. Law No. 825 of October 9, 1971, on tax reform; Decree Law No. 636 of October 26, 1972, on tax courts and procedure, as amended. Decree Law No. 603 of September 29, 1973, on the collection of direct taxes. Before the 1971-1972 tax reform, the system of taxes was as follows. The state levied basically seven direct taxes and a number of indirect taxes. The direct taxes were four real taxes and three personal taxes. The real taxes were: the land tax (*imposta fondiaria*); tax on the income from the use of structures, excepting structures used in agriculture (*imposta sul reddito dei fabbricati*); tax on income from agricultural use of land (*imposta sul reddito agrario*); and tax on income from movable property (*imposta sui redditi di ricchezza mobile*). The personal taxes were: income tax (*imposta complementare sul reddito*); corporation tax (*imposta sulle società*); and payment tax (*imposta sulle obbligazioni*). The indirect taxes were either taxes on the transfer of property or on the sale of goods intended for consumption. The tax on the transfer of property (*imposta sui transferimenti*) was levied on inheritances and gifts, mortgages, stocks, and so forth. The sale of goods tax (*imposta sui consumi*) was imposed on liquor, sugar, beer, electricity, and the like. The authorities of local autonomy, i.e., the regions, provinces and communities, also levied taxes. These taxes were mainly a fraction added to the existing state taxes, expecially to the income tax (*imposta complementare sul reddito*), which was known as the family tax (*imposta di famiglia*). They also added to the land tax (*imposta fondiaria*) and to the tax on the income from the use of structures (*imposta sul reddito dei fabbricati*). They further levied other taxes, like the communal tax on industries, commerce, arts, and professions (*imposta comunale sulle industrie, i comerci, le arti e le professioni*). This was a counterpart of the state tax on the income from movable property (*imposta statale sul reddito di ricchezza mobile*).

89. Decree Law No. 597 of September 29, 1973, as amended.

90. Decree Law No. 598 of September 29, 1973, as amended.

91. Decree Law No. 599 of September 29, 1973, as amended.

92. Decree Law No. 643 of October 26, 1972, as amended.

93. Decree Law No. 633 of October 26, 1972, as amended.

94. The Only Text of communal and provincial law approved by Legislative Decree No. 383 of April 3, 1934, as amended.

95. Municipalities obtain a return of the ILOR (*imposta locale sui redditi*) equivalent to 6 to 8.5 percent levied on net income of individuals and corporations realized within the municipality. The actual percentage of the tax between the 6 and 8.5 percent is determined every year by the municipality. They obtain the total revenue produced by the INVIM (*imposta comunale sull'incremento di valore degli immobili*) applied to the increased value of real property located in the municipality realized by the owner at the time of its transfer. These are the two major sources of municipal income. In addition, municipalities may levy a tax on signs displayed within the municipality (*imposta sulla pubblicità*), a rate on posters affixed (*tassa sulle pubbliche affissioni*), a rate on the right of occupation of land owned by the municipality (*tassa di occupazione di aree pubbliche*), a rate on services of weighing and measuring, and on the renting of public stands (*tassa per servizi di peso e misura e di apprestamento di banchi nei mercati*), a garbage fee (*tributo per il funzionamento del servizio di raccolta e transporto dei rifiuti solidi urbani*), a rate on dogs (*imposta sui cani*), and the like. All such rates must be approved and allowed to be levied by a national statute.

96. Constitution of Italy, Arts. 128, 129. The Only Text of communal and provincial law approved by Legislative Decree No. 383 of April 3, 1934, as amended.

97. The main income of the provinces is derived from a return of the ILOR (*imposta locale sui redditi*), equivalent to 1.5 to 2.5 percent levied on net income of individuals and corporations realized within the province. The actual percentage of the tax between 1.5 and 2.5 percent is determined every year by the province. Provinces may levy a rate on the occupation of land owned by the province (*tassa di occupazione di aree pubbliche*) and they derive further income by fees charged for services they perform to the general public.

98. Constitution of Italy, Arts. 114-133, dealing with regions, provinces and communities; Law No. 62 of February 10, 1953, as amended; Law No. 108 of February 17, 1968, as amended; and Law No. 281 of May 16, 1970, as amended.

99. Constitution of Italy, Art. 122; Law No. 108 of February 17, 1968, on ordinary regions; Law No. 1257 of August 5, 1962, on the Val d'Aosta.

100. The main income of the regions is derived from a return of the ILOR (*imposta locale sui redditi*) equivalent to 1 to 2 percent levied on net income of individuals and corporations realized within the region. The actual percentage of the tax between 1 to 2 percent is determined every year by the region. Regions may levy the following taxes: (1) tax on the use of inalienable state land (*imposta sulle concessioni su beni dello Stato demaniali e patrimoniali indisponibili*); (2) tax on regional licenses (*tassa sulle concessioni regionali*); (3) tax on motor vehicles (*tassa di circolazione dei veicoli e degli autoscafi*), in addition to the existing state tax; (4) tax on the right of occupation of land owned by the region (*tassa per l'occupazione di aree pubbliche di proprietà della regione*).

101. What is meant is that any person against whom an administrative act is directed has standing in administrative courts as contrasted with just a general interest in the proper functioning of administrative bodies by persons against whom no administrative acts are directed.

102. Law No. 1034 of December 6, 1971, on the creation of regional administrative courts. Regional administrative courts are set up in all regions, including special regions. The administrative courts previously set up in special regions are now defunct with the exception of the Sicilian council of administrative justice which sits as an appellate administrative court from the divisions of the Sicilian regional administrative court.

103. The provincial administrative council (*giunta provinciale amministrativa*) was the

traditional first instance administrative court in Italian administration with one in every province. It was constituted by five members, including its presiding officer. It was presided over by the prefect, and the other members were the two senior officers ranking immediately below the prefect in the prefectoral office and the two members of the provincial assembly who received the most votes in elections (in case of parity, the older ones). The G.P.A. had jurisdiction to hear appeals (*ricorsi*) against administrative organs of local and provincial administration and decided not only on the legitimacy of the act, but also on the merits. Its decisions were reviewable by the Council of State. The *ricorso* to the G.P.A. had to be filed within thirty days after notification of the administrative act appealed from, and the *appello* to the Council of State from the decision of the G.P.A. had to be filed also within thirty days. The function of the G.P.A. has been taken over by the regional administrative courts.

104. Constitution of Italy, Art. 100. The Only Text on the Council of State, Decree Law No. 1054 of June 26, 1924, as amended.

105. It may be contrasted with the advice the government may obtain from the *avvocatura dello stato* (office of government counsel). The *Avvocatura* handles the legal business of the state in the courts, and has branches in every seat of a court of appeal. Its head office in Rome is the *Avvocatura Generale dello Stato*, which is headed by the *Avvocato Generale dello Stato*. It is directly subordinated to the presidency of the council of ministers and has to act in accordance with directions obtained from the Prime Minister.

106. Exceptionally, on some matters, e.g., on reacquisition of Italian citizenship, the government must request the advice and it is bound by it.

107. Constitution of Italy, Art. 100.

108. Before regional administrative courts have taken over from provincial administrative councils, the Council of State would hear appeals (*appelli*) against decisions of these provincial administrative councils (*giunte provinciali amministrative*).

109. It is regulated by the Only Text on the Court of Accounts, the Decree Law of June 28, 1941, as amended. The basic provision concerning the Court may be found in Art. 100 of the Italian Constitution.

110. Another organ of government control is the *Ragioneria Generale dello Stato*, which is integrated within the ministry of treasury (*ministero del tesoro*) and controls government expenditures and the observance of proper methods of accountancy. It has officers within every ministry, known as *ragionerie centrali*, within every region, known as *ragionerie regionali*, and within every province, known as *ragionerie provinciali*.

111. The statute on the water courts is the Only Text of laws on public waters and electrical works, Royal Decree No. 1775 of December 11, 1933, as amended.

112. Law No. 825 of October 9, 1971, on tax reform; Decree No. 636 of the President of the Republic of October 26, 1972, on tax courts and procedure, as amended; Decree Law No. 603 of September 29, 1973, on the collection of direct taxes. Before the 1971-72 tax reform, disputes as to the assessment and levy of taxes were handled by the following organs. Commissions of assessment (*commissioni censuarie*) were set up at the communal level as communal commissions of assessment (*commissioni censuarie comunali*) and were appointed by the intendant of finance (*intendante di finanza*). At the provincial and central levels they were provincial commissions of assessment (*commissioni censuarie provinciali*) and the central commission of assessment (*commissione censuaria centrale*). They were appointed by the Minister of Finance (*Ministro per le Finanze*). They handled disputes on land tax (*imposta fondiaria*) and the tax on income from the use of structures (*imposta sul reddito dei fabbricati*). The administrative commissions for direct and indirect taxes (*commissioni amministrative*

per le imposte dirette e indirette) handled disputes concerning all the other taxes, with a few exceptions. They were again set up at three levels: district (*distrettuali*), province (*provinciali*), and central (*commissione centrale*). The district commissions were appointed by the intendant of finance and the other commissions by the Minister of Finance. Cases before the commissions generally started at the local level. Parties before each commission had to be represented by advocates (*avvocati*) or attorneys (*procuratori*), with the exception of the central administrative commission for direct and indirect taxes where they had to be represented by counsel admitted to appear before the commission. Having exhausted the appeal by having obtained a decision from the central commission, the petitioner was then entitled to initiate proceedings in ordinary civil courts where he could have obtained a declaration that the decision of the commission was illegal. In fact, the petitioner was free to initiate action in ordinary civil courts immediately after an adverse decision had been given at the local level or at any later stage.

113. Code of Civil Procedure, Arts. 395, 396. *See* procedure before the Council of State.
114. Rules as to administrative procedure, in addition to the rules of civil procedure contained in the Code of Civil Procedure, may be found in several special statutes, e.g., in the Only Text of communal and provincial law approved by Legislative Decree No. 383 of April 3, 1934, as amended.
115. Recourses (*ricorsi*) are either *amministrativi*, i.e., brought to an administrative authority from a decision of a subordinated or the same administrative authority (*ricorso per opposizione*), or *giurisdizionali amministrativi*, brought to an administrative court.
116. Procedure before *tribunali amministrativi regionali* is governed by Law No. 1034 of December 6, 1971, as amended.
117. In proceedings before the former provincial administrative councils (*giunte provinciali amministrative*), the parties could act for themselves and they were not bound to appoint counsel. The petition could have been signed by the party.
118. If the authority orders, e.g., a building to be demolished and the petitioner files a *ricorso* and petitions for a stay of execution, the administrative court will grant it because irreparable injury would be done to the interests of the petitioner if the building is demolished.
119. The Only Text on the Council of State, Decree Law No. 1054 of June 26, 1924, as amended; Regulation of judicial procedure before the Council of State, Royal Decree No. 642 of August 17, 1907, as amended.
120. Decree No. 636 of the President of the Republic of October 26, 1972, on tax courts and procedure, as amended.
121. The fundamental provisions on judges are: Constitution of Italy, Arts. 101-113; *Ordinamento Giudiziario, Regio decreto 30 gennaio 1941, n. 12*, as amended; *Legge 24 marzo 1958, n. 195.—Norme sulla costituzione e sul funzionamento del consiglio superiore della Magistratura; R.D.L. 31 maggio 1946, n. 511.—Guarentigie della Magistratura.*
122. The procurator general of the republic and eight members elected by a secret ballot as follows: five members from among appellate judges and three members from among judges of courts of general jurisdiction. The elected members hold office for two years.
123. Constitution of Italy, Arts. 104-107; *Legge 24 marzo 1958, n. 195.—Norme sulla costituzione e sul funzionamento del consiglio superiore della Magistratura; Ordinamento Giudiziario, Regio decreto 30 gennaio 1941, n. 12*, as amended.
124. *Ordinamento Giudiziario, Regio decreto 30 gennaio 1941, n. 12*, Arts. 69-84, as amended.
125. Also, officers of the office of government counsel (*avvocatura dello stato*) are

government lawyers who represent the state in suits where the state is a party and who give the government and its agencies legal advice. They are not comprised within the *pubblico ministero*.

126. The basic provision concerning the legal profession is Royal Legislative Decree No. 1578 of November 27, 1933, as amended.

127. The basic provisions concerning notaries are: Law No. 89 of February 16, 1913, on Notaries and Notarial Archives; Royal Decree No. 1326 of September 10, 1914, executing Law No. 89 of February 16, 1913, as amended.

The Spanish Law

I. INTRODUCTION

The present law of Spain rests on foundations laid by Roman law and by canon law with Germanic influences. Spanish law developed from these foundations in the leading Spanish kingdoms of Castile, Aragon, Catalonia and Navarre. It produced an early Roman-Germanic compilation known as the *Lex Romana Visigothorum* in the fifth century, and the well-known *Código de las Siete Partidas* in the thirteenth century; the latter attained royal recognition in 1348. Spain was, however, ruled by the *fueros*, which were local compilations applicable in a particular city or in a larger area, like a province. A compilation of the existing law was produced in the digest known as the *Nueva Recopilación* of 1805. Modern codification begins in the nineteenth century, first by the unification of laws on given subjects, and then in the codes. All codes took a considerable time to draft and to enact. The Civil Code was finally enacted in 1889 and it is still in power as amended. The Commercial Code is as of 1885, but it was preceded by another one of 1829. The Code of Civil Procedure was enacted in 1881 and is in power as amended. The Penal Code actually dates from 1848, but it was revised and modified in the reforms of 1850, 1870, 1928, 1932 and 1944. The 1944 version is in power as amended. The first Code of Criminal Procedure dates from 1835, but it was thoroughly revised in 1870 and 1872. The present version of the Code dates from 1882 and it is in power as further amended.

II. THE SYSTEM AND ADMINISTRATION OF CIVIL LAW

A. THE SUBSTANTIVE CIVIL LAW

The Civil Code of 1889 is in power as amended. It has 1976 articles. It is introduced by sixteen articles on laws, their effects and application, and the introduction is followed by four books dealing with: Book 1. Persons; Book 2. Property; Book 3. Acquisition of Property; and Book 4. Obligations and Contracts.

Book 1 (Persons) has the following titles: I. Spaniards and foreigners; II. Birth and the extinction of civil personality; III. Domicile; IV. Marriage; V. Paternity and affiliation; VI. Alimony and support; VII. Paternal power; VIII. Absence; IX. Guardianship; X. Family council; XI. Emancipation and full age; and XII. Civil register.

Book 2 (Property) has the following titles: I. Classification of property; II. Property; III. Concurrent ownership; IV. Special types of property; V. Possession; VI. Usufruct, use and right to use premises; VII. Easements; and VIII. Register of property.

Book 3 (Acquisition of Property) has the following titles: I. Occupation; II. Gifts; and III. Succession.

Book 4 (Obligations and Contracts) has the following titles: I. Obligations; II. Contracts; III. Matrimonial contracts; IV. Contract of purchase and sale; V. Barter; VI. Lease; VII. Emphyteusis; VIII. Partnership; IX. Agency; X. Loan; XI. Bailment; XII. Aleatory contracts; XIII. Settlement and compromise; XIV. Surety; XV. Pledge, mortgage and antichresis; XVI. Contracts formed without agreement; XVII. Ranking and priorities of debts; and XVIII. Prescription.

Further important statutes are listed in the appendix to the Civil Code. They deal, e.g., with adoption, arbitration, eminent domain, and naturalization.

The following are topics selected from the Spanish substantive civil law.

1. Domicile (*Domicilio*)[1]

The domicile of a person is the place where he habitually resides, and it is further determined by the Code of Civil Procedure. The domicile of a diplomat who resides abroad in the exercise of his official functions and who enjoys the right of exterritoriality is the last one he had in Spain.

If it has not been determined by the law under which they were set up or under other statutes and rules, the domicile of juridical persons is the place where they established their office for legal purposes or their head office.

The domicile of married women who are not legally separated is that of their husbands. The domicile of minors is that of their parents; the domicile of minors or incompetents under guardianship is that of their guardians.[2] The domicile of military persons on active duty is the place where the unit to which they belong was located at the time they were drafted.[3]

NOTES AND QUESTIONS

1. Consider the provisions concerning residence and domicile in the French,

the German and the Italian law. Is there a distinction between the two in these systems?

2. Is the meaning of domicile in Spanish law different from that in the French and the Italian law? How does it differ from the meaning of *Wohnsitz* in German law? Does the Spanish law make a fundamental distinction between residence and domicile?

3. Is there a significant distinction between the meaning of domicile in Spanish law and in Anglo-American law? *See,* Ramsey v. Liverpool Royal Infirmary [1930] A.C. 588 (H.L.).

---

2. Marriage (*Matrimonio*)[4]

The law recognizes two kinds of marriage: the canonical and the civil. Where at least one party to the marriage is Catholic, they must be married canonically. Where neither party is Catholic, they will be married civilly.

(a) Provisions applicable to both kinds of marriage (*Disposiciones comunes a las dos clases de matrimonio*). The following may not marry: (1) a minor not emancipated by a previous marriage who has not obtained the consent from those entitled to give it; (2) a widow for 301 days from the death of her husband, or before giving birth if pregnant, and a woman whose marriage has been annulled, similarly counting from the legal separation; (3) a guardian and a person under his guardianship until the termination of his office and the approval of his accounts, unless the marriage was authorized by the father of the ward in his will or a notarized document.[5]

Consent is given to legitimate children by the father or, failing him, by the mother, then by the paternal grandfather and, in descending order, by the maternal grandfather, paternal grandmother, and maternal grandmother. Failing all the above, consent is given by the family council. The same applies to legitimated children. Adopted persons must obtain the consent of the adopting parent or, failing him, of the family council. An illegitimate child must obtain consent from his mother, if known, or, failing her, from the maternal grandparents; failing all, consent must be obtained from the family council. The heads of foundling homes give their consent to those reared therein. The consent must be notarized or certified by the office of the civil registry. Should consent be denied, it may be granted by the bishop in his diocese or by the president of the court of appeal within his judicial district.

Should a marriage be celebrated in contradiction to the above provisions of Art. 45 of the Civil Code, it is nonetheless valid; the parties are, however, subject to the rules of separation of property and not to those of community property. Further, a minor will not be entitled to administer his property until he reaches majority; and where one party to the marriage was the guardian and the other the ward, the guardian will be removed from office as of the date of the marriage.[6]

Marriage contracted by a party already legally married produces no effect. Marriage is dissolved by the death of one of the spouses.[7] The husband is the administrator of the property of both spouses, but the wife is the administrator of her personal (paraphernal) property.

(b) Canonical marriage (*Matrimonio canónico*). Canonical marriage is governed by provisions of the canon law. It produces a full civil effect immediately upon its celebration. It should be registered in the civil register within five days from its celebration but if it is not so registered, the lack of registration will not affect rights lawfully acquired by third parties. The spouses are required to have their marriage registered, but it may be registered by any interested party at any time, even after the spouses die. Petitions for the annulment of a canonical marriage or for judicial separation are heard by ecclesiastical courts. The decisions of ecclesiastical authorities in these matters will be executed by civil authorities.

(c) Civil marriage (*Matrimonio civil*). The following may not marry: (1) males below the age of fourteen and females below the age of twelve. Yet a marriage entered into by parties below the minimum age is automatically validated as soon as they reach that age and continue to live together without contesting the validity of the marriage, or if the woman becomes pregnant before reaching that age or before she contests the validity of the marriage. (2) persons of unsound mind; (3) impotent persons; (4) religious persons bound by the vow of chastity, unless they obtain a dispensation from the Catholic Church; and (5) those already married.[8]

The following also may not marry: (1) ascendants and descendants related by blood or marriage; (2) legitimate collaterals by blood up to the fourth degree; (3) legitimate collaterals by marriage up to the fourth degree; (4) illegitimate collaterals up to the second degree; (5) adopting father or mother and the adopted, the adopted and the spouse of the surviving adopting father or mother, and the adopting father or mother and the surviving spouse of the adopted; (6) legitimate descendants of the adopting parent and the adopted as long as the relation created by adoption subsists; and (7) those convicted as principals or principal and accessory to the death of a spouse and the surviving spouse.[9]

A dispensation may be obtained from impediments between legitimate collaterals by marriage, and from impediments concerning the descendants of adopting parents.

Those wishing to enter into a civil marriage must file with the civil registry of their domiciles a form giving their full names, occupations, and the domiciles or residences of their parents. They must attach their certificates of birth, consents if required, and dispensations if necessary. The municipal judge of the locality involved then orders the publication of the petition for fifteen days in all places where the applicants have lived for the last two years with the request that all those aware of some impediment should come forward. He will also certify that the publication requirements have been met. A foreigner who has not resided in Spain for two years must produce a certificate from a competent authority stating that announcement of his intention to marry was made in all places where he resided in the last two years. If no impediment is brought to the attention of the municipal judge, he may celebrate the marriage forthwith; but it must be celebrated within a year, otherwise a new publication is required. If an objection is made, it is conveyed to the public ministry (*ministerio fiscal*); if found substantiated, the public ministry will file and prosecute an opposition. Only interested parties may file an opposition on their own. If the opposition is dismissed, the person filing it is liable in damages to the parties.

Marriage is celebrated before a municipal judge in the presence of both parties, or in the presence of only one party and another person to whom the absent party has given a special power, and in the further presence of two adult witnesses. The municipal judge then reads to the parties Articles 56 and 57 of the Civil Code,[10] and asks them whether they wish to be married. Upon their affirmative answer, he declares them man and wife and executes the marriage certificate, which is signed by the municipal judge, the spouses, the witnesses and the court secretary. Spanish consuls and vice-consuls exercise the powers of municipal judges and may celebrate marriage of Spanish citizens abroad.[11]

(d) Nullity of marriage (*Nulidad del matrimonio*). The following civil marriages are null and void: (1) marriages celebrated contrary to the prohibition of Articles 83 and 84 of the Civil Code, unless a dispensation has been obtained; (2) marriages entered into by error in the person, by coercion or by duress; (3) marriage between the abductor and the abducted while she is in his power; and (4) marriages not celebrated before a competent municipal judge or as authorized by him, or without the presence of the witnesses required by Article 100 of the Civil Code.

A suit for annulment of marriage may be initiated by the spouses, the public ministry, or any interested party. In the case of abduction, error, coercion or duress, only the spouse making the allegation may bring suit. In the case of impotence, suit may be brought by either spouse and by any interested party. Where the parties have lived together for six months after the discovery of the error, the ceasing of coercion or duress or the recovery of freedom by the abducted, the defect in the marriage is validated and no suit may be brought. Petitions for annulment are brought in the courts of general jurisdiction (*tribunales civiles*).

(e) Separation of spouses (*Separación*). A petition for the separation of spouses married civilly may be brought in the courts of general jurisdiction (*tribunales civiles*). The grounds for separation are: (a) adultery; (b) mistreatment, serious injury or abandonment; (c) force applied by one spouse to the other to induce him to change his religion; (d) proposal by the husband to prostitute the wife; (e) endeavor of either spouse to corrupt the sons or to prostitute the daughters, or his connivance in connection therewith; and (f) conviction for serious crime to *reclusión mayor*.[12]

Only the innocent spouse may petition for separation. The effect of separation is the termination of cohabitation and the partition of community property. The innocent spouse retains, and the guilty spouse loses, his right to alimony. The innocent spouse has custody of the children and can enforce his claim to alimony and support by attachment, garnishment or any other means. If both spouses are guilty, the judge will appoint a guardian to the children. Unless otherwise provided, the mother has custody of children below the age of seven years. In case of death of the spouse having custody, it passes to the other spouse if the ground for separation was not one affecting morality; but a guardian will have to be appointed. In case of reconciliation, the proceedings for separation come to an end. Where separation has already been pronounced, it will have no effect. If the ground for the petition was the corruption of sons or prostitution of daughters, the court will make proper provisions for their protection.

NOTES AND QUESTIONS

1. Note the distinction between canonical and civil marriages. Is any such distinction made in Italian law? How are marriages entered into under provisions of the French and of the German law? For Anglo-American law, *see*, e.g., Texas Family Code, Chapter 1.

2. Note the minimum age for entering into marriage. Compare it with the Italian and the German law. For Anglo-American law *see*, e.g., Texas Family Code §1.51ff.

3. Compare the Spanish consanguinity rule with similar rules in France and Italy. *See also* Texas Family Code §2.21ff.

4. What are the rules governing marriages of foreigners in Spain? Compare them with the French rules. Are there any special rules governing marriages of foreigners in Anglo-American law?

5. What are the Spanish provisions concerning the annulment of marriage? On which grounds may a marriage be annulled? Annulment of marriage must be pronounced by a competent court. Compare the German and the French provisions. *See also* Texas Family Code, Chapter 2.

6. Note the grounds for the separation of spouses. Are they similar to the grounds for divorce applicable in other countries? Compare the French and the Italian law.

---

3.   Civil Register (*Registro del estado civil*)[13]

The civil register carries records and annotations of births, marriages, emancipations, recognitions and legitimations, deaths, and naturalizations. Municipal judges and other officers are in charge of civil registers in Spain, and Spanish diplomatic and consular officers exercise their powers abroad. The records are proof of the facts recorded and these facts cannot be proved otherwise, except when there is no record or where the books have disappeared or where the records are challenged in court. It is the duty of the parties to convey to the proper officer of the civil registry the necessary information upon their entering into a canonical marriage so that it may be recorded. Naturalizations must be recorded in order to be valid and those not so recorded are invalid. Any breach of the provisions concerning recording is subject to a fine assessed by municipal judges or judges of first instance courts.

NOTES AND QUESTIONS

Note the wide scope of the Spanish civil register. In other countries, the civil register keeps mainly the records of births, deaths and marriages. *See,* e.g., French Civil Code, Arts. 34ff.; Italian Civil Code, Arts. 449ff.

Who keeps similar records in Anglo-American countries? *See,* e.g., V.A. Texas Civ. St. Art. 4477, Rules 34(a)-55(a), as to the Registrars of Vital Statistics.

---

4. Property *(Propiedad)*

(a) Ownership of property *(Bienes y la propiedad).*[14]   Property is the right to enjoy and dispose of a thing with only such limitations as are established by law. The owner has an action against the holder and possessor thereof. No one may be deprived of his property except by the proper authority on the ground of public need and for a proper compensation paid beforehand. If these conditions are not met, the courts will put the owner back in possession.

The owner of land owns both the surface and the subsoil. He may build, plant or excavate as he pleases, observing easements and the laws on mining and water as well as relevant police regulations. A hidden treasure belongs to the owner of the land. Where it is found by accident on someone else's land or on state-owned land, the finder will receive one half thereof. If the objects found are of interest to science or the arts, the state may acquire them by paying a just price to those entitled as provided above. By treasure, the law means money, jewelry or other valuables that have been concealed and whose owner is unknown. Any citizen or foreigner may excavate on public lands to a depth of ten meters and for an equal length for the purpose of searching for minerals. He must advise the local authorities before he begins prospecting. For excavation on private land, the permission of the owner is required. Further details are governed by the law of mining.[15]

(b) Land register *(Registro de la propiedad).*[16]   The land register contains the records and annotations of documents and contracts with respect to title and other rights to immovables. Title to land and other rights to immovables that are not properly recorded or annotated in the land register do not affect third parties. The land register is public. The rules of recording appear in the law of mortgages.[17]

(c) Acquisition of property *(Adquisición de la propiedad).*[18]   Property may be acquired by occupation, gift, succession testate or intestate, contract and prescription. Property that by its nature has no owner, such as animals subject to hunting or fishing, a hidden treasure or abandoned movables, may be acquired by occupation. A gift is an act by which a person disposes of a thing free of charge to another person who accepts it.

NOTES AND QUESTIONS

1. Note the definition of property in Spanish law. Compare the French and the

Italian law. What is the Spanish rule with respect to finding and to treasure trove? Compare it with the French and the German law. *See also* Calif. C.C.A. §2080ff. as to Anglo-American law.

2. Note the Spanish rule as to eminent domain. It falls within administrative law. *See* the section on expropriation below. Compare also the French law of eminent domain. How is eminent domain regulated in Anglo-American law? *See* the American Uniform Eminent Domain Code.

3. Spanish title registration and the recording of other dealings like incumbrances and mortgages is very similar to registration in other civil law countries. In Germany, the matter is dealt with by a special statute, the *Grundbuchordnung* of March 24, 1897 (RGB1. S. 139), as amended; in France, by the Decree of January 4, 1955, as further amended, on the Land Register; in Italy, by Arts. 2673ff. of the Civil Code.

How is the registration of land handled in Anglo-American countries? *See,* e.g., Calif. C.C.A. §1169ff.

4. Title to property, both movable and immovable, is acquired by the standard methods known to civil law. Compare the German and the Italian law. Compare the detailed provisions of the French law on the different modes of acquisition of property, especially by gift and by intestate succession. How is property acquired in Anglo-American law? *See,* e.g., Calif. C.C.A. §1000ff.

----

5.   Wills and Estates (*Sucesiones*)[19]

Any person can make a will unless expressly prohibited by law. Minors below fourteen years of age and persons of unsound mind, whether permanently or temporarily, are not competent to make a will. A will made under duress, undue influence or fraud is void. A person exercising such duress, undue influence or fraud upon the testator may not inherit. Every testamentary disposition is understood literally unless it clearly appears that the testator meant otherwise. When in doubt, the literal meaning of words will be followed, subject to the intention of the testator apparent in the will. The testator may not provide that his will cannot be contested in cases where the law itself declares the testament void.

(a)   Kinds of wills (*Forma de los testamentos*).   A will (*testamento*) may be either ordinary (*común*) or special (*especial*). The ordinary will may be holographic, open or closed. The special will may be military, or it may be made aboard ship or in a foreign country.

A holographic will (*testamento ológrafo*) is written by the hand of the testator and is subscribed by him. It may be made only by adults and it must give the day, month and year of its making. Foreigners may make it in their own language.

An open will (*testamento abierto*) is made before a notary and three witnesses who must certify it.

A closed will (*testamento cerrado*) is handed by the testator to the notary in a sealed envelope in the presence of five witnesses. The notary will endorse the envelope with the notarial act of the reception of the will therein enclosed and will sign the endorsement together with the witnesses and the testator. The will itself may be either holographic or it may be prepared by another person at the testator's request and signed by the testator.

Military testament (*testamento militar*) may be made by military and civil personnel of the armed forces in the field in time of war. It may be open or closed and it is made before an officer of the rank of captain or above and two witnesses. Sick or wounded persons may make it also before the chaplain and two witnesses. Military wills become null and void four months after the testator returns from the field.

A testament made aboard ship (*testamento marítimo*) is made before the purser and two witnesses, in the case of naval vessels, and marked as seen by the ship's captain or his deputy. In the case of other ships, it is made before the master or his deputy and two witnesses. The wills are either open or closed. They become null and void four months after the ship reaches the first Spanish port.

In a foreign country, Spanish citizens may make wills (*testamento hecho en país extranjero*) in accordance with the law of the country where they are located. They may also make wills aboard ship in accordance with the law of the country to which the ship belongs. They may also make holographic wills in accordance with Spanish law even in countries that do not recognize such wills. A will made jointly by two or more persons, or one made by two or more persons in one instrument, is not valid in Spain even though the will is reciprocal or for the benefit of a third person and even though it is valid in the foreign country where it was made. Spaniards abroad may also make an open or a closed will before a Spanish diplomatic or consular officer. The officer acts as a notary in accordance with Spanish law. Spanish citizens may also deposit their holographic wills with their diplomatic or consular officers.

(b) Revocation (*Revocación*). All testamentary provisions are revocable even though the testator provides in his will that he will not revoke them. All stipulations to the contrary are void. A will may be revoked in full or in part only under the same formalities of making a will. A later will revokes a prior one, unless the testator provides in the later will that the prior one should stand in full or in part. A prior will is revived when the testator revokes the later will and declares that the prior will should stay in power.

A closed will is presumed revoked if it is found in the testator's home opened or with its seals undone or with the signatures crossed out, erased or amended. The testament is considered valid, however, if it can be shown that what happened occurred without the wish or knowledge or the testator or when he was of unsound mind. Where a closed testament is found opened or with its seals broken, its authenticity also must be established. If the testament is found in the possession of another person, its damaged condition is presumed to have been caused by that person and its authenticity must be established. However, where the envelope and seals are intact but the signatures are crossed out, erased or amended, the testatment is considered valid if it is shown that it was in that condition when it was handed in by the testator.

(c) Capacity to inherit (*Capacidad para suceder*). Any person may inherit unless prohibited by law. Stillborn children who do not live for more than twenty-four hours, and partnerships and corporations not permitted by the law may not inherit. A testamentary provision in favor of a person who may not inherit is null and void.

The following may not inherit because of indignity: (1) parents who abandon their children or who prostitute their daughters; (2) a person who is convicted of an attempt on the life of the decedent, his spouse, descendants and ascendants; (3) a person who falsely accuses the decedent of a crime punishable by law; (4) an heir of full age who is aware of the decedent's violent death and does not inform the authorities within one month therefrom; (5) a person who is found guilty of adultery with the decedent's wife; (6) a person who with threats, fraud or force makes the decedent make or alter a will; and (7) a person who by the same means prevents the decedent from making or revoking a will or makes him revoke, hide or alter a will.[20]

(d) Forced heirs (*Herederos forzosos*). Forced heirs are legitimate children and descendants in relation to their parents and ascendants, and vice versa; one spouse in relation to the other; and children legitimated by recognition or by royal decree in relation to their father and mother, and vice versa.

The forced share (*legitima*) to which legitimate children and descendants are entitled amounts to two thirds of the father's or mother's estate. The father and mother may dispose freely of the remaining one third. The surviving spouse is entitled to a usufruct in two ninths of the estate taken from the two thirds that form the forced share of the legitimate children and descendants. The forced share to which parents and ascendants are entitled from the estate of their children or descendants amounts to one half thereof, but where there is a surviving spouse of such child or descendant, they are entitled to one third of the estate. The forced share due to parents is divided in two, with one half due to each of them. If only one survives, he receives the whole share. If there are no surviving parents but there are ascendants both paternal and maternal of the same degree, the paternal receive one half and the maternal the other. If the ascendants are of a different degree, the closer relatives receive the whole share whether they are paternal or maternal. Where there are no descendants but only ascendants, the surviving spouse is entitled to a usufruct in one half of the estate. Where there are neither descendants nor ascendants, he is entitled to a usufruct in two thirds of the estate.

(e) Disinheritance (*Desheredación*). A person may be disinherited only for cause expressly stipulated by law. Disinheritance may be effected only in a will expressly stating the ground. The heirs must make proof if the disinherited denies the act. If they are unsuccessful, the disinherited takes his forced share. The grounds for disinheritance are enumerated in Article 756 (1-6) above.

Children and descendants may also be disinherited for: (1) denying support without any legal ground to their father or another ascendant or mistreating them by acts or words; (2) prostituting their daughters or granddaughters; or (3) being convicted of a crime that carries with it the loss of civil rights.[21]

Parents and ascendants may be disinherited also for: (1) being deprived of their parental powers by a court order; (2) denying support to their children or descendants without any legal ground; or (3) making an attempt on the life of the other parent when there is no reconciliation.

A spouse may be disinherited on the grounds enumerated in Article 756 (2)(3)(6) above, as well as on the following grounds: (1) on the ground of separation; (2) where he is deprived of his parental power by a court order; (3) where he denies support to his children or to his spouse; or (4) where he makes an attempt on the life of the other spouse and there is no reconciliation.

(f) Intestacy (*Sucesión intestada*). Intestacy takes place: (1) where a person dies without leaving a will, leaving a void will or one declared void later; (2) where the will does not appoint an heir as to the whole or as to a part of the estate or where it does not dispose of all the estate (in such a case, intestacy takes effect only with respect to the property not disposed of); (3) where the appointment of the heir depends on a condition precedent and the condition was not complied with, or where the heir predeceases the testator, or where he repudiates his appointment; or (4) where the heir lacks the capacity to inherit.

On intestacy, the direct ascending line takes first. Failing legitimate children and descendants of the deceased, the ascendants (collaterals excepted) take the estate. Failing legitimate descendants and ascendants, illegitimate children of the deceased properly legitimated by recognition or by royal decree take the whole estate. Failing all of the above, the collaterals (brothers and sisters of the decedent and their descendants) take, and failing them, the surviving spouse takes the estate. Where there are the above collaterals, the surviving spouse takes a usufruct in two thirds of the estate.

NOTES AND QUESTIONS

1. Note the minimum age required by Spanish law for a person to make a will. Compare the French and the German law. What is the minimum age requirement in Anglo-American law? *See,* e.g., V.A. Texas S. Probate Code §57.

2. What kinds of wills exist in Spanish law? Compare them with those of the German and the French law. Does Anglo-American law sanction holographic wills? *See,* e.g., V.A. Texas S. Probate Code §60.

3. Wills may be deposited for safekeeping with a notary. Compare the Spanish safekeeping provisions with those of the German, the Italian and the French law. As to Anglo-American law *see,* e.g., V.A. Texas S. Probate Code §71.

4. How is a will revoked in Spanish law? Compare with the French and the German law. For Anglo-American law *see,* e.g., V.A. Texas S. Probate Code §63.

5. Note the Spanish provisions dealing with incapacity to inherit. In addition to the obvious condition that the beneficiary must survive the testator or the intestate, the law lists grounds on which the law will not allow a person to take from the decedent. Are these grounds identical with those of disinheritance? Compare the provisions of the French and the German law. How does Anglo-American law deal with the matter? *See,* e.g., Calif. Prob. C.A. §258. The problem is connected with that of forced shares. Who is entitled to a forced share under Spanish law? Compare the French and the Italian law. Are there any forced shares in Anglo-American law?

6. What are the Spanish rules of succession on intestacy? Compare them with the French and the German rules. For Anglo-American law *see*, e.g., V.A. Texas S. Probate Code §37ff.

---

6.   Obligations (*Obligaciones*).[22]

Every obligation consists in giving, doing or not doing a thing. Obligations arise from the law, from contracts and quasi-contracts, from illicit acts and omissions, and from such acts and omissions in which fault or negligence intervenes. Obligations are extinguished by payment or performance, by destruction of the thing due, by remission of the debt, by the union of the rights of creditor and debtor, by compensation, and by novation.

(a)   Contracts (*Contratos*).   There is a contract when one or more persons obligate themselves with respect to another person or persons to give a thing or to render some service. The essentials of contracts are: (1) agreement of the parties; (2) a certain subject matter as the substance of the contract; and (3) the *causa* of the contract.[23] Contracts *sine causa* or with an illicit *causa* produce no effects. By an illicit *causa*, it is meant one contrary to law or morals.

The following must be made in a public document:[24] (1) acts or contracts that create, transfer, modify or extinguish rights in immovables; (2) lease of immovables for six or more years whenever it may affect the rights of third parties; (3) marriage contracts and the setting up or increase of dowry if intended to have effect against third parties; (4) assignment, repudiation or renunciation of the right to inherit or of matrimonial property rights; (5) proxy to enter into marriage and power of attorney to represent in court, to administer property or to execute a document or a public document or one that may affect third parties; and (6) assignment of actions or rights contained in a public document.

Also, all contracts exceeding a certain minimum value (1,500 pesetas) must be made in writing (private writing).

(b)   Rescission of contracts (*rescisión de los contratos*).   Valid contracts may be rescinded for causes provided for by law. The following contracts may be rescinded: (1) contracts entered into by guardians without authorization of the family council whereby the ward lost property in excess of one fourth of the value of the subject matter thereof; (2) contracts made on behalf of persons absent and of unknown whereabouts under the same conditions as under (1) above; (3) contracts made in fraud of creditors; (4) contracts made *pendente lite* without the knowledge or approval of the parties or of the court; and (5) all other contracts determined by law. All payments made by insolvents may also be rescinded.

The action for rescission is a subsidiary one. It may be brought only where no other means of recovery subsist. Rescission brings about the restitution of property, i.e., the restitution of the subject matter of the contract together with its increments, or the restitution of the price with interest. Consequently, it may take place only where the property may be restituted. Equally, there may be no rescission where the property is lawfully in the possession of third parties who have not acted in bad faith. Damages are recoverable in such cases. The action for rescission must be brought within four years. In the case of persons under guardianship, time begins to run only after they gain full capacity; in the case of persons absent, only after their place of abode is known.

(c) Nullity of contracts (*Nulidad de los contratos*). Contracts may be annulled for causes provided for by law. Suit must be brought within four years. Time begins to run in the case of duress or force from the day when it ceases; in the case of error or fraud from the making of the contract. Where the action is brought to invalidate a contract made by a married woman without proper authorization, time runs from the dissolution of marriage. With respect to contracts entered into by minors or incompetents, time runs from the day when they become of age or when they regain full capacity. Persons of full capacity may not base their claim on the ground that the other party lacked capacity. Similarly those who applied duress, force, error or fraud may not base their suit thereon.

Where a contract is annulled, parties must restitute all that they have received thereunder with increments and interest. Where nullity is based on the lack of capacity of one of the parties, the incompetent must make restitution only to the extent of his enrichment. Where nullity is based on illegality and the act amounts to a criminal offense committed by both parties, neither may claim against the other. Where the act constitutes a criminal offense by one party only, the innocent party may reclaim all that he has given but he is not required to perform. Where nullity is based on illegality and the act does not constitute any criminal offense, and where the fault lies with both parties, neither may reclaim what he has given nor demand performance. Where the fault lies with one party only, he may not reclaim what he has given nor may he claim performance. The innocent party may reclaim what he has given and he is not required to perform. Whenever restitution cannot be had because of the destruction of the subject matter, its value at the time of destruction, together with interest, must be paid.

Action for an annulment is extinguished upon affirmation of the contract. Only contracts validly entered into in accordance with Article 1261 above may be affirmed.

NOTES AND QUESTIONS

1. Spanish law deals first with obligations in general and then proceeds to the treatment of individual contracts. This is the standard approach adopted in the civil law. How does it compare with the French and German approaches.

2. What are the essentials of contract in Spanish law? Compare the French and the German law.

3. Note the distinction in Spanish law between contracts to be made in writing and those which must be made in a public form in order to be enforceable. Compare the Italian and the German law. How does the Spanish rule compare with an Anglo-American Statute of Frauds? *See,* e.g., V. Texas C.A. Bus. & C. §26.01.

4. On which grounds may a contract be rescinded? Compare the grounds of the Spanish law with those of the French and the German law. How does

Anglo-American law deal with rescission? *See,* e.g., Restatement, Contracts §406ff.; Corbin on Contracts, One Volume Ed., 1952, §§301ff. and 1236.

5. **On which grounds may a contract be annulled? Note the distinction made** in Spanish law between rescission and annulment. Do other legal systems make a similar distinction? Compare the French and the Italian law. *See also* Restatement, Contracts, §492ff.

6. Note that Spanish law may also enforce performance of contracts similarly to the Anglo-American specific performance. This is provided in the Spanish Civil Code, Art. 1096ff. It covers the delivery of property as well as injunctions to do or to abstain. The Spanish rule is fully equivalent to the German and Italian rules.

---

7. Marriage Contracts (*Contratos sobre bienes con ocasión del matrimonio*)[25]

Parties entering into marriage may stipulate before the celebration thereof by a marriage contract how their property, present and future, should be regulated during marriage. If the parties do not make a marriage contract, their property relations are governed by the law of community property (*sociedad legal de gananciales*). Minors may make marriage contracts only with the consent of those whose consent is required for them to enter into marriage. Failing such consent, their property relations are governed by the law of community property. No modification of the property arrangement is possible after the celebration of marriage. The marriage contract must be made in a public document.

Where a Spanish man marries a Spanish woman abroad without making a marriage contract, their property relations are governed by the law of community property. The same applies to a marriage of a Spanish man with a foreign woman. But where a Spanish woman marries a foreign man under the law of a foreign country, their property relations are governed by the law of that country.

All gifts between spouses during marriage are void, with the exception of small gifts made at family occasions.

(a) **Dowry** (*Dote*). The dowry is composed of the property and rights that the wife brings into the marriage at the time of its celebration and of such other property and rights which she acquires during marriage by gift or inheritance and which are earmarked as dowry. Property acquired during marriage with property constituted as dowry is itself dowry. Dowry is given before or after the celebration of marriage by the parents and relatives of the spouses or by other persons. It may also be given by the husband but only before the celebration of marriage.

The parents or the surviving parent must give a dowry to their legitimate daughters except where minor daughters marry without their consent and the authorization of the authorities that takes its place has not been obtained.[26] The obligatory dowry amounts to one half of the presumed forced share to which the daughter would be entitled on her parents' death.[27] But where the daughter has property of her own amounting to one half of the presumed forced share, the obligation of the parents to provide a dowry is extinguished. Where the daughter has property of her own not amounting to the required amount, her parents must make up for the difference as a dowry. A detailed investigation of the property position of the parents may not be undertaken and reliance must be placed on the statements of the parents and on those of the two closest relatives of the daughter, one paternal and the other maternal.

Dowry is either valued and its worth determined or it is not valued.

Title to property comprised in a valued dowry passes to the husband and he is bound to restitute its value. Where dowry is not valued, the wife retains title to the property and the husband is obligated to restitute the very property.

With respect to valued dowry, the husband must give a mortgage to the wife over the immovables given as dowry, and further, he must give her a mortgage over his own immovables as security for movables given as a dowry.

The husband is the administrator and usufructuary of the not valued dowry. He must enter the immovable property in the land register in the name of his wife as not valued dowry and he must give her a mortgage over his own land as security for the management, the usufruct and the restitution of movables brought in as not valued dowry. The wife has title to the not valued dowry and the husband is liable only for negligence. The wife may sell or encumber property pertaining to not valued dowry with the husband's permission. Where such property is sold, the husband must give security for the proceeds as in the case of valued dowry. The husband may not lease land pertaining to not valued dowry for a term longer than six years without his wife's consent.

The dowry will be restituted to the wife or to her heirs: (1) on dissolution or annulment of the marriage; (2) on the transfer of administration of the dowry to the wife in case of the husband's incompetence; and (3) where it is so ordered by a court.

As to valued dowry, the amount at which it was valued when received by the husband will be refunded, reduced by the amount that the wife gave to her daughters as dowry and by the amount of the wife's debts contracted before marriage and paid by the husband.

As to not valued dowry, immovables will be restituted in the condition in which they are. If they were sold, their value will be refunded less whatever was spent on the discharge of obligations entered into by the wife. Movables and immovables must be restituted promptly after the dissolution of marriage. Money, perishable goods and valuable papers that are not on hand in full or in part at the dissolution of marriage may be demanded only one year after the dissolution of marriage. Until they are restituted, their increment and interest must be paid. Whenever the actual pieces of property are not returned, the refund must be in money. Movables and perishable goods may, however, be returned in kind. From the refund of the not valued dowry are deducted the following items, if they were paid by the husband: (1) the expenses of recovery and defense of the dowry; (2) the debts of the dowry; and (3) debts incurred by the wife.

Where the dowry is restituted, the husband is entitled to restitution of the gifts, if any, he made to the wife upon entering into the marriage.

Where the marriage is dissolved by the death of the wife, interest and increments of the dowry go to her heirs as of the date of the dissolution of marriage. Where it is dissolved by the husband's death, the wife is entitled to interest and increments of the dowry for one year; or she may obtain, if she so chooses, alimony from the entire estate of the husband for one year.

(b) Paraphernal property (*Bienes parafernales*). Paraphernal property is all of the property that the wife brings into the marriage apart from the dowry or that which she acquires after marriage but does not add to the dowry. The wife has title to her paraphernal property. The husband has no power over such property except with the consent of the wife. The wife administers her paraphernal property but she may pass its administration to the husband by a notarized act. In that case, the husband must give security as provided for in the administration of the dowry. The proceeds of paraphernal property accrue to the marital community and may be applied to the expenses of the marriage. Personal debts of the husband may not be satisfied from the proceeds of paraphernal property, unless it is shown that such proceeds are not needed for the upkeep of the family. The wife may not alienate nor encumber her paraphernal property nor litigate with respect to it without the consent of her husband or without judicial authorization.

NOTES AND QUESTIONS

1. Note the Spanish law as to marriage contracts. How does it compare with the French and the Italian law on the subject? May a marriage contract be modified after the celebration of marriage? What are the reasons given as to why it may not be so modified? As to marriage contracts in Anglo-American law, *see*, e.g., Texas Family Code §5.41.

2. Note the elaborate provisions as to the dowry in the Spanish law. Do dowries exist in the French and the Italian law? Would an Anglo-American trust perform the function of the Spanish dowry?

3. What is the paraphernal property of the wife? Is it in fact equivalent to the separate property of the wife under the community property system? As to kinds of marital property in American community property systems, *see*, e.g., Texas Family Code, Chapter 5.

----

8.   Marital Property (*Bienes de los conyuges*)

(a) Community property (*Bienes gananciales*).[28] Community property is set up on the day of the celebration of the marriage. It may not be renounced during marriage except in cases of judicial separation and the dissolution or annulment of the marriage. The renunciation is made by a public act without prejudice to the rights of creditors, if any. Community property is governed by the provisions applicable to partnerships unless provided otherwise in the Civil Code. On dissolution of the marriage, the husband and wife share equally all gains and profits obtained by both of them in community during marriage.

Community property consists of: (1) whatever has been acquired for value during marriage at the expense of the marital community, even if acquired for one spouse only; (2) whatever has been acquired due to the industry, salary, wages or work of the spouses; and (3) whatever has been obtained as proceeds, income or interest during marriage from community property or separate property of the spouses.

The right to usufruct or pension for life or in perpetuity of a spouse is his separate property, but other proceeds, pensions or interests acquired during marriage are community property. Whatever is obtained by a spouse as winnings in games or from other sources where restitution is not required belongs to the community. Generally, all property of the spouses is reputed community property, unless it is shown that it belongs separately to one of them.

The husband is the administrator of the community property. He may alienate or encumber it for value. His dispositions of immovables or business property require approval of his wife or, failing such approval, a judicial authorization. In his will, the husband may dispose of only one half of the community property. He may make moderate gifts to charity, but he may not make gifts to children of the marriage to set them up in life.

The wife may not bind community property without the consent of the husband, except where she is charged with its administration.

Community property comes to an end upon dissolution of the marriage, annulment of the marriage, or separation of matrimonal property by a court order. The spouse who by his bad faith caused the annulment of the marriage may not share in the community property.[29]

An inventory of the community property is made upon its dissolution. It is not made, however, where one of the spouses has renounced his share therein, where separation of matrimonal property has already been effected, or where one of the spouses has forfeited his right to it as provided in Article 1417 of the Civil Code.

After the inventory is made, the dowry and paraphernal property of the wife is repaid first, then debts of the community are paid. Where assets are lacking to effectuate these payments, the rules provided for in Title 17 of Book 4 of the Civil Code, on the ranking and priorities of debts, are applied. After all the debts of the community are paid, the capital of the husband is repaid, and whatever remains is divided equally between husband and wife or their heirs.

While the inventory is being prepared and the community property distributed, support to the surviving spouse and children is paid from the assets of the estate until it reaches their share of the estate.

(b) Separate property (*Bienes propios*). The separate property of each of the spouses consists of: (1) whatever he brings into the marriage as separate property; (2) whatever he acquires during marriage by gift or inheritance; (3) whatever he acquires in exchange for his separate property; and (4) whatever he buys with his own money.

Property given to the spouses by will, jointly or in common, accrues to the dowry of the wife and to the capital of the husband in equal shares. Where unequal shares are indicated by the testator, it accrues in the proportions so indicated.

(c) Separation of marital property (*Separación de los bienes de los conyuges*). Should the spouses fail to provide in the marriage contract for the separation of property, it is obtainable during marriage only by a judicial order, except as provided in Article 50 of the Civil Code.[30] A spouse may petition for separation of property and the petition must be granted where the other spouse is convicted to punishment that carries with it the loss of civil rights, where he is declared missing, or where he gives the petitioner a cause for separation. The decree of separation of property dissolves the community property, and it will be distributed as provided in the Civil Code. Yet, the spouses must support each other and their children in accordance with their means.

Where separation is granted on the husband's petition, he continues to administer the marital property and the wife has no claim to community property acquired thereafter, but the husband must restitute the dowry.

Where the separation is granted on the wife's petition on the grounds of the disappearance of her husband or his giving her cause for separation, the wife takes over the administration of her dowry and of all other property falling to her upon distribution of community property.

The petition and the order of separation are recorded in the land register if immovables are affected. The separation is without prejudice to rights of creditors previously acquired.

Where separation comes to an end by reconciliation or by the removal of the cause for separation, property relations of the spouses are governed by the rules applicable before the separation, without prejudice to transactions legally effected in the meantime.

The administration of marital property will be transferred to the wife: (1) where she is appointed guardian of her husband; (2) where she petitions for him to be declared missing; or (3) where he is deprived of his civil rights.

The court must also transfer the administration to the wife, subject to any limitations it may deem proper to impose, where the husband is a fugitive from justice or where he is unable to attend to the administration. While administering marital property, the wife may not alienate nor encumber immovables without a court order. The order will be made where such action is convenient or necessary.

NOTES AND QUESTIONS

1. Compare the Spanish community property system with those of France and Italy. What are the main differences? How does the Spanish community property system compare with those of California and Texas? *See* Calif. C.C.A. §5100ff.; Texas Family Code, Chapter 5.

2. How does the Spanish law define the separate property of the spouses? Compare Spanish separate property with separate property in the French and Italian law. Does Spanish separate property differ from the separate property of the spouses in California or Texas? *See* Calif. C.C.A. §§5107, 5108; Texas Family Code §5.01ff.

3. Which property becomes community property in Spanish law? Does Spanish community property comprise the same kind of property as French or Italian community property? How does it compare with California or Texas community property? *See* Calif. C.C.A. §5104ff.; Texas Family Code §5.01ff. Who manages community property? Compare the Spanish rule with that of France and Italy. How is community property dissolved in the Spanish, the French and the Italian law?

4. Compare the Spanish system of separation of marital property with those of France and Italy. Is the system of separation of marital property in community

property countries similar to the system of marital property current in British countries and in American common law states? Note that in community property countries the spouses may by marriage contract provide for the separation of marital property.

---

9. Prescription (*Prescripción*)[31]

Title and rights to immovables may be acquired by prescription. Conversely, rights and actions may be extinguished by prescription. Persons capable of acquiring rights or property by other legitimate means may acquire them by prescription. The rights and actions are extinguished after the term provided for by the law has run. Prescription accruing to one co-owner benefits all others. All things *intra commercium* are subject to prescription.

(a) Prescription of title and other property rights (*Prescripción del dominio y demás derechos reales*). To acquire title, a person must be in possession in good faith under a just title for a term determined by law. Such possession must be as the owner and open, peaceful and uninterrupted. Acts of possessory character undertaken by virtue of a license of the owner or in which the owner acquiesces do not qualify.

Possession may be interrupted naturally or civilly. Natural interruption takes place where possession ceases for more than one year for any reason. Civil interruption is produced by the service of process on the possessor even from a court lacking jurisdiction. Service of process will not cause interruption where: (1) the citation is void because of form; (2) the plaintiff withdraws his action or abandons his case; or (3) the possessor prevails in the suit. Civil interruption also occurs by settlement of the dispute. An admission, whether express or tacit, by the possessor of the right of the owner interrupts the possession.

Prescription does not run against titles recorded in the land register to the prejudice of third parties but only in favor of another recorded title. Time then runs from the recording of the second title.

Title to movables is prescribed by uninterrupted possession in good faith for three years. It is also prescribed by uninterrupted possession for six years without any other requirement. The owner of chattels lost or of which he was wrongfully deprived may repossess them irrespective of prescription. If such chattels were acquired by another person in good faith in a public sale, he may retake them only if he pays that person the amount paid therefor.[32]

Title to immovables is prescribed by possession in good faith under a just title for ten years between persons present, and for twenty years between person absent. Persons residing abroad or beyond the seas are considered absent. If a person was partly present and partly absent, every two years of absence count as one year of presence. Absences for a time shorter than one year are disregarded.

Title to immovables is also prescribed by an uninterrupted possession for thirty years without any requirement of good faith or just title and without any distinction between persons present and absent.

As to the computation of time, the time of succeeding possessors may be tacked. It is presumed that a present possessor who has been in possession at an earlier time has also been in possession in the interim unless shown otherwise; and the first day of possession is counted as a full day, but the last day of possession must be fully completed to be counted.

(b) Limitation of actions (*Prescripción de las acciones*). Actions to recover movables prescribe in six years from the loss of possession unless the possessor has acquired title to them in a shorter time as provided in Article 1955 of the Civil Code. Actions to recover stolen chattels are not subject to prescription as against the thief and his accessories.

Actions to recover immovables prescribe in thirty years without prejudice to acquisition of title by prescription. An action to recover money secured by a mortgage (*acción hipotecaria*) prescribes in twenty years. Personal actions for which no special term is given prescribe in fifteen years.

A limitation of five years applies to suits to recover: (1) alimony; (2) rent, whether in rural or urban tenancy; and (3) and other payments to be made by years or in shorter intervals.

A limitation of three years applies to suits for payments due to: (1) courts, attorneys, registrars, notaries, scribes, experts and agents for their fees and disbursements; (2) pharmacists for medicines supplied and teachers for instruction given; (3) servants and laborers for their work and disbursements; and (4) innkeepers for food and lodging, and shopkeepers for goods sold. Time runs as from the completion of the service given.

A limitation of one year applies to suits: (1) to recover or retain possession; and (2) for defamation, and to enforce liability for fault or negligence. As to (2), time runs from the time when the aggrieved person learned of the defamation or injury.

Whenever it is not specifically indicated when the limitation begins to run, it will begin to run on the day on which the action could have been brought.

The running of time is interrupted by the bringing of legal action in court, by an extrajudicial claim made by the creditor, and by any act of acknowledgement of the debt by the debtor. The interruption of prescription in the case of joint actions or obligations affects all creditors and debtors as well as the heirs of the debtors. Where a creditor claims from a particular debtor only his corresponding share, the time running against the other joint debtors is not interrupted.

Interruption of prescription in favor of a debtor by the filing of suit interrupts also the time running in favor of his surety. But extrajudicial claims by the creditor or a private acknowledgement by the debtor does not interrupt the time running in favor of the surety.

NOTES AND QUESTIONS

1. The law of prescription is governed by statutory provisions even in the common law countries. The civil law statutes cover under prescription subjects treated in the common law countries both under limitation and acquisition of title by adverse possession. *See*, e.g., Calif. C.C.P.A. §§315-363.

2. How does limitation of time operate in the case of lost chattels found by another person? May the finder acquire title to lost chattels? How does the Spanish rule compare with the law applicable in your state?

3. Does the Spanish three-year term of prescription occur in the French, the

Italian and the German law? If so, is the subject treated similarly or are there considerable differences?

4. Compare the Spanish rules of acquisition of title by adverse possession with those of France. How does the Spanish ten-year prescription compare with that of France? How do the thirty-year prescriptions compare in these two countries? What are the differences?

B. THE COMMERCIAL LAW

The Spanish Commercial Code of 1885 is in power as amended. It is supplemented by a number of statutes. The Code has 955 articles presented in four books dealing with: Book 1. Merchants and commerce in general; Book 2. Special commercial contracts; Book 3. Maritime commerce; and Book 4. Suspension of payments, bankruptcy and prescription.

Book 1 (Merchants and commerce in general) has the following titles: I. Merchants and acts of commerce; II. Commercial register; III. Commercial books and bookkeeping; IV. General provisions concerning commercial contracts; V. Places and establishments of commercial contracting; and VI. Commercial agents and their duties.

Book 2 (Special commercial contracts) has the following titles: I. Commercial partnerships and corporations; II. Financial participation in the business of others; III. Commercial commission; IV. Commercial depositum; V. Commercial loans; VI. Commercial sale and barter and the transfer of nonendorsable credits; VII. Commercial contracts of carriage of goods on land; VIII. Contracts of insurance; IX. Commercial guarantees; X. Contracts and bills of exchange; XI. Drafts, promissory notes and checks; XII. Commercial paper payable to bearer, and theft or loss of commercial paper and its effects on the bearer; and XIII. Letters of credit.

Book 3 (Maritime commerce) has the following titles: I. Vessels; II. Persons engaging in maritime commerce; III. Particular contracts of maritime commerce; IV. Risks, losses and accidents of maritime commerce; and V. Adjustment and settlement of claims.

Book 4 (Suspension of payments, bankruptcy and prescription) has the following titles: I. Suspension of payments and bankruptcy in general; II. Prescription; and III. General provisions.

The following are selected topics from the Spanish commercial law.

1. Merchants (*Comerciantes*)[33]

Merchants are: (1) those who have legal capacity to engage in commerce and exercise it habitually as their profession; and (2) commercial or industrial corporations set up in accordance with provisions of the Commercial Code.

Acts of commerce, whether or not undertaken by merchants and whether or not defined in the Commercial Code, are governed by it. Failing such provisions in the Commercial Code, they are governed by the general rules of commerce; failing such rules, they are governed by the provisions of the civil law. Acts of commerce are such as are defined in the Commercial Code, including any analogous acts.

Persons of full age not subject to parental power nor to marital authority and having full right of disposition of their property have the legal capacity to engage in commerce. Minors and incompetents may continue the business exercised by their parents or predecessors through their guardians. If the guardians lack legal capacity to engage in commerce, they must appoint one or more agents who must comply with the legal requirements.

A married woman over twenty-one years of age may engage in commerce with the authorization of her husband executed in a public act and recorded in the commercial register. A married woman who engages in commerce with the knowledge of her husband is presumed to have obtained his authorization. The husband may by public act revoke the authorization; such action must be recorded in the commercial register and published in the official gazette of the place where the business is located. The revocation will not affect rights acquired before its publication. Where a married woman engages in business with her husband's consent, her dowry and paraphernal property as well as the community property of both spouses is jointly liable for her management and she may alienate and encumber both her separate and community property. Separate property of the husband may be made subject to this arrangement if the husband authorizes it.

A married woman of full age may also engage in commerce on any of the following conditions: (1) where she obtains judicial separation; (2) where her husband is under guardianship; (3) where her husband has disappeared and his place of abode is unknown and his return not expected; or (4) where her husband is deprived of the exercise of his civil rights by order of the court.

The following may not engage in commerce nor hold office in commercial or industrial corporations: (1) those sentenced to the loss of their civil rights, until rehabilitated; (2) bankrupts, until rehabilitated or authorized to engage in commerce by the general meeting of creditors approved by the court; and (3) those prohibited from engaging in commerce by special laws.

The following may not engage in commerce directly or indirectly nor hold office in commercial or industrial corporations: (1) judges and officers of public ministries in active service (this provision does not apply to mayors, municipal judges and municipal prosecutors); (2) heads of administrative, economic and military districts, provinces or units; (3) government appointed officers for the collection of taxes and the administration of funds; (4) stockbrokers of all kinds; and (5) those who by provision of special laws may not engage in commerce in a particular place.

Foreigners and foreign corporations may engage in commerce in Spain. They are subject to the laws of their respective countries concerning their capacity to enter into contracts, and to the provisions of the Spanish Commercial Code with respect to their business in Spain. To that extent, they are also subject to the jurisdiction of Spanish courts.

2.   Commercial Register (*Registro mercantil*)[34]

The commercial register is located in all provincial capitals. It is composed of two sets of books holding individual merchants, and partnerships and corporations. In maritime provinces a third set of books is kept containing records of vessels.

Registration of individual merchants is optional but that of partnerships and corporations and vessels is obligatory. An unregistered merchant may not record any document in the register nor may he take advantage of the effects of registration.

Registration is effected in chronological order. The record must contain the following information: name and kind of business; day of commencement of business; seat of business with addresses of branches; charter; modifications; rescission or dissolution of partnerships and corporations; powers granted and their revocation; authority of husband to the wife to engage in commerce; authority of wife to administer her property during absence or incapacity of husband; revocation of authority of the wife to engage in commerce; arrangements as to dowry, marital contracts and paraphernal property of wives of merchants; emissions of stock, bonds and obligations by corporations or by individual merchants; and patents and trademarks. In addition, foreign partnerships and corporations must file certificates, made by Spanish consuls, stating that they are properly constituted in their respective countries.

The register of vessels contains the following recordings: (1) name of vessel, motive system, power of engines, year of construction, material of construction, dimensions, gross tonnage and net tonnage, names and addresses of owners; (2) any changes in the vessel and in the ownership; and (3) any encumbrances.

Records are made on the strength of notarized documents filed with the registry.

All records take effect upon their recording with respect to third parties. Unrecorded instruments of partnerships and corporations have effect among members but may not prejudice third parties who may, however, use them to their advantage. Unrecorded powers have effect between the parties but they may not be used to the prejudice of third parties, who may, however, use them to their advantage.

The commercial register is public. The registrar will assist anyone in obtaining information therefrom and will make copies therefrom when requested.

The registrar also keeps a daily record of stock values and stock transactions on the stock exchange. These records form the basis of proof of such dealings on the given dates.

3. Commercial Books (*Libros de los comerciantes*)[35]

Merchants must keep the following books: a book of inventories and balances, a book of daily entries, a ledger, copies of all correspondence, and all other books required by special laws. In addition, partnerships and corporations must keep books recording decisions made by the general assembly and the board of directors. They may keep other useful and convenient books.

Properly bound books are presented to the proper municipal judge who will make an entry on the first page, thereof, under his signature and seal, authorizing entries to be made therein.

The book of inventories and balances begins with the inventory at the beginning of the business. It lists all individual assets and their value, all debts and liabilities, and the difference between the assets and the liabilities. In addition, a balance sheet including all the above must be entered in the book annually and must be signed by the merchant. The book of daily entries carries all day-by-day transactions; they are then entered into the ledger under individual accounts. In the book of copies, copies of all correspondence sent out are kept in chronological order. All correspondence received is collected in the same way.

Books must be kept in good order; that is, in chronological order of entries without blanks, interpolations or erasures. Sheets may not be substituted or torn out or in any way altered. Errors in entries must be rectified upon discovery by an appropriate entry and the correction must indicate in the margin the erroneous or missed entry.

Commercial books have probative value as follows: (1) they make irrebutable proof against the merchant; his adversary, on accepting the merchant's books as proof, is subject to entries both favorable and unfavorable to his claim; (2) where books of two merchants are in conflict and those of one of them are properly kept and those of the other are defective in some respect, those properly kept make proof unless shown otherwise by other means of proof; (3) where one of the merchants does not produce his books or claims not to have them, those of the adversary make proof against him if properly kept unless he can show that the loss occurred due to superior force. Entries in the adversary's books may be contradicted by any other means of proof; (4) where books of both opponents are properly kept but are in conflict, the court will decide in accordance with other means of proof in conformity with the law.

Books must be kept for fifteen years from the date of the last entry therein. They may not be destroyed before the term of limitation has run on any action based on the entries therein. Books relevant in business or to litigation must be kept for five years from the completion of that business or from the sentence given in that litigation. In case of litigation, the court may order the production of the books. Books of dissolved partnerships and corporations are kept by order of the registrar of the commercial register at a safe place in accordance with the above provisions and for the time therein stipulated.

NOTES AND QUESTIONS

1. How does the Spanish Commercial Code compare with the French and German Codes of Commerce? How does it compare with the Uniform Commercial Code? Note that Italy does not have a separate commercial code and that the corresponding provisions are either to be found in the Italian Civil Code or in special statutes.

2. Who are merchants under the Spanish law? Does an act of commerce in Spanish law correspond to similar acts in German and French law? To engage in commerce, must a person be of full age and capacity? Compare UCC 2-104.

3. Note the Spanish provisions concerning foreigners engaging in commerce in Spain. Are they subject to any limitations?

4. Must all merchants be registered in the commercial register? What is recorded in the commercial register? Compare the Spanish commercial register with those of France and Germany.

5. Merchants must keep commercial books. Note the detailed rules of the Spanish law concerning commercial books and the care with which they must be kept. What proof do entries in the commercial books make? For how long must the

books be preserved after they have been filled with entries? What are the French and German rules concerning commercial books?

---

4. Partnerships and Corporations (*Compañías mercantiles*)[36]

A contract of partnership or incorporation is a commercial contract whenever it is made under the provisions of the Commercial Code. Once set up, the partnership or corporation has a legal personality. Before a commercial partnership or corporation engages in business, it must file its constitution and rules in a notarized document with the commercial register. All additional acts adding to, amending or modifying the original act must also be filed with the commercial register in a notarized form. No contracts among members may be made except those that are made in the above form and filed with the commercial register. Commercial partnerships and corporations are governed by their constitutions and rules and on points not determined therein by the provisions of the Commercial Code.

Generally, partnerships and corporations are of the following kinds: (a) general partnership; (b) commandite partnership; (c) stock corporation; and (d) corporation with limited liability.

(a) General partnership (*Compañía colectiva*).[37] The document of the partnership must state: the names and addressess of all partners; the firm name, the names of partners who manage the firm and may sign for it; the capital in money or other form and its value; the duration of the partnership; the reward to which managing partners are entitled; and any other contracts and conditions the partners desire to make. All partners, some of them, or one partner only may be authorized to sign for the partnership; in the last two cases, the words "and company" must be added after the name or names of the signing partners. This will constitute the firm name, which may never contain the name of a person who is not presently a partner. Those whose names appear in the firm name are jointly liable with other partners in the partnership business.

All partners, whether managing or not, are personally and jointly liable with all their property for the business of the partnership carried out in the name thereof and under the signature of an authorized person. Partners not properly authorized to sign for the firm do not bind the partnership thereby but bear exclusive liability for such acts.

Unless otherwise provided in the partnership contract, all partners must take part in the management and must agree on any particular step to be taken in the partnership business. No step should be taken against the direct wishes of any partner; if it is so taken, it is valid, but those who have taken it must compensate the partnership for any loss thereby incurred. Where one or more partners are charged with management, the others may not intervene therein. Where a partner is charged with management in the partnership contract, he may not be removed for bad management; but the partners may appoint a co-managing partner who will jointly manage the firm or they may petition for the dissolution of the partnership in court, which must dissolve it on proof of loss.

All partners, whether managing or not, have the right to inquire into the firm's business and accounting and to make recommendations.

Any business entered into by partners on their own, in their own names, and with their own property does not affect the firm. Should they, however, use firm funds or the firm name in their own business, they must give credit to the firm for all profits so made while forfeiting their share therein and are liable for all losses. In partnerships with no fixed commercial activity, partners may engage in business on their own only with the consent of the partnership. Those who break this rule must account for all profits made but bear all losses themselves.[38] Where the nature of commercial activity of the partnership is determined in the partnership contract, partners may engage on their own in all business of a nature other than that carried on by the partnership unless otherwise agreed upon.[39]

A partner who brings in no capital and contributes only his work may not participate in the partnership business without an express permission of the partnership, and if he does so, he may be expelled from the partnership and be deprived of all benefits due to him.[40]

No partner may take from the common funds more than the share allotted to him, and if he does so, he may be compelled to refund it.

If no provision as to the sharing of profits is made, partners participate in accordance with their interest in the partnership. Those who contribute only their work take a share of the same size as the partner with the smallest capital investment. Losses are incurred in the same proportion, but those who contribute only their work do not participate in the sharing thereof.

The partnership must pay the expenses of partners and indemnify them for losses incurred in the partnership business assigned to them, but it is not liable for losses they incurred by their own fault or by accident or by any other cause unconnected with that business.

No partner may assign his interest in the partnership to another person or substitute another person for himself without the consent of the partners.

A loss caused to the partnership by malice, abuse of powers or gross negligence of a partner makes him liable to make it good at the request of the other partners, and such conduct may not be approved or ratified by the other partners.[41]

(b) Commandite partnership (*Sociedad en comandita*).[42] The partnership contract must give the same information as a partnership contract of the general partnership. The firm name is constituted by the names of the general partners who are authorized to sign for the partnership. If only some or one is so authorized, the words "and Company" must follow the names of the signing partner or partners, and in all cases the words "Commandite Partnership" (*Sociedad en Comandita*) must follow thereafter. The names of the commandite partners may not appear in the firm name. Should the name of a commandite partner appear in the firm name, he would be liable as a managing partner while not acquiring any rights additional to those held by commandite partners.

All general partners, whether managing or not, are personally and jointly liable for the business of the firm as partners of a general partnership. They also have the same rights and duties. Commandite partners are liable only with the funds they have brought in. They may not take part in the management of the partnership even as agents for the managing partners. All partners, whether general or commandite, are subject to the provisions of Article 144 of the Commercial Code.

Commandite partners may not inquire into the business and accounts of the firm except as provided in the partnership contract. If no such provision is made, they are entitled at the end of every business year to a balance sheet and to any documents that will enable them to evaluate the business of the firm for the past year.

(c) Stock corporation (*Sociedad Anónima*).[43]   The act of incorporation of a stock corporation must indicate: the names and addresses of founding members; the name of the corporation; the name or names of persons who will administer the corporation and a method for filling vacancies; the capital of the corporation; the number of shares constituting the capital; payments by which the unpaid part of the capital at the founding of the corporation is to be paid; the duration of the corporation; the terms and method of convocation of general meetings, both ordinary and extraordinary; and any other agreements and conditions provided for by the members. The name of the corporation must fit its objectives. No name of an already existing corporation may be adopted.

The liability of the shareholders for debts and losses of the corporation is limited to their investment therein. The capital of the corporation, together with its further accumulation, is responsible for obligations properly incurred by an authorized person in accordance with the corporation's rule and regulations. The administrators of a corporation are appointed by the shareholders as determined by the corporation's rules and regulations. They are agents for the corporation and when they act in accordance with the rules and regulations they are not personally liable for its business. But if they act in breach of law or in breach of the rules and regulations of the corporation or contrary to provisions made in the general assembly and incur losses thereby, each of them must answer proportionally for the loss.

Stock corporations must publish their balance sheets annually in the government gazette. The shareholders may not inquire into the administration of the corporation except as provided in the rules and regulations.

The capital of a commandite partnership and of a stock corporation may be held in stock or other documents. The shares may be to order or to bearer. A record of the order shares must be kept by the corporation together with entries of transfers. The bearer shares must be numbered and records thereof kept by the corporation. No new series of shares may be issued until the previously issued shares are fully subscribed.

Stock corporations may buy their own shares only for the purpose of their amortization. They may not borrow money under guaranty of their own shares.

The general assembly of shareholders, meeting especially for that purpose, may increase or decrease the corporation capital, modify the act of association, or dissolve the corporation. These measures may not be taken in ordinary meetings unless proper notice of the subject of discussion is given. The decision at the meeting of the general assembly must be taken by two thirds of the shareholders and two thirds of the capital. Where the shares are bearer shares, two thirds of the capital must be in favor. Where the required majority is not reached, a subsequent meeting may be held, unless prohibited by the corporation rules, in order to deal exclusively with those matters. There a simple majority of all shareholders and of the capital is required for a decision, and where the shares are bearer shares, the majority of the capital must be in favor.

(d)   Corporation with limited liability (*Sociedad de responsabilidad limitada*).[44] The corporation must have a fixed capital divided into equal shares that may not be negotiated nor called stock. It must have at least two, and not more than fifty, members. Members are not personally liable for the debts of the corporation. The name of the corporation may not be identical with that of another partnership or corporation, and must be followed by the words "Corporation with Limited Liability" (*Sociedad de Responsabilidad Limitada*) or "Corporation Limited" (*Sociedad Limitada*). The capital of the corporation may not exceed five million pesetas and must be fully paid before the opening of business. Whatever its objective, a corporation with limited liability is a commercial corporation subject to the provisions of the Law of July 17, 1953, on corporations with limited liability, as amended, and further subject to the provisions of the Commercial Code applicable to partnerships and corporations.

The corporation is set up by a public document and must be entered into the commercial register. When so entered, it has legal personality. Contracts entered into by the corporation before its registration may be ratified by the corporation within three months of its registration. Failing ratification, those who acted for the corporation are jointly liable on such contracts.

The document of constitution of the corporation must indicate: the names, citizenship and addresses of members, and whether they are physical or legal persons; the name of the corporation and its line of business, duration; principal seat, branches and agencies, and capital and shares; the participation of each member in the capital; appointment of a director or directors; the manner of making decisions; the constitution and convocation of the meeting of members; and any other agreements members desire to make. The capital and shares must be in Spanish currency.

The corporation is managed by one or more persons (directors), whether members or not, who represent it in all matters. Any limitations imposed on them are ineffective against third parties. The appointments are effective as of acceptance, and the names of the directors must be entered in the commercial register. They may be removed by members holding a majority of the capital of the corporation; but if they are appointed in the constitution, they may be removed only by a majority of members holding two thirds of the corporation's capital. The directors may not engage in business on their own in the line of business of the corporation. The directors are liable to the corporation for losses caused by intent, gross negligence or noncompliance with the law or the corporate constitution. Suit may be brought by members holding the majority of the corporate capital. Each director is liable for his own acts; where two or more are liable, they are liable jointly.

The corporation is governed by a majority vote of the members holding over one half of the corporation's capital. Where there are more than fifteen members or where required by the constitution, the vote will be taken in the general assembly; otherwise, the vote may be taken by correspondence or by any other means. A general assembly is called by the directors, who must indicate the matters to be discussed. Directors must call the meeting when they are requested to do so by members holding at least one fourth of the capital. A general assembly may be held, however, whenever all members are present and decide to hold it, irrespective of notice. Unless otherwise provided in the constitution, a member may have another member represent him in the general assembly but a power in writing must be given to such person expressly empowering him to so act in that meeting.

A qualified majority, namely a majority of members together with a two-thirds majority of capital, is required to increase or decrease the capital, extend the duration of the corporation, or effect its merger, dissolution or modification. Where such majority is not reached, a second meeting requires only two thirds of the capital to vote affirmatively. Any such decision must be entered in the commercial register.

An intention to transfer shares to nonmembers must be communicated in writing to the directors, who then notify all members. Members may buy such shares within thirty days. If several members are interested, they buy in proportion to their existing shares. If no one is interested, the corporation may buy such shares in another thirty days and reduce its capital thereby. If this term runs fruitlessly, the shares may be sold to nonmembers.

On the death of a member, his heir will become the member, but the constitution may provide for the acquisition of such shares by the remaining members in proportion to their existing shares.

Within five months from the end of any business year, the directors must present a profit and loss account and a balance sheet. Unless otherwise provided in the constitution, the business year ends on December 31. Members may examine the accounts during the time specified in the constitution. The accounts must be approved by members holding the majority of the corporation's capital.

The corporation is dissolved in the following cases: (1) by the running of time stipulated in the contract; (2) by the attaining of the stipulated objective or by the manifest impossibility of attaining it; (3) by loss of more than two thirds of the capital, unless it is reduced; (4) by merger; (5) by dissolution of the corporation by decision of its members; and (6) by any other reason provided for in the contract. The corporation will also be dissolved by a judicial order decreeing dissolution on bankruptcy.

The corporation may be partially dissolved by excluding one or more members for reasons provided in sections (1), (2) and (7) of Article 218 of the Commercial Code, or by excluding a director who engages in business on his own in the line of the corporation's business. Partial dissolution also occurs in cases provided in Article 219 of the Commercial Code.

Corporations with limited liability are otherwise dissolved and liquidated in accordance with the provisions of the Commercial Code below.

(e) Dissolution of partnerships and corporations (*Liquidación de las compañías mercantiles*).[45]   A general partnership and a commandite partnership are partially dissolved in the following circumstances: (1) where a partner uses the partnership capital or name in his own business; (2) where a partner who is not entitled to manage the partnership pursuant to the partnership contract assumes its administration; (3) where a managing partner is guilty of fraud in the management or bookkeeping of the partnership; (4) where a partner does not bring in the capital he promised to bring in in the partnership contract after having been requested to do so; (5) where a partner engages in business in his own name in breach of Articles 136, 137 and 138 of the Commercial Code; (6) where a partner who is bound to act personally in the partnership business absents himself and does not return upon request; and (7) where a partner fails to comply with any other provision stipulated in the partnership contract.[46]

Upon partial dissolution, the guilty partner is considered excluded from the partnership. He is responsible for losses and excluded from profits until all business pending at the time of his exclusion is finalized.[47] Until the exclusion is entered in the commercial register, both the excluded partner and the partnership are liable for all transactions.

All partnerships and corporations are fully dissolved in the following circumstances: (1) by the running of time stipulated in the contract or by the attaining of the stipulated objective; (2) by total loss of its capital; and (3) by bankruptcy.

General partnerships and commandite partnerships are in addition fully dissolved for the following reasons: (1) by the death of a partner unless the partnership contract expressly provides for the continuation of the partnership with the heirs of the decedent or by the remaining partners; (2) insanity or any other cause that prevents a partner from administering his property; and (3) bankruptcy of a general partner. They may also be dissolved at the request of any partner. The other partners may not oppose the request for dissolution unless it is made in bad faith. There is bad faith where the petitioning partner will realize a profit upon dissolution that he would not have made if the partnership were not dissolved. The outgoing partner may not prevent the partnership from properly concluding all of its pending business. Partition of the partnership property may be effected only thereafter.

The dissolution of commercial partnerships and corporations cannot produce any adverse effects on third parties until it is recorded in the commercial register.

As soon as the partnership or corporation declares its dissolution, no new obligations may be incurred and the managing partners or managing officers become the liquidators thereof. A general meeting may appoint liquidators other than the managing partners or officers. The liquidators must: (1) submit an inventory and balance sheet to the partners or members within twenty days; and (2) report every month on the liquidation. After liquidating the business of the partnership or corporation, the liquidators must distribute the net assets among the members. A member who believes himself injured thereby may initiate proceedings in court.

NOTES AND QUESTIONS

1. What kinds of partnerships and corporations are there in Spain? What is the main reason for the virtual uniformity of partnerships and corporations in civil law countries? Compare the Spanish law with the French and the Italian law.

2. How does a general partnership come into existence? What must a

document of partnership contain? Must a partnership be registered in the commercial register? What is the liability of the partners? What kinds of partners are there and what are their shares in the partnership? For Anglo-American law, compare the Uniform Limited Partnership Act and the Uniform Partnership Act. *See*, e.g., Texas Vernon's Ann. Civ. St. Arts. 6132(a) and 6132(b), respectively.

3. How would you define a commandite partnership? What is the distinction between a general and a commandite partner? What are the rights of commandite partners? Compare the Spanish commandite partnership with those of Italy and France. How does the Spanish commandite partnership compare with an American limited partnership in accordance with the Uniform Limited Partnership Act?

4. Is the Spanish stock corporation a counterpart of German and Italian stock corporations? Does it perform the same function as the American corporation? *See*, e.g., V.A. Texas S. Bus. Corp. Act. How does a stock corporation come into being? Compare, e.g., V.A. Texas S. Bus. Corp. Act, Art. 3.01ff. Who are the officers of the corporation and what organs does it have? Compare, e.g., V.A. Texas S. Bus. Corp. Act, Art. 2.24ff.

5. What are the main features of the Spanish corporation with limited liability? How does it compare with those of the Italian and the French law? How does it differ from the Spanish stock corporation? How many members must it have and is there an upper limit imposed on membership? Is there any limit imposed on the holding of capital by the Spanish corporation with limited liability? How does the Spanish corporation with limited liability compare with an American corporation?

6. How are partnerships and corporations dissolved in the Spanish law? Note the detailed provisions of the Spanish law dealing with the dissolution of partnerships and corporations. For Anglo-American law, *see*, e.g., as to partnerships, Texas Vernon's Ann. Civ. St. Art. 6132(b), Sec. 29ff; as to corporations, V.A. Texas S. Bus. Corp. Act, Art. 6.01ff.

---

5. The Law of Exchange (*Letras de cambio y cheques*)

Spain has signed but never ratified the Geneva Conventions of June 7, 1930, on bills of exchange, and March 19, 1931, on checks. Consequently, the rules dealing with the subject established in Articles 443-566 of the Spanish Commercial Code of 1885 are still in power. Since they are the rules which have traditionally governed European banking, they are greatly similar to the uniform law of the Geneva Conventions.

6. The Law of Bankruptcy (*Suspensión de pagos y las quiebras*)

Spanish law deals separately with the suspension of payments and with bankruptcy.

(a) Suspension of payments (*Suspensión de pagos*).[48] A businessman who has sufficient assets to meet his obligations, but who can foresee that he will be unable to make payments when they come due, may take advantage of the provisions of the law with respect to suspension of payments. He may also do so within forty-eight hours after failing to pay a debt that comes due.

He will have to file a petition with the judge of the court of first instance requesting a declaration of suspension of payments. He must attach a balance sheet and a request to his creditors to accept payment in full within no more than three years. The judge will then make an order issuing the declaration. The creditors will then meet and if they disapprove of the plan of payment, the whole scheme comes to an end. They may then proceed in bankruptcy. The advantage of the suspension of payments scheme is that the debtor manages his business under the supervision of court-appointed supervisors (*interventores*) and the creditors are paid in full. Partnerships and corporations are eligible to apply.

(b) Bankruptcy (*Quiebra*).[49] The subject is dealt with under general provisions, classes of bankruptcy, accord of settlement of the bankrupt with his creditors, rights of creditors, and rehabilitation of the bankrupt.

(i) GENERAL PROVISIONS. A businessman, including partnerships and corporations, who is unable to meet his current obligations is considered bankrupt. Declaration of bankruptcy may be made at the request of the bankrupt or at that of a creditor. Once made, the bankrupt may not administer his property.

(ii) CLASSES OF BANKRUPTCY. Bankruptcy is accidental, culpable or fraudulent. Accidental bankruptcy (*insolvencia fortuita*) is due to misfortune in trading. Culpable bankruptcy (*insolvencia culpable*) occurs when it is found that there are excessive personal expenditures, losses through gambling, imprudent investment, or the sale of property for less than it was bought for within six weeks prior to the declaration of bankruptcy; when, since the last inventory, debts due at any time exceed twice the amount of available cash; when books are not properly kept; or when the petition for suspension of payments is not made within forty-eight hours after a due debt was not met.

Fraudulent bankruptcy (*insolvencia fraudulenta*) takes place when the books do not reflect the true position unless proved otherwise. Fraudulent bankruptcy is also presumed when the bankrupt disappears with some or all of his assets; when fictitious entries are made in the books; when books are not kept; when entries are not properly made, when books are altered or manipulated, when transactions are simulated or assets transferred to an *alter ego*; when payments are made in anticipation of bankruptcy to the detriment of creditors; or when dissipation of assets occurs after the declaration of bankruptcy.

Culpable and fraudulent bankruptcy are offenses proceeded against within the order of criminal law.

(iii) ACCORD OF SETTLEMENT. Once the claims of the various creditors have been proved, they may make an accord with the bankrupt as they see fit. No accord may be made with a fraudulent bankrupt. The accord must be made by the meeting of creditors. Individual deals between the bankrupt and one or more creditors are void. Where the creditors make an accord with the bankrupt, his debts to them are extinguished by virtue thereof and he must discharge his obligations under the accord, which is substituted for his debts. The creditors always agree to take only a dividend. Where the debtor does not keep the accord, the accord may be rescinded and the bankruptcy reopened.

(iv) RIGHTS OF CREDITORS. Any property in the possession of the bankrupt, the title of which did not pass fully to the bankrupt is considered owned by the transferor and must be returned to him. This includes all property, movable and immovable, irrespective of whether it was acquired by sale or by negotiation.

From the mass of movable property, payments are made first to specially privileged creditors in the following order: burial, funeral and administration expenses, if any; alimentary expenses to feed the bankrupt and his family; common labor bills for labor done within six months prior to .the bankruptcy; and any subsidies received by the bankrupt from public funds within six months before bankruptcy. Payments are next made to preferred creditors so designated by the Commercial Code, next to creditors so designated by other laws, then to creditors by commercial title through the intervention of an agent or broker, then to common creditors by virtue of commercial law, and finally to common creditors by virtue of civil law.

From immovable property, the first to be satisfied are mortgagees. If there is a surplus, it is available to creditors under the rules of distribution of movable property referred to above.

The assets are used to pay one class at a time beginning with the first. If the class is paid in full, the remainder is applied to the next class, and so on. Where there is no descending order of taking within a class, the participating interests take a pro rata dividend. Payments are made without regard to the date when the claims arise with the exception of mortgagees where the first mortgagee has preference over the second, and so forth, and with the further exception of claims of creditors by commercial title through the intervention of an agent or broker where the earlier title has preference over a later one.

(v) REHABILITATION OF THE BANKRUPT. A bankrupt if fully rehabilitated after he fully complies with the accord of settlement with his creditors. Where there is no accord of settlement, the bankrupt obtains his rehabilitation when he discharges all the claims made against him in the bankruptcy proceedings. A fraudulent bankrupt may not be rehabilitated.

NOTES AND QUESTIONS

1. Note that the Spanish law makes provision for composition with creditors, and it provides for bankruptcy only if composition does not succeed. Is this approach common in civil law countries? Compare the French and the Italian law. For American law, *see* Federal Code Annotated 11 §701ff.

2. Which courts handle bankruptcy cases in Spain? Are there any special commercial or bankruptcy courts in Spain? Compare the French and the German law. *See also* F.C.A. 11 §11.

3. What are the different kinds of bankruptcy in Spanish law? Are there similar kinds of bankruptcy in Italian law?

4. What is the order of payment made to creditors? What are the preferred claims? Compare F.C.A. 11§104.

5. On which conditions may a bankrupt be rehabilitated? Compare the French and the German law. *See also* F.C.A. 11 §32ff; Bankruptcy Rules, Rules 404-409.

---

7.   Maritime Law (*Derecho marítimo*)[50]

Apart from special statutes dealing with particular matters, maritime law is dealt with in the Commercial Code under vessels; persons; maritime contracts; and risks, damages, and accidents.

(a)   Vessels (*Buques*).   Ships are considered movables. An interest therein may be acquired by sale and purchase in writing. A sale has effect against third parties only when recorded in the commercial register.

A forced sale of a vessel may be ordered by a court of law. The sale is by public auction. It must be properly advertised and may not be held earlier than twenty days after the announcement.

Where a forced sale is held for the benefit of creditors, the ranking of the claims is as follows: (1) taxes; (2) judicial costs; (3) fees of pilotage and such as are levied by ports (port taxes); (4) expenses of maintenance of the vessel, including wages for guards from her entry into port up to the sale; (5) rent for safekeeping of ship equipment, if any; (6) wages of the master and the crew; (7) reimbursement for cargo sold by the master in order to raise money to make urgent repairs to the vessel, where such sale was approved by a court order; (8) the remainder of the purchase price of the ship, if it has not been fully paid, to be paid to the previous owner or to the shipbuilder as the case may be, and also claims for ship repair and equipment and for the supply of food and fuel for the last voyage; (9) ship mortgages and bottomry bonds properly recorded, and insurance premiums due; and (10) indemnity due to shippers for loss or damage to cargo for which the ship is responsible by order of court or by arbitral award.

Where the proceeds of the sale are not sufficient to pay all the claims in a given class, they are paid pro rata. When the record of the forced sale is entered in the commercial register, all claims in rem (liens) against the ship are extinguished.

In the case of an ordinary sale, all liens against the ship are intact for three months after the ship returns to her home port or from the entry of the record of sale in the commercial register.

(b)   Person (*personas*).   Persons involved in maritime commerce are the owner, the ship's husband, the master, the ship's officers, engineers, the purser, and the crew.

(i)   THE OWNER AND THE SHIP'S HUSBAND.   The owner (*propietario*) may be a partnership or a corporation. The ship's husband (*naviero*) is a person appointed by the owner with full powers to represent the ship. Both the owner and the ship's husband are civilly responsible for the acts of the master, even if the master acts beyond the scope of his authority as long as his acts benefit the ship. Co-owners are liable in proportion to their interest in the vessel only and may discharge their liability by giving up their interest in the ship by a notarized document. They contribute also in proportion to their interests. The ship's husband represents the owner of the ship. He manages the ship and appoints the master.

(ii) THE MASTER. The master (*capitán*) must be Spanish and must possess the qualifications required by law to command a ship. The master commands the ship and also manages her in the absence of the ship's husband. Before he sails, the master must have on board an inventory of the ship, its equipment and appurtenances; a certificate of seaworthiness of the ship; the ship's registration, showing ownership and incumbrances; copies of charter parties and bills of lading; and a list of passengers. He must have aboard a copy of the Commercial Code and must keep the log book, the book of accounts, and the book of cargo. In the log book (*diario de navegación*), he must enter daily all events pertaining to navigation and any supervening damage to ship or cargo. He enters in the books of accounts (*libro de contabilidad*) all payments made by the ship, including wages of the crew. He enters details concerning the loading and unloading of cargo, in the book of cargo (*libro de cargamento*) and also makes entries concerning the embarkation and disembarkation of passengers. In the case of the loss of the ship, he must attempt to save the ship's documents.

The master must stay with his ship in the case of danger and may not give an order to abandon ship unless such decision is made in the council of officers (*junta de oficiales*) by the majority of the ship's officers, the master having a casting vote. He is civilly responsible, together with the ship's husband, for damage caused to the ship by his negligence and for loss caused by theft of the crew. He is not liable for damage or loss to ship and cargo by *force majeure*.

(iii) SHIP'S OFFICERS AND CREW. The first officer (*piloto*) is next in line of command and substitutes for the master. His chief duty is the navigation of the ship. The second officer (*contramaestre*) is next in line of command and his chief duty is the supervision of the crew. The third, and other officers have duties assigned to them under the command of the master and the first and second officers. The engineering part of the ship's operation is headed by the chief engineer (*maquinista jefe*), and staffed by the second and other engineers (*maquinistas*). The purser (*sobrecargo*) and his staff handle matters concerning cargo and passengers. They carry the books of accounts and cargo for the master, leaving him with nominal supervision only.

The crew (*tripulación*) must be Spanish with not more than one fifth thereof foreign. Crew members serve on the ship by virtue of a contract made with each sailor. The sailor may be discharged only for cause. If the master does not want a particular sailor aboard before the expiration of the contract, he may let him stay in the home port, but with full pay. The sailor may leave the service at any time with permission of the master. Sailors are entitled to maintenance and cure while sick.

(c) **Maritime contracts** (*Contratos especiales del comercio marítimo*). Maritime contracts are mainly charter parties, affreightment contracts under bills of lading, contracts for the transport of passengers, ship mortgages and bottomry bonds, and marine insurance.

A charter party (*contrato de fletamento por entero*) provides for the charterer (*fletador*) to take over the ship for a certain voyage or time. A bill of lading (*conocimiento*) is issued by the master after the cargo is loaded, and it may be made to bearer or to order of the shipper (*cargador*). It gives the name, registration, and home port of the ship; the name of the master and his address; the port of loading and discharge; the name of the shipper; the name of the consignee, if given; the quantity, quality, number of bales, and brand of the goods; and the freight.

The law regulates contracts for the transport of passengers. Passengers are entitled to a full refund of money plus damages if the voyage is cancelled but only to a refund where the reason for the cancellation is an act of God or *force majeure*. The same rule governs abandonment of the voyage *in itinere*, but the ship retains a portion of the fare in proportion to the distance covered. Where the passenger does not show up at the announced time of departure, the ship is entitled to the fare.

Ship mortgages and bottomry bonds must be made in writing and must be recorded in the commercial register.

Marine insurance may be issued to cover any maritime risk. Policies must be in writing and must be signed by the insurer. The Commercial Code deals in considerable detail with marine insurance and the above subjects.

(d) Risks, damages and accidents of maritime commerce (*Riesgos, daños y accidentes del comercio marítimo*).   The law deals with average, entry into port in distress, collision, shipwreck and salvage.

Average (*averías*) means an extraordinary expense incurred during a voyage for the preservation of the ship, the cargo or both. Average is particular where the expense does not benefit all concerned, and general where it does. The law contains detailed provisions concerning the calculation of average.

Entry into port in distress (*arribada forzosa*) is made by decision taken in the council of officers (*junta de oficiales*) by a simple majority, the master having a casting vote. It is taken when they believe that the ship cannot proceed to the port of destination because of a condition that makes it impossible, e.g., an embargo, presence of pirates, damages to the ship, or danger that the cargo would spoil. In port, the ship requests instructions from the owners with respect to further dispositions. Cargo may be discharged and even sold by order of the court. The owners or the charterers are responsible for the expense of entry into port but not for damage to cargo where the entry was proper as decided by a court.

In collisions (*abordajes*), each ship is liable in proportion to their respective fault in causing the collision. Where the collision occurred due to act of God or *force majeure*, each ship bears its own loss. A ship that does not make it to port or must run aground in order to save itself after a collision is considered lost in the collision. The civil liability of owners for loss caused in a collision is limited to their interest in the ship and the freight of the voyage. Where the fund so established is insufficient to pay all claims, claims for loss of life and for personal injuries are paid first.

Losses caused by shipwreck (*naufragio*) to ship and cargo are borne by the owners thereof in proportion to their interests. In the same way, they participate in the property salvaged. Salvaged property is subject to the payment of salvage.

NOTES AND QUESTIONS

1. How does Spanish law treat the subject of maritime law? Is the division into ships, persons, maritime contracts, average, risks, damages and accidents typical for the treatment of the subject? Compare the French and the German law. How does Anglo-American law approach the subject? Is the Anglo-American maritime law codified?

2. What is the ranking of claims of creditors upon a forced sale of a ship? Does such a sale extinguish all liens clinging to the ship and does the buyer receive a clean title? *See*, e.g., Gilmore and Black on Admiralty, 2nd ed., pp. 586ff.

3. How is ownership of vessels regulated in Spanish law? What is the function of the master and the crew?

4. Note the Spanish provisions concerning charter parties and the carriage of goods and passengers by sea. How does the Spanish law compare with the German and the French law? Does it virtually apply the provisions of the American Harter Act and the Carriage of Goods by Sea Act? *See*, e.g., Gilmore and Black on Admiralty, 2nd ed., pp. 93ff.

5. Does the Spanish law apply the provisions of the Brussels Convention of September 23, 1910, as to collisions? Is the United States a party to the convention? *See*, e.g., the German law and Gilmore and Black on Admiralty, 2nd ed., pp. 503ff.

6. How is the liability of owners limited in the case of the loss of ship and cargo? Compare the Limitation of Shipowners' Liability Act, 46 U.S.C.A. §§181-189; the Harter Act, 46 U.S.C.A. §§190-195; and the Carriage of Goods by Sea Act, 46 U.S.C.A. §§1300-1312.

C. THE SYSTEM OF CIVIL COURTS

The civil courts are: courts of the peace (*juzgados de paz*), municipal and country courts (*juzgados municipales y comarcales*), courts of first instance (*juzgados de primera instancia e instrucción*), courts of civil appeal (*audiencias territoriales*) and the Supreme Court of Justice (*Tribunal Supremo de Justicia*).[51] There are no separate commercial courts. Commercial matters are handled by the civil courts. There is, however, a hierarchy of labor courts.

1. Courts of the Peace (*Juzgados de paz*)

These are purely village courts. They are constituted by one lay justice of the peace sitting alone. They are set up in small communities that are not seats of public administration. Justices of the peace may undertake acts of conciliation, and they have jurisdiction to decide disputes up to a fixed small value (250 pesetas). They are supervised by the municipal and country courts and their services are honorary.

2.   Municipal and Country Courts
(*Juzgados municipales y comarcales*)

They are set up in all municipalities with thirty thousand or more inhabitants and in rural towns that are the seats of public administration, known as the *comarca*, irrespective of their size. In larger municipalities, several municipal courts are set up.

They are courts of limited jurisdiction, with their jurisdiction extending up to a certain fixed value (50,000 pesetas). The court is constituted by one judge sitting alone. An appeal against a judgment of the court may be made to the same court within three days for transmittal to the proper court of first instance. Parties before the court may appear by themselves, but they also may be represented by attorneys (*procuradores*) or by counsel (*abogados*). Legal representation is, however, compulsory whenever the value of the subject matter in dispute exceeds a certain minimum sum (1,000 pesetas). The public ministry (*ministerio fiscal*) is represented by officers of the municipal and country procurator (*fiscal municipal y comarcal*).

3.   Courts of First Instance (*Juzgados de primera instancia e instrucción*)

These are courts of general jurisdiction having original jurisdiction in all matters not especially attributed to other courts. They are constituted by one judge sitting alone. The proceedings are summary, known as proceedings of *menor cuantía*, where the value of the subject matter is below a certain fixed sum (500,000 pesetas). Regular proceedings are held where the value of the subject matter exceeds that sum and are known as proceedings in matters of *mayor cuantía*. An appeal against a judgment of a court of first instance must be lodged with that court within five days from the notification; it then is transmitted to the court of civil appeal.

In the exercise of their appellate jurisdiction, courts of first instance hear appeals against judgments of municipal and country courts. No further appeal nor a petition for cassation lies against their judgments in these cases.

There is one court of first instance in every territorial district (*cabeza de partido*); in provincial capitals and large cities, there may be two or more.

Parties before the court must be represented by attorneys (*procuradores*) and also by counsel (*abogados*). The public ministry (*ministerio fiscal*) is represented by officers of the procurator of the court of civil appeal (*fiscal de la audiencia territorial*).

4.   Courts of Civil Appeal (*Audiencias territoriales*)

Courts of civil appeal are set up to hear appeals from judgments of courts of first instance in matters heard by these courts in the exercise of their original jurisdiction. In addition, courts of civil appeal have jurisdiction in matters specially assigned to them, such as determining jurisdiction of lower courts or hearing suits against judges of courts of first instance.

There are fifteen courts of civil appeal in Spain.[52] The court is presided over by a president and has as many presidents of chambers are there are chambers, a number of judges and an administrative staff. The actual panel hearing an appeal is presided over by a president of a chamber and has another two, but not more than four, judges. Three affirmative votes are required for a decision.

The court may hold a plenary session, which is presided over by the president and is composed of all the judges, as well as the president of the *audiencia provincial* located in the seat of the *audiencia territorial* and the procurator. It decides by simple majority specifically designated matters, such as the jurisdiction of lower courts or the disqualification of a judge to sit in a particular case.

The court sits also as the *sala de gobierno*, which is composed of the president, presidents of chambers, the president of the *audiencia provincial* located in the seat of the *audiencia territorial*, and the procurator. In this composition, it exercises within its territory the functions that the *sala de gobierno* in the Supreme Court of Justice exercises in the entire country. It has, however, the authority to appoint justices of the peace (*jueces de paz*) and procurators of the peace (*fiscales de paz*) within its territory. The *sala de gobierno*, minus the procurator, sits as a disciplinary court over all judges, attorneys and counsel within its territory.

No further appeal lies against decisions of the court, but a petition for cassation of the judgment may be lodged with the court within ten days from the notification of the judgment for transmittal to the Supreme Court.

Parties before the court must be represented by attorneys (*procuradores*) and also by counsel (*abogados*). The public ministry (*ministerio fiscal*) is represented by the procurator of the court of civil appeal (*fiscal de la audiencia territorial*) and the staff of his office.

5. Supreme Court of Justice (*Tribunal Supremo de Justicia*)

There is one Supreme Court of Justice in Spain; its seat is in Madrid. It is the court of final resort in civil, criminal and administrative matters. It is headed by a president and is subdivided into six chambers: (1) civil, (2) criminal, (3), (4), and (5) administrative, and (6) welfare and labor. Each chamber is presided over by a president of chamber and has a number of judges on its staff. The Court, as well as every chamber, has its secretariat.

Civil matters are handled by the first chamber (*sala primera*), which is divided in sections. Each section has its president and four judges. Regular business is handled by two united section. The actual panel hearing a case has a presiding judge and four, but not more than six other judges. As a general rule, ordinary cases are heard by five judges, one of them presiding, while cases of special importance are heard by seven judges, one of them presiding. The panel is formed by any of the judges irrespective of their membership in particular sections. The presiding judge is either the president of the civil chamber or the most senior judge. In matters heard by a panel of five judges, three affirmative votes on all points are required for a decision. In matters heard by a panel of seven judges, four affirmative votes on all points are required for a decision.

The Court hears petitions for the cassation of judgments pronounced by courts of civil appeal (*audiencias territoriales*). It further hears petitions for the cassation of arbitration awards. It also hears petitions for the revision of judgments in power of law given by any civil court as well as other matters specifically assigned to it, such as the disqualification of its own judges to hear a particular case.

The petition for cassation must be filed with the court that pronounced the judgment within ten days from its notification for transmittal to the Supreme Court.

The Court may also sit in a plenary session with all the judges of the Court and the procurator. In this composition, it will attend to nonjudicial business, like swearing in judges, giving advice to the government on legislative reforms concerning the judiciary, or any other matter assigned to it by the president of the Court. Without the procurator, it will hear, as a court of first and final instance, cases of civil responsibility brought against the president of the council of ministers of individual ministers.

The Supreme Court of Justice also attends to matters of its own administration and other matters of a supervisory nature. In this capacity it forms a panel known as the *sala de gobierno*, which is presided over by the president of the Court and is attended by the presidents of chambers and by the procurator. In this composition it distributes business among the chambers, supervises the administration of law in the country, advises the government on the administration of justice with recommendations of measures to be taken, and the like. The *sala de gobierno*, minus the procurator, sits as the supreme disciplinary court over all judges, attorneys and counsel.

Parties before the Court must be represented by attorneys (*procuradores*) and also by counsel (*abogados*). The public ministry is represented by the procurator of the Supreme Court (*fiscal del Tribunal Supremo*) and the staff of his office.

6.   Labor Courts (*Magistraturas de trabajo*)

Labor courts specialize in labor, workmen's compensation and social security matters. There is a labor court (*magistratura de trabajo*) in every province with additional labor courts in larger cities. Labor courts are staffed by judges of the civil judicial system. Cases are heard by one judge sitting alone. The procedure is governed by provisions of the Code of Civil Procedure. Parties may appear themselves or they may be represented by attorneys (*procuradores*). To plead the case before the court, they must obtain the services of counsel (*abogados*). The public ministry is represented by its regular officers.

Appeals against decisions of labor courts proceed to the central labor court (*tribunal central del trabajo*) situated in Madrid. This court has a presiding judge, known as director general of the labor jurisdiction (*Director general de Jurisdicción del Trabajo*), and a number of judges. It is subdivided into chambers. Each chamber has a president of chamber and four judges. Appeals are heard by panels of three judges, one of them presiding.

Petitions for cassation of judgments of labor courts and of the central labor court may be made to the sixth chamber of the Supreme Court (*sala sexta del Tribunal Supremo*). The chamber also has jurisdiction to hear petitions for the revision of any labor court judgments that already have entered into the power of law. It will further hear petitions filed by the procurator of the Supreme Court against decisions of the central labor court in the interest of the law when it considers the decision of that court erroneous as to the law applied.

Labor courts have jurisdiction in all disputes between labor and management. Public employees are also considered labor and may sue the government and the provincial or municipal administration. Labor courts also have jurisdiction in matters of workmen's compensation and social security.

The particular labor court having jurisdiction is the court sitting in the district where the petitioner resides.

NOTES AND QUESTIONS

1. Note the jurisdiction of municipal and country courts. How does it compare with that of German *Amtsgerichte*? Is legal representation in these courts compulsory? To which courts may decisions of municipal and country courts be appealed? May such cases be pursued to yet higher courts?

2. Are courts of first instance general jurisdiction courts? With which courts of the French court system can they be compared? Note that whenever the jurisdiction of a court is limited by a sum of money, such sum is subject to a frequent upgrading due to inflation. To keep courts of limited jurisdiction in business and to assure that only cases of greater importance reach courts of general jurisdiction, the value which the subject matter in dispute must have may be raised frequently by proper legislation.

3. What is the jurisdiction of Spanish courts of appeal? How do they compare with Italian courts of appeal? What is the composition of the court? What kind of majority is required for a decision? Is there any remedy against decisions of courts of appeal? Who must represent the parties in the proceedings?

4. Note the powers of the Spanish Supreme Court. Does it deal only with civil and criminal cases like the typical supreme court in civil law countries? What further powers does it exercise as compared with the French Court of Cassation? How many chambers does it have and what business do they handle? How does the Spanish Supreme Court compare with the United States Supreme Court or with the highest state courts?

5. Note the system of Spanish labor courts. What is the scope of their jurisdiction? Are Spanish labor courts subject to the jurisdiction of the Spanish Supreme Court? How do Spanish labor courts compare with German labor courts? Which courts handle labor disputes in Anglo-American jurisdictions?

D. THE LAW OF CIVIL PROCEDURE

The Spanish Code of Civil Procedure (*Ley de Enjuiciamiento Civil*) dates from 1881, as supplemented and amended by later provisions. It has 2182 articles presented in three books: Book 1. Provisions common to contested and uncontested jurisdiction; Book 2. Contested jurisdiction; and Book 3. Uncontested jurisdiction.

Book 1 (Provisions common to contested and uncontested jurisdiction) has thirteen titles: I. Appearance before the courts; II. Jurisdiction; III. Disputes of jurisdiction; IV. Joinder of actions; V. Disqualifications; VI. Judicial acts and terms; VII. Proceedings, hearings, voting and decision of cases; VIII. Substance and form of judicial decisions; IX. Remedies against judicial decisions and their effects; X. Lapse of time for failure of prosecution; XI. Taxing of costs; XII. Allocation of business; and XIII. Disciplinary powers of courts.

Book 2 (Contested jurisdiction) has twenty-two titles: I. Acts of conciliation; II. Judicial proceedings; III. Connected matters; IV. Proceedings on default; V. Arbitration and conciliation; VI. Appellate proceedings; VII. Suits of civil responsibility against judges; VIII. Execution of judgments; IX. Intestacy proceedings; X. Testamentary proceedings; XI. Class gifts proceedings; XII. Suspension of payments; XIII. Proceedings in bankruptcy; XIV. Attachment and seizure of property; XV. Execution proceedings; XVI. Execution proceedings in commercial matters; XVII. Dispossession proceedings; XVIII. Provisional support; XIX. Preemptive rights; XX. Injunctions; XXI. Petitions for cassation; and XXII. Petitions for revision.

Book 3 (Uncontested jurisdiction) has two parts. The first part has sixteen titles: I. General provisions; II. Adoption; III. Appointment of guardians; IV. Provisional orders of separation and support; V. Parental consent to marriage; VI. Procedure to have an oral will or codicil written as a public act; VII. Opening of closed testaments; VIII. Dispensation of law; IX. Authority to minors and married women to appear in court; X. Preservation of testimony; XI. Alienation of property of minors and the incapacitated; XII. Declaration of disappearance and of death; XIII. Voluntary auction sales; XIV. Provisional possession of land; XV. Surveying and delimitation of land; and XVI. Surveying and apportionment of income from land.

The second part of Book 3 deals with voluntary jurisdiction in commercial matters and has eight titles: I. General provisions; II. Storage of goods and inspection by experts; III. Provisional sequestration and deposit of bills of exchange; IV. Proceedings in general average; V. Unloading, abandonment and inspection of cargo, insurance of cargo; VI. Urgent sale of cargo and ship repairs; VII. Other acts of commerce requiring peremptory judicial action; and VIII. Appointment of arbiters and experts in insurance contract matters.

The following are topics selected from the Spanish law of civil procedure.

1.   Procedure in Municipal and Country Courts.
(*Juzgados municipales y comarcales*)[53]

The procedure is of two types: summary proceedings in matters not exceeding a certain fixed value (10,000 pesetas), known as *juicio verbal o de minima cuantía*, and ordinary proceedings in matters up to a certain fixed value (50,000 pesetas), known as *juicio de cognición*.

(a)   Summary proceedings (*Juicio verbal*).   Summary proceedings are initiated by the plaintiff presenting to the court clerk (*secretario*) as statement of claim in writing. It must contain: the names, addresses and occupations of the plaintiff and the defendant; the claim that is made; the date; and the signature of the plaintiff. The plaintiff must supply as many copies as there are defendants. The municipal or country judge will set a day and time for a hearing within the next six days. The statement of claim, together with the citation, is served on the defendant by an officer of the court. If the plaintiff does not appear at the hearing, the case is dismissed with costs after the defendant is heard. If the defendant does not appear, proceedings are continued in his absence. At the hearing, the parties orally state their claims and present proof by witnesses or documents. The case is heard by a municipal or country judge sitting alone. A record of the hearing is made and subscribed to by parties and witnesses. The judge gives judgment on the same day or on the next day.

The judgment is appealable to a court of first instance. The appeal must be lodged within three days from notification of the judgment with the municipal or country court that pronounced it. The court will transmit the papers to the proper court of first instance for further proceedings.

(b) Regular proceedings (*Juicio de cognición*). In ordinary or regular proceedings, known as *juicio de cognición,* the value of the subject matter in dispute exceeds a certain fixed sum (10,000 pesetas) but is below another fixed sum (50,000 pesetas). The statement of claim must contain: the name of the court; the names, addresses, and occupations of the plaintiff and the defendant; a statement of claim giving the facts and the applicable law in a clear form; the petition stating clearly what the plaintiff desires the court to order; the date; and the signature of the plaintiff and his counsel (*abogado*). All documents of proof must be filed with the statement of claim. All must be filed with as many copies as there are defendants.

The clerk of court will hand the papers to a judge who will consider whether he has jurisdiction. If so, he orders a copy to be served on the defendant and cites him to file an appearance within six days. If he rules that he lacks jurisdiction, the judge makes an order to that effect after hearing the procurator (*fiscal*). The order is appealable within three days to the court of first instance. If the defendant appears, he has three days to file an answer. It must be drawn in accordance with the same rules applicable to the statement of claim. Where the defendant does not file an answer, the allegations of the plaintiff are deemed admitted. The same occurs where he does not appear. The defendant may challenge the jurisdiction of the court in his answer and the court will make a ruling in the judgment.

The day after the filing of the answer, or after the defendant has been declared in default for not appearing or filing an answer, the judge will set a hearing to take place within five days. If the plaintiff does not appear, he will not be allowed to prove his case and the court will hear the defendant and his proof. The same applies in the case of the nonappearance of the defendant. If neither party appears, the court will make an order that the case is ready for judgment and then gives a judgment dismissing the plaintiff's claim.

Where the parties appear, the court will first hear the plaintiff and then the defendant so as to ascertain their respective positions and to determine the issues that the court will have to decide. This done, the parties offer their proof. Where expert opinion is sought, experts are appointed by a court order. The court will rule on the propriety or impropriety of the proof offered and will admit it or reject it. The ruling is appealable to the same court within three days. Against a decision on that appeal, known as *recurso de reposición,* a further appeal may be taken to the court of first instance, but only as an integral part of an appeal against the final judgment given by the municipal or country court in that matter. The court will then adjourn the hearing for not more than ten days to hear the proof. At the hearing, witnesses and experts, if any, are heard, and documents are examined.

Several hearings may be so held, always not later than ten days from the preceding hearing. The hearings are oral. A record in writing is made of the hearings by the court clerk (*secretario*). After the parties have made proof, the court will declare the proceedings closed and will give judgment within three days from the closing. The victorious party is entitled to costs. Where the judgment is split, each party pays his own costs. Expenses jointly incurred are shared equally. The court makes an order as to costs in the judgment.

The judgment is appealable to the court of first instance in the same way as that given in summary proceedings.

NOTES AND QUESTIONS

What kinds of proceedings may be held in municipal and country courts? What is the distinction between summary and regular proceedings? Could it be said that German courts of limited jurisdiction hold summary proceedings? How do Spanish regular proceedings compare with those held in Italian courts of limited jurisdiction? Do Anglo-American courts of limited jurisdiction proceed summarily? *See*, e.g., 28 U.S.C.A. §636 as to U.S. Magistrates.

----

2.   Procedure in Courts of First Instance
(*Juzgados de primera instancia e instrucción*)

The procedure is either regular or summary; in either case, the court is constituted by one judge.

(a) Regular proceedings (*Juicio ordinario de mayor cuantía*).[54] Regular proceedings are held whenever the subject matter in dispute exceeds a certain fixed sum (500,000 pesetas).

(i) PLEADINGS.   Proceedings are initiated by the filing of a petiton with the clerk of court. The petition must contain all the relevant facts, the law to be applied to those facts, and the claim made by the plaintiff. It must be filed with as many copies as there are defendants. The petition is then served by an officer of the court on the defendant, together with a citation commanding him to file an appearance within nine days. If the defendant does not appear, the statement of claim is deemed to have been admitted and the plaintiff may move for a default judgment. Where the defendant appears, he has twenty days from his appearance to file an answer to the plaintiff's petition.

The defendant may, within six days from his appearance, contest the jurisdiction of the court and file other privileged defenses, namely, alleging lack of legal capacity of the plaintiff or the defendant, lack of proper legal representation, *lis pendens* in the same matter between the parties in another court, legal insufficiency of the claim (that the claims fails to state a cause of action). If he does so, a copy thereof is given to the plaintiff within three days. The judge will then hear the objection and give his ruling in the matter. The ruling is appealable to the court of appeal. If the objection is upheld, the case is dismissed. If the objection is overruled, the defendant has ten days from notification of the overruling of his objection to file an answer to the plaintiff's petition.

Where the defendant does not file an answer, the plaintiff may move for a default judgment.

In his answer, which is subject to the same rules as the statement of claim, the defendant may raise all the privileged defenses if he has not done so previously; but in such case, the court will rule on them only in the final judgment. The answer is served on the plaintiff and he has ten days to file a replication, and the defendant another ten days to file a rejoinder. The plaintiff may decline to file a replication, however, in which case the defendant has no opportunity to file a rejoinder and the matter is ready for proof.

(ii) PROCEEDINGS ON PROOF. The parties may admit to each other's allegations and dispense with all proof. If so, the case is ready for judgment.

The parties have twenty days from the conclusion of pleadings to request proceedings on proof and an immediately following term of thirty days to make proof. The court may, at the request of the parties, reduce the time to ten and fifteen days respectively. An extraordinary term on proof is allowed in cases where proof is to be made in foreign countries, but such term may not exceed eight months.

Proceedings on proof are held when all parties request them. When a party opposes the proceedings, the court will rule on the opposition. There is no appeal against the ruling granting the proceedings, but the ruling denying proof is appealable within five days to the same court. If the court upholds its decision to deny proof, there is no further appeal; but the matter may be raised again on appeal from the final judgment.

When the proceedings on proof are held, the parties must prove the allegations made in their pleadings. The court will not allow proof of allegations not made therein, unless such allegations are admitted as to new facts coming to the knowledge of the parties after conclusion of the pleadings. The court will also reject proof that it considers improper or not to the point. There is no appeal against the admission of proof, but a rejection of proof is appealable within five days to the same court. If the court upholds its decision to reject the proof, there is no further appeal; but the matter may be raised again on appeal from the final judgment.

The means of proof are: confession on oath, public documents, private documents, books of commerce, expert testimony, viewing of parts, and witnesses.

Confession on oath is brought about at the request of one party directed to the opponent to admit or deny certain allegations on oath. The oath may be decisive or indecisive by the party requesting it. The admission or denial of allegations on a decisive oath has the power of full proof. On an indecisive oath, an admission goes only to the prejudice of the party making the admission.

Public documents are those executed by public officers in the exercise of their official functions. They make proof unless challenged. If challenged, their authenticity must be established by certification of the office that issued them.

Private documents must be produced in their originals if in possession of litigants. Certified copies are admissible when in possession of third parties or when they form part of books, like commercial papers. Commercial books make proof as provided in the Code of Commerce.[55]

Expert testimony may be obtained whenever convenient. The parties may agree to have one or three experts approved. If they do not agree, the judge will determine the number of experts. The parties may then agree on the actual expert or experts to be appointed. If they do not agree, three times as many experts as are required are submitted by the court from an official list of experts and the expert or experts are selected by drawing lots. The expert or experts so selected may be challenged for cause. The expert or experts then prepare his or their opinion, which is then submitted by him or them in writing. A hearing is held where parties may question him or them and his or their expert opinion. The court considers the opinion in accordance with the rules of evidence without being bound to give it credence.

The viewing of parts may be ordered by the court whenever convenient. The court may set a time to inspect a place or a thing in the presence of the parties.

Parties may submit a list of witnesses whom they wish to have called. They may call as many as they like, but each party must pay the expenses of those called by him above the number of six. Together with the names and addresses of the witnesses, the party must submit a list of questions to be asked of them. Lists of witnesses are exchanged by the parties. The parties may submit additional questions to be asked of witnesses before the opening of the hearing. The court may reject any question it deems improper. The lists must be filed within ten days from the ruling of the court admitting proof by witnesses. The court then sets a date for the hearing to take place as soon as three days have run from the service of the notice. At the hearing, the judge asks the witnesses those questions submitted by the parties, and he may ask further questions on his own. The parties may not submit new questions, but they may request the court to ask again a question already submitted so as to clarify a matter or a point avoided by the witness or one on which the witness contradicted himself. All questions are asked by the court, the parties may not directly question the witness. All witnesses give evidence on oath except those below the age of fourteen. A witness may not consult anyone or anything in giving his answers. Whenever the question refers to documents, accounts, books or other papers, however, the witness may consult those papers. The witness may also make a prepared statement, which he may read.

A record of the evidence so presented is taken by the court. The court has all the usual powers to compel attendance of witnesses.

Within four days after the hearing, each party may challenge the witnesses and their evidence for the following causes: because of relation to the party up to the fourth degree; because the witness is an associate or an employee of the party; because he has an interest in the outcome of the suit; because he was previously convicted of false testimony; or because he is a close friend or an opponent of one of the parties. The petition must be filed in writing with the court and may contain an offer of proof to rebut the evidence given. A hearing is then set by the court where such evidence is heard. The hearing must take place within the original thirty days allowed for the proceedings of proof; however, the court may allow additional time, not exceeding ten days, to hear such a challenge.

(iii) FINAL STATEMENTS AND FINAL HEARING.   After the proceedings on proof are concluded, the court makes a ruling to this effect. Within three days of the notification thereof, the parties may request a final oral hearing. Where neither party requests it, the court will order that each party in succession be handed the court files for not less than ten and not more than twenty days in order to prepare a final statement. The final statement must consist of numbered sections and must contain the claims of the party in view of the proof. It must further contain the facts as established by the proof made by the opponent and the law to be applied by the court in the opinion of the party. After both parties file their final statements, the court will make a ruling that the case is ready for judgment and will give such judgment within twelve days of the ruling.

Where both parties request a final hearing, the court will order that each party in succession be handed the court files for not less than ten days and not more than twenty days in order to prepare for the final hearing. Where only one party requests the final hearing, the court will decide whether to hold it or whether to order the parties to file final statements only. There is no recourse against the decision. Where a final hearing is ordered, no final statements are filed. After the time for the preparation for the final hearing expires, and the parties have returned the court files, the court will set a day for the final hearing to take place within the next eight days.

At the hearing, the court will hear what the parties have to say, which is along the lines of what would have been otherwise contained in their final statements. After the hearing concludes, the court will give judgment within twelve days.

(iv) JUDGMENT.   The judgment is written by the judge and is typed in its final form by the office. It is signed by the judge and is read by him in open court. It is then published by the court clerk.

The judgment must contain the following generalia: the place and date; the name of the court and the judge that pronounced the judgment; the names, addresses and occupations of the parties and in what capacity they sued; the names of their attorneys and counsel; and the object of the suit. The claims and facts are contained in a separate, second section, beginning with the word *Resultando*, wherein the claims of the parties are summarized together with the facts on which they are founded. The law is contained in a third section, beginning with the word *Considerando*, in which the points of law made by the parties, together with their reasons and legal propositions, are given. Finally, the fourth section contains the decision. The decision must give judgment for the plaintiff or the defendant and decide all the points in issue clearly and systematically; the court may not avoid any issue raised; it must clearly provide for interests and damages, if any, and for costs.

The judgment may be appealed within five days from its notification to the court that pronounced it. The court orders the transmittal of all the papers to the proper court of appeal, which must be accomplished within six days, and it issues a citation ordering the parties to appear in the court of appeal within twenty days.

(b) Summary proceedings (*Juicio de menor cuantía*).[56]   Summary proceedings are held whenever the subject matter in dispute exceeds a certain fixed sum (50,000 pesetas), but is below another higher sum (500,000 pesetas). The procedure follows that of *mayor cuantía*, but it is simplified in some details. Unless so simplified by a direct provision of law, the rules applicable to regular procedure apply.

Proceedings are initiated by the plaintiff filing a petition. It is served on the defendant together with a citation to appear within nine days. If he does not appear, the plaintiff may move for a default judgment. If the defendant appears, he has six days to file an answer.

The defendant may object to the plaintiff's selection of proceedings of *menor cuantía* within four days from the service of the citation on the ground that proceedings of *mayor cuantía* should be held due to the higher value of the subject matter in dispute. Where the objection is filed, the court sets a day for the hearing to take place within six days. If the parties do not agree on the valuation, each may appoint an expert, and the court will appoint a third one, to value the subject matter in dispute. After the valuation is made, the court will decide within two days from the filing of the report of experts which procedure is to be followed. There is no appeal against a ruling ordering the procedure of *mayor cuantía*, but there is an appeal against that ordering the procedure of *menor cuantía*. A notice of appeal must be filed within three days and the appeal itself must be made together with any other grounds of appeal after judgment is given.

In his answer, the defendant may object to the jurisdiction of the court and may file any privileged defenses together with his answer to the plaintiff's statement of claim. The court will rule on the objections and the defenses only in the final judgment. Where the answer of the defendant requires a replication by the plaintiff, he may make it within four days, limiting himself to that matter.

Where the parties agree on the facts but disagree on the law, the court will set a hearing to take place within the next six days and will hear the parties thereon. If only one of the parties appears, the court will hear him in the absence of the nonappearing party. In either case, the court will give judgment within three days from such hearing. If neither party appears, the court will give judgment within three days. A record of the hearing is made.

Where the parties disagree on facts, the court will order them to offer proof within six days. If neither party requests proceedings on proof within that time, the court will set a hearing to take place within the next six days. The court will hear the parties, or the one that appears, and will give judgment within three days whether or not they appeared.

Where a party requests presentation of proof, the court orders proceedings on proof in accordance with the rules for proceedings in *mayor cuantía*, but all proof must be made within twenty days.

After the proceedings on proof are concluded, the court will immediately set a day for a final hearing where it will hear the parties; it will give judgment within five days from such hearing.

The judgment is appealable within five days from its notification. Any objections to the rulings of the court must be made on the grounds of an appeal. An appeal on the grounds that proceedings of *mayor cuantía* should have been held, known as a nullity appeal (*recurso de nulidad*), must now be made.

Where an appeal is filed, the court transmits the files to the proper court of appeal and cites the parties to appear there within ten days.

(c) Procedure on appeal from municipal and country courts (*Recurso de apelación en los juicios de congnición*).[57] Appeals against judgments of municipal and country courts may be lodged in writing or orally within three days from notification of the judgment and must be made to the clerk of court (*secretario*) of the municipal or country court that pronounced it. Where the appeal is lodged orally, the clerk of court will reduce it to writing. If there is any doubt as to the admissibility of the appeal, the municipal or country court will rule on the admissibility the next day.

Where the court refuses to admit the appeal, the appellant may, within twenty-four hours from notification of the refusal, indicate that he wishes to file a complaint (*queja*) against the refusal. The municipal or country court then issues a certification of the refusal and orders the appellant to file his complaint in writing, indicating his reasons therefor, with the proper court of the first instance within ten days. The court of first instance will hear the appellant and will finally rule on the admissibility of his appeal on the same or the next day. Where admissibility is denied, the court of first instance will notify the municipal or country court with the direction to execute the judgment.

Where the appeal is admitted, the files are transmitted to the proper court of first instance with an order to the parties to appear there within ten days. Where the appellant appears, the court of first instance will set a day for a hearing, summoning the parties. The appeal will usually be heard at one hearing without adjournment. However, the court may allow a party to make proof that he could not make in the court below and this may be done within ten days. In that case, the hearing will be adjourned. After the hearing is concluded, the court of first instance will give judgment within three days. The judgment will finally decide the matter as to substance. Where the appeal complained of the breach of an essential formal requirement and where it is found substantiated, the court of first instance will quash the judgment of the court below and remit the case to it for new proceedings from the moment when the breach was committed. No further appeal nor a petition for cassation lies against the decision of the court of first instance.

NOTES AND QUESTIONS

1. Note that the court of general jurisdiction holds regular or summary proceedings in accordance with the value of the subject matter in dispute. What is the main difference between these two proceedings?

2. How are the proceedings initiated? What are the procedural steps taken until the taking of proof? What must the briefs of the parties contain? Compare the Italian law and also, e.g., F.R.C.P. Rule 5.

3. What are the means of proof? How do they compare with those of the French law? Compare also the Anglo-American means of proof.

4. Note that the proceedings consist of successive hearings before a single

judge. After all the proof has been taken, is a final hearing in the case obligatory? Compare the German and the Italian law. Are there any juries in the Spanish civil system?

5. What are the contents of a judgment? Must the court adhere strictly to the rules concerning judgments?

6. Note the procedure on appeal from municipal and country courts. Does any further remedy lie against the decision of a court of first instance?

---

3. Procedure in Courts of Civil Appeal
(*Audiencias territoriales*)[58]

Procedure in courts of civil appeal is either regular procedure on appeal from proceedings of *mayor cuantía* in courts of first instance, or summary procedure on appeal from proceedings of *menor cuantía* in those same courts. In either case, the court of civil appeal is composed of at least three, and of not more than five, judges.

(a) **Summary proceedings** (*Apelaciones de las sentencias y autos dictados en incidentes en los juicios que no sean de mayor cuantía*).   After the files from the court of first instance are received and the appellant appears within ten days from notification of the judgment as cited, the clerk of the court of appeal refers the matter to a proper chamber and the president of that chamber appoints one of the judges to act as rapporteur (*magistrado ponente*). The appellee may file his brief within the next six days, and either party may request proceedings on proof. Where the appellee does not appear, the appeal may proceed in his absence. Where the appellant does not appear, the appeal is summarily dismissed with costs to be paid by the appellant and the files are returned to the court of first instance with instructions to execute the judgment.

Proof may be had only: (1) where the proof was rejected by the trial court; (2) where the party was unable to make proof in the trial proceedings for reasons beyond his control; (3) where new facts appeared after proof in the trial proceedings already was made; (4) where the party learned only then of facts previously existing and swears not to have known of them previously; and (5) where the defendant in default appeared only after proof in the trial court was made.

Where proof is requested, the chamber will rule on the request. If it is granted, the chamber will allow time for proof, which may not exceed twenty days. In accordance with the rules applicable to proceedings of *mayor cuantía* in courts of first instance, proof is then made before the rapporteur sitting alone. He may, however, have the proof made before the court of first instance.

Proof having been made, the rapporteur takes the files and studies them for not more than six days. Where no proof is requested, the rapporteur receives the files from the clerk of the chamber and studies them for not more than six days. He then returns the files to the clerk of court. The chamber immediately sets a day and time for a hearing. Ten days must elapse between the service of the citation and the hearing, during which time the parties may inspect the files in preparation for the hearing.

At the hearing, the chamber will hear the parties in accordance with the rules of regular appellate procedure. The chamber will give judgment within five days of the hearing. It affirms, modifies or reverses the judgment of the trial court or decides on the nullity appeal (*recurso de nulidad*). Where the judgment is reversed or modified, the chamber gives a new or modified judgment in the case. Where the judgment is affirmed or the judgment of the court of appeal is more favorable to the appellee, the appellant must pay the costs of the appellate proceedings.

The judgment of the court of appeal is then communicated to the court of first instance for its execution. No further appeal lies against the decision of the court of appeal in a matter of *menor cuantía*, but a petition for the cassation of the judgment for breach of law or legal doctrine may be brought to the Supreme Court when the value of the subject matter exceeds a certain minimum sum (300,000 pesetas); a petition for breach of form may always be brought.

(b) **Regular proceedings** (*Apelaciones de sentencias definitivas dictadas en pleitos de mayor cuantía*).[59]

(i) PROCEDURE UP TO THE FINAL HEARING. After receiving the files from the court of first instance, the clerk of the court of appeal refers the case to the proper chamber. Where the appellant appears within twenty days from notification of the judgment as cited, the president of the chamber appoints a rapporteur (*magistrado ponente*) from among its members to report to the chamber on the case.

Where the appellant fails to appear, the appeal is summarily dismissed with costs and the files are returned to the court of first instance with instructions to execute the judgment. Where the appellant appears, the appellee may join the proceedings at any time and may take part in them as from the time of his actual appearance. Each party may withdraw from the proceedings at any time by paying his opponent's costs of the appellate proceedings.

Where both parties appear, the files are given to the appellant for a period of not less than ten and not more than twenty days to study the case, and then to the appellee for an equal time. At the expiration of that time, each party must file his brief. In his brief, the appellee may join in the appeal and may indicate how he has been harmed by the judgment.

Where the court of first instance is alleged to have broken a rule of procedure that would entitle a party to petition for the cassation of the judgment, and the party objected to this alleged breach in the court below but his objection was overruled by that court, and where the party now alleges this breach in his appellate brief, the chamber will rule on the objection. The files are handed to the rapporteur (*magistrado ponente*) who studies the objection for a time equal to that allowed previously to the parties for studying the files and reports to the chamber. A hearing is set immediately thereafter before the chamber. The chamber will hear the parties and decide on that and any other objection the parties may have made against proceedings in the court below. The chamber may overrule the objection or objections, or it may uphold them. If the objection is upheld, the chamber will rectify the error by applying the rules of procedure applicable to proceedings of *mayor cuantía* in courts of first instance, as the court below should have done.

In their briefs, the parties may also request proof. Proof may be had only on the grounds enumerated in summary procedure above. Without requesting proof, a party may request, up to the issuance of the citation for the final hearing, the administration of a decisive or nondecisive oath to his opponent on facts that were not raised in the proceedings in the court below. In addition, he may request production of documents of a later date than that of the proceedings in the court below and also documents that the parties did not know existed or which they were unable to obtain at that time.

Where the appellant requests proof in his brief, the appellee must agree or object to it in his brief. Where the appellee requests proof in his brief, the appellant has three days from the receipt of the appellee's brief to object. The chamber will allow proceedings of proof when they are warranted by law and when both parties agree that proof should be made. Where the parties are not in agreement, the matter is referred to the rapporteur for six days to study it and report to the chamber, which will decide within the next three days. There is no appeal against the decision admitting proceedings on proof; but there is an appeal, known as the *recurso de súplica*, against an order denying such proceedings. The appeal must be made to the same chamber within five days from notification of the decision denying proceedings on proof. The opponent has three days to oppose the appeal. The chamber will then decide within three days. Where it upholds its decision to deny proceedings on proof, the aggrieved party may use the denial as a ground for the cassation of the final judgment to be given in the case. The same proceedings are used where a particular proof is denied to a party.

Where proof is admitted, it is made before the rapporteur sitting alone and in accordance with the rules of procedure applicable to proceedings of *mayor cuantía* in courts of first instance. The rapporteur may, however, have the proof made in the court of first instance.

After the proof is made, each party takes the files in turn for six days and files a statement pointing out defects, if any.

The case is then referred to the rapporteur, who studies it for a time equal to that previously allowed to the parties for studying the files before the submission of their briefs. The same occurs where proof is not requested or is denied. The rapporteur reports to the chamber, and the chamber will decide whatever is proper. It will cure any defects that occurred in the proceedings in the court below which do not entitle the aggrieved party to cassation. After disposing of all the requests and objections of the parties, and with the case thus ready for a final hearing, the chamber will set a date for the final hearing.

(ii) FINAL HEARING AND JUDGMENT.   At the hearing, the rapporteur gives his report first, giving a brief history of the case and referring to the points in dispute to be decided by the court. Then counsel for the appellant takes the floor and immediately thereafter counsel for the appellee. They refer to the facts and the law to be applied and urge the court to decide accordingly. With permission of the presiding judge, they may speak again to clarify or correct their statements. The parties themselves, by leave of the presiding judge, also may address the court. The presiding judge conducts the hearing in accordance with the rules of civil procedure. After the subject matter is exhausted to the satisfaction of the court, the presiding judge concludes the hearing by pronouncing the word *"Visto."*

A record of the final hearing is made by the court clerk. It gives the names of the judges, counsel, and attorneys, and the times of the opening and conclusion of the hearing.

Immediately after the final hearing, the court may make an order, known as the *providencia para mejor proveer*, requiring a party or parties to produce further documents, make an admission on a point that has not been proved, or undergo further investigation or valuation. The order fixes the time within which it must be complied with. For that time and until compliance, the time of fifteen days, counted from the day after the final hearing, within which the court must give judgment is suspended. There is no recourse against such an order except to the very court that pronounced it. After the order is complied with, the court will give judgment without any further hearing.

If no order (*providencia para mejor proveer*) as above is made, immediately after the final hearing the court retires to consider judgment. The deliberation may also take place later, as determined by the court, but the court must give judgment within fifteen days counted from the day after the final hearing. The deliberation is closed to the public and is held during usual business hours.

The deliberation is opened by the report of the rapporteur (*magistrado ponente*). He outlines the facts of the case and the applicable law necessary for the decision to be made without suggesting a particular decision. The discussion thus opened is carried on by the judges until they are ready to vote. Once voting begins, the session may not be interrupted except for unavoidable causes. The rapporteur votes first, then other judges in their inverse order of seniority; the presiding judge votes last. Three affirmative votes are required for a decision. The court usually is composed of five members, including the presiding judge, so that there usually are three affirmative votes. In the case of an interlocutory order, a simple majority vote is sufficient. Should a judge be unable to vote, e.g., because of illness, and if he becomes incapacitated after the conclusion of the final hearing, he may vote in writing. If he cannot vote at all, e.g., because of illness or death, and if the remaining judges do not provide three affirmative votes, a new final hearing must be held.

Where the court is composed of three or four judges only, or where, although composed of five judges, three affirmative votes to decide the case are not forthcoming even on a second ballot, the court will declare its inability to decide the case and order a new final hearing with more judges present. Only those points on which three affirmative votes have not been reached are decided. Two additional judges are added to the court where the number of the judges was uneven, and three where it was even. The individual judges to be added are appointed by the president of the court of appeal and their names are communicated to the parties so that the parties can exercise their right to object to the appointments. Where three affirmative votes are not forthcoming on a particular point even then, only the two opinions that obtained the most votes are taken to a new vote.

The judgment is prepared by the rapporteur. Where he is not one of the majority, the presiding judge may appoint one of the majority to prepare the judgment. It is then typed by the office in final form. All judges sign it, even if they voted against it. It is then read in open court by the rapporteur or the presiding judge, and it is published in writing under the signature of the court clerk. The dissenting votes are separately listed and are communicated together with the dissenting opinions to the court of cassation in case a petition for the cassation of the judgment is made. The form and contents of the judgment must follow the general rules concerning judgments.[60]

No further appeal lies against the judgment, but it is subject to a petition for its cassation. Notice of an intention to file the petition must be given to the court of appeal that pronounced the judgment within ten days, counted from the day after notification of the judgment on the parties. The court of appeal will certify all the documents relative to the proceedings in the case, beginning with proceedings in the trial court, and will transmit them to the Supreme Court of Justice.It will also summon the parties to appear in the Supreme Court of Justice within forty days from the certification where the case originated in continental Spain and the Baleares, and within fifty days where it originated in the Canary Islands, when a petition for the cassation of the judgment for breach of law or legal doctrine is involved and within fifteen and thirty days respectively in the case of a petition for the cassation of the judgment for the breach of formal requirements. The above time is counted from the day after the certification is handed to the parties.

When no notice of the intention to file a petition for the cassation of the judgment is filed, the judgment enters into the power of law. The judgment is certified under the signature of the clerk of the court of appeal and communicated by him to the trial court for its execution by that court. Even where the notice of intention to file a petition for the cassation of the judgment is filed, and even where the petition is actually filed in the Supreme Court, the court of civil appeal may order the execution of the judgment on the motion by the party obtaining it if that party files a bond set by the court in an amount which would make good all losses incurred by the opponent if the petition for the cassation of the judgment is successful.

NOTES AND QUESTIONS

1. Note that Spanish procedure calls for a distinction between regular and summary proceedings even on the appellate level. What is the composition of the court?

2. Are the appellate proceedings in fact a trial *de novo*? What is the function of the rapporteur in the proceedings? Compare the Italian law.

3. What is the procedure at the final hearing? Compare the French and the German law. *See also*, e.g., F.R. App. P. Rule 34ff.

4. Since the court is a collegiate court, deliberation before judgment is necessary. How is the decision of the court arrived at? Compare the German and the Italian law. Does the Spanish appellate court always give a new judgment without any remission?

---

4. Procedure in the Supreme Court of Justice
(*Tribunal Supremo de Justicia*)

All civil matters are heard by the first chamber (*sala primera*) of the Supreme Court of Justice. Cases heard are of two kinds: petitions for the cassation of a judgment (*recurso de casación*), and petition for the revision of a judgment (*recurso de revisión*). The court is composed of five, but not more than seven, judges.

(a) **Petitions for the cassation of judgments** (*Recurso de casación*).[61] Petitions for the cassation of judgments may be brought for an alleged breach of law or legal doctrine (*por infracción de ley o de doctrina legal*), for an alleged breach of formal requirements (*por quebrantamiento de forma*), and for an alleged breach of both the above in the same judgment. A petition may also be brought for the cassation or annulment of an award made by arbitrators. The petition may be brought by the parties or by the public ministry.

(i) PETITIONS FOR THE CASSATION OF JUDGMENTS FOR BREACH OF LAW OR LEGAL DOCTRINE (*por infracción de ley o de doctrina legal*)

(aa) *Procedures on admission of petitions.* The petition is admissible where the judgment suffers from the violation, erroneous interpretation, or improper application of the law or a legal doctrine; where it does not dipose of claims properly made by the parties; where it grants more than has been requested or does not dispose of a claim made in the pleadings; where it makes contradictory provisions; where the judgment is contrary to the evidence; where jurisdiction was improperly assumed or denied; or where evidence was wrongfully admitted or rejected.

The petition is inadmissible in cases originating with courts of first instance in matters of *menor cuantía* except where the value of the subject matter exceeds a certain minimum sum (300,000 pesetas); it is also inadmissible in all indigent cases where the decision of the trial court was affirmed on appeal. A petition for breach of form (*por quebrantamiento de forma*) is admissible, however, in all these cases.

Proceedings are initiated by the filing of a notice of intention to file a petition for the cassation of a judgment with the court of civil appeal (*audiencia territorial*) that pronounced the judgment as stated above.[62] The court of civil appeal certifies the judgment and states that the notice was filed in time; and on the same day during which it issues this certification to the parties, it hands over all necessary files to the Supreme Court. Where the petitioner does not appear within the time stipulated, the judgment of the court of civil appeal enters into the power of law. The appearance is filed under the signature of an attorney (*procurador*). Within the same time, the petitioner must file a certified copy of the contested judgment and file the petition for the cassation of the judgment in as many copies as there are parties. Where the decision of the trial court was affirmed on appeal, he must also pay a fixed deposit of money, unless he is declared indigent; no deposit is payable where the decision of the trial court was reversed or modified on appeal. In the petition, which is drawn up in separate numbered sections, the petitioner must state clearly which law or legal doctrine has been violated in the judgment.

Where the petition is filed in time and is formally in order, the files are handed to the procurator (*fiscal*) for ten days to rule on the admissibility of the petition. When the procurator is of the opinion that the petition should be admitted for consideration by the Court, he returns the files to the court clerk (*secretario*) with the word "*Visto*" written under his signature. Where he advises the Court not to admit the petition, he gives his reasoned opinion and explains in detail why the petition should not be admitted. Copies of his opinion are given to the parties.

As soon as the procurator returns the files, the court clerk immediately hands them to the rapporteur appointed by the chamber president for six days of study. The rapporteur's advice on whether or not to admit the petition is given orally at a session of the Court constituted by seven judges and known as the admission chamber (*sala de admisión*).

Where the procurator rules that the petition is inadmissible because it was filed out of time, because the petitioner's attorney was not properly appointed, because a certified copy of the contested judgment was not filed, or because the required deposit was not made, the admission chamber will decide in private on the admission of the petition without hearing the parties. Where the procurator rules that the petition is inadmissible in full or in part for any other reason, the admission chamber will set a hearing on admission. A hearing will also be set when due to the advice of the rapporteur, the majority of the admission chamber has doubts as the admissibility of the petition. Where the majority of the admission chamber has no doubts as to the admissibility of the petition, it will admit it without any hearing.

At the admission hearing, if any, first the judgment complained of is read, together with the reasons for its cassation alleged by the petitioner. The counsel for the petitioner takes the floor, followed by counsel for the respondent. Thereafter, the public ministry addresses the admission chamber; its address, however, is discretionary. The arguments are limited to the question of the admission of the petition; the merits of the petition may not be discussed.

The admission chamber announces its decision within ten days from the hearing. It will either deny admission, admit the petition, or admit some of its grounds and deny others. Admission may be denied on the grounds referred to above and also because the petition does not indicate the laws that have been infringed, because the laws alleged to have been infringed are not relevant to the case, because the petition does not contain a claim, and because the alleged principle of law is not considered by the admission chamber to merit that classification. The petition is admitted where the admission chamber does not find any ground for its rejection. It is admitted on some grounds and denied on others under the same considerations above.

There is no remedy against decisions of the admission chamber.

(bb) *Hearing on the merits.*   After the petition for the cassation of the judgment is admitted by the Supreme Court, the files are given to the petitioner for ten days to study the case, and after he returns them, they are given to all other parties in turn for the same period of time. The Court will then set a day for a hearing on the merits.

The Court hearing the petition is presided over by the president of the first chamber (*sala primera*), by the president of the Supreme Court, or more likely, by the most senior judge. It is further composed of another six judges, one of whom is the rapporteur.

The rapporteur prepares a report in writing that deals with all the points of fact and law contained in the record and the judgment of the court of civil appeal that are of importance in connection with the petition. It also mentions any dissenting opinion and refers to the laws and legal doctrines that are alleged to have been infringed. Copies of the rapporteur's report are given to all the judges and to the parties two days before the hearing.

The hearing is opened by the reading of the rapporteur's report. Then counsel for the petitioner addresses the court; he is followed by counsel for the respondent. The presiding judge then declares the hearing closed.

The Court gives judgment within fifteen days, counted from the day after the hearing. Four concurrent votes are required for a decision on all points.

Where the Court is of the opinion that the court below committed a breach of law or legal doctrine, it will set aside the judgment and order the deposit refunded to the petitioner. Then in a continuing but separate act, it will give a new judgment in the case deciding the matter on the merits.

Where the Court does not find the grounds for the petition substantiated, it will deny the petition and order the petitioner to pay the costs of the petition and to forfeit his deposit.

(ii) PETITIONS FOR THE CASSATION OF JUDGMENTS FOR BREACH OF FORM (*por quebrantamiento de forma*). The petition must be filed within ten days from notification of the judgment in the court of civil appeal that pronounced it. It must be based on one of the following grounds: failure to give notice of the proceedings in the first or second instance to necessary parties; lack of proper legal representation; improper rejection of evidence; failure to give notice of a hearing on proof or of the pronouncement of judgment; denial of proof, which may have caused a party to be deprived of a defense; lack of jurisdiction; participation in the judgment of a judge who should have disqualified himself; or lack of the proper number of judges on the Court. The petition must further allege and show that the petitioner has requested in vain that the court which committed the breach rectify it. Where it was impossible to request rectification in the trial court, the request must be made in the appellate proceedings. Only where the alleged breach was committed by the appellate court and it is impossible to petition for its rectification there may the petition be made in the Supreme Court.

Where the decision of the trial court was affirmed on appeal, the petitioner must pay, together with the petition, a fixed deposit of money, unless he is indigent. No deposit is payable if the decision of the trial court was reversed or modified on appeal.

The court of civil appeal will consider the petition and will examine whether the contested judgment is a final judgment, whether the petition was filed in time, whether it is founded on a ground provided for by law as pointed out above, and whether correction of the alleged breach was requested in vain in the prior proceedings. Where these requirements have been complied with, the court will make an order within three days from the filing of the petition admitting the petition and will summon the parties to appear in the Supreme Court within fifteen days where the case originated in continental Spain and the Baleares, or within thirty days where it originated in the Canary Islands. It will also transmit the files to the Supreme Court.

Where the court of civil appeal considers the requirements for admission not to have been complied with, it will deny admission of the petition and will issue a certified copy of the order to the petitioner with indication of the date of service. The petitioner may then appeal the denial to the admission chamber of the Supreme Court within fifteen days for cases arising in continental Spain and the Baleares, or within thirty days for cases arising in the Canary Islands. Time runs from the day after the day of service. Where no such appeal is made, the admission of the petition is finally barred.

The admission chamber will consider the appeal without any hearing within five days and will make an order within the same time against which there is no further recourse. It will either vacate the order denying admission, admit the petition and request the files from the court of civil appeal, or it will affirm the order denying admission.

Where the petitioner appears, the parties are handed the files in turn for ten days each. After the files are returned, the court sets a day for hearing and issues a summons to the parties.

The court is composed as for the hearing of petitions for breach of law or legal doctrine and the procedure is identical except that the court must give judgment within ten days from the day after the hearing. Where the judgment is set aside, the case is remanded to the court of civil appeal and returned to the point where the error occurred. The court of civil appeal will then cure the error and proceed.

(iii)   PETITIONS FOR THE CASSATION OF JUDGMENTS FOR BREACH OF FORM (*por quebrantamiento de forma*) AND AT THE SAME TIME FOR BREACH OF LAW OR LEGAL DOCTRINE (*por infracción de ley o de doctrina legal*).   The procedure follows that for breach of formal requirements as given above, except the petitioner declares in his petition that he will later file another petition for breach of law or legal doctrine. In case the petition for breach of formal requirements is denied, the petitioner has twenty days, counted from the day after notification, to file a petition for breach of law or legal doctrine. If the respondent requests it, costs of the unsuccessful petition for breach of form are then taxed. If no such request is made, it shall await the outcome of the petition for breach of law or legal doctrine.

The petition for breach of law or legal doctrine then proceeds in accordance with its own rules.

(iv)   PETITIONS FOR THE CASSATION OR ANNULMENT OF ARBITRATION AWARDS (*Recursos contra los fallos de los arbitros*).   Arbitration[63] is of two kinds. The first is known as legal arbitration (*arbitraje de derecho*), where the arbitrators are bound to apply the rules of law as set in the arbitration agreement. The second is equitable arbitration (*arbitraje de equidad*), where the arbitrators may decide *ex equo et bono*. Awards made in legal arbitration are subject to cassation for breach of law or legal doctrine and also for breach of form. The petition is made to the first chamber of the Supreme Court. The applicable procedure follows *mutatis mutandis* that for breach of law or legal doctrine or breach of form in the case of judgments. Awards made in equitable arbitration are subject only to a petition for annulment filed with the first chamber of the Supreme Court. The procedure is the same in both cases.

The petition may be presented only on the following grounds: (1) the award was made after the time provided for in the arbitration agreement has run; (2) the award deals with matters not submitted by the parties for decision; (3) the matter is not one of civil law; (4) the award deals with political or honorific matters, personal privileges, affiliation, paternity, capacity and other matters affecting the status of persons that may not be submitted to arbitration; and (5) it deals with matters in which the public ministry must intervene.

Together with the petition, the petitioner must file the following: the arbitration agreement; the award; a fixed deposit of money; and, where the petition alleges that the award was made out of time, the agreement on the extension of time, if any, within which the award was to be made.

The petition must be filed within twenty days, counted from the day after notification of the award on the petitioner, in cases where the award was made anywhere in Spain except the Canary Islands and within forty days where it was made in the Canary Islands. The Court will summon all other interested parties to appear within fifteen days, or within thirty days where the matter comes from the Canary Islands. The procedure followed is that provided for in the cassation of judgments for breach of form unless otherwise provided. Where the court finds that the award was made out of time, it will annul the award and refund the deposit. Where it finds that the award dealt with points not submitted to the arbitrators in the agreement, it will annul the award only on those points and refund the deposit.

(v) PETITIONS FOR THE CASSATION OF JUDGMENTS INITIATED BY THE PUBLIC MINISTRY (*ministerio fiscal*).   The public ministry may file petitions for the cassation of judgments in cases in which it intervened without being required to make a deposit. It may also file a petition without any time limit in the interest of law (*en interés de la ley*) for breach of law or legal doctrine in cases in which it did not take part. In that case, parties in the action are summoned to appear in the Supreme Court within twenty days, if they wish to do so. Judgments given in these cases serve only the purposes of the law and have no effect on the matter already decided nor on the parties.

All petitions are filed directly in the Supreme Court and are handled by the first chamber. In cases where the parties have appeared and where the petition interposed by the public ministry is denied, the costs to such parties are paid from the proceeds realized by the forfeiture of deposits. Claims are paid in chronological order as soon as there are funds available. The same occurs where the public ministry withdraws the petition.

(b)   Petitions for the revision of judgments (*Recurso de revisión*).[64]   A petition for the revision of a judgment pronounced by any court may be filed in the first chamber of the Supreme Court. The Supreme Court thus has exclusive jurisdiction.

Grounds for revision are: discovery of documents of decisive importance; the judgment was based on documents, the falsity of which was not known to the petitioner or the falsity of which was later established; the judgment relied on the testimony of witnesses who were later convicted of perjury in connection therewith; and the judgment was obtained by bribery, force or any fraudulent practices. Only final judgments that have entered into power of law may be contested.

The petition may be filed within three months from the discovery of documents, from the discovery of fraud, or from a judgment declaring such fraud, but not later than five years from the publication of the contested judgment. The petitioner must also make a fixed deposit of money.

After receiving the petition, the Supreme Court will obtain the files from the court that pronounced the contested judgment and will summon the parties to appear within forty days. The procedure follows the rules of civil procedure. The public ministry must be heard before judgment.

Filing of the petition does not suspend execution of the contested judgment if it has not already been executed, but the Court may order suspension thereof upon the petitioner giving bond in an amount determined by the Court; such amount must equal the value of the subject matter together with the loss caused by the delay in the event the petition is denied. Where criminal proceedings are instituted on the same facts, proceedings in the Supreme Court are suspended until a final decision is given in the criminal proceedings. In that case, the term of five years within which the petition for revision must be brought is also suspended. .

Where the Supreme Court grants the petition, it will rescind the judgment in full or in part. It will then return the files to the court that pronounced the judgment. The matter will rest there unless the parties initiate further proceedings in that court. The points decided by the Supreme Court are *res judicata* and may not be relitigated. The costs of the revision proceedings are assessed against the respondent and the petitioner is refunded his deposit.

Where the Supreme Court denies the petition, the petitioner must pay the costs of the proceedings and forfeits his deposit.

No remedy lies against decisions of the Supreme Court in the revision of judgments proceedings.

NOTES AND QUESTIONS

1. Which chamber of the Spanish Supreme Court hears civil cases? What types of petitions for the cassation of judgments are available to the parties? What allegations must be made in a petition for cassation for breach of law? What allegations must be made in a petition for cassation for breach of form?

2. Do cases reach the Supreme Court by leave only? What is the procedure for admission of a petition?

3. When a petition is admitted, what further proceedings are then held? What is the function of the rapporteur?

4. Under what circumstances would the Supreme Court remit a case to the court of civil appeal for further proceedings?

5. Note that the Supreme Court also hears petitions for the cassation of arbitration awards.

6. Under what conditions may the public ministry file a petition for the cassation of a judgment in the interest of the law?

7. Compare the procedure in the Spanish Supreme Court with that in the French Court of Cassation and that in the Italian Supreme Court of Cassation. How does such procedure compare with that before the court of final resort in the Anglo-American civil courts system? *See,* e.g., 28 U.S.C.A. §2101ff. as to the United States Supreme Court.

8. Note the Spanish rules on petitions for the revision of judgments. What are the grounds for revision? Compare the French rules as to the revision of judgments, which appear in Arts. 593ff. of the French Code of Civil Procedure. Compare also

the German law on the reopening of proceedings, including the notes. *See also* F.R.C.P. Rule 60.

III. THE SYSTEM AND ADMINISTRATION OF CRIMINAL LAW

A. THE SUBSTANTIVE CRIMINAL LAW

The substantive criminal law is governed by the Penal Code and by a number of other statutes. The Penal Code originates from 1848 but it was revised in major reforms in 1850, 1870, 1928, 1932, and 1944. The 1944 version is in power as further amended. The Code has 604 articles contained in three books dealing with: Book 1. General provisions with respect to crimes and infractions, persons responsible and punishment; Book 2. Crimes and their punishment; and Book 3. Infractions and their punishment.

Book 1 (General provisions with respect to crimes and infractions, persons responsible and punishment) has the following titles: I. Crimes and infractions and circumstances that relieve, reduce or increase criminal responsibility; II. Persons responsible for crimes and infractions; III. Punishment; IV. Civil responsibility and court costs; V. Extinction of responsibility and its effects; and VI. General provisions.

Book 2 (Crimes and the punishment) has the following titles: I. Crimes against the external security of the state; II. Crimes against the internal security of the state; III. Counterfeiting and falsification; IV. Crimes against the administration of justice; V. Infractions against the peace of the deceased, and crimes against the safety of traffic and against public health; VI. Illegal gaming; VII. Crimes committed by public officers in the exercise of their functions; VIII. Crimes against the person; IX. Crimes against honesty; X. Crimes against honor; XI. Crimes against the civil status of persons; XII. Crimes against liberty and security; XIII. Crimes against property; and XIV. Criminal negligence.

Book 3 (Infractions and their punishment) has the following titles: I. Infractions by printed word and infractions against the public order; II. Infractions against general interest and those against city regulations; III. Infractions against persons; IV. Infractions against property; and V. Provisions general to infractions.

In addition to the Penal Code, there are numerous statutes that provide for the punishment of crimes and infractions of a specific nature. They deal, for instance, with railroads, waters, protection of birds, hunting, motor vehicle traffic, and weights and measures.

The following are topics selected from the Spanish substantive criminal law.

1. Crimes and Infractions (*Delitos y faltas*)[65]

Crimes and infractions are voluntary acts and omissions punishable by law. Acts and omissions punishable by law are always considered voluntary unless proved otherwise. A person who voluntarily commits a crime or an infraction is criminally responsible even though the effect produced differs from that actually intended.

Where a court has knowledge of the commission of an act that is not punishable by law but, in its opinion, should be made punishable, it will refer the matter to the government with a reasoned opinion as to why such acts should be made punishable. In the same way, it will call the attention of the government to punishable acts which, in its opinion, should be made not punishable or where the punishment stipulated is excessive.

The following are punishable: a completed crime, a frustrated crime, an attempt and a conspiracy to commit a crime, an incitement to commit a particular crime, and in incitement to commit crimes in general.

Only completed infractions are punishable with the exception of frustrated infractions against persons and property, which are punishable.

Crimes (*delitos*) are offenses punishable by grave punishments (*penas graves*) and infractions (*faltas*) are offenses punishable by light punishments (*penas leves*).

NOTES AND QUESTIONS

1. Note the definition of crime and of infraction. Spanish law thus has only two categories of criminal offenses. Compare this division with those of the French and the Italian law. How is the matter regulated in the German law? *See also*, e.g., Texas Penal Code §12.02ff.

2. What attempts are punishable in Spanish law? Compare the French law. *See also*, e.g., Texas Penal Code §15.01.

---

2.   Punishment (*Penas*)[66]

Crimes and infractions may be punished only with punishments provided for by law before their perpetration. Penal laws have retroactive effect only when they favor the person who committed a crime or an infraction even though he was convicted and is serving his term.

Punishments are: grave punishments (*penas graves*), light punishments (*penas leves*), punishments common to both the above categories, and additional punishments.

Grave punishments (*penas graves*) are: *reclusión mayor, reclusión menor, presidio mayor, prisión mayor, presidio menor, prisión menor, arresto mayor, extrañamiento, confinamiento, destierro*, public censure, loss of Spanish citizenship, loss of public rights, loss of particular public rights, and suspension of public rights. The above-enumerated punishments beginning with *reclusión mayor* and ending with *arresto mayor* are imprisonments of different severity and length from the most severe to the lightest in descending order. *Reclusión mayor* ranges from twenty years and one day to thirty years of imprisonment, and *arresto mayor* from one month and one day to six months.

Extrañamiento consists of expulsion from Spain for a certain time. *Confinamiento* consists of confinement in a designated locality in full liberty under observation for a stipulated time. Public censure (*reprensión pública*) consists of censure being pronounced in a public session of court. Only naturalized persons may be deprived of Spanish citizenship.

Light punishments (*penas leves*) are: *arresto menor*, and private censure. *Arresto menor* consists of light imprisonment of from one day to thirty days. Private censure (*reprensión privada*) consists of censure being pronounced in a closed session of court.

Punishments common to both grave and light punishments are: a fine, the withdrawal of a driver's license, and the giving of security. Additional punishments include civil interdiction and the confiscation of tools used in the commission of an offense.

An attempt to commit a crime (*delito*) is punishable by punishment one or two grades lower than that provided for the completed crime in the discretion of the court. Accessories before the fact (*cómplices*) are punishable by punishment one grade lower than that provided for the completed crime, and accessories after the fact (*encubridores*) are punishable by punishment two grades lower than that provided for the completed crime.[67]

NOTES AND QUESTIONS

1. Spanish criminal law rigorously applies the principle *Nullum crimen sine lege*. This is so in all civil law systems. May penal laws have retroactive effect in favor of the person who committed an act that ceased to be punishable after he committed it? Compare the German law. *See also*, e.g., Texas Penal Code §1.03.

2. What kinds of punishment does the Spanish law permit? Note that there is no death penalty in Spain. Compare the French and the Italian law. Is there a death penalty in the criminal law of your state? *See*, e.g., Texas Penal Code §12.31.

3. Does Spanish law provide for imprisonment for life? Compare the Italian law. *See also*, e.g., Texas Penal Code §12.31.

4. Consider the different time periods given to heavy punishments in the Spanish law. Each of the punishments provides for a different length of imprisonment within the minimum and maximum terms. How does this approach compare with that adopted by the French and the German law? *See also*, e.g., Texas Penal Code §12.31ff.

5. Note the light punishments and additional punishments provided in the Spanish law. How do they compare with those of the Italian and the French law? *See also*, e.g., Texas Penal Code §12.21ff.

6. What is the punishment for an attempt? How does it compare with the French and the Italian law? *See also*, e.g., Texas Penal Code §15.01.

---

3. Minors (*Menores*)[68]

A person who at the time of the commission of an offense has not yet completed sixteen years of age is not imputable. The fact that a person has completed sixteen years of age but not yet eighteen years of age is taken as an attenuating circumstance. In such as case, the court will reduce punishment by one or two grades, and it may order the minor detained in a special institution. A person who has completed eighteen years of age is fully imputable.

NOTES AND QUESTIONS

When does imputability begin in Spanish law? At what age is a person fully imputable? How does the French and the German law regulate the matter? Note the special category created by the Spanish law concerning persons between the ages of sixteen and eighteen. Do similar categories exist in other legal systems? Note the differing age requirements in the laws of the several countries. *See also* the Texas Penal Code §8.07.

---

4.   Repeaters (*Reiterantes y reincidentes*)[69]

There are two kinds of repeaters: *reiterantes*, those who were convicted before of a crime that carries an equal or heavier punishment or of two or more crimes carrying lesser punishments; and *reincidentes*, those who were convicted before of one or more crimes listed in the same title of the Penal Code. Both instances of recidivism are taken as aggravating circumstances. The rules applicable to repeaters do not apply to infractions (*faltas*) but apply only to crimes (*delitos*).

Where there is one aggravating circumstance, the punishment is imposed in the maximum grade. Where there are also attenuating circumstances, the court will balance them against the aggravating circumstances. Irrespective of the number of aggravating circumstances, the court may not impose a heavier punishment than that indicated in the Penal Code as heaviest in the maximum grade with the only exception of *reincidencia* where, beginning with the second reincidence, the court may impose a punishment heavier by one or two grades.

NOTES AND QUESTIONS

Note that the Spanish law distinguishes two different kinds of repeaters, namely, those who engage in crimes of the same type and those who engage in crimes of a different type. Does this distinction have merit in the subsequent treatment of the offender? Do other legal systems consider this feature of importance? Compare the Italian law. *See,* e.g., Texas Penal Code §12.42.

Note also that the Spanish provisions as to repeaters apply only to crimes and not to infractions. Is the same approach taken in the French and the Italian law? *See also* Texas Penal Code §12.43. Is it desirable to let petty criminals continue their criminal activities without any stern action? Compare the treatment of repeaters in Italian law.

---

5.   Accomplices (*Cómplices*)[70]

Those involved in the commission of a punishable act are either principals (*autores*), accessories before the fact (*cómplices*) or accessories after the fact (*encubridores*). *Autores* are those who take direct part in the act, force or induce others to carry it out, or cooperate in its execution so that without their cooperation it would not be carried out. *Cómplices* are those who, without being *autores*, cooperate in the execution of the act by prior or simultaneous acts. *Encubridores* are those who help *autores* profit from the commission of the act by concealing or destroying the evidence of the act in order to prevent its discovery or by sheltering *autores* or enabling them to escape.

Autores are punishable in accordance with the law, *cómplices* by punishment one grade lower than that provided for the completed offense, and *encubridores* by punishment two grades lower than that provided for the completed offense. The above rules apply both to crimes (*delitos*) and infractions (*faltas*).

NOTES AND QUESTIONS

Spanish law applies the theoretical distinction between principals and accessories before and after the fact. This approach is universally recognized by both the civil and the common law. What inroads in the principle have been made? How are the parties to an offense treated with respect to punishment? Compare the German, the Italian, and the French law. May it be said that the distinction between principals and accessories is sound if it can be established as a fact? *See also,* e.g., Texas Penal Code §7.01, and 18 U.S.C.A. §2-4.

---

6. Homicide (*Homicidio*)[71]

Homicide is either parricide, assassination, simple homicide, or negligent homicide.

Parricide (*parricidio*) consists of killing one's father, mother, child or any other ascendant or descendant, legitimate or illegitimate, or one's spouse. The punishment is *reclusión mayor.*[72]

Assassination (*asesinato*) consists of killing a person under one of the following circumstances: by treachery; for hire; by drowning, arson, poison or explosives; with premeditation; or by torture increasing unnecessarily the pain of the victim. The punishment is *reclusión mayor.*[73]

Simple homicide (*homicidio*) is punishable by *reclusión menor.*[74]

Negligent homicide (*muerte a consecuencia de impericia o negligencia*)[75] is punishable by *arresto mayor* or *prisión menor.*[76] Where death is caused by lack of experience or by professional negligence, the punishment is imposed in the highest grade; and in cases of special gravity, it may be increased by one or two grades.

NOTES AND QUESTIONS

1. What different kinds of homicide are known to the Spanish law? How do these kinds of homicide compare with those of the Italian and the German law? Note that the Spanish law specifically lists parricide as does the French law, which lists parricide in Art. 299 of the French Penal Code, and the Italian law, which lists

it in Arts. 576 and 577 of the Italian Penal Code. Parricide is treated as an aggravating circumstance.

2. Does the Spanish definition of assassination differ from that of the French law? Does it come close to the definition of capital murder in the Texas Penal Code §19.03?

3. Simple homicide in Spanish law comes close to the concept of manslaughter in Anglo-American law and to the concept of not further qualified homicide in the civil law. *See,* e.g., Texas Penal Code §19.04.

4. Negligent homicide is now generally recognized in most legal systems. Compare the German and the Italian law. *See also* Texas Penal Code §19.05 on Involuntary Manslaughter and §19.07 on Criminally Negligent Homicide.

---

7.   Wounding and Bodily Harm (*Lesiones*)[77]

Wounding and bodily harm is punishable by *prisión mayor* where the victim becomes weak of mind, impotent or blind in consequence. It is punishable by *prisión menor* and a fine of from 5,000 to 50,000 pesetas where the victim loses an eye or a principal organ of his body or where he is unable to perform work that he heretofore had performed. It is punishable by *prisión menor* where the victim is disfigured or loses a nonessential member of his body or where he is incapacitated for over ninety days. It is punishable by *arresto mayor* and a fine of from 5,000 to 25,000 pesetas where the victim is incapacitated for over thirty days.

Where, however, the offense is committed against a person enumerated in Art. 405 of the Penal Code (mentioned under parricide above) or under the circumstances enumerated in Art. 406 of the Penal Code (mentioned under assassination above), the punishments are increased to *reclusión menor* in the case mentioned first in the above paragraph, to *prisión mayor* and a fine of from 5,000 to 25,000 pesetas in the second case, to *prisión mayor* in the third case, and to *prisión menor* in the fourth case.[78]

NOTES AND QUESTIONS

Wounding and bodily harm covers a vast range of injuries with an equally extensive range of punishments. Compare the gradation of the offense in the French, the Italian and the German law, especially with respect to punishment. Which of the above systems provides for the most severe punishment? How is the matter treated in Anglo-American law? *See,* e.g., Texas Penal Code §22.01ff. Would you agree that severe punishment is proper in cases where injuries are inflicted that leave the victim incapacitated and where he only narrowly escapes death?

---

8.   Theft (*Hurtos*)

Theft is dealt with under the headings of robbery, larceny, and robbery and larceny of the use of motor vehicles.

(a) Robbery (*Robo*).[79]   A person commits robbery when he, with a view to his gain, takes movable property not his own by violence or intimidation of a person or by the application of force against property.

A person guilty of robbery by violence or intimidation of a person is liable to punishment by *reclusión mayor* where homicide occurs in connection with the commission of the crime, where the victim is mutilated, where he becomes weak of mind, impotent or blind in consequence, where the victim is held for ransom or for more than one day, or where the kidnapping of a person is intended; by *reclusión menor* where the victim loses an eye or a principal organ of his body or where he is unable to perform work that he heretofore had performed; by *presidio mayor* where the violence or intimidation applied was manifestly unnecessary to the execution of the crime, or where the victim is disfigured or loses a nonessential member of his body, or where he is incapacitated for over thirty days; and by *presidio menor* in other cases. The above-enumerated punishments are imposed in their maximum grades where the offender makes use of arms or other dangerous means or where he attacks those who come to the victim's aid or those who pursue him.[80] Where the above-enumerated crimes are committed by a fully or partially armed gang of four or more members, the ringleader thereof is punished by the immediately higher punishment. All members of a gang present at the site of a crime committed by it (*en cuadrilla*) are punished as principals (*autores*) unless they prove that they tried to prevent the commission thereof.

Robbery by the application of force against property is committed where one of the following elements is present: scaling of walls; breaking of a wall, roof or ground, door or window; forcing of closets or drawers or closed or sealed containers or their locks, or taking such locked objects away to force them elsewhere; or use of false keys, picklocks and similar instruments. The offender is punished by *arresto mayor* where the value of the property taken does not exceed 2,500 pesetas, with *presidio menor* where it exceeds 2,500 pesetas but does not exceed 25,000 pesetas, and by *presidio mayor* where it exceeds 25,000 pesetas.[81] The punishment prescribed by law is assessed in its maximum grade in any of the following circumstances: where the offender is armed; or where the offense takes place in an inhabited building, a public building, or one used for religious purposes. Where both of the above circumstances occur, the immediately higher punishment is imposed. The punishment is further assessed in its maximum grade where the crime is committed by attacking a train, ship, airplane, automobile or another vehicle; where it is committed against a bank, savings bank, commercial institution or any other institution where valuable papers are held or against persons who keep or transport them.

(b) Larceny (*Hurto*).[82]   A person commits larceny when he, with a view to his gain, without violence or intimidation of a person and without the application of force against property, takes movable property not his own without the consent of its owner. Larceny is also committed by the finder of lost property if he keeps it with a view to his gain; and further by those who keep or use the proceeds of the loss caused in the value indicated below. Offenders guilty of larceny are punished with *presidio mayor* where the value of the property stolen exceeds 100,000 pesetas, with *presidio menor* where it exceeds 25,000 pesetas but is below 100,000 pesetas, with *arresto mayor* where it exceeds 2,500 pesetas but is below 25,000 pesetas, and also where it does not exceed 2,500 pesetas but where the offender has already been con-

victed once of the crime of robbery, larceny, fraud, larceny by a bailee, or the passing
of a valueless check, or where he has already been twice convicted of the infraction of
fraud, larceny, or larceny by a bailee.[83]

Larceny will be punished with punishments immediately higher than those
indicated above where the thing stolen is used in a religious service or where the act
is committed during a religious service or in a building used for such service; where
the offense is committed by a domestic servant, or where there is abuse of
confidence; or where the offender has already been convicted three times of offenses
within the same title of the Penal Code (*reincidencia*).

(c) Robbery and larceny in the use of motor vehicles (*Robo y hurto de uso de
vehículos de motor*).[84] Whosoever uses a motor vehicle not his own without
permission but without an intention to appropriate it is punished with *arresto
mayor* or only with a fine from 5,000 to 50,000 pesetas. Where force against property
is applied, the punishment is assessed in the maximum grade.

Where the offender does not return or abandon the motor vehicle within
twenty-four hours, he will be punished for larceny as per Article 515 of the Penal
Code above where no force against property is applied, and for róbbery as per
Article 505 of the Penal Code above where force against property is applied.

Where violence or intimidation of a person is applied in the act, the
punishment imposed is that provided for in Article 501 of the Penal Code above.

NOTES AND QUESTIONS

1. What is the definition of robbery in Spanish law? How does it compare with
the French, the Italian and the German law? How is robbery defined in
Anglo-American law? *See*, e.g., Texas Penal Code §29.02. Can it be said that robbery
is actually larceny by force? Do the statutory definitions in the various laws refer to
larceny while adding the element of taking by force?

2. Note also the several kinds of robbery foreseen by the Spanish law. Note also
that some kinds of offenses cover the same field covered by housebreaking and
burglary in Anglo-American law.

3. How is larceny defined in Spanish law? Compare the definitions given in
the French, the Italian and the German law. How does the Spanish definition of
larceny compare with that current in Anglo-American law? *See*, e.g., Texas Penal
Code §31.03. Is the punishment usually commensurate with the value of the
property taken?

4. Do penal laws make a routine distinction between the theft or robbery of a
motor vehicle and theft or robbery limited only to the use of a motor vehicle?
Compare the rule of the Spanish law with that of the German law. How does the
law distinguish between the two kinds of taking? Is the Spanish approach, which
makes the distinction depend on the time for which the vehicle is used, meritorious?
As to Anglo-American law, *see*, e.g., Texas Penal Code §31.07.

9. Probation (*Remisión condicional*)[85]

The court may grant probation in pursuance of its own power or by order of law.

In pursuance of its own power (*por si*), the court may grant probation where the offender is first convicted, where he appears properly as summoned, and where the punishment to be imposed for the crime (*delito*) or infraction (*falta*) does not exceed one year of imprisonment whether imposed directly or in conversion of a fine in case of inability to pay. Where the above conditions concur, the court may grant probation after having considered all attending circumstances, such as age and the past life of the offender. Where there is one or more attenuating circumstance, the court may grant probation where the punishment to be imposed does not exceed two years of imprisonment.

The court will grant probation by order of law (*por ministerio de la ley*) where a number of features appear which, if present in full, would have exempted the offender from criminal liability altogether,[86] and also where, in offenses prosecuted privately by the aggrieved person, the offended person requests that probation be granted.

NOTES AND QUESTIONS

Probation is called in Spanish law the conditional remission of punishment. Other civil law countries use similar terminology.

Note that to be eligible for probation, the offender may not have any prior convictions. Further, the offense committed may not be of any gravity since the punishment foreseen by the law may not exceed one or possibly two years. Does the French law apply similar principles? How does the Italian or the German law deal with the matter? Is the Anglo-American approach more favorable to the accused? *See*, e.g., Texas Code of Criminal Procedure, Art. 42.12 B.

---

10. Parole (*Libertad condicional*)[87]

A person sentenced to a term of imprisonment exceeding one year will be considered for parole. He may be paroled after serving three fourths of his term if he merits it by good conduct in prison and gives high hope for good conduct after being set free. The term of parole is the remainder of his term of imprisonment. If he commits an offense or is guilty of objectionable conduct within that time, his parole will be revoked and he will have to serve the time remaining of his sentence, returning to the point of time when he was set free on parole; thus, he will not be given any credit for the time spent on parole.

NOTES AND QUESTIONS

How much time must a convict serve of his sentence to be eligible for parole? Are similar conditions imposed in the French and the German law? *See also* the Texas Code of Criminal Procedure, Art. 42.12 C.

Since the prisoner is paroled for good behavior, he must continue so behaving once out of prison. If he breaks the rules on which he was paroled, his parole will be revoked. The regime of conditional liberty, as parole is called in Spanish law, ends when the remainder of the term has run without revocation. This is a rule common to all systems.

B. THE SYSTEM OF CRIMINAL COURTS

The courts that exercise civil jurisdiction are also invested with criminal jurisdiction so that all that was said about the civil courts in the section on the system of civil courts above applies also *mutatis mutandis* to their criminal jurisdiction with the exception of *audiencias provinciales*, which are chiefly criminal courts. Criminal courts are: courts of the peace (*juzgados de paz*), municipal and country courts (*juzgados municipales y comarcales*), courts of instruction (*juzgados de instrucción*), courts of criminal appeal (*audiencias provinciales*), and the Supreme Court of Justice (*Tribunal Supremo de Justicia*).

1. Courts of the Peace (*Juzgados de paz*)

Courts of the peace are set up in localities where there is no municipal or country court. They are constituted by one justice of the peace, a layman, sitting alone. Their jurisdiction extends only to infractions (*faltas*) against the public order and against the government of their localities, except those infractions that deal with the unauthorized exercise of a profession or are against public health. They also have jurisdiction over specifically enumerated infractions against persons and property, like abusive language, battery, trespass, and cattle trespass. They are supervised by municipal and country courts and their services are honorary.

2. Municipal and Country Courts
(*Juzgados municipales y comarcales*)

They are constituted by one professional judge sitting alone. In the exercise of their criminal authority, their jurisdiction extends to infractions (*faltas*) of any description. An appeal against their judgments may be lodged in the same court at the latest on the day after final notification of the judgment for transmittal to the court of instruction against the decision of which there is no further remedy.

The accused may handle his own defense or he may be represented by an attorney (*procurador*) and by counsel (*abogado*). The public ministry (*ministerio fiscal*), which acts as prosecutor, is represented by officers of the municipal and country procurator (*fiscal municipal y comarcal*).

3. Courts of Instruction (*Juzgados de Instrucción*)

Courts of instruction are the criminal branch of courts of first instance. They are constituted by one judge sitting alone. Their name is derived from their chief function; that is, to act as courts of instruction in cases decided by *audiencias provinciales.* They also have original criminal jurisdiction over minor crimes (*delitos*) that are punishable at the most by *arresto mayor*, the cancellation of a driver's license, or a fine not exceeding a certain amount (50,000 pesetas). They further exercise appellate jurisdiction from judgments of municipal and country courts and courts of the peace. An appeal against their decisions in the exercise of their original jurisdiction lies to an *audiencia provincial* and must be filed within five days from notification of the decision. There is no further remedy against their decisions in the exercise of their appellate jurisdiction.

Cases before the court are prosecuted by the public ministry (*ministerio fiscal*), which is represented by officers of the office of the provincial procurator (*fiscal provincial*). The accused before the court in its original jurisdiction must be represented by an attorney (*procurador*) and by counsel (*abogado*); on appeal from municipal and country courts and courts of the peace, he may appear by himself.

4. Courts of Criminal Appeal (*Audiencias provinciales*)

The name "courts of criminal appeal" does not properly characterize these courts so they will be called rather by their Spanish name, *audiencias provinciales.* They hear appeals from courts of instruction in matters in which these courts exercise original jurisdiction. They also act as trial courts of general jurisdiction in crimes (*delitos*) above those which are tried by the courts of instruction. In these cases, they use judges of instruction (*jueces de instrucción*) to do the instruction, i.e., to prepare the cases for trial.

In addition, they are also invested with some civil jurisdiction, namely, to hear appeals in certain special matters against judgment of courts of first instance and against those of municipal and country courts.[88]

There is one *audiencia provincial* in every province. The court is headed by a president and has presidents of chambers, judges, a court clerk (*secretario*) and further staff. The actual panel hearing a case is composed of three judges. The decision is by simple majority.

The court may hold a plenary session and it is then composed of all the judges and the procurator. The function of the plenary session is nonjudicial, e.g., swearing in judges and advising the government on legislative reforms concerning the judiciary. The court may also sit as a *junta de gobierno*, which is composed of the president, presidents of chambers and the procurator. Its function is administrative, e.g., distribution of business among chambers, supervision of lower courts, and inspection of prisons within its territory. Minus the procurator, the *junta de gobierno* sits as a disciplinary court over all judges and advocates within its territory.

No appeal nor a further appeal lies against decisions of the court, but a petition for cassation of the judgment may be filed with the court within five days from notification thereof for transmittal to the second chamber of the Supreme Court.

The accused must be represented by an attorney (*procurador*) and by counsel (*abogado*). The public ministry prosecuting in the court is represented by the procurator of the *audiencia provincial* (*fiscal de la audiencia provincial*) and his staff.

5. Supreme Court of Justice (*Tribunal Supremo de Justicia*)

Whatever was said on the Supreme Court of Justice under the system of civil courts above applies also to its function in criminal matters.

The criminal business of the Court is handled by its second chamber (*sala segunda*). It is presided over by a president of chamber and has a number of judges on its staff. Cases are heard by panels consisting of five judges. Decision is by simple majority.

The chamber hears petitions for the cassation of judgments for breach of law (*por infracción de ley*) and for breach of form (*por quebrantamiento de forma*) given by *audiencias provinciales*, and further, petitions for the revision of judgments (*recursos de revisión*) given by any criminal court, and matters specially assigned to it, such as disqualification of its own judges to hear a particular case. It further hears, as a trial court, criminal cases against certain enumerated high judges, procurators and officers of state.

The accused must be represented by an attorney (*procurador*) and by counsel (*abogado*). The public ministry prosecuting in the court is represented by the procurator of the Supreme Court (*fiscal del Tribunal Supremo*) and the staff of his office.

NOTES AND QUESTIONS

1. Consider the hierarchy of Spanish criminal courts. Note that, as in other civil law countries, the criminal courts are chiefly the criminal branch of a unified system of civil and criminal courts. Is there any exception to this rule in the Spanish criminal system?

2. Courts of the peace are only of minor importance. Their chief function is to settle minor disputes between neighbors and impose minor fines for breach of the peace.

3. Municipal and country courts are courts of limited jurisdiction. May they be compared with German *Amtsgerichte*, French police courts and Italian praetorial courts? With which Anglo-American courts may they best be compared? *See*, e.g., Texas Code of Criminal Procedure, Art. 4.11, as to justice courts and Art. 4.14, as to corporation courts. What is the composition of municipal and country courts? May the accused handle his own defense or does he require an attorney to defend him?

4. How would you characterize the standing of the courts of instruction within the Spanish system of criminal courts? Can you point to their counterparts in the French, Italian and German systems? Note that they have some original jurisdiction and also an appellate jurisdiction. What is, however, their main function? Do similar courts exist in Anglo-American jurisdictions?

5. Consider the jurisdiction of *audiencias provinciales*. How are they linked with courts of instruction and to what extent do they cooperate? Note that the *audiencia* exercises full criminal powers. What would be its counterpart in the Italian and German court systems? Which Anglo-American criminal court would

best fit into its place in the Spanish system? *See,* e.g., Texas Code of Criminal Procedure, Art. 4.05, as to district courts, and 18 U.S.C.A. §3231, as to United States district courts. What is the remedy against decisions of the *audiencia?*

6. Does the Spanish system have courts of criminal appeal similar to appellate courts in other civil law countries and in common law countries? Which courts in the Spanish system exercise appellate criminal jurisdiction?

7. What is the jurisdiction of the Spanish Supreme Court in criminal matters? Is it purely a court of error? How does it compare with the French and the Italian Courts of Cassation? Compare it with the highest courts in the Anglo-American system of criminal courts.

For judges, prosecutors and attorneys, *see* the section on legal officers below.

C. THE LAW OF CRIMINAL PROCEDURE

The law of criminal procedure is governed by the Code of Criminal Procedure of 1882, which is in power as amended and as supplemented by further statutes. It has 998 articles presented in seven books: Book 1. General provisions; Book 2. Preliminary proceedings; Book 3. Oral proceedings; Book 4. Special proceedings; Book 5. Cassation and revision; Book 6. Proceedings in infractions; and Book 7. Execution of sentences.

Book 1 (General provisions) has the following titles: I. Preliminaries; II. Jurisdiction of judges and courts in criminal matters; III. Disqualification of judges and officers of public ministry; IV. Persons entitled to initiate suits originating from crimes and infractions; V. Right to defense and indigent defendants; VI. Orders and judgments and the breaking of ties; VII. Notifications, citations and dates; VIII. Letters rogatory; IX. Judicial terms; X. Appeals against decisions of judges of instruction; XI. Costs; XII. Duties of judges and courts concerning statistics; and XIII. Disciplinary punishments (contempt).

Book 2 (Preliminary proceedings) has the following titles: I. Information; II. Complaint; III. Judicial police; IV. Instruction; V. Verification of the commission of the offense and identification of the delinquent; VI. Citation, arrest and provisional detention; VII. Bail; VIII. Searches and seizure of documents; IX. Security and attachment of property; X. Civil responsibility of third parties; XI. Closing of preliminary proceedings and the suspension of proceedings; and XII. General provisions applicable to this book.

Book 3 (Oral proceedings) has the following titles: I. Filing of charges; II. Special defenses; and III. Oral proceedings.

Book 4 (Special proceedings) has the following titles: I. Proceedings against senators and congressmen; II. Proceedings prior to the institution of proceedings against judges; III. Summary proceedings for certain offenses; IV. Proceedings for defamation; V. Proceedings for offenses committed by printed letter, recording or other mechanical means of publication; VI. Proceedings for extradition; and VII. Proceedings against absent offenders.

Book 5 (Cassation and revision) has the following titles: I. Cassation; and II. Revision.

Book 6 (Proceedings in infractions) has the following titles: I. Proceedings at trial level; and II. Proceedings at appellate level.

Book 7 (Execution of sentences) is not subdivided in titles.

The following are topics selected from the Spanish law of criminal procedure.

1. Procedure in Courts of the Peace
    (*Juzgados de paz*) and Municipal and Country
    Courts (*Juzgados municipales y comarcales*)

Procedure in both sets of courts proceeds along the same lines.[89]

Whenever the commission of an infraction (*falta*) comes to the attention of a justice of the peace or a municipal or country judge, he will set a hearing within three days, or at a later day if necessary, and will summon the procurator, the civil party, if any, the suspect and the witnesses. Twenty-four hours must elapse between the service of the citation and the hearing where the person cited resides within the municipal limits. One full day is added for each twenty kilometers of distance from the municipal limits. A person who fails to appear may be fined and a new date for the hearing may be set. Also, a person who fails to appear may be brought before the court by force. Together with the citation, a copy of the complaint is served. Parties, including the suspect, who reside outside the circumscription of the court may give their testimony on deposition.

The hearing is open to the public unless it is closed by decision of the court for reasons of morality or public order. At the hearing, the allegations of the civil party, if any, the information, and the record of steps previously undertaken are read first. Then the witnesses are examined and proof requested by the civil party and the informant is made. Then the accused is heard and his witnesses are examined. Thereafter the procurator may speak, if he is present, and following him the civil party and the informer take the floor. Then the accused may speak. He always has the last word. The court makes a detailed record of the proceedings.

Judgment is given at the end of the hearing or within three days thereafter. It gives a summary of the positions taken by the procurator, the civil party, and the accused; it includes the proof taken; and it pronounces the sentence. Where the court finds that the offense committed is, because of the seriousness of the matter, beyond its competence, it will transmit the record to the court of instruction for further proceedings.

Judgments of courts of the peace and municipal and country courts are appealable to the court of instruction. The appeal may be made in writing or orally either to the court clerk or at the time of notification of judgment to the particular court officer who notifies the accused. It must be made at the latest the day after notification of the judgment to the court that pronounced it. The files are then transmitted to the proper court of instruction. Where no appeal is filed, the judgment becomes executory.

NOTES AND QUESTIONS

Since the jurisdiction of municipal and country courts is limited to infractions, the suspect is only rarely arrested; instead, a summons much like that in civil proceedings is issued. The procedure follows that in higher courts, but it is simplified. How does the procedure compare with that in French police courts or that in Italian praetorial courts? Compare it also with the procedure in Anglo-American justice courts, corporation courts or county courts. *See*, e.g., Texas Code of Criminal Procedure, Art. 54.01ff.

---

2. Procedure in Courts of Instruction (*Juzgados de instrucción*)

(a) Appellate proceedings (*Juicio sobre faltas en segunda instancia*).[90] The court hears appeals against judgments of courts of the peace, and municipal and country courts. The court from which the appeal proceeds issues a summons to all parties to file an appearance in the court of instruction within five days. Where the appellant does not file an appearance, the appeal is considered abandoned and files are returned to the court against whose decision the appeal was filed.

Where the appellant files an appearance, parties are summoned for a hearing. Forty-eight hours must elapse between the service of the summons and the time of the hearing.

At the hearing, first the orders made in the case by the court below are read. Then the procurator takes the floor. The presence of the procurator is always necessary where the infraction is one prosecuted ex officio; it is not necessary in cases of private prosecution. Then the appellant and the appellee are heard, if present. Judgment is given immediately at the conclusion of the hearing. If further proof is requested, it must be made within ten days. Only proof that could not have been made in the proceedings below may be made. The proceedings then resume at a date set by the court and judgment is given at the close of the hearing.

Where the appeal alleges breach of form, and the judgment is set aside on that ground, the case is returned to the court below to take it up from the moment when the defect was committed.

After the judgment of the court of instruction is given, the files are returned to the court below for execution thereof.

No further remedy lies against the judgment of the court of instruction.

(b) Original jurisdiction proceedings (*Procedimiento para delitos cuyo fallo compete a los juzgados de instrucción*).[91] In the exercise of their original jurisdiction, courts of instruction prepare cases for final hearing and judgment to be given by the *audiencia provincial*. Here, however, they hold the final hearing and give judgment themselves. The proceedings are also simplified in view of the less serious nature of the crimes prosecuted. An appeal lies to the *audiencia provincial* against their judgments. It must be filed within five days from notification of the judgment.

(c) Preparation of cases for decision of the *audiencia provincial* (*Sumario*).[92]
    (i) INITIATION OF PROCEEDINGS. Proceedings are initiated by information, by notification of the authorities on the part of the victim of crime who may appear as the civil party, or by arrest of the offender in the act. In all cases, notice of the commission of the crime (*delito*) reaches the judge of instruction (*juez de*

instrucción), who notifies the provincial procurator (*fiscal provincial*). The procurator may have already been notified by the police.

The judge of instruction immediately opens preliminary proceedings in the matter, known as the *sumario*, which is conducted in cooperation with the procurator. The judge of instruction proceeds on his own, but he must undertake acts requested by the procurator or by the private party unless he considers such acts useless or prejudicial. Where he denies a request, the ruling may be appealed to the *audiencia provincial* but even if denied there, the request may be renewed at the hearing before the *audiencia provincial.* The proceedings should not last longer than one month and where they have not been concluded within that time, the judge of instruction must give a weekly report to the *audiencia provincial* on the case explaining the reason for the delay so that the *audiencia* may give instructions, if any, for the speedy conclusion of the proceedings. The proceedings are conducted in secret so that the persons involved are not adversely affected. The judge of instruction acts always in the presence of the court clerk (*secretario*), who keeps a record of the proceedings.

Where the crime has left traces of its commission, the judge of instruction inspects the site of the crime and makes a record thereof. He also draws a plan of the place, if convenient, and has pictures taken of the site of the crime and of the victims. The record is signed by the judge of instruction, the procurator, if he was present, the court clerk, and any other persons present. Where the person suspected of having committed the crime is known and the inspection of the site of the crime is made in his presence, he may be represented by counsel and may make his observations, which are included in the record. Any weapons, instruments or objects found at the site of the crime or elsewhere and connected with the crime are impounded. The judge of instruction may appoint experts to advise on such weapons, instruments or objects. Where the victim of crime was injured, the judge of instruction will appoint medical experts to advise on the injuries. Where the victim was killed, an autopsy will be performed by medical experts appointed by the judge of instruction. Where the suspect is known and criminal proceedings have been instituted against him, he may always designate an expert of his choice to participate in the examination with the court-appointed expert or experts.

(ii) **PERSON PROCEEDED AGAINST** (*Procesado*).   Where a person suspected of having committed a crime is known, the judge of instruction will summon such person to appear before him to be heard. If he does not appear, the judge of instruction will issue an order for his detention. Where the suspect is arrested in the act or thereafter, he must be handed over to the judge of instruction or another judge within twenty-four hours. The judge of instruction will order the suspect detained where a crime has been committed for which the criminal code prescribes as punishment a term of imprisonment exceeding six years, i.e., when it exceeds the punishment of *prisión menor,* and where there is reason to believe that the suspect committed that crime. The judge of instruction may order the detention even in the case of a lesser crime unless bail is given. Conversely, the judge of instruction may release the suspect on bail even in the case of a more serious crime where the suspect is a person of good repute and is not expected to abscond.

Those who bring criminal charges against a particular person must properly identify him. The judicial identification is made in a line-up with the suspect surrounded by persons of similar features and appearance. The person bringing the charges is then asked to indicate whether he can see the suspect among those present. He must be able to identify the suspect without any doubt.

Whenever proceedings are instituted against a person, he may immediately appoint counsel to conduct his defense. The person so proceeded against may request the judge of instruction to stop the proceedings. The request, known as the *recurso de reforma,* must be made within three days from notification of the institution of proceedings. Against an order denying the request, an appeal lies to the *audiencia.* It must be filed within five days from the notification of the denial. The *recurso de reforma* lies also against an order of the judge of instruction refusing to institute the proceedings, but no further appeal lies from an order denying the *recurso.*

The judge of instruction must hear the person proceeded against within twenty-four hours after such person is delivered to him. For good reasons, the time to hear the person may be extended for another forty-eight hours. Such reasons must be given in an order making the extension. The person is not sworn in, thus the statement he gives is unsworn. He is only asked to tell the truth. Questions asked by the judge of instruction must be direct, suggestive questions and questions designed to entrap the person are prohibited. No undue influence, threats or force may be applied. Where the handwriting of the person is of importance, the judge of instruction may request him to give a sample of his handwriting. The judge of instruction may hear the person as many times as is required and the person may request to be so heard. The statement is reduced to writing by the court clerk and read to the person. All present then sign the record. Where the person confesses to having committed the crime, the judge of instruction must still proceed and establish the facts irrespective of the confession. Where contradictions appear, the judge of instruction must clear them up by further questioning.

Where the judge of instruction notices that the person proceeded against may suffer from a mental ailment, he must appoint medical experts to examine the person and submit a report. He will also request a record of prior convictions, if any, from the central register of convictions on all persons proceeded against.

(iii) TESTIMONY OF WITNESSES AND EXPERTS. Witnesses are summoned by the judge of instruction. If they do not appear, a fine may be imposed. If they do not appear when summoned again, they may be proceeded against for refusal to give testimony.

Witnesses are heard by the judge of instruction in the presence of the clerk of court; no other person may be present with the exception of an interpreter. They are asked to give their own accounts and only after they have ended may the judge of instruction ask questions to clarify the testimony. The testimony is reduced to writing and the witness is asked to read it, make additions and corrections, if any, and sign it. The testimony is also signed by the judge of instruction and the clerk.

Where contradictions appear in the statements of the person proceeded against and the witnesses, or in those of the witnesses, the judge of instruction may confront them so that such contradictions are cleared up.

Testimony of adult witnesses is given on oath. Minors are not sworn in but are requested to tell the truth.

Ascendants and descendants in the direct line of the person proceeded against are exempted from giving testimony, as are his spouse, brothers, half brothers, sisters, half sisters, and collaterals up to and including the second degree. They may, however, give testimony if they so desire.

Whenever a report by experts is desirable, the judge of instruction may appoint experts by his own decision or at the request of the parties. Two experts are always appointed, normally from among persons holding the government required qualifications for the exercise of a particular profession, science or art. Failing such experts, persons having special knowledge in such fields may be appointed. They may be challenged for cause by the parties. The civil party and the person proceeded against may each appoint an expert who will take part in the expertise. The experts are subject to the same rules as witnesses. The judge of instruction gives them the exact topic of the expertise. The experts are given time to submit a report. When they submit it, the judge of instruction may ask them questions clarifying their conclusions on his own initiative or at the request of the parties. Where the opinions of the two court appointed experts are in conflict, another expert will be appointed to give a report.

(iv) CONCLUSION OF THE PROCEEDINGS. After the judge of instruction undertakes all of the investigation required by law, he will make an order to that effect, has the files transmitted to the *audiencia* for further proceedings, and orders the parties to appear there within ten days. Where he is of the opinion that only an infraction has been committed, he will have his ruling approved by the *audiencia* and order the parties to appear in the proper municipal or country court within five days. The files will be transmitted there for further proceedings.

Where the civil party or the procurator is of the opinion that the judge of instruction has accumulated sufficient material to enable the *audiencia* to proceed, they may make a motion to that effect to the judge of instruction requesting him to conclude his proceedings.

NOTES AND QUESTIONS

1. Consider the appellate procedure on appeal to courts of instruction. It is handled in the simplified form similar to proceedings in municipal and country courts. How does the procedure compare with that on appeal from the *Amtsgericht* to the *Landgericht* in the German criminal procedure? How does it compare with similar procedure in the Anglo-American system? *See*, e.g., Texas Code of Criminal Procedure Arts. 45.10 and 44.01ff.

2. What is the original jurisdiction of courts of instruction and what is the procedure applied? Is it the regular procedure? May it be then compared with procedures used in the French and the German courts of general criminal jurisdiction and with that applied in Anglo-American courts of general criminal jurisdiction?

3. Consider the procedure used in the court of instruction to prepare cases for trial in the *audiencia*.

Note the provisions as to arrest and first hearing before the judge of instruction. Compare, e.g., Texas Code of Criminal Procedure Arts. 14.01ff. and 16.01ff. Note that the person proceeded against may immediately appoint counsel.

The judge of instruction collects the evidence in order to make the case ready for a decision as to whether the person should actually be charged or the proceedings against him stopped. Who will eventually make that decision? Does the Spanish judge of instruction have the same powers as the French or the Italian judge of instruction?

After the judge of instruction has concluded his investigation, he will hand over the files to the *audiencia* for further proceedings.

---

3. Procedure in the *Audiencia Provincial*

(a) Regular proceedings (*Juicio oral*).[93]

(i) PROCEEDINGS PRELIMINARY TO TRIAL. The files received from the court of instruction in the *audiencia provincial* are handed by the court clerk to the rapporteur (*magistrado ponente*). As soon as the time for appearance of the parties has run, the rapporteur hands the files to the procurator for a term of three to ten days as determined by the court; he then hands them for an equal term to the attorneys for the civil party, if any, and to those for the person proceeded against. In involved cases, the term allowed may be doubled, but it may not exceed twenty days. When files are returned to the court clerk, the parties may make motions, e.g., to reopen the proceedings in the court of instruction, to proceed to trial, to suspend the proceedings, and so forth. The files are then handed for a period of three days to the rapporteur, who then reports to the court. The court decides either to confirm the order of the court of instruction to conclude the proceedings, in which case it will within another three days rule on any motion to set the case for trial or suspend the proceedings; or to revoke the order and reopen the proceedings, in which case it will return the files to the court of instruction with directions to take further steps in the preliminary proceedings.

The court will suspend the proceedings where it appears that no offense has been committed or that an offense has been committed but the persons proceeded against did not commit it or are exempt from criminal liability. Where it appears that only an infraction may have been committed, the court will order the case transmitted to the proper municipal or country court. The proceedings will also be suspended where an offense has been committed but there is no one to be linked with it as having committed it (an unknown perpetrator).

The only remedy available against an order suspending the proceedings (*sobreseimiento*) is a petition for its cassation.

At the motion of the person proceeded against, the court may reserve its right to proceed against the civil party for malicious prosecution. The court may also proceed ex officio against the civil party for having made false accusations.

Where an order to proceed to trial is made, the files are handed to the procurator for five days to file the charges; they are then handed for an equal time first to the civil party, who must sign by his attorney (*procurador*) and counsel (*abogado*), and finally to the person proceeded against. Where the person proceeded against has not yet appointed an attorney (*procurador*) and counsel (*abogado*), he must do so now.

In their statements, the parties must indicate the proof they wish to make and give a list of experts and witnesses they wish to call. The proceedings are public from the time the order for trial is made.

The files are handed to the rapporteur for three days to advise. The court then makes an order allowing all proof that it considers proper to be made and rejecting the rest. No remedy lies against admission of proof. Against its rejection, a petition for the cassation of the order may be filed. The court will also set a date for the trial in the same order. The court will order the issuance of citations to parties and witnesses.

(ii) THE TRIAL.   The trial court is composed of the presiding judge and another two judges. The trial is conducted by the presiding judge. He maintains order; he may fine and expell those who disturb and may hand over for prosecution those who commit offenses in the courtroom. Where the accused misbehaves, he may be expelled and the trial may proceed in his absence.

After the trial is opened by the presiding judge and in all cases where the prosecution demands punishment up to *presidio* or *prisión menores* in the scale of punishments taken from below, the presiding judge will ask the accused whether he considers himself guilty of the charge brought against him in writing by the prosecution and whether he considers himself civilly responsible for restitution or for the payment of damages as provided in the statement of the charge by the prosecution.

Where the accused pleads guilty to the criminal charge but denies his civil responsibility or admits it only partially, the proceedings will be concerned only with the responsibility the accused has not admitted. Where the accused pleads not guilty to the criminal charge or does not answer at all, or where the defense counsel so demands, the trial must proceed on all points. This will also occur in all cases where the punishment demanded is *presidio* or *prisión menores* or higher.

The court clerk opens up by reading the charges and giving a summary of the proceedings undertaken up to then. He will then read a list of witnesses and experts summoned.

Witnesses are then called and examined. The rules applicable to witnesses are common to all criminal trials and proceedings before judges of instruction. The witnesses are called in the order given on the list, first those for the prosecution and then those for the defense, but the order may be changed by the presiding judge. Each witness gives his story; after he has concluded, the presiding judge, and with his leave the other judges and parties may ask him questions to clarify the matter. The witness must give reasons for his statements, e.g., he was present when the events took place or he was told by a particular person. No hearsay rule exists. The court will evaluate for itself the evidence given. Where the evidence given differs from what the witness alleged in the preliminary proceedings, the evidence he gave then may be read and an explanation demanded.

The presiding judge will not allow the witness to answer any question that he considers is designed to entrap the witness, is suggestive or is impertinent. A ruling of the presiding judge not to allow a question may be used as a ground for cassation of the judgment eventually given. The party requesting such question to be asked must request the noting of the exact wording of the question in the record, together with the adverse ruling of the presiding judge, so that the record can be reviewed by the court of cassation.

The testimony of witnesses above the age of fourteen is taken on oath. Where the witness refuses to testify, he may be fined; and if he persists, he may be prosecuted for refusal to give testimony.[94]

Experts are heard in accordance with those rules applicable to them in criminal proceedings that are common to criminal trials and proceedings before judges of instruction.

After the proceedings on proof are concluded, the parties may modify their positions as to the classification of the offense alleged to have been committed by the accused. The prosecution may charge the accused with additional offenses and it may upgrade or reduce the charge. If this is done, the parties must file in writing new conclusions in their briefs. An adjournment may then be necessary.

After the parties have complied with the above, or where no change in the position of the parties occurred, the presiding judge invites the procurator to address the court. He will state the facts that he considers have been proved and what offense, in his opinion, has been committed by the accused and what his position is with respect to civil liability. Then counsel for the civil party addresses the court with respect to the civil claim for damages against the accused. Then counsel for the defense takes the floor and, finally, counsel for the party civilly responsible, if any. Thereafter the presiding judge asks the accused whether he would like to address the court, and if the accused so desires, he may speak. Then the presiding judge declares the trial closed.

(iii) JUDGMENT. Judgment is always reserved and it is not given immediately at the close of the proceedings. It must be given within three days. After the presiding judge declares the trial closed, the court retires to consider judgment. Should this come close to the end of usual business hours, the court will meet to consider judgment the first thing on the next business day, or it may decide to continue. The deliberation is held in private. The judgment must resolve all issues raised, including civil liability. The discussion is declared open by the presiding judge and the rapporteur first gives his report and suggests a judgment to be given. Discussion follows on the proposal. After deliberation, the court begins to vote on all of the issues. First the rapporteur votes and then the other judges in inverse order of seniority. The presiding judge votes last. A simple majority is required. Where there are several opinions and a majority is not reached on an issue, a new vote is taken after new discussion. When the next vote is also deadlocked, a new vote is taken with only the two opinions most favorable to the accused voted on. The judgment is then written by the rapporteur. If he is not one of the majority, another judge who voted with the majority will write the opinion. In that case, the rapporteur will write his dissenting opinion. The judgment is then written up by the office in its final form and is signed by all the judges of the panel. It is then communicated to the parties and read by the rapporteur in open court. Once signed, the judgment may not be modified, but errors therein may be rectified on the day after notification at the latest.

The judgment must state the name of the court; the place and the date; the names of the parties; personal information on the accused, such as his age, address, profession and marital status; and the names of the judges with the indication of who acted as rapporteur. The statement of facts determined by the court and the summaries of the positions taken by the parties then follow. Next are numbered sections, beginning with the word *"Considerando,"* dealing with the legal qualifications of those facts the court found as proved, with the participation of the accused in the case, with aggravating and attenuating circumstances or exemption from criminal liability, and with civil liability. Finally the judgment itself is pronounced, absolving the accused of liability or convicting him and imposing punishment. All the counts of the charges must be disposed of.

In every session, the court clerk makes a record of what transpires. At the end of each session, the record is read and is amended or implemented as required by the parties by permission of the court. The record is signed by the members of the court, by the procurator and by counsel for the parties.

(b)   Urgent (summary) proceedings (*Procedimiento de urgencia*).[95]   Prosecution of crimes (*delitos*) punishable with *presidio* or *prisión menores* and *mayores* in which the offender was apprehended *in flagranti* proceeds in accordance with the provisions for urgent (summary) proceedings. The proceedings proceed along the lines set for ordinary proceedings but are simplified in view of the fact that the principle that a person is considered innocent until found guilty cannot apply to the accused with equal force because he was apprehended *in flagranti*. Time allotted to the proceedings is shortened so that it proceeds at a brisker pace. Time allowed for proof and time within which witnesses have to appear is shortened. The order concluding preliminary proceedings (*sumario*) orders the parties to appear in the *audiencia* within five days rather than the regular ten days. Also, an order by the *audiencia* to reopen the *sumario*, if made, can be made only at the request of the procurator. In the *audiencia*, parties studying the files must return them within a shorter time and are fined for every day they delay their return. Where expert testimony is ordered, only one may be appointed.

Against the decisions of the *audiencia*, a petition for cassation lies to the Supreme Court as in regular proceedings, but cases handled in urgent proceedings have preference over those dealt with in accordance with regular proceedings.

NOTES AND QUESTIONS

1. Can the *audiencia* be best described as a trial court of serious offenses? With which French or Italian court could it best be compared? Note that there are no juries in Spanish criminal courts. Note also that proceedings are either regular or summary. Is the justification for summary proceedings well founded?

2. What is the first subject matter of the procedure when the files are received in the *audiencia* from the court of instruction? Consider the procedure by which the court arrives at a decision as to whether the person proceeded against should actually stand trial or be released and the case against him dropped.

3. What is the procedure after the court has ordered the person proceeded against to stand trial? From when on will the proceedings be public? What are the functions of the procurator and the rapporteur? Note that there is no plea bargaining. The process is geared to finding the truth; if it appears that there is enough evidence to charge the person proceeded against with a particular offense, he will be so charged. For Anglo-American law compare, e.g., Texas Code of Criminal Procedure, Arts. 23-32.

4. What is the composition of the trial court and how does it conduct the trial? What are the functions of the presiding judge? In which cases is the accused required to plead (guilty or not guilty)? How is evidence produced in court? Is the evidence given by witnesses on oath? Do the attorneys for the prosecution and the defense question witnesses? Does the hearsay rule apply? Compare trial procedure in German and Italian criminal trials. For Anglo-American law, *see*, e.g., Texas Code of Criminal Procedure, Arts. 33-39.

5. How does the court decide on the judgment? Note the Spanish voting procedure. Compare it with the deliberation and voting procedures in French and German trials. What is the form of the judgment? Is judgment given immediately at the close of the proceedings, or is it reversed? For Anglo-American law, *see*, e.g., Texas Code of Criminal Procedure, Art. 42.

---

4. Procedure in the Supreme Court of Justice (*Tribunal Supremo de Justicia*)[96]

(a) Cassation proceedings (*Recurso de casación*).

(i) PETITION FOR CASSATION OF A JUDGMENT.   A petition for cassation of a judgment lies against all judgments pronounced by *audiencias*. The petition for cassation may be for breach of law, known as *recurso de casación por infracción de ley*, or for breach of form, known as *recurso de casación por quebrantamiento de forma*.

A petition for cassation for breach of law (*por infracción de ley*) may be brought where the lower court infringed a fundamental legal principle or broke a legal norm that must be observed in the application of criminal law, or where in the evaluation of proof it committed an error of fact and the error was not cured.

A petition for cassation for breach of form (*por quebrantamiento de forma*) may be brought where evidence was ruled inadmissible; where a necessary party was not served with process unless he actually appeared; or where the presiding judge directed a witness not to answer a question because it was, in his opinion, improper, designed to entrap, suggestive or impertinent. The petition may further be brought in cases where the judgment does not state clearly which acts were considered established by proof, where there is some contradiction between them, where the court did not rule on all points brought up by the prosecution and the defense, where the accused was convicted of a more serious offense than that with which he was charged, where the trial court was improperly constituted, where the required majority of votes was not obtained, or where a judge who should have disqualified himself took part in the proceedings.

A petition for cassation of a judgment may be filed by the public ministry (*ministerio fiscal*), by all parties and all those who although not parties are made liable in the judgment, and by the heirs of all such parties and persons.

(ii) PETITION FOR LEAVE TO FILE A PETITION FOR CASSATION.   A petition for leave to file a petition for cassation of a judgment must be made in writing, signed by an attorney (*procurador*) and by counsel (*abogado*), to the court that pronounced the judgment within five days from notification thereof on the parties. The petition must request a certified copy of the judgment and must indicate the legal ground for cassation without giving any further reasons.

The court will consider the petition for leave within three days from its filing without hearing the parties. It will grant leave to file the petition for cassation of the judgment whenever the petition for leave was made in time and indicated a legal ground for cassation; otherwise, it will deny the petition for leave.

The order granting leave will direct the clerk to transmit within three days to the second chamber of the Supreme Court a certified copy of the judgment together with any dissenting opinion. The clerk will also forward to the second chamber of the Supreme Court a summary of the record of the case. The order will also summon the parties to appear before the second chamber of the Supreme Court within fifteen days when the court sits in Spain, within twenty days when it sits in the Baleares, and within thirty days when it sits in the Canary Islands.

The judgment does not enter into the power of law until the petition for its cassation is disposed of. Where the judgment was one of acquittal, the accused is set free irrespective of a petition for its cassation. The prosecution of the petition may be abandoned at any time by the petitioner.

Where the petition for leave to file a petition for the cassation of a judgment has been denied, the petitioner may file a complaint (*queja*) against such denial to the same court within two days. The court then orders a certified copy of the order denying the leave to be transmitted to the second chamber of the Supreme Court and issues a summons to the parties to appear there within the time, referred to above, allowed for appearance where leave to file the petition was granted.

Where the complainant does not appear, the second chamber of the Supreme Court will make an order declaring the complaint abandoned and it will confirm the order of the court below denying leave to file a petition for cassation.

Where the complainant appears, he must within the same time file a brief by his attorney (*procurador*) and by his counsel (*abogado*) to substantiate his complaint. The file will be given to the public ministry (*ministerio fiscal*) for three days to submit its brief, and then it will be given to the rapporteur (*magistrado ponente*).

The rapporteur will report to the second chamber and it will rule on the complaint (*queja*) on the basis of the briefs presented without any hearing. Where it grants the complaint, it rescinds the order of the court below denying leave to file the petition for cassation, and it will order the court below to grant the leave and summon the parties to appear before it. Where it dismisses the complaint, it will do so with costs, and where it finds that the allegations of the complainant were untrue, it may fine him in addition. No remedy lies against the order disposing of the complaint (*queja*).

Within the time allowed for appearance, the petitioner must also file his brief by his attorney (*procurador*) and counsel (*abogado*) with the second chamber of the Supreme Court. The brief must state in numbered articles the legal doctrines relied upon for the cassation of the judgment, the articles of the Code of Criminal Procedure on which the petition is founded and which authorize the petition, and the efforts of the petitioner in the court below to remedy the error alleged to have been committed by that court. Where the petitioner does not file his brief in time, the petition is considered abandoned and the second chamber will make an order to that effect with costs.

Where the petitioner files his brief in time, the second chamber will appoint a rapporteur and will direct the clerk to prepare within ten days a record of the proceedings, which must include an exact copy of the part of the judgment complained of, a summary of the petition for cassation and anything of importance for the decision of the petition. Within the same time, the parties may challenge the granting of the leave to file the petition for cassation. Where this is done, a separate brief attacking the granting of the leave must be filed with as many copies as there are parties. All parties may, within three days after receiving such brief, file their answer thereto. The petitioner may state in his brief that he does not require the second chamber to hold a hearing; in such a case, the other parties must state whether they agree or disagree.

After all of the above is concluded, the record and briefs are added to the files and they are passed to the rapporteur for his study for ten days. Immediately after hearing the report of the rapporteur, the second chamber will make an order on the admissibility of the petition. It will either admit the petition for decision on the merits with or without a hearing, or it will deny admission. To deny admission, the decision of the five-judge panel of the second chamber dealing with the case must be unanimous. Admission will be denied when, in the opinion of the panel, the petition is not well founded on the articles of the Code of Criminal Procedure that authorize the petition or where the petitioner has not made any effort to bring the error to the attention of the court that committed it. The decision to admit the petition for decision without a hearing must also be unanimous.

No remedy lies against the decision admitting or denying the petition.

(iii) PROCEEDINGS ON THE PETITION FOR CASSATION. Where the second chamber admits the petition for decision without a hearing (because the parties have not requested it), it will give judgment within ten days.

Where it admits the petition for decision after a hearing, it will set a day for the hearing. The hearing is public. Should the defense counsel fail to appear, the court may proceed in his absence if it so desires. The panel hearing the case has five judges.

The hearing is opened by the clerk (*secretario*) who gives a summary of the case. Then counsel for the petitioner takes the floor and following him counsel for any other party who has joined in the petition. Thereafter counsel for the respondent addresses the court. The public ministry is either petitioner or respondent, and it is subject to the same rules of procedure, whether it appears on one side of the case or the other, as any other party. The presiding judge and other judges may ask questions and counsel must reply. All parties may speak again in the same order to clarify their respective positions in view of statements made by others. Only issues of law may be discussed and no questions of fact may be raised. The presiding judge then declares the hearing closed.

The court must give judgment within ten days. It may, however, at the suggestion of the rapporteur or on its own motion, require the court that gave the judgment now challenged to submit the entire record of the case; if so, the ten-day limit will not apply, in order to enable the panel to study the case further.

Judgment is given in accordance with the rules of the Code of Criminal Procedure that are discussed above in the section on procedure in the *audiencia provincial.*

The judgment is headed "Second Chamber of the Supreme Court." It gives the date, the offense prosecuted, the names of parties, the name of the court that gave the judgment, the case number, and the name of the rapporteur handling the case. It further relates all the facts found as proved by the court below, the reasons for the petition for cassation of the judgment alleged by the petitioner, the reasons for the decision, and finally the decision itself.

Where the court grants the petition, having found it substantiated, it will annul the judgment with costs. Where it denies the petition, not having found any grounds for granting it, it will do so with costs. Costs of the case, however, may not be imposed on the public ministry; thus, where the public ministry loses the case, each party pays its own costs.

Where the judgment of the court below is annulled because of breach of form, the Supreme Court will remit the case to the same court that pronounced the judgment to cure the defect and proceed on from the moment when the error was committed. Where both error of form and error of law are alleged, and the Supreme Court finds no error of form but an error of law, it will so rule and it will grant the petition on that ground. Where the petition is granted because of breach of law, the Supreme Court will separately give a new judgment in the case in accordance with the law, but it cannot increase the sentence embodied in the petition for cassation.

Where the accused is the petitioner and the new judgment is given in his favor, all other codefendants in the same position are benefited thereby.

No further remedy lies against the decision of the Supreme Court. The judgment of the Court is then published in the law reports known as the *Colección Legislativa.*

(b) Revision proceedings (*Recurso de revisión*).[97] Revision proceedings are held before the second chamber of the Supreme Court and follow the rules prescribed for the proceedings for cassation of judgments for breach of law.

The petition may be filed without any time limit on the following grounds: where two or more persons are convicted of an offense that could not have been committed by more than one person; where the accused is convicted in connection with a homicide and the alleged victim is found alive; where the conviction is founded on documentary evidence or testimony which was in later criminal proceedings found to have been false, or where a confession was obtained by improper means; and where new evidence comes to light which establishes the innocence of the person convicted.

The petition may be filed by the person convicted and also by his spouse, descendants and ascendants, both during the lifetime of the convicted person and also after his death. It is filed with the ministry of justice (*ministerio de justicia*). The ministry may then order the procurator of the Supreme Court (*fiscal del Tribunal Supremo*) to bring the petition before the second chamber of the Supreme Court, but the procurator may do so on his own initiative whenever facts meriting the filing of a petition for revision of a judgment come to his attention.

Where the innocence of the convicted person is established, the second chamber will annul the conviction, and it will instruct the court that pronounced the judgment to proceed in the matter further where someone else has actually committed the offense. The person falsely convicted has a claim for compensation against the state, but the state may recover against the judge or judges who pronounced the sentence or against the person or persons found responsible for the conviction.

NOTES AND QUESTIONS

1. On which ground may a petition for the cassation of a judgment be brought? Note the distinction between breach of law and breach of form. Considering the grounds for cassation, would you say that the opportunity for bringing a petition is very great? May an appeal be brought against judgments of the *audiencia*? Who may file a petition for cassation? Compare the French and Italian procedures. For Anglo-American procedure, *see*, e.g., Texas Code of Criminal Procedure, Art. 44.

2. Note that a leave to bring the petition is necessary. What is the procedure on the petition to obtain such leave? Which court will eventually decide whether the leave will be granted?

3. Where the petition for cassation is admitted, must an oral hearing actually be held? If there is a hearing, how does it proceed? How is the judgment of the court arrived at? If the court sets aside the judgment of the court below, will it give a new judgment or will it remit the case to the court below?

4. Note the procedure on a petition for the revision of a judgment. Is there any time limit imposed within which the petition must be brought? Who may file the petition? Compare the French, Italian and German proceedings. As to Anglo-American law, *see*, e.g., F.R.Crim.P. Rule 33.

---

5. Bail (*Libertad provisional*)[98]

Bail may be granted by the judge or the court handling the case where a suspect is proceeded against for a crime (*delito*) which is punishable by punishment below that of *prisión menor* and he does not appear to be unlikely to show up when summoned. Bail may be granted in the case of infractions (*faltas*). The judge or court may admit a person to bail with or without a security. The order granting or denying the petition is communicated to the petitioner, the public ministry, and other parties, if any, and is appealable to the proper superior court.

Where the suspect is proceeded against for an offense committed by driving a motor vehicle and is free on bail, the judge may provisionally impound his driver's license so as to prevent him from driving.

The type and value of the security is determined in accordance with the nature of the offense committed, the economic position of the suspect, and any other circumstances that may have a bearing on the possibility of his not appearing when required. The security may be in money or valuables, movables or immovables, actually owned by the suspect or by another person who would vouch for his appearance.

The suspect who is unable to meet the terms of bail is held in jail unless the judge orders his release without bail.

Where the suspect is released on bail and does not appear when summoned without a valid excuse, the court will forfeit the security. Where there is a person vouching for the accused, he will be ordered to produce him within ten days, and where he does not comply, the security will be forfeited. Such person has no recourse against the state for having forfeited the security, but he may claim the value thereof from the suspect. Property other than money given as security will be sold by public auction upon its forfeiture.

Bail will also come to an end where the person vouching for the suspect so requests and produces him at the same time, where the suspect is put in jail, where proceedings against him are discontinued, or where he dies.

NOTES AND QUESTIONS

What is the purpose of bail in Spanish law? Is it the same as in Anglo-American law? *See,* e.g., Texas Code of Criminal Procedure, Art. 17.01. Is the person proceeded against actually required to give security or may he be released without giving any security? How does bail in Spanish law compare with bail in the French, the Italian and the German law?

Compare also 18 U.S.C.A. §3141ff.; F.R.Crim.P. Rule 46; and Texas Code of Criminal Procedure, Art. 17.

IV.　THE SYSTEM AND ADMINISTRATION OF ADMINISTRATIVE LAW

A.　THE SUBSTANTIVE ADMINISTRATIVE LAW

The Spanish administrative law is composed of a great number of statutes and regulations. It governs the relations between the state as the holder of public authority and the citizens. It embraces the wide area of public administration, including central, intermediate and local administrative bodies; public servants; the police; mails and telecommunications; transport; highways, waterways, maritime and aerial navigation; tourism; hotels and restaurants; markets; hunting and fishing; gas and electricity; public welfare; publice health; public property; printing and the press; public education; and taxation.

Many leading statutes, together with further regulations and orders dealing with a given area of law, are published in separate publications. They are sometimes referred to as codes, e.g., The Code of Food Supply (*Código Alimentario*), or the Code of Traffic (*Código de la Circulación*). Sometimes all the provisions pertaining to a particular subject are consolidated in one publication, like the Laws of Eminent Domain (*Expropriación Forzosa*), the Mining Laws (*Ley y Reglamento de Montes*), or the Civil Register (*Registro Civil*).

The following are topics selected from the Spanish substantive administrative law.

1. Spanish Code of Food Supply (*Código Alimentario Español*)

All food supplied in Spain is regulated by the above code.[99] The Code deals with food, seasonings, stimulants, and beverages; with the substances from which the above are made; and with all the substances used for human and animal consumption. The Code defines those substances and sets minimum standards for foods. It also sets standards to be observed in the manufacture, preparation, conservation, distribution and transport of food. The provisions of the Code are very detailed and call for strict observance. The Code is administered by the administrative system.

The Code has five parts: 1. General provisions; 2. General rules applicable to substances, processing and personnel dealing with food, food establishments and food industries; 3. Food and beverages; 4. Additives and impurities in foodstuffs; and 5. Animal feed and products related to food, like fertilizers and pesticides, cosmetics, soaps, candles, and so forth. The Code is further subdivided into chapters and sections.

The Code provides that all foodstuffs must be made from substances authorized by the Code; that they must be kept and transported so as not to enter in contact with toxic substances or be contaminated; that no foreign substances may be added to foodstuffs or beverages, except as approved; that additives may not exceed the permitted limit; and that the stated composition of foodstuffs and beverages may not be altered.

Chapter 30, Section 3, of the Spanish Code of Food Supply deals with wine. It defines wine as an alcoholic beverage produced by the total or partial fermentation of fresh grapes or their must. Wine is ordinary, mixed, green or special. Ordinary wine is produced by the fermentation of must without any special treatment. It must contain at least 9 percent of alcohol by volume. Mixed wine is that which is obtained by mixing different wines which, by being so mixed, lose their individual character. Green wine is made by the usual process of fermentation of must, but of grapes that due to climate or weather conditions do not properly ripen. Its alcoholic content may fall below 9 percent by volume. Special wines are such by their specific properties, the types of grapes used, or the technique of their making. Special wines are: fine table wine, dry wine, sweet wine, liquor wine, sparkling wine, soda wine and rough wine.

Fine table wine is dry or sweet and it is made by the application of special skills and techniques. Its sugar content is prescribed; it may not exceed 14 percent of alcohol by volume. Dry wine is produced by traditional methods with the optional addition of further wine alcohol. Its alcoholic content must exceed 14 percent by volume and its sugar content must be below 5 grams per liter. Sweet wine is produced by traditional methods with the optional addition of further wine alcohol. It must contain at least 17 percent alcohol by volume and 50 grams of sugar per liter. Liquor wine is that to which, in addition to wine alcohol, further concentrates are added. The greater part of its alcoholic content, however, must originate from the fermentation of sugar in the must. Its alcoholic content may vary between 14 and 23 percent by volume, and it must contain a minimum of 150 grams of sugar per liter.

Sparkling wine is usually made inside a bottle. On opening, it produces a lasting natural fine foam caused by the loosening of carbonic acid gas from the second fermentation of the natural sugar of wine or of additives. The pressure inside the bottle must be at least of 4 atmospheres at 20 degrees centigrade of temperature. Sparkling wine may also be produced in large containers and then bottled. Soda wine has a foam which is produced by the loosening of carbonic acid gas added to it in the process of production. Rough wine is that which, because of the type of grapes used or because of the technique of its making, retains a part of its carbonic acid gas from the fermentation. On opening, it sparkles mildly without producing a lasting foam.

There also are aromatic wines, which must contain at least 75 percent of wine with the remainder additives. Their alcoholic content is between 15 and 18 percent by volume. Their dry extract may not fall below 50 grams per liter, with the exception of dry vermouth. Their total sugar content may not fall below 40 points of saccharosis per liter, with the exception of dry vermouth. Aromatic wines are then called in accordance with the flavor added.

NOTES AND QUESTIONS

Note that the Spanish Code of Food Supply governs the entire production of food and beverages as well as the production of related products for human use. It also regulates production of animal feed. It actually sets standards to be maintained. In that, it is similar to legislation in all countries. Note especially the provisions dealing with wine since Spain is a significant wine growing and producing country. How do the Spanish provisions compare with the U.S. Federal Food, Drug, and Cosmetic Act? *See*, 21 U.S.C.A. §301ff.

----

2.   Spanish Universities (*Universidades españolas*)

Spanish universities are governed by the General Law of Education[100] and by further statutes. The General Law of Education governs all education, university education being a part thereof.

The highest organs in education are the ministry of education and its advisory body, the National Council of Education (*Consejo Nacional de Educación*), and as far as university education is concerned, the National Board of Universities (*Junta Nacional de Universidades*).

The National Board of Universities is composed of the rectors and chairmen of the boards of trustees (*presidentes de patronatos*) of all universities. It is presided over by the Minister of Education or his deputy. It has its own secretariat headed by the secretary of the board. The board functions in a general assembly, as a permanent commission, and as preparatory committees. In a general assembly, the board must be consulted by the ministry of education on university planning; creation or dissolution of universities; creation or dissolution of faculties, schools and departments in the universities; or distribution of funds among the universities. It must give its advice on any topic submitted to it by the Minister.

The permanent commission is composed of all rectors. It must be consulted on matters of standards required for the attainment of university degrees, on equivalents with foreign degrees, on agreements universities may enter into with other entities, on appointment committees in the process of selection of university teachers, on appointments of chairholding professors, on university regulations. It will advise on any matter submitted to the National Board of Universities that is not submitted to the general assembly for its consideration.

Preparatory committees are working groups engaged in research. They submit their studies to the general assembly or the permanent commission.

Individual universities are autonomous bodies, with legal personalities and full legal capacities. They handle their own financial matters. Each is governed by a special statute regulating its organization, structure, proceedings and rules. The National Board of Universities coordinates their actions.

The highest officer of a university is the rector. He is elected by chairholding professors from among themselves in accordance with the university statute and is then appointed by the Minister of Education. He holds his office for a term determined in the university statute, usually three years. The rector directs and supervises all university activity. There also are two or more vice rectors appointed by the Minister of Education from among chairholding professors at the proposal of the rector. The university has a head of its financial management, the general manager (*gerente*), who is appointed by the Minister of Education by agreement with the rector and after hearing from the board of trustees (*patronato*).

The deans (*decanos*) are heads of the various faculties. They are in charge of the academic aspect of university education. They are elected by the chairholding professors in a given faculty from among themselves in accordance with the university statute. They are then appointed by the Minister of Education. There also are one or more vice deans in every faculty, appointed by the Minister from among chairholding professors in the faculty at the proposal of the dean. The term of their office, usually three years, is determined in the university statute.

Directors of university institutes are appointed by the Minister of Education from among chairholding professors of that university at the proposal of the rector in accordance with the university statute. Directors of university colleges are appointed in the same way. The university has a secretariat headed by the secretary-general.

The basic unit in university education is a department. Every department is integrated in a particular faculty. It is headed by a director. He must be a chairholding professor. If there are two or more chairholding professors within a department, the rector appoints one of them director after hearing from the university council (*junta de gobierno*). There also is a departmental council (*consejo*), which is constituted by all chairholding professors in the department and by representatives of the other professors and doctoral candidates in the department. The departmental council meets not less than every three months within the school year. It is an advisory body to the director.

In addition to the above unipersonal organs, the university has collegiate organs, namely, the board of trustees (*patronato*), the university assembly (*claustro*), and the university council (*junta de gobierno*).

The board of trustees serves as liaison between the university and the general public. Through it, the general public may participate in university life. It has not more than twenty members appointed in accordance with the university statute by the Minister of Education from among persons of local importance active in local government, members of Parliament representing the area, professional organizations, trade organizations, associations of parents of students, students, alumni, and other persons suggested by the board of trustees itself or by the university council. All must reside within the area. The president of the board may not hold public office in the area. The functions and powers of the board are regulated by the university statute. The board is advisory to the rector.

The university assembly (*claustro*) is the highest collegiate organ of the university. It is regulated by the university statute as to its composition and function. It is generally composed of all chairholding professors and of representatives of all other professors and students. It acts in assembly or in committees. Its function is advisory to the rector.

The university council (*junta de gobierno*) advises the rector on a day-to-day basis. It is constituted as provided in the university statute. Generally, it is composed of the rector, who presides over its meetings, and of all vice rectors, deans, and directors of institutes, and representatives of students. The council may invite any officer of the university to participate when such participation may benefit the meeting. These same three collegiate organs are reproduced on a faculty level in every faculty as a commission of the board of trustees (*comisión del patronato*), the faculty assembly (*claustro de la faculdad*), and the faculty council (*junta de faculdad*).

Students participate in the university government at all of its levels. They elect their representatives by secret, direct ballot from among themselves. Elections are held the first month of the school year. They are regulated by the university statute. Generally, each class elects three representatives to represent it before the professor teaching a course. They then, in the second month, elect from among themselves representatives to the university collegiate organs, first within the department and faculty and then within the whole university. Students are covered by health and social security insurance. They enjoy full academic freedom.

Admission to study is regulated in accordance with the particular subject of study by the general law of education and further provisions, and by the university statute of each university. An applicant must hold the bachelor's degree (*bachillerato*) or its equivalent and successfully conclude an admission course (*curso de orientación*). Those who pass the course are admitted as regular students (*alumnos oficiales*); those who do not pass it may enter as external students (*alumnos libres*). External students may not attend classes, tutorials, and the like, but must study externally and submit themselves to examinations in order to receive their degrees.

The study is conducted in three phases or cycles (*ciclos*). The first cycle takes three years of basic study and the second two years of specialization. The third cycle is the academic preparation for teaching and is purely optional.

Those who conclude the study of the first cycle plus additional required professional courses, and those who conclude their studies in a particular university school (*escuela universitaria*), receive their diplomas and the title of *Diplomado* or Technical Engineer (*Ingeniero Técnico*) or Technical Artist (*Arquitecto Técnico*). Those who conclude the second cycle obtain the full university degree of *Licenciado, Ingeniero* or *Arquitecto*. Those who conclude the third cycle, which requires the presentation of a thesis, receive the degree of *Doctor*.

Classes are held in every subject, followed by tutorials in small groups where the discussion method is applied and tests are conducted. Students are graded in tutorials and their grades are computed into their final examination results, which are of a supplementary nature only.

Professors are: (1) chairholding professors (*catedráticos*), (2) professors (*profesores agregados*), (3) adjunct professors (*profesores adjuntos*), and (4) assistant professors (*profesores ayudantes*). Their selection is governed by the general law of education and further provisions and by the university statute of a particular university. Generally, chairholding professors are selected by a university appointments ccommittee in public competition. First preference is given to chairholding professors from the particular university or other universities who enter in the competition. If no one is so selected, professors who apply are considered. Professors are selected similarly, with first preference given to professors from that or other universities; if no selection is so made, candidates who have doctorates in their specialties and have taught in their specialties in a university or have engaged in research for at least four years may be selected. Adjunct professors are selected similarly from among applicants who hold doctorates in their specialties and have taught as assistant professors for at least two years or have engaged in research in an equivalent capacity. Assistant professors are selected from among candidates who have full degrees in their specialties and adequate experience, and who are successful in tests administered by the university. All selections are made strictly on academic merit.

As far as their decision-making process is concerned, universities fall within the framework of the administrative system and are subject to administrative review. Their decisions are subject to an appeal by the proper party to the National Council of Education (*Consejo Nacional de Educación*), with a further appeal to the ministry of education and administrative courts.

NOTES AND QUESTIONS

The Spanish system of university education is similar to that existing in other civil law countries. Universities are state owned and maintained; however, they are fully autonomous and are regulated by statutes and regulations. The system is merit oriented, which means that it relies on qualifications that may be objectively determined by examinations. Note the appointment of university teachers, which is strictly on qualifications of a national competition. The whole system is a part of the administrative system with full recourse to administrative courts.

What is the highest organ of education in Spain? How are rectors and deans elected and for how long may they stay in office? Note that since the universities and their individual schools are regulated by law and university statutes, the internal government falls entirely to the faculty and students. The terms of rectors and deans are short so as to allow all professors to share in the honor. The system is designed to promote independent scientific research and teaching, headed by nationally recognized specialists who themselves had to progress through the system on merit.

How does the Spanish system of higher education differ from that in Anglo-American countries? Compare, e.g., 20 U.S.C.A., Chapter 21—Higher Educational Facilities; and the laws of the individual states, e.g., Texas Public Education, V.A. Civ. St. Art. 2584 on the University of Texas.

---

3. Eminent Domain (*Expropriación forzosa*)

Eminent domain is governed by the statute on the subject, by regulations issued thereunder, and by further provisions.[101] Expropriation of property may be had on the ground of public utility or social need and for an adequate compensation, which must be paid prior to the taking. Both immovables and movables may be expropriated.

(a) **General safeguards** (*Principios generales*). The Spanish Constitution of 1978, Art. 33(3),[102] provides that an act of eminent domain may be undertaken only for purposes of public utility or social need and for proper compensation to be paid before the taking, both in conformity with the law. Only the state, the province, and the municipality have the power of eminent domain.

(b) **Proceedings** (*Procedimiento*). The proper authority must first obtain a declaration of public utility or social need with respect to the piece of property it wishes to expropriate. In the case of immovables, the declaration must be made in the form of a statute passed by Parliament (*Cortes*). The same applies in the case of movables; but if a statute has already provided for the expropriation of movables of particular description, a decision by the council of ministers suffices with respect to a particular piece.

The declaration made, the beneficiary of the expropriation—the state, province or municipality, their agencies, entities or public utilities— must submit a detailed request outlining the project and dealing with all aspects of the taking and the rights involved. The request is submitted to the office of the governor of the province, which will hold public hearings on the matter within fifteen days of its receipt. Notice of the hearings is given in the proper official gazettes and in the daily press. Any person may attend and challenge the proposed expropriation on merit or on form. After the hearings are concluded, the governor will decide within twenty days in a written, reasoned decision on the necessity for the taking, on the property subject to it, and on the right of ownership, identifying those having legal interest therein. Where the decision approves of the expropriation, the approval will indicate the actual proceedings of expropriation. The decision is published in the same way as the original notice and those having legal interest in the property are served personally.

Those having legal interest and all those who actually challenged the taking at the hearings may appeal the decision to the proper ministry within ten days from the notification. The appeal suspends further proceedings. The ministry will rule on the appeal within twenty days, and no further appeal may be taken at this stage of the proceedings.

The next step is the determination of the proper compensation. The parties may now agree on the proper price and the owner may sign a transfer of title. This may take place at any later time. Where no agreement is reached within fifteen days, proceedings to determine proper compensation are initiated before the proper expropriating authority, whether state, provincial or municipal. The authority will send a request to the owner for a substantiated claim of value to be submitted to it within twenty days. It should be supported by opinion of expert valuers. The expropriating authority must within twenty days either accept or reject the claim so submitted. If accepted, the value is finally determined. If rejected, the authority must at the same time submit to the owner its valuation, which the owner may accept or reject within ten days. Where he rejects it, he should state his reasons. The matter is then submitted to the provincial jury of expropriation (*jurado provincial de expropriación*) for decision.

(c) Provincial jury of expropriation (*Jurado provincial de expropriación*). A provincial jury of expropriation is set up in the capital of every province. It is presided over by a judge appointed by the president of the local *audiencia* and has another four members: the legal counsel (*abogado del estado*) of the local delegation of the ministry of finance (*ministerio de hacienda*); a technical expert appointed by the provincial office dealing with the subject, e.g., an agronomist, a highway engineer, a hydraulic or mining engineer, or an architect; an officer of the National Council of Trade; and a notary appointed by the local chamber of notaries.

The provincial jury on expropriation must decide within eight days, and in involved cases within fifteen days, from the submission to it of the matter. It studies all the documents, inspects the property and considers the arguments of the parties. It decides by majority vote. The decision determining just compensation must be reasoned, giving in detail the criteria followed. Its decision terminates proceedings before administrative organs and leaves the parties to take the case to administrative courts in case they do not wish to abide by its decision.

(d) Payment and taking of possession (*Pago y toma de posesión*). Where the just compensation is finally determined, the expropriating authority may within six months pay it to the owner as a condition precedent to taking possession and take possession. The sum paid is free of any tax whatsoever. Where the owner refuses to accept the money, it is paid into the proper court deposit for him. A certificate of payment is drawn up, and upon the actual taking of possession, a certificate of taking possession is drawn up. These two documents are sufficient to register the transfer of title in the proper register.

Should the authority fail to act within the above-mentioned period of six months, the expropriation lapses. Should the authority fail to carry out the project for which the property was expropriated, the owner or his successor may recover the property upon refund of the compensation. The administration will, of its own initiative, notify the owner that it has abandoned the project and that he may, if he so wishes, recover his property. If more than two years have run since the expropriation when the project is abandoned, and the owner wishes to recover his property, special rules provide for the refund of the compensation, the payment of lost revenue, and damages, if any, etc., by the authority to the owner.

The usual reason for expropriation is the need of land for the construction of roads and other public works.

NOTES AND QUESTIONS

Spanish laws on eminent domain are very similar to those in other civil law countries. Compare the French law on eminent domain.

What are the steps to be taken to obtain expropriation of property? On what ground may property be expropriated? Which authorities have the power to expropriate property? Where property is expropriated, what is the procedure to determine proper compensation? What is the function of the provincial jury of expropriation? Note that the system of eminent domain falls within the administrative system and decisions are subject to appeal to administrative courts.

How does the Spanish law of eminent domain compare with the Anglo-American law on the subject? *See,* e.g., the Uniform Eminent Domain Code and the individual state laws on eminent domain. Compare, e.g., the Texas Law of Eminent Domain, V.A. Civ. St. Art. 3264ff.

B. THE SYSTEM OF ADMINISTRATIVE AUTHORITIES (OFFICES AND COURTS)

Administrative authorities are local (communities and cities), intermediate (the provinces), and central (the highest offices of public administration, like ministries and the head of the state). Administrative courts are of two levels. The administrative tribunals are at the lower level, and the Supreme Court in the exercise of its administrative jurisdiction, is at the final level. In addition, there are several administrative courts exercising jurisdiction over matters specially assigned to them by law.

1. Local Administration[103]

Local administration is conducted on three levels according to the size of the community. There are localities, municipalities, and large cities.

(a) Localities (*Entidades locales menores*).   These are very small localities. The head of the locality is the mayor (*alcalde pedáneo*), who is assisted by the council (*junta vecinal*). The council is presided over by the mayor and has two councilors (*vocales*). They are elected and function like their counterparts in the municipalities.

(b) Municipalities (*Municipios*).   Municipalities are the fundamental entities of local public administration. Local government embodies the principles of local autonomy and of central administration. The authorities of the municipality are: the mayor (*alcalde*), the municipal council (*ayuntamiento*), and the permanent commission (*comisión permanente*), which is set up in municipalities of over five thousand inhabitants only.

The mayor (*alcalde*) is the head of the municipality. He is also the head of the municipal council (*ayuntamiento*), of the permanent commission (*comisión permanente*), and of the municipal administration (*jefe de la administración municipal*). The mayor must be Spanish, twenty-five years of age, of full capacity, without a criminal record, and a local resident. The mayor is elected for a term of four years by the city councilors from among themselves by secret ballot. To be elected, the candidate must receive an absolute majority of the votes of all councilors. The office carries no stipend and is honorary. In municipalities with over ten thousand inhabitants, the municipal council may grant the mayor his incurred expenses in a fixed sum not exceeding one percent of the city income. The mayor is the head and representative of the municipality in all its dealings.

The municipal council (*ayuntamiento*) is the highest organ of the municipality; it represents and personifies the municipality. It is presided over by the mayor and is composed of a number of councilors (*consejales*) and of a secretary (*secretario*). The number of councilors varies with the size of the municipality, from a minimum of six to a maximum of thirty-six. They must be local residents of full age and capacity, with no criminal record. They may be either men or women. The incompatibilities and excuses for holding the office of councilor are similar to those applicable to the office of the mayor. The office is honorary, but they are entitled to expenses.

Councilors are elected for a four-year term in municipal elections by direct and secret ballot.

The municipal council (*ayuntamiento*) is presided over by the mayor. He calls the meetings and has a casting vote in case of a tie. He must carry out the decisions of the council. The council is the legislative body of the municipality. It approves all city ordinances and budgetary provisions, but it also has many administrative functions; that is, the administration of municipal property, acquisitions and sales, city planning, building and eminent domain, all financial matters, administration of public services, and so forth.

The permanent commission (*comisión permanente*) is set up only in municipalities with over five thousand inhabitants. It is presided over by the mayor and is composed of all deputy mayors (*tenientes de alcalde*) appointed in the municipality. One deputy mayor is appointed for every municipal district, (*distrito municipal*). Where there is only one district, two deputy mayors are appointed; but in cases where the municipality has no permanent commission because it does not comply with the over five thousand inhabitants requirement, only one deputy mayor is appointed. Deputy mayors are appointed by the mayor from among the councilors. There may not be more deputy mayors than one third of the councilors. The permanent commission must attend to all urgent business that cannot be immediately handled by the municipal council. It also has administrative functions of its own, namely, the supervision of the daily operations of the municipal administration. Deputy mayors assist the mayor in his office and are his substitutes. The mayor may delegate to them the performance of his functions.

(c) Large cities (*Grandes ciudades*). There are four large cities in Spain: Madrid, Barcelona, Bilbao and Valencia.[104] Only Madrid and Barcelona have some special features in their city governments that differ from the rules governing the municipalities referred to above.[105] Unless otherwise provided, the rules governing municipalities apply. The special features are, however, nearly identical for both Madrid and Barcelona.

In Madrid, the organs of city administration are: the mayor (*alcalde*), deputy mayors (*tenientes de alcalde*), the full municipal council (*ayuntamiento pleno*), the commission of municipal government (*comisión municipal de gobierno*), and municipal district councils (*juntas municipales de distrito*).

There are three deputy mayors and they are appointed as first, second and third deputy mayors. They substitute for the mayor in that order. There are fifty-nine city councilors (*consejales*). The public services provided by the city are grouped in six divisions, each of which is headed by a *delegado de servicios* appointed by the mayor. These six *delegados* together with six municipal councilors designated by the municipal council, all three deputy mayors, and the presiding mayor form the commission of municipal government.

There is one municipal district council in every district. It is composed of municipal councilors elected in that district.

In Barcelona, the full municipal council is termed *consejo pleno* rather than *ayuntamiento pleno*, and the municipal commission is termed *comisión municipal ejecutiva* rather than *comisión municipal de gobierno*. The city councilors who sit on the *comisión municipal ejecutiva* are designated by the mayor rather than by the municipal council.

In addition, in both cities, special commissions are set up to facilitate relations with the ministries of central administration, like the planning commission and the commission of urban development. The purpose of the special administration is to improve services and make city life more pleasant in view of the large size of the cities.

NOTES AND QUESTIONS

1. Note that Spanish local administration distinguishes three types of units in accordance with size in terms of population. The system of government, however, is standardized and is basically regulated by the law on local government. Compare the Spanish system with those existing in Italy and France. On Anglo-American law, *see*, e.g., the Texas V.A.Civ. St. Art. 961ff.

2. Who are the officers and what are the bodies governing cities? How are they elected? For what terms are they elected? Is the election held in a particular month of the year? Compare the German and the French law. *See also*, e.g., Texas V.A.Civ.St. Art. 977ff.

3. What are the powers of the mayor and the city council? Compare the Italian and the French law. *See*, e.g., Texas V.A.Civ. St. Arts. 993ff. and 1007ff.

4. Note that cities have the power to pass local ordinances, levy city rates, have city employees, run the public utilities, and maintain peace and order. Compare the French and the German law. *See also*, e.g, Texas V.A.Civ.St. Arts. 1026ff., 1106ff., 1165ff., 1269(m)ff.

5. Is there any substantial difference between the organization and government of most Spanish cities and that of the few big cities in Spain? Compare the French and the German law.

---

2.   Intermediate Administration

Spanish intermediate administration is carried out by the provinces (*provincias*).[106] It combines the principles of central administration and local autonomy. The organs of provincial administration are: the governor (*gobernador civil*), · the president of the council (*presidente de la diputación*), the council (*diputación provincial*), and the provincial commission of technical services (*comisión provincial de servicios técnicos*).

The governor (*gobernador civil*) is the permanent representative of the government, the head of the government administration, and the head of the local administration in the province. He is appointed and removed by the head of the state at the recommendation of the Minister of Home Affairs (*Ministro de Gobernación*) after deliberation in the council of ministers. He must be Spanish and over twenty-five years of age, with a fully completed university education. He holds his post until removed. His rank within the government structure is equivalent to the director general in the ministries, with the exception of the governors in the provinces of Madrid and Barcelona, whose rank is equivalent to that of undersecretaries (*subsecretarios*). He may also preside over the council and the provincial commission of technical services. He is the visible head of the provincial administration. Whenever necessary, a deputy governor (*subgobernador civil*) is appointed. A deputy governor must have the same qualifications as the governor. He is appointed and removed by the council of ministers. The deputy governor, whenever appointed, substitutes for the governor and exercises functions delegated to him by the governor. Where no deputy governor is appointed, the duty to substitute for the governor when he is absent or ill falls first on the president of the council (*presidente de la diputación*), then on the president of the court of criminal appeal (*presidente de la audiencia provincial*), and then on the secretary-general of the governor's office (*secretario general del gobierno civil*).

The president of the council (*presidente de la diputación*) is also the vice-president of the provincial commission of technical services. He is elected for a term of four years by the provincial councilors from among themselves by secret ballot. To be elected, he must receive an absolute majority of the votes of all councilors. The president of the council calls, presides over and dismisses the sessions of the council. In the case of a tie, he has a casting vote. He is the chief representative of the council and has the duty to see to it that its decisions are published and carried out. He appoints from among the councilors a vice-president who is his substitute.

The council (*diputación provincial*) is composed of the president and the councilors (*diputados*). The number of councilors varies with the size of population in the province, from a minimum of eighteen to a maximum of thirty-six. Councilors are elected in provincial elections by direct and secret ballot for a term of four years. The office of councilor is honorary, but they are entitled to expenses.

The council is the legislative body of the province. It votes on all ordinances, rules and provisions applicable in the province. It may set up and dissolve institutions and bodies within the province; it appoints provincial officers unless the power rests in a higher authority; it administers provincial property and may acquire and dispose of it; it enacts provincial taxes; and it supervises the provincial financial administration. The council has a number of committees. The following are obligatory: welfare; health; city planning and housing; agriculture and forestry; education, sports and tourism; public works; and finance and economy. Each committee is presided over by a councilor but the president of the council may preside. The office of the council is headed by the secretary-general (*secretario general de la diputación*).

The provincial commission of technical services (*comisión provincial de servicios técnicos*) is headed by the governor with the president of the council as vice-president. Members of the commission include: the mayor of the provincial capital, the provincial head of health, the provincial representative of every ministry, and the head of the provincial office of government counsel (*abogado del estado jefe*). The governor may further invite to meetings on a particular topic any other person whose participation he considers beneficial. The secretary-general of the governor's office is the secretary of the commission. The commission forms several committees, the following being obligatory: economics, transport and communications, culture, health, and welfare.

The commission supervises the use of public funds provided by the state or derived from other sources for the promotion of provincial development, and it coordinates the work of all government agencies in the province.

In addition to the individual provinces, there is a regime of special autonomy in operation in the Catalan, the Basque, the Aragon, the Galicia, the Valencia, the Andalusia, the Asturias, the Estremadura and the Castile-Leon regions, in the Canary Islands and in the Balearic Islands.

NOTES AND QUESTIONS

Spanish provinces combine the principles of central administration and local autonomy. How do they compare with Italian provinces and French departments? What are the organs of the provinces? How are they constituted? What is the term of the provincial council? What are its functions? How do the organs of Spanish provinces compare with the organs of French departments and those of Italian provinces?

May the Spanish provinces be best compared with Anglo-American counties? *See,* e.g., Texas V.A. Civ. St. Art. 1539ff.

---

3. Central Administration

Offices of central administration are those of actual public administration and those that are consultative and of control.

(a) Offices of central public administration.[107]

(i) PRIME MINISTER (*Presidente del Gobierno*). The Prime Minister is the chairman of the council of ministers (*consejo de ministros*). He calls, presides over and dismisses the meetings of the council. He directs the work of the government and sees to it that its decisions are implemented. He recommends to the head of the state the appointment and dismissal of ministers. He is charged with the proper functioning of the public administration. His office is known as the *Presidencia del Gobierno* and is headed by the minister undersecretary of the presidency of government (*ministro subsecretario de la presidencia del gobierno*). One or more deputy prime ministers (*vicepresidente del gobierno*) may be appointed. The deputy prime ministers are appointed and hold office as other ministers. The Prime Minister is appointed and relieved of his functions by the head of state.

(ii) COUNCIL OF MINISTERS (*Consejo de ministros*). The council of ministers comprises all ministers and is presided over by the Prime Minister or by a deputy prime minister. The minister undersecretary of the presidency of government acts as secretary. The council is collectively responsible for the carrying out of govermental function. It recommends to the head of state the approval of laws and decrees, submits bills of laws to congress and exercises all functions assigned to it by law. All its decisions are signed by the presiding minister or by the minister within whose competence the subject matter falls.

The council forms committees dealing with special subjects through which, by delegation, the council exercises its function in these matters. The committees are known as the *Comisiones Delegadas del Gobierno*. They are, e.g., the *Comisión Delegada de Asuntos Económicos; de Transportes y Comunicaciones;* and *de Sanidad y Asuntos Sociales.* Members of the committees are the concerned ministers. The *Junta de Defensa Nacional,* which is also a committee of the council, has in addition to the concerned ministers the chief of the general staff and the chiefs of staff of the army, navy and air force on the committee. The committees coordinate cooperation among the several ministries and study matters of concern to several ministries. They are presided over by the Prime Minister, a deputy prime minister or by the minister undersecretary of the presidency of government. They report to the council on the matters dealt with, but they may decide themselves on those matters which, by decision of the Prime Minister, need not be brought before the council because of their lesser importance.

(iii) MINISTERS *(Ministros)*.   Ministers are appointed by the head of state at the proposal of the Prime Minister. They cease to be ministers whenever a new prime minister is appointed. They may resign, but their resignation must be accepted by the head of state at the proposal of the Prime Minister. They may always be relieved of their functions by decision of the head of state at the proposal of the Prime Minister. As heads of the various ministries, they direct the operations of the sector of public administration entrusted to them. They suggest to the council of ministers proposals for new laws and regulations within their competence, and they regulate and supervise the running of the ministry under their direction. As heads of public administration, they must decide appeals in the administrative process brought to the ministries against the decisions of subordinate administrative offices. In the council of ministers, they represent that sector of public administration which they head.

(iv) UNDERSECRETARIES AND DIRECTORS GENERAL *(Subsecretarios y directores generales)*.   The undersecretary is the head of the ministry directly subordinate to the minister. One or more may be appointed in the same ministry. The undersecretary is the deputy of the minister and the administrative head of the ministry.

The directors general are heads of departments within ministries, subordinate to the undersecretary. They are responsible for the running of their particular departments and must recommend to the minister and the undersecretary what measures or decisions should be taken in their respective spheres of public administration.

(v) PROVINCIAL DELEGATES *(Delegados provinciales)*.   Each ministry maintains in the capital of every province an office headed by its provincial delegate. The office supervises the function of the ministry in the province.

(b) Central consultative offices and offices of control.   There are a considerable number of advisory bodies in the public administration, called councils, commissions, committees, and the like. The more important are: the Council of State, the directorate general of litigation, legal departments of the various ministries, and offices of the government counsel. The function of control is built into all ministries and is exercised by the ministry of finance *(ministerio de hacienda)*. There is, however, an independent organ of control known as the Court of Accounts *(**Tribunal de Cuentas**)*.

(i) COUNCIL OF STATE *(Consejo de Estado)*.[108]   The Council of State is the highest advisory body in the country. It is headed by a president, who is appointed by the head of state for a six-year term and may be reappointed. The Council is further composed of councilors *(consejeros)*, who are appointed by the head of state from among persons who hold high political or administrative offices. They are appointed for three-year terms and may be reappointed. The Council further has many officers who form the *cuerpo de letrados* and are career legal officers in the service of the Council. The Council has a number of sections, each presided over by a councilor. It also has a secretariat headed by the secretary-general.

The Council gives advice to the government on any matter of general interest or administration submitted to it by the government or on its own initiative.

The Council sits also in a plenary session. The plenum must be consulted by the government whenever a law so demands and also on international treaties, proposed legislative decrees, interpretation of contracts of great importance entered into by the state, important administrative matters, and the dismissal of councilors of state. In addition, the government may submit any matter of importance for consideration by the plenum.

The Council of State also has a permanent commission (*comisión permanente*). It is composed of the president of the Council, all presidents of sections and the secretary-general. The permanent commission must be consulted by the government before it issues any decrees of a fiscal nature or any executive regulations and before it rules on jurisdictional conflicts between branches of public administration. It must be consulted further on contracts entered into by the government, their interpretation or rescission.

(ii) DIRECTORATE GENERAL OF LITIGATION (*Dirección general de lo contencioso*) AND OFFICES OF GOVERNMENT COUNSEL (*Abogacias del estado*).[109]　The central office of government counsel is known as the *dirección general de lo contencioso* and the offices of government counsel located in the provinces, one in each province, are known as *abogacias del estado*. They advise the central and the provincial administration on legal matters and actually represent the state in court as both plaintiff and defendant.

(iii) LEGAL DEPARTMENTS IN THE VARIOUS MINISTRIES (*Asesorias jurídicas de los distintos departamentos ministeriales*).　Every ministry has a legal department which is routinely consulted on any matter of legal portent handled by the ministry.

(iv) COURT OF ACCOUNTS (*Tribunal de Cuentas*).[110]　The Court of Accounts is an independent body modeled on the Supreme Court of Justice. It gives advice to the government and to congress on fiscal matters, especially as to whether or not the government has complied with fiscal provisions of the various laws and with the budget. It examines government accounts and reports to the government and to congress. It is the highest body of control of operations of the public administration.

In addition, the Court of Accounts acts as the supreme court in fiscal matters, hearing appeals (*recursos*) against decisions of the offices of central administration. The petitions are for the cassation (*casación*) or revision (*revisión*) of the orders complained of. The Court has a president appointed by the head of state and a number of councilors. It has several sections. It forms trial and appellate panels in the same manner as the Supreme Court of Justice. The state is represented by the public ministry of accounts (*ministerio fiscal de cuentas*). Parties must have the same representation as required in the Supreme Court of Justice.

NOTES AND QUESTIONS

1. Central offices of Spanish government are either administrative or consultative. Both are very similar to those in other civil law countries.

2. Note the consultative offices. What is the function of the Spanish Council of

State? Note that it is limited to consultative function. How does it compare with the Italian and French Councils of State?

3. The Spanish Court of Accounts performs a function similar to the French and Italian Courts of Accounts. Which American department performs a similar function? *See*, e.g., 31 U.S.C.A. §41ff. concerning the United States General Accounting Office.

---

4. Administrative Courts

Administrative courts are the administrative chambers within *audiencias territoriales,* the administrative chambers and the administrative revision chamber within the Supreme Court of Justice, and other administrative courts.

(a) Administrative chambers within *audiencias territoriales* (*Salas de lo contencioso-administrativo de las audiencias territoriales*)[111] There is one administrative chamber (*sala de lo contencioso-administrativo*) within every *audiencia territorial;* more may be set up if required. The chamber is constituted by a presiding judge and another two judges.

They hear appeals (*recursos*) against decisions of organs of public administration within their territorial jurisdiction which may not be appealed to higher administrative bodies, further appeals against decisions given by central organs of public administration at a lower than ministerial level in matters of public servants and eminent domain, appeals against decisions of such organs in fiscal matters, and appeals by public authorities and public servants against decisions of organs of public administration within their territorial jurisdiction where such decisions hold these public authorities or public servants responsible for acts done in the exercise of their official functions.

An appeal against their rulings (*recurso de súplica*) or against their judgments (*recurso de apelación*) and a petition for the revision of their judgments (*recurso de revisión*) lies to the administrative chambers within the Supreme Court of Justice and must be brought in the first two cases within five days to the court that pronounced the decision complained of.

The *recurso de apelación* will, however, not lie in the following cases: where the value of the subject matter does not exceed a certain fixed sum (500,000 pesetas); in matters of personnel, except in the case of the removal of a permanent officer; in cases of approval or modification of ordinances of local entities setting dues; and in cases disputing the validity of election of provincial councilors. An appeal always lies, irrespective of value or the subject matter, whenever it is alleged that the public authority abused its powers (*desviación de poder*).

The *recurso de revisión* is brought against judgments that have entered into the power of law on the following grounds: where the dispositive part of the judgment is contradictory; where irreconcilable decisions were made by the same or different courts in similar circumstances; where new evidence came to light; where documents or testimony given was adjudged false; where there was fraud, violence or undue influence; and where the court exceeded its powers by granting more than the parties demanded. The *recurso de revisión* must be brought within three months from the discovery of new evidence or of the falsehood, and within one month in the case of contradiction, irreconcilable decisions and excess of power.

In addition to the above, the office of government counsel (*abogacia del estado*) may, within three months, appeal in the interest of the law (*en interés de la ley*) any decision given by administrative chambers of *audiencias territoriales* in which it had not intervened and could not thus have brought a regular appeal.

Parties before the court must be represented by counsel (*abogado*). The public authority is represented by the office of government counsel (*abogacia del estado*) in the seat of the court.

Being a chamber of the *audiencia territorial*, the court is subject to rules governing the *audiencia* unless expressly provided otherwise.

(b) Administrative chambers within the Supreme Court of Justice (*Salas de lo contencioso-administrativo del Tribunal Supremo de Justicia*).[112]   There are three administrative chambers (*salas de lo contencioso-administrativo*), Nos. 3, 4, and 5, each presided over by a president of chamber and comprised of a number of judges. The chambers are divided into sections (*secciones*). The panel actually hearing a case is presided over by a presiding judge and has, in accordance with the subject matter of the case and the nature of the hearing (e.g., a formal final hearing in open court or a decision taken in the absence of the parties in closed session), a varying number of judges. Thus, for a decision without an actual public hearing in open court, a panel of three judges is formed to decide, for example, matters of personnel and less important cases, and a five judge panel is formed to decide all other cases. The decision is by simple majority.

Where there is a formal final hearing held in open court, the presiding judge and six other judges must concur in order to decide on cases dealing with annulment, appeals, cases dealing with administrative acts involving the Council of State in plenary session, or matters on which there are prior divergent opinions of the chambers.

The presiding judge and two other judges must concur in the above-referred to cases of personnel and less important cases whenever the decision is given after a formal hearing in open court, and the presiding judge and four judges must concur in all other such cases. Consequently, a greater number of judges must hear all such cases without any fixed number of those present being imposed.

A plenary session of the chamber must be called to decide a *recurso de revisión* against a decision of the administrative chamber within an *audiencia territorial*.

The chambers hear appeals (*recursos*) against administrative decisions of organs of central administration that have jurisdiction over the entire national territory; against decisions in matters of public administration of the council of ministers, its committees and individual ministers; against administrative decisions made with the advice of the Council of State; and against administrative decisions made by or on the advice of the Supreme Council of Military Justice (*Consejo Supremo de Justicia Militar*).

As courts of appeal, the chambers hear appeals (*recursos de súplica*) against rulings of administrative chambers within *audiencias territoriales* as well as appeals (*recursos de apelación*) against their judgments and petitions for revision of judgments (*recursos de revisión*) pronounced by them.

No further appeal lies against decisions of the chambers, but a petition for revision of their judgments (*recurso de revisión*) may be brought to the administrative revision chamber within the Supreme Court on the same grounds and within the same time as it may be brought against decisions of administrative chambers within *audiencias territoriales.*

Parties before the chambers must be represented by counsel (*abogado*). The public authority is represented by the directorate general of litigation (*dirección general de lo contencioso*).

Being chambers of the Supreme Court of Justice, the administrative chambers are subject to the rules governing the Supreme Court unless otherwise provided.

(c)   Administrative revision chamber within the Supreme Court of Justice (*Sala de revisión de lo contencioso-administrativo del Tribunal Supremo de Justicia*).[113] An administrative revision chamber is formed within the Supreme Court of Justice to hear petitions for the revision of judgments (*recursos de revisión*) against judgments of the administrative chambers within the Supreme Court. It is presided over by the president of the Supreme Court and has as its members the presidents and most senior judges of each of the three administrative chambers. A seven-judge panel is thus formed.

Parties before the chamber must be represented by counsel (*abogado*). The public authority is represented by the directorate general of litigation (*dirección general de lo contencioso*).

Being a chamber of the Supreme Court of Justice, it is subject to the rules governing the Supreme Court unless otherwise provided.

NOTES AND QUESTIONS

1. What is the hierarchical organization of administrative courts in Spain? Note that the administrative chambers form part of the regular court system. What is the jurisdiction of administrative chambers within *audiencias territoriales*? Does an appeal lie against their decisions? With which Italian and French administrative courts may they be compared?

Does the private party need legal representation in the proceedings? Who represents the public authority?

2. What is the jurisdiction of the administrative chambers within the Supreme Court? Note that they have both original and appellate jurisdiction. What is the composition of the chambers? How many judges do the panels hearing cases have? Does an appeal lie against their decisions? How do the chambers compare with those of the French and Italian Councils of State?

3. What is the function of the administrative revision chamber within the Spanish Supreme Court? Does a comparable organ exist in the Italian and the French administrative courts systems?

4. Compare the Spanish system of administrative courts with the system of German administrative courts. How does the Spanish system compare with the Anglo-American system of administrative law? May a meaningful comparison be made due to fundamental differences in system and approach?

(d) Other administrative courts. They are chiefly the Court of Accounts (*Tribunal de Cuentas*), mentioned above under central consultative offices and offices of control, taxation juries (*jurados tributarios*), and economic-administrative courts (*tribunales económico-administrativos*). The latter two are both tax courts. Tax assessments are handled by the system of tax authorities headed by the ministry of finance (*ministerio de hacienda*); disputes, however, are handled by different organs, namely, taxation juries and economic-administrative courts.

(i) TAXATION JURIES (*Jurados tributarios*).[114]   Whenever a dispute arises between the tax administration and a taxpayer as to a question of fact that attracts the imposition of a tax, the dispute is submitted for decision to the taxation jury system. Taxation juries establish the basis on which a tax is levied. After the decision is made, the matter is remitted to tax authorities for the imposition of the tax. The jurisdiction of taxation juries extends to all taxes.

Taxation juries operate at two levels, territorial and central. Territorial taxation juries (*jurados tributarios territoriales*) are set up in major centers and have jurisdiction over several provinces. There are nine territorial districts. They decide without any appeal all disputes where the value of the base does not exceed a certain fixed sum (500,000 pesetas) or where the value is in doubt. Against their decisions in matters exceeding that amount, an appeal (*recurso de alzada*) lies to the central taxation jury. They are composed of a president and four members. The president and two members are appointed by the Minister of Finance from among taxation officers; the other two members also are appointed by the Minister of Finance, each from among three persons whose names are submitted to the Minister by the syndical organization. In cases of a city tax (*contribución territorial urbana*) and a personal income tax (*impuesto sobre rendimiento del trabajo personal*), only one member is appointed at the proposal of the syndical organization, and the other is appointed from among three persons suggested by the proper taxpayers' association. Territorial taxation juries decide by a simple majority, the president having a casting vote. The quorum is three. Each territorial taxation jury has a secretary who is a government counsel (*abogado del estado*). His duty is to see to it that they proceed in accordance with the law.

The central taxation jury (*jurado central tributario*) has its seat in the ministry of finance in Madrid and its jurisdiction extends over all the country. It hears, as a tribunal of first instance, cases of national scope and importance; as a tribunal of appeal, it hears appeals from the territorial taxation juries. It has a president and twelve members. They are appointed by decree, with the selection having been approved by the council of ministers. The president and six members are selected from taxation officers, the other six members from taxpayers' associations. They function in sections in accordance with the tax under consideration. There are nine sections. Each section is presided over by a member designated by the president and has another four members, two taken from taxation officers and two from taxpayers' associations. Cases are decided by the sections but the president may reserve a case for the decision of the plenum of all twelve members, he himself presiding. The quorum of the plenum is seven, of a section three. They decide by simple majority, the president having a casting vote. The central taxation jury has a secretary-general and his staff, who are government counsel (*abogados del estado*).

No further appeal lies against decisions of the central taxation jury. This applies as to the substance. As to form, taxation juries must apply the rules of economic-administrative procedure. For an alleged breach of such rules, an appeal lies to an economic-administrative court.

(ii) ECONOMIC-ADMINISTRATIVE COURTS (*Tribunales económico-administrativos*).[115] Economic-administrative courts hear complaints against decisions of taxation authorities. The function of economic-administrative courts is performed by the following bodies: the Minister of Finance, the central economic-administrative court, provincial economic-administrative courts, and customs courts.

(aa) Minister of Finance (Ministro de Hacienda). ·The Minister of Finance decides all complaints against those decisions of taxation authorities that are made with the advice of the Council of State; that are in connection with the payment of costs awarded against the state; that are referred to him by the central economic-administrative court; and that were not properly decided in the central economic-administrative court because the vote was divided and neither opinion was supported by three votes. The decision of the Minister exhausts the administrative way. An appeal lies to the administrative chambers within the Supreme Court of Justice.

(bb) Central economic-administrative court (Tribunal económico-administrativo central). The central economic-administrative court decides in the first and final instance complaints against decisions of the central offices of financial administration; in the second instance, it decides appeals (*recursos de alzada*) against decisions of provincial economic-administrative courts and against decisions of customs courts; it also decides petitions for the remission of fines. It is located in the ministry of finance in Madrid. It has a president, a vice-president, six members and a secretary-general. All are appointed by decree, with the selection first approved by the council of ministers at the proposal of the Minister of Finance. The court has three chambers; the first two deal with tax complaints, the third with customs complaints. The first two chambers hear cases presided over by the president of the court or another member and has three additional members. The customs chamber is presided over by the vice-president or another member and has three additional members. The plenum sits with the president and all six members. The president, the vice-president and two members must be lawyers. Only they may preside. The other members are financial experts taken from different branches of financial administration.

The court is governed by the rules of economic-administrative procedure, which follow the standard rules of procedure in administrative courts (*procedimiento contencioso-administrativo*). The court decides by majority vote; the presiding officer has a casting vote. Parties before the court must be represented by counsel. The decision of the court exhausts the administrative way. An appeal against its decisions lies to the administrative chambers within the Supreme Court of Justice.

(cc) Provincial economic-administrative courts (Tribunales económico-administrativos provinciales). These courts are set up in every province. They have a president, who is the delegate of the ministry of finance in the province, and the following members: the inspector of finance in the province, the head of the

office of public administration that issued the order complained of, a government counsel, and the provincial head of the office of inspection dealing with the particular kind of tax, if any. The court thus has a president and three or four members in accordance with the matter before it.

The court decides all appeals against decisions of the provincial taxation administration. An appeal (*recurso de alzada*) lies against its decisions to the central economic-administrative court only where the value of the subject matter exceeds a certain fixed sum (500,000 pesetas). The court is governed by the rules of economic-administrative procedure, which follow the standard rules of procedure in administrative courts. The court decides by majority vote; the presiding officer has a casting vote. Parties before the court must be represented by counsel. Where an appeal against the decision of the court to the central economic-administrative court is excluded, the decision exhausts the administrative way and an appeal lies to the administrative chamber within the proper *audiencia territorial*.

    (dd) Customs courts (Juntas arbitrales de aduanas). Customs courts are set up in every province. They have a president, who is the provincial administrator of customs, and the second in command and another officer of customs as members.

The court decides all appeals against decisions of the provincial customs administration. An appeal (*recurso de alzada*) lies against its decisions to the central economic-administrative court only where the value of the subject matter exceeds a certain fixed sum (500,000 pesetas). The court is governed by the rules of economic-administrative procedure, which follow the standard rules of procedure in administrative courts. The court decides by majority vote; the presiding officer has a casting vote. Parties before the court must be represented by counsel. Where an appeal against the decision of the court to the central economic-administrative court is excluded, the decision exhausts the administrative way and an appeal lies to the administrative chamber within the proper *audiencia territorial*.

NOTES AND QUESTIONS

1. What is the function of taxation juries? At how many levels do they operate? Are they independent bodies or organs of the government tax administration? How do they compare with Italian tax commissions?

2. Note the various organs that function as economic-administrative courts. What is the jurisdiction of customs courts? What is their composition? What are the remedies against their decisions? Do parties appearing before them need legal representation?

3. What is the jurisdiction of provincial economic-administrative courts? What is their composition and what remedies lie against their decisions? Compare them with Italian tax commissions and German tax courts.

4. What is the function of the central economic-administrative court within the taxation system? What is its composition and what remedies lie against its decisions? May it be compared with the United States Tax Court? *See* 28 U.S.C.A. §7441ff.

5. Note the function of the Minister of Finance who, as the head of his department, also acts as a body with the nature of an economic-administrative court.

C. ADMINISTRATIVE PROCEDURE AND PROCEDURE BEFORE ADMINISTRATIVE COURTS

1. Administrative Procedure (*Procedimiento administrativo*)[116]

Whatever has been said previously concerning administrative procedure in the General Part, Section III. C. in the chapter on an overview of the law applies generally to Spanish administrative procedure. Spanish public administration functions at three levels. Process may be initiated at any level depending on the matter at issue. It is usually initiated at the local or provincial level with an appeal to the higher level. The person must exhaust his administrative remedies before he can appeal to administrative courts.

Administrative procedure parallels that before civil courts, but it is less formal. It is conducted in writing and the party is free to orally consult with the officers of public administration. The party does not require any representation. The public authority must find the facts, have them proved, and give a reasoned decision.

The administrative remedy against decisions of the public administration is the administrative appeal (*recurso administrativo*), which includes the *recurso de alzada*, the *recurso de reposición*, the *recurso de súplica*, and the *recurso de revisión*.

(a) *Recurso de alzada*.   The *recurso de alzada* is the regular appeal against a decision of a lower administrative office to its hierarchical superior. It may be brought only once and it exhausts the appeal. It may not be brought against decisions of the central administration. The *recurso* must be brought within fifteen business days from notification of the decision. It is brought either to the office that pronounced it or to its hierarchical superior. The office that rendered the decision must, within ten days, submit the files to its hierarchical superior together with its comments. The reviewing authority may affirm, modify or revoke the decision complained of. Its decision is in turn subject to further remedies. Time to file a further remedy runs from notification of the decision on the party. However, should no decision be made within three months from the filing of the *recurso*, it is deemed denied by administrative silence.

(b) *Recurso de reposición*.   The *recurso de reposición* may be brought against decisions of central authorities and against decisions of authorities that decide *recursos de alzada*. The *recurso* is thus brought to the same administrative organ that made the decision complained of with the purpose of giving that authority a chance to reconsider its decision. It must be filed within thirty days from notification of the decision. It is a prerequisite for a recourse to administrative courts and must be filed before the party may proceed to an administrative court. If the authority makes no reply within thirty days from the filing of the *recurso*, the party may take his case to the proper administrative court.

(c) *Recurso de súplica.* The *recurso de súplica* is an extension of the *recurso de alzada*, but it may be brought only on the strength of a statute providing expressly for it. Where such an authority exists, the *recurso de súplica* is brought to the council of ministers, ministerial committees, or the presidency of government as provided therein. It is thus a special administrative appeal against the decision of an administrative office that denies a *recurso de alzada* and is brought to its hierarchical superior. The time within which to bring the *recurso* is the same as that provided for the *recurso de alzada*.

(d) *Recurso de revisión.* The *recurso de revisión* aims at a revision of a decision already entered into the power of law. It is brought to the proper minister in order to correct an error that exists in the decision or to set the decision aside because of the discovery of new evidence, because evidence given in the proceedings was adjudged false in a court of law, or because of fraud, duress or undue influence. On the ground of error, the *recurso* must be brought within four years from notification of the decision; on other grounds, it must be brought within three months from the discovery, the legal decision, or the cessation of undue influence, as the case may be.

NOTES AND QUESTIONS

Spanish administrative procedure governs proceedings in all matters transacted by public authorities. It is of uniform application throughout the country. Compare it with the German and French administrative procedures. The principles of administrative procedure are of general application in all countries governed by civil law.

Note the different kinds of appeals available against decisions of public authorities. Once the administrative way has been exhausted, the party may proceed to administrative courts. How does the Spanish administrative procedure compare with the U.S. administrative procedure? *See* 5 U.S.C.A. §500ff.

---

2. Procedure before Administrative Courts
(*Procedimiento contencioso-administrativo*)[117]

Procedure before administrative courts consists of preliminary proceedings, procedure before courts of first or the only level, appellate procedure, and procedure for the revision of judgments already in the power of law.

(a) Preliminary proceedings (*Diligencias preliminares*). The filing of the *recurso de reposición* with the authority that made the decision complained of is a prerequisite for the initiation of proceedings in administrative courts, as mentioned above. There is no need to file the *recurso de reposición* where the authority denied the prior petition by administrative silence, where its decision was not communicated in writing, where the measure complained of was of general character and was not made in bilateral proceedings, where the authority approved a fiscal measure originating from another authority, or where an act of the authority was already impliedly decided adversely to the petitioner.

The appeal (*recurso*) must be filed with the proper administrative court within two months from notification of the decision of the *recurso de reposición*, or within one year from the filing of the *recurso de reposición* in the case of administrative silence. Where the filing of the *recurso de reposición* is not required, the appeal must be brought within two months from the notification or from the last act of the authority in the matter. In the case of administrative silence, the appeal must be brought within one year from the time when the matter was deemed decided adversely to the appellant by administrative silence.[118]

(b)   Procedure before courts of the first or the only level (*Procedimiento de primera o única instancia*).   After the appeal (*recurso*) is received, the court orders the authority to file the record of the case with the court within twenty days. It has a notice of the filing appear in the government gazette (*Boletín Oficial del Estado*) in the case of the Supreme Court, or in the provincial gazette in the case of the *audiencia territorial*. If the authority does not comply, a further time of ten days is given. If the authority does not comply even then, a fine is imposed and collected personally from the head thereof and the case proceeds further.

The court will reject the appeal if it does not comply with formal requirements; but where the defect can be corrected, it will give ten days to the appellant to cure it. Against a denial of the appeal, the *recurso de súplica* lies to the court; if the court is the *audiencia territorial* and it denies the *recurso de súplica*, an appeal (*apelación*) to the Supreme Court may be brought.

After the formal requirements of the appeal are satisfied and the defendant authority supplies its record, the record is handed to the appellant for twenty days to file his brief. The file, together with the appellant's brief, is then given to the authority for an equal time of twenty days to file its brief. The appellant may request that the authority should supply further information on the ground that the supplied record is not exhaustive. Such a request must be made to the court within ten days from receipt of the record, and the court will rule on the request within three days. Noncompliance by the authority results in an extension of time and in a fine as mentioned above.

The briefs must state with precision the facts and the law to be applied and the demand made. All necessary documents must be attached or, when held by others, their production must be requested. Documents not mentioned in the briefs will not be admitted.

If a party desires to contest the jurisdiction of the court or admissibility of the appeal, he must do so within five days from his appearance. The statement of objection will be handed over to the opponent to file his comments within five days. If he admits the defect, he will have ten days to cure it. The court will rule on the motion. No remedy lies against denial of the motion. Against a ruling granting the motion and dismissing the case, the *recurso de súplica* lies to the court; if the court is the *audiencia territorial* and it denies the *recurso de súplica*, a further appeal lies to the Supreme Court.

Proof will be admitted only when the parties differ on material facts. Where admitted, it will be made within thirty days, in accordance with the Code of Civil Procedure, and before a judge of the court or before a judge of the court of first instance.

A formal final hearing is held only when both parties request it or when the court thinks it necessary. If it is held, the court will set a day. The proceedings at the hearing, the deliberation and the voting are governed by the Code of Civil Procedure.

Where no formal final hearing is held, the court, in making the order, requests the parties to file within fifteen days their written conclusions, which must sum up the facts, the proof, the legal principles involved and their petitions, in as many copies as there will be judges deciding the case. After the written conclusions are filed, the court will set a day for the decision to be made in the case and in the absence of the parties.

No new matters may be raised at the formal final hearing or in the written conclusions. If the court desires additional matters to be raised, it will so notify the parties and will give them an additional three days to prepare for the final hearing or to include such matters in the conclusions.

The decision must be given within ten days from the formal final hearing or from the decision of the case in the absence of the parties.

The decision will declare the appeal inadmissible where the court lacks jurisdiction, where the appellant lacks capacity to appeal, where no appeal is permissible, where the matter is already *res judicata*, where the *recurso de reposición* was not filed although it should have been filed, where the appeal was filed out of time, and where the proper requirements as to form were not observed.

The decision will deny the appeal where the act of the authority complained of was in accordance with the law.

The decision will allow the appeal where the act or provision of the authority complained of is found to be in breach of the law or when abuse of power is found. Where the appeal is allowed, the act or provision is set aside in full or in part. Where the petitioner so demands, the parties will be placed back in the positions they had before the proceedings were initiated. Where the petitioner proves his damages, the court may award them; where not, they will be awarded in further proceedings. The decision will also provide for costs.

(c) Appellate procedure (*Recursos contra sentencias*). An appeal (*recurso de apelación*) may be brought to the administrative chambers within the Supreme Court of Justice against decisions of the administrative chambers of the *audiencia territorial*. The appeal must be filed within five days from notification of the decision to the court that pronounced the decision. Where formally in order, the court will summon the parties to appear in the Supreme Court within thirty days. The parties must submit their briefs to the Supreme Court within the same time. If they desire a formal public hearing, they must so indicate therein. The parties must also state in their briefs whether they wish further proof to be taken where such proof was denied in the court below or where they allege that no proper proof was allowed. Where the Supreme Court rules to have proof taken, the proceedings proceed as in the *audiencia territorial*.

Where the appellee contends that the appeal was wrongly admitted, a day in court is set within three days to hear the allegation and the Supreme Court will decide forthwith. Where the case is formally in order, the Supreme Court will set a day for the formal public hearing or rules that it will decide the appeal without any such hearing. Proceedings at the formal public hearing, e.g., the decision and voting, proceed as in the *audiencia territorial*.

The Supreme Court always decides the matter on the merits. This is also the case where the Supreme Court reverses the *audiencia* on its decision disclaiming jurisdiction or denying admission of the *recurso* on formal grounds.

The decision of the Supreme Court is final. No further remedy lies against its decisions.

(d) Procedure for the revision of judgments (*Recurso de revisión*). A petition for the revision of a judgment that has entered into the power of law (*recurso de revisión*) may be brought to the court that pronounced the judgment on the grounds and within the time referred to above. This may be either the administrative chamber of an *audiencia territorial* or one of the administrative chambers of the Supreme Court.

When formally correct, the *recurso de revisión* will be heard by one of the administrative chambers of the Supreme Court where the decision complained of is that of an *audiencia territorial* and by the administrative revision chamber within the Supreme Court where the decision complained of is that of one of the administrative chambers of the Supreme Court.

The proceedings follow the rules governing procedure before these courts as mentioned above.

NOTES AND QUESTIONS

1. Note the preliminary proceedings that must be undertaken to bring a case before an administrative court. Within what time must the appeal against the decision of the administrative authority be brought to the administrative court? Note the rule as to administrative silence.

2. Procedure in trial courts is basically identical whether the trial court happens to be an administrative chamber in the *audiencia* or one in the Supreme Court. The procedure relies heavily on the Code of Civil Procedure with the above-mentioned differences. Compare it with procedures in Italian regional administrative courts and the Italian Council of State, and in French administrative courts and the French Council of State. How does the Spanish procedure compare with that in German administrative courts? Note that the courts give decisions on the merits and exercise the powers of a full administrative review.

3. Note the procedure on appeal from decisions of the administrative chamber of the *audiencia*. Does any appeal lie against decisions of the administrative chamber of the Supreme Court sitting as a trial court? Compare the Spanish appellate procedure with appellate procedure in the German and the Italian administrative law.

4. Procedure for the revision of judgments follows the rules of the Code of Civil Procedure with the modifications applicable to administrative procedure as mentioned above.

V. LEGAL OFFICERS

A. JUDGES (*Magistrados*)[119]

Whatever has been said previously concerning judges in the General Part, Section IV. A. in the chapter on an overview of the law applies also to the Spanish legal system.

Admission into the judiciary is by public competition conducted by the ministry of justice. An applicant must be Spanish, of full age and capacity, of either sex, and of good moral character. The applicant must hold the degree of *Licenciado* or *Doctor* of Law from a Spanish university. The competition is held annually in October for a fixed number of positions in the judicial and procuratorial service as advertised. A practical written examination and two theoretical oral examinations are given to the applicants on all aspects of the law. Those making the best grades are admitted into the judicial school, which opens immediately after the results are published. Courses and examinations take over one year. They are given by professors of law and by judges and procurators. Those who conclude the courses satisfactorily are appointed aspirants in the judicial or procuratorial service. While in judicial school, they receive a salary. After a short orientation practice, they are appointed judges or procurators.

Once appointed, judges are irremovable. They are promoted on seniority, with the exception of judgeships in the Supreme Court and the office of the presidents of *audiencias territoriales* and *provinciales,* all of which are filled in accordance with special rules.

Presidents of *audiencias territoriales* and *provinciales* are appointed from among judges without regard to the seniority system.

Judges of the Supreme Court are appointed from among: (1) highest ranking judges (*magistrados de termino*) or (2) highest ranking procurators; chairholding professors of law, and counsel of twenty years' standing. Appointments are in the proportion of six from the first group above to one from the second group.

Presidents of chambers of the Supreme Court are selected from among judges of the Supreme Court. The president of the Supreme Court is appointed by decree at the proposal of the General Council of the Judiciary from among jurists of national standing who hold judgeships or procuratorships and from among counsel or chairholding professors of law.

Judges of the administrative chambers of the Supreme Court (*salas de lo contencioso-administrativo*) are appointed as follows: One third of the judgeships is filled by promotion from lower courts on seniority basis; another third is filled by administrative judges of at least ten years' standing on a seniority basis. The last third is taken from: (1) chairholding professors of law, (2) counsel to the Council of State, (3) government counsel, (4) counsel in the ministry of justice and counsel in the directorate general of registers and notaries, (5) counsel to congress, (6) military judges with the rank of general, (7) senior heads of public administration with at least fifteen years of service, (8) senior heads of local administration with at least twenty years of service, and (9) counsel with at least twenty years of practice.

Judges serve until retirement at the age of seventy-two years, but they may continue to serve from year to year until the age of seventy-five years.

Judges are subject to discipline by the president of the court on which they sit, but any disciplinary measure must be imposed by the *sala de gobierno* of the Supreme Court with respect to judges of that court, and by the *sala de gobierno* of the proper *audiencia territorial* with respect to other judges. They may be removed for cause. Removal proceedings must be instituted in the *sala de gobierno* of the Supreme Court. If it recommends removal, it will send its recommendation to the Minister of Justice, who then may recommend removal to the council of ministers. The council of ministers, after hearing the advice of the Council of State, may then remove the judge by decree.

NOTES AND QUESTIONS

The selection and appointment of judges follows the system generally current in civil law countries. A law graduate must apply for admission into the service as a young person immediately after graduation. Selection is made on the basis of an examination and those scoring best in the examination are taken into the service. After further training, they are then appointed to positions as beginners in the system and are promoted on seniority. Provision is also made for distinguished jurists who wish to join the service at a later time.

Compare the Spanish system with those of Germany, Italy and France. How does it compare with that customary in Anglo-American countries? *See*, e.g., Texas V.A. Civ. St. Arts. 1715ff. and 1884ff. as to the Texas judiciary.

B. THE PUBLIC MINISTRY (*Ministerio fiscal*)[120]

There is considerable similarity between qualifications for the office of judge and of procurator. The way to become a procurator is identical with that to become a judge. Conditions of their status are also very similar, except that judges are independent while procurators are subordinate to their superiors within the hierarchy.

The head of the structure of procurators (*fiscales*) is the procurator of the Supreme Court (*fiscal del Tribunal Supremo*), and below him are procurators general (*fiscales generales*), procurators (*fiscales*), advocates-procurators (*abogados-fiscales*), municipal and country procurators (*fiscales municipales y comarcales*), and procurators of courts of the peace (*fiscales de los juzgados de paz*).

Procuratorial offices are: The *fiscalia del tribunal supremo, fiscalias de las audiencias territoriales,* and *fiscalias de las audiencias provinciales. Fiscalias de las audiencias provinciales* appear in trial courts.

Procurators in municipal and country courts and in courts of the peace are not within the professional career group of procurators of the higher courts. They are recruited locally and their qualifications are below those of career procurators.

The main function of *fiscalias* is to prosecute criminal cases but they also fullfil other functions. They supervise and enforce compliance with the law in the administration of justice; maintain disciplinary proceedings against legal officers; ensure that sentences pronounced are properly carried out; instruct judicial police in the conduct of criminal investigations; and act for the state whenever it is not represented by the office of the government counsel (*abogacia del estado*). They also represent and protect minors and persons incapacitated or absent until their representation is assured by guardians, and they may bring suit in the interest of the law to set aside judgments obtained in breach of the Law.

In addition to procurators (*fiscales*), there are government counsel (*abogados del estado*)[121] who represent the state in court whenever it appears as a litigant and advise on legal matters. Officers of this service are recruited by public competition from among candidates holding the degree of *Licenciado* or *Doctor* of Law. This service is separate from that of procurators. The head office of the service is the directorate general of litigation (*dirección general de lo contencioso del estado*) in the ministry of justice, and the service maintains offices of government counsel (*abogacias del estado*) in the capital city of every province.

NOTES AND QUESTIONS

The Spanish public ministry is organized like similar ministries in other civil countries. Compare the French and German public ministries. The method of selection and training of officers of the public ministry is identical with that of judges, with whom they actually form one body of judicial officers.

How do officers of the public ministry and the system of public ministry compare with that customary in Anglo-American countries? *See,* e.g., Texas V.A. Civ. St. Art. 321ff.

C. LEGAL PRACTITIONERS

There are two kinds of legal practitioners, attorneys (*procuradores*) and advocates (*abogados*). Their functions are mutually exclusive and very similar to those of English solicitors on the one hand and barristers on the other.

1. Attorneys (*Procuradores*)[122]

The *procurador* represents the person of the party for whom he acts and needs a power of attorney from him. Having been so retained by the party, he handles the matter and watches over any deadlines for filing suit; he takes the necessary procedural steps and avoids being closed out by some statute of limitations. To handle the matter in court, he engages the services of an advocate. He must secure an advance payment from the party as he is responsible to the advocate for the payment of his fee.

To become a *procurador*, a person must be Spanish, be twenty-one years of age, and have conferred on him by the ministry of justice a license to practice. The ministry confers the license as a matter of right on any *Licenciado* in law of good repute who has the above qualifications of citizenship and age. It may also confer it on a person not holding the degree of *Licenciado* in law, but such practice is limited to small places below the rank of a provincial capital. In order to engage in practice, the *procurador* must join the bar organization in the place where he wishes to practice and be entered on its roll, make a bond of his financial responsibility, and take an oath before the highest court in the locality. His practice is then limited to the courts in that locality.

There is a local bar of *procuradores* (*colegio de procuradores*) in every locality where there are more than ten practitioners. In localities with fewer than ten practitioners, they are on the roll of the nearest bar. Each bar has its organization statute approved by the ministry of justice. They elect a council (*junta de gobierno*) and a dean (*decano*), who is the president of the local bar and chairman of the council. In every province, there is a provincial organization with a dean and council. At the national level, there is a national council (*Junta Nacional de los Colegios de Procuradores*) to represent the profession nationally and protect its interests. It is headed by a president, has a vice-president, secretary, vice-secretary, treasurer and another fourteen members (*consejeros*).

The discipline of the bar is exercised by the proper *junta*, with the *Junta Nacional* being the highest organ of discipline of the entire bar. A further appeal lies to the ministry of justice.

2. Advocates (*Abogados*)[123]

Advocates, also known as counsel (*letrados*), may exercise the profession of advocacy in any court and before any office. Their qualifications are: full age and capacity, Spanish citizenship, and the degree of *Licenciado* or *Doctor* of Law. They must be of good repute. No other license or permit is needed. To practice, the applicant must be entered on the roll of the bar of advocates (*colegio de abogados*) in the locality where he wishes to practice. Against a denial of enrollment, an appeal (*recurso de reposición*) lies to the *junta de gobierno* of the bar where he is applying, with a further appeal (*recurso de súplica*) to the general council of advocacy; and from a further denial, an appeal (*recurso de alzada*) may be taken to the ministry of justice, and from there to the Supreme Court by way of the *recurso de agravios*.

The newly enrolled advocate may engage in the practice of law without being required to undergo any further training, such as an apprenticeship. In practice, however, advocates read with an experienced advocate who introduces them into the routine, or they enroll in courses given by seasoned advocates to gain the necessary experience. The courses are given in private schools known as the *escuelas de prática jurídica*.

There is a bar of advocates (*colegio de abogados*) in every capital of a province and in any locality having at least twenty advocates. Every bar has a dean, a treasurer, a librarian, and a secretary. These officers, together with not less than two and not more than ten members (*diputados*) of the bar, form the council (*junta de gobierno*) of the bar. The number of the members on the council varies in accordance with the size of the bar. The council is elected by the general assembly (*junta general*) in accordance with the statute of the particular bar. The local bar protects the interests of its members and exercises disciplinary powers over them.

To coordinate the work of the individual bars, there is a general council of advocacy (*Consejo General de la Abogacia Española*) set up as a representative organ of advocacy at the national level.

Disciplinary powers over advocates are exercised by the *juntas de gobierno* of every bar, with an appeal (*recurso de súplica*) to the *Consejo General*.

NOTES AND QUESTIONS

The Spanish bar distinguishes two kinds of legal pratitioners, *procuradores* and *abogados*. How do they differ? How do they compare with the Italian division of the bar into attorneys and advocates and with the English division into solicitors and barristers? Is their function mutually exclusive? Must a party be represented by both a *procurador* and an *abogado*?

How does the Spanish bar compare with those of Germany and France? Compare their respective organizational and disciplinary provisions.

Is there a term of apprenticeship prescribed for candidates who desire to become legal practitioners? Is a bar examination required? Compare the French and Mexican systems.

For the American system, compare, e.g., Texas V.A. Civ. St. Art. 304ff. as to Texas attorneys, and the Code of Professional Responsibility promulgated by the American Bar Association.

D. NOTARIES (*Notarios*)[124]

Notaries are public officers whose function it is to legalize documents, contracts and other transactions in accordance with the law. They keep copies of all documents executed and legalized by them and issue copies and extracts therefrom. They also perform all other functions assigned to them by law. They must take out a bond as security for monies received by them in the exercise of their official functions.

To become a notary, a person must hold Spanish citizenship, be twenty-three years of age, be of good repute, hold the degree of *Licenciado* or *Doctor* of Law, and pass the notarial examination.

The examination is held in a designated seat of a chamber of notaries (*colegio notarial*) by an examination committee set up by the ministry of justice through its directorate general of registers and notaries (*dirección general de los registros y del notariado*). It is presided over by the director general or the deputy director general of the above directorate general or by the dean of the chamber of notaries of the place where the examination is held. It has another six members of whom three are notaries, one is a registrar of property (*registrador de propiedad*), one a chairholding professor law (*catedrático de derecho*), and one a legal counsel in the above directorate general. The examination is public and consists of an oral and two written parts. The examination turns on Spanish law applicable in the profession of a notary and on the drafting of notarial acts. Those who pass the examination are ranked in order of merit in accordance with the examination results.

Whenever an actual vacancy occurs, it is filled by those who qualify in accordance with specific rules. The notarial offices are of three categories, first, second and third, in accordance with the importance of the locality. Madrid and Barcelona have special standing within the first category. Vacancies occurring in Madrid, Barcelona, other first-category places, and second-category places are filled so that out of every six vacancies in each category, three are filled on seniority in the service, two on seniority in the particular category, and one by public competition. Vacancies occurring in third-category places are filled by public competition. Public competition means an examination closely following the rules applicable to notarial examinations for the initial qualification as a notary.

It may be seen that the system provides for promotion of notaries from smaller places to larger places and finally to Barcelona and Madrid. The appointments are made by the Minister of Justice and are published in the government gazette (*Boletín Oficial del Estado*). Notaries hold office until retirement at age seventy-five.

Each notary must exercise his office at the designated place and may undertake notarial acts in his particular district. There are several notaries in every notarial district so that the public has a choice of notaries. Every Spanish province has several notarial districts, and several provinces are grouped together to form a chamber of notaries (*colegio notarial*). Such chambers have their seats in major cities. Notaries holding office within the area of a particular *colegio notarial* are members thereof.

The *colegio notarial* meets in general assembly (*junta general*). The notaries elect a dean, two censors, a treasurer and a secretary by simple majority vote. Each holds office for three years and may be reelected only once. These five form the *junta directiva*. It represents the notaries and also is the disciplinary body of the profession in its area.

The several *colegios notariales* form a national association of their deans, known as the *Junta de Decanos de los Colegios Notariales*, with its seat in Madrid. The association meets in a plenary session of all the deans. It has a permanent committee (*comisión permanente*) composed of the president, the vice-president, the secretary and another three members, and also a delegated committee (*comisión delegada*), which is composed of the first three officers only.

The function of the *Junta de Decanos* is to represent the profession nationally, advise the government in matters pertaining to the interest of its members, promote cooperation among notaries, and the like.

Notaries may be disciplined by their *juntas directivas*. The punishments are an admonishment, a fine, and finally forcible transfer to a lesser ranked locality. An appeal against the discipline may be filed with the directorate general of registers and notaries, with a further appeal to the Minister of Justice. Forcible transfer may be decreed only by the Minister of Justice. All appeals must be filed within fifteen days. No further appeal lies against the decision of the Minister. Notaries may be entirely removed from their offices only by the Minister of Justice at the request of the directorate general of registers and notaries which, in turn, acts upon a request for removal formulated by the particular *colegio notarial*.

NOTES AND QUESTIONS

Like notaries in the civil system, Spanish notaries are fully qualified lawyers who by futher training and examinations qualify for the office. Since the office is a public office, they must be appointed by the government.

How are Spanish notaries appointed to particular vacant offices? Is there a provision made for promotion from smaller places to larger towns where the practice has more prestige and where it generates more income?

What are the main functions of notaries?

Note the organization of notaries existing in Spain. Compare it with the organization of notaries in France and in Germany.

Note also the disciplinary provisions. Compare them with similar provisions in Italy and in Germany.

How does the profession of Spanish notary compare with Anglo-American notaries public? *See,* e.g,. Texas V.A. Civ. St. Art. 5949ff. as to Texas notaries public.

VI. DECISIONS OF SPANISH COURTS

NOTE: *Cases have been selected to allow an insight into the legal system and the life of the country under consideration.*

Note the approach taken by the various courts in handling the matters considered.

Note also the time needed to bring the case from the trial court through the several hierarchically superimposed courts to the court of last resort.

A. DECISIONS OF CIVIL COURTS IN CIVIL AND COMMERCIAL MATTERS

DON PEDRO B.T. v. DON MIGUEL B.R.

Supreme Court, Civil Chamber, Judgment of January 12, 1970, Rapporteur *Excmo. Sr. D.* Jacinto Garcia Monge y Martín. (*Aranzadi, Repertorio de Jurisprudencia,* 1970, Vol. XXXVII, Case No. 167).

Don Miguel B.R. and Don Pedro B.T. made a contract in writing whereby they submitted to arbitration a dispute concerning the boundaries of their farms.

Don Pedro B.T. brought a petition for the annulment of the award made by the arbiter.

The Supreme Court denied the petition.

The Supreme Court

Considering that the three grounds for annulment were based on Art. 1691 (3) of the Code of Civil Procedure, in that the award decided points not submitted for the decision of the arbiter. The subject matter submitted to the arbiter as per the arbitration agreement was to draw the boundary between the overlapping farms of Messrs. B. and B. It appears from a detailed study of the land in the award, of the titles and allegations of the parties concerning individual parcels of land, and of the efforts of the arbiter to identify such parcels on the plan which he was using, that the line which separates the farm of Mr. B. from that of Mr. B., as found by the arbiter, is the wall situated Northeast from parcel D. on the plan. To reach that conclusion, the arbiter relied on documents and allegations of the parties. It may not be supposed that he exceeded his powers considering that there was a controversy and uncertainty as to the boundary. From the material submitted and from the terms of the award, it does not appear that the arbiter made pronouncements with respect to matters not submitted to him and exceeding the limits imposed by the agreement. This leads us to deny the petition on all the grounds on which it is founded and to dismiss the claim based on such grounds. Costs are taxed against the petitioner. He also loses his deposit.

NOTES AND QUESTIONS

Article 1691 (3) of the Code of Civil Procedure provides that a petition for the cassation of an arbitration award may be brought on the ground that the award was made out of the time set in the arbitration agreement or that it decided matters not submitted to arbitration.

The jurisdiction of the civil chamber of the Supreme Court is based on Art. 1688 (3) of the Code of Civil Procedure, which provides that the chamber has jurisdiction to hear petitions for the cassation of arbitration awards.

Note that the words *Excmo. Sr. D.* before the name of the rapporteur justice stand for *Excelentísimo Señor Don* (Most Excellent Sir).

On what grounds may arbitration awards be challenged in Anglo-American law? In which courts may action be brought contesting arbitration awards? *See also* Scherk v. Alberto-Culver Co., 417 U.S. 506 (1974).

DON AUGUSTIN B.V. v. DOÑA DOLORES O.C.

Supreme Court, Civil Chamber, Judgment of January 15, 1970, Rapporteur *Excmo. Sr. D.* Juan Antonío Linares Fernández. (*Aranzadi, Repertorio de Jurisprudencia,* 1970, Vol. XXXVII, Case No. 168).

The plaintiff, a merchant and citizen of the city of Barcelona, brought suit in Municipal Court No. 9 of Barcelona against the defendant residing in Tarrateig (Valencia) to recover a fixed sum of money.

The defendant appeared in the Country Court of Albaida and challenged the jurisdiction of the Barcelona court.

Having considered the question of jurisdiction, the Supreme Court ruled in favor of Municipal Court No. 9 of Barcelona as the court having jurisdiction of the matter.

The Supreme Court

Considering that it appears from the allegations of the parties and from the documents produced that the sum demanded from Doña Dolores O.C. is constituted by the total of several payments made to her by the plaintiff, Don Augustín B.V., in fulfillment of a contract of sale of a café-bar located in Barcelona where the plaintiff began to pay the purchase price and where he continuted the said business, and since the claim is founded on the breach of the contract of sale by the vendor, it must be held that the judge of the place where the parties began to perform the contract is competent to hear all the disputes arising from its breach in accordance with the provisions of Art. 62 (1) of the Code of Civil Procedure and repeated holdings of this chamber. The dispute as to jurisdiction must therefore be resolved in favor of Municipal Court No. 9 of Barcelona to which all the files are remitted together with a certification of this judgment and its notification on the Country Court of Albaida.

Considering that with respect to costs the challenge to jurisdiction is not to be taken as frivolous.

NOTES AND QUESTIONS

Article 62 (1) of the Code of Civil Procedure provides that in actions in personam, jurisdiction is vested in the court of the place where the obligation is to be performed or, failing such a place, at the discretion of the plaintiff, either at the place where the defendant resides or at the place where the contract was made if the defendant is served there with process. The defendant may be served there even if his presence there is accidental.

A challenge to jurisdiction may be either inhibitory or declinatory. Inhibitory challenge is brought by the defendant in the court that he thinks has jurisdiction. The defendant must persuade such court that it has jurisdiction rather than the court where the plaintiff brought his action. If so, the court of the defendant's selection has then to induce the court where the plaintiff filed suit to declare itself without jurisdiction and transmit the case to the court of the defendant's selection. If the courts disagree, the dispute as to jurisdiction will be decided by the common superior of both courts involved. In this particular case, the respective courts are located within the areas of territorial competence of two different courts of appeal and, consequently, their only common superior is the Supreme Court. This is how the matter reached the Supreme Court. The inhibitory challenge gives the defendant the advantage of staying within his jurisdiction and not being required to appear in a far away court to challenge its jurisdiction.

Declinatory challenge is brought by the defendant in the court in which the plaintiff brought suit. If the court overrules the objection to its jurisdiction, the defendant can use all his remedies. If the court declines jurisdiction, it will designate a court which in its opinion has jurisdiction, usually the court indicated by the defendant. The question of jurisdiction is then decided by the common superior of these two courts as in the inhibitory challenge.

How are questions of jurisdiction decided in Anglo-American law? Does the Anglo-American law apply the principle of inhibitory challenge used in the Spanish law? Is the Anglo-American approach more like the Spanish declinatory challenge? Is the principle of the common superior court applied in Anglo-American law?

DON ANTONIO NICOLÁS N.G. AND OTHERS v.
DON JOSÉ MARIA M. Y R. DE T.

Supreme Court, Civil Chamber, Judgment of February 5, 1970, Rapporteur *Excmo. Sr. D.* Manuel Prieto Delgado. (*Aranzadi, Repertorio de Jurisprudencia,* 1970, Vol. XXXVII, Case No. 677).

Don Antonio Nicolás M.G., Don Armando G.V. and Don Máximo P.F. brought suit in the court of first instance of Benavente in its jurisdiction of *menor cuantia* against Don José Maria M. y R. de T. claiming damages.

The plaintiffs, the fathers of three minors who drowned in the river Esla when a small boat belonging to the defendant capsized while it was taking them together with other workmen across the river from the shore at *Santa Coloma de las Carabias* to work at the farm *Valdelapuerca* owned by the defendant. They alleged that the boat was unsuitable for the purpose for which it was being used and claimed damages of 150,000 pesetas each or an amount determined by the court as compensation for the loss suffered together with costs.

The defendant alleged that the boat was suitable for the purpose for which it was being used and that the accident was caused by an act of God since on the day of the accident the river carried twice as much water as on the preceding day.

The judge of first instance gave judgment for the plaintiffs and ordered the defendant to pay to each plaintiff the sum of 75,000 pesetas as damages. On appeal, the court of appeal affirmed and assessed all the costs of the proceedings against the appellant.

The appellant brought petition for cassation of the judgment for breach of law on the grounds stated further below. The Supreme Court denied the petition.

The Supreme Court

Considering that the first ground of the petition relies on Art. 1692 (7) of the Code of Civil Procedure and alleges error in law in the evaluation of proof, in that the court of first instance did not give effect to the cause of the act of God, which consisted in the fact that the river Esla carried twice the volume of water from one day to the other, an event that was properly attested to by the Duero Valley Authority and an event that interrupted the chain of causation required by Art. 1902 of the Civil Code. The petition cannot succeed on this ground because, as this chamber has repeatedly held, an error of law is committed only when a rule of proof is infringed, i.e., when a particular proof is not given the effect given to it by the law. It is clear that in order to determine whether such error was committed, the party must allege which particular rule of law was so infringed. The petitioner did not comply with this requirement in this case.

Considering that the second ground of the petition must also be denied because the documents that are alleged to establish an error of fact do not meet the requirements of cassation. They are a certification dated May 11, 1968, given by the Commissioner in Chief of the Duero Valley Authority, which certifies the volume of water carried by the river Esla on the day of the accident and on the days before and after the accident, and a certification given by the clerk of court of the court of first instance of Benavente of the viewing of the place of the accident by the said court in the proceedings. Both documents were examined and considered by the court of first instance and their contents are not in a manifest contradiction to the facts found in the judgment.

Considering that the third and last ground of the petition, which alleges improper application of Art. 1902 of the Civil Code, must also be denied since such an error is committed when the factual premise of the judgment does not call for the application of the legal norm actually applied. In order to determine whether such an error was committed, this court must consider the facts proved. . . . The court of first instance, in applying Art. 1902, considered the objective, subjective and causal elements of tortious liability, all of which were proved. Consequently, the proper application of the law to the facts by the court cannot be doubted. The argument used by the petitioner concerning this ground shows merely that he is attempting to set up facts other than those found as proved and to substitute his own criteria for those of the court of first instance.

This court orders the application of Art. 1748 of the Code of Civil Procedure as to the costs and to the deposit.

NOTES AND QUESTIONS

For jurisdiction of *menor cuantia, see* courts of first instance in the section on civil courts above.

Article 1692 (7) of the Code of Civil Procedure provides that a petition of cassation for breach of law or legal doctrine may be brought when error of law was committed in the evaluation of proof, and also when error of fact was so committed if such error appears from documents or official acts of the court.

Article 1902 of the Civil Code provides that whoever, by his act or omission, causes damage to another through his fault or negligence must make good the loss caused.

Article 1748 of the Code of Civil Procedure provides that the judgment which denies a petition of cassation must assess all costs of the proceedings against the petitioner, and that the petitioner should also forfeit his deposit if one was made.

What principles of law would govern a similar situation in Anglo-American law? Would the plaintiff have to rely on a death statute? Could the case be brought in admiralty jurisdiction? *See,* e.g., Spencer Kellogg & Sons, Inc., v. Hicks, 285 U.S. 502 (1932).

DOÑA EULOGIA O.M. AND DON JUAN JOSÉ N.O. v. DON JOSÉ M.A. AND DOÑA JOSEFINA S.A.

Supreme Court, Civil Chamber, Judgment of June 17, 1970, Rapporteur *Excmo. Sr. D. Manuel Prieto Delgado. (Aranzadi, Repertorio de Jurisprudencia,* 1970, Vol. XXXVII, Case No. 2977).

Doña Eulogia O.M. and Don Juan José N.O. brought suit in the Court of First Instance No. 2 of Alicante in its jurisdiction of *mayor cuantia* against Don José M.A. and his wife Doña Josefina S.A. for partition of property.

The plaintiffs alleged that their deceased husband and father, respectively, bought from the defendants a one-half interest in a pharmacy owned by the defendants. They petitioned for the termination of the co-ownership while recognizing that the pharmacy was indivisible and could not be physically partitioned.

The defendants brought countersuit and alleged that the contract was not a contract of sale but a usurious loan disguised as a sale.

The judge of first instance gave judgment for the plaintiffs without costs. On appeal, the court of appeal set the judgment aside, held the defendants not liable and gave judgment in part on the counterclaim without costs, holding that the contract was a loan of 115,000 pesetas on 19 percent interest.

On a petition of cassation for breach of law brought on the grounds stated further below, the Supreme Court denied the petition.

The Supreme Court

Considering that the first ground of the petition, which relies on Art. 1692 (7) of the Code of Civil Procedure, cannot succeed when it alleges an error of law in the evaluation of proof. The petitioners allege the violation of Art. 1218 of the Civil Code but fail to state any reasons. They refer to the documents produced, one public instrument and one private document, in order to deduce therefrom that what the parties actually intended does indeed appear from those documents. The error they allege to have been committed by the court of first instance is thus not the result of the application of the above-mentioned principle of evaluation of proof by public documents, which would be an error of law but an error in the interpretation of a contract, a concept different from that alleged by the petitioners.

Considering that the second and last ground of cassation based on Art. 1692 (1) of the Code of Civil Procedure, may also not succeed when it alleges the violation of Arts. 1281, 1282 and 1285 of the Civil Code, in that the court of first instance did not base its decision on an interpretation of the said documents but on indirect proof by presumption, which may be used only when the facts cannot be established by direct proof.

The court of first instance held that the dealing embodied in the private document of August 24, 1944, was so intricate and secretive that the document would never make a more or less direct proof but only a very circumstantial proof of what the parties intended because the truth appears in it only to a very slight extent. The judgment found a number of facts that were not contradicted and may not now be challenged; and considering their meaning together with the contents of the documents produced, it is evident that the conclusion of the court that the dealing was a loan is logical, rational and likely. For these reasons, the petition is denied.

This court orders the application of Art. 1748 of the Code of Civil Procedure as to costs. No order as to the deposit is required since no deposit was made.

NOTES AND QUESTIONS

For jurisdiction of *mayor cuantia*, *see* courts of first instance in the section on civil courts above.

Article 1692 (7) of the Code of Civil Procedure is given in the notes to the previous decision.

Article 1692 (1) of the Code of Civil Procedure provides that a petition of cassation for breach of law or legal doctrine may be brought when the decision contains a violation or an erroneous interpretation or the improper application of laws or legal doctrines applicable to the case in question.

Articles 1281 of the Civil Code provides that when the terms of a contract are clear and leave no doubt as to the intention of the contracting parties, the contract will be interpreted in accordance with the literal meaning of its provisions. Where the words appear contrary to the obvious intent of the contracting parties, the intent will prevail over them.

Article 1282 of the Civil Code provides that in order to discover the intent of the contracting parties, their conduct at the time of the making of the contract and after its making should mainly be considered.

Article 1285 of the Civil Code provides that the provisions in a contract must be interpreted one by the other, so as to give to those doubtful provisions the meaning that appears from all the provisions as a whole.

Article 1748 of the Code of Civil Procedure is cited in the previous decision.

The judgment of the Supreme Court thus left the judgment of the court of appeal stand.

May a lender recover on a usurious contract in Anglo-American law? What penalties may be imposed on the usurious lender? *See,* e.g., Texas V.A.C. St. Art. 5069. Spanish law punishes usury by fines and imprisonment in Arts. 542-546 of the Penal Code.

DOÑA GUADALUPE G.H. AND OTHERS v. DON MANUEL A.G.

Supreme Court, Civil Chamber, Judgment of December 2, 1970, Rapporteur *Excmo. Sr. D.* Manuel Lojo Tato. (*Aranzadi, Repertorio de Jurisprudencia,* 1970, Vol. XXXVII, Case No. 5253).

Doña Guadalupe G.H., acting for herself and for her children Maria Cristina, José and Manuel A.G., brought suit in the Court of First Instance No. 1 of Salamanca in its jurisdiction of *mayor cuantia* against Don Manuel A.G. to determine permanent alimony.

The plaintiff, who is legally separated from her husband, the defendant, considers the provisional alimony awarded to her inadequate and petitions for its increase at the occasion of setting permanent alimony.

The judge of the court of first instance gave judgment in part for the plaintiff, held that the defendant was bound to pay permanent alimony, and awarded the plaintiff for herself and her minor children alimony to be paid to her at the rate of 20,000 pesetas monthly by the defendant as of the day of service of the suit on the defendant without costs. . . . On appeal, the court of appeal affirmed, with costs of the appeal to be assessed against the defendant.

On a petition of cassation for breach of law brought on the grounds stated further below, the Supreme Court denied the petition.

The Supreme Court

Considering that the petition of cassation for breach of law is based on four grounds and only the first one alleges error of law in the evaluation of proof relying on Art. 1692 (7) of the Code of Civil Procedure in that Art. 1232 of the Civil Code was not applied with respect to the answers given by the plaintiff to questions submitted by the defendant concerning alimony. . . . But it must be noted that the plaintiff only stated the amounts of money she received at different occasions from her husband while he still lived in the matrimonial home. She stated that ultimately he paid her 10,000 pesetas per month. . . . The trial court carefully considered many points, including the financial condition of the parties, from which a trial court has to come to a conclusion without making the admission of the wife the decisive element of its decision. The defendant wishes, however, the court to base its decision exclusively on the wife's admission. It follows that the first ground of the petition cannot succeed.

Considering that the second and third grounds of the petition allege violation of Art. 142 of the Civil Code by stressing the words "all that is indispensable" in the said article and by giving it a restrictive interpretation. They also allege violation of Art. 146 of the Civil Code, insisting that alimony must be limited to what is indispensable and that it is paid for necessities and for nothing else. But this thesis is untenable because we are dealing here with alimony due to a wife and three minor children of the very defendant and a distinction must be made, as it follows from Arts. 142 and 143, between civil or full alimony and that necessary for subsistence to which the last two subsections of Art. 143 refer, and which is called natural or restrictive alimony. Article 146 of the Civil Code deals with civil or full alimony, the amount of which is determined by the need of the recipients as well as by the ability to pay of the person liable. The restrictive interpretation suggested by the defendant is contrary to both the general doctrine and the decided cases and is untenable since we are dealing with spouses and legitimate children and not with persons listed in Art. 143 (4). This is in accordance with the duties imposed upon the husband by marriage and paternity. It follows that the petition cannot succeed.

Considering that in accordance with the well-known doctrine expounded by this chamber, it is for the courts of first instance to determine, within the limits of Art. 146 of the Civil Code in the exercise of their prudent discretion, the amount due as alimony. The determination of the trial court may not be challenged except when considering the need of the recipient and the ability to pay of the obligated person in accordance with the standing of the family in society (on which point a special stress was laid by the trial court in this case), the alimony awarded is clearly excessive. It must be noted that the trial court did not offend any legal rule and that the amount of money awarded as alimony is not excessive. . . . These are additional reasons why the first three grounds of error cannot succeed.

Considering that the fourth ground of the petition alleges the misapplication of Art. 148 of the Civil Code. . . . The judgment of the court of appeal, which affirmed that of the court of first instance, proceeded in accordance with the law when it ordered the payment of permanent alimony as from the service of the statement of claim on the defendant, i.e., as from the time when the defendant acquired knowledge of the demand made against him. Consequently, the fourth ground of the petition must also be denied.

Considering that none of the four grounds of cassation meet with success, the petition is denied with costs to be assessed against the petitioner. He also loses his deposit.

NOTES AND QUESTIONS

For jurisdiction of *mayor cuantia, see* courts of first instance in the section on civil courts above. Article 1692 (7) of the Code of Civil Procedure is cited above in the notes to the decision on Don Antonio Nicolás M.G. v. Don José Maria M. y R. de T.

Article 1232 of the Civil Code provides that an admission makes proof against the party making it except when compliance with the law could be avoided by making an admission.

Article 142 of the Civil Code provides that by alimony (support), it is meant everything that is indispensable for maintenance, shelter, clothing and medical assistance in accordance with the social standing of the family. Alimony includes also the education and upbringing of a minor recipient.

Article 143 of the Civil Code provides that those obligated to give alimony (support) to each other to the full extent of Art. 142 are: (1) spouses; (2) legitimate ascendants and descendants; (3) parents and their children legitimated by royal decree and their legitimate descendants; and (4) parents and their recognized illegitimate children and their legitimate descendants.

Parents and their illegitimate children must give each other support necessary for subsistence. Parents are further obligated to give such children elementary educations and provide them with professions, trades or occupations.

Brothers and sisters, including half brothers and half sisters by the same father or mother, are bound to give each other the help necessary to sustain life when, because of any reason not imputable to the recipient, he is unable to support himself. The help also includes the necessary expense of elementary education and the acquisition of a profession, trade or occupation.

Article 146 of the Civil Code provides that the amount of alimony (support) due in the cases enumerated in Art. 143 (1) through (4) inclusive, must be in accordance with the means of those who give it and with the needs of those who receive it.

Article 148 of the Civil Code provides that the obligation to give alimony (support) may be demanded by the entitled person as of the time of need; but it will be awarded only from the date on which suit is brought.

Is the Anglo-American law in agreement with the Spanish law concerning the obligation of the husband and father to support his wife and children? Consider Texas Family Code §4.02, which provides: "Each spouse has the duty to support his or her minor children. The husband has the duty to support the wife, and the wife has the duty to support the husband when he is unable to support himself. A spouse who fails to discharge a duty of support is liable to any person who provides necessaries to those to whom support is owed." What elements does an Anglo-American court consider in assessing the amount of support? Are the Anglo-American and the Spanish criteria virtually identical?

DON EDUARDO M.S. v. CELAYA ESPERANZA Y GALDOS, S.A.

Supreme Court, Civil Chamber, Judgment of April 30, 1970, Rapporteur *Excmo. Sr. D.* Baltasar Rull Villar. (*Aranzadi, Repertorio de Jurisprudencia*, 1970, Vol. XXXVII, Case No. 2054).

Don Eduardo M.S. brought suit in the Court of First Instance No. 1 of La Coruña against the Celaya Esperanza y Galdos, S.A. for the dissolution of a contract of lease of premises.

The facts of the case appear from the judgment.

The judge of first instance gave judgment for the plaintiff and held the contract of lease terminated with costs. On appeal, the court of appeal affirmed without making any award as to costs of appeal.

On a petition of cassation on the ground of an obvious injustice, the Supreme Court denied the petition.

The Supreme Court

Considering that the function of courts consists of the defense of legally protected interests and may not be converted into a game of pure legal speculation by pressing claims relying on hypothetical grounds of marginal merit. An action in our system of civil procedure must be based on facts that are constitutive of a cause of action and on facts established by the defense. We have to start in the case before us from the premise that the suit is founded on Art. 114 (7) of the Law of Lease of Premises (*Ley de Arrendamientos Urbanos*) and that the plaintiff-landlord claims that the defendant-tenant carried out work on the rented premises, which made structural changes in the premises, without the consent of the landlord and that the tenant denies having made such changes.

Considering that the contested judgment holds: (1) that the allegation of the plaintiff concerning the work carried out on the premises was fully established; (2) that such work modified the structure of the premises; and (3) that the work was done by the defendant-tenant.

Considering that all six grounds of error must be dismissed since none of them constitutes a proper defense and does not deny the execution of the work by the defendant but all deal only with pure hypothesis of a kind referred to by this court above and must be declared inadmissible. All these grounds were already submitted to the court of appeal and proved unsuccessful. The petition is denied, and with respect to costs, it is considered frivolous.

NOTES AND QUESTIONS

The provision of Art. 114 (7) of the Law of Lease of Premises appears in the text of the decision above.

The defendant is a stock corporation. For stock corporations, *see* the section on commercial law above.

The defendant did not have any legitimate defense for his suit, yet he was able to bring the case before the court of appeal and then before the Supreme Court. Costs of the proceedings were thus assessed against him.

May a tenant make structural changes in rented premises without the consent of the landlord in Anglo-American law? If he carries out such changes, is it a ground for the determination of the lease? Would an Anglo-American court give a similar judgment on the facts of the case?

EL BANCO EXTERIOR DE ESPAÑA v. DON JUAN A.F.

Supreme Court, Civil Chamber, Judgment of April 24, 1970, Rapporteur *Excmo. Sr. D.* Antonio Peral Garcia. (*Aranzadi, Repertorio de Jurisprudencia,* 1970, Vol. XXXVII, Case No. 2039).

The Banco Exterior de España brought suit in the Court of First Instance No. 1 of Alicante in its jurisdiction of *mayor cuantia* against Don Juan A.F. for a fixed sum of money.

The facts of the case appear from the judgment.

The judge of first instance gave judgment for the plaintiff and ordered the defendant to pay the plaintiff the sum of 2,800,000 pesetas with interest as from the day of protest of the bills of exchange and 6,812 pesetas as expenses of the protest without costs. He denied the counterclaim and absolved the plaintiff of any liability without costs. On appeal, the court of appeal affirmed and assessed the costs of the appeal against the appellant.

On a petition of cassation for breach of law, the Supreme Court denied the petition.

The Supreme Court

Considering that the court of appeal in its judgment upheld the obligation of the defendant to pay the value of the bills of exchange in question on the action of the holder in due course by endorsement. The acceptor of the bills of exchange petitions for cassation on the ground of lack of proper endorsement and alleges the failure of the court to apply Art. 447 of the Commercial Code since the endorsements did not specify that the persons signing were empowered to do so. But the endorsements were made by the president of the corporation with the indication of his position in some of the bills and by the secretary of the corporation with the indication of her position in other bills, and the corporate seal was affixed to their signatures in all endorsements. Don Louis G.V. and Doña Ute S. were appointed president and secretary, respectively, of the corporation as of the date of the founding of the corporation and it is obvious that the endorsement of bills of exchange falls within their powers and is authorized by the memorandum of association of the corporation. The endorsements thus comply fully with the requirements of Art. 447 of the Commercial Code since the two officers not only hold the power to act for the Loyte S.A., but they are also members of its board of administration. Whenever a firm or a corporation endorses a bill of exchange, it is sufficient if the endorsement is made by a representative thereof and the firm or corporate seal is affixed to the bill. . . . It follows that the several grounds for cassation cannot succeed.

Considering that the dismissal of the counterclaim brought by the defendant does not violate any legal doctrine. As the counterclaim does not deal with the matter raised in the action, it may not prevent the prosecution of the claim against the party actually liable. . . . The petition is denied. Article 1748 of the Code of Civil Procedure applies as to costs.

NOTES AND QUESTIONS

For jurisdiction of *mayor cuantia, see* the courts of first instance in the section on civil courts above.

Article 447 of the Commercial Code provides that those who sign bills of exchange for another, such as drawers, endorsers or acceptors, must be authorized by the persons for whom they sign and the authority must appear in the act. The drawers and holders of bills of exchange have the right to demand that those who sign produce their authorization. Administrators of corporations are authorized by the fact of their appointment.

Article 1748 is cited above in the notes to the decision on Don Antonio Nicolás M.G. v. Don José Maria M. y R. de T.

For corporations, *see* the section on stock corporations above.

How do corporations execute documents in Anglo-American law? Is the signature of the executive officer, like a secretary, with the indication of his authority and the seal of the corporation all that is required? Is then Anglo-American law in agreement with the requirements of Art. 447 of the Spanish Commercial Code?

DON ADOLFO H.D. v. SOCIEDAD GAMA, S.A.

Supreme Court, Civil Chamber, Judgment of November 25, 1970, Rapporteur *Excmo. Sr. D.* Antonio Cantos Guerrero. (*Aranzadi, Repertorio de Jurisprudencia,* 1970, Vol. XXXVII, Case No. 4904).

Don Adolfo H.D. brought suit in the Court of First Instance No. 14 of Barcelona against the Sociedad Gama S.A. for cancellation of the registration of a trademark.

The plaintiff, holder of the trademark "Festina" for watches, petitioned for cancellation of the registration of the trademark granted to the defendant corporation under the name "Festina" for stockings, socks, and the like.

The court of appeal held for the plaintiff and ordered cancellation of the registration of the trademark with costs.

On a petition of cassation for breach of law on the grounds appearing in the decision, the Supreme Court granted the petition, set aside the judgment of the court of appeal and gave judgment dismissing the action with costs.

The Supreme Court

With respect to the first judgment:

Considering that the first two grounds of the petition rely on Art. 1692 (7) of the Code of Civil Procedure and contest the findings of fact and allege an error of law in the evaluation of proof referring to the same two documents: the certificate of the Registry of Industrial Property, Folio 95, in relation to a similar certificate, Folio 83.

Considering that the third ground of the petition relies on Art. 1692 (1) of the Code of Civil Procedure and alleges the improper application of Art. 124 (1) of the Law of Industrial Property and brings before the court the important legal question of whether under an identical name under which certain objects were registered, it is possible to register later other totally different objects by a different holder. The view expounded in the petition is that the protection of the registration does not extend to phonetic identity of the trademark where the object protected by the new registration is totally different from the object already registered. This is because the confusion referred to in Art. 124 (1) cannot arise.

Considering that in order to decide the question the court of appeal considered the nature of the protection given by registration and stated that it ensures the exclusive use of the registered product, and that the phonetic and graphic appearance of the trademark makes it an exclusive symbol which becomes a piece of property separate from the registered object; that it has economic value to its holder and that it would be unjust to allow its use free of charge to others, even to mark different objects.

Considering that although the principle expounded by the court of appeal is meritorious, it is certain that by the mandates of Art. 124 (1) of the Law of Industrial Property . . . the protection given by registration applies only to registered products in order to prevent another product in the same or related class of products from being marketed under the same or similar name or under a name that is similar to it phonetically or graphically so as to induce confusion. But the law does not protect a name itself as a separate piece of property, making it the exclusive property of the one who first registered it, so as to prohibit its use by another holder with reference to different objects. It follows that the third ground of error succeeds and that the judgment must be set aside.

With respect to the second judgment:

Considering that by provisions of Art. 270 of the Law of Industrial Property as republished on March 5, 1930, the costs of the proceedings must be assessed against the defeated party.

NOTES AND QUESTIONS

For stock corporations, *see* the section dealing with stock corporations above.

Article 1692 (7) of the Code of Civil Procedure is cited above in the notes to the decision on Don Antonio Nicolás M.G. v. Don José Maria M. y R. de T. Article 1692 (1) of the same Code is cited above in the notes to the decision on Doña Eulogia O.M. and al. v. Don José M.A. and al.

Article 124 (1) of the Law of Industrial Property appears in the text of the decision.

How is the protection of trademarks accomplished in different countries? *See* 15 U.S.C.A. §1051ff. as to the U.S. trademark law. What is the definition of a trademark? What is the main purpose of registration of trademarks?

B.   DECISIONS OF CRIMINAL COURTS

JOSÉ B.F.

Supreme Court, Criminal Chamber, Judgment of January 15, 1970, Rapporteur *Excmo. Sr. D.* Fidel de Oro Pulido. (*Aranzadi, Repertorio de Jurisprudencia,* 1970, Vol. XXXVII, Case No. 5).

José B.F. was found guilty of the crime of abandonment of family pursuant to the provision of Art. 487 (1), point 1, of the Penal Code and was convicted to three months of imprisonment (*arresto mayor*) and a fine of 10,000 pesetas. He petitioned for cassation on the ground of improper application of the above provision The Supreme Court denied the petition.

The Supreme Court
Considering that the crime of abandonment of family in Art. 487 (1) of the Penal Code foresees two incidents; that is, willful abandonment of the family home or abandonment because of the disorderly conduct of the accused. It appears from the facts proved that there is sufficient evidence for a conviction on the first ground, since it is proved that the accused walked out of the family home abandoning his wife and daughter and ceased to fullfil his parental and matrimonial obligations. The abandonment is willful since it resulted in a total failure of support, this being the only meaning in which the word willful may be understood and this being the meaning attributed to it by the trial court. Consequently, the only ground of error based on Art. 849 (1) of the Code of Criminal Procedure must be dismissed and the petition must be denied.

NOTES AND QUESTIONS

Article 487 (1) of the Penal Code provides that a person who ceases to discharge his legal duties arising out of paternal power, protection of the family or marriage, although he could have done so, will be punished with *arresto mayor* and a fine of from 5,000 to 25,000 pesetas if: (1) he willfully abandons the family home or (2) his disorderly conduct is the reason for the cessation of his legal obligation of support.

Article 849 (1) of the Code of Criminal Procedure provides that a petition of cassation for breach of law may be brought when a principle of substantive penal law, or another norm of similar nature that must be observed in the application of penal law, is infringed.

For *arresto mayor, see* the section on punishment above.

The Supreme Court thus found no error.

Is the abandonment of family punishable in Anglo-American law? Is the law mainly concerned with the failure to support the family? *See,* e.g., California Pen. C.A. §270ff.

AURELIO F.N.

Supreme Court, Criminal Chamber, Judgment of June 15, 1970, Rapporteur *Excmo. Sr. D.* Alfredo Garcia Tenorio y San Miguel. (*Aranzadi, Repertorio de Jurisprudencia,* 1970, Vol. XXXVII, Case No. 2820).

The *audiencia* found the accused guilty of the crime of larceny pursuant to the provisions of Arts. 514 (1), 515 (1) and 516 (2) of the Penal Code and convicted him to eleven years of imprisonment (*presidio mayor*).

The accused petitions for cassation for improper application of the above articles and the inapplication of Art. 535 of the Penal Code.

The Supreme Court granted the petition; it set aside the judgment of the *audiencia,* gave a new judgment finding the accused guilty of embezzlement without aggravating circumstances, and convicted him to six years and one day of imprisonment *(presidio mayor).*

The Supreme Court

Considering that . . . the distinction between larceny and embezzlement must be sought in the provisions of Arts. 514 and 535 of the Penal Code, in accordance with which larceny is committed when, without violence or intimidation of persons or force being applied to property, movables belonging to another are taken without the consent of their owner with a view to gain; embezzlement is committed when money, valuables or any other movable thing is appropriated or dissipated to the loss of another by a person who receives it into custody, commission or administration or on any other ground and is obligated to deliver or return it. In addition to the different meaning of the verbs "take" and "receive" used in the above provisions, it must be noted that in larceny the actor proceeds actively and unilaterally, taking the things without the consent of their owner, whereas in embezzlement he receives what is not his from another quite passively and holds it lawfully until he incorporates it into his own property. The breach of the law arises only then on the ground of breach of contract pursuant to which he received the thing. In larceny, however, the actor never holds the property lawfully and the offense is committed at the moment of the taking.

Since it has been proved that the petitioner was employed by a firm as a cashier and his duties consisted of accepting money from its customers, and that with the intent to gain he appropriated a certain amount of it, it appears that he committed the crime of embezzlement and not larceny for which he was punished by the *audiencia.* Consequently, the first ground of the petition, which relies on Art. 849 (1) of the Code of Criminal Procedure and alleges the improper application of Arts. 514 (1), 515 (1), and 516 (2) of the Penal Code and the inapplication of Art. 535 in relation to Art. 528 of the same Code, succeeds.

NOTES AND QUESTIONS

Article 514 (1) of the Penal Code provides that a person commits larceny if he, with a view to gain, without violence or intimidation of a person and without application of force against property, takes movable property not his own, without the consent of its owner.

Article 515 (1) of the Penal Code provides that the punishment for larceny is *presidio mayor* where the value of the thing stolen exceeds 100,000 pesetas.

Article 516 (2) of the Penal Code provides that larceny is punished by penalties prescribed in the next higher grade of punishment when the actor is an employee of his victim or is guilty of abuse of confidence.

Article 535 of the Penal Code provides that those who, to the loss of another, appropriate or dissipate money, valuables or any other movable things they receive into their custody, commission or administration or on any other ground and are obligated to deliver or return such things, or who deny having received them, shall be punished with the punishments provided for in Arts. 528 or 530, as the case may be. The punishment will be imposed in its maximum grade in the case of necessaries.

Article 528 of the Penal Code provides for punishment in accordance with the value of the property embezzled. Article 530 provides for punishment of repeaters. Article 849 (1) of the Code of Criminal Procedure is cited above in the notes to the decision on José B.F. For the *audiencia*, *see* the section on the system of criminal courts above.

For *presidio mayor*, *see* the section on punishment above.

For theft, *see* the section on theft under the Spanish substantive criminal law above.

What is the distinction between larceny and embezzlement in the Anglo-American law? Is the Anglo-American law in full agreement with the Spanish law on the matter? *See*, e.g., Calif. Pen. C.A. §484ff. as to theft and §503ff. as to embezzlement.

JOSÉ R.O. AND JUAN F.R.

Supreme Court, Criminal Chamber, Judgment of January 17, 1970, Rapporteur *Excmo. Sr. D.* Jesús Riano Goiri. (*Aranzadi, Repertorio de Jurisprudencia*, 1970, Vol. XXXVII, Case No. 9).

The *audiencia* found the accused, José R.O. and Juan F.R., guilty of the crime of robbery with violence and intimidation of persons pursuant to Arts. 500 and 501 (5) of the Penal Code and convicted each of them to six months and one day of imprisonment (*presidio menor*).

The public ministry petitioned for cassation of the judgment alleging infringement of the last subsection of the above-cited Art. 501 because of its inapplication.

The Supreme Court granted the petition and gave a new judgment finding the accused guilty of the crime of robbery with violence and intimidation of persons from which light injuries resulted and convicted each of them to four years, two months and one day of imprisonment (*presidio menor*).

The Supreme Court

Considering that the taking of a movable property of another with violence against a person is punished in accordance with the injuries and loss caused, and by provision of Art. 501 (2) of the Penal Code the punishment is increased when weapons or other dangerous means are applied. The accused carried a club and two knives, one of which they set at the throat of the victim to rob him of 300 pesetas and his wallet. The court gives a description of the means applied, but it does not increase the penalty to its maximum grade. It thus infringes the provision referred to by the public ministry as its only ground for cassation. The petition thus succeeds.

NOTES AND QUESTIONS

Article 500 of the Penal Code provides that a person commits robbery if he, with a view to gain, takes movable property not his own by violence or intimidation of a person or by applying force to property.

Article 501 of the Penal Code provides for the punishment of robbery. The punishment ranges from *presidio menor* to *reclusión mayor* in accordance with the seriousness of the offense. Article 501 (5) provides that robbery is punished by *presidio menor* as a minimum. The last subsection of Art. 501 provides that punishments are imposed in their maximum grades where the offender makes use of arms or other dangerous means or where he attacks those who come to the victim's aid or those who pursue him

For robbery, *see* the section on robbery in the substantive criminal law above.

For *presidio menor, see* the section on punishment in the substantive criminal law above.

How is robbery defined and punished in Anglo-American law? *See*, e.g., Calif. Pen. C.A. §211ff. How do the punishments provided for in Spanish law compare with those of Anglo-American law? May an Anglo-American court of final resort increase the punishment on the appeal or petition of the prosecution?

ANTONIO E.F.

Supreme Court, Criminal Chamber, Judgment of January 19, 1970, Rapporteur *Excmo. Sr. D.* José Espinosa Herrera. (*Aranzadi, Repertorio de Jurisprudencia*, 1970, Vol. XXXVII, Case No. 10).

Pursuant to Art. 565 (1) of the Penal Code, the accused was found guilty of criminal negligence resulting in death and loss of property and was convicted to six months and one day of imprisonment (*prisión menor*) and to the suspension of his driver's license for one year. On a petition for cassation brought by the accused for misapplication of the provision referred to above, the Supreme Court denied the petition.

The Supreme Court

Considering that the accused did not stop at a stop sign when arriving at a crossing of a minor road with a major highway. The stop sign requires the driver to stop even though there happens to be no traffic on the road into which one enters. This measure is adopted by the traffic authorities because of the danger presented by the entry without caution on major roads where vehicles are allowed to travel at high speed. The accused did not obey this order of caution since he traveled at an excessive speed and was unable to stop his car. He entered the major road and placed himself in the way of an oncoming truck which, in order to avoid collision, swerved sharply to the left placing itself into the way of another automobile, which collided with the truck with the above-mentioned consequences. The criminal negligence of the accused is obvious since a reasonable person would have avoided the accident by obeying the order to stop and would have entered the highway only with due care and not at an excessive speed as was done by the accused.

NOTES AND QUESTIONS

Article 565 (1) of the Penal Code provides that a person who by criminal negligence brings about an event which, if committed willfully, would be a crime shall be punished with *prisión menor*.

For *prisión menor, see* the section on punishment above.

Is criminal negligence in the driving of vehicles punishable in Anglo-American law? *See,* e.g., Calif. Pen. C.A. §192 (3), Manslaughter in the Driving of a Vehicle, and the California Vehicle Code. Would the accused be punishable on the facts of the case in Anglo-American law?

JOSÉ F.M.

Supreme Court, Criminal Chamber, Judgment of March 7, 1970, Rapporteur *Excmo. Sr. D.* José Espinosa Herrera. (*Aranzadi, Repertorio de Jurisprudencia,* 1970, Vol. XXXVII, Case No. 1193).

The accused, José F.M., was found guilty of the crime of swindling pursuant to Art. 528 (3) of the Penal Code and was assessed the proper penalty. He petitioned for cassation on the ground of misapplication of the above provision. The Supreme Court denied the petition.

The Supreme Court

Considering that swindling to be criminally punishable requires the representation of something as true which is not true, and it must be so presented as to make the victim act upon the representation and accept that which is offered to him as good in exchange for value that passes to the swindler and whereby the swindler realizes a gain.

The petitioner knew that his victim would buy antique coins and he offered him some which he claimed were antique Spanish coins although he knew that they were imitations of recent making. He succeeded in misleading his victim into believing them to be genuine and into paying for them the value that he appropriated. The offense was thus fully consummated. It is of no importance that the accused did not state when the coins were supposed to have been minted. . . . It is sufficient that the coins were not genuine, that he knew this fact, and that he defrauded his victim. Consequently, the petition for cassation is denied.

NOTES AND QUESTIONS

Article 528 (3) of the Penal Code provides that a person who defrauds another in the substance, quantity or quality of things which he hands over to the other in compliance with an obligation will be punished with *arresto mayor* when the loss exceeds 2,500 pesetas but is below 25,000 pesetas.

How is swindling treated in Anglo-American law? Is it a separate offense or does it usually fall under theft or obtaining by false pretenses? *See,* e.g., Calif. Pen. C.A. §§484 and 532.

GASPAR G.C.

Supreme Court, Criminal Chamber, Judgment of January 19, 1970, Rapporteur *Excmo. Sr. D.* José Maria González Diaz. (*Aranzadi, Repertorio de Jurisprudencia,* 1970, Vol. XXXVII, Case No. 13).

The Supreme Court denied a petition of cassation for breach of form and breach of law brought by the accused, Gaspar G.C., against the judgment of the *audiencia,* which found him guilty of the crime defined in Art. 531 (1) of the Penal Code and convicted him to *arresto mayor* of one month and one day and to a fine of 100,000 pesetas.

The Supreme Court

Considering that the first ground of error relies on Art. 851 (1) of the Code of Criminal Procedure and alleges an error as to form in that legal concepts determinative of the offense were treated as facts. The error is not well founded since the public ministry, in prosecuting the offense under Art. 531 (1), did not make any such statements but simply related the facts using common language for whose understanding no special knowledge is required. It appears that the accused sold a piece of land by a contract of sale, claiming to be the owner although the land did not belong to him since his father had sold it to another person five years earlier.

Considering that the second ground of error relies on Art. 849 (1) of the Code of Criminal Procedure and alleges breach of Art. 531 of the Penal Code with respect to the fine imposed in that the court did not determine the amount of loss suffered by the purchaser. This ground is not well founded since the court found that the purchaser paid the accused 100,000 pesetas as a deposit on the purchase of the land. This is a finding of economic loss and the determination of the amount. The fact is admitted by the accused since the court also found that the accused repaid the full amount to the purchaser one day before the trial. The error is manifestly unfounded since had there not been any economic loss, the accused would not have felt obliged to indemnify the purchaser.

NOTES AND QUESTIONS

Article 531 (1) of the Penal Code provides that a person who shall pretend to be the owner of an immovable and shall alienate, rent or incumber it will be punished with *arresto mayor* and a fine amounting to three times the amount appropriated but not less than 5,000 pesetas. Article 531 (2) provides the same punishment for a person who would sell land as unencumbered although he knows it to be encumbered.

Article 849 (1) is cited above in the notes to the decision on José B.F.

Article 851 (1) provides that a petition of cassation may be brought when the judgment does not contain the facts which were found as proved by the court, when there is an obvious contradiction between such facts, or where legal concepts determinative of the offense were treated as facts.

The offense under Art. 531 falls within swindling and similar frauds.

For *arresto mayor, see* the section on punishment under substantive criminal law above.

Would the above-described offense in Spanish law fall within theft or obtaining by false pretenses in Anglo-American law? Does Anglo-American law specifically punish fraudulent conveyances or selling land twice? *See,* e.g., Calif. Pen. C.A. §§531 and 533. Would the accused be punishable under Anglo-American law?

C. DECISIONS OF ADMINISTRATIVE COURTS

CAMPSA v. DIRECTORATE GENERAL OF NAVIGATION

Supreme Court, Administrative Chamber (No. 4), Judgment of February 27, 1970, Rapporteur *Excmo. Sr. D.* José Samuel Roberes Garcia. (*Aranzadi, Repertorio de Jurisprudencia,* 1970, Vol. XXXVII, Case No. 658).

The corporation CAMPSA appeals the decision of the Directorate General of Navigation of January 16, 1966, which affirmed on a *recurso de alzada* an order of the Naval Command in Bilbao assessing a fine against the above corporation for having discharged oil wastes into the sea. The Supreme Court dismissed the appeal.

The Supreme Court

Considering that the factory of the corporation CAMPSA in Santurce was fined by the above decision for having discharged oil wastes into the sea. The corporation denies having done so. The investigating judge of the Naval Command in Bilbao found that the oil wastes were discharged into the sea through the drainage system which said factory constructed in the outer parts of the jetty in Santurce. The corporation did not bring any proof to the contrary in view of the testimony of the numerous witnesses who observed the discharge and of the two inspections made by the investigating judge, one in the presence of representatives of the corporation. The corporation later suggested that the discharge may have been made by someone else, but it did not even attempt to bring any proof substantiating its allegation. The investigating judge made a detailed investigation in this regard and found the allegations of the corporation unsubstantiated. The corporation did not give any information on the strength of which it could have been absolved of liability for the discharge for which it was fined 10,000 pesetas by the Naval Command of Bilbao; the fine was affirmed by decision of the Directorate General of Navigation of January 16, 1966. Considering that the decision appealed from was made in conformity with the Order of the Presidency of the Government of June 1, 1963 (R. 1138 y Ap. 51-66, 7178) for the prevention of sea water pollution by oil, the present appeal must be dismissed without costs.

NOTES AND QUESTIONS

For the *recurso de alzada, see* the section on administrative procedure above.

The Supreme Court has three administrative chambers, Nos. 3, 4, and 5. For procedure in the Supreme Court, *see* the section on administrative procedure above.

How did the case reach the Spanish Supreme Court? Through which jurisdictional levels did the case proceed? Was there another way to reach the Supreme Court?

Do Anglo-American countries prohibit the discharge of oil into the sea? Would similar proceedings be held in Anglo-American countries to impose a fine on the person or entity responsible for water pollution? Would the proceedings be administrative or judicial?

DON ALEJANDRO I. v. THE MINISTRY OF COMMERCE

Supreme Court, Administrative Chamber (No. 4), Judgment of May 26, 1970, Rapporteur *Excmo. Sr. D.* Juan Becerril y Antón-Miralles. (*Aranzadi, Repertorio de Jurisprudencia,* 1970, Vol. XXXVII, Case No. 2964).

On December 1, 1965, market inspection agents appeared in the factory "Embutidos M." located in Zaragoza and owned by Don Alejandro I. They took three samples of 150 grams each of the minced beef that was being used to make sausages. An analysis made by the Provincial Inspector of Health disclosed that the minced meat also contained horse meat. The defendant denied the charge, whereupon the governor appointed an independent expert who analyzed the samples and confirmed the prior analysis. The governor then imposed a fine of 15,000 pesetas against Don I., who brought a *recurso de alzada* to the ministry of commerce. The *recurso* was denied by decision of July 19, 1966. Don I. then appealed to the Supreme Court, which dismissed the appeal.

The Supreme Court

Considering that the question to be determined is whether on the facts of the case established as proved, the administrative act that imposed on Don I. the fine of 15,000 pesetas for breach of market regulations was made in accordance with the law.

Considering that the appeal relies on two grounds; the first alleges breach of the rules of procedure in connection with form and expertise. This ground is unfounded. The meticulous objectivity of the expertise carried out by the public administration cannot be denied and its results were fully corroborated by an independent expertise. The proceedings were carried out in accordance with the Law of Administrative Procedure.

Considering that the second ground with respect to the merits of the case is also unsuccessful in view of the outcome of the proceedings on proof which established the infraction. Consequently, the administrative act issued by the Department of Market Inspection and the decision of the ministry of commerce of July 19, 1966, affirming it were made in accordance with the law. It follows that the appeal must be dismissed without costs.

NOTES AND QUESTIONS

For the *recurso de alzada* and for procedure in the Supreme Court, *see* the section on administrative procedure above.

Through which jurisdictional levels did the case proceed? What other remedies were available to the defendant?

DON PELAYO R.Z. AND OTHERS v.
DIRECTORATE GENERAL OF HEALTH

Supreme Court, Administrative Chamber (No. 4), Judgment of October 30, 1970, Rapporteur *Excmo. Sr. D.* Luis Bermudez Acero. (*Aranzadi, Repertorio de Jurisprudencia*, 1970, Vol. XXXVII, Case No. 4736).

Don Pelayo R.Z. and others brought an appeal against a tacit denial and an express denial of November 7, 1968, by the Directorate General of Health of their *recurso de reposición* brought by them on July 15, 1968, to contest a decision of the said Directorate General of March 30, 1968, which authorized the pharmacist Doña Ramona C.V. to open a pharmacy at 24 Carolinas Street in the city of Barcelona. The Supreme Court dismissed the appeal.

The Supreme Court

Considering that two questions are to be decided, the first being whether the appeal was brought in time. We hold that it was. The plaintiffs brought the *recurso de reposición* on July 15, 1968. It was decided on November 7 of that year and the order notifying the plaintiffs was issued by the Directorate General on November 21 of that year from which it appears that the appeal was brought in time. Even in cases where the *recurso de reposición* needs not be brought but it is actually brought, and where it is not decided by the authority within two months, it is considered denied by administrative silence and the time to bring an appeal to the administrative courts is not two months but one year unless the authority makes a decision within that time. In that case, the term of two months begins to run from notification of the express decision. All of this is in accordance with provisions of Art. 126 (2) of the Law of Administrative Procedure and Art. 58 of the Law Governing Administrative Justice. Consequently, the present appeal was brought in time.

The second question to be decided is whether the decision of the Directorate General of March 30, 1968, was made in accordance with the law. The authorization given to Doña Ramona C.V. to open a pharmacy at 24 Carolinas Street was contested by Don Mariano S.F., who has a pharmacy at 25 Guillermo Tell Street, Doña Maria Rosa T.B., who has a pharmacy at 41 Principe de Asturias Street, and Don Pelayo R.Z., whose pharmacy is located at 167 Mayor de Gracia Street, all in the city of Barcelona. The question to be determined is whether the distance given in the plans between 24 Carolinas Street and 25 Guillermo Tell Street was correctly measured and whether it exceeds the distance of 225 meters required by the Decree of May 31, 1957 (R. 834 y Ap. 51-66, 6050) applicable to Barcelona. The distance between 24 Carolinas Street and the pharmacies of the other plaintiffs notoriously exceeds 225 meters. The measurement carried out on behalf of Doña Ramona C.V. gives the distance at 239 meters and 20 centimeters, and that made by the city architect at 204 to 205 meters. In view of the discrepancy, the Directorate General, on a *recurso de alzada* of the said Doña Romana C.V., appointed Don Juan Carlos C.G., one of three architects whose names were submitted to the Directorate General by the chamber of architects, to make a new measurement. He did so in the presence of the plaintiffs. He measured the distance from the center of the frontage of the existing pharmacy to that of the new pharmacy and found the distance between them to be 220.45 meters. And he understood that he was not supposed to include in the total the distance from the respective frontages to the middle of the street, which was 4.25 meters each. The Directorate General included those distances to make a total distance of 229.65 meters, which thus exceeded the minimum distance required of 225 meters. The Directorate General therefore granted the *recurso de alzada* and gave authorization to open the new pharmacy. The decision of the Directorate General is in accordance with the law because to reach one pharmacy going from the other, one must cross the street, at least Principe de Asturias Street, and that distance must be included in the total. Consequently, the distance between 24 Carolinas Street and 25 Guillermo Tell Street exceeds the required minimum.

Considering that it appears from the above that the appeal must be dismissed because the decision appealed from was given in accordance with the law. The appeal is dismissed without costs as there is no bad faith on the part of the appellants.

NOTES AND QUESTIONS

For the *recurso de reposición* and the *recurso de alzada, see* the section on administrative procedure above.

The contents of Art. 126 (2) of the Law of Administrative Procedure and Art. 58 of the Law Governing Administrative Justice appear in the text of the decision.

Note that by provision of a decree regulating pharmacies in the city of Barcelona, no new pharmacy may be opened unless it is located at least 225 meters from an existing pharmacy.

How did the case reach the Spanish Supreme Court? What were the prior proceedings?

How are pharmacies regulated in Anglo-American Law? What is the requirement for opening a new pharmacy? To which court or courts may the applicant appeal the administrative decision denying him a license to open a new pharmacy? *See,* e.g., Vernon's Ann. Civ. St. Art. 454(a)ff. as to Texas law.

VIAJES MELIÁ, S.A. v. DIRECTORATE GENERAL OF TOURISM

Supreme Court, Administrative Chamber (No. 3), Judgment of December 14, 1970, Rapporteur *Excmo. Sr. D.* Victor Servan Mur. (*Aranzadi, Repertorio de Jurisprudencia,* 1970, Vol. XXXVII, Case No. 5227).

A foreign tourist filed a complaint with the Directorate General of Tourism complaining that the travel agency Viajes Meliá, S.A. did not provide their tourist group with an air-conditioned bus as stated in the offer of services. The agency denied the charge and stated that the travel contract did not provide for an air-conditioned bus.

The Directorate General fined the travel agency with a fine of 5,000 pesetas. Its *recurso de alzada* was denied by the Ministry of Information and Tourism.

On appeal, the Supreme Court granted the appeal and held that no fine could be imposed on the travel agency as it did not break the contract.

The Supreme Court

Considering that the administrative act of the Directorate General of Tourism which imposed a fine upon the travel agency Viajes Meliá, S.A. was affirmed on a *recurso de reposición* by an Order of the Ministry of Information and Tourism of

September 23, 1969. The decision relies on the complaint of Mr. Joseph H. of Chicago, an American citizen. It states that the travel agent who made the reservation for the tour assured him, after having read the prospectus of Meliá, that the bus was to be air-conditioned.

Considering that the provisions quoted in the ministerial order as legal grounds for the imposition of the fine . . . provide that an enterprise of tourism is bound to provide services in accordance with the contract and in accordance with regulations or, failing such provisions, in accordance with current use and custom. In this particular case, the travel agency was bound to provide specific services agreed upon by contract.

Considering that the reasoning of the ministry to the effect that the terms of the contract provided for an air-conditioned bus cannot be accepted. . . . The complainant, Mr. Joseph H., himself claims that he contracted for the service with the agency Trip Inc. of Chicago on the strength of the prospectus of Meliá offering a tour named "Fiesta Iberia." . . . As the prospectus describing the tour does not state that the bus would be air-conditioned, Art. 59 of the Regulation of Travel Agencies of February 26, 1963, cannot be infringed since it decrees that the travel agency is bound to provide its customers with services in accordance with the contract.

After carefully studying the prospectus of Meliá, as is stated in the complaint, it is apparent that Viajes Meliá may not be held responsible for the statement made by an employee of the Chicago travel agency with which Mr. H. made the contract that the bus would be air-conditioned since no such statement appears in the prospectus. Mr. H. never asked the travel agent to show him the actual conditions of the tour so that he could read them himself, which he could have done since the prospectus is written in English.

Considering that it follows that the decision of the Directorate General of Tourism of October 7, 1968, and that of the Ministry of Information and Tourism of September 23, 1969, affirming the first were not given in accordance with the law. The appeal therefore succeeds without costs.

NOTES AND QUESTIONS

For the *recurso de alzada* and the *recurso de reposición, see* the section on administrative procedure above.

The contents of Art. 59 of the Regulation of Travel Agencies appear in the text of the decision.

Through which jurisdictional levels did the case proceed in order to reach the Supreme Court? How were the proceedings initiated? On the strength of which provision was the fine imposed?

DON JOSÉ MANUEL V.G. v. THE MINISTRY OF LABOR

Supreme Court, Administrative Chamber (No. 5), Judgment of November 14, 1970, Rapporteur *Excmo. Sr. D.* Francisco Camprubí y Páder. (*Aranzadi, Repertorio de Jurisprudencia,* 1970, Vol. XXXVII, Case No. 4734).

Don José Manuel V.G., an Inspector of Labor, appealed a decision of the Ministry of Labor of November 23, 1968, which denied his petition concerning triennal increments in the computation of his salary concerning the services he rendered as an officer of emigration prior to his joining the department of labor. The Supreme Court granted the appeal and held that the plaintiff was entitled to have such time included in the computation.

The Supreme Court

Considering that the plaintiff joined the civil service by public competition as an officer of emigration in accordance with the Civil Service Law of October 13, 1928, and was assigned to the Inspectorate General of Emigration by appointment of September 6, 1930. The appointment was subject to one year of probation. His appointment became permanent by order of the said Inspectorate General on March 20, 1932. By Order of the Ministry of Labor he was transferred in 1940 to the department of labor as subinspector 2nd class and assumed his functions as of January 30, 1940. After the enactment of the Law of Public Officers of May 4, 1965, he was not given credit for the services he rendered as an officer of emigration until 1935. He requested the Ministry of Labor to include the time so spent in the computation of his salary, but his request was denied by decision of the undersecretary of the said ministry on November 23, 1968. No reason for the decision was given except that according to a report of the department of finance in the ministry, a new rule concerning trieenal increments was under study. Plaintiff's *recurso de reposición* was also denied, contrary to the advice of the legal department of the ministry.

Considering that it appears from the above that the plaintiff was a public officer as from the time of his appointment as an officer of emigration. . . . and that he is entitled that the time spent by him in that service be computed for the purpose of triennal salary increments since that time was already fully credited to him on February 19, 1936, for the purpose of a five-year salary increment. This right cannot be denied to him on the flimsy ground that a new rule as to triennal increments was under study; such rule in any event could not affect rights already acquired. The plaintiff is therefore entitled to have the time spent in the service computed as from the date of his appointment in September 1930.

Considering that the present appeal must be granted and the decisions complained of must be set aside. This court holds that the plaintiff is entitled to have the time spent in the service from September 1930 to the present included in the computation of his salary for the purpose of triennal increments and that he must be paid the amount which he did not receive as from the enactment of the new remuneration system. No special determination as to costs is being made.

NOTES AND QUESTIONS

For a *recurso de reposición, see* the section on administrative procedure above. For the function of an undersecretary, *see* the section on central administration above.

Through which instances did the petition of the plaintiff proceed? Was the plaintiff required to file a *recurso de reposición* or was he actually free to file an appeal with the Supreme Court immediately after denial of his petition by the ministry.

COMPAÑÍA ANÓNIMA DE SECUROS v. ADMINISTRATION OF PUBLIC REVENUE OF BARCELONA

Supreme Court, Administrative Chamber (No. 3), Judgment of February 25, 1970, Rapporteur *Excmo. Sr. D.* Valentín Silva Melero. (*Aranzadi, Repertorio de Jurisprudencia*, 1970, Vol. XXXVII, Case No. 960).

The Compañía Anónima de Seguros appealed the decisions of the provincial economic-administrative court of Barcelona and of the central economic-administrative court. The Supreme Court granted the appeal and held null and void the assessment made by the Administration of Public Revenue of Barcelona concerning the appellant.

The Supreme Court

Considering that the Administration alleges that the appeal should be denied because of lack of form in that the appellant did not attach to the statement of appeal a receipt of payment of tax made to the treasury as required by Art. 57 (2) (e) and Art. 82 (f) of the Law Governing Administrative Justice. The objection cannot be sustained. A certificate of payment of the sum in question to the treasury made by the Bank of Santander was attached to the statement of claim in compliance with the mandates of the above provisions.

Considering that the question to be determined on the merits is whether the appellant has to pay tax on the total amount received in payment of premiums on insurance policies in the years 1958 to 1961 at the rate of 4.10 percent as demanded by the Administration or at the rate of 1.30 percent as actually paid by the appellant.

Considering that this chamber held in its prior decisions that the Order of the Ministry of Finance of March 3, 1965, which set the rate of tax at 4.10 percent, cannot be.applied retroactively. No retroactive application of the Order is possible as such application would be contrary to the fundamental principles of law, and it would also infringe the mandate of Art. 3 of the Civil Code. The rate of tax applicable prior to the Order referred to above was 1.30 percent and the tax was properly paid by the appellant. The proper course of public administration does not admit any ex post facto laws. This principle has been followed for years. It follows that the appeal succeeds. No special order as to costs is made.

NOTES AND QUESTIONS

Article 57 (2) (e) of the Law Governing Administrative Justice provides that an action in administrative courts is initiated by a statement of claim which must refer to the administrative act challenged. A certificate of payment of tax must be attached.

Article 82 (f) of the same law provides that the action will be dismissed if the statement of claim is filed after the time set for its filing has run or if it is defective as to form.

Article 3 of the Civil Code provides that laws do not have retroactive effect unless they expressly so provide.

Through which courts did the case proceed? What is the function of the economic-administrative courts and at what levels do they operate? May a law be retroactively applied? Is the Spanish law in full agreement with the Anglo-American law on this point?

FOOTNOTES

1. Civil Code, Arts. 40-41.
2. Code of Civil Procedure, Art. 64.
3. *Ibid.*, Art. 68.
4. Civil Code, Arts. 42-107.
5. *Ibid.*, Art. 45.
6. *Ibid.*, Art. 50.
7. There is still no divorce in Spain, but legislation providing for divorce is expected soon.
8. Civil Code, Art.83.
9. *Ibid.*, Art. 84.
10. Civil Code, Art. 56 reads: "Spouses are bound to live together, maintain matrimonial fidelity and support one another." Article 57 reads: "The husband must protect the wife and she must obey her husband."
11. Civil Code, Art. 100.
12. *Ibid.*, Art. 105. *Reclusión mayor* provides for imprisonment of from twenty years and one day to thirty years.
13. Civil Code, Arts. 325-332.
14. *Ibid.*, Arts. 333-608.
15. Law on Mines of July 19, 1944, and its Regulations of August 9, 1946.
16. Civil Code, Arts. 605-608.
17. Law on Mortgages of February 8, 1946, and its Regulations of February 14, 1947.
18. Civil Code, Arts. 609-1087.
19. *Ibid.*, Arts. 657-1087.
20. *Ibid.*, Art. 756.
21. Penal Code, Art. 43 provides that the loss of civil rights (*interdicción civil*) brings about the loss of paternal power, guardianship, membership in the family council, powers of the husband, administration of property, and the power to dispose of one's property *inter vivos.*
22. Civil Code, Arts. 1088-1314.
23. *Ibid.*, Art. 1261. All things that are not *extra commercium* may form the subject matter of a contract. Under *causa* is meant the performance or promise of a thing or service by both parties, the service or labor by one paid by the other, or a mere gift by the donor.
24. Civil Code, Art. 1280. A public document is one legalized by a notary or by a proper public officer observing the formalities prescribed by law.
25. Civil Code, Arts. 1315-1444.
26. *Ibid.*, Arts. 45-50; *see* the section on marriage above.
27. *See* the section on wills and estates (forced heirs), Civil Code, Art. 808ff.
28. Civil Code, Art. 1392-1431.
29. *Ibid.*, Art. 1417.
30. *See* the section on marriage above.
31. Civil Code, Arts. 1930-1975.
32. *Ibid.*, Art. 1955.
33. Commercial Code, Arts. 1-15.
34. *Ibid.*, Arts. 16-32.
35. *Ibid.*, Arts. 33-49.
36. *Ibid.*, Arts. 116-238.
37. *Ibid.*, Arts. 125-144.
38. *Ibid.*, Art. 136.
39. *Ibid.*, Art. 137.
40. *Ibid.*, Art. 138.
41. *Ibid.*, Art. 144.
42. *Ibid.*, Arts. 145-150.

43. *Ibid.*, Arts. 151-159.
44. The Law of July 17, 1953, as amended.
45. Commercial Code, Arts. 218-238.
46. *Ibid.*, Art. 218.
47. *Ibid.*, Art. 219.
48. Suspension of payments is governed by Commercial Code, Arts. 870-873, and by the Law on Suspension of Payments (*Ley de Suspensión de Pagos*) of June 26, 1922, all as amended.
49. Bankruptcy is governed by Commercial Code, Arts. 874-941, as supplemented by further provisions, and by title XII and XIII of the Code of Civil Procedure, Arts. 1130-1428, as amended.
50. Maritime law is governed by Book 3 of the Code of Commerce, and by a great number of particular statutes.
51. The fundamental statutes governing the jurisdiction of Spanish courts are the Organic Law on the Judiciary of September 15, 1870, and the Law Amending the Organic Law on the Judiciary of October 14, 1882, as further amended.
52. They are located in Albacete, Barcelona, Burgos, Cáceres, La Coruña, Granada, Madrid, Las Palmas, Palma de Mallorca, Oviedo, Pamplona, Sevilla, Valencia, Valladolid and Zaragoza.
53. Procedure in municipal and country courts is governed by numerous provisions, especially by the Decree of January 24, 1947, as amended by the Decree of November 21, 1952; the Law of July 17, 1948, amending the Law of May 21, 1936; the Decree of November 21, 1952, implementing the Law of July 19, 1944; the Law of July 23, 1966, amending the Code of Civil Procedure; Code of Civil Procedure, Arts. 715-740.
54. Rules of regular procedure are scattered throughout the Code of Civil Procedure (*Ley de Enjuiciamiento Civil*) but the basis thereof appears in Arts. 524-679 therein.
55. *See* Commercial Law, 3. on commercial books and bookkeeping above in Part B.
56. Summary procedure is governed by the Code of Civil Procedure, Arts. 680-714.
57. The Decree of November 21, 1952, on Municipal Justice, Arts. 22, 24, 25, 62, as amended.
58. Appellate procedure is governed by the provisions of title 6, Arts. 840-902 of the Code of Civil Procedure.
59. Code of Civil Procedure, Arts. 855-886.
60. *See* section 2 (a) (iv) under the Law of Civil Procedure, above (Procedure in courts of first instance, regular proceedings, judgment).
61. *Recursos de casación* are handled in title 21, Arts. 1686-1795 of the Code of Civil Procedure.
62. *See* section 3 (b) (ii) under the Law of Civil Procedure above (Procedure in the courts of civil appeal, regular procedure, final hearing and judgment).
63. Arbitration is governed by the Law of December 12, 1953, on arbitration in private law.
64. *Recursos de revisión* are handled in title 22, Arts. 1796-1810 of the Code of Civil Procedure.
65. Penal Code, Arts. 1-7.
66. *Ibid.*, Arts. 23-100. The death penalty was abolished in Spanish criminal law. It remains, however, in Spanish military law but may be pronounced only in time of war (Spanish Constitution of 1978, Art. 15).
67. All the above-enumerated kinds of imprisonment, from *reclusión mayor* to *arresto mayor*, are given in three grades: minimum, medium and maximum. Thus, e.g., *reclusión menor* and *extrañamiento* in their minimum grade range from twelve years and one day to fourteen years and eight months; in the medium grade from fourteen years, eight months and one day to seventeen years and four months; and in the maximum grade from seventeen years, four months and one day to twenty years.
68. Penal Code, Arts. 8, 9, 65.

69. *Ibid.*, Arts. 10, 61, 601.
70. *Ibid.*, Arts. 12-18, 53-54.
71. *Ibid.*, Arts. 405-409.
72. *Ibid.*, Art. 405.
73. *Ibid.*, Art. 406.
74. *See* footnote 67.
75. Penal Code, Art. 565.
76. *Arresto mayor* ranges from one month and one day to six months, including all three grades, and *prisión menor* from six months and one day to six years, including all three grades.
77. Penal Code, Arts. 418-428.
78. *Prisión mayor* ranges from six years and one day to twelve years, including all three grades.
79. Penal Code, Arts. 500-513.
80. Penal Code, Art. 501. *Presidio mayor* ranges from six years and one day to twelve years, including all three grades. *Presidio menor* ranges from six months and one day to six years, including all three grades. The terms are thus identical with those provided for under *prisión mayor* and *menor*, respectively, but *presidio* is a stricter kind of imprisonment.
81. Penal Code, Art. 505.
82. *Ibid.*, Arts. 514-516.
83. *Ibid.*, Art. 515.
84. *Ibid.*, Art. 516 bis.
85. *Ibid.*, Arts. 92-97.
86. Circumstances that exempt a person from criminal liability are enumerated in Penal Code, Art. 8. They are, e.g., insanity, minority below 16 years of age, self-defense or that of others, etc.
87. Penal Code, Arts. 98-100.
88. This occurred by the Law of June 20, 1968. Previously, they had no civil jurisdiction and the grant thereof is considered erroneous by the legal profession.
89. The Decree of November 21, 1952, which expounds basis 10 of the Law of July 19, 1944, dealing with procedural rules applicable to municipal justice.
90. Appellate proceedings against judgment of courts of the peace and municipal and country courts that are held in courts of instruction are also governed by the Decree of November 21, 1952, which expounds basis 10 of the Law of July 19, 1944.
91. Proceedings are held in accordance with the provisions for the so-called "urgent proceedings," Code of Criminal Procedure, Arts. 790-792. *See* section 3 (b) above for urgent proceedings in *Audiencias Provinciales*.
92. The *sumario* is governed by provisions of Book 2 of the Code of Criminal Procedure.
93. Regular proceedings in *audiencias provinciales* are governed chiefly by provisions of Book 3 of the Code of Criminal Procedure.
94. Prosecution lies under Penal Code, Art. 237 for serious disobedience to authority. Punishment is a fine and/or *arresto mayor* (imprisonment of from one month and one day to six months).
95. Urgent (summary) proceedings are dealt with in title 3 of Book 4 of the Code of Criminal Procedure. Urgent proceedings in *audiencias provinciales* are dealt with especially in the Code of Criminal Procedure, Arts. 793-802.
96. Procedure in the Supreme Court is dealt with in Book 5 of the Code of Criminal Procedure.
97. Revision proceedings are governed by the Code of Criminal Procedure, Arts. 954-961.
98. Code of Criminal Procedure, Arts. 528-544 and 589-614.

99. Decree No. 2484 of September 21, 1967, approving the text of the Code of Food Supply (*Código Alimentario Español*).

100. Law 14/1970 of August 4, 1970, the General Law of Education.

101. The Law of December 16, 1954, on Eminent Domain, and the regulations made thereunder.

102. Spanish Constitution of December 29, 1978, Art. 33(3).

103. Local administration is governed by the Law of Local Administration (*Ley de Administración Local*) of November 19, 1975, as amended and is based on Arts. 140-142 of the Spanish Constitution of 1978.

104. They were made legally big cities (*grandes ciudades*) by the Law of Greater Madrid of November 25, 1944, as published on March 1, 1946; the Law of Greater Bilbao of July 17, 1945, as published on March 1, 1946; and the Law of Greater Valencia of December 18, 1946, as published on October 14, 1948. The regime of Barcelona depends on the Law of Delegation of November 7, 1957, and on the Delegated Law of May 23, 1960. All the above are as amended.

105. The Law of November 7, 1957, provides for a special regime for Madrid and Barcelona and for any other big city where such a regime would prove advisable. In accordance with this Law, the Decree of July 11, 1963, established a special regime for Madrid, and the Decree of May 23, 1960, for Barcelona.

106. Provincial administration is based on Art. 141 of the Spanish Constitution of 1978.

107. The highest offices of state are governed by Title IV. of the Spanish Constitution of 1978.

108. The Council of State is governed by Art. 107 of the Spanish Constitution of 1978.

109. The directorate general of litigation is governed by the Regulation of July 27, 1943, and the Decrees of June 11, 1948, and April 25, 1958, as amended. These provisions also govern the offices of the government counsel.

110. The Court of Accounts is governed by Art. 136 of the Spanish Constitution of 1978.

111. Administrative chambers within *audiencias territoriales* are governed by the Law Governing Administrative Justice (*Ley Reguladora de la Jurisdicción Contencioso-administrativa*) of December 27, 1956, as amended by the Law of March 17, 1973, and by further provisions.

112. They are governed by the same statutes as are administrative chambers within *Audiencias Territoriales, see* above.

113. It is governed by the same statutes as are administrative chambers within *Audiencias Territoriales, see* above.

114. Taxation juries are governed by the General Tax Law (*Ley General Tributaria*) of December 28, 1963; by Decree 1881/1964 of June 25, 1964, on the Organization of Taxation Juries; by the Order of the ministry of finance on their organization of July 31, 1964; and by Decree 1292/1965 of May 6, 1965, on the Unification of Procedure before taxation juries; all as amended.

115. They are governed by the Decree of November 26, 1959, which approves the Rules of Economic-Administrative Procedure (*Reglamento de Procedimiento Económico-administrativo*), as amended.

116. Administrative procedure is governed by the Law of Administrative Procedure (*Ley de Procedimiento Administrativo*) of July 17, 1958, as amended and supplemented by further provisions.

117. Procedure in administrative courts is governed by the Law Governing Administrative Justice (*Ley Reguladora de la Jurisdicción Contencioso-administrativa*) of December 27, 1956 as amended by the Law of March 17, 1973, and by further provisions. Whatever is not regulated by these provisions is governed by the various laws governing procedures in *audiencias territoriales* and in the Supreme Court of Justice, especially by the Code of Civil Procedure.

118. Where a petition or request of any sort is filed with an administrative authority and no answer is forthcoming within three months, the party may file a reminder with that authority with the effect that if the authority does not answer within three months from the date of the reminder, the party is entitled to presume that the matter was decided adversely to him by administrative silence. The party may then take all other steps at his disposal. Law Governing Administrative Justice, Art. 38.

119. The office and function of judgeship is based on Title VI. of the Spanish Constitution of 1978 and is governed mainly by the Organic Law on the Judiciary of September 15, 1870; by the Law of May 26, 1944, on the Judicial School; and by the Organic Regulations of December 28, 1967, on the Judicial Career and on Magistrates of the Supreme Court; all as amended.

120. The office and function of procuratorship is based on Art. 124 of the Spanish Constitution of 1978 and is governed by the Organic Law on the Judiciary of September 15, 1870; by the Statute of the Public Ministry (*Estatuto del Ministerio Fiscal*) of June 21, 1926, and its Organic Regulations of February 27, 1969; all as amended.

121. The function and office of government counsel (*abogados del estado*) is governed by the Statute of the Directorate General of Litigation (*Estatuto de la Dirección General de lo Contencioso*) of January 21, 1925, and by Regulations (*Reglamento*) of July 27, 1943, all as amended.

122. The office of the *procurador* is governed by the Organic Law on the Judiciary of September 15, 1870; by the General Statute of the *Procuradores* (*Estatuto General de Procuradores de los Tribunales*) of December 19, 1947; and by further provisions; all as amended.

123. The profession of advocacy is governed by the Organic Law on the Judiciary of September 15, 1870; by the General Statute of Advocacy (*Estatuto General de la Abogacia*) of June 28, 1946; by the General Statute of the Bars of Advocates (*Estatuto General de los Colegios de Abogados*) of February 3, 1947; and by further provisions; all as amended.

124. The office of notaries is governed by the Notarial Law (*Ley del Notariado*) of May 28, 1862, as amended, by the Decree of June 2, 1944, which approves and introduces the Regulation of the Organization and Function of the Notarial Office (*Reglamento de la Organización y Regimen del Notariado*), as amended, and by additional provisions.

NOTES ON LEGAL SYSTEMS OF
ADDITIONAL COUNTRIES

The Austrian Law

I. INTRODUCTION

Modern Austrian law developed from fragmentary rules territorially applied and greatly influenced by Roman law.

As far as civil law is concerned, the Civil Code of 1811 is in power as amended. The Civil Code is one of the best ever produced in its field, and it has served as a model for legislation in many other countries. It represents a great advance over its predecessor in Austria, the *Codex Theresianus*, which remained a draft only, however, not being enacted with the exception of its family law part, which became law under Joseph II.

In commercial law, the law was based on custom and fragmentary rules until the promulgation of the Commercial Code in 1862, which actually was the German Commercial Code of 1861. This code, as amended, was in power in Austria until March 1, 1939, when the German Commercial Code of 1897 entered in power due to the German occupation of Austria. This code remained in power after World War II, and it is still in operation as amended.

In civil procedure, the present code, which was enacted in 1895, is in power as amended. It is a modern code and replaces its predecessor, the Code of Civil Procedure of 1781.

Modern criminal law has its beginning with the *Constitutio Criminalis Theresiana* of 1768 and the Criminal Code of 1787. A new criminal code was brought into operation in 1804, which, with minor changes, was reenacted as the Criminal Code 1852, which was extensively amended and republished as the Criminal Code of 1945. It is still in power as amended.

Modern criminal procedure also begins with the *Constitutio Criminalis*

Theresiana of 1768, which embodied both substantive and procedural criminal law, and with the Code of Criminal Procedure of 1788. A new and modern Code of Criminal Procedure was enacted in 1873. It was overhauled and reenacted as the Code of Criminal Procedure of 1960 and is still in power as amended.

Austrian administrative law is a leader in its field. It goes back to the practice of government offices in the eighteenth century. It has been regulated by a great number of decrees and orders. The administrative procedure was consolidated in the Administrative Procedure Statute of 1925. Its present version originates in 1950, and it is in power as amended.

II. THE SYSTEM AND ADMINISTRATION OF CIVIL LAW

The civil law field comprises substantive civil law, commercial law, the system of civil courts, and the law of civil procedure.

A. THE SUBSTANTIVE CIVIL LAW

The substantive civil law is governed by the Civil Code of 1811, as amended, and by a great mass of individual statutes. The Civil Code is presented in three parts dealing with persons, property, and provisions common to persons and property. Under persons, it deals with the rights of persons, family law and guardianship. Under property, it deals with possession and title, acquisition of property, wills and estates, intestacy, easements, contracts in general, and particular contracts (e.g., sales, gifts, partnerships, and damages). Under provisions common to persons and property, it deals with the securing of rights and obligations (e.g., suretyship), with the modification of rights and obligations (e.g., novation, assignment, and cession), with the extinction of rights and obligations by performance and with limitations and adverse possession.

B. THE COMMERCIAL LAW

The commercial law is governed by the Commercial Code of 1897, which is in power as of March 1, 1939, as amended, and by many additional statutes. The Commercial Code is given in four books dealing with merchants, corporations, commercial contracts, and maritime commerce. Under merchants, it deals with businessmen, agency, mercantile register, books and bookkeeping, and brokers. Under corporations, it deals with partnerships and various types of corporations. Under commercial contracts, it deals with penalties, interest, damages, sales, carriage of goods, and warehouse transactions. Under maritime commerce, it deals with shipowners and personnel, carriage of goods and passengers by sea, collision, marine insurance, general average, salvage, liens and ship mortgages.

In addition to the Commercial Code, there are many statutes dealing with commercial matters, the most important being the statute on corporations with limited liability, the several statutes on cooperatives, the patents and trademarks legislation, and the unfair competition statute.

C. THE SYSTEM OF CIVIL COURTS

The system of civil courts comprises courts of limited, general and appellate jurisdiction, and one court of final resort. The limited jurisdiction court is the county court (*Bezirksgericht*). It is a single judge court with jurisdiction limited by the value of the subject matter in dispute, and also with jurisdiction over specifically enumerated causes of action of limited importance, such as paternity actions, alimony and support, possession of land, and disputes between innkeeper and guest. An appeal against decisions of the court may be filed within fourteen days from notification of the decision with the district court (*Kreisgericht*). Parties before the *Bezirksgericht* may appear by themselves.

The district court (*Kreisgericht*) is a general jurisdiction court. It has unlimited jurisdiction above the limit of the *Bezirksgericht*. It is a single judge court in cases where the value of the subject matter in dispute is below a certain determined sum, and a three judge court where it exceeds that sum. Parties may agree to have the case heard by a single judge even where the subject matter in dispute exceeds the determined sum. The *Kreisgericht* also hears appeals against decisions of the *Bezirksgericht*. In its appellate jurisdiction, it sits as a three judge court. An appeal against decisions of the *Kreisgericht* in its trial jurisdiction may be filed within fourteen days from notification of the decision on the parties with the proper court of appeal (*Oberlandesgericht*). Against decisions of the *Kreisgericht* in its appellate jurisdiction, a further appeal lies on the same conditions to the Supreme Court (*Oberster Gerichtshof*), but only in cases where the value of the subject matter in dispute exceeds a certain minimum sum. Parties before the *Kreisgericht* must be represented by attorneys.

The court of appellate jurisdiction is the *Oberlandesgericht*. It sits in senates of three judges and hears appeals against decisions of the district court (*Kreisgericht*) and the commercial court (*Handelsgericht*) in its original jurisdiction. Against decisions of the *Oberlandesgericht*, an appeal may be filed within fourteen days from notification thereof on the parties to the Supreme Court (*Oberster Gerichtshof*). Parties before the *Oberlandesgericht* must be represented by attorneys.

The *Oberster Gerichtshof* is the court of final resort. It sits in senates of five judges and hears appeals against decisions of courts of appeal (*Oberlandesgerichte*) and also against decisions of *Kreisgerichte* and *Handelsgerichte* where these courts hear cases on appeal from *Bezirksgerichte*.

There also are commercial courts (*Handelsgerichte*). They are set up at the limited jurisdiction level and at the general jurisdiction level within the *Bezirks* and *Kreisgerichte*. They are composed of two judges and one lay judge who is a businessman elected for a term by the business community. Where the volume of business warrants it, independent commercial courts (*Handelsgerichte*) are set up. At the limited jurisdiction level, there is only one such independent *Handelsgericht*, called the *Bezirksgericht für Handelssachen;* it sits in Vienna.

The term *Handelsgericht* means a commercial court at the general jurisdiction level. These courts are fitted within the framework of civil courts. An appeal from decisions of a limited jurisdiction commercial court goes to the *Handelsgericht*, and from there to the *Oberster Gerichtshof*. An appeal against decisions of the *Handelsgericht* in its original jurisdiction goes to the *Oberlandesgericht* and then, if a further appeal is filed, to the *Oberster Gerichtshof*. Appeals are governed by the usual rules of civil procedure.

D. THE LAW OF CIVIL PROCEDURE

Civil procedure is governed by the Code of Civil Procedure, the Statute on the Jurisdiction of Courts, and several additional statutes.

The Statute on the Jurisdiction of Courts of 1895, as amended, governs jurisdiction of all civil courts in all matters. The Code of Civil Procedure of 1895, as amended, deals with provisions applicable to all civil courts, like parties, service of process, and proceedings before courts in general. It further deals with the procedure in trial courts, including briefs; proof by witnesses, documents and experts; and rulings and judgments. It also deals with procedure on appeal; nullity proceedings, and special proceedings, such as those in cases dealing with negotiable instruments.

Of the additional statutes on procedure, the more important is the one governing procedure in separation and divorce proceedings (Law No. 244 of July 6, 1938; Law No. 302 of July 27, 1938) and the one governing actions against the state for damages caused by the state and its organs in the exercise of their official functions (Law No. 60 of March 21, 1952; Law No. 218 of November 7, 1956).

III. THE SYSTEM AND ADMINISTRATION OF CRIMINAL LAW

The criminal law field comprises the substantive criminal law, the system of criminal courts and the law of criminal procedure.

A. THE SUBSTANTIVE CRIMINAL LAW

The criminal law is governed by the Criminal Code of 1945, as amended, and by a number of further statutes. The Criminal Code is presented in two parts, which deal separately with felonies and with misdemeanors and infractions. The first part, dealing with felonies, provides for provisions applicable to felonies in general, for punishment, and for aggravating and attenuating circumstances. It further deals with individual felonies from treason and offenses against the public authority to murder, manslaughter, bodily harm, arson, theft, robbery, swindling and bigamy. These provisions are followed by the limitation statutes. The second part, dealing with misdemeanors and infractions, first carries provisions applicable in general and then deals with punishment and with individual misdemeanors and infractions, from disturbing public order to those against the person and property; it is followed by the limitation statutes.

B. THE SYSTEM OF CRIMINAL COURTS

The system of criminal courts comprises courts of limited, general and appellate jurisdictions, and one of final resort. The same courts at each level exercise both civil and criminal jurisdiction in their civil and criminal branches, respectively. Only where the volume of business warrants it, are entirely separate criminal courts set up. There is only one court of final resort, the Supreme Court, which deals with both civil and criminal matters in separate civil and criminal senates.

The limited jurisdiction court is the county court (*Bezirksgericht*). It is a single judge court with jurisdiction limited to infractions (*Übertretungen*). An appeal against decisions of the court may be filed within three days from notification of the decision with the proper district court, known as the *Gerichtshof erster Instanz*. The defendant may defend himself without legal representation.

The *Gerichtshof erster Instanz* is the general jurisdiction court. It is a court of many functions. It has a number of judges of instruction (*Untersuchungsrichter*) who handle preliminary proceedings for the court and prepare cases for trial. It has chambers of three judges (*Ratskammern*) to supervise and hear appeals against rulings of judges of instruction. It has an appellate senate of three judges to hear appeals against decisions of the *Bezirksgericht*. In the exercise of its function as a trial court, it sits as a single judge court in cases where the prosecution demands a term of imprisonment of less than one year, or a fine. In more serious cases, it sits as the *Schöffengericht*, which has two judges and two lay judges; one of the judges presides. If the votes are equally divided, the opinion more favorable to the accused prevails.

In very serious offenses, where the penalty provided in the Criminal Code exceeds ten years of imprisonment, the court sits as the *Geschworenengericht*, a jury trial court. It is composed of three judges and a jury of eight jurors. The jury decides separately each question of fact by a simple majority. Where the votes are equally divided, the opinion more favorable to the accused prevails. Persons appearing before the district court must be represented by attorneys.

Appeals against decisions of district courts must be filed within three days from notification to the court of appeal, known as the *Gerichtshof zweiter Instanz*. Petitions for the nullity of a judgment must be filed within three days for transmission to the Supreme Court (*Oberster Gerichtshof*). No further appeal lies from decisions of the district court in its appellate jurisdiction, but a petition for the annulment of the judgment to the Supreme Court is available.

The *Gerichtshof zweiter Instanz* is the appellate jurisdiction court. It sits in senates of three judges. It hears appeals against decisions of district courts (*Gerichtshöfe erster Instanz*) within their trial jurisdiction, and also appeals against decisions of the *Ratskammer*. The decision is by majority vote. Persons before the court must be represented by attorneys. Further appeal against decisions of the court in cases tried in the *Schöffengericht* or the *Geschworenengericht* version of the district court in the first instance may be made to the Supreme Court (*Oberster Gerichtshof*), as may a petition for the annulment of any judgment given by the court of appeal. The time within which to file is always three days.

The court of final resort is the *Oberster Gerichtshof*. It sits in senates of five judges. It hears appeals against decisions of *Gerichtshöfe zweiter Instanz* in cases indicated above and all petitions for the annulment of judgments coming from any court. Parties before the Supreme Court must be represented by attorneys admitted to practice before the Court.

C. THE LAW OF CRIMINAL PROCEDURE

Criminal procedure is governed by the Code of Criminal Procedure and by several additional statutes.

The Code of Criminal Procedure of 1960 is in power as amended. It deals with the jurisdiction of all courts; with the prosecution and the defense; with the disqualification of judges and prosecutors; with statutes of limitation; with preliminary proceedings; and with proof, experts, witnesses, documents, and summonses. It has detailed provisions on proceedings concerning trials before criminal courts, decisions, rulings, appeals, and nullity petitions.

IV. THE SYSTEM AND ADMINISTRATION OF ADMINISTRATIVE LAW

The administrative law field comprises substantive administrative law, the system of administrative authorities and courts, and the law of administrative procedure.

A. THE SUBSTANTIVE ADMINISTRATIVE LAW

Substantive administrative law is statutory and appears whenever the state, as holder of the sovereign power, regulates its relations with the citizenry. It is the very extensive area of law that remains after taking out all civil and criminal law from the legal structure. It is governed by a great mass of statutes regulating particular subject matters. It deals, e.g., with public administration, public servants, mails, transport, tourism, hotels and restaurants, markets, public welfare, public health, education, taxation, and eminent domain.

Substantive administrative law is mainly civil, but there is also administrative criminal law dealing with offenses committed by the breach of substantive administrative law. It is governed by the Administrative Criminal Statute of 1950, as amended. Punishments are provided for such breach in the particular statutes and may consist of a fine or imprisonment. Imprisonment may be for any term between six hours and fourteen days, unless otherwise provided.

In administrative criminal proceedings, punishment is imposed by the proper administrative authorities. The prisoner is ordered to suffer imprisonment in his own place of residence, being prohibited from leaving it for the imposed term.

Should he break the order, he is held by the authority in a place specially provided for that purpose by the police department.

B. THE SYSTEM OF ADMINISTRATIVE AUTHORITIES AND COURTS

Administrative authorities are local, intermediate and central. The local authorities are the county administrative authorities (*Bezirksverwaltungsbehörden*), one in every county (*Bezirk*). The intermediate authorities are the district administrative authorities (*Landeshauptmannschaften*), and the central authorities are the proper ministries in Vienna in accordance with the subject matter. The direct superior in public administration of the *Landeshauptmannschaft* is the ministry of the interior (*Bundesministerium für Inneres*). Administrative authorities are thus large government offices handling all public administration in the country. Proceedings normally start at the local level, with appeals to the intermediate and central levels. Parties may appear in person or by legal representatives. Attorneys admitted to practice in courts of law are also admitted to practice before the administrative system.

There is one Supreme Administrative Court (*Verwaltungsgerichtshof*) superimposed over the structure of administrative authorities. It hears appeals (*Beschwerden*) against decisions of the central administration. It sits in senates of five judges. It may also sit in a plenary session comprising all judges, with two thirds being a quorum. The *Verwaltungsgerichtshof* is headed by a president, and has one vice-president, several presidents of senates, and judges. Parties before the Court must be represented by attorneys admitted to practice before it.

C. THE LAW OF ADMINISTRATIVE PROCEDURE

The law of administrative procedure is governed by the Administrative Procedure Statute (*Verwaltungsverfahrensgesetz*) of 1950, as amended; by the Statute Governing the Execution of Administrative Orders (*Verwaltungsvollstreckungsgesetz*) of 1950, as amended; and by several other statutes.

The Administrative Procedure Statute of 1950, as amended, deals with administrative authorities, parties, summonses, procedure before administrative authorities, proof, decision, appeal, costs, and the like. The Statute Governing the Execution of Administrative Orders of 1950, as amended, provides that orders directing a positive act or a negative duty to abstain from interference will be enforced by fines or imprisonment which may not exceed four weeks. It is similar to the enforcement of decrees by contempt in common law countries.

Administrative criminal procedure is governed by the Administrative Criminal Statute of 1950, as amended, which embodies the administrative criminal procedure. It deals with jurisdiction, apprehension, bail, proceedings before the hearing, proof, proceedings at the hearing, the decision, appeal, execution, and so forth.

Procedure before the Supreme Administrative Court (*Verwaltungsgerichtshof*) is governed by the Supreme Administrative Court Act (*Verwaltungsgerichtshof-*

gesetz) of 1965, as amended. The statute deals both with the Court and the procedure before it.

V. LEGAL OFFICERS

Legal officers are chiefly judges, officers of the public ministry, attorneys and notaries. Whatever has been said about them previously in the General Part, Section IV of the chapter "An Overview of the Law," applies with special force to the Austrian legal system.

A. JUDGES AND THE PUBLIC MINISTRY

Judges (*Richter*) and officers of the public ministry are in fact one group. The time to embark upon this career is immediately after graudation from law school. Every year, the ministry of justice announces the number of law graduates it will employ in the judicial and procuratorial service and applicants are invited to apply. Applicants are ranked in accordance with merit and the highest placed are accepted. They become judicial assessors (*Richteramtsanwärter*) and undergo professional training for as long as seven years. They must pass a judicial examination, which is both oral and written, dealing with the routine handling of matters in judicial and procuratorial offices. They are then appointed to the beginning category of judges and procurators. They are appointed for life (until retirement) and are irremovable. Promotion is on seniority.

Procurators (*Prokuratoren*) prosecute criminal cases before criminal courts. Their hierarchy is structured along that of the criminal courts before whom they appear. At the head of the structure is the procurator general, who appears before the Supreme Court, and below him are the procurators in courts of appeal and district courts and their staffs, both legal and clerical.

There are also offices of the government counsel (*Finanzprokurator*). They are similarly structured and handle civil matters of the state whenever the state appears as a litigant.

B. ATTORNEYS

The profession of attorney is governed by a number of statutory provisions, the fundamental being the Statute Regulating the Profession of Attorney (*Rechtsanwaltsordnung*) of 1868, as amended. To join the profession, a candidate must have a law degree and a doctorate in law, and must undergo professional training for seven years before being admitted to practice. One year must be spent with the judicial service in civil and criminal courts, the other six years may be spent with an attorney, with an office of the government counsel, or in the judicial service, either civil or criminal. An examination must be taken, which is both oral and written, on the professional tasks of an attorney. Membership in the bar is compulsory. An attorney (*Rechtsanwalt*) may practice in any court, civil or criminal, and before administrative authorities. The profession is united; there is no division between pleaders and practitioners. The profession favors individual practice, but partnerships of two attorneys are also common.

C. NOTARIES

Notaries (*Notare*) are similar to attorneys in their qualifications. They must have a law degree and must undertake seven years of practice, of which at least three years must be in a notary's office as a *Notariatskandidat*. The other four years may be taken in practice at the same places required for admission as an attorney (*Rechtsanwalt*), as mentioned above. They must pass an examination, both oral and written, on the professional tasks of a notary. They must then wait for an opening. Notaries are appointed by the Minister of Justice to a particular district by public competition. Until then, they work as fully qualified notaries in the office of a notary. When appointed, they must take out a bond as security for monies held by them in the exercise of their official functions.

Notaries certify and legalize documents, keep records, and are asked frequently by parties to draw up the contracts and documents that must be legalized by them. They draw up wills. They are appointed court commissioners in probate and administration matters so that they handle all uncontested probate and administration for the courts. Membership in the bar of notaries is compulsory. Although they are appointed for a particular district, they may undertake notarized acts anywhere in Austria. They serve until retirement at the age of seventy-two. The profession is governed by many statutes, the fundamental being the Statute Regulating the Profession of Notary (*Notariatsordnung*) of 1871, as amended.

The Swiss Law

I. INTRODUCTION

Swiss law goes back to the mediaeval German law from which it takes its origin as far as the German-speaking part of Switzerland is concerned. The influence of Roman law was keenly felt and it entered into Swiss law both through the German law and directly as the law of the Romanic population of Switzerland. The Swiss states were knit together as a confederation from the 1300's to 1798, then they set up a unitary state, the Helvetian Republic, which lasted only until 1803 when the present confederation was established. Present Switzerland has twenty-three cantons. The majority of the cantons are predominantly German; six are predominantly French, namely, Genève, Vaud, Valais, Neuchâtel, Fribourg and Jura; and one is predominantly Italian, namely, Ticino. As a confederation, Switzerland has federal and cantonal law. Federal law is mainly constitutional, but also civil and criminal, procedural and administrative. Cantonal law is mainly constitutional, procedural and administrative.

In civil law, some predominantly German cantons never codified their customary law, some codified it on the model of the Austrian Code of 1811, others introduced their own codifications. The predominantly French cantons and the canton of Ticino either adopted the Code Napoleon of 1804 or closely followed it in their own enactments. Finally, a Civil Code for all of Switzerland was enacted in 1907; it entered into force on January 1, 1912.

In civil procedure, all of the cantons, as well as the confederation, have their own codes, although they do not differ greatly from one another.

In criminal law, a unification was achieved under the Helvetian Republic, and a Criminal Code applicable to all of Switzerland was enacted in 1799. A number of

698

cantons kept it for some time, even after the demise of the Republic; others enacted their own codes. From the mid-nineteenth century on, all of the cantons had their own individual criminal codes; a new unification was achieved by the Criminal Code enacted in 1937 and in power from January 1, 1942.

In criminal procedure, the cantons, as well as the federation, have their own individual codes. In administrative law also, the cantons, as well as the federation, have their own individual laws. The administrative law is very uniform throughout the country, however.

II. THE SYSTEM AND ADMINISTRATION OF CIVIL LAW

The civil law field comprises substantive civil law, commercial law, the system of civil courts, and the law of civil procedure.

A. THE SUBSTANTIVE CIVIL LAW

In substantive civil law, the Civil Code of 1907 is in power as amended. It has four parts, which deal with the law of persons, family law, the law of inheritance, and the law of property. Its fifth part, dealing with the law of contracts and commercial law, was enacted in 1911 and entered in force, together with the other parts, in 1912. It is still in power as amended. It is a modern code of great juristic merit.

The fifth part of the Civil Code is known as the law of obligations. It deals, as mentioned above, with contract and commercial law. As to its commercial law aspect, it deals with agency, commission merchants, carriage of goods, warehouse contracts, partnerships and corporations of several types, the commercial register, bookkeeping, and sales. It further deals with the whole law of exchange, including checks and all types of commercial paper. The commercial law is thus an integral part of the civil law. The law of bankruptcy is governed by a separate federal statute, the Law of April 11, 1889, as amended.

The cantons have their own civil law statutes. They contain provisions that are applicable only in the respective cantons and are additional to the Civil Code.

B. THE SYSTEM OF CIVIL COURTS

The system of civil courts comprises cantonal courts and one federal court, the *Bundesgericht*. The cantonal courts are organized in accordance with the language prevalent in the canton. Thus, in German-speaking cantons, the system of courts resembles the Austrian system; in French-speaking cantons, the French system; and in the Italian-speaking canton of Ticino, the Italian system. The actual system of courts in every canton is a matter for that canton's decision, so that there is no uniformity among the cantons of a particular prevailing language, only a resemblance on general lines. Also, some of the smaller cantons do not have court systems as complex as those in the larger cantons.

1.   Civil Courts in German-Speaking Cantons

In German-speaking cantons, there are justices of the peace (*Friedensrichter*) with conciliatory jurisdiction and very limited ordinary jurisdiction.

Individual judges of county courts (*Bezirksgerichte*) sit as single judges of limited jurisdiction. They need a special commission to sit in that capacity, with the exception of the chief judge of the county court (*Präsident des Bezirksgerichts*) who can sit as a single judge ex officio. The commission is granted by the court of appeal (*Obergericht*). There is thus always one, and sometimes several, single judges in every judicial district of a canton. Their jurisdiction is limited by the value of the subject matter in dispute. In addition, they handle a few matters specifically assigned to them within bankruptcy proceedings. Appeals against their judgments lie to the court of appeal (*Obergericht*) and must be filed with the county court (*Bezirksgericht*) within ten days from notification of the judgment. A nullity petition to the *Obergericht* is always availabe within ten years of the judgment. Proceedings before single judges (*Einzelrichter*) are summary, and parties may represent themselves or may be represented by others under power of attorney. An attorney (*Rechtsanwalt*) is not required.

The county court (*Bezirksgericht*) is a court of general jurisdiction; there is one in every district. It has a chief judge (*Präsident*) and several judges (*Richter*). The actual court panel hearing a case has five members, three making a quorum. The decision is by simple majority. An appeal against judgments of the *Bezirksgericht* lies to the *Obergericht* and must be filed with the *Bezirksgericht* within ten days from notification of the judgment. A nullity petition to the *Obergericht* is always available within ten years of the judgment. Parties before the court may represent themselves, but if they do not, they must be represented by attorneys (*Rechtsanwälte*).

There is one court of appeal (*Obergericht*) in each canton. It has a chief justice (*Präsident*) and several justices (*Räte*). The actual court panel hearing a case has five members. The decision is by simple majority. The *Obergericht* hears appeals against rulings and judgments of single judges (*Einzelrichter*) and against those of the *Bezirksgericht*, and against rulings of the commercial court (*Handelsgericht*). It also hears nullity petitions against rulings and decisions of the *Einzelrichter* and *Bezirksgerichte*. An appeal against rulings and judgments must be filed within ten days from notification to the court that pronounced it. The nullity petition must be filed within thirty days under the same conditions, or within thirty days after discovery of the ground for nullity at any time within ten years. No further appeal lies against decisions of the *Obergericht*, but a nullity petition may be filed with the Court of Cassation (*Kassationsgericht*) within thirty days from notification, or within thirty days of discovery of the ground for nullity at any time within ten years. Parties before the *Obergericht* may represent themselves, but if they do not, they must be represented by attorneys (*Rechtsanwälte*).

The commercial court (*Handelsgericht*), one in each canton, has a chief justice (*Präsident*), one or more deputy chief justices (*Vize-Präsidente*) and several justices (*Räte*), all of whom are professional judges, and a number of business judges (*kaufmännische Richter*). The professional judges are member of the *Obergericht*. An actual panel hearing a case has two professional judges and three to five business judges. They decide by simple majority. Where the number of members of a panel is even and the votes are evenly divided, the presiding judge (a professional judge) has the casting vote. Business judges are selected for six-year terms by the government of the canton from a list submitted by the business community. From this established pool of business judges, the actual panel members are appointed in accordance with a rotating order made by the *Obergericht*.

The *Handelsgericht* hears cases between registered businessmen over a fixed minimum value, and all patent and trademark cases. The subject matter of the dispute must concern commerce. Matters not concerning commerce may not be brought before the court. Where the plaintiff is not a registered businessman, he may sue in ordinary courts. No appeal lies against judgments of the court, but a nullity petition lies under the above-mentioned conditions to the *Kassationsgericht*. Against rulings of the court, an appeal lies to the *Obergericht;* it must be filed with the *Handelsgericht* within ten days of the notification. Parties may act by themselves, but otherwise they must be represented by attorneys (*Rechtsanwälte*).

There is one Court of Cassation (*Kassationsgericht*). It has a chief justice (*Präsident*), a deputy chief justice (*Vize-Präsident*) and several members (*Räte*). The actual panel hearing a case has seven members. Decision is by simple majority. The court hears nullity petitions against decisions of the *Obergericht* and the *Handelsgericht*. Parties may represent themselves, but if they do not, they must be represented by attorneys (*Rechtsanwälte*).

2. Civil Courts in French-Speaking Cantons

There are justices of the peace (*juges de paix*) with conciliatory jurisdiction and very limited ordinary jurisdiction.

There is a court of general jurisdiction, known as the court of the first instance (*tribunal de première instance*) in every judicial district. It has a president and several judges. The court is a single judge court. An appeal against decisions of the court lies to the court of appeal (*cour de justice civile*). It must be filed with the *tribunal de première instance* within twenty days from the notification. There is no appeal in matters below a certain small value of the subject matter in dispute. A petition for the interpretation or revision of the judgment may be brought to the court that pronounced the judgment complained of within twenty days of the notification, or within two months of the discovery of the ground for interpretation or revision. Parties before the court may appear by themselves, but if they do not, they must be represented by attorneys (*avocats*).

There is one court of appeal (*cour de justice civile*). It has a president, a vice-president and several judges (*juges*). The actual panel hearing an appeal is composed of five members. They decide by simple majority. No further appeal lies against decisions of the *cour de justice civile*, but a petition for the interpretation or revision of the judgment may be brought to the court within twenty days from notification of the judgment, or within two months of the discovery of the ground for interpretation or revision. Parties before the court may appear by themselves, but if they do not, they must be represented by attorneys (*avocats*).

3. Civil Courts in the Canton of Ticino

There are justices of the peace (*giudici di pace*) with conciliatory jurisdiction and very limited ordinary jurisdiction.

There are single judges known as praetors (*pretori*), at least one in every judicial district. They have general civil jurisdiction. In matters below a certain specified value of the subject matter in dispute, no appeal lies against their decisions. Otherwise, an appeal lies to the court of appeal (*tribunale di appello*). It must be filed within fifteen days from notification to the *pretore* who pronounced the judgment. A petition for the cassation of a judgment is always available against all decisions of a praetor and must be filed within the same time (fifteen days). Parties before the praetor may appear by themselves, but if they do not, they must be represented by attorneys (*avvocati*).

There is one court of appeal (*tribunale di appello*). It has a president, vice-president and several judges (*giudici*). The actual panel hearing an appeal has five members. The decision is by simple majority. The court also forms a panel of three members to hear petitions for the cassation of those judgments pronounced by justices of the peace and praetors that are not appealable because of the low value of the subject matter in dispute. The court also sits as a trial court in cases of patents, trademarks, and certain commercial matters. No appeal lies against decisions of the court, but a petition for the interpretation or revision of its judgments may be brought within fifteen days from the notification to the same court. Parties before the court may appear by themselves, but if they do not, they must be represented by attorneys (*avvocati*).

4. Federal Court (*Bundesgericht*)

The *Bundesgericht* is the highest court in the land with civil, criminal and administrative jurisdiction. It has a president, a vice-president and a number of judges (*Räte*). It has a number of sections. There are two civil sections. The actual panel hearing a civil case has five members. There is a separate bankruptcy section, and the panel hearing such a case has three members. Decision is by simple majority in all cases.

In its civil jurisdiction, as a one instance court, the court hears disputes between the federation and a canton or between cantons, claims against the federation by private parties where the value of the subject matter in dispute exceeds a certain minimum, cases referred to it by a canton through cantonal legislation approved by the federal parliament, and disputes brought before the court by agreement of the parties where the value of the subject matter in dispute exceeds a certain minimum. It also hears disputes between a canton and a private party at the request of one of the parties and where the value of the subject matter in dispute exceeds a certain minimum.

As a court of appeal, the *Bundesgericht* hears appeals from decisions of cantonal courts in the following instances: where no further appeal lies in the canton; where a federal law is involved; in patent, trademark and copyright cases; in cases concerning the use of a firm name; in cases dealing with commercial papers, like bills of exchange, checks, stock and insurance policies; and in any case where the value of the subject matter in dispute exceeds a certain minimum. The appeal must be filed with the court that pronounced the judgment within twenty days from the notification.

In cases in which an appeal would not lie, a petition for the nullity of the decision is always available on the ground of nonapplication of the proper federal law, or its misapplication. The petition must be filed within twenty days from notification with the court that pronounced the judgment. No further remedy lies against the decisions of the *Bundesgericht*.

Parties before the *Bundesgericht* may appear by themselves, but if they do not, they must be represented by attorneys (*Rechtsanwälte, avocats, avvocati*). The court may direct a party to appoint an attorney where the party is not properly handling its case, and when the party does not do so, the court may appoint an attorney ex officio.

C. THE LAW OF CIVIL PROCEDURE

Each canton, as well as the *Bundesgericht*, has its own Code of Civil Procedure. These codes carry all the provisions usually found in such codes; they deal with, for instance, parties, jurisdiction, proceedings before trial, trial, proof, judgment, appeal, and cassation.

III. THE SYSTEM AND ADMINISTRATION OF CRIMINAL LAW

The criminal law field comprises the substantive criminal law, the system of criminal courts and the law of criminal procedure.

A. THE SUBSTANTIVE CRIMINAL LAW

The Criminal Code of 1937 is in power as amended and applies in all Switzerland. It is presented in three books. The first book deals with general provisions, jurisdiction, penalties, minors, and most of the infractions. The second book deals with felonies, misdemeanors and some infractions. The third book deals with the application of the Code, the jurisdiction of the cantonal courts and the federal courts, the criminal register, and prisons. The cantons have their own criminal law statutes. They contain provisions that are applicable only in their respective cantons and are additional to the Criminal Code.

B. THE SYSTEM OF CRIMINAL COURTS

The system of criminal courts comprises cantonal courts and federal courts. The courts have generally both civil and criminal jurisdiction. They become criminal courts in the exercise of their criminal jurisdiction.

1. Criminal Courts in German-Speaking Cantons

The individual judges (*Einzelrichter*) of the *Bezirksgericht* mainly hear infractions (*Übertretungen*). They also hear specifically enumerated minor felonies (*Verbrechen*) and misdemeanors (*Vergehen*) where the accused pleads guilty. In any event, they may not impose a penalty of imprisonment exceeding two months or a fine exceeding a certain limited amount. An appeal against decisions of individual judges lies to the *Obergericht* and must be filed within five days from notification of the decision. A petition for the nullity of their judgments lies to the *Obergericht* in all cases where an appeal would not lie. It must be filed within five days from notification of the decision or from discovery of the ground for nullity.

The county court (*Bezirksgericht*) hears cases in panels of three to five judges; the decision is by simple majority. It has jurisdiction over those felonies and misdemeanors that are not specially reserved for the jury court (*Geschworenengericht*), and it further hears all infractions that exceed the authority of individual judges. With respect to felonies and misdemeanors, an appeal against its decisions lies to the *Obergericht*. With respect to infractions, an appeal lies to the *Obergericht* only where the judgment is for imprisonment or for a fine exceeding a certain amount. It must be filed within five days from the notification. A petition for nullity lies to the *Obergericht* under the same conditions as from the individual judges.

The court of appeal (*Obergericht*) sits in panels of five members. Its decision is by simple majority. It hears appeals and nullity petitions against decisions of individual judges and against county courts. Appeals must be filed with the court that pronounced the decision under the conditions referred to above. The same applies to nullity petitions. No further appeal lies against the decision of the court, but a petition for the nullity of its decisions lies to the Court of Cassation (*Kassationsgericht*). It must be filed within five days from notification of the decisions or from discovery of the ground for cassation.

The jury court (*Geschworenengericht*) is composed of three judges and nine lay judges. Judges forming the professional panel are appointed for each session by the *Obergericht* from among judges of the *Obergericht* or the *Bezirksgericht*. Lay judges are selected in accordance with the usual principles for the selection of juries. They sit together and decide as one body. For a judgment of guilty, there must be at least eight votes. When they are not reached, and in all questions of a tie, the opinion more favorable to the accused prevails. Other questions are decided by a simple majority. In voting, the lay judges vote first, in order of their selection, and then the two professional judges vote; the presiding judge votes last.

The jury court hears all specially enumerated more serious cases of felonies and misdemeanors. No appeal lies against its decisions, but a petition for the nullity of its judgments may be brought to the Court of Cassation. It must be filed within five days from notification of the decision or from discovery of the ground for cassation.

The Court of Cassation (*Kassationsgericht*) sits in panels of seven members. It decides by simple majority. It hears petitions for the nullity of decisions of the *Obergericht* and of the *Geschworenengericht*. No remedy lies against decisions of the *Kassationsgericht*.

Parties before all criminal courts may act for themselves or be represented by others under power of attorney. They also may be represented by attorneys (*Rechtsanwälte*). The accused must have a defender before the *Geschworenengericht* or where a term of imprisonment of over one year may be imposed, or where he is deaf or dumb or of reduced competence. Where he does not appoint a defender, the court must appoint an attorney (*Rechtsanwalt*) to defend him. The prosecution is handled by the office of the public ministry.

2. Criminal Courts in French-Speaking Cantons

The police court (*tribunal de police*) is the criminal branch of the *tribunal de première instance*. It is a single judge court. It deals with infractions and with specifically enumerated misdemeanors (*délits*). It may not impose a term of imprisonment exceeding six months. An appeal against its decisions lies to the court of criminal appeal (*cour de justice criminelle*) and must be filed within fourteen days from notification of the judgment. It may be brought in any case where imprisonment is imposed or a fine exceeding a certain small amount. The appeal also includes grounds for cassation. No independent petition for the cassation of a judgment may be brought, but a petition for the revision of a judgment may be brought to the Court of Cassation (*Cour de Cassation*) whenever appropriate.

The correctional court (*cour correctionnelle*) is a branch of the court of criminal appeal (*cour de justice criminelle*). It normally sits as a jury court, composed of a presiding judge and six jurors. The jury is selected according to usual principles for the selection of juries. The jury decides questions of fact by a simple majority; in the case of a tie, the opinion more favorable to the accused prevails. It is a jury trial along the lines traditionally applied. The court will sit without a jury where the accused so demands, and it is then composed of three judges. The court hears all cases that exceed the powers of the *tribunal de police* but do not fall within the jurisdiction of the *cour d'assises*. No appeal lies against decisions of the court, but a petition for the cassation of judgments and rulings of the court may be brought within three days to the *Cour de Cassation*.

The assize court (*cour d'assises*) is a jury court and a branch of the *cour de justice criminelle*. It is presided over by a judge and has twelve jurors. The trial proceeds according to the same rules as the jury trial before the correctional court. It hears cases where the prosecution demands a penalty exceeding five years of imprisonment. No appeal lies against decisions of the court, but a petition for the cassation of its decisions may be brought within three days to the Court of Cassation.

The *Cour de Cassation* is the court of final resort in criminal matters. It has a president and four members. The actual panel hearing a petition for the nullity of a judgment, ruling, or a petition for the revision of a judgment, is composed of three judges. It hears such petitions brought against decisions of the correctional court and the assize court as well as against those of the chamber of accusation (*chambre d'accusation*), which must approve the imposition of arrest and release on bail. No further remedy lies against decisions of the Court of Cassation.

The suspect or accused in criminal proceedings may act by himself, but if not, he must be represented by an attorney (*avocat*). The accused must be represented by an attorney in proceedings before the assize court and the Court of Cassation. The prosecution is handled by the office of the public ministry.

3. Criminal Courts in the Canton of Ticino

The praetor (*pretore*) hears all cases dealing with infractions (*contravvenzioni*) and those cases of misdemeanors (*delitti*) where the prosecution does not demand a term of imprisonment exceeding fifteen days or a fine exceeding a certain amount. No appeal lies against decisions of praetors (*pretori*) but a petition for the cassation of their judgments may be brought within ten days from the notification to the Court of Cassation (*Corte di Cassazione*), and a petition for the revision of their judgments may be brought to the Court of Cassation at any time.

The court of appeal in the exercise of its criminal jurisdiction forms a criminal chamber (*camara criminale*) composed of three members. One judge and three lay judges form the correctional assize court (*assise correzionali*), which hears all cases of misdemeanors (*delitti*) that exceed the authority of the *pretore,* and those minor felonies (*crimini*) that are not punishable with the imprisonment in a penitentiary known as *reclusione.* The court decides by a simple majority; in the case of a tie, the opinion more favorable to the accused prevails. Lay judges are selected in accordance with rules routinely applied for the selection of jurors.

The criminal chamber and five lay judges form the criminal assize court (*assise criminali*). The court hears all cases of serious felonies (*crimini*) where the prosecution demands the imprisonment known as *reclusione.* The court decides by simple majority; in the case of a tie, the opinion more favorable to the accused prevails. Lay judges are selected in accordance with the rules routinely applied for the selection of jurors.

No appeal lies against decisions of the two assize courts, but a petition for the cassation of their judgments may be brought within ten days from the notification to the Court of Cassation, and a petition for the revision of their judgments may be brought to the Court of Cassation at any time.

The Court of Cassation (*Corte di Cassazione*) is composed of three judges of the court of appeal. It hears petitions for the cassation and revision of judgments pronounced by all three lower courts, namely, the *pretore, assise correzionali* and *assise criminali.* No further remedy lies against the decision of the court.

The person proceeded with before the criminal courts may represent himself, or he may be represented by an attorney (*avvocato*). Once he is formally accused of a criminal act, however, he must be represented by an attorney (*avvocato*). This happens when the document of accusation (*atto di accusa*) is filed by the prosecution. The prosecution is handled by the office of the public ministry.

4. Federal Criminal Courts

The federal court (*Bundesgericht*) forms a criminal chamber (*Kriminalkammer*) composed of three judges.

The *Kriminalkammer* and two other judges from the *Bundesgericht* form the *Bundesstrafgericht* (federal criminal court), which thus has five members. It decides by simple majority. It hears all cases specifically assigned to it; such cases are not serious enough to be heard by the federal assize court. These are mainly crimes committed with explosives and offenses against the federation, such as interference with elections or the defacing of currency and federal emblems.

The *Kriminalkammer* of three judges together with twelve jurors form the federal assize court (*Bundesassisen*). Jurors are selected in accordance with the usual principles for the selection of juries. The jury decides questions of fact by a simple majority; in the case of a tie, the opinion more favorable to the accused prevails. It is a traditional jury trial. The court decides specifically enumerated most serious crimes against the federation, like treason or insurrection.

No appeal lies against decisions of the *Bundesstrafgericht* and the *Bundesassisen*, but a petition for the cassation of their judgments may be brought within ten days from the notification to the Special Federal Court of Cassation *(Ausserordentlicher Kassationshof)*, and a petition for the revision of their judgments may be brought to the same court at any time.

The Special Federal Court of Cassation *(Ausserordentlicher Kassationshof)* sits with seven judges of the *Bundesgericht*. No further remedy lies against its decisions. The Court of Cassation *(Kassationshof)* sits with five judges of the *Bundesgericht* and decides petitions for the cassation of judgments pronounced by cantonal criminal courts in federal criminal cases. No further remedy lies against its decisions. Both cassation courts decide by simple majority.

The accused before a federal criminal court may represent himself, but if not, he must be represented by an attorney *(Rechtsanwalt, avocat, avvocato)*. The prosecution is handled by the office of the federal public ministry.

C. THE LAW OF CRIMINAL PROCEDURE

Each canton, as well as the federation, has its own Codes of Criminal Procedure. These codes carry all the provisions usually found in such codes; they deal with, for instance, parties, representation, jurisdiction, proceedings before trial, trial, proof, judgment, appeal, cassation, and revision.

IV. THE SYSTEM AND ADMINISTRATION OF ADMINISTRATIVE LAW

The system comprises substantive administrative law, the system of administrative authorities and courts, and the law of administrative procedure. Each canton, as well as the federation, has its own administrative law, but the pattern is one of great similarity throughout the country.

A. THE SUBSTANTIVE ADMINISTRATIVE LAW

Substantive administrative law governs the relations of the state with the citizens where the state appears as the holder of sovereign power. It is regulated by a great number of statutes. It deals, for instance, with public administration, public servants, taxation, public works, public welfare, health, education, and eminent domain.

B. ADMINISTRATIVE AUTHORITIES

Administrative authorities are cantonal and federal. Within the cantons, the usual pattern is a system of local, intermediate and central authorities. The local authorities are the communities *(Gemeinden)*, the intermediate ones are the county offices *(Bizirksämter)*, and the central authorities are the several departments of the particular canton under the direction of the cantonal government *(Regierungsrat)*.

Proceedings usually start at the local or the intermediate level with appeals to the central level. It is an informal procedure before administrative officers.

From the final decision of the central level, an appeal lies to the cantonal administrative court (*Verwaltungsgericht, tribunal administratif, tribunale amministrativo*). The cantonal administrative court has a president, a vice-president, and several judges. The actual panel hearing a case is usually composed of five members. The decision is by simple majority. The time to appeal to the administrative court is usually fifteen days from notification of the final administrative decision. The time to appeal within the administrative system of offices is always stated on the decision, but it is usually fifteen or thirty days. Parties may appear by themselves, but if they do not, they must be represented by attorneys before all higher offices and administrative courts.

Federal administrative authorities are set up along the same scheme referred to above. They act within the constitutional sphere of federal authority, e.g., armed forces, railways, mails, customs, currency, federal taxation, federal public servants, and so forth. The offices of central administration (*Departemente*) under the direction of the federal government (*Bundesrat*) are located in Bern. From their decisions, an appeal lies to the *Bundesgericht* in the exercise of its administrative jurisdiction. The administrative chamber (*verwaltungsrechtliche Kammer*) has five members and decides by a simple majority. The appeal (*Beschwerde*) must be filed directly with the court within thirty days from notification of the administrative decision. The court also sits as a trial court and a court of final decision in specially enumerated matters, which deal mainly with federal property and taxation. The court also hears appeals against decisions of cantonal authorities where this is allowed constitutionally.

Parties before federal administrative authorities, including the *Bundesgericht*, may represent themselves, but if they do not, they must be represented by attorneys (*Rechtsanwälte, avocats, avvocati*).

C.   THE LAW OF ADMINISTRATIVE PROCEDURE

Each canton, as well as the federation, has its own law of administrative procedure. They frequently apply many provisions of their codes of civil procedure to the administrative procedure.

V.   LEGAL OFFICERS

Legal officers are chiefly judges, officers of the public ministry, attorneys and notaries.

A.   JUDGES

Judges in Switzerland are elected into office. The mode of election and of their terms in office vary from canton to canton. In some cantons, judges are elected by general suffrage; in others, by the cantonal parliament; in yet others, the lower judges are elected by general suffrage and the higher by the cantonal parliament. Sometimes they are elected until retirement, normally at the age of seventy, but usually they are elected for a term only, and the term most frequently used is six years. They are reeligible. The presidents and vice-presidents are elected from among the judges by the cantonal parliament for terms of usually two years and are not immediately reeligible to preside, or they are elected by the judges themselves for similar terms. The requirement for eligibility is to be an attorney of the particular canton or to hold the degree of a law graduate or of a doctor of law. Judges of the federal court (*Bundesgericht*) are elected for terms of six years by the federal parliament; the president and vice-presidents are elected by the federal parliament from among judges of the court for terms of two years.

B.   THE PUBLIC MINISTRY

Officers of the public ministry represent the state, i.e., the canton or the federation, in criminal prosecution and also in all matters provided for by law. They are elected under similar conditions as are judges. They are elected usually for terms of three years and are reeligible. There always is one head officer of the public ministry in a canton (*Staatsanwalt, procureur général, procuratore pubblico*) and several of his deputies. County offices are headed by a *Bezirksanwalt, procureur,* or *sostituto procuratore pubblico*. The public ministry at the *Bundesgericht* is headed by the *Bundesanwalt* with deputies for territories of all languages of the country. They hold office for three years and are reeligible.

C.   ATTORNEYS

Attorneys (*Rechtsanwälte, avocats, avvocati*) must hold a law degree, have practical training in an attorney's office for one or two years, and pass a bar examination. The conditions differ slightly from canton to canton, but they are fairly uniform. The main difference consists in the term of practical experience before admission, which takes one year in some cantons and two years in others. When an attorney wishes to practice in another canton, he must usually undertake a normal or shortened term of practical experience and pass the cantonal bar examination. Any attorney may act before federal authorities and the *Bundesgericht*. The profession is united, there is no division between pleaders and practitioners. Membership in the organized bar is compulsory. The profession favors individual practice, but partnerships are also common.

D.   NOTARIES

Notaries (*Notare, notaires, notai*) are similar to attorneys in their qualifications, which also vary slightly from canton to canton. They must have a law degree and must undertake usually four years of practice in the office of a notary. They must pass a professional examination. In some cantons, it is possible to become a notary without obtaining a law degree, but those without it must take a number of oral examinations on Swiss law in order to qualify for admission to the written examinations that every candidate, including those holding law degrees, must pass. The written examinations are on the professional tasks of a notary. After fully qualifying, the notary must wait for a vacancy to occur. Notaries are usually appointed for particular districts, but they may undertake notarial acts in the entire canton. In some cantons, they are appointed by the government of the canton, in others by the highest cantonal court. They usually hold office for life. When appointed, they must take out a bond as security for monies held by them in the exercise of their official functions. They certify and legalize documents, and keep records. They are frequently asked by parties to draw up the documents that are to be legalized by them. They draw up wills, contracts, and the like, and also act as court commissioners in probate and administration of estates.

The Mexican Law

I. INTRODUCTION

The present Mexican law developed from the Spanish law introduced into Mexico in the sixteenth century. After its independence in 1821, Mexico continued to develop its law on its Spanish foundations; but the Mexican law also absorbed ideas of other European civil law systems as well as many notions of the Anglo-American common law system, especially in the area of constitutional law. Mexico is a federal state, its structure of government being greatly influenced by that of the United States. The Mexican constitution in many respects resembles that of the United States. The division of powers into legislative, executive and judicial, the organs holding those powers, the congress, the president, and the supreme court, resemble those of the United States in considerable detail. The constitution also contains a bill of rights guaranteeing individual freedom and liberty to every Mexican citizen.

Each state in Mexico has its own civil and criminal law as well as the law of civil and criminal procedure. The Federal District (*Distrito Federal*) and the Federal Territories (*Territorios Federales*) also have their own laws. Since the Federal District includes Mexico City, it is, due to the size of its population and its importance as the seat of the federal government, probably the most influential territorial unit within the federation. Its codes and laws serve as models for the individual states. They are enacted by the Federal Congress, and the Federal District and the Federal Territories are governed directly by the federal government. In commercial law, there is only one code applicable to all Mexico. Administrative law also follows one pattern, that applied by the federal government. The law of the federation is thus the preponderant law in the country. Politically, the federation overshadows the states completely and this is reflected in the law.

II. THE SYSTEM AND ADMINISTRATION OF CIVIL LAW

The civil law field comprises substantive civil law, commercial law, the system of civil courts, the law of civil procedure, and the *amparo* legislation.

A. THE SUBSTANTIVE CIVIL LAW

The substantive civil law in the Federal District and the Federal Territories is governed by the Civil Code of 1928, which entered into operation as of October 1, 1932, and is in power as amended, and by a number of other statutes. The Civil Code also applies in the federal courts. The individual states have their own civil codes, but they are modeled on the above Code. It is presented in four books, dealing with persons, property, succession and obligations. Under persons, it deals with physical and juridical persons, domicile, civil register, marriage, support, paternity and affiliation, guardianship, and the like. Under property, which is classified as movables and immovables, it includes possession, title, usufruct, easements, and prescription. Under succession, it deals with wills and testate succession, then with intestate succession, and finally with provisions applicable to both. Under obligations it deals with contracts, unilateral declarations, unjust enrichment, agency, different types of obligations, cession and subrogation, performance, extinction of obligations, and the different types of contracts, like sales, barter, bailment, and mortgages. It also deals with the public register and with transactions that must be registered therein in order to be valid against third parties.

B. THE COMMERCIAL LAW

The commercial law is governed by the Commercial Code of 1889, which entered into operation as of January 1, 1890, and many additional statutes. The Code itself has been extensively amended. It applies in all Mexico since the Federal Constitution of 1917, presently in power, in Article 73 (X), gives the federation the power to regulate commerce. The original provisions of the Commercial Code that are still in operation deal with merchants, the mercantile register, commercial contracts, and proceedings in commercial matters before courts. Later statutes govern partnerships and corporations, the law of bills of exchange and cheques, the banking business, the insurance business, bankruptcy, and maritime law.

C. THE SYSTEM OF CIVIL COURTS

The civil system includes state and federal courts. State courts and courts of the Federal District and the Federal Territories are of limited, general, and appellate jurisdiction.

Justice of the peace courts (*juzgados de paz*) are courts of limited jurisdiction. They are single judge courts with jurisdiction limited by the value of the subject matter in dispute. No appeal lies against judgments of the judge, except a special petition, known as the *recurso de responsabilidad*, to the civil court alleging negligence or ignorance on the part of the judge. It must be filed within one year from the judgment.

Civil courts (*juzgados de lo civil*) are courts of general jurisdiction. They are single judge courts. They have full civil jurisdiction. Appeals against their judgments may be lodged within five days, and those against their rulings within three days, to the *tribunal superior*.

There is usually one court of appeal in the states, as well as in the Federal District and Federal Territories, which is also a court of final resort. In the Federal District, it is the *tribunal superior*, which hears cases from the Federal District and Federal Territories. It has a president, several presidents of chambers, and a number of judges. It sits in its plenum and in several numbered chambers. The quorum of the plenum is fifteen members. Each chamber (*sala*) has three members. Decision is by simple majority in all cases. The plenum mainly has functions of an administrative nature, like appointing judges of lower courts and designating its own members to individual chambers. The judicial business of the court is transacted in the chambers. The first five chambers hear appeals against decisions of civil courts. No further appeal lies against decisions of the *tribunal superior*.

Federal courts include district courts, circuit courts, and the Supreme Court of Justice. They handle cases involving federal law and international treaties to which Mexico is a party. When the matter involves only the interests of the parties, the plaintiff may at his election bring the action in state courts, or in the courts of the Federal District if they are territorially applicable.

Federal district courts (*juzgados de distrito*) are single judge courts. They hear matters of federal law, matters affecting federally owned propery, matters concerning diplomats and consuls, and matters of the *amparo*. Appeals against their judgments in matters exceeding a certain limited value may be filed with the court within five days for transmission to the proper circuit court. Appeals against their rulings may be filed under the same rules within three days. In some cases of the *amparo*, e.g., where a statute is attacked as unconstitutional, a direct appeal lies to the Supreme Court of Justice.

Federal circuit courts (*tribunales de circuito*) sit either as single judge courts or as collegiate courts in panels of three members. They sit as single judge courts to hear appeals against decisions of district courts. They sit in panels of three members in cases of *amparo* provided for by the *amparo* legislation. They decide by simple majority. An appeal against their decisions lies to the Supreme Court under the above conditions applicable to appeals in the federal system.

The Supreme Court of Justice (*Suprema Corte de Justicia*) has a president, several presidents of chambers, and a number of justices. It sits in plenary session in matters specially assigned to it, like disputes between federal entities, between federal and state (local) entities, between federal and state courts, and the like. The plenum comprises all members of the Court, but fifteen members make a quorum. It decides by simple majority. The Court transacts its normal judicial business in four chambers (*salas*) of five members each. The first chamber has criminal business, the second administrative, the third civil, and the fourth conciliation and arbitration business. Decisions are taken by simple majority. No further remedy lies against decisions of the Court.

Parties before all Mexican civil courts may act by themselves, have themselves represented by others under power of attorney, or be represented by attorneys.

D. THE LAW OF CIVIL PROCEDURE

Each state, the Federal District and Federal Territories, and the federal courts all have their own codes of civil procedure. The Code of Civil Procedure for the Federal District and Federal Territories serves as a model for the state codes. The present Code of Civil Procedure dates from 1931 and is in power as of October 1, 1932, as amended. It has fifteen titles and a special title. It deals with actions, general rules (capacity, notifications, costs, etc.), jurisdiction, preparation of trial, proceedings on trial, summary proceedings, arbitration proceedings, proceedings on default, proceedings in divorce by mutual consent, appellate proceedings, proceedings in bankruptcy, proceedings in probate and administration matters, and uncontested proceedings (guardianship, adoption, etc.). The special title deals with proceedings in justice of peace courts.

The Federal Code of Civil Procedure of 1942 is in power as amended. It has three books: Book 1. General Provisions; Book 2. Proceedings; and Book 3, Special Proceedings. It deals with parties, jurisdiction, proceedings on trial, appellate proceedings, proceedings in bankruptcy and in succession to property to which the federal government is entitled, and with uncontested matters (involving minors or persons absent). It governs procedure in civil and administrative matters before the federal courts.

E. THE *AMPARO* LEGISLATION

The *amparo* legislation is constitutional in its nature and extends to all law, civil, criminal and administrative. It consists in the judicial review of statutes and measures violating the constitutional guarantees and legal order. It is based on Articles 103 and 107 of the Federal Constitution and on the Organic Statute of January 8, 1936, as amended, elaborating on the application of these two articles and providing the procedural rules for their application. Subject to the *amparo* are all state and federal statutes and measures that violate individual constitutional guarantees (Chapter 1, Articles 1-29 of the Federal Constitution), all federal statutes and measures that violate or restrict the rights of states, and all statutes and measures of states that invade the constitutional sphere of federal authority. The word "measures" also includes decisions of courts. Cases of *amparo* are always brought by the aggrieved party to the federal courts, with the Supreme Court of Justice being the final authority in the matter.

III. THE SYSTEM AND ADMINISTRATION OF CRIMINAL LAW

The criminal law field comprises the substantive criminal law, the system of criminal courts, the law of criminal procedure, and the *amparo* legislation.

A. THE SUBSTANTIVE CRIMINAL LAW

Substantive criminal law is governed by the Criminal Code for the Federal District and Federal Territories of 1931, which is in power as of September 17, 1931, as amended, and by a number of additional statutes. The Code also applies in federal courts. The several states have their own criminal codes, which are modeled on the above. The Code is presented in two books. The first deals with criminal responsibility, punishments, execution of punishments, probation, extinction of cr:minal responsibility, and criminal responsibility of minors. Book two deals with individual offenses. They are offenses against the exterior security of the nation (treason, espionage, and conspiracy), against the security of the nation (rebellion, sedition, and disturbance of public order), against international law (piracy, violation of neutrality, and mistreatment of prisoners), and against public security (aiding the escape of prisoners, possession of prohibited weapons, etc.) There are offenses in connection with public communications and mails; offenses against public authority, public health, and public morals; offenses which may be committed by officers of public administration; offenses committed in breach of the rules of professional responsibility; sexual offenses; offenses against life, corporal integrity or honor; and such other offenses as kidnapping, thefts, frauds, and threats.

B. THE SYSTEM OF CRIMINAL COURTS

Criminal courts are state and federal courts. State courts and courts of the Federal District and Federal Territories are of limited, general and appellate jurisdiction. The hierarchy of criminal courts corresponds to that of civil courts, the same courts exercising both civil and criminal jurisdiction.

In the Federal District, courts of limited jurisdiction are justice of the peace courts (*juzgados de paz*). They are single judge courts with jurisdiction limited to fines and imprisonment of up to six months. Appeals against their rulings and judgments may be filed with the *tribunal superior*. Appeals against rulings may be filed within three days; those against judgments, within five days.

Criminal courts (*juzgados de lo penal*) are courts of general jurisdiction. They are single judge courts. In all cases where the prosecution demands punishment exceeding one year of imprisonment, they sit as jury courts in conformity with the mandate of Article 20 of the Federal Constitution. In that case, the court is presided over by a judge and has a jury of seven jurors. They sit separately, the jury deciding the questions of fact submitted to it by the jduge, known as the *presidente de debates*. The jury decides by simple majority. An appeal against rulings and judgments of the court lies to the *tribunal superior* and must be filed within three days as to rulings, and within five days as to judgments.

The *tribunal superior*, in the exercise of its criminal jurisdiction, hears appeals from lower criminal courts in the Federal District and Federal Territories. Its criminal business is transacted by its sixth, seventh and eighth chambers. No further appeal lies against its decisions.

In the federal system, federal district courts (*juzgados de distrito*) hear all criminal cases assigned to them by federal law. They are mainly offenses committed abroad, as far as they are punishable in Mexico; offenses committed abroad by officers of the Mexican foreign service, and those committed in Mexico in foreign diplomatic missions; offenses committed against the federation; and offenses committed by federal officers in the exercise of their functions. *Juzgados de distrito* also hear cases of *amparo* against decisions of any state or Federal District and Federal Territories court. In cases where the prosecution demands imprisonment for a term exceeding one year, they sit as jury courts in accordance with the mandate of Article 20 of the Federal Constitution. The jury consists of seven jurors. It decides questions of fact submitted to it by the district judge. It decides by simple majority.

Judgments and rulings of district courts are appealable to the proper federal circuit court. The appeal must be filed within three days as to rulings and within five days as to judgments. In some *amparo* cases, e.g., where a statute is alleged to be unconstitutional, there is a direct appeal to the federal Supreme Court.

Whatever has been said about federal circuit courts in the exercise of their civil authority applies also to the exercise of their criminal functions. An appeal against decisions of *tribunales de circuito* lies to the federal Supreme Court as provided for by law under the above conditions applicable to appeals in the federal system.

The federal Supreme Court of Justice (*Suprema Corte de Justicia*) acts through its first chamber in the exercise of its criminal jurisdiction. Whatever has been said above about the Court in the exercise of its civil jurisdiction applies also to its criminal jurisdiction. No further remedy lies against its decisions.

In proceedings before justice of the peace courts (*juzgados de paz*), the accused may represent himself, or he may appoint another person to defend him, or an attorney. In all higher criminal courts, the accused must have a defender. He may appoint another person to defend him, or an attorney. If he does not appoint one, the court will appoint an attorney ex officio.

C. THE LAW OF CRIMINAL PROCEDURE

Each state, the Federal District and Federal Territories, and the federal courts all have their own codes of criminal procedure. The Code of Criminal Procedure for the Federal District and Federal Territories serves as a model for the state codes. The present Code of Criminal Procedure for the Federal District and Federal Territories is in power as of September 17, 1931, as amended. It has seven titles dealing with general provisions, proceedings before trial, trial proceedings, remedies against decisions, diverse provisions dealing with bail, civil claims, cumulation and separation of proceedings, execution of judgments, and jurisdiction and organization of courts.

The Federal Code of Criminal Procedure is in power as of October 18, 1934, as amended. It has thirteen titles dealing with general rules, initiation of proceedings, criminal prosecution, instruction, proof, judgment, remedies against decisions, bail, civil claims, cumulation and separation of proceedings, and the execution of judgment.

D. THE *AMPARO* LEGISLATION

Whatever has been said above as to the *amparo* legislation and matters of civil law applies with equal force in matters of criminal law.

IV. THE SYSTEM AND ADMINISTRATION OF ADMINISTRATIVE LAW

Mexican administrative law is based fully on the American model. It adopted the Anglo-American approach to administrative law and virtually copied the system of public administration of the United States. It thus has very little in common with the system of administrative law as it exists in European countries.

A. THE SUBSTANTIVE ADMINISTRATIVE LAW

Many statutes and rules and regulations issued by administrative authorities on their strength cover the field usually covered by administrative law in European countries. They are either state or federal provisions. They fall within the executive branch of the government, which is entrusted with their administration.

B. THE SYSTEM OF ADMINISTRATIVE AUTHORITIES AND COURTS

The system of administrative authorities resembles that of the United States. There is no uniform system of public administration as it exists in European countries.

The basic unit of public administration is the municipality (*municipio*). It is an independent unit of public administration endowed with a legal personality. It is headed by the municipal council (*ayuntamiento*), elected by universal suffrage and presided over by the municipal president (*presidente municipal*). It administers all federal and state laws as well as its own regulations. Its administrative decisions are subject only to judicial review, the *amparo* review before the proper state or federal court, as provided for by state and federal law.

The states and the Federal District and Federal Territories are administrative units of public administration. Their rights, duties and powers are regulated by constitutions, both federal and state. Administrative acts issued by them are subject to judicial review only as provided for by federal and state laws. By mandate of Article 15 (I) of the Federal Constitution, no intermediate authorities may be set up between municipalities and state governments.

The federal government is headed by a president, elected by universal suffrage for a term of six years. He may not succeed himself in office. He is the head of the federal executive branch of government. He appoints in his discretion the secretaries who head the several government departments (*secretarias*). There is no department of justice in the European sense; rather, an attorney general (*procurador general de la República*) heads the law offices of the government, as in the United States. The president is the direct head of the administration of the Federal District and he appoints a head of the Federal District administration (*Jefe del Departamento del Distrito Federal*) who is the immediate superior of the administration in the Federal District. The president also appoints governors (*gobernadores*) for the Federal Territories.

In addition to the *secretarias,* there are several departments of state (*departmentos de estado*), e.g., the *Departamento del Distrito Federal,* as mentioned above, and the Department of Tourism (*Departamento de Turismo*).

Further, there are commissions, modeled on those existing in the United States, such as the Electricity Commission (*Comisión Federal de Electricidad*), the Securities Commission (*Comisión Nacional de Seguros*), and the Mining Commission (*Comisión de Fomento Minero*).

There are also government institutions, like the Mexican Institute of Social Security (*Instituto Mexicano del Seguro Social*), the National Railways of Mexico (*Ferrocarriles Nacionales de Mexico*), and Mexican Gasoline, Inc. (*Petroleos Mexicanos, S.A.*).

The above federal government departments, commissions and institutions operate throughout the national territory from their central offices in Mexico City. They also establish administrative dependencies (*dependencias administrativas*), which are located throughout the national territory and are subordinate to the central offices.

The administrative acts of all these authorities are subject to the judicial review of the *amparo* before the federal court system, namely, federal district courts, circuit courts, and the federal Supreme Court. No genuine administrative review along the lines of European administrative authorities and courts exists in Mexico, with the exception of the Federal Taxation Court (*Tribunal Fiscal de la Federación*), which reviews final administrative decisions of the fiscal nature made by the Department of Treasury (*Secretaria de Hacienda y Credito Público*). Against its decisions, an appeal (*recurso de revisión*) lies to the second chamber of the federal Supreme Court.

Whatever has been said above about the federal district and circuit courts and the federal Supreme Court in connection with their civil and criminal functions applies also to their administrative functions. The administrative business that comes to the federal Supreme Court is handled by its second chamber. No further remedy lies against decisions of the Supreme Court.

Parties before all Mexican administrative authorities and civil courts undertaking judicial review of administrative acts may act by themselves, they may be represented by others under power of attorney, or they may be represented by attorneys.

C. THE LAW OF ADMINISTRATIVE PROCEDURE

No systematic law of administrative procedure is in existence apart from individual regulations issued by the particular departments of federal, state and municipal administration for the ordering of business transacted by them. Notable among these regulations is the Federal Fiscal Code (*Código Fiscal de la Federación*) of 1938, which is in power as of January 1, 1939, as amended. It contains the federal fiscal law and the rules of procedure before federal fiscal authorities and the *Tribunal Fiscal de la Federación*. The judicial review of administrative acts is possible by the way of the *amparo* on constitutional grounds. Administrative authorities generally apply the procedural rules contained in the respective codes of civil procedure. Federal courts apply the Federal Code of Civil Procedure to administrative cases heard by them.

D.   THE *AMPARO* LEGISLATION

Whatever has been said about the *amparo* legislation applicable to matters of civil law, and also to those matters of administrative law discussed above, applies to the administrative law. The *amparo* against administrative acts of any authority, whether state or federal, may be brought to federal courts, namely, federal district and circuit courts and the federal Supreme Court of Justice, as provided by law. The administrative business in the federal Supreme Court is handled by its second chamber. No further remedy lies against the decisions of the Supreme Court.

V.   LEGAL OFFICERS

Legal officers are chiefly judges, officers of the public ministry, attorneys, and notaries.

A.   JUDGES

Judges of all Mexican courts are appointed from among attorneys (*abogados*). Their other requirements and the method of appointment differ slightly with respect to the position held.

In the Federal District and Federal Territories, judges of all lower courts below the *tribunal superior* are appointed by the plenary session of the *tribunal superior* for terms of six years, counted from January 1, 1935. A judge appointed for the remainder of a term (e.g., replacing a judge who has died) serves only to the end of the term of his predecessor. All judges may be reappointed or promoted at the discretion of the plenum of the *tribunal superior*. They must be Mexican citizens by birth and thirty years or older, but not over sixty-five years of age, on the day of their appointment. They must be of good moral character, never convicted by a criminal court. All judges above justices of the peace (*jueces de paz*) must be attorneys (*abogados*) of at least five years' standing, while the requirement for a justice of the peace is only to be an attorney (*abogado*).

Judges (*magistrados*) of the *tribunal superior* are appointed by the President of the Republic with the consent of the House of Deputies (*Cámara de Diputados*) for six-year terms as above. They must possess the same qualifications required of judges as described above. They may be reappointed at the discretion of the President acting together with the Secretary of Government (*Secretario de Gobernación*) who must countersign the appointment. The president of the *tribunal superior* is elected by secret ballot for one calendar year in the first session of the court in January by all the judges of the court from among themselves. He may be reelected. The presidents of chambers are similarly elected for one calendar year by the judges of the particular chambers from among themselves; they also may be reelected.

In the federal system, all judges must possess the above-mentioned qualifications with the following exceptions and additions.

1. Judges of Federal District Courts
(*Jueces de Distrito*)

They must be at least twenty-five years old and be attorneys (*abogados*) of at least three years' standing on the day of the appointment. There is no upper age limit. They are each appointed by the plenum of the federal Supreme Court of Justice for a first term of four years. If a judge is reappointed or promoted at the expiration of this first term, the new appointment is for life, but he may be retired at the age of seventy.

2. Judges of Federal Circuit Courts
(*Magistrados de Circuito*)

They must be at least thirty years of age and attorneys (*abogados*) of at least five years' standing on the day of the appointment. They are appointed by the plenum of the federal Supreme Court on the same conditions as are district judges. They elect from among themselves the president of the particular circuit court for a term of one calendar year. He may be reelected.

3. Judges of the Federal Supreme Court
(*Ministros*)

They are appointed for life by the President of the Republic with the consent of the Senate (*Cámara de Senadores*). They may be retired by the plenum of the court after they have reached the age of seventy. They must be at least thirty-five years old, but not over sixty-five years of age, and attorneys (*abogados*) of at least five years' standing at the time of the appointment. They elect from among themselves a president for one calendar year, and he may be reelected. Judges of the several chambers (*salas*) elect from among themselves the president of the chamber for one calendar year, and he may be reelected.

B. THE PUBLIC MINISTRY

The public ministry (*ministerio público*) is organized on the American model of the attorney general and his offices. Each state, the Federal District and Federal Territories, and the federation have their own attorney general offices.

The public ministry for the Federal District and Federal Territories is headed by an attorney general (*procurador general de justicia*) who has two deputy attorneys general (*subprocuradores*), known as first (*primero*) and second (*segundo*) *subprocuradores*, and further officers. The *procurador general* is appointed and removed by the President of the Republic. The two *subprocuradores* are appointed and removed by the *procurador general* with the consent of the President of the Republic. Other officers are appointed and removed by the *procurador general*. The *procurador general* and the two *subprocuradores* must possess the qualifications of a judge of the *tribunal superior*, their immediate deputies (*auxiliares*) must be attorneys (*abogados*) of three years' standing, and the other officers must be *abogados*. All must be Mexicans by birth and of good moral conduct.

The public ministry acts through their officers in the prosecution of criminals before criminal courts, but it also represents the state in civil courts. The offices are centrally organized. The *procurador general* is the legal officer of the President of the Republic in the exercise of his functions as the head of the government in the Federal District and Federal Territories.

The public ministry for the federation is headed by an attorney general (*procurador general de la República*) and his first (*subprocurador primero substituto del procurador*) and second (*subprocurador segundo substituto del procurador*) deputies. The *Procurador* is appointed and removed by the President of the Republic. The two *subprocuradores* are appointed and removed by the President at the request of the *Procurador*. All three must have the qualifications of a judge of the federal Supreme Court. All other officers are appointed and removed by the President of the Republic at the request of the *Procurador* and must be attorneys (*abogados*), Mexican by birth, of good conduct, and twenty-five years of age. The immediate deputies of the *subprocuradores* must be attorneys (*abogados*) of at least three years' standing.

The attorney general and other officers of the federal public ministry represent the federation before federal courts in all matters brought before such courts. The service is centrally organized, and the attorney general is the legal advisor to the President of the Republic and of the federal government.

C. ATTORNEYS (*Abogados*)

To become an attorney, a person must complete his legal studies and obtain the degree of *Licenciado de derecho*. Thereupon he must present his degree to the proper authority licensing professions in his state or the Federal District and Federal Territories, together with evidence of Mexican citizenship and possession of his civil rights. In the Federal District and Federal Territories, the licensing authority is the *Dirección general de profesiones de la secretaria de educación pública* which will, as a matter of routine, issue the license (*patente de ejercicio*) whereupon the person may engage in the exercise of the legal profession. Nothing else is required.

The statute regulating the licensing of all professions, including the legal profession, is one enacted on the basis of Articles 4 and 5 of the Federal Constitution, which guarantee the unimpeded exercise of professions. In the Federal District and Federal Territories, the statute is the *Ley reglamentaria de los articulos cuatro y cinco constitucionales, relativos al ejercicio de las profesiones*, in power as of October 1, 1945, as amended. The states follow the practice established in the Federal District and Federal Territories. Persons so licensed may represent parties before all courts and authorities in the respective states of their registration, or in the Federal District and Federal Territories, if registered there. The profession is thus united, with no distinction between pleaders and solicitors, as is customary in British countries.

There is also no compulsory membership in any association resembling the bar as it exists in the United States, the British countries, or other civil law countries. There is, however, a voluntary bar in Mexico in which some of those who practice law as a profession and who carry the title of *abogado* participate. Its function is mainly educational and cultural. In Mexico City, the well-known association of *abogados* is the *Ilustre y Nacional Colegio de Abogados de Mexico*.

D. NOTARIES

To become a notary (*notario*), a person must be an attorney (*abogado*) and must comply with further requirements determined by his state or by the Federal District and Federal Territories. The profession is protected by the constitutional guarantees contained in Articles 4 and 5 of the Federal Constitution and its regulation is very uniform throughout the country.

In the Federal District and Federal Territories, the candidate must be an attorney (*abogado*) and Mexican by birth; he must be at least twenty-five, but not over seventy, years of age on the day of his appointment; and he must have practiced for eight months in the office of a notary and passed an examination on the office and functions of a notary. The examination is written and is followed by an oral examination on the topic of the written examination, which consists of the preparation of a notarial act in a designated area of law. The examination is given by an examination commission of the Council of Notaries (*Consejo de notarios*) and is presided over by a representative of the government.

After passing the examination, the successful candidate receives a license of an aspirant to exercise the office of a notary (*patente de aspirante al ejercicio del notariado*), and he is eligible to apply for appointment to fill a particular vacancy whenever it might occur. In the meantime, he works in the office of a notary. When such a vacancy occurs, it is properly advertised and all those who apply must pass another examination before another equally composed examination commission in order to determine the order of merit among the applicants. The one placed first is then appointed by the government to the vacant office. He is appointed for life to a particular notarial district. When appointed, he must take out a bond as security for monies held by him in the exercise of his official functions. In the Federal District, he may perform notarial acts in the whole territory of the district. In the Federal Territories, he may perform such functions only in his notarial district. The notarial districts and their number are determined by the government.

Notaries execute notarial acts, i.e., certify documents that either need official legalization by law or which the party or parties wish to have legalized. They may draft documents and obtain their registration, if required, for a party. They keep copies of all documents they execute and records of all transactions.

All notaries within the Federal District and Federal Territories form a bar (*El Colegio de Notarios del Distrito Federal y Territorios Federales*), the membership of which is compulsory. They elect a council (*consejo*) of ten officers, beginning with the president (*presidente*), the treasurer (*tesorero*) and the secretary (*secretario*) and ending with the seventh councilor (*vocal*). The officers hold office for two years. Elections are held annually for one half of the seats. The officers are elected by public vote in writing of the members and may be reelected.

The council watches over compliance with the notarial law in the Federal

District and Federal Territories and advises the government on any matter concerning notaries and their functions.

In the Federal District and Federal Territories the office and functions of notaries are governed by statute, the *Ley del Notariado para el Distrito Federal y T·rritorios Federales* of 1946, as amended, by the Regulation of the Council of Notaries (*Reglamento del Consejo de Notarios del Distrito y Territorios Federales*) of 1946, as amended, and by further provisions.

Provisions regulating the exercise and function of notaries in the Mexican states follow closely the pattern set up in the Federal District and Federal Territories.

The Law of Other Spanish- and Portuguese-Speaking Countries of the American Continent

Since the sixteenth century, Latin America has been chiefly under Spanish and Portuguese influence. The proportion between the Spanish and the Portuguese spheres is slightly in favor of the Spanish element, and the Spanish-speaking countries hold slightly over one half of the territory and of the population. The fact that the Portuguese element is represented by one country only—Brazil—brings out the enormous size of that country in both area and population.

The various Latin American countries have a great many things in common. They were all settled by the Spanish and the Portuguese in the sixteenth century; they were governed by their mother countries until independence, which they all acquired early in the nineteenth century; they established a republican form of government under constitutions modeled on that of the United States; and their legal systems began to develop independently from their Spanish and Portuguese foundations.

They are all part of the civil law system as it developed in Europe. Virtually the only outside influence is in the area of constitutional law, where they adopted constitutions on the American model, as mentioned above. This is especially apparent in the case of the federal states of Argentina, Brazil and Venezuela, where the influence of the United States constitution is strongest.

Until independence, the law in power in Latin America was the law of Spain and Portugal, respectively, as applied in the mother countries with some special legislation designed for the American settlements only. The system of courts also followed the familiar pattern of municipal courts, courts of the first instance, appellate courts, and a court of final resort. The courts of the first three levels were locally established, whereas the court of final resort was in the respective mother country. Administratively, the home pattern also was kept, with final authority resting in the royal offices in the home countries.

Since independence, the law has followed the path of codification, which set in during the early nineteenth century in the civil law countries. Just as the various French codes served as models for other countries within the civil law system, they also exercised their influence on codifications in Latin America. Today, in civil and criminal law, the system of five separate codes is current. The several Latin American countries have their civil and commercial codes, criminal codes, and codes of civil and criminal procedure. In administrative law, the prevailing system is that of Spain, Portugal or France, selectively applied from country to country.

The civil court system is comprised of courts of limited jurisdiction, usually called municipal courts or justice of the peace courts, courts of general jurisdiction, usually termed first instance courts or district courts; appellate courts, known as courts of appeal or *audiencias;* and one supreme court on the top of the structure. The dualistic system of federal and state courts that exists in Mexico and the United States is not in existence in any other Latin American country. The three above-mentioned federal states—Argentina, Brazil and Venezuela—use a unitary court system, similar to the other Latin American countries. Criminal courts follow the pattern of Civil courts, as is customary in the civil law system.

True administrative courts are in operation in some countries, e.g., Colombia and Uruguay, while a number of other countries, e.g., Brazil and Venezuela, use the regular civil court system to hear administrative cases.

As to legal officers, judges are appointed from fully qualified attorneys, usually of senior standing, along the pattern in power in Mexico and discussed above. Officers of the public ministry hold office and exercise their functions in the manner as is usual in the civil law countries, and also as exemplified by the Mexican system. The same applies to attorneys and notaries.

The Geographical Extent of the Common Law and Its Dominant Features

The common law as developed in England extends today over large portions of the globe. This is due to the vast extent of British power which, beginning with the sixteenth century, began to spread out of the British Isles in all directions by way of the developing English supremacy over the seas. English explorers were in most cases followed by settlers, who actually settled in the newly acquired territories of which the explorers took possession on behalf of the Crown.

America was a place of early English interest, and permanent English settlements were established in North America in the early seventeenth century, leading eventually to the creation of the present United States of America and Canada. In due time, Britain also acquired a number of islands in the Americas, especially in the Caribbean area, as well as British Honduras and British Guyana.

Another area of early English interest was India, which the English first penetrated in the early seventeenth century, and Ceylon, where they arrived at the end of the eighteenth century. By that time, they were occupying islands all over the seas of the entire world.

The object of further British interest was Australia, New Zealand, and the Pacific Ocean area, where they began to establish settlements by the end of the eighteenth century. From the same time, they began to extend their influence over Malaya.

In the nineteenth century, Britain took possession of vast territories in Africa and, at the same time, extended and tightened its rule over those areas of all the world that British interests had previously occupied. By the end of the nineteenth and the beginning of the twentieth centuries, the process of British colonization and settlement was completed, one of the last territories acquired being the area of South Africa.

Wherever the British came, they established the system of government developed in Britain, an order based on the English common law. The process is described by Blackstone (Blackstone, Commentaries, Intro. Section 4) as follows:

> 'It hath been held that if an uninhabited country be discovered and planted by English subjects all the English laws then in being, which are the birthright of every English subject, are immediately in force. But this must be understood with very many and very great restrictions. Such colonists carry with them only so much of the English law as is applicable to their new situation and the condition of an infant colony, such, for instance, as the general rules of inheritance and of protection from personal injuries. The artificial distinctions and refinements, incident to the property of a great and commercial people, the laws of police and revenue (such especially as are enforced by penalties), the mode of maintenance for the established clergy, the jurisdiction of spiritual courts, and a multitude of other provisions, are neither necessary nor convenient for them and therefore are not in force. What shall be admitted and what rejected, at what times and under what restrictions, must in case of dispute be decided in the first instance by their own provincial judicature, subject to the decision and control of the King-in-Council; the whole of their constitution being also liable to be newly modelled and reformed by the general superintending power of the legislature in the mother country.'

The English settlers brought the English common law with them not only to uninhabited countries, as described by Blackstone, but also to all the other countries that they drew into their sphere of dominant influence, like India and Malaya. Although the settlers were careful not to displace local customs and laws, the English law, due to the superiority of its development at the time of its introduction, gradually took over the legal systems of those countries. The English common law was thus adopted by such countries and became the law of many nations, whose leaders also adopted the English language as their second language. English became the language of government, the language of commerce, and the language of the law. English law was always introduced in the English language and penetrated through it into the life of nations; thus, the knowledge of English law presupposed the mastery of the English language and so contributed significantly to the spread of English.

As a result of this development, the most significant legal systems in the world today are the civil law system on one hand, and the common law system on the other. This is apart from the religious law that developed in some parts of the world, most notably in the Arabic countries, but which is, even in those countries, overshadowed by the civil or the common law. The civil law system extended from Europe over the world in the languages of the nations of continental Europe, especially in French and Spanish, and took its hold mainly in countries and territories formerly held by France and Spain. In addition, it was adopted by other nations who were not within the British, English-speaking orbit. The tie between the English common law and the English language thus becomes well apparent.

The English common law stands, however, in a close relationship to the civil law. The development of the law on the continent of Europe and in England proceeded along closely similar lines until the sixteenth century when the trend for the codification of the law began on the continent. Up to then, the various continental countries applied a largely customary law, which exhibited the same features as the English common law.

The influence of Roman law was significant in both systems. In the early period of the development of English law, the time of Glanvil (in the reigns of Henry II and Richard I) and of Brackton (in the reign of Henry III), Roman law flowed freely into English law, and its influx continued for centuries thereafter (compare, e.g., quasi-contract and unjust enrichment in English law). Also, Roman law entered the continent of Europe and Britain together with the Latin language, which dominated the sources of European learning well into the seventeenth century and still plays a significant part today in both the civil and the common law.

It is the codification of the law in civil law countries and the use of languages other than the English language that are the main distinguishing features between the civil and the common law. This is not to say that the civil law is all codified or that the common law is entirely uncodified. In the civil law system, only those parts of the law are codified that are not likely to change very often, encompassing chiefly fundamentals of the substantive civil law, procedural civil law, substantive criminal law, procedural criminal law, and commercial law; the other vast areas of the law are governed by individual statutes. Within the common law, there is a pronounced trend toward the statutory consolidation of large parts of the common law, reaching especially procedural and criminal law, but also commercial law and administrative and constitutional law, to give only a few examples. It is thus rather the all-statutory nature of the civil law system that distinguishes it from the common law system, which still recognizes other than statutory law, the judge made common law as a rule of decision.

Both the civil law and the common law spring from a common source, the legal thought of European nations. They followed a closely similar path for centuries of development, sometimes moving closer and at other times becoming more divergent. The present position is one of the stabilization of the established order, with a noticeable trend of an approximation of the common law to the civil law by the progressing statutory consolidation, if not an outright codification, of the common law. This trend will in all probability continue and may well increase in its intensity due to the worldwide tightening of government control over the lives of nations.

The Law of the Soviet Union and the Countries of the Soviet Orbit in Central and Eastern Europe

It is not contemplated to give a survey of the law and of the legal institutions of these several countries due to the excessive scope of the subject. It is rather proposed to inquire briefly into the meaning of law and its application in the Soviet orbit, since it differs fundamentally from the notion of law in Western countries even though a similar terminology is used.

It is the political system that determines the nature and function of the law in the Soviet Union. All power there is vested in the communist party, a fact that is prominently stated in the constitution and the law. The communist party is ruled by its central committee and the central committee, in turn, is dominated by its presidium. Virtually all power is concentrated in the hands of the secretary-general of the party, who is at the head of the party apparatus of secretariats. He makes all important decisions and no decision of any weight can be made without his express consent.

The Soviet Union is ruled by the communist party through a descending structure of party secretariats. Decisions of the presidium of the central committee are communicated as orders by secret circulars through the office of the secretary-general of the party to the subordinate secretariats at the republic, regional, provincial and district levels. Such secretariats are responsible for the execution of these decisions in their respective areas. Decisions at lower levels are made by the republic, regional, provincial, and district committees of the party and are communicated in the same way to the subordinate units of the party organization by the respective secretariats.

State organs (like the presidium of the supreme soviet, the council of ministers, the governments of the several republics, and the regional, provincial and district soviets), as distinct from party organs, are the executive organs of the party, responsible for the proper execution of the party's orders. Thus the party, in its pyramidal structure, is the policy-making body, whereas the state apparatus, which is staffed and managed by party members, is the executive branch of the party's will. Under these circumstances, judicial power is of relatively minor importance; all important matters and disputes are settled directly by the party and are immediately carried into effect by the Department of the Interior through its branches of the uniformed and secret police, which is the real source of the party's power. Judges are thus the executive organs of the will of the party in the settlement of disputes assigned to them by the party; thus the party, or rather the presidium of its central committee or its secretary-general, is at the same time the supreme lawmaker, the supreme executive and the supreme judge for the entire country.

Before the communists came to power in Russia, the country belonged to the civil law system. It had a legal system based on codes modeled on the French codes and a similarly well-functioning system of courts. The communist party abolished that existing legal system and built one of its own along the lines referred to above.

There are civil codes, codes of civil procedure, criminal codes and codes of criminal procedure in existence in the several republics of the Soviet Union. The leading ones are those of the Russian Soviet Federated Socialist Republic (R.S.F.S.R.). Those of the other republics are modeled thereon and are virtually identical. The codes reflect the party ideology and differ fundamentally from those of the civil law countries.

All laws (statutes, edicts, decrees, regulations and orders) are made by the party through its executive organs and are put in effect and administered by the party through the same organs. There is an important difference between the meaning of the law in civil or common law countries and in the Soviet Union. Whereas in civil and common law countries the law is equally and absolutely binding on everyone, in the Soviet Union, laws that are actually published are meant largely as instructions, principles or guidelines for the guidance of the respective state organs so that variations in application may be made in appropriate circumstances. All laws are interpreted so as to lead to the furtherance of the will of the "working class," which in Soviet terminology means the furtherance of the objectives of the party since the party is the sole and exclusive spokesman of the "working class."

There also is a system of courts at the district, provincial, regional, and republic levels, with the Supreme Court of the Soviet Union superimposed over them. Within a republic, the decision of its supreme court is final. It may, however, be reviewed by the Supreme Court of the Soviet Union at the request of the procurator general or at that of the president of the Supreme Court of the Soviet Union. The courts, however, deal only with a small fraction of legal business. In terms of civil law, they are limited mainly to family matters and inheritances; and as for criminal law, the courts hear only those matters passed to them by the party. Since a person may own only items of personal use, the area of the law of contracts and property as known in the civil and common law is not dealt with by the courts but by administrative proceedings, known as "arbitration," which handles disputes between national enterprises. Similarly, a vast area of criminal law is handled administratively by the Ministry of the Interior and its branches throughout the country.

An overwhelming part of all law in the Soviet Union thus somewhat resembles the administrative law found in civil and common law countries; but it is all made by administrative organs, and it is also enforced by them. A large part thereof is not published and is inaccessible to the general public.

As to legal officers, there are persons legally trained who then may hold legal positions; but legal training is not necessarily required, even for the position of a professional judge. Judges are appointed by the soviet of the administrative unit coextensive with the court's jurisdiction and may be freely removed by it. Trial courts are composed of a single judge sitting together with two lay assessors as a panel. Appellate courts are staffed with professional judges only.

There also are attorneys. They are public servants under the supervision of the Ministry of Justice. Although they are now legally trained, attorneys do not require legal education in a university as a qualification for legal practice. They are grouped in Colleges of Advocates and they give legal aid to persons requesting it. Their offices somewhat resemble legal aid offices in common law countries. The office charges fees for services to persons requesting legal aid, and the attorneys are then paid from the proceeds.

An examination of the legal order in the other countries of the Soviet orbit in Central and Eastern Europe reveals that the political and legal structure of the Soviet Union is the model which the other communist countries strive to assimilate by adopting and applying the Soviet prototype to their particular conditions. Thus a continuous process of assimilation is distinctly noticeable throughout these countries. The system exhibits the same dominant features with an allowance for local geographic, economic and ethnic differences.

APPENDIX

The Administrative Structure and Legal System of Malaya*

I. INTRODUCTION

As early as the sixteenth century, the Malay Peninsula attracted the attention of European traders. First the Portuguese,[1] later the English[2] and the Dutch[3] came to trade and to look for suitable sites to establish settlements. Unlike Portuguese[4] and Dutch[5] influence, which was confined chiefly to Malacca and of which only very few traces now remain, the English influence extended over the whole of the peninsula and impressed a permanent mark on the political and legal institutions of the country.

The original foothold of the British was the island of Penang, which was acquired in 1786.[6] Later, in 1891, Singapore was acquired,[7] and in 1824, Malacca became part of the British possessions. The Straits Settlements, as they became known, were subordinate to Fort William in Bengal, but as of August 1, 1851, they were placed under the Government of India, and on April 1, 1867, became a separate colony.[8] Although the British possessions comprised only a small part of the Malay Peninsula, their influence over it soon became decisive. The states of Perak, Selangor, Pahang and Negri Sembilan accepted British protection, and the remaining states of Kelantan, Trengganu, Kedah, Johore and Perlis followed suit.[9]

As was customary in all British possessions, English law was introduced into the Straits Settlements and became the law of the land. In the several states of Malaya, however, the local law has survived to a certain degree up to the present time, notwithstanding the influx of the English law. The old law of Malaya was the customary *adat*. It was an agglomeration of principles and sayings which were

*George E. Glos, "The Administrative and Legal System of Malaya" in *Zeitschrift für auslandisches öffentliches Recht und Völkerrecht*, (Stuttgart, Kohlhammer), v. 25: no. 1, Jan., 1965.

orally transmitted from generation to generation and which, as the time went on, absorbed many elements of Hindu and Muslim law. Some *adat* law appeared also in written form, but it is rather vague with no precise limits of application. There are two types of *adat*, the *adat perpateh* and the *adat temenggong*.

II. THE ADAT

A. *ADAT PERPATEH*

Adat perpateh first appeared in Malaya around the fifteenth century in Negri Sembilan, having been introduced there by the Minangkabaus from Sumatra.[10] It is chiefly unwritten, but there are three *adat* digests in existence, one from Sungai Ujong in Perak, another, the Minangkabau legal digest from Perak, and the third from Kuala Pilah in Negri Sembilan.[11] *Adat perpateh* envisages a matrilineal tribal structure and the female line of descent is all important. Yet only men are allowed to be heads in the tribal organization. They must, however, guard and protect the rights of their wives.[12] The tribal organization itself is structured on an ascending line and exhibits many democratic features. The basic unit is the family in a larger sense, which is headed by the mother's eldest brother, the *mamak*. The *mamaks* of related families form a family group, the *perut*, and elect a head, whom they call the *bapa*. The *bapas* of the tribe elect the tribal head, the *lembaga*. The *lembagas* of a given area choose the territorial chief, who is called the *undang* or the *penghulu*, and the *undangs* elect the ruler, whose title is *Yang di-Pertuan Besar*. The power of the various heads, which is now only nominal, is limited to their respective units. Formerly, however, the *undangs*, who stand in rank immediately below the ruler, exercised the widest authority in public matters, leaving the ruler himself with mostly ceremonial powers.[13] Apart from their administrative authority, the *bapas* were entrusted with only petty civil and criminal jurisdiction, and the *lembagas* with intermediate jurisdiction. Full judicial powers rested with the *undangs*, who were the most important administrative and judicial officers.

The *adat* has provisions dealing with all matters likely to arise in the community. It regulates the election, the status and the powers of public officers; it deals with matters of movable and immovable property, with family law, including marriage and divorce, with disposition of property upon death, and with the punishment of offenders.[14] It also provides for the insignia of rank, marks of dignity of public officers, and privileges, and it lays down rules of precedence to be observed at ceremonies.[15]

The *adat* recognized that the aborigines, who were the only inhabitants in Negri Sembilan prior to the arrival of the Minangkabaus, had the right to all land. They used it, however, only for hunting. The *adat* therefore provided that whenever the jungle was cleared and the land was cultivated, it passed to the cultivators upon payment of a small annual compensation to the aborigines for the loss of their hunting rights.[16] Evidence of ownership was supplied by long ancestral possession.[17] All ancestral land belonged to the women, but the men cultivated it and were entitled to maintenance out of the proceeds. Apart from ancestral property, property individually owned by the groom and the bride before marriage was held by each of them during marriage and followed its owner in the case of divorce. Similarly, property jointly acquired during marriage was divided equally in the event of divorce.[18]

A man was a member of his mother's tribe until he left the village and settled in that of his wife's on marriage. He had to marry out of the family group, the *perut*. A woman, on the other hand, stayed and inherited the ancestral land.[19] A man's position in the family was thus rather weak; if he did not behave to the satisfaction of the family, he ran the risk of being divorced and expelled.[20] It is not surprising, therefore, that under these circumstances the men of Negri Sembilan proved to be the most industrious of all Malaya.

As to wrongs and offenses, the underlying idea of the *adat* was compensation. The family needed its breadwinner, so that every offense was likely to be rectified by providing compensation. Only men for whom the tribe would not accept responsibility were exposed to punishment, and consequently, to divorce and expulsion.[21]

The *adat perpateh* was a very kind system of law, lenient and understanding. It aimed at restitution rather than at punishment. By substituting family responsibility for individual responsibility, it tended to encourage the family to use its influence with the offending member and so to avert difficulties and trouble. It was reasonable and humane in all its rules and yet so simple, popularized in customary sayings, that it was readily understood by the community. It was, no doubt, much superior to the *adat temenggong*.

B. *ADAT TEMENGGONG*

The *adat temenggong* is merely a variation of the *adat perpateh*. It developed from the *adat perpateh* in the Palembang state (Sri Vijaya) from where it was introduced into the Malay Peninsula, together with the entire Palembang customs and culture.[22] The reason why the *adat perpateh* stood unchanged in the Minangkabau highlands in Sumatra, while it was affected by profound changes in Palembang, can be explained by its exposure to Hindu, and later Muslim, influences. Due to these influences, it changed from a matrilineal and democratic system to a patriarchal and despotic one. Yet, since these influences did not operate evenly throughout the Malay Peninsula, the *adat temenggong* in some areas continued to exhibit some matrilineal elements.[23] With all the power concentrated in the hands of the *raja* and the chiefs, the *adat* ceased to be administered in the customary way, and the absolute discretion of the powerful prevailed.[24] This being so, the family was no longer able to protect its members, and with the passing of time, the sense of collective responsibility that made *adat perpateh* what it was, was supplanted by individual responsibility. The *raja*, who under Muslim influence became the sultan, was omnipotent. His chief aids were the *bendahara*, who was also the head of the armed force, and the *temenggong*, who held an office similar to that of a minister of interior and a chief of police combined. The transaction of other important business was entrusted to several *menteri*, whose offices could be likened to those of ministers, and *mandulika*, who administered provinces as governors.[25] The authority of these officers was supreme and was weakened only by their internal rivalries and power struggles. They exacted services and payments from the population without any limit whatsoever and oppressed the people as they pleased.[26] The unfettered pleasure of the rulers thus became the chief feature of the *adat temenggong.*

III. HINDU AND MUSLIM INFLUENCES

Hindu law made its way to the Malay Peninsula, together with the Hindu culture and customs, at the beginning of the Christian era. It gained considerable influence in the Palembang state (Sri Vijaya), which finally disintegrated under the pressure of the Javanese of Majapahit in the second half of the fourteenth century.[27] The Hindu influence on law and government was not uprooted with the downfall of the Palembang state but survived in the peninsula. The Hindu law introduced to Sumatra, Java and Malaya was that prevailing in India at the time of its introduction. It was chiefly customary and unwritten. Later, however, Hindu law in written form, as expounded in the Dharmasutras in prose and in the Dharmasastra in verse, was introduced.[28] The structure of Hindu society was patriarchal and autocratic. The country was ruled by *rajas* and their lieutenants, with the people having no say in the administration whatsoever. In matters of succession, males were preferred to females, while the *lex talionis,* varied by the caste distinction, provided the rule in criminal matters. It was this type of Hindu influence that was responsible for the decay of the *adat perpateh* and its degeneration into the much inferior *adat temenggong.*

Similar to the Hindu influence, the Muslim religion and law, together with the Muslim world outlook and way of life, found their way into Malaya around the fourteenth century and eventually established an overlasting foothold in the country.[29] The authorities of Muslim law are the Koran; the oral tradition of rulings, decisions and sayings attributed to the prophet, which are called the Hadith; and the Ijma, i.e., an exposition of the law by the four great jurists of Islam (AbuHanifa, Malik, Shafei, and IbnHanbal) on points on which these authorities were in agreement. Apart from these unquestioned authoritative sources, the legal views of the four great jurists on points on which they differed are also of importance. And as the views of one of them prevailed over those of the other three in certain Muslim countries, the whole Muslim world may be divided in areas according to the applicable law.[30] In Malaya, the views of Shafei prevailed over those of his learned colleagues.

Notwithstanding the influence of Muslim law in Malaya, it did not supplant the local *adat* in its entirety. It was accepted in religious matters, in family law and in the law of succession; but in other matters, the *adat* prevailed, with only some Muslim additions incorporated in it in the course of centuries.[31]

IV. THE EVOLUTION OF LAW AND STATE

English law spread throughout Malaya from Penang, which was the original English possession in the peninsula.[32] According to the general rule that, when

Englishmen establish themselves in an uninhabited or barbarous country, they carry with them the laws and the sovereignty of their own country,[33] the law of England became the law of Penang in as far as it was suitable and as modified as it was in its application by the circumstances.[34] Within a few years after the arrival of the British, thousands of Malays and Chinese settled on the island, yet there was no proper authority in existence to administer justice. Captain Light's power was limited to the preservation of good order, and he did so by administering justice according to his conscience.[35] Proper government was set up in Penang only in 1800, when a Lieutenant-Governor assumed office.[36] In the same year, the administration acquired a large strip of land on the mainland of Malay opposite Penang, which became known as Province Wellesley and became part of the Penang settlement.[37] The rapid development of the settlement made the establishment of adequate judicial machinery a necessity. In 1807, a Charter of Justice[38] was granted by the Crown establishing a Court of Judicature in Penang[39] with the jurisdiction and powers of an English superior court, and the several justices, judges and barons thereof, as far as circumstances would admit, and those of an ecclesiastical court, as far as the several religions, manners and customs of the inhabitants would admit.[40] The law that the Court was to apply was the law of England with the necessary modifications.[41] From decisions of the Court, an appeal lay to the King in Council.

A. THE STRAITS SETTLEMENTS

The Penang settlement being too far to the north of the straits, and Malacca being held by the Dutch, it became of importance to establish another settlement to command the straits. The place selected was Singapore.[42] The success of the Singapore settlement was quite spectacular, and the city developed with such speed that the introduction of a regular administration of justice was highly desirable. In the meantime in 1824, Malacca was finally abandoned by the Dutch and was acquired by Great Britain.[43] The joining of the three settlements under one administration then became only a matter of time and was actually effected in 1826.[44] In these circumstances, the Second Charter of Justice was granted in 1826,[45] extending the jurisdiction of the Court of Judicature in Penang to Singapore and Malacca.[46] A political and legal unity of the Straits Settlements was thus established.

The center of gravity within the Straits Settlements shifted rapidly from Penang to Singapore, and it was no surprise when the seat of government was moved to Singapore in 1832. The development of the Straits Settlements went on at a rapid pace, so that within another thirty-five years their growing importance gradually led to their independence from both Fort William and the Government of India. Finally, on April 1, 1867, they became a separate colony.[47] In the field of law, the Court of Judicature was granted admiralty jurisdiction,[48] and a fresh charter of justice, the Third Charter of Justice of August 10, 1855, confirmed its jurisdiction and powers.[49] In 1867, the Recorder of the Court became its Chief Justice, and the following year, the Court itself was reconstituted as the Supreme Court of the Straits Settlements.[50] In a further reconstruction in 1873, the Court was given appellate jurisdiction.[51]

Since 1867, the status of the Straits Settlements was that of a Crown Colony, the powers of government being vested in the several constitutionally established organs of administration. The Crown retained and exercised its prerogatives to pass laws, to make peace and war, to create courts of justice, to be the instance of last appeal, to pardon offenses, to coin money, to have allegiance, fealty and homage, and to impose taxes.[52]

Legislative powers of the Crown were delegated to the Legislative Council,[53] yet the Crown retained the power to legislate by Order in Council[54] and the power to disallow any ordinance passed by the Legislative Council.[55] Nonetheless, the Legislative council had vast, unrestricted powers of legislation within the colony, similar to those exercised by the Parliament at Westminster,[56] with the one exception that some bills were reserved for Royal Assent, which would be given by an Order in Council.[57] Additional powers were, however, conferred on the Legislative Council by various Imperial Acts.[58] As a result, legislation in the Straits Settlements were effected by the Ordinances of the Legislative Council,[59] by Orders of the King in Council and by Acts of the Imperial Parliament.[60]

Executive power in the colony was exercised by the Governor and the Executive Council. The Governor, representing the King, was appointed and held office during His Majesty's pleasure.[61] His powers were delimited in his commission and the various letters patent and instructions.[62] His principal functions consisted in convoking and proroguing the Legislative and Executive Councils; in initiating legislation; in assenting to, vetoing, or reserving bills for Royal Assent; in appointing judges, and judicial or other officers; in dismissing certain officers; in remitting fines and granting pardons; and in the general responsibility for the administration of the colony.

The Executive Council was designed to assist the Governor in the exercise of his duties. It consisted of the most senior officers of the colony, some ex officio, some by appointment. Two other persons not holding office in the public service were added by appointment.[63] Its function was to advise the Governor on matters of public administration. Certain important powers, however, had to be exercised by the Governor in Council, in which case the function of the council was more than advisory. These powers related chiefly to the removal of officers[64] and the banishment of persons from the colony.[65]

Administration of justice was in the hands of the Supreme Court, district courts and magistrates courts.[66] From a decision of the full court of appeal, a further appeal lay to the King in Council. Judges of the Supreme Court were appointed by the Crown, district judges and magistrates by the Governor.[67] Legal practitioners in the colony were termed advocates and solicitors, the two professions having been fused in the colony.[68]

B. THE MALAY STATES

In several Malay states, evolution took a similar although much more independent course. Although the first British settlement on the Malay Peninsula was established in 1786, and the influence of British administration on the peninsula was great, there was no actual British intervention in the internal affairs of the Malay states until about ninety years later. The intervention itself, however, was prompted by the desire to protect rather than to annex. The reason for the intervention lay in the chaos and general disorder which characterized the management of the Malay states and which contrasted disfavourably with the good order prevailing in the flourishing colony of the Straits Settlements. It so happened that the people themselves desired more order and stability, which they knew would be established under British protection and which would secure to them the fruits of their industry and labor. The first state to be protected was Perak. By the Treaty of Pangkor of January 20, 1874, the state of Perak accepted British protection.[69] In 1875, Selangor followed suit;[70] later in 1887, Pahang came under British protection;[71] and in 1889, British protection was extended to Negri Sembilan.[72] British residents assumed office in these states with the immediate result that these states were then actually administered by them. The rulers, who before wielded unlimited power, could act only through the residents, who in turn acted under instructions from the British government. In 1895, a treaty of federation[73] was concluded among these four above-mentioned states, pursuant to which the four rulers agreed to receive a Resident-General as the head of all public administration.[74] In 1909, a Federal Council was set up with legislative and executive power over the four federated states,[75] while local legislation and administration was exercised by the residents in council, although nominally by the rulers in council acting upon the advice of the residents.[76]

In addition to the Federated Malay States, British influence was increasingly felt in the northern part of the peninsula. The states of Kedah, Kelantan, Perlis and Trengganu were, however, under Thai suzerainty, and it was only in 1909 that Thailand transferred her rights to Great Britain.[77] Agreements similar to those with each of the four federated states were then made.[78] These states, which became known as the Unfederated Malay States, received British advisers who advised the rulers on the government along lines similar to the administration existing in the Federated Malay States. Only local custom and religion were exempted from the authority of the advisers.

The only Malay state with a largely independent government was Johore. The British government had had official dealings with Johore since 1818,[79] but it had not officially advised nor interfered in the internal matters of the state. The reason may well have been the efficiency of the sultan and his administration and his friendly relations with the government of the Straits Settlements. Mutual relations were regulated by the Agreement of December 11, 1885,[80] whereby Great Britain undertook to protect Johore from external attacks, and Johore placed the management of her external relations in the hands of the British government. The internal order in Johore was greatly enhanced by the enactment of a constitution given by Sultan Abubakar on April 14, 1895.[81] It provided for an orderly exercise of legislative, executive and judicial powers, and for the regulation of important state matters. The sultan acted on the advice of experienced British advisers whom he had asked to come and who were in his service. Only as of May 12, 1914, did Johore agree to accept British advice in the internal business of the state, yet the power of the British adviser was much less than that exercised by advisers in other Malay states.[82]

C. THE FEDERATION OF MALAYA

The above-outlined situation existed until it was forcibly disrupted by Japanese military occupation during the Second World War.[83] The Japanese held the country for too short a time to be able to introduce changes in the administration, however, and very little was changed.[84] Immediately after the termination of hostilities, the British government unfolded its plan for a Malayan Union, which reflected ideas expounded before the war and which was based chiefly on economic considerations. The rulers of the several Malay states signed agreements by which they ceded full jurisdiction to the British government, and the British government proceeded to weld the Malay states into one country under one administration.[85] Another innovation was that the settlements of Penang and Malacca were included in the Malayan Union, so that the Straits Settlements came to an end, and Singapore became a separate Crown Colony. The new arrangement entered into operation on April 1, 1946.[86] However, considerable opposition to the arrangement continued, and fresh negotiations were held. As a result, the Malayan Union was abrogated, and the Federation of Malaya came into being as of February 1, 1948.[87] The Federation was self-governing but not independent. Full independence was granted to the Federation by Great Britain on August 31, 1957, and the Federation chose to remain within the Commonwealth.[88]

Furthermore, Singapore advanced in its status from a colony to statehood. An elected legislative assembly was created in 1955,[89] and a state of Singapore, fully self-governing with only the external affairs and defense being handled by Great Britain, was established on June 3, 1959.[90] Negotiations for the merger of Singapore, along with other states, into the Federation of Malaya were carried on for several years, and an agreement[91] was reached for Singapore to enter the Federation on August 31, 1963. The entry of Singapore into the Federation was, however, slightly delayed due to the many problems connected with the formation of Malaysia, which was to comprise the Federation of Malaya, Singapore, Sarawak and North Borneo, so that Singapore actually entered Federation of Malaya and the newly formed Malaysia on September 16, 1963.[92]

V. THE PRESENTLY APPLICABLE LAW

As to the law applicable in the several Malay states, the *adat*, influenced by Hindu law and in many instances supplanted by Muslim law, was the law of the land. The law was, however, not uniform but differed from state to state, and its application depended on the pleasure of the rulers and the powerful of the time.[93] With the arrival of the British residents in the last quarter of the nineteenth century, the Malay states opened their doors to the increasing influence of the English law. The way the English law entered was by legislation. The British residents in the several Malay states saw to it that legislation by orders, regulations or ordinances was enacted to regulate the important business, transactions and affairs in the state. The legal provisions were invariably based on English law, so that a large portion of the law of England was thus introduced. The enactments provided for the administration of justice, the introduction of the substance of the law of contracts, sale of goods, bills of exchange, commercial law, criminal law and procedure, the law of evidence, land law, labor law, and the regulation of many matters of public interest. When the legislation grew complex, a law revision was undertaken, and a consolidated edition of the law in power was published in a majority of the states.[94]

Nonetheless, there were many gaps in the law that needed filling, and so English common law was applied by English-trained judges whenever the need arose.[95]

The influx of English law into the Federated Malay States[96] was further enhanced by the Civil Law Enactment, 1937, which introduced the whole body of English common law and rules of equity with minor modifications.[97] The application of the Enactment was extended to all of Malaya in 1951;[98] and in 1956, a new provision was made that introduced the whole of the common law of England and the rules of equity into the Federation of Malaya, subject to such qualifications as local circumstances rendered necessary.[99] In this way, English law became the law of Malaya.[100] Yet, there were additions and differences. Although the law of England is of general application, local provisions based on old tribal and religious law survived to a certain extent in those areas traditionally excluded from the overwhelming influence of English law—the law of property and succession, and of marriage and divorce.[101] In view of the importance and the close relationship of these provisions to public law, public order and administration, their salient features are now briefly stated.

A. THE LAW OF PROPERTY AND SUCCESSION

Tenure of land according to the old *adat* rule is now to be found only in Negri Sembilan.[102] It is, however, systematized and regulated by a statute, the Customary Tenure Enactment of 1926.[103] The land so held is entered in land registers kept in each of the three existing districts, Kuala Pilah, Jelebu and Tampin, and may be dealt with only according to custom, which implies matrilineal succession. Only females can hold customary land, and the consent of the *lembaga* (tribal head) is necessary to effect a transfer, charge, or lease of the land. There are restrictions imposed on forced sales to enforce payment of debts, as only female purchasers of the local tribe are eligible bidders. Failing daughters in any given family, sons may hold a life estate in the family land, the land itself being transferred to the female heir according to custom.

Tenure of land throughout the Federation of Malaya is now governed by the respective land codes enacted in every state.[104] The land belongs to the ruler, from whom it may be held in fee or for a term of years. He also holds the reversion on failure of successors. Furthermore, the property in, and the control of, the waters of all rivers is vested in the ruler. Title to land is acquired by registration. The system of registration is that known as the Torrens system, which is currently used in the several Australian states.

The Malays are benefited by the enactment of certain privileges in the tenure of land, designed to secure to them their interests in the land.[105] The government[106] may declare any land a Malay reservation, with the effect that such land may be held only by Malays. The object of this enactment is to prevent land from passing out of the hands of the traditional population into the hands of newcomers and foreigners. The definition of a Malay varies slightly from state to state, but it always includes a person belonging to any Malayan race who habitually speaks the Malay language or any Malayan language and professes the Muslim religion.[107]

Legislative provision for the protection of tenure of land by the aboriginal tribes was also made.[108] The matter is governed by the Aboriginal Peoples

Ordinance of 1954.[109] An area that is exclusively inhabited by aborigines may be declared an aboriginal reserve. Such land cannot be alienated and is reserved for the aborigines who live on it. An area that is predominantly inhabited by aborigines may be declared an aboriginal area. It is divided into cantons to provide a separate canton for each ethnic group. Land in this area may be freely alienated only to aborigines living there. Government approval must be obtained for alienation to other persons.

As to the law of succession, local enactments closely follow English provisions as to wills, intestate succession, probate and administration, so that there is very little divergence between the law of England and that of the Federation of Malaya and Singapore.[110] The existing additions consist of the recognition of polygamous marriages in the case of persons lawfully practicing polygamy, the recognition of Muslim religious rules of succession to be applied to Muslims, and the recognition of the local *adat* law concerning succession wherever applicable.

The rules as to wills, intestate succession, and probate and administration are practically identical with those of England, but they are modified to provide for wives of polygamous marriages and their children.[111] None of the rules, however, apply to persons professing the Muslim religion. In Singapore, where no provision comparable to the Federation of Malaya Distribution Ordinance was made, the English Statute of Distributions[112] is applied with such modifications as to include wives and children of polygamous marriages.[113]

The Muslim law of succession as applied in the Federation of Malaya and in Singapore was outlined in the section on Hindu and Muslim influences above. The proper heirs are those falling within the twelve groups enumerated in the Koran, and then the agnates and the cognates. Failing all of them, the property goes to the state in which it is situated. In Singapore, both movables and land go to the state. According to the Singapore Muslims Ordinance, 1957,[114] the court may ascertain the rules of the law of Islam in one or all specifically enumerated books on the subject and accept as proof of the law of Islam any definite statement appearing therein.[115] The court is thus given guidance in this matter.

Furthermore, the *adat* law is recognized to govern the law of succession in communities subject to it.[116] Succession to *adat* land is governed by the Customary Tenure Enactment of 1926,[117] but a few *adat* rules of succession still apply to improve the position of a widow or a divorcée as compared with Muslim law.[118]

B.   THE LAW OF MARRIAGE AND DIVORCE

Monogamous and polygamous marriages exist side by side in Malaya and Singapore. Monogamous marriages may be solemnized according to provisions of the respective statutory enactments, which are based on the English Matrimonial Causes Act of 1959.[119] There are provisions for civil and Christian marriages,[120] and for the dissolution of marriages so solemnized.[121] Yet only Christians and some non-Christian Chinese may enter into monogamous marriages. The Malays, however, are Muslims without exception and follow their own religious rules in questions of marriage and divorce.[122] Consequently, the statutory provisions governing monogamous marriages do not apply to them. To regulate the matter, the several Malay states and Singapore enacted statutes governing Muslim marriages and divorces.[123] These provisions are designed to give effect to the

Muslim law on the subject. They provide for the registration of Muslim marriages and divorces, the revocation of divorces, and the establishment of *shariat* courts (Muslim religious tribunals) to hear disputes arising therefrom.

Non-Christian Chinese may marry and divorce according to their customary rules. A non-Christian Chinese man may marry as many wives as he wishes. He can have only one principal wife, the *tsai*, but he may have a number of secondary wives, the *tsips*.[124] Divorce is by mutual consent. The parties agree to dissolve the marriage and make further provisions in order to settle all other important points arising therefrom. The agreement is made in writing under seal. It invariably contains a statement that the wife has no claim for maintenance from the husband and that the parties are free to remarry; it also contains a provision as to the custody of the children, if any. Apart from divorce by mutual consent, there is also divorce by repudiation, but it seems that this form of divorce applies only to secondary wives.[125]

Like the Chinese, the various Indians (e.g., Tamils, Hindus, Bengalis) living in Malaya and Singapore are free to follow their own religious and customary rules as to marriage and divorce, and they may practice polygamy. This also applies to any other non-Christians.

VI. CONCLUSION

Like the population of the Malay Peninsula, which originates from many countries and incorporates many racial groups, the law of the Federation of Malaya and of the State of Singapore springs from various sources. It is founded on *adat* law, Hindu and Muslim law, and it continues its development by the adoption of the English legal system. English ideas of order, justice, state and public administration were introduced in the country and a legal order was set up which, although consonnant with the English point of view, gives full scope to the realisation of aspirations of a multiracial community. The immense progress and development of Malaya and Singapore in the last hundred years, and especially since the last World War, bears an adequate testimony to the suitability, effectiveness and efficiency of the existing legal order, and there seems to be no doubt that the work so well begun will continue to achieve favourable results in the future.

FOOTNOTES

Abbreviations: A.C. = Appeal Cases; C.J. = Chief Justice; F.M. = Federation of Malaya; F.M.S. = Federated Malay States; F.M.S.L.R. = Federated Malay States Law Reports; J.M.B.R.A.S. = Journal of Malayan Branch of the Royal Asiatic Society; Ky. = J. W. Norton Kyshe (Reporter, see footnote 100); L.R. = Law Reports; Leic. = Stephen Leicester (Reporter, see footnote 100); M.L.J. = Malayan Law Journal; P.C. = Privy Council; R. = Recorder; S.C.S.S. = Supreme Court of the Straits Settlements; S.S. = Straits Settlements; S.S.L.R. = Straits Settlements Law Reports.

1. Portuguese ships called in Malacca in 1509. *See also* D.K. Bassett, European Influence in the Malay Peninsula 1571-1786, Journal of the Malayan Branch of the Royal Asiatic Society, 1960, Vol. 33, Part 3, p. 9.

2. Sir Francis Drake came to Malaya in 1578.

3. In 1594, the Houtman's Dutch expedition first traded in Malaya.

4. Malacca was conquered in 1511 by Alfonso d'Albuquerque, and the Portuguese held their settlement up to 1641.

5. The Dutch wrested Malacca from the Portuguese in 1641 and held it up to 1795, when it was taken by the British. The Dutch held it again from 1801 to 1807, and from 1818 to 1824 when, by the Treaty of March 17, 1824, between Holland and Great Britain, Malacca was handed over to Great Britain (Hertslet's Treaties, Vol. 3, p. 284).

6. Captain Light landed in Penang on July 15, 1786. On August 11, 1786, the eve of the birthday of the Prince of Wales, he called the island Prince of Wales's Island, but the new name did not become a permanent feature, and the island is still known as Penang. The Sultan of Kedah, who agreed to Captain Light's taking possession of the island, formally ceded it to the British by virtue of the Treaty of May 1, 1791 (Sir William George Maxwell and William Sumner Gibson: Treaties and Engagements affecting the Malay States and Borneo, London, Truscott & Son, 1924, pp. 95-98), and the cession was acknowledged by the King of Siam, whose tributary the Sultan of Kedah was, by the Treaty of Bangkok of June 20, 1926 (Hertslet's Treaties, Vol. 8, p. 707). *See also* L.A. Mills, Penang 1786-1830; Singapore 1819-1826; British Malaya 1824-1867; J.M.B.R.A.S. 1960, Vol. 33, Pt. 3, pp. 36; 60; 86.

7. The acquisition of Singapore was effected by a preliminary agreement between Sir Stamford Raffles and the Dato Temenggong, the Ruler of Singapore, made on January 30, 1819 (Maxwell & Gibson Treaties, p. 116), by the Treaty of February 6, 1819, between Sir Stamford Raffles and the Sultan of Johore and the Dato Temenggong (Maxwell & Gibson Treaties, p. 117), and by the Treaty of August 2, 1824, between John Crawfurd, the British Resident in Singapore with full powers of William Pitt, the Governor-General of Bengal, and the Sultan of Johore and the Dato Temenggong (Maxwell & Gibson Treaties, p. 122).

8. The Government of the Straits Settlements Act, 1866. 29 & 30 Vic. c. 115. Order in Council of Dec. 28, 1866, Statutory Rules & Orders Revised to Dec. 31, 1903, London, H.M. Stationery Office, 1904.

9. The northern part of Malaya was for a long time under Siamese suzerainty, and it was only by the Anglo-Siamese Treaty of March 10, 1909 (State Papers, Vol. 102, p. 126), that Siam renounced her claim to the states of Kelantan, Trengganu, Kedah and Perlis in favor of Great Britain.

10. *Adat perpateh* seems to be the original form of the *adat*. It is supposed to have been the law of the Minangkabau people, who lived in the highlands of Sumatra at the beginning of the Christian era. It flourished also in South East Sumatra and in Java prior to the foundation of the Palembang State (Sri Vijaya) in about the 7th century. The strong Hindu influence exercised on it from the arrival of the Indians in the beginning of the Christian era culminated in the Palembang State (Sri Vijaya) and was responsible for the formation of the *adat temenggong*, which gained ground throughout the entire Malay Peninsula. *Adat perpateh* was, however, continuously applied in the Minangkabau (Padang) highlands in Sumatra, from where it was brought to Negri Sembilan by Minangkabau settlers in the 15th and 16th centuries. *See* R.J. Wilkinson, Papers on Malay Subjects, Kuala Lumpur, F.M.S. Government Press, 1908, Vol. 2, Pt. 1, pp. 2, 8; Richard O. Windstedt, A History of Malaya, Singapore, Marican & Sons, 1962, pp. 29-43, 155; Patrick Edward de Josselin de Jong, Minangkabau and Negri Sembilan Socio-Political Structure in Indonesia, Leiden, Eduard Ijdo, 1951, pp. 7-9.

11. *See* footnote 14.

12. The *adat* says: Ancestral property belongs to the woman, but the man protects her rights. *See* E.N. Taylor, Customary Law of Rembau, J.M.B.R.A.S. 1929, Vol. 7, Pt. 1, p. 31.

13. *Adat* sayings define the administrative structure: The man rules his house; the *bapa* rules his family; the *lembaga* rules his tribe; the *undang* (*penghulu*) his province; and the *Yang di-Pertuan Besar* (*raja*, under Hindu influence) his world. The *raja* has majesty, the *penghulu* has honor; the *raja* decrees, the *penghulu* orders; the *raja* rules the world; the *penghulu* rules his tribe. See R.J. Wilkinson, *op cit.*, Vol. 2, Pt. 1, p. 24.

14. Sir Richard Winstedt and P.E. de Josselin de Jong, A digest of customary law from Sungai Ujong, J.M.B.R.A.S. 1954, Vol. 27, Pt. 3, p. 1; Sir Richard Winstedt, An old Minangkabau legal digest from Perak, J.M.B.R.A.S. 1953, Vol. 26, Pt. 1, p. 1; R.J. Wilkinson, *op. cit.*, Vol. 2, Pt. 1, p. 8; J.J. Shehan and Abdul Aziz bin Khamis, Adat Kuala Pilah, J.M.B.R.A.S. 1936, Vol. 14, Pt. 3, p. 190.

15. So, e.g., the marriage festivities were fixed to last one day in the ordinary man's family, two days in a *bapa's* family, three days in that of a *lembaga* and five days in the *undang's* family.

16. E.N. Taylor, Customary Law of Rembau, J.R.M.B.R.A.S. 1929, Vol. 7, Pt. 1, p. 31; R.J. Wilkinson, *op. cit.*, Vol. 2, Pt. 1, p. 28.

17. The relevant *adat* rule says: When the areca palms have grown tall, and the coconut palms are ancient, and the line of owner's graves grows larger and larger. See R.J. Wilkinson, *op. cit.*, Vol. 2, Pt. 1, p. 30.

18. E.N. Taylor, Customary Law of Rembau, J.R.M.B.R.A.S. 1929, Vol. 7, Pt. 1, pp. 21-29, 31.

19. The *adat* says: The man seeks his fate, the woman awaits hers. E.N. Taylor, Customary Law of Rembau, J.M.B.R.A.S. 1929, Vol. 7, Pt. 1, pp. 7-8; R.J. Wilkinson, *op. cit.*, Vol. 2, Pt. 1, p. 30.

20. The *adat* says: The married man shall be subservient to his mother-in-law; if he is clever I will try to cajole him, if he is stupid I will see that he works; like the buttress of a big tree he shall shelter me, like the thick foliage he shall shade me. R.J. Wilkinson, *op. cit.*, Vol. 2, Pt. 1, p. 12.

21. Capital crimes known to the *adat* were: treason, incest, robbery, arson, theft, cheating, poisoning, stabbing; but the penalty was averted if compensation was paid. Sir R. Winstedt and P.E. de Josselin de Jong, *op. cit.*, p. 15.

22. *See* footnote 10.

23. This is so especially with respect to acquisition of land and succession to property. In Perak, land descended to the daughters equally; personal property was divided between the sons. But men could also hold land by clearing and cultivating it. Sir William Maxwell, Malay land tenure, Journal of the Straits Asiatic Society, Vol. 13, p. 75, p. 127. In Perak and Malacca, proprietary right to land was created by clearing and cultivation and continued with occupation. Sir William Maxwell, *op. cit.*, p. 77.

24. Nonetheless there are several digests of the *adat temenggong* in existence, such as the Malacca Code (R.J. Wilkinson, *op. cit.*, Vol. 2, Pt. 1, p. 39), the Kedah digest (R.O. Winstedt, Kedah Laws, J.M.B.R.A.S. 1928, Vol. 6, Pt. 2, p. 1), and the Ninety-nine laws of Perak (J. Rigby, The Ninety-nine laws of Perak, in R.J. Wilkinson, *op. cit.*, Vol. 2, Pt. 2, p. 1).

25. R.J. Wilkinson, *op. cit.*, Vol. 2, Pt. 1, pp. 42ff.

26. They were forced to work on the land of the chiefs without reward, to serve in the armed force and provide all kinds of services. Services sometimes varied with the district, so that one district had to supply timber, others servants and musicians, yet others boats. All were bound to repair roads, build bridges, carry messages, etc. Sir William Maxwell, *op. cit.*, p. 108.

27. Richard O. Winstedt, *op. cit.*, pp. 29-43. R.J. Wilkinson, *op. cit.*, Vol. 2, Pt. 1, p. 34.

28. Julius Jolly, Hindu law and custom, Calcutta, Greater India Society, 1928, pp. 1-27; Mayne's Treatise on Hindu Law and usage, Madras, Higginbothams Ltd., 1953, 11th ed. Reprint, p. 21; Mulla on Hindu law, Bombay, Tripathi, 1959, 12th ed. pp. 13-14.

29. The oldest record of Muslim law in the Malay Peninsula, dating back to 1326 or 1386,

was found in Trengganu. Richard O. Winstedt, *op. cit.*, p. 40. It is interesting to note that at present, out of the nine rulers in Malaya, seven call themselves sultans (the Sultans of Johore, Kedah, Kelantan, Pahang, Perak, Selangor, Trengganu), one *raja* (the Raja of Perlis), and one *yang di-pertuan besar* (the Yang di-Pertuan Besar of Negri Sembilan).

30. Aziz Ahmad, Islamic Law in theory and practice, Lahore, All-Pakistan Legal Decisions, 1956, pp. 24-105; Kashi Prasad Saksena, Muslim Law as administered in India and Pakistan, Lucknow, Eastern Book Co., 1954, 3rd ed., pp. 20ff.

31. R.J. Wilkinson, *op. cit.*, Vol. 2, Pt. 1, p. 48. Even in family law and the law of succession, there are many *adat* rules that are still observed and mingled with Muslim law. As to marriage, a Muslim may have four wives at a time, but they must be Muslim, Christian or Jewish. A Muslim woman may marry only a Muslim. [There are detailed rules of affinity which make it unlawful to marry within the prohibited degree (Khalil Ibn Ishak, A manual of the law of marriage, London, Kegan Paul, Trench, Trubner Co., 18?, p. 31ff.). No woman can be married without the consent of her ascending agnate—father or grandfather—or if they are no longer alive, without that of a guardian (Khalil Ibn Ishak, *op. cit.*, p. 5ff.; Kashi Prasad Saksena, *op. cit.* above note 30, p. 153)] The ritual of a proper Muslim wedding ceremony is adhered to in Malaya, but a local Malay wedding ritual is added. It includes the *henna-staining* festivity, the sitting in state of the bride and bridegroom on a throne before family and invited guests, called the *bersanding,* and the ceremonial ablutions of the newly married pair. [R.J. Wilkinson, *op. cit.*, Vol. 2, Pt. 1, p. 52]. The rule as to dowry, the *mahr,* is applied with local variations. The husband is required to give his wife a dowry. It consists of a sum of money given at the time of the marriage or, if the dowry is deferred, paid to the wife if the husband divorces her without a good ground. [Apart from the *mahr,* the bride's parents also present her with a gift]. Thus a check on divorce is provided, and the woman is ensured of means of subsistence if the divorce is final. There are two main forms of divorce: by the husband, which is called the *talak,* and by the wife, which is called the *khula.* The husband can irrevocably divorce his wife by repeating three times the divorce formula (divorce by *talak*). Similarly, the wife is entitled to be released by the husband if she returns to him the amount of the *mahr* (divorce by *khula*).

The pronouncement of the divorce formula only once results in an incomplete divorce, and the husband may recall his wife within one hundred days, called the *iddah.* But he can so divorce and recall her only twice, for after the third *talak* is pronounced, the divorce is final, which is also the case if the husband does not recall his wife during the *iddah.* If the parties wish to remarry, they must go through a fresh marriage ceremony all over again, but the divorced wife must, before she is remarried to her former husband, marry another man and that marriage must be fully consummated before they are divorced. This operates as a check on hasty divorces and it happens only very rarely that parties choose to remarry. (Khalil Ibn Ishak, *op. cit.*, pp. 134ff.; K.P. Saksena, *op. cit.*, pp. 261ff.) If the wife desires a divorce, she can obtain one if she returns to the husband the amount of the *mahr.* This is called divorce by *khula.* In Malaya, by custom, the double of the *mahr* must be paid so that this practice is rarely encountered, but the woman uses other methods to scandalize her husband and so force him to divorce her by *talak.* (Khalil Ibn Ishak, *op. cit.*, pp. 112ff.; K.P. Saksena, *op. cit.*, pp. 266ff.; R.J. Wilkinson, *op. cit.*, Vol. 2, Pt. 1, p. 58). In the case of divorce by *talak,* the husband must pay a sum for maintenance. There is, however, a type of divorce by mutual consent which does not require either party to pay any money, so that the parties remain in the *status quo ante* (Aziz Ahmad, *op. cit.*, p. 203; K.P. Saksena, *op. cit.*, p. 268).

As to devolution of property on death [see Sir William Maxwell, *op. cit.*, pp. 124-132], all children share in the father's estate, but a man's share is twice the share of a woman. Nearer relatives exclude the more remote, and inheritance is *per capita* and not *per stirpes*. [The effect of the rule is that as long as there is a surviving child, no grandchild may receive anything, and further the share within a given class of descendants is equal so that if a man leaves no surviving children but has four grandsons, all receive an equal share, although three of them are his grandsons by one son and the fourth that by another son (inheritance *per capita*). Aziz Ahmad, *op. cit.,* pp. 506ff.]. Apart from these rules, a man may dispose of one third of his property by will, but this applies only to enable gifts to be made to religious bodies. He cannot disinherit, nor can he leave a larger share to one and a smaller one to another. [This can be done only by agreement among the beneficiaries. Aziz Ahmad, *op. cit.,* pp. 477ff.; K.P. Saksena, *op. cit.,* pp. 770ff.]. This is a wise rule which prevents disputes as to inheritance. A widower is entitled to one half of the estate if there are no surviving children or agnates, otherwise to one fourth only. A widow is entitled to one fourth, but if there are children or agnates she gets only one eighth of the estate. The *adat*, with considerable Hindu and Muslim additions, was for centuries the law of the Malay states. Only after the end of the 18th century was it decisively affected and to a large extent supplanted by English law.

32. *See* footnote 6.

33. *Fatimah* v. *Logan* (1871) 1 Ky. 255, Hackett J., Supreme Court of the Straits Settlements.

34. *Yeap Cheah Neo* v. *Ong Cheng Neo* (1875) L.R. 6 P.C. 381. *See also R.* v. *Willans* (1858) 3 Ky. 16, Maxwell R., S.C.S.S., where Sir Benson Maxwell held that as the island of Penang was not a deserted island but was inhabited by four Malay families at the time of Captain Light's landing, the law of England could not have been made the *lex loci* but was only the personal law of the garrison and its followers. Yet as no known body of law was in fact in existence in Penang, the law of England was to be applied.

35. The only instructions Captain Light received were the Regulations of 1794, dealing with criminal matters, which Lord Teignmouth, the Governor-General of Bengal forwarded to him in that year. Roland Braddell, The Law of Straits Settlements, 2nd ed., Singapore, Kelly & Walsh, 1931, Vol. 1, pp. 7-9.

36. The operation of the Statute 13 Geo. III. c.63 was extended in 1800 by the Statute 39 & 40 Geo. III. c.79, s.20 to apply to all places administered by the Bengal Presidency. Penang, which was administered from Bengal, was made a Lieutenant Governorship. The first Lt.-Governor, Sir George Leith, Bart., assumed office on April 19, 1800.

37. Province Wellesley was acquired by cession from the Sultan of Kedah by the Treaty of June 6, 1800 (Maxwell & Gibson Treaties, p. 98). Later, in 1805, Penang became a separate Presidency headed by a Governor and council.

38. Letters Patent establishing the Court of Judicature in Penang bear the date of March 25, 1807. The document is referred to as the First Charter of Justice.

39. Members of the Court were: the Governor, three councilors and a recorder. Sir Edmund Stanley was the first recorder. Braddell, *op. cit.,* Vol. 1, p. 11.

40. The Court was constituted as a Court of Record with general jurisdiction in civil and criminal matters, including authority over persons and estates of infants and lunatics. It had power to grant probate and letters of administration. Accordingly, quarter sessions were held from June 11, 1808, and sessions of oyer and terminer from September 5, 1808. The Court was constituted a Court of Requests by proclamation from May 20, 1809. Braddell, *op. cit.,* Vol. 1, p. 19.

41. The *punctum temporis* of application of the law of England to the settlement was July 15, 1786, the day of landing of Captain Light. *Yeap Cheah Neo* v. *Ong Cheng Neo* (1875) L.R. 6 P.C. 381. To dispel all doubts as to its application, the Court held that it was so introduced, but in any event by the Charter of 1807 at the latest, and became the law of the land, and that all who settled there became subject to it. *Regina* v. *Willans* (1858) 3 Ky. 16, 25, Sir Benson Maxwell R.; *Fatimah* v. *Logan* (1871) 1 Ky. 255, Hackett J.

42. *See* footnote 7.

43. *See* footnote 5.

44. By Statute 5 Geo. IV. c. 108 of June 24, 1824, Singapore and Malacca weré transferred to the East India Company and became automatically subordinate to Fort William in Bengal by virtue of the Statue 39 & 40 Geo. III. c.79. By the Statute 6 Geo. IV. c.85 of July 5, 1825, the King was empowered to make provisions for the administration of justice in Singapore and Malacca, and the directors of the East India Company were authorized to annex both settlements to Penang. By Treaty of October 18, 1826, with the Sultan of Perak, the island of Pangkor and the Sembilan Islands were acquired (Maxwell & Gibson Treaties, p. 23), and by the Treaty of Pangkor of January 20, 1874, an additional piece of territory, known as the Dindings, was brought under British sovereignty (Maxwell & Gibson Treaties, p. 28).

45. Letters Patent of November 27, 1826, establishing the Court of Judicature at Penang, Singapore and Malacca.

46. The legal situation in Singapore prior to the Second Charter of Justice was analogous to that at Penang prior to the First Charter. In Malacca, the Dutch law applied prior to the Second Charter. *Rodyk* v. *Williamson* (1834) 2 Ky. Ec.9, Sir Benjamin Malkin R.; *R.* v. *Willans* (1858) 3 Ky. 16, 36, Sir Benson Maxwell R.

47. *See* footnote 8. The Government of Straits Settlements Act, 1866, gave the Queen power to establish laws, institutions and ordinances, and to make provisions for the courts and administration of justice generally for the good government of the Straits Settlements. The Queen delegated legislative authority in the Straits Settlements to the Legislative Council of the Straits Settlements and other executive powers to the Governor and the Executive Council by Letters Patent of February 4, 1867.

48. Statute 6 & 7 Wm. IV. c.53. Letters Patent of February 25, 1837.

49. Braddell, *op. cit.*, Vol. 1, p. 232. The granting of the Charter was ratified by Statute 18 & 19 Vic. c.93, s. 4.

50. Straits Settlements Act III. of 1867; Ordinance V. of 1868. Acts and Ordinances of the S.S. 1867-98, Garrard's ed.

51. Ordinance V. of 1873, Pt. 4. It provided for an appeal from the divisional court to a full court of appeal of not less than three judges.

52. *R.* v. *Hampden* (1637) 3 State Tr. 826.

53. Government of S.S. Act, 1866, s.2; Order in Council of December 28, 1866; Letters Patent of February 4, 1867, and of February 17, 1911.

54. Government of S.S. Act, 1866, proviso to s.3.

55. Letters Patent of February 17, 1911, art. IX.

56. *Powell* v. *Apollo Candle Co.* [1885] L.R. 10 A.C. 282; Letters Patent of February 17, 1911, art. VIII.

57. Letters Patent of February 17, 1911, art. XI. In other, unreserved cases, the Governor had power to give his assent, art. X.

58. Braddell, *op. cit.*, Vol. 1, pp. 113-115, where the acts are enumerated.

59. The composition and powers of the Legislative Council are laid down in the Instructions of August 18, 1924, art. XV.-XLIV. (Braddell, *op. cit.*, Vol. 1, pp. 314ff.), and in the Standing Rules and Orders of the Legislative Council as of June 1, 1925 (*ibid.*, pp.330ff.). It consisted of eleven ex officio members (senior officers of public administration), two official members appointed by the Governor on instructions from the Seretary for Colonies, two unofficial members elected by the Chamber of Commerce, and eleven unofficial members nominated by the Governor. There were 26 members altogether excluding the Governor, who was the president of the Council.

60. The Parliament at Westminster can legislate for the colonies, but it is presumed to legislate only for the United Kingdom, unless by express words it makes its will clear.

61. The office of the Governor was constituted and his powers delimited in Letters Patent of

February 4, 1867; in Letters Patent of February 17, 1911; in Letters Patent of August 18, 1924; and in the Instructions of August 18, 1924 (Braddell, *op. cit.*, Vol. 1, p. 307).

62. *Musgrave* v. *Pulido* [1879] L.R. 5 A.C. 102, 111. He had no sovereign authority delegated to him, so that he did not enjoy any *prima facie* immunity and could be sued in the local courts. *Cameron* v. *Kyte* (1835) 3 Knapp. 332.

63. The constitution and powers of the Executive Council are laid down in the Instructions of August 18, 1924, art. II.-XIV. (Braddell, *op. cit.*, Vol. 1, p. 307).

64. Colonial Leave of Absence Act, 1782, 22 Geo. III. c.75, s.2.

65. Ordinance IV. of 1888. Acts and Ordinances of the S.S. 1867-1898, Garrard's ed.

66. *See* footnotes 50 and 51. Ordinance III. of 1878 (Courts). Acts and Ordinances of the S.S. 1867-1898, Garrard's ed.

67. Ordinance III. of 1878 (Courts).

68. *Ibid.*

69. Article VI. of the Treaty of Pangkor reads: "That the Sultan receive and provide a suitable residence for a British Officer to be called Resident, who shall be accredited to his Court, and whose advice must be asked and acted upon on all questions other than those touching Malay Religion and Custom" (Maxwell & Gibson Treaties, p. 28).

70. No treaty was signed. By exchange of letters, the Sultan agreed to receive a British Resident who would assist him in running the government.

71. Treaty with Pahang of October 8, 1887 (Maxwell & Gibson Treaties, p. 66).

72. Agreements of July 13, 1889, and of August 8, 1895 (Maxwell & Gibson Treaties, pp. 63 and 64).

73. Maxwell & Gibson Treaties, p. 70.

74. Article 4 of the Treaty provided that only matters touching the Mohammedan religion would not be dealt with by the Resident-General.

75. Agreement for the constitution of a Federal Council, 1909 (Roland Braddell, Legal Status of the Malay States, Singapore, Malaya Publishing House, 1931, p. 40). Agreement for the reconstitution of the Federal Council, 1927 (Braddell, *op. cit.*, Vol. 1, p. 43).

76. Braddell, Legal Status, *op. cit.*, p. 13.

77. *See* footnote 9.

78. Agreements, with Trengganu of April 22, 1910; with Kelantan of October 22, 1910; with Kedah of November 1, 1923 (Maxwell & Gibson Treaties, pp. 112, 109, 104); Agreement with Perlis of April 28, 1930 (State Papers, Vol. 132, p. 216).

79. *See* footnote 7 (Maxwell & Gibson Treaties, p. 115ff.).

80. .Maxwell & Gibson Treaties, p. 132.

81. Malayan Constitutional Documents, 2nd ed., Kuala Lumpur, Government Press, 1962, Vol. 2, p. 1.

82. Correspondence between the Sultan of Johore and the High Commissioner for the Malay States (Maxwell & Gibson Treaties, p. 134). Agreement of May 12, 1914 (Maxwell & Gibson Treaties, p. 136).

83. The Japanese were in full control of Malaya on February 15, 1942, the day of the capitulation of Singapore, and they remained in occupation until September 5, 1945. The British Military Administration, which took over the administration of the country after the Japanese surrender, ended on March 31, 1946, whereupon the civil administration was fully reinstated on April 1, 1946.

84. Sudhir Kumar Das, Japanese occupation and ex post facto legislation in Malaya. Singapore, Malayan Law Journal, 1960.

85. *See* Statement of Policy for the Future Constitution of the Malayan Union and the Colony of Singapore, Singapore, Dept. of Publicity and Printing of the British Military Administration, 1945; Sir Harold MacMichael, Report on a Mission to Malaya, Kuala Lumpur, Government Press, 1946; Richard O. Winstedt, *op. cit.*, Ch. XV.

86. Straits Settlements (Repeal) Act, 1946, 9 & 10 Geo. 6. c. 37; Straits Settlements (Repeal) Order in Council, 1946 (1946, No. 462); Malayan Union Order in Council, 1946 (1946, No. 463).

87. Federation of Malaya Agreement, 1948, Kuala Lumpur, Government Printer, 1948; Federation of Malaya Order in Council, 1948, (G.N. 5 of 1948); Richard O. Winstedt, *op. cit.*, Ch. XV.

88. Federation of Malaya Independence Act, 1957, 5 & 6 Eliz. 2, c.60; Federation of Malaya Independence Order in Council, 1957 (1957 No. 1533), [The Federation of Malaya Agreement of August 5, 1957, and the Constitution of the Federation of Malaya appear in the annex and First Schedule respectively to the said Order in Council]. The Federation of Malaya (Adaptation of Enactments) Order in Council, 1957 (1957, No. 1534).

89. The Singapore Colony (Electoral Provisions) Order in Council, 1954 (1954, No. 1377); The Singapore Colony Order in Council, 1955 (1955, No. 187).

90. State of Singapore Act, 1958, 6 & 7 Eliz. 2, c.59.

91. Agreement Relating to Malaysia, concluded between the United Kingdom of Great Britain and Northern Ireland, the Federation of Malaya, North Borneo, Sarawak and Singapore, signed at London on July 9, 1963 (Cmnd. 2094), including as Annex D the Constitution of the State of Singapore (*loc. cit.*, pp. 133-174), with Supplementary Agreement of July 9, 1963 (Cmnd. 2150).

92. Commonwealth Survey, A Record of United Kingdom and Commonwealth Affairs, Vol. 9, No. 18, p. 742, No. 20, p. 809.

93. Compare the section on the *Adat* and on Hindu and Muslim influences above.

94. A revised edition of the laws of the Federated Malay States (Negri Sembilan, Perak, Pahang and Selangor) covers all the law in force on December 31, 1934. Similarly, a consolidation of the laws of Johore was undertaken with respect to all law in force on January 1, 1935, and a consolidation of the laws of Kedah on July 13, 1934, was made. No consolidation was undertaken in the remaining three states, Kelantan, Trengganu and Perlis.

95. *See, e.g., Kandasamy v. Suppiah* (1919) 1 F.M.S.L.R. 381, 381-2; Re Yap Kwam Seng's Will (1924) 4 F.M.S.L.R. 313, 316-18; *Mohamed Gunny v. Vadwang Kuti* (1930) 7 F.M.S.L.R. 170, 171.

96. *See* footnote 94.

97. Civil Law Enactment, 1937 (No. 3 of 1937) F.M.S. s. 2(i) provided: "Save in so far as other provision has been or may hereafter be made by any written law in force in the Federated Malay States the common law of England, and the rules of equity, as administered in England at the commencement of this Enactment (March 12, 1937), other than any modifications of such law or any such rules enacted by statute, shall be in force in the Federated Malay States: Provided always that the said common law and rules of equity shall be in force in the Federated Malay States so far only as the circumstances of the Federated Malay States and its inhabitants permit and subject to such qualifications as local circumstances render necessary".

98. The Federation of Malaya Civil Law (Extension) Ordinance, 1951 (No. 49 of 1951) s. 2. provided: "Section 2 of the Civil Law Enactment, 1937 of the F.M.S. is hereby extended to the States of Johore, Kedah, Kelantan, Perlis and Trengganu and shall have effect in all the Malay States".

99. The Federated Malaya Civil Law Ordinance, 1956 (No. 5 of 1956) s. 3(i) provided: "Save in so far as other provision has been made or may hereafter be made by any written law in force in the Federation or any part thereof, the Court shall apply the common law of England and the rules of equity as administered in England at the date of the coming into force of this Ordinance (April 7, 1956): Provided always that the said common law and rules of equity shall be applied so far only as the circumstances of the States and

Settlements comprised in the Federation and their respective inhabitants permit and subject to such qualifications as local circumstances render necessary".

100. Proper administration of justice is enhanced by the existence of a well-organized system of law reporting. The following law reports appeared: Wood's Oriental Cases, a selection of cases decided in the Supreme Court of the S.S. before 1869, reprinted by Sweet & Maxwell, London, 1911; Straits Law Reports, a collection of cases decided between 1827-77 in the Supreme Court of the S.S., collected by Stephen Leicester and printed in Penang in 1877; J.W. Norton Kyshe, 4 vols. covering the period 1808-1890, Supreme Court of the S.S.; The Straits Law Journal, 4 vols. 1888-1891, by S.R. Groom; The Straits Law Rep., New Series, 1891-1892; The S.S. Law Reports, Old series, 15 vols., 1893-1922, published under the direction of the Singapore Bar Committee; New Series, 1926-1942, cited by year of volume; The Law Reports of the Federated Malay States 1922-1931, Kuala Lumpur; New Series 1932-1941, last volume published in 1947; The Malayan Law Journal, 1932-current, edited in Singapore by Bashir A. Mallal; Malayan Union Law Reports, 2 vols., 1946-47; Singapore Law Reports, 4 vols., 1946-49, published by Bashir A. Mallal; Malayan Law Reports, 5 vols., 1950-54, edited by M. Edgar and L. Rayner; Colony of Singapore Law Reports, 1953-56, by A.H. Simpson.

101. An outline of the local law of property, marriage, divorce and succession appears in footnote 31 above.

102. *See* E.N. Taylor, Inheritance in Negri Sembilan, 1948, 21 J.M.B.R.A.S. Pt. 2, p. 1.

103. Customary Tenure Enactment, 1926 (No. 1 of 1926) Negri Sembilan, now incorporated in chapter 215 of the Revised Laws of the F.M.S. 1935, as amended.

104. The Land Code, Revised Laws of the F.M.S. 1935, c. 138. Land codes are in existence in all Malay states. A new land code, which would unify the land law throughout the Federation, is expected in the near future. In the State of Singapore, registration of land is governed by the Land Titles Ordinance, 1956 (No. 21 of 1956), which is based on the Torrens system as applied in New South Wales in Australia.

105. Malay Reservations Enactment, 1935, Revised Laws of the F.M.S. 1935, c. 142. Similar legislation was passed in all Malay states.

106. In the state of Johore, the landowner himself may do so in certain circumstances. Johore Malay Reservations Enactment, 1936 (No. 1 of 1936).

107. Malay Reservations Enactment, 1935, Rev. Laws of the F.M.S., c.142, s.2. A company registered under the Companies Enactment is deemed to be Malayan if every member thereof is a Malay and the transfer of shares therein is restricted to Malays. Malay Reservations (Amendment) (No. 2) Enactment, 1936 (F.M.S. No. 51 of 1936).

108. There are well over 40,000 aborigines in Malaya. They are of three chief ethnic groups: the Jakun; the Negritos; and several tribes of Caucasoid extraction, known as the Teniar, the Semai, the Sisek and the Semelai. The 1957 census established figures as follows: Jakun 4,213, Negrito 841, Temiar 9, 408, Semai 12,451, Semelai 2,821, other 11,626, a total of 41, 360. (1957 Population Census of the Fed. of Malaya, Report No. 14, Dept. of Statistics, Kuala Lumpur.)

109. Federation of Malaya (No. 3 of 1954).

110. Federation of Malaya Wills Ordinance, 1959 (No. 38 of 1959); F.M. Distribution Ordinance, 1958 (No. 1 of 1958); Probate and Administration Enactment, 1935 (Rev. Laws of the F.M.S., 1935, c. 8). Singapore Wills Ordinance, 1955 (Rev. Laws, 1955, c. 35); Singapore Conveyancing and Law of Property Ordinance, 1955 (Rev. Laws, 1955, c. 243, s. 35); Singapore Probate and Administration Ordinance, 1955 (Rev. Laws, 1955, c. 17).

111. *See* footnote 110.

112. Statute of Distributions, 1671, 22 & 23 Car. II. c. 10 (an act for the better settling of intestates' estates).

113. In the Goods of Lao Leong An (1867) Leic. 418; *Khoo Tiang Bee* v. *Tan Beng Guat*

(1877) 1 Ky. 413; *Lee Joo Neo* v. *Lee Eng Swee* (1887) 4 Ky. 325; *Khoo Hooi Leong* v. *Khoo Hean Kwee* [1926] A.C. 529.

114. No. 25 of 1957. Muslim (Amendment) Ordinance, 1960 (No. 40 of 1960).

115. That is to say: (1) English translation of the Koran by A. Yusof Ali or Marmaduke Pickthall; (2) Mohammedan Law by Syed Ameer Ali; (3) Howard's translation of Vanden Berg's French translation of the Minhaj Et Talibin, a manual of Muhammadan Law according to the School of Shafi, by Nawawi; (4) Digest of Moohummudan Law by Neil B.E. Baillie; (5) Anglo-Muhammadan Law by Sir Roland Knyvet Wilson; (6) Outlines of Muhammadan Law by A.A. Fyzee; (7) Muhammadan Law by F.B. Tyobji. [Muslims Ordinance, 1957, (No. 25 of 1957), s. 44 (i)].

116. An outline of the *adat* law was given in the section on the *adat* above.

117. *See* footnote 103.

118. Her share in the estate is set at one half if it was jointly acquired, and at one third if it was acquired solely by the husband. E.N. Taylor, Inheritance in Negri Sembilan, 1948, 21 J.M.B.R.A.S., Pt. 2, p. 49.

119. Matrimonial Causes Act, 1950, 14 Geo. 6, c. 25.

120. Federation of Malaya Civil Marriage Ordinance, 1952 (No. 44 of 1952); Christian Marriage Ordinance, 1956 (No. 33 of 1956). Singapore Civil Marriage Ordinance (Rev. Laws, 1955, c. 38); Christian Marriage Ordinance (Rev. Laws, 1955, c. 37).

121. Federation of Malaya Divorce Ordinance, 1952 (No. 74 of 1952). Singapore Divorce Ordinance (Rev. Laws, 1955, c. 40).

122. For a brief outline of Malay marriage and divorce, *see* the section on Hindu and Muslim influences above.

123. E.g., Muslim Law and Malay Custom (Determination) Enactment, 1935 (Rev. Laws of the F.M.S., 1935, c. 196); Muhammadan Marriage and Divorce Registration Enactment, 1935 (Rev. Laws of the F.M.S., 1935, c. 197); Muhammadan Marriage and Divorce Registration Enactment, 1935 (Rev. Laws of Johore, 1935 No. 17); Offences by Muhammadans Enactment, 1935 (Rev. Laws of Johore, 1935 No. 47); Singapore Muslims Ordinance, 1957 (No. 25 of 1957).

124. As to the ceremony of a Chinese marriage, *see Choo Ang Chee* v. *Neo Chan Neo* (1908) 12 S.S.L.R. 120; *Cheong Thye Phin* v. *Tan Ah Loy* [1920] A.C. 369; Re Yeow Kian Kee's Estate (1949) 15 M.L.J. 171; and also Maurice Freedman, Chinese Family and Marriage in Singapore, Report to the Colonial Social Research Council (Scheme R. 281), London, Colonial Office, 1953.

125. *In re* Sim Siew Guan's Estate (1924) 1 M.L.J. 95, 96, Shaw C.J. heard evidence of the Chinese Consul-General to the effect that a husband was entitled to divorce his secondary wife if she was disobedient to him, or his principal wife if she did not conform to the household regulations or was guilty of immoral conduct. He had, however, no such right if she has borne him a son during the marriage. *See also Khoo Hooi Leong* v. *Khoo Chong Yeok* [1930] A.C. 346, 353.

Contemporary Trends in Continental
and British Legal Education*

I. INTRODUCTION

It is a well-known fact that no science or method of instruction can remain stationary but that it must advance in order to keep abreast of the standard of knowledge at any particular time. There can be no doubt that such considerations apply to legal education. From time to time, views are expressed suggesting possible changes and improvements in the existing system of legal education. On many occasions, these claims are based on experiences in other countries, mainly those of Continental Europe, or Britain and the British Commonwealth. The following presents a brief appraisal of these two systems of legal education.

Nobody will dispute that the standard of legal education is one of utmost importance. The law schools, the legal profession, the students themselves, and the general public, all are interested in sound legal education. It is in the greatest interest of law schools to give their graduates good instruction in order to prepare them adequately for their tasks in life, since the reputation of a law school rises or declines with the success or failure of its graduates. Similarly, the legal profession, organized in legal associations, has an active interest in admitting to its ranks only such persons who, on their student records, give assurance of satisfactory performance. The trust of the public in the legal profession would be shaken should lawyers, or at least the young ones, be found inadequately prepared for their function in society. Also the students themselves are eager to undergo good legal training, for their success will depend largely on what they learn in law school. Finally, the general public being, so to speak, a reservoir of potential clients, is

*George E. Glos, "Contemporary Trends in Continental and British Legal Education" in *South Texas Law Journal* (Houston, South Texas Law Journal, Inc.) v. 11: no. 3, 1970.

vitally interested in the training and academic qualities of lawyers. Further, as judges are drawn only from lawyers, the public has an essential interest in the wisdom and learning of those who are called upon to pass on their claims in the process of settlement of disputes.

It can therefore be asserted that the entire community is eminently interested in the standard of legal education, which is both the gate and the key to a legal career. This is so not only in America and in Europe, but everywhere in the world. The object is identical, only the ways and methods applied to achieve it vary with time and place.

II. PRELEGAL EDUCATION

In order to embark on a legal career, the student must have a sound general education.

The typical Continental education is obtained in a college, lycee or gymnasium school. The course of study proceeds at two levels: the lower, which takes four years, and the upper, which takes three to four years and corresponds roughly to the American college. The study culminates with the taking of the bachelor's examinations, i.e., the Baccalaureate of Maturity examinations.[1] There is also a choice of subjects, although never as wide as in an American college. In the final year of their studies, students usually have to choose between subjects related to the sciences (e.g., mathematics, physics, or chemistry) and those related to the liberal arts; subjects such as languages and history are taught in both branches. The two divisions, the sciences and the liberal arts, thus do not differ as much as to subjects as they do to the number of hours devoted to instruction in these subjects.[2] A bachelor's examination taken in the science branch entitles the student to admission to a university of technology or to the study of mathematics and other sciences in the university; that taken in the liberal or philosophy branch is a prerequisite for admission to a university course in all "nontechnical" branches of the university, such as philosophy, law, medicine and so forth.[3]

The corresponding British education leading to admission to a university is obtained in the grammar school or the comprehensive or bilateral school. The course in all these schools, which is comparable in its nature and subjects taken to study in the Continental lycee or gymnasium school, is geared toward examinations for the acquisition of the General Certificate of Education (Advanced Level). This is the counterpart of the Continental Baccalaureate and Maturity Degree and is a prerequisite for admission to the university. Prelegal education throughout the Commonwealth generally follows the British model, with the final examination generally called the Matriculation examination.

III. ADMISSION TO LAW SCHOOL

After successfully concluding his baccalaureate studies, the student must arrange for admission to a law school.

In Continental countries, the matter is quite simple. All that is required is to present the necessary evidence of having acquired the appropriate degree which entitles him to study in a law school, and the candidate is thereupon admitted. There is no quota system or *numerus clausus*. Continental universities are nonresidential, university dormitories being provided only for students from out of town and usually only for the needy ones; those who can afford to do so rent their own rooms in town. The problem of limiting the number of students is not likely to arise, because the codified law system of Continental countries does not make much demand on the law library; everybody, as a matter of course, acquires his own copies of the codes and textbooks, which are relatively inexpensive and easy to get. Further, attendance in classes is not only not enforced, it is, on the contrary, absolutely voluntary with the result that only a small portion of the student body attends classes regularly. This enables the law school to admit a practically unlimited number of students.

In Britain and the Commonwealth, the position is similar in that the applicant is entitled to admission on presentation of his General Certificate of Education (Advanced Level) or his Certificate of Matriculation.[4] There is, however, a significant difference between the Continental and the British systems in that the British legal structure is based on the doctrine of precedent. This being so, the student must make extensive use of the law library in order to master his daily assignments. The necessity of providing a seat in the law library for every student who can reasonably be expected to make use of the library at any particular time carries with it the necessity for a quota system in every law school. In the majority of British and Commonwealth law schools, the ceiling has not yet been reached; but where there are more applicants than open places, the law school selects its students on the basis of the results achieved by them in the Matriculation examination and also on the strength of a test administered by the law school.[5] The universities are largely non-residential so that the seating capacity in classrooms and libraries determines the number of students who can be admitted in any given year. Attendance in classes is usually not strictly enforced, and this also allows the law school certain flexibility in its admission policy.

In Continental countries, the standards, reputation and method of instruction in the various law schools do not differ greatly. Similarly, the prospect of graduates getting suitable employment does not depend greatly on the fame of the particular law school attended. Instruction is governed by statutes and regulations that apply equally to all law schools in any given country. Universities are usually state-owned and state run. Although they are academically independent, the state provides either all, or the most significant portion, of the university's income. It is therefore not of any particular importance to the student where he is going to study. Personal reasons are the strongest. Generally, the student attends the law school of easiest geographic access, the one nearest to his home. It is very rare indeed to find a student from a place where there is a law school studying at another place far away. Only country students who have to leave their homes in any event sometimes select, for their own specific reasons, a law school farther away from their home than one of an easier access. The capital city of a country has, of course, its attraction so that sometimes even students from places where there are law schools prefer to study in the country's capital.[6] Since the government is a potential employer of lawyers, big centers of government, such as the capital city and the main centers of government administration, are preferred over cities with limited employment prospects. Similarly, business centers are preferred to quiet provincial towns. On the Continent of Europe, then, the student's choice is influenced mainly by his personal feeling of present or future advantage as to the geographic location of the school.

The situation in Britain and the Commonwealth does not differ a great deal from that on the Continent. Although the universities are largely private institutions of learning, the government contributes heavily to their budgets. Since the law is uniform throughout the country (e.g., England, Wales, Scotland or any state within the Commonwealth that constitutes a unit) and the curricula in the several schools are practically identical, it does not matter in which particular law school study is undertaken. Eventually, a great number of graduates will practice as barristers or solicitors, and as admission to membership in these legal professions is governed by the respective law societies with fixed admission standards, uniformity in the required legal education is adequately ensured. Under these circumstances, students tend to go to the law school nearest to their home. In the Commonwealth countries, student must study in a law school situated within the jurisdiction in which they wish to practice, since study in the local law school is a prerequisite for admission to the local bar.[7] It can thus be said that, contrary to the American practice, on the Continent of Europe and in Britain and the Commonwealth, the student selects the law school rather then the law school selecting the student.

IV. LAW SCHOOLS

A. LAW SCHOOLS IN CONTINENTAL EUROPE

Like its American counterpart, the Continental curriculum proceeds by semesters.[8] However, unlike the general American practice where the entire course takes six semesters, i.e., three school years, and where each subject is fully disposed of in one semester with examinations at the end, in Continental law schools the law course takes generally eight to ten semesters, i.e., a full four to five years.[9] As final examinations are held only thereafter, the course extends well over four, and often up to six, years of study. It is however, dangerous to generalize as the position may vary from country to country. The length of the course, the subjects of instruction, the method of teaching, and the examination may differ slightly, but yet one factor is common to all Continental law schools: the law is codified and the doctrine of precedent, so characteristic for the Anglo-American legal system, has no application.

Subjects offered in Continental law schools cover the entire field of law.[10] Practically all of the subjects are compulsory; there are, however, certain elective subjects. The study is usually divided into three major groups: first, Roman law and the history of law; second, civil law; and third, public law. Subjects pertaining to these three groups are usually taken in this order.

The study of Roman law is of considerable importance as the Continental legal system is built on Roman law. Thus the student is acquainted with the system that served as a model for the presently existing legal order. The study of legal history is essential as it gives the student the necessary legal background and, since the course is nearly always conducted on a comparative basis, it provides the student with an exposition of the law applicable in other countries.

The civil law group of subjects embraces all presently applicable law with the exception of public law. Thus the civil law in the narrow sense (i.e., contracts, torts, personal and real property, devolution of estates, etc.), conflict of laws, commercial law, civil procedure, and criminal law and procedure form part of this group.

Public law deals with the relationship between the state and the citizen and is traditionally dealt with in the subjects of constitutional law, administrative law, the science of finance, and taxation.

Public international law is studied either as an independent subject or as part of the public law division. Most law schools also conduct compulsory courses in political economy, some offer courses in canon law and in the relationship of state and church. The subjects are studied in a logical sequence. Roman law and legal history first, followed by the several subjects of civil law and finally by the subjects of the public law group.

Individual subjects are often carried over a period ranging from one to three or four semesters according to the extent of the subject. Relevant examinations are held thereafter so that the times of examinations vary. Yearly examinations are not generally held.[11] The first examinations taken in a law school are those in the historical subjects, and they are usually held only in the second year of study, i.e., after the completion of the first year.[12] The successful passing of these examinations enables the student to continue his studies in the various subjects of the law applicable between citizen and citizen and between citizen and the state. Courses in all these subjects invariably extend over two or three semesters so that the period of long vacations is necessarily included in the time available for study before any examinations are taken.[13] This is very beneficial as the student is given time to master the law; and since he has to be simultaneously proficient in many subjects, he is led to study and appreciate the law as one cohesive whole.

B. LAW SCHOOLS IN BRITAIN AND THE COMMONWEALTH

Contrary to the Continental practice, in Britain and the Commonwealth, the law is based on the doctrine of precedent so that decisions of courts of justice are studied. It does not follow, however, that decisions of courts are never studied in Continental law schools. In the various European countries, only decisions of the highest court or those of the few highest courts in the country are reported but as these decisions have usually only persuasive authority, their study cannot be compared in importance with the study of decisions in the Anglo-American legal system.

The presently existing legal order in Britain and the Commonwealth, like the American legal system, is built upon the common law of England. It exhibits the same range of subjects encountered in American law schools.[14] Even the course in Roman law, while not offered in all Commonwealth law schools,[15] is still offered in British law schools.[16] As the British legal system is not directly founded on Roman law, its omission from the curriculum in some law schools is not very surprising. In contrast to the American practice, however, a strong course in legal history is offered in every British and Commonwealth law school. Both on the Continent of Europe and in British countries all over the world, the course in legal history is carefully designed to give the student the necessary background for the study of the currently applicable law. It is, however, plain that there is a far greater need for the study of legal history in the Anglo-American legal system than in the Continental legal system. The system of codified law needs a course in legal history only to acquaint the student with the previous codes and the evolution which, starting in the dark ages of antiquity, culminated in the establishment of the presently existing legal order. But looked upon as a whole, no knowledge of legal history is necessary to the successful study of the codes and the entire legal system. The Anglo-American legal system is quite different in this point. The doctrine of precedent, whereby decisions given even several centuries ago might still be of importance, makes the study of legal history imperative. The knowledge of history and evolution in every branch of the law, be it the law of property, torts, contracts, equity, criminal law, procedure, and so forth, is needed to give the student the necessary background and understanding of the presently applicable law. The subjects themselves are living evidence of the necessity of a historical presentation.

Another difference between the Anglo-American and the Continental systems consists in the fact that no courses in economics and the science of finance are offered in the former. Every law school in a civil law country offers a course in economics which is centered on political economy and which gives the student a good insight into the management of the state. As states and their public services are invariably run by lawyers, the knowledge of economics is of utmost importance. Similarly public budgeting, operations of the government treasury and of the national bank, currency, foreign exchange, stocks and the stock exchange, taxation policy, methods of levying taxes, and the influence and effect of taxation on the economic situation in the country are all of considerable importance to the lawyer. It is true that the share of the Anglo-American lawyer in the management of public affairs is a much smaller one than that of the Continental jurist, but it is inescapable that the range of functions of lawyers in English-speaking countries is increasing and that being conversant with the above-mentioned problems would definitely be an asset to any lawyer.

Also, contrary to the Continental division of subjects into groups of historical introduction and civil and public law, no such division is usually made in British and Commonwealth law schools. The subjects are, however, given in a logical sequence: introductory subjects first, followed by subjects of private and public law. But the course may also start immediately with subjects of the currently applicable law so that subjects of both private and public law may be taken simultaneously in any one year of study.

C. TEACHING METHODS

The method of teaching applied in Continental law schools and in those of Britain and the Commonwealth, although very similar, is not absolutely uniform. The Continental method consists of holding lectures, revision classes and seminars. The student is expected to listen to the lectures and master the materials referred to by the professor. Sometimes revision classes are held where the matter previously lectured on is revised and various topics of the subject are stressed and discussed. Seminars are held to give the student an opportunity to discuss with the professor the more involved points referred to in the course of instruction and to enable the student to obtain the necessary clarification on any matter.

The method of teaching applied in British and Commonwealth law schools comes very close to that used in the Continental countries. The first instruction is given in lectures. The various topics are then discussed in more detail in tutorials, where students ask questions and obtain clarification on matters not fully understood, and in seminars, which usually specialize in the treatment of specific, selected topics.

Curious as it may sound, the Socratic method of instruction has not been adopted either on the Continent of Europe or in Britain and the Commonwealth. It is in fact not surprising. European law schools are all of a very ancient origin and tradition. They are the direct successors of the old Italian law schools in Ravenna, Bologna and Pavia and embody in themselves the learning, scholarship and teaching methods of old Rome and Greece. The Socratic method has never been applied in any of them. Although connected with the name of Socrates, it has apparently never been used beyond the area of philosophy even in ancient Greece. The chief European objection to the use of the Socratic method can be summarized as follows: The Socratic method is not superior to the traditional teaching method. Continental universities have in their development long passed the state where the Socratic method could usefully be applied.

The Socratic method stands or falls with the conscientious preparation of the student for each class. If the entire instruction is given only in classes without any further tutorials and seminars held in any given subject, the benefit students derive from such instruction depends on the degree of their preparation for classes. If they work hard, they reap the benefit; if not, the profit they derive from their participation in class decreases and may on the contrary, turn into a liability. The time students spend in the classroom is lost if they are unprepared and therefore unable to follow the instructions. The European system of lectures is designed to ensure that the students know how and what to study[17] and that they are allowed sufficient time to master their assignments. Having been allowed time to study and to digest the material expounded in the lectures, they are ready for tutorials and seminars where the colloquial or discussion method is used. The distinction between the Continental and the British and Commonwealth law schools on this point consists in that whereas in the British and Commonwealth law schools the professor usually addresses questions to students, much like in an American classroom, the Continental student, consonant with his status of academic freedom in the university participates in the active discussion only if he so chooses. The professor thus addresses himself to the whole group, and the student volunteers to answer or to participate in the discussion. In fact, it is the student who asks the question, which in the course of group discussion is finally authoritatively answered by the professor. The whole exercise thus takes the form of a learned disputation and not of personal questioning, which is highly objectionable to Continental students.

A teaching method very much akin to the Socratic method is used in Europe, especially in secondary education. There is a quota admission system; compulsory attendance in class is strictly enforced; there are frequent oral and written tests. There are no tutorials nor seminars, all instruction is given in class. Students are supposed to study the assigned materials and the teacher then addresses student after student with questions pertinent to the assignment. A discussion is thus opened in which the whole class participates. The object of such instruction is to teach the student to stand on his own feet and to promote individual thinking, of which the supreme and final test is the Baccalaureate or Maturity examination. The graduate is then considered a mature man able to face university study with confidence. This method of instruction is, however, not carried forward in to the university and is not considered of university level.

In the university, the student is an academic citizen, free to pursue his own course of conduct. He may or may not attend classes, tutorials and seminars. If he attends, he may speak up or prefer to be silent. He is given all the opportunity; it is up to him to make his choice.

The European division of the course in every subject into a lecture-study period and a post-study discussion period embodies in fact the best of both the Socratic and the lecture methods. It ensures that the student is prepared when he attends the revision class, tutorial or seminar, and it gives him an excellent chance to derive benefit from the learned disputation. To do this, more time is, of course, required. But the Continental law course takes five years on the average and the student is supposed to study the whole year, including the long vacation.

D. COURSES AND EXAMINATIONS

The law course in Continental law schools takes a full four to five years, and final examinations may be attempted only at the end of the final year of study. Therefore, it easily takes another year before the candidate actually takes all his examinations and receives his degree. There are generally no yearly examinations,[18] but examinations are taken successively in the broadly grouped historical subjects, and civil and public law subjects. It is the general practice for the student to devote a large part of his summer vacation to study as success in examinations, which are taken on many occasions right after the long vacation, depends on preparation. Successfully passing examinations in the historical part of the course is a prerequisite for the continuation of study. Having enrolled and listened to all the prescribed subjects, the student is free to present himself for examination. It is therefore essential to a speedy termination of his studies to be well prepared when that time comes. The student who has studied for the whole duration of the course, including the long vacation, may receive his degree in much shorter time than one who begins a serious preparation for examinations only then.[19]

The school year is divided into semesters. The Fall Semester begins in October and ends in January, and the Spring Semester runs from February to the end of June. Subjects always spread over at least two semesters, the larger ones over three or four. As examinations are generally not held immediately upon the termination of lectures, the student is given ample time to master his materials. Experience has shown that much better results are obtained if the number of hours devoted to study is spread over larger periods of time.[20] Another advantage consists in the inability of the student to present himself for examination in a subject before he has taken all compulsory subjects in any of the three divisions. Thus the student must master all the history of law, all private law and all public law before he can attempt the examination in any one subject within that particular division. In this way he learns to understand and to appreciate the law as one cohesive whole. He is aware of the interrelation among individual subjects to the substantive law and of the relationship of the substantive law to the law of procedure. The justification for this approach lies in the realization that if the other method is used and the student is required to master an extensive mass of law within a relatively short period of time (e.g., within one semester), he has really no time to digest it properly; and even if he manages to grasp all the necessary law to pass the examinations, he tends to forget quickly what he has learned.[21] In addition, the law does not then appear to the student as one cohesive whole but as a haphazard series of independent subjects. Thus, the method of teaching applied in Continental law schools is designed to give the student every opportunity to do his work properly without unnecessary haste and to prepare him well for his work as a jurist.

Continental law schools hold examinations generally after the student has been given an opportunity to attend all lectures and to do his seminar work in all the subjects within any of the several groups of subjects. Sometime both oral and written examinations are held, but the emphasis is on oral examinations, the written examination being the preliminary step and a prerequisite for admission to the oral one. Yearly examinations are held in British and Commonwealth law schools. They are invariably written.

Both written and oral examinations have certain advantages and disadvantages. The advantage of a written examination over an oral one is that each student is required to answer identical questions.[22] Thus the ability and proficiency of students may be better assessed and a class list in order of merit may be prepared. In any event, a written examination rules out the possibility of complaints that one candidate was asked an easier or a more difficult question than the other. The time allotted for written examinations is the same for all students whereas an oral examination may take more time with respect to one student and less with respect to another.[23] Not only may the duration of an oral examination vary, but candidates also are asked different questions. Furthermore, the number and caliber of questions are necessarily uneven. Oral examinations nonetheless have the advantage that an impromptu analysis of a given problem must be given. This reveals the aptitude of the candidate for quick and accurate reasoning and for a coherent and impressive presentation such as is needed for the arguing of cases in court.[24]

As a general rule, the law course in British and Commonwealth law schools takes three to four full years. The study is pursued by school years rather than by semesters. In various Commonwealth universities, the school year begins and ends at different times of the year to suit local conditions.[25]

The school year is divided into trimesters rather than semesters and all subjects run throughout the school year. A bigger subject may be taught for four hours per week, while a smaller subject may be taught only at a rate of one or two hours per week. Subjects are taken in logical sequence with introductory subjects first, such as introduction to law and legal history, then the subjects of private law, and finally those of public law. Each course is fully disposed of during the school year and the examination is held at the end of the course. The usual examination period is May or early June in the northern hemisphere and November in the southern hemisphere.

Although the British system does not incorporate all the above-mentioned features characteristic of the Continental law schools, the fact that each course runs throughout the entire school year before examinations are held gives the student a reasonable opportunity to prepare himself adequately for the examination. The spreading of the course over the whole school year rather than over one semester only has excellent results over the semester system where examinations are held at the end of each semester.

In Continental law schools, all examinations are held before an examining committee composed of three members as a minimum. They are appointed not only from among professors of the law school, but also from among members of the bar, judges, and government officers; such other members in fact form the majority of the examining committee.[26] The examination procedure is usually as follows: If the examination is written, each paper is read by one of the members and the committee acts on his recommendation.[27] If the mark is a failing mark, two members must read the paper. If the examination is oral, all members may ask questions or they may act as examiners in succession while the others listen. They vote on the mark. The mark is the average of grades given by individual members.[28]

If the number of candidates warrants it, several examining committees may be in session at any given time. Examinations are held at a designated time, usually twice a year, in May and June, and in October. Due to the number of candidates, the October session is a very long one indeed, extending sometimes over the great part of the school year. After studying all of the relevant subjects, the candidate is free to present himself for examination whenever he feels he is ready. Examinations are thus not given at the end of each course, but at each student's request whenever he applies. This gives the student additional time to study and to prepare well for the examination.[29]

All oral examinations are public and the student body is invited to attend. Since watching other people taking a given examination is the best preparation for the examination, every candidate spends many hours in the examination room before he takes the examination himself.

In Britain and the Commonwealth countries, all examinations are written with only a possibility of an oral examination, which nearly never materializes. Examinations are held immediately at the end of each course at the end of the school year. There are generally two examiners in every subject who read all papers: the internal examiner, who is the professor giving the course, and an external examiner, who usually is a member of the local bar. The mark is generally arrived at by agreement between the two examiners, but sometimes the average is taken, or the mark of the external examiner prevails.[30] The examination is given by the University Registrar and is quite a formal matter. The giving of examinations is minutely regulated and supervised so that any possible informalities are entirely ruled out.[31] After the examinations are over, the examination papers are reprinted and published for the benefit of students. Study of past examination papers in any given subject is an excellent preparation for the examination. Every student will study and attempt to answer examination papers for the last ten years at the least. The whole pattern of the examination becomes familiar to the students. They discover how examination questions are formulated and which are the topics most frequently examined upon; they are thus in the position to develop a sound examination technique. The study of examination papers given in the past in any given subject takes the place, and is the equivalent, of the Continental practice of students attending oral examinations as spectators before presenting themselves to the examination.

The formality of examinations both in Britain and the Commonwealth and in the Continental law schools may seem somewhat overbearing, but it is a system which works justly and flawlessly. It has a considerable advantage over any more informal system in that it avoids in advance any irregularities that might otherwise occur and thus does not give the student any ground for possible complaint.[32]

E.   THE STUDENT AND LAW SCHOOL

As far as student life is concerned, the practice also differs from country to country and from university to university.

In the Continental countries, the fact that long vacations should be devoted to study and that examinations are usually held at a date after the termination of classes accounts for the law student having more spare time during the school year than his British colleagues.[33] As in British and Commonwealth law schools, presence in classes is not enforced but, contrary to the British and Commonwealth practice, where most of the student attend their classes, many students in Continental law schools do not attend every class. Consequently, every Continental law school anticipates a certain margin of absenteeism in classes. This attitude is characteristic of Continental law schools. The student is regarded a mature person and it is for him to attend or not. If he wants to get his degree, he must present himself for examination, and it is of no concern how he acquires the necessary knowledge. The secondary school method of teaching is necessarily left with the secondary school and is not carried to the university.[34]

In British and Commonwealth law schools, instruction is given by school years and yearly examinations are taken at the end of each school year. This, of course, leaves the long vacation free to the student. The students could use some of this free time to prepare ahead and study the subjects for which they are going to enroll in the coming school year, but this is not done. This is partly because the courses are so set up that conscientious study during the school year will secure the student a satisfactory grade in the end-of-year examinations. Also, by studying from books without the benefit of the professor's guidance, the student risks doing a lot of unnecessary work and may drift off the proper course. There being no need to study in the summer months, students use the long vacation to enjoy life or, more habitually, to earn money. They usually engage in summer employment much on the American pattern. In the endeavor to find suitable summer employment, they are assisted by their own associations, which frequently organize an information service on employment for the summer months. The employment they engage in is nearly always unconnected with their line of study.

It is also interesting to note that the law school placement service, which forms a characteristic feature of the services offered by every American law school, is significantly absent both in Continental and in British and Commonwealth law schools. No trace of such activity exists on the Continent of Europe. The duty of a Continental law school to the student ends at graduation and it is the graduate's own worry to secure a position. In Britain and the Commonwealth countries, law schools place on the notice board any requests from potential employers for graduates; but they do not, as a rule, engage in any active placement activities on behalf of their graduates.

V. THE DEGREE AND ADMISSION TO THE BAR

After going through all the prescribed examinations, the student receives his law degree. The degree awarded on the Continent of Europe is that of a law graduate, or there is no degree awarded at all with the successful candidate being issued a certificate indicating that he passed all the prescribed examinations.[35] On the strength of this certificate, the young lawyer may engage in a legal calling.[36] He may join the public service or the business world, or he may undertake further practical training in order to become an advocate. Whereas in Britain and the Commonwealth, where every law graduate becomes a member of the local bar,[37] on the Continent, only those actually engaging in advocacy take the bar examination. Thus, upon deciding to practice law, the law graduate must become a member of the bar. To that end, he must first serve as a junior advocate with a senior advocate and then take the presribed bar examination.[38]

As in America, in civil law countries there is no division resembling the British division between barristers and solicitors. Whereas the British and Commonwealth trend favors large firms with several partners and employee lawyers, carrying with it a corresponding degree of specialization, the civil law system favors one-man practices. The Continental advocate deals with the client, prepares the case for presentation in court and argues it in court. If the decision is appealed from, he continues to handle the case and argues the appeal right up to the highest tribunal.[39]

Both the British and Commonwealth and the Continental universities offer higher law degrees, which are not required, however, except for a law teaching career. The degrees of Master of Laws, Master of Civil Law, Doctor of Civil Law and the like are conferred by the British and Commonwealth law schools, and the degree of Doctor of Laws by the Continental law schools.[40]

Contrary to Continental practice, the legal profession in Britain and the Commonwealth is composed of two branches, barristers and solicitors. In Britain, the legal education necessary for admission to the bar (to become a barrister) is given in the Inns of Court School of Law, and that required for admission to the law society (to become a solicitor) is given in the Law Society School of Law. The instruction is in the first case under the control and direction of the Council of Legal Education and the four Inns of Court, and in the second case under that of the Law Society. The entire law course takes three years. No degrees are awarded, but the call to the bar or admission to practice as a solicitor in the Supreme Court takes the place of graduation. A student may study law in a university law school and there obtain a proper law degree.[41] In order to be admitted as a barrister or a solicitor, however, he must apply to one of the Inns of Court[42] (for prospective barristers) or to the Law

Society (for future solicitors). On the strength of his law degree, he will be exempted from examinations in subjects he has already passed in the university. The exemption will account for at least one half of the requirements for admission.

After being admitted, the student must undertake his practical training. Freshly admitted barristers must read in chambers for a period of twelve months, and freshly admitted solicitors must be articled for a period of three years.[43] They are fully qualified only after they have complied with this requirement and only then may they engage in the exercise of their profession.

The position with respect to a legal profession in the Commonwealth countries is similar to that in Britain, but there is a substantial difference in the system of legal education. In the Commonwealth countries, all legal education is obtained in university law schools. Examinations are given under the supervision of the bar and are at the same time both university and bar examinations. After passing all of the examinations prescribed for admission to practice in the Supreme Court as a barrister or as a solicitor,[44] the student then undertakes his practical training, i.e., twelve months of reading in chambers to become a barrister or twelve months of articles of clerkship to become a solicitor. Admission to practice takes place only after the candidate has complied with all these requirements.[45] As in the United States, admission to the bar in the Commonwealth marks the completion of legal studies; only then does the candidate become a fully qualified lawyer.

The insistence on admission to the bar in Britain and the Commonwealth can be easily reconciled with the insistence on state examinations in the Continental system. Both these tests are imposed to ensure uniformity of standards in legal education. In Britain and the Commonwealth, many law schools are private institutions of learning not bound by any minimum standards so that a government or a government supervised uniform aptitude test must ultimately be imposed. In the Continental countries on the other hand, the teaching itself, its standards and examinations, are prescribed and supervised by the state and the bar so that no further test is required.

The British division of the legal profession into barristers and solicitors[46] applies with equal strength to the Commonwealth countries. In some Commonwealth countries, the legal profession is legally united so that candidates are admitted to practice as both barristers and solicitors.[47] In such countries, however, those members of the bar who practice exclusively as barristers, renounce their right to practice as solicitors and form their own bar association which, by custom, has all the rights and privileges of the bar in England, so that even in these countries the profession is in fact divided.[48]

VI. SELECTION AND APPOINTMENT OF JUDGES

Since the successful functioning of the legal system depends largely on the learning, skill and efficiency of judges, the method of their selection is of the greatest importance. Although the systems adopted in the Continental countries and in Britain and the Commonwealth differ widely, both are very efficient and have functioned very well for centuries.

In the Continental countries, the time to decide whether to embark on a judicial career is right after graduation. This is not to say that a legal practitioner cannot at a later date enter the judicial service and a judge become a legal practitioner. It is, indeed, possible; but it is only very rarely done because the loss of seniority and income involved is so considerable as to make it impractical.[49] The judicial service is administered by the Department of Justice and the graduate has to apply there. Judicial service is generally composed of three branches: courts (judges), offices for handling of criminal matters (procurators), and offices for handling of civil matters (government counsel). If there is a vacancy and the graduate's application is successful, he will be assigned in succession to all three branches as an assistant. After a period of training of about three years,[50] he will receive his first appointment to a subordinate position.[51] Only after a further period of three to five years will he be appointed an independent single judge, procurator or government counsel and assigned to a lower tribunal.[52] Promotion in rank and the corresponding elevation to higher tribunals proceeds on seniority and merit so that judges of appellate tribunals and courts of final resort are never below fifty years of age on their appointments.[53] A judge is thus gradually promoted from a judgeship in a court of limited jurisdiction to a court of general jurisdiction and then to a court of appellate level and lastly to a court of final resort. A judge on the bench of the court of final resort must have necessarily worked his way through the entire judicial hierarchy. He will be a man of extreme capability and experience, tested by some thirty years of service on the bench.

In Britain and the Commonwealth, judges of both superior and lower courts are drawn from barristers.[54] Stipendiary magistrates, who are the judicial officers sitting in the lowest courts (generally called courts of petty sessions), are appointed by the Crown from barristers of at least five or ten years' standing.[55] Judges sitting in courts of limited civil and criminal jurisdiction (usually called county courts and courts of general sessions, respectively), are drawn from barristers of senior standing, sometimes even from Queen's counsel. Justices of the High Court in England and of the Supreme Court in the Commonwealth countries, which are courts of general jurisdiction, are appointed exclusively from Queen's counsel of senior standing. Lord Justices, who are judges sitting on the bench of the English Court of Appeal, are selected from Justices of the High Court of senior standing, and the Lords who are judges sitting on the bench of the House of Lords are appointed from the Lord Justices. The appointees are selected by the Crown and are appointed by the Queen but the selection is not within the Crown's discretion. All appointments are in fact made by agreement of the bench and the bar and the candidate agreed upon is appointed. It is therefore not an exaggeration to say that all appointments are made by members of the legal profession themselves.[56]

It is apparent that both the Continental and the British and Commonwealth judicial systems are so designed as to appoint the right men to the right positions. It is also plain that the British and Commonwealth system ensures that only pronounced leaders of the bar become judges. Both systems proceed on the principle that only judges of lower courts are eligible for appointment to higher tribunals and that judges sitting on the bench of the court of final resort must have risen through the entire hierarchy. Their learning, erudition and experience is such as to be beyond any doubt.[57] Judicial appointments made in this manner ensure quality and absolute impartiality.

VII. SELECTION AND APPOINTMENT OF LAW TEACHERS

The selection and appointment of law teachers is another matter of utmost importance in legal education. There are many similarities but also some dissimilarities in the Continental and the British and Commonwealth approaches. The Continental approach is in no way exclusively related to the structure and the method of teaching of the civil law. It is a method or system of selection that could be applied in any legal system just as the British method could be successfully applied elsewhere.

In the Continental countries, a high academic standing evidenced by a Doctor's degree is a condition precedent to a teaching appointment. Thus, an applicant with the basic law degree would not stand a chance.[58] Further, considerable experience in the practice of law at the bar, in public service or in another legal capacity is essential. As law schools and their standards are government controlled, a license to teach law from the Department of Education is required. The license is in fact the first teaching appointment. It is issued on the strength of a treatise which the candidate must publish and which must satisfy the faculty of law to which it is submitted for approval. The Department of Education then may, on the recommendation of the faculty, grant the teaching license which is, however, issued as a matter of course. The successful candidate thus becomes a reader (lecturer) within a given law school. He has the right to lecture and is asked to do so if need for his services arises. He devotes only a small part of his time to lecturing; otherwise, he follows his calling of law practitioner or government officer.

In this way, a pool of candidates for professorships is established. It is very rare indeed for a candidate to secure the teaching license before the age of thirty or thirty-five and to be appointed professor before the age of forty or forty-five. Professors are drawn exclusively from candidates holding law teaching licenses for many years. The appointment to a professorship being one of great prestige, only candidates of illustrious achievement in the practice of law are appointed.[59] All university vacancies are properly advertised and competition among candidates develops. The selection is made by an appointment board strictly on the basis of academic merit and achievement in the practice of law.[60] The appointment itself is then made usually by the head of the state.[61] Professors are appointed for life, i.e., until retirement (usually at the age of seventy) and enjoy the judicial privilege of irremovability.

The faculty of a law school is composed of professors and readers (lecturers).[62] The law school is governed by the faculty, the head of which is the dean. Generally, professors succeed to the deanship in order of seniority and hold office for one school year. The dean becomes the vice-dean for one school year immediately after his term as dean has expired. All important matters are decided by vote of faculty members.

In Britain and the Commonwealth, the universities are free to devise their own rules for the selection and appointment of law teachers. Consequently, one would expect a variety of methods to be used to fill existing vacancies; yet, the methods actually applied are fairly similar. All law teachers are drawn from barristers or solicitors only, and previous experience in the practice of law is a condition precedent to an appointment.[63] A higher university degree, while highly desirable, is not absolutely essential for an initial appointment.[64]

All vacancies are widely advertised and suitable persons are invited to apply. The qualifications of the applicants are evaluated by the university appointments committee and the selection, which has the form of a recommendation, is made on merit. The selection has to be approved by the governing body of bodies of the university and after such approval is given, the selected applicant is appointed by the university.

The first teaching appointment is to the post of assistant lecturer,[65] but applicants with experience in the practice of law and holding a higher law degree are invariably appointed to the higher rank of lecturer or senior lecturer.[66] The higher rank of reader is attainable by promotion or by a new appointment. Professorial vacancies are always advertised and filled by new appointment. The selection and appointment procedure is basically identical with that applied in the filling of lower posts, only somewhat more rigorous care and attention is given to the appointment.[67]

When the appointment is made, a formal contract is drawn up and signed by the appointee and the university, each holding a copy. The contract embodies the conditions of the appointment and the rights, privileges and duties of both parties. All appointments, with the exception of those of assistant lecturers,[68] are made until retirement (usually at the age of sixty-five or seventy), and the appointee has the right to terminate the contract by giving notice in writing of his intention to resign.[69]

There are relatively few positions of professorial rank within a typical British or Commonwealth law school, usually only three or four and sometimes even fewer than that. Consequently, professors are in the minority on the average faculty, the great majority of members being of lower academic rank. The faculty is composed of both full-time and part-time members.[70] The head of the law school is the dean, who is elected by the faculty from among faculty members for a term of up to five years. He then appoints a faculty member to the office of sub-dean.[71] In some law schools, there is also the office of vice-dean in addition to that of sub-dean. If so, the vice-dean is elected by the faculty from among its members in a way similar to that used for the election of the dean and for the same term.

VIII. CONCLUSION

A brief analysis of the Continental and the British and Commonwealth approaches to prelegal education, admission to law school, courses of instruction, examinations, teaching methods, admission to practice, and methods of selection of judges and law teachers reveals that the British and Commonwealth answer to these problems would, in most cases, stand midway between the Continental and American positions. As to the system of prelegal education and the method of admission to legal curriculum, the Continental and generally the civil law practice is much more akin to the British than to the American practice. The characteristic features of the British system of courses of instruction, techniques of examination and teaching methods are reflected both in America and in the Continental countries, yet the British methods of admission to legal practice and of selection and appointment of judges and law teachers have hardly a parallel elsewhere.

Widely divergent as they may seem, the Continental and the British and Commonwealth systems constitute a positive contribution to legal education. Obviously, the fact that some features of these systems do not seem at first glance useful or worth following does not necessarily imply that they would not be likely or able to render good services and reward any system of legal education with satisfying results. The American method of selection of students for admission to law school, which is conducive to the raising of class standard, may be contrasted with the Continental method, which is aimed at a uniform standard of instruction thus obliterating substantially the distinctions between individual law schools. Again, the British and American teaching techniques lead to a closer contact between the faculty and the students, which is very desirable. On the other hand, the Continental method, which grants the student absolute freedom, exercises a considerable influence on the formation of his independent judgment, teaching him not to rely on anyone but himself. Or again, the system of end of semester examinations, as practiced in the United States, operates as a stimulus to master as much as possible in a short time, whereas the Continental system stresses the importance of an evenly distributed effort and the appreciation of the law as one cohesive whole. The British and American method of written examinations makes possible a more accurate evaluation of the work of every student, whereas the Continental emphasis on oral examinations rather tests the student's ability for quick reasoning and effectiveness of presentation.

It is quite plain that many useful ideas and suggestions may originate from the impact of many generations of thought abroad and that a study of the diverse foreign systems of legal education may prove beneficial to the molding and formation of future developments. To this end, the fostering and promotion of an exchange of views and opinions on legal education among members of the teaching profession in the various countries of the world is a necessary prerequisite. Meetings, discussion of the many burning problems, on the spot study of the several systems of legal education, and a comparison of the results achieved by the various methods applied, would certainly clarify a great many obscurities and provide fitting answers to many previously unanswered questions. Such steps and activities would also contribute to the promotion of international understanding and cooperation so badly needed in relations among nations.

FOOTNOTES

1. The terms Baccalaureate and Maturity are interchangeable and both connote the same type of general examination. The terms college, lycée and Baccalaureate are used in French-speaking countries, whereas the terms gymnasium school and Maturity are used in non-French-speaking countries. Thus a student in a lycée, college or lyceum takes Baccalaureate examinations, and one in the gymnasium school, Maturity examinations.
2. Yet the division is never complete as it consists mainly in the sharp increase of the weekly load in science subjects in the science branch at the expense of subjects of a liberal nature and vice versa in the increase of weekly hours of instruction in liberal subjects in the philosophy branch at the expense of mathematices, physics and the like.

But a certain minimum of philosophy and mathematices is always taught in both branches.

3. It is interesting to note that classes in the Continental lycée and gymnasium schools are held six days a week and six hours per day as a minimum. The school year usually starts at the very beginning of September and ends at the very end of June. Christmas and Easter vacations are about ten days and six days, respectively. Instruction is given at a very intense pace so that students study all the day and sometimes even on Sundays.

4. In Canada, admission is predicated on two further years of study in an approved university or college after matriculation. On the whole, Canadian requirements with respect to both prelegal education and legal education come very close to those applicable in the United States. In the Republic of South Africa, a Bachelor's Degree in Arts or Commerce is required for admission to law school.

5. E.g., in the University of Melbourne in Australia, the yearly admission quota stands at present at 250. Selection is based on academic merit as disclosed by the results of the Matriculation Examination, but a further admission test may be given by the law school.

6. Thus students from Bordeaux and Marseilles study in Paris, or those from Valencia or Sevilla in Madrid, from Genoa and Naples in Rome, or from Frankfurt or Hamburg in Bonn, those from Innsbruck in Vienna, and so forth.

7. E.g., in order to be admitted to the Victorian Bar in Australia, the candidate must have done his studies in a Victorian law school. This is so because the law school examinations are at the same time bar examinations. But once admitted to the Victorian Bar, he is entitled to admission to any other Australian or New Zealand bar without further examination.

8. I.e., half years. This differs from the British and Commonwealth system of school years whereby yearly courses are offered and yearly examinations are usually held. The school year is subdivided into three terms but the subjects proceed throughout the entire school year without interruption.

9. There are two semesters in any one year, the Fall and the Spring semesters. The Fall semester usually starts at the beginning of October, and runs up to the end of January, the Spring semester starts in February and ends at the end of June.

10. Typical Continental subjects are: legal history, legal philosophy, Roman law, church law (canon law), civil law, civil procedure, criminal law, criminal procedure, commercial law, labor law, private international law, constitutional law, administrative law, public international law, economics, financial law and taxation. Many other subjects are, however, offered on an elective basis. Students take certain compulsory subjects and elect to take some other subjects.

11. As an exception to the general rule, some Continental law schools have lately adopted a system more akin to the British system of study by years with examinations held at the end of each school year or thereafter. Such is the case of the French, Italian and Spanish law schools where instruction is given by school years and yearly examinations are held in all subjects.

12. In or after the third semester.

13. Some universities, e.g., those of Austria, allow the candidate to take his final examinations in civil and public law only after the conclusion of lectures in all subjects within each of these two groups, so that the candidate may carry these subjects over two long vacations before he can present himself for examination.

14. The typical British and Commonwealth subjects are: introduction to law, legal history, contracts, torts, criminal law, real property, commercial (mercantile) law, conveyancing, equity, evidence, civil procedure, criminal procedure, law relating to executors and trustees, company law, industrial (labor) law, domestic relations, taxation, private international law, constitutional law, administrative law, jurisprudence, and

professional conduct. Further subjects are sometimes offered at an elective basis.

15. Roman law is taught in South Africa, accounting thus for the Afrikaans (Dutch) element in the South African law. Although not a member of the British Commonwealth, the Republic of South Africa is referred to in this article.

16. It is in fact, a required subject for admission to the English Bar.

17. Lectures in European law schools do not consist of the exposition of that which students can read for themselves in law books. They are rather designed to draw the attention of the students to important matters and to guide the students so that in their reading and study they keep on the right track. The professor explains the difficult points, so to speak, in advance, thus saving the student much time and effort in his study.

18. *See* note 11.

19. The student may present himself for examinations at practically any time during the school year. Examinations are held on application on a day and hour specified by the examiners.

20. The student has a much better grasp of a subject if he spends, *e.g.*, one hundred hours in the study of a subject spread over two years than the same one hundred hours congested in three or four months, the length of a semester.

21. The experience of centuries of teaching is neatly summarized in the maxim: "Quickly learned, quickly forgotten".

22. It is generally believed that the student has more time to think in a written examination, but this is not necessarily so since the paper is invariably packed. Thus the student may, on the contrary, experience a considerable time shortage.

23. An oral examination may take, *e.g.*, half an hour with respect to one candidate and a full hour with respect to another.

24. Written examinations may also present a certain aspect of these elements; but even if they do not, the defect is easily remedied by the holding of moot court as part of regular instruction as is done in every British and Commonwealth law school. Other problems may arise, however. For instance, the problem of keeping secret the questions set for a written examination must be faced, as examination questions must be ready many days before the test and are usually printed or mimeographed. Also, the setting and correcting of papers is time consuming, placing a heavy burden on the examiners. In oral examinations, the danger of leakage obviously does not arise, but oral examinations may be as time consuming as the correcting of examination papers.

25. The school year may begin and end so as to avoid the period of rain or intense heat. In the University of Singapore the school year begins in May and ends in January, and in the University of Khartoum it begins in July and ends in March.

26. Examiners are drawn from specialists in their field of study so that apart from members of the bar known to specialize in a given area, judges are frequently committee members in private law and procedure examinations, whereas government officers and judges of administrative tribunals serve on the committees examining public law.

27. All members are examiners-rapporteurs with respect to a part of the papers. If they are, *e.g.*, three, each of them reads and reports on one third of the papers.

28. The scale of grades is usually as follows: excellent, very good, good, pass, and the failing mark. If grades are given in Latin, the scale runs as follows: summa cum laude, magna cum laude, cum laude, rite, and the failing mark. In France, the scale runs from 0-20 points: 17 and better is very good, 15-17 is good, 13-15 is satisfactory, 10-13 is pass, below 10 is failing mark.

29. This is a substantial advantage over the end of course examinations where the student must take the examination or fail the course. The Continental system, whereby the student selects the time of his examinations, gives him all the opportunity to be well prepared. It is also consonnant with the academic freedom accorded to the student in

that he cannot be required to take an examination before he himself indicates his intention of taking it.

30. The scale of grades runs usually from 0-100 points. A passing grade is usually 40 and over or 51 and over. First, second and third class honors are awarded. If the passing grade is 40, third class honors run usually from 55 to 64, second class from 65 to 74 and first class from 75 up. If the passing grade is 51, third class honors run usually from 65 to 74, second class from 75 to 84 and first class from 85 up. The actual range of points may differ from law school to law school, but the difference consists only in arithmetic. So in the 40 pass system, it is very difficult to score over 70, and in the 51 pass system, over 80. Examination results are given as pass and honors. In the three honors groups, candidates are usually classed in order of merit so that they know which place they actually took within their class. Since the results appear only under numbers and no names are given, the student will find his grade but not those of other students. The actual number of points scored by each candidate is not given. The student can find out if he inquires in the Registrar's Office. He will be given the result on payment of a fee.

31. The usual examination procedure is as follows, although variations of the routine occur. The examinations are given and are supervised by the University Registrar and his staff, and faculty members are not present unless they volunteer to act as supervisors. Students are allowed to enter the examination room ten minutes before the beginning of the examination. There they find the examination paper and the book in which to write their answers. Each student is given his number and his seat number by the Registrar's Office several weeks before the examination. Within the ten minutes, students are allowed to study the examination paper but are not allowed to write answers. The examination begins right on the hour and ends three hours later with precision. A warning is given ten and five minutes before the time is out. Examination papers are immediately collected, counted, a record of the examination is made and signed by the supervisors. The examination is heavily supervised and cheating is unheard of. Every student writes his name and number on the cover of the examination book, but results are published under numbers only. The Registrar hands the papers to the proper examiners who return the papers to him. The papers are then kept in the Registrar's Office for a number of years. Marks are recorded in the Registrar's Office before they are published and a list is then made and sent to the law school where the marks are again recorded on each student's history card. If a student desires to look over his paper with the examiners, he has to file an application with the Registrar and pay the prescribed fee. The Registrar arranges a meeting of the student with the examiners in the Registrar's Office. Students, however, never avail themselves of this privilege since there is no benefit to be expected to come to them from the exercise. The mark can in no event be altered.

32. In the British and Commonwealth system, the professor giving the course is never present in the examination room when his examination is given and he will also act as only one of two or several examiners of the subject. By not being present in the examination room, he is saved any possible embarrassment he may otherwise face should students ask him questions with respect to the examination paper.

33. In practice, only a short period of the long vacation is used for recreation since the students in many cases take their examinations immediately thereafter.

34. In this connection, it is interesting to note that the necessary trapping of the Socratic method, which consists in the teacher's having a list of names of students so that he may call them to answer his questions and may take a roll call if he wishes, would sound absurd to any Continental university. The student would regard it rather as an insult to be called to answer in class in the same way as he was bound to in primary and secondary school. Also contrary to the British and Commonwealth practice, where the student finds himself frequently subject to the authority of registrars, bursars,

librarians and their staffs, nothing of this sort would be possible in a Continental university. The university is an association of professors and students who rule the university and the employees are there to serve and assist them. There is a very strong feeling of academic freedom and the students, as individuals and through their organizations, exercise a considerable influence on what is going on.

35. The second alternative is the usual one. As to the first alternative, which is used, *e.g.*, in France, the French law graduates are called "licenciés," having passed all the state prescribed examinations and having received the state license to engage in the exercise of the legal profession.

36. Examinations taken by law students are prescribed and supervised by the state. Consequently, they are usually called "state examinations." The successful passing of these examinations gives the candidate the right to exercise the legal profession. Nobody is allowed to follow a legal calling in any capacity, be it the practice of law at the bar, in the public service, in corporations, in business, or as a teacher of law, unless he has passed the prescribed state examinations. As this is all that is required, any other examinations (e.g., university examinations) are not necessary outside of the teaching career. Thus the state examinations correspond to the British, Commonwealth and American first degree, i.e., the LL.B., B.C.L. and J.D. degree.

37. In Britain and the Commonwealth countries, legal education is completed by admission to the bar either as a barrister or as a solicitor, or as both. Graduation from a law school is not a complete legal education and, consequently, a person holding the LL.B. or B.C.L. degree from a university, but not admitted to the bar, is not a qualified lawyer.

38. Both the length of junior advocacy and the nature of the bar examination differ from country to country. It takes about three years, but during that time the candidate is not just an apprentice in the sense of reading in chambers or doing articles of clerkship as in Britain and the Commonwealth countries where the candidate has no right to appear in court. The candidate for full membership at the bar—the junior counsel—has equal rights and duties as any full member, but is usually debarred from appearing in a few of the highest courts in the country. The bar examination, which is taken before the expiration of the period of junior advocacy, is a practical examination. It is both written, as to the drafting of writs and legal documents, and oral, in the art of advocacy. No question on substantive law or procedure is asked as this has been finally disposed of in the state examinations.

39. It is interesting to note that contrary to the practically uniform Continental practice of advocacy, in France there is a functional division between the advocate who specializes in pleading in court and the *avoué* who deals with the client on a line similar to the English solicitor. Admission in France is not to the bar in general, but to a given jurisdiction headed by a given appellate tribunal. The number of members admitted to practice before a given court is limited. In the highest French tribunal, the Court of Cassation, only 60 advocates are admitted to practice. Their practice is limited to arguing cases before the Court of Cassation and the Council of State, so that on appeal to these tribunals a new advocate must be hired. Since the appeal is on a matter of law only, the services of an *avoué* are not required and the advocate alone is in charge.

40. The Continental Doctor of Laws degree is usually conferred on the passing of many oral and written examinations, the submission of papers and a doctoral dissertation, which must be publicly defended. The rules for the acquisition of this degree vary from country to country and from law school to law school. It is a university degree as distinguished from a state degree so that the rules are, on many occasions, set by the university authorities without state interference.

41. The LL.B. or the B.C.L. degree.

42. There are four Inns of Court: the Societies of Lincoln's Inn, the Inner Temple, the

Middle Temple and Gray's Inn. They have a monopoly on the call to the bar in England and Wales. Scotland and Northern Ireland have their own societies, the Faculty of Advocates of Scotland and the Hon. Society of the Inn of Court of Northern Ireland.

43. Reading in chambers and articles of clerkship are designed to give the student an introduction into his profession and to show him the daily routine. A student barrister is thus being taught the art of advocacy by a senior barrister of not less than five years' standing and a student solicitor receives his practical instruction in a solicitor's office from a senior solicitor again of not less than five years' standing.

44. A university law degree is not required for admission to the bar. A certain minimum of basic subjects qualifies the candidate for admission. This minimum may be taken in three years as compared with the four-year course required for the LL.B. degree. This is to keep the admission standards uniform with those existing in Britain.

45. It will be noted that whereas in the Commonwealth countries, admission to the bar is the final step fully qualifying the candidate to practice, the call to the bar in England does not amount to full qualification, since the reading in chambers must then be undertaken. The reason for the distinction between England and the Commonwealth is historical. Law has been taught in England only in the Inns of Court, university law schools being of recent origin only. The first legal instruction outside the Inns of Court was given in the second half of the eighteenth century (Blackstone in the University of Oxford in 1753). This accounts for the fact that legal education in England is closely associated with the Inns of Court. No Inns of Court having ever existed in the Commonwealth countries, students from those countries had to travel to England to study law, be admitted in England and return to their home countries to practice. To remedy the situation, law schools were established within universities to give instruction in law in the Commonwealth countries. Admission to the bar was then regulated by the Supreme Court in each particular country on the English pattern, the admission being always the final step granting the candidate permission to engage in legal practice.

46. Barristers (counsel) have an exclusive right of audience in the House of Lords, the Judicial Committee of the Privy Council and in the Court of Appeal as well as in the High Court but there their monopoly does not extend to bankruptcy and hearings in chambers. They usually argue cases, even in the inferior courts. Solicitors may argue cases in the inferior courts but their task is to handle the case and to instruct, *i.e.*, to hire a counsel to argue it in court. Solicitors have law offices where they receive clients and do all the work required in the case, with the exception of appearance in court. Barristers, on the other hand, have chambers (usually one room only) in a building which is occupied by Barristers only. They have a reception office with adequate staff to handle their typing and other office work and they share in the payment of the expenses. Barristers are the superior type of lawyers. Judges are drawn exclusively from their ranks. Judges of the superior courts are appointed invariably from Queen's counsel (Q.C. or K.C. for King's Counsel, as the case may be) who are the acknowledged senior barristers and who are also known as "Silks," being entitled to wear a silk gown.

47. *E.g*, in Victoria and South Australia in Australia, in Singapore and in Malaya.

48. Judges are drawn from Q.C.'s who in turn are appointed exclusively from barristers, *i.e.*, those members of the bar who renounced their right to practice as solicitors.

49. The privilege is limited to legal practitioners and members of the judicial service (judges, procurators and government counsel). Those lawyers who work in corporations and in business in general or who serve in the public service and who have not been admitted to the bar would have to start from the beginning if they decided to become legal practitioners or to join the judicial service. This being so, a judicial career is in practice open only to those who join immediately after graduation, and further to

legal practitioners who are always given some credit for the time they spent in legal practice on their joining the judicial service. The loss of seniority involved in the switch from legal practice to a judicial career is, however, so pronounced that very few legal practitioners ever take this course.

50. The period corresponds to that required by a junior advocate to become a full member of the bar.

51. A position where he can exercise judicial discretion only under supervision, *e.g.*, a judge of instruction in criminal proceedings.

52. The appointment is for life or until retirement, usually at 70.

53. Ranks in the three branches of judicial administration are interchangeable so that promotions and transfers occur from branch to branch.

54. This does not include justices of the peace who are not judges in the proper meaning of the word and who are not legally trained. They may exercise some minor judicial functions.

55. The vacant position is advertised, applications are invited, and the selection and appointment are made on merit.

56. The appellate bench in the Commonwealth countries is composed of Supreme Court Justices sitting as a panel of three or more, called the Full Court. Justices of the High Court in England and Justices of the Supreme Court in the Commonwealth countries sit as single judges and the appeal from their decisions is taken in England to the Court of Appeal sitting in panels of three Lord Justices and in the Commonwealth countries to the Full Court. Further appeal may, in proper cases, be taken in England to the House of Lords and in the Commonwealth countries to a higher appellate tribunal, if any, or to the Judicial Committee of the Privy Council.

57. It is interesting to note that the system of electing judges or leaving it to the discretion of the government to appoint judges is practically unknown on the Continent, and has not existed in Britain and the Commonwealth in modern times. Both these methods of selection are manifestly inferior to those presently existing. The present system is carefully designed to avoid nepotism and favoritism, as well as politically motivated appointments. It was not established overnight but only after many centuries of struggle. While the method of electing judges is not directly objectionable if they are elected for life, it is nonetheless not the best method to fill judicial vacancies. It in no way ensures the competence of the candidate while it makes him accessible to political pressure and outside influences. It also places him in a dire predicament in the conduct of his electoral campaign. He must necessarily imply that he is better qualified than his opponent, *i.e.*, that his opponent is not well qualified. This is not only embarrassing but it must create the impression in the electorate that the legal profession is divided in its opinion on the relative merits of the candidates and that, not being able to agree, it submits the matter for decision to the layman who professedly is in no position to decide the matter on merit. The method of electing judges probably originated in ancient Greece where the judges were, however, not learned in law in the present meaning of the word, but were elders who just pledged to render decisions in accordance with their conscience. The communities were very small and the candidates were personally known to the electorate. The electorate did not elect one or the other on the strength of his legal learning but just on his general record of honesty and uprightness. The foundations on which the system rested having disappeared, the system was soon abandoned in ancient Greece.

58. He would not be eligible to apply for the license to teach law in the first place as the application requirement consists in the submission of a major legal work by a candidate of post-doctoral standing.

59. Publication of a legal work is essential for the acquisition of the teaching license, but a frequent publication of articles in law reviews is not required and is not practiced.

There is only a handful of law reviews concentrating on the expounding of newly arising matters of interest, like comments on new legislation or proposed new legislation and the like. An article must be a positive contribution to legal science and cannot consist only in the rearrangement of known facts. In teaching appointments, emphasis is laid on the learning of the candidate as evidenced by high degrees, on his successful practice at the bar, or generally in the exercise of his legal profession, and on his ability to teach as evidenced by his experience as lecturer.

60. Thus successful practice of law and successful previous teaching under teaching license issued by the Department of Education are essential, but the consideration of matters unrelated to academic record, such as references or any other extra-curricular considerations, would be contrary to the ethics of appointment.

61. The above method of appointment is practically of uniform application throughout all countries of the Continent of Europe, with the exception of the Communist-controlled countries. There are, of course, slight differences and an absolutely accurate position in any given country can be readily obtained by having recourse to the relevant rules. The position in France differs slightly from that in the other countries in that appointments to teaching positions are made from among the successful candidates in the *concours d'agrégation,* a competitive examination and a series of lectures delivered in one of the following groups of subjects: private law and criminal law; Roman law and French legal history; public law; or political economy. As a prerequisite for admission to the competition, the candidate must hold the degree of *licencié, i.e.,* his LL.B. and his doctor's degree, which is obtainable by specialization in one of the above-mentioned four groups of subjects. He must also take several written and oral examinations, undertake independent research and present and defend a dissertation. He must further give evidence of his prior accomplishment in the practice of law or, generally, in the exercise of his legal calling and also submit a list of his publications. If successful in the *concours d'agrégation,* the candidate is appointed to a professorship (*professeur chargé de cours*) in a university where a vacancy exists in one of the subjects within the group of subjects in which he qualified. With time, he will be appointed to a chair (*professeur titulaire*) and further promoted to chairs in more illustrious universities, finishing his career, *e.g.,* in the University of Paris. All appointments are made by the President of the Republic.

62. Professor means full professor. The distinction between ordinary and extraordinary professor is just that the former holds a specifically instituted chair in a given subject whereas an extraordinary professor holds no such chair. The distinction is important mainly because only ordinary professors, also called titular professors or simply chair-holding professors, are eligible to become deans. A reader (lecturer) is a faculty member who is not a full professor. Readers are normally called docents (because they teach) or professors *agrégés* or *agregados* to indicate that they were successful in the public competition for appointment to professorships and are now teaching pursuant to the license to teach so acquired.

63. The greater the experience in the practice of law, the higher the academic rank to which the candidate is appointed. So a minimum experience of two or three years of legal practice may suffice for an appointment to the rank of assistant lecturer, while a more extensive experience will warrant appointment to the rank of lecturer, or senior lecturer.

64. Applicants for teaching appointments are university graduates who, in most cases, hold an advanced law degree, usually the LL.M. or the Ph.D. (Law) degree. The LL.B. degree is not regarded as sufficient for a permanent teaching appointment; in cases where an applicant holding only the LL.B. degree is appointed, he has to acquire a higher law degree within reasonable time. Legal practitioners who are not university graduates do not engage in the teaching of law in university law schools.

65. The post of assistant lecturer is a probationary appointment for a period of three years and is followed by promotion to the rank of lecturer, which is a permanent appointment.

66. The ranks usually encountered in British and Commonwealth law schools are: professor, reader, lecturer, assistant lecturer; or professor, reader, senior lecturer, lecturer. The second variety occurs frequently in the Commonwealth. Where it is adopted, the rank of lecturer means then a part-time lecturer.

67. Successful applicants invariably hold advanced law degrees and have balanced experience in the practice of law and law teaching, as well as a superior academic record. Their competence in legal research must be evidenced by adequate legal writing.

68. *See* note 65.

69. A three-to-six months' notice is usually required and the resignation must be timed to coincide with the end of the school year.

70. In addition to the full-time faculty, every British and Commonwealth law school employs a considerable number of part-time teaching staff. Part-time law teachers are termed lecturers. Each of them teaches one subject only. They are distinguished barristers or solicitors known to specialize in the subject they are invited to teach. They bring their superior experience in the practice of law into the classroom and are an invaluable asset to the law school faculty. Their method of presentation of the subject tends to concentrate on the practical application of law in court with constant illustrations from cases they actually handled or argued. Part-time lecturers usually teach subjects in which they can display their superior skills, such as evidence, civil and criminal procedure, legal ethics, taxation, and conveyancing, but they may also teach commercial law, criminal law, contracts, etc.

71. The dean is invariably one of the professors, although a faculty member of a lower rank could be elected. The sub-dean holds office until a new dean is elected.

Index

A

Abandonment of family:
  Spanish law, 667
Accomplices:
  French law, 131
  German law, 292
  Italian law, 432
  Spanish law, 598
Administrative authorities:
  in general, 25
  Austrian law, 695
  French law, 164
  German law, 323
  Italian law, 459
  Mexican law, 717
  Spanish law, 630
  Swiss law, 707
Administrative courts:
  in general, 25
  Austrian, 695
  French, 169
  German, 331
  Italian, 466
  Mexican, 717
  Spanish, 638
  Swiss, 707
Administrative law:
  in general, 25
  Austrian, 694
  French, 159
  German, 318

Administrative law *(cont.)*
  Italian, 452
  Mexican, 717
  Spanish, 623
  Swiss, 707
Administrative procedure:
  in general, 27
  Austrian, 695
  French, 173
  German, 337
  Italian, 474
  Mexican, 718
  Spanish, 644
  Swiss, 708
Admiralty, *see* Maritime law
Adverse possession:
  French law, 98, 99
  German law, 238
  Italian law, 398
  Spanish law, 553
Airplanes:
  French law, 91
Alibi:
  German law, 369
Alimony:
  French law, 46, 184
  German law, 245
  Italian law, 391, 489
  Spanish law, 539, 661
Amparo:
  Mexican law, 714, 716, 719

Animals:
  French law, 91
  Italian law, 398, 404
Annulment of marriage:
  French law, 39
  German law, 243
  Italian law, 390
  Spanish law, 539
Arbitration:
  Spanish law, 655
Assault:
  French law, 197
Astreinte:
  French law, 81
Attorneys:
  in general, 29
  Austrian, 696
  French, 179
  German, 345
  Italian, 486
  Mexican, 721
  Spanish, 651
  Swiss, 709
Auction:
  French law, 63
  German law, 229, 235, 239,
    240
Austrian law:
  in general, 689
  administrative authorities,
    695

781

Austrian law *(cont.)*
  administrative courts, 695
  administrative law, 694
  administrative procedure,
    695
  attorneys, 696
  civil courts, 691
  civil law, 690
  civil procedure, 692
  commercial law, 690
  criminal courts, 693
  criminal law, 692
  criminal procedure, 694
  judges, 696
  notaries, 697
  public ministry, 696

B

Bail:
  French law, 142
  German law, 307, 312
  Italian law, 451
  Spanish law, 622
Bankruptcy:
  in general, 9
  French law, 107, 192
  German law, 263
  Italian law, 415
  Spanish law, 565
Bills of Exchange:
  in general, 9
  French law, 107
  German law, 262
  Italian law, 415
  Spanish law, 565
Books of commerce, *see*
    Commercial books

C

Carriage of goods and pas-
    sengers by sea, *see* Mari-
    time law
Causa in contract:
  French law, 79
  German law, 229
  Italian law, 401, 402
  Spanish law, 546
Checks:
  in general, 9
  French law, 107
  German law, 262
  Italian law, 415
  Spanish law, 565

Civil courts:
  in general, 11
  Austrian, 691
  French, 113
  German, 271
  Italian, 418
  Mexican, 712
  Spanish, 571
  Swiss, 699
Civil law:
  in general, 5
  Austrian, 690
  French, 36
  German, 224
  Italian, 387
  Mexican, 712
  Spanish, 536
  Swiss, 699
Civil procedure:
  in general, 14
  Austrian, 692
  French, 118
  German, 278
  Italian, 421
  Mexican, 714
  Spanish, 575
  Swiss, 703
Claims against the state:
  French law, 205, 209
Codes, *see* Civil law, Crimi-
    nal law, Civil proce-
    dure, etc.
Commercial books:
  French, 102
  German, 253
  Spanish, 557
Commercial courts:
  in general, 14
  Austrian, 693
  French, 114
  German, 272, 273
  Swiss, 700
Commercial law:
  in general, 7
  Austrian, 690
  French, 101
  German, 251
  Italian, 387
  Mexican, 712
  Spanish, 555
  Swiss, 699
Commercial register:
  French law, 102
  German law, 253
  Italian law, 412
  Spanish law, 556

Common law, 726
Communities and cities:
  French law, 164
  German law, 323
  Italian law, 459
  Spanish law, 631
Community property:
  French law, 92
  Italian law, 393
  Spanish law, 550
Comparative negligence:
  French law, 187
  Italian law, 404, 406
Conditional obligations:
  French law, 82
Conflict of laws:
  French law, 48
Contracts:
  French law, 77
  German law, 228
  Italian law, 401
  Spanish law, 546
Contracts to be made in
    writing (Stat. of Frauds):
  German law, 233
  Italian law, 401, 405
  Spanish law, 546
Corporations:
  in general, 8
  French law, 103
  German law, 254
  Italian law, 406
  Spanish law, 559
Council of State:
  French law, 170, 175
  Italian, 468
  Spanish, 636
Courts, *see* Administrative,
    Civil, Commercial,
    Criminal
Court of Accounts:
  French, 180
  German, 330, 335
  Italian, 455, 470
  Spanish, 637
Courts of Appeal (Civil):
  in general, 13
  French, 116
  German, 274
  Italian, 419
  Spanish, 572
Courts of Appeal (Criminal):
  in general, 20
  French, 137
  German, 304
  Italian, 439

Courts of Appeal (Criminal) *(cont.)*
  Spanish, 605
Courts of final resort (Civil):
  in general, 13
  French, 116
  German, 274
  Italian, 419
  Spanish, 573
Courts of final resort (Criminal):
  in general, 20
  French, 138
  German, 304
  Italian, 439
  Spanish, 606
Courts of general jurisdiction (Civil):
  in general, 12
  French, 114
  German, 272
  Italian, 419
  Spanish, 572
Courts of general jurisdiction (Criminal):
  in general, 20
  French, 136
  German, 302
  Italian, 437
  Spanish, 604
Courts of limited jurisdiction (Civil):
  in general, 11
  French, 113
  German, 271
  Italian, 419
  Spanish, 571
Courts of limited jurisdiction (Criminal):
  in general, 19
  French, 135
  German, 301
  Italian, 437
  Spanish, 604
Criminal courts:
  in general, 19
  Austrian, 693
  French, 135
  German, 301
  Italian, 437
  Mexican, 715
  Spanish, 604
  Swiss, 703
Criminal law:
  in general, 17
  Austrian, 692

Criminal law *(cont.)*
  French, 128
  German, 289
  Italian, 428
  Mexican, 714
  Spanish, 595
  Swiss, 703
Criminal procedure:
  in general, 21
  Austrian, 694
  French, 138
  German, 306
  Italian, 440
  Mexican, 716
  Spanish, 607
  Swiss, 707
Custody of children:
  French law, 46
Customs:
  German law, 371

D

Decisive oath:
  in general, 16
  French law, 122
  German law, 281
  Italian law, 423
  Spanish law, 579, 586
Defamation:
  French law, 200
  Italian law, 493
Departments:
  French law, 166
Deposit:
  German law, 235
Divorce:
  French law, 42
  German law, 244
  Italian law, 391
  Spanish law, 537
Domicile (Residence):
  French law, 37
  German law, 224
  Italian law, 388
  Spanish law, 536

E

Easements:
  French law, 54
Electricity:
  German law, 299, 354
  Italian law, 434, 524
Eminent domain:
  French law, 160

Eminent domain *(cont.)*
  Spanish law, 628
  English law, 726
Evidence, *see* Procedure

F

False advertising:
  French law, 201
Finding:
  French law, 57
  German law, 239
  Italian law, 398
  Spanish law, 541
Fire:
  French law, 90
Food supply:
  Italian law, 510
  Spanish law, 623
Forced shares, *see* Unavoidable heirs
Foreigners:
  French law, 162
Forum selection clauses:
  French law, 193
Freedom of assembly:
  German law, 321
French law:
  in general, 35
  administrative authorities, 164
  administrative courts, 169
  administrative law, 159
  administrative procedure, 173
  attorneys, 179
  civil courts, 113
  civil law, 36
  civil procedure, 118
  commercial law, 101
  criminal courts, 135
  criminal law, 128
  criminal procedure, 138
  judges, 176
  judicial decisions, 183
  maritime law, 109
  notaries, 181
  public ministry, 178

G

German law:
  in general, 223
  adminstrative authorities, 323

German law *(cont.)*
  administrative courts, 331
  administrative law, 318
  administrative procedure, 337
  attorneys, 345
  civil courts, 271
  civil law, 224
  civil procedure, 278
  commercial law, 251
  criminal courts, 301
  criminal law, 289
  criminal procedure, 306
  judges, 343
  judicial decisions, 350
  maritime law, 267
  notaries, 348
  public ministry, 344
Gifts:
  French law, 66

H

Hearsay rule:
  German law, 280

I

Immigration laws:
  French law, 162
Immovables, *see* Property
Injunctions:
  French law, 81
  German law, 234
  Italian law, 405
  Spanish law, 548
Intestacy:
  French law, 58
  German law, 246
  Italian law, 397
  Spanish law, 545
Italian law:
  in general, 386
  administrative authorities, 459
  administrative courts, 466
  administrative law, 452
  administrative procedure, 474
  attorneys, 486
  civil courts, 418
  civil law, 387
  civil procedure, 421
  commercial law, 387
  criminal courts, 437

Italian law *(cont.)*
  criminal law, 428
  criminal procedure, 440
  judges, 483
  judicial decisions, 489
  maritime law, 417
  notaries, 488
  public ministry, 485

J

Joint liability:
  French law, 84
Judges:
  in general, 28
  Austrian, 696
  French, 176
  German, 343
  Italian, 483
  Mexican, 719
  Spanish, 649
  Swiss, 708
Judges of Instruction (Civil):
  French, 120, 123
  German, 279
  Italian, 422
Judges of Instruction (Criminal):
  French, 140
  German, 312
  Italian, 442
  Spanish, 604, 609
Judicial decisions (Administrative):
  French, 203
  German, 370
  Italian, 517
  Spanish, 674
Judicial decisions (Civil and Commercial):
  French, 183
  German, 350
  Italian, 489
  Spanish, 655
Judicial decisions (Criminal):
  French, 195
  German, 363
  Italian, 507
  Spanish, 667
Judicial separation of spouses:
  French law, 47
  Italian law, 391
  Spanish law, 539

L

Labor courts:
  German law, 276
  Spanish law, 574
Land registration:
  French law, 542
  German law, 237, 240
  Italian law, 400
  Spanish law, 541
Latin American law, 724
Law schools, *see* Legal education
Legal education, 755
Lesione:
  Italian law, 402, 405
Limitation of actions, *see* Prescription

M

Manslaughter:
  French law, 132
  German law, 297
  Italian law, 433
  Spanish law, 599
Maritime law:
  in general, 10
  Austrian, 690
  French, 109
  German, 267
  Italian, 417
  Mexican, 712
  Spanish, 568
Marriage:
  French law, 38
  German law, 241
  Italian law, 389
  Spanish law, 537
Marriage of foreigners:
  French law, 38
  German law, 241
  Italian law, 390
  Spanish law, 538
Mens rea:
  Italian law, 510
Merchants:
  in general, 8
  Austrian law, 690
  French law, 101
  German law, 252
  Italian law, 412
  Mexican law, 712
  Spanish law, 555
  Swiss law, 699

Merger, *see* Obligations (extinction)
Mexican law:
  in general, 711
  administrative authorities, 717
  administrative courts, 717
  administrative law, 717
  administrative procedure, 718
  amparo 714, 716, 719
  attorneys, 721
  civil courts, 712
  civil law, 712
  civil procedure, 714
  commercial law, 712
  criminal courts, 715
  criminal law, 714
  criminal procedure, 716
  judges, 719
  notaries, 722
  public ministry, 720
Military service:
  German law, 370
  Italian law, 519
Minors (criminal law):
  French law, 131
  German law, 291
  Italian law, 430
  Spanish law, 597
Motor vehicles:
  French law, 90
  German law, 299, 352, 377
  Italian law, 404, 406, 512
  Spanish law, 602, 671
Movables, *see* Property
Murder:
  French law, 132
  German law, 297
  Italian law, 432
  Spanish law, 599
Muslim law, 738, 744, 745

N

Notaries:
  in general, 30
  Austrian, 697
  French, 181
  German, 348
  Italian, 488
  Mexican, 722

Notaries *(cont.)*
  Spanish, 653
  Swiss, 709
Novation, *see* Obligations (extinction)

O

Oath, *see* Procedure, Decisive oath
Obligations:
  in general, 7
  French law, 77
  German law, 226
  Italian law, 400
  Spanish law, 546
Ombudsman, 31
Ownership:
  French law, 50
  German law, 237
  Italian law, 398
  Spanish law, 541

P

Paris, city of, 165
Parole:
  French law, 158
  German law, 296
  Italian law, 436
  Spanish law, 603
Partition of land:
  French law, 63
Partnerships:
  in general, 8
  French law, 103
  German law, 254
  Italian law, 406
  Spanish law, 559
Passports:
  German law, 318;
Penal clauses:
  French law, 86
  German law, 231
Pleading, *see* Procedure
Pollution, protection against:
  German law, 319
  Spanish law, 674

Possession:
  French law, 97
  German law, 237
Praetor:
  Italian law, 419, 437
Prescription (limitation of actions):
  French law, 97
  German law, 225
  Italian law, 413
  Spanish law, 553
Printing and periodical publications:
  French law, 161
Probation:
  French law, 142
  German law, 295
  Italian law, 435
  Spanish law, 603
Procedure (civil) before courts of appellate jurisdiction:
  in general, 16
  French, 124
  German, 284
  Italian, 425
  Spanish, 584
Procedure (criminal) before courts of appellate jurisdiction:
  in general, 23
  French, 151
  German, 313
  Italian, 446
  Spanish, 613
Procedure (civil) before courts of final resort:
  in general, 16
  French, 126
  German, 286
  Italian, 426
  Spanish, 588
Procedure (criminal) before courts of final resort:
  in general, 23
  French, 154
  German, 314
  Italian, 448
  Spanish, 617
Procedure (civil) before courts of general jurisdiction:
  in general, 15
  French, 119
  German, 279

Procedure (civil) before courts of general jurisdiction *(cont.)*
Italian, 422
Spanish, 578
Procedure (criminal) before courts of general jurisdiction:
in general, 21
French, 146
German, 302
Italian, 441
Spanish, 609
Procedure (civil) before courts of limited jurisdiction:
in general, 15
French, 118
German, 278
Italian, 421
Spanish, 576
Procedure (criminal) before courts of limited jurisdiction:
in general, 21
French, 149, 152
German, 301
Italian, 440
Spanish, 608
Property:
in general, 6
French law, 49
German law, 237
Italian law, 398
Spanish law, 541
Prosecutors, *see* Public ministry and Procedure (criminal)
Provinces:
Italian, 461
Spanish, 633
Public domain:
French law, 49
Italian law, 398, 399
Public ministry:
in general, 29
Austrian, 696
French, 178
German, 344
Italian, 485
Mexican, 720
Spanish, 650
Swiss, 709
Public servants:
French, 203
Italian, 454, 525
Spanish, 678

Punishment:
French law, 129
German law, 293
Italian law, 429
Spanish law, 596
Purchaser for value without notice:
French law, 100
Italian law, 399, 400

Q

Quasi-contract:
French law, 89

R

Rape:
Italian law, 507
Regions:
French, 167
Italian, 462
Release:
French law, 87
German law, 236
Religions:
French law, 159
Remission of debt, *see* Obligations (extinction)
Repeaters:
French law, 130
German law, 294
Italian law, 431
Spanish law, 598
Representation:
French law, 58
Rescission of contract:
French law, 88
German law, 231
Residence (domicile):
French law, 37
German law, 224
Italian law, 388
Spanish law, 536
Restitution:
French law, 88
German law, 231, 234
Italian law, 403
Spanish law, 547
Retirement:
Italian law, 522, 525
Roads:
French law, 204

Roads *(cont.)*
German law, 377
Italian law, 456
Robbery:
French law, 134
German law, 299
Italian law, 435
Spanish law, 601

S

Set-off:
French law, 88
German law, 236
Ships, *see* Maritime law
Spanish law:
in general, 535
administrative authorities, 630
administrative courts, 638
administrative law, 623
administrative procedure, 644
attorneys, 651
civil courts, 571
civil law, 536
civil procedure, 575
commercial law, 555
criminal courts, 604
criminal law, 595
criminal procedure, 607
judges, 649
judicial decisions, 655
maritime law, 568
notaries, 653
public ministry, 650
Specific performance:
French law, 79, 81
German law, 234
Italian law, 405
Spanish law, 548
Soviet law, 729
Succession:
in general, 6
French law, 58
German law, 246
Italian law, 397
Spanish law, 545
Sunday Observance Act:
Italian law, 514
Swindling:
French law, 198
German law, 365
Spanish law, 672, 673

Swiss law:
  in general, 698
  administrative authorities,
    707
  administrative courts, 707
  administrative law, 707
  administrative procedure,
    708
  attorneys, 709
  civil courts, 699
  civil law, 699
  civil procedure, 703
  commercial law, 699
  criminal courts, 703
  criminal law, 703
  criminal procedure, 707
  judges, 708
  notaries, 709
  public ministry, 709

T

Taxation:
  French law, 208
  German law, 374
  Italian law, 457
  Spanish law, 680
Tax courts:
  French, 169
  German, 336
  Italian, 471
  Spanish, 641

Television in the courtroom:
  French law, 147, 149
  German law, 366
Theft:
  French law, 134
  German law, 298
  Italian law, 434
  Spanish law, 600
Torts:
  French law, 90, 91, 183,
    185, 190, 207
  German law, 406, 352, 354
  Italian law, 403, 406, 491,
    493
  Spanish law, 658
Trademarks:
  Spanish law, 666

U

Unavoidable heirs:
  French law, 67, 68, 71
  German law, 250
  Italian law, 396, 397
  Spanish law, 544
Unfair competition:
  Italian law, 504
Universities:
  Spanish law, 625
  see also Legal education
Unjust enrichment:
  French law, 87, 90

Unjust enrichment *(cont.)*
  German law, 230, 233
  Italian law, 403, 406
  Spanish law, 547
Unworthiness to inherit:
  French law, 58
  German law, 251
  Italian law, 396, 397
  Spanish law, 544
Usufruct:
  French law, 51
  Italian law, 500

W

Water courts:
  Italian, 470
Welfare courts:
  German law, 335
Wills:
  French law, 71
  German law, 247
  Italian law, 396
  Spanish law, 542
Wine:
  Spanish law, 623
Witnesses, *see* Procedure,
  Wills
Wounding:
  French law, 133
  German law, 297
  Italian law, 434
  Spanish law, 600